FEMINIST FRONTIERS III

LAUREL RICHARDSON
The Ohio State University

VERTA TAYLOR
The Ohio State University

McGRAW-HILL, INC.

New York   St. Louis   San Francisco   Auckland
Bogotá   Caracas   Lisbon   London   Madrid
Mexico   Milan   Montreal   New Delhi   Paris
San Juan   Singapore   Sydney
Tokyo   Toronto

FEMINIST FRONTIERS III

Copyright © 1993 by McGraw-Hill, Inc. All rights reserved. Previously published under the title of *Feminist Frontiers II: Rethinking Sex, Gender, and Society.* Copyright © 1989, 1986 by McGraw-Hill, Inc. All rights reserved. Printed in the United States of America. Except as permitted under the United States Copyright Act of 1976, no part of this publication may be reproduced or distributed in any form or by any means, or stored in a data base or retrieval system, without the prior written permission of the publisher.

2 3 4 5 6 7 8 9 0 DOH   DOH 9 0 9 8 7 6 5 4 3

ISBN 0-07-052298-7

This book was set in Times Roman by The Clarinda Company.
The editors were Phillip A. Butcher and Katherine Blake;
the production supervisor was Louise Karam.
The cover was designed by Rafael Hernandez.
R. R. Donnelley & Sons Company was printer and binder.

Library of Congress Cataloging–in–Publication Data

Feminist frontiers III / [edited by] Laurel Richardson, Verta Taylor.
        p.   cm.
    Includes bibliographical references.
    ISBN 0-07-052298-7
        1. Feminism—United States.   2. Women—United States.
3. Sex role—United States.   4. Women—Cross-cultural studies.
I. Richardson, Laurel.   II. Taylor, Verta A.   III. Title: Feminist
frontiers III.
HQ1426.F472   1993
305.42—dc20   92-18801

ABOUT THE AUTHORS

LAUREL RICHARDSON is a Professor of Sociology and Graduate Faculty of Women's Studies at The Ohio State University. She received her B.A. from the University of Chicago, where she was a Ford Fellow and a University Honors Fellow, and her Ph.D. from the University of Colorado, where she held a University Graduate Fellowship and a National Science Foundation Dissertation Fellowship. She has been the recipient of many grants and fellowships, including support from the National Endowment of the Humanities, the National Institute of Education, and the National Institute of Mental Health, and various state and local awards. She introduced a women's studies course in 1970, and has taught and written about gender extensively since then.

Professor Richardson is the author of *The Dynamics of Sex and Gender* (currently in its third edition), *Gender and University Teaching, Writing Strategies: Reaching Diverse Audiences,* and *The New Other Woman,* which has been translated into Portuguese, Japanese, and German. In addition, her work has appeared in many journals, including the *American Sociological Review, Social Forces, Symbolic Interaction, Journal of Contemporary Ethnography, Sociological Theory, Qualitative Sociology,* and *Gender & Society.* She is a frequent presenter on topics of gender to national and international meetings. She has served on the editorial boards of *The National Women's Studies Journal, Gender & Society, Journal of Contemporary Ethnography*, and *Sociological Quarterly.* Currently she is studying the sociological implications of women's narratives and social scientific narratives. This work will eventuate in a book, *Feminine Endings/Feminist Beginnings.*

VERTA TAYLOR is Associate Professor of Sociology at The Ohio State University, where she teaches courses on gender and women's studies, the women's movement, social movements, and qualitative research methods. She held a joint faculty appointment with the Center for Women's Studies at Ohio State from 1982 to 1984, served as acting director of Women's Studies in 1984, and is currently a member of the Graduate Faculty in Women's Studies. She has won several departmental graduate teaching awards, an Ohio State University Distinguished Teaching Award, and a multicultural teaching award.

Professor Taylor has recently coauthored (with Leila Rupp) *Survival in the Doldrums: The American Women's Rights Movement, 1945 to the 1960s,* which received scholarly research awards from the Collective Behavior and Social Movement Section of the American Sociological Association and the North Central Sociological Association. Her writings have appeared in numerous scholarly collections and in journals such as *Gender & Society, Signs, Journal of Marriage and the Family, Mass Emergencies,* and the *American Sociological Review.* She has served as investigator of grants from the National Science Foundation, the National Institute of Mental Health, the National Endowment for the Humanities, and the Ohio Department of Mental Health. She has been Advisory Editor for the *National Women's Studies Association Journal* and *Gender & Society* and is currently Associate Editor of *Gender & Society.* In addition to her continuing research on women's movements, Taylor lectures frequently at national and international meetings on feminism and women's movements. Currently she is studying lesbian feminist communities and is also working on a book on the self-help movement to combat postpartum depression.

To our mothers,
Rose Foreman Richardson
and Alice F. Houston,
and to our sisters
Jessica Richardson Phillips
and Betty Jo Hudson

C O N T E N T S

SECTION THREE: Socialization

PART THREE:

SOCIAL ORGANIZATION OF GENDER

SECTION FOUR: Explanations of Gender Inequality

SECTION FIVE: Work   181

SECTION SIX: Families   235

SECTION SEVEN: Intimacy and Sexuality   279

SECTION EIGHT: Health and Medicine   327

SECTION ELEVEN: Social Protest and the Feminist Movement   497

P R E F A C E

The first edition of *Feminist Frontiers* was conceived in the late 1970s, at a time when many women inside and outside academia were beginning to recognize and challenge male domination. The anthology was published in the early 1980s, just as a backlash swelled against feminism. At the time of its publication, only a handful of books and anthologies written for classroom use presented a feminist perspective on women's status. The evolution of this book through three editions reflects both the successes of the women's movement and the development of feminist scholarship over the past two decades. Women's studies courses have blossomed and spread to campuses in even the most conservative regions of the country. Feminist scholars in the meantime have refined and enlarged our understanding of how gender inequality operates and how it intersects with other systems of domination based on race, ethnicity, nationality, class, and sexuality. There is no doubt that the situation of women has changed since the publication of the first edition of *Feminist Frontiers*. Gender inequality has not, however, disappeared.

With pride and excitement we write this preface to *Feminist Frontiers III*. We are proud to be part of the continuing women's movement which struggles to reform the structure and culture of male dominance; and we are excited by the burgeoning of knowledge about diversity and differences among women. We feel fortunate to be writing, teaching, and learning at a time when feminist thought and research are flourishing and deepening. It is simultaneously a time to enjoy the bounty of feminist scholarship and to sow new feminist seeds.

Feminist thought seeks to transform, in fundamental and profound ways, all the old patriarchal ways of seeing, defining, and understanding our experiences and the social world. Feminists view the accomplishment of this transformation as a global activity that must take account of differences and diversity. The articles in *Feminist Frontiers III* underscore the pervasive cultural, racial, ethnic, and other differences that interact with gender. The experience of being disadvantaged is not the same for different groups of women.

We developed this book for use as the major or supplementary text in courses on the sociology of women, women's studies, gender studies, or sex roles. In addition, because the book offers a general framework for analyzing women's status, it can be used as a supplementary text in introductory sociology courses and in courses on social problems, foundations of society, comparative studies, and American studies. Although we have retained some of the articles from the first and second editions of *Feminist Frontiers*, particularly writings that have become feminist classics, approximately half of the readings are new to this edition. We have sought out new cross-cultural and comparative articles and selections that focus on diverse groups of women. In choosing such works, we have looked for material that lends itself to discussion by people with little previous knowledge of the culture and groups under consideration.

Feminist Frontiers III is organized into four parts, each introduced by a sociological-feminist analysis. Part One, "Introduction to Feminist Research," deals with feminist approaches to diversity and difference and outlines the parameters of feminist theoretical and methodological approaches. Part Two, "Learning Gender," has two sections, "Language, Images, and Culture" and "Socialization." The six sections of Part Three, "Social Organization of Gender," provide theoretical explanations of gender inequality and readings on work, families, intimacy and sexuality, health and medicine, and violence against women. Part Four, "Social Change," includes articles on the state and international politics and on social protest and the feminist movement.

As we set about the task of selecting articles for this edition, we found an abundance of excellent pieces. We used the following criteria for choosing what to include. First, we wanted each selection to be engagingly written and accessible in style and language to readers from different disciplinary backgrounds. Second, as a testament to the tremendous growth in depth and understanding of feminist scholarship, we sought selections exploring a wide range of theoretical and substantive issues. Third, we wanted the anthology to reflect a diversity of racial, ethnic, generational, sexual, and cultural experiences. Fourth, we sought to capture the cross-disciplinary nature of gender research. The result is a collection that links well-written and significant articles within a general feminist sociological perspective.

We gratefully acknowledge the support, skill, and help of many people. We extend thanks to contributing authors, not only for writing the selected pieces but also for allowing us to reprint them here. At McGraw-Hill, we especially thank our executive editor, Phil Butcher, for believing in and supporting this project, Kathy Blake for shepherding the book through its developmental phases, Laura Warner for overseeing the final manuscript through editing and production, and Barbara Hale, permissions editor. Amber Ault and Bridget Anderson have worked untold hours on the manuscript; their help and advice have been invaluable. Ursula Anderson provided the necessary clerical support. We express our appreciation to students in our sociology of women and women's studies classes, who have contributed to the development of this anthology by their critical responses to proposed articles. In addition, Mary Margaret Fonow, Claire Robertson, and Nancy Whittier have given us valuable feedback on their teaching experiences with earlier editions of *Feminist Frontiers*. Barrie Thorne and Michael Kimmel provided insight and encouragement for our revision.

The following reviewers read the manuscript and improved it by their expert and generous comments: Marjorie DeVault, Syracuse University; Lowell Krokoff, University of Wisconsin–Madison; Patricia MacCorquodale, University of Arizona–Tucson; Susan Marshall, University of Texas–Austin; Judith Rollins, Simmons College; Beth Schneider, University of California–Santa Barbara; and Susan Shoemaker, University of Illinois–Urbana.

Special thanks go to those close to us who inspired both the work and the authors. Ernest Lockridge has been steadfast in his belief in and support for the project. Leila Rupp critically reviewed the entire collection at every stage of the revision, spent endless hours helping to prepare the manuscript for production, and offered the friendship and support needed to carry out the project. To them and to the many others who touched our lives positively, we express our gratitude.

Finally, we are full coeditors; our names are listed in alphabetical order.

Laurel Richardson
Verta Taylor

P A R T   O N E

Introduction to Feminist Research

How are women alike? How do women differ? Does the common experience of patriarchy unite us across our differences? Feminist scholars look at *both* commonalities *and* differences. Women everywhere suffer similar restrictions, oppression, and discrimination because they are women living in patriarchal societies. Yet, differences in race, ethnicity, class, sexuality, age, region, nation, and so on, inflect those seemingly similar experiences. Furthermore, diversity exists within the "categories of difference" (such as race, class, and sexual orientation); for example, there are considerable differences in experiences among such "women of color" as Asian Americans, African Americans, Native Americans, and Hispanic Americans. There are considerable differences within such groups as well; the experiences of the Korean-American woman, for example, are not the same as those of the Chinese-American woman. Moreover, categories of difference intersect each other. Lesbians of different ages, social classes, races, ethnicities, and religions, for example, have different experiences. In addition, each of us has multiple alliances and identifications with different groups that shift through time and social context. The religious identity of childhood may be shunted aside during young adulthood, only to be reclaimed again in later years. As biracial or bicultural or mixed religion daughters, we might variously identify with either parent's heritage or that of both, depending upon the social context.

If matters were not complex enough—categories of commonality and difference, diversity, and shifting identities—feminist scholars recognize that individuals have unique constellations of experiences: we each have our own story to tell. Large cultural forces such as sexism, racism, heterosexism, and classism shape our biographies, but we experience our lives and make sense of them as individuals. Individuals do not easily attribute their experiences to class, race, or gender as *separate* or *separable* entities. They rarely see their own biographies as sociohistorically situated.

In the midst of all these considerations, feminist scholarship is flourishing. It flourishes because feminist research builds upon and links two levels of analysis: structure and biography. The *structural* level looks at social institutions and cultural practices which create and sustain gender inequalities and links those inequalities to other systems of oppression such as racism, ageism, and homophobia. The *biographical* level honors individual women's expressions of their own experiences. It makes available individual self-representation and personal voice. Because feminist scholarship links structural understandings with personal biography, we learn how difference and commonality are structurally induced and personally experienced. We can see how larger social forces affect our own and others' lives. Feminist scholarship thus leads us to rethink the structural changes necessary to meet the needs of actual women.

Given the issues of diversity and difference, how do feminist researchers approach their work? How do they actually do feminist research? Although there is considerable variation among feminist scholars, there are some identifiable commonalities in feminist approaches to research. Building upon and adding to Judith Cook and Mary Margaret Fonow's analysis of feminist methodology, we will discuss five central "feminist ways of knowing."

1. *Acknowledging the pervasive influence of gender.* Gender and gender asymmetry are basic features of social life. Women, their worlds, and their subjective experiences, including their relationships to men and to gender inequality, are the focus. Subject to critique are claims about "human" behavior based on research on men. Indeed, the entire academic enterprise is subject to critique. How do claims to scientific and scholarly objectivity disguise male bias? How do the social conditions and practices of doing research reinscribe gender inequities? Central problems for feminist scholars include how research is done, how it is analyzed, and who does it in what kind of social settings with financial support from whom.

2. *Uncovering the links between gender and other asymmetric systems.* Feminist researchers understand systems of oppression as interlinking: race, class, ethnicity, sexual orientation, and other systems of domination inflect how one experiences gender oppression. Therefore, although gender asymmetry is a basic fact of social life, it is differently experienced by women situated differently in society. These differences in women's experiences are not to be ignored or dismissed, but uncovered. Just as feminist researchers challenge knowledge claims based on research on men, they question knowledge about "women" based on research on white women. In a highly self-reflexive manner, feminists question how their own scholarly practices and social locations (such as in an all-white academic department) bias their research and lead to false generalities.

3. *Focusing on consciousness-raising.* Consciousness-raising refers to the experience of recognizing through contact with other women (reading, research, discussion) how male-centeredness has affected the individual woman. Feminist research alters the consciousness of researchers. As members of a society, feminist researchers have incorporated cultural understandings about women; as feminists, they have analyzed official and inherited understandings in ways that reveal their implications for women's oppression. They have, therefore, as Liz Stanley and Sue Wise put it, "double vision". Women's lives are seen simultaneously through the old lens of patriarchy and the new lens of feminism. Having double vision helps feminist researchers to recognize the diversity of responses to oppression, and the contradictions between consciousness and action. Much feminist research looks at crisis points and transitions in women's lives, such as divorce, rape, coming out, pregnancy, menopause, sexual harassment, and career shifts. A transition ruptures the taken-for-granted world; at such times the "normalcy" of patriarchy is revealed to women, giving them an opportunity to rethink their lives.

4. *Rethinking the relationship between researcher and researched.* Scientific research assumes that there is a separation between the "researched" and the "researcher" and that this separation produces "objective" and "valid" knowledge. Feminist researchers challenge this tenet. Treating women as "objects" of research contravenes feminist goals for equality by elevating the researcher and the researcher's agenda above the researched and her agenda. One of the hottest areas of feminist thought is about how to do research that empowers both the researcher and the researched. How do we create social research practices that reduce the power of the researcher to collect, categorize, and name the experiences of other women? For some, the solution has been to work on their own biographies; some focus on how they have written their own biases into their work on other women;

some study the groups with which they are allied; others engage in "dialogic" research in which the interplay between the researcher and the researched is the research topic; and still others do "participatory research" where the "researcher" and the "researched" determine together the topics, methods, goals, and political action to follow from the research, so that the academic is a participant in the project, but not its leader.

The relationships between researcher and researched, moreover, are not only pragmatic or theoretical concerns. For contemporary feminist researchers these are salient *ethical* questions. What right does a scholar have to study and write about another woman's life? For whom should she write? Who should her audiences be? What do you do if, through your interviewing, for example, you have raised the consciousness of a woman but cannot change her life circumstances? How can feminist scholars use the skills and privileges of academic practice to improve the life opportunities of other women? Feminist research is thus characterized by a constant critique of the morality of its labors.

5. *Emphasizing empowerment and transformation.* Almost as a corollary to the above, feminist researchers are concerned with how their research can be used to improve the lives of women through individual empowerment or social change. Often this is embedded in the nature of the research problem and the method chosen to study it. For example, studies of battered women will often be based on interviews with women in battered women's shelters. The texts then tell the stories of individual women and the positive impact that the battered women's shelter movement has had on their lives. The results will be disseminated through different media with the hope of reaching other women caught in abusive relationships. The topics for feminist research are legion because the sites in need of transformation—such as work, family, sexual socialization, schooling, health care, and political arenas—are everywhere. Therefore, the opportunities for empowering women through one's research are, also, everywhere.

We invite you to engage in reading and doing feminist research. We hope that through that engagement, you will find how gender has shaped your life, and how gender intersects other systems of inequality that affect your life. We hope that you will share your understandings with others, becoming yourself a researcher of your own and others' lives so that we might all be empowered and society transformed.

Diversity and Difference

Conducting research about women has been the focus of feminist scholars from the 1960s to the present. In recent years, researchers have looked especially closely at the differences and commonalities among women. Scholars are interested in knowing about the rich complexities of women's lives and in discovering ways of knowing that stand true to women's experiences and also offer the prospect of effecting positive change. Differences among women include those which come from a variety of experiences based on race, class, sexual orientation, age, geographical region, and so on. Commonalities include living with the ubiquitous "monotone" of male advantage, in all its manifestations. Researchers constantly grapple with the twin problems of "*what* we know" and "*how* we know" it. As a result, these are exciting times to do feminist research because the topics and methods bring scholars into contact with a historical tradition concerning research on women and with multiple and newly evolving methods of knowing about women. The notion of "diversity and difference," then, applies not only to "other" women but to every woman and to every way of knowing about women's experiences. The notion itself raises the question of the bases of comparison and the grounds for affiliation.

One source of "commonality" that has attracted and shaped feminist understanding is the idea of *oppression*. As a concept, oppression has had a long history in contemporary feminist scholarship. What does it mean? Why is it important to think about it? The first selection, "Oppression," answers these questions and raises some others. In that article, Marilyn Frye defines oppression as "living one's life confined and shaped by forces and barriers which are not accidental or occasional and hence avoidable, but are systematically related to each other in such a way as to catch one between and among them and restrict or penalize motion in any direction." There are, then, multiple sources of interrelated oppressions making it difficult for people to recognize how the systems of oppression impinge on their lives or the lives of others. Knowing about the larger social forces, however, helps one to understand the shape of one's life and the difference between "suffering" and "suffering from oppression."

The difficulties of sensitively and accurately identifying how systems of oppression affect a person's life are further amplified in "The Master's Tools Will Never Dismantle the Master's House." In this article, Audre Lorde argues that feminists must critically examine their own use of patriarchal concepts in their analyses of women's lives. Will the "regular" methods of scholarship and science be adequate to the task of understanding the diversity between women? Will new tools be necessary? Furthermore, she argues that encouraging women to relate at the points of their differences promotes growth, creativity, and social change. Women, she proposes, gain more through celebrating their differences than in trying to erase them.

The feminist concern with "*how* we know" is a recurrent theme amongst scholars. The relevance of the question is not, however, simply "academic."

What feminist scholars are struggling with are questions concerning who has the authority to call "something" knowledge, and where that authority comes from. Science is one of the systems of knowledge that is being challenged. In "After the Science Question in Feminism," Sandra Harding explicates feminist critiques of science. She discusses the dilemmas raised by those critiques and identifies five specific issues that need to be rethought. She concludes that science is but one way of understanding the world, a set of "beliefs and practices" used by people of the modern West, and that we must understand its limitations and power in order to challenge its role in perpetuating inequities.

Making visible a black woman's standpoint is the goal of Patricia Hill Collins's article, "The Social Construction of Black Feminist Thought." Hill Collins posits that African-American women's political and economic experiences have allowed them to develop a particular analysis of racism and sexism in the United States, as well as specific strategies of resistance. Hill Collins's analysis challenges the notions that oppressed groups are not conscious of their oppression and are somehow less capable than their oppressors of understanding the relations of ruling.

Linking the ideas of "how we know" and "what we know" to underexamined systems of oppression, Rosalinda Méndez González discusses "Distinctions in Western Women's Experience: Ethnicity, Class, and Social Change." In her article, she reconsiders the meaning of the "winning of the West" (whose win? whose loss?) and "women going west" (which women? from where?). González alerts us to the ways in which historical and social-scientific research, including early feminist research, has unconsciously picked up the "master's tools," rendering invisible the experiences of nondominant women. She argues that one way to overcome the problems is to understand how large-scale systems of oppression have created commonalities of experience for minority women.

Oppression

MARILYN FRYE

It is a fundamental claim of feminism that women are oppressed. The word 'oppression' is a strong word. It repels and attracts. It is dangerous and dangerously fashionable and endangered. It is much misused, and sometimes not innocently.

The statement that women are oppressed is frequently met with the claim that men are oppressed too. We hear that oppressing is oppressive to those who oppress as well as to those they oppress. Some men cite as evidence of their oppression their much-advertised inability to cry. It is tough, we are told, to be masculine. When the stresses and frustrations of being a man are cited as evidence that oppressors are oppressed by their oppressing; the word 'oppression' is being stretched to meaninglessness; it is treated as though its scope includes any and all human experience of limitation or suffering, no matter the cause, degree or consequence. Once such usage has been put over on us, then if ever we deny that any person or group is oppressed, we seem to imply that we think they never suffer and have no feelings. We are accused of insensitivity; even of bigotry. For women, such accusation is particularly intimidating, since sensitivity is one of the few virtues that has been assigned to us. If we are found insensitive, we may fear we have no redeeming traits at all and perhaps are not real women. Thus are we silenced before we begin: the name of our situation drained of meaning and our guilt mechanisms tripped.

But this is nonsense. Human beings can be miserable without being oppressed, and it is perfectly consistent to deny that a person or group is oppressed without denying that they have feelings or that they suffer. . . .

"Oppression," copyright © 1983 by Marilyn Frye from *The Politics of Reality,* The Crossing Press, Freedom, Ga.

The root of the word 'oppression' is the element 'press'. *The press of the crowd; pressed into military service; to press a pair of pants; printing press; press the button.* Presses are used to mold things or flatten them or reduce them in bulk, sometimes to reduce them by squeezing out the gasses or liquids in them. Something pressed is something caught between or among forces and barriers which are so related to each other that jointly they restrain, restrict or prevent the thing's motion or mobility. Mold. Immobilize. Reduce.

The mundane experience of the oppressed provides another clue. One of the most characteristic and ubiquitous features of the world as experienced by oppressed people is the double bind—situations in which options are reduced to a very few and all of them expose one to penalty, censure or deprivation. For example, it is often a requirement upon oppressed people that we smile and be cheerful. If we comply, we signal our docility and our acquiescence in our situation. We need not, then, be taken note of. We acquiesce in being made invisible, in our occupying no space. We participate in our own erasure. On the other hand, anything but the sunniest countenance exposes us to being perceived as mean, bitter, angry or dangerous. This means, at the least, that we may be found "difficult" or unpleasant to work with, which is enough to cost one one's livelihood; at worst, being seen as mean, bitter, angry or dangerous has been known to result in rape, arrest, beating and murder. One can only choose to risk one's preferred form and rate of annihilation.

Another example: It is common in the United States that women, especially younger women, are in a bind where neither sexual activity nor sexual inactivity is all right. If she is heterosexually active, a woman is open to censure and punishment for being loose, unprincipled or a whore. The "punishment" comes in the form of criticism, snide and embarrassing remarks, being treated as an easy lay by men, scorn from her more restrained female friends. She may have to lie and hide her behavior from her parents. She must juggle the risks of unwanted pregnancy and dangerous contraceptives. On the other hand, if she refrains from heterosexual activity, she is fairly constantly harassed by men who try to persuade her into it and pressure her to "relax" and "let her hair down"; she is threatened with labels like "frigid," "uptight," "man-hater," "bitch" and "cocktease." The same parents who would be disapproving of her sexual activity may be worried by her inactivity because it suggests she is not or will not be popular, or is not sexually normal. She may be charged with lesbianism. If a woman is raped, then if she has been heterosexually active she is subject to the presumption that she liked it (since her activity is presumed to show that she likes sex), and if she has not been heterosexually active, she is subject to the presumption that she liked it (since she is supposedly "repressed and frustrated"). Both heterosexual activity and heterosexual nonactivity are likely to be taken as proof that you wanted to be raped, and hence, of course, weren't *really* raped at all. You can't win. You are caught in a bind, caught between systematically related pressures.

Women are caught like this, too, by networks of forces and barriers that expose one to penalty, loss or contempt whether one works outside the home or not, is on welfare or not, bears children or not, raises children or not, marries or not, stays married or not, is heterosexual, lesbian, both or neither. Economic necessity; confinement to racial and/or sexual job ghettos; sexual harassment; sex discrimination; pressures of competing expectations and judgments about *women, wives* and *mothers* (in the society at large, in racial and ethnic subcultures and in one's own mind); dependence (full or partial) on husbands, parents or the state; commitment to political ideas; loyalties to racial or ethnic or other "minority" groups; the demands of self-respect and responsibilities to others. Each of these factors exists in complex tension with every other, penalizing or prohibiting all of the apparently available options. And nipping at one's heels, always, is the endless pack of little things. If one dresses one way, one is subject to the assumption that one is advertising one's sexual availability; if one dresses another way, one appears to "not care about oneself" or to be "unfeminine." If one uses "strong language," one invites categorization as a whore or slut; if one does not, one invites categorization as a "lady"—one too delicately constituted to cope with robust speech or the realities to which it presumably refers.

The experience of oppressed people is that the living of one's life is confined and shaped by forces and barriers which are not accidental or occasional and hence avoidable, but are systematically related to each other in such a way as to catch one between and among them and restrict or penalize motion in any direction. It is the experience of being caged in: all avenues, in every direction, are blocked or booby trapped.

Cages. Consider a birdcage. If you look very closely at just one wire in the cage, you cannot see the other wires. If your conception of what is before you is determined by this myopic focus, you could look at that one wire, up and down the length of it, and be unable to see why a bird would not just fly around the wire any time it wanted to go somewhere. Furthermore, even if, one day at a time, you myopically inspected each wire, you still could not see why a bird would have trouble going past the wires to get anywhere. There is no physical property of any one wire, *nothing* that the closest scrutiny could discover, that will reveal how a bird could be inhibited or harmed by it except in the most accidental way. It is only when you step back, stop looking at the wires one by one, microscopically, and take a macroscopic view of the whole cage, that you can see why the bird does not go anywhere; and then you will see it in a moment. It will require no great subtlety of mental powers. It is perfectly *obvious* that the bird is surrounded by a network of systematically related barriers, no one of which would be the least hindrance to its flight, but which, by their relations to each other, are as confining as the solid walls of a dungeon.

It is now possible to grasp one of the reasons why oppression can be hard to see and recognize: one can study the elements of an oppressive structure with great care and some good will without seeing the structure as a whole, and hence without seeing or being able to understand that one is looking at a cage and that there are people there who are caged, whose motion and mobility are restricted, whose lives are shaped and reduced.

The arresting of vision at a microscopic level yields such common confusion as that about the male door-opening ritual. This ritual, which is remarkably widespread across classes and races, puzzles many people, some of whom do and some of whom do not find it offensive. Look at the scene of the two people approaching a door. The male steps slightly ahead and opens the door. The male holds the door open while the female glides through. Then the male goes through. The door closes after them. "Now how," one innocently asks, "can those crazy womenslibbers say that is oppressive? The guy *removed* a barrier to the lady's smooth and unruffled progress." But each repetition of this ritual has a place in a pattern, in fact in several patterns. One has to shift the level of one's perception in order to see the whole picture.

The door-opening pretends to be a helpful service, but the helpfulness is false. This can be seen by noting that it will be done whether or not it makes any practical sense. Infirm men and men burdened with packages will open doors for able-bodied women who are free of physical burdens. Men will impose themselves awkwardly and jostle everyone in order to get to the door first. The act is not determined by convenience or grace. Furthermore, these very numerous acts of unneeded or even noisome "help" occur in counterpoint to a pattern of men not being helpful in many practical ways in which women might welcome help. What *women* experience is a world in which gallant princes charming commonly make a fuss about being helpful and providing small services when help and services are of little or no use, but in which there are rarely ingenious and adroit princes at hand when substantial assistance is really wanted either in mundane affairs or in situations of threat, assault or terror. There is no help with the (his) laundry; no help typing a report at 4:00 a.m.; no help in mediating disputes among relatives or children. There is nothing but advice that women should stay indoors after dark, be chaperoned by a man, or when it comes down to it, "lie back and enjoy it."

The gallant gestures have no practical meaning. Their meaning is symbolic. The door-opening and similar services provided are services which really are needed by people who are for one reason or another incapacitated—unwell, burdened with parcels, etc. So the message is that women are incapable. The detachment of the acts from the concrete realities of what women need and do not need is a vehicle for the message that women's actual needs and interests are unimportant or irrelevant. Finally, these gestures imitate the behavior of servants toward masters and thus mock women, who are in most respects the servants and caretakers of men. The message of the false helpfulness of male gallantry is female dependence, the invisibility or insignificance of women, and contempt for women.

One cannot see the meanings of these rituals if one's focus is riveted upon the individual event in all its particularity, including the particularity of the individual man's present conscious intentions and motives and the individual woman's conscious perception of the event in the moment. It seems sometimes that people take a deliberately myopic view and fill their eyes with things seen microscopically in order not to see macroscopically. At any rate, whether it is deliberate or not, people can and do fail to see the oppression of women because they fail to see macroscopically and hence fail to see the various elements of the situation as systematically related in larger schemes.

As the cageness of the birdcage is a macroscopic phenomenon, the oppressiveness of the situations in which women live our various and different lives is a macroscopic phenomenon. Neither can be *seen* from a microscopic perspective. But when you look macroscopically you can see it—a network of forces and barriers which are systematically related and which conspire to the immobilization, reduction and molding of women and the lives we live.

READING 2

The Master's Tools Will Never Dismantle the Master's House

AUDRE LORDE

I agreed to take part in a New York University Institute for the Humanities conference a year ago, with the understanding that I would be commenting upon papers dealing with the role of difference within the lives of american [sic] women: difference of race, sexuality, class, and age. The absence of these considerations weakens any feminist discussion of the personal and the political.

It is a particular academic arrogance to assume any discussion of feminist theory without examining our many differences, and without a significant input from poor women, Black and Third World women, and lesbians. And yet, I stand here as a Black lesbian feminist, having been invited to comment within the only panel at this conference where the input of Black feminists and lesbians is represented. What this says about the vision of this conference is sad, in a country where racism, sexism, and homophobia are inseparable. To read this program is to assume that lesbian and Black women have nothing to say about existentialism, the erotic, women's culture and silence, developing feminist theory, or heterosexuality and power. And what does it mean in personal and political terms when even the two Black women who did present here were literally found at the last hour? What does it mean when the tools of a racist patriarchy are used to examine the fruits of that same patriarchy? It means that only the most narrow perimeters of change are possible and allowable.

The absence of any consideration of lesbian consciousness or the consciousness of Third World women leaves a serious gap within this conference and within the papers presented here. For example, in a paper on material relationships between women, I was conscious of an either/or model of nurturing which totally dismissed my knowledge as a Black lesbian. In this paper there was no examination of mutuality between women, no systems of shared support, no interdependence as exists between lesbians and women-identified women. Yet it is only in the patriarchal model of nurturance that women "who attempt to emancipate themselves pay perhaps too high a price for the results," as this paper states.

For women, the need and desire to nurture each other is not pathological but redemptive, and it is within that knowledge that our real power is rediscovered. It is this real connection which is so feared by a patriarchal world. Only within a patriarchal structure is maternity the only social power open to women.

Interdependency between women is the way to a freedom which allows the *I* to *be*, not in order to be used, but in order to be creative. This is a difference between the passive *be* and the active *being*.

Advocating the mere tolerance of difference between women is the grossest reformism. It is a total denial of the creative function of difference in our lives. Difference must be not merely tolerated, but seen as a fund of necessary polarities between which our creativity can spark like a dialectic. Only then does the necessity for interdependency become unthreatening. Only within that interdependency of different strengths, acknowledged and equal, can the power to seek new ways of being in the world generate, as well as the courage and sustenance to act where there are no charters.

Copyright © 1984 by Audre Lorde, excerpted from *Sister Outsider*, published by the Crossing Press and reprinted with permission from the Charlotte Sheedy Literary Agency Inc.

Within the interdependence of mutual (nondominant) differences lies that security which enables us to descend into the chaos of knowledge and return with true visions of our future, along with the concomitant power to effect those changes which can bring that future into being. Difference is that raw and powerful connection from which our personal power is forged.

As women, we have been taught either to ignore our differences, or to view them as causes for separation and suspicion rather than as forces for change. Without community there is no liberation, only the most vulnerable and temporary armistice between an individual and her oppression. But community must not mean a shedding of our differences, nor the pathetic pretense that these differences do not exist.

Those of us who stand outside the circle of this society's definition of acceptable women; those of us who have been forged in the crucibles of difference—those of us who are poor, who are lesbians, who are Black, who are older—know that *survival is not an academic skill.* It is learning how to stand alone, unpopular and sometimes reviled, and how to make common cause with those others identified as outside the structures in order to define and seek a world in which we can all flourish. It is learning how to take our differences and make them strengths. *For the master's tools will never dismantle the master's house.* They may allow us temporarily to beat him at his own game, but they will never enable us to bring about genuine change. And this fact is only threatening to those women who still define the master's house as their only source of support.

Poor women and women of Color know there is a difference between the daily manifestations of marital slavery and prostitution because it is our daughters who line 42nd Street. If white american [sic] feminist theory need not deal with the differences between us, and the resulting difference in our oppressions, then how do you deal with the fact that the women who clean your houses and tend your children while you attend conferences on feminist theory are, for the most part, poor women and women of Color? What is the theory behind racist feminism?

In a world of possibility for us all, our personal visions help lay the groundwork for political action. The failure of academic feminists to recognize difference as a crucial strength is a failure to reach beyond the first patriarchal lesson. In our world, divide and conquer must become define and empower.

Why weren't other women of Color found to participate in this conference? Why were two phone calls to me considered a consultation? Am I the only possible source of names of Black feminists? And although the Black panelist's paper ends on an important and powerful connection of love between women, what about interracial cooperation between feminists who don't love each other?

In academic feminist circles, the answer to these questions is often, "We did not know who to ask." But that is the same evasion of responsibility, the same cop-out, that keeps Black women's art out of women's exhibitions, Black women's work out of most feminist publications except for the occasional "Special Third World Women's Issue," and Black women's texts off your reading lists. But as Adrienne Rich pointed out in a recent talk, white feminists have educated themselves about such an enormous amount over the past ten years, how come you haven't also educated yourselves about Black women and the differences between us—white and Black—when it is key to our survival as a movement?

Women of today are still being called upon to stretch across the gap of male ignorance and to educate men as to our existence and our needs. This is an old and primary tool of all oppressors to keep the oppressed occupied with the master's concerns. Now we hear that it is the task of women of Color to educate white women—in the face of tremendous resistance—as to our existence, our differences, our relative roles in our joint survival. This is a diversion of energies and a tragic repetition of racist patriarchal thought.

Simone de Beauvoir once said: "It is in the knowledge of the genuine conditions of our lives that we must draw our strength to live and our reasons for acting."

Racism and homophobia are real conditions of all our lives in this place and time. *I urge each one of us here to reach down into that deep place of knowledge inside herself and touch that terror and loathing of any difference that lives there. See whose face it wears.* Then the personal as the political can begin to illuminate all our choices.

After the Science Question in Feminism

SANDRA HARDING

The feminist discussions of science, technology, and theories of knowledge occur at a moment of rising skepticism about the benefits that the sciences and their technologies can bring to society. Calls for reforms and transformations have arisen from many different groups. However, these discussions also occur when intellectuals in the fields of science and technology are gaining more and more power in higher education and in government.

Feminists themselves are of at least three minds about the sciences. They (we) criticize not only "bad science" but also the problematics, agendas, ethics, consequences, and status of what has come to be called "science-as-usual." The criticisms of science-as-usual are made in the context of a call for better science: important tendencies within feminism propose to provide empirically more adequate and theoretically less partial and distorted descriptions and explanations of women, men, gender relations, and the rest of the social and natural worlds, including how the sciences did, do, and could function. From theorists who draw on European philosophy, however, comes criticism of the very idea of trying to reconstruct science, whether or not in feminist ways. These feminists appear to be arguing that there is no baby to be found in the bath water we would throw out. Additionally, analyses flow from not just one but many feminisms, each increasingly well developed in both theoretical and historical terms. Consequently, feminist analysts of science, technology, and epistemology disagree with one another over many important aspects of these issues.

Reprinted from Sandra Harding, *Whose Science? Whose Knowledge? Thinking from Women's Lives.* Copyright © 1991 by Cornell University. Used by permission of the publisher, Cornell University Press.

FEMINISM AND SCIENCE: A CONFUSING MOMENT

Skepticism about the Sciences

Modern Western sciences and their technologies have always been regarded with both enthusiasm and dread. On the one hand, we tend to attribute to them at least some responsibility for the high standards of living that many in the West enjoy—especially if we are white and middle or upper class. It is unimaginable to us that we could want to give up the food and clothing, medical treatment, cars and airplanes, computers, television sets, and telephones that have become available through scientific and technological development. On the other hand, just who or what is responsible for atomic bombs, Agent Orange, industrial exploitation, polluted air and vast oil spills, dangerous contraceptives such as Dalkon shields, inappropriate uses of Valium, health profiteering, high infant mortality in the United States, famine in Ethiopia, and the development of a black underclass in the United States? Conventionalists insist that science get full credit for the good aspects of the "Western way of life" but that such "misuses and abuses" are entirely the fault either of politicians or of the industries that apply supposedly pure information in socially irresponsible ways.

The insistence on this separation between the work of pure scientific inquiry and the work of technology and applied science has long been recognized as one important strategy in the attempt of Western elites to avoid taking responsibility for the origins and consequences of the sciences and their technologies or for the interests, desires, and values they promote. From a sociological perspective, it is virtually irresistible to regard contemporary science as fundamentally a social problem. Sal Restivo has argued that it should be conceptualized as no different in this respect from alcoholism, crime, excessive drug use, and poverty.[1] The name "Frankenstein," which Mary Shelley gave to the scientist in her dystopian novel, has in popular thought migrated to the monster he inadvertently created. How the monster actually got created—and gets nourished and reproduced day after day—retreats into the shadows, as if there are no persons or institutional practices that we can hold responsible for the shape of the sciences and the kind of social order with which they have been in partnership.

These kinds of issues have been raised by feminists . . . but they are certainly not what is unique about feminist analyses. In one form or another, such concerns are voiced by the ecology and environmental movement, the peace movement, the animals rights movement, leftist and worker movements, and antiracist and antiimperialist movements in both the West and the Third World. Even "postmodernist" criticisms of the philosophical foundations of Western rationality should be regarded as part of the counterculture of science. What is at issue for all these critics, including feminists, is not only the easily identifiable theories, methods, institutions, and technological consequences of the sciences but also something harder to describe: the Western scientific world view or mind-set. The "indigenous peoples" of the modern West—those most at home in Western societies—have culturally distinctive belief patterns in which scientific rationality plays a central role. These "natives," like all others, have trouble even recognizing that they exhibit culturally distinctive patterns of belief; it is like discovering that one speaks a distinctive genre—prose. From an anthropological perspective, faith in scientific rationality is at least partly responsible for many of the Western beliefs and behaviors that appear most irrational to people whose life patterns and projects do not so easily fit with those of the modern West. From the perspective of women's lives, scientific rationality frequently appears irrational.

Still, scientific rationality certainly is not as monolithic or determinist as many think or as the description above suggests. Nor is it all "bad." It has been versatile and flexible enough throughout its history to permit constant reinterpretation of what should count as legitimate objects and processes of scientific research; it is itself shaped by cultural transformations and must struggle within them; and it is inherently no better or worse than other widespread social assumptions that have appealed to groups with different and sometimes conflicting agendas. Perhaps even liberalism and feminism would provide examples, since both have at times been associated with racist and bourgeois projects, even though at other times they have advanced struggles against racism and class exploitation. It is one theme of this book that modern Western science contains both progressive and regressive tendencies, and that our task must be to advance the former and block the latter. Indeed, scientific rationality can make possible the transformation of its own agendas; critics from feminist and other scientific countercultures certainly intend to use it for this purpose.

The Rising Status of the Intellectuals in Science and Technology

Increased participation in the countercultures of the sciences occurs just when the prestige of the intellectuals in science and technology is rising in higher education and the government. Scientists have been held in high regard since Sputnik, of course—indeed, even since Newton[2]—but the flood of industrial and federal funds that pours into scientific and technological projects in universities these days is truly astounding. It is a long time since scientific research could be regarded as significantly isolated in real life from the goals of the state and industry—if it ever could. Scientific research is an important part of the economic base of modern Western societies.

No doubt envy plays a certain role in the criticism of science. Scholars from the humanities and social sciences perceive themselves increasingly working in offices cramped into university attics and basements as new science and engineering buildings open; they lose what they think are too many of the best graduate students to the sciences and engineering as they lose support for graduate programs. More and more they find themselves reporting to deans, provosts, presidents, chancellors, and trustees whose backgrounds are in science and engineering and who intend to take universities where the money is flowing. How could they justify not doing so, these administrators ask.

Intellectuals in science and technology do not see their situation as rosy. One can hardly open a science journal or even an airline magazine without finding hand-wringing projections of a shortage of scientists and engineers. It has gotten so bad, they say, that in order to "keep America strong" they are even willing to develop special programs to recruit women and minorities to science, mathematics, and engineering departments. This institutional setting needs to be kept in mind when one thinks about the "postmodernist" criticisms of the philosophical foundations of modern science. The attractions of the postmodernist critique are many,[3] but among them are surely its perceived usefulness as a means to restore status to the humanities, status that has stolen away to science and technology without public discussion of the benefits and losses of such a move.[4] The intellectual fundamentalism of Allan Bloom and the "back to the classics" movement in the United States is another critical response to the rise in status of science and technology. The countercultures of science have at least the beginnings of a realistic assessment of possible futures for the West, an assessment that is lacking in intellectual fundamentalism.

The Need for New Sciences

It is at this moment that feminism and other liberatory social movements appear on the scene with agendas that include generating new sciences. Women need sciences and technologies that are *for* women and that are for women in *every class, race, and culture.* Feminists (male and female) want to close the gender gap in scientific and technological literacy, to invent modes of thought and learn the existing techniques and skills that will enable women to get more control over the conditions of their lives. Such sciences can and must benefit men, too—especially those marginalized by racism, imperialism, and class exploitation; the new sciences are not to be *only* for women. But it is time to ask what sciences would look like that were *for* "female men," all of them, and not primarily for the white, Western, and economically advantaged "male men" toward whom benefit from the sciences has disproportionately tended to flow. Moreover, it is time to examine critically the conflicting interests in science that women in opposing classes and races may well have; women's interests are not homogeneous. Feminism insists that questions be asked of nature, of social relations, and of the sciences different from those that "prefeminists" have asked, whether conventional or countercultural. How can women manage their lives in the context of sciences and technologies designed and directed by powerful institutions that

appear to have few interests in creating social relations beneficial to anyone but those in the dominant groups?

Thus, though it would be foolish to deny that science is a major social problem, we can ask who benefits from regarding it as *nothing but* a social problem. Possible scientific beliefs and practices are not limited to those that have already existed, let alone to that subset that has existed in the modern West. It is complicitous with the dominant ideology to assert that everything deserving the name of science has been done in the modern West. Nevertheless, we must contend realistically with what the West has done with its sciences. It is important for the countercultures to struggle with science and technology on the existing social terrains while they also try to envision and plan different social environments for science in the future.

The Diversity of Feminist Analyses

Feminist analyses of science, technology, and knowledge are not monolithic. There is no single set of claims beyond a few generalities that could be called "feminism" without controversy among feminists. (The same could be said about sexism or androcentrism or nonfeminism, which can also claim diverse historical frameworks and projects: Aristotle is not Freud.) The feminist science discussions are both enriched and constrained by the different political, practical, and conceptual perspectives that they bring to bear on science, its beliefs, practices, and institutions.

This is a good place to note that the term "feminism" is itself a contested zone not only within feminism but also between feminism and its critics. It is widely used as a critical epithet in the Second and Third Worlds and in some Western subcultures, by women as well as by men, to prevent women from organizing across class, race, and national borders and even just to "keep women in their place."[5] It is also important to note that widespread tendency in the West, at least, for women and men to insist that they are absolutely not feminists but then to advance the very same intellectual and political programs that are promoted by others under the label of feminism. These nonfeminists too are for ending violence against women, the sexual exploitation of women, women's poverty, job discrimination against women, the exclusion of women from public office, unequal educational opportunities, sexist biological and sociological and historical claims, and so on. For these people, "feminism" appears a handy label for those elements in feminism from which they wish to distance themselves—and it is the Eurocentric, racist, bourgeois, and heterosexist elements in feminism, as well as the vigorous opposition to them, from which different groups wish to distance themselves.

I think it is important to try to distinguish regressive from progressive tendencies in peoples' actions and beliefs and to support the progressive tendencies, whether or not others think about them in just the way I do. What appears to be radical and progressive from the perspective of some women's lives may be too conservative, too dangerous, or just irrelevant from the perspective of other women's lives. If feminism is a term people find appropriate to their attempts to improve women's conditions, they will use it. It would be regressive and ethnocentric for me to decide for them that they should adopt a term I find useful in my world. Nevertheless, I do use the word throughout this book, since I can assume that the majority of readers will find it appropriate here.

Several distinctive traditions of thought within which feminists have analyzed human nature, the fundamental causes of women's inferior conditions, and what should be done to change those conditions generate different issues about science, technology, and epistemology. Most important are the "grand theory" traditions that borrow from Western political theory: liberal feminism and traditional Marxist feminism. We should also include in this group the African American feminism that has strong roots, we are now learning, in the nineteenth-century struggles of African American women.[6] Then there are the now well-developed feminisms that emerged in the politics of the 1960s: radical feminism, socialist feminism, and the feminisms of racially marginalized women both in the West and in the Third World, some associated with national liberation struggles.[7] Other feminist political orientations and traditions can be located within and alongside these: anarchist feminism, Jewish feminism, lesbian and gay feminisms, antimilitarist feminism, ecology-focused feminism, and others. Most of these feminists also work in other intellectual and political movements, as their compound identities indicate. Each of these "movement" orientations brings unique concerns and approaches to discussions of gender, science, and knowledge.

Moreover, feminists work in diverse social settings. In the United States we work in battered women's shelters and rape crisis centers, in agencies for international development and mainstream political organizations, in law and medicine, in child-care and organizational management, in factories and secretarial pools, in computer programming and therapy—not to mention in laboratories and women's studies programs. And we experience the consequences of developments in science and technology not only at work but also as pregnant women and mothers, as sick or old, as pedestrians or drivers, and every time we eat or even breathe. We experience science and technology in our everyday lives, in the struggles for dignity and survival that women engage in daily on behalf of their kin and community as well as themselves.[8] In Western Europe and the Second and Third Worlds, there are other culturally specific daily activities of women that produce distinctive experiences of Western science and technology. It is in different and conflicting ways that women experience modern science and technology in each of these locations. Analyses from these different social perspectives have contributed insights—sometimes contradictory ones—to our understanding of the sciences and their technologies.

Additionally, the conceptual frameworks and current agendas of our disciplines and the various approaches within them have provided important resources for feminist science discussions. Feminist analyses have drawn from the history of science, focused on intellectual or social history, formal and informal institutions, economic history, or the history of individuals; from the sociology of science, focused on the structure of occupations, the workings of institutions, the legitimation of erroneous belief, the class structure of science, the sociology of knowledge, or the microstructure of laboratory life; from the philosophy of science, informed by traditional rationalist and empiricist agendas, Marxist epistemology, critical theory, the postmodernism of Jean-François Lyotard, Michel Foucault, Richard Rorty. All these theoretical and disciplinary frameworks—and others, such as literary criticism, psychoanalysis, and even art history—have provided rich resources for the study of gender and science.[9] At the same time, the "prefeminist" schemes have limited or obscured important ways in which the relations between women, gender, and science could and should be analyzed.

A Complex and Changing Environment for Discussion

The joint action of these various competing and inter-acting forces in the terrain in which feminism also operates—indeed, feminism is also part of all of these other tendencies—will have consequences different from those one might imagine from the perspective of the feminist critiques alone. It is as if we were at the point at which bands of men and women leave the familiar streets of their different neighborhoods to join an ongoing march down a boulevard. We watch each band struggle to maintain its identity and carry its banners forward as it is jostled by boisterous groups with similar intent. As the crowd surges forward, some people leave their group to join others; some groups merge, and others disappear. The words of anthems change, and the inadvertent harmonies and dishar-monies created when one hears two bands playing at once suggest previously unimaginable musical possi-bilities—not all of them desirable. The necessity to struggle to advance their goals in the environment of everyone else's equally determined efforts creates configurations different from those of individual groups marching alone. Similarly, feminist tendencies must struggle against, with, and within these other streams of contemporary intellectual, political, and social life. The consequences of these interactions can-not but be surprising to everyone.

Challenges

Five issues that are at present emerging in one form or another from recent analyses of science, technology, epistemology, and feminism shape my concerns. . . . The challenge in each case is to develop conceptual frameworks that are theoretically rich enough and empirically adequate to enable us to think what appear at first to be contradictory thoughts.

(1) Science is politics by other means, and it also generates reliable information about the empirical world. Science is more than politics, of course, but it is that. It is a contested terrain and has been so from its origins. Groups with conflicting social agendas have struggled to gain control of the social resources that the sciences—their "information," their technologies, and their prestige—can provide. For those who have suffered from what seem to be the consequences of the sciences, their technologies, and their forms of ration-ality, it appears absurd to regard science as the value-free, disinterested, impartial, Archimedean *arbiter* of conflicting agendas, as conventional mythology holds.

And yet sciences created through political struggles, which are the only ones we have ever had, usually do produce reliable information about nature and social relations—reliable, that is, for some group or another's purposes. They are no less sciences for being driven by particular historical and political projects.

There are few resources in the conventional philos-ophy of science, epistemology, or sociology of science, however, which permit the articulation and exploration of these seemingly contradictory understandings. It is a challenge for feminism and other countercultures of science to develop conceptual frameworks that encour-age widespread discussion of this apparently contradic-tory character of science.

(2) Science contains both progressive and regressive tendencies. So does feminism. To say this about sci-ence is to oppose the view that "science is inherently good, although it is sometimes applied in regressive ways." And it is to oppose the view that "science is inherently value-neutral, although it can be used in progressive or regressive ways." It is to oppose both views because they refuse to recognize that the social origins of science and the values it carries suffuse scientific projects. A critical examination of these origins and values can be carried out as part of the project of science, however. The very scientific ration-ality that has been the object of criticism from so many quarters contains the resources for its own transforma-tion. Thus, what science becomes in any historical era depends upon what we make of it.

The same can be said of feminism. It too contains both progressive and regressive tendencies. It is not usefully conceptualized without qualification as inher-ently good—and of course no one characterizes it as value-neutral—because its origins and the values it carries clearly shape its projects. Those of its ten-dencies that focus on male supremacy and gender rela-tions without giving equal weight to other important aspects of social relations can provide resources for Eurocentrism, racism, imperialism, compulsory hetero-sexism, and class exploitative beliefs and practices—whether or not such a result is overtly or consciously intended. But it also contains tendencies that can con-tribute sturdy resources to the elimination of these forms of oppression, exploitation, and domination.

It is a challenge for feminism and other contemporary countercultures of science to figure out just which are the regressive and which the progressive tendencies brought into play in any particular scientific or feminist project, and how to advance the progressive and inhibit the regressive ones. The countercultures of science must elicit and address these contradictory elements in the sciences and scientific consciousness (and feminists must continue to do so with their various feminisms). The alternative is that regressive forces in the larger society manipulate these contradictory features and mobilize the progressive tendencies for their own ends. For example, international financiers appeal to belief in scientific and technological progress to gain support for technology transfers to the Third World which deteriorate the power of people there to control their lives. In the West it appears that there must be something wrong with "those people" if they cannot progress even when "gifted" with the supposed fruits of First World science and technology. Industries appeal to feminist themes about the importance of new health standards for women in order to produce profit from the sales of sporting goods, cosmetics, and so-called "health food."

(3) The observer and the observed are in the same causal scientific plane. An outpouring of recent studies in every area of the social studies of the sciences forces the recognition that all scientific knowledge is always, in every respect, socially situated.[10] Neither knowers nor the knowledge they produce are or could be impartial, disinterested, value-neutral, Archimedean. The challenge is to articulate how it is that knowledge has a socially situated character denied to it by the conventional view, and to work through the transformations that this conception of knowledge requires of conventional notions such as objectivity, relativism, rationality, and reflexivity.

Another way to put the issue is to note that if science is created only within political struggles, as mentioned above, then our "best beliefs," not just the least defensible ones, have social causes.[11] This means that observers and their subject matters are in the same social, political, economic, and psychological scientific planes. If, as the social sciences hold, class and race and gender relations must be called on to explain observable patterns in the social beliefs and behaviors of other people—of health profiteers, or the Ku Klux Klan, or rapists—then other aspects of those very kinds of relations have probably shaped the "empirically supported," "confirmed by evidence," and therefore less

false results of our own fine research projects as well. We should think of the social location of our own research—the place in race, gender, and class relations from which it originates and from which it receives its empirical support—as part of the implicit or explicit evidence for our best claims as well as our worst ones.

One consequence of this claim is that we can understand how inanimate nature *simulates* encultured humans in that it always comes to us culturally preconstructed as a possible object of knowledge, just as do humans. Humans construct themselves as possible objects of knowledge and have also constructed inanimate nature as a possible object of knowledge. We cannot "strip nature bare" to "reveal her secrets," as conventional views have held, for no matter how long the striptease continues or how rigorous its choreography, we will always find under each "veil" only nature-as-conceptualized-within-cultural-projects; we will always (but not only) find more veils. Moreover, the very attempt to strip nature bare weaves more veils, it turns out. Nature-as-an-object-of-knowledge simulates culture, and science is part of the cultural activity that continually produces nature-as-an-object-of-knowledge in culturally specific forms.

Neither the conventional nor the countercultural science discussions have developed conceptually rich enough or empirically adequate frameworks to enable critical thought about the fact or consequences of recognizing that observers and observed are in the same scientific field. This understanding brings into sight a new kind of agent of both knowledge and history.

(4) It is necessary to decenter white, middle-class, heterosexual, Western women in Western feminist thought and yet still generate feminist analyses from the perspective of women's lives. Feminists have argued for the decentering of masculinity in society's thoughts and practices: no longer should manliness (however that is culturally defined) be the standard for the so-called human; no longer should masculinity and its widespread expressions across the canvas of cultural life be the preoccupation of everyone's anxious attention. The centering of men's needs, interests, desires, visions ensures only partial and distorted understandings and social practices. (And it *must* be possible for women to criticize this institutionalization of masculinity without being thought to "hate men.")

But then it is also necessary to decenter the preoccupations of white, economically advantaged, heterosexual, and Western feminists in the thinking and politics of feminists with these characteristics. No longer should their needs, interests, desires, and visions be permitted to set the standard for feminist visions of the human or to enjoy so much attention in feminist writings. How can this decentering be enacted in the discussions and practices of feminist science and technology? What will be feminist about them if they are not grounded in the presumed common lives of women?

One way to approach this issue is to keep in mind the argument of Jane Flax and others that gender is fundamentally a relation, not a thing.[12] That is, masculine and feminine are always defined "against each other," though the "content" of womanliness and manliness can vary immensely. Furthermore, as Judith Butler argues, gender is not an "interior state" but a performance that each of us acts and reenacts daily.[13] Moreover, we can see that the relationship picked out by "woman" or "man" is always a historically situated one. It is not constructed by relations between men and women in general, for there are no such persons and therefore no such relations. Nor are the gender relations between men and women in any particular group shaped only by the men and women in that group, for those relations too are always shaped by how men and women are defined in every other race, class, or culture in the environment. Gender relations in any particular historical situation are always constructed by the entire array of hierarchical social relations in which "woman" or "man" participates. The femininity prescribed for the plantation owner's wife was exactly what was forbidden for the black slave woman.[14] The forms of femininity required of Aryan women in Nazi Germany were exactly what was forbidden—and in fact eliminated—for women who were Jews, Gypsies, or members of other "inferior races."[15] So we cannot meaningfully talk about "women and science" or "women and knowledge" without exploring the different meanings and practices that accumulate in the life of someone who is a woman at any particular historical intersection of race, class, and culture. There are as many relationships between women and science as there are cultural configurations of womanhood (and of science).

Being white or Western or economically advantaged or heterosexual, however, need not be the scientific and epistemological disadvantage that one might expect it to be when one thinks about these identities as parallel to *andocentric* ways of being a man in gender relations. To decenter manliness does not mean that men can make no contributions to feminism or can generate no original feminist insights out of their own particular historical experiences. At least some have already done so. Similarly, white women can (and do) generate original antiracist insights out of their particular historical experiences as white women. We can demand of ourselves that we do so as a condition of producing analyses and politics adequate to feminism in a global context. But just what we are to demand of ourselves from such apparently contradictory social situations as "male feminist" and "white antiracist" requires more analysis than it has yet received.[16]

(5) The natural sciences are illuminatingly conceptualized as part of the social sciences. What kind of theoretical framework will enable us to understand sciences-in-society and the consequent society-in-sciences? According to one influential tendency in conventional thought, there is only one standard for what counts as science, and that is provided by the natural sciences. Physics, with its reliance on quantitative methods and its positivist ethos, is supposed to be accorded the highest rank among the natural sciences, with chemistry and then the more abstract areas of biology following behind. The social sciences are even lower on this scale. The "harder" social sciences such as economics and behaviorist psychology (cognitive psychology would now probably be substituted for behaviorism) lead the "softer" fields (softer to the extent that they rely more on "qualitative" studies) such as anthropology, sociology, and history. Some writers have even thought that the natural sciences should be the model for all knowledge, certainly for anything deserving such prestigious words as "scientific," "rational," and "objective." The sciences are fundamentally one, and the model for that one is physics. This internal ordering reflects fairly accurately the power and prestige accorded different fields of research within the sciences today.

Such a conception, however, prevents us from developing *natural* as well as social sciences that are not systematically blinded to the ways in which their descriptions and explanations of their subject matters are shaped by the origins and consequences of their research practices and by the interests, desires, and values promoted by such practices. How can the natural and social sciences be led to take responsibility for their social locations and thus for their origins, values, and consequences? To ask this is to ask a social science question. Adequate *social* studies of the sciences turn out to be the necessary foundations upon which more comprehensive and less distorted descriptions and explanations of nature can be built. This conclusion is demanded by recognition that the culture "knows" a great deal that we individuals do not. The culture remains the "authoritative knower" of all those things about us for which we neglect or refuse personal and institutional responsibility. It "knows" the Eurocentrism and androcentrism that "natives" in the culture routinely express but cannot detect. If androcentric or Eurocentric beliefs and practices are part of the evidence for one hypothesis over another (inadvertently or not), then as part of scientific practice we must learn how to detect and eliminate them. Although the outcome of the natural sciences is shaped by how well this job is done, the methods of the natural sciences have been the wrong kind to do it. Consequently, it makes good sense to think of the natural sciences as a subfield of the critical social sciences. We will all have to think further about what this counter-intuitive proposal would mean in practice. Obviously, few fields of contemporary social science have methodologies, institutional structures, or agendas that are competent to identify the kinds of almost culturewide interests, values, and assumptions that end up functioning as evidence "behind the back" of the natural and social sciences, so to speak. Thus, it is one challenge to remedy this situation in the social sciences and another to conceptualize and then institutionalize a relationship between the natural and social sciences that will enable the former to get control of more of their evidence than they can now manage to do.

The Zairean philosopher V. Y. Mudimbe argues that just as European and American imperialists invented an Africa that would serve their purposes (they said they discovered it), so must Africans now invent a West that serves Africans' purposes. The imperialists claimed to discover in Africa a primitiveness, a prelogicality, an immorality that could serve as the opposite of the purportedly civilized West they were simultaneously inventing. But such an approach can be usefully developed by the other side as well, Mudimbe points out. For Africans today, he argues, a "critical reading of the Western experience is simultaneously a way of 'inventing' a foreign tradition in order to master its techniques and an ambiguous strategy for implementing alterity."[17]

The feminist discussions of science and epistemology are similarly engaged: we must "invent" the very Western sciences and institutions of knowledge in which we participate (and which pay some of our salaries) as bizarre beliefs and practices of the indigenous peoples who rule the modern West. We must master their techniques as we simultaneously continue to "discover" the ways in which they are "other" to ourselves and our agendas.

If we in the West can reinvent this part of the West, Western culture can learn things about itself and about the "others" against which it has built mighty conceptual and institutional fortresses. Of course, that will require different practices as well as different thoughts.

NOTES

1. Sal Restivo, "Modern Science as a Social Problem," *Social Problems* 35:3 (1988).

2. See, e.g., Wolfgang Van den Daele, "The Social Construction of Science," in *The Social Production of Scientific Knowledge,* ed. Everett Mendelsohn, Peter Weingart, and Richard Whitley (Dordrecht: Reidel, 1977).

3. And so are the problems with it, many will say. . . .

4. Philosopher Cornel West made this point in the plenary session "What Is Cultural Studies?" at the conference sponsored by the Committee for Cultural Studies, City University of New York, May 11, 1989.

5. The designations First, Second, and Third Worlds have been constructed by the West. They distort global politics in many ways, all to the benefit of the West, but I use them for lack of better terms.

6. See, e.g., Hazel Carby, *Reconstructing Womanhood* (New York: Oxford University Press, 1987); Angela Davis, *Women, Race, and Class* (New York: Random House, 1981);

Paula Giddings, *When and Where I Enter: The Impact of Black Women on Race and Sex in America* (New York: Bantam Books, 1985).

7. See Alison Jaggar, *Feminist Politics and Human Nature* (Totowa, N.J.: Rowman & Allenheld, 1983).

8. See Bettina Aptheker, *Tapestries of Life: Women's Work, Women's Consciousness, and the Meaning of Daily Life* (Amherst: University of Massachusetts Press, 1989).

9. One good place for newcomers to start in this literature is the collection of essays in Sandra Harding and Jean O'Barr, eds., *Sex and Scientific Inquiry* (Chicago: University of Chicago Press, 1987). . . .

10. Donna Haraway focuses on the importance of his insight and supplies the useful term: "Situated Knowledges: *The Science Question in Feminism* and the Privilege of Partial Perspective," *Feminist Studies* 14:3 (1988).

11. The last part of this claim is the contention of the "strong programme" in the sociology of knowledge . . . with which I agree in this respect, though not in others. See, e.g., David Bloor, *Knowledge and Social Imagery* (London: Routledge & Kegan Paul, 1977).

12. See Jane Flax, *Thinking Fragments: Psychoanalysis, Feminism, and Postmodernism in the Contemporary West* (Berkeley: University of California Press, 1990).

13. Judith Butler, *Gender Trouble: Feminism and the Subversion of Identity* (New York: Routledge, 1990).

14. Davis, *Women, Race, and Class.*

15. Gisela Boch, "Racism and Sexism in Nazi Germany: Motherhood, Compulsory Sterilization, and the State," *Signs* 8:3 (1983).

16. Questions have been raised (by me, among others) about the ability of the feminist standpoint epistemology to deal with differences between women's lives. Here, however, I defend the theory against these and related skeptical questions.

17. V. Y. Mudimbe, *The Invention of Africa: Gnosis, Philosophy, and the Order of Knowledge* (Bloomington: Indiana University Press, 1988), 171.

R E A D I N G   4

The Social Construction of Black Feminist Thought

PATRICIA HILL COLLINS

Sojourner Truth, Anna Julia Cooper, Ida Wells Barnett, and Fannie Lou Hamer are but a few names from a growing list of distinguished African-American women activists. Although their sustained resistance to Black women's victimization within interlocking systems of race, gender, and class oppression is well known, these women did not act alone.[1] Their actions were nurtured by the support of countless, ordinary African-American women who, through strategies of everyday resistance, created a powerful foundation for this more visible Black feminist activist tradition.[2] Such support has been essential to the shape and goals of Black feminist thought.

The long-term and widely shared resistance among African-American women can only have been sustained by an enduring and shared standpoint among Black women about the meaning of oppression and the actions that Black women can and should take to resist it. Efforts to identify the central concepts of this Black women's standpoint figure prominently in the works of contemporary Black feminist intellectuals.[3] Moreover, political and epistemological issues influence the social construction of Black feminist thought. Like other subordinate groups, African-American women not only have developed distinctive interpretations of Black women's oppression but have done so by using alternative ways of producing and validating knowledge itself. . . .

Excerpts from "The Social Construction of Black Feminist Thought" by Patricia Hill Collins, in *Signs: Journal of Women in Culture and Society*, vol. 14, no. 4, 1989. Copyright © 1989 by The University of Chicago Press. All rights reserved.

THE CONTOURS OF AN AFROCENTRIC FEMINIST EPISTEMOLOGY

Africanist analyses of the Black experience generally agree on the fundamental elements of an Afrocentric standpoint. In spite of varying histories, Black societies reflect elements of a core African value system that existed prior to and independently of racial oppression.[4] Moreover, as a result of colonialism, imperialism, slavery, apartheid, and other systems of racial domination, Blacks share a common experience of oppression. These similarities in material conditions have fostered shared Afrocentric values that permeate the family structure, religious institutions, culture, and community life of Blacks in varying parts of Africa, the Caribbean, South America, and North America.[5] This Afrocentric consciousness permeates the shared history of people of African descent through the framework of a distinctive Afrocentric epistemology.[6]

Feminist scholars advance a similar argument. They assert that women share a history of patriarchal oppression through the political economy of the material conditions of sexuality and reproduction.[7] These shared material conditions are thought to transcend divisions among women created by race, social class, religion, sexual orientation, and ethnicity and to form the basis of a women's standpoint with its corresponding feminist consciousness and epistemology.[8]

Since Black women have access to both the Afrocentric and the feminist standpoints, an alternative epistemology used to rearticulate a Black women's standpoint reflects elements of both traditions.[9] The search for the distinguishing features of an alternative epistemology used by African-American women reveals that values and ideas that Africanist scholars identify as being characteristically "Black" often bear remarkable resemblance to similar ideas claimed by feminist scholars as being characteristically "female."[10] This similarity suggests that the material conditions of oppression can vary dramatically and yet generate some uniformity in the epistemologies of subordinate groups. Thus, the significance of an Afrocentric feminist epistemology may lie in its enrichment of our understanding of how subordinate groups create knowledge that enables them to resist oppression.

The parallels between the two conceptual schemes raise a question: Is the worldview of women of African descent more intensely infused with the overlapping feminine/Afrocentric standpoints than is the case for either African-American men or white women?[11] While an Afrocentric feminist epistemology reflects elements of epistemologies used by Blacks as a group and women as a group, it also paradoxically demonstrates features that may be unique to Black women. On certain dimensions, Black women may more closely resemble Black men, on others, white women, and on still others, Black women may stand apart from both groups. Black feminist sociologist Deborah K. King describes this phenomenon as a "both/or" orientation, the act of being simultaneously a member of a group and yet standing apart from it. She suggests that multiple realities among Black women yield a "multiple consciousness in Black women's politics" and that this state of belonging yet not belonging forms an integral part of Black women's oppositional consciousness.[12] Bonnie Thornton Dill's analysis of how Black women live with contradictions, a situation she labels the "dialectics of Black womanhood," parallels King's assertions that this "both/or" orientation is central to an Afrocentric feminist consciousness.[13] Rather than emphasizing how a Black women's standpoint and its accompanying epistemology are different than those in Afrocentric and feminist analyses, I use Black women's experiences as a point of contact between the two.

Viewing an Afrocentric feminist epistemology in this way challenges analyses claiming that Black women have a more accurate view of oppression than do other groups. Such approaches suggest that oppression can be quantified and compared and that adding layers of oppression produces a potentially clearer standpoint. While it is tempting to claim that Black women are more oppressed than everyone else and therefore have the best standpoint from which to understand the mechanisms, processes, and effects of oppression, this simply may not be the case.[14]

African-American women do not uniformly share an Afrocentric feminist epistemology since social class introduces variations among Black women in seeing, valuing, and using Afrocentric feminist perspectives. While a Black women's standpoint and its accompanying epistemology stem from Black women's consciousness of race and gender oppression, they are not simply the result of combining Afrocentric and female values—standpoints are rooted in real material conditions structured by social class.[15]

Concrete Experience as a Criterion of Meaning

Carolyn Chase, a thirty-one-year-old inner city Black woman, notes, "My aunt used to say, 'A heap see, but a few know.' "[16] This saying depicts two types of knowing, knowledge and wisdom, and taps the first dimension of an Afrocentric feminist epistemology. Living life as Black women requires wisdom since knowledge about the dynamics of race, gender, and class subordination has been essential to Black women's survival. African-American women give such wisdom high credence in assessing knowledge.

Allusions to these two types of knowing pervade the words of a range of African-American women. In explaining the tenacity of racism, Zilpha Elaw, a preacher of the mid-1800s, noted: "The pride of a white skin is a bauble of great value with many in some parts of the United States, who readily sacrifice their intelligence to their prejudices, and possess more knowledge than wisdom."[17] In describing differences separating African-American and white women, Nancy White invokes a similar rule: "When you come right down to it, white women just *think* they are free. Black women *know* they ain't free."[18] Geneva Smitherman, a college professor specializing in African-American linguistics, suggests that "from a black perspective, written documents are limited in what they can teach about life and survival in the world. Blacks are quick to ridicule 'educated fools,' . . . they have 'book learning' but no 'mother wit,' knowledge, but not wisdom."[19] Mabel Lincoln eloquently summarizes the distinction between knowledge and wisdom: "To black people like me, a fool is funny—you know, people who love to break bad, people you can't tell anything to, folks that would take a shotgun to a roach."[20]

Black women need wisdom to know how to deal with the "educated fools" who would "take a shotgun to a roach." As members of a subordinate group, Black women cannot afford to be fools of any type, for their devalued status denies them the protections that white skin, maleness, and wealth confer. This distinction between knowledge and wisdom, and the use of experience as the cutting edge dividing them, has been key to Black women's survival. In the context of race, gender, and class oppression, the distinction is essential since knowledge without wisdom is adequate for the powerful, but wisdom is essential to the survival of the subordinate.

For ordinary African-American women, those individuals who have lived through the experiences about which they claim to be experts are more believable and credible than those who have merely read or thought about such experiences. Thus, concrete experience as a criterion for credibility frequently is invoked by Black women when making knowledge claims. For instance, Hannah Nelson describes the importance that personal experience has for her: "Our speech is most directly personal, and every black person assumes that every other black person has a right to a personal opinion. In speaking of grave matters, your personal experience is considered very good evidence. With us, distant statistics are certainly not as important as the actual experience of a sober person."[21] Similarly, Ruth Shays uses her concrete experiences to challenge the idea that formal education is the only route to knowledge: "I am the kind of person who doesn't have a lot of education, but both my mother and my father had good common sense. Now, I think that's all you need. I might not know how to use thirty-four words where three would do, but that does not mean that I don't know what I'm talking about . . . I know what I'm talking about because I'm talking about myself. I'm talking about what I have lived."[22] Implicit in Shays's self-assessment is a critique of the type of knowledge that obscures the truth, the "thirty-four words" that cover up a truth that can be expressed in three.

Even after substantial mastery of white masculinist epistemologies, many Black women scholars invoke their own concrete experiences and those of other Black women in selecting topics for investigation and methodologies used. For example, Elsa Barkley Brown subtitles her essay on Black women's history, "how my mother taught me to be an historian in spite of my academic training."[23] Similarly, Joyce Ladner maintains that growing up as a Black woman in the South gave her special insights in conducting her study of Black adolescent women.[24]

Henry Mitchell and Nicholas Lewter claim that experience as a criterion of meaning with practical images as its symbolic vehicles is a fundamental epistemological tenet in African-American thought-systems.[25] Stories, narratives, and Bible principles are selected for their applicability to the lived experiences of African-Americans and become symbolic representations of a whole wealth of experience. For example, Bible tales are told for their value to common life, so their interpretation involves no need for scientific historical verification. The narrative method requires that the story be "told, not torn apart in analysis, and trusted as core belief, not admired as science."[26] Any biblical story contains more than characters and a plot—it presents key ethical issues salient in African-American life.

June Jordan's essay about her mother's suicide exemplifies the multiple levels of meaning that can occur when concrete experiences are used as a criterion of meaning. Jordan describes her mother, a woman who literally died trying to stand up, and the effect that her mother's death had on her own work:

> I think all of this is really about women and work. Certainly this is all about me as a woman and my life work. I mean I am not sure my mother's suicide was something extraordinary. Perhaps most women must deal with a similar inheritance, the legacy of a woman whose death you cannot possibly pinpoint because she died so many, many times and because, even before she became your mother, the life of that woman was taken. . . . I came too late to help my mother to her feet. By way of everlasting thanks to all of the women who have helped me to stay alive I am working never to be late again.[27]

While Jordan has knowledge about the concrete act of her mother's death, she also strives for wisdom concerning the meaning of that death.

Some feminist scholars offer a similar claim that women, as a group, are more likely than men to use concrete knowledge in assessing knowledge claims. For example, a substantial number of the 135 women in a study of women's cognitive development were "connected knowers" and were drawn to the sort of knowledge that emerges from first-hand observation. Such women felt that since knowledge comes from experience, the best way of understanding another person's ideas was to try to share the experiences that led the person to form those ideas. At the heart of the procedures used by connected knowers is the capacity for empathy.[28]

In valuing the concrete, African-American women may be invoking not only an Afrocentric tradition, but a women's tradition as well. Some feminist theorists suggest that women are socialized in complex relational nexuses where contextual rules take priority over abstract principles in governing behavior. This socialization process is thought to stimulate characteristic

ways of knowing.[29] For example, Canadian sociologist Dorothy Smith maintains that two modes of knowing exist, one located in the body and the space it occupies and the other passing beyond it. She asserts that women, through their child-rearing and nurturing activities, mediate these two modes and use the concrete experiences of their daily lives to assess more abstract knowledge claims.[30]

Amanda King, a young Black mother, describes how she used the concrete to assess the abstract and points out how difficult mediating these two modes of knowing can be:

> The leaders of the ROC [a labor union] lost their jobs too, but it just seemed like they were used to losing their jobs. . . . This was like a lifelong thing for them, to get out there and protest. They were like, what do you call them—intellectuals. . . . You got the ones that go to the university that are supposed to make all the speeches, they're the ones that are supposed to lead, you know, put this little revolution together, and then you got the little ones . . . that go to the factory everyday, they be the ones that have to fight. I had a child and I thought I don't have the time to be running around with these people. . . . I mean I understand some of that stuff they were talking about, like the bourgeoisie, the rich and the poor and all that, but I had surviving on my mind for me and my kid.[31]

For King, abstract ideals of class solidarity were mediated by the concrete experience of motherhood and the connectedness it involved.

In traditional African-American communities, Black women find considerable institutional support for valuing concrete experience. Black extended families and Black churches are two key institutions where Black women experts with concrete knowledge of what it takes to be self-defined Black women share their knowledge with their younger, less experienced sisters. This relationship of sisterhood among Black women can be seen as a model for a whole series of relationships that African-American women have with each other, whether it is networks among women in extended families, among women in the Black church, or among women in the African-American community at large.[32]

Since the Black church and the Black family are both woman-centered and Afrocentric institutions,

African-American women traditionally have found considerable institutional support for this dimension of an Afrocentric feminist epistemology in ways that are unique to them. While white women may value the concrete, it is questionable whether white families, particularly middle-class nuclear ones, and white community institutions provide comparable types of support. Similarly, while Black men are supported by Afrocentric institutions, they cannot participate in Black women's sisterhood. In terms of Black women's relationships with one another then, African-American women may indeed find it easier than others to recognize connectedness as a primary way of knowing, simply because they are encouraged to do so by Black women's tradition of sisterhood.

The Use of Dialogue in Assessing Knowledge Claims

For Black women, new knowledge claims are rarely worked out in isolation from other individuals and are usually developed through dialogues with other members of a community. A primary epistemological assumption underlying the use of dialogue in assessing knowledge claims is that connectedness rather than separation is an essential component of the knowledge-validation process.[33]

The use of dialogue has deep roots in an African-based oral tradition and in African-American culture.[34] Ruth Shays describes the importance of dialogue in the knowledge-validation process of enslaved African-Americans: "They would find a lie if it took them a year . . . the foreparents found the truth because they listened and they made people tell their part many times. Most often you can hear a lie. . . . Those old people was everywhere and knew the truth of many disputes. They believed that a liar should suffer the pain of his lies, and they had all kinds of ways of bringing liars to judgement."[35]

The widespread use of the call and response discourse mode among African-Americans exemplifies the importance placed on dialogue. Composed of spontaneous verbal and nonverbal interaction between speaker and listener in which all of the speaker's statements or "calls" are punctuated by expressions or "responses" from the listener, this Black discourse mode pervades African-American culture. The fundamental requirement of this interactive network is active participation of all individuals.[36] For ideas to be

tested and validated, everyone in the group must participate. To refuse to join in, especially if one really disagrees with what has been said is seen as "cheating."[37]

June Jordan's analysis of Black English points to the significance of this dimension of an alternative epistemology.

> Our language is a system constructed by people constantly needing to insist that we exist. . . . Our language devolves from a culture that abhors all abstraction, or anything tending to obscure or delete the fact of the human being who is here and now/the truth of the person who is speaking or listening. Consequently, *there is no passive voice construction possible in Black English.* For example, you cannot say, "Black English is being eliminated." You must say, instead, "White people eliminating Black English." The assumption of the presence of life governs all of Black English . . . every sentence assumes the living and active participation of at least two human beings, the speaker and the listener.[38]

Many Black women intellectuals invoke the relationships and connectedness provided by use of dialogue. When asked why she chose the themes she did, novelist Gayle Jones replied: "I was . . . interested . . . in oral traditions of storytelling—Afro-American and others, in which there is always the consciousness and importance of the hearer."[39] In describing the difference in the way male and female writers select significant events and relationships, Jones points out that "with many women writers, relationships within family, community, between men and women, and among women—from slave narratives by black women writers on—are treated as complex and significant relationships, whereas with many men the significant relationships are those that involve confrontations—relationships outside the family and community."[40] Alice Walker's reaction to Zora Neale Hurston's book, *Mules and Men,* is another example of the use of dialogue in assessing knowledge claims. In *Mules and Men,* Hurston chose not to become a detached observer of the stories and folktales she collected but instead, through extensive dialogues with the people in the communities she studied, placed herself at the center of her analysis. Using a similar process, Walker tests the truth of Hurston's knowledge claims: "When I read *Mules and Men* I was delighted. Here was this perfect book! The 'perfection' of which I immediately tested on my relatives, who are such typical Black Americans they are useful for every sort of political, cultural, or economic survey. Very regular people from the South, rapidly forgetting their Southern cultural inheritance in the suburbs and ghettos of Boston and New York, they sat around reading the book themselves, listening to me read the book, listening to each other read the book, and a kind of paradise was regained."[41]

Their centrality in Black churches and Black extended families provides Black women with a high degree of support from Black institutions for invoking dialogue as a dimension of an Afrocentric feminist epistemology. However, when African-American women use dialogues in assessing knowledge claims, they might be invoking a particularly female way of knowing as well. Feminist scholars contend that males and females are socialized within their families to seek different types of autonomy, the former based on separation, the latter seeking connectedness, and that this variation in types of autonomy parallels the characteristic differences between male and female ways of knowing.[42] For instance, in contrast to the visual metaphors (such as equating knowledge with illumination, knowing with seeing, and truth with light) that scientists and philosophers typically use, women tend to ground their epistemological premises in metaphors suggesting speaking and listening.[43]

While there are significant differences between the roles Black women play in their families and those played by middle-class white women, Black women clearly are affected by general cultural norms prescribing certain familial roles for women. Thus, in terms of the role of dialogue in an Afrocentric feminist epistemology, Black women may again experience a convergence of the values of the African-American community and woman-centered values.

The Ethic of Caring

"Ole white preachers used to talk wid dey tongues widdout sayin' nothin', but Jesus told us slaves to talk wid our hearts."[44] These words of an ex-slave suggest that ideas cannot be divorced from the individuals who create and share them. This theme of "talking with the heart" taps another dimension of an alternative epistemology used by African-American women, the ethic of caring. Just as the ex-slave used the wisdom in his heart to reject the ideas of the preachers who talked "wid dey

tongues widdout sayin' nothin'," the ethic of caring suggests that personal expressiveness, emotions, and empathy are central to the knowledge-validation process.

One of three interrelated components making up the ethic of caring is the emphasis placed on individual uniqueness. Rooted in a tradition of African humanism, each individual is thought to be a unique expression of a common spirit, power, or energy expressed by all life.[45] This belief in individual uniqueness is illustrated by the value placed on personal expressiveness in African-American communities.[46] Johnetta Ray, an inner city resident, describes this Afrocentric emphasis on individual uniqueness: "No matter how hard we try, I don't think black people will ever develop much of a herd instinct. We are profound individualists with a passion for self-expression."[47]

A second component of the ethic of caring concerns the appropriateness of emotions in dialogues. Emotion indicates that a speaker believes in the validity of an argument.[48] Consider Ntozake Shange's description of one of the goals of her work: "Our [Western] society allows people to be absolutely neurotic and totally out of touch with their feelings and everyone else's feelings, and yet be very respectable. This, to me, is a travesty. . . . I'm trying to change the idea of seeing emotions and intellect as distinct faculties."[49] Shange's words echo those of the ex-slave. Both see the denigration of emotion as problematic, and both suggest that expressiveness should be reclaimed and valued.

A third component of the ethic of caring involves developing the capacity for empathy. Harriet Jones, a sixteen-year-old Black woman, explains why she chose to open up to her interviewer: "Some things in my life are so hard for me to bear, and it makes me feel better to know that you feel sorry about those things and would change them if you could."[50]

These three components of the ethic of caring—the value placed on individual expressiveness, the appropriateness of emotions, and the capacity for empathy—pervade African-American culture. One of the best examples of the interactive nature of the importance of dialogue and the ethic of caring in assessing knowledge claims occurs in the use of the call and response discourse mode in traditional Black church services. In such services, both the minister and the congregation routinely use voice rhythm and vocal inflection to convey meaning. The sound of what is being said is just as important as the words themselves in what is, in a sense, a dialogue between reason and emotions. As a result, it is nearly impossible to filter out the strictly linguistic-cognitive abstract meaning from the socio-cultural psycho-emotive meaning.[51] While the ideas presented by a speaker must have validity, that is, agree with the general body of knowledge shared by the Black congregation, the group also appraises the way knowledge claims are presented.

There is growing evidence that the ethic of caring may be part of women's experience as well. Certain dimensions of women's ways of knowing bear striking resemblance to Afrocentric expressions of the ethic of caring. Belenky, Clinchy, Goldberger, and Tarule point out that two contrasting epistemological orientations characterize knowing—one, an epistemology of separation based on impersonal procedures for establishing truth, and the other, an epistemology of connection in which truth emerges through care. While these ways of knowing are not gender specific, disproportionate numbers of women rely on connected knowing.[52]

The parallels between Afrocentric expressions of the ethic of caring and those advanced by feminist scholars are noteworthy. The emphasis placed on expressiveness and emotion in African-American communities bears marked resemblance to feminist perspectives on the importance of personality in connected knowing. Separate knowers try to subtract the personality of an individual from his or her ideas because they see personality as biasing those ideas. In contrast, connected knowers see personality as adding to an individual's ideas, and they feel that the personality of each group member enriches a group's understanding.[53] Similarly, the significance of individual uniqueness, personal expressiveness, and empathy in African-American communities resembles the importance that some feminist analyses place on women's "inner voice."[54]

The convergence of Afrocentric and feminist values in the ethic-of-care dimension of an alternative epistemology seems particularly acute. While white women may have access to a women's tradition valuing emotion and expressiveness, few white social institutions except the family validate this way of knowing. In contrast, Black women have long had the support of the Black church, an institution with deep roots in the African past and a philosophy that accepts and encourages expressiveness and an ethic of caring. While Black men share in this Afrocentric tradition, they must resolve the contradictions that distinguish abstract, unemotional Western masculinity from an Afrocentric

ethic of caring. The differences among race/gender groups thus hinge on differences in their access to institutional supports valuing one type of knowing over another. Although Black women may be denigrated within white-male-controlled academic institutions, other institutions, such as Black families and churches, which encourage the expression of Black female power, seem to do so by way of their support for an Afrocentric feminist epistemology.

The Ethic of Personal Accountability

An ethic of personal accountability is the final dimension of an alternative epistemology. Not only must individuals develop their knowledge claims through dialogue and present those knowledge claims in a style proving their concern for their ideas, people are expected to be accountable for their knowledge claims. Zilpha Elaw's description of slavery reflects this notion that every idea has an owner and that the owner's identity matters: "Oh, the abominations of slavery! . . . every case of slavery, however lenient its inflictions and mitigated its atrocities, indicates an oppressor, the oppressed, and oppression."[55] For Elaw, abstract definitions of slavery mesh with the concrete identities of its perpetrators and its victims. Blacks "consider it essential for individuals to have personal positions on issues and assume full responsibility for arguing their validity."[56]

Assessments of an individual's knowledge claims simultaneously evaluate an individual's character, values, and ethics. African-Americans reject Eurocentric masculinist beliefs that probing into an individual's personal viewpoint is outside the boundaries of discussion. Rather, all views expressed and actions taken are thought to derive from a central set of core beliefs that cannot be other than personal.[57] From this perspective, knowledge claims made by individuals respected for their moral and ethical values will carry more weight than those offered by less respected figures.[58]

An example drawn from an undergraduate course composed entirely of Black women, which I taught, might help clarify the uniqueness of this portion of the knowledge-validation process. During one class discussion, I assigned the students the task of critiquing an analysis of Black feminism advanced by a prominent Black male scholar. Instead of dissecting the rationality of the author's thesis, my students demanded facts about the author's personal biography. They were especially interested in concrete details of his life such as his relationships with Black women, his marital status, and his social class background. By requesting data on dimensions of his personal life routinely excluded in positivist approaches to knowledge validation, they were invoking concrete experience as a criterion of meaning. They used this information to assess whether he really cared about his topic and invoked this ethic of caring in advancing their knowledge claims about his work. Furthermore, they refused to evaluate the rationality of his written ideas without some indication of his personal credibility as an ethical human being. The entire exchange could only have occurred as a dialogue among members of a class that had established a solid enough community to invoke an alternative epistemology in assessing knowledge claims.[59]

The ethic of personal accountability is clearly an Afrocentric value, but is it feminist as well? While limited by its attention to middle-class, white women, Carol Gilligan's work suggests that there is a female model for moral development where women are more inclined to link morality to responsibility, relationships, and the ability to maintain social ties.[60] If this is the case, then African-American women again experience a convergence of values from Afrocentric and female institutions.

The use of an Afrocentric feminist epistemology in traditional Black church services illustrates the interactive nature of all four dimensions and also serves as a metaphor for the distinguishing features of an Afrocentric feminist way of knowing. The services represent more than dialogues between the rationality used in examining biblical texts/stories and the emotion inherent in the use of reason for this purpose. The rationale for such dialogues addresses the task of examining concrete experiences for the presence of an ethic of caring. Neither emotion nor ethics is subordinated to reason. Instead, emotion, ethics, and reason are used as interconnected, essential components in assessing knowledge claims. In an Afrocentric feminist epistemology, values lie at the heart of the knowledge-validation process such that inquiry always has an ethical aim. . . .

ACKNOWLEDGMENTS

Special thanks go out to the following people for reading various drafts of this manuscript: Evelyn Nakano Glenn, Lynn Weber Cannon, and participants in the 1986 Research Institute, Center for Research on Women, Memphis State University; Elsa Barkley Brown, Deborah K. King, Elizabeth V. Spelman, and Angelene Jamison-Hall; and four anonymous reviewers at *Signs*.

NOTES

1. For analyses of how interlocking systems of oppression affect Black women, see Frances Beale, "Double Jeopardy: To Be Black and Female," in *The Black Woman,* ed. Toni Cade (New York: Signet, 1970); Angela Y. Davis, *Women, Race and Class* (New York: Random House, 1981); Bonnie Thornton Dill, "Race, Class, and Gender: Prospects for an All-Inclusive Sisterhood," *Feminist Studies* 9, no. 1 (1983): 131–50; bell hooks, *Ain't I a Woman? Black Women and Feminism* (Boston: South End Press, 1981); Diane Lewis, "A Response to Inequality: Black Women, Racism, and Sexism," *Signs: Journal of Women in Culture and Society* 3, no. 2 (Winter 1977): 339–61; Pauli Murray, "The Liberation of Black Women," in *Voices of the New Feminism,* ed. Mary Lou Thompson (Boston: Beacon, 1970), 87–102; and the introduction in Filomina Chioma Steady, *The Black Woman Cross-Culturally* (Cambridge, Mass.: Schenkman, 1981), 7–41.

2. See the introduction in Steady for an overview of Black women's strengths. This strength-resiliency perspective has greatly influenced empirical work on African-American women. See, e.g., Joyce Ladner's study of low-income Black adolescent girls, *Tomorrow's Tomorrow* (New York: Doubleday, 1971); and Lena Wright Myers's work on Black women's self-concept, *Black Women: Do They Cope Better?* (Englewood Cliffs, N.J.: Prentice-Hall, 1980). For discussions of Black women's resistance, see Elizabeth Fox-Genovese, "Strategies and Forms of Resistance: Focus on Slave Women

in the United States," in *In Resistance: Studies in African, Caribbean and Afro-American History,* ed. Gary Y. Okihiro (Amherst, Mass.: University of Massachusetts Press, 1986), 143–65; and Rosalyn Terborg-Penn, "Black Women in Resistance: A Cross-Cultural Perspective," in Okihiro, ed., 188–209. For a comprehensive discussion of everyday resistance, see James C. Scott, *Weapons of the Weak: Everyday Forms of Peasant Resistance* (New Haven, Conn.: Yale University Press, 1985).

3. See Patricia Hill Collins's analysis of the substantive content of Black feminist thought in "Learning from the Outsider Within: The Sociological Significance of Black Feminist Thought," *Social Problems* 33, no. 6 (1986): 14–32.

4. For detailed discussions of the Afrocentric worldview, see John S. Mbiti, *African Religions and Philosophy* (London: Heinemann, 1969); Dominique Zahan, *The Religion, Spirituality, and Thought of Traditional Africa* (Chicago: University of Chicago Press, 1979); and Mechal Sobel, *Trabelin' On: The Slave Journey to an Afro-Baptist Faith* (Westport, Conn.: Greenwood Press, 1979), 1–76.

5. For representative works applying these concepts to African-American culture, see Niara Sudarkasa, "Interpreting the African Heritage in Afro-American Family Organization," in *Black Families,* ed. Harriette Pipes McAdoo (Beverly Hills, Calif.: Sage, 1981); Henry H. Mitchell and Nicholas Cooper Lewter, *Soul Theology: The Heart of American Black Culture* (San Francisco: Harper & Row, 1986); Robert Farris Thompson, *Flash of the Spirit: African and Afro-American Art and Philosophy* (New York: Vintage, 1983); and Ortiz M. Walton, "Comparative Analysis of the African and the Western Aesthetics," in *The Black Aesthetic,* ed. Addison Gayle (Garden City, N.Y.: Doubleday, 1971), 154–64.

6. One of the best discussions of an Afrocentric epistemology is offered by James E. Turner, "Foreword: Africana Studies and Epistemology; a Discourse in the Sociology of Knowledge," in *The Next Decade: Theoretical and Research Issues in Africana Studies,* ed. James E. Turner (Ithaca, N.Y.: Cornell University Africana Studies and Research Center, 1984), v–xxv. See also Vernon Dixon, "World Views and Research Methodology," summarized in Sandra Harding, *The Science Question in Feminism* (Ithaca, N.Y.: Cornell University Press, 1986), 170.

7. See Hester Eisenstein, *Contemporary Feminist Thought* (Boston: G. K. Hall, 1983). Nancy Hartsock's *Money, Sex, and Power* (Boston: Northeastern University Press, 1983), 145–209, offers a particularly insightful analysis of women's oppression.

8. For discussions of feminist consciousness, see Dorothy Smith, "A Sociology for Women," in *The Prism of Sex: Essays in the Sociology of Knowledge,* ed. Julia A. Sherman and Evelyn T. Beck (Madison: University of Wisconsin Press, 1979); and Michelle Z. Rosaldo, "Women, Culture, and Society: A Theoretical Overview," in *Woman, Culture, and Society,* ed. Michelle Z. Rosaldo and Louise Lamphere (Stanford, Calif.: Stanford University Press, 1974), 17–42. Feminist epistemologies are surveyed by Alison M. Jaggar, *Feminist Politics and Human Nature* (Totowa, N.J.: Rowan & Allanheld, 1983).

9. One significant difference between Afrocentric and feminist standpoints is that much of what is termed women's culture is, unlike African-American culture, created in the context of and produced by oppression. Those who argue for a women's culture are electing to value, rather than denigrate, those traits associated with females in white patriarchal societies. While this choice is important, it is not the same as identifying an independent, historic culture associated with a society. I am indebted to Deborah K. King for this point.

10. Critiques of the Eurocentric masculinist knowledge-validation process by both Africanist and feminist scholars illustrate this point. What one group labels "white" and "Eurocentric," the other describes as "male-dominated" and "masculinist." Although he does not emphasize its patriarchal and racist features, Morris Berman's *The Reenchantment of the World* (New York: Bantam, 1981) provides a historical discussion of Western thought. Afrocentric analyses of this same process can be found in Molefi Kete Asante, "International/Intercultural Relations," in *Contemporary Black Thought,* ed. Molefi Kete Asante and Abdulai S. Vandi (Beverly Hills, Calif.: Sage, 1980), 43–58; and Dona Richards, "European Mythology: The Ideology of 'Progress,'" in Asante and Vandi, eds., 59–79. For feminist analyses, see Hartsock, *Money, Sex, and Power.* Harding also discusses this similarity (see chap. 7, "Other 'Others' and Fractured Identities: Issues for Epistemologists," 163–96).

11. Harding, 166.

12. Deborah K. King, "Race, Class, and Gender Salience in Black Women's Womanist Consciousness" (Dartmouth College, Department of Sociology, Hanover, N.H., 1987, typescript).

13. Bonnie Thornton Dill, "The Dialectics of Black Womanhood," *Signs* 4, no. 3 (Spring 1979): 543–55.

14. One implication of standpoint approaches is that the more subordinate the group, the purer the vision of the oppressed group. This is an outcome of the origins of standpoint approaches in Marxist social theory, itself a dualistic analysis of social structure. Because such approaches rely on quantifying and ranking human oppressions—familiar tenets of positivist approaches—they are rejected by Blacks and feminists alike. See Harding (n. 6 above) for a discussion of this point. See also Elizabeth V. Spelman's discussion of the fallacy of additive oppression in "Theories of Race and Gender: The Erasure of Black Women," *Quest* 5, no. 4 (1982): 36–62.

15. Class differences among Black women may be marked. For example, see Paula Giddings's analysis in *When and Where I Enter: The Impact of Black Women on Race and Sex in America* (New York: William Morrow, 1984) of the role of

social class in shaping Black women's political activism; or Elizabeth Higginbotham's study of the effects of social class in Black women's college attendance in "Race and Class Barriers to Black Women's College Attendance," *Journal of Ethnic Studies* 13, no. 1 (1985): 89–107. Those African-American women who have experienced the greatest degree of convergence of race, class, and gender oppression may be in a better position to recognize and use an alternative episte-mology.

16. John Langston Gwaltney, *Drylongso: A Self-Portrait of Black America* (New York: Vintage, 1980), 83.

17. William L. Andrews, *Sisters of the Spirit: Three Black Women's Autobiographies of the Nineteenth Century* (Bloomington: Indiana University Press, 1986), 85.

18. Gwaltney, 147.

19. Geneva Smitherman, *Talkin and Testifyin: The Language of Black America* (Detroit: Wayne State University Press, 1986), 76.

20. Gwaltney, 68.

21. Ibid., 7.

22. Ibid., 27, 33.

23. Elsa Barkley Brown, "Hearing Our Mothers' Lives" (paper presented at the Fifteenth Anniversary Faculty Lecture Series, African-American and African Studies, Emory University, Atlanta, 1986).

24. Ladner (n. 2 above).

25. Mitchell and Lewter (n. 5 above). The use of the narrative approach in African-American theology exemplifies an inductive system of logic alternately called "folk wisdom" or a survival-based, need-oriented method of assessing knowledge claims.

26. Ibid., 8.

27. June Jordan, *On Call: Political Essays* (Boston: South End Press, 1985), 26.

28. Mary Belenky, Blythe Clinchy, Nancy Goldberger, and Jill Tarule, *Women's Ways of Knowing* (New York: Basic, 1986), 113.

29. Hartsock, *Money, Sex and Power* (n. 7 above), 237; and Nancy Chodorow, *The Reproduction of Mothering* (Berkeley and Los Angeles: University of California Press, 1978).

30. Dorothy Smith, *The Everyday World as Problematic* (Boston: Northeastern University Press, 1987).

31. Victoria Byerly, *Hard Times Cotton Mill Girls: Personal Histories of Womanhood and Poverty in the South* (New York: ILR Press, 1986), 198.

32. For Black women's centrality in the family, see Steady (n. 1 above): Ladner (n. 2 above); Brown (n. 23 above); and McAdoo, ed. (n. 5 above). See Cheryl Townsend Gilkes, " 'Together and in Harness:' Women's Traditions in the Sanctified Church," *Signs* 10, no. 4 (Summer 1985): 678–99, for Black women in the church; and chap. 4 of Deborah Gray White, *Ar'n't I a Woman? Female Slaves in the Plantation South* (New York: Norton, 1985). See also Gloria Joseph, "Black Mothers and Daughters: Their Roles and Functions in American Society," in *Common Differences: Conflicts in Black and White Feminist Perspectives,* ed. Gloria Joseph and Jill Lewis (Garden City, N.Y.: Anchor, 1981), 75–126. Even though Black women play essential roles in Black families and Black churches, these institutions are not free from sexism.

33. As Belenky et al. note, "Unlike the eye, the ear requires closeness between subject and object. Unlike seeing, speaking and listening suggest dialogue and interaction" (18).

34. Thomas Kochman, *Black and White: Styles in Conflict* (Chicago: University of Chicago Press, 1981); and Smitherman (n. 19 above).

35. Gwaltney (n. 16 above), 32.

36. Smitherman, 108.

37. Kochman, 28.

38. Jordan (n. 27 above), 129.

39. Claudia Tate, *Black Women Writers at Work* (New York: Continuum, 1983), 91.

40. Ibid., 92.

41. Alice Walker, *In Search of Our Mothers' Gardens* (New York: Harcourt Brace Jovanovich, 1974), 84.

42. Evelyn Fox Keller, *Reflections on Gender and Science* (New Haven, Conn.: Yale University Press, 1985); Chodorow (n. 29 above).

43. Belenky et al. (n. 28 above), 16.

44. Thomas Webber, *Deep Like the Rivers* (New York: Norton, 1978), 127.

45. In her discussion of the West African Sacred Cosmos, Mechal Sobel (n. 4 above) notes that Nyam, a root word in many West African languages, connotes an enduring spirit, power, or energy possessed by all life. In spite of the pervasiveness of this key concept in African humanism, its definition remains elusive. She points out, "Every individual analyzing the various Sacred Cosmos of West Africa has recognized the reality of this force, but no one has yet adequately translated this concept into Western terms" (13).

46. For discussions of personal expressiveness in African-American culture, see Smitherman (n. 19 above); Kochman (n. 34 above), esp. chap. 9; and Mitchell and Lewter (n. 5 above).

47. Gwaltney (n. 16 above), 228.

48. For feminist analyses of the subordination of emotion in Western culture, see Arlie Russell Hochschild, "The Sociology of Feeling and Emotion: Selected Possibilities," in *Another Voice: Feminist Perspectives on Social Life and Social Science,* ed. Marcia Millman and Rosabeth Kanter (Garden City, N.Y.: Anchor, 1975), 280–307; and Chodorow.

49. Tate (n. 39 above), 156.

50. Gwaltney, 11.

51. Smitherman, 135 and 137.

52. Belenky et al. (n. 28 above), 100–130.

53. Ibid., 119.

54. See ibid., 52–75, for a discussion of inner voice and its role in women's cognitive styles. Regarding empathy, Belenky et al. note: "Connected knowers begin with an interest in the

facts of other people's lives, but they gradually shift the focus to other people's ways of thinking. . . . It is the form rather than the content of knowing that is central. . . . Connected learners learn through empathy" (115).

55. Andrews (n. 17 above), 98.

56. Kochman (n. 34 above), 20 and 25.

57. Ibid, 23.

58. The sizable proportion of ministers among Black political leaders illustrates the importance of ethics in African-American communities.

59. Belenky et al. discuss a similar situation. They note, "People could critique each other's work in this class and accept each other's criticisms because members of the group shared a similar experience. . . . Authority in connected knowing rests not on power or status or certification but on commonality of experience" (118).

60. Carol Gilligan, *In a Different Voice* (Cambridge, Mass.: Harvard University Press, 1982). Carol Stack critiques Gilligan's model by arguing that African-Americans invoke a similar model of moral development to that used by women (see "The Culture of Gender: Women and Men of Color," *Signs* 11, no. 2 [Winter 1986]: 321–24). Another difficulty with Gilligan's work concerns the homogeneity of the subjects whom she studied.

R E A D I N G 5

Distinctions in Western Women's Experience: Ethnicity, Class, and Social Change

ROSALINDA MÉNDEZ GONZÁLEZ

The issues of ethnicity, class, and social change as they relate to women in western history and to historical reevaluation derive in part from the social-change movements of the 1950s and 1960s. Until then academic research had tended to neglect the experiences of minorities, women, and the laboring classes or to justify their subordinate social condition. Then the civil rights, feminist, and nationalist movements raised challenges to these approaches.

The new research born of the rebellions of those exciting years sought to uncover and document the historical facts of the neglected groups; to critique the existing myths, stereotypes, and paradigms that veiled or rationalized the inequalities and the historical contributions of the affected social groups; and to examine and expose the structures of domination and subordination in our society.

At first, these investigations took a rigidly protec-

From *The Women's West,* edited by Susan Armitage and Elizabeth Jameson. Copyright © 1987 by the University of Oklahoma Press.

tive stance toward their subjects. Black or Chicano nationalist analyses tended to question all traditional assumptions and to defend all that was black or brown; women's analyses attacked institutions and ideologies as patriarchal without distinction as to class or ethnic inequalities; radicals imbued with class analysis criticized imperialism abroad and class structures at home without considering the ramifications of sex or ethnic discrimination. Those who sought to integrate the analyses of the various forms of social inequality were at first in the minority.

By the 1970s the diverse groups had successfully documented the importance of their subjects' contributions to historical development and demonstrated the existence of social structures of domination over each group. An effort began then to integrate this analysis and to arrive at a more complex, fundamental explanation of the interconnections among these distinct social-historical experiences.

The process of including women's history, black history, Indian, Chicano, Asian, immigrant, and labor histories in the chronicles of United States history has been a first step toward an integrated history. Now we are confronted with the next step of jointly interpreting our interrelated histories. This requires going beyond the empirical combination of facts, names, and dates to the conceptual problem of seeking an explanation of how the diverse experiences were daily woven by individual human beings into a single and common historical reality.

In outlining the factors involved in these interconnected experiences, we must be careful to search for both the subjective, cultural conditions that motivated the individual woman's experiences and perceptions, and the objective, political-economic conditions that shaped the experiences of each social group.

The use of diaries, personal testimonies, oral histories, and literature have proved to be effective for uncovering the first set of conditions: women's personal or subjective experiences. But there are shortcomings to this approach. Women of the poor, slave, or laboring classes do not tend to leave diaries. Different methods and different questions have to be posed if one is to recapture the personal experiences of Indian, Hispanic, black, Asian, and poor white women of the laboring classes.

To find a conceptual interpretation of these diverse personal experiences, we must address the objective conditions of western life. This involves first challenging the traditional Turnerian interpretation of western history as the "frontier" period. The evolution of the West spans hundreds of years of Indian society before the American frontier. It is important to understand Indian social relations and the role of women before the Europeans imposed a class society.

Four centuries of Spanish conquest and settlement left a legacy of cultural development and social relations which is still in force today as, for example, in the legislation of western states.[1] Then, overlapping the three decades of Mexican rule over large parts of the West, comes the relatively brief period of United States conquest, the "frontier" period which has so absorbed myopic western historians. Finally, it is important to keep in mind that western history also comprises the twentieth century development of women in the West.[2]

THE QUESTION OF CLASS

In studying western history since European penetration, one of the most obvious but often ignored condi-

tions is the existence of social classes.[3] A class system was first introduced in the sixteenth century by the conquering Spaniards into the area that is now the southwestern United States.

Acknowledging the class character of Spanish and Mexican society in the Southwest penetrates the mist of generalizations which inaccurately assume classless homogeneity. Albert Camarillo's study of the Chicano communities in Santa Barbara and Los Angeles, California, delineates the four classes that comprised Mexican society: the elite rich "Californios," wealthy land-owning ranchers whose holdings averaged 25,000 acres; the middle class of small property owners and ranchers; the majority class of artisans and laborers living in humble dwellings; and the Indian population which was converted into laborers for the missions and menial servants for the wealthy Californios.[4]

In this society, what would it mean to talk about the life cycles of women? Certainly women's lives would appear different within the same household, where the wealthy Californios lived with their slave-like Indian female servants. Historian Elinor Burkett encountered this problem when she set out to study the relations of class, race, and sex in Spanish colonial South America. In feminist studies, Burkett notes, we often assume that:

> sex is as important a force in the historical process as class. Thus, we deal with the domestic squabbles of the aristocracy and the survival trials of the black female in the same conference without feeling uncomfortable; frequently forget that the position of the one is maintained only through the exploitation of the other and that such a relationship leaves little concrete room for sisterhood.[5]

If western historians raised these questions they might uncover in verbal records the gulf between the experiences of women of different classes. For example, the following black lullaby from the southern United States laments a black mother's inability to be with her newborn child through early motherhood and nursing because she had to tend to the baby of her mistress.[6]

All the Pretty Little Horses

Hushaby, don't you cry.
Go to sleepy, little baby.
When you wake, you shall have cake,
And all the pretty little horses.

Blacks and bays, dapples and grays,
Coach and six-a little horses.
Way down yonder in the meadow,
There's a poor little lambie;
The bees and the butterflies pickin' out his eyes,
The poor little thing cries, "Mammy."
Hushaby, don't you cry,
Go to sleepy, little baby.

The evidence of working class women's experience is there, but the prevailing orientations of studying history, even women's history, steer us toward elite or educated women and their written records; then from this limited and class-biased evidence generalizations are drawn and applied to all women.[7]

In fact, if one looks at history through the eyes of the majority of women, the poor and the laboring classes, a very different picture of society emerges; the picture is far more complete, for elite eyes take *their* world as the standard and assume that all society exists, or should exist, in their image.

But to see through the eyes of the women on the bottom, is to see not only the lives of the vast majority, but also to look upward through all levels of society; the flaws and contradictions of the upper classes and of the social structure they maintain become exposed from this perspective. The elite class perspective tends to be biased, myopic, and class-centered; the majority laboring class perspective tends to be more critical and encompassing.

WESTWARD EXPANSION

A second major historical consideration in studying the objective conditions that shaped women's experiences is the process of United States "westward expansion" which ultimately resulted in the appropriation of Indian, French, Spanish, and Mexican territories by the United States and the subordination of local ethnic groups as dispossessed cultural or national "minorities."

The process of westward expansion brings into play a host of major economic, political, and social developments. In a historical and economic sense the conquest of the West can be interpreted as corresponding to the similar process undergone by the western European countries in the sixteenth, seventeenth, and eighteenth centuries; known as the original or "primitive" accumulation of land and resources, this process constituted the preliminary stage for the development of industrial capitalist society.[8] In what sense is the conquest of the West a primitive accumulation?[9] And what is the significance of this process for women's experiences in the West?

Frederick Jackson Turner wrote that "the existence of an area of free land, its continuous recession, and the advance of American settlement westward, explain American development." Yet in the process of westward expansion the leading political actors clearly recognized the true character of that expansion: not an acquisition of an unclaimed territory free for the taking, not the expansion of "free land," but a military and political conquest of an already inhabited territory.[10]

Without the United States Army, in fact, the West could never have been "taken" by the settlers and pioneers. What effect did the army, both in the conquest and in its subsequent preservation, have on women in the West? What effect did it have on creating, altering, or maintaining class, ethnic, or racial divisions? Indian reservations in California were inevitably placed next to army posts and outposts.[11] What impact did the army have on Indian women who survived the devastating wars of extermination against their people?

The railroads were also instrumental in the penetration of the West. The building of the railroads was a key to expansion, not just as a means of military transportation but more fundamentally because of what lay behind the conquest: the penetration of the West by eastern capital. Linking the West Coast to the East Coast not only opened up the ports and raw materials of the West for exploitation by eastern bankers, industrialists, and land speculators but, far beyond that, opened up the Asian subcontinent for exploitation in such a way that it placed the United States at the crossroads of international commerce between the Far East and western Europe. Thus, the military conquest of the Indian and Mexican West and the construction of the transcontinental railroads opened up both a national market and an international empire for giant eastern capitalists.[12]

The building of the transcontinental railroads affected women of diverse ethnic and class backgrounds in a variety of ways; the full effects remain to be studied. We know, for example, that the railroads, after the military, provided one of the most effective ways of destroying American Indian people's subsistence on the Plains, by establishing the policy of paying sharpshooters to kill the buffalo.

The railroads stimulated mass immigration from Europe into the United States and mass migration into the West and Southwest. The construction of the railroads was accomplished by exploiting immigrant laborers: the Chinese, Japanese, and Mexicans on the West Coast, the Irish and European immigrants on the East Coast.[13]

Yet the treatment of European immigrant laborers was qualitatively different, in a political sense, from that of the Asian and Mexican immigrants.[14] Chinese laborers, for example, were brought in as bound labor, as "coolies," a politically unfree form of contract labor. They were forbidden to bring their wives or families. This restriction had a negative and long-lasting impact on the development of Chinese communities in the West, and it led to the importation of Chinese women in the most brutal form of "white slave traffic," an experience quite distinct from that of European immigrant women in the East.[15]

The importation of Mexican labor by the railroads has also left a deep legacy. As with the placement of Indian reservations next to Army forts, maps show that the *colonias* or Mexican settlements in the first half of the twentieth century were invariably located along the railroad routes, since whole Mexican families were imported by the companies to clear, lay, and maintain the tracks. The railroad companies would segregate their work force along ethnic lines and establish Mexican colonies of boxcar residences in certain places along the track; thus, the phrase "the wrong side of the tracks" came to be applied to Mexican barrios.[16] In the growing search for roots among Chicanas and Chicanos, the oral histories and family records that are surfacing reveal, in instance after instance, the ties to the railroads among our parents, grandparents, and great-grandparents.[17]

Today many Chicano barrios are still alongside the "wrong side of the tracks." They developed on the original sites of the old railroad-track Mexican colonies; in cities throughout the Southwest from California to Texas, these barrios are still distinguished by adobe houses, unpaved dirt streets, lack of sidewalks, often in direct proximity to walled, modern, Anglo middle-class housing tracts with multitiered, air-conditioned, carpeted homes.

PROPERTY, PATRIARCHY, AND THE NUCLEAR FAMILY

What did the settlement of the land itself mean for women of different classes and ethnicity? Much of the preliminary analysis on women in the West focuses on pioneer women, and their lives are studied through the diaries or literature they left behind. But the majority of women in the nineteenth-century West neither read nor wrote English. Barbara Mayer Wertheimer points out that the ordinary American could not pack up and head West. "It took capital, about $1,500, to outfit a wagon, buy supplies, and tide the family over until the land began to produce. This was an impossible sum for most working-class families to come by."[18]

Without detracting from the courage and endurance of these pioneer women, we have to ask what the takeover and settlement of western lands really represents for the majority of Indian, Mexican, and immigrant women in the West. A more comprehensive answer has to be found by studying first what western conquest and settlement represented in American economic and historical development. The West was not really developed by individual pioneering men and women seeking land. Rather, the West was made economically exploitable by federal intervention in the form of massive land grants to railroads, mining companies, timber companies, and land speculators, and by virtue of federal legislation and funding that subsidized these private profit-making ventures and speculators at public expense.[19]

Industrial and financial magnates did not operate simply out of greed for lucrative profits; they were driven by the economic necessity for expansion, which is at the heart of this system of competition and property. When the United States broke away from England in 1783, capitalist expansion was faced with three obstacles: the plantation slave economy of the South which held onto a bound labor force, raw materials, and productive lands; the Indian tribes and nations which had been pushed together into the West; and the Mexican Northwest.

These barriers could only be overcome by the usurpation and appropriation that have characterized the birth of capitalism wherever it has appeared. This process essentially involves breaking up the existing economic system (e.g., feudalism, tribal societies, peasant communities), concentrating land and wealth in the hands of a few entrepreneurs, and uprooting the native peoples from their land and mode of living to provide a source of wage labor.

A bloody Civil War was launched to remove the first obstacle. Wars against the Indians removed the second, and an unprovoked war against Mexico eliminated the third obstacle. After the defeat of the slave plantation economy, Indian tribal societies, and Mexican feudalism in the Southwest, the United States engaged in accelerated expansion and conquest of western territories. This process involved plunder, massacres, swindling, and bribery. It succeeded in imposing capitalist private property and, equally important, individualism and the patriarchal nuclear family which is so necessary to sustain this form of property.

Various methods were used to impose this system of property and family in the West. In the accumulation of Indian lands, force was not the only technique applied. Andrew Jackson and subsequent presidents attempted to deprive the Indians of their lands by refusing to deal with them as tribes or to negotiate treaties with them as nations. Instead the government forced the Indians, through bribery, treachery, and legislation, to deal with the government as individuals; this policy set them up against each other with the incentive of immediate cash payment to individuals selling plots of land. By forcing the foreign system of private property onto them, the government was attempting to destroy the fundamental communal basis of Indian tribes.

The General Allotment Act, or Dawes Act, of 1883 sought to push the Indians out of the way of western penetration and open up their lands to exploitation, by alloting parcels of tribal land to individuals. The bill was condemned by Senator Henry Teller of Colorado as "a bill to despoil the Indians of their lands and to make them vagabonds on the face of the earth," yet Congress passed it with the justification that "Indians needed to become competitive." Senator Henry Dawes, principal proponent of the measure, argued that Indians "needed to become selfish."[20]

Two centuries earlier the French colonizers in Canada had been amazed at the egalitarianism and freedom among the women and men of the Montagnais tribe, at their disdain for formal authority and domination, and at the respect and independence between husbands and wives. Yet the Jesuit policy of colonization sought to "give authority to one of them to rule the others," and to teach them "to elect and obey 'Captains,' inducing them to give up their children for schooling, and above all, attempting to introduce the principle of binding monogamy and wifely fidelity and obedience to male authority."[21]

In a similar manner the United States recognized that to break down Indian resistance it was necessary to undermine the tribal and clan social organization of the Indians and to enforce upon them the individual nuclear family, with the husband the authority figure over the women and children. This attempt had the multiple purposes of forcing the Indians to alienate their communal tribal lands, breaking their economic and social clan organization, transforming them into individualist and competitive capitalist farmers, and providing the nuclear family institution through which the ideology of private property, individualism, and dominant-subordinate relations could be passed on.

Other American people—the small farmers, European immigrants, and settlers—also were subject to official policies promoting individualism in the process of westward expansion. The Homestead Act of 1862, which preceded the Dawes Act by almost three decades, forced individuals and individual families to settle independently; no land was made available for whole communities. On the other hand, huge tracts of land were made available only to the big companies penetrating the West: the railroads, banks, land speculators, and mining companies. While the individual homesteaders were told, "The government bets 160 acres against the entry fee of $14 that the settler can't live on the land for five years without starving to death,"[22] the financial and industrial giants were granted all the land they wanted; the government even provided capital for the infrastructural construction they needed to operate and extract their private profits.

The fostering of private property, individualism, and the nuclear family in the West thus resulted on the one hand in the breakup of the population into individual, isolated, competitive miniscule units:—nuclear families; and the concentration of wealth and power in the hands of an increasingly smaller elite on the other—monopolies. For monopolization to take place, it was necessary to fragment the population through the imposition of private property.

The United States government promoted this process in the West. Neither the government's nor the monopolies' intention, however, was to perpetuate small-scale production and independence. Rather, they brought people in to clear the land, develop the resources, and make the area productive and, when this was done, usurped this settled population from their small plots and transformed them into the wage-labor force needed in the West. Both stages were accomplished by fostering private property, individual ownership of land, and the privatization of the nuclear family.

EXPLOITATION OF WOMEN'S DOMESTIC LABOR

The patriarchal nuclear family was important, not just as a means of preserving and transferring private property and the values associated with it, but also, for the families of the laboring classes, as a means of privately producing through the domestic labor of women the goods and services necessary to sustain the agricultural or industrial labor force needed by capitalist enterprises.[23]

Among Mexican immigrant families in the early twentieth-century Southwest, women's domestic labor was exploited indirectly by large employers as a means of subsidizing the payment of discriminatory and substandard wages to their Mexican workers.[24] This policy was refined by the monopolies engaged in developing the Southwest; these companies in the extractive, infrastructural, and agricultural industries first imported Mexican immigrants in large numbers at the turn of the century.[25]

The monopolistic pattern of southwestern land ownership and industry in many places retained vestiges of the feudal system, such as tenant or sharecropping systems in agriculture or debt peonage in company mining towns. These practices retarded the assimilation of Mexican immigrants into the working class, and had the effect of perpetuating the bondage of the wife and children under the patriarchal family. Patriarchal family relations were particularly strong in rural areas. Women who were hired as agricultural laborers to pick cotton were never paid their own wages; rather, these were paid to the father, husband, or brother. Because of this system of "family wages," feudal relations in the countryside were not easily broken down, and wage labor did not offer women the economic independence that weakened patriarchal relations as did urban or industrial employment.[26]

Even in urban areas, Mexican families found themselves segregated and living in boxcars or makeshift housing. Mario Garcia, in a study of Mexican families in El Paso, Texas, at the turn of the century, documented how their reduced standard of living provided a justification for the payment of wages far below the "American standard." Mexican families were forced to live "75 percent cheaper than Americans" by a series of economic and political mechanisms. Racial discrimination and starvation wages confined Mexicans to the worst slums, with overcrowded, inferior housing in adobes or shacks. These settlements were denied public services (water, paved streets, electricity, sewers) because the Anglo property owners refused to pay taxes to provide them and because the city, in turn, argued that Mexican residents were not property owners and taxpayers, and therefore not entitled to services.[27]

Given this living situation, the domestic labor of women and children was particularly arduous. They hauled water long distances from the river in buckets, hand-ground corn for hours, gathered and chopped wood for fuel, to make up for the lack of adequate wages and public services.

This extreme exploitation of family labor and the intense immiseration of the laboring communities caused high infant-mortality rates, infectious diseases, and malnourishment, while providing the justification for lower wages. It also provided a pool of severely underpaid Mexican female servants whose dusk-to-dawn exploitation in the homes of Anglo-American families freed the women of these families to seek outside employment and enter the industrial world. The economic advancement of many Anglo-American women in the Southwest was carried out on the backs of Mexican-American women, as it was in the South on the backs of black women, and the immediate beneficiaries were the banks and monopolies dominating the South and West.

THE QUESTION OF RESEARCH AND SOCIAL CHANGE

My discussion has not centered on individual heroines of different ethnic or class backgrounds nor on the important subject of women's struggles to change the conditions of ethnic, class, racial, or sex discrimination. I have sought to demonstrate the necessity of taking into consideration the larger, more fundamental political-economic forces in the development of the West, which must be studied if one is to understand the experiences of *all* women.

The forces that had come to dominate the West at the end of the nineteenth century have continued to shape the experiences of women in the twentieth century, the more so as economic concentration and its influence through the growth of government power has expanded. In 1962, the wealthiest 10 percent of the United States population controlled close to 70 percent of all personal wealth, while the other 90 percent of the population shared a little over 30 percent.[28] Even this small share of the pie was unevenly divided. Poverty in the United States was concentrated in the South and West, and among blacks and Mexican-Americans. In 1960, for example, official figures showed that in the Southwest 35 percent of the Spanish-surnamed families and 42 percent of nonwhite families were living in poverty. Among Anglo families, only 16 percent were listed in poverty, and yet this represented a very large number, since Anglos comprised 66 percent of all poor in the Southwest.[29]

Today we know that poverty and unemployment have worsened, that two out of every three persons in poverty are women, and that black women and Chicanas are among those most affected. This situation continues as the "minority" peoples of the Southwest are rapidly becoming the majority.

The trend toward greater inequality is growing. Richard M. Cyert, president of Pittsburgh's Carnegie-Mellon University, which houses the most advanced research and experimentation center in the robotics fields, recently stated, "I don't think there's any question that we're moving toward a society where income distribution will be even more unequal than it is at present and where unemployment is going to be even greater than it is now."[30]

The issue of inequality confronts anyone seeking to develop a historically accurate, comprehensive analysis that integrates the experiences of the majority of poor and working-class women, the experiences of black, Chicana, Indian, Asian, and immigrant women. We have been dealing with the divisions among us: while these divisions of race and class have existed, we also have to deal with the fundamental unity among us.

Our task is to discover both the causes of the artificial, socially created divisions that have kept us apart and ways to make our fundamental unity a reality. If we are concerned with social change, if our research is to involve a commitment to shedding light on the historical roots of contemporary problems and inequalities so that these inequalities can be abolished, then our research will have to address the issues of inequality, exploitation, and the related political question of democracy. For the history of the West, as the history of the United States, is a history of exploitation of the labor, land, and resources of diverse groups of peoples: Indians, indentured servants, black slaves, farmers, the working class, immigrants, and, not least, the exploitation of women in the home.

For this reason it is also a history of the unfolding struggle over democratic rights and against the powerful minority of anti-democratic forces who have sought to monopolize political power to ensure their economic concentration. This struggle for democracy has involved the Indians' struggle for their land and sovereignty; the struggle of immigrants, of blacks, of Chicanos; working-class and socialist struggles; and, integral to all of these, women's struggle for equality and political emancipation.

ACKNOWLEDGMENTS

Special thanks to Nancy Paige Fernandez, of the Program in Comparative Culture at the University of California at Irvine, for her thoughtful critique of my first draft, and to Lisa Rubens, Lyn Reese, Deanne Thompson, and all the other women at the Women's West Conference whose warm encouragement and extensive discussions and comments enlightened my analysis and understanding.

NOTES

1. E.g., community-property laws for married couples in many southern and western states (especially in former Spanish and French territories); and the Texas "cuckoo law," which allowed a husband to kill his wife's lover if he caught them "in the act." On community property consult Barbara Allen Babcock et al., *Sex Discrimination and the Law* (Boston: Little, Brown, 1975), pp. 604–13. On the Texas "cuckoo law" see "The 'Equal Shooting Rights,'" *Texas Observer,* 16 Mar. 1965; and "Origins of the Cuckoo Law," 2 Apr. 1965. The latter article observes, "Like so many of our

especially Texan legal institutions (our homestead law, our venue statute, the independent executor, our adoption law, and our community property system), our legal attitude toward the cuckold's right to take vengeance for an affront to his conjugal honor is Spanish in origin." More accurately, they are feudal in origin.

2. If we include the twentieth century, certain "academic" problems are resolved, such as that there were few black women in "the West" narrowly defined as the frontier period. If we define the West more fully, the presence of black women emerges as a real issue. How, for example, did the development of Jim Crow in the South in the early twentieth century under the sponsorship of the large propertied and monied interests affect women when Jim Crow was imposed on black, Mexican, and Asian communities in the West?

3. Louis M. Hacker, in "Sections—or Classes?" *The Nation* 137, no. 355 (26 July 1933): 108–10 leveled a sharp critique at the Turnerian thesis of a unique and democratic frontier environment in the West. See also Barry D. Karl, "Frederick Jackson Turner: The Moral Dilemma of Professionalization," *Reviews in American History* 3 (March 1975): 1–7.

4. Albert Camarillo, *Chicanos in a Changing Society: From Mexican Pueblos to American Barrios in Santa Barbara and Southern California, 1848–1930* (Cambridge, Mass.: Harvard University Press, 1979). Other studies of sixteenth- to nineteenth-century Mexican families or women include Leonard Pitt, *The Decline of the Californios: A Social History of the Spanish-Speaking Californians, 1846–1890* (Berkeley: University of California Press, 1971); Richard Griswold del Castillo, *The Los Angeles Barrio, 1850–1890: A Social History* (Berkeley: University of California Press, 1979); Richard Griswold del Castillo, *La Familia: Chicano Families in the Urban Southwest, 1848 to the Present* (Notre Dame, Ind.: University of Notre Dame Press, 1984); Frances Leon Swadesh, *Los Primeros Pobladores, Hispanic Americans of the Ute Frontier* (Notre Dame, Ind.: University of Notre Dame Press, 1974); Ramon A. Gutierrez, *Marriage, Sex, and the Family: Social Change in Colonial New Mexico, 1690–1846* (Ph.D. diss., University of Wisconsin, Madison, 1980); Ramon A. Gutierrez, "From Honor to Love: Transformation of the Meaning of Sexuality in Colonial New Mexico," in Raymond T. Smith, ed., *Love, Honor, and Economic Fate: Interpreting Kinship Ideology and Practice in Latin America* (Chapel Hill: University of North Carolina Press, 1983); Ramon A. Gutierrez, "Marriage and Seduction in Colonial New Mexico," in Adelaida del Castillo, ed., *Mexicana/Chicana Women's History*, Chicana Studies Research Center (forthcoming); Gloria E. Miranda, *"Gente De Razon* Marriage Patterns in Spanish and Mexican California: A Case Study of Santa Barbara and Los Angeles," *Southern California Quarterly* 39 no. 1 (March 1957): 149–66; Jane Dysart, "Mexican Women in San Antonio, 1830–1860: The Assimilation Process," *Western Historical Quarterly* 7 no. 4 (October

1976): 365–75; Fray Angelico Chavez, "Dona Tules, Her Fame and Her Funeral," *Palacio* 57 (August 1950): 227–34; Marcela Lucero Trujillo, "The Spanish Surnamed Woman of Yester Year," in José Otero and Evelio Echevarria, eds., *Hispanic Colorado* (Fort Collins, Colo.: Centennial Publications, 1977); Daniel J. Garr, "A Rare and Desolate Lane: Population and Race in Hispanic California," *Western Historical Quarterly* 6, no. 2 (April, 1975): 133–48. A masterful bibliography on the "Borderlands," containing hundreds of references for further research, is Charles C. Cumberland, *The United States–Mexican Border: A Selective Guide to the Literature of the Region*, published by *Rural Sociology* as vol. 25, no. 2 (June 1970): 230 pp. The work includes references to Spanish-Indian relations in the region.

5. Elinor C. Burkett, "In Dubious Sisterhood: Race and Class in Spanish Colonial South America," *Latin American Perspectives* 4 nos. 1–2 (Winter–Spring, 1977): 18–26.

6. "All the Pretty Little Horses," in Middleton Harris et al., *The Black Book* (New York: Random House, 1974), p. 65. The book is a photographic documentary history of the black experience in the United States, including documents and graphics of blacks in the West.

7. For example, Barbara Welter's "The Cult of True Womanhood: 1820–1860," *American Quarterly* 18, no. 2 (1966): 151–74, reprinted in Michael Gordon, ed., *The American Family in Socio-Historical Perspective* (New York: St. Martin's Press, 1973). Welter assumes an upper-class, native WASP homogeneity of all women in America: "It was a fearful obligation, a solemn responsibility, which the nineteenth century *American woman* had—to uphold the pillars of the temple with her frail *white hand*" (p. 225, emphasis added). Her article provides no discussion of property or of women and the family's relation to property. In her only (indirect) reference to the economic character of American society and its class divisions, she blithely passes by without acknowledging these contradictions: "America was a land of precarious fortunes. . . . the woman who had servants today, might tomorrow, because of a depression or panic, be forced to do her own work. . . . she was to be the same cheerful consoler of her husband in their cottage as in their mansion" (p. 238).

In fact, this section contains the only references to the existence of other classes of women: ". . . the value of a wife in case of business reverses . . . of course she had a little help from 'faithful Dinah' who absolutely refused to leave her beloved mistress" (pp. 238–239). Welter cites quotations linking the Cult of True Womanhood to a certain order of society ("that a stable order of society depended upon her maintaining her traditional place in it" [p. 242]), yet she never questions that order, never examines that society and why its maintenance depended on women's domestic subordination.

8. Cf. Leo Huberman, *Man's Worldly Goods: The Story of the Wealth of Nations* (New York: Monthly Review Press, 1936); Maurice Dobb, *Studies in the Development of Capital-*

ism (New York: International Publishers, 1947). An incisive presentation of primitive accumulation and its devastating impact on peasant families in Europe is found in Karl Marx, *Capital,* vol. 1, part 8 "The So-Called Primitive Accumulation."

9. Raul A. Fernandez, in *The United States–New Mexico Border: A Politico-Economic Profile* (Notre Dame, Ind.: University of Notre Dame Press, 1977), presents an analysis of the complex character of this process in the Southwest. Ray Allen Billington's classic *Westward Expansion* traces the historical facts of the process of westward expansion, though from the perspective of Frederick Jackson Turner's "frontier thesis."

10. Both Jefferson Davis and Captain Randolph B. Marcy compared the conquest of the West with the French imperialist conquest of Algeria, and both argued that the United States Army should apply the French tactics in that conquest to the conquest of the Indians in the West. Walter Prescott Webb, *The Great Plains* (Lincoln: University of Nebraska Press, ca. 1931), pp. 194, 195, 196.

11. Lynwood Carranco, *Genocide and Vendetta: The Round Valley Wars in Northern California* (Norman: University of Oklahoma Press, 1981). An excellent survey of government-Indian relations is found in D'Arcy McNichols, *Native American Tribalism: Indian Survivals and Renewals* (published for the Institute of Race Relations, London, by Oxford University Press, 1973). Indian women's resistance in the face of both the Spanish and United States conquests is presented in Victoria Brady, Sarah Crome, and Lyn Reese's "Resist and Survive, Aspects of Native Women of California," (MS Sarah Crome, Institute for the Study of Social Change, University of California, Berkeley, Calif.)

12. For a very explicit account of the connections between this internal conquest and the creation of a foreign empire by the United States, see Scott Nearing, *The American Empire* (New York: Rand School of Social Science, 1921). See also Leo Huberman, *We, the People* (New York, London: Harper Brothers, 1947).

13. A good overview of immigration in the United States is found in Barbara Kaye Greenleaf, *America Fever: The Story of American Immigration* (New York: New American Library, 1974).

14. Rosalinda M. González, "Capital Accumulation and Mexican Immigration to the United States" (Ph.D. diss., University of California at Irvine, 1981) offers a political-economic analysis of the discriminatory treatment of Asian and Mexican immigrants that differs from the traditional explanations in terms of racism.

15. Dorothy Gray, "Minority Women in the West, Juanita, Biddy Mason, Donaldina Cameron," in *Women of the West* (Millbrae, Calif.: Les Femmes Publishing, 1976), pp. 62–75; *Asian Women* (Berkeley: University of California, Dwinelle Hall, 1971); Ruthanne Lum McCunn, *An Illustrated History of the Chinese in America* (San Francisco: Design Enterprises, 1979).

16. Case studies of these barrios and their twentieth-century development appear in Arthur J. Rubel, *Across the Tracks: Mexican-Americans in a Texas City* (Austin: University of Texas Press, 1966); and Ricardo Romo, *East Los Angeles, History of a Barrio* (Austin: University of Texas Press, 1983). The historical development of the Chicano people is examined in Carey McWilliams's classic *North from Mexico: The Spanish Speaking People of the United States* (New York: Greenwood Press, 1968); Rodolfo Acuna, *Occupied America: A History of Chicanos* (New York: Harper & Row, 1981); and the excellent bilingual pictorial history by Chicano Communications Center, *450 Years of Chicano History in Pictures* (South Pasadena, Calif.: Bilingual Educations Services, n.d.). A case study of how monopoly-motivated reforms of the Progressive Era were applied to Mexican immigrant communities at the turn of the century is found in Gilbert G. Gonzalez, *Progressive Education: A Marxist Interpretation* (Minneapolis: Marxist Educational Press, 1982). A historical analysis of Chicanas is presented in Martha P. Cotera, *Diosa y Hembra: The History and Heritage of Chicanas in the U.S.* (Austin, Tex.: Information Systems Development, 1976).

17. See, e.g., the beautiful and poignant description in Jose Lona's "Biographical Sketch of the Life of an Immigrant Woman," in Maria Linda Apodaca, "The Chicana Woman: An Historical Materialist Analysis," *Latin American Perspectives* 4, nos. 1–2: p. 70–89. The Institute of Oral History at the University of Texas at El Paso has a growing collection of over 500 taped interviews, many of which relate to the railroads.

18. Barbara Mayer Wertheimer, *We Were There: The Story of Working Women in America* (New York: Pantheon Books, 1977), pp. 249. Lillian Schlissel, in *Women's Diaries of the Westward Journey* (New York: Schocken Books, 1982), pointed out that most of the western pioneers were landowners and that their parents had also been landowners, "a class of 'peasant proprietors' " (pp. 10–11).

19. See, e.g., Gabriel Kolko, *Railroads and Regulation* (Westport, Conn.: Greenwood Press, 1976); Robert Wiebe, *The Search for Order, 1877–1920* (New York: Hill and Wang, 1968); James Weinstein, *The Corporate Idea in the Liberal State, 1900–1918* (Boston: Beacon Press, 1968); Matthew Josephson, *The Robber Barons* (New York: Harcourt Brace, 1934); and Matthew Josephson, *The Money Lords* (New York: Weybright and Talley, 1972).

20. McNichols, *Native American Tribalism.* For a brief description of the negative effects on tribal solidarity from the imposition of individualism and the nuclear family on Indian society, see the first two chapters of Keith Basso's *The Cibecue Apache* (New York: Holt, Rinehart and Winston, 1970).

21. Eleanor Leacock, "Women in Development: Anthropological Facts and Fictions," *Latin American Perspectives* 4, nos. 1–2.

22. Sheryll and Gene Pattersen-Black, *Western Women in History and Literature* (Crawford, Neb.: Cottonwood Press, 1978), p. 5.

23. An important article by Joan Jensen, "Cloth, Bread, and Boarders: Women's Household Production for the Market," *The Review of Radical Political Economics* 12, no. 2 (Summer 1980): 14–24, examines women's household production from the late-eighteenth to early-twentieth centuries. Jensen concludes that it increased the economic productivity of the family through women's provision of services and the home production of produce for domestic consumption and for local and regional markets. In rural areas the domestic labor of women allowed men to increase production of cash crops for urban markets without increasing food costs. "Low food costs combined with taking in boarders allowed the males of American urban families to work for lower wages than they might have required had women not contributed to the family income."

24. Rosalinda M. González, "Mexican Immigrants in the United States: Cultural Conflict and Class Transformation," *Labor History,* forthcoming; and Rosalinda M. González, "Chicanas and Mexican Immigrant Families, 1920–1940" in Joan Jensen and Lois Scharf, eds., *Decades of Discontent: The Women's Movement, 1920–1940* (Westport, Conn.: Greenwood Press, 1983).

25. Many of the leading entrepreneurs in western expansion also had their stakes in foreign conquest. In the Southwest, for example, Adolph Spreckles, who built his fortune in California and Hawaii sugar plantations, merged with Henry C. Havemeyer, the eastern sugar king, to form the sugar trust, which was obtaining concessions in Mexico to grant it complete monopolization. Spreckles was a close friend of the Southern Pacific Railroad, which under the leadership of Henry Huntington and subsequently under William Harriman was gobbling up railroads in the United States and Mexico and absorbing steamship lines and ports. John Kenneth Turner, *Barbarous Mexico* (Austin: University of Texas Press, 1969); Carey McWilliams, *Factories in the Field* (Santa Barbara, Calif.: Peregrine Publishers, 1971).

26. Ruth Allen, *The Labor of Women in the Production of Cotton* (Austin, Tex.: University of Texas Press, 1931).

27. Mario T. Garcia, *Desert Immigrants: The Mexicans of El Paso, 1880–1920* (New Haven, Conn.: Yale University Press, 1981).

28. Institute for Labor Education and Research, *What's Wrong with the U.S. Economy?* (Boston: South End Press, 1982), pp. xi, 32.

29. Leo Grebler et al., in "A Preview of Socioeconomic Conditions," *The Mexican American People* (New York: The Free Press, 1970), pp. 13–34.

30. Donald Dewey, "Robots Reach Out," *United* (August 1983): 92–99.

P A R T   T W O

Learning Gender

Everyone is born into a *culture*—a set of shared ideas about the nature of reality, the nature of right and wrong, the evaluation of what is good and desirable, and the nature of good and desirable versus the bad and undesirable. These ideas are manifested in behaviors and artifacts. As totally dependent infants we are *socialized*—taught the rules, roles, and relationships of the social world we will inherit. We exchange our infant hedonism for love, protection, and the attention of others; in the process, we learn to think, act, and feel as we are "supposed to."

One of the earliest and most deeply seated ideas to which we are socialized is that of gender identity: the idea that "I am a boy" or "I am a girl." Because the culture, moreover, has strong ideas about what boys and girls are like, we learn to identify our gender identity (our "boyness" or "girlness") with behaviors that are sex-assigned in our culture. Thus, for example, a girl who plays with dolls is viewed as behaving in an appropriate and "feminine" manner and a boy who plays with trucks as behaving appropriately "masculine." Sometimes consciously and sometimes unconsciously, children are categorized, differentially responded to and regarded, and encouraged to adopt behaviors and attitudes on the basis of their sex. We raise, in effect, two different kinds of children: boys and girls.

Parents (or surrogate parents) are strong socializing influences, and they provide the first and most deeply experienced socialization experiences. Despite claims to the contrary, American parents treat their infant girls and boys differently. Boys have "boy toys," "boy names," "boy room decor," and are played with in more "boylike" ways than girls. Even if parents monitor their actions in the hope of preventing sexism from affecting their child, their endeavors will not succeed, because *other* socializing influences bear down on the child.

One of the primary socializing influences is *language*. In learning to talk we acquire the thought patterns and communication styles of our culture. Those patterns and styles in all languages perpetuate and reinforce differentiation by sex and sex stereotyping, albeit the kind of stereotyping may vary from culture to culture. If a child is reared bilingually, then she or he acquires two cultures' notions of sex stereotyping, which may not be compatible with each other, but will then require the child to negotiate the cultural rifts, including learning how the dominant culture speaks about the nondominant culture. A "gendered" person is thus created through different linguistic and cultural contexts.

All languages teach deep-seated ideas about men and women. They do it "naturally": as one learns a language, one learns the viewpoint of their culture. In the English language, for example, the generic *man* is supposed to include males and females, as well as blacks and whites; but in linguistic practice it does not. People other than white and male are linguistically tagged in writing and in speech. For example, occupational categories are sex-tagged if the person's sex or race does not fit cultural stereotypes about who will be in those occupations. Consider: doctor/woman doctor/black woman doctor; nurse/male nurse/Asian male nurse. What is being taught is the centricity of "white men" in a socially prescribed system of inequity.

As societies become more complex, increasingly the mass media have become centralized agents for the transmission of dominant cultural beliefs. Movements toward cultural heterogeneity are thwarted through the homogenizing effects of television, in particular. The media present sex stereotypes in their purest and simplest forms. For example, whether the program is about African-American families, Hispanic families, or white families, the sex-stereotyping messages are endlessly repetitive. Children in the United States spend more time watching television than they spend in school or interacting with parents or peers. Moreover, they believe that what they see on television is an accurate representation of how the world is and should be organized. White middle-class male dominance is the repetitive theme.

The socialization effected by the family and by language (including that of the mass media) is supplemented by the educational system. Educational institutions are formally charged with teaching the young. While teaching them reading, writing, and arithmetic, however, the schools also imbue them with sexist values. They do so through the pattern of staffing (male principals and custodians, female teachers and food servers), the curriculum materials, the sex segregation of sports and activities, and differential *expectations* of boys and girls. No child can avoid this socialization experience.

Through powerful social institutions, then, children learn a culture. The culture they learn is one that views malehood as superior to femalehood; it is a system that differentially assigns behaviors and attitudes to males and females.

Socialization—whether through the home, the school, language, or the mass media—creates and sustains gender differences. Boys are taught that they will inherit the privileges and prestige of manhood, while girls are taught that they are less socially valuable than boys. Both are expected to view their status as right, moral, and appropriate. Moreover, socialization never ends. As adults we continue to be resocialized by the books we read, the movies we see, and the people we spend time with.

The readings in this part of *Feminist Frontiers III* illustrate and explain different aspects of the socialization process and provide the reader with conceptual frameworks and perspectives for understanding the implications of gender.

Language, Images, and Culture

Language—both verbal and nonverbal—affects the way we view ourselves and our relationships to each other and to the world around us. Language reflects and perpetuates the values of a society. The English language teaches that males and masculine values, behaviors, and goals are more important than females and the values, behaviors, and goals associated with girls and women. In addition to images created by language, visual images in various media surround us with cultural messages about the power differences between women and men. This section explores images of women and men expressed in language and visual media.

Laurel Richardson's "Gender Stereotyping in the English Language" demonstrates six major ways in which sexism pervades the structure and standard usage of modern American English. Her analysis reveals differential expectations of men and women embedded in the language; offers insights on how we internalize and reinforce gender differences as we read, write, and speak English or hear it spoken; and implicitly raises questions about the relationships between language and social life, including connections between linguistic and social change.

In "Hablando cara a cara/Speaking Face to Face: An Exploration of Ethnocentric Racism," María Lugones explores racism, ethnocentrism, and the points of convergence and divergence between them. She argues that to love one's people does not necessitate assumption of racial superiority. Writing in both Spanish and English, Lugones emphasizes the importance of white Anglo women recognizing their own ethnicities in order to form honest and meaningful alliances with women of color and to counter racist oppression sensitively and effectively.

Paula Gunn Allen situates herself between Anglo and American Indian cultures and, from that vantage point, analyzes images of women and images of Indians in each context. In "Where I Come From Is Like This," she provides insight on the psychological and social conflicts created by the bicultural experiences of many Indian women. In particular, she reveals the incongruity of the images of women embedded in Anglo and American Indian cultures.

Because of women's common economic dependence upon men, many women must strive to meet male-defined standards of femininity and beauty in order to obtain male financial support and protection. An account of women's suffering to meet male-prescribed standards of beauty appears in Andrea Dworkin's "Gynocide: Chinese Footbinding." Her analysis, easily extended to other cultural contexts, incisively reveals the relationships between cultural ideologies and social practices, particularly as they function to restrict women's lives.

We cannot emphasize too strongly the importance of language and images in the construction of our understandings about women's positions in society. We are continuously exposed to ideas of women as subordinate to men. Moreover, since the language we have acquired and the images we use are so deeply rooted and inseparable, it is very difficult for us to break from them, to see and describe the world and our experiences in nonsexist ways. The power to define has a major influence on our perceptions of ourselves and others.

43

Gender Stereotyping in the English Language

LAUREL RICHARDSON

Everyone in our society, regardless of class, ethnicity, sex, age, or race, is exposed to the same language, the language of the dominant culture. Analysis of verbal language can tell us a great deal about a people's fears, prejudices, anxieties, and interests. A rich vocabulary on a particular subject indicates societal interests or obsessions (e.g., the extensive vocabulary about cars in America). And different words for the same subject (such as *freedom fighter* and *terrorist, passed away* and *croaked, make love* and *ball*) show that there is a range of attitudes and feelings in the society toward that subject.

It should not be surprising, then, to find differential attitudes and feelings about men and women rooted in the English language. Although the English language has not been completely analyzed, six general propositions concerning these attitudes and feelings about males and females can be made.

First, in terms of grammatical and semantic structure, women do not have a fully autonomous, independent existence; they are part of man. The language is not divided into male and female with distinct conjugations and declensions, as many other languages are. Rather, *women* are included under the generic *man.* Grammar books specify that the pronoun *he* can be used generically to mean *he* or *she.* Further, *man,* when used as an indefinite pronoun, grammatically refers to both men and women. So, for example, when we read *man* in the following phrases we are to interpret it as applying to both men and women: "man the oars," "one small step for man, one giant step for mankind," "man, that's tough," "man overboard," "man the toolmaker," "alienated man," "garbageman."

Adapted from Laurel Richardson, *The Dynamics of Sex and Gender: A Sociological Perspective* (New York: Harper & Row, 1987), by permission of the author.

Our rules of etiquette complete the grammatical presumption of inclusivity. When two persons are pronounced "man and wife," Miss Susan Jones changes her entire name to Mrs. Robert Gordon (Vanderbilt, 1972). In each of these correct usages, women are a part of man; they do not exist autonomously. The exclusion of women is well expressed in Mary Daly's ear-jarring slogan "the sisterhood of man" (1973:7–21).

However, there is some question as to whether the theory that *man* means everybody is carried out in practice (see Bendix, 1979; Martyna, 1980). For example, an eight-year-old interrupts her reading of "The Story of the Cavemen" to ask how we got here without cavewomen. A ten-year-old thinks it is dumb to have a woman post*man*. A beginning anthropology student believes (incorrectly) that all shamans ("witch doctors") are males because her textbook and professor use the referential pronoun *he*.

But beginning language learners are not the only ones who visualize males when they see the word *man*. Research has consistently demonstrated that when the generic *man* is used, people visualize men, not women (Schneider & Hacker, 1973; DeStefano, 1976; Martyna, 1978; Hamilton & Henley, 1982). DeStefano, for example, reports that college students choose silhouettes of males for sentences with the word *man* or *men* in them. Similarly, the presumably generic *he* elicits images of men rather than women. The finding is so persistent that linguists doubt whether there actually is a semantic generic in English (MacKay, 1983).

Man, then, suggests not humanity but rather male images. Moreover, over one's lifetime, an educated American will be exposed to the prescriptive *he* more than a million times (MacKay, 1983). One consequence is the exclusion of women in the visualization, imagination, and thought of males and females. Most likely this linguistic practice perpetuates in men their feelings of

A MONUMENTAL OVERSIGHT

EDITORIAL STAFF, WOMEN RIGHT NOW, *GLAMOUR MAGAZINE*

A few weeks after **Betsy Gotbaum** . . . became New York City's parks and recreation commissioner (the first female to hold the position), someone asked her how many statues of women were in the city's parks. "I said I wasn't sure, but I'd find out," Gotbaum says. What she found was that *there isn't a single statue of an American woman in New York City.* In fact, of the Park Department's 417 monuments considered significant in terms of size, subject or artist, only three depict individual and identifiable females: Joan of Arc, Alice in Wonderland and Mother Goose. "I counted Mother Goose because she's a mother and I was trying to make sure I was getting everybody in," says Gotbaum. "But I was also making a point."

Part of the problem is that most of the monuments and statues in New York City were erected between 1876 and 1917. "Before the women's movement, women were not considered on a par with men in terms of their accomplishments," Gotbaum says. "There's a visual domination of males in our society."

Procuring more statues of women won't be easy, but Gotbaum's a fighter—and she's already getting results. "The owner of an art gallery read about what our department is trying to do and donated a statue of Gertrude Stein," she says. "It's going to go into Bryant Park, next to the public library, within the next few months." Also in the works are a plaque dedicated to Emma Lazarus (the writer of the Statue of Liberty sonnet) and the Eleanor Roosevelt Memorial, a landscape that will include a bronze sculpture and panels of quotes from the first lady.

"Maybe if women read about what we're doing here in New York, they'll be inspired to do it in their cities," says Gotbaum. "I'd love to get a whole movement going."

Courtesy *Glamour.* Copyright © 1991 by The Conde Nast Publications Inc.

dominance over and responsibility for women, feelings that interfere with the development of equality in relationships.

Second, in actual practice, our pronoun usage perpetuates different personality attributes and career aspirations for men and women. Nurses, secretaries, and elementary school teachers are almost invariably referred to as *she;* doctors, engineers, electricians, and presidents as *he.* In one classroom, students referred to an unidentified child as *he* but shifted to *she* when discussing the child's parent. In a faculty discussion of the problems of acquiring new staff, all architects, engineers, security officers, faculty, and computer programmers were referred to as *he;* secretaries and file clerks were referred to as *she.* Martyna (1978) has noted that speakers consistently use *he* when the referent has a high-status occupation (e.g., doctor, lawyer, judge) but shift to *she* when the occupations have lower status (e.g., nurse, secretary).

Even our choice of sex ascription to nonhuman objects subtly reinforces different personalities for males and females. It seems as though the small (e.g., kittens), the graceful (e.g., poetry), the unpredictable (e.g., the fates), the nurturant (e.g., the church, the school), and that which is owned and/or controlled by men (e.g., boats, cars, governments, nations) represent the feminine, whereas that which is a controlling forceful power in and of itself (e.g., God, Satan, tiger) primarily represents the masculine. Even athletic teams are not immune. In one college, the men's teams are called the Bearcats and the women's teams the Bearkittens.

Some of you may wonder whether it matters that the female is linguistically included in the male. The inclusion of women under the pseudogeneric *man* and the prescriptive *he,* however, is not a trivial issue. Language has tremendous power to shape attitudes and influence behavior. Indeed, MacKay (1983) argues that the prescriptive *he* "has all the characteristics of a highly effective propaganda technique": frequent repetition, early age of acquisition (before age 6), covertness (*he* is not thought of as propaganda), use by high-prestige sources (including university texts and professors), and indirectness (presented as though it were a matter of common knowledge). As a result, the prescriptive affects females' sense of life options and feelings of well-being. For example, Adamsky (1981) found that women's sense of power and importance was enhanced when the prescriptive *he* was replaced by *she.*

Awareness of the impact of the generic *man* and prescriptive *he* has generated considerable activity to change the language. One change, approved by the Modern Language Association, is to replace the prescriptive *he* with the plural *they*—as was accepted practice before the 18th century. Another is the use of *he or she.* Although it sounds awkward at first, the *he or she* designation is increasingly being used in the media and among people who have recognized the power of the pronoun to perpetuate sex stereotyping. When a professor, for example, talks about "the lawyer" as "he or she," a speech pattern that counteracts sex stereotyping is modeled. This drive to neutralize the impact of pronouns is evidenced further in the renaming of occupations: a policeman is now a police officer, a postman is a mail carrier, a stewardess is a flight attendant.

Third, linguistic practice defines females as immature, incompetent, and incapable and males as mature, complete, and competent. Because the words *man* and *woman* tend to connote sexual and human maturity, common speech, organizational titles, public addresses, and bathroom doors frequently designate the women in question as *ladies.* Simply contrast the different connotations of *lady* and *woman* in the following common phrases:

Luck, be a lady (woman) tonight.
Barbara's a little lady (woman).
Ladies' (Women's) Air Corps.

In the first two examples, the use of *lady* desexualizes the contextual meaning of *woman.* So trivializing is the use of *lady* in the last phrase that the second is wholly anomalous. The male equivalent, *lord,* is never used; and its synonym, *gentleman,* is used infrequently. When *gentleman* is used, the assumption seems to be that certain culturally condoned aspects of masculinity

(e.g., aggressivity, activity, and strength) should be set aside in the interests of maturity and order, as in the following phrases:

A gentlemen's (men's) agreement.
A duel between gentlemen (men).
He's a real gentleman (man).

Rather than feeling constrained to set aside the stereotypes associated with *man,* males frequently find the opposite process occurring. The contextual connotation of *man* places a strain on males to be continuously sexually and socially potent, as the following examples reveal:

I was not a man (gentleman) with her tonight.
This is a man's (gentleman's) job.
Be a man (gentleman).

Whether males, therefore, feel competent or anxious, valuable or worthless in particular contexts is influenced by the demands placed on them by the expectations of the language.

Not only are men infrequently labeled *gentlemen,* but they are infrequently labeled *boys.* The term *boy* is reserved for young males, bellhops, car attendants, and as a putdown to those males judged inferior. *Boy* connotes immaturity and powerlessness. Only occasionally do males "have a night out with the boys." They do not talk "boy talk" at the office. Rarely does our language legitimize carefreeness in males. Rather, they are expected, linguistically, to adopt the responsibilities of manhood.

On the other hand, women of all ages may be called *girls.* Grown females "play bridge with the girls" and indulge in "girl talk." They are encouraged to remain childlike, and the implication is that they are basically immature and without power. Men can become men, linguistically, putting aside the immaturity of childhood; indeed, for them to retain the openness and playfulness of boyhood is linguistically difficult.

Further, the presumed incompetence and immaturity of women are evidenced by the linguistic company they keep. Women are categorized with children ("women and children first"), the infirm ("the blind, the lame, the women"), and the incompetent ("women, convicts, and idiots"). The use of these categorical designations is not accidental happenstance; "rather these selectional groupings are powerful forces behind the actual expressions of language and are based on distinctions which are not regarded as trivial by the speakers of the language" (Key, 1975:82). A total language analysis of categorical groupings is not available, yet it seems likely that women tend to be included in groupings that designate incompleteness, ineptitude, and immaturity. On the other hand, it is difficult for us to conceive of the word *man* in any categorical grouping other than one that extends beyond humanity, such as "Man, apes, and angels" or "Man and Superman." That is, men do exist as an independent category capable of autonomy; women are grouped with the stigmatized, the immature, and the foolish. Moreover, when men are in human groupings, males are invariably first on the list ("men and women," "he and she," "man and wife"). This order is not accidental but was prescribed in the 16th century to honor the worthier party.

Fourth, in practice women are defined in terms of their sexual desirability (to men); men are defined in terms of their sexual prowess (over women). Most slang words in reference to women refer to their sexual desirability to men (e.g., *dog, fox, broad, ass, chick*). Slang about men refers to their sexual prowess over women (e.g., *dude, stud, hunk*). The fewer examples given for men is not an oversight. An analysis of sexual slang, for example, listed more than 1,000 words and phrases that derogate women sexually but found "nowhere near this multitude for describing men" (Kramarae, 1975:72). Farmer and Henley (cited in Schulz, 1975) list 500 synonyms for *prostitute,* for example, and only 65 for *whoremonger.* Stanley (1977) reports 220 terms for a sexually promiscuous woman and only 22 for a sexually promiscuous man. Shuster (1973) reports that the passive verb form is used in reference to women's sexual experiences (e.g., *to be laid, to be had, to be taken*), whereas the active tense is used in reference to the male's sexual experience (e.g., *lay, take, have*). Being sexually attractive to males is culturally condoned for women and being sexually powerful is approved for males. In this regard, the slang of the street is certainly not countercultural; rather it perpetuates and reinforces different expectations in females and males as sexual objects and performers.

Further, we find sexual connotations associated with neutral words applied to women. A few examples should suffice. A male academician questioned the title of a new course, asserting it was "too suggestive." The title? "The Position of Women in the Social Order." A male tramp is simply a hobo, but a female tramp is a slut. And consider the difference in connotation of the following expressions:

> It's easy.
> He's easy.
> She's easy.

In the first, we assume something is "easy to do"; in the second, we might assume a professor is an "easy grader" or a man is "easygoing." But when we read "she's easy," the connotation is "she's an easy lay."

In the world of slang, men are defined by their sexual prowess. In the world of slang and proper speech, women are defined as sexual objects. The rule in practice seems to be: If in doubt, assume that *any* reference to a women has a sexual connotation. For both genders, the constant bombardment of prescribed sexuality is bound to have real consequences.

Fifth, women are defined in terms of their relations to men; men are defined in terms of their relations to the world at large. A good example is seen in the words *master* and *mistress.* Originally these words had the same meaning—"a person who holds power over servants." With the demise of the feudal system, however, these words took on different meanings. The masculine variant metaphorically refers to power over something; as in "He is the master of his trade"; the feminine variant metaphorically (although probably not in actuality) refers to power over a man sexually, as in "She is Tom's mistress." Men are defined in terms of their power in the occupational world, women in terms of their sexual power over men.

The existence of two contractions for Mistress (*Miss* and *Mrs.*) and but one for Mister (*Mr.*) underscores the cultural concern and linguistic practice: women are defined in relation to men. Even a divorced woman is defined in terms of her no-longer-existing relation to a man (she is still *Mrs. Man's Name*). But apparently the divorced state is not relevant enough to the man or to the society to require a label. A divorced woman is a *divorcee,* but what do you call a divorced man? The recent preference of many women to be called *Ms.* is an attempt to provide for women an equivalency title that is not dependent on marital status.

Sixth, a historical pattern can be seen in the meanings that come to be attached to words that originally were neutral: those that apply to women acquire obscene and/or debased connotations but no such pattern of derogation holds for neutral words referring

WOMEN RAP BACK

MICHELE WALLACE

Like many black feminists, I look on sexism in rap as a necessary evil. In a society plagued by poverty and illiteracy, where young black men are as likely to be in prison as in college, rap is a welcome articulation of the economic and social frustrations of black youth.

It offers the release of creative expression and historical continuity; it draws on precedents as diverse as jazz, reggae, calypso, Afro-Cuban, African and heavy-metal, and its lyrics include rudimentary forms of political, economic, and social analysis.

But though there are exceptions, like raps advocating world peace (The W.I.S.E. Guyz's "Time for Peace") and opposing drug use (Ice T's "I'm Your Pusher"), rap lyrics can be brutal, raw, and, where women are the subject, glaringly sexist.

Though styles vary—from that of the X-rated Ice T to the sybaritic Kwamé to the hyperpolitics of Public Enemy—what seems universal is how little male rappers respect sexual intimacy and how little

From *Ms.* Magazine 1, no. 3 (November–December 1990): 61.

regard they have for the humanity of the black woman.

At present there is only a small platform for black women to address the problems of sexism in rap and in their community. For a black feminist to chastise misogyny in rap publicly would be viewed as divisive and counterproductive. The charge is hardly new. Such a reaction greeted Ntozake Shange's play *For Colored Girls Who Have Considered Suicide When the Rainbow Is Enuf,* my own essays, *Black Macho and the Myth of the Superwoman,* and Alice Walker's novel *The Color Purple,* all of which were perceived as being critical of black men.

Rap is rooted not only in the blaxploitation films of the 1960s but also in an equally sexist tradition of black comedy. In the use of four-letter words and explicit sexual references, both Richard Pryor and Eddie Murphy, who themselves drew upon the earlier examples of Redd Foxx, Pigment Markham, and Moms Mabley, are conscious reference points for the 2 Live Crew. Black comedy, in turn, draws on an oral tradition in which black men trade "toasts," stories in which dangerous badmen and

to men. The processes of *pejoration* (the acquiring of an obscene or debased connotation) and *amelioration* (the reacquiring of a neutral or positive connotation) in the English language in regard to terms for males and females have been studied extensively by Muriel Schulz (1975).

Leveling is the least derogative form of pejoration. Through leveling, titles that originally referred to an elite class of persons come to include a wider class of persons. Such democratic leveling is more common for female designates than for males. For example, contrast the following: *lord–lady (lady); baronet–dame (dame); governor–governess (governess).*

Most frequently what happens to words designating women as they become pejorated, however, is that they

come to denote or connote sexual wantonness. *Sir* and *mister,* for example, remain titles of courtesy, but at some time *madam, miss,* and *mistress* have come to designate, respectively, a brothelkeeper, a prostitute, and an unmarried sexual partner of a male (Schulz, 1975:66).

Names for domestic helpers, if they are females, are frequently derogated. *Hussy,* for example, originally meant "housewife." *Laundress, needlewoman, spinster* ("tender of the spinning wheel"), and *nurse* all referred to domestic occupations within the home, and all at some point became slang expressions for prostitute or mistress.

Even kinship terms referring to women become denigrated. During the 17th century, *mother* was used trickster figures like Stackolee and Dolomite sexually exploit women and promote violence among men.

Rap remains almost completely dominated by black males and this mind-set. Although women have been involved in rap since at least the mid-1980s, record companies have only recently begun to promote them. And as women rappers like Salt-N-Pepa, Monie Love, M.C. Lyte, L.A. Star, and Queen Latifah slowly gain more visibility, rap's sexism may emerge as a subject for scrutiny. Indeed, the answer may lie with women, expressing in lyrics and videos the tensions between the sexes in the black community.

Today's women rappers range from a high ground that refuses to challenge male rap on its own level (Queen Latifah) to those who subscribe to the same sexual high jinks as male rappers (Oaktown 3.5.7.). M.C. Hammer launched Oak-town 3.5.7., made up of his former backup dancers. These female rappers manifest the worst-case scenario: their skimpy, skintight leopard costumes in the video of "Wild and Loose (We Like It)" suggest an exotic animalistic sexuality. Clearly, their bodies are more important than rapping. And in a field in which writing one's own rap is crucial, their lyrics are written by their former boss, M.C. Hammer.

Most women rappers constitute the middle ground: they talk of romance, narcissism, and parties. On the other hand, Salt-N-Pepa on "Shake Your Thang" uses the structure of the 1969 Isley Brothers song "It's Your Thing" to insert a proto-feminist rap response: "Don't try to tell me how to party. It's my dance and it's my body." M.C. Lyte, in a dialogue with Positive K on "I'm Not Havin' It," comes down hard on the notion that women can't say no, and criticizes the shallowness of the male rap.

Queen Latifah introduces her video "Ladies First," performed with the English rapper Monie Love, with photographs of black political heroines like Winnie Mandela, Sojourner Truth, Harriet Tubman, and Angela Davis. With a sound that resembles scat as much as rap, Queen Latifah chants "Stereotypes they got to go" against a backdrop of newsreel footage of the apartheid struggle in South Africa. The politically sophisticated Queen Latifah seems worlds apart from the adolescent, buffoonish sex orientation of most rap. In general, women rappers seem so much more grown up.

Can they inspire a more beneficent attitude toward sex in rap?

What won't subvert rap's sexism is the actions of men; what will is women speaking in their own voice.

---

to mean "a bawd"; more recently *mother* (*mothuh f——*) has become a common derogatory epithet (Cameron, 1974). Probably at some point in history every kinship term for females has been derogated (Schulz, 1975:66).

Terms of endearment for women also seem to follow a downward path. Such pet names as Tart, Dolly, Kitty, Polly, Mopsy, Biddy, and Jill all eventually became sexually derogatory (Schulz, 1975:67). *Whore* comes from the same Latin root as *care* and once meant "a lover of either sex."

Indeed, even the most neutral categorical designations—*girl, female, woman, lady*—at some point in their history have been used to connote sexual immorality. *Girl* originally meant "a child of either sex"; through the process of semantic degeneration it eventually meant "a prostitute." Although *girl* has lost this meaning, *girlie* still retains sexual connotations. *Woman* connoted "a mistress" in the early 19th century; *female* was a degrading epithet in the latter part of the 19th century; and when *lady* was introduced as a euphemism, it too became deprecatory. "Even so neutral a term as *person,* when it was used as substitute for *woman,* suffered [vulgarization]" (Mencken, 1963: 350, quoted in Schulz, 1975:71).

Whether one looks at elite titles, occupational roles, kinship relationships, endearments, or age-sex categorical designations, the pattern is clear. Terms referring to females are pejorated—"become negative in the middle instances and abusive in the extremes" (Schulz, 1975:69). Such semantic derogation, however, is not evidenced for male referents. *Lord, baronet, father, brother, nephew, footman, bowman, boy, lad, fellow, gentleman, man, male,* and so on "have failed to undergo the derogation found in the history of their corresponding feminine designations" (Schulz, 1975:67). Interestingly, the male word, rather than undergoing derogation, frequently is replaced by a female referent when the speaker wants to debase a male. A weak man, for example, is referred to as a *sissy* (diminutive of *sister*), and an army recruit during basic training is called a *pussy*. And when one is swearing at a male, he is referred to as a *bastard* or a *son-of-a-bitch*—both appellations that impugn the dignity of a man's mother.

In summary, these verbal practices are consistent with the gender stereotypes that we encounter in everyday life. Women are thought to be a part of man, nonautonomous, dependent, relegated to roles that require few skills, characteristically incompetent and immature, sexual objects, best defined in terms of their relations to men. Males are visible, autonomous and independent, responsible for the protection and containment of women, expected to occupy positions on the basis of their high achievement or physical power, assumed to be sexually potent, and defined primarily by their relations to the world of work. The use of the language perpetuates the stereotypes for both genders and limits the options available for self-definition.

REFERENCES

Adamsky, C. 1981. "Changes in pronominal usage in a classroom situation." *Psychology of Women Quarterly* 5:773–79.

Bendix, J. 1979. "Linguistic models as political symbols: Gender and the generic 'he' in English." In J. Orasanu, M. Slater, and L. L. Adler, eds., *Language, sex and gender: Does la différence make a difference?* pp. 23–42. New York: New Academy of Science Annuals.

Cameron, P. 1974. "Frequency and kinds of words in various social settings, or What the hell's going on?" In M. Truzzi, ed., *Sociology for pleasure,* pp. 31–37. Englewood Cliffs, N.J.: Prentice-Hall.

Daly, M. 1973. *Beyond God the father.* Boston: Beacon Press.

DeStefano, J. S. 1976. Personal communication. Columbus: Ohio State University.

Hamilton, N., & Henley, N. 1982. "Detrimental consequences of the generic masculine usage." Paper presented to the Western Psychological Association meetings, Sacramento.

Key, M. R. 1975. *Male/female language.* Metuchen, N.J.: Scarecrow Press.

Kramarae, Cheris. 1975. "Woman's speech: Separate but unequal?" In Barrie Thorne and Nancy Henley, eds., *Language and sex: Difference and dominance,* pp. 43–56. Rowley, Mass.: Newbury House.

MacKay, D. G. 1983. "Prescriptive grammar and the pronoun problem." In B. Thorne, C. Kramarae, and N. Henley, eds., *Language, gender, and society,* pp. 38–53. Rowley, Mass.: Newbury House.

Martyna, W. 1978. "What does 'he' mean? Use of the generic masculine." *Journal of Communication* 28:131–38.

Martyna, W. 1980. "Beyond the 'he/man' approach: The case for nonsexist language." *Signs* 5:482–93.

Mencken, H. L. 1963. *The American language.* 4th ed. with supplements. Abr. and ed. R. I. McDavis. New York: Knopf.

Schneider, J., & Hacker, S. 1973. "Sex role imagery in the use of the generic 'man' in introductory texts: A case in the sociology of sociology." *American Sociologist* 8:12–18.

Schulz, M. R. 1975. "The semantic derogation of women." In B. Thorne and N. Henley, eds., *Language and sex: Difference and dominance,* pp. 64–75. Rowley, Mass.: Newbury House.

Shuster, Janet. 1973. "Grammatical forms marked for male and female in English." Unpublished paper. Chicago: University of Chicago.

Stanley, J. P. 1977. "Paradigmatic woman: The prostitute." In D. L. Shores, ed., *Papers in language variation.* Birmingham: University of Alabama Press.

Vanderbilt, A. 1972. *Amy Vanderbilt's etiquette.* Garden City, N.Y.: Doubleday.

Hablando cara a cara/Speaking Face to Face: An Exploration of Ethnocentric Racism

MARÍA LUGONES

Esta es escritura hablada cara a cara. This is writing spoken face to face. *Escritura solitaria por falta de compañía que busca solaz en el dialogo.* Writing that is solitary for lack of company and looks for solace in dialogue. *Monólogo extendido hacia afuera y hablado en muchas lenguas.* Monologue spoken outwardly and in tongues.*

Empazaré monologándoles en mi lengua ancestral para hacerle honor, para prepararme y prepararlas a hablar con comprensión† de las dificultades de nuestros diálogos y para recrearlas con el precioso son de una de las lenguas vivas de este país.

From "Hablando cara a cara/Speaking Face to Face: An Exploration of Ethnocentric Racism," by Maria Lugones, in *Making Face, Making Soul/Haciendo Caras*, ed. Gloria Anzaldúa. Copyright © 1990. Reprinted by permission of aunt lute books.

*Inglés and several varieties of Spanish. If you do not read Spanish, see footnote below.
†Porque si compartes mis lenguas, entonces comprendes todos los niveles de mi intención.* And if you do not understand my many tongues, you begin to understand why I speak them. It is truly not just to be understood by you. I speak them because I want to point to the possibility of becoming playful in the use of different voices and because I want to point to the possibility of coming to appreciate this playfulness. Here I exercise this playful practice. The appreciation of my playfulness and its meaning may be realized when the possibility of becoming playful in this way has been collectively realized, when it has become realized by us. It is here to be appreciated or missed and both the appreciation and the missing are significant. The more fully this playfulness is appreciated, the less broken I am to you, the more dimensional I am to you. But I want to exercise my multidimensionality even if you do not appreciate it. To do otherwise would be to engage in self-mutilation, to come to be just the person that you see. To play in this way is then an act of resistance as well as an act of self-affirmation.

La soledad de mi escritura me pesa en la multitud de sus significados. Por eso, porque no quiero estar sola, invocaré a dos hermanas poetizas que me han guiado y acompañado en esta tarea. Marina Rivera, poetiza de Arizona, y Margarita Cota-Cárdenas, poetiza de California, me espantaron la soledad de lejos.
Dice Marina:[1]

Quedo solamente yo
persona de en medio
que luché en vida color de café
luché en vida color blanco
y me hice fuerte
bastante para decir
no me llamen por la chicana
ni por el chicano
ni por las mujeres

y Margarita:[2]

Todas aguantaron
. . .y yo
*   yo no quise*
no acepté
. . . no quería que una débil tarde
vieras tus antiguas penas bordadas en mi cara
. . .yo quise
. . .volar altísimo
definir mis entrañas
. . .yo ya no pude
que mis hijas y sus hijas y sus hijas no
dolorosa . . .
di que comprendes
*   resucita conmigo*

ya era tiempo
de abortar los mitos
de un solo sentido

¡Qué bonita la coincidencia que no es azarosa! La relación íntima entre el abortar los mitos de un solo sentido y el romper espejos que nos muestran rotas, despedazadas. We want to be seen unbroken, we want to break cracked mirrors that show us in many separate, *unconnected* fragments.

Soy de la gente de colores, soy mestiza, latina, porteña, indita, mora criollita, negra. Soy de piel morena y labios color ciruela. Soy vata, mujer, esa. To know me unbroken requires the kind of devotion that makes empathetic and sympathetic thinking possible. I think it is possible for White/Anglo women to think empathetically and sympathetically about those who are harmed seriously by racism and about their lives held in communities where culture flourishes through struggle. But I do think that this takes the devotion of friendship. In becoming conscious and critical of the ways of thinking about racism and ethnocentrism, I thought it realistic to reserve sympathetic and empathetic thinking for the rarity of deep friendship. But anyone who is not self-deceiving about racist ethnocentrism can begin to see us unbroken through engaged thinking that takes seriously her own participation in an ethnocentric culture in a racial state. Such thinking requires that she become and think as a self-conscious critical practitioner of her culture and a self-conscious and critical member of the racial state. Furthermore, such thinking is possible because she is a participant in both.

Resucita conmigo y llámame por mi misma.[3] Come back to life with me and call me for myself, or don't call me at all.

RACISM AND ETHNOCENTRISM

To speak another language and another culture are not the same as being racialized. One can be ethnocentric without being racist. The existence of races as the products of racialization presupposes the presence of racism, but the existence of different ethnicities does not presuppose ethnocentrism, even if ethnocentrism is universal. So we should conclude that ethnicity is not the same as race and ethnocentrism is not the same as racism.

Ethnocentrism: the explicit and arrogantly held action-guiding belief that one's culture and cultural ways are superior to others'; or the disrespectful, lazy, arrogant indifference to other cultures that devalues them through not seeing appreciatively *any* culture or cultural ways except one's own when one could do otherwise; or the disrespectful, lazy, arrogant indifference that devalues other cultures through stereotyping of them or through non-reflective, self-satisfied acceptance of such stereotypes.

Thus if I lead you to recognize your own and my ethnicity, I would not yet have led you to recognize that we are differently racialized, that we occupy very different positions in the racial state and that our ethnicities may be contaminated to some small or maximal degree with racism. But, on the other hand, unless there is a very high degree of assimilation, racism always seems to be accompanied and in part expressed by ethnocentrism.

Investigating collectively one's ethnocentrism and its roots may lead one to locate it in one's racism.

Racism: one's affirmation of or acquiescence to or lack of recognition of the structures and mechanisms of the racial state; one's lack of awareness of or blindness or indifference to one's being racialized; one's affirmation of, indifference or blindness to the harm that the racial state inflicts on some of its members.*

Racist ethnocentrism: ethnocentrism that is expressive of racism.

*We need to produce a theory of the racial state and its mechanisms. So far, the following seems to me true of the racial state:
i. It produces a classification of people that gives rise to race.
ii. The classification is not a rational ordering based on any 'natural' phenomena.
iii. The classification is historically variable.
iv. The classification has a strong normative force in the form of custom or in the form of positive law.
v. The classification is presupposed (explicitly or not) by many other legal and customary norms.
vi. The classification imposes on people a false identity and arrogates the power of self-definition, even though the history of the classification may include the search and the hegemonical struggle for identity and self-definition by particular groups.
vii. The classification is given meaning by particular organizations of social, political and economic interaction that regulate relations among people who are differently classified.
viii. The racial state also produces ideologies that create the illusion that both the classification and the organization of life that accompany and give meaning to it are justified. (These

Hablando cara a cara/
SPEAKING FACE TO FACE:
MUTING AND DISENGAGEMENT

I am thinking about cracked mirrors that reflect us falsely because I want to lead you into the spaces where I explore racist ethnocentrism with White/Anglas or with White-assimilated-to-Anglo women.† In this context bi-lingualism and bi-culturalism or multiculturalism are very hard to express because they, as well as the racialization of everyone in the learning space, are muted: our ethnicities and races are muted. Since these mutings are not heard, they are not heard as related. This three-fold muting is a central feature of the context of inquiry, one which needs to be overcome collectively simply because so long as it is present, we cannot really hear or speak about what is muted. Within this silence White/Anglo women can see themselves as simply human or simply women. I can bring you to your senses *con el tono de mi voz,* with the sound of my—to you—alien voice.

Precisely because thinking about this feature of the context of inquiry collectively presupposes a recognition of it and because I cannot assume this recognition, I speak to you in tongues. But as I speak in tongues, *me siento separada como por una pared en el presentarme frente a los demás.* As I speak to you in the many incarnations of my native tongue, one of the live tongues of this country, I feel isolated from you as if by a thick wall. *Pero no lo hago para romper la pared, lo hago tan solo para reconocerla.* My intention is not to break the wall down, just to recognize it. This recognition is *a* first step to an honest understanding of ethnocentric racism and of the connections between the two.

---

claims about the racial state were provoked by Michael Omi's and Howard Winant's "By the Rivers of Babylon: Race in the United States," *Socialist Review* 71 and 72. I think that Omi and Winant would find fault in my formulation of (vi) because it does not give enough attention to competing racially defined political projects. My intent in formulating (vi) is to take these competing projects into account, but I am uncomfortable with the lack of clarity of this formulation on this particular point.)

†I have in mind the institutional academic classroom and other intellectual contexts that are predominantly White/Anglo. I also discuss racism and ethnocentrism in predominantly raza contexts, and in contexts that are predominantly peopled by Third World interlocutors. But this paper is not located in the latter contexts. The understanding of racism and ethnocentrism in the latter contexts proceeds in a very different manner than the one delineated in this essay.

So the central and painful questions for *me* in this encounter become questions of speech: *¿En qué voz* with which voice, *anclada en qué lugar* anchored in which place, *para qué y porqué* why and to what purpose, do I trust myself to you . . . *o acaso juego un juego de* cat and mouse just for your entertainment . . . *o por el mío?* I ask these questions out loud because they need to be asked. Asking them in this way *demands* recognition and places the burden (?) of answering them *actively* on your and not just on my shoulders.

So we can see that *si pudiera decir todo "derecho viejo"* if I could say everything straightforwardly *lo diría mal* I would be saying it falsely, so I can't, *porque me hace mal* because it harms me. It harms me to be clean and easy when it is a pretense, a pretense imposed on me because double talk is supposed to be more efficient and more educational than bi-lingual talk. So, for "our" sake, for the sheer possibility *de un "nosotras,"* I will swallow my tongue *"a medias,"* half-way.

We have begun to see that one cannot think well about racism and ethnocentrism or challenge and reconstruct the racial state or the ethnocentrism in one's culture and in oneself without an awareness of one's ethnicity, or one's being racialized as well as of the ties between the two. It is one's competence and the competence of the other investigators as inquirers that is at stake. Being unaware of one's own ethnicity and racialization commits the inquirer to adopt a disengaged stance, one from outside the racial state and the ethnocentric culture looking in. *But it is one's culture and one's society that one is looking at.* Such a disengaged inquirer is committed either to dishonest study or to ignoring deep meanings and connections to which she has access only as a self-conscious member of the racial state and as a sophisticated practitioner of the culture: she is committed to ethnocentric racism.

Everyone who is racialized is a member of and participant in at least one culture. One's position in the racial state may be maintained by beliefs of cultural superiority or by either active or passive devaluation, erasure or stereotyping of cultures other than one's own.* That is, ethnocentrism may be one of the mechanisms of the racial state. Ethnocentrism may be part of

---

*When one's position in the racial state is that of a victim of racism, then that position may be partially maintained by beliefs of cultural inferiority or by either active or passive devaluation, erasure or stereotyping of one's own culture.

the *ideology* of the racial state. Dis-engagement as a sanctioned ethnocentric racist strategy works as follows: you do not see me because you do not see yourself and you do not see yourself because you declare yourself outside of culture. But declaring yourself outside of culture is self-deceiving. The deception hides your seeing only through the eyes of your culture. So dis-engagement is a radical form of passivity toward the ideology of the ethnocentric racial state which privileges the dominant culture as the only culture to "see with" and conceives this seeing as to be done non-self-consciously.

Reading *Drylongso*,[4] *White Over Black*,[5] *I Know Why the Caged Bird Sings*,[6] *They Called Them Greasers*,[7] *The Woman Warrior*,[8] *Invisible Man*,[9] etc. is not helpful in exploring racism and ethnocentrism *unless* these works are read from this engaged position. When read from the engaged position, these works can help the White/Angla become self-consciously White/Anglo in the racial and ethnic senses of the words: they can help her unravel the connections between racism, ethnocentrism, White/Anglo self-esteem, polite arrogance, polite condescension and a troubled sense of responsibility in the face of people of color.

Para interrupción, un son:

Todo cada cual con su cada cuala
doblando la espalda o volviendo la cara.
Miras en mis ojos y te ves mirada,
me tocas la mano y ya estás tocada.
Si no miras, vata, nunca verás nada.

Lo nuestro

Thinking back about the claim that ethnocentrism may be universal, as it is sometimes claimed, I think it is worth making a distinction between two phenomena which, because they are expressed similarly, are often taken to exemplify ethnocentrism. I think one of them does not.

"¡Ay qué linda mi gente (o mi cultura, o mi comunidad, o mi tierra), qué suave, si, la más suave!" "Ah, how beautiful my people (or my culture, or my community, or my land), how beautiful, the most beautiful!" I think this claim is made many times non-comparatively. It is expressive of the centrality that one's people, culture, community or language have to the subject's sense of self and her web of connections.

It expresses her fondness for them. In these cases, the claim does not mean "better than other people's," but "dearer to me than other people's communities, etc., are to me." It is like a mother saying *"¡Qué bella mi niña, la más bella!"* "How beautiful my child, the most beautiful!" and expressing the centrality of this child in her affection. Similar claims are made many times comparatively and invidiously and I think that *only then* are they ethnocentric.

It is worth noticing that rarely have I heard White/Anglos make such claims in the first way, though I have heard similar claims used by White/Anglos to convey the second meaning. Many White/Anglos seem to me disaffected from, or indifferent to, or unaware of, or chauvinistically proud of their culture, people, communities.

In making this distinction I do not mean to imply that one cannot make judgements about a people, culture, etc., that are not chauvinistic, not ethnocentric, and yet critical. Indeed, becoming aware of racism through an understanding of one's own ethnicity and the extent to which it is expressive of racism presupposes the possibility of making non-ethnocentric critical judgements about one's own culture.

But sometimes Third World peoples in this country are accused of ethnocentrism and chauvinism when we are expressing our fundamental ties to "lo nuestro." Keeping this distinction in mind may result in an undermining of the claim that ethnocentrism is universal. It may also help White/Anglos in exploring their ethnicity. In this exploration it may be helpful to see the extent to which White/Anglos do or can make the first kind of claim. One may be too quick to assume an ethnocentric interpretation of one's claims and too quick to see the whole of one's culture and cultural ways as tainted with ethnocentrism. This distinction should be helpful in keeping that tendency in check.

INFANTILIZATION OF JUDGEMENT

I think it is essential that in exploring racism and ethnocentrism, the White/Angla challenge and be challenged in her own sense of incompetence. So far I have directed my attention to the particular incompetence that results from the three-fold muting mentioned at the beginning of this essay and which leads the inquirer, when the muting is not heard, to a disengaged position in the inquiry. I would like to conclude by addressing another source of incompetence in the White/Anglo exploration of racism and ethnocentrism: infantilization of judgement.

I have encountered this phenomenon so many times and in so many people of good judgement in other matters, that it is frequently disconcerting: *Se han vuelto como niños, incapaces de juzgar, evitando el compromiso, paralizados en tantos seres responsables.* They have turned into children, incapable of judgement, avoiding all commitment except against racism in the abstract, paralyzed as responsible beings, afraid of hostility and hostile in their fear, wedded to their ignorance and arrogant in their guilty purity of heart.

Infantilization of judgement is a dulling of the ability to read critically, and with maturity of judgement, those texts and situations in which race and ethnicity are salient. It appears to me as a flight into a state in which one cannot be critical or responsible: a flight into those characteristics of childhood* that excuse ignorance and confusion, and that appeal to authority. If the description "child" is an appropriate description of White/Anglas in the context of racism and ethnocentrism, then to ascribe responsibility to them for the understanding and undoing of these phenomena is inappropriate. If a child, the White/Angla can be guilty of racism and ethnocentrism innocently, unmarked and untouched in her goodness, confused with good reason, a passive learner because she cannot exercise her judgement with maturity. But, of course, she is not a child. She is an ethnocentric racist.

Infantilization of judgement is a form of ethnocentric racism precisely because it is a self-indulgent denial of one's understanding of one's culture and its express-

ing racism. One of the features of this denial is the denial that racism is a two-party affair, an interactive phenomenon. In infantilization of judgement the racist attempts to hide that she understands racism as a participant.

Infantilization is broken if one squarely and respectfully sets the White/Anglo inquirer in the position of seeing herself as a competent practitioner of her culture and a racialized member of the racial state and if one also blocks the possibility of escape into lack of engagement. She cannot then take refuge into incompetence, for this presupposes that racialization and the having of a culture are what happens to others who are not her people and whom she can know only abstractly. One cannot disown one's culture. One can reconstruct it in struggle.

One's experience of time, of movement through space, one's sense of others and of oneself are all culturally formed and informed:

> *Siempre hay tiempo para los amigos.*
>> I'll see you next Tuesday
>> at 5:15.
> *Vente y tomamos un café y charlamos*
> *mientras plancho la ropa.*
>> I'll call you Monday
>> evening to let you know for sure
>> that I am coming.
> *Ay mujer, te ves triste,*
> *¿te sientes bien?*
> *Me duele mucho la cabeza y*
> *estoy un poco sola y cansada.*
> *Dura la vida, ¿no?*
>> Hi, how are you? Fine, and you?
>> Fine, thank you.

My suggestions here are directed to the breaking down of traits in the inquirer that make the inquiry pointless, an exercise in self-deception or an exercise in further domination, and adorns the inquirer with dishonesty.

> *Ya era tiempo*
> *de abortar los mitos*
> *de un solo sentido.*[10]

---

*I use the word "child" here not because I think that young human beings are incapable of judgement, but because young human beings are *alleged* to be incapable of judgement *and* because women have been thought to be like children in this respect. Any women who rejects this attribution but falls into infantilization with respect to racism should be struck by the inconsistency of her stance. (Thanks to Sarah Hoagland for eliciting this note from me with her criticism of my use of the word "child" to make my point.)

NOTES

1. Marina Rivera, "Mestiza: poema en cinco partes," *Mestiza* (Tucson: Grilled Flowers, 1977).

2. Margarita Cota-Cárdenas, "A una Madre de Nuestros Tiempos," *Noches Despertando Inconciencias* (Tucson: Scorpion Press, 1977).

3. Marina Rivera, ibid.

4. I chose these texts because they are and should be examples of classics in the contemporary White/Angla bibliography on racism. J. Gwaltney, *Drylongso: A Self Portrait of Black America* (New York: Random House, Vintage Books, 1980).

5. Winthrop D. Jordan, *White Over Black* (Chapel Hill: University of North Carolina Press, 1968; Baltimore: Penguin Books, 1971).

6. Maya Angelou, *I Know Why the Caged Bird Sings* (New York: Bantam Books, 1969).

7. Arnoldo de Leon, *They Called Them Greasers* (Austin: University of Texas Press, 1983).

8. Maxine Hong Kingston, *The Woman Warrior* (New York: Vintage Books, 1976).

9. Ralph Ellison, *Invisible Man* (New York: Vintage Books, 1963).

10. Margarita Cota-Cárdenas, ibid.

R E A D I N G   8

Where I Come From Is Like This

PAULA GUNN ALLEN

I

Modern American Indian women, like their non-Indian sisters, are deeply engaged in the struggle to redefine themselves. In their struggle they must reconcile traditional tribal definitions of women with industrial and postindustrial non-Indian definitions. Yet while these definitions seem to be more or less mutually exclusive, Indian women must somehow harmonize and integrate both in their own lives.

An American Indian woman is primarily defined by her tribal identity. In her eyes, her destiny is necessarily that of her people, and her sense of herself as a woman is first and foremost prescribed by her tribe. The definitions of woman's roles are as diverse as tribal cultures in the Americas. In some she is devalued, in others she wields considerable power. In some she is a familial/clan adjunct, in some she is as close to autonomous as her economic circumstances and psy-

chological traits permit. But in no tribal definitions is she perceived in the same way as are women in western industrial and postindustrial cultures.

In the west, few images of women form part of the cultural mythos, and these are largely sexually charged. Among Christians, the madonna is the female prototype, and she is portrayed as essentially passive: her contribution is simply that of birthing. Little else is attributed to her and she certainly possesses few of the characteristics that are attributed to mythic figures among Indian tribes. This image is countered (rather than balanced) by the witch-goddess/whore characteristics designed to reinforce cultural beliefs about women, as well as western adversarial and dualistic perceptions of reality.

The tribes see women variously, but they do not question the power of femininity. Sometimes they see women as fearful, sometimes peaceful, sometimes omnipotent and omniscient, but they never portray women as mindless, helpless, simple, or oppressed. And while the women in a given tribe, clan, or band may be all these things, the individual woman is provided with a variety of images of women from the

From *The Sacred Hoop* by Paula Gunn Allen. Copyright © 1986. Reprinted by permission of Beacon Press.

interconnected supernatural, natural, and social worlds she lives in.

As a half-breed American Indian woman, I cast about in my mind for negative images of Indian women, and I find none that are directed to Indian women alone. The negative images I do have are of Indians in general and in fact are more often of males than of females. All these images come to me from non-Indian sources, and they are always balanced by a positive image. My ideas of womanhood, passed on largely by my mother and grandmothers, Laguna Pueblo women, are about practicality, strength, reasonableness, intelligence, wit, and competence. I also remember vividly the women who came to my father's store, the women who held me and sang to me, the women at Feast Day, at Grab Days, the women in the kitchen of my Cubero home, the women I grew up with; none of them appeared weak or helpless, none of them presented herself tentatively. I remember a certain reserve on those lovely brown faces; I remember the direct gaze of eyes framed by bright-colored shawls draped over their heads and cascading down their backs. I remember the clean cotton dresses and carefully pressed hand-embroidered aprons they always wore; I remember laughter and good food, especially the sweet bread and the oven bread they gave us. Nowhere in my mind is there a foolish woman, a dumb woman, a vain woman, or a plastic woman, though the Indian women I have known have shown a wide range of personal style and demeanor.

My memory includes the Navajo woman who was badly beaten by her Sioux husband; but I also remember that my grandmother abandoned her Sioux husband long ago. I recall the stories about the Laguna woman beaten regularly by her husband in the presence of her children so that the children would not believe in the strength and power of femininity. And I remember the women who drank, who got into fights with other women and with the men, and who often won those battles. I have memories of tired women, partying women, stubborn women, sullen women, amicable women, selfish women, shy women, and aggressive women. Most of all I remember the women who laugh and scold and sit uncomplaining in the long sun on feast days and who cook wonderful food on wood stoves, in beehive mud ovens, and over open fires outdoors.

Among the images of women that come to me from various tribes as well as my own are White Buffalo Woman, who came to the Lakota long ago and brought them the religion of the Sacred Pipe which they still practice; Tinotzin the goddess who came to Juan Diego to remind him that she still walked the hills of her people and sent him with her message, her demand and her proof to the Catholic bishop in the city nearby. And from Laguna I take the images of Yellow Woman, Coyote Woman, Grandmother Spider (Spider Old Woman), who brought the light, who gave us weaving and medicine, who gave us life. Among the Keres she is known as Thought Woman who created us all and who keeps us in creation even now. I remember Iyatiku, Earth Woman, Corn Woman, who guides and counsels the people to peace and who welcomes us home when we cast off this coil of flesh as huskers cast off the leaves that wrap the corn. I remember Iyatiku's sister, Sun Woman, who held metals and cattle, pigs and sheep, highways and engines and so many things in her bundle, who went away to the east saying that one day she would return.

II

Since the coming of the Anglo-Europeans beginning in the fifteenth century, the fragile web of identity that long held tribal people secure has gradually been weakened and torn. But the oral tradition has prevented the complete destruction of the web, the ultimate disruption of tribal ways. The oral tradition is vital; it heals itself and the tribal web by adapting to the flow of the present while never relinquishing its connection to the past. Its adaptability has always been required, as many generations have experienced. Certainly the modern American Indian woman bears slight resemblance to her forebears—at least on superficial examination—but she is still a tribal woman in her deepest being. Her tribal sense of relationship to all that is continues to flourish. And though she is at times beset by her knowledge of the enormous gap between the life she lives and the life she was raised to live, and while she adapts her mind and being to the circumstances of her present life, she does so in tribal ways, mending the tears in the web of being from which she takes her existence as she goes.

My mother told me stories all the time, though I often did not recognize them as that. My mother told me stories about cooking and childbearing; she told me stories about menstruation and pregnancy; she told me stories about gods and heroes, about fairies and elves, about goddesses and spirits; she told me stories about the land and the sky, about cats and dogs, about snakes and spiders; she told me stories about climbing trees and exploring the mesas; she told me stories about going to dances and getting married; she told me stories about dressing and undressing, about sleeping and waking; she told me stories about herself, about her mother, about her grandmother. She told me stories about grieving and laughing, about thinking and doing; she told me stories about school and about people; about darning and mending; she told me stories about turquoise and about gold; she told me European stories and Laguna stories; she told me Catholic stories and Presbyterian stories; she told me city stories and country stories; she told me political stories and religious stories. She told me stories about living and stories about dying. And in all of those stories she told me who I was, who I was supposed to be, whom I came from, and who would follow me. In this way she taught me the meaning of the words she said, that all life is a circle and everything has a place within it. That's what she said and what she showed me in the things she did and the way she lives.

Of course, through my formal, white, Christian education, I discovered that other people had stories of their own—about women, about Indians, about fact, about reality—and I was amazed by a number of startling suppositions that others made about tribal customs and beliefs. According to the un-Indian, non-Indian view, for instance, Indians barred menstruating women from ceremonies and indeed segregated them from the rest of the people, consigning them to some space specially designed for them. This showed that Indians considered menstruating women unclean and not fit to enjoy the company of decent (nonmenstruating) people, that is, men. I was surprised and confused to hear this because my mother had taught me that white people had strange attitudes toward menstruation: they thought something was bad about it, that it meant you were sick, cursed, sinful, and weak and that you had to be very careful during that time. She taught me that menstruation was a normal occurrence, that I could go swimming or hiking or whatever else I wanted to do during my period. She actively scorned women who took to their beds, who were incapacitated by cramps, who "got the blues."

As I struggled to reconcile these very contradictory interpretations of American Indians' traditional beliefs concerning menstruation, I realized that the menstrual

taboos were about power, not about sin or filth. My conclusion was later borne out by some tribes' own explanations, which, as you may well imagine, came as quite a relief to me.

The truth of the matter as many Indians see it is that women who are at the peak of their fecundity are believed to possess power that throws male power totally out of kilter. They emit such force that, in their presence, any male-owned or -dominated ritual or sacred object cannot do its usual task. For instance, the Lakota say that a menstruating woman anywhere near a yuwipi man, who is a special sort of psychic, spirit-empowered healer, for a day or so before he is to do his ceremony will effectively disempower him. Conversely, among many if not most tribes, important ceremonies cannot be held without the presence of women. Sometimes the ritual woman who empowers the ceremony must be unmarried and virginal so that the power she channels is unalloyed, unweakened by sexual arousal and penetration by a male. Other ceremonies require tumescent women, others the presence of mature women who have borne children, and still others depend for empowerment on postmenopausal women. Women may be segregated from the company of the whole band or village on certain occasions, but on certain occasions men are also segregated. In short, each ritual depends on a certain balance of power, and the positions of women within the phases of womanhood are used by tribal people to empower certain rites. This does not derive from a male-dominant view; it is not a ritual observance imposed on women by men. It derives from a tribal view of reality that distinguishes tribal people from feudal and industrial people.

Among the tribes, the occult power of women, inextricably bound to our hormonal life, is thought to be very great; many hold that we possess innately the blood-given power to kill—with a glance, with a step, or with a judicious mixing of menstrual blood into somebody's soup. Medicine women among the Pomo of California cannot practice until they are sufficiently mature; when they are immature, their power is diffuse and is likely to interfere with their practice until time and experience have it under control. So women of the tribes are not especially inclined to see themselves as poor helpless victims of male domination. Even in those tribes where something akin to male domination was present, women are perceived as powerful, socially, physically, and metaphysically. In times past, as in times present, women carried enormous burdens with aplomb. We were far indeed from the "weaker sex," the designation that white aristocratic sisters unhappily earned for us all.

I remember my mother moving furniture all over the house when she wanted it changed. She didn't wait for my father to come home and help—she just went ahead and moved the piano, a huge upright from the old days, the couch, the refrigerator. Nobody had told her she was too weak to do such things. In imitation of her, I would delight in loading trucks at my father's store with cases of pop or fifty-pound sacks of flour. Even when I was quite small I could do it, and it gave me a belief in my own physical strength that advancing middle age can't quite erase. My mother used to tell me about the Acoma Pueblo women she had seen as a child carrying huge ollas (water pots) on their heads as they wound their way up the tortuous stairwell carved into the face of the "Sky City" mesa, a feat I tried to imitate with books and tin buckets. ("Sky City" is the term used by the Chamber of Commerce for the mother village of Acoma, which is situated atop a high sand-stone table mountain.) I was never very successful, but even the attempt reminded me that I was supposed to be strong and balanced to be a proper girl.

Of course, my mother's Laguna people are Keres Indian, reputed to be the last extreme mother-right people on earth. So it is no wonder that I got notably nonwhite notions about the natural strength and prowess of women. Indeed, it is only when I am trying to get non-Indian approval, recognition, or acknowledgment that my "weak sister" emotional and intellectual ploys get the better of my tribal woman's good sense. At such times I forget that I just moved the piano or just wrote a competent paper or just completed a financial transaction satisfactorily or have supported myself and my children for most of my adult life.

Nor is my contradictory behavior atypical. Most Indian women I know are in the same bicultural bind: we vacillate between being dependent and strong, self-reliant and powerless, strongly motivated and hopelessly insecure. We resolve the dilemma in various ways: some of us party all the time; some of us drink to excess; some of us travel and move around a lot; some of us land good jobs and then quit them; some of us engage in violent exchanges; some of us blow our brains out. We act in these destructive ways because we suffer from the societal conflicts caused by having to identify with two hopelessly opposed cultural definitions of women. Through this destructive dissonance

we are unhappy prey to the self-disparagement common to, indeed demanded of, Indians living in the United States today. Our situation is caused by the exigencies of a history of invasion, conquest, and colonization whose searing marks are probably ineradicable. A popular bumper sticker on many Indian cars proclaims: "If You're Indian You're In," to which I always find myself adding under my breath, "Trouble."

III

No Indian can grow to any age without being informed that her people were "savages" who interfered with the march of progress pursued by respectable, loving, civilized white people. We are the villains of the scenario when we are mentioned at all. We are absent from much of white history except when we are calmly, rationally, succinctly, and systematically dehumanized. On the few occasions we are noticed in any way other than as howling, bloodthirsty beings, we are acclaimed for our noble quaintness. In this definition, we are exotic curios. Our ancient arts and customs are used to draw tourist money to state coffers, into the pocketbooks and bank accounts of scholars, and into support of the American-in-Disneyland promoters' dream.

As a Roman Catholic child I was treated to bloody tales of how the savage Indians martyred the hapless priests and missionaries who went among them in an attempt to lead them to the one true path. By the time I was through high school I had the idea that Indians were people who had benefited mightily from the advanced knowledge and superior morality of the Anglo-Europeans. At least I had, perforce, that idea to lay beside the other one that derived from my daily experience of Indian life, an idea less dehumanizing and more accurate because it came from my mother and the other Indian people who raised me. That idea was that Indians are a people who don't tell lies, who care for their children and their old people. You never see an Indian orphan, they said. You always know when you're old that someone will take care of you—one of your children will. Then they'd list the old folks who were being taken care of by this child or that. No child is ever considered illegitimate among the Indians, they said. If a girl gets pregnant, the baby is still part of the family, and the mother is too. That's what they said, and they showed me real people who lived according to those principles.

Of course the ravages of colonization have taken

their toll; there are orphans in Indian country now, and abandoned, brutalized old folks; there are even illegitimate children, though the very concept still strikes me as absurd. There are battered children and neglected children, and there are battered wives and women who have been raped by Indian men. Proximity to the "civilizing" effects of white Christians has not improved the moral quality of life in Indian country, though each group, Indian and white, explains the situation differently. Nor is there much yet in the oral tradition that can enable us to adapt to these inhuman changes. But a force is growing in that direction, and it is helping Indian women reclaim their lives. Their power, their sense of direction and of self will soon be visible. It is the force of the women who speak and work and write, and it is formidable.

Through all the centuries of war and death and cultural and psychic destruction have endured the women who raise the children and tend the fires, who pass along the tales and the traditions, who weep and bury the dead, who are the dead, and who never forget. There are always the women, who make pots and weave baskets, who fashion clothes and cheer their children on at powwow, who make fry bread and piki bread, and corn soup and chili stew, who dance and sing and remember and hold within their hearts the dream of their ancient peoples—that one day the woman who thinks will speak to us again, and everywhere there will be peace. Meanwhile we tell the stories and write the books and trade tales of anger and woe and stories of fun and scandal and laugh over all manner of things that happen every day. We watch and we wait.

My great-grandmother told my mother: Never forget you are Indian. And my mother told me the same thing. This, then, is how I have gone about remembering, so that my children will remember too.

R E A D I N G   9

Gynocide: Chinese Footbinding

ANDREA DWORKIN

FOOTBINDING EVENT

Instructions before Reading Chapter

1. Find a piece of cloth 10 feet long and 2 inches wide
2. Find a pair of children's shoes
3. Bend all toes except the big one under and into the sole of the foot. Wrap the cloth around these toes and then around the heel. Bring the heel and toes as close together as possible. Wrap the full length of the cloth as tightly as possible

4. Squeeze foot into children's shoes
5. Walk
6. Imagine that you are 5 years old
7. Imagine being like this for the rest of your life

The origins of Chinese footbinding, as of Chinese thought in general, belong to that amorphous entity called antiquity. The 10th century marks the beginning of the physical, intellectual, and spiritual dehumanization of women in China through the institution of footbinding. That institution itself, the implicit belief in its necessity and beauty, and the rigor with which it was practiced lasted another 10 centuries. There were sporadic attempts at emancipating the foot—some artists, intellectuals, and women in positions of power were

"Gynocide: Chinese Footbinding," from *Woman Hating* by Andrea Dworkin. Copyright © 1974 by Andrea Dworkin. Used by permission of the publisher, Dutton, an imprint of New American Library, a division of Penguin Books USA Inc.

the proverbial drop in the bucket. Those attempts, modest as they were, were doomed to failure: footbinding was a political institution which reflected and perpetuated the sociological and psychological inferiority of women; footbinding cemented women to a certain sphere, with a certain function—women were sexual objects and breeders. Footbinding was mass attitude, mass culture—it was the key reality in a way of life lived by real women—10 centuries times that many millions of them.

It is generally thought that footbinding originated as an innovation among the dancers of the Imperial harem. Sometime between the 9th and 11th centuries, Emperor Li Yu ordered a favorite ballerina to achieve the "pointed look." The fairy tale reads like this:

Li Yu had a favored palace concubine named Lovely Maiden who was a slender-waisted beauty and a gifted dancer. He had a six-foot-high lotus constructed for her out of gold; it was decorated lavishly with pearls and had a carmine lotus carpet in the center. Lovely Maiden was ordered to bind her feet with white silk cloth to make the tips look like the points of a moon sickle. She then danced in the center of the lotus, whirling about like a rising cloud.[1]

From this original event, the bound foot received the euphemism "Golden Lotus," though it is clear that Lovely Maiden's feet were bound loosely—she could still dance.

A later essayist, a true foot gourmand, described 58 varieties of the human lotus, each one graded on a 9-point scale. For example:

Type: Lotus petal, New moon, Harmonious bow, Bamboo shoot, Water chestnut
Specifications: plumpness, softness, fineness
Rank: Divine Quality (A-1), perfectly plump, soft and fine
Wondrous Quality (A-2), weak and slender
Immortal Quality (A-3), straight-boned, independent
Precious Article (B-1), peacocklike, too wide, disproportioned
Pure Article (B-2), gooselike, too long and thin
Seductive Article (B-3), fleshy, short, wide, round (the disadvantage of this foot was that its owner *could* withstand a blowing wind)

Excessive Article (C-1), narrow but insufficiently pointed
Ordinary Article (C-2), plump and common
False Article (C-3), monkeylike large heel (could climb)

The distinctions only emphasize that footbinding was a rather hazardous operation. To break the bones involved or to modify the pressure of the bindings irregularly had embarrassing consequences—no girl could bear the ridicule involved in being called a "large-footed demon" and the shame of being unable to marry.

Even the possessor of an A-1 Golden Lotus could not rest on her laurels—she had to observe scrupulously the taboo-ridden etiquette of bound femininity: (1) do not walk with toes pointed upwards; (2) do not stand with heels seemingly suspended in midair; (3) do not move skirt when sitting; (4) do not move feet when lying down. The same essayist concludes his treatise with this most sensible advice (directed to the gentlemen, of course):

Do not remove the bindings to look at her bare feet, but be satisfied with its external appearance. Enjoy the outward impression, for if you remove the shoes and bindings the aesthetic feeling will be destroyed forever.[2]

Indeed. The real feet looked like Figure 1.

FIGURE 1   Feet: 3 to 4 inches in length

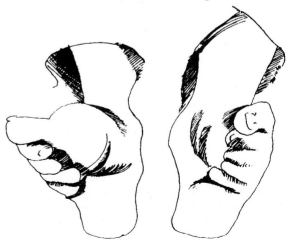

The physical process which created this foot is described by Howard S. Levy in *Chinese Footbinding: The History of a Curious Erotic Custom:*

The success or failure of footbinding depended on skillful application of a bandage around each foot. The bandage, about two inches wide and ten feet long, was wrapped in the following way. One end was placed on the inside of the instep, and from there it was carried over the small toes so as to force the toes in and towards the sole. The large toe was left unbound. The bandage was then wrapped around the heel so forcefully that heel and toes were drawn closer together. The process was then repeated from the beginning until the entire bandage had been applied. The foot of the young child was subjected to a coercive and unremitting pressure, for the object was not merely to confine the foot but to make the toes bend under and into the sole and bring the heel and sole as close together as physically possible.[3]

A Christian missionary observed:

The flesh often became putrescent during the binding and portions sloughed off from the sole; sometimes one or more toes dropped off.[4]

An elderly Chinese woman, as late as 1934, remembered vividly her childhood experience:

Born into an old-fashioned family in P'ing-hsi, I was inflicted with the pain of footbinding when I was seven years old. I was an active child who liked to jump about, but from then on my free and optimistic nature vanished. Elder Sister endured the process from six to eight years of age [this means that it took Elder Sister two years to attain the 3-inch foot]. It was in the first lunar month of my seventh year that my ears were pierced and fitted with gold earrings. I was told that a girl had to suffer twice, through ear piercing and footbinding. Binding started in the second lunar month; mother consulted references in order to select an auspicious day for it. I wept and hid in a neighbor's home, but Mother found me, scolded me, and dragged me home. She shut the bedroom door, boiled water, and from a box withdrew binding, shoes, knife, needle and thread. I begged for a one-day postponement, but Mother refused: "Today is a lucky day," she said. "If bound today, your feet will never hurt; if bound tomorrow they will." She washed and placed alum on my feet and cut the toenails. She then bent my toes toward the plantar with a binding cloth ten feet long and two inches wide, doing the right foot and then the left. She finished binding and ordered me to walk, but when I did the pain proved unbearable.

That night, Mother wouldn't let me remove the shoes. My feet felt on fire and I couldn't sleep; Mother struck me for crying. On the following days, I tried to hide but was forced to walk on my feet. Mother hit me on my hands and feet for resisting. Beatings and curses were my lot for covertly loosening the wrappings. The feet were washed and rebound after three or four days, with alum added. After several months, all toes but the big one were pressed against the inner surface. Whenever I ate fish or freshly killed meat, my feet would swell, and the pus would drip. Mother criticized me for placing pressure on the heel in walking, saying that my feet would never assume a pretty shape. Mother would remove the bindings and wipe the blood and pus which dripped from my feet. She told me that only with the removal of the flesh could my feet become slender. If I mistakenly punctured a sore, the blood gushed like a stream. My somewhat fleshy big toes were bound with small pieces of cloth and forced upwards, to assume a new-moon shape.

Every two weeks, I changed to new shoes. Each new pair was one- to two-tenths of an inch smaller than the previous one. The shoes were unyielding, and it took pressure to get into them. Though I wanted to sit passively by the K'ang, Mother forced me to move around. After changing more than ten pairs of shoes, my feet were reduced to a little over four inches. I had been in binding for a month when my younger sister started; when no one was around, we would weep together. In summer, my feet smelled offensively because of pus and blood; in winter, my feet felt cold because of lack of circulation and hurt if they got too near the K'ang and were struck by warm air currents. Four of the toes were curled in like so many dead caterpillars; no outsider would ever have believed that they belonged to a human being. It took two years to achieve the three-inch model. My toenails pressed against the flesh like thin paper. The heavily creased plantar couldn't be scratched when it itched or soothed when it ached. My shanks were thin, my feet became humped, ugly, and odiferous; how I envied the natural-footed![5]

Bound feet were crippled and excruciatingly painful. The woman was actually "walking" on the outside of toes which had been bent under into the sole of the foot. The heel and instep of the foot resembled the sole and heel of a high-heeled boot. Hard callouses formed; toenails grew into the skin; the feet were pus-filled and bloody; circulation was virtually stopped. The footbound woman hobbled along, leaning on a cane, against a wall, against a servant. To keep her balance she took very short steps. She was actually falling with every step and catching herself with the next. Walking required tremendous exertion.

Footbinding also distorted the natural lines of the female body. It caused the thighs and buttocks, which were always in a state of tension, to become somewhat swollen (which men called "voluptuous"). A curious belief developed among Chinese men that footbinding produced a most useful alteration of the vagina. A Chinese diplomat explained:

> The smaller the woman's foot, the more wondrous become the folds of the vagina. (There was the saying: the smaller the feet, the more intense the sex urge.) Therefore marriages in Ta-t'ung (where binding is most effective) often take place earlier than elsewhere. Women in other districts can produce these folds artificially, but the only way is by footbinding, which concentrates development in this one place. There consequently develop layer after layer (of folds within the vagina); those who have personally experienced this (in sexual intercourse) feel a supernatural exaltation. So the system of footbinding was not really oppressive.[6]

Medical authorities confirm that physiologically footbinding had no effect whatsoever on the vagina, although it did distort the direction of the pelvis. The belief in the wondrous folds of the vagina of footbound woman was pure mass delusion, a projection of lust onto the feet, buttocks, and vagina of the crippled female. Needless to say, the diplomat's rationale for finding footbinding "not really oppressive" confused his "supernatural exaltation" with her misery and mutilation.

Bound feet, the same myth continues, "made the buttocks more sensual,[and] concentrated life-giving vapors on the upper part of the body, making the face more attractive."[7] If, due to a breakdown in the flow of these "life-giving vapors," an ugly woman was footbound and still ugly, she need not despair, for an A-1 Golden Lotus could compensate for a C-3 face and figure.

But to return to her story, how did our Chinese ballerina become the millions of women stretched over 10 centuries? The transition from palace dancer to population at large can be seen as part of a class dynamic. The emperor sets the style, the nobility copies it, and the lower classes climbing ever upward do their best to emulate it. The upper class bound the feet of their ladies with the utmost severity. The Lady, unable to walk, remained properly invisible in her boudoir, an ornament, weak and small, a testimony to the wealth and privilege of the man who could afford to keep her—to keep her idle. Doing no manual labor, she did not need her feet either. Only on the rarest of occasions was she allowed outside of the incarcerating walls of her home, and then only in a sedan chair behind heavy curtains. The lower a woman's class, the less could such idleness be supported: the larger the feet. The women who had to work for the economic survival of the family still had bound feet, but the bindings were looser, the feet bigger—after all, she had to be able to walk, even if slowly and with little balance.

Footbinding was a visible brand. *Footbinding did not emphasize the differences between men and women—it created them,* and they were then perpetuated in the name of morality. Footbinding functioned as the Cerberus of morality and ensured female chastity in a nation of women who literally could not "run around." Fidelity, and the legitimacy of children, could be reckoned on.

The minds of footbound women were as contracted as their feet. Daughters were taught to cook, supervise the household, and embroider shoes for the Golden Lotus. Intellectual and physical restriction had the usual male justification. Women were perverse and sinful, lewd and lascivious, if left to develop naturally. The Chinese believed that being born a woman was payment for evils committed in a previous life. Footbinding was designed to spare a woman the disaster of another such incarnation.

Marriage and family are the twin pillars of all patriarchal cultures. Bound feet, in China, were the twin pillars of these twin pillars. Here we have the joining together of politics and morality, coupled to produce their inevitable offspring—the oppression of women based on totalitarian standards of beauty and a rampant sexual fascism. In arranging a marriage, a male's parents inquired first about the prospective bride's feet, then about her face. Those were her human, recognizable qualities. During the process of footbinding, mothers consoled their daughters by conjuring up the luscious marriage possibilities dependent on the beauty of the bound foot. Concubines for the Imperial harem were selected at tiny-foot festivals (forerunners of Miss America pageants). Rows upon rows of women sat on benches with their feet outstretched while audience and judges went along the aisles and commented on the size, shape and decoration of foot and shoes. No one, however, was ever allowed to touch the merchandise. Women looked forward to these festivals, since they were allowed out of the house.

The sexual aesthetics, literally the art of love, of the bound foot was complex. The sexual attraction of the foot was based on its concealment and the mystery surrounding its development and care. The bindings were unwrapped and the feet were washed in the woman's boudoir, in the strictest privacy. The frequency of bathing varied from once a week to once a year. Perfumes of various fragrances and alum were used during and after washing, and various kinds of surgery were performed on the callouses and nails. The physical process of washing helped restore circulation. The mummy was unwrapped, touched up, and put back to sleep with more preservatives added. The rest of the body was never washed at the same time as the feet, for fear that one would become a pig in the next life. Well-bred women were supposed to die of shame if men observed them washing their feet. The foot consisted, after all, of smelly, rotted flesh. This was naturally not pleasing to the intruding male, a violation of his aesthetic sensibility.

The art of the shoes was basic to the sexual aesthetics of the bound foot. Untold hours, days, months went into the embroidery of shoes. There were shoes for all occasions, shoes of different colors, shoes to hobble in, shoes to go to bed in, shoes for special occasions like birthdays, marriages, funerals, shoes which denoted age. Red was the favored color for bed shoes because it accentuated the whiteness of the skin of the calves and thighs. A marriageable daughter made about 12 pairs of shoes as a part of her dowry. She presented two specially made pairs to her mother-in-law and father-in-law. When she entered her husband's home for the first time, her feet were immediately examined by the whole family, neither praise nor sarcasm being withheld.

There was also the art of the gait, the art of sitting, the art of standing, the art of lying down, the art of adjusting the skirt, the art of every movement which involves feet. Beauty was the way feet looked and how they moved. Certain feet were better than other feet, more beautiful. Perfect three-inch form and utter uselessness were the distinguishing marks of the aristocratic foot. These concepts of beauty and status defined women: as ornaments, as sexual playthings, as sexual constructs. The perfect construct, even in China, was naturally the prostitute.

The natural-footed woman generated horror and repulsion in China. She was anathema, and all the forces of insult and contempt were used to obliterate her. Men said about bound feet and natural feet:

A tiny foot is proof of feminine goodness. . . .

Women who don't bind their feet look like men, for the tiny foot serves to show the differentiation. . . .

The tiny foot is soft and, when rubbed, leads to great excitement. . . .

The graceful walk gives the beholder mixed feelings of compassion and pity. . . .

Natural feet are heavy and ponderous as they get into bed, but tiny feet lightly steal under the coverlets. . . .

The large-footed woman is careless about adornment, but the tiny-footed frequently wash and apply a variety of perfumed fragrances, enchanting all who come into their presence. . . .

The natural foot looks much less aesthetic in walking. . . .

Everyone welcomes the tiny foot, regarding its smallness as precious. . . .

Men formerly so craved it that its possessor achieved harmonious matrimony. . . .

Because of its diminutiveness, it gives rise to a variety of sensual pleasures and love feelings. . . .[8]

Thin, small, curved, soft, fragrant, weak, easily inflamed, passive to the point of being almost inanimate—this was footbound woman. Her bindings created extraordinary vaginal folds; isolation in the bedroom increased her sexual desire; playing with the shriveled, crippled foot increased everyone's desire. Even the imagery of the names of various types of foot suggest, on the one hand, feminine passivity (lotuses, lilies, bamboo shoots, water chestnuts) and, on the other hand, male independence, strength, and mobility (lotus boats, large-footed crows, monkey foot). It was unacceptable for a woman to have those male qualities denoted by large feet. This fact conjures up an earlier assertion: footbinding did not formalize existing differences between men and women—it created them. One sex became male by virtue of having made the other sex some thing, something other, something completely polar to itself, something called female. In 1915, a satirical essay in defense of footbinding, written by a Chinese male, emphasized this:

> The bound foot is the condition of a life of dignity for man, of contentment for woman. Let me make this clear. I am a Chinese fairly typical of my class. I pored too much over classic texts in my youth and dimmed my eyes, narrowed my chest, crooked my back. My memory is not strong, and in an old civilization there is a vast deal to learn before you can know anything. Accordingly among scholars I cut a poor figure. I am timid, and my voice plays me false in gatherings of men. But to my footbound wife, confined for life to her house except when I bear her in my arms to her palanquin, my stride is heroic, my voice is that of a roaring lion, my wisdom is of the sages. To her I am the world; I am life itself.[9]

Chinese men, it is clear, stood tall and strong on women's tiny feet.

The so-called art of footbinding was the process of taking the human foot, using it as though it were insensible matter, molding it into an inhuman form. Footbinding was the "art" of making living matter insensible, inanimate. We are obviously not dealing here with art at all, but with fetishism, with sexual psychosis. This fetish became the primary content of sexual experience for an entire culture for 1,000 years. The manipulation of the tiny foot was an indispensable prelude to all sexual experience. Manuals were written elaborating various techniques for holding and rubbing the Golden Lotus. Smelling the feet, chewing them, licking them, sucking them, all were sexually charged experiences. A woman with tiny feet was supposedly more easily maneuvered around in bed and this was no small advantage. Theft of shoes was commonplace. Women were forced to sew their shoes directly into their bindings. Stolen shoes might be returned soaked in semen. Prostitutes would show their naked feet for a high price (there weren't many streetwalkers in China). Drinking games using cups placed in the shoes of prostitutes or courtesans were favorite pastimes. Tiny-footed prostitutes took special names like Moon Immortal, Red Treasure, Golden Pearl. No less numerous were the euphemisms for feet, shoes, and bindings. Some men went to prostitutes to wash the tiny foot and eat its dirt, or to drink tea made from the washing water. Others wanted their penises manipulated by the feet. Superstition also had its place—there was a belief in the curative powers of the water in which tiny feet were washed.

Lastly, footbinding was the soil in which sadism could grow and go unchecked—in which simple cruelty could transcend itself, without much effort, into atrocity. These are some typical horror stories of those times:

> A stepmother or aunt in binding the child's foot was usually much harsher than the natural mother would have been. An old man was described who delighted in seeing his daughters weep as the binding was tightly applied. . . . In one household, everyone had to bind. The main wife and concubines bound to the smallest degree, once morning and evening, and once before retiring. The husband and first wife strictly carried out foot inspections and whipped those guilty of having let the binding become loose. The sleeping shoes were so painfully small that the women had to ask the master to rub them in order to bring relief. Another rich man would flog his concubines on their tiny feet, one after another, until the blood flowed.[10]
>
> . . . About 1931 . . . bound-foot women unable to flee had been taken captive. The bandits, angered because of their captives' weak way of walking and inability to keep in file, forced the women to remove the bindings and socks and run about barefoot. They cried out in pain and were unable to move on in spite of the beatings. Each of the bandits grabbed a woman and forced her to dance about on a wide field covered with sharp rocks. The harshest treatment was meted out to prostitutes. Nails were driven through their hands and feet; they cried aloud for several days before expiring. One form of torture was to tie up a woman so that her legs dangled in midair and place bricks around each toe, increasing the weight until the toes straightened out and eventually dropped off.[11]

END OF FOOTBINDING EVENT

One asks the same questions again and again, over a period of years, in the course of a lifetime. The questions have to do with people and what they do—the how and the why of it. How could the Germans have murdered 6,000,000 Jews, used their skins for lampshades, taken the gold out of their teeth? How could white people have bought and sold black people, hanged them and castrated them? How could "Americans" have slaughtered the Indian nations, stolen the land, spread famine and disease? How could the Indochina genocide continue, day after day, year after year? How is it possible? Why does it happen?

As a woman, one is forced to ask another series of hard questions: Why, everywhere, the oppression of women throughout recorded history? How could the Inquisitors torture and burn women as witches? How could men idealize the bound feet of crippled women? How and why?

The bound foot existed for 1,000 years. In what terms, using what measure, could one calculate the enormity of the crime, the dimensions of the transgression, the *amount* of cruelty and pain inherent in that 1,000-year herstory? In what terms, using what vocabulary, could one penetrate to the meaning, to the reality, of that 1,000-year herstory?

Here one race did not war with another to acquire food, or land, or civil power; one nation did not fight with another in the interest of survival, real or imagined; one group of people in a fever pitch of hysteria did not destroy another. None of the traditional explanations or justifications for brutality between or among peoples applies to this situation. On the contrary, here one sex mutilated (enslaved) the other in the interest of the *art* of sex, male–female *harmony,* role-definition, beauty.

Consider the magnitude of the crime.

Millions of women, over a period of 1,000 years, were brutally crippled, mutilated, in the name of erotica.

Millions of human beings, over a period of 1,000 years, were brutally crippled, mutilated, in the name of beauty.

Millions of men, over a period of 1,000 years, reveled in love-making devoted to the worship of the bound foot.

Millions of men, over a period of 1,000 years, worshiped and adored the bound foot.

Millions of mothers, over a period of 1,000 years, brutally crippled and mutilated their daughters for the sake of a secure marriage.

Millions of mothers, over a period of 1,000 years, brutally crippled and mutilated their daughters in the name of beauty.

But this thousand-year period is only the tip of an awesome, fearful iceberg: an extreme and visible expression of romantic attitudes, processes, and values organically rooted in all cultures, then and now. It demonstrates that man's love for woman, his sexual adoration of her, his human definition of her, his delight and pleasure in her, require her negation: physical crippling and psychological lobotomy. That is the very nature of romantic love, which is the love based on polar role definitions, manifest in herstory as well as in fiction—he glories in her agony, he adores her deformity, he annihilates her freedom, he will have her as sex object, even if he must destroy the bones in her feet to do it. Brutality, sadism, and oppression emerge as the substantive core of the romantic ethos. That ethos is the warp and woof of culture as we know it.

Women should be beautiful. All repositories of cultural wisdom from King Solomon to King Hefner agree: women should be beautiful. It is the reverence for female beauty which informs the romantic ethos, gives it its energy and justification. Beauty is transformed into that golden ideal, Beauty—rapturous and abstract. Women must be beautiful and Woman is Beauty.

Notions of beauty always incorporate the whole of a given societal structure, are crystallizations of its values. A society with a well-defined aristocracy will have aristocratic standards of beauty. In Western "democracy" notions of beauty are "democratic": even if a woman is not born beautiful, she can make herself *attractive.*

The argument is not simply that some women are not beautiful, therefore it is not fair to judge women on the basis of physical beauty; or that men are not judged on that basis, therefore women also should not be judged on that basis; or that men should look for character in women; or that our standards of beauty are too parochial in and of themselves; or even that judging women according to their conformity to a standard of beauty serves to make them into products, chattels, differing from the farmer's favorite cow only in terms of literal form. The issue at stake is different, and crucial. Standards of beauty describe in precise terms the relationship that an individual will have to her own body. They prescribe her mobility, spontaneity, posture, gait,

IN MAGAZINES (I FOUND SPECIMENS OF THE BEAUTIFUL)

EKUA OMOSUPE

Once
I looked for myself
between the covers of
Seventeen
Vogue
Cosmopolitan
among blue eyes, blonde hair, white skin, thin
   bodies,
this is beauty.
I hated this shroud of
Blackness
that makes me invisible
a negative print
some other one's
nightmare.

In a store front window
against a white back drop
I saw a queenly head of nappy hair
and met this chiseled face
wide wondering eyes,
honey colored, bronzed skin
a mouth with thick lips
bowed   painted red
smiled purple gums and shining pearls
I turned to leave
but this body of
curvacious hips
strong thighs
broad ass
long legs
called me back to look again at likenesses of
African Queens, Dahomey Warriors, statuesque
   Goddesses.
I stand outside those covers meet
Face to Face
Myself
I am the Beautiful

From "In Magazines (I Found Specimens of the Beautiful),"
by Ekua Omosupe, in *Making Face, Making Soul/Haciendo
Caras*, ed. Gloria Anzaldúa. Copyright © 1990. Reprinted by
permission of aunt lute books.

the uses to which she can put her body. *They define precisely the dimensions of her physical freedom.* And, of course, the relationship between physical freedom and psychological development, intellectual possibility, and creative potential is an umbilical one.

In our culture, not one part of a woman's body is left untouched, unaltered. No feature or extremity is spared the art, or pain, of improvement. Hair is dyed, lacquered, straightened, permanented; eyebrows are plucked, penciled, dyed; eyes are lined, mascaraed, shadowed; lashes are curled, or false—from head to toe, every feature of a woman's face, every section of her body, is subject to modification, alteration. This alteration is an ongoing, repetitive process. It is vital to the economy, the major substance of male–female role differentiation, the most immediate physical and psychological reality of being a woman. From the age of 11 or 12 until she dies, a woman will spend a large part of her time, money, and energy on binding, plucking, painting, and deodorizing herself. It is commonly and wrongly said that male transvestites through the use of makeup and costuming caricature the women they would become, but any real knowledge of the romantic ethos makes clear that these men have penetrated to the core experience of being a woman, a romanticized construct.

The technology of beauty, and the message it carries, is handed down from mother to daughter. Mother teaches daughter to apply lipstick, to shave under her arms, to bind her breasts, to wear a girdle and high-heeled shoes. Mother teaches daughter concomitantly her role, her appropriate behavior, her place. Mother teaches daughter, necessarily, the psychology which defines womanhood: a woman must be beautiful, in order to please the amorphous and amorous Him. What we have called the romantic ethos operates as vividly in 20th-century America and Europe as it did in 10th-century China.

This cultural transfer of technology, role, and psychology virtually affects the emotive relationship between mother and daughter. It contributes substantially to the ambivalent love-hate dynamics of that relationship. What must the Chinese daughter/child have felt toward the mother who bound her feet? What does any daughter/child feel toward the mother who forces her to do painful things to her own body? The mother takes on the role of enforcer: she uses seduction, command, all manner of force to coerce the daughter to conform to the demands of the culture. It is because this role becomes her dominant role in the mother–daughter relationship that tensions and difficulties between mothers and daughters are so often unresolvable. The daughter who rejects the cultural norms enforced by the mother is forced to a basic rejection of her own mother, a recognition of the hatred and resentment she felt toward that mother, an alienation from mother and society so extreme that her own womanhood is denied by both. The daughter who internalizes those values and endorses those same processes is bound to repeat the teaching she was taught—her anger and resentment remain subterranean, channeled against her own female offspring as well as her mother.

Pain is an essential part of the grooming process, and that is not accidental. Plucking the eyebrows, shaving under the arms, wearing a girdle, learning to walk in high-heeled shoes, having one's nose fixed, straightening or curling one's hair—these things *hurt*. The pain, of course, teaches an important lesson: no price is too great, no process too repulsive, no operation too painful for the woman who would be beautiful. *The tolerance of pain and the romanticization of that tolerance begins here,* in preadolescence, in socialization, and serves to prepare women for lives of childbearing, self-abnegation, and husband-pleasing. The adolescent experience of the "pain of being a woman" casts the feminine psyche into a masochistic mold and forces the adolescent to conform to a self-image which bases itself on mutilation of the body, pain happily suffered, and restricted physical mobility. It creates the masochistic personalities generally found in adult women: subservient, materialistic (since all value is placed on the body and its ornamentation), intellectually restricted, creatively impoverished. It forces women to be a sex of lesser accomplishment, weaker, as underdeveloped as any backward nation. Indeed, the effects of that prescribed relationship between women and their bodies are so extreme, so deep, so extensive, that scarcely any area of human possibility is left untouched by it.

Men, of course, like a woman who "takes care of herself." The male response to the woman who is made up and bound is a learned fetish, societal in its dimensions. One need only refer to the male idealization of the bound foot and say that the same dynamic is operating here. Romance based on role differentiation, superiority based on a culturally determined and rigidly enforced inferiority, shame and guilt and fear of women and sex itself: all necessitate the perpetuation of these oppressive grooming imperatives.

The meaning of this analysis of the romantic ethos surely is clear. A first step in the process of liberation (women from their oppression, men from the unfreedom of their fetishism) is the radical redefining of the relationship between women and their bodies. The body must be freed, liberated, quite literally: from paint and girdles and all varieties of crap. Women must stop mutilating their bodies and start living in them. Perhaps the notion of beauty which will then organically emerge will be truly democratic and demonstrate a respect for human life in its infinite, and most honorable, variety.

NOTES

1. Howard S. Levy, *Chinese footbinding: The history of a curious erotic custom* (New York: W. Rawls, 1966), p. 39. Mr. Levy's book is the primary source for all the factual, historical information in this chapter.

2. Ibid., p. 112.

3. Ibid., pp. 25–26.

4. Ibid., p. 26.

5. Ibid., pp. 26–28.

6. Ibid., p. 141.

7. Ibid.

8. Ibid., p. 182.

9. Ibid., p. 89.

10. Ibid., p. 144.

11. Ibid., pp. 144–45.

Socialization

We are born into cultures that have definite ideas about males and females and their appropriate attitudes, values, and behaviors. Dominant American culture valuates men's behaviors, occupations, and attitudes more highly than those associated with women. It assumes that what men do is right and normal. Women are judged in accordance with how well they conform to the male standard. This way of thinking is known as *androcentrism*.

Carol Gilligan in "Woman's Place in Man's Life Cycle," shows how androcentric thinking about human development has failed to take account of women's experiences. Theories of the "life cycle" have valued the autonomy and achievement associated with men's goals more highly than the attachment and intimacy associated with women's goals. To achieve a more balanced conception of human development, Gilligan suggests, both theory and research should direct more systematic attention to women's lives.

Learning about our culture begins in the family. We learn about gender not only from what our parents say but also from what they do. Some theorists argue that women's universal mothering role has consequences for both the development of gender-related personality differences and the unequal social status of women and men. Nancy Chodorow, in "Family Structure and Feminine Personality," proposes that because women do the mothering, men are socioculturally superior but psychologically defensive and insecure. Women's secondary social value is somewhat countered, however, by their gains in psychological strength and security.

Because the culture differentiates not only along the basis of gender but on the bases of race and ethnicity as well, our experiences differ along these lines. What a black mother, for example, needs to teach her sons and daughters to enable them to survive in a white-male-dominated society is different from what a white mother has to teach her children. These kinds of racial differences, in turn, are compounded by differences in class status.

In "'The Means to Put My Children Through': Child-Rearing Goals and Strategies among Black Female Domestic Servants," Bonnie Thornton Dill writes about the complexity of race and gender issues by focusing on the experiences of black female domestic workers. Contrasting the race and class advantages available to white employers' children with the goals these women held for their own children, Dill outlines the reactions and responses of black female servants who reared white children to provide income but who reared their own children to enter the middle class.

The family, then, provides an environment in which interactions establish deep-seated ideas about gender and gender-appropriate behavior. Today many parents claim that they raise their boys and girls without gender bias, but considerable evidence indicates that such claims have little validity. Letty Cottin Pogrebin, in "The Secret Fear That Keeps Us from Raising Free Children," discusses a common but empirically unsupported fear of many parents:

that if their children are allowed sex-role freedom, they may grow up to be gay or lesbian.

Gender socialization is carried out in schools as well as homes. By the time children are in school, they not only have been socialized into their gender but are able to negotiate how and in which situations gender will be socially salient. Barrie Thorne, in "Girls and Boys Together . . . But Mostly Apart: Gender Arrangements in Elementary Schools," argues for this more complex idea of gender as a socially constructed variable. In her observations of social relations among children in elementary school,

she finds that the organization of one's sex and gender depends on the particular situation, and that children socialize each other.

Throughout these readings we come to understand that families, schools, and peers continuously socialize and resocialize us into our culture. We invite you to reflect upon your own socialization experiences. How have the members of your family, the teachers and staff in your school system, and your friends, coworkers, and classmates influenced your ideas about sex and gender. Reciprocally, how have you influenced theirs?

Woman's Place in Man's Life Cycle

CAROL GILLIGAN

In the second act of *The Cherry Orchard,* Lopakhin, the young merchant, describes his life of hard work and success. Failing to convince Madame Ranevskaya to cut down the cherry orchard to save her estate, he will go on, in the next act, to buy it himself. He is the self-made man, who, in purchasing "the estate where grandfather and father were slaves," seeks to eradicate the "awkward, unhappy life" of the past, replacing the cherry orchard with summer cottages where coming generations "will see a new life" (Act III). Elaborating this developmental vision, he describes the image of man that underlies and supports this activity: "At times when I can't go to sleep, I think: Lord, thou gavest us immense forests, unbounded fields and the widest horizons, and living in the midst of them we should indeed be giants." At which point, Madame Ranevskaya interrupts him, saying, "You feel the need for giants—They are good only in fairy tales, anywhere else they only frighten us" (Act II).

Conceptions of the life cycle represent attempts to order and make coherent the unfolding experiences and perceptions, the changing wishes and realities of everyday life. But the truth of such conceptions depends in part on the position of the observer. The brief excerpt from Chekhov's play (1904/1956) suggests that when the observer is a woman, the truth may be of a different sort. This discrepancy in judgment between men and women is the center of my consideration.

This essay traces the extent to which psychological theories of human development, theories that have informed both educational philosophy and classroom practice, have enshrined a view of human life similar to

Carol Gilligan, "Woman's Place in Man's Life Cycle," *Harvard Educational Review,* 49:4, pp. 431–446. Copyright © 1979 by the President and Fellows of Harvard College. All rights reserved.

Lopakhin's while dismissing the ironic commentary in which Chekhov embeds this view. The specific issue I address is that of sex differences, and my focus is on the observation and assessment of sex differences by life-cycle theorists. In talking about sex differences, however, I risk the criticism which such generalization invariably invites. As Virginia Woolf said, when embarking on a similar endeavor: "When a subject is highly controversial—and any question about sex is that—one cannot hope to tell the truth. One can only show how one came to hold whatever opinion one does hold" (1929:4).

At a time when efforts are being made to eradicate discrimination between the sexes in the search for equality and justice, the differences between the sexes are being rediscovered in the social sciences. This discovery occurs when theories formerly considered to be sexually neutral in their scientific objectivity are found instead to reflect a consistent observational and evaluative bias. Then the presumed neutrality of science, like that of language itself, gives way to the recognition that the categories of knowledge are human constructions. The fascination with point of view and the corresponding recognition of the relativity of truth that has informed the fiction of the twentieth century begin to infuse our scientific understanding as well when we begin to notice how accustomed we have become to seeing life through men's eyes.

A recent discovery of this sort pertains to the apparently innocent classic by Strunk and White (1959), *The Elements of Style.* The Supreme Court ruling on the subject of discrimination in classroom texts led one teacher of English to notice that the elementary rules of English usage were being taught through examples which counterposed the birth of Napoleon, the writings of Coleridge, and statements such as "He was an interesting talker, a man who had traveled all over the world and lived in half a dozen countries" (p. 7) with "Well, Susan, this is a fine mess you are in" (p. 3) or, less drastically, "He saw a woman accompanied by two children, walking slowly down the road" (p. 8).

Psychological theorists have fallen as innocently as Strunk and White into the same observational bias. Implicitly adopting the male life as the norm, they have tried to fashion women out of a masculine cloth. It all goes back of course, to Adam and Eve, a story which shows, among other things, that if you make a woman out of a man, you are bound to get into trouble. In the life cycle, as in the Garden of Eden, it is the woman who has been the deviant.

The penchant of developmental theorists to project a masculine image, and one that appears frightening to women, goes back at least to Freud (1905/1961), who built this theory of psychosexual development around the experiences of the male child that culminate in the Oedipus complex. In the 1920s, Freud struggled to resolve the contradictions posed for his theory by the different configuration of female sexuality and the different dynamics of the young girl's early family relationships. After trying to fit women into his masculine conception, seeing them as envying that which they missed, he came instead to acknowledge, in the strength and persistence of women's pre-Oedipal attachments to their mothers, a developmental difference. However, he considered this difference in women's development to be responsible for what he saw as women's developmental failure.

Deprived by nature of the impetus for a clear-cut Oedipal resolution, women's superego, the heir to the Oedipus complex, consequently was compromised. It was never, Freud observed, "so inexorable, so impersonal, so independent of its emotional origins as we require it to be in men" (1925/1961:257). From this observation of difference, "that for women the level of what is ethically normal is different from what it is in men" (p. 257), Freud concluded that "women have less sense of justice than men, that they are less ready to submit to the great exigencies of life, that they are more often influenced in their judgments by feelings of affection and hostility" (pp. 257–58).

Chodorow (1974, 1978) addresses this evaluative bias in the assessment of sex differences in her attempt to account for "the reproduction within each generation of certain general and nearly universal differences that characterize masculine and feminine personality

and roles" (1974:43). Writing from a psychoanalytic perspective, she attributes these continuing differences between the sexes not to anatomy but rather to "the fact that women, universally, are largely responsible for early child care and for (at least) later female socialization" (1974:43). Because this early social environment differs for and is experienced differently by male and female children, basic sex differences recur in personality development. As a result, "in any given society, feminine personality comes to define itself in relation and connection to other people more than masculine personality does. (In psychoanalytic terms, women are less individuated than men; they have more flexible ego boundaries)" (1974:44).

In her analysis, Chodorow relies primarily on Stoller's research on the development of gender identity and gender-identity disturbances. Stoller's work indicates that male and female identity, the unchanging core of personality formation, is "with rare exception firmly and irreversibly established for both sexes by the time a child is around three" (Chodorow, 1978:150). Given that for both sexes the primary caretaker in the first three years of life is typically female, the interpersonal dynamics of gender identity formation are different for boys and girls. Female identity formation takes place in a context of ongoing relationship as "mothers tend to experience their daughters as more like, and continuous with, themselves. Correspondingly, girls tend to remain part of the dyadic primary mother–child relationship itself. This means that a girl continues to experience herself as involved in issues of merging and separation, and in an attachment characterized by primary identification and the fusion of identification and object choice" (1978:166).

In contrast, "mothers experience their sons as a male opposite" and, as a result, "boys are more likely to have been pushed out of the preoedipal relationship and to have had to curtail their primary love and sense of empathic tie with their mother" (1978:166). Consequently, boys' development entails a "more emphatic individuation and a more defensive firming of ego boundaries." For boys, but not for girls, "issues of differentiation have become intertwined with sexual issues" (1978:167).

Thus Chodorow refutes the masculine bias of psychoanalytic theory, claiming that the existence of sex differences in the early experiences of individuation and relationship "does not mean that women have 'weaker ego boundaries' than men or are more prone to psychosis" (1978:167). What it means instead is that "the earliest mode of individuation, the primary construction of the ego and its inner object-world, the earliest conflicts and the earliest unconscious definitions of self, the earliest threats to individuation, and the earliest anxieties which call up defenses, all differ for boys and girls because of differences in the character of the early mother–child relationships for each" (1978:167). Because of these differences, "girls emerge from this period with a basis for 'empathy' built into their primary definition of self in a way that boys do not" (1978:167). Chodorow thus replaces Freud's negative and derivative description of female psychology with a more positive and direct account of her own:

> Girls emerge with a stronger basis for experiencing another's needs and feelings as one's own (or of thinking that one is so experiencing another's needs and feelings). Furthermore, girls do not define themselves in terms of the denial of preoedipal relational modes to the same extent as do boys. Therefore, regression to these modes tends not to feel as much a basic threat to their ego. From very early, then, because they are parented by a person of the same gender . . . girls come to experience themselves as less differentiated than boys, as more continuous with and related to the external object world, and as differently oriented to their inner object-world as well. [1978:167].

Consequently, "issues of dependency, in particular, are handled and experienced differently by men and women" (Chodorow, 1974:44). For boys and men, separation and individuation are critically tied to gender identity since separation from the mother is essential for the development of masculinity. "For girls and women, by contrast, issues of femininity or feminine identity are not problematic in the same way (1974:44); they do not depend on the achievement of separation from the mother or on the progress of individuation. Since, in Chodorow's analysis, masculinity is defined through separation while femininity is defined through attachment, male gender identity will be threatened by intimacy while female gender identity will be threatened by individuation. Thus males will tend to have difficulty with relationships while females will tend to have problems with separation. The quality of embeddedness in social interaction and personal relationships that characterizes women's lives in contrast to men's,

however, becomes not only a descriptive difference but also a developmental liability when the milestones of childhood and adolescent development are described by markers of increasing separation. Then women's failure to separate becomes by definition a failure to develop.

The sex differences in personality formation that Chodorow delineates in her analysis of early childhood relationships, as well as the bias she points out in the evaluation of these differences, reappear in the middle childhood years in the studies of children's games. Children's games have been considered by Mead (1934) and Piaget (1932/1965) as the crucible of social development during the school years. In games children learn to take the role of the other and come to see themselves through another's eyes. In games they learn respect for rules and come to understand the ways rules can be made and changed.

Lever (1976), considering the peer group to be the agent of socialization during the elementary school years and play to be a major activity of socialization at that time, set out to discover whether there were sex differences in the games that children play. Studying 181 fifth-grade, white, middle-class Connecticut children, ages 10 and 11, she observed the organization and structure of their playtime activities. She watched the children as they played during the school recess, lunch, and in physical education class, and, in addition, kept diaries of their accounts as to how they spent their out-of-school time.

From this study, Lever reports the following sex differences: boys play more out of doors than girls do; boys more often play in large and age-heterogeneous groups; they play competitive games more often than girls do, and their games last longer than girls' games (Lever, 1976). The last is in some ways the most interesting finding. Boys' games appeared to last longer not only because they required a higher level of skill and were thus less likely to become boring, but also because when disputes arose in the course of a game, the boys were able to resolve the disputes more effectively than the girls: "During the course of this study, boys were seen quarrelling all the time, but not once was a game terminated because of a quarrel and no game was interrupted for more than seven minutes. In the gravest debates, the final word was always to 'repeat the play,' generally followed by a chorus of 'cheater's proof'" (1976:482). In fact, it seemed that the boys enjoyed the legal debates as much as they did the game itself, and even marginal players of lesser size or skill participated equally in these recurrent squabbles. In contrast, the eruption of disputes among girls tended to end the game.

Thus Lever extends and corroborates the observations reported by Piaget (1932/1965) in his naturalistic study of the rules of the game, where he found boys becoming increasingly fascinated with the legal elaboration of rules and the development of fair procedures for adjudicating conflicts, a fascination that, he noted, did not hold for girls. Girls, Piaget observed, had a more "pragmatic" attitude toward rules, "regarding a rule as good as long as the game repaid it" (p. 83). As a result, he considered girls to be more tolerant in their attitudes toward rules, more willing to make exceptions, and more easily reconciled to innovations. However, and presumably as a result, he concluded that the legal sense which he considered essential to moral development "is far less developed in little girls than in boys" (p. 77).

This same bias that led Piaget to equate male development with child development also colors Lever's work. The assumption that shapes her discussion of results is that the male model is the better one. It seems, in any case, more adaptive, since, as Lever points out, it fits the requirements Riesman (1961) describes for success in modern corporate life. In contrast, the sensitivity and care for the feelings of others that girls develop through their primarily dyadic play relationships have little market value and can even impede professional success. Lever clearly implies that, given the realities of adult life, if a girl does not want to be dependent on men, she will have to learn to play like a boy.

Since Piaget argues that children learn the respect for rules necessary for moral development by playing rule-bound games, and Kohlberg (1971) adds that these lessons are most effectively learned through the opportunities for role-taking that arise in the course of resolving disputes, the moral lessons inherent in girls' play appear to be fewer than for boys. Traditional girls' games like jump rope and hopscotch are turn-taking games where competition is indirect in that one person's success does not necessarily signify another's failure. Consequently, disputes requiring adjudication are less likely to occur. In fact, most of the girls whom Lever interviewed claimed that when a quarrel broke out, they ended the game. Rather than elaborating a system of rules for resolving disputes, girls directed their efforts instead toward sustaining affective ties.

Lever concludes that from the games they play boys learn both independence and the organizational skills necessary for coordinating the activities of large and diverse groups of people. By participating in controlled and socially approved competitive situations, they learn to deal with competition in a relatively forthright manner—to play with their enemies and compete with their friends, all in accordance with the rules of the game. In contrast, girls' play tends to occur in smaller, more intimate groups, often the best-friend dyad, and in private places. This play replicates the social pattern of primary human relationships in that its organization is more cooperative and points less toward learning to take the role of the generalized other than it does toward the development of the empathy and sensitivity necessary for taking the role of the particular other.

Chodorow's analysis of sex differences in personality formation in early childhood is thus extended by Lever's observations of sex differences in the play activities of middle childhood. Together these accounts suggest that boys and girls arrive at puberty with a different interpersonal orientation and a different range of social experiences. While Sullivan (1953), tracing the sequence of male development, posits the experience of a close same-sex friendship in preadolescence as necessary for the subsequent integration of sexuality and intimacy, no corresponding account is available to describe girls' development at this critical juncture. Instead, since adolescence is considered a crucial time for separation and individuation, the period of "the second individuation process" (Blos, 1967), it has been in adolescence that female development has appeared most divergent and thus most problematic.

"Puberty," Freud said, "which brings about so great an accession of libido in boys, is marked in girls by a fresh wave of repression" (1905/1961:220) necessary for the transformation of the young girls' "masculine sexuality" into the "specifically feminine" sexuality of her adulthood. Freud posits this transformation on the girl's acknowledgment and acceptance of "the fact of her castration." In his account puberty brings for girls a new awareness of "the wound to her narcissism" and leads her to develop, "like a scar, a sense of inferiority" (1925/1961:253). Since adolescence is, in Erikson's expansion of Freud's psychoanalytic account, the time when the ego takes on an identity which confirms the individual in relation to society, the girl arrives at this juncture in development either psychologically at risk or with a different agenda.

The problem that female adolescence presents for

psychologists of human development is apparent in Erikson's account. Erikson (1950) charts eight stages of psychosocial development, in which adolescence is the fifth. The task of this stage is to forge a coherent sense of self, to verify an identity that can span the discontinuity of puberty and make possible the adult capacity to love and to work. The preparation for the successful resolution of the adolescent identity crisis is delineated in Erikson's description of the preceding four stages. If in infancy the initial crisis of trust versus mistrust generates enough hope to sustain the child through the arduous life cycle that lies ahead, the task at hand clearly becomes one of individuation. Erikson's second stage centers on the crisis of autonomy versus shame and doubt, the walking child's emerging sense of separateness and agency. From there, development goes on to the crisis of initiative versus guilt, successful resolution of which represents a further move in the direction of autonomy. Next, following the inevitable disappointment of the magical wishes of the Oedipal period, the child realizes with respect to his parents that to bear them he must first join them and learn to do what they do so well. Thus in the middle childhood years, development comes to hinge on the crisis of industry versus inferiority, as the demonstration of competence becomes critical to the child's developing self-esteem. This is the time when children strive to learn and master the technology of their culture in order to recognize themselves and be recognized as capable of becoming adults. Next comes adolescence, the celebration of the autonomous, initiating, industrious self through the forging of an identity based on an ideology that can support and justify adult commitments. But about whom is Erikson talking?

Once again it turns out to be the male child—the coming generation of men like George Bernard Shaw, William James, Martin Luther, and Mahatma Gandhi—who provide Erikson with his most vivid illustrations. For the woman, Erikson says, the sequence is a bit different. She holds her identity in abeyance as she prepares to attract the man by whose name she will be known, by whose status she will be defined, the man who will rescue her from emptiness and loneliness by filling "the inner space" (Erikson, 1968). While for men, identity precedes intimacy and generativity in the optimal cycle of human separation and attachment, for women these tasks seem instead to be fused. Intimacy precedes, or rather goes along with, identity as the female comes to know herself as she is known, through her relationships with others.

Two things are essential to note at this point. The first is that, despite Erikson's observation of sex differences, his chart of life-cycle stages remains unchanged: identity continues to precede intimacy as the male diagonal continues to define his life-cycle conception. The second is that in the male life cycle there is little preparation for the intimacy of the first adult stage. Only the initial stage of trust versus mistrust suggests the type of mutuality that Erikson means by intimacy and generativity and Freud by genitality. The rest is separateness, with the result that development itself comes to be identified with separation and attachments appear as developmental impediments, as we have repeatedly found to be the case in the assessment of women.

Erikson's description of male identity as forged in relation to the world and of female identity as awakened in a relationship of intimacy with another person, however controversial, is hardly new. In Bettelheim's discussion of fairy tales in *The Uses of Enchantment* (1976) an identical portrayal appears. While Bettelheim argues, in refutation of those critics who see in fairy tales a sexist literature, that opposite models exist and could readily be found, nevertheless the ones upon which he focuses his discussion of adolescence conform to the pattern we have begun to observe.

The dynamics of male adolescence are illustrated archetypically by the conflict between father and son in "The Three Languages" (Bettelheim, 1976). Here a son, considered hopelessly stupid by his father, is given one last chance at education and sent for a year to study with a famous master. But when he returns, all he has learned is "what the dogs bark" (p. 97). After two further attempts of this sort, the father gives up in disgust and orders his servants to take the child into the forest and kill him. The servants, however, those perpetual rescuers of disowned and abandoned children, take pity on the child and decide simply to leave him in the forest. From there, his wanderings take him to a land beset by furious dogs whose barking permits nobody to rest and who periodically devour one of the inhabitants. Now it turns out that our hero has learned just the right thing: he can talk with the dogs and is able to quiet them, thus restoring peace to the land. The other knowledge he acquires serves him equally well, and he emerges triumphant from his adolescent confrontation with his father, a giant of the life-cycle conception.

In contrast, the dynamics of female adolescence are depicted through the telling of a very different story. In

the world of the fairy tale, the girl's first bleeding is followed by a period of intense passivity in which nothing
seems to be happening. Yet in the deep sleep of Snow
White and Sleeping Beauty, Bettelheim sees that inner
concentration which he considers to be the necessary
counterpart to the activity of adventure. The adolescent heroines awaken from their sleep not to conquer
the world but to marry the prince. Their feminine identity is inwardly and interpersonally defined. As in
Erikson's observation, for women, identity and intimacy are more intricately conjoined. The sex differences
depicted in the world of the fairy tales, like the fantasy
of the woman warrior in Maxine Hong Kingston's
(1977) autobiographical novel (which in turn echoes
the old stories of Troilus and Cressida and Tancred
and Chlorinda) indicate repeatedly that active adventure is a male activity, and if women are to embark on
such endeavors, they must at least dress like men.

These observations about sex difference support the
conclusion reached by McClelland, that "sex role turns
out to be one of the most important determinants of
human behavior. Psychologists have found sex differences in their studies from the moment they started
doing empirical research" (1975:81). But since it is difficult to say "different" without saying "better" or
"worse," and since there is a tendency to construct a
single scale of measurement, and since that scale has
been derived and standardized on the basis of men's
observations and interpretations of research data predominantly or exclusively drawn from studies of males,
psychologists have tended, in McClelland's words, "to
regard male behavior as the 'norm' and female behavior as some kind of deviation from that norm" (p. 81).
Thus when women do not conform to the standards of
psychological expectation, the conclusion has generally
been that something is wrong with the women.

What Horner (1972) found to be wrong with
women was the anxiety they showed about competitive
achievement. From the beginning, research on human
motivation using the Thematic Apperception Test
(TAT) was plagued by evidence of sex differences
which appeared to confuse and complicate data analysis. The TAT presents for interpretation an ambiguous
cue—a picture about which a story is to be written or
a brief story stem to be completed. Such stories in
reflecting projective imagination are considered to
reveal the ways in which people construe what they
perceive—that is, the concepts and interpretations they
bring to their experience and thus presumably the kind

of sense that they make of their lives. Prior to Horner's
work, it was clear that women made a different kind of
sense than men of situations of competitive achievement, that in some way they saw the situation differently or the situation aroused in them some different
response.

On the basis of his studies of men, McClelland
(1961) had divided the concept of achievement motivation into what appeared to be its two logical components, a motive to approach success ("hope success")
and a motive to avoid failure ("fear failure"). When
Horner (1972) began to analyze the problematic projective data on female achievement motivation, she
identified as a third category the unlikely motivation to
avoid success ("fear success"). Women appeared to
have a problem with competitive achievement, and
that problem seemed, in Horner's interpretation, to
emanate from a perceived conflict between femininity
and success, the dilemma of the female adolescent who
struggles to integrate her feminine aspirations and the
identifications of her early childhood with the more
masculine competence she has acquired at school.
Thus Horner reports, "When success is likely or possible, threatened by the negative consequences they
expect to follow success, young women become anxious and their positive achievement strivings become
thwarted" (1972:171). She concludes that this fear
exists because for most women, the anticipation of
success in competitive achievement activity, especially
against men, produces anticipation of certain negative
consequences, for example, threat of social rejection
and loss of femininity.

It is, however, possible to view such conflicts about
success in a different light. Sassen (forthcoming), on
the basis of her reanalysis of the data presented in
Horner's thesis, suggests that the conflicts expressed by
the women might instead indicate "a heightened perception of the 'other side' of competitive success, that
is, the great emotional costs of success achieved
through competition, or an understanding which, while
confused, indicates an awareness that something is rot-
ten in the state in which success is defined as having
better grades than everyone else." Sassen points out
that Horner found success anxiety to be present in
women only when achievement was directly competitive, that is, when one person's success was at the
expense of another's failure.

From Horner's examples of fear of success, it is
impossible to differentiate between neurotic or realistic

anxiety about the consequences of achievement, the questioning of conventional definitions of success, and the discovery of personal goals other than conventional success. The construction of the problem posed by success as a problem of identity and ideology that appears in Horner's illustrations, if taken at face value rather than assumed to be derivative, suggests Erikson's distinction between a conventional and neohumanist identity, or, in cognitive terms, the distinction between conventional and postconventional thought (Loevinger & Wessler, 1970; Inhelder & Piaget, 1958; Kohlberg, 1971; Perry, 1968).

In his elaboration of the identity crisis, Erikson discusses the life of George Bernard Shaw to illustrate the young person's sense of being co-opted prematurely by success in a career he cannot wholeheartedly endorse. Shaw at seventy, reflecting upon his life, describes his crisis at the age of twenty as one caused not by lack of success or the absence of recognition, but by too much of both:

> I made good in spite of myself, and found, to my dismay, that Business, instead of expelling me as the worthless imposter I was, was fastening upon me with no intention of letting me go. Behold me, therefore, in my twentieth year, with a business training, in an occupation which I detested as cordially as any sane person lets himself detest anything he cannot escape from. In March, 1876, I broke loose. [Quoted in Erikson, 1968:143]

At which point Shaw settled down to study and to write as he pleased. Hardly interpreted as evidence of developmental difficulty, of neurotic anxiety about achievement and competition, Shaw's refusal suggested to Erikson "the extraordinary workings of an extraordinary personality coming to the fore" (1968:144).

We might on these grounds begin to ask not why women have conflicts about succeeding but why men show such readiness to adopt and celebrate a rather narrow vision of success. Remembering Piaget's observation, corroborated by Lever, that boys in their games are concerned more with rules while girls are more concerned with relationships, often at the expense of the game itself; remembering also that, in Chodorow's analysis, men's social orientation is positional and women's orientation is personal, we begin to understand why, when Anne becomes John in Horner's tale of competitive success and the stories are written by

men, fear of success tends to disappear. John is considered by other men to have played by the rules and won. He has the *right* to feel good about his success. Confirmed in his sense of his own identity as separate from those who, compared to him, are less competent, his positional sense of self is affirmed. For Anne, it is possible that the position she could obtain by being at the top of her medical school class may not, in fact, be what she wants.

"It is obvious," Virginia Woolf said, "that the values of women differ very often from the values which have been made by the other sex" (1929:76). Yet, she adds, it is the masculine values that prevail. As a result, women come to question the "normality" of their feelings and to alter their judgments in deference to the opinion of others. In the nineteenth-century novels written by women, Woolf sees at work "a mind slightly pulled from the straight, altering its clear vision in the anger and confusion of deference to external authority" (1929:77). The same deference that Woolf identifies in nineteenth-century fiction can be seen as well in the judgments of twentieth-century women. Women's reluctance to make moral judgments, the difficulty they experience in finding or speaking publicly in their own voice, emerge repeatedly in the form of qualification and self-doubt, in intimations of a divided judgment, in public and private assessments which are fundamentally at odds (Gilligan, 1977).

Yet the deference and confusion that Woolf criticizes in women derive from the values she sees as their strength. Women's deference is rooted not only in their social circumstances but also in the substance of their moral concern. Sensitivity to the needs of others and the assumption of responsibility for taking care lead women to attend to voices other than their own and to include in their judgment other points of view. Women's moral weakness, manifest in an apparent diffusion and confusion of judgment, is thus inseparable from women's moral strength, an overriding concern with relationships and responsibilities. The reluctance to judge can itself be indicative of the same care and concern for others that infuses the psychology of women's development and is responsible for what is characteristically seen as problematic in its nature.

Thus women not only define themselves in a context of human relationship but also judge themselves in terms of their ability to care. Woman's place in man's life cycle has been that of nurturer, caretaker, and helpmate, the weaver of those networks of relationships on which she in turn relies. While women have thus taken care of men, however, men have in their theories of psychological development tended either to assume or devalue that care. The focus on individuation and individual achievement that has dominated the description of child and adolescent development has recently been extended to the depiction of adult development as well. Levinson, in his study *The Seasons of a Man's Life* (1978), elaborates a view of adult development in which relationships are portrayed as a means to an end of individual achievement and success. In the critical relationships of early adulthood, the "Mentor" and the "Special Woman" are defined by the role they play in facilitating the man's realization of his "Dream." Along similar lines Vaillant (1977), in his study of men, considers altruism a defense, characteristic of mature ego functioning and associated with successful "adaptation to life," but conceived as derivative rather than primary, in contrast to Chodorow's analysis, in which empathy is considered "built in" to the woman's primary definition of self.

The discovery now being celebrated by men in midlife of the importance of intimacy, relationships, and care is something that women have known from the beginning. However, because that knowledge has been considered "intuitive" or "instinctive," a function of anatomy coupled with destiny, psychologists have neglected to describe its development. In my research, I have found that women's moral development centers on the elaboration of that knowledge. Woman's moral development thus delineates a critical line of psychological development whose importance for both sexes becomes apparent in the intergenerational framework of a life-cycle perspective. While the subject of moral development provides the final illustration of the reiterative pattern in the observation and assessment of sex differences in the literature on human development, it also indicates more particularly why the nature and significance of women's development has for so long been obscured and considered shrouded in mystery.

The criticism that Freud (1961) makes of women's sense of justice, seeing it as compromised in its refusal to blind impartiality, reappears not only in the work of Piaget (1934) but also in that of Kohlberg (1958). While girls are an aside in Piaget's account of *The Moral Judgment of the Child* (1932), an odd curiosity to whom he devotes four brief entries in an index that omits "boys" altogether because "the child" is assumed to be male, in Kohlberg's research on moral develop-

ment, females simply do not exist. Kohlberg's six stages that describe the development of moral judgment from childhood to adulthood were derived empirically from a longitudinal study of eighty-four boys from the United States. While Kohlberg (1973) claims universality for his stage sequence and considers his conception of justice as fairness to have been naturalistically derived, those groups not included in his original sample rarely reach his higher stages (Edwards, 1975; Gilligan, 1977). Prominent among those found to be deficient in moral development when measured by Kohlberg's scale are women whose judgments on his scale seemed to exemplify the third stage in his six-stage sequence. At this stage morality is conceived in terms of relationships, and goodness is equated with helping and pleasing others. This concept of goodness was considered by Kohlberg and Kramer (1969) to be functional in the lives of mature women insofar as those lives took place in the home and thus were relationally bound. Only if women were to go out of the house to enter the arena of male activity would they realize the inadequacy of their Stage Three perspective and progress like men toward higher stages where morality is societally or universally defined in accordance with a conception of justice as fairness.

In this version of human development, however, a particular conception of maturity is assumed, based on the study of men's lives and reflecting the importance of individuation in their development. When one begins instead with women and derives developmental constructs from their lives, then a different conception of development emerges, the expansion and elaboration of which can also be traced through stages that comprise a developmental sequence. In Loevinger's (1966) test for measuring ego development that was drawn from studies of females, fifteen of the thirty-six sentence stems to complete begin with the subject of human relationships (for example, "Raising a family . . . ; If my mother . . . ; Being with other people . . . ; When I am with a man . . . ; When a child won't join in group activities . . . ") (Loevinger & Wessler, 1970:141). Thus ego development is described and measured by Loevinger through the conception of relationships as well as by the concept of identity that measures the progress of individuation.

Research on moral judgment has shown that when the categories of women's thinking are examined in detail (Gilligan, 1977) the outline of a moral conception different from that described by Freud, Piaget, or Kohlberg begins to emerge and to inform a different description of moral development. In this conception, the moral problem is seen to arise from conflicting responsibilities rather than from competing rights and to require for its resolution a mode of thinking that is contextual and inductive rather than formal and abstract.

This conception of morality as fundamentally concerned with the capacity for understanding and care also develops through a structural progression of increasing differentiation and integration. This progression witnesses the shift from an egocentric through a societal to the universal moral perspective that Kohlberg described in his research on men, but it does so in different terms. The shift in women's judgment from an egocentric to a conventional to a principled ethical understanding is articulated through their use of a distinct moral language, in which the terms "selfishness" and "responsibility" define the moral problem as one of care. Moral development then consists of the progressive reconstruction of this understanding toward a more adequate conception of care.

The concern with caring centers moral development around the progressive differentiation and integration that characterize the evolution of the understanding of relationships just as the conception of fairness delineates the progressive differentiation and balancing of individual rights. Within the responsibility orientation, the infliction of hurt is the center of moral concern and its considered immoral whether or not it can otherwise be construed as fair or unfair. The reiterative use of the language of selfishness and responsibility to define the moral problem as a problem of care sets women apart from the men whom Kohlberg studied and from whose thinking he derived his six stages. This different construction of the moral problem by women may be seen as the critical reason for their failure to develop within the constraints of Kohlberg's system.

Regarding all constructions of responsibility as evidence of a conventional moral understanding, Kohlberg defines the highest stages of moral development as deriving from a reflective understanding of human rights. That the morality of rights differs from the morality of responsibility in its emphasis on separation rather than attachment, in its consideration of the individual rather than the relationship as primary, is illustrated by two quotations that exemplify these different orientations. The first comes from a twenty-five-year-old man who participated in Kohlberg's longitudinal study. The quotation itself is cited by Kohlberg to illustrate the principled conception of morality that he

scores as "integrated [Stage] Five judgment, possibly moving to Stage Six."

[What does the word morality mean to you?] Nobody in the world knows the answer. I think it is recognizing the right of the individual, the rights of other individuals, not interfering with those rights. Act as fairly as you would have them treat you. I think it is basically to preserve the human being's right to existence. I think that is the most important. Secondly, the human being's right to do as he pleases, again without interfering with somebody else's rights.

[How have your views on morality changed since the last interview?] I think I am more aware of an individual's rights now. I used to be looking at it strictly from my point of view, just for me. Now I think I am more aware of what the individual has a right to. [Note 1, p. 29]

"Clearly," Kohlberg states,

these responses represent attainment of the third level of moral theory. Moving to a perspective outside of that of his society, he identifies morality with justice (fairness, rights, the Golden Rule), with recognition of the rights of others as these are defined naturally or intrinsically. The human's right to do as he pleases without interfering with somebody else's rights is a formula defining rights prior to social legislation and opinion which defines what society may expect rather than being defined by it. [Note 1, pp. 29–30]

The second quotation comes from my interview with a woman, also twenty-five years old and at the time of the interview a third-year student at Harvard Law School. She described her conception of morality as follows:

[Is there really some correct solution to moral problems or is everybody's opinion equally right?] No, I don't think everybody's opinion is equally right. I think that in some situations . . . there may be opinions that are equally valid and one could conscientiously adopt one of several courses of action. But there are other situations which I think there are right and wrong answers, that sort of inhere in the nature of existence, of all individuals here who need to live with each other to live. We need to depend on each other and hopefully it is not only a physical need but a need of fulfillment in ourselves, that a person's life is enriched by cooperating with other people and striving to live in harmony with everybody else, and to that end, there are right and wrong, there are things which promote that end and that move away from it, and in that way, it is possible to choose in certain cases among different courses of action, that obviously promote or harm that goal.

[Is there a time in the past when you would have thought about these things differently?] Oh, yah. I think that I went through a time when I thought that things were pretty relative, that I can't tell you what to do and you can't tell me what to do, because you've got your conscience and I've got mine. . . .

[When was that?] When I was in high school. I guess that it just sort of dawned on me that my own ideas changed and because my own judgments changed, I felt I couldn't judge another person's judgment . . . but now I think even when it is only the person himself who is going to be affected, I say it is wrong to the extent it doesn't cohere with what I know about human nature and what I know about you, and just from what I think is true about the operation of the universe, I could say I think you are making a mistake.

[What led you to change, do you think?] Just seeing more of life, just recognizing that there are an awful lot of things that are common among people . . . there are certain things that you come to learn promote a better life and better relationships and more personal fulfillment than other things that in general tend to do the opposite and the things that promote these things, you would call morally right.

These responses also represent a reflective reconstruction of morality following a period of relativistic questioning and doubt, but the reconstruction of moral understanding is based not on the primacy and universality of individual rights, but rather on what she herself describes as a "very strong sense of being responsible to the world." Within this construction, the moral dilemma changes from how to exercise one's rights without interfering with the rights of others to how "to

lead a moral life which includes obligations to myself and my family and people in general." The problem then becomes one of limiting responsibilities without abandoning moral concern. When asked to describe herself, this woman says that she values

having other people that I am tied to and also having people that I am responsible to. I have a very strong sense of being responsible to the world, that I can't just live for my enjoyment, but just the fact of being in the world gives me an obligation to do what I can to make the world a better place to live in, no matter how small a scale that may be on.

Thus while Kohlberg's subject worries about people interfering with one another's rights, this woman worries about "the possibility of omission, of your not helping others when you could help them."

The issue this law student raises is addressed by Loevinger's fifth "autonomous" stage of ego development. The terms of its resolution lie in achieving partial autonomy from an excessive sense of responsibility by recognizing that other people have responsibility for their own destiny (Loevinger, 1968). The autonomous stage in Loevinger's account witnesses a relinquishing of moral dichotomies and their replacement with "a feeling for the complexity and multifaceted character of real people and real situations" (1970:6).

Whereas the rights conception of morality that informs Kohlberg's principled level (Stages Five and Six) is geared to arriving at an objectively fair or just resolution to the moral dilemmas to which "all rational men can agree" (Kohlberg, 1976), the responsibility conception focuses instead on the limitations of any particular resolution and describes the conflicts that remain. This limitation of moral judgment and choice is described by a woman in her thirties when she says that her guiding principle in making moral decisions has to do with "responsibility and caring about yourself and others, not just a principle that once you take hold of, you settle [the moral problem]. The principle put into practice is still going to leave you with conflict."

Given the substance and orientation of these women's judgments, it becomes clear why a morality of rights and noninterference may appear to women as frightening in its potential justification of indifference and unconcern. At the same time, however, it also becomes clear why, from a male perspective, women's judgments appear inconclusive and diffuse, given their insistent contextual relativism. Women's moral judgments thus elucidate the pattern that we have observed in the differences between the sexes, but provide an alternative conception of maturity by which these differences can be developmentally considered. The psychology of women that has consistently been described as distinctive in its greater orientation toward relationships of interdependence implies a more contextual mode of judgment and a different moral understanding. Given the differences in women's conceptions of self and morality, it is not surprising that women bring to the life cycle a different point of view and that they order human experience in terms of different priorities.

The myth of Demeter and Persephone, which McClelland cites as exemplifying the feminine attitude toward power, was associated with the Eleusinian Mysteries, celebrated in ancient Greece for over two thousand years (1975:96). As told in *The Homeric Hymn* (1971), the story of Persephone indicates the strengths of "interdependence, building up resources and giving" (McClelland, 1975:96) that McClelland found in his research on power motivation to characterize the mature feminine style. Although, McClelland says, "it is fashionable to conclude that no one knows what went on in the Mysteries, it is known that they were probably the most important religious ceremonies, even partly on the historical record, which were organized by and for women, especially at the onset before men by means of the cult of Dionysus began to take them over" (p. 96). Thus McClelland regards the myth as "a special presentation of feminine psychology." It is, as well, a life-cycle story par excellence.

Persephone, the daughter of Demeter, while out playing in the meadows with her girl friends, sees a beautiful narcissus which she runs to pick. As she does so, the earth opens and she is snatched away by Pluto, who takes her to his underworld kingdom. Demeter, goddess of the earth, so mourns the loss of her daughter that she refuses to allow anything to grow. The crops that sustain life on earth shrivel and dry up, killing men and animals alike, until Zeus takes pity on man's suffering and persuades his brother to return Persephone to her mother. But before she leaves, Persephone eats some pomegranate seeds which ensures that she will spend six months of every year in the underworld.

The elusive mystery of women's development lies in its recognition of the continuing importance of attachment in the human life cycle. Woman's place in man's life cycle has been to protect this recognition while the developmental litany intones the celebration of separation, autonomy, individuation, and natural rights. The myth of Persephone speaks directly to the distortion in this view by reminding us that narcissism leads to death, that the fertility of the earth is in some mysterious way tied to the continuation of the mother–daughter relationship, and that the life cycle itself arises from an alternation between the world of women and that of men. My intention in this essay has been to suggest that only when life-cycle theorists equally divide their attention and begin to live with women as they have lived with men will their vision encompass the experience of both sexes and their theories become correspondingly more fertile.

REFERENCES

Bettelheim, B. 1976. *The uses of enchantment.* New York: Knopf.

Blos, P. 1967. "The second individuation process of adolescence." In A. Freud, ed., *The psychoanalytic study of the child,* vol. 22, New York: International Universities Press.

Chekhov, A. 1904/1956. *The cherry orchard.* Stark Young, trans. New York: Modern Library.

Chodorow, N. 1974. Family structure and feminine personality. In M. Rosaldo and L. Lamphere, eds., *Women, culture, and society.* Stanford, Calif.: Stanford University Press.

Chodorow, N. 1978. *The reproduction of mothering.* Berkeley: University of California Press.

Edwards, C. P. 1975. "Societal complexity and moral development: A Kenyan study." *Ethos* 3:505–527.

Erikson, E. 1950. *Childhood and society.* New York: Norton.

Erikson, E. 1968. *Identity: Youth and crisis.* New York: Norton.

Freud, S. 1931/1961. "Female sexuality." In J. Strachey, ed., *The standard edition of the complete psychological works of Sigmund Freud,* vol. 21. London: Hogarth Press.

Freud, S. 1925/1961. "Some psychical consequences of the anatomical distinction between the sexes." In J. Strachey, ed., *The standard edition of the complete psychological works of Sigmund Freud,* vol. 19. London: Hogarth Press.

Freud, S. 1905/1961. "Three essays on sexuality." In J.

Strachey, ed., *The standard edition of the complete psycho-logical works of Sigmund Freud,* vol. 7., London: Hogarth Press.

Gilligan, C. 1977. "In a different voice: Women's conceptions of the self and of morality." *Harvard Educational Review* 47:481–517.

The Homeric Hymn. 1971. C. Boer, trans. Chicago: Swallow Press.

Horner, M. 1972. "Toward an understanding of achievement-related conflicts in women." *Journal of Social Issues* 28:157–74.

Inhelder, B., & Piaget, J. 1958. *The growth of logical thinking from childhood to adolescence.* New York: Basic Books.

Kingston, M. H. 1977. *The woman warrior.* New York: Vintage Books.

Kohlberg L. 1971. "From is to ought; How to commit the nat-uralistic fallacy and get away with it in the study of moral development." In T. Mischel, ed., *Cognitive development and epistemology.* New York: Academic Press.

Kohlberg, L. 1973. "Continuities and discontinuities in child-hood and adult moral development revisited." Unpub-lished manuscript, Harvard University.

Kohlberg L., & Kramer, R. 1969. "Continuities and disconti-nuities in childhood and adult moral development." *Human Development* 12:93–120.

Lever, J. 1976. "Sex differences in the games children play." *Social Problems* 23:478–87.

Levinson, D. 1978. *The seasons of a man's life.* New York: Knopf.

Loevinger, J., & Wessler, R. 1970. *The meaning and measure-ment of ego development.* San Francisco: Jossey-Bass.

McClelland, D. 1961. *The achieving society.* New York: Van Nostrand.

McClelland, D. 1975. *Power: The inner experience.* New York: Irvington.

Mead, G. H. 1934. *Mind, self, and society.* Chicago: University of Chicago Press.

Perry, W. 1968. *Forms of intellectual and ethical development in the college years.* New York: Holt, Rinehart & Winston.

Piaget, J. 1932/1965. *The moral judgment of the child.* New York: Free Press.

Riesman, D. 1961. *The lonely crowd.* New Haven: Yale University Press.

Sassen, G. "Success-anxiety in women: A constructivist theory of its sources and its significance." *Harvard Educational Review.*

Strunk, W., & White, E. B. 1959. *The elements of style.* New York: Macmillan.

Sullivan, H. S. 1953. *The interpersonal theory of psychiatry.* New York: Norton.

Vaillant, G. 1977. *Adaptation to life.* Boston: Little, Brown.

Woolf, V. 1929. *A room of one's own.* New York: Harcourt, Brace.

R E A D I N G I I

Family Structure and Feminine Personality

NANCY CHODOROW

I propose here[1] a model to account for the reproduc-tion within each generation of certain general and nearly universal differences that characterize mascu-line and feminine personality and roles. My perspec-tive is largely psychoanalytic. Cross-cultural and social-psychological evidence suggests that an argument

Reprinted from *Women, Culture, and Society,* edited by Michelle Zimbalist Rosaldo and Louise Lamphere, with the permission of the publishers, Stanford University Press. Copy-right © 1974 by the Board of Trustees of the Leland Stanford Junior University. Some notes have been renumbered.

drawn solely from the universality of biological sex dif-ferences is unconvincing.[2] At the same time, explana-tions based on patterns of deliberate socialization (the most prevalent kind of anthropological, sociological, and social-psychological explanation) are in themselves insufficient to account for the extent to which psycho-logical and value commitments to sex differences are so emotionally laden and tenaciously maintained, for the way gender identity and expectations about sex roles and gender consistency are so deeply central to a person's consistent sense of self.

This paper suggests that a crucial differentiating experience in male and female development arises out of the fact that women, universally, are largely responsible for early child care and for (at least) later female socialization. This points to the central importance of the mother–daughter relationship for women, and to a focus on the conscious and unconscious effects of early involvement with a female for children of both sexes. The fact that males and females experience this social environment differently as they grow up accounts for the development of basic sex differences in personality. In particular, certain features of the mother–daughter relationship are internalized universally as basic elements of feminine ego structure (although not necessarily what we normally mean by "femininity").

Specifically, I shall propose that, in any given society, feminine personality comes to define itself in relation and connection to other people more than masculine personality does. (In psychoanalytic terms, women are less individuated than men; they have more flexible ego boundaries.)[3] Moreover, issues of dependency are handled and experienced differently by men and women. For boys and men, both individuation and dependency issues become tied up with the sense of masculinity, or masculine identity. For girls and women, by contrast, issues of femininity, or feminine identity, are not problematic in the same way. The structural situation of child rearing, reinforced by female and male role training, produces these differences, which are replicated and reproduced in the sexual sociology of adult life.

The paper is also a beginning attempt to rectify certain gaps in the social-scientific literature, and a contribution to the reformulation of psychological anthropology. Most traditional accounts of family and socialization tend to emphasize only role training, and not unconscious features of personality. Those few that rely on Freudian theory have abstracted a behaviorist methodology from this theory, concentrating on isolated "significant" behaviors like weaning and toilet training. The paper advocates instead a focus on the ongoing interpersonal relationships in which these various behaviors are given meaning.[4]

More empirically, most social-scientific accounts of socialization, child development, and the mother–child relationship refer implicitly or explicitly only to the development and socialization of boys and to the mother–son relationship. There is a striking lack of systematic description about the mother–daughter relationship, and a basic theoretical discontinuity between,

on the one hand, theories about female development, which tend to stress the development of "feminine" qualities in relation to and comparison with men, and on the other hand, theories about women's ultimate mothering role. This final lack is particularly crucial, because women's motherhood and mothering role seem to be the most important features in accounting for the universal secondary status of women (Chodorow, 1971; Ortner, Rosaldo, this volume). The present paper describes the development of psychological qualities in women that are central to the perpetuation of this role.

In a formulation of this preliminary nature, there is not a great body of consistent evidence to draw upon. Available evidence is presented that illuminates aspects of the theory—for the most part psychoanalytic and social-psychological accounts based almost entirely on highly industrialized Western society. Because aspects of family structure are discussed that are universal, however, I think it is worth considering the theory as a general model. In any case, this is in some sense a programmatic appeal to people doing research. It points to certain issues that might be especially important in investigations of child development and family relationships, and suggests that researchers look explicitly at female vs. male development, and that they consider seriously mother–daughter relationships even if these are not of obvious "structural importance" in a traditional anthropological view of that society.

THE DEVELOPMENT OF GENDER PERSONALITY

According to psychoanalytic theory,[5] personality is a result of a boy's or girl's social-relational experiences from earliest infancy. Personality development is not the result of conscious parental intention. The nature and quality of the social relationships that the child experiences are appropriated, internalized, and organized by her/him and come to constitute her/his personality. What is internalized from an ongoing relationship continues independent of that original relationship and is generalized and set up as a permanent feature of the personality. The conscious self is usually not aware of many of the features of personality, or of its total structural organization. At the same time, these are important determinants of any person's behavior, both that which is culturally expected and that which is idiosyncratic or unique to the individual. The conscious aspects of personality, like a person's general self-concept and, importantly, her/his gender identity, require and depend upon the consistency and stability of its unconscious organization. In what follows I shall describe how contrasting male and female experiences lead to differences in the way the developing masculine or feminine psyche resolves certain relational issues.

Separation and Individuation (Preoedipal Development)

All children begin life in a state of "infantile dependence" (Fairbairn, 1952) upon an adult or adults, in most cases their mother. This state consists first in the persistence of primary identification with the mother: the child does not differentiate herself/himself from her/his mother but experiences a sense of oneness with her. (It is important to distinguish this from later forms of identification, from "secondary identification," which presuppose at least some degree of experienced separateness by the person who identifies.) Second, it includes an oral-incorporative mode of relationship to the world, leading, because of the infant's total helplessness, to a strong attachment to and dependence upon whoever nurses and carries her/him.

Both aspects of this state are continuous with the child's prenatal experience of being emotionally and physically part of the mother's body and of the exchange of body material through the placenta. That this relationship continues with the natural mother in most societies stems from the fact that women lactate. For convenience, and not because of biological necessity, this has usually meant that mothers, and females in general, tend to take all care of babies. It is probable that the mother's continuing to have major responsibility for the feeding and care of the child (so that the child interacts almost entirely with her) extends and intensifies her/his period of primary identification with her more than if, for instance, someone else were to take major or total care of the child. A child's earliest experience, then, is usually of identity with and attachment to a single mother, and always with women.

For both boys and girls, the first few years are preoccupied with issues of separation and individuation. This includes breaking or attenuating the primary identification with the mother and beginning to develop an individuated sense of self, and mitigating the totally dependent oral attitude and attachment to the mother. I would suggest that, contrary to the traditional psy-

choanalytic model, the preoedipal experience is likely to differ for boys and girls. Specifically, the experience of mothering for a woman involves a double identification (Klein & Rivière, 1937). A woman identifies with her own mother and, through identification with her child, she (re)experiences herself as a cared-for child. The particular nature of this double identification for the individual mother is closely bound up with her relationship to her own mother. As Deutsch expresses it, "In relation to her own child, woman repeats her own mother–child history" (1944:205). Given that she was a female child, and that identification with her mother and mothering are so bound up with her being a woman, we might expect that a woman's identification with a girl child might be stronger; that a mother, who is, after all, a person who is a woman and not simply the performer of a formally defined role, would tend to treat infants of different sexes in different ways.

There is some suggestive sociological evidence that this is the case. Mothers in a women's group in Cambridge, Massachusetts (see note 1), say that they identified more with their girl children than with boy children. The perception and treatment of girl vs. boy children in high-caste, extremely patriarchal, patrilocal communities in India are in the same vein. Families express preference for boy children and celebrate when sons are born. At the same time, Rajput mothers in North India are "as likely as not" (Minturn & Hitchcock, 1963) to like girl babies better than boy babies once they are born, and they and Havik Brahmins in South India (Harper, 1969) treat their daughters with greater affection and leniency than their sons. People in both groups say that this is out of sympathy for the future plight of their daughters, who will have to leave their natal family for a strange and usually oppressive postmarital household. From the time of their daughters' birth, then, mothers in these communities identify anticipatorily, by reexperiencing their own past, with the experiences of separation that their daughters will go through. They develop a particular attachment to their daughters because of this and by imposing their own reaction to the issue of separation on this new external situation.

It seems, then, that a mother is more likely to identify with a daughter than with a son, to experience her daughter (or parts of her daughter's life) as herself. Fliess's description (1961) of his neurotic patients who were the children of ambulatory psychotic mothers presents the problem in its psychopathological extreme. The example is interesting, because, although Fliess claims to be writing about people defined only by the fact that their problems were tied to a particular kind of relationship to their mothers, an overwhelmingly large proportion of the cases he presents are women. It seems, then, that this sort of disturbed mother inflicts her pathology predominantly on daughters. The mothers Fliess describes did not allow their daughters to perceive themselves as separate people, but simply acted as if their daughters were narcissistic extensions or doubles of themselves, extensions to whom were attributed the mothers' bodily feelings and who became physical vehicles for their mothers' achievement of autoerotic gratification. The daughters were bound into a mutually dependent "hypersymbiotic" relationship. These mothers, then, perpetuate a mutual relationship with their daughters of both primary identification and infantile dependence.

A son's case is different. Cultural evidence suggests that insofar as a mother treats her son differently, it is usually by emphasizing his masculinity in opposition to herself and by pushing him to assume, or acquiescing in his assumption of, a sexually toned male-role relation to her. Whiting (1959) and Whiting et al. (1958) suggest that mothers in societies with mother–child sleeping arrangements and postpartum sex taboos may be seductive toward infant sons. Slater (1968) describes the socialization of precarious masculinity in Greek males of the classical period through their mothers' alternation of sexual praise and seductive behavior with hostile deflation and ridicule. This kind of behavior contributes to the son's differentiation from his mother and to the formation of ego boundaries (I will later discuss certain problems that result from this).

Neither form of attitude or treatment is what we would call "good mothering." However, evidence of differentiation of a pathological nature in the mother's behavior toward girls and boys does highlight tendencies in "normal" behavior. It seems likely that from their children's earliest childhood, mothers and women tend to identify more with daughters and to help them to differentiate less, and that processes of separation and individuation are made more difficult for girls. On the other hand, a mother tends to identify less with her son, and to push him toward differentiation and the taking on of a male role unsuitable to his age, and undesirable at any age in his relationship to her.

For boys and girls, the quality of the preoedipal relationship to the mother differs. This, as well as differences in development during the oedipal period, accounts for the persisting importance of preoedipal issues in female development and personality that many psychoanalytic writers describe.[6] Even before the establishment of gender identity, gender personality differentiation begins.

Gender Identity (Oedipal Crisis and Resolution)

There is only a slight suggestion in the psychological and sociological literature that preoedipal development differs for boys and girls. The pattern becomes explicit at the next developmental level. All theoretical and empirical accounts agree that after about age three (the beginning of the "oedipal" period, which focuses on the attainment of a stable gender identity) male and female development becomes radically different. It is at this stage that the father, and men in general, begin to become important in the child's primary object world. It is, of course, particularly difficult to generalize about the attainment of gender identity and sex-role assumption, since there is such wide variety in the sexual sociology of different societies. However, to the extent that in all societies women's life tends to be more private and domestic, and men's more public and social . . . we can make general statements about this kind of development.

In what follows, I shall be talking about the development of gender personality and gender identity in the tradition of psychoanalytic theory. Cognitive psychologists have established that by the age of three, boys and girls have an irreversible conception of what their gender is (see Kohlberg, 1966). I do not dispute these findings. It remains true that children (and adults) may know definitely that they are boys (men) or girls (women), and at the same time experience conflicts or uncertainty about "masculinity" or "femininity," about what these identities require in behavioral or emotional terms, etc. I am discussing the development of "gender identity" in this latter sense.

A boy's masculine gender identification must come to replace his early primary identification with his mother. This masculine identification is usually based on identification with a boy's father or other salient adult males. However, a boy's father is relatively more remote than his mother. He rarely plays a major caretaking role even at this period in his son's life. In most societies, his work and social life take place farther from the home than do those of his wife. He is, then, often relatively inaccessible to his son, and performs his male role activities away from where the son spends most of his life. As a result, a boy's male gender identification often becomes a "positional" identification, with aspects of his father's clearly or not-so-clearly defined male role, rather than a more generalized "personal" identification—a diffuse identification with his father's personality, values, and behavioral traits—that could grow out of a real relationship to his father.[7]

Mitscherlich (1963), in his discussion of Western advanced capitalist society, provides a useful insight into the problem of male development. The father, because his work takes him outside of the home most of the time, and because his active presence in the family has progressively decreased, has become an "invisible father." For the boy, the tie between affective relations and masculine gender identification and role learning (between libidinal and ego development) is relatively attenuated. He identifies with a fantasied masculine role, because the reality constraint that contact with his father would provide is missing. In all societies characterized by some sex segregation (even those in which a son will eventually lead the same sort of life as his father), much of a boy's masculine identification must be of this sort, that is, with aspects of his father's role, or what he fantasies to be a male role, rather than with his father as a person involved in a relationship to him.

There is another important aspect to this situation, which explains the psychological dynamics of the universal social and cultural devaluation and subordination of women.[8] A boy, in his attempt to gain an elusive masculine identification, often comes to define this masculinity largely in negative terms, as that which is not feminine or involved with women. There is an internal and external aspect to this. Internally, the boy tries to reject his mother and deny his attachment to her and the strong dependence upon her that he still feels. He also tries to deny the deep personal identification with her that has developed during his early years. He does this by repressing whatever he takes to be feminine inside himself, and, importantly, by denigrating and devaluing whatever he considers to be feminine in the outside world. As a societal member, he also appropriates to himself and defines as superior particular social activities and cultural (moral, religious, and creative) spheres—possibly, in fact, "society" and "culture" themselves.[9]

Freud's description of the boy's oedipal crisis speaks to the issues of rejection of the feminine and identification with the father. As his early attachment to his mother takes on phallic-sexual overtones, and his father enters the picture as an obvious rival (who, in the son's fantasy, has apparent power to kill or castrate his son), the boy must radically deny and repress his attachment to his mother and replace it with an identification with his loved and admired, but also potentially punitive, therefore feared, father. He internalizes a superego.[10]

To summarize, four components of the attainment of masculine gender identity are important. First, masculinity becomes and remains a problematic issue for a boy. Second, it involves denial of attachment or relationship, particularly of what the boy takes to be dependence or need for another, and differentiation of himself from another. Third, it involves the repression and devaluation of femininity on both psychological and cultural levels. Finally, identification with his father does not usually develop in the context of a satisfactory affective relationship, but consists in the attempt to internalize and learn components of a not immediately apprehensible role.

The development of a girl's gender identity contrasts with that of a boy. Most important, femininity and female role activities are immediately apprehensible in the world of her daily life. Her final role identification is with her mother and women, that is, with the person or people with whom she also has her earliest relationship of infantile dependence. The development of her gender identity does not involve a rejection of this early identification, however. Rather, her later identification with her mother is embedded in and influenced by their ongoing relationship of both primary identification and preoedipal attachment. Because her mother is around, and she has had a genuine relationship to her as a person, a girl's gender and gender-role identification are mediated by and depend upon real affective relations. Identification with her mother is not positional—the narrow learning of particular role behaviors—but rather a personal identification with her mother's general traits of character and values. Feminine identification is based not on fantasied or externally defined characteristics and negative identification, but on the gradual learning of a way of being familiar in everyday life, and exemplified by the person (or kind of people—women) with whom she has been most involved. It is continuous with her early childhood identifications and attachments.

The major discontinuity in the development of a girl's sense of gender identity, and one that has led Freud and other early psychoanalysts to see female development as exceedingly difficult and tortuous, is that at some point she must transfer her primary sexual object choice from her mother and females to her father and males, if she is to attain her expected heterosexual adulthood. Briefly, Freud considers that all children feel that mothers give some cause for complaint and unhappiness: they give too little milk; they have a second child; they arouse and then forbid their child's sexual gratification in the process of caring for her/him. A girl receives a final blow, however: her discovery that she lacks a penis. She blames this lack on her mother, rejects her mother, and turns to her father in reaction.

Problems in this account have been discussed extensively in the general literature that has grown out of the women's movement, and within the psychoanalytic tradition itself. These concern Freud's misogyny and his obvious assumption that males possess physiological superiority, and that a woman's personality is inevitably determined by her lack of a penis.[11] The psychoanalytic account is not completely unsatisfactory, however. A more detailed consideration of several theorists[12] reveals important features of female development, especially about the mother–daughter relationship, and at the same time contradicts or mitigates the absoluteness of the more general Freudian outline.

These psychoanalysts emphasize how, in contrast to males, the female oedipal crisis is not resolved in the same absolute way. A girl cannot and does not completely reject her mother in favor of men, but continues her relationship of dependence upon and attachment to her. In addition, the strength and quality of her relationship to her father is completely dependent upon the strength and quality of her relationship to her mother. Deutsch suggests that a girl wavers in a "bisexual triangle" throughout her childhood and into puberty, normally making a very tentative resolution in favor of her father, but in such a way that issues of separation from and attachment to her mother remain important throughout a woman's life (1944:205):

It is erroneous to say that the little girl gives up her first mother relation in favor of the father. She only gradually draws him into the alliance, develops from the mother–child exclusiveness toward the triangular parent–child relationship and continues the latter, just as she does the former, although in a weaker and less elemental form, all her life. Only the principal part changes: now the mother, now the father plays it. The ineradicability of affective constellations manifests itself in later repetitions.

We might suggest from this that a girl's internalized and external object-relations become and remain more complex, and at the same time more defining of her, than those of a boy. Psychoanalytic preoccupation with constitutionally based libidinal development, and with a normative male model of development, has obscured this fact. Most women are genitally heterosexual. At the same time, their lives always involve other sorts of equally deep and primary relationships, especially with their children, and, importantly, with other women. In these spheres also, even more than in the area of heterosexual relations, a girl imposes the sort of object-relations she has internalized in her preoedipal and later relationship to her mother.

Men are also for the most part genitally heterosexual. This grows directly out of their early primary attachment to their mother. We know, however, that in many societies their heterosexual relationships are not embedded in close personal relationship but simply in relations of dominance and power. Furthermore, they do not have the extended personal relations women have. They are not so connected to children, and their relationships with other men tend to be based not on particularistic connection or affective ties, but rather on abstract, universalistic role expectations.

Building on the psychoanalytic assumption that unique individual experiences contribute to the formation of individual personality, culture and personality theory has held that early experiences common to members of a particular society contribute to the formation of "typical" personalities organized around and preoccupied with certain issues: "Prevailing patterns of child-rearing must result in similar internalized situations in the unconscious of the majority of individuals in a culture, and these will be externalized back into the culture again to perpetuate it from generation to generation" (Guntrip, 1961:378). In a similar vein, I have tried to show that to the extent males and females, respectively, experience similar interpersonal environments as they grow up, masculine and feminine personality will develop differently.

I have relied on a theory which suggests that features of adult personality and behavior are determined, but which is not biologically determinist. Culturally expected personality and behavior are not simply "taught," however. Rather, certain features of social structure, supported by cultural beliefs, values, and perceptions, are internalized through the family and the child's early social object-relationships. This largely unconscious organization is the context in which role training and purposive socialization take place.

SEX-ROLE LEARNING AND ITS SOCIAL CONTEXT

Sex-role training and social interaction in childhood build upon and reinforce the largely unconscious development I have described. In most societies (ours is a complicated exception) a girl is usually with her mother and other female relatives in an interpersonal situation that facilitates continuous and early role learning and emphasizes the mother–daughter identification and particularistic, diffuse, affective relationships between women. A boy, to a greater or lesser extent, is also with women for a large part of his childhood, which prevents continuous or easy masculine role identification. His development is characterized by discontinuity.

Ariès (1962:61), in his discussion of the changing concept of childhood in modern capitalist society, makes a distinction that seems to have more general applicability. Boys, he suggests, became "children" while girls remained "little women." "The idea of childhood profited the boys first of all, while the girls persisted much longer in the traditional way of life which confused them with the adults: we shall have cause to notice more than once this delay on the part of the women in adopting the visible forms of the essentially masculine civilization of modern times." This took place first in the middle classes, as a situation developed in which boys needed special schooling in order to prepare for their future work and could not begin to do this kind of work in childhood. Girls (and working-class boys) could still learn work more directly from their parents, and could begin to participate in the adult economy at an earlier age. Rapid economic change and development have exacerbated the lack of male generational role continuity. Few fathers now have either the opportunity or the ability to pass on a profession or skill to their sons.

Sex-role development of girls in modern society is more complex. On the one hand, they go to school to prepare for life in a technologically and socially complex society. On the other, there is a sense in which this schooling is a pseudo-training. It is not meant to interfere with the much more important training to be "feminine" and a wife and mother, which is embedded in the girl's unconscious development and which her mother teaches her in a family context where she is clearly the salient parent.

This dichotomy is not unique to modern industrial society. Even if special, segregated schooling is not necessary for adult male work (and many male initiation rites remain a form of segregated role training), boys still participate in more activities that characterize them as a category apart from adult life. Their activities grow out of the boy's need to fill time until he can begin to take on an adult male role. Boys may withdraw into isolation and self-involved play or join together in a group that remains more or less unconnected with either the adult world of work and activity or the familial world.

Jay (1969) describes this sort of situation in rural Modjokuto, Java. Girls, after the age of five or so, begin gradually to help their mothers in their work and spend time with their mothers. Boys at this early age begin to form bands of age mates who roam and play about the city, relating neither to adult men nor to their mothers and sisters. Boys, then, enter a temporary group based on universalistic membership criteria, while girls continue to participate in particularistic role relations in a group characterized by continuity and relative permanence.

The content of boys' and girls' role training tends in the same direction as the context of this training and its results. Barry, Bacon, and Child, in their well-known study (1957), demonstrate that the socialization of boys tends to be oriented toward achievement and self-reliance and that of girls toward nurturance and responsibility. Girls are thus pressured to be involved with and connected to others, boys to deny this involvement and connection.

ADULT GENDER PERSONALITY AND SEX ROLE

A variety of conceptualizations of female and male personality all focus on distinctions around the same issue, and provide alternative confirmation of the developmental model I have proposed. Bakan

(1966:15) claims that male personality is preoccupied with the "agentic," and female personality with the "communal." His expanded definition of the two concepts is illuminating:

I have adopted the terms "agency" and "communion" to characterize two fundamental modalities in the existence of living forms, agency for the existence of an organism as an individual and communion for the participation of the individual in some larger organism of which the individual is a part. Agency manifests itself in self-protection, self-assertion, and self-expansion; communion manifests itself in the sense of being at one with other organisms. Agency manifests itself in the formation of separations; communion in the lack of separations. Agency manifests itself in isolation, alienation, and aloneness; communion in contact, openness, and union. Agency manifests itself in the urge to master; communion in noncontractual cooperation. Agency manifests itself in the repression of thought, feeling, and impulse; communion in the lack and removal of repression.

Gutmann (1965) contrasts the socialization of male personalities in "allocentric" milieux (milieux in which the individual is part of a larger social organization and system of social bonds) with that of female personalities in "autocentric" milieux (in which the individual herself/himself is a focus of events and ties).[13] Gutmann suggests that this leads to a number of systematic differences in ego functioning. Female ego qualities, growing out of participation in autocentric milieux, include more flexible ego boundaries (i.e., less insistent self–other distinctions), present orientation rather than future orientation, and relatively greater subjectivity and less detached objectivity.[14]

Carlson (1971) confirms both characterizations. Her tests of Gutmann's claims lead her to conclude that "males represent experiences of self, others, space, and time in individualistic, objective, and distant ways, while females represent experiences in relatively interpersonal, subjective, immediate ways" (p. 270). With reference to Bakan, she claims that men's descriptions of affective experience tend to be in agentic terms and women's in terms of communion, and that an examination of abstracts of a large number of social-psychological articles on sex differences yields an overwhelming confirmation of the agency/communion hypothesis.

Cohen (1969) contrasts the development of "analytic" and "relational" cognitive style, the former characterized by a stimulus-centered, parts-specific orientation to reality, the latter centered on the self and responding to the global characteristics of a stimulus in reference to its total context. Although focusing primarily on class differences in cognitive style, she also points out that girls are more likely to mix the two types of functioning (and also to exhibit internal conflict about this). Especially, they are likely to exhibit at the same time both high field dependence and highly developed analytic skills in other areas. She suggests that boys and girls participate in different sorts of interactional subgroups in their families: boys experience their family more as a formally organized primary group; girls experience theirs as a group characterized by shared and less clearly delineated functions. She concludes (p. 836): "Since embedded responses covered the gamut from abstract categories, through language behaviors, to expressions of embeddedness in their social environments, it is possible that embeddedness may be a distinctive characteristic of female sex-role learning in this society regardless of social class, native ability, ethnic differences, and the cognitive impact of the school."

Preliminary consideration suggests a correspondence between the production of feminine personalities organized around "communal" and "autocentric" issues and characterized by flexible ego boundaries, less detached objectivity, and relational cognitive style, on the one hand, and important aspects of feminine as opposed to masculine social roles, on the other.

Most generally, I would suggest that a quality of embeddedness in social interaction and personal relationships characterizes women's life relative to men's. From childhood, daughters are likely to participate in an intergenerational world with their mother, and often with their aunts and grandmothers, whereas boys are on their own or participate in a single-generation world of age mates. In adult life, women's interaction with other women in most societies is kin-based and cuts across generational lines. Their roles tend to be particularistic, and to involve diffuse relationships and responsibilities rather than specific ones. Women in most societies are *defined* relationally (as someone's wife, mother, daughter, daughter-in-law; even a nun becomes the bride of Christ). Men's association (although it too may be kin-based and intergenerational) is much more likely than women's to cut across kinship units, to be restricted to a single generation, and to be recruited according to universalistic criteria and involve relationships and responsibilities defined by their specificity.

EGO BOUNDARIES AND THE MOTHER–DAUGHTER RELATIONSHIP

The care and socialization of girls by women ensures the production of feminine personalities founded on relation and connection, with flexible rather than rigid ego boundaries, and with a comparatively secure sense of gender identity. This is one explanation for how women's relative embeddedness is reproduced from generation to generation, and why it exists within almost every society. More specific investigation of different social contexts suggests, however, that there are variations in the kind of relationship that can exist between women's role performance and feminine personality.

Various kinds of evidence suggest that separation from the mother, the breaking of dependence, and the establishment and maintenance of a consistently individuated sense of self remain difficult psychological issues for Western middle-class women (i.e., the women who become subjects of psychoanalytic and clinical reports and social-psychological studies). Deutsch (1944, 1945) in particular provides extensive clinical documentation of these difficulties and of the way they affect women's relationships to men and children and, because of their nature, are reproduced in the next generation of women. Mothers and daughters in the women's group mentioned in note 1 describe their experiences of boundary confusion or equation of self and other, for example, guilt and self-blame for the other's unhappiness; shame and embarrassment at the other's actions; daughters' "discovery" that they are "really" living out their mothers' lives in their choice of career; mothers' not completely conscious reactions to their daughters' bodies as their own (overidentification and therefore often unnecessary concern with supposed weight or skin problems, which the mother is really worried about in herself); etc.

A kind of guilt that Western women express seems to grow out of and to reflect lack of adequate self/other distinctions and a sense of inescapable embeddedness in relationships to others. Tax describes this well (1970:2; italics mine):

Since our awareness of others is considered our duty, the price we pay when things go wrong is guilt and self-hatred. And things always go wrong. We respond with apologies; we continue to apologize long after the event is forgotten—and *even if it had no causal relation to anything we did to begin with.* If the rain spoils someone's picnic, we apologize. We apologize for taking up space in a room, for living.

As if the woman does not differentiate herself clearly from the rest of the world, she feels a sense of guilt and responsibility for situations that did not come about through her actions and without relation to her actual ability to determine the course of events. This happens, in the most familiar instance, in a sense of diffuse responsibility for everything connected to the welfare of her family and the happiness and success of her children. This loss of self in overwhelming responsibility for and connection to others is described particularly acutely by women writers (in the work, for instance, of Simone de Beauvoir, Kate Chopin, Doris Lessing, Tillie Olsen, Christina Stead, Virginia Woolf).

Slater (1961) points to several studies supporting the contention that Western daughters have particular problems about differentiation from their mother. These studies show that though most forms of personal parental identification correlate with psychological adjustment (i.e., freedom from neurosis or psychosis, *not* social acceptability), personal identification of a daughter with her mother does not. The reason is that the mother–daughter relation is the one form of personal identification that, because it results so easily from the normal situation of child development, is liable to be excessive in the direction of allowing no room for separation or difference between mother and daughter.

The situation reinforces itself in circular fashion. A mother, on the one hand, grows up without establishing adequate ego boundaries or a firm sense of self. She tends to experience boundary confusion with her daughter, and does not provide experiences of differentiating ego development for her daughter or encourage the breaking of her daughter's dependence. The daughter, for her part, makes a rather unsatisfactory and artificial attempt to establish boundaries: she projects what she defines as bad within her onto her mother and tries to take what is good into herself. (This, I think, is the best way to understand the girl's oedipal "rejection" of her mother.) Such an arbitrary mechanism cannot break the underlying psychological unity, however. Projection is never more than a temporary solution to ambivalence or boundary confusion.

The implication is that, contrary to Gutmann's suggestion (see note 3), "so-called ego pathology" may not be "adaptive" for women. Women's biosexual experiences (menstruation, coitus, pregnancy, childbirth, lactation) all involve some challenge to the boundaries of her body ego ("me"/"not-me" in relation to her blood or milk, to a man who penetrates her, to a child once part of her body). These are important and fundamental human experiences that are probably intrinsically meaningful and at the same time complicated for women everywhere. However, a Western woman's tenuous sense of individuation and of the firmness of her ego boundaries increases the likelihood that experiences challenging these boundaries will be difficult for her and conflictive.

Nor is it clear that this personality structure is "functional" for society as a whole. The evidence presented in this paper suggests that satisfactory mothering, which does not reproduce particular psychological problems in boys and girls, comes from a person with a firm sense of self and of her own value, whose care is a freely chosen activity rather than a reflection of a conscious and unconscious sense of inescapable connection to and responsibility for her children.

SOCIAL STRUCTURE AND THE MOTHER–DAUGHTER RELATIONSHIP

Clinical and self-analytic descriptions of women and of the psychological component of mother–daughter relationships are not available from societies and subcultures outside of the Western middle class. However, accounts that are primarily sociological about women in other societies enable us to infer certain aspects of their psychological situation. In what follows, I am not claiming to make any kind of general statement about what constitutes a "healthy society," but only to examine and isolate specific features of social life that seem to contribute to the psychological strength of some members of a society. Consideration of three groups with matrifocal tendencies in their family structure (Tanner, 1971) highlights several dimensions of importance in the developmental situation of the girl.

Young and Willmott (1957) describe the daily visit-

ing and mutual aid of working-class mothers and daughters in East London. In a situation where household structure is usually nuclear, like the Western middle class, grown daughters look to their mothers for advice, for aid in childbirth and child care, for friendship and companionship, and for financial help. Their mother's house is the ultimate center of the family world. Husbands are in many ways peripheral to family relationships, possibly because of their failure to provide sufficiently for their families as men are expected to do. This becomes apparent if they demand their wife's disloyalty toward or separation from her mother: "The great triangle of childhood is mother–father–child; in Bethnal Green the great triangle of adult life is Mum–wife–husband" (p. 64).

Geertz (1961)[15] and Jay (1969) describe Javanese nuclear families in which women are often the more powerful spouse and have primary influence upon how kin relations are expressed and to whom (although these families are formally centered upon a highly valued conjugal relationship based on equality of spouses). Financial and decision-making control in the family often rests largely in the hands of its women. Women are potentially independent of men in a way that men are not independent of women. Geertz points to a woman's ability to participate in most occupations, and to own farmland and supervise its cultivation, which contrasts with a man's inability, even if he is financially independent, to do his own household work and cooking.

Women's kin role in Java is important. Their parental role and rights are greater than those of men; children always belong to the woman in case of divorce. When extra members join a nuclear family to constitute an extended family household, they are much more likely to be the wife's relatives than those of the husband. Formal and distant relations between men in a family, and between a man and his children (especially his son), contrast with the informal and close relations between women, and between a woman and her children. Jay and Geertz both emphasize the continuing closeness of the mother–daughter relationship as a daughter is growing up and throughout her married life. Jay suggests that there is a certain amount of ambivalence in the mother–daughter relationship, particularly as a girl grows toward adulthood and before she is married, but points out that at the same time the mother remains a girl's "primary figure of confidence and support" (1969:103).

GENDER IN THE CONTEXT OF RACE AND CLASS: NOTES ON CHODOROW'S "REPRODUCTION OF MOTHERING"

ELIZABETH V. SPELMAN

. . . Much of feminist theory has proceeded on the assumption that gender is indeed a variable of human identity independent of other variables such as race and class, that whether one is a woman is unaffected by what class or race one is.[1] Feminists have also assumed that sexism is distinctly different from racism and classism, that whether and how one is subject to sexism is unaffected by whether and how one is subject to racism or classism.

The work of Nancy Chodorow has seemed to provide feminist theory with a strong foundation for these arguments. It has explicitly and implicitly been used to justify the assumption that there is nothing problematic about trying to examine gender independently of other variables such as race, class, and ethnicity. Though Chodorow's writings have received sometimes scathing criticism from feminists, more often they have been seen by feminist scholars in many different disciplines as providing a particularly rich understanding of gender.[2] Indeed, Chodorow offers what appears to be a very promising account of the relations between gender identity and other important aspects of identity such as race and class. For while she treats gender as separable from race and class, she goes on to suggest ways in which the sexist oppression intimately connected to gender differences is related to racism and classism.

. . . While Chodorow's work is very compelling, it ought to be highly problematic for any version of feminism that demands more than lip service to the significance of race and class, racism and classism, in the lives of the women on whom Chodorow focuses. The problem, as I see it, is not that feminists have taken Chodorow seriously, but that we have not taken her seriously enough. Her account points to a more complicated understanding of gender and the process of becoming gendered than she herself develops. She tells us to look at the social context of mothering in order to understand the effect of mothering on the acquisition of gender identity in

From *Inessential Woman* by Elizabeth V. Spelman. Copyright © 1988 by Elizabeth Spelman. Reprinted by permission of Beacon Press.

children; but if we follow her advice, rather than her own practice, we are led to see that gender identity is not neatly separable from other aspects of identity such as race and class. They couldn't be if, as Chodorow insists, the acquisition of gender occurs in and helps perpetuate the "hierarchical and differentiated social worlds" we inhabit. . . . It is a general principle of feminist inquiry to be sceptical about any account of human relations that fails to mention gender or consider the possible effects of gender differences: for in a world in which there is sexism, obscuring the workings of gender is likely to involve—whether intentionally or not—obscuring the workings of sexism. We thus ought to be sceptical about any account of gender relations that fails to mention race and class or to consider the possible effects of race and class differences on gender: for in a world in which there is racism and classism, obscuring the workings of race and class is likely to involve—whether intentionally or not—obscuring the workings of racism and classism.

For this reason alone we may have a lot to learn from the following questions about any account of gender relations that presupposes or otherwise insists on the separability of gender, race, and class: Why does it seem possible or necessary to separate them? Whatever the motivations for doing so, does it serve the interests of some people and not others? Does methodology ever express race or class privilege—for example, do any of the methodological reasons that might be given for trying to investigate gender in isolation from race and class in fact serve certain race or class interests?

These questions are not rhetorical. For very good and very important reasons, feminists have insisted on asking how gender affects or is affected by every branch of human inquiry (even those such as the physical sciences, which seem to have no openings for such questions). And with very good reason we have been annoyed by the absence of reference to gender in inquires about race or class, racism and classism. Perhaps it seems the best response, to such a state of affairs, first to focus on gender and sexism and then to go on to think about how gender and sexism are related to race and racism, class and classism. Hence the appeal of the work of Nancy Chodorow and the variations on it by others. But however logically, methodologically, and politically sound such inquiry seems, it obscures the ways in which race and class identity may be intertwined with gender identity. Moreover, since in a racist and classist society the racial and class identity of those who are subject to racism and classism are not obscured, all it can really mask is the racial and class identity of white middle-class women. It is because white middle-class women have something at stake in not having their racial and class identity made and kept visible that we must question accepted feminist positions on gender identity.

If feminism is essentially about gender, and gender is taken to be neatly separable from race and class, then race and class don't need to be talked about except in some peripheral way. And if race and class are peripheral to women's identities as women, then racism and classism can't be of central concern to feminism. Hence the racism and classism some women face and other women help perpetuate can't find a place in feminist theory unless we keep in mind the race and class of all women (not just the race and class of those who are the victims of racism and classism). I have suggested here that one way to keep them in mind is to ask about the extent to which gender identity exists in concert with these other aspects of identity. This is quite dif-ferent from saying either (1) we need to talk about race and class instead of gender or (2) we need to talk about race and class in addition to gender. Some feminists may be concerned that focus on race and class will deflect attention away from gender and from what women have in common and thus from what gives feminist inquiry its distinctive cast. This presupposes not only that we ought not spend too much time on what we don't have in common but that we have gender in common. But do we have gender identity in common? In one sense, of course, yes: all women are women. But in another sense, no: not if gender is a social construction and females become not simply women but particular kinds of women. If I am justified in thinking that what it means for me to be a woman must be exactly the same as what it means for you to be a woman (since we both are women), I needn't bother to find out anything from you or about you in order to find out what it means for you to be a woman: I can simply deduce what it means from my own case. On the other hand, if the meaning of what we apparently have in common (being women) depends in some ways on the meaning of what we don't have in common (for example, our different racial or class identities), then far from distracting us from issues of gender, attention to race and class in fact helps us to understand gender. In this sense it is only if we pay attention to how we differ that we come to an understanding of what we have in common.[3]

NOTES

[1] Notice how different this is from saying that whether one is *female* is unaffected by what race or class one is.

[2] Among the philosophers and political theorists who have incorporated Chodorow's work into their own analyses are Jane Flax, "Political Philosophy and the Patriarchal Unconscious: A Psychoanalytic Perspective on Epistemology and Metaphysics," Nancy C. M. Hartsock, "The Feminist Standpoint: Developing the Ground for a Specifically Feminist Historical Materialism," Naomi Scheman, "Individualism and the Objects of Psychology," and Sandra Harding, "Why Has the Sex/Gender System Become Visible Only Now?"—all in *Discovering Reality,* ed. Harding and Hintikka. See also Isaac D. Balbus, *Marxism and Domination* (Princeton: Princeton University Press, 1982). Chodorow's work also has been incorporated into the literary criticism of Judith Kegan Gardiner, "On Female Identity and Writing by Women," *Critical Inquiry* 8, no. 2 (1981): 347–61, and of Elizabeth Abel, "(E)Merging Identities: The Dynamics of Female Friendship in Contemporary Fiction by Women," *Signs* 6, no. 3 (1981): 413–35. Students of psychoanalysis such as Jessica Benjamin and Evelyn Fox Keller have found Chodorow's work helpful in explaining their own positions, Benjamin in "Master and Slave: The Fantasy of Erotic Domination," in *Powers of Desire: The Politics of Sexuality,* ed. Ann Snitow, Christine Stansell, and Sharon Thompson (New York: Monthly Review Press, 1983), 280–99; Keller in "Gender and Science," *Psychoanalysis and Contemporary Thought* 2, no. 3 (1978): 409–33. Chodorow's work has also influenced the far-reaching work of Carol Gilligan, *In a Different Voice* (Cambridge: Harvard University Press, 1982). Chodorow's book and earlier articles were the subject of a critical symposium in *Signs 6,* no. 3 (1981), with comments from Judith Lorber, Rose Laub Coser, Alice S. Rossi, and a response from Chodorow. Iris Young recently has expressed doubts about the wisdom of Flax's, Hartsock's, and Harding's use of Chodorow, in "Is Male Gender Identity the Cause of Male Domination?" in *Mothering: Essays in Feminist Theory,* ed. Joyce Trebilcot (Totowa, N.J.: Rowman and Allanheld, 1983). In the *Mothering* volume also appears Pauline Bart's highly critical review of Chodorow's book, a review first found in *off our backs* 11, no. 1 (1981). Adrienne Rich has pointed out the heterosexist bias in *The Reproduction of Mothering* in "Compulsory Heterosexuality and Lesbian Existence," *Signs 5,* no. 4 (1980): 631–60. As discussed below, Gloria Joseph has addressed the fact of the absence of a discussion of race and racism in accounts like Chodorow's.

[3] Thanks to Helen Longino, Monica Jakuc, and Marilyn Schuster for helpful comments on a very early draft of this chapter.

Siegel (1969) describes Atjehnese families in Indonesia in which women stay on the homestead of their parents after marriage and are in total control of the household. Women tolerate men in the household only as long as they provide money, and even then treat them as someone between a child and a guest. Women's stated preference would be to eliminate even this necessary dependence on men: "Women, for instance, envision paradise as the place where they are reunited with their children and their mothers; husbands and fathers are absent, and yet there is an abundance all the same. Quarrels over money reflect the women's idea that men are basically adjuncts who exist only to give their families whatever they can earn" (p. 177). A woman in this society does not get into conflicts in which she has to choose between her mother and her husband, as happens in the Western working class (see above; also Komarovsky, 1962), where the reigning ideology supports the nuclear family.

In these three settings, the mother–daughter tie and other female kin relations remain important from a woman's childhood through her old age. Daughters stay closer to home in both childhood and adulthood, and remain involved in particularistic role relations. Sons and men are more likely to feel uncomfortable at home, and to spend work and play time away from the house. Male activities and spheres emphasize universalistic, distancing qualities: men in Java are the bearers and transmitters of high culture and formal relationships; men in East London spend much of their time in alienated work settings; Atjehnese boys spend their time in school, and their fathers trade in distant places.

Mother–daughter ties in these three societies, described as extremely close, seem to be composed of companionship and mutual cooperation, and to be positively valued by both mother and daughter. The ethnographies do not imply that women are weighed down by the burden of their relationships or by overwhelming guilt and responsibility. On the contrary, they seem to have developed a strong sense of self and self-worth, which continues to grow as they get older and take on their maternal role. The implication is that "ego strength" is not completely dependent on the firmness of the ego's boundaries.

Guntrip's distinction between "immature" and "mature" dependence clarifies the difference between mother–daughter relationships and women's psyche in the Western middle class and in the matrifocal societies described. Women in the Western middle class are caught up to some extent in issues of infantile dependence, while the women in matrifocal societies remain in definite connection with others, but in relationships characterized by mature dependence. As Guntrip describes it (1961:291): "*Mature dependence* is characterized by full differentiation of ego and object (emergence from primary identification) and therewith a capacity for valuing the object for its own sake and for giving as well as receiving; a condition which should be described not as independence but as mature dependence." This kind of mature dependence is also to be distinguished from the kind of forced independence and denial of need for relationship that I have suggested characterizes masculine personality, and that reflects continuing conflict about infantile dependence (Guntrip, 1961:293; my italics): "Maturity is not equated with independence though it includes a certain capacity for independence. . . . The independence of the mature person is simply that he does not collapse when he has to stand alone. It is not an independence of needs for other persons with whom to have relationship: *that would not be desired by the mature.*"

Depending on its social setting, women's sense of relation and connection and their embeddedness in social life provide them with a kind of security that men lack. The quality of a mother's relationship to her children and maternal self-esteem, on the one hand, and the nature of a daughter's developing identification with her mother, on the other, make crucial differences in female development.

Women's kin role, and in particular the mother role, is central and positively valued in Atjeh, Java, and East London. Women gain status and prestige as they get older; their major role is not fulfilled in early motherhood. At the same time, women may be important contributors to the family's economic support, as in Java and East London, and in all three societies they have control over real economic resources. All these factors give women a sense of self-esteem independent of their relationship to their children. Finally, strong relationships exist between women in these societies, expressed in mutual cooperation and frequent contact. A mother, then, when her children are young, is likely to spend much of her time in the company of other women, not simply isolated with her children.

These social facts have important positive effects

on female psychological development. (It must be emphasized that all the ethnographies indicate that these same social facts make male development difficult and contribute to psychological insecurity and lack of ease in interpersonal relationships in men.) A mother is not invested in keeping her daughter from individuating and becoming less dependent. She has other ongoing contacts and relationships that help fulfill her psychological and social needs. In addition, the people surrounding a mother while a child is growing up become mediators between mother and daughter, by providing a daughter with alternative models for personal identification and objects of attachment, which contribute to her differentiation from her mother. Finally, a daughter's identification with her mother in this kind of setting is with a strong woman with clear control over important spheres of life, whose sense of self-esteem can reflect this. Acceptance of her gender identity involves positive valuation of herself, and not an admission of inferiority. In psychoanalytic terms, we might say it involves identification with a preoedipal, active, caring mother. Bibring points to clinical findings supporting this interpretation: "We find in the analysis of the women who grew up in this 'matriarchal' setting the rejection of the feminine role less frequently than among female patients coming from the patriarchal family culture" (1953:281).

There is another important aspect of the situation in these societies. The continuing structural and practical importance of the mother–daughter tie not only ensures that a daughter develops a positive personal and role identification with her mother, but also requires that the close psychological tie between mother and daughter become firmly grounded in real role expectations. These provide a certain constraint and limitation upon the relationship, as well as an avenue for its expression through common spheres of interest based in the external social world.

All these societal features contrast with the situation of the Western middle-class woman. Kinship relations in the middle class are less important. Kin are not likely to live near each other, and, insofar as husbands are able to provide adequate financial support for their families, there is no need for a network of mutual aid among related wives. As the middle-class woman gets older and becomes a grandmother, she cannot look forward to increased status and prestige in her new role.

The Western middle-class housewife does not have an important economic role in her family. The work she does and the responsibilities that go with it (household management, cooking, entertaining, etc.) do not seem to be really necessary to the economic support of her family (they are crucial contributions to the maintenance and reproduction of her family's class position, but this is not generally recognized as important either by the woman herself or by the society's ideology). If she works outside the home, neither she nor the rest of society is apt to consider this work to be important to her self-definition in the way that her housewife role is.

Child care, on the other hand, is considered to be her crucially important responsibility. Our post-Freudian society in fact assigns to parents (and especially to the mother)[16] nearly total responsibility for how children turn out. A middle-class mother's daily life is not centrally involved in relations with other women. She is isolated with her children for most of her workday. It is not surprising, then, that she is likely to invest a lot of anxious energy and guilt in her concern for her children and to look to them for her own self-affirmation, or that her self-esteem, dependent on the lives of others than herself, is shaky. Her life situation leads her to an overinvolvement in her children's lives.

A mother in this situation keeps her daughter from differentiation and from lessening her infantile dependence. (She also perpetuates her son's dependence, but in this case society and his father are more likely to interfere in order to assure that, behaviorally, at least, he doesn't *act* dependent.) And there are no other people around to mediate in the mother–daughter relationship. Insofar as the father is actively involved in a relationship with his daughter and his daughter develops some identification with him, this helps her individuation, but the formation of ego autonomy through identification with and idealization of her father may be at the expense of her positive sense of feminine self. Unlike the situation in matrifocal families, the continuing closeness of the mother–daughter relationship is expressed only on a psychological, interpersonal level. External role expectations do not ground or limit it.

It is difficult, then, for daughters in a Western middle-class family to develop self-esteem. Most psychoanalytic and social theorists[17] claim that the mother inevitably represents to her daughter (and son) regression, passivity, dependence, and lack of orientation to reality, whereas the father represents progression, activity, independence, and reality orientation.[18] Given the value implications of this dichotomy, there are advantages for the son in giving up his mother and identifying with his father. For the daughter, feminine gender identification means identification with a devalued, passive mother, and personal maternal identification is with a mother whose own self-esteem is low. Conscious rejection of her oedipal maternal identification, however, remains an unconscious rejection and devalation of herself, because of her continuing preoedipal identification and boundary confusion with her mother.

Cultural devaluation is not the central issue, however. Even in patrilineal, patrilocal societies in which women's status is very low, women do not necessarily translate this cultural devaluation into low self-esteem, nor do girls have to develop difficult boundary problems with their mother. In the Moslem Moroccan family, for example, a large amount of sex segregation and sex antagonism gives women a separate (domestic) sphere in which they have a real productive role and control, and also a life situation in which any young mother is in the company of other women.[19] Women do not need to invest all their psychic energy in their children, and their self-esteem is not dependent on their relationship to their children. In this and other patrilineal, patrilocal societies, what resentment women do have at their oppressive situation is more often expressed toward their sons, whereas daughters are seen as allies against oppression. Conversely, a daughter develops relationships of attachment to and identification with other adult women. Loosening her tie to her mother therefore does not entail the rejection of all women. The close tie that remains between mother and daughter is based not simply on mutual overinvolvement but often on mutual understanding of their oppression.

CONCLUSION

Women's universal mothering role has effects both on the development of masculine and feminine personality and on the relative status of the sexes. This paper has described the development of relational personality in women and of personalities preoccupied with the denial of relation in men. In its comparison of different societies it has suggested that men, while guaranteeing to themselves sociocultural superiority over women, always remain psychologically defensive and insecure. Women, by contrast, although always of secondary social and cultural status, may in favorable circumstances gain psychological security and a firm sense of worth and importance in spite of this.

Social and psychological oppression, then, is perpetuated in the structure of personality. The paper enables us to suggest what social arrangements contribute (and could contribute) to social equality between men and women and their relative freedom from certain sorts of psychological conflict. Daughters and sons must be able to develop a personal identification with more than one adult, and preferably one embedded in a role relationship that gives it a social context of expression and provides some limitation upon it. Most important, boys need to grow up around men who take a major role in child care, and girls around women who, in addition to their child-care responsibilities, have a valued role and recognized spheres of legitimate control. These arrangements could help to ensure that children of both sexes develop a sufficiently individuated and strong sense of self, as well as a positively valued and secure gender identity that does not bog down either in ego-boundary confusion, low self-esteem, and overwhelming relatedness to others or in compulsive denial of any connection to others or dependence upon them.

NOTES

1. My understanding of mother–daughter relationships and their effect on feminine psychology grows out of my participation beginning in 1971 in a women's group that discusses mother–daughter relationships in particular and family relationships in general. All the women in this group have contributed to this understanding. An excellent dissertation by Marcia Millman (1972) first suggested to me the importance of boundary issues for women and became a major organizational focus for my subsequent work. Discussions with Nancy Jay, Michelle Rosaldo, Philip Slater, Barrie Thorne, Susan Weisskopf, and Beatrice Whiting have been central to the development of the ideas presented here. I am grateful to George Goethals, Edward Payne, and Mal Slavin for their comments and suggestions about earlier versions of this paper.

2. Margaret Mead provides the most widely read and earliest argument for this viewpoint (cf., e.g., 1935 and 1949); see also Chodorow (1971) for another discussion of the same issue.

3. Unfortunately, the language that describes personality structure is itself embedded with value judgment. The implication in most studies is that it is always better to have firmer ego boundaries, that "ego strength" depends on the degree of individuation. Gutmann, who recognizes the linguistic problem, even suggests that "so-called ego pathology may have adaptive implications for women" (1965:231). The argument can be made that extremes in either direction are harmful. Complete lack of ego boundaries is clearly pathological, but so also, as critics of contemporary Western men point out (cf., e.g., Bakan, 1966, and Slater, 1970), is individuation gone wild, what Bakan calls "agency unmitigated by communion," which he takes to characterize, among other things, both capitalism based on the Protestant ethic and aggressive masculinity. With some explicit exceptions that I will specify in context, I am using the concepts solely in the descriptive sense.

4. Slater (1968) provides one example of such an investigation. LeVine's recent work on psychoanalytic anthropology (1971a, b) proposes a methodology that will enable social scientists to study personality development in this way.

5. Particularly as interpreted by object-relations theorists (e.g., Fairbairn, 1952, and Guntrip, 1961) and, with some similarity, by Parsons (1964) and Parsons and Bales (1955).

6. See, e.g., Brunswick, 1940; Deutsch, 1932, 1944; Fliess, 1948; Freud, 1931; Jones, 1927; and Lampl-de Groot, 1927.

7. The important distinction between "positional" and "personal" identification comes from Slater, 1961, and Winch, 1962.

8. For more extensive arguments concerning this, see, e.g., Burton & Whiting (1961), Chodorow (1971), and Slater (1968).

9. The processes by which individual personal experiences and psychological factors contribute to or are translated into social and cultural facts, and, more generally, the circularity of explanations in terms of socialization, are clearly very complicated. A discussion of these issues, however, is not within the scope of this paper.

10. The question of the universality of the oedipus complex as Freud describes it is beyond the scope of this paper. Bakan (1966, 1968) points out that in the original Oedipus myth, it was the father who first tried to kill his son, and that the theme of paternal infanticide is central to the entire Old Testament. He suggests that for a variety of reasons, fathers probably have hostile and aggressive fantasies and feelings about their children (sons). This more general account, along with a variety of psychological and anthropological data, convinces me that we must take seriously the notion that members of both generations may have conflicts over the inevitable replacement of the elder generation by the younger, and that children probably feel both guilt and (rightly) some helplessness in this situation.

11. These views are most extreme and explicit in two papers (Freud, 1925, 1933) and warrant the criticism that has been directed at them. Although the issue of penis envy in women is not central to this paper, it is central to Freud's theory of female development. Therefore I think it worthwhile to mention three accounts that avoid Freud's ideological mistakes while allowing that his clinical observations of penis envy might be correct.

Thompson (1943) suggests that penis envy is a symbolic expression of women's culturally devalued and underprivileged position in our patriarchal society; that possession of a penis symbolizes the possession of power and privilege. Bettelheim (1954) suggests that members of either sex envy the sexual functions of the other, and that women are more likely to express this envy overtly, because, since men are culturally superior, such envy is considered "natural." Balint (1954) does not rely on the fact of men's cultural superiority, but suggests that a little girl develops penis envy when she realizes that her mother loves people with penises, i.e., her father, and thinks that possession of a penis will help her in her rivalry for her mother's attentions.

12. See, e.g., Brunswick, 1940; Deutsch, 1925, 1930, 1932, 1944; Freedman, 1961; Freud, 1931; Jones, 1927.

13. Following Cohen (1969), I would suggest that the external structural features of these settings (in the family or in school, for instance) are often similar or the same for boys and girls. The different kind and amount of adult male and female participation in these settings accounts for their being experienced by children of different sexes as different sorts of milieux.

14. Gutmann points out that all these qualities are supposed to indicate lack of adequate ego strength, and suggests that we ought to evaluate ego strength in terms of the specific demands of different people's (e.g., women's as opposed to men's) daily lives. Bakan goes even further and suggests that modern male ego qualities are a pathological extreme. Neither account is completely adequate. Gutmann does not consider the possibility (for which we have good evidence) that the everyday demands of an autocentric milieu are unreasonable: although women's ego qualities may be "functional" for their participation in these milieux, they do not necessarily contribute to the psychological strength of the women themselves. Bakan, in his (legitimate) preoccupation with the lack of connection and compulsive independence that characterize Western masculine success, fails to recognize the equally clear danger (which, I will suggest, is more likely to affect women) of communion unmitigated by agency—of personality and behavior with no sense of autonomous control or independence at all.

I think this is part of a more general social-scientific mistake, growing out of the tendency to equate social structure and society with male social organization and activities within a society. This is exemplified, for instance, in Erikson's idealistic conception of maternal qualities in women (1965) and, less obviously, in the contrast between Durkheim's extensive treatment of "anomic" suicide (1897) and his relegation of "fatalistic" suicide to a single footnote (p. 276).

15. This ethnography and a reading of it that focuses on strong female kin relations (Siegel, 1969) were brought to my attention by Tanner (1971).

16. See Slater (1970) for an extended discussion of the implications of this.

17. See, e.g., Deutsch, 1944, *passim;* Erikson, 1964:162; Klein & Rivière, 1937:18; Parsons, 1964, *passim;* Parsons & Bales, 1955, *passim.*

18. Their argument derives from the universal fact that a child must outgrow her/his primary identification with and total dependence upon the mother. The present paper argues that the value implications of this dichotomy grow out of the particular circumstances of our society and its devaluation of relational qualities. Allied to this is the suggestion that it does not need to be, and often is not, relationship to the father that breaks the early maternal relationship.

19. Personal communication from Fatima Mernissi, based on her experience growing up in Morocco and her sociological fieldwork there.

REFERENCES

Ariès, P. 1962. *Centuries of childhood: A social history of family life.* New York.

Bakan, D. 1966. *The duality of human existence: Isolation and communion in Western man.* Boston.

———. 1968. *Disease, pain, and sacrifice: Toward a psychology of suffering.* Boston.

Balint, A. 1954. *The early years of life: A psychoanalytic study.* New York.

Barry, H., Bacon, M., & I. Child. 1957. "A cross-cultural survey of some sex differences in socialization." *Journal of Abnormal and Social Psychology* 55:327–32.

Bettelheim, B. 1954. *Symbolic wounds: Puberty rites and the envious male.* New York.

Bibring, G. 1953. "On the 'passing of the Oedipus complex' in a matriarchal family setting." In R. Lowenstein, ed., *Drives, affects and behavior: Essays in honor of Marie Bonaparte,* pp. 278–84. New York.

Brunswick, R. 1940. "The preoedipal phase of the libido development." In R. Fliess, ed., pp. 231–53.

Burton, R., & Whiting, J. 1961. "The absent father and cross-sex identity." *Merrill-Palmer Quarterly of Behavior and Development* 7 (2):85–95.

Carlson, R. 1971. "Sex differences in ego functioning: Exploratory studies of agency and communion." *Journal of Consulting and Clinical Psychology* 37:267–77.

Chodorow, N. 1971. "Being and doing. A cross-cultural examination of the socialization of males and females." In V. Gornick & B. Moran, eds., *Woman in sexist society: Studies in power and powerlessness.* New York.

Cohen, R. 1969. "Conceptual styles, culture conflict, and nonverbal tests of intelligence." *American Anthropologist* 71:828–56.

Deutsch, H. 1925. "The psychology of woman in relation to the functions of reproduction." In R. Fliess, ed., pp. 165–79.

———. 1930. "The significance of masochism in the mental life of women." In R. Fliess, ed., pp. 195–207.

———. 1932. "On female homosexuality." In R. Fliess, ed., pp. 208–30.

———. 1944, 1945. *Psychology of women.* Vols. I & II. New York.

Durkheim, E. 1897. *Suicide.* New York, 1968.

Erikson, E. 1964. *Insight and responsibility.* New York.

———. 1965. "Womanhood and the inner space." In R. Lifton, ed., *The woman in America.* Cambridge, Mass.

Fairbairn, W. 1952. *An object-relations theory of the personality.* New York.

Fliess, R. 1948. "Female and preoedipal sexuality: A historical survey." In R. Fliess, ed., pp. 159–64.

———. 1961. *Ego and body ego: Contributions to their psychoanalytic psychology.* New York, 1970.

Fliess, R., ed. 1969. *The psychoanalytic reader: An anthology of essential papers with critical introductions.* New York. Originally published in 1948.

Freedman, D. 1961. "On women who hate their husbands." In H. Ruitenbeek, ed., pp. 221–37.

Freud, S. 1925. "Some psychological consequences of the anatomical distinction between the sexes." In J. Strachey, ed., *The standard edition of the complete psychological works of Sigmund Freud,* Vol. XIX, pp. 248–58. London.

———. 1931. "Female sexuality." In H. Ruitenbeek, ed., pp. 88–105.

———. 1933. "Femininity." In *New introductory lectures in psychoanalysis,* pp. 112–35. New York, 1961.

Geertz, H. 1961. *The Javanese family: A study of kinship and socialization.* New York.

Guntrip, H. 1961. *Personality structure and human interaction: The developing synthesis of psycho-dynamic theory.* New York.

Gutmann, D. 1965. "Women and the conception of ego strength." *Merrill-Palmer Quarterly of Behavior and Development* 2:229–40.

Harper, E. 1969. "Fear and the status of women." *Southwestern Journal of Anthropology* 25:81–95.

Jay, R. 1969. *Javanese villagers: Social relations in rural Modjokuto.* Cambridge, Mass.

Jones, E. 1927. "The early development of female sexuality." In H. Ruitenbeek, ed., pp. 21–35.

Klein, M., & Rivière, J. 1937. *Love, hate and reparation.* New York, 1964.

Kohlberg, L. 1966. "A cognitive-developmental analysis of children's sex-role concepts and attitudes." In E. Maccoby, ed., *The development of sex differences,* pp. 82–173. Stanford, Calif.

Komarovsky, M. 1962. *Blue-collar marriage,* New York, 1967.

Lampl-de Groot, J. 1927. "The evolution of the Oedipus complex in women." In R. Fliess, ed., pp. 180–94.

LeVine, R. 1971a. "The psychoanalytic study of lives in natural social settings." *Human Development* 14:100–109.

————. 1971b. "Re-thinking psychoanalytic anthropology." Paper presented at the Institute on Psychoanalytic Anthropology, 70th Annual Meeting of the American Anthropological Association, New York.

Mead, M. 1935. *Sex and temperament in three primitive societies.* New York, 1963.

————. 1949. *Male and female: A study of sexes in a changing world.* New York, 1968.

Millman, M. 1972. "Tragedy and exchange: Metaphoric understandings of interpersonal relationships." Ph.D. dissertation, Department of Sociology, Brandeis University.

Minturn, L., & Hitchcock, J. 1963. "The Rajputs of Khalapur, India." In B. Whiting, ed., *Six cultures: Studies in child rearing.* New York.

Mitscherlich, A. 1963. *Society without the father.* New York, 1970.

Parsons, T., 1964. *Social structure and personality.* New York.

Parsons, T., & Bales, R. 1955. *Family, socialization and interaction process.* New York.

Ruitenbeek, H., ed. 1966. *Psychoanalysis and female sexuality.* New Haven.

Siegel, J. 1969. *The rope of God.* Berkeley, Calif.

Slater, P. 1961. "Toward a dualistic theory of identification." *Merrill-Palmer Quarterly of Behavior and Development* 7:113–26.

————. 1968. *The glory of Hera: Greek mythology and the Greek family.* Boston.

————. 1970. *The pursuit of loneliness: American culture at the breaking point.* Boston.

Tanner, N. 1971. "Matrifocality in Indonesia and among Black Americans." Paper presented at the 70th Annual Meeting of the American Anthropological Association, New York.

Tax, M. 1970. *Woman and her mind: The story of daily life.* Boston.

Thompson, C. 1943. "'Penis envy' in women." In H. Ruitenbeek, ed., pp. 246–51.

Whiting, J. 1959. "Sorcery, sin and the superego: A cross-cultural study of some mechanisms of social control." In C. Ford, ed., *Cross-cultural approaches: Readings in comparative research,* pp. 147–68. New Haven, 1967.

Whiting, J., Kluckhohn, R., & Anthony, A. 1958. "The function of male initiation rites at puberty." In E. Maccoby, T. Newcomb, & E. Hartley, eds., *Readings in social psychology,* pp. 359–70. New York.

Winch, R. 1962. *Identification and its familial determinants.* New York.

Young, M., & Willmott, P. 1957. *Family and kinship in East London.* London, 1966.

R E A D I N G   1 2

"The Means to Put My Children Through": Child-Rearing Goals and Strategies among Black Female Domestic Servants

BONNIE THORNTON DILL

This essay explores the family and child-rearing strategies presented by a small group of Afro-American women who held jobs as household workers while raising their children. The data are drawn from a study of the relationship of work and family among American-born women of African descent who were private household workers (domestic servants) for most of their working lives.

The primary method of data collection was life histories, collected through open-ended, in-depth interviews with 26 women living in the northeastern United States. All participants were between 60 and 80 years old. A word of caution in reading this essay: The conclusions are not meant to apply to all Black female domestic servants, but represent only my interpretation of the experiences of these 26 women.

The life history method is particularly useful in studying Black female domestic workers whose stories and experiences have largely been distorted or ignored in the social science literature.* According to Denzin (1970:220), the method "presents the experiences and definitions held by one person, group or organization as that person, group or organization interprets those experiences." As such, it provides a means of exploring the processes whereby people construct, endure, and create meaning in both the interactional and structural aspects of their lives. It aids in the identification and definition of concepts appropriate to a sociological understanding of the subject's experience, and moves toward building theory that is grounded in imagery and meanings relevant to the subject. Collected through in-depth interviews, life histories are active processes of rendering meaning to one's life—its conflicts, ambiguities, crises, successes, and significant interpersonal relationships. Subjects are not merely asked to "report" but rather to reconstruct and interpret their choices, situations and experiences.* The study of Black Americans cries out for such a sensitized approach to their lives.

The child-rearing goals and strategies adopted by the women who participated in this study are particularly revealing of the relationship of work and family. As working mothers, they were concerned with providing safe and secure care for their children while they were away from home. As working-class people, seeking to advance their children beyond their own occupational achievements, they confronted the problem of guiding them toward goals that were outside of their own personal experience. These issues, as well as others, take on a particular form for women who were

---

Reprinted from La Frances Rodgers-Rose, ed., *The Black Woman.* Copyright © 1980 by Sage Publications, Inc. Reprinted by permission of Sage Publications, Inc.

*There is a very limited body of literature directly focused upon Black women in domestic service in the United States. Many of these studies are confined to the Southern experience. Among the most important containing data on Black women in northern cities are Haynes (1923), Eaton (1967), and Chaplin (1964). Some discussion of the subject was also found in community studies, particularly those conducted before World War II (Drake & Cayton, 1945; Ovington, 1969). Labor studies provided a third source of data (among these were Green & Woodson, 1930, and Haynes, 1912).

* This discussion is largely drawn from a paper by Dill and Joselin (1977).

household workers primarily because of the nature of their work.

Unlike many other occupations, domestic work brings together, in a closed and intimate sphere of human interaction, people whose paths would never cross were they to conduct their lives within the socio-economic boundaries to which they were ascribed. These intimate interactions across the barriers of income, ethnicity, religion, and race occur within a sphere of life that is private and has little public exposure—the family.

As household workers, these women often become vital participants in the daily lives of two separate families: their employer's and their own. In fact, they have often been described as being "like one of the family" (Childress, 1956), and yet the barriers between them and their employers are real and immutable ones. In addition, working-class Black women employed by middle- and upper-class white families observe and experience vast differences in the material quality of life in the two homes. With regard to child-rearing, employers could provide luxuries and experiences for their children that were well beyond the financial means of the employee.

This essay, therefore, presents some of the ways in which the women talked about their reactions and responses to the discrepancies in life chances between those of their children and those of their employers. To some extent, these discrepancies became the lens through which we viewed their goals for their children and their child-rearing practices. At the same time, the contrast in objective conditions provides a background against which the women's perceptions of similarities between themselves and their employers are made more interesting.

The data from this study indicate that the relationship between the employee's family life and her work was shaped by four basic factors. First, there was the structure of the work. Whether she worked full-time or part-time and lived in, lived out, or did day work determined the extent to which she became involved in the employer's day-to-day life. It also determined the amount of time she had to share with her own family. Second were the tasks and duties she was assigned. With regard to her own child-rearing goals and strategies, the intermingling of employer and employee lifestyles occurred most frequently among those women who took care of the employer's children. It is through their discussion of these activities that the sim-

ilarities and differences between the two families are most sharply revealed. A third factor is the degree of employer–employee intimacy. An employee who cared for the employer's children was more likely to have an intimate relationship with her employing family, but not always. Though the employer–employee relationship in domestic service is characterized as a personalized one when compared with other work relationships, this does not presume intimacy between the two parties; that is, a reciprocal exchange of interests and concerns. Among the women who participated in this study, those who did not share much of their own life with their employers appeared to minimize the interaction of work and family. Finally were the employee's goals for her children. Those women who felt that their employers could aid them in achieving the educational or other goals they had set for their children were more likely to encourage an intermingling of these two parts of their lives.

On domestic work and upward mobility:

> Strangely enough, I never intended for my children to have to work for anybody in the capacity that I worked. Never. And I never allowed my children to do any babysitting or anything of the sort. I figured it's enough for the mother to do it and in this day and time you don't have to do that. . . . So they never knew anything about going out to work or anything. They went to school.

Given the low social status of the occupation, the ambivalent and defensive feelings many of the women expressed about their work and the eagerness with which women left the occupation when other opportunities were opened to them, it is not at all surprising that most of the women in this study said they did not want their children to work in domestic service. Their hopes were centered upon "better" jobs for their children: jobs with more status, income, security, and comfort. Pearl Runner* recalled her goals for her children:

> My main goal was I didn't want them to follow in my footsteps as far as working. I always wanted them to please go to school and get a good job because it's important. That was really my main object.

* The names used for the participants in the study are fictitious.

Lena Hudson explained her own similar feelings this way:

> They had a better chance than I had, and they shouldn't look back at what I was doing. They had a better chance and a better education than I had, so look out for something better than I was doing. And they did. I haven't had a one that had to do any housework or anything like that. So I think that's good.

The notion of a better chance is a dominant one in the women's discussions of their goals for their children. They portray themselves as struggling to give their children the skills and training they did not have; and as praying that opportunities which had not been open to them would be open to their children. In their life histories, the women describe many of the obstacles they encountered in this quest. Nevertheless, there are dilemmas which, though not discussed explicitly, are implicit in their narratives and a natural outgrowth of their aspirations.

First of these is the task of guiding children toward a future over which they had little control and toward occupational objectives with which they had no direct experience. Closely tied to this problem was their need to communicate the undesirability of household work and at the same time maintain their personal dignity despite the occupation. While these two problems are not exceptional for working-class parents in an upwardly mobile society, they were mediated for Black domestic workers through the attitudes toward household work held by members of the Black communities in which the women lived and raised their children.

Had domestic work not been the primary occupation of Black women and had racial and sexual barriers not been so clearly identifiable as the reason for their concentration in this field of employment, these problems might have been viewed more personally and the women's histories might have been more self-deprecating than in fact they were. This particular set of circumstances would suggest that the women at least had the option of directing their anger and frustration about their situation outward upon the society rather than turning it inward upon themselves. Drake and Cayton (1945) confirm this argument in their analysis of domestic work, saying that "colored girls are often bitter in their comments about a society which condemns them to the 'white folks' kitchen" (p. 246). In addition, attitudes in the Black community toward domestic ser-

vice work mediated some of the more negative attitudes which were prevalent in the wider society. Thus, the community could potentially become an important support in the child-rearing process, reinforcing the idea that while domestic service was low-status work, the people who did it were not necessarily low-status people.

The data in this study do not include the attitudes of the children of domestic servants toward their mothers' occupation. To my knowledge, there has been no systematic study of this issue. However, some biographies and community studies have provided insight into the range of feelings children express. Drake and Cayton (1945), for example, cite one woman who described her daughter as being "bitter against what she calls the American social system." DuBois talks about feeling an instinctive hatred toward the occupation (1920:110). I have had employers tell me that their domestics' children hated their children because the employer's kids got the best of their mother's time. I have also heard Black professionals speak with a mixture of pride, anger, and embarrassment about the fact that their mother worked "in the white folks' kitchen" so that they could get an education. Clearly, these issues deserve further study.

Throughout these histories, the women identified education as the primary means through which mobility could be achieved. As with many working-class people, education was seen as a primary strategy for upward mobility; a means to a better-paying and more prestigious job. Most of the women who participated in this study had not completed high school (the mean years of schooling completed for the group was 9.2 years). They reasoned that their limited education in combination with racial discrimination had hindered their own chances for upward mobility. Zenobia King explained her attitudes toward education in this way:

> In my home in Virginia, education, I don't think, was stressed. The best you could do was a school teacher. It wasn't something people impressed upon you you could get. I had an aunt and cousin who were trained nurses and the best they could do was nursing somebody at home or something. They couldn't get a job in a hospital. . . . I didn't pay education any mind really until I came to New York. I'd gotten to a certain stage in domestic work in the country and I didn't see the need for it. When I came, I could see opportunities that I could have

had if I had a degree. People said it's too bad I didn't have a diploma.

From Mrs. King's perspective and from those of some of the other women, education for a Black woman in the South before World War II did not seem to offer any tangible rewards. She communicates the idea that an education was not only unnecessary but could perhaps have been a source of even greater frustration and dissatisfaction. This idea was reemphasized by other women who talked about college-educated women they knew who could find no work other than domestic work. In fact, both Queenie Watkins and Corrinne Raines discussed their experiences as trained teachers who could not find suitable jobs and thus took work in domestic service. Nevertheless, Corrinne Raines maintained her belief in education as a means of upward mobility, a belief that was rooted in her family of orientation. She said:

I am the 12th child [and was] born on a farm. My father was—at that day, you would call him a successful farmer. He was a man who was eager for his children to get an education. Some of the older ones had gotten out of school and were working and they were able to help the younger ones. That's how he was able to give his children as much education as he gave them, because the older ones helped him out.

Given this mixed experience with education and social mobility, it might be expected that many of the women would have expressed reservations about the value of an education for their children's mobility. However, this was not the case. Most of them, reflecting on their goals for their children, expressed sentiments similar to Pearl Runner's:

This is the reason why I told them to get an education. . . . If they want to go to college it was fine because the higher you go the better jobs you get. They understood that because I always taught that into them. Please try to get an education so you can get a good job 'cause it was hard for colored girls to get jobs, period. They had to have an education.

Mrs. Runner's statement is important because it contains the rudiments of an explanation for why she and other women stressed education in the face of discriminatory practices that frequently discounted even their best efforts. Opallou Tucker elaborates on this theme and provides a somewhat more detailed explanation:

It's [domestic work] all right if you want to do it and if you can't do anything else, but it's not necessary now. If you prepare yourself for something that's better, the doors are open now. I know years ago there was no such thing as a Black typist. I remember girls who were taking typing when I was going to school. They were never able to get a job at it. So it really [was] for their own personal use. My third child, and a niece, after they got up some size, started taking typing. And things began to open up after she got grown up. But in my day and time you could have been the greatest typist in the world, but you would never have gotten a job. It's fine to prepare yourself so that when opportunity knocks, you'll be able to catch up.

In these statements, Mrs. Runner and Mrs. Tucker convey a complex and subtle understanding of the interaction of racism and opportunity. They recognize the former as a real and tangible barrier, but they do not give in to it. They describe themselves as having taught their children to be prepared. Education was seen as a means of equipping oneself for whatever breaks might occur in the nation's patterns of racial exclusion. Thus, key to their aspirations for their children was the hope and belief that opportunities would eventually open and permit their children to make full use of the skills and knowledge they encouraged them to attain.

Nevertheless, maintaining these hopes could not have been as easy and unproblematic as hindsight makes it seem. The fact that many of the women who expressed this strong commitment to education at the time of the interview had seen their children complete a number of years of schooling and enter jobs which would never have been open to them when they were young was clearly a source of pride and satisfaction which could only have strengthened their beliefs. Thus, as they recalled their goals and aspirations for their children, they tended to speak with a sense of self-affirmation about their choices; confidence that may not have been present years earlier. As Mrs. Runner expressed,

I tell you I feel really proud and I really feel that with all the struggling that I went through, I feel happy and proud that I was able to keep helping my children, that they listened and that they all went to high school. So when I look back, I really feel proud, even though at times the work was very hard and I came home very tired. But now, I feel proud about it. They all got their education.

Perhaps reflective of their understanding of the complex interaction of racism and opportunity, most of the women described limited and general educational objectives for their children. Although a few women said they had wanted their children to go to college and one sent her son to a private high school with the help of scholarships, most women saw high school graduation as the concrete, realizable objective which they could help their children attain. Willie Lee Murray's story brings out a theme that was recurrent in several other histories:

> My children did not go to college. I could not afford to send them to college. And they told me, my younger one especially, he said: Mommy, I don't want to go to college at your expense. When I go to college, I'll go on my own. I would not think of you workin' all your days—sometimes you go sick and I don't know how you gonna get back. You put us through school and you gave us a beautiful life. We'll get to college on our own.

Mrs. Murray seems to indicate that while she would have liked her children to go to college, she limited her goals and concentrated her energies upon their completing high school.

In addition to limited educational objectives, most of the women did not describe themselves as having had a specific career objective in mind for their children. They encouraged the children to get an education in order to get a better job. Precisely what those jobs would be was left open, to be resolved through the interaction of their son or daughter's own luck, skill, perseverance, and the overall position of the job market vis-à-vis Black entrants.

Closely related to the goals the women expressed about their children's future position in society were their goals relative to their child's development as a person. Concern that their children grow up to be good, decent, law-abiding citizens was a dominant theme in these discussions. Most of the women in the study described their employers as having very specific career goals for their children, usually goals that would have the children following their parents' professional

footsteps. In characterizing the differences between their goals and those of their employers, the women stressed the differences in economic resources. Johnnie Boatwright was quite explicit on this point:

> There was a lot of things they [employers] did that I wanted to do for mine, but I just couldn't afford it. . . . Like sending them to school. Then they could hire somebody; child slow, they could hire a tutor for the child. I wish I could have been able to do what they done. And then too, they sent them to camps, nice camps, not any camp but one they'd pick out. . . . So that's what I wished I could had did for him [her son]. . . . See whether it was right or wrong, mines I couldn't do it because I didn't have the money to do it. I wasn't able to do it. So that's the way it was. I did what I could and that was better than nothing.

In light of these discrepancies in resources, personal development was an important and realizable goal which may have been an adaptive response to the barriers which constricted the women's range of choices. This was an area over which the women had greater influence and potential control. It was also an area in which they probably received considerable community support, since values in the Black community, as pointed out above, attribute status to success along personal and family dimensions in addition to the basic ones of occupation, education, and income.

While Mrs. Boatwright conveys a sense of resignation and defeat in discussing her inability to do for her son what the employers did for theirs, Pearl Runner is more optimistic and positive about what she was able to do for her children.

> Their money may be a little more, but I felt my goal was just as important as long as they [the children] got their education. They [employers] had the money to do lots more than I did, but I felt that if I kept working, my goals was just as important. I felt my children were just as important.

Feelings like those expressed by both Mrs. Runner and Mrs. Boatwright are reflected throughout the data in the women's comparisons of their aspirations and expectations for their children's future with those of their employers. However, it also seems apparent that their intimate participation in families in which the husbands were doctors, lawyers, stockbrokers, college professors, writers, and housewives provided considerable support for their more limited educational objectives. While not everyone had the specific experience of Lena Hudson, whose employer provided an allowance for her daughter which permitted the girl to stay in high school, the model of the employer's life with regard to the kinds of things they were able to give their children was a forceful one and is repeatedly reflected in the women's discussions of their child-rearing goals.

When asked: "What do you think were the goals that the Wallises [her employers] had for their children? What did they want for their children? What did they want them to become in life?" Lena Hudson replied:

> Well, for *their* children, I imagine they wanted them to become like they were, educators or something that like. What they had in mind for *my* children, they saw in me that I wasn't able to make all of that mark. But raised my children in the best method I could. Because I wouldn't have the means to put *my* children through like they could for *their* children. And they see I wasn't the worst person in the world, and they saw I meant *some* good to my family, you see, so I think that was the standard with them and my family.

Her answers provide insight into the personal and social relationship between the two families and into her recognition of the points of connectedness and distance between them. The way in which she chose to answer the question reflects her feelings about working for the Wallis family and how that helped her accomplish the goals which she had set for her own family.

MRS. HUDSON: And in the meantime, they owned a big place up in Connecticut. And they would take my children, and she, the madam, would do for my children just what she did for theirs.

INTERVIEWER: What kinds of things do you think your children learned from that, from the time that they spent with them?

MRS. HUDSON: Well, I think what they learnt from them, to try to live a decent life themselves, and try to make the best out of their life and the best out of the education they had. So I think that's what they got from them.

INTERVIEWER: What would you say you liked most about the work that you did?

MRS. HUDSON: Well, what I liked most about it, the things that I weren't able to go to school to do for my children. I could kinda pattern from the families that I worked for, that I could give my children the best of my abilities. And I think that's the thing I got from them, though they [her children] couldn't become professors, but they could be good in whatever they did.

The warm personal relationship between the two families was based not only on the direct assistance which the Wallises gave Mrs. Hudson, but also on the ways in which she was able to utilize her position in their family to support and sustain her personal goals. Thus, we can understand why she saw work as an ability rather than a burden. Work was a means for attaining her goals; it provided her with the money she needed to be an independent person, and it exposed her and her children to "good" things—values and a style of life which she considered important. To some extent, Lena Hudson found the same things in her work that she found in her church; reinforcement for the standards which she held for her children and for herself.

The women who stressed education for their children and saw their children attain it were most frequently women like Mrs. Hudson who were closely tied to one or two employing families for a long period of time. For the most part, they were the women who had careers in domestic service. However, ties with employers were not crucial even within this small group, because some women said they had received very little support from their employers along these lines. Several women, as indicated above, pointed to a strong emphasis upon education in their families of orientation. Additionally, education as a means of upward mobility is a fundamental element in American social ideology. It appears, therefore, that the importance of the employer–employee relationship was in the support and reinforcement these middle-class families' goals, aspirations, and style of life provided the women. The amount of support varied, of course, with the particular relationship the employee had with her employer's family and the degree of the employer's interest in and commitment to the employee's personal life. On the spectrum presented by the women in this study, Mrs. Hudson's relationship with the Wallis family would be at one end; the relationship between Georgia Sims and the family for whom she worked longest at the other. The following segment of the interview with Mrs. Sims is a good example of a minimally interactive employer–employee relationship:

INTERVIEWER: What were your goals for your children?

MRS. SIMS: Well, to be decent, law-abiding men. That's all.

INTERVIEWER: Do you think there were any similarities between your goals for your children and the goals your employers, the Peters, had for their children?

MRS. SIMS: On, sure! Oh, yes, because I mean you must remember, they had the money; now I didn't have it. Oh, definitely there was different goals between us. [*Note:* Mrs. Sims obviously understood the question to be about *differences* rather than similarities, so the question was asked again.]

INTERVIEWER: Do you think there were any things that were alike in terms of your goals for your children and their goals for their children?

MRS. SIMS: No. Nothing.

INTERVIEWER: Nothing at all?

MRS. SIMS: No.

INTERVIEWER: What kinds of goals did they have for their children?

MRS. SIMS: Oh, I mean education, going on to be, you know, upstanding citizens, and they had the jobs—My children couldn't get up, I mean when they become 20, 21, they couldn't get up and go out and say, well, I'm gonna get an office job, I'm gonna get this kind of job. No. The best thing they could do is go and be a porter in the subway.

Mrs. Sims was very detached from her occupation. She was not a career household worker. In fact, she described herself as having had very limited contact with her employers, arriving when they were all on their way to work and school and often departing before they returned home. She said that she had no specific child-care duties. Thus, her description of the employers' goals for their children is probably more of a projection on her part than it is based on discussion or direct participation in the employers' life.

Two types of child-rearing goals have been identified thus far: goals regarding the child's future position in the society and goals regarding his or her personal development. In addition to these two types of goals, the women aspired to provide their children with some accoutrements of a middle-class lifestyle. Their discussion of these desires often reflects the discrepancies between their lives and those of their employers. Jewell Prieleau describes her employer's children as follows:

> Her children always dress nice. Whenever her daughter was going to music school or anyplace, I had to take her in a taxi. Whenever she finish, she had to be picked up. I had to go get her.

In describing her own grandchildren, she said:

> I went to three nice department stores and I opened up credit for them so I could send them to school looking nice. I got up early in the morning and sent them off to school. After school I would pick them up in a taxi and bring them here [the job].

Mrs. Prieleau is not the only woman in this study who talked about going into debt to give her children some of the material things that she never had and that were part of her image of a "better life" for her children. Willa Murray told the following story:

> I remember when my sons wanted that record player. I said I'm gonna get a record player; I'm gonna do days work. But I had to get AC current for this record player. I called up this lady [her employer] and I said, I'm goin' to Household Finance this morning. If they call you for a reference would you give me some reference. She said, sure. I sat down and the man said come in. He said, Miz Murray, do you have a co-signer. I said, no. He said, well what's your collateral? I said something about the furniture. He said, do you work? I said, yeah, I do days work. He said, days work? You don't have a steady job? I said yes sir, days work. He said, who do you work for? I told him. He said, we'll see what we can do. He gave the hundred and fifty dollars. I came home, phone the electric company, told them they could send the man to put the current in.

In these statements and some of the ones quoted earlier, we begin to see how the employer's style of life influenced these women. However, it cannot be assumed that the women's desires were merely an outgrowth of the employer–employee relationship. The material products which they sought are so widely available in the culture that they are considered general symbols of upward mobility. Upward mobility for their children was the basic goal of most of the women who participated in this study. It was a goal which seems to have existed prior to and apart from their work situation and the values of their employers. Nevertheless, in some cases the women found reinforcement for and regeneration of these goals within the work situation, just as they found supports within their community and family lives.

RAISING THE "WHITE FOLKS" CHILDREN

The women's discussion of child-rearing strategies, particularly such issues as discipline, exemplify both the class and cultural differences between employer and employee. For private household workers, these differences are expressed within a relationship of inequality. The data collected in this study permitted an examination of employer parent–child interactions as it was perceived and constructed by the household workers. This has benefits as well as liabilities. As outsiders whose child-rearing practices and lifestyle differed from those of the employers, the women in this study provide a particularly revealing picture of parent–child relationships in the employing family. However, they were not mere observers of the process; they participated in it and thereby restructured it. The women's insights, therefore, offer a unique critical perspective that is found only in subordinates' characterizations of their superiors. However, as participants in the process, their observations are limited to the time frame in which they were present and make it virtually impossible to assess the women's impact on the process. Nevertheless, their stories about their own role in rearing the employer's children provide considerable understanding of how they saw their work and, more importantly, how their work affected their own style of parenting. Willa Murray's comments illuminate this:

Throughout, the people that I worked for taught their children that they can talk back. They would let them [the children] say anything they wanted to say to them. I noticed a lot of times they [the children] would talk back or something and they [the parents] would be hurt. They would say to me, I wish they [the children] wouldn't. I wish they

were more like your children. They allowed them to do so much. But they taught them a lot of things. I know one thing, I think I got a lot of things from them. . . . I think I've learnt a lot about [how to do] with my children by letting them do and telling them—like the whites would tell them—that I trust you. I think a lot of Black mothers when we come along, they didn't trust us. They were telling us what we were gonna do. . . . But I think they [whites] talk to their children about what's in life, what's for them, what not to do. And they let them talk, they tell them all the things that we didn't tell our children. We're beginning to tell our children. . . . The alternative is that I told my children straight, that if a boy and a girl have sexual intercourse—I learned that from the white people—and you don't have anything to protect it, that girl will get a baby. So my children were looking out for that. I learned that from my people. I listened to what they tell [their children].

Talk between parents and children is a dominant theme of Mrs. Murray's comments. She is critical of her employers for permitting their children to "talk back" to them; to question their instructions, to respond impertinently or otherwise mock or demean the parents' authority. Yet, talking *with* the children, reasoning with them, explaining things and hearing their thoughts and opinions on various matters, is behavior which she admired enough to try to emulate. Telling the children that you "trust them" places greater emphasis upon self-direction than upon following orders. Clearly, the line between letting the children talk and permitting them to "talk back" is a difficult one to draw, yet Mrs. Murray draws it in transferring her work-learned behavior to her own child-rearing circumstances.

It should not be surprising that there would be behavioral characteristics which employers would admire in employee children, just as there were traits which Mrs. Murray and others admired in their employers' interactions with their children. In fact, it is striking that each would admire aspects of the other and seek to incorporate them within their own lives while the circumstances that generated those particular patterns were quite different. Nevertheless, reorienting the parent–child relationship in the employer's family was frequently described as a regular part of the worker's child-care activity. In fact, the women's discussions

of their experiences in caring for their employers'
children are variations upon the stories of resistance
which characterized their establishing themselves in
the employer–employee relationship. Queenie Watkins' description of the following child-care incident
provides a good example:

> One morning I was feeding Stevie oatmeal and I
> was eating oatmeal. His uncle, the little girl and I
> were all sitting at the table together eating. He said,
> I don't want this and I'm gonna spit it out. I said,
> you better not, Stevie. With that he just let it all
> come into my face. I took myself a big mouthful and
> let it go right back in his face. He screamed, and his
> uncle said, what did you do that for? I said, you
> fight fire with fire. My psychology is to let a child
> know he can't do to you what you can't do to him.
> The mother came running. I said, this ends my work
> here but she said, just wash Stevie's face. I said, I'm
> not gonna wash it; let him wash it himself—he
> wasn't two years old. Finally, I said, I'll take him
> and wash his face but who's gonna wash my face?
> His mother started to laugh and said, you're some
> character. And you know what, he never did that
> again. He ate his food and I never had to chastise
> Stevie about anything after that.

Zenobia King told a slightly different story about
the way in which she inserted her values into the
parent–child relationship of an employing family:

> One time the daughter went out and she stayed all
> day. She didn't tell her mother where she was. And
> when she came back, her mother jumped on her in a
> really bad way. She told her she wished she had
> died out there, etc., etc., and her daughter said if her
> mother had loved her she would have asked where
> she was going. So, I separated them. I sent the
> daughter to one room and the mother to the other
> and talked to both of them and I brought them back
> together.

In both of these stories, as in others in this genre, the
women see themselves as the instructor of both the
children and the parents. They characterize themselves
as helping the parent learn how to parent while simultaneously setting rules and regulations as to the kind
of treatment they should expect from the children.
Queenie Watkins' philosophy of fighting fire with fire

was reiterated by Oneida Harris in describing her relations with one of the children whom she cared for:

> He was nine years old and he rate me the worst
> maid they'd ever had because I wouldn't take any of
> his foolishness. If he kicked me in the shins, I'd kick
> him back. . . . I said he hasn't any bringing up, and
> if I stay here he's gonna listen. I said to his mother,
> if you don't want me, tell me tomorrow and I'll go.
> So anyway, the next day he would bring me up a lit-
> tle bit; she's the next-to-the-worst maid we ever
> had. Each week I came up till I was the best one.

As in the stories of resistance, both Queenie Watkins
and Oneida Harris depict themselves as setting guidelines for respect from the children in the same way
respect was established in the employer–employee
relationship. The additional dimension of instructing
parents in the ways of handling their children was
another recurrent theme in the life histories.

Through these and other similar anecdotes which
the women used to describe their participation in caring for their employers' children, they communicate
a perception of their employers as uncomfortable in
exercising the power associated with the parenting
role. To a large degree, they depict their employers as
either inconsistent and afraid of their children or ignorant of child-rearing strategies that would develop obedience and respect. The women see this as their forte;
in many instances they describe themselves as exercising power on behalf of the parents and teaching the
children to obey them and respect their parents. In so
doing, they also present themselves as teaching the
parents. Willa Murray is keenly aware of the paradoxical nature of this situation when she says: "Now I'm
the maid, not the mistress." In the maid–mistress relationship, the latter gives instructions which the former
carries out. In a sense, Willa Murray's story presents a
role reversal, one which she finds both surprising and
amusing but also appropriate. It is akin to the anecdote
in which she described herself telling her employers
that they had more education than she did but their
behavior was not intelligent. These presentations
suggest that despite stereotypic conceptions of the
maid–mistress relationship, women in these roles could
gain considerable power and influence within a family,
particularly where they had worked for a number of
years and had considerable responsibility.

The household worker's impact on the parent–child

relationship is only one aspect of their child-care role. The other, equally important, aspect of this role is their relationship with the children they cared for and the fact, implicit in our earlier discussion, that they describe themselves as surrogate mothers for these children:

There's a long time she [the child] use to thought I was her mamma. She would ask me why is my skin white and yours brown, you my mamma? I tell her I'm not your mamma and I see the hurt coming in her eye. You know like she didn't want me to say that. I said there's your mamma in there, I'm just your nurse. She said no, you my mamma. [Mattie Washington]

I took care of the children. In fact, the children would call me when they had a problem or something, before they would call her [their mother]. [Zenobia King]

He [the boy] looked at me as a mother. When he went away to school he just would not come home if I wasn't there. And even when he was at home, if he was out playing with the boys he'd come in, his mother, grandmother and father would be sitting around, he'd say, where is everybody? His mother would look around and say well if you mean Oneida, I think she's upstairs. Upstairs he'd come. And they couldn't get that. It was sad, you see. They give him everything in the world but love. [Oneida Harris]

I was more like a mother to them, and you see she didn't have to take too much time as a mother should to know her children. They were more used to me because I put them to bed. The only time she would actually be with them was like when I'm off Thursday and on Sundays. They would go out sometime, but actually I was really the mother because I raised them from little. [Pearl Runner]

Without exception, the women in this study who had child-care responsibilities talked about themselves as being "like a mother" to the employers' children. Their explanations of the development of this kind of relationship tended to follow those of Oneida Harris and Pearl Runner: their employers were frequently unavailable and spent less time with the children than

they did. Because they interacted with the children on a daily basis and often had responsibility for their care, discipline, play, and meals, their role was a vital and important one in the eyes of both child and parent. This explains, in part, some of their power in affecting the parent–child relationship, as discussed above. The fact that the women had such an important and pivotal role in the development of the employer's children and at the same time held a job in which they could be replaced gave the entire relationship of parent, child, and housekeeper a particularly intense quality. For the most part, workers developed their strongest emotional ties to the children in the employing family.

Because the women saw themselves as surrogate mothers, the children whom they cared for could easily become their surrogate children. This is particularly apparent when we compare their comments and discussions about their own and their employers' children. One of the most prevalent patterns was to talk with pride and satisfaction about the accomplishments of their surrogate children. In general, the women would talk about how frequently they heard from these children and whether they got cards, letters, or money at Mothers' Day or Christmas. In addition, they would describe the (now grown) children's occupation and family and, if they had pictures available, they would show them to me. This type of commentary provided an interesting parallel to their discussions of their own children. But even more important, it was designed to communicate the closeness that they felt existed between them and the children they had raised; closeness which was maintained over a number of years even after the children were grown.

Surrogate mothering, as pointed out in Opallou Tucker's case study, had the prospect of tying the worker into the emotional life of the employing family. For the women who lived outside the employer's household and were actively engaged in rearing their own children and caring for their own families, as were most of the women in this study, the prospect was minimized. However, for a woman like Mattie Washington, who lived in for most of the 30 years that she worked for one family, the potential for becoming enveloped in their life, at the expense of her own, was much greater.

In most instances, the women described themselves as caretakers, playmates, disciplinarians, confidantes, and friends of the employer's children. Nevertheless, it is clear from their discussions that in most cases the real ties of affection between themselves and their employer came through the children.

The children, therefore, provided the ties that bound the women to their employers as well as the mark of their difference. The role of surrogate mother allowed the women to cross these barriers and, for a fleeting moment, express their love and concern for a child without regard to the obstacles that lay ahead. Also, because most young children readily return love that is freely given and are open and accepting of people without regard to status factors that have meaning for their parents, the workers probably felt that they were treated with greater equality and more genuine acceptance by the children of the household.

REFERENCES

Chaplin, D. 1964. "Domestic service and the Negro." In A. Shostak and W. Gamberg, eds., *Blue Collar World.* Englewood Cliffs, N.J.: Prentice-Hall.

Childress, A. 1956. *Like one of the family.* Brooklyn: Independence Publishers.

Denzin, N. K. 1970. *The research act.* Chicago: AVC.

Dill, B.T., & Joselin, D. 1977. "The limit of quantitative methods: The need of life histories." Paper presented at the Society for the Study of Social Problems Annual Meetings, Chicago.

Drake, S. C., & Cayton, H. 1945. *Black metropolis.* New York: Harper & Row.

DuBois, W. E. B. 1920. *Darkwater.* New York: Harcourt Brace.

Eaton, I. 1967. "Negro domestic service in Seventh Ward Philadelphia." In W. E. B. DuBois, *The Philadelphia Negro.* New York: Schocken.

Greene, L. J., & Woodson, C. G. 1930. *The Negro wage earner.* Washington, D.C.: Association for the Study of Negro Life and History.

Haynes, G. 1912. *The Negro at work in New York City: A study in economic progress.* New York: Longmans.

Haynes, G. 1923. "Negroes in domestic service in the United States." *Journal of Negro History* 8:384–442.

Ovington, M. W. 1969. *Half a man.* New York: Schocken.

R E A D I N G   1 3

The Secret Fear That Keeps Us from Raising Free Children

LETTY COTTIN POGREBIN

In the 19th century when women of all races began their drive for the vote, what was the argument most often used against them?

From *Growing Up Free: Raising Your Child in the '80s* by Letty Cottin Pogrebin. Reprinted by permission of The Wendy Weil Agency, Inc. Copyright © 1980 by Letty Cottin Pogrebin.

That voting was a masculine concern, and that therefore women who attempted it would become (or already were) "mannish," "unwomanly," and "unnatural." In short, sexually suspect.

In the 20th century when young men objected to the rationale for the American military presence in Vietnam, what was the argument most used to discredit their protest?

That refusing a masculine enterprise like war made them "like a woman," "soft," "scared," and therefore sexually suspect.

It's time we faced head-on the most powerful argument that authoritarian forces in any society use to keep people—male or female—in line: the idea that you are not born with gender but must earn it, and thus the threat that if you don't follow orders you will not be a "real man" or "real woman."

Even those of us who have long since stopped worrying about this conformity for ourselves may find that our own deepest conditioning takes over in the emotional landscape inhabited by our children and our feelings about child-rearing. It is this conditioning that the right wing plays on to prevent change, no matter how life-enhancing. And it is these fears that sometimes inhibit pro-child attitudes in the most well-intentioned parents; the fear

1. that sex roles determine sexuality;
2. that specific ingredients *make* a child homosexual; and
3. that homosexuality is one of the worst things that can happen.

ASSUMPTION I: SEX ROLES DETERMINE SEXUALITY

It was inevitable that the cult of sex differences would lead us to the familiar romantic bromide—*opposites attract.* Most people truly believe that the more "masculine" you are, the more you'll love and be loved by females, and the more "feminine" you are, the more you'll love and be loved by males.

If you believe this quid pro quo, you will systematically raise your daughters and sons differently so that they become magnets for their "opposites," and you will fear that resistance to stereotyped sex roles might distort their behavior in bed as adults.

Clever, this patriarchy. In return for conformity, it promises a "normal" sex life for our children. But it can't deliver on that promise, because all available evidence proves that *sex role does not determine sexual orientation.*

During the last decade thousands of homosexual men and women have "come out" from behind their "straight" disguises, and we discovered that except for choice of sex partner, they look and act so much the same as everyone else that as sexologist Dr. Wainright

Churchill put it, "they may not be identified as homosexuals even by experts." Most female and male homosexuals have tried heterosexual intercourse; many have been married and have children; and sometimes they are remarkable only for being so *unlike* the "gay" stereotype.

Take a quintessential "man's man," David Kopay—six feet one, 205 pounds, 10-year veteran of pro football. "I was the typical jock," writes Kopay in his autobiography (*The David Kopay Story;* Bantam). "I was tough. I was successful. And all the time I knew I preferred sex with men."

And great beauties, such as Maria Schneider, the sex bomb of *Last Tango in Paris;* "feminine-looking" women, married women, mothers of many children have, for centuries, had lesbian love affairs with one another, disproving the opposites-attract theory with a vengeance, and reminding us again that sex roles do not determine sexuality.

ASSUMPTION 2: SPECIFIC INGREDIENTS *MAKE* A CHILD HOMOSEXUAL

Although no one knows what causes homosexuality, there is no shortage of theories on the subject. Sociobiologists and other behavioral scientists pursue the idea that "genetic loading" can create a predisposition toward homosexuality, a theory that will remain farfetched until researchers find many sets of identical twins both members of which became homosexual although reared separately.

Proponents of *hormone theory* have tried to find a definitive connection between testosterone level and homosexual orientation. However, various biochemical studies of the last decade show directly contradictory results, and even when hormonal differences are found, no one knows whether hormones cause the homosexuality, or the homosexual activities cause the hormone production.

The biochemical "explorers," like the geneticists, perpetuate the idea that homosexuals are a different species with a hormonal disturbance that chemistry might "cure." So far, attempts to alter sexual orientation with doses of hormones have only succeeded in increasing the *amount* of sex drive, not in changing its direction.

The *conditioned-response theory* holds that sexual orientation depends not on biology or "instincts" but on learning from experience, from the same reward-

and-punishment process as any other acquired behavior, and from sexual trigger mechanisms, such
as pictures, music, or certain memories, that set off
homosexual or heterosexual responses the way the bell
set off Pavlov's dog salivating.

The conditioning theory, logical as far as it goes,
leads us down several blind alleys. Why might one
child experience a certain kind of stroking as pleasurable when a same-sex friend does it but *more* pleasurable when a friend of the other sex does it, while
another child feels the reverse? Why do some children
"learn to" overcome the effects of a frightening early
sexual experience, while others may be hurt by it forever, and still others "learn" to merge pain with
pleasure?

Doesn't cultural pressure itself "teach" children to
avoid a particular sexual response, no matter what the
body has learned to like? Otherwise, how do millions
of adolescents move from masturbation to homosexual
experimentation—often the *only* interpersonal sexual
pleasure they have known—to heterosexuality?

Perhaps the conditioned-response theory can explain the man who has felt homosexual since childhood, but how does it account for the woman who,
after 20 years as an orgasmic, exclusive heterosexual,
had a lesbian encounter and found she didn't have to
"learn" to like it?

One research psychiatrist reminds us that we don't
yet understand the basic mechanism of sexual arousal
in the human central nervous system, and until we do,
questions about homosexual or heterosexual arousal
are entirely premature.

Psychoanalytic theory, the most steadfast and intimidating of all the causation theories, is the one that
"blames" homosexuality on the family. To challenge it,
we must begin at the beginning.

In 1905, Sigmund Freud declared that human
beings are innately *bisexual* at birth and their early
psychosexual experiences tip the scales one way or
the other.

To ensure a heterosexual outcome, the child is supposed to identify with the same-sex parent, to "kill
them off," so to speak, as an object of sexual interest.
For example, a girl's psychodynamic is "I become like
Mother, therefore I no longer desire Mother; I desire
Father, but I can't have him so I desire those who are
like him."

If instead the girl identifies with the other-sex parent ("I become like Father"), he is killed off as object

choice ("therefore I do not desire Father"), and the
girl will be a lesbian ("I desire Mother or those who
are like her"). For the boy, obviously, the same psychodynamic is true in reverse.

According to this theory, female homosexuality
derived mainly from too much *hostility* toward the
mother for passing on her inferior genital equipment.
The lesbian girl identifies with the Father and compen-
sates for her hatred of the inferior mother by loving
women, while rejecting "femininity" (meaning passivity, masochism, inferiority) for herself.

Male homosexuality derives mainly from too much
attachment to the mother, i.e., a Momma's Boy can't
be a woman's man.

Although many contemporary psychologists now
believe otherwise, and despite the fact that Freud's
views are unsupported by objective evidence, it is his
ideas that millions of lay people have accepted—the
view that human beings grow "healthy" by the Oedipal
resolution: fearing and thus respecting one parent
(Dad) and disdaining the other (Mom). Since our parents stand as our first models of male and female, this
primal fear and disdain tends to form a paradigm for
lifelong sexual enmity, suspicion, betrayal, and rejection.

Father is supposed to represent reality and Mother
is associated with infant dependency. In order to gain
their independence, both girls and boys must form an
alliance with Father against Mother. Politically, this
translates to male supremacy ("alliance with Father")
and cultural misogyny ("against Mother"). Psychologically, the message is conform or you might turn
out "queer."

The hitch is, as we've noted, that sex role and sexual
orientation have been shown to be totally unrelated.
Modern practitioners may know this, but since they
have not loudly and publicly revised psychoanalytic
theories on homosexuality, they are in effect supporting the old lies. What's more, their silence leaves un-
challenged these contradictions within psychoanalytic
theory itself:

- A human *instinct,* by definition, should be the same
  for everyone, everywhere; yet in societies where sex
  stereotypes do not exist, the supposedly instinctual
  Oedipal psychodrama doesn't exist either.
- If the castration complex, the fear of losing the
  penis, is the founding element of "masculinity," how
  is it that Dr. Robert Stoller, professor of psychiatry

at UCLA Medical School, found boys who were born without penises believed themselves boys anyway?

- How do we account for millions of children who become heterosexual though raised in father-absent homes? How do these mothers arouse fear and respect in the boy and the requisite penis envy in the girl?

- Why do batteries of psychological tests *fail to show any significant difference* between lesbians and heterosexuals on the psychological criteria that are supposed to "cause" female homosexuality?

- How can one say that male homosexuals identify with Mother and take on "feminine" ways, when mothers of homosexuals are supposedly "masculine," dominant, and aggressive?

- If a woman's compensation for her missing penis is a baby boy, then of course she'll overprotect her son as a hedge against a *second* castration—losing him. It's a cruel tautology to posit motherhood in these terms and, at the same time, to hold Mother responsible for overprotection of the one treasure she's supposedly spent her whole life seeking.

- Could it be that girls and women envy the *privileges* that accrue to people whose distinguishing feature happens to be the penis, without envying the penis?

- Freud declared the "vaginal orgasm" to be the diploma of heterosexual maturity, yet in *Human Sexual Response,* William Masters and Virginia Johnson have proved the clitoris to be the physiological source of all female orgasms. Why require a girl to unlearn clitoral pleasure when in every other instance Freud believed that "urges dissipate when they become satisfied"? Is it because the clitoral orgasm is active, not receptive; because it doesn't require a penis and it doesn't result in procreation? Was the promotion of the "vaginal orgasm" patriarchy's way of keeping females passive, male-connected, and frequently pregnant?

We could devote pages and pages to poking holes in psychoanalytic theory, but these final points should do the trick: studies show that the classic "homosexual-inducing" family produces plenty of "straight" children; other kinds of families raise both heterosexual and homosexual siblings under the same roof; and totally "straight" family constellations rear homosexual kids.

And so, all speculations have been found wanting, and we are left with one indisputable fact: *no one knows what causes homosexuality.*

ASSUMPTION 3: HOMOSEXUALITY IS ONE OF THE WORST THINGS THAT CAN HAPPEN TO ANYONE

Studies show that the majority of American people want homosexuality "cured." Yet the facts—when this volatile subject can be viewed factually—prove that homosexuality is neither uncommon, abnormal, nor harmful to its practitioners or anyone else.

When the "naturalness" of heterosexuality is claimed via examples in the animal kingdom, one can point to recorded observations of homosexuality among seagulls, cows, mares, sows, primates, and many other mammals. But more important, among humans, "there is probably no culture from which homosexuality has not been reported," according to Drs. Clellan Ford and Frank Beach in *Patterns of Sexual Behavior* (Harper). And no matter what moral or legal prohibitions have been devised through the ages, none has ever eliminated homosexuality. In fact, the incidence of homosexuality is greater in countries that forbid it than in those that don't. With all the fluctuations of public morality, many sources confirm that 10 percent of the entire population consider themselves exclusively homosexual at any given place and time.

Aside from choosing to love members of their own sex, lesbians and homosexual males have been found no different from heterosexuals in gender identity or self-esteem, in drinking, drug use, suicide rates, relationships with parents and friends, and general life satisfaction. One study actually found lower rates of depression among lesbians; another study measured higher competence and intellectual efficiency; still another found more lesbians (87 percent) than heterosexual women (18 percent) experienced orgasm "almost always"; and two important recent reports revealed that homosexuals seem clearly far *less* likely than heterosexuals to commit child abuse or other sexual crimes. In short, many homosexuals "could very well serve as models of social comportment and psychological maturity." And yet, parents feel obliged to protect their children from it.

Why?

In a word, *homophobia*—fear and intolerance of homosexuality. Despite the facts just enumerated, millions still believe homosexuality *is* the worst thing. In one study, nearly half of the college students questioned labeled it more deviant than murder and drug addiction. Others reveal their homophobia by sitting an average of 10 inches further away from an interviewer of the same sex wearing a "gay and proud" button than from an interviewer wearing no button. Another group said they wouldn't be able to form a close friendship with a gay person.

In a society that works as hard as ours does to convince everyone that Boys are Better, homosexual taunts whether "sissy" or "faggot," say *nonboy*. In pure form, the worst insult one boy can scream at another is "You girl!" That curse is the coming home to roost of the cult of sex differences. Indeed, sexism and homophobia go hand in hand. The homophobic male *needs* sharp sex-role boundaries to help him avoid transgressing to the "other side." His terror is that he is not different enough from the "opposite" sex, and that his "masculine" facade may not always protect him from the "femininity" within himself that he learned as a boy to hate and repress. Among men, homophobia is rooted in contempt for everything female.

A homophobic man cannot love a woman with abandon, for he might reveal his vulnerability; he cannot adore and nurture his children because being around babies is "sissy" and child care is "women's work." According to his perverse logic, making women pregnant is "masculine," but making children happy is a betrayal of manhood. One man complained that his child wouldn't shake hands and was getting too old for father–son kissing. How old was "too old"? Three.

Homophobia, the malevolent enforcer of sex-role behavior, is the enemy of children because it doesn't care about children, it cares about conformity, differences, and divisions.

If women seem to be less threatened by homosexuality than men and less obsessed with latent homosexual impulses, it's because the process of "becoming" a

woman is considered less arduous for the female and less important to society than the process of "proving" one's manhood. "Masculinity" once won is not to be lost. But a girl needn't guard against losing that which is of little value.

Like male homosexuals, the lesbian doesn't need the other sex for physical gratification. But the lesbian's crime goes beyond sex: she doesn't need men at all. Accordingly, despite the relative unimportance of female sexuality, lesbianism is seen as a hostile alternative to heterosexual marriage, family, and patriarchal survival.

Before children have the vaguest idea about who or what is a homosexual, they learn that homosexuality is something frightening, horrid, and nasty. They become homophobic long before they understand what it is they fear. They learn that "What are you, a sissy?" is the fastest way to coerce a boy into self-destructive exploits.

While homophobia cannot prevent homosexuality, its power to destroy female assertiveness and male sensitivity is boundless. For children who, for whatever reason, would have been homosexual no matter what, homophobia only adds external cruelty to their internal feelings of alienation. And for those who become the taunters, the ones who mock and harass "queers," homophobia is a clue to a disturbed sense of self.

It's all so painful. And so unnecessary. Eliminate sex-role stereotypes and you eliminate homophobia. Eliminate homophobia and you eliminate the power of words to wound and the power of stigma to mold a person into something she or he was never meant to be. So here's my best advice on the subject: *Don't worry how to raise a heterosexual child; worry about how not to be a homophobic parent.*

Girls and Boys Together . . . But Mostly Apart: Gender Arrangements in Elementary Schools

BARRIE THORNE

Throughout the years of elementary school, children's friendships and casual encounters are strongly separated by sex. Sex segregation among children which starts in preschool and is well established by middle childhood, has been amply documented in studies of children's groups and friendships (e.g., Eder & Hallinan, 1978; Schofield, 1981) and is immediately visible in elementary school settings. When children choose seats in classrooms or the cafeteria, or get into line, they frequently arrange themselves in same-sex clusters. At lunchtime, they talk matter-of-factly about "girls' tables" and "boys' tables." Playgrounds have gendered turfs, with some areas and activities, such as large playing fields and basketball courts, controlled mainly by boys, and others—smaller enclaves like jungle-gym areas and concrete spaces for hopscotch or jumprope—more often controlled by girls. Sex segregation is so common in elementary schools that it is meaningful to speak of separate girls' and boys' worlds.

Studies of gender and children's social relations have mostly followed this "two worlds" model, separately describing and comparing the subcultures of girls and boys (e.g., Lever, 1976; Maltz & Borker, 1983). In brief summary: Boys tend to interact in larger, more age-heterogeneous groups (Lever, 1976; Waldrop & Halverson, 1975; Eder & Hallinan, 1978). They engage in more rough and tumble play and physical fighting (Maccoby & Jacklin, 1974). Organized sports are both

Reprinted from Willard W. Hartup and Zick Rubin, eds., *Relationships and Development* (Hillsdale, N.J.: Lawrence Erlbaum Associates, 1986). Volume sponsored by the Social Science Research Council. Copyright © 1986 by Lawrence Erlbaum Associates. Reprinted by permission of the publisher and the author.

a central activity and a major metaphor in boys' subcultures; they use the language of "teams" even when not engaged in sports, and they often construct interaction in the form of contests. The shifting hierarchies of boys' groups (Savin-Williams, 1976) are evident in their more frequent use of direct commands, insults, and challenges (Goodwin, 1980).

Fewer studies have been done of girls' groups (Foot, Chapman, & Smith, 1980; McRobbie & Garber, 1975), and—perhaps because categories for description and analysis have come more from male than female experience—researchers have had difficulty seeing and analyzing girls' social relations. Recent work has begun to correct this skew. In middle childhood, girls' worlds are less public than those of boys; girls more often interact in private places and in smaller groups or friendship pairs (Eder & Hallinan, 1978; Waldrop & Halverson, 1975). Their play is more cooperative and turn-taking (Lever, 1976). Girls have more intense and exclusive friendships, which take shape around keeping and telling secrets, shifting alliances, and indirect ways of expressing disagreement (Goodwin, 1980; Lever, 1976; Maltz & Borker, 1983). Instead of direct commands, girls more often use directives which merge speaker and hearer, e.g., "let's" or "we gotta" (Goodwin, 1980).

Although much can be learned by comparing the social organization and subcultures of boys' and of girls' groups, the separate worlds approach has eclipsed full, contextual understanding of gender and social relations among children. The separate worlds model essentially involves a search for group sex differences, and shares the limitations of individual sex difference research. Differences tend to be exaggerated and similarities ignored, with little theoretical attention to the integration of similarity and difference (Unger, 1979). Statistical findings of difference are often portrayed as dichotomous, neglecting the considerable individual variation that exists; for example, not all boys fight, and some have intense and exclusive friendships. The sex difference approach tends to abstract gender from its social context, to assume that males and females are qualitatively and permanently different (with differences perhaps unfolding through separate developmental lines). These assumptions mask the possibility that gender arrangements and patterns of similarity and difference may vary by situation, race, social class, region, or subculture.

Sex segregation is far from total, and is a more complex and dynamic process than the portrayal of separate worlds reveals. Erving Goffman (1977) has observed that sex segregation has a "with-then-apart" structure; the sexes segregate periodically, with separate spaces, rituals, groups, but they also come together and are, in crucial ways, part of the same world. This is certainly true in the social environment of elementary schools. Although girls and boys do interact as boundaried collectivities—an image suggested by the separate worlds approach—there are other occasions when they work or play in relaxed and integrated ways. Gender is less central to the organization and meaning of some situations than others. In short, sex segregation is not static, but is a variable and complicated process.

To gain an understanding of gender which can encompass both the "with" and the "apart" of sex segregation, analysis should start not with the individual, nor with a search for sex differences, but with social relationships. Gender should be conceptualized as a system of relationships rather than as an immutable and dichotomous given. Taking this approach, I have organized my research on gender and children's social relations around questions like the following: How and when does gender enter into group formation? In a given situation, how is gender made more or less salient or infused with particular meanings? By what rituals, processes, and forms of social organization and conflict do "with-then-apart" rhythms get enacted? How are these processes affected by the organization of institutions (e.g., different types of schools, neighborhoods, or summer camps), varied settings (e.g., the constraints and possibilities governing interaction on playgrounds vs. classrooms), and particular encounters?

METHODS AND SOURCES OF DATA

This study is based on two periods of participant observation. In 1976–1977 I observed for 8 months in a largely working-class elementary school in California, a school with 8% Black and 12% Chicana/o students. In 1980 I did fieldwork for 3 months in a Michigan elementary school of similar size (around 400 students), social class, and racial composition. I observed in several classrooms—a kindergarten, a second grade, and a combined fourth-fifth grade—and in school hallways, cafeterias, and playgrounds. I set out to follow the round of the school day as children experience it, recording their interactions with one another, and with adults, in varied settings.

Participant observation involves gaining access to everyday, "naturalistic" settings and taking systematic notes over an extended period of time. Rather than starting with preset categories for recording, or with fixed hypotheses for testing, participant observers record detail in ways which maximize opportunities for discovery. Through continuous interaction between observation and analysis, "grounded theory" is developed (Glaser & Strauss, 1967).

The distinctive logic and discipline of this mode of inquiry emerges from: (1) theoretical sampling—being relatively systematic in the choice of where and whom to observe in order to maximize knowledge relevant to categories and analysis which are being developed; and (2) comparing all relevant data on a given point in order to modify emerging propositions to take account of discrepant cases (Katz, 1983). Participant observation is a flexible, open-ended and inductive method, designed to understand behavior within, rather than stripped from, social context. It provides richly detailed information which is anchored in everyday meanings and experience.

DAILY PROCESSES OF SEX SEGREGATION

Sex segregation should be understood not as a given, but as the result of deliberate activity. The outcome is dramatically visible when there are separate girls' and boys' tables in school lunchrooms, or sex-separated groups on playgrounds. But in the same lunchroom one can also find tables where girls and boys eat and talk together, and in some playground activities the sexes mix. By what processes do girls and boys separate into gender-defined and relatively boundaried collectivities? And in what contexts, and through what processes, do boys and girls interact in less gender-divided ways?

In the school settings I observed, much segregation happened with no mention of gender. Gender was implicit in the contours of friendship, shared interest, and perceived risk which came into play when children chose companions—in their prior planning, invitations, seeking of access, saving of places, denials of entry, and allowing or protesting of "cuts" by those who violated the rules for lining up. Sometimes children formed mixed-sex groups for play, eating, talking, working on a classroom project, or moving through space. When adults or children explicitly invoked gender—and this was nearly always in ways which separated girls and boys—boundaries were heightened and mixed-sex interaction became an explicit arena of risk.

In the schools I studied, the physical space and curricula were not formally divided by sex, as they have been in the history of elementary schooling (a history evident in separate entrances to old school buildings, where the words "Boys" and "Girls" are permanently etched in concrete). Nevertheless, gender was a visible marker in the adult-organized school day. In both schools, when the public address system sounded, the principal inevitably opened with: "Boys and girls . . . ," and in addressing clusters of children, teachers and aides regularly used gender terms ("Heads down, girls"; "The girls are ready and the boys aren't"). These forms of address made gender visible and salient, conveying an assumption that the sexes are separate social groups.

Teachers and aides sometimes drew upon gender as a basis for sorting children and organizing activities. Gender is an embodied and visual social category which roughly divides the population in half, and the separation of girls and boys permeates the history and lore of schools and playgrounds. In both schools—although through awareness of Title IX, many teachers had changed this practice—one could see separate girls' and boys' lines moving, like caterpillars, through the school halls. In the fourth–fifth-grade classroom the teacher frequently pitted girls against boys for spelling and math contests. On the playground in the Michigan school, aides regarded the space close to the building as girls' territory, and the playing fields "out there" as boys' territory. They sometimes shooed children of the other sex away from those spaces, especially boys who ventured near the girls' area and seemed to have teasing in mind.

In organizing their activities, both within and apart from the surveillance of adults, children also explicitly invoked gender. During my fieldwork in the Michigan school, I kept daily records of who sat where in the lunchroom. The amount of sex segregation varied: it was least at the first-grade tables and almost total among sixth-graders. There was also variation from classroom to classroom within a given age, and from day to day. Actions like the following heightened the gender divide: In the lunchroom, when the two second-grade tables were filling, a high-status boy walked by the inside table, which had a scattering of both boys and girls, and said loudly, "Oooo, too many girls," as he headed for a seat at the far table. The boys at the inside table picked up their trays and moved, and no other boys sat at the inside table, which the pronouncement had effectively made taboo. In the end, that day (which was not the case every day), girls and boys ate at separate tables.

Eating and walking are not sex-typed activities, yet in forming groups in lunchrooms and hallways children often separated by sex. Sex segregation assumed added dimensions on the playground, where spaces, equipment, and activities were infused with gender meanings. My inventories of activities and groupings on the playground showed similar patterns in both schools: boys controlled the large fixed spaces designated for team sports (baseball diamonds, grassy fields used for football or soccer); girls more often played closer to the building, doing tricks on the monkey bars (which, for sixth-graders, became an area for sitting and talking) and using cement areas for jumprope, hopscotch, and group games like four-square. (Lever, 1976, provides a good analysis of sex-divided play.) Girls and boys most often played together in kickball, and in group (rather than team) games like four-square, dodgeball, and handball. When children used gender to exclude others from play, they often drew upon beliefs connecting boys to some activities and girls to others: A first-grade boy avidly watched an all-female game of jumprope. When the girls began to shift positions, he recognized a means of access to the play and he offered, "I'll swing it." A girl responded, "No way, you don't know how to do it, to swing it. You gotta be a girl." He left without protest. Although children sometimes ignored pronouncements about what each sex could or could not do, I never heard them directly challenge such claims.

When children had explicitly defined an activity or a group as gendered, those who crossed the boundary—especially boys who moved into female-marked space—risked being teased. ("Look! Mike's in the girls' line!"; "That's a girl over there," a girl said loudly, pointing to a boy sitting at an otherwise all-female table in the lunchroom.) Children, and occasionally adults, used teasing—especially the tease of "liking" someone of the other sex, or of "being" that sex by virtue of being in their midst—to police gender boundaries. Much of the teasing drew upon heterosexual romantic definitions, making cross-sex interaction risky, and increasing social distance between boys and girls.

RELATIONSHIPS BETWEEN THE SEXES

Because I have emphasized the "apart" and ignored the occasions of "with," this analysis of sex segregation falsely implies that there is little contact between girls and boys in daily school life. In fact, relationships between girls and boys—which should be studied as fully as, and in connection with, same-sex relationships—are of several kinds:

1. "Borderwork," or forms of cross-sex interaction which are based upon and reaffirm boundaries and asymmetries between girls' and boys' groups.
2. Interactions which are infused with heterosexual meanings.
3. Occasions where individuals cross gender boundaries to participate in the world of the other sex.
4. Situations where gender is muted in salience, with girls and boys interacting in more relaxed ways.

Borderwork

In elementary school settings boys' and girls' groups are sometimes spatially set apart. Same-sex groups sometimes claim fixed territories such as the basketball court, the bars, or specific lunchroom tables. However, in the crowded, multifocused, and adult-controlled environment of the school, groups form and disperse at a rapid rate and can never stay totally apart. Contact between girls and boys sometimes lessens sex segregation, but gender-defined groups also come together in ways which emphasize their boundaries.

"Borderwork" refers to interaction across, yet based upon and even strengthening gender boundaries. I have drawn this notion from Fredrik Barth's (1969) analysis of social relations which are maintained across ethnic boundaries without diminishing dichotomized ethnic status.* His focus is on more macro, ecological arrangements; mine is on face-to-face behavior. But the insight is similar: groups may interact in ways which strengthen their borders, and the maintenance of ethnic (or gender) groups can best be understood by examining the boundary that defines the groups, "not the cultural stuff that it encloses" (Barth, 1969:15). In elementary schools there are several types of borderwork: contests or games where gender-defined teams compete; cross-sex rituals of chasing and pollution; and group invasions. These interactions are asymmetrical, challenging the separate-but-parallel model of "two worlds."

Contests   Boys and girls are sometimes pitted against each other in classroom competitions and playground games. The fourth–fifth-grade classroom had a boys' side and a girls' side, an arrangement that reemerged each time the teacher asked children to choose their own desks. Although there was some within-sex shuffling, the result was always a spatial moiety system—boys on the left, girls on the right—with the exception of one girl (the "tomboy" whom I'll describe later), who twice chose a desk with the boys and once with the girls. Drawing upon and reinforcing the children's self-segregation, the teacher often pitted the boys against the girls in spelling and math competitions, events marked by cross-sex antagonism and within-sex solidarity. The teacher introduced a math game; she would write addition and subtraction problems on the board, and a member of each team would race to be the first to write the correct answer. She wrote two score-keeping columns on the board: "Beastly Boys" . . . "Gossipy Girls." The boys yelled out, as several girls laughed, "Noisy girls! Gruesome girls!" The girls sat in a row on top of their desks; sometimes they moved collectively, pushing their hips or whispering "Pass it on." The boys stood along the wall, some reclining against desks. When members of either group came back victorious from the front of the room, they

*I am grateful to Frederick Erickson for suggesting the relevance of Barth's analysis.

would do the "giving five" hand-slapping ritual with their team members.

On the playground a team of girls occasionally played a team of boys, usually in kickball or team two-square. Sometimes these games proceeded matter-of-factly, but if gender became the explicit basis of team solidarity, the interaction changed, becoming more antagonistic and unstable. Two fifth-grade girls played against two fifth-grade boys in a team game of two-square. The game proceeded at an even pace until an argument ensued about whether the ball was out or on the line. Karen, who had hit the ball, became annoyed, flashed her middle finger at the other team, and called to a passing girl to join their side. The boys then called out to other boys, and cheered as several arrived to play. "We got five and you got three!" Jack yelled. The game continued, with the girls yelling, "Bratty boys! Sissy boys!" and the boys making noises—"Weee haw," "Ha-ha-ha"—as they played.

Chasing   Cross-sex chasing dramatically affirms boundaries between girls and boys. The basic elements of chase and elude, capture and rescue (Sutton-Smith, 1971) are found in various kinds of tag with formal rules, and in informal episodes of chasing which punctuate life on playgrounds. These episodes begin with a provocation (taunts like "You can't get me!" or "Slobber monster!"; bodily pokes or the grabbing of possessions). A provocation may be ignored, or responded to by chasing. Chaser and chased may then alternate roles. In an ethnographic study of chase sequences on a school playground, Christine Finnan (1982) observes that chases vary in number of chasers to chased (e.g., one chasing one or five chasing two); form of provocation (a taunt or a poke); outcome (an episode may end when the chased outdistances the chaser, or with a brief touch, being wrestled to the ground, or the recapturing of a hat or a ball); and in use of space (there may or may not be safety zones).

Like Finnan (1982) and Sluckin (1981), who studied a playground in England, I found that chasing has a gendered structure. Boys frequently chase one another, an activity which often ends in wrestling and mock fights. When girls chase girls, they are usually less physically aggressive; they less often, for example, wrestle one another to the ground.

Cross-sex chasing is set apart by special names— "girls chase the boys"; "boys chase the girls"; "the chase"; "chasers"; "chase and kiss"; "kiss chase";

"kissers and chasers"; "kiss or kill"—and by children's animated talk about the activity. The names vary by region and school, but contain both gender and sexual meanings (this form of play is mentioned, but only briefly analyzed, in Finnan, 1982; Sluckin, 1981; Parrott, 1972; and Borman, 1979).

In "boys chase the girls" and "girls chase the boys" (the names most frequently used in both the California and Michigan schools) boys and girls become, by definition, separate teams. Gender terms override individual identities, especially for the other team ("Help, a girl's chasin' me!"; "C'mon, Sarah, let's get that boy"; "Tony, help save me from the girls"). Individuals may also grab someone of their sex and turn them over to the opposing team: Ryan grabbed Billy from behind, wrestling him to the ground. "Hey, girls, get 'im," Ryan called.

Boys more often mix episodes of cross-sex with same-sex chasing. Girls more often have safety zones, places like the girls' restroom or an area by the school wall, where they retreat to rest and talk (sometimes in animated postmortems) before new episodes of cross-sex chasing begin.

Early in the fall in the Michigan school, where chasing was especially prevalent, I watched a second-grade boy teach a kindergarten girl how to chase. He slowly ran backwards, beckoning her to pursue him, as he called, "Help, a girl's after me." In the early grades chasing mixes with fantasy play, e.g., a first-grade boy who played "sea monster," his arms outflung and his voice growling, as he chased a group of girls. By third grade, stylized gestures—exaggerated stalking motions, screams (which only girls do), and karate kicks—accompany scenes of chasing.

Names like "chase and kiss" mark the sexual meanings of cross-sex chasing, a theme I return to later. The threat of kissing—most often girls threatening to kiss boys—is a ritualized form of provocation. Cross-sex chasing among sixth-graders involves elaborate patterns of touch and touch avoidance, which adults see as sexual. The principal told the sixth-graders in the Michigan school that they were not to play "pom-pom," a complicated chasing game, because it entailed "inappropriate touch."

Rituals of Pollution   Cross-sex chasing is sometimes entwined with rituals of pollution, as in "cooties," where specific individuals or groups are treated as contaminating or carrying "germs." Children have rituals for transfering cooties (usually touching someone else and shouting, "You've got cooties!"), for immunization (e.g., writing "CV" for "cootie vaccination" on their arms), and for eliminating cooties (e.g., saying "no gives" or using "cootie catchers" made of folded paper) (described in Knapp & Knapp, 1976). While girls may give cooties to girls, boys do not generally give cooties to one another (Samuelson, 1980).

In cross-sex play, either girls or boys may be defined as having cooties, which they transfer through chasing and touching. Girls give cooties to boys more often than vice versa. In Michigan, one version of cooties is called "girl stain"; the fourth-graders whom Karkau (1973) describes used the phrase "girl touch." "Cootie queens" or "cootie girls" (there are no "kings" or "boys") are female pariahs, the ultimate school untouchables, seen as contaminating not only by virtue of gender, but also through some added stigma such as being overweight or poor.* That girls are seen as more polluting than boys is a significant asymmetry, which echoes cross-cultural patterns, although in other cultures female pollution is generally connected to menstruation, and not applied to prepubertal girls.

Invasions Playground invasions are another asymmetric form of borderwork. On a few occasions I saw girls invade and disrupt an all-male game, most memorably a group of tall sixth-grade girls who ran onto the playing field and grabbed a football which was in play. The boys were surprised and frustrated, and, unusual for boys this old, finally tattled to the aide. But in the majority of cases, boys disrupt girls' activities rather than vice versa. Boys grab the ball from girls playing four-square, stick feet into a jumprope and stop an ongoing game, and dash through the area of the bars where girls are taking turns performing, sending the rings flying. Sometimes boys ask to join a girls' game and then, after a short period of seemingly earnest play, disrupt the game. Two second-grade boys begged to "twirl" the jumprope for a group of second-grade girls who had been jumping for some time. The girls agreed, and the boys began to twirl. Soon, without announcement, the boys changed from "seashells, cockle bells" to "hot peppers" (spinning the rope very

fast), and tangled the jumper in the rope. The boys ran away laughing.

Boys disrupt girls' play so often that girls have developed almost ritualized responses: they guard their ongoing play, chase boys away, and tattle to the aides. In a playground cycle which enhances sex segregation, aides who try to spot potential trouble before it occurs sometimes shoo boys away from areas where girls are playing. Aides do not anticipate trouble from girls who seek to join groups of boys, with the exception of girls intent on provoking a chase sequence. And indeed, if they seek access to a boys' game, girls usually play with boys in earnest rather than breaking up the game.

A close look at the organization of borderwork—or boundaried interactions between the sexes—shows that the worlds of boys and girls may be separate, but they are not parallel, nor are they equal. The worlds of girls and boys articulate in several asymmetric ways:

1. On the playground, boys control as much as ten times more space than girls, when one adds up the area of large playing fields and compares it with the much smaller areas where girls predominate. Girls, who play closer to the building, are more often watched over and protected by the adult aides.

2. Boys invade all-female games and scenes of play much more than girls invade boys. This, and boys' greater control of space, correspond with other findings about the organization of gender, and inequality, in our society: compared with men and boys, women and girls take up less space, and their space and talk are more often violated and interrupted (Greif, 1982; Henley, 1977; West & Zimmerman, 1983).

3. Although individual boys are occasionally treated as contaminating (e.g., a third-grade boy who both boys and girls said was "stinky" and "smelled like pee"), girls are more often defined as polluting. This pattern ties to themes that I discuss later: it is more taboo for a boy to play with (as opposed to invade) girls, and girls are more sexually defined than boys.

A look at the boundaries between the separated worlds of girls and boys illuminates within-sex hierarchies of status and control. For example, in the sex-divided seating in the fourth–fifth-grade classroom, several boys recurrently sat near "female space": their desks were at the gender divide in the classroom, and they were more likely than other boys to sit at a predominantly female table in the lunchroom. These boys—two nonbilingual Chicanos and an overweight "loner" boy who was afraid of sports—were at the bot-

*Sue Samuelson (1980) reports that in a racially mixed playground in Fresno, California, Mexican-American but not Anglo children gave cooties. Racial as well as sexual inequality may be expressed through these forms.

tom of the male hierarchy. Gender is sometimes used as a metaphor for male hierarchies; the inferior status of boys at the bottom is conveyed by calling them "girls." Seven boys and one girl were playing basketball. Two younger boys came over and asked to play. While the girl silently stood, fully accepted in the company of players, one of the older boys disparagingly said to the younger boys, "You girls can't play."*

In contrast, the girls who more often travel in the boys' world, sitting with groups of boys in the lunchroom or playing basketball, soccer, and baseball with them, are not stigmatized. Some have fairly high status with other girls. The worlds of girls and boys are asymmetrically arranged, and spatial patterns map out interacting forms of inequality.

Heterosexual Meanings

The organization and meanings of gender (the social categories "woman/man," "girl/boy") and of sexuality vary cross-culturally (Ortner & Whitehead, 1981)—and, in our society, across the life course. Harriet Whitehead (1981) observed that in our (Western) gender system, and that of many traditional North American Indian cultures, one's choice of a sexual object, occupation, and dress and demeanor are closely associated with gender. However, the "center of gravity" differs in the two gender systems. For Indians, occupational pursuits provide the primary imagery of gender; dress and demeanor are secondary, and sexuality is least important. In our system, at least for adults, the order is reversed: heterosexuality is central to our definitions of "man" and "woman" ("masculinity/femininity") and the relationships that obtain between them, whereas occupation and dress/demeanor are secondary.

Whereas erotic orientation and gender are closely linked in our definitions of adults, we define children as relatively asexual. Activities and dress/demeanor are more important than sexuality in the cultural meanings of "girl" and "boy." Children are less heterosexually defined than adults, and we have nonsexual imagery for relations between girls and boys. However, both children and adults sometimes use heterosexual lan-

guage—"crushes," "like," "goin' with," "girlfriends," and "boyfriends"—to define cross-sex relationships. This language increases through the years of elementary school; the shift to adolescence consolidates a gender system organized around the institution of heterosexuality.

In everyday life in the schools, heterosexual and romantic meanings infuse some ritualized forms of interaction between groups of boys and girls (e.g., "chase and kiss") and help maintain sex segregation. "Jimmy likes Beth" or "Beth likes Jimmy" is a major form of teasing, which a child risks in choosing to sit by or walk with someone of the other sex. The structure of teasing and children's sparse vocabulary for relationships between girls and boys are evident in the following conversation which I had with a group of third-grade girls in the lunchroom. Susan asked me what I was doing, and I said I was observing the things children do and play. Nicole volunteered, "I like running, boys chase all the girls. See Tim over there? Judy chases him all around the school. She likes him." Judy, sitting across the table, quickly responded, "I hate him. I like him for a friend." "Tim loves Judy," Nicole said in a loud, sing-song voice.

In the younger grades, the culture and lore of girls contains more heterosexual romantic themes than that of boys. In Michigan, the first-grade girls often jumped rope to a rhyme which began: "Down in the valley where the green grass grows, there sat Cindy [name of jumper], as sweet as a rose. She sat, she sat, she sat so sweet. Along came Jason, and kissed her on the cheek. First comes love, then comes marriage, then along comes Cindy with a baby carriage." Before a girl took her turn at jumping, the chanters asked her, "Who do you want to be your boyfriend?" The jumper always proffered a name, which was accepted matter-of-factly. In chasing, a girl's kiss carried greater threat than a boy's kiss; "girl touch," when defined as contaminating, had sexual connotations. In short, starting at an early age, girls are more sexually defined than boys.

Through the years of elementary school, and increasing with age, the idiom of heterosexuality helps maintain the gender divide. Cross-sex interactions, especially when children initiate them, are fraught with the risk of being teased about "liking" someone of the other sex. I learned of several close cross-sex friendships, formed and maintained in neighborhoods and church, which went underground during the school day.

By the fifth grade a few children began to affirm,

---

*This incident was recorded by Margaret Blume, who, for an undergraduate research project in 1982, observed in the California school where I earlier did fieldwork. Her observations and insights enhanced my own, and I would like to thank her for letting me cite this excerpt.

rather than avoid, the charge of having a girlfriend or a boyfriend; they introduced the heterosexual courtship rituals of adolescence. In the lunchroom in the Michigan school, as the tables were forming, a high-status fifth-grade boy called out from his seat at the table: "I want Trish to sit by me." Trish came over, and almost like a king and queen, they sat at the gender divide—a row of girls down the table on her side, a row of boys on his. In this situation, which inverted earlier forms, it was not a loss but a gain in status to publicly choose a companion of the other sex. By affirming his choice, the boy became unteasable (note the familiar asymmetry of heterosexual courtship rituals: the male initiates). This incident signals a temporal shift in arrangements of sex and gender.

Traveling in the World of the Other Sex

Contests, invasions, chasing, and heterosexually defined encounters are based upon and reaffirm boundaries between girls and boys. In another type of cross-sex interaction, individuals (or sometimes pairs) cross gender boundaries, seeking acceptance in a group of the other sex. Nearly all the cases I saw of this were tomboys—girls who played organized sports and frequently sat with boys in the cafeteria or classroom. If these girls were skilled at activities central in the boys' world, especially games like soccer, baseball, and basketball, they were pretty much accepted as participants.

Being a tomboy is a matter of degree. Some girls seek access to boys' groups but are excluded; other girls limit their "crossing" to specific sports. Only a few—such as the tomboy I mentioned earlier, who chose a seat with the boys in the sex-divided fourth–fifth grade—participate fully in the boys' world. That particular girl was skilled at the various organized sports which boys played in different seasons of the year. She was also adept at physical fighting and at using the forms of arguing, insult, teasing, naming, and sports-talk of the boys' subculture. She was the only Black child in her classroom, in a school with only 8% Black students; overall that token status, along with unusual athletic and verbal skills, may have contributed to her ability to move back and forth across the gender divide. Her unique position in the children's world was widely recognized in the school. Several times, the teacher said to me, "She thinks she's a boy."

I observed only one boy in the upper grades (a

fourth-grader) who regularly played with all-female groups, as opposed to "playing at" girls' games and seeking to disrupt them. He frequently played jump-rope and took turns with girls doing tricks on the bars, using the small gestures—for example, a helpful push on the heel of a girl who needed momentum to turn her body around the bar—which mark skillful and earnest participation. Although I never saw him play in other than an earnest spirit, the girls often chased him away from their games, and both girls and boys teased him. The fact that girls seek and have more access to boys' worlds than vice versa, and the fact that girls who travel with the other sex are less stigmatized for it, are obvious asymmetries, tied to the asymmetries previously discussed.

Relaxed Cross-Sex Interactions

Relationships between boys and girls are not always marked by strong boundaries, heterosexual definitions, or interacting on the terms and turfs of the other sex. On some occasions girls and boys interact in relatively comfortable ways. Gender is not strongly salient nor explicitly invoked, and girls and boys are not organized into boundaried collectivities. These "with" occasions have been neglected by those studying gender and children's relationships, who have emphasized either the model of separate worlds (with little attention to their articulation) or heterosexual forms of contact.

Occasions when boys and girls interact without strain, when gender wanes rather than waxes in importance, frequently have one or more of the following characteristics:

1. The situations are organized around an absorbing task, such as a group art project or creating a radio show, which encourages cooperation and lessens attention to gender. This pattern accords with other studies finding that cooperative activities reduce group antagonism (e.g., Sherif & Sherif, 1953, who studied divisions between boys in a summer camp; and Aronson et al., 1978, who used cooperative activities to lessen racial divisions in a classroom).

2. Gender is less prominent when children are not responsible for the formation of the group. Mixed-sex play is less frequent in games like football, which require the choosing of teams, and more frequent in games like handball or dodgeball, which individuals can join simply by getting into a line or a circle. When adults organize mixed-sex encounters—which they fre-

quently do in the classroom and in physical education periods on the playground—they legitimize cross-sex contact. This removes the risk of being teased for choosing to be with the other sex.

3. There is more extensive and relaxed cross-sex interaction when principles of grouping other than gender are explicitly invoked—for example, counting off to form teams for spelling or kickball, dividing lines by hot lunch or cold lunch, or organizing a work group on the basis of interests or reading ability.

4. Girls and boys may interact more readily in less public and crowded settings. Neighborhood play, depending on demography, is more often sex and age integrated than play at school, partly because with fewer numbers, one may have to resort to an array of social categories to find play partners or to constitute a game. And in less crowded environments there are fewer potential witnesses to "make something of it" if girls and boys play together.

Relaxed interactions between girls and boys often depend on adults to set up and legitimize the contact.* Perhaps because of this contingency—and the other, distancing patterns which permeate relations between girls and boys—the easeful moments of interaction rarely build to close friendship. Schofield (1981) makes a similar observation about gender and racial barriers to friendship in a junior high school.

IMPLICATIONS FOR DEVELOPMENT

I have located social relations within an essentially spatial framework, emphasizing the organization of children's play, work, and other activities within specific settings and in one type of institution, the school. In contrast, frameworks of child development rely upon temporal metaphors, using images of growth and transformation over time. Taken alone, both spatial and temporal frameworks have shortcomings; fitted together, they may be mutually correcting.

Those interested in gender and development have relied upon conceptualizations of "sex-role socialization" and "sex differences." Sexuality and gender, I have argued, are more situated and fluid than these individualist and intrinsic models imply. Sex and gen-

der are differently organized and defined across situations, even within the same institution. This situational variation (e.g., in the extent to which an encounter heightens or lessens gender boundaries, or is infused with sexual meanings) shapes and constrains individual behavior. Features which a developmental perspective might attribute to individuals and understand as relatively internal attributes unfolding over time may, in fact, be highly dependent on context. For example, children's avoidance of cross-sex friendship may be attributed to individual gender development in middle childhood. But attention to varied situations may show that this avoidance is contingent on group size, activity, adult behavior, collective meanings, and the risk of being teased.

A focus on social organization and situation draws attention to children's experiences in the present. This helps correct a model like "sex-role socialization" which casts the present under the shadow of the future, or presumed "endpoints" (Speier, 1976). A situated analysis of arrangements of sex and gender among those of different ages may point to crucial disjunctions in the life course. In the fourth and fifth grades, culturally defined heterosexual rituals ("goin' with") begin to suppress the presence and visibility of other types of interaction between girls and boys, such as nonsexualized and comfortable interaction and traveling in the world of the other sex. As "boyfriend/girlfriend" definitions spread, the fifth-grade tomboy I described had to work to sustain "buddy" relationships with boys. Adult women who were tomboys often speak of early adolescence as a painful time when they were pushed away from participation in boys' activities. Other adult women speak of the loss of intense, even erotic ties with other girls when they entered puberty and the rituals of dating, that is, when they became absorbed into the situation of heterosexuality (Rich, 1980). When Lever (1976) describes best-friend relationships among fifth-grade girls as preparation for dating, she imposes heterosexual ideologies onto a present which should be understood on its own terms.

As heterosexual encounters assume more importance, they may alter relations in same-sex groups. For example, Schofield (1981) reports that for sixth- and seventh-grade children in a middle school, the popularity of girls with other girls was affected by their popularity with boys, while boys' status with other boys did not depend on their relations with girls. This is an asymmetry familiar from the adult world; men's rela-

---

*Note that in daily school life, depending on the individual and the situation, teachers and aides sometimes lessened and at other times heightened sex segregation.

tionships with one another are defined through varied activities (occupations, sports), while relationships among women—and their public status—are more influenced by their connections to individual men.

A full understanding of gender and social relations should encompass cross-sex as well as within-sex interactions. "Borderwork" helps maintain separate, gender-linked subcultures, which, as those interested in development have begun to suggest, may result in different milieux for learning. Daniel Maltz and Ruth Borker (1983), for example, argue that because of different interactions within girls' and boys' groups, the sexes learn different rules for creating and interpreting friendly conversation, rules which carry into adulthood and help account for miscommunication between men and women. Carol Gilligan (1982) fits research on the different worlds of girls and boys into a theory of sex differences in moral development. Girls develop a style of reasoning, she argues, which is more personal and relational; boys develop a style which is more positional, based on separateness. Eleanor Maccoby (1982), also following the insight that because of sex segregation, girls and boys grow up in different environments, suggests implications for gender-differentiated prosocial and antisocial behavior.

This separate worlds approach, as I have illustrated, also has limitations. The occasions when the sexes are together should also be studied, and understood as contexts for experience and learning. For example, asymmetries in cross-sex relationships convey a series of messages: that boys are more entitled to space and to the nonreciprocal right of interrupting or invading the activities of the other sex; that girls are more in need of adult protection, lower in status, more defined by sexuality, and may even be polluting. Different types of cross-sex interaction—relaxed, boundaried, sexualized, or taking place on the terms of the other sex—provide different contexts for development.

By mapping the array of relationships between and within the sexes, one adds complexity to the overly static and dichotomous imagery of separate worlds. Individual experiences vary, with implications for development. Some children prefer same-sex groupings; some are more likely to cross the gender boundary and participate in the world of the other sex; some children (e.g., girls and boys who frequently play "chase and kiss") invoke heterosexual meanings, while others avoid them.

Finally, after charting the terrain of relationships, one can trace their development over time. For example, age variation in the content and form of borderwork, or of cross- and same-sex touch, may be related to differing cognitive, social, emotional, or physical capacities, as well as to age-associated cultural forms. I earlier mentioned temporal shifts in the organization of cross-sex chasing, from mixing with fantasy play in the early grades to more elaborately ritualized and sexualized forms by the sixth grade. There also appear to be temporal changes in same- and cross-sex touch. In kindergarten, girls and boys touch one another more freely than in fourth grade, when children avoid relaxed cross-sex touch and instead use pokes, pushes, and other forms of mock violence, even when the touch clearly expresses affection. This touch taboo is obviously related to the risk of seeming to *like* someone of the other sex. In fourth grade, same-sex touch begins to signal sexual meanings among boys as well as between boys and girls. Younger boys touch one another freely in cuddling (arm around shoulder) as well as mock-violence ways. By fourth grade, when homophobic taunts like "fag" become more common among boys, cuddling touch begins to disappear for boys, but less for girls.

Overall, I am calling for more complexity in our conceptualizations of gender and of children's social relationships. Our challenge is to retain the temporal sweep, looking at individual and group lives as they unfold over time, while also attending to social structure and context and to the full variety of experiences in the present.

ACKNOWLEDGMENTS

I would like to thank Jane Atkinson, Nancy Chodorow, Arlene Daniels, Peter Lyman, Zick Rubin, Malcolm Spector, Avril Thorne, and Margery Wolf for comments on an earlier version of this paper. Conversations with Zella Luria enriched this work.

REFERENCES

Aronson, E., et al. 1978. *The jigsaw classroom.* Beverly Hills, Calif.: Sage.

Barth, F., ed. 1969. *Ethnic groups and boundaries.* Boston: Little, Brown.

Borman, K. M. 1979. "Children's interactions in playgrounds," *Theory into Practice* 18:251–57.

Eder, D., & Hallinan, M. T. 1978. "Sex differences in children's friendships." *American Sociological Review* 43:237–50.

Finnan, C. R. 1982. "The ethnography of children's spontaneous play." In G. Spindler, ed., *Doing the ethnography of schooling,* pp. 358–80. New York: Holt, Rinehart & Winston.

Foot, H. C.; Chapman, A. J.; & Smith, J. R. 1980. "Introduction." *Friendship and social relations in children,* pp. 1–14. New York: Wiley.

Gilligan, C. 1982. *In a different voice: Psychological theory and women's development.* Cambridge: Harvard University Press.

Glaser, B. G., & Strauss, A. L. 1967. *The discovery of grounded theory.* Chicago: Aldine.

Goffman, E. 1977. "The arrangement between the sexes." *Theory and Society* 4:301–36.

Goodwin, M. H. 1980. "Directive-response speech sequences in girls' and boys' task activities." In S. McConnell-Ginet, R. Borker, & N. Furman, eds., *Women and language in literature and society,* pp. 157–73. New York: Praeger.

Greif, E. B. 1982. "Sex differences in parent-child conversations." *Women's Studies International Quarterly* 3:253–58.

Henley, N. 1977. *Body politics: Power, sex, and nonverbal communication.* Englewood Cliffs, N.J.: Prentice-Hall.

Karkau, K. 1973. *Sexism in the fourth grade.* Pittsburgh: KNOW, Inc. (pamphlet).

Katz, J. 1983. "A theory of qualitative methodology: The social system of analytic fieldwork." In R. M. Emerson, ed., *Contemporary field research,* pp. 127–48. Boston: Little, Brown.

Knapp, M., & Knapp, H. 1976. *One potato, two potato: The secret education of American children.* New York: W. W. Norton.

Lever, J. 1976. "Sex differences in the games children play." *Social Problems* 23:478–87.

Maccoby, E. 1982. "Social groupings in childhood: Their relationship to prosocial and antisocial behavior in boys and girls." Paper presented at conference on The Development of Prosocial and Antisocial Behavior, Voss, Norway.

Maccoby, E., & Jacklin, C. 1974. *The psychology of sex differences.* Stanford, Calif.: Stanford University Press.

McRobbie, A., & Garber, J. 1975. "Girls and subcultures." In S. Hall & T. Jefferson, eds., *Resistance through rituals,* pp. 209–23. London: Hutchinson.

Maltz, D. N., & Borker, R. A. 1983. "A cultural approach to male–female miscommunication." In J. J. Gumperz, ed., *Language and social identity,* pp. 195–216. New York: Cambridge University Press.

Ortner, S. B., & Whitehead, H. 1981. *Sexual meanings.* New York: Cambridge University Press.

Parrott, S. 1972. "Games children play: Ethnography of a second-grade recess." In J. P. Spradley & D. W. McCurdy, eds., *The cultural experience,* pp. 206–19. Chicago: Science Research Associates.

Rich, A. 1980. "Compulsory heterosexuality and lesbian existence." *Signs,* 5:631–60.

Samuelson, S. 1980. "The cooties complex." *Western Folklore* 39:198–210.

Savin-Williams, R. C. 1976. "An ethological study of dominance formation and maintenance in a group of human adolescents." *Child Development* 47:972–79.

Schofield, J. W. 1981. "Complementary and conflicting identities: Images and interaction in an interracial school." In S. R. Asher & J. M. Gottman, eds., *The development of children's friendships,* pp. 53–90. New York: Cambridge University Press.

Sherif, M., & Sherif, C. 1953. *Groups in harmony and tension.* New York: Harper.

Sluckin, A. 1981. *Growing up in the playground.* London: Routledge & Kegan Paul.

Speier, M. 1976. "The adult ideological viewpoint in studies of childhood." In A. Skolnick, ed., *Rethinking childhood,* pp. 168–86. Boston: Little, Brown.

Sutton-Smith, B. 1971. "A syntax for play and games." In R. E. Herron and B. Sutton-Smith, eds., *Child's play,* pp. 298–307. New York: Wiley.

Unger, R. K. 1979. "Toward a redefinition of sex and gender." *American Psychologist* 34:1085–94.

Waldrop, M. F., & Halverson, C. F. 1975. "Intensive and extensive peer behavior: Longitudinal and cross-sectional analysis." *Child Development* 46:19–26.

West, C., & Zimmerman, D. H. 1983. "Small insults: A study of interruptions in cross-sex conversations between unacquainted persons." In B. Thorne, C. Kramarae, & N. Henley, eds., *Language, gender, and society.* Rowley, Mass.: Newbury House.

Whitehead, H. 1981. "The bow and the burden strap: A new look at institutionalized homosexuality in Native America." In S. B. Ortner & H. Whitehead, eds., *Sexual meanings,* pp. 80–115. New York: Cambridge University Press.

P A R T   T H R E E

Social Organization of Gender

The processes of gender socialization that begin in early childhood work to prepare us for participation in society as males or females throughout the course of childhood, adolescence, and adulthood. Socialization alone, however, cannot account for the differences in power and prestige apparent between men and women in almost all societies. Indeed, socialization continues as a dynamic process throughout our lives. Because most people in contemporary societies have experiences that lead them to challenge the beliefs inherent in their socialization, socialization alone cannot ensure that adults will conform to the patterns of belief and behavior dictated by the social groups to which they belong.

In this part of *Feminist Frontiers III,* we consider the structural bases of women's subordination to men and feminist approaches for identifying, analyzing, and challenging these sources of oppression. When we consider social structural components of patriarchy, we look for relatively stable and predictable patterns of behavior which situate women as a group or category in disadvantaged positions relative to men. Key to feminist analyses of the social organization of gender inequality is an understanding of the role of a society's *institutions* in perpetuating sexual inequality.

Like other forms of social inequality, *gender inequality* can be regarded as a function of the unequal distribution of rights to control three kinds of valued commodities. First, inequality results from differential access to power, defined as the ability to carry out one's will despite opposition. Second, differential access to the sources of prestige—defined as the ability to command respect, honor, and deference—creates structural inequalities. Third, differential access to wealth, or economic and material resources, serves as a source of inequality. Those who have access to any of these resources— power, wealth, or prestige—occupy a position from which they are likely to achieve access to the others and thereby reinforce their status over those who have less. In the case of gender-stratified social systems, men's greater access to wealth, power, and prestige enhances their opportunities to exploit women and decreases women's ability to resist.

Institutions which express and enhance male dominance appear in a variety of forms. Economic and legal systems, political, educational, medical, religious, and familial institutions, public media, and the institutions of science and technology in male-dominated societies reinforce male dominance. How? Fundamentally, the control of these institutions usually rests in the hands of men, and social scientists understand that dominant groups tend to behave in ways that enhance their own power. Such institutions, therefore, engage in practices which discriminate against women, exclude women's perspectives, and perpetuate images of the "naturalness" of male dominance.

In addition, such institutions establish various kinds of rewards and punishments which encourage women to behave in submissive ways, and such behavior perpetuates the idea that women should submit. For example, a complex social system in the United States exerts strong pressures on women to marry heterosexually: families train daughters to be wives and mothers; high school events require opposite-sex dates; college fraternities and sororities promote heterosexual coupling; widespread violence against women encourages them, ironically, to seek male protection; and the combination of men's higher incomes and tax incentives for married couples means that heterosexual marriage tends to improve a woman's standard of living. A woman's failure to marry constitutes a violation of social prescriptions and often leaves women economically disadvantaged and socially suspect. On the other hand, despite women's increasing participation in the paid labor force, heterosexual marriage still usually allows the burden of domestic labor to fall disproportionately to women, a dynamic that helps maintain the inequality between men and women.

It is important to realize that gender stratification is not the only form of social inequality affecting women's lives. Social institutions that disadvantage particular races, older people, the physically disabled, the poor, or particular religious or class-based groups also discriminate against women who belong to those groups. Understanding women's oppression as a function of the social organization of gender necessitates understanding how the convergence of sexism and other forms of subordination by dominant groups works to disadvantage women in different positions in society.

In the following articles, we present various feminist theoretical explanations of the social organization of gender, as well as examinations of particular institutions involved in the processes of enforcing women's submission to male control.

Explanations of Gender Inequality

Scholars have struggled to explain why gender or sex-based stratification is so ubiquitous. Their explanations fall into two basic schools of thought: the biogenetic and the biocultural. The *biogenetic* argument holds that the behaviors of men and women are rooted in biological and genetic factors, including differences in hormonal patterns, physical size, aggressiveness, the propensity to "bond" with members of the same sex, and the capacity to rear children or to lead. Whether they view such differences as innate or as a natural outgrowth of human evolution, biogeneticists contend that sex-based inequality and the natural superiority of the male are inevitable, immutable, and necessary for the survival of the species. For the biogeneticist, the sexual division of labor in human societies is rooted in the sexual determination to be found in all species, from ants to deer to felines to primates.

The second school of thought, the *biocultural* approach, bases its position on a growing body of historical and anthropological research that points to wide variations in gender behavior and in the sexual division of labor among human societies throughout time. Bioculturalists contend that the diversity of cultural adaptations to biological differences in the sexes is so great that biological factors do not sufficiently explain universal male dominance. They argue that one of the reasons the superiority of males appears to be inevitable is that in societies of all types a cultural idea or belief has arisen to justify and perpetuate sex-based stratification systems that entitle men to greater power, prestige, and wealth than women. This ideology is known as *patriarchalism*. While patriarchy does not cause gender inequality, it certainly justifies it as natural.

Why patriarchalism arose in the first place is difficult to determine, but social scientists have long understood that it is common for groups to propagate beliefs that aggrandize themselves, and it is equally common for the subordinated group to accept the dominant group's definition as natural and inevitable. The important point is that ideas are culturally produced and, therefore, always subject to revision. If, however, we are to refute the inevitability of male dominance, we must understand the complex structures and social processes through which it is perpetuated. The biocultural perspective holds that it is within the context of universal social stratification, or institutionalized social inequality, that gender inequality occurs and can be understood.

In "A Theory of Gender Stratification," Joan Huber agrees that traditional stratification theories in the social sciences, by defining women as appendages to men, do not adequately address the question of gender inequality. Huber's evolutionary analysis emphasizes the effect that subsistence technology has had on the evolution of the division of labor between women and men. Three principles form the core of Huber's theory of gender stratification: (1) family members who produce goods enjoy more power and prestige than those who consume them, (2) women's tasks must be compatible with pregnancy and lactation if societies are to replace themselves, and (3) the people who control the distribution of valued resources outside the family have the greatest power and prestige.

The next two readings focus on gender stratification in particular social contexts. Evelyn Blackwood, in "Sexuality and Gender in Certain Native American Tribes: The Case of Cross-Gender Females," examines a subsistence-level economy with an egalitarian kinship system in which some women assumed the male role permanently and were allowed to marry other women. She demonstrates in a striking way the cultural bases of sex and gender and provides evidence that not all societies conceive of male and female gender as dictating invariably opposed roles.

"'The Status of Women' in Indigenous African Societies," by Niara Sudarkasa, demonstrates that although some precolonial societies assigned different roles to men and women, the status of those roles was not unequal. Sudarkasa examines the roles of women in precolonial African societies and concludes that gender was not a basis for inequality. Rather, the colonial experience was significant in the creation of hierarchical relations between the sexes.

Finally, in "Compulsory Heterosexuality and Lesbian Existence," Adrienne Rich argues that one of the primary means of perpetuating male dominance is what she conceptualizes as the social institution of heterosexuality. A significant contribution of this article is its power to force us to consider heterosexuality as a cultural ideology and social institution that proscribes and devalues all forms of female friendship and community as it perpetuates women's subordination to men.

A Theory of Gender Stratification

JOAN HUBER

In the long view of history, most theories of social stratification have been theological. The world was thus because God (or the gods) wanted it that way. In the words of a popular hymn,

> The rich man in his castle,
> The poor man at his gate,
> God made them high and lowly
> And ordered man's estate.

By the time that stanza was dropped from the hymn about all creatures great and small, God was being given less credit for stratal design than he used to be. Industrialization in Europe and North America during the nineteenth century had spawned grand theories about class differences in power and prestige. These theories came to permeate twentieth-century consciousness.

Gender differences in power and privilege, in contrast, were still taken for granted. Before 1970 the major theory of gender stratification was biological: sex differences in power and prestige stemmed from inborn characteristics. One was categorical: no man could bear or breastfeed a child. Other differences overlapped. Men tended to come in larger sizes with heavier muscles. Many mental differences also overlapped. The extent to which they were inborn or the result of experience was (and still is) unknown.

Industrialization reduced the functional importance of many sex differences. The importance of men's inability to breastfeed a child diminished after 1910, when techniques of sterilization enabled babies to survive on bottled milk. Women's lesser muscular strength mattered less as machines increasingly replaced human power. Today, for example, a man's

Reprinted by permission of Joan Huber.

brawn gives him little advantage in a white-collar job, the kind where brains count. Brawn still gives marginal advantage in such activities as shoveling heavy wet snow, but prudent men do not press it too hard. They tend to suffer vascular problems earlier than women do.

Industrialization also lessened the credibility of some alleged sex differences. Myths about women's mental weakness which justified their exclusion from positions of power were thwarted by the spread of compulsory education. It became harder to define women as less able than men when girls did as well as boys in school. In fact, they often did better. Ever since colleges admitted women, it has been hard to preserve a balanced sex ratio when the same admission standards are applied to both sexes. Historically, many colleges separated the applicant pools, reserving a larger quota for men. Some used the same yardstick but required higher scores for girls. In the 1960s, for example, the New York City Colleges required a grade average of 85 for men but 90 for women lest the system be swamped with women. Using the same yardstick for both sexes, North Carolina at Chapel Hill now has more women undergraduates than men, a development that has alarmed some of the trustees (Greene, 1987).

The need to replace biological theories of sex stratification became apparent around 1970 (Huber, 1986). A new wave of the women's movement threw into relief many anomalies that had surfaced in the wake of industrialization. Sex-role behaviors clearly followed no logical pattern based on biological differences. Even though men possessed the requisite skills, for example, they were much less likely than women to bottle-feed babies. Similarly, the hours that fully employed wives spent washing dishes and cleaning toilets stemmed from no demonstrable biological imperative. It dawned on scholars that gender stratification was a form of social stratification to which biology contributed but which biology alone could not explain.

In 1970, however, the data needed for a theory were hard to find in the relevant disciplines (Huber & Spitze, forthcoming). Anthropologists had long gathered data on foraging and hoe cultures, but most anthropologists, being men, had not been able to mix freely with native women going about their work. In consequence, the data about women's behavior and beliefs were sketchy. Moreover, interpretations tended to stem from the Western sex-role ideologies that male anthropologists carried in their heads as part of their intellectual equipment.

Historians had long studied the great men and great events of diplomatic history to the neglect of social history, the study of the daily lives of ordinary people. Since the historical record included few great queens and female warriors, women were nearly invisible.

Sociologists had analyzed women as wives and mothers in the study of the family or as prostitutes in the study of deviance. The literature on stratification defined women only as appendages to their husbands. A basic problem was that stratification theories, whether influenced by Karl Marx or Max Weber, defined social class as a market relationship. The household was a black box. Neither Marx nor Weber (nor, for that matter, Emile Durkheim) had conceptualized the household division of labor as part of the division of labor in society. In consequence, neither European nor American theories of society had much to contribute to a theory of gender stratification.

Nonetheless, the earliest social theories of gender stratification were the work of scholars who were influenced by Marx or Weber. The focus was primarily on occupations. Little attention was given to the long-term changes in fertility that had greatly altered women's life chances. The theories influenced by Marx were almost entirely the work of women scholars. They were the first to appear.

Marxism had been rather isolated from social science in the United States until the late 1960s, when some of the under-thirties crowd rediscovered an extensive literature. A common thread was the idea that the working class had been done in by the capitalists. Early Marxist feminists, invoking the concept of patriarchal capitalism, tried to show that working-class women had been done in even more thoroughly than working-class men. Over time, however, Marxist feminist thought divided into two identifiable streams.

One view implicitly or explicitly held that women are subordinated only in class societies; gender is simply an aspect of class stratification. The other held that sex was the original and basic class division. Marx was not incorrect but incomplete (Crompton, 1986). In point of fact, patriarchal socialism strongly resembles patriarchal capitalism. The position of women relative to men in the people's democracies of Eastern Europe seems remarkably akin to that in the Western democracies.

In the early 1970s the Weberian tradition in U.S. sociology was making its way through a new and quite different channel: measuring the effects of fathers' educational and occupational attainment on the attainment of their sons had come to dominate stratification research. When the models were extended to women in the mid-1970s, it was found that both sexes experienced similar rates of occupational mobility but, anomalously, women earned less. Later it was reported that the standard indicators of socioeconomic status do not tap the attributes of sex-typed occupations (Bose & Rossi, 1983). In sum, neither Marxist nor Weberian theories could adequately explain women's status in industrial societies. A basic problem was that neither theorist, understandably, had perceived the part that a dramatic decline in fertility would play in determining women's life chances. In consequence, the study of occupations was conceptualized as being quite apart from the study of fertility.

The interaction of occupations and fertility became more evident during the 1970s. New data appeared, a result of interest in the trends that had stimulated a massive expansion of the women's movement. Historical demography and sociology, social history, and anthropology greatly enriched knowledge about fertility and women's labor-force participation. One research stream culminated in the life-course perspective, a mix of history, social psychology, and demography that addressed events of the industrial period. Sophisticated analytic techniques and large longitudinal data sets enabled researchers to address previously unanswerable questions.

Another stream was influenced by comparative sociology—or social anthropology, which was separated artificially from sociology in those Western countries where preindustrial peoples were wiped out (e.g., native Americans) or incorporated much earlier (e.g., European peasants) (Goody, 1982:2). This stream includes the work of the anthropologists Ernestine

Friedl (1975) and Jack Goody (1976); the sociologists Gerhard Lenski (1970), Rae Lesser Blumberg (1978, 1984), and Janet Saltzman Chafetz (1984); the demographers Ron Lesthaeghe (1980) and John Caldwell (1980); and the economist Ester Boserup (1970).

The theory outlined below draws heavily on this second stream. It obviously needs to be fleshed out with more data. Its purpose is not to lay out a tidy set of answers but rather to suggest the potential of this research strategy.

Gender stratification is a subset of social stratification. A theory of stratification must begin with what men and women do each day to secure food, clothing, and shelter, analyzing how their work is organized around the tools available to do it. It must also consider the physical conditions that affect human ability to sustain life—climate, soil, temperature, and other ecological variables. This approach is not new. Although such factors are often overshadowed by the abiding fascination with personal interactions as prime movers in human affairs, from its very beginnings much sociological analysis has implicitly or explicitly stressed the importance of ecology and technology.*

This view of the importance of subsistence technology is not deterministic. A given technology only permits certain events to occur; it does not require that they occur. Nor can this approach claim to answer all the significant questions about the human condition. But it is a necessary first step. Analyses that focus primarily on thought, feeling, and belief can yield important knowledge but they are unlikely to provide much insight into the causes and effects of stratification systems, which are inextricably intertwined with material reality (Harris, 1979). Humankind does not live by bread alone, but without bread no one can live at all.

The most complete analysis of the anthropological literature showing the interaction of ecology, technology, and the organization of work is in Lenski's *Power and Privilege* (1966) and his macrosociology text (1970), indebted to Gordon Childe (1951) and Walter Goldschmidt (1959). The approach is called evolutionary because improvements in tool efficiency result in an increase in food supply.

The anthropologist Ernestine Friedl (1975) used an ecological approach to examine the effect of subsistence tools on gender stratification in hunting-and-

gathering and hoe cultures, thereby suggesting two principles of gender stratification. The following three principles represent a modification of her analysis. First, at the family level, the people who produce goods tend to have more power and prestige than those who consume them. It is better to be able to give than to have to receive.

But what determines who gets to do the most productive work in a given society? Men and women can perform a wide range of tasks, yet in all societies most tasks are allocated by sex. The answer stems from the fact that one sex cannot perform two tasks central to group survival: no man can bear or breastfeed a child. If societies are to survive, most women must bear and suckle children. This fact suggests a second principle: women's tasks must be compatible with pregnancy and lactation if the population is to be replaced.

The emphasis on population replacement makes my formulation differ somewhat from Friedl's (1975) and Blumberg's (1984) dictum that the work women do shapes the mode of child-rearing and not the other way round. Their view has merit in that it corrects for the tendency to assume that throughout human history child-rearing activities have comprised women's primary task, a common mistake in postwar American sociology. Also, it is probably true that the lower the level of living, the more women must perform certain tasks, no matter how these activities affect population replacement. It is not widely known, for example, that early in the nineteenth century the work that many French wives had to do in order to feed their families significantly increased infant mortality.

French cities had grown quickly because of rapid rural population increase, as Sussman (1982) has shown. But industrialization was slow, and the resulting high rents, low working-class incomes, and persistence of the household as the unit of production imposed more work on wives. Since safe methods of artificial infant feeding had not yet been invented, wet-nursing was widely adopted (hiring another woman to suckle one's child for pay). Working-class families followed the examples of the nobility, who for a century or more and for different reasons had put their children out to nurse. Early in the nineteenth century the majority of Lyonnais babies were sent out (Garden, 1975); only one Parisian baby in 30 was nursed by its own mother (Sussman, 1982:183). Even though the death rate was much higher among wetnursed babies than among babies nursed by their mothers, the cus-

*O. D. Duncan's (1964) statement remains the best description of this perspective in modern sociology.

tom ceased only when household production of textiles became unprofitable.

The third principle in my gender theory comes from general stratification theory: in any society the most power and prestige accrue to the people who control the distribution of valued goods beyond the family. In foraging societies, for example, these are the hunters; in plow societies, the warrior nobility; and in industrial societies, the top bureaucrats in the political, economic, and military arenas.

Together, these principles comprise a theory that can explain how ecological conditions and tool use interacted with childbearing and suckling to shape gender stratification in five of the most important of the ten basic types of societies that Lenski (1970) analyzed. The oldest type was based on hunting and gathering. Throughout most of our species' history, the entire human population lived in such societies. This period of relative technological uniformity ended only within the last 10,000 to 12,000 years (Lenski & Lenski, 1982:87). Hoe cultures first appeared in the Middle East about 9,000 years ago. Plow societies appeared about 5,000 years ago, with herding societies somewhere in between. The most modern type of society is based on industrial technology.

In hunting-and-gathering societies the tools consisted of wooden spears, rocks, and human hands. As such tools yielded a meager food supply, these groups were small, averaging about 50. The level of equality was high. Slim pickings flatten the distribution of power and privilege. Men hunted large animals. Women and children gathered nuts, berries, insects, and small animals. A woman could typically gather enough nuts and berries to feed only her immediate family. The hunters, in contrast, could distribute a large animal to the entire group. Men therefore tended to have more power and prestige than women did. Their dominance was greatest when hunting was almost the only source of food, as in Eskimo societies. Men and women were more equal when both sexes contributed to subsistence tasks (Friedl, 1975:32).

Polygyny was permitted in most of these societies but it was rare. Food was too scarce to enable a hunter to supply more than one set of affinal relatives. Divorce was fairly common, since it had little effect on the subsistence of either spouse or of the children. Premarital sexual relations were usually permitted.

Why didn't women hunt? They could readily master the necessary skills. Success in hunting depended far more on cooperation, patience, and dexterity than on brute strength. The functional requirements of hunting, however, conflicted with those of child-rearing. A hunt requires an uncertain number of days away from camp. To offset the wastage of a high death rate, women were pregnant or breastfeeding during most of their productive years. Children were breastfed to age 4 to increase the probability of their survival. A woman could not carry a suckling on a hunt nor could she readily return to camp to feed it. Thus the need for population replacement ultimately excluded women from the task that yielded the most power and prestige.

What induced a shift to plant cultivation as the basis for subsistence? Gerhard and Jean Lenski (1982:135) observe that until recently it was thought that the benefits of a more advanced technology were obvious to early peoples. New evidence, however, shows that between 22,000 and 7,000 years ago the number of large animals declined and human diet shifted. In North America, for example, 32 genera of large animals became extinct, including horses, giant bison, oxen, elephants, camels, and giant rodents. The pattern was similar in northern Europe, where the woolly mammoth, woolly rhinoceros, steppe bison, and giant elk vanished. People in these areas increasingly relied on fish, crabs, birds, snails, nuts, and wild grains and legumes. The shift may have resulted from the striking advances in weapons technology that began 20,000 years ago. The increase in kills of large animals led, in turn, to an increasing human population, which had a feedback effect on the big-game kills. In consequence (and perhaps in combination with a climate change), large mammals' reproductive rates could no longer match kill rates. One species after another was exterminated. The resulting food shortage induced peoples to opt for a more sedentary lifestyle wherever plants and animals could be domesticated. Despite the extra work, plant cultivation was attractive because it yielded so much more food per unit of land.

Simple hoe cultures appeared in the area where Eurasia abuts Africa about 9,000 years ago. The major tool, a wooden digging stick, did not dig deeply enough to raise soil nutrients or eradicate weeds. Consequently, groups had to move every few years to find fertile soil. Subsistence was supplemented by hunting, herding, or gathering in various combinations. Nonetheless, the digging stick produced enough surplus to enable these groups to number about 95 persons (Lenski & Lenski, 1982:91). The only such societies that remain today are on Pacific islands and in pockets of the New World.

Advanced hoe cultures appeared about 6,000 years ago, when the invention of metallurgy permitted the making of metal tools and weapons. Such societies appeared in North and South America (the Aztecs, Mayas, and Incas), Asia, and Europe. Today almost all remaining ones are in sub-Saharan Africa, where they are in transitional status (Robertson, 1984). Metal tools and weapons were so much more efficient than wooden ones that a greatly increased food surplus enabled these societies to be about 60 times larger than their predecessors.

Thus the introduction of the hoe, especially with a metal tip, marked the beginnings of modern social stratification. The hoe enabled people to settle in one place and thus to accumulate more goods. Dwellings became more substantial, settlements grew larger and more dense, and the creation of a stable economic surplus made occupational specialization common, which in turn increased the level of social inequality. Kinship systems, which represented social security, became extremely complex. Since the use of metal made weapons more effective, for the first time in human history war became a profitable alternative to technological innovation as a means of increasing a surplus.

For our purposes the most important aspect of hoe technology is that women on average produce about half of the food, giving them half the economic power (Blumberg, 1984:29). Care of a garden-size plot meshes readily with pregnancy and lactation. There is no simple division of labor, however, with men producing one kind of food and women another, and no universal pattern of women's producing one type of craft object and men another, except that routine domestic cooking tends to be women's work and metallurgy men's. Men monopolized land clearing in simple hoe cultures. In advanced hoe cultures they monopolized war (Friedl, 1975:53–60), thus gaining an advantage over women in the right to distribute valued goods beyond the family.

One would expect women's substantial contribution to food production to improve their status in relation to men. Indeed, the data show that the incidence of matrilineality (the tracing of descent in the mother's line) and matrilocality (newlyweds move in with her family) is greater in hoe cultures, although such practices occur only in a minority of them. Both practices improve women's status. The extent to which a woman

must operate as an initially powerless bride in her husband's extended kin household, isolated from support from her natal kin, tends to depress her status (Mason, 1984:72).

Women's contribution to food production also affects the divorce rate. In hoe cultures it tends to be high, higher on average than in the United States today. A high divorce rate is more common when the dissolution of a marriage does not interfere with the subsistence of either spouse or of their children.

Women's ability to feed their children also permits what I have elsewhere called populist polygyny (Huber & Spitze, forthcoming), as in sub-Saharan Africa. In this type of polygyny, nearly everyone marries. Such societies solve the sex-ratio problem by having women marry young and men marry when they are older. A postpartum taboo on sexual relations decreases child mortality by ensuring longer birth intervals. As an appropriation of female labor and sexual gratification by those who by virtue of age, sex, and descent form the ruling group, the system serves male gerontocratic control (Lesthaeghe, 1980:531). The need for women's productive work, however, ensures the wives a measure of freedom of movement.

Herding societies are found where mountains, low rainfall, or a short season makes agriculture impractical, as in Central Asia and the Middle East. The roles, norms, and ideologies of such societies have acquired importance because the Jewish, Christian, and Muslim religions originally developed in herding cultures; their beliefs and rules affect communities all over the world. The need for water and grazing rights made war an important means of acquiring a surplus and enabled elites to control economy and polity. Since warfare and herding both involve absence from home over long periods, they are incompatible with pregnancy and nursing. Women therefore lack access to the major tools of food production. These circumstances make it possible to practice elite polygyny—only rich men have plural wives (Huber & Spitze, forthcoming). In contrast to the sub-Saharan African women, the wives of elite polygynists tend to be secluded, free to interact only with other wives and children, as in much of the Arab world.

Plow societies are of special importance because they immediately preceded the industrial societies that developed in Europe and Asia. The laws, customs, and beliefs that have governed men's and women's behavior in all of the industrialized societies were therefore directly inherited from those of the plow kingdoms and empires of Eurasia.

The earliest plows were made of wood. After the invention of techniques to smelt iron, which was commonly available, the plow was equipped with an iron blade, which greatly increased its efficiency. The effect on the food supply was fantastic. The plow could dig much deeper than the hoe, bringing plant nutrients to the surface and killing weeds. It stimulated the domestication of draft animals. Confining oxen in stalls to prevent their wandering away in turn encouraged the collection of manure to fertilize fields, further increasing food production. Eurasian stratification patterns assumed the pyramidal form that characterized feudal societies: a tiny political and economic elite, artisans and craftworkers of lesser rank, and swarms of peasants, serfs, or slaves. The plow's effect on the status of ordinary people was devastating. The presence of a food surplus in the countryside coupled with the availability of iron weapons tempted elites to extract as much as possible from impoverished peasants. The flatter and richer the land, the worse off the common people, probably worse off than their hunting-and-gathering ancestors (Lenski & Lenski, 1978:206).

For two reasons the plow had an enormous effect on patterns of gender stratification. First, whenever it was introduced, men monopolized its use—as they do in Africa today (Boserup, 1970). Larger fields a substantial distance from home make it hard to arrange work to suit a nursing baby (Blumberg, 1978:50). Women therefore supplied a much lower proportion of food in plow than in hoe cultures (Giele & Smock, 1977).

The effect of the plow on women's status, however, went well beyond what was implied by women's reduced participation in food production. The basic reason was that the use of the plow required a particular kind of inheritance pattern, which in turn affected marriage and sexual behavior. Landownership became the basis for social stratification. The plow makes land the chief form of wealth because its use permits land to be used indefinitely and so increases its value. Hoe peoples, by contrast, had to move when the soil's fertility was exhausted.

Unlike gold and silver trinkets, cowrie beads, or money, land is an impartible inheritance. At a given level of technology a piece of land can support only a given number of persons. Therefore, the number of legal heirs must be controlled. The dominant form

of marriage must be monogamy because polygyny permits the uncontrolled proliferation of legal heirs. Divorce must become difficult or impossible because serial monogamy regulates the number of legal heirs less efficiently than does lifetime marriage. Women's premarital and marital sexual behavior must be governed by law and custom lest a man's property go to another man's child. Wealthy Eurasian men can in effect practice polygyny by keeping mistresses or concubines whose children have few or no inheritance rights. The concern with women's sexual purity derives from their status as transmitters of male property (Goody, 1976:97, 15). Friedrich Engels' insight about the effect of private property on women's status still rings true.

Severe constraints, such as footbinding and suttee, governed women's behavior in Asian plow kingdoms. Clitoridectomy occurs in Muslim countries of mixed plow and herding culture.*

The custom of binding a little girl's feet arose about a thousand years ago, during a period marked by change in the direction of controlling women's behavior. An emperor was said to have admired a dancer's feet. Loosely bound in linen cloths, they resembled those of a ballerina (Levy, 1966). The rationale for the custom was that the resulting hobbled gait so tightened the muscles in the genital region that sleeping with a woman with bound feet was like sleeping with a virgin. Western physicians report that no evidence supports such a belief. Whatever the rationale, women with bound feet certainly did little running around.

The mother applied the bindings when the little girl was three to five years old, depending on how small a foot was desired. The richer the girl's family, the less work she would have to do, and the smaller the foot could be. Rich women were so crippled that they could not walk at all. The pain resulted primarily from bending the four smaller toes underneath the foot, then successively tightening the bindings until the toes were broken and, finally, atrophied.

The custom was widespread in China (Gamble, 1943), especially in the colder and drier regions of the north, where wheat was the main crop. In the south, where rice, a much more labor-intensive crop, was the main staple, the entire family was needed to work in

---

*These discussions follow the accounts in Huber and Spitze (1983). Footbinding is also discussed at length in Andrea Dworkin's "Gynocide: Chinese Footbinding."

the paddies—work that girls and women with crippled feet could not do. Early in the industrial period, opposition to the custom increased. Footbinding was outlawed in 1911.

The Hindu custom of suttee requires a widow to be burned alive on her husband's funeral pyre. Some widows climbed up willingly. Others had to be tied down. The rationalization was that a widow, by sinning in a previous life, caused her husband to die first. Her death also gave the husband's male relatives undisputed influence over the children and precluded her lifetime rights in the estate. The incidence of suttee was low in comparison with that of footbinding, as only rich women were at risk.

Clitoridectomy, apparently widespread in Egypt, Yemen, Ethiopia, Somalia, Sudan, Kenya, and Muslim West Africa (Hosken, 1979; El Saadawi, 1982), shows the importance of protecting a daughter's reputation for chastity (Paige, 1982). It is often called female circumcision, but this is a euphemism because it is like slicing off the glans penis or the entire penis. The operation, extremely painful, is practiced on prepubertal girls. Its purpose is to prevent sexual pleasure so that women will find it easier to remain chaste. A popular belief holds that women by nature are so lascivious that chastity is inordinately difficult for them.

The operation takes three forms. In traditional circumcision the clitoral prepuce and tip of the clitoris are removed. In excision, the entire clitoris is removed. Infibulation involves removal of the clitoris, the labia minora, and part of the labia majora. The two sides of the vulva are partially sliced or scraped raw and then sewn together, so that the entrance to the vagina is closed except for a tiny posterior opening to allow urine and, later, menstrual blood to drain. Primary fatalities result from hemorrhage, shock, and septicemia. Long-term problems include urinary disturbance due to chronic infection and difficulties in coitus and childbirth.

So far as I know, European women during the plow era suffered no restraints that were so severe or that affected so many women. But if not, why not? Recent work of the anthropologist Jack Goody (1983) suggests that European women's greater freedom may have been an unplanned outcome of efforts by the Roman Catholic church to increase its wealth. The church sought to influence inheritance patterns by instituting controls on marriage and the legitimation of children. After A.D. 325 it established a series of measures that

reduced a person's supply of close relatives in an effort to persuade the pious to bequeath it their land. The church encouraged celibacy, prohibited close cousin marriage and adoption (both widespread in biblical and Roman times), condemned polygyny and divorce, and discouraged remarriage. The church also emphasized mutual consent as a requirement for valid marriage, which decreased the incidence of child marriage and also reduced the probability that a marriage would serve family interests. Furthermore, unlike Chinese or Indian women, European women could avoid marriage altogether by entering the cloister, a possibility that tended to increase their control over property.

Such measures arguably gave European women more freedom than Asian women for more than a millennium before the Industrial Revolution. In principle, this relative freedom should have made European women better able than Asian women to adapt to new circumstances and seize new opportunities. It would be ironic were historians one day to find that the spirit of capitalism in Europe was spurred less by the Protestant ethic than by a Catholic ethic that incidentally permitted women a modest measure of control over property.

Industrialization ended the plow era in Europe during the nineteenth century. The primary event was the invention of machines that made cheap cotton cloth. Rapid acceleration in the development of machines that replaced human labor stimulated a train of events that sharply altered the work men and women did. Over time, changes in behavior led to changes in beliefs.

Men's work behavior changed first. The factory system transformed erstwhile peasants, serfs, and slaves into urban wage workers, giving rise to a series of men's movements that voiced the claims of ordinary men for a fair share of a rapidly increasing surplus. These movements represented men's response to the changes that industrialization had wrought in the conditions of their lives. However, historians do not refer to these struggles as the men's movement. They write instead about the socialist and labor movements that swept nineteenth-century Europe, labels that tend to obscure the fact that women played little part in them. A mass movement that would represent women's occupational claims would appear only after women had entered the labor market in large numbers. They could not do so until three trends spawned by industrialization had irrevocably altered the conditions of their lives: the first two, a decrease in mortality and the attainment of widespread literacy, preceded the third, a decrease in fertility. The stage is set for a massive increase in the labor-force participation of married women only when these three trends are well under way.

Mortality, primarily of infants, declined in response to improved nutrition, reduced exposure to disease, and (in the twentieth century) medical measures (Collins, 1982). The mortality decline reduced the average number of births per woman needed to ensure population replacement. Then after 1910 the invention of sterilization techniques permitted safe bottle-feeding; for the first time in history artificially fed babies had the same survival probabilities as babies nursed by their mothers. Population replacement now poses few constraints on women's work.

Education was compulsory in most Western countries by 1880. As John Caldwell (1980) notes, education restructures family relations by redirecting generational wealth flows and thereby profoundly affects fertility. In preindustrial societies family wealth flowed from children to parents. Mass education redirects these flows by reducing the child's potential for employment outside the home. When children cannot earn, the cost of raising them is increased far beyond the fees that must be paid. Schools place indirect demands on families. The children's appearance must enable them to participate equally with others. Third, schooling speeds cultural change by propagating the values not of local families but of the Western middle classes. The main message of schooling is not spelled out in textbooks. It is assumed. Schools destroy the corporate identity of the family for those members previously the most submissive: children and women (Caldwell, 1980:241). Schooling causes parents to lose control over their children's labor (Lesthaeghe, 1980).

The fertility decline was triggered by the mortality decline, the spread of mass education, and rapid economic growth. A rapid increase in real income—it doubled in the West between 1860 and 1910—fuels individual aspirations and opens up new opportunities, creating an impression of lowered economic vulnerability. This self-confidence in turn allows individuals to be more independent. The net outcome is an alteration in preference maps. Since the new maps require legitimation, periods of economic growth also generate various emancipation movements (Lesthaeghe, 1983:430).

Fertility declined from more than seven to fewer than three children with the use of methods that re-

quired considerable, self-discipline and courage: abstinence, withdrawal, and abortion, which has been a major means of birth control in nearly all industrializing societies until women learn other means of fertility control (Mohr, 1978). The decline also occurred despite massive opposition from church and state. When people are motivated to reduce fertility, they find ways of doing so.

From early in the industrial period women had worked for pay, but the typical worker was either young and unmarried or poor. Young women who expect to be briefly employed are unlikely to be aware of discrimination. Moreover, young women and poor women lack political clout. What matters politically is the participation of educated women who expect to remain in the work force. Such women entered the labor force in ever larger numbers after 1950 in response to strong demand for female labor (Blau & Ferber, 1986), and their rates of participation are still rising (Mott, 1982). Although most women work in heavily feminized occupations (Rytina & Bianchi, 1984), the wage gap is beginning to close. A generation ago most highly educated men were employed and most of their female counterparts were housewives. This pattern is reversing. The higher a woman's level of education, the more likely she is to be employed. From now to the end of the century young women's wage rates are expected to rise about 15 percent faster than young men's (Smith & Ward, 1984).

In sum, these trends have irrevocably altered the social stratification systems of plow societies. Declines in mortality and fertility have reduced the proportion of time the average woman spends in pregnancy or breastfeeding. Increases in educational levels and employment rates have enabled women to provide a sizable share of family income. These trends increased the centrality of individual goal attainment in the Western ideational system (Lesthaeghe, 1983:429). The ideology of equal opportunity which pervades all modern societies finally applies to women too.

Still in question is the extent to which women will hold a fair share of top positions, those whose incumbents control the distribution of valued goods. The outcome will hinge on the division of household labor. Housework is to gender stratification as market work is to class stratification. Women cannot become men's social equals until the most talented women can aspire as realistically as their male counterparts to contribute in proportion to their talents.

To date, the household division of labor has changed little, but I predict substantial change on the basis of American beliefs about fairness. A generation or two ago husbands did not want their wives to be employed, hence wives' household obligations seemed fair. Today men like their wives to work for pay. This change gives wives leverage for a little friendly persuasion.

Incentives to share housework should be strongest for highly paid doctors, lawyers, and merchant chiefs who are married to highly paid doctors, lawyers, and merchant chiefs. People who think great thoughts and push paper all day need the healthful relaxation that comes from scrubbing kitchen floors, cleaning up after the dog, and preparing meals that contain all four essential nutrients. Housework may even improve mental health. Ross and colleagues (1983) report that the more spouses share housework, the lower their depression scores. Housework may even account for women's longevity: its varied physical activities lower cholesterol, keep the arteries free of crud, and increase cardiac output. If housework be the perfect form of exercise, surely equity requires that it be equally shared.

REFERENCES

Blau, F., & Ferber, M. 1986. *The economics of women, men, and work.* Englewood Cliffs, N.J.: Prentice-Hall.

Blumberg, R. L. 1978. *Stratification: Socioeconomic and sexual inequality.* Dubuque: William C. Brown.

Blumberg, R. L. 1984. "A general theory of gender stratification." In R. Collins, ed., *Sociological theory.* San Francisco: Jossey-Bass.

Bose, C., & Rossi, P. 1983. "Gender and jobs: Prestige standings of occupations and gender." *American Journal of Sociology* 48:316–330.

Boserup, E. 1970. *Women's role in economic development.* London: George Allen & Unwin.

Caldwell, J. 1980. "Mass education as a determinant of fertility decline timing." *Population and Development Review* 6:225–256.

Chafetz, J. S. 1984. *Sex and advantage.* Towtowa, N.J.: Rowman & Allenheld.

Childe, G. 1951. *Man makes himself.* New York: Mentor.

Collins, J. 1982. "The contribution of modern medicine to mortality decline." *Demography* 19:409–427.

Crompton, R. 1986. "Women and the 'service class.'" In R. Crompton and M. Mann, eds., *Gender stratification.* Oxford: Polity Press.

Duncan, O. D. 1964. "Social organization and the ecosystem." In R. E. L. Faris, ed., *Handbook of modern sociology.* Chicago: Rand McNally.

El Saadawi, N. 1982. *The hidden face of Eve.* Boston: Beacon Press.

Friedl, E. 1975. *Women and men: An anthropologist's view.* New York: Holt, Rinehart & Winston.

Gamble, S. 1943. "The disappearance of footbinding in Tinghsien." *American Journal of Sociology* 49:181–183.

Garden, M. 1975. *Lyon et les lyonnais au XVIIIe siècle.* Paris: Flammarion.

Giele, J. Z., & Smock, A. C. 1977. *Women: Roles and status in eight countries.* New York: Wiley.

Goldschmidt, W. 1959. *Man's way.* New York: Holt.

Goody, J. 1976. *Production and reproduction.* Cambridge: Cambridge University Press.

Goody, J. 1982. *Cooking, cuisine, and class.* Cambridge: Cambridge University Press.

Goody, J. 1983. *The development of family and marriage in Europe.* Cambridge: Cambridge University Press.

Greene, E. 1987. "Too many women?" *Chronicle of Higher Education* 28 (January 28, 1987):27–28.

Harris, M. 1979. *Cultural materialism.* New York: Random House.

Hosken, F. 1979. *The Hosken report.* Lexington, Mass.: Women's Network News.

Huber, J. 1986. "Trends in gender stratification, 1970–1985." *Sociological Forum* 1:476–495.

Huber, J., & Spitze, G. 1983. *Sex stratification.* New York: Academic Press.

Huber, J., & Spitze, G. Forthcoming. "Family sociology." In N. Smelser & R. Burt, eds., *The revised handbook of sociology.* Beverly Hills: Sage.

Lenski, G. 1966. *Power and privilege.* New York: McGraw-Hill.

Lenski, G. 1970. *Human societies.* New York: McGraw-Hill.

Lenski, G., & Lenski, J. 1978. *Human societies,* 3rd ed. New York: McGraw-Hill.

Lesthaeghe, R. 1980. "On the social control of reproduction." *Population and Development Review* 6:527–548.

Lesthaeghe, R. 1983. "A century of demographic and cultural change in Western Europe." *Population and Development Review* 9:411–435.

Levi, H. 1966. *Chinese footbinding.* New York: Walton Rawls.

Mason, K. 1984. *The status of women: A review of its relation-*

ships to fertility and mortality. New York: Rockefeller Foundation.

Mohr, J. 1978. *Abortion in America.* New York: Oxford University Press.

Mott, F. 1982. *The employment revolution.* Cambridge: MIT Press.

Paige, K. 1982. "Patterns of excision and excision rationale in Egypt." Mimeo. University of California at Davis.

Robertson, C. 1984. *Sharing the same bowl: A history of women and class in Accra, Ghana.* Bloomington: Indiana University Press.

Ross, C., Mirowsky, J., & Huber, J. 1983. "Marriage patterns and depression." *American Sociological Review* 48:809–823.

Rytina, N., & Bianchi, S. 1984. "Occupational reclassification and changes in distribution by gender." *Monthly Labor Review* 107:11–17.

Smith, J., & Ward, M. 1984. *Women's wages and work in the twentieth century.* Santa Monica: Rand Corporation.

Sussman, G. 1982. *Selling mothers' milk: The wet-nursing business in France 1715–1914.* Urbana: University of Illinois Press.

R E A D I N G   1 6

Sexuality and Gender in Certain Native American Tribes: The Case of Cross-Gender Females

EVELYN BLACKWOOD

Ideological concepts of gender and sexuality arise from cultural constructions and vary from culture to culture. The female cross-gender role in certain Native American tribes constituted an opportunity for women to assume the male role permanently and to marry women. Its existence challenges Western assumptions about gender roles. Some feminist anthropologists assume that it is in the nature of sex and gender systems to create asymmetry in the form of male dominance and female subservience and to enforce corresponding forms of sexual behavior.[1] Because kinship and marriage are closely tied to gender systems, these social structures are implicated in the subordination of women. The existence of the female cross-gender role, however, points to the inadequacies of such a view and helps to clarify the nature of sex and gender systems.

This study closely examines the female cross-gender

role as it existed historically in several Native American tribes, primarily in western North America and the Plains. It focuses on western tribes that shared a basically egalitarian mode of production in precolonial times,[2] and for which sufficient data on the female role exist. Although there were cultural differences among these groups, prior to the colonial period they all had subsistence-level economies that had not developed significant forms of wealth or rank. These tribes include the Kaska of the Yukon Territory, the Klamath of southern Oregon, and the Mohave, Maricopa, and Cocopa of the Colorado River area in the Southwest. The Plains tribes, by contrast, are noteworthy for the relative absence of the female cross-gender role. Conditions affecting the tribes of the Plains varied from those of the western tribes, and thus analysis of historical-cultural contexts will serve to illuminate the differing constraints on sex and gender systems in these two areas.

Ethnographic literature has perpetuated some misconceptions about the cross-gender role. Informants frequently describe the institution in negative terms,

Reprinted from *Signs: Journal of Women in Culture and Society* 10, no. 1 (1984): 27–42. Copyright © 1984 by The University of Chicago. All rights reserved. Some footnotes have been renumbered.

stating that berdache were despised and ridiculed.[3] But ethnographers collected much of the data in this century; it is based on informants' memories of the mid- to late 1800s. During this period the cross-gender institution was disappearing rapidly. Thus, twentieth-century informants do not accurately represent the institution in the precontact period. Alfred Kroeber found that "while the [berdache] institution was in full bloom, the Caucasian attitude was one of repugnance and condemnation. This attitude . . . made subsequent personality inquiry difficult, the later berdache leading repressed or disguised lives."[4] Informants' statements to later ethnographers or hostile white officials were far different from the actual attitude toward the role that prevailed in the precolonial period. An analysis of the cross-gender role in its proper historical context brings to light the integral nature of its relationship to the larger community.

CULTURAL SIGNIFICANCE OF THE FEMALE CROSS-GENDER ROLE

Most anthropological work on the cross-gender role has focused on the male berdache, with little recognition given to the female cross-gender role. Part of the problem has been the much smaller data base available for a study of the female role. Yet anthropologists have overlooked even the available data. This oversight has led to the current misconception that the cross-gender role was not feasible for women. Harriet Whitehead, in a comprehensive article on the berdache, states that, given the small number of cross-gender females, "the gender-crossed status was more fully instituted for males than for females."[5] Charles Callender and Lee Kochems, in a well-researched article, base their analysis of the role predominantly on the male berdache.[6] Evidence from thirty-three Native American tribes indicates that the cross-gender role for women was as viable an institution as was the male berdache role.[7]

The Native American cross-gender role confounded Western concepts of gender. Cross-gender individuals typically acted, sat, dressed, talked like, and did the work of the other sex. Early Western observers described the berdache as half male and half female, but such a description attests only to their inability to accept a male in a female role or vice versa. In the great majority of reported cases of berdache, they assumed the social role of the other sex, not of both

sexes.[8] Contemporary theorists, such as Callender and Kochems and Whitehead, resist the idea of a complete social role reclassification because they equate gender with biological sex. Native gender categories contradict such definitions.

Although the details of the cross-gender females' lives are scant in the ethnographic literature, a basic pattern emerges from the data on the western tribes. Recognition and cultural validation of the female cross-gender role varied slightly from tribe to tribe, although the social role was the same. Among the Southwestern tribes, dream experience was an important ritual aspect of life and provided success, leadership, and special skills for those who sought it. All cross-gender individuals in these tribes dreamed about their role change. The Mohave *hwame* dreamed of becoming cross-gender while still in the womb.[9] The Maricopa *kwiraxame* dreamed too much as a child and so changed her sex.[10] No information is available for the development of the female cross-gender role *(tw!nnaek)* among the Klamath. It was most likely similar to the male adolescent transformative experience, which was accomplished through fasting or diving.[11] Dreaming provided an avenue to special powers and also provided sanction for the use of those powers. In the same way, dreams about the cross-gender role provided impetus and community sanction for assumption of the role.

The female candidate for cross-gender status displayed an interest in the male role during childhood. A girl avoided learning female tasks. Instead, as in the case of the Cocopa *warrhameh,* she played with boys and made bows and arrows with which to hunt birds and rabbits.[12] The Mohave *hwame* "[threw] away their dolls and metates, and [refused] to shred bark or perform other feminine tasks."[13] Adults, acknowledging the interests of such girls, taught them the same skills the boys learned. Among the Kaska, a family that had all female children and desired a son to hunt for them would select a daughter (probably the one who showed the most inclination) to be "like a man." When she was five, the parents tied the dried ovaries of a bear to her belt to wear for life as protection against conception.[14] Though in different tribes the socializing processes varied, girls achieved the cross-gender role in each instance through accepted cultural channels.

Upon reaching puberty, the time when girls were considered ready for marriage, the cross-gender female was unable to fulfill her obligations and duties as a woman in marriage, having learned the tasks assigned to men. Nonmarriageable status could have presented a disadvantage both to herself and to her kin, who would be called upon to support her in her later years. But a role transfer allowed her to enter the marriage market for a wife with whom she could establish a household. The Mohave publicly acknowledged the new status of the woman by performing an initiation ceremony. Following this ceremony she assumed a name befitting a person of the male sex and was given marriage rights.[15] At puberty, the Cocopa *warrhameh* dressed her hair in the male style and had her nose pierced like the men, instead of receiving a chin tattoo like other women.[16] These public rites validated the cross-gender identity, signifying to the community that the woman was to be treated as a man.

In adult life cross-gender females performed the duties of the male gender role. Their tasks included hunting, trapping, cultivating crops, and fighting in battles. For example, the Cocopa *warrhameh* established households like men and fought in battle.[17] The Kaska cross-gender female "dressed in masculine attire, did male allocated tasks, often developing great strength and usually becoming an outstanding hunter."[18] The Mohave *hwame* were known as excellent providers, hunting for meat, working in the fields, and caring for the children of their wives.[19] Cross-gender females also adhered to male ritual obligations. A Klamath *tw!nnaek* observed the usual mourning when her long-time female partner died, wearing a bark belt as did a man.[20] Mohave *hwame* were said to be powerful shamans, in this case especially good at curing venereal disease.[21] Many other cross-gender females were considered powerful spiritually, but most were not shamans, even in the Southwest. Cross-gender females did not bear children once they took up the male role. Their kin considered them nonreproductive and accepted the loss of their childbearing potential, placing a woman's individual interests and abilities above her value as a reproducer.[22]

In most cases ethnographers do not discuss the ability of cross-gender females to maintain the fiction of their maleness. Whitehead suggests that women were barred from crossing over unless they were, or at least pretended to be, deficient physically.[23] However, despite some reports that cross-gender women in the Southwest had muscular builds, undeveloped secondary sexual characteristics, and sporadic or absent menstruation,[24] convincing physical evidence is noticeably lacking. In fact, the Mohave *hwame* kept a hus-

band's taboos with regard to her menstruating or pregnant wife and ignored her own menses.[25] That such may have been the case in other tribes as well is borne out by the practice of the Ingalik cross-gender female. Among the Alaskan Ingalik, the *kashim* was the center of men's activities and the place for male-only sweat baths. The cross-gender female participated in the activities of the *kashim,* and the men were said not to perceive her true sex.[26] Cornelius Osgood suggests that she was able to hide her sex, but, as with the Mohave, the people probably ignored her physical sex in favor of her chosen role. Through this social fiction, then, cross-gender females dismissed the physiological functions of women and claimed an identity based on their performance of a social role.

GENDER EQUALITY

Women's ability to assume the cross-gender role arose from the particular conditions of kinship and gender in these tribes. The egalitarian relations of the sexes were predicated on the cooperation of autonomous individuals who had control of their productive activities. In these tribes women owned and distributed the articles they produced, and they had equal voice in matters affecting kin and community. Economic strategies depended on collective activity. Lineages or individuals had no formal authority; the whole group made decisions by consensus. People of both sexes could achieve positions of leadership through skill, wisdom, and spiritual power. Ultimately, neither women nor men had an inferior role but rather had power in those spheres of activity specific to their sex.[27]

Among these tribes, gender roles involved the performance of a particular set of duties. Most occupations necessary to the functioning of the group were defined as either male or female tasks. A typical division of labor allocated responsibilities for gathering, food preparation, child rearing, basket weaving, and making clothes to women, while men hunted, made weapons, and built canoes and houses. The allocation of separate tasks to each sex established a system of reciprocity that assured the interdependence of the sexes. Because neither set of tasks was valued more highly than the other, neither sex predominated.

Gender-assigned tasks overlapped considerably among these people. Many individuals engaged in activities that were also performed by the other sex without incurring disfavor. The small game and fish that Kaska and Klamath women hunted on a regular basis were an important contribution to the survival of the band. Some Klamath women made canoes, usually a man's task, and older men helped women with food preparation.[28] In the Colorado River area, both men and women collected tule pollen.[29] Engaging in such activities did not make a woman masculine or a man feminine because, although distinct spheres of male and female production existed, a wide range of tasks was acceptable for both sexes. Because there was no need to maintain gender inequalities, notions of power and prestige did not circumscribe the roles. Without strict gender definitions, it was then possible for some Native American women to take up the male role permanently without threatening the gender system.

Another factor in creating the possibility of the cross-gender role for women was the nature of the kinship system. Kinship was not based on hierarchical relations between men and women; it was organized in the interest of both sexes. Each sex had something to gain by forming kin ties through marriage,[30] because of the mutual assistance and economic security marital relations provided.[31] Marriage also created an alliance between two families, thereby broadening the network of kin on whom an individual could rely. Thus, marriage promoted security in a subsistence-level economy.

The marriage customs of these tribes reflected the egalitarian nature of their kinship system. Since status and property were unimportant, marriage arrangements did not involve any transfer of wealth or rank through the female. The small marriage gifts that were exchanged served as tokens of the woman's worth in the marriage relationship.[32] Furthermore, because of the unimportance of property or rank, individuals often had a series of marriages, rather than one permanent relationship; divorce was relatively easy and frequent for both women and men.[33] Marriages in these tribes became more permanent only when couples had children. Women were not forced to remain in a marriage, and either partner had the right to dissolve an unhappy or unproductive relationship.

This egalitarian kinship system had important ramifications for the cross-gender female. A daughter's marriage was not essential for maintenance of family rank; that is, a woman's family did not lose wealth if she abandoned her role as daughter. As a social male, she had marriage rights through which she could establish a household and contribute to the subsistence of the group. Additionally, because of the frequency of

divorce, it was possible for a married cross-gender female to raise children. Evidence of cross-gender females caring for their wives' offspring is available only for the Mohave *hwame*. Women in other tribes, however, could also have brought children into a cross-gender marriage, since at least younger offspring typically went with the mother in a divorce.[34] A cross-gender woman might acquire children through marriage to a pregnant woman, or possibly through her wife's extramarital relationships with men. Cross-gender couples probably also adopted children, a practice common among heterosexual couples in many tribes.

Details from the Mohave help to illuminate the cross-gender parent/child relationship. The Mohave believed that the paternity of an unborn child changed if the pregnant woman had sex with another partner; thus, the cross-gender female claimed any child her wife might be carrying when they married. George Devereux states that such children retained the clan affiliation of the previous father.[35] But the clan structure of the Mohave was not strongly organized and possessed no formal authority or ceremonial functions.[36] The significant relationships were those developed through residence with kin. Thus, children raised in a cross-gender household established strong ties with those parents. The investment of parental care was reciprocated when these children became adults. In this way the cross-gender female remained a part of the network of kin through marriage.

SEXUAL RELATIONS IN THE CROSS-GENDER ROLE

Sexual behavior was part of the relationship between cross-gender females and the women they married. Although the cross-gender female was a social male, Native Americans did not consider her sexual activity an imitation of heterosexual behavior. Her sexual behavior was recognized as lesbian—that is, as female homosexuality. The Mohave were aware of a range of sexual activities between the cross-gender female and her partner—activities that were possible only between two physiological females. Devereux recorded a Mohave term that referred specifically to the lesbian love-making of the *hwame* and her partner.[37] The Native American acceptance of lesbian behavior among cross-gender females did not depend on the presence of a male role-playing person; their acceptance derived instead from their concept of sexuality.

Native American beliefs about sexuality are reflected in the marriage system. Theorists such as Gayle Rubin have implicated marriage as one of the mechanisms that enforce and define women's sexuality. According to Rubin, the division of labor "can . . . be seen as a taboo against sexual arrangements other than those containing at least one man and one woman, thereby enjoining heterosexual marriage."[38] Yet in certain Native American tribes other sexual behavior, both heterosexual and homosexual, was available and permissible within and outside of marriage. Homosexual behavior occurred in contexts within which neither individual was cross-gender, nor were such individuals seen as expressing cross-gender behavior.[39] Premarital and extramarital sexual relations were also permissible.[40] Furthermore, through the cross-gender role, women could marry one another. Sexuality clearly was not restricted by the institution of marriage.

Native American ideology disassociated sexual behavior from concepts of male and female gender roles and was not concerned with the identity of the sexual partner. The status of the cross-gender female's partner is telling in this respect. She was always a traditional female; that is, two cross-gender females did not marry. Thus, a woman could follow the traditional female gender role, yet marry and make love with another woman without being stigmatized by such behavior. Even though she was the partner of a cross-gender female, she was not considered homosexual or cross-gender. If the relationship ended in divorce, heterosexual marriage was still an option for the ex-wife. The traditional female gender role did not restrict her choice of marital/sexual partners. Consequently, individuals possessed a gender identity, but not a corresponding sexual identity, and thus were allowed several sexual options. Sexuality itself was not embedded in Native American gender ideology.

WOMEN ON THE PLAINS

The conditions that supported the development and continuation of the cross-gender role among certain western tribes were not replicated among the Plains tribes. Evidence of cross-gender females there is scant while reports of male berdache are numerous. Whitehead suggests that the absence of cross-gender females resulted from the weakness of the cross-gender institution for women.[41] A more plausible explanation

involves the particular historical conditions that differentiate the Plains tribes from the western tribes. Yet it is precisely these conditions that make accurate interpretation of women's roles and the female cross-gender role much more difficult for the Plains tribes.

The Plains Indian culture of nomadic buffalo hunting and frequent warfare did not develop until the late eighteenth and early nineteenth centuries as tribes moved west in response to the expansion and development of colonial America. The new mode of life represented for many tribes a tremendous shift from an originally settled and horticultural or hunting and gathering life-style. With the introduction of the horse and gun, the growth of the fur trade, and pressure from westward-moving white settlers, tribes from the east and north were displaced onto the Plains in the late 1700s.[42] As the importance of hide trade with Euro-Americans increased in the early 1800s, it altered the mode of production among Plains tribes. Increased wealth and authority were accessible through trade and warfare. Individual males were able to achieve greater dominance while women's social and economic autonomy declined.[43] With the growing importance of hides for trade, men who were successful hunters required additional wives to handle the tanning. Women's increasing loss of control in this productive sphere downgraded their status and tied them to marital demands. Recent work on the Plains tribes, however, indicates that this process was not consistent; women maintained a degree of autonomy and power not previously acknowledged.[44]

Early ethnographic descriptions of Plains Indian women were based on a Western gender ideology that was contradicted by actual female behavior. Although traditional Plains culture valued quiet, productive, nonpromiscuous women, this was only one side of the coin. There was actually a variability in female roles that can only be attributed to women's continued autonomy. Beatrice Medicine provides an excellent discussion of the various roles open to women among the Blackfoot and Lakota. Such roles included the "manly-hearted woman," the "crazy woman" (who was sexually promiscuous), the Sun Dance woman, and the chief woman or favorite wife.[45] According to Ruth Landes, Lakota women served in tribal government and were sometimes appointed marshals to handle problems among women. Most Plains tribes had women warriors who accompanied war parties for limited purposes on certain occasions, such as avenging the death of kin, and who received warrior honors for their deeds.[46] As Medicine states, "These varied role categories . . . suggest that the idealized behavior of women was not as rigidly defined and followed as has been supposed."[47]

The presence of a variety of socially approved roles also suggests that these were normative patterns of behavior for women that need not be construed as "contrary" to their gender role. Warrior women were not a counterpart of the male berdache, nor were they considered cross-gender.[48] Ethnographers' attributions of masculinity to such behavior seem to be a product of Western beliefs about the rigid dichotomization of gender roles and the nature of suitable pursuits for women. That men simply accepted females as warriors and were not threatened by such behavior contradicts the notion that such women were even temporarily assuming the male role.[49] The men's acceptance was based on recognition of the women warriors' capabilities as women.

There were individual Plains women in the nineteenth century whose behavior throughout their lives exemplified a cross-gender role. They did not always cross-dress, but, like Woman Chief of the Crow, neither did they participate in female activities. They took wives to handle their households and were highly successful in hunting and raiding activities. They were also considered very powerful. Of these women, the Kutenai cross-gender woman always dressed in male attire and was renowned for her exploits as warrior and mediator and guide for white traders. Running Eagle of the Blackfoot lived as a warrior and married a young widow. Woman Chief became the head of her father's lodge when he died and achieved the third highest rank among the Crow. She took four wives.[50] Particularly since no records of earlier cross-gender women have been found, these few examples seem to constitute individual exceptions. What then was the status of the female cross-gender role among Plains tribes?

Part of the difficulty with answering this question stems from the nature of the data itself. Nineteenth-century observers rarely recorded information on Plains Indian women, "considering them too insignificant to merit special treatment."[51] These observers knew few women and only the more successful males. "Those who did become known were women who had acted as go-betweens for the whites and Indians,"[52] such as the Kutenai cross-gender female. Running Eagle and Woman Chief were also exceptional enough to be noticed by white traders. Except for the Kutenai

woman, none of the women are identified as berdache in nineteenth-century reports, although all were cross-gender. Observers seem to have been unable to recognize the female cross-gender role. Indeed, no nineteenth-century reports mention cross-gender females among even the western tribes, although later ethnographers found ample evidence of the role.

Ethnographers had no solid evidence of the female cross-gender role among Plains Indians. Several factors may help to explain this discrepancy. White contact with Plains tribes came earlier than with the western tribes and was more disruptive. The last cross-gender females seem to have disappeared among Plains tribes by the mid-nineteenth century, while in the Southwest this did not occur until the end of the century, much closer to the time when ethnographers began to collect data. Discrepancies also arise in informants' stories. The Kutenai denied the existence of cross-gender females among them, in contradiction with earlier evidence, and yet willingly claimed that such women lived among the Flathead and Blackfoot.[53] The Arapaho told Alfred Kroeber that the Lakota had female berdache, but there is no corroborating evidence from the Lakota themselves.[54] Informants were clearly reticent or unwilling to discuss cross-gender women. In her article on Native American lesbians, Paula Gunn Allen suggests that such information was suppressed by the elders of the tribes.[55] Most information on Plains Indian women was transmitted from elder tribesmen to white male ethnographers. But men were excluded from knowledge of much of women's behavior;[56] in this way much of the data on cross-gender females may have been lost.

The record of Plains cross-gender females remains limited. Certain social conditions may have contributed to the small number of women who assumed the role in the nineteenth century. During the 1800s the practice of taking additional wives increased with the men's need for female labor. This phenomenon may have limited women's choice of occupation. The pressures to marry may have barred women from a role that required success in male tasks only. The practice of sororal polygyny particularly would have put subtle pressures on families to assure that each daughter learned the traditional female role. Indeed, there were said to be no unmarried women among the Lakota.[57] Furthermore, given the constant state of warfare and loss of able-bodied men, the tribes were under pressure merely to survive. Such conditions in the 1800s discouraged women from abandoning their reproductive abilities through the cross-gender role. In fact, among the Lakota, women who insisted on leading men's lives were ostracized from the group and forced to wander by themselves.[58] Knowledge of the female cross-gender role may have persisted, but those few who actually lived out the role were exceptions in a changing environment.

THE DEMISE OF THE CROSS-GENDER ROLE

By the late nineteenth century the female cross-gender role had all but disappeared among Native Americans. Its final demise was related to a change in the construction of sexuality and gender in these tribes. The dominant ideology of Western culture, with its belief in the inferior nature of the female role and its insistence on heterosexuality, began to replace traditional Native American gender systems.

Ideological pressures of white culture encouraged Native American peoples to reject the validity of the cross-gender role and to invoke notions of "proper" sexuality that supported men's possession of sexual rights to women. Communities expressed disapproval by berating the cross-gender female for not being a "real man" and not being properly equipped to satisfy her wife sexually. In effect, variations in sexual behavior that had previously been acceptable were now repudiated in favor of heterosexual practices. Furthermore, the identity of the sexual partner became an important aspect of sexual behavior.

The life of the last cross-gender female among the Mohave, Sahaykwisa, provides a clear example of this process. According to Devereux, "Sahaykwisa . . . was born toward the middle of the last century and killed . . . at the age of 45. Sahaykwisa had at a certain time a very pretty wife. Other men desired the woman and tried to lure her away from the *hwame.*" The men teased Sahaykwisa in a derogatory manner, suggesting that her love-making was unsatisfactory to her wife in comparison to that of a "real man." They ridiculed her wife and said, "Why do you want a transvestite for your husband who has no penis and pokes you with the finger?"[59] Such derision went beyond usual joking behavior until finally Sahaykwisa was raped by a man who was angered because his wife left him for Sahaykwisa. The community no longer validated the cross-gender role, and Sahaykwisa herself eventually abandoned it, only to be killed later as a witch. By accusing the cross-gender female of sexual inadequacy, men of the tribe claimed in effect that they had sole rights to women's sexuality, and that sexuality was appropriate only between men and women.

CONCLUSION

In attempting to fit the Native American cross-gender role into Western categories, anthropologists have disregarded the ways in which the institution represents native categories of behavior. Western interpretations dichotomize the two sexes' gender roles because of erroneous assumptions about, first, the connection between biology and gender and, second, the nature of gender roles. Callender and Kochems state, "The transformation of a berdache was not a complete shift from his or her *biological* gender to the opposite one, but rather an approximation of the latter in some of its social aspects.[60] They imply that anatomy circumscribed the berdache's ability to function in the gender role of the other sex. Whitehead finds the anatomical factor particularly telling for women, who were supposedly unable to succeed in the male role unless deficient physically as females.[61] These theorists, by claiming a mixed gender status for the berdache, confuse a social role with a physical identity that remained unchanged for the cross-gender individual.

Knowing the true sex of the berdache, Native Americans accepted them on the basis of their social attributes; physiological sex was not relevant to the gender role. The Mohave, for example, did not focus on the biological sex of the berdache. Nonberdache were said to "feel toward their possible transvestite mate as they would feel toward a true woman, [or] man."[62] In response to a newly initiated berdache, the Yuma "began to feel toward him as to a woman."[63] These tribes concurred in the social fiction of the cross-gender role despite the obvious physical differences, indicating the unimportance of biological sex to the gender role.[64]

Assumptions regarding the hierarchical nature of Native American gender relations have created serious problems in the analysis of the female cross-gender role. Whitehead claims that few females could have been cross-gender because she assumes the asymmetrical nature of gender relations.[65] In cultures with an egalitarian mode of production, however, gender does not create an imbalance between the sexes. In the western North American tribes discussed above, neither gender role nor sexuality was associated with an ideology of male dominance. Women were not barred from the cross-gender role by rigid gender definitions; instead, they filled the role successfully. Although cross-gender roles are not limited to egalitarian societies, the historical conditions of nonegalitarian societies, in which increasing restrictions are placed on women's productive and reproductive activities, strongly discourage them from taking on the cross-gender role.

Anthropologists' classification of gender roles as dichotomous has served to obscure the nature of the Native American cross-gender role. For Whitehead, the male berdache is "less than a full man" but "more than a mere woman."[66] suggesting a mixed gender role combining elements of both the male and the female. Similarly, Callender and Kochems suggest that the berdache formed an intermediate gender status.[67] Native conceptualizations of gender, particularly in the egalitarian tribes, do not contain an invariable opposition of two roles. The Western ideology of feminine and masculine traits actually has little in common with these Native American gender systems, within which exist large areas of overlapping tasks.

The idea of a mixed gender role is particularly geared to the male berdache and assumes the existence of a limited traditional female role. Such a concept does not account for the wide range of behaviors possible for both the male and female gender roles. By contrast, the term "cross-gender" defines the role as a set of behaviors typifying the attributes of the other sex, but not limited to an exact duplication of either role. Attributes of the male berdache that are not typical of the female role—for example, certain ritual activities—do not indicate a mixed gender category. These activities are specialized tasks that arise from the spiritual power of the cross-gender individual.

The term "cross-gender," however, is not without its problems. Sue-Ellen Jacobs suggests that a person who from birth or early childhood fills this variant role may not be "crossing" a gender boundary. She prefers the term "third gender" because, as among the Tewa, the berdache role may not fit either a male or female gender category but may be conceived instead as another gender.[68] Kay Martin and Barbara Voorheis also explore the possibility of more than two genders.[69] Certainly the last word has not been spoken about a role that has confounded researchers for at least one hundred years. But it is imperative to develop an analysis of variant gender roles based on the historical conditions that faced particular tribes, since gender systems vary in different cultures and change as modes of production change.

ACKNOWLEDGMENTS

I am particularly grateful to Naomi Katz, Mina Caulfield, and Carolyn Clark for their encouragement, support, and suggestions during the development of this article. I would also like to thank Gilbert Herdt, Paula Gunn Allen, Sue-Ellen Jacobs, Walter Williams, Luis Kemnitzer, and Ruby Rohrlich for their insightful comments on an earlier version.

NOTES

1. Sherry B. Ortner and Harriet Whitehead, eds., *Sexual Meanings: The Cultural Construction of Gender and Sexuality* (Cambridge: Cambridge University Press, 1981); Gayle Rubin, "The Traffic in Women: Notes on the 'Political Economy' of Sex," in *Toward an Anthropology of Women,* ed. Rayna R. Reiter (New York: Monthly Review Press, 1975), pp. 157–210.

2. Much feminist debate has focused on whether male dominance is universal, or whether societies with egalitarian relations exist. For a more comprehensive discussion of egalitarian societies, see Mina Davis Caulfield, "Equality, Sex and Mode of Production," in *Social Inequality: Comparative and Developmental Approaches,* ed. Gerald D. Berreman (New York: Academic Press, 1981), pp. 201–19; Mona Etienne

and Eleanor Leacock, eds., *Women and Colonization: Anthropological Perspectives* (New York: J. F. Bergin, 1980); Eleanor Burke Leacock, *Myths of Male Dominance: Collected Articles on Women Cross-Culturally* (New York: Monthly Review Press, 1981); Karen Sacks, *Sisters and Wives: The Past and Future of Sexual Inequality* (Westport, Conn.: Greenwood Press, 1979); Rayna R. Reiter, ed., *Toward an Anthropology of Women* (New York: Monthly Review Press, 1975); and Eleanor Burke Leacock and Nancy O. Lurie, eds., *North American Indians in Historical Perspective* (New York: Random House, 1971).

3. The term "berdache" is the more common term associated with the cross-gender role. It was originally applied by Europeans to Native American men who assumed the female role, and was derived from the Arabic *bardaj,* meaning a boy slave kept for sexual purposes. I prefer the term "cross-gender," first used by J. M. Carrier, particularly for the female role. See J. M. Carrier, "Homosexual Behavior in Cross-Cultural Perspective," in *Homosexual Behavior: A Modern Reappraisal,* ed. Judd Marmor (New York: Basic Books, 1980), pp. 100–122.

4. Alfred L. Kroeber, "Psychosis or Social Sanction," *Character and Personality* 8, no. 3 (1940): 204–15, quote on p. 209.

5. Harriet Whitehead, "The Bow and the Burden Strap: A New Look at Institutionalized Homosexuality in Native North America," in Ortner and Whitehead, eds. (n. 1 above), pp. 80–115, quote on p. 86.

6. Charles Callender and Lee M. Kochems, "The North American Berdache," *Current Anthropology* 24, no. 4 (1983): 443–56.

7. These tribes by area are as follows: Subarctic—Ingalik, Kaska; Northwest—Bella Coola, Haisla, Lillooet, Nootka, Okanagon, Queets, Quinault; California/Oregon—Achomawi, Atsugewi, Klamath, Shasta, Wintu, Wiyot, Yokuts, Yuki; Southwest—Apache, Cocopa, Maricopa, Mohave, Navajo, Papago, Pima, Yuma; Great Basin—Ute, Southern Ute, Shoshoni, Southern Paiute, Northern Paiute; Plains—Blackfoot, Crow, Kutenai.

8. See S. C. Simms, "Crow Indian Hermaphrodites," *American Anthropologist* 5, no. 3 (1903): 580–81; Alfred L. Kroeber, "The Arapaho," *American Museum of Natural History Bulletin* 18, no. 1 (1902): 1–150; Royal B. Hassrick, *The Sioux: Life and Customs of a Warrior Society* (Norman: University of Oklahoma Press, 1964); Ronald L. Olson, *The Quinault Indians* (Seattle: University of Washington Press, 1936); Ruth Murray Underhill, *Social Organization of the Papago Indians* (1939; reprint, New York: AMS Press, 1969).

9. George Devereux, "Institutionalized Homosexuality of the Mohave Indians," *Human Biology* 9, no. 4 (1937): 498–527.

10. Leslie Spier, *Yuman Tribes of the Gila River* (Chicago: University of Chicago Press, 1933).

11. Leslie Spier, *Klamath Ethnography,* University of

California Publications in American Archaeology and Ethnology, vol. 30 (Berkeley: University of California Press, 1930).

12. E. W. Gifford, *The Cocopa,* University of California Publications in American Archaeology and Ethnology, vol. 31, no. 6 (Berkeley: University of California Press, 1933).

13. Devereux (n. 9 above), p. 503.

14. John J. Honigmann, *The Kaska Indians: An Ethnographic Reconstruction,* Yale University Publications in Anthropology, no. 51 (New Haven, Conn.: Yale University Press, 1954), p. 130.

15. Devereux (n. 9 above), pp. 508–9.

16. Gifford (n. 12 above).

17. Ibid., p. 294.

18. Honigmann (n. 14 above), p. 130.

19. Devereux (n. 9 above).

20. Spier, *Klamath Ethnography* (n. 11 above), p. 53.

21. Devereux (n. 9 above).

22. Ibid.; Gifford (n. 12 above); Honigmann (n. 14 above).

23. Whitehead (n. 5 above), pp. 92–93.

24. C. Daryll Forde, *Ethnography of the Yuma Indians,* University of California Publications in American Archaeology and Ethnology, vol. 28, no. 4 (Berkeley: University of California Press, 1931), p. 157; Gifford (n. 12 above), p. 294; Devereux (n. 9 above), p. 510.

25. Devereux (n. 9 above), p. 515.

26. Cornelius Osgood, *Ingalik Social Culture,* Yale University Publications in Anthropology, no. 53 (New Haven, Conn.: Yale University Press, 1958).

27. Based on ethnographic data in Honigmann (n. 14 above); Gifford (n. 12 above); Leslie Spier, *Cultural Relations of the Gila and Colorado River Tribes,* Yale University Publications in Anthropology, no. 3 (New Haven, Conn.: Yale University Press, 1936), *Klamath Ethnography* (n. 11 above), and *Yuman Tribes* (n. 10 above); Theodore Stern, *The Klamath Tribe* (Seattle: University of Washington Press, 1966); Alfred L. Kroeber, *Mohave Indians: Report on Aboriginal Territory and Occupancy of the Mohave Tribe,* ed. David Horr (New York: Garland Publishing, 1974), and *Handbook of the Indians of California,* Bureau of American Ethnology Bulletin no. 78 (Washington, D.C.: Government Printing Office, 1925); William H. Kelly, *Cocopa Ethnography,* Anthropological Papers of the University of Arizona, no. 29 (Tucson: University of Arizona Press, 1977); Lorraine M. Sherer, *The Clan System of the Fort Mohave Indians* (Los Angeles: Historical Society of Southern California, 1965).

28. Julie Cruikshank, *Athapaskan Women: Lives and Legends* (Ottawa: National Museums of Canada, 1979); Spier, *Klamath Ethnography* (n. 11 above).

29. Gifford (n. 12 above).

30. The five tribes discussed here varied in forms of kinship, but this variation did not have a significant effect on the relations between the sexes. Lacking rank or wealth, kinship groups were not the focus of power or authority, hence

whether a tribe was matrilineal or patrilineal was not as important as the overall relationship with kin on either side.

31. John J. Honigmann, *Culture and Ethos of Kaska Society,* Yale University Publications in Anthropology, no. 40 (New Haven, Conn.: Yale University Press, 1949), and *Kaska Indians* (n. 14 above).

32. Spier, *Klamath Ethnography* (n. 11 above); J. A. Teit, "Field Notes on the Tahltan and Kaska Indians: 1912–15," *Anthropologica* 3, no. 1 (1956): 39–171; Kroeber, *Handbook* (n. 27 above); Gifford (n. 12 above).

33. Kelly (n. 27 above); Spier, *Klamath Ethnography* (n. 11 above).

34. Kelly (n. 27 above).

35. Devereux (n. 9 above), p. 514.

36. Kelly (n. 27 above); Forde (n. 24 above).

37. Devereux (n. 9 above), pp. 514–15.

38. Rubin (n. 1 above), p. 178.

39. See Forde (n. 24 above), p. 157; Honigmann, *Kaska Indians* (n. 14 above), 127.

40. Spier, *Klamath Ethnography* (n. 11 above), and *Yuman Tribes* (n. 10 above); Kroeber, *Handbook* (n. 27 above).

41. Whitehead (n. 5 above), p. 86.

42. Gene Weltfish, "The Plains Indians: Their Continuity in History and Their Indian Identity," in Leacock and Lurie, eds. (n. 2 above).

43. Leacock and Lurie, eds. (n. 2 above); Alan Klein, "The Political Economy of Gender: A 19th-Century Plains Indian Case Study," in *The Hidden Half: Studies of Plains Indian Women,* ed. Patricia Albers and Beatrice Medicine (Washington, D.C.: University Press of America, 1983), pp. 143–73.

44. See Albers and Medicine, eds.

45. Beatrice Medicine, "'Warrior Women'—Sex Role Alternatives for Plains Indian Women," in Albers and Medicine, eds., pp. 267–80; see also Oscar Lewis, "Manly-Hearted Women among the North Piegan," *American Anthropologist* 43, no. 2 (1941): 173–87.

46. Ruth Landes, *The Mystic Lake Sioux* (Madison: University of Wisconsin Press, 1968).

47. Medicine, p. 272.

48. Sue-Ellen Jacobs, "The Berdache," in *Cultural Diversity and Homosexuality,* ed. Stephen Murray (New York: Irvington Press, in press); Medicine, p. 269.

49. On male acceptance of women warriors, see Landes.

50. Edwin Thompson Denig, *Of the Crow Nation,* ed. John C. Ewers, Smithsonian Institution, Bureau of American Ethnology, Bulletin no. 151, Anthropology Papers no. 33 (Washington, D.C.: Government Printing Office, 1953), and *Five Indian Tribes of the Upper Missouri,* ed. John C. Ewers

(Norman: University of Oklahoma Press, 1961); Claude E. Schaeffer, "The Kutenai Female Berdache: Courier, Guide, Prophetess, and Warrior," *Ethnohistory* 12, no. 3 (1965): 193–236.

51. Patricia Albers, "Introduction: New Perspectives on Plains Indian Women," in Albers and Medicine, eds. (n. 43 above), pp. 1–26, quote on p. 3.

52. Katherine Weist, "Beasts of Burden and Menial Slaves: Nineteenth Century Observations of Northern Plains Indian Women," in Albers and Medicine, eds. (n. 43 above), pp. 29–52, quote on p. 39.

53. Harry H. Turney-High, *Ethnography of the Kutenai,* Memoirs of the American Anthropological Association, no. 56 (1941; reprint, New York: Kraus Reprint, 1969), and *The Flathead Indians of Montana,* Memoirs of the American Anthropological Association, no. 48 (1937; reprint, New York: Kraus Reprint, 1969).

54. Kroeber, "The Arapaho" (n. 8 above), p. 19.

55. Paula Gunn Allen, "Beloved Women: Lesbians in American Indian Cultures," *Conditions: Seven* 3, no. 1 (1981): 67–87.

56. Alice Kehoe, "The Shackles of Tradition," in Albers and Medicine, eds. (n. 43 above), pp. 53–73.

57. Hassrick (n. 8 above).

58. Jeannette Mirsky, "The Dakota," in *Cooperation and Competition among Primitive Peoples,* ed. Margaret Mead (Boston: Beacon Press, 1961), p. 417.

59. Devereux (n. 9 above), p. 523.

60. Callender and Kochems (n. 6 above), p. 453 (italics mine).

61. Whitehead (n. 5 above), p. 92.

62. Devereux (n. 9 above), p. 501.

63. Forde (n. 24 above), p. 157.

64. Data on the Navajo *nadle* are not included in this article because the Navajo conception of the berdache was atypical. The *nadle* was considered a hermaphrodite by the Navajo—i.e., of both sexes physically—and therefore did not actually exemplify a cross-gender role. See W. W. Hill. "The Status of the Hermaphrodite and Transvestite in Navaho Culture." *American Anthropologist* 37, no. 2 (1935): 273–79.

65. Whitehead (n. 5 above), p. 86.

66. Ibid., p. 89.

67. Callender and Kochems (n. 6 above), p. 454.

68. Sue-Ellen Jacobs, personal communication, 1983, and "Comment on Callender and Kochems," *Current Anthropology* 24, no. 4 (1983): 459–60.

69. M. Kay Martin and Barbara Voorheis, *Female of the Species* (New York: Columbia University Press, 1975).

The "Status of Women" in Indigenous African Societies

NIARA SUDARKASA

INTRODUCTION

Long before the women's movement ushered in an era of renewed concern with the "status of women" in various societies and cultures, a number of writers had addressed the question of the "status of women" in various African societies.[1] Some writers characterized women in African societies as "jural minors" for most of their lives, falling under the guardianship first of their fathers and then their husbands. Other writers stressed the independence of African women, noting their control over their own lives and resources.

From my own readings on Africa and my research among the Yoruba in Nigeria and other parts of West Africa, it appears that except for the highly Islamized societies in Sub-Saharan Africa, in this part of the world more than any other, in precolonial times women were conspicuous in high places. They were queen-mothers; queen-sisters; princesses; chiefs; and holders of other offices in towns and villages; occasional warriors; and, in one well known case, that of the Lovedu, the supreme monarch. Furthermore, it was almost invariably the case that African women were conspicuous in the economic life of their societies, being involved in farming, trade, or craft production.

The purviews of female and male in African societies were often described as separate and complementary.[2] Yet, whenever most writers compared the lot of women and men in Africa, they ascribed to men a bet-

ter situation, a higher status. Women were depicted as saddled with home and domesticity; men were portrayed as enjoying the exhilaration of life in the outside world. For me, the pieces of the portrait did not ring true. Not only was there an obvious distortion of the ethnographic reality—women were outside the home as well as in it—but there was also something inappropriate about the notion that women and men were everywhere related to each other in a hierarchical fashion, as was implied in the most common usage of the concept of status of women.

The *status* of women is often used simultaneously in the two conceptual meanings that it has in social science. On the one hand, the term is used in Ralph Linton's sense to mean the collection of rights and duties that attach to particular positions. According to this usage, *status,* which refers to a particular position itself, contrasts with *role,* which refers to the behavior appropriate to a given status.[3] On the other hand, the concept of the status of women is also used to refer to the placement of females relative to males in a dual-level hierarchy. In this sense, the term *status* connotes stratification and invites comparison with other systems of stratification. It was this notion of sexual stratification that seemed inappropriate for describing the relationships between females and males in most of the African societies I had studied.

Martin K. Whyte concludes his cross-cultural survey, *The Status of Women in Preindustrial Societies,* with a similar observation. After discussing the status of women in the hierarchical sense used above, Whyte's first major finding is that there is a general absence of covariation among the different indicators of status in this hierarchical usage. He notes that one cannot assume "that a favorable position for women in

"The Status of Women in Indigenous African Societies" by Niara Sudarkasa from *Women in Africa and the African Diaspora,* edited by Rosalyn Tergborg-Penn, Sharon Harley, and Andrea Benton Rushing. Copyright © 1987 by Rosalyn Tergborg-Penn, Sharon Harley, and Andrea Benton Rushing. Reprinted by permission of Howard University Press.

any particular area of social life will be related to favorable positions in other areas." Similarly, there is no best indicator or key variable that will yield an overall assessment of the status of women relative to men.[4]

More to the point of the present argument is Whyte's observation that this lack of covariation in the indicators of the status of women signals a difference between this area and other areas where stratification is a known feature of the social structure. "This lack of association between different measures of the role and status of women relative to men still constitutes something of a puzzle. . . . In the study of stratification we ordinarily expect indicators of status at the individual level to be positively, although not perfectly, associated with one another." Drawing on Simone de Beauvoir's distinction between the position of women and that of oppressed national or racial groups, Whyte concludes that "powerful factors" in all preindustrial societies lead to the perception by females and males that women's statuses differ from those of men but in a manner that does not imply the hierarchical relationship characteristic of those linking occupational and ethnic groups. Going further, Whyte states that "the lack of association between different aspects of the role and status of women relative to men is due largely to the fact that women as a group [in preindustrial societies] are fundamentally different from status groups and classes."[5]

This observation by Whyte seems to make sense of the data from most African societies. Although his cross-cultural study dispels a number of treasured notions about "*the* status of women," it points to a critical research problem that should be pursued, namely, the problem of determining the conditions under which women's relationship to men *does* take on the characteristics of a hierarchical relationship. I should hasten to point out that conceptually, this is a *different* problem from that which seeks to ascertain when an egalitarian relationship between the sexes gives way to a subordinate-superordinate relationship. The very concept of an egalitarian relationship between women and men implies that the female and male are unitary categories that are measured, or "sized-up," one against the other in the societies described. Here, I will attempt to show that there are societies for which such a conceptualization does not accurately reflect the social and ideological reality of the peoples concerned. The data gathered from some African societies suggest a reason for this. As I will attempt to demonstrate,

female and male are not so much statuses, in Linton's sense, as they are clusters of statuses for which gender is only one of the defining characteristics. Women and men might be hierarchically related to each other in one or more of their reciprocal statuses, but not in others. Because contradiction, as much as congruence, characterized the status-clusters termed female and male, many African societies did not or could not consistently stratify the categories one against the other, but, rather, codified the ambiguities.

The argument put forth in this article suggests that Engels and a number of his adherents may have missed the mark in arguing that private property and production for exchange served to lower the status of women. It also suggests that Karen Sacks's reformulation of Engels, which, in any case, rests on a controversial interpretation of the African data, also misses the mark by arguing that the critical, or key, variable in the subordination of women in class societies was their confinement to production within the domestic sphere and their exclusion from "social production for exchange."[6] I am suggesting here that various conditions, including most probably the development of private property and the market or exchange economy, *created conditions where female and male became increasingly defined as unitary statuses that were hierarchically related to one another.* Such conditions appear to have been absent in various precolonial African societies and possibly in other parts of the world as well.[7]

In recent years, the postulation of separate, non-hierarchically related—and, therefore, complementary—domains for women and men has been disputed by anthropologists who argued that women occupied the "domestic domain" and men the "public domain" and that, because power and authority were vested in the public domain, women had *de facto* lower status than men.[8] It has always seemed to me that in many African societies a more appropriate conception (and by that I mean one that makes sense of more of the realities of those societies) was to recognize two domains, one occupied by men and another by women—both of which were internally ordered in a hierarchical fashion and both of which provided personnel for domestic and extradomestic (or public) activities. I have already argued in another article that there was considerable overlap between the public and domestic domains in preindustrial African societies.[9]

In the remainder of this paper, I will examine the roles of women in families and descent groups, in the economy, and in the political process in West Africa.

Potentially nonhierarchical models of relationships between females and males are indicated and contrasted with ones that are hierarchical. The data are used from stateless societies, such as the Ibo and Tallensi, and from preindustrial state societies, such as the Asante (Ashanti), Nupe, and Yoruba.

Before turning to the data, note that there is no question that status, in the hierarchical sense, attaches to sex (or gender) in contemporary Africa. Ester Boserup is the best known exponent of the view that the forces of modernization and development have denied African women equal access to formal education and have undermined their contribution to the political and economic arenas of their countries.[10] Annie M. D. Lebeuf was one of the first writers to make this point and was the one who demonstrated it most conclusively for the political sphere.[11] Other scholars have taken up and elaborated the same theme. The fact of the present-day linkage between gender and stratification in West Africa and elsewhere on the continent and the realization that most of the studies from which we have to take our data were carried out *after* the onset of the colonial period, should be borne in mind as the following discussion unfolds.[12]

WOMEN IN AFRICAN KIN GROUPS

In West Africa, as in most parts of the continent, the three basic kin groups to which females and males belong are (1) corporate unilineal descent groups, which we term lineages; (2) domiciled extended families made up of certain lineage members and their spouses and dependent children; and (3) conjugally based family units that are subdivisions of the extended family and within which procreation and primary responsibilities for socialization rest.[13] Within their lineages, African women have rights and responsibilities toward their kinsmen and kinswomen that are independent of males. As far as their responsibilities are concerned, female members of the lineage are expected to meet certain obligations in the same way that males are. For example, women offer material assistance to their sisters and brothers; they also do their part (that is, they make the appropriate financial or material outlay) at the time of important rites of passage such as naming ceremonies, marriages, and funerals. Within patrilineages, women, as father's sisters, sisters, and daughters, generally do not hold formal

leadership positions—although they do take part in most discussions of lineage affairs—and the more advanced in age they are, the more influence they wield. As mothers, sisters, and daughters within the matrilineages, some women hold leadership positions and exercise authority equivalent to that of men.[14]

In both patrilineages and matrilineages, interpersonal relations on a daily basis tend to be regulated by seniority as determined by order of birth rather than by gender. Hence, senior sisters outrank junior brothers. Where males prostrate before their elders, they do so for females, as well as males.

In the extended family, women occupy roles defined by consanguinity, as well as conjugality. They are mothers and daughters, as well as wives and cowives. The position of "wife" refers not only to the conjugal relationship to a husband, but also to the affinal (or in-law) relationship to all members—female as well as male—in the husband's compound and lineage. (Among the Yoruba, for example, female members of a lineage refer to their brother's wives as their own "wives," a formulation which signals that certain reciprocal responsibilities and behavior are entailed in the relationship of the women to each other.)

If there is one thing that is conspicuous in discussions of "the status of women" in Africa (and elsewhere in the world), it is the tendency to assess that status only in relation to the conjugal roles of wife or cowife. Interestingly, in Whyte's cross-cultural study of the status of women in ninety-three societies, of the twenty-seven indicators of status as related to gender and the family, twenty (74 percent) of the variables had to do specifically with behavior or rights within or related to the conjugal (marital) relationship. The focus on the conjugal roles of women to the near exclusion of analyses of their functioning in consanguineal roles derives, as I have tried to show elsewhere, from the obsession of Western scholars with analyses of the nuclear family and the operation of the principle of conjugality in determining kin relations. In other words, the emphasis derives from an attempt to analyze kinship in other societies from the viewpoint of and with paradigms appropriate to Western kin groups.[15] African *extended* families, which are the normal coresidential form of family in indigenous precolonial African societies, are *built around* consanguineal relationships; failure to recognize this has led to misrepresentation of many aspects of African kinship. One consequence of the focus on conjugal families and the concern with breaking down polygynous families into "constituent nuclear families" is the distortion of an understanding of the roles of women as wives, cowives, and mothers.[16]

Women as *wives* generally exhibit overt signals of deference to their husbands in patrilineal African societies. In matrilineal societies, the patterns may not be as pronounced, but wives still defer to their husbands. In other kinship roles, especially those of mother and senior consanguineal kinswoman, women are the recipients of deference and the wielders of power and authority.

Western students of African societies have not only focused unduly on the husband-wife relationship in describing African kinship, they have also sought to define that conjugal relationship in terms of parameters found in Western societies. This has led to a misrepresentation of the essence and implications of what is generally called "woman-to-woman" marriage. This complex institution cannot be described at length here, but I would make the following observations: First, the institution of "woman marriage" signifies most of all that gender is not the sole basis for recruitment to the "husband" role in Africa; hence, the authority that attaches to that role is not gender-specific. Second, the institution must be understood in the context of the meaning of concepts of husband and wife in African societies, not in Western societies. Third, in African societies, the term *wife* has two basic referents: female married to a given male (or female) and female married into a given compound or lineage. Thus, for example, among the Yoruba, a husband refers to his spouse as "wife"; a woman refers to her cowife as "wife" or "mate," and as noted earlier, female, as well as male, members of the lineage refer to the in-marrying spouses as their "wives." The term *husband* refers specifically to a woman's spouse but also generally to the males (and females) in her husband's lineage. Again, among the Yoruba, a woman refers to her own spouse, and in certain contexts, to his lineage members, including her own children, as "husband."

Given these usages, it is important to recognize that the terms *husband* and *wife* connote certain clusters of affinal relations, and in women marriage the principles concerned emphasize certain *jural* relations. (They do not, as all writers point out, imply a sexual component to the relationship as in heterosexual conjugal unions.)

If the concept of conjugal relations in Africa were not circumscribed to those common in the West, it would be appreciated that the unifying factor in the various kinds of woman-to-woman marriage is that everywhere it serves a procreative function, either on behalf of the female husband herself, or on behalf of her male spouse or male kinsmen. Because marriage is the institution and the idiom through which procreation is legitimated in Africa, it must be entered into by women (as by men) who want to acquire rights over a woman's childbearing capacity.[17] The existence of woman-to-woman marriage in Africa is consistent with a general deemphasis on gender and an emphasis on seniority and personal standing (usually but not always determined by wealth) in recruitment to positions of authority.

This brief discussion of African families and kin groups is intended to suggest that male gender predictably calls forth deferential behavior only within the conjugal relationship. The case of woman-to-woman marriage demonstrates, however, that male gender does not exclusively determine entry into the husband role, which is the more authoritative of the two conjugal roles. But even though patterns of deference emphasize subordination of the wife's role, the decision-making process and the control *over resources* within the conjugal relationship in many West African societies, including those of the Yoruba, Ibo, Ashanti, and Nupe, indicate parallel and complementary control by husbands and wives. In the consanguineal aspects of African kinship, as I have indicated, seniority and personal attributes (especially accumulated resources) rather than gender, serve as the primary basis of status in the hierarchical sense.

WOMEN IN THE POLITICAL PROCESS IN INDIGENOUS AFRICAN SOCIETIES

Any investigation of women in the political process in precolonial Africa should begin with the excellent article by Annie Lebeuf in Denise Paulme's *Women of Tropical Africa*.[18] Here I only want to highlight certain facts that might aid in addressing the question of whether the relationship of females and males within the political domain is most appropriately conceptualized as a hierarchical one.

Africa is noted for the presence of women in very high positions in the formal governmental structure.[19] Africa is also noted for having parallel chieftaincies, one line made up of males, the other of females. One way of interpreting these facts has been to dismiss the female chieftaincies as simply women controlling women (and after all, if women are subordinate anyway, of what significance is it that they have chieftaincies or sodalities among themselves?). The presence of women at the highest levels of indigenous government has been dismissed as an instance of women distinguishing themselves individually by entering the "public world of men."[20] I would suggest that a formulation that makes an *a priori judgment* that any participation of women in the public sphere represents entry into the world of men simply begs the question. For in West Africa, the "public domain" was not conceptualized as *the world of men*. Rather, the public domain was one in which both sexes were recognized as having important roles to play.[21]

Indeed, the positing of distinct public and domestic domains does not hold true for precolonial West Africa. The distinction is also not very useful for looking at the rest of the continent. As many writers on African political structure have shown, even in states in which monarchs were elevated to statuses "removed from their kin groups," the lineage (and the compound) remained important aspects of political organization in all localities where they existed.[22] Compounds were generally the courts of the first instance and the bases for mobilizing people for public works and public services; lineages were the units through which the land was allocated and were the repository of titles to offices in many African societies. Women held formal leadership roles in matrilineages and were influential in decision-making patrilineages. Their participation in the affairs of their affinal compounds, (within which women in patrilineal societies lived most of their adult lives), was channeled through an organizational structure in which women were most often ranked according to order of marriage into the group.

To answer the question of whether women's participation in the political process should be conceptualized as subordinate to that of men, I would propose that one examine the kind of political decisions and activities in which women were involved and ask from what kind they were excluded. Throughout most of West Africa, women controlled their own worlds. For example, they had trade and craft guilds, and they spoke on matters of taxation and maintenance of public facilities (such as markets, roads, wells, and streams). They also testified on their own behalf in any court or hearing. Thus, in internal political affairs, women were general-

ly consulted and had channels through which they were represented. External affairs were largely in the hands of men, but in any crisis, such as war, women were always involved—minimally as suppliers of rations for troops but in some instances as leaders of armies and as financiers of campaigns.[23]

The question then arises, from what political processes were they excluded? They could not participate in the male secret societies that were important in the political process in some Western African states. They were also excluded from certain councils of chiefs, although this was rare. Much more common was representation on the council by one or more of the women who headed the hierarchy of women chiefs. In all cases, however, it seems that women were consulted on most governmental affairs. Their participation through their spokespersons paralleled the participation of males through theirs. And of course in cases in which the chief rulers were female and male (for example, the queen-mother and monarch-son), the complementarity of the relationship between the sexes was symbolized and codified in the highest offices of the land.

THE INVOLVEMENT OF WOMEN IN PRODUCTION AND DISTRIBUTION IN AFRICAN SOCIETIES

It is well known that African women were farmers, traders, and crafts producers in different parts of the continent. It is equally well documented that their economic roles were at once public and private. Women worked outside the home in order to meet the responsibilities placed upon them in their roles as mothers, wives, sisters, daughters, members of guilds, chiefs, or citizens.[24] In the economic sphere, more than in any other, it is easy to show that women's activities were complementary to those of men and that women producers and traders were not subordinate to men. In most African societies, as elsewhere, the division of labor among sexual lines promoted a reciprocity of effort. If men were farmers, women were food processors and traders. Where women and men were engaged in the same productive activity (such as farming or weaving), they produced different items. Among the Ibo, females and males grew different crops; among the Yoruba, the female and male weavers produced different types of cloth on different types of looms. Where both females and males traded, there was usually a sexual bifurcation along commodity lines. Normally, too, men predominated in long-distance trade, and women were predominant in local markets. I have never heard of an indigenous African society in which differential value was attached to the labor of women and men working in the same line or in which women and men were differentially rewarded for the products of their labor.

In the management and disposal of their incomes, the activities of African women and men also were separate but coordinated. Within the conjugal family unit, women and men had different responsibilities that were met from the proceeds of their separate economic pursuits. A husband might be primarily responsible for the construction and upkeep of the home and the provision of staple foods, while the wife (or more probably the wives) assumed responsibility for nonstaple foods and the daily needs of her children.

> The separate management of "the family purse" definitely appeared to be a response to a situation in which the members of conjugal units had independent obligations to persons outside these groups. However, it was also a way of minimizing the risks involved in the expenditure (of resources) by disbursing [them] among potentially beneficial investment options, as perceived from the vantage point of the different persons concerned.[25]

IMPLICATIONS FOR FUTURE RESEARCH ON AFRICAN/AFRICAN-AMERICAN WOMEN

I have tried to show that a "neutral" complementarity, rather than subordination/superordination, more accurately describes the relationship between certain female and male roles in various precolonial African societies. In the process, I have argued that the preconceived notion of a unitary status for female and male, respectively, is probably what led many students of African societies to paint such misleading pictures of *the* status of African women.

The data presented in this brief discussion are only an indication of those that must be considered in any serious research into the issues raised here. I have always been intrigued by what appear to be linguistic clues into the "neutrality" of gender in many African societies. The absence of gender in the pronouns of many African languages and the interchangeability of first names among females and males strike me as possibly related to a societal deemphasis on gender as a designation for behavior. Many other areas of traditional culture, including personal dress and adornment, religious ceremonials, and intragender patterns of comportment, suggest that Africans often deemphasize gender in relation to seniority and other insignia of status.

Only brief mention can be made of the fact that in contemporary Africa, the relationship between women and men has moved decidedly in the direction of a hierarchical one. In understanding the change in the nature of these relationships from the precolonial, preindustrial context to the present, it is important that we not presume the movement from an egalitarian relationship to a nonegalitarian one. Rather, it has been suggested that the domains of women and men in many indigenous African societies should not be conceptualized in terms of ranking at all (which is implied in the concept of egalitarianism because each concept entails its opposite). It is suggested that the changes that occurred with the onset of colonialism (and capitalism, its economic corrolate) were ones that created hierarchical relations between the sexes. It is therefore appropriate in the modern context to investigate causes and characteristics of the status of women in Africa.

This effort to recast the study of the statuses and roles of women in indigenous precolonial African societies has important implications for the study of the roles that the descendants of these women came to play in the American context. Over the past two decades, most historians of blacks in America have come to accept the premise that in order to understand that history, one must understand the implications of saying it was "enslaved Africans," rather than "slaves," who came to these shores in chains. This implies that these Africans brought with them their beliefs and values; varying degrees of knowledge of their political, economic, technological, religious, artistic, recreational and familial organization; and codes governing interpersonal behavior between such societal groupings as chiefs and citizenry, old and young, and female and male.

Given this context, to understand the roles that black women came to play in America, it is necessary to understand the tradition of female independence and responsibility within the family and wider kin groups in Africa, and the tradition of female productivity and leadership in the extra-domestic, or public, domain in African societies. It is understood, of course, that the context of slavery did not permit the exact replication of African patterns, but the forms of behavior that did emerge had their roots in those patterns.

A brief reference to black American women's roles in three spheres will suffice to indicate the directions in which research into the linkage with Africa might take. I refer to women's activities as leaders on the plantations and in their communities at later periods; as workers helping to provide economic support for their families; and as key figures in the intergenerational kinship units that formed (and still form) the core of many black families.

Much has been written about the heroism of women such as Harriet Tubman and Sojourner Truth. Precisely because of their extraordinary deeds, they are portrayed as being unique among black women. It would seem, however, that these are but the most famous of the black female leaders whose assumption of their roles came out of a tradition where women were always among the leaders in a community. A reassessment of the roles of the so-called Mammies in the Big House; of the elderly women who looked after children on the plantation while younger people worked in the fields; of women who planned escapes and insurrections; and of female religious leaders should reveal that there was a complementarity and parallelism in the historical roles of male and female leaders among black Americans that bore clear relationship to what existed in Africa.

The roles of black women in the economic sphere have long been remarked upon, but most of the analyses have presumed that these women worked outside the home because of economic necessity, rather than because of choice or tradition. In other words, the presumption of the literature seems to be that where possible, the black woman, like her white counterpart before the era of "women's liberation," would choose the role of housewife and mother over that of working wife and mother.

The present analysis suggests that we should take another look at the phenomenon of black women in the world of work, with a view to examining the continuities that this represents with African traditions wherein women were farmers, craftswomen, and entrepreneurs par excellence. It is noteworthy that in Africa, unlike Europe, women of privileged statuses (such as the kings' or chiefs' wives, daughters, sisters,

and mothers) were not removed from the world of work. On the contrary, their rank in society often conferred special access to certain economic activities. For example, among the Yoruba, the kings' wives were the premier long-distance traders among the women, as was remarked upon by some of the first European visitors to Yoruba kingdoms in the nineteenth century. Given these traditions, one might expect, therefore, that middle- or upper-class status would not necessarily incline black women in America to prefer a life of relative leisure to that of the workaday world. In other words, it would not incline middle- or upper-class black women to choose the relative confinement of the domestic domain over the public world of work. What we know about black women entrepreneurs and professionals in the nineteenth and early twentieth centuries suggests that regardless of socioeconomic status, Afro-American women were more likely to be employed outside the home than were their Euro-American counterparts.

Finally, I would suggest that a reexamination of the statuses and roles of women and men in African kin groups can help to unravel the antecedents of a number of patterns of African-American kinship that emerged in the context of slavery and evolved into the forms of family organization we see today. The importance of age and seniority in conferring authority on African females, as well as males, for example, helps to explain the authoritative roles of elderly women, as well as elderly men, in black American families. The African emphasis on consanguinity, as opposed to conjugality, helps to explain much of black American kinship, including, for example, the formation of households around two- or three-generational clusters of "blood relatives" (such as a woman and her adult daughters and their children); the transresidential extended family networks that characterized black family organization in the past and still remain in some areas today; the special obligations for mutual assistance and support that characterized relationships between sisters, regardless of their marital statuses; and the tendency, until recently, for unmarried black women with children to reside with their "blood" relatives, rather than in households of their own.[26]

Much work remains before we can confidently trace the multifaceted connections between African and African-American behavioral patterns, including those concerning the roles and statuses of women and their relationships to the men in their families and communities. The intention of this brief review of some of the possible linkages is to point to areas where research might be fruitfully pursued. I have suggested that many of the activities and attributes that have been taken to be characteristic of black women in America have their roots in Africa. These characteristics—leadership in the community, as well as in the home; prominence in the world of work; independence and pride in womanhood—are usually pointed to as evidence of the strength of black American women. What I have tried to show in this paper is that this strength had its roots in African societies where women were literally expected to "shoulder their own burdens," and where, in many contexts, respect and responsibility, as well as rights and privileges, were accorded without reference to gender.

NOTES

1. M. Perlman and M. P. Moal, in *Women of Tropical Africa,* ed. Denise Paulme, trans. H. M. Wright (Berkeley: University of California Press, 1963), 231–93.

2. Paulme, *Women of Tropical Africa,* Introduction, 1–16.

3. Ralph Linton, *The Study of Man,* (New York: Appleton-Century, 1936), 113–31.

4. Martin K. Whyte, *The Status of Women in Preindustrial Societies* (Princeton, N.J.: Princeton University Press, 1978), 170.

5. Ibid., 176, 179–80.

6. Karen Sacks, "Engels Revisited: Women, the Organization of Production, and Private Property," in *Woman, Culture, and Society,* ed. Michelle Z. Rosaldo and Louise Lamphere (Stanford: Stanford University Press, 1974), 207–22.

7. Here the term *precolonial* refers to the period before the mid- and late-nineteenth century from which European colonization is conventionally dated. Some information concerning African social life in precolonial times is gleaned from contemporaneous written sources, but most information comes from anthropological constructions of "traditional life," using oral history and ethnographic techniques. Due allowance must be made for possible distortions in these ethnographies but, for the most part, they are all we have to rely on for descriptions of Africa's sociocultural past.

8. Gloria Marshall (Niara Sudarkasa), "In a World of Women: Field Work in a Yoruba Community," in *Women in the Field,* ed. Peggy Golde (Chicago: Aldine Publishing Co., 1970); and Niara Sudarkasa, *Where Women Work: A Study of Yoruba Women in the Market Place and in the Home* (Ann Arbor, Museum of Anthropology, University of Michigan, 1973).

9. Niara Sudarkasa, "Female Employment and Family Organization in West Africa," in *The Black Woman Cross-Culturally,* ed. Filomina C. Steady (Cambridge, Mass.: Schenkman Publishing Co., 1981), 49–64.

10. Ester Boserup, *Women's Role in Economic Development* (London; Allen & Unwin, 1970).

11. Annie M. D. Lebeuf, "The Role of Women in the Political Organization of African Societies," in Paulme, *Women of Tropical Africa.*

12. Marjorie Mbilinyi, "The 'New Woman' and Traditional Norms in Tanzania," *Journal of Modern African Studies* 10 (January 1972): 57–72; Judith Van Allen, "Women in Africa: Modernization Means More Dependency," *Center Magazine* 7 (March 1974): 60–67; Audrey Smock, "The Impact of Modernization on Women's Position in the Family in Ghana," in *Sexual Stratification: A Cross-Cultural View,* ed. Alice Schlegel (New York: Columbia University Press, 1977), 192–214; Niara Sudarkasa, "The Effects of Twentieth-Century Social Change, Especially of Migration, on Women of West Africa," in *Proceedings of the West Africa Conference,* ed. Patricia Paylore and Richard Haney (Tucson: Office of Arid Lands Studies, University of Arizona, 1976), 102–10; and Niara Sudarkasa, "Sex Roles, Education, and Development in Africa," *Anthropology and Education Quarterly* 13 (Fall 1982): 279–89.

13. Niara Sudarkasa, "African and Afro-American Family Organization," in *Anthropology for the Eighties: Introductory Readings,* ed. Johnetta B. Cole (New York: Free Press, 1982), 132–60; and Sudarkasa, "Female Employment and Family Organization in West Africa," 49–64. See these authors on Asante: K. A. Busia, *The Position of the Chief in the Modern Political System of the Ashanti* (London: Oxford University Press, 1951); Meyer Fortes and E. E. Evans-Pritchard, eds. *African Political Systems* (Oxford: Oxford University Press, 1980); and R. S. Rattray, *Ashanti Law and Constitution* (Oxford: Clarendon Press, 1929).

14. Niara Sudarkasa, "An Exposition on the Value Premise Underlying Black Family Studies," *Journal of the National Medical Association* 67 (March 1975): 235–39; and Niara Sudarkasa, "African and Afro-American Family Organization," *Anthropology for the Eighties,* 132–60.

15. Sudarkasa, "An Exposition on the Value Premise Underlying Black Family Studies"; "Female Employment and

Family Organization in West Africa"; and "African and Afro-American Family Organization."

16. Bamidele Agbasegbe, "Is There Marriage between Women in Africa?" in *Sociological Research Symposium V,* ed. J. S. Williams et al. (Richmond: Virginia Commonwealth University, Department of Sociology, 1975); and Denise O'Brien, "Female Husbands in Southern Bantu Societies," in Schlegel, *Sexual Stratification: A Cross-Cultural View.*

17. See Lebeuf.

18. Ibid.

19. Michele Z. Rosaldo, "Woman, Culture, and Society: A Theoretical Overview," in Rosaldo and Lamphere, *Woman, Culture, and Society.*

20. Sudarkasa, "Female Employment and Family Organization in West Africa."

21. See Fortes and Evans-Pritchard.

22. Paulme, *Women of Tropical Africa;* Sudarkasa, *Where Women Work;* Victor Uchendu, *The Igbo [Ibo] of Southeast Nigeria* (New York: Holt, Rinehart, & Winston, 1965); and Bolanle Awe, "The Iyalode in the Traditional Yoruba Political System" in Schlegel, *Sexual Stratification: A Cross-Cultural View.*

23. Sudarkasa, *Where Women Work;* and "Female Employment and Family Organization in West Africa."

24. Sudarkasa, "Female Employment and Family Organization in West Africa," 60.

25. Ibid.

26. Niara Sudarkasa, "Interpreting the African Heritage in Afro-American Family Organization," in *Black Families,* ed. Harriette P. McAdoo (Beverly Hills: Sage Publishing Co., 1981): 37–53.

R E A D I N G   1 8

Compulsory Heterosexuality and Lesbian Existence
ADRIENNE RICH

FOREWORD

I want to say a little about the way "Compulsory Heterosexuality" was originally conceived and the context in which we are now living. It was written in part to challenge the erasure of lesbian existence from so much of scholarly feminist literature, an erasure which I felt (and feel) to be not just antilesbian but antifeminist in its consequences, and to distort the experience of heterosexual women as well. It was not written to widen divisions but to encourage heterosexual feminists to examine heterosexuality as a political institution which disempowers women—and to change it. I also hoped that other lesbians would feel the depth and breadth of woman identification and woman bonding that has run like a continuous though stifled theme

Reprinted from *Blood, Bread, and Poetry, Selected Prose, 1979-1985,* by Adrienne Rich, by permission of W. W. Norton & Company, Inc. Copyright © 1986 by Adrienne Rich.

through the heterosexual experience, and that this would become increasingly a politically activating impulse, not simply a validation of personal lives. I wanted the essay to suggest new kinds of criticism, to incite new questions in classrooms and academic journals, and to sketch, at least, some bridge over the gap between *lesbian* and *feminist.* I wanted, at the very least, for feminists to find it less possible to read, write, or teach from a perspective of unexamined heterocentricity.

Within the three years since I wrote "Compulsory Heterosexuality"—with this energy of hope and desire—the pressures to conform in a society increasingly conservative in mood have become more intense. The New Right's messages to women have been, precisely, that we are the emotional and sexual property of men, and that the autonomy and equality of women threaten family, religion, and state. The institutions by which women have traditionally been controlled—patriarchal motherhood, economic exploitation, the nuclear family, compulsory heterosexuality—are being strengthened by legislation, religious fiat, media imagery, and efforts at censorship. In a worsening economy, the single mother trying to support her children confronts the feminization of poverty which Joyce Miller of the National Coalition of Labor Union Women has named one of the major issues of the 1980s. The lesbian, unless in disguise, faces discrimination in hiring and harassment and violence in the street. Even within feminist-inspired institutions such as battered-women's shelters and Women's Studies programs, open lesbians are fired and others warned to stay in the closet. The retreat into sameness—assimilation for those who can manage it—is the most passive and debilitating of responses to political repression, economic insecurity, and a renewed open season on difference.

I want to note that documentation of male violence against women—within the home especially—has been accumulating rapidly in this period (see note 9). At the same time, in the realm of literature which depicts woman bonding and woman identification as essential for female survival, a steady stream of writing and criticism has been coming from women of color in general and lesbians of color in particular—the latter group being even more profoundly erased in academic feminist scholarship by the double bias of racism and homophobia.[1]

There has recently been an intensified debate on female sexuality among feminists and lesbians, with lines often furiously and bitterly drawn, with *sado-masochism* and *pornography* as key words, which are variously defined according to who is talking. The depth of women's rage and fear regarding sexuality and its relation to power and pain is real, even when the dialogue sounds simplistic, self-righteous, or like parallel monologues.

Because of all these developments, there are parts of this essay that I would word differently, qualify, or expand if I were writing it today. But I continue to think that heterosexual feminists will draw political strength for change from taking a critical stance toward the ideology which *demands* heterosexuality, and that lesbians cannot assume that we are untouched by that ideology and the institutions founded upon it. There is nothing about such a critique that requires us to think of ourselves as victims, as having been brainwashed or totally powerless. Coercion and compulsion are among the conditions in which women have learned to recognize our strength. Resistance is a major theme in this essay and in the study of women's lives, if we know what we are looking for.

I

Biologically men have only one innate orientation—a sexual one that draws them to women—while women have two innate orientations, sexual toward men and reproductive toward their young.[2]

I was a woman terribly vulnerable, critical, using femaleness as a sort of standard or yardstick to measure and discard men. Yes—something like that. I was an Anna who invited defeat from men without ever being conscious of it. (But I am conscious of it. And being conscious of it means I shall leave it all behind me and become—but what?) I was stuck fast in an emotion common to women of our time, that can turn them bitter, or Lesbian, or solitary. Yes, that Anna during that time was . . .

[Another blank line across the page:][3]

The bias of compulsory heterosexuality, through which lesbian experience is perceived on a scale ranging from deviant to abhorrent or simply rendered invisible, could be illustrated from many texts other than the two just preceding. The assumption made by Rossi, that women are "innately" sexually oriented only toward men, and that made by Lessing, that the lesbian is simply acting out of her bitterness toward men, are by no means theirs alone; these assumptions are widely current in literature and in the social sciences.

I am concerned here with two other matters as well: first, how and why women's choice of women as passionate comrades, life partners, co-workers, lovers, community has been crushed, invalidated, forced into hiding and disguise; and second, the virtual or total neglect of lesbian existence in a wide range of writings, including feminist scholarship. Obviously there is a connection here. I believe that much feminist theory and criticism is stranded on this shoal.

My organizing impulse is the belief that it is not enough for feminist thought that specifically lesbian texts exist. Any theory of cultural/political creation that treats lesbian existence as a marginal or less "natural" phenomenon, as mere "sexual preference," or as the mirror image of either heterosexual or male homosexual relations is profoundly weakened thereby, whatever its other contributions. Feminist theory can no longer afford merely to voice a toleration of "lesbianism" as an "alternative life style" or make token allusion to lesbians. A feminist critique of compulsory heterosexual orientation for women is long overdue. In this exploratory paper, I shall try to show why.

I will begin by way of examples, briefly discussing four books that have appeared in the last few years, written from different viewpoints and political orientations, but all presenting themselves, and favorably reviewed, as feminist.[4] All take as a basic assumption that the social relations of the sexes are disordered and extremely problematic, if not disabling, for women; all seek paths toward change. I have learned more from some of these books than from others, but on this I am clear: each one might have been more accurate, more powerful, more truly a force for change had the author dealt with lesbian existence as a reality and as a source of knowledge and power available to women, or with the institution of heterosexuality itself as a beachhead of male dominance.[5] In none of them is the question ever raised as to whether, in a different context or other things being equal, women would *choose* heterosexual coupling and marriage; heterosexuality is presumed the "sexual preference" of "most women," either implicitly or explicitly. In none of these books, which concern themselves with mothering, sex roles, relationships, and societal prescriptions for women, is compulsory heterosexuality ever examined as an institution powerfully affecting all these, or the idea of "preference" or "innate orientation" even indirectly questioned.

In *For Her Own Good: 150 Years of the Experts' Advice to Women* by Barbara Ehrenreich and Deirdre English, the authors' superb pamphlets *Witches, Midwives and Nurses: A History of Women Healers and Complaints and Disorders: The Sexual Politics of Sickness* are developed into a provocative and complex study. Their thesis in this book is that the advice given to American women by male health professionals, particularly in the areas of marital sex, maternity, and child care, has echoed the dictates of the economic marketplace and the role capitalism has needed women to play in production and/or reproduction. Women have become the consumer victims of various cures, therapies, and normative judgments in different periods (including the prescription to middle-class women to embody and preserve the sacredness of the home—the "scientific" romanticization of the home

itself). None of the "experts" advice has been either particularly scientific or women-oriented; it has reflected male needs, male fantasies about women, and male interest in controlling women—particularly in the realms of sexuality and motherhood—fused with the requirements of industrial capitalism. So much of this book is so devastatingly informative and is written with such lucid feminist wit that I kept waiting as I read for the basic proscription against lesbianism to be examined. It never was.

This can hardly be for lack of information. Jonathan Katz's *Gay American History*[6] tells us that as early as 1656 the New Haven Colony prescribed the death penalty for lesbians. Katz provides many suggestive and informative documents on the "treatment" (or torture) of lesbians by the medical profession in the nineteenth and twentieth centuries. Recent work by the historian Nancy Sahli documents the crackdown on intense female friendships among college women at the turn of the present century.[7] The ironic title *For Her Own Good* might have referred first and foremost to the economic imperative to heterosexuality and marriage and to the sanctions imposed against single women and widows—both of whom have been and still are viewed as deviant. Yet, in this often enlightening Marxist-feminist overview of male prescriptions for female sanity and health, the economics of prescriptive heterosexuality go unexamined.[8]

Of the three psychoanalytically based books, one, Jean Baker Miller's *Toward a New Psychology of Women,* is written as if lesbians simply do not exist, even as marginal beings. Given Miller's title, I find this astonishing. However, the favorable reviews the book has received in feminist journals, including *Signs* and *Spokeswoman,* suggest that Miller's heterocentric assumptions are widely shared. In *The Mermaid and the Minotaur: Sexual Arrangements and the Human Malaise,* Dorothy Dinnerstein makes an impassioned argument for the sharing of parenting between women and men and for an end to what she perceives as the male/female symbiosis of "gender arrangements," which she feels are leading the species further and further into violence and self-extinction. Apart from other problems that I have with this book (including her silence on the institutional and random terrorism men have practiced on women—and children—throughout history,[9] and her obsession with psychology to the neglect of economic and other material realities that help to create psychological reality), I find Dinnerstein's view of the relations between women and men as "a collaboration to keep history mad" utterly ahistorical. She means by this a collaboration to perpetuate social relations which are hostile, exploitative, and destructive to life itself. She sees women and men as equal partners in the making of "sexual arrangements," seemingly unaware of the repeated struggles of women to resist oppression (their own and that of others) and to change their condition. She ignores, specifically, the history of women who—as witches, *femmes seules,* marriage resisters, spinsters, autonomous widows, and/or lesbians—have managed on varying levels *not* to collaborate. It is this history, precisely, from which feminists have so much to learn and on which there is overall such blanketing silence. Dinnerstein acknowledges at the end of her book that "female separatism," though "on a large scale and in the long run wildly impractical," has something to teach us: "Separate, women could in principle set out to learn from scratch—undeflected by the opportunities to evade this task that men's presence has so far offered—what intact self-creative humanness is."[10] Phrases like "intact self-creative humanness" obscure the question of what the many forms of female separatism have actually been addressing. The fact is that women in every culture and throughout history *have* undertaken the task of independent, nonheterosexual, woman-connected existence, to the extent made possible by their context, often in the belief that they were the "only ones" ever to have done so. They have undertaken it even though few women have been in an economic position to resist marriage altogether, and even though attacks against unmarried women have ranged from aspersion and mockery to deliberate gynocide, including the burning and torturing of millions of widows and spinsters during the witch persecutions of the 15th, 16th, and 17th centuries in Europe.

Nancy Chodorow does come close to the edge of an acknowledgment of lesbian existence. Like Dinnerstein, Chodorow believes that the fact that women, and women only, are responsible for child care in the sexual division of labor has led to an entire social organization of gender inequality, and that men as well as women must become primary carers for children if that inequality is to change. In the process of examining, from a psychoanalytic perspective, how mothering by women affects the psychological development of girl and boy children, she offers documentation that men are "emotionally secondary" in women's lives, that

"women have a richer, ongoing inner world to fall back on . . . men do not become as emotionally important to women as women do to men."[11] This would carry into the late 20th century Smith-Rosenberg's findings about 18th- and 19th-century women's emotional focus on women. "Emotionally important" can, of course, refer to anger as well as to love, or to that intense mixture of the two often found in women's relationships with women—one aspect of what I have come to call the "double life of women" (see below). Chodorow concludes that because women have women as mothers, "the mother remains a primary internal object [*sic*] to the girl, so that heterosexual relationships are on the model of a nonexclusive, second relationship for her, whereas for the boy they re-create an exclusive, primary relationship." According to Chodorow, women "have learned to deny the limitations of masculine lovers for both psychological and practical reasons."[12]

But the practical reasons (like witch burnings, male control of law, theology, and science, or economic nonviability within the sexual division of labor) are glossed over. Chodorow's account barely glances at the constraints and sanctions which historically have enforced or ensured the coupling of women with men and obstructed or penalized women's coupling or allying in independent groups with other women. She dismisses lesbian existence with the comment that "lesbian relationships do tend to re-create mother–daughter emotions and connections, but most women are heterosexual" (implied: more mature, having developed beyond the mother–daughter connection?). She then adds: "This heterosexual preference and taboos on homosexuality, in addition to objective economic dependence on men, make the option of primary sexual bonds with other women unlikely—though more prevalent in recent years."[13] The significance of that qualification seems irresistible, but Chodorow does not explore it further. Is she saying that lesbian existence has become more *visible* in recent years (in certain groups), that economic and other pressures have changed (under capitalism, socialism, or both), and that consequently more women are rejecting the heterosexual "choice"? She argues that women want children because their heterosexual relationships lack richness and intensity, that in having a child a woman seeks to re-create her own intense relationship with her mother. It seems to me that on the basis of her own findings, Chodorow leads us implicitly to conclude that heterosexuality is *not* a "preference" for women, that, for one thing, it fragments the erotic from the emotional in a way that women find impoverishing and painful. Yet her book participates in mandating it. Neglecting the covert socializations and the overt forces which have channeled women into marriage and heterosexual romance, pressures ranging from the selling of daughters to the silences of literature to the images of the television screen, she, like Dinnerstein, is stuck with trying to reform a manmade institution—compulsory heterosexuality—as if, despite profound emotional impulses and complementarities drawing women toward women, there is a mystical/biological heterosexual inclination, a "preference" or "choice" which draws women toward men.

Moreover, it is understood that this "preference" does not need to be explained unless through the tortuous theory of the female Oedipus complex or the necessity for species reproduction. It is lesbian sexuality which (usually, and incorrectly, "included" under male homosexuality) is seen as requiring explanation. This assumption of female heterosexuality seems to me in itself remarkable: it is an enormous assumption to have glided so silently into the foundations of our thought.

The extension of this assumption is the frequently heard assertion that in a world of genuine equality, where men are nonoppressive and nurturing, everyone would be bisexual. Such a notion blurs and sentimentalizes the actualities within which women have experienced sexuality; it is a liberal leap across the tasks and struggles of here and now, the continuing process of sexual definition which will generate its own possibilities and choices. (It also assumes that women who have chosen women have done so simply because men are oppressive and emotionally unavailable, which still fails to account for women who continue to pursue relationships with oppressive and/or emotionally unsatisfying men.) I am suggesting that heterosexuality, like motherhood, needs to be recognized and studied as a *political institution*—even, or especially, by those individuals who feel they are, in their personal experience, the precursors of a new social relation between the sexes.

II

If women are the earliest sources of emotional caring and physical nurture for both female and male children, it would seem logical, from a feminist perspective at least, to pose the following questions: whether the search for love and tenderness in both sexes does not originally lead toward women; *why in fact women would ever redirect that search;* why species survival, the means of impregnation, and emotional/erotic relationships should ever have become so rigidly identified with each other; and why such violent strictures should be found necessary to enforce women's total emotional, erotic loyalty and subservience to men. I doubt that enough feminist scholars and theorists have taken the pains to acknowledge the societal forces which wrench women's emotional and erotic energies away from themselves and other women and from woman-identified values. These forces, as I shall try to show, range from literal physical enslavement to the disguising and distorting of possible options.

I do not assume that mothering by women is a "sufficient cause" of lesbian existence. But the issue of mothering by women has been much in the air of late, usually accompanied by the view that increased parenting by men would minimize antagonism between the sexes and equalize the sexual imbalance of power of males over females. These discussions are carried on without reference to compulsory heterosexuality as a phenomenon, let alone as an ideology. I do not wish to psychologize here but rather to identify sources of male power. I believe large numbers of men could, in fact, undertake child care on a large scale without radically altering the balance of male power in a male-identified society.

In her essay "The Origin of the Family," Kathleen Gough lists eight characteristics of male power in archaic and contemporary societies which I would like to use as a framework: "men's ability to deny women sexuality or to force it upon them; to command or exploit their labor to control their produce; to control or rob them of their children; to confine them physically and prevent their movement; to use them as objects in male transactions; to cramp their creativeness; or to withhold from them large areas of the society's knowledge and cultural attainments."[14] (Gough does not perceive these power characteristics as specifically enforcing heterosexuality, only as producing sexual inequality.) Below, Gough's words appear in italics; the elaboration of each of her categories, in brackets, is my own.

Characteristics of male power include *the power of men*

1. *to deny women* [their own] *sexuality*—[by means of clitoridectomy and infibulation; chastity belts; pun-

ishment, including death, for female adultery; punishment, including death, for lesbian sexuality; psychoanalytic denial of the clitoris; strictures against masturbation; denial of maternal and postmenopausal sensuality; unnecessary hysterectomy; pseudo-lesbian images in the media and literature; closing of archives and destruction of documents relating to lesbian existence]

2. or to force it [male sexuality] upon them—[by means of rape (including marital rape) and wife beating; father–daughter, brother–sister incest; the socialization of women to feel that male sexual "drive" amounts to a right;15 idealization of heterosexual romance in art, literature, the media, advertising, etc.; child marriage; arranged marriage; prostitution; the harem; psychoanalytic doctrines of frigidity and vaginal orgasm; pornographic depictions of women responding pleasurably to sexual violence and humiliation (a subliminal message being that sadistic heterosexuality is more "normal" than sensuality between women)]

3. *to command or exploit their labor to control their produce*—[by means of the institutions of marriage and motherhood as unpaid production; the horizontal segregation of women in paid employment; the decoy of the upwardly mobile token woman; male control of abortion, contraception, sterilization, and childbirth; pimping; female infanticide, which robs mothers of daughters and contributes to generalized devaluation of women]

4. *to control or rob them of their children*—[by means of father right and "legal kidnaping";[16] enforced sterilization; systematized infanticide; seizure of children from lesbian mothers by the courts; the malpractice of male obstetrics; use of the mother as "token torturer"[17] in genital mutilation or in binding the daughter's feet (or mind) to fit her for marriage]

5. *to confine them physically and prevent their movement*—[by means of rape as terrorism, keeping women off the streets; purdah; foot binding; atrophying of women's athletic capabilities, high heels and "feminine" dress codes in fashion; the veil; sexual harassment on the streets; horizontal segregation of women in employment; prescriptions for "full-time" mothering at home; enforced economic dependence of wives]

6. *to use them as objects in male transactions*—[use of women as "gifts"; bride price; pimping; arranged marriage; use of women as entertainers to facilitate male deals—e.g., wife–hostess, cocktail waitress required to dress for male sexual titillation, call girls, "bunnies," geisha, *kisaeng* prostitutes, secretaries]

7. *to cramp their creativeness*—[witch persecutions as campaigns against midwives and female healers, and as pogrom against independent, "unassimilated" women;[18] definition of male pursuits as more valuable than female within any culture, so that cultural values become the embodiment of male subjectivity; restriction of female self-fulfillment to marriage and motherhood; sexual exploitation of women by male artists and teachers; the social and economic disruption of women's creative aspirations;[19] erasure of female tradition][20]

8. *to withhold from them large areas of the society's knowledge and cultural attainments*—[by means of noneducation of females; the "Great Silence" regarding women and particularly lesbian existence in history and culture;[21] sex-role tracking which deflects women from science, technology, and other "masculine" pursuits; male social/professional bonding which excludes women; discrimination against women in the professions]

These are some of the methods by which male power is manifested and maintained. Looking at the schema, what surely impresses itself is the fact that we are confronting not a simple maintenance of inequality and property possession, but a pervasive cluster of forces, ranging from physical brutality to control of consciousness, which suggests that an enormous potential counterforce is having to be restrained.

Some of the forms by which male power manifests itself are more easily recognizable as enforcing heterosexuality on women than are others. Yet each one I have listed adds to the cluster of forces within which women have been convinced that marriage and sexual orientation toward men are inevitable—even if unsatisfying or oppressive—components of their lives. The chastity belt; child marriage; erasure of lesbian existence (except as exotic and perverse) in art, literature, film; idealization of heterosexual romance and marriage—these are some fairly obvious forms of compulsion, the first two exemplifying physical force, the second two control of consciousness. While clitoridectomy has been assailed by feminists as a form of woman torture,[22] Kathleen Barry first pointed out that it is not simply a way of turning the young girl into a "marriageable" woman through brutal surgery. It intends that women in the intimate proximity of polygynous marriage will not form sexual relationships with each other, that—from a male, genital-fetishist perspective—female erotic connections, even in a sex-segregated situation, will be literally excised.[23]

The function of pornography as an influence on consciousness is a major public issue of our time, when a multibillion-dollar industry has the power to disseminate increasingly sadistic, women-degrading visual images. But even so-called soft-core pornography and advertising depict women as objects of sexual appetite devoid of emotional context, without individual meaning or personality—essentially as a sexual commodity to be consumed by males. (So-called lesbian pornography, created for the male voyeuristic eye, is equally devoid of emotional context or individual personality.) The most pernicious message relayed by pornography is that women are natural sexual prey to men and love it, that sexuality and violence are congruent, and that for women sex is essentially masochistic, humiliation pleasurable, physical abuse erotic. But along with this message comes another, not always recognized: that enforced submission and the use of cruelty, if played out in heterosexual pairing, is sexually "normal," while sensuality between women, including erotic mutuality and respect, is "queer," "sick," and either pornographic in itself or not very exciting compared with the sexuality of whips and bondage.[24] Pornography does not simply create a climate in which sex and violence are interchangeable; *it widens the range of behavior considered acceptable from men in heterosexual intercourse*— behavior which reiteratively strips women of their autonomy, dignity, and sexual potential, including the potential of loving and being loved by women in mutuality and integrity.

In her brilliant study *Sexual Harassment of Working Women: A Case of Sex Discrimination,* Catharine A. MacKinnon delineates the intersection of compulsory heterosexuality and economics. Under capitalism, women are horizontally segregated by gender and occupy a structurally inferior position in the workplace. This is hardly news, but MacKinnon raises the question why, even if capitalism "requires some collection of individuals to occupy low-status, low-paying positions . . . such persons must be biologically female," and goes on to point out that "the fact that male employers often do not hire qualified women, *even when they could pay them less than men,* suggests that more than the profit motive is implicated" [emphasis added].[25] She cites a wealth of material documenting the fact that women are not only segregated

in low-paying service jobs (as secretaries, domestics, nurses, typists, telephone operators, child-care workers, waitresses), but that "sexualization of the woman" is part of the job. Central and intrinsic to the economic realities of women's lives is the requirement that women will "market sexual attractiveness to men, who tend to hold the economic power and position to enforce their predilections." And MacKinnon documents that "sexual harassment perpetuates the interlocked structure by which women have been kept sexually in thrall to men at the bottom of the labor market. Two forces of American society converge: men's control over women's sexuality and capital's control over employees' work lives."[26] Thus, women in the workplace are at the mercy of sex as power in a vicious circle. Economically disadvantaged, women—whether waitresses or professors—endure sexual harassment to keep their jobs and learn to behave in a complaisantly and ingratiatingly heterosexual manner because they discover this is their true qualification for employment, whatever the job description. And, MacKinnon notes, the woman who too decisively resists sexual overtures in the workplace is accused of being "dried up" and sexless, or lesbian. This raises a specific difference between the experiences of lesbians and homosexual men. A lesbian, closeted on her job because of heterosexist prejudice, is not simply forced into denying the truth of her outside relationships or private life. Her job depends on her pretending to be not merely heterosexual, but a heterosexual *woman* in terms of dressing and playing the feminine, deferential role required of "real" women.

MacKinnon raises radical questions as to the qualitative differences between sexual harassment, rape, and ordinary heterosexual intercourse. ("As one accused rapist put it, he hadn't used 'any more force than is usual for males during the preliminaries.'") She criticizes Susan Brownmiller[27] for separating rape from the mainstream of daily life and for her unexamined premise that "rape is violence, intercourse is sexuality," removing rape from the sexual sphere altogether. Most crucially she argues that "taking rape from the realm of 'the sexual,' placing it in the realm of 'the violent,' allows one to be against it without raising any questions about the extent to which the institution of heterosexuality has defined force as a normal part of 'the preliminaries.'"[28] "Never is it asked whether, under conditions of male supremacy, the notion of 'consent' has any meaning."[29]

The fact is that the workplace, among other social institutions, is a place where women have learned to accept male violation of their psychic and physical boundaries as the price of survival; where women have been educated—no less than by romantic literature or by pornography—to perceive themselves as sexual prey. A woman seeking to escape such casual violations along with economic disadvantage may well turn to marriage as a form of hoped-for protection, while bringing into marriage neither social nor economic power, thus entering that institution also from a disadvantaged position. MacKinnon finally asks:

What if inequality is built into the social conceptions of male and female sexuality, of masculinity and femininity, of sexiness and heterosexual attractiveness? Incidents of sexual harassment suggest that male sexual desire itself may be aroused by female vulnerability. . . . Men feel they can take advantage, so they want to, so they do. Examination of sexual harassment, precisely because the episodes appear commonplace, forces one to confront the fact that sexual intercourse normally occurs between economic (as well as physical) unequals . . . the apparent legal requirement that violations of women's sexuality appear out of the ordinary before they will be punished helps prevent women from defining the ordinary conditions of their own consent.[30]

Given the nature and extent of heterosexual pressures—the daily "eroticization of women's subordination," as MacKinnon phrases it[31]—I question the more or less psychoanalytic perspective (suggested by such writers as Karen Horney, H. R. Hayes, Wolfgang Lederer, and, most recently, Dorothy Dinnerstein) that the male need to control women sexually results from some primal male "fear of women" and of women's sexual insatiability. It seems more probable that men really fear not that they will have women's sexual appetites forced on them or that women want to smother and devour them, but that women could be indifferent to them altogether, that men could be allowed sexual and emotional—therefore economic— access to women *only* on women's terms, otherwise being left on the periphery of the matrix.

The means of assuring male sexual access to women have recently received searching investigation by Kathleen Barry.[32] She documents extensive and appalling evidence for the existence, on a very large scale, of international female slavery, the institution once known as "white slavery" but which in fact has involved, and at this very moment involves, women of every race and class. In the theoretical analysis derived from her research, Barry makes the connection between all enforced conditions under which women live subject to men: prostitution, marital rape, father –daughter and brother–sister incest, wife beating, pornography, bride price, the selling of daughters, purdah, and genital mutilation. She sees the rape paradigm—where the victim of sexual assault is held responsible for her own victimization—as leading to the rationalization and acceptance of other forms of enslavement where the woman is presumed to have "chosen" her fate, to embrace it passively, or to have courted it perversely through rash or unchaste behavior. On the contrary, Barry maintains, "female sexual slavery is present in ALL situations where women or girls cannot change the conditions of their existence; where regardless of how they got into those conditions, e.g., social pressure, economic hardship, misplaced trust or the longing for affection, they cannot get out; and where they are subject to sexual violence and exploitation."[33] She provides a spectrum of concrete examples, not only as to the existence of a widespread international traffic in women, but also as to how this operates—whether in the form of a Minnesota pipeline" funneling blonde, blue-eyed midwestern runaways to Times Square, or the purchasing of young women out of rural poverty in Latin America or Southeast Asia, or the providing of *maisons d'abattage* for migrant workers in the eighteenth arrondissement of Paris. Instead of "blaming the victim" or trying to diagnose her presumed pathology, Barry turns her floodlight on the pathology of sex colonization itself, the ideology of "cultural sadism" represented by the pornography industry and by the overall identification of women primarily as "sexual beings whose responsibility is the sexual service of men."[34]

Barry delineates what she names a "sexual domination perspective" through whose lens sexual abuse and terrorism of women by men has been rendered almost invisible by treating it as natural and inevitable. From its point of view, women are expendable as long as the sexual and emotional needs of the male can be satisfied. To replace this perspective of domination with a universal standard of basic freedom for women from gender-specific violence, from constraints on movement, and from male right of sexual and emotional access is the political purpose of her book. Like Mary Daly in *Gyn/Ecology,* Barry rejects structuralist and other cultural-relativist rationalizations for sexual torture and antiwoman violence. In her opening chapter, she asks of her readers that they refuse all handy escapes into ignorance and denial. "The only way we can come out of hiding, break through our paralyzing defenses, is to know it all—the full extent of sexual violence and domination of women. . . . In *knowing,* in facing directly, we can learn to chart our course out of this oppression, by envisioning and creating a world which will preclude sexual slavery."[35]

"Until we name the practice, give conceptual definition and form to it, illustrate its life over time and in space, those who are its most obvious victims will also not be able to name it or define their experience."

But women are all, in different ways and to different degrees, its victims; and part of the problem with naming and conceptualizing female sexual slavery is, as Barry clearly sees, compulsory heterosexuality.[36] Compulsory heterosexuality simplifies the task of the procurer and pimp in worldwide prostitution rings and "eros centers," while, in the privacy of the home, it leads the daughter to "accept" incest/rape by her father, the mother to deny that it is happening, the battered wife to stay on with an abusive husband. "Befriending or love" is a major tactic of the procurer, whose job it is to turn the runaway or the confused young girl over to the pimp for seasoning. The ideology of heterosexual romance, beamed at her from childhood out of fairy tales, television, films, advertising, popular songs, wedding pageantry, is a tool ready to the procurer's hand and one which he does not hesitate to use, as Barry documents. Early female indoctrination in "love" as an emotion may be largely a Western concept; but a more universal ideology concerns the primacy and uncontrollability of the male sexual drive. This is one of many insights offered by Barry's work:

> As sexual power is learned by adolescent boys through the social experience of their sex drive, so do girls learn that the locus of sexual power is male. Given the importance placed on the male sex drive in the socialization of girls as well as boys, early adolescence is probably the first significant phase of male identification in a girl's life and development. . . . As a young girl becomes aware of her

own increasing sexual feelings . . . she turns away from her heretofore primary relationships with girlfriends. As they become secondary to her, recede in importance in her life, her own identity also assumes a secondary role and she grows into male identification.[37]

We still need to ask why some women never, even temporarily, turn away from "heretofore primary relationships" with other females. And why does male identification—the casting of one's social, political, and intellectual allegiances with men—exist among lifelong sexual lesbians? Barry's hypothesis throws us among new questions, but it clarifies the diversity of forms in which compulsory heterosexuality presents itself. In the mystique of the overpowering, all-conquering male sex drive, the penis-with-a-life-of-its-own, is rooted the law of male sex right to women, which justifies prostitution as a universal cultural assumption on the one hand, while defending sexual slavery within the family on the basis of "family privacy and cultural uniqueness" on the other.[38] The adolescent male sex drive, which, as both young women and men are taught, once triggered cannot take responsibility for itself or take no for an answer, becomes, according to Barry, the norm and rationale for adult male sexual behavior: a condition of *arrested sexual development.* Women learn to accept as natural the inevitability of this "drive" because they receive it as dogma. Hence, marital rape; hence, the Japanese wife resignedly packing her husband's suitcase for a weekend in the *kisaeng* brothels of Taiwan; hence, the psychological as well as economic imbalance of power between husband and wife, male employer and female worker, father and daughter, male professor and female student.

The effect of male identification means

> internalizing the values of the colonizer and actively participating in carrying out the colonization of one's self and one's sex. . . . Male identification is the act whereby women place men above women, including themselves, in credibiiity, status, and importance in most situations, regardless of the comparative quality the women may bring to the situation. . . . Interaction with women is seen as a lesser form of relating on every level.[39]

What deserves further exploration is the doublethink

many women engage in and from which no woman is permanently and utterly free: However woman-to-woman relationships, female support networks, a female and feminist value system are relied on and cherished, indoctrination in male credibility and status can still create synapses in thought, denials of feeling, wishful thinking, a profound sexual and intellectual confusion.[40] I quote here from a letter I received the day I was writing this passage: "I have had very bad relationships with men—I am now in the midst of a very painful separation. I am trying to find my strength through women—without my friends, I would not survive." How many times a day do women speak words like these or think them or write them, and how often does the synapse reassert itself?

Barry summarizes her findings:

Considering the arrested sexual development that is understood to be normal in the male population, and considering the numbers of men who are pimps, procurers, members of slavery gangs, corrupt officials participating in this traffic, owners, operators, employees of brothels and lodging and entertainment facilities, pornography purveyors, associated with prostitution, wife beaters, child molesters, incest perpetrators, johns (tricks) and rapists, one cannot but be momentarily stunned by the enormous male population engaging in female sexual slavery. The huge number of men engaged in these practices should be cause for declaration of an international emergency, a crisis in sexual violence. But what should be cause for alarm is instead accepted as normal sexual intercourse.[41]

Susan Cavin, in a rich and provocative, if highly speculative, dissertation, suggests that patriarchy becomes possible when the original female band, which includes children but ejects adolescent males, becomes invaded and outnumbered by males; that not patriarchal marriage, but the rape of the mother by the son, becomes the first act of male domination. The entering wedge, or leverage, which allows this to happen is not just a simple change in sex ratios; it is also the mother-child bond, manipulated by adolescent males in order to remain within the matrix past the age of exclusion. Maternal affection is used to establish male right of sexual access, which, however, must ever after be held by force (or through control of conscious-

ness) since the original deep adult bonding is that of woman for woman.[42] I find this hypothesis extremely suggestive, since one form of false consciousness which serves compulsory heterosexuality is the maintenance of a mother–son relationship between women and men, including the demand that women provide maternal solace, nonjudgmental nurturing, and compassion for their harassers, rapists, and batterers (as well as for men who passively vampirize them).

But whatever its origins, when we look hard and clearly at the extent and elaboration of measures designed to keep women within a male sexual purlieu, it becomes an inescapable question whether the issue feminists have to address is not simple "gender inequality" nor the domination of culture by males nor mere "taboos against homosexuality," but the enforcement of heterosexuality for women as a means of assuring male right of physical, economic, and emotional access.[43] One of many means of enforcement is, of course, the rendering invisible of the lesbian possibility, an engulfed continent which rises fragmentedly into view from time to time only to become submerged again. Feminist research and theory that contribute to lesbian invisibility or marginality are actually working against the liberation and empowerment of women as a group.[44]

The assumption that "most women are innately heterosexual" stands as a theoretical and political stumbling block for feminism. It remains a tenable assumption partly because lesbian existence has been written out of history or catalogued under disease, partly because it has been treated as exceptional rather than intrinsic, partly because to acknowledge that for women heterosexuality may not be a "preference" at all but something that has had to be imposed, managed, organized, propagandized, and maintained by force is an immense step to take if you consider yourself freely and "innately" heterosexual. Yet the failure to examine heterosexuality as an institution is like failing to admit that the economic system called capitalism or the caste system of racism is maintained by a variety of forces, including both physical violence and false consciousness. To take the step of questioning heterosexuality as a "preference" or "choice" for women— and to do the intellectual and emotional work that follows—will call for a special quality of courage in heterosexually identified feminists, but I think the rewards will be great: a freeing-up of thinking, the exploring of new paths, the shattering of another great silence, new clarity in personal relationships.

III

I have chosen to use the terms *lesbian existence* and *lesbian continuum* because the word *lesbianism* has a clinical and limiting ring. *Lesbian existence* suggests both the fact of the historical presence of lesbians and our continuing creation of the meaning of that existence. I mean the term *lesbian continuum* to include a range—through each woman's life and throughout history—of woman-identified experience, not simply the fact that a woman has had or consciously desired genital sexual experience with another woman. If we expand it to embrace many more forms of primary intensity between and among women, including the sharing of a rich inner life, the bonding against male tyranny, the giving and receiving of practical and political support, if we can also hear it in such associations as *marriage resistance* and the "haggard" behavior identified by Mary Daly (obsolete meanings: "intractable," "willful," "wanton," and "unchaste," "a woman reluctant to yield to wooing"),[45] we begin to grasp breadths of female history and psychology which have lain out of reach as a consequence of limited, mostly clinical, definitions of *lesbianism.*

Lesbian existence comprises both the breaking of a taboo and the rejection of a compulsory way of life. It is also a direct or indirect attack on male right of access to women. But it is more than these, although we may first begin to perceive it as a form of naysaying to patriarchy, an act of resistance. It has, of course, included isolation, self-hatred, breakdown, alcoholism, suicide, and intrawoman violence; we romanticize at our peril what it means to love and act against the grain, and under heavy penalties; and lesbian existence has been lived (unlike, say, Jewish or Catholic existence) without access to any knowledge of a tradition, a continuity, a social underpinning. The destruction of records and memorabilia and letters documenting the realities of lesbian existence must be taken very seriously as a means of keeping heterosexuality compulsory for women, since what has been kept from our knowledge is joy, sensuality, courage, and community, as well as guilt, self-betrayal, and pain.[46]

Lesbians have historically been deprived of a political existence through "inclusion" as female versions of male homosexuality. To equate lesbian existence with male homosexuality because each is stigmatized is to erase female reality once again. Part of the history of lesbian existence is, obviously, to be found where lesbians, lacking a coherent female community, have shared a kind of social life and common cause with homosexual men. But there are differences: women's lack of economic and cultural privilege relative to men; qualitative differences in female and male relationships—for example, the patterns of anonymous sex among male homosexuals, and the pronounced ageism in male homosexual standards of sexual attractiveness. I perceive the lesbian experience as being, like motherhood, a profoundly *female* experience, with particular oppressions, meanings, and potentialities we cannot comprehend as long as we simply bracket it with other sexually stigmatized existences. Just as the term *parenting* serves to conceal the particular and significant reality of being a parent who is actually a mother, the term *gay* may serve the purpose of blurring the very outlines we need to discern, which are of crucial value for feminism and for the freedom of women as a group.[47]

As the term *lesbian* has been held to limiting, clinical associations in its patriarchal definition, female friendship and comradeship have been set apart from the erotic, thus limiting the erotic itself. But as we deepen and broaden the range of what we define as lesbian existence, as we delineate a lesbian continuum, we begin to discover the erotic in female terms: as that which is unconfined to any single part of the body or solely to the body itself; as an energy not only diffuse but, as Audre Lorde has described it, omnipresent in "the sharing of joy, whether physical, emotional, psychic," and in the sharing of work; as the empowering joy which "makes us less willing to accept powerlessness, or those other supplied states of being which are not native to me, such as resignation, despair, self-effacement, depression, self-denial."[48] In another context, writing of women and work, I quoted the autobiographical passage in which the poet H. D. described how her friend Bryher supported her in persisting with the visionary experience which was to shape her mature work:

> I knew that this experience, this writing-on-the-wall before me, could not be shared with anyone except the girl who stood so bravely there beside me. This girl said without hesitation, "Go on." It was she really who had the detachment and integrity of the Pythoness of Delphi. But it was I, battered and dis-

sociated . . . who was seeing the pictures, and who was reading the writing or granted the inner vision. Or perhaps, in some sense, we were "seeing" it together, for without her, admittedly, I could not have gone on.[49]

If we consider the possibility that all women—from the infant suckling at her mother's breast, to the grown woman experiencing orgasmic sensations while suckling her own child, perhaps recalling her mother's milk smell in her own, to two women, like Virginia Woolf's Chloe and Olivia, who share a laboratory,[50] to the woman dying at ninety, touched and handled by women—exist on a lesbian continuum, we can see ourselves as moving in and out of this continuum, whether we identify ourselves as lesbian or not.

We can then connect aspects of woman identification as diverse as the impudent, intimate girl friendships of eight or nine year olds and the banding together of those women of the 12th and 15th centuries known as Beguines who "shared houses, rented to one another, bequeathed houses to their room-mates . . . in cheap subdivided houses in the artisans' area of town," who "practiced Christian virtue on their own, dressing and living simply and not associating with men," who earned their livings as spinsters, bakers, nurses, or ran schools for young girls, and who managed—until the Church forced them to disperse—to live independent both of marriage and of conventual restrictions.[51] It allows us to connect these women with the more celebrated "Lesbians" of the women's school around Sappho of the 7th century B.C., with the secret sororities and economic networks reported among African women, and with the Chinese marriage-resistance sisterhoods—communities of women who refused marriage or who, if married, often refused to consummate their marriages and soon left their husbands, the only women in China who were not foot-bound and who, Agnes Smedley tells us, welcomed the births of daughters and organized successful women's strikes in the silk mills.[52] It allows us to connect and compare disparate individual instances of marriage resistance: for example, the strategies available to Emily Dickinson, a 19th-century white woman genius, with the strategies available to Zora Neale Hurston, a 20th-century Black woman genius. Dickinson never married, had tenuous intellectual friendships with men, lived self-convented in her genteel father's house in Amherst, and wrote a lifetime of passionate letters to

her sister-in-law Sue Gilbert and a smaller group of such letters to her friend Kate Scott Anthon. Hurston married twice but soon left each husband, scrambled her way from Florida to Harlem to Columbia University to Haiti and finally back to Florida, moved in and out of white patronage and poverty, professional success, and failure; her survival relationships were all with women, beginning with her mother. Both of these women in their vastly different circumstances were marriage resisters, committed to their own work and selfhood, and were later characterized as "apolitical." Both were drawn to men of intellectual quality; for both of them women provided the ongoing fascination and sustenance of life.

If we think of heterosexuality as *the* natural emotional and sensual inclination for women, lives such as these are seen as deviant, as pathological, or as emotionally and sensually deprived. Or, in more recent and permissive jargon, they are banalized as "life styles." And the work of such women, whether merely the daily work of individual or collective survival and resistance or the work of the writer, the activist, the reformer, the anthropologist, or the artist—the work of self-creation—is undervalued, or seen as the bitter fruit of "penis envy" or the sublimation of repressed eroticism or the meaningless rant of a "man-hater." But when we turn the lens of vision and consider the degree to which and the methods whereby heterosexual "preference" has actually been imposed on women, not only can we understand differently the meaning of individual lives and work, but we can begin to recognize a central fact of women's history: that women have always resisted male tyranny. A feminism of action, often though not always without a theory, has constantly re-emerged in every culture and in every period. We can then begin to study women's struggle against powerlessness, women's radical rebellion, not just in male-defined "concrete revolutionary situations"[53] but in all the situations male ideologies have not perceived as revolutionary—for example, the refusal of some women to produce children, aided at great risk by other women,[54] the refusal to produce a higher standard of living and leisure for men (Leghorn and Parker show how both are part of women's unacknowledged, unpaid, and ununionized economic contribution). We can no longer have patience with Dinnerstein's view that women have simply collaborated with men in the "sexual arrangements" of history. We begin to observe behavior, both in history and in individual biography, that has hitherto been invisible or misnamed, behavior which often constitutes, given the limits of the counterforce exerted in a given time and place, radical rebellion. And we can connect these rebellions and the necessity for them with the physical passion of woman for woman which is central to lesbian existence: the erotic sensuality which has been, precisely, the most violently erased fact of female experience.

Heterosexuality has been both forcibly and subliminally imposed on women. Yet everywhere women have resisted it, often at the cost of physical torture, imprisonment, psychosurgery, social ostracism, and extreme poverty. "Compulsory heterosexuality" was named as one of the "crimes against women" by the Brussels International Tribunal Crimes against Women in 1976. Two pieces of testimony from two very different cultures reflect the degree to which persecution of lesbians is a global practice here and now. A report from Norway relates:

A lesbian in Oslo was in a heterosexual marriage that didn't work, so she started taking tranquillizers and ended up at the health sanatorium for treatment and rehabilitation. . . . The moment she said in family group therapy that she believed she was a lesbian, the doctor told her she was not. He knew from "looking into her eyes," he said. She had the eyes of a woman who wanted sexual intercourse with her husband. So she was subjected to so-called "couch therapy." She was put into a comfortably heated room, naked, on a bed, and for an hour her husband was to . . . try to excite her sexually. . . . The idea was that the touching was always to end with sexual intercourse. She felt stronger and stronger aversion. She threw up and sometimes ran out of the room to avoid this "treatment." The more strongly she asserted that she was a lesbian, the more violent the forced heterosexual intercourse became. This treatment went on for about six months. She escaped from the hospital, but she was brought back. Again she escaped. She has not been there since. In the end she realized that she had been subjected to forcible rape for six months.

And from Mozambique:

I am condemned to a life of exile because I will not deny that I am a lesbian, that my primary commit-

ments are, and will always be to other women. In the new Mozambique, lesbianism is considered a left-over from colonialism and decadent Western civilization. Lesbians are sent to rehabilitation camps to learn through self-criticism the correct line about themselves. . . . If I am forced to denounce my own love for women, if I therefore denounce myself, I could go back to Mozambique and join forces in the exciting and hard struggle of rebuilding a nation, including the struggle for the emancipation of Mozambiquan women. As it is, I either risk the rehabilitation camps, or remain in exile.[55]

Nor can it be assumed that women like those in Carroll Smith-Rosenberg's study, who married, stayed married, yet dwelt in a profoundly female emotional and passional world, "preferred" or "chose" heterosexuality. Women have married because it was necessary, in order to survive economically, in order to have children who would not suffer economic deprivation or social ostracism, in order to remain respectable, in order to do what was expected of women, because coming out of "abnormal" childhoods they wanted to feel "normal" and because heterosexual romance has been represented as the great female adventure, duty, and fulfillment. We may faithfully or ambivalently have obeyed the institution, but our feelings—and our sensuality—have not been tamed or contained within it. There is no statistical documentation of the numbers of lesbians who have remained in heterosexual marriages for most of their lives. But in a letter to the early lesbian publication *The Ladder,* the playwright Lorraine Hansberry had this to say:

I suspect that the problem of the married woman who would prefer emotional-physical relationships with other women is proportionally much higher than a similar statistic for men. (A statistic surely no one will ever really have.) This because the estate of women being what it is, how could we ever begin to guess the numbers of women who are not prepared to risk a life alien to what they have been taught all their lives to believe was their "natural" destiny—AND—their only expectation for ECONOMIC security. It seems to be that this is why the question has an immensity that it does not have for male homosexuals. . . . A woman of strength and honesty may, if she chooses, sever her marriage and marry a new male mate and society will be upset that the divorce rate is rising so—but there are few places in the United States, in any event, where she will be anything remotely akin to an "outcast." Obviously this is not true for a woman who would end her marriage to take up life with another woman.[56]

This *double life*—this apparent acquiescence to an institution founded on male interest and prerogative—has been characteristic of female experience: in motherhood and in many kinds of heterosexual behavior, including the rituals of courtship; the pretense of asexuality by the 19th-century wife; the simulation of orgasm by the prostitute, the courtesan, the 20th-century "sexually liberated" woman.

Meridel LeSueur's documentary novel of the depression, *The Girl,* is arresting as a study of female double life. The protagonist, a waitress in a St. Paul working-class speakeasy, feels herself passionately attracted to the young man Butch, but her survival relationships are with Clara, an older waitress and prostitute, with Belle, whose husband owns the bar, and with Amelia, a union activist. For Clara and Belle and the unnamed protagonist, sex with men is in one sense an escape from the bedrock misery of daily life, a flare of intensity in the gray, relentless, often brutal web of day-to-day existence:

> It was like he was a magnet pulling me. It was exciting and powerful and frightening. He was after me too and when he found me I would run, or be petrified, just standing in front of him like a zany. And he told me not to be wandering with Clara to the Marigold where we danced with strangers. He said he would knock the shit out of me. Which made me shake and tremble, but it was better than being a husk full of suffering and not knowing why.[57]

Throughout the novel the theme of double life emerges; Belle reminisces about her marriage to the bootlegger Hoinck:

> You know, when I had that black eye and said I hit it on the cupboard, well he did it the bastard, and then he says don't tell anybody. . . . He's nuts, that's what he is, nuts, and I don't see why I live with him, why I put up with him a minute on this earth. But listen kid, she said, I'm telling you something. She looked at me and her face was wonderful.

> She said, Jesus Christ, Goddam him I love him that's why I'm hooked like this all my life, Goddam him I love him.[58]

After the protagonist has her first sex with Butch, her women friends care for her bleeding, give her whiskey, and compare notes.

> My luck, the first time and I got into trouble. He gave me a little money and I come to St. Paul where for ten bucks they'd stick a huge vet's needle into you and you start it and then you were on your own. . . . I never had no child. I've just had Hoinck to mother, and a hell of a child he is.[59]

> Later they made me go back to Clara's room to lie down. . . . Clara lay down beside me and put her arms around me and wanted me to tell her about it but she wanted to tell about herself. She said she started it when she was twelve with a bunch of boys in an old shed. She said nobody had paid any attention to her before and she became very popular. . . . They like it so much, she said, why shouldn't you give it to them and get presents and attention? I never cared anything for it and neither did my mama. But it's the only thing you got that's valuable.[60]

Sex is thus equated with attention from the male, who is charismatic though brutal, infantile, or unreliable. Yet it is the women who make life endurable for each other, give physical affection without causing pain, share, advise, and stick by each other. (*I am trying to find my strength through women—without my friends, I could not survive.*) LeSueur's *The Girl* parallels Toni Morrison's remarkable *Sula,* another revelation of female double life:

> Nel was the one person who had wanted nothing from her, who had accepted all aspects of her. . . . Nel was one of the reasons Sula had drifted back to Medallion. . . . The men . . . had merged into one large personality: the same language of love, the same entertainments of love, the same cooling of love. Whenever she introduced her private thoughts into their rubbings and goings, they hooded their eyes. They taught her nothing but love tricks, shared nothing but worry, gave nothing but money. She had been looking all along for a friend, and it

took her a while to discover that a lover was not a comrade and could never be—for a woman.

But Sula's last thought at the second of her death is "Wait'll I tell Nel." And after Sula's death, Nel looks back on her own life:

> "All that time, all that time, I thought I was missing Jude." And the loss pressed down on her chest and came up into her throat. "We was girls together," she said as though explaining something. "O Lord, Sula," she cried, "Girl, girl, girlgirlgirl!" It was a fine cry—loud and long—but it had no bottom and it had no top, just circles and circles of sorrow.[61]

The Girl and *Sula* are both novels which examine what I am calling the lesbian continuum, in contrast to the shallow or sensational "lesbian scenes" in recent commercial fiction.[62] Each shows us woman identification untarnished (till the end of LeSueur's novel) by romanticism; each depicts the competition of heterosexual compulsion for women's attention, the diffusion and frustration of female bonding that might, in a more conscious form, reintegrate love and power.

IV

Woman identification is a source of energy, a potential springhead of female power, curtailed and contained under the institution of heterosexuality. The denial of reality and visibility to women's passion for women, women's choice of women as allies, life companions, and community, the forcing of such relationships into dissimulation and their disintegration under intense pressure have meant an incalculable loss to the power of all women *to change the social relations of the sexes, to liberate ourselves and each other.* The lie of compulsory female heterosexuality today afflicts not just feminist scholarship but every profession, every reference work, every curriculum, every organizing attempt, every relationship or conversation over which it hovers. It creates, specifically, a profound falseness, hypocrisy, and hysteria in the heterosexual dialogue, for every heterosexual relationship is lived in the queasy strobe light of that lie. However we choose to identify ourselves, however we find ourselves labeled, it flickers across and distorts our lives.[63]

The lie keeps numberless women psychologically trapped, trying to fit mind, spirit, and sexuality into a prescribed script because they cannot look beyond the parameters of the acceptable. It pulls on the energy of such women even as it drains the energy of "closeted" lesbians—the energy exhausted in the double life. The lesbian trapped in the "closet," the woman imprisoned in prescriptive ideas of the "normal" share the pain of blocked options, broken connections, lost access to self-definition freely and powerfully assumed.

The lie is many-layered. In Western tradition, one layer—the romantic—asserts that women are inevitably, even if rashly and tragically, drawn to men; that even when that attraction is suicidal (e.g., *Tristan and Isolde,* Kate Chopin's *The Awakening*), it is still an organic imperative. In the tradition of the social sciences it asserts that primary love between the sexes is "normal"; that women *need* men as social and economic protectors, for adult sexuality, and for psychological completion; that the heterosexually constituted family is the basic social unit, that women who do not attach their primary intensity to men must be, in functional terms, condemned to an even more devastating outsiderhood than their outsiderhood as women. Small wonder that lesbians are reported to be a more hidden population than male homosexuals. The Black lesbian-feminist critic Lorraine Bethel, writing on Zora Neale Hurston, remarks that for a Black woman—already twice an outsider—to choose to assume still another "hated identity" is problematic indeed. Yet the lesbian continuum has been a life line for Black women both in Africa and the United States.

> Black women have a long tradition of bonding together . . . in a Black/women's community that has been a source of vital survival information, psychic and emotional support for us. We have a distinct Black woman-identified folk culture based on our experiences as Black women in this society; symbols, language and modes of expression that are specific to the realities of our lives. . . . Because Black women were rarely among those Blacks and females who gained access to literary and other acknowledged forms of artistic expression, this Black female bonding and Black woman-identification has often been hidden and unrecorded except in the individual lives of Black women through our own memories of our particular Black female tradition.[64]

Another layer of the lie is the frequently encountered implication that women turn to women out of hatred for men. Profound skepticism, caution, and righteous paranoia about men may indeed be part of any healthy woman's response to the misogyny of male-dominated culture, to the forms assumed by "normal" male sexuality, and to *the failure even of "sensitive" or "political" men to perceive or find these troubling.* Lesbian existence is also represented as mere refuge from male abuses, rather than as an electric and empowering charge between women. One of the most frequently quoted literary passages on lesbian relationship is that in which Colette's Renée, in *The Vagabond,* describes "the melancholy and touching image of two weak creatures who have perhaps found shelter in each other's arms, there to sleep and weep, safe from man who is often cruel, and there to taste *better than any pleasure, the bitter happiness of feeling themselves akin, frail and forgotten* [emphasis added]."[65] Colette is often considered a lesbian writer. Her popular reputation has, I think, much to do with the fact that she writes about lesbian existence as if for a male audience; her earliest "lesbian" novels, the Claudine series, were written under compulsion for her husband and published under both their names. At all events, except for her writings on her mother, Colette is a less reliable source on the lesbian continuum than, I would think, Charlotte Brontë, who understood that while women may, indeed must, be one another's allies, mentors, and comforters in the female struggle for survival, there is quite extraneous delight in each other's company and attraction to each others' minds and character, which attend a recognition of each others' strengths.

By the same token, we can say that there is a *nascent* feminist political content in the act of choosing a woman lover or life partner in the face of institutionalized heterosexuality.[66] But for lesbian existence to realize this political content in an ultimately liberating form, the erotic choice must deepen and expand into conscious woman identification—into lesbian feminism.

The work that lies ahead, of unearthing and describing what I call here "lesbian existence," is potentially liberating for all women. It is work that must assuredly move beyond the limits of white and middle-class Western Women's Studies to examine women's lives, work, and groupings within every racial, ethnic, and political structure. There are differences, moreover, between "lesbian existence" and the "lesbian continuum," differences we can discern even in the movement of our own lives. The lesbian continuum, I suggest, needs delineation in light of the "double life" of

women, not only women self-described as heterosexual but also of self-described lesbians. We need a far more exhaustive account of the forms the double life has assumed. Historians need to ask at every point how heterosexuality as institution has been organized and maintained through the female wage scale, the enforcement of middle-class women's "leisure," the glamorization of so-called sexual liberation, the withholding of education from women, the imagery of "high art" and popular culture, the mystification of the "personal" sphere, and much else. We need an economics which comprehends the institution of heterosexuality, with its doubled workload for women and its sexual divisions of labor, as the most idealized of economic relations.

The question inevitably will arise: Are we then to condemn all heterosexual relationships, including those which are least oppressive? I believe this question, though often heartfelt, is the wrong question here. We have been stalled in a maze of false dichotomies which prevents our apprehending the institution as a whole: "good" versus "bad" marriages; "marriage for love" versus arranged marriage; "liberated" sex versus prostitution; heterosexual intercourse versus rape; *Liebeschmerz* versus humiliation and dependency. Within the institution exist, of course, qualitative differences of experience; but the absence of choice remains the great unacknowledged reality, and in the absence of choice, women will remain dependent upon the chance or luck of particular relationships and will have no collective power to determine the meaning and place of sexuality in their lives. As we address the institution itself, moreover, we begin to perceive a history of female resistance which has never fully understood itself because it has been so fragmented, miscalled, erased. It will require a courageous grasp of the politics and economics, as well as the cultural propaganda, of heterosexuality to carry us beyond individual cases or diversified group situations into the complex kind of overview needed to undo the power men everywhere wield over women, power which has become a model for every other form of exploitation and illegitimate control.

AFTERWORD

In 1980, Ann Snitow, Christine Stansell, and Sharon Thompson, three Marxist-feminist activists and scholars, sent out a call for papers for an anthology on the politics of sexuality. Having just finished writing

"Compulsory Heterosexuality" for *Signs,* I sent them that manuscript and asked them to consider it. Their anthology, *Powers of Desire,* was published by the Monthly Review Press New Feminist Library in 1983 and included my paper. During the intervening period, the four of us were in correspondence, but I was able to take only limited advantage of this dialogue due to ill health and resulting surgery. With their permission, I reprint here excerpts from that correspondence as a way of indicating that my essay should be read as one contribution to a long exploration in progress, not as my own "last word" on sexual politics. I also refer interested readers to *Powers of Desire* itself.

Dear Adrienne,
. . . In one of our first letters, we told you that we were finding parameters of left-wing/feminist sexual discourse to be far broader than we imagined. Since then, we have perceived what we believe to be a crisis in the feminist movement about sex, an intensifying debate (although not always an explicit one), and a questioning of assumptions once taken for granted. While we fear the link between sex and violence, as do Women Against Pornography, we wish we better understood its sources in ourselves as well as in men. In the Reagan era, we can hardly afford to romanticize any old norm of a virtuous and moral sexuality.

In your piece, you are asking the question, what would women choose in a world where patriarchy and capitalism did *not* rule? We agree with you that heterosexuality is an institution created between these grind stones, but we don't conclude, therefore, that it is entirely a male creation. You only allow for female historical agency insofar as women exist on the lesbian continuum while we would argue that women's history, like men's history, is created out of a dialectic of necessity and choice.

All three of us (hence one lesbian, two heterosexual women) had questions about your use of the term "false consciousness" for women's heterosexuality. In general, we think the false-consciousness model can blind us to the necessities and desires that comprise the lives of the oppressed. It can also lead to the too easy denial of others' experience when that experience is different from our own. We posit, rather, a complex social model in which all erotic life is a continuum, one which therefore includes relations with men.

Which brings us to this metaphor of the continuum. We know you are a poet, not an historian, and we look forward to reading your metaphors all our lives—and standing straighter as feminists, as women, for having read them. But the metaphor of the lesbian continuum is open to all kinds of misunderstandings, and these sometimes have odd political effects. For example, Sharon reports that at a recent meeting around the abortion-rights struggle, the notions of continuum arose in the discussion several times and underwent divisive transformation. Overall, the notion that two ways of being existed on the same continuum was interpreted to mean that those two ways were the *same.* The sense of range and gradation that your description evokes disappeared. Lesbianism and female friendship became exactly the same thing. Similarly, heterosexuality and rape became the same. In one of several versions of the continuum that evolved, a slope was added, like so:

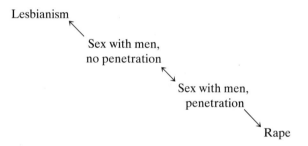

This sloped continuum brought its proponents to the following conclusion: An appropriate, workable abortion-rights strategy is to inform all women that heterosexual penetration is rape, whatever their subjective experiences to the contrary. All women will immediately recognize the truth of this and opt for the alternative of nonpenetration. The abortion-rights struggle will thus be simplified into a struggle against coercive sex and its consequences (since no enlightened woman would voluntarily undergo penetration unless her object was procreation—a peculiarly Catholic-sounding view).

The proponents of this strategy were young women who have worked hard in the abortion-rights movement for the past two or more years. They are inexperienced but they are dedicated. For this reason, we take their reading of your work seriously. We don't think, however, that it comes solely, or even at all, from the work itself. As likely a source is the tendency to dichotomize that has plagued the women's movement. The source of that tendency is harder to trace.

In that regard, the hints in "Compulsory" about the double life of women intrigue us. You define the double life as "the apparent acquiescence to an institution founded on male interest and prerogative." But that definition doesn't really explain your other references—to, for instance, the "intense mixture" of love and anger in lesbian relationships and to the peril of romanticizing what it means "to love and act against the grain." We think these comments raise extremely important issues for feminists right now; the problem of division and anger among us needs airing and analysis. Is this, by any chance, the theme of a piece you have in the works?

. . . We would still love it if we could have a meeting with you in the next few months. Any chance? . . . Greetings and support from us—in all your undertakings.

We send love,
Sharon, Chris, and Ann

New York City
April 19, 1981

Dear Ann, Chris, and Sharon,

. . . It's good to be back in touch with you, you who have been so unfailingly patient, generous, and persistent. Above all, it's important to me that you know that ill health, not a withdrawal because of political differences, delayed my writing back to you. . . .

"False consciousness" can, I agree, be used as a term of dismissal for any thinking we don't like to adhere to. But, as I tried to illustrate in some detail, there is a real, identifiable system of heterosexual propaganda, of defining women as existing for the sexual use of men, which goes beyond "sex role" or "gender" stereotyping or "sexist imagery" to include a vast number of verbal and nonverbal messages. And this I call "control of consciousness." The possibility of a woman who does not exist sexually for men—the lesbian possibility—is buried, erased, occluded, distorted, misnamed, and driven underground. The feminist books—Chodorow, Dinnerstein, Ehrenreich and English, and others—which I discuss at the beginning of my essay contribute to this invalidation and erasure, and as such are part of the problem.

My essay is founded on the belief that we all think from within the limits of certain solipsisms—usually linked with privilege, racial, cultural, and economic as well as sexual—which present themselves as "the universal," "the way things are," "all women," etc., etc. I

wrote it equally out of the belief that in becoming conscious of our solipsisms we have certain kinds of choices, that we can and must re-educate ourselves. I never have maintained that heterosexual feminists are walking about in a state of "brainwashed" false consciousness. Nor have such phrases as "sleeping with the enemy" seemed to me either profound or useful. *Homophobia* is too diffuse a term and does not go very far in helping us identify and talk about the sexual solipsism of heterosexual feminism. In this paper I was trying to ask heterosexual feminists to examine their experience of heterosexuality critically and antagonistically, to critique the institution of which they are a part, to struggle with the norm and its implications for women's freedom, to become more open to the considerable resources offered by the lesbian-feminist perspective, to refuse to settle for the personal privilege and solution of the individual "good relationship" within the institution of heterosexuality.

As regards "female historical agency," I wanted, precisely, to suggest that the victim model is insufficient; that there *is* a history of female agency and choice which has actually challenged aspects of male supremacy; that, like male supremacy, these can be found in many different cultures. . . . It's not that I think all female agency has been solely and avowedly lesbian. But by erasing lesbian existence from female history, from theory, from literary criticism . . . from feminist approaches to economic structure, ideas about "the family," etc., an enormous amount of female agency is kept unavailable, hence unusable. I wanted to demonstrate that that kind of obliteration continues to be acceptable in seriously regarded feminist texts. What surprised me in the responses to my essay, including your notes, is how almost every aspect of it has been considered, except this—to me—central one. I was taking a position which was neither lesbian/separatist in the sense of dismissing heterosexual women nor a "gay civil rights" plea for . . . openness to lesbianism as an "option" or an "alternate life style." I was urging that lesbian *existence* has been an unrecognized and unaffirmed claiming by women of their sexuality, thus a pattern of resistance, thus also a kind of borderline position from which to analyze and challenge the relationship of heterosexuality to male supremacy. And that lesbian existence, when recognized, demands a conscious restructuring of feminist analysis and criticism, not just a token reference or two.

I certainly agree with you that the term *lesbian con-*

tinuum can be misused. It was, in the example you report of the abortion-rights meeting, though I would think anyone who had read my work from *Of Woman Born* onward would know that my position on abortion and sterilization abuse is more complicated than that. My own problem with the phrase is that it can be, is, used by women who have not yet begun to examine the privileges and solipsisms of heterosexuality, as a safe way to describe their felt connections with women, without having to share in the risks and threats of lesbian existence. What I had thought to delineate rather complexly as a continuum has begun to sound more like "life-style shopping." *Lesbian continuum*—the phrase—came from a desire to allow for the greatest possible variation of female-identified experience, while paying a different kind of respect to *lesbian existence*—the traces and knowledge of women who have made their primary erotic and emotional choices for women. If I were writing the paper today, I would still want to make this distinction, but would put more caveats around *lesbian continuum.* I fully agree with you that Smith-Rosenberg's "female world" is not a social ideal, enclosed as it is within prescriptive middle-class heterosexuality and marriage.

My own essay could have been stronger had it drawn on more of the literature by Black women toward which Toni Morrison's *Sula* inevitably pointed me. In reading a great deal more of Black women's fiction I began to perceive a different set of valences from those found in white women's fiction for the most part: a different quest for the woman hero, a different relationship both to sexuality with men and to female loyalty and bonding. . . .

You comment briefly on your reactions to some of the radical-feminist works I cited in my first footnote.[67] I am myself critical of some of them even as I found them vitally useful. What most of them share is a taking seriously of misogyny—of organized, institutionalized, normalized hostility and violence against women. I feel no "hierarchy of oppressions" is needed in order for us to take misogyny as seriously as we take racism, anti-Semitism, imperialism. To take misogyny seriously needn't mean that we perceive women merely as victims, without responsibilities or choices; it does mean recognizing the "necessity" in that "dialectic of necessity and choice"—identifying, describing, refusing to turn aside our eyes. I think that some of the apparent reductiveness, or even obsessiveness, of some white radical-feminist theory derives from racial and/or class solipsism, but also from the immense effort of trying to render women hating visible amid so much denial. . . .

Finally, as to poetry and history: I want both in my life; I need to see through both. If metaphor can be misconstrued, history can also lead to misconstrual when it obliterates acts of resistance or rebellion, wipes out transformational models, or sentimentalizes power relationships. I know you know this. I believe we are all trying to think and write out of our best consciences, our most open consciousness. I expect that quality in this book which you are editing, and look forward with anticipation to the thinking—and the actions—toward which it may take us.

In sisterhood,
Adrienne

Montague, Massachusetts
November 1981

NOTES

1. See, for example, Paula Gunn Allen, *The Sacred Hoop: Recovering the Feminine in American Indian Traditions* (Boston: Beacon, 1986); Beth Brant, ed., *A Gathering of Spirit: Writing and Art by North American Indian Women* (Montpelier, Vt.: Sinister Wisdom Books, 1984); Gloria Anzaldúa and Cherrie Moraga, eds., *This Bridge Called My Back: Writings by Radical Women of Color* (Watertown, Mass.: Persephone, 1981; distributed by Kitchen Table/ Women of Color Press, Albany, N.Y.); J. R. Roberts, *Black Lesbians: An Annotated Bibliography* (Tallahassee, Fla.: Naiad, 1981); Barbara Smith, ed., *Home Girls: A Black Feminist Anthology* (Albany, N.Y.: Kitchen Table/Women of Color Press, 1984). As Lorraine Bethel and Barbara Smith pointed out in *Conditions 5: The Black Women's Issue* (1980), a great deal of fiction by Black women depicts primary relationships between women. I would like to cite here the work of Ama Ata Aidoo, Toni Cade Bambara, Buchi Emecheta, Bessie Head, Zora Neale Hurston, Alice Walker. Donna Allegra, Red Jordan Arobateau, Audre Lorde, Ann Allen Shockley, among others, write directly as Black lesbians. For fiction by other lesbians of color, see Elly Bulkin, ed., *Lesbian Fiction: An Anthology* (Watertown, Mass.: Persephone, 1981).

See also, for accounts of contemporary Jewish-lesbian existence, Evelyn Torton Beck, ed., *Nice Jewish Girls: A Lesbian Anthology* (Watertown, Mass.: Persephone, 1982; distributed by Crossing Press, Trumansburg, N.Y. 14886); Alice Bloch, *Lifetime Guarantee* (Watertown, Mass.: Persephone, 1982); and Melanie Kaye-Kantrowitz and Irena Klepfisz, eds., *The Tribe of Dina: A Jewish Women's Anthology* (Montpelier, Vt.: Sinister Wisdom Books, 1986).

The earliest formulation that I know of heterosexuality as an institution was in the lesbian-feminist paper *The Furies,* founded in 1971. For a collection of articles from that paper, see Nancy Myron and Charlotte Bunch, eds., *Lesbianism and the Women's Movement* (Oakland, Calif.: Diana Press, 1975; distributed by Crossing Press, Trumansburg, N.Y. 14886).

2. Alice Rossi, "Children and Work in the Lives of Women," paper delivered at the University of Arizona, Tucson, February 1976.

3. Doris Lessing, *The Golden Notebook,* 1962 (New York: Bantam, 1977), p. 480.

4. Nancy Chodorow, *The Reproduction of Mothering* (Berkeley: University of California Press, 1978); Dorothy Dinnerstein, *The Mermaid and the Minotaur: Sexual Arrangements and the Human Malaise* (New York: Harper & Row, 1976); Barbara Ehrenreich and Deirdre English, *For Her Own Good: 150 Years of the Experts' Advice to Women* (Garden City, N.Y.: Doubleday, Anchor, 1978); Jean Baker Miller, *Toward a New Psychology of Women* (Boston: Beacon, 1976).

5. I could have chosen many other serious and influential recent books, including anthologies, which would illustrate the same point: e.g., *Our Bodies, Ourselves,* the Boston Women's Health Book Collective's best seller (New York: Simon and Schuster, 1976), which devotes a separate (and inadequate) chapter to lesbians, but whose message is that heterosexuality is most women's life preference; Berenice Carroll, ed., *Liberating Women's History: Theoretical and Critical Essays* (Urbana: University of Illinois Press, 1976), which does not include even a token essay on the lesbian presence in history, though an essay by Linda Gordon, Persis Hunt, et al. notes the use by male historians of "sexual deviance" as a category to discredit and dismiss Anna Howard Shaw, Jane Addams, and other feminists ("Historical Phallacies: Sexism in American Historical Writing"); and Renate Bridenthal and Claudia Koonz, eds., *Becoming Visible: Women in European History* (Boston: Houghton Mifflin, 1977), which contains three mentions of male homosexuality but no materials that I have been able to locate on lesbians. Gerda Lerner, ed., *The Female Experience: An American Documentary* (Indianapolis: Bobbs-Merrill, 1977), contains an abridgment of two lesbian-feminist–position papers from the contemporary movement but no other documentation of lesbian existence. Lerner does note in her preface, however, how the charge of deviance has been used to fragment women and discourage women's resistance. Linda

Gordon, in *Woman's Body, Woman's Right: A Social History of Birth Control in America* (New York: Viking, Grossman, 1976), notes accurately that "it is not that feminism has produced more lesbians. There have always been many lesbians, despite the high levels of repression; and most lesbians experience their sexual preference as innate" (p. 410).

[A. R., 1986: I am glad to update the first annotation in this footnote. *"The New" Our Bodies, Ourselves* (New York: Simon and Schuster, 1984) contains an expanded chapter on "Loving Women: Lesbian Life and Relationships" and furthermore emphasizes *choices* for women throughout— in terms of sexuality, health care, family, politics, etc.]

6. Jonathan Katz, ed., *Gay American History: Lesbians and Gay Men in the U.S.A.* (New York: Thomas Y. Crowell, 1976).

7. Nancy Sahli, "Smashing Women's Relationships before the Fall," *Chrysalis: A Magazine of Women's Culture* 8 (1979): 17–27.

8. This is a book which I have publicly endorsed. I would still do so, though with the above caveat. It is only since beginning to write this article that I fully appreciated how enormous is the unasked question in Ehrenreich and English's book.

9. See, for example, Kathleen Barry, *Female Sexual Slavery* (Englewood Cliffs, N.J.: Prentice-Hall, 1979); Mary Daly, *Gyn/Ecology: The Metaethics of Radical Feminism* (Boston: Beacon, 1978); Susan Griffin, *Woman and Nature: The Roaring inside Her* (New York: Harper & Row, 1978); Diana Russell and Nicole van de Ven, eds., *Proceedings of the International Tribunal of Crimes against Women* (Millbrae, Calif.: Les Femmes, 1976); and Susan Brownmiller, *Against Our Will: Men, Women and Rape* (New York: Simon and Schuster, 1975); *Aegis: Magazine on Ending Violence against Women* (Feminist Alliance against Rape, P.O. Box 21033, Washington, D.C. 20009).

[A. R., 1986: Work on both incest and on woman battering has appeared in the 1980s which I did not cite in the essay. See Florence Rush, *The Best-kept Secret* (New York: McGraw-Hill, 1980); Louise Armstrong, *Kiss Daddy Goodnight: A Speakout on Incest* (New York: Pocket Books, 1979); Sandra Butler, *Conspiracy of Silence: The Trauma of Incest* (San Francisco: New Glide, 1978); F. Delacoste and F. Newman, eds., *Fight Back!: Feminist Resistance to Male Violence* (Minneapolis: Cleis Press, 1981); Judy Freespirit, *Daddy's Girl: An Incest Survivor's Story* (Langlois, Ore.: Diaspora Distribution, 1982); Judith Herman, *Father-Daughter Incest* (Cambridge, Mass.: Harvard University Press, 1981); Toni McNaron and Yarrow Morgan, eds., *Voices in the Night: Women Speaking about Incest* (Minneapolis: Cleis Press, 1982); and Betsy Warrior's richly informative, multipurpose compilation of essays, statistics, listings, and facts, the *Battered Women's Directory* (formerly entitled *Working on Wife Abuse*), 8th ed. (Cambridge, Mass.: 1982).]

10. Dinnerstein, p. 272.

11. Chodorow, pp. 197–198.

12. Ibid., pp. 198–199.

13. Ibid., p. 200.

14. Kathleen Gough, "The Origin of the Family," in *Toward an Anthropology of Women,* ed. Rayna [Rapp] Reiter (New York: Monthly Review Press, 1975), pp. 69–70.

15. Barry, pp. 216–219.

16. Anna Demeter, *Legal Kidnapping* (Boston: Beacon, 1977), pp. xx, 126–128.

17. Daly, pp. 139–141, 163–165.

18. Barbara Ehrenreich and Deirdre English, *Witches, Midwives and Nurses: A History of Women Healers* (Old Westbury, N.Y.: Feminist Press, 1973); Andrea Dworkin, *Woman Hating* (New York: Dutton, 1974), pp. 118–154; Daly, pp. 178–222.

19. See Virginia Woolf, *A Room of One's Own* (London: Hogarth, 1929), and ibid., *Three Guineas* (New York: Harcourt Brace, [1938] 1966); Tillie Olsen, *Silences* (Boston: Delacorte, 1978); Michelle Cliff, "The Resonance of Interruption" *Chrysalis: A Magazine of Women's Culture* 8 (1979): 29–37.

20. Mary Daly, *Beyond God the Father* (Boston: Beacon, 1973), pp. 347–351; Olsen, pp. 22–46.

21. Daly, *Beyond God the Father*, p. 93.

22. Fran P. Hosken, "The Violence of Power: Genital Mutilation of Females," *Heresies: A Feminist Journal of Art and Politics* 6 (1979): 28–35; Russell and van de Ven, pp. 194–195.

[A. R., 1986: See especially "Circumcision of Girls," in Nawal El Saadawi, *The Hidden Face of Eve: Women in the Arab World* (Boston: Beacon, 1982), pp. 33–43.]

23. Barry, pp. 163–164.

24. The issue of "lesbian sadomasochism" needs to be examined in terms of dominant cultures' teachings about the relation of sex and violence. I believe this to be another example of the "double life" of women.

25. Catharine A. MacKinnon, *Sexual Harassment of Working Women: A Case of Sex Discrimination* (New Haven, Conn.: Yale University Press, 1979), pp. 15–16.

26. Ibid., p. 174.

27. Brownmiller, *Against Our Will.*

28. MacKinnon, p. 219. Susan Schecter writes: "The push for heterosexual union at whatever cost is so intense that . . . it has become a cultural force of its own that creates battering. The ideology of romantic love and its jealous possession of the partner as property provide the masquerade for what can become severe abuse" (*Aegis: Magazine on Ending Violence against Women* [July–August 1979]: 50–51).

29. MacKinnon, p. 298.

30. Ibid., p. 220.

31. Ibid., p. 221.

32. Barry, *Female Sexual Slavery.*

[A. R., 1986: See also Kathleen Barry, Charlotte Bunch, and Shirley Castley, eds., *International Feminism: Networking against Female Sexual Slavery* (New York: International Women's Tribune Center, 1984).]

33. Barry, p. 33.

34. Ibid., p. 103.

35. Ibid., p. 5.

36. Ibid., p. 100.

[A. R., 1986: This statement has been taken as claiming that "all women are victims" purely and simply, or that "all heterosexuality equals sexual slavery." I would say, rather, that all women are affected, though differently, by dehumanizing attitudes and practices directed at women as a group.]

37. Ibid., p. 218.

38. Ibid., p. 140.

39. Ibid., p. 172.

40. Elsewhere I have suggested that male identification has been a powerful source of white women's racism and that it has often been women already seen as "disloyal" to male codes and systems who have actively battled against it (Adrienne Rich, "Disloyal to Civilization: Feminism, Racism, Gynephobia," in *On Lies, Secrets, and Silence: Selected Prose, 1966–1978* [New York: W. W. Norton, 1979]).

41. Barry, p. 220.

42. Susan Cavin, "Lesbian Origins" (Ph.D. diss., Rutgers University, 1978), unpublished, ch. 6.

[A. R., 1986: This dissertation was recently published as *Lesbian Origins* (San Francisco: Ism Press, 1986).]

43. For my perception of heterosexuality as an economic institution I am indebted to Lisa Leghorn and Katherine Parker, who allowed me to read the unpublished manuscript of their book *Woman's Worth: Sexual Economics and the World of Women* (London and Boston: Routledge & Kegan Paul, 1981).

44. I would suggest that lesbian existence has been most recognized and tolerated where it has resembled a "deviant" version of heterosexuality—e.g., where lesbians have, like Stein and Toklas, played heterosexual roles (or seemed to in public) and have been chiefly identified with male culture. See also Claude E. Schaeffer, "The Kuterai Female Berdache: Courier, Guide, Prophetess and Warrior," *Ethnohistory* 12, no. 3 (Summer 1965): 193–236. (Berdache: "an individual of a definite physiological sex [m. or f.] who assumes the role and status of the opposite sex and who is viewed by the community as being of one sex physiologically but as having assumed the role and status of the opposite sex" [Schaeffer, p. 231].) Lesbian existence has also been relegated to an upper-class phenomenon, an elite decadence (as in the fascination with Paris salon lesbians such as Renée Vivien and Natalie Clifford Barney), to the obscuring of such "common women" as Judy Grahn depicts in her *The Work of a Common Woman* (Oakland, Calif.: Diana Press, 1978) and *True to Life Adventure Stories* (Oakland, Calif.: Diana Press, 1978).

45. Daly, *Gyn/Ecology,* p. 15.

46. "In a hostile world in which women are not supposed to survive except in relation with and in service to men, entire

communities of women were simply erased. History tends to bury what it seeks to reject" (Blanche W. Cook, "'Women Alone Stir My Imagination': Lesbianism and the Cultural Tradition," *Signs: Journal of Women in Culture and Society* 4, no. 4 [Summer 1970]: 719–720). The Lesbian Herstory Archives in New York City is one attempt to preserve contemporary documents on lesbian existence—a project of enormous value and meaning, working against the continuing censorship and obliteration of relationships, networks, communities in other archives and elsewhere in the culture.

47. [A. R., 1986: The shared historical and spiritual "crossover" functions of lesbians and gay men in cultures past and present are traced by Judy Grahn in *Another Mother Tongue: Gay Words, Gay Worlds* (Boston: Beacon, 1984). I now think we have much to learn both from the uniquely female aspects of lesbian existence and from the complex "gay" identity we share with gay men.]

48. Audre Lorde, "Uses of the Erotic: The Erotic as Power," in *Sister Outsider* (Trumansburg, N.Y.: Crossing Press, 1984).

49. Adrienne Rich, "Conditions for Work: The Common World of Women," in *On Lies, Secrets, and Silence,* p. 209; H. D., *Tribute to Freud* (Oxford: Carcanet, 1971), pp. 50–54.

50. Woolf, *A Room of One's Own,* p. 126.

51. Gracia Clark, "The Beguines: A Mediaeval Women's Community," *Quest: A Feminist Quarterly* 1, no. 4 (1975): 73–80.

52. See Denise Paulmé, ed., *Women of Tropical Africa* (Berkeley: University of California Press, 1963), pp. 7, 266–267. Some of these sororities are described as "a kind of defensive syndicate against the male element," their aims being "to offer concerted resistance to an oppressive patriarchate," "independence in relation to one's husband and with regard to motherhood, mutual aid, satisfaction of personal revenge." See also Audre Lorde, "Scratching the Surface: Some Notes on Barriers to Women and Loving" in *Sister Outsider,* pp. 45–52; Marjorie Topley, "Marriage Resistance in Rural Kwangtung," in *Women in Chinese Society,* ed. M. Wolf and R. Witke (Stanford, Calif.: Stanford University Press, 1978), pp. 67–89; Agnes Smedley, *Portraits of Chinese Women in Revolution,* ed. J. MacKinnon and S. MacKinnon (Old Westbury, N.Y.: Feminist Press, 1976), pp. 103–110.

53. See Rosalind Petchesky, "Dissolving the Hyphen: A Report on Marxist-Feminist Groups 1–5," in *Capitalist Patriarchy and the Case for Socialist Feminism,* ed. Zillah Eisenstein (New York: Monthly Review Press, 1979), p. 387.

54. [A. R., 1986: See Angela Davis, *Women, Race and Class* (New York: Random House, 1981), p. 102; Orlando Patterson, *Slavery and Social Death: A Comparative Study* (Cambridge: Harvard University Press, 1982), p. 133.]

55. Russell and van de Ven, pp. 42–43, 56–57.

56. I am indebted to Jonathan Katz's *Gay American History* for bringing to my attention Hansberry's letters to *The Ladder* and to Barbara Grier for supplying me with copies of relevant pages from *The Ladder,* quoted here by permission of Barbara Grier. See also the reprinted series of *The Ladder,* ed. Jonathan Katz et al. (New York: Arno, 1975), and Deirdre Carmody, "Letters by Eleanor Roosevelt Detail Friendship with Lorena Hickok." *New York Times* (October 21, 1979).

57. Meridel LeSueur, *The Girl* (Cambridge, Mass.: West End Press, 1978), pp. 10–11. LeSueur describes, in an afterword, how this book was drawn from the writings and oral narrations of women in the Workers Alliance who met as a writers' group during the depression.

58. Ibid., p. 20.

59. Ibid., pp. 53–54.

60. Ibid., p. 55.

61. Toni Morrison, *Sula* (New York: Bantam, 1973), pp. 103–104, 149. I am indebted to Lorraine Bethel's essay "'This Infinity of Conscious Pain': Zora Neale Hurston and the Black Female Literary Tradition," in *All the Women Are White, All the Blacks Are Men, but Some of Us Are Brave: Black Women's Studies,* ed. Gloria T. Hull, Patricia Bell Scott, and Barbara Smith (Old Westbury, N.Y.: Feminist Press, 1982).

62. See Maureen Brady and Judith McDaniel, "Lesbians in the Mainstream: The Image of Lesbians in Recent Commercial Fiction," *Conditions* 6 (1979): 82–105.

63. See Russell and van de Ven, p. 40: "Few heterosexual women realize their lack of free choice about their sexuality, and few realize how and why compulsory heterosexuality is also a crime against them."

64. Bethel, "'This Infinity of Conscious Pain.'"

65. Dinnerstein, the most recent writer to quote this passage, adds ominously: "But what has to be added to her account is that these 'women enlaced' are sheltering each other not just from what men want to do to them, but also from what they want to do to each other" (Dinnerstein, p. 103). The fact is, however, that woman-to-woman violence is a minute grain in the universe of male-against-female violence perpetuated and rationalized in every social institution.

66. Conversation with Blanche W. Cook, New York City, March 1979.

67. See note 9, above.

S E C T I O N   F I V E

Work

"Work for pay" influences many aspects of our lives: our economic prosperity, our social status, our relationships with family members and friends, our health, and (often) even our access to health care. Our work experiences influence how we come to view others, ourselves, and the social world around us. Reciprocally, how we are situated in society often influences the kinds of work we do and our compensation for that work. In traditional societies, division of labor based on sex and age did not necessarily correspond to differences in the importance assigned to different kinds of work. In societies like ours, however, social divisions of labor based on gender, race, and age reflect and perpetuate power differences among groups.

This section begins with Alice Kessler-Harris's examination of the historical justifications of pay inequities between women and men. In "The Wage Conceived: Value and Need as Measures of a Woman's Worth," we begin to understand the ideological bases of the differential economic rewards available to men and women, and the implications of both gender ideologies and economic practices for women's participation in society.

Barbara F. Reskin's article, "Bringing the Men Back In: Sex Differentiation and the Devaluation of Women's Work," further examines the political nature of sex segregation in the labor force. Reskin argues that two commonly posed solutions to the persistent problem of sex segregation—comparable worth and sex-integrating occupations—will not succeed because the men who retain a vested interest in maintaining male power ultimately define the terms of such reform efforts.

The remaining articles in this section offer focused examinations of the work experiences of particular groups of women. Beverly W. Jones reveals the interplay of race, class, and gender in "Race, Sex, and Class: Female Tobacco Workers in Durham, North Carolina, 1920–1940, and the Development of Female Consciousness." Jones describes a tobacco company's relegation of black women to unhealthy working conditions because of race and to the lowest-paying jobs because of sex. In response to their oppression, black women tobacco workers developed a class identity, and from it emerged a sisterhood of struggle, support, dignity, and resistance.

Just as women in traditionally female occupations face particular work-related difficulties, women who enter male-dominated fields encounter distinct challenges. In a case study called "Occupation/ Steelworker: Sex/Female," Mary Margaret Fonow documents the problems encountered by women in one male-dominated industry.

As these articles demonstrate, women's ethnicities, ages, and class backgrounds affect both the structural opportunities available to women in the labor force and women's interpretations of those experiences. The final article in this section introduces another factor in women's work lives: sexuality.

Women face additional problems in the workplace as a result of heterosexual privilege and "the heterosexual assumption." The cultural belief that all women desire and will ultimately obtain access to a man's paycheck through heterosexual marriage rationalizes paying men a "family wage," regardless of their sexual orientation or familial status, and paying women considerably less, regardless of their sexual orientation or partnership status.

While most women suffer the effects of the heterosexual assumption in the labor market, lesbians encounter particular challenges at work because of heterosexual privilege. In "Peril and Promise: Lesbians' Workplace Participation," Beth Schneider discusses specific problems and pressures lesbians experience in their jobs, as well as the strategies used to integrate their lesbian social identity and their work lives. Schneider's analysis clarifies the connections between economics, social values, and women's oppression.

The Wage Conceived:
Value and Need as Measures of a Woman's Worth

ALICE KESSLER-HARRIS

When a person complains that a certain wage rate is unduly low, he may be making that judgment in the light of what he thinks is due the kind of person *performing that work, e.g. a married man. Others may regard the same rate as not unreasonable in view of the kind of work* it is.

—Henry A. Landsberger[1]

In 1915 New York State's Factory Investigating Commission asked some seventy-five prominent individuals—economists, social reformers, businessmen, and publicists among them—what factors determined the rate of wages. The answers varied. Some suggested that workers' organizations were most important; others believed the size of a business's profits could enhance or restrain the wages of employees. Another key factor was the standard of living anticipated by workers. But the majority of those interviewed believed the efficiency of the worker and the supply of labor constituted by far the two most powerful determinants of wages.[2] These traditional explanations for wage rates would have found favor with the proponents of the economic theory then popular.

Widely accepted wage theory at the turn of the century was rooted in, though not limited to, the law of supply and demand. If that phrase, as economic historian Arnold Tolles implies, does not do economists jus-

tice, it does, at least, convey the economists' belief "that the reward for every kind of human effort is controlled by some kind of impersonal and irresistible force, similar to the force of gravity."[3] Theory held that wages would rise or fall in response to employers' fluctuating willingness to pay. That willingness in turn was predicated on what employers thought they could earn from labor as well as on how much labor was available at different wage rates. Thus, in theory, the demand for labor (measured by the additional revenue labor could produce) and the supply (which took into account the differences in education and training of the worker) together determined the wage.[4]

Despite the apparent certainty of economists such as Professor Roy Blakely of Cornell who testified before the commission that "wages tend to approximate the value of what they produce,"[5] the theory left room for a substantial degree of subjective judgment on the part of employers as to the value of particular workers. A critical part of the chemical mix that determined the wages of workers in general involved something intangible called "custom." If a male worker was paid according to some formula that reflected the value of what he produced and the difficulty of replacing him, he was also paid according to what he and other workers thought he was worth. Custom, or tradition, played an acknowledged but uncalculated role in regulating the wage. But custom and tradition were gendered. They influenced male and female wages in different ways. And especially in the female wage, they played a far larger role than we have earlier been willing to concede. The women's wage, at least for the early twentieth century, rested in large measure on conceptions of what women needed.

From *A Woman's Wage: Historical Meanings and Social Consequences* by Alice Kessler-Harris. Copyright © 1990 by Alice Kessler-Harris. Used by permission of The University Press of Kentucky.

The distinction alerts us to the rich possibilities contained in the wage conceived as a social rather than as a theoretical construct. If the wage is, as most economists readily acknowledge, simultaneously a set of ideas about how people can and should live and a marker of social status, then it contains within it a set of social messages and a system of meanings that influence the way women and men behave. We are all familiar with the capacity of these social meanings to reduce the wages of recent immigrants, of African-Americans, and of other groups. But, partly because it is so apparently natural, the capacity of the wage to speak to issues of gender is less clear. Yet the language with which the women's wage is conceived throws into relief the same process that exists for men. The wage frames gendered messages; it encourages or inhibits certain forms of behavior; it can reveal a system of meaning that shapes the expectations of men and women and anticipates their struggles over power; it participates in the negotiations that influence the relationships of the sexes inside and outside the family. In all these capacities, the wage functions as a terrain of contest over visions of fairness and justice. This essay will attempt to illustrate some of these processes in the early twentieth century.

The structure of wages that emerged in the course of industrialization in the late nineteenth century reflected a long tradition that revolved around what has become known as the family wage—the sum necessary to sustain family members. That sum had been earned by several family members for most of the history of capitalism. Family income was typically pooled and then redistributed by one family member. But the dream of a family wage that could be earned by a male breadwinner alone had long been an object of struggle among organized working people who thought of it as a mechanism for regulating family life and allowing women to work in their own homes.[6] Ideally, and sometimes in practice, the family wage was a male wage, a wage that went to a male breadwinner.[7]

What then of a woman's wage? It reflected not what was but what ought to be. That men ought to be able to support wives and daughters implied that women need not engage in such support. They ought to be performing home duties. Thus, if a woman earned wages, the normal expectation was that she did so to supplement those of other family wage earners. Theoretically, at least, the decision as to who would and would not earn was regulated by the family unit. The wage belonged to

her family. Until the third quarter of the nineteenth century, U.S. law and practice reflected these assumptions. Typically, a woman's wage was legally the property of her husband or father. The average wage of women workers was little more than half of the male wage. And even the most skilled women rarely earned as much as two-thirds of the average paid to unskilled men. If a woman lived independently, her wage was normally not sufficient to support her. Nor was it intended to do so.

The nineteenth century fight for a family wage was thus simultaneously a fight for a social order in which men could support their families and receive the services of women; and women, dependent on men, could stay out of the labor force. Historians have debated the advantages and disadvantages of this mode of thinking, but for our purposes it is important to note only that the family wage reflected popular thinking—a sense of what was right and just.[8] Widely supported by working class men and women at the end of the nineteenth century, it rested on what seemed to many to be a desirable view of social order.

Its incarnation in the form of the living wage more clearly isolated the female role. Though the content of a living wage varied, like the family wage, it was imbued with gendered expectations. John Ryan, the Catholic priest who was the United States' most prolific exponent of the living wage, for example, asserted the laborer's right to a "decent and reasonable" life that meant to him "the right to exercise one's primary faculties, supply one's essential needs, and develop one's personality."[9] Others were somewhat more specific. British economist William Smart thought the living wage ought to pay for "a well-drained dwelling, with several rooms, warm clothing with some changes of underclothing, pure water, a plentiful supply of cereal food with a moderate allowance of meat and milk and a little tea, etc., some education, and some recreation, and lastly sufficient freedom for his wife from other work to enable her to perform properly her maternal and her household duties."[10] John Mitchell, head of the United Mine Workers union, was somewhat more ambitious. The wage, he thought, ought to be enough to purchase "the American standard of living." This included, but was not limited to, "a comfortable house of at least six rooms," which contained a bathroom, good sanitary plumbing, parlor, dining room, kitchen, sleeping rooms, carpets, pictures, books, and furniture.[11]

For Ryan, as for other proponents of the living

wage, the "love and companionship of a person of the opposite sex"[12] was an essential element of what a living wage should purchase. The bottom line, according to Ryan, was the laborer's capacity "to live in a manner consistent with the dignity of a human being."[13] The *Shoe Workers' Journal* proposed that "everything necessary to the life of *a normal man* be included in the living wage: the right to marriage, the right to have children and to educate them."[14]

As the family wage held the promise of female homemaking, the living wage, which explicitly incorporated wife and children, excluded the possibility that female dignity could inhere either in a woman's ability to earn wages or in her capacity to support a family. Because the living wage idealized a world in which men had the privilege of caring for women and children, it implicitly refused women that privilege. And, because it assumed female dependency, to imagine female independence impugned male roles and male egos. Ground rules for female wage earners required only self-support, and even that was estimated at the most minimal level. Champions of the living wage for women counted among her necessities food, clothing, rent, health, savings, and a small miscellaneous fund.[15] Nothing in the arguments for a female living wage vitiates the harsh dictum of John Stuart Mill. The wages of single women, asserted that famous economist, "must be equal to their support, but need not be more than equal to it; the minimum in their case is the pittance absolutely required for the sustenance of one human being."[16] "Women who are forced to provide their own sustenance have a right," echoed Ryan, "to what is a living wage *for them*." Their compensation, he argued, with apparent generosity, "should be sufficient to enable them to live decently."[17]

At the time Ryan wrote, women constituted close to 25 percent of the industrial work force. More than one-third of wage-earning women in urban areas lived independently of their families, and three-quarters of those living at home helped to support other family members. False conceptions of women who needed only to support themselves did a particular disservice to Black women, who were eight times as likely to earn wages as white women. For Black women racial discrimination and its attendant poverty meant that more that one-third of those who were married would continue to earn wages, and virtually all of those who earned wages participated in family support.[18] Yet the real needs of these women were rarely acknowledged. Nor did the brief, dismissive commentary on "a

woman's living wage" mention recreation or comfort or human dignity or the capacity to care for others.

Ryan readily conceded that men without families to support and/or with other means of support were entitled to draw a living wage because "they perform as much labor as their less fortunate fellows."[19] His proposals generously allocated a living wage to men who never intended to marry because "rights are to be interpreted according to the average conditions of human life."[20] But the same generosity was not evident in notions of the living wage for women workers. Rather, it seemed fair to reduce women to the lowest levels of bestiality. Advocates of the living wage confidently explained that women's "standard of physical comfort, in other words, their standard of life" was lower than that of men." While her ideals were "naturally higher than those of men," her physical wants are simpler. The living wage for a woman is lower than the living wage for a man because it is possible for her as a result of her traditional drudgery and forced tolerance of pain and suffering to keep alive upon less."[21] Women, with a single set of exceptions, were to be paid only according to their most minimal needs. Only to women who were employed in the same jobs as men did Ryan concede the need for equal pay because, he argued, "when women receive less pay than men, the latter are gradually driven out of the occupation."[22]

Ryan failed to acknowledge that in attributing to women "average conditions" that reflected social myth rather than reality he undermined his own cause. While his vision and that of most living wage advocates came from a desire to protect the home, not from antagonism to the pitiable condition of those women who worked for wages, his proposals left the home vulnerable. "The welfare of the whole family," he noted, "and that of society likewise, renders it imperative that the wife and mother should not engage in any labor except that of the household. When she works for hire, she can neither care properly for her own health, rear her children aright, nor make her home what it should be for her husband, her children, herself."[23] Theoretically, that might have been true; but in practice, by reducing women's potential capacity to earn adequate incomes, he diminished their ability to support themselves and their homes.

Without negating the good intentions of Ryan and others on behalf of the family and without imposing anachronistic judgments about their desire to protect the family and to place family needs ahead of women's individual rights, one can still see that the consequences of their rhetoric for women who earned wages were no mere abstractions. They assumed a hard and concrete reality, for example, in discussions of the minimum wage for women that took place between about 1911 and 1913. To alleviate the plight of women workers, social reformers attempted to pass legislation that would force employers to pay a wage sufficient to meet a woman's minimal needs. Between 1912 and 1923, thirteen states and the District of Columbia passed such legislation in one form or another. Each statute was preceded by a preamble that declared the legislators' intentions to offer protection that ranged from providing a sum "adequate for maintenance" to ensuring enough to "maintain the worker in health" and guaranteeing her "moral well-being." Whatever the language of the preamble, and whatever the mechanism by which the wage was ultimately to be decided, the minimum was invariably rooted in what was determined to be a "living" wage for women workers.[24] But the discussion required some estimate of what a living wage might be. Elizabeth Beardsley Butler who surveyed working women in Pittsburgh in 1907 suggested that a woman could "not live decently and be self supporting" at a wage of less than $7 a week. Three years later Louise Bosworth estimated the living wage of Boston's women ranged from $9 to $11 a week—the first amount would keep a woman from dying of cold or hunger; the second provided the possibility of efficiency at work and some minimal recreation.[25] The question, said social pundit Thomas Russell, was whether "it is to be an amount that shall provide only the bare necessaries of life or shall it include some provision for comforts, recreation and the future?"[26]

The budgets drawn up by experts generally opted only for the necessities. Arrived at after extensive surveys to uncover the actual expenditures of "working girls," and heavily reliant on language and imagery that reduced women to perpetual girlhood, they included almost nothing beyond the barest sustenance.[27] A typical survey was undertaken by Sue Ainslee Clark in 1908 and published by Clark and Edith Wyatt in the pages of *McClure's* magazine in 1910.[28] The authors focused on the effortful struggle to make ends meet, turning survival itself into a praiseworthy feat. They exuded sympathy for the girl who "ate no breakfast," whose "luncheon consisted of coffee and rolls for ten cents," and who, as "she had no convenient place for doing her own laundry, . . . paid 21 cents a week to have it done. Her regular weekly expenditure was as

follows: lodging, 42 cents; board, $1.40; washing, 21 cents; clothing and all other expenses, $1.97: total, $4."[29] Such estimates encouraged social investigators to define precisely how much a female wage earner might spend for everything from undergarments to gifts.

The debate over the minimum wage revealed what this outward order dictated: to live alone required the strictest exercise of thrift, self-discipline, and restraint. The budgets warned fiercely against expectations of joy, spontaneity, pleasure, or recreation. Even the carfare that might provide access to a walk in the country was rigidly restricted. The wage prescribed a spartan life-style, sufficient, it was hoped, to preserve morality for those destined to earn but not so generous as to tempt those in families to live outside them. It limited fantasy to the price of survival and held open the door of ambition only to a meagre independence. Its effects are grimly reflected in a series of snippets selected by and published in *Harper's Bazar* in 1908 under the title "The Girl Who Comes to the City."[30]

Offering to pay $5 for each one it used, the magazine solicited brief essays "written by those girl readers who have gone through the experience of coming to the city, and either succeeding or failing there during the last ten years."[31] Success, in these pieces, is measured in small and treasured doses. Mere survival emerges as a potent source of satisfaction. In a period when most experts estimated a living wage at around $9 a week, a pay envelope that amounted to $10 a week could yield happiness. A $2 a week raise, accompanied by a kind boss, and perhaps the chance to improve oneself by reading occasionally at work seemed to be the height of ambition.[32] At the top of the wage scale, a bookkeeper could aspire to $65 a month, enough to ensure a small cash balance in the bank if one limited social excursions to one night a week and carefully selected clothes from among sale items.[33] The stories reveal justified pride and accomplishment in the ability to sustain oneself. But they also tell us something of the limits imposed on women's aspirations. "I had," boasted one contributor about the period before she returned home, "made both ends meet financially for five months and I had saved a modest sum for the purchase of a winter suit."[34] Even women who needed help in the form of occasional contributions of clothing felt they had managed very nicely.

And yet, in practice, survival was the best, not the worst, that the wage embodied. The estimates made by well-intentioned reformers and the efforts of the most well-meaning women were compromised by the refusal of most employers to concede a woman's need even to support herself. Evidence for this is part of the folklore of the female labor market before World War II and has frequently been recorded by historians.[35] The *Harper's Bazar* series is no exception. There, as elsewhere, women recalled how difficult it was to ask for reasonable compensation. A stenographer described how a lawyer had refused to pay more because "he expected young women had friends who helped them out." A budding news reporter was told by a potential employer that his "rule is never to employ a woman who must depend entirely upon my salaries."[36]

The aspirations of young women thus fell victim to the self-confirming myths that enforced their dependence. Nineteenth century British economist William Smart described the process succinctly. Part of the reason a woman's wage is low, he suggested, was "because she does not require a high wage, whether it be because her father partly supports her, or because her maintenance does not cost so much."[37] Employers routinely acted upon this myth. "We try to employ girls who are members of families," a box manufacturer told social investigator and economist Elizabeth Butler, "for we don't pay the girls a living wage in this trade."[38] Historian Joanne Meyerowitz summed up the prevailing attitude this way: "Employers assumed that all working women lived in families where working males provided them with partial support. It profited employers to use this idealized version of the family economy to determine women's wages."[39]

For all the elaborate theory justifying low wages, the bottom line turned out almost always to be the employer's sense of what was acceptable. Men, as Elizabeth Butler noted, came into occupations at a wage paid for the job. Women came into them at a wage deemed appropriate for female workers—not, that is to say, at the customary wage level of the occupation but "at a level analogous to that paid women generally in other occupations."[40] New York City social worker Mary Alden Hopkins told the Factory Investigating Commission that the sex of the employee was one of the most important influences on women's wages. "In laundry work, factory work, some mercantile establishments and home work, efficiency has little and often no effect upon wages," she declared.[41] The hardest woman's job, in her judgment, was the lowest paid, and an increase in worker productivity and

employer profits led less often to rewarding workers than to discharging high-paid workers in favor of those who could be paid for less. The young Scott Nearing summarized the process this way: "No one even pretends that there is a definite relation between the values produced by the workers and the wage which he secures."[42] Samuel Gompers would have agreed: "Everyone knows that there is little connection between the value of services and wages paid; the employer pays no more than he must."[43]

While from the economist's perspective this may be a gross oversimplification, employers, workers, and observers all accepted the critical importance of custom in the wage structure. A vice-president of the Pullman Company, speaking before the commission that investigated the great strike of 1894, acknowledged as much. Piece rates, he said, were based on the company's estimates of a "reasonable wage for ten hours . . . for a competent workman." If the company discovered "that at the piece price fixed the known less competent and less industrious workmen are regularly making an unreasonable day's wage, it becomes apparent that the piece price allotted is too large."[44] At issue here was what was "reasonable" and "unreasonable," not the productivity or efficiency of the worker. In this context, that part of the content of custom should rest on the sex of the worker appears to be merely natural. An official of International Harvester, testifying before an Illinois investigating commission in 1912, described his company's efforts to set a minimum wage for female employees. His company's desire, he claimed, "was to establish a minimum that would be fair and reasonable." But the constraints of what was deemed reasonable were established as much by the nature and characteristics of the worker as by the company's financial spread sheets. "The girls affected by lower wages," he said in mitigation, "are mostly of foreign birth. They are not required to dress up for their employment. Many of those to whom we will pay $8 could not earn a dollar downtown."[45] Presumably, the same kind of reasoning led to paying Black women less than white women. Although occupational segregation accounts for most of the wage differential between Black and white women, Black women who worked on the same kinds of jobs routinely received one dollar a week less.

Nor was the weight of custom in setting wages a hidden dimension. Rather, the comments of employers and others reveal it to have been quite conscious and available. Several respondents to the Factory

Investigating Commission's survey noted its influence in setting wage rates, pointing out that wages could not be set without reference to such factors as the "needs of the individual and family," the influence of "local or trade union conditions," and the differential requirements of "pin-money workers." Edward Page, an officer of the Merchants' Association of New York, thought that the "customary or habitual rate of wages which prevails in the group to which the workingman belongs and which is usual in the industry under consideration . . . is by far the most important factor in the determination of wages."[46] On their face these factors were gender neutral. But since each embodied deeply rooted aspects of gendered expectations, the wage both reflected and perpetuated gendered behavior.

If the role of custom in fixing wages is not surprising, and we can take for granted that sex played a part, then we need ask only to what degree the sex of the worker influenced custom. When it came to women, one might argue that custom played not the smallest but the largest part in determining the wage. William Smart placed the factors that determined the wages of women in the category of "wants." The wage scale in a modern industrial economy, he suggested, was typically determined by "what a worker does." But for a woman "what the worker is" was the gauge of wages. The difference made him uneasy. "If a male worker," he asked, "is supposed to get a high wage when he produces much, a low wage when he produces little, why should a woman's wage be determined by another principle? We cannot hunt with the individualist hounds and run with the socialist hare."[47]

Yet women's wages at the turn of the century clung stubbornly to what Smart would have called her "wants" rather than to either the value of the product or the level of the worker's productivity. For if custom was inscribed into the wage and the wage was conceived male, what women earned was not in the same sense as males a "wage." In the minds of employers and of male workers, the wage was to be paid to those who supported families.[48] If part of its function was to reflect the value of the product made, another and equally important part was to make a statement about the value of the worker who made the product. As long as female workers were not—could not be—male workers, their wages could not hope to touch those of their male peers.

We can guess that employers thought of it that way

by their responses to questions about how much they paid women. Louise Bosworth cited the case of a woman who told her employer, "We cannot live on what we earn," and was asked in response, "Then what wages can you live on?"[49] The same paternalistic assumptions appear among employers who testified before the commission that investigated Illinois's white slave traffic in 1912. The employers interviewed reported unhesitatingly that they paid their male and female workers on the basis of what they estimated each needed. Julius Rosenwald, head of Sears, Roebuck and Company, then a mail-order house, told an investigative commission that "the concern made it a point not to hire girls not living at home at less than $8 a week."[50] A Montgomery Ward vice-president echoed the sentiment: "We claim that all our employees without homes are on a self-supporting basis, and if we discover they are not we will put them there in an hour."[51] One department store executive described how his store asked all job applicants to sign a form "giving their estimate of necessary expenses in addition to family particulars. The girls who are not receiving sufficient to live on come to us. There are many instances of such receiving an increase." No one ever investigated the accuracy of the application forms, and even the commission chair was dubious as to who the procedure protected. A girl might readily lie about home support, he noted, "to assure herself of a job."[52] But at bottom, this was less the issue than the prevailing assumption that "girls" could and should be paid at a minimum that relied on family subsidy rather than on what their labor was worth.

If employers and popular opinion are any guide, and the question of what appeared to be reasonable lay at the heart of the wage structure, then all wages—not only those of women—contained a greater proportion of wants than most of us have recognized. Women's wages, then, are only uniquely vulnerable in the sense that they participate in popular definitions of gender that denigrate the needs of one sex. The wage simultaneously framed job-related expectation in the light of existing gender roles and shaped gender experiences to avoid disappointment in view of the prevailing wage structure. More than exploitation of women, or paternalism towards them, the wage reflected a rather severe set of injunctions about how men and women were to live. These injunctions could be widely negated only at the peril of social order. Thus, part of the function of the female wage was to ensure attachment to family. The male wage, in contrast, provided incentives to individual achievement. It promoted geographical mobility and sometimes hinted at the possibility of social mobility as well. The female wage allowed women to survive; the male wage suggested a contribution to national economic well-being. These messages affirmed existing values and integrated all the parties into a set of understandings that located the relationships of working men and women to each other.

Some of these messages are powerful. Existing wage fund theory posited a limited sum available for all wages. It reduced the incentive to provide a higher wage for women by suggesting that their gain would come at the cost of male raises and therefore threaten the family's well-being. Smart put it this way: "Women's wages are, after all, part and parcel of the one share in the distribution of income which falls to labor."[53] What followed from that, of course, was that raising women's wages would merely reduce those of the men in their class by a similar proportion, leaving families in the same place economically and depriving them of maternal care to boot. Samuel Gompers translated this into a warning to members of the American Federation of Labor: "In industries where the wives and children toil, the man is often idle because he has been supplanted, or because the aggregate wages of the family are no higher than the wages of the adult man—the husband and father of the family."[54]

If women's wage gains could come only at the cost of the family, then their low wages affirmed and supported existing family life. As the renowned economist Alfred Marshall put it, a higher wage for women might be "a great gain in so far as it tends to develop their faculties, but an injury in so far as it tempts them to neglect their duty of building up a true home, and of investing their efforts in the personal capital of their children's character and abilities."[55] To Marshall the clear social choice implicit in the wage payment was between individual achievement and family well-being. His statement affirms the use of wages to preserve what is desirable to him: that all women are or will be married, that marriage is a normal state, that women will be continuously supported by men with sufficient wages, and that under these circumstances a wage that might be translated into an incentive not to marry or remain within families poses a challenge. Moreover, Marshall's view reflected the prevailing belief that a man was entitled to a wife to serve him and their home.

It contained the assumption that a female who did not have a husband had erred. The differential female wage thus carried a moral injunction, a warning to women to follow the natural order.

The absence, by choice or necessity, of a family of her own did not excuse a woman from adherence to familial duties or morals, nor did it impel a more generous attitude toward wages. In fact, the level of the wage, which signaled an affirmation of family life, simultaneously threw out a challenge to preserve morality. In a March 1913 letter to the *New York Herald,* the head of Illinois's vice commission commented that "our investigations . . . show conclusively that thousands of good girls are going wrong every year merely because they can not live upon the wages paid them by employers."[56] But this was not necessarily an invitation to raise wages. Since not to live within a family was itself immoral, and the wage was seen as primarily a contribution to family life, a higher wage would only contribute to immorality. An ongoing debate over the fine line between a wage high enough to tempt women into supporting themselves and one so low that it could push the unwary into prostitution placed the wage in thrall to morality. Social worker Jeannette Gilder found herself in the awkward position of testifying against a pay raise for working women because "it seems to me to be paying a pretty poor compliment to the young women of this country to suggest that their virtue hangs upon such a slender thread that its price can be fixed somewhere between $6 and $8 a week."[57] And yet those who insisted that a low wage was an invitation to prostitution dominated the debate.

The wage also transmitted messages about the work force. Employers feared that a rise in women's wages would trigger a demand for higher wages for men. As the wage captured social restrictions on female aspirations at work, so it conveyed the male potential for advancement, promotion, loyalty, and persistence. Contemporaries understood this well. When Elizabeth Butler remarked that "boys are often preferred to girls . . . because they can be relied on to learn the trade and women cannot,"[58] she captured the notion that implicit in the wage is the assumption that a man's wage is an investment in the future, while a woman's wage assumes only that the work at hand will be done. Economist Francis Walker said this in a different way. If a man marries, he "becomes a better and more notable workman on that account." In contrast, if a woman marries, "it is most probable that she will . . . be a less desirable laborer than she was before."[59] Yet these statements promote the self-fulfilling function they simultaneously reflect. Lacking a man's wage, women were not normally given the opportunity to demonstrate that they too could be an investment in the future. Such experiments would be dangerous. Not only would a higher wage for women convey an inaccurate estimate of the potential occupational mobility of females, but it might inhibit the employer's capacity to use wages to construct the work force to his liking.

Finally, the wage made a familiar statement about female personality. Holding the stereotypical male as the norm, it claimed recompense for the costs of translating female qualities into the marketplace. Francis Walker exaggerated but caught the point when he insisted that the wage reflected women's character traits as well as their domestic orientation. It took account, he noted, of personalities that were "intensely sensitive to opinion, [and] shrink from the familiar utterances of blame." Coldness and indifference alone, he thought, were often sufficient to repress women's "impulses to activity."[60] These qualities of character exacted supervisory costs of the employer that were recaptured in the lower pay of women. As Charles Cheney, a South Manchester, Connecticut, manufacturer, put it, part of the reason women were paid less than men was because "they are sensitive and require extraordinarily tactful and kindly treatment and much personal consideration."[61]

Restrictive as the messages thrown out by a woman's wage were clearly intended to be, they were by no means the only messages that reached women. The very existence of a wage, the possibility of earning income evoked a contrary set of images: images that derived some support from the promise of American success. The same wage that evoked a struggle to survive and placed a lid on social mobility, the same wage that obscured women's visions of independence and citizenship had the capacity to conjure contrary images as well. It could even point the way to potential equality for women. These tensions are visible in the huge strikes that wracked the garment industry beginning in 1909–10, in the energy of young female labor leaders, and in the quest of more affluent women for lives that combined career and motherhood. Such events indicate that the notion of wages rooted in wants existed in a contested sphere—tempered by a broader ideology of individualism. They lead us to wonder about the role played by a woman's wage in a period of changing wants and rising levels of personal ambition.

The wage that in some measure helped to affirm and construct gendered expectations in the period before World War I continued to play that role afterward. But the dramatic social changes that came during and after the war, particularly the rise of a consumer culture, created their own pressures on the structure of gender. Because for most people the wage offered access to consumption, it mediated some of the tensions in gender roles that emerged in the 1920s. While public perception of a woman's wage remained conceptually "needs-based," continuing to limit female expectations, it quickly became clear that changing needs demanded some concessions to women's individual aspirations. These mixed messages contributed to arguments among women about who deserved a wage.[62]

In the statistical tables, the war appears as a small blip in the history of working women. New entrants into the labor force were relatively few, and the teens ended with little apparent increase in the numbers of women who earned wages. But the big surprise lay in the numbers of women who switched jobs. About half a million women, it seemed, chose to move into men's jobs. The *New York Times* commented on these figures with surprise: "The world of men woke up and took a second look at the world of women during the World War. It is still looking." And, it continued, "the Great War has in many cases been responsible for a change of premise as well as job."[63]

The primary explanation for these job shifts seems to have been the attraction of the male wage. Historian Maurine Greenwald estimates, for example, that women who became streetcar conductors immediately increased their wages by about one-third over those they had earned in traditional female jobs.[64] Daniel Nelson, who has explored the transformation of the factory, notes that after 1915 "the wages offered by machinery and munitions makers" drew an increasing number of women who had worked in traditional women's fields.[65] Though women's productivity was frequently acknowledged to be as high as that of the men they replaced, women were not, on principle, offered the same wage. A twenty-six city survey by the New York State Industrial Commission at the end of the war revealed that less than 10 percent of the women who replaced men received pay equal to that of the men who had preceded them. The commission reported that "in many cases the production of women was equal to that of men, in others it was greater, and in still others, less. The wages paid had little, if anything, to do with productive efficiency."[66] Since women who were paid less than men still earned far more than they could have at women's jobs, few of those who benefited from wartime opportunities complained. But the pressure of a dual wage structure on male wages posed a problem. Fearing a breakdown of social order, men and women began to call for a wage paid for the job—or equal pay. This slogan, as we will see later, was designed primarily to reduce pressure on men's wages.

Though most of the wartime job shifts proved to be temporary, they signaled an incipient dissatisfaction among some wage-earning women over the issue of wages—a dissatisfaction that could no longer be contained by rationalizations over social role. These struggles frequently pitted women who earned wages against those who did not, revealing something about contested definitions of womanhood among white women. For example, when female streetcar conductors in several large cities waged largely futile battles to hang on to their high-paying jobs, they were fighting not only the men who wanted their jobs back but a conception of womanliness that restricted access to outdoor work. And the female printers in New York State who successfully struggled to exempt themselves from legislation that precluded their working during the lucrative night hours simultaneously attacked rigid conceptions of family life.

Such campaigns were opposed by clear signals from government and corporations to women not to expect too much. The Women's Bureau of the Department of Labor offers a case in point. In 1920, when the bureau was created, it received a meagre $75,000 lump-sum appropriation and distributed it as effectively as it could. In 1922 a House proviso "stipulated that no salary in the Women's Bureau should be more than $1800, except three at $2000, and the director's and assistant director's salaries which have been fixed by statute." If effected, the proviso, as the Women's Bureau pointed out, would have left it with "no staff of technically trained, experienced people to direct and supervise its work." But more important, the bureau noted that other agencies of the government paid their male employees with the same qualifications "very much higher salaries than any that have even been suggested by the Women's Bureau—twice as much in many instances."[67]

Such policies were routine in industry. In the electrical industry of the 1920s, Ronald Schatz reports that "corporations maintained separate pay scales for men and women. Male wage keysheets began where female keysheets left off; the least skilled male workers earned more than the most capable female employee."[68] Still, the point for women was that even this low pay exceeded that of such traditionally female jobs as laundry work and waiting on tables. "For this reason, many young women preferred jobs in electrical factories." When the Ford Motor Company instituted a $5 day for its male employees after the war, it deliberately omitted women workers. According to Vice-President James Couzens, women "are not considered such economic factors as men."[69]

Corporations carefully distinguished between the kinds of social welfare programs offered as extensions of cash wages to women and men. General Electric and Westinghouse offered men programs that stressed financial and job security such as a 5 percent bonus every six months after five years of service; a pension after twenty years, and group life insurance and paid vacations after ten years of service. Women, for whom longevity was not encouraged and for whom it was thought not to matter, got programs that emphasized sociability such as "dances, cooking classes, secretarial instruction, picnics, clubs, and summer camps."[70]

The not-so-subtle relationship between policy and practice is beautifully illustrated in the self-confirming apparatus in effect at the General Electric company where President Gerard Swope defended his policies on the grounds that "our theory was that women did not recognize the responsibilities of life and were hoping to get married soon and would leave us, and therefore, this insurance premium deduction from the pay would not appeal to them."[71] As historian Ronald Schatz notes, because GE compelled women to quit if they married, women rarely acquired enough seniority to obtain pensions or vacations with pay. Women's aspirations could not be entirely stilled by these measures. The Ford Motor Company, according to historian Stephen Meyer III, "considered all women, regardless of their family stakes, as youths: that is as single men under twenty-two without dependents, and therefore ineligible for Ford profits." Yet "as the result of criticism from women's rights advocates, the company eventually allowed some women, who were the heads of households, to participate in its welfare plan."[72]

One result of such policies and an instrument in

their perpetuation as well was that women carefully rationalized their increasing work force participation and defended themselves by comparing their wages only to those of other women. The model was familiar. The numerous investigating commissions of the prewar period had already asserted the injustice of paying women as much as men. Thus, investigators exploring the feasibility of a higher wage for women raised such issues as what, for instance, a firm would "have to pay a man with a family if it paid $2 a day to girls with no one but themselves to support?"[73] This does not seem to have inhibited women's desire for higher incomes. But it seems to have channeled their grievances away from men who earned far more than they and toward women instead. Among Western Electric workers interviewed in the late 1920s, a typical female who complained about wages tended to be distressed not at her absolute wage but at how it compared with those of other women. As one female employee complained, "the girl next to me, her job pays $39.80 per hundred, and mine pays $28.80 and I work just as hard as she does. I don't see how they figure that out. She makes ten cents more on every one she makes."[74]

These powerful and sometimes explicit barriers extended across race lines and to the social wages offered by modern corporations. In their presence Black women were paid less than white women for the same or similar jobs. Employers utilized them to sanction distinctions in the amenities they offered to Black and white women. An early survey of the tobacco industry in Virginia reflects the value of such circumscribed comparisons. "Tuesday and Friday," the report noted matter of factly, "the white girls have 15 minutes extra in order to dance, but the 15 minutes is paid for by the firm."[75]

What kept the "wage" pot bubbling, then, was not women's desire to achieve male pay but their urge to satisfy more concrete wants. As mass production jobs and clerical work opened up to white women, some factory jobs became available to Black women. New, relatively well-paying jobs and rising real wages for both men and women contributed to the advent of the consumer society and helped to create a new definition of wants that drew on a prevailing individualism from which women could hardly be excluded. Marketing techniques, installment buying, and the increasing value placed on consumption replaced thrift and postponed gratification as appropriate spirits of the time. New definitions of wants attracted new groups of women to the work force and suggested new rationales for staying there.

The changing population of female workers challenged perceptions of a wage that spoke to simpler needs. To women for whom the prewar women's wage had offered little apart from the despair of poverty, the wage now stretched to encompass the hope of individual achievement measured by material goals. Defined in prewar practice as the minimum required to sustain a single woman partially supported by her family, the postwar wage at least suggested the capacity to earn a living.[76] Ronald Edsforth, who studied auto workers in the 1920s, notes that government investigators discovered among the women working in auto factories in the 1920s a "genuinely modern level of individual materialism . . . guiding . . . life-shaping decisions." They concluded that "jobs in the auto factories were most desired simply because auto workers' earnings were high."[77] But even the rising wage was clearly inadequate to reconcile the competing needs of an increasingly heterogeneous group of female wage earners. Less immigrant than native born, containing a small but steadily growing proportion of married women, and with a still tiny but slowly growing representation of Black women in mainstream jobs that had long been closed to them, women with competing views of the wage attempted to participate in what some called the "American standard of living." In the process they helped to establish a new set of gendered definitions about self and others.

For middle class, single, adventurous women, work and a wage meant escape from boredom, a bit of rebellion, a purpose in life—the means to a relatively autonomous existence. Fuelled by the rhetoric of the women's movement and energized by a successful campaign for the vote, single women, no longer subsidized by families and increasingly eager to live outside them, craved the independence that wages potentially offered. To some, participation in wage work offered to contribute economic equality to the political citizenship they had won with suffrage.[78] To others, as economist Theresa Wolfson suggested, the wage bought the liberty to live "comparatively free lives outside of their working hours."[79]

For poorer women, including immigrants and women of color, and for most of the married women who earned, the wage became a measure of the capacity to participate in an increasingly pervasive consumer society. "I would like to work," commented one young assembly line worker, "until I get my furniture paid for. My husband is young and hasn't got much of a start yet and I want to help him."[80] A woman's wage represented, still, a supplement to male earnings—an extension of family life. Less a vehicle to sheer survival in the 1920s, it promised access to the new wants generated by an ethic of consumption. If it still continued to preclude freedom for most women, it offered a way to sustain and even enhance family life and exacted, in return, the price of women's continuing commitment to the work force.[81] It should not surprise us then that the changing material content of the wage did not diminish either the effort to earn it or its importance in women's lives. And it dramatically expanded the numbers of women willing and able to earn wages. A young woman who had worked at the Western Electric company for a year complained that her feet swelled on the job. She didn't want to sit down, however, because "I can't turn out the rates when I sit down." She had, she said, returned to Western Electric after a year at another job because "I couldn't earn near as much money, and I couldn't save any."[82]

Because a woman's wage had to serve the increasingly fragmented needs of a diverse array of women, the rhetoric surrounding it became more complex. It is best uncovered in the efforts of the newly created Women's Bureau of the Department of Labor to represent women workers of all kinds. The bureau's official position consistently upheld wages for women based on the value of the job. Yet its public posture simultaneously affirmed the need for a minimum wage based on the needs of the worker. Wages, wrote Mary Anderson, head of the bureau, "should be established on the basis of occupation and not on the basis of sex or race." At the same time, she added, the minimum wage rate that was available to women only, if at all, "should cover the cost of living in health and decency, instead of a bare existence, and should allow for dependents and not merely for the individual."[83]

The compromise, then, appeared to lie not in abandoning a needs-based assessment of women's wages so much as in an effort to understand that any definition of "wants" encompassed a broad range of human needs. While fewer than 15 percent of all married women, and about 30 percent of Black married women, with wage-earning husbands were regularly employed before the 1930s, those who earned wages had a complicated series of wants. For example, well-paid male and female hosiery workers in the Piedmont

Valley of North Carolina and Tennessee flaunted their capacity to buy consumer goods.[84] In the same region, the poorly paid white textile workers could and frequently did hire Black women to take care of their children while white husbands and wives worked in the mills.[85] Black women used their tiny pay to feed and clothe their children and to support those who cared for them in their absence. Such enormous differences in the uses of wages notwithstanding, the image of women paid at a rate regulated by public perceptions of abstract needs helped to perpetuate the sense that, in the competition for jobs among women, what was at stake was not skill or the nature of work but the capacity to contribute to family support. This image perpetuated a low wage for all women. In exactly the way that employers had earlier chosen to believe that young, single women were supported by their parents, so, in the period after World War I, an idealized image of marriage with its attendant financial subsidy served to define a woman's role and threatened to regulate the level of wages for all women.

Partly in consequence, single women, inside and outside the Women's Bureau, were haunted by visions of married women subsidized by their husbands and therefore able to accept lower wages. Public debate over the wage question in the 1920s turned on the issue of whose needs the wage was intended to meet—the married woman working for "pin money" or the independent self-supporting woman of all classes. Neither category encompassed the reality of women workers, more than three-quarters of whom, according to contemporary studies, supported themselves and their families. While in the prewar period, questions about "workers who are in part supported by parents or other members of the family"[86] had captured a certain unease about independent women who transcended traditional roles, the 1920s attack on "pin money" workers focused on the distress of single working women who feared competition from women whose families partially supported them. The competition, muted by the prosperity of the 1920s, did not explode until the 1930s. In the meantime, the question of married women in industry was argued pro and con, with such stalwart champions of working women as Mary Gilson, Melinda Scott, and Sophonisba Breckinridge protesting that married women ought not to be in the labor force. Breckinridge proposed instead "a living wage for men based on their own needs and those of their wives and a standard family of three children; disciplinary measures for husbands who are unwilling to work, and state aid for wives of those who cannot work."[87]

In the face of the commitment to a needs-based wage, proponents of individualism and some champions of the Women's Bureau fought a losing battle for "a rate for the job." The new consumerism required a more complex set of messages than simple individualism. While it offered support for raising the wage enough to accommodate both new social relations and new needs, it would not, and did not, challenge conceptions of the wage that sustained family life. Thus, one group of women struggled to elevate a woman's wage by asking that all workers receive value for the job, while a second declared itself in need of protective legislation and advocated a minimum wage to legitimate women's capacity to work at all. A woman's wage still refused to incorporate the capacity to earn a living. At most, it offered a fling at independence to those who did not need to contribute to family support. For the poor it could enhance a family's standard of living. But in no sense was a woman's wage intended to promote the desire for a self-sufficient existence.

Yet to women who worked, the capacity to improve the standard of living was not mere ideology. The reification of an "American" standard of living offered a rationale for continuing wage work among married women. As consumer expectations rose, the purchase of what some might have called pin money goods became not luxuries but part of the quality of life. Because a woman's wage appeared as largely contributory, it neither undermined male egos nor fomented female independence. Men understood the wage as an indication of whether they were "getting ahead." Women understood it as an indication of whether they could keep up with their work, their status among their peers, and their position in the eyes of the boss. And yet women's capacity to enhance the family standard contributed to denuding the notion that the family wage either could or should be earned by men alone. At the same time, women established new sources of comparisons that enabled them to maintain status and self-esteem even as they continued to earn less than two-thirds of the wage of the average male worker.

But women's wages, restricted by an ethos of need and locked into comparisons with other women, still could not rise high enough to compete with the wages of men. If the message of the wage differed for men and women, it failed to prevent women from seeking the same kinds of material gains acquired by men. At some level the "woman's wage" decisively relegated females to a plateau of citizenship that could not be equated with that of men. As much as suffrage had seemed to extend citizenship to women, a woman's wage suggested the limits of their aspirations and assigned them to sometimes objectionable social roles. A "rate for the job"—a wage equivalent to that of similarly situated men working in the same firm—would have trumpeted a message of aspiration and ambition that few in the 1920s were ready to hear. But the value that a woman worker created was never the central issue of women's wage work. Rather, the wage sought to identify the boundaries within which economic inequality could be used to constrain the prerogatives of citizenship. The sex of a worker remained safely more important than what that worker did. With some few exceptions, equality was not at issue; the wage did not contest male prerogatives in the workplace. Rather, it symbolized the limits of political citizenship.

NOTES

1. Henry A. Landsberger, *Hawthorne Revisited: Management and the Worker, Its Critics, and the Developments in Human Relations in Industry* (Ithaca, N.Y.: Cornell University, 1958), 19.

2. New York State, *Factory Investigating Commission, Fourth Report* (Albany: S.B. Lyon Co., 1915), vol. 1, app. 3, passim. (Hereinafter referred to as FIC.)

3. N. Arnold Tolles, *Origins of Modern Wage Theories* (Englewood Cliffs, N.J.: Prentice-Hall, 1964), 8.

4. This theory, known as marginal productivity theory, was predicated on the assumption of perfect competition and emphasized the demands of employers in calculating the wage. Its classic exposition is John Bates Clark, *The Distribution of Wealth* (New York: Macmillan, 1899).

5. FIC, Fourth Report, vol. 4, 435.

6. In the United States, organized workers agitated for the idea beginning in the 1830s.

7. Melton McLaurin, *Paternalism and Protest: Southern*

Cotton Mill Workers and Organized Labor, 1875–1905 (Westport, Conn.: Greenwood Press, 1971), 23, describes how the notion of a family wage that rested on the labor of all family members could contribute to expectations of female and child labor. In southern textile mills, "mill management argued that the total annual income of a mill family was far greater than that of a farm family. Thus the 'family wage' was used as a cover for the low wages paid individuals" (23). But this is not the usual understanding. See Martha May, "The Historical Problem of the Family Wage: The Ford Motor Company and the Five Dollar Day," *Feminist Studies,* 8 (Summer 1982), 394–424.

8. For access to the opposing positions, see Jane Humphries, "The Working Class Family, Women's Liberation, and Class Struggle: The Case of Nineteenth Century British History," *Review of Radical Political Economics,* 9 (Fall 1977), 25–41; Michelle Barrett and Mary McIntosh, "The Family Wage: Some Problems for Socialists and Feminists," *Capital and Class,* 11 (1980), 51–72; and Hilary Land, "The Family Wage," *Feminist Review,* 6 (1980), 55–78.

9. John A. Ryan, *A Living Wage: Its Ethical and Economic Aspects* (New York: Macmillan, 1906), 117.

10. William Smart, *Studies in Economics* (London: Macmillan, 1985), 34. Smart added that "in addition perhaps some consumption of alcohol and tobacco, and some indulgence in fashionable dress are, in many places, so habitual that they may be said to be 'conventionally necessary'"(34).

11. Cited by Ryan, *Living Wage,* 130, from the *American Federationist,* 1898.

12. Ryan, *Living Wage,* 117.

13. Ibid., vii.

14. Italics mine. Quoted in May, "Historical Problem of the Family Wage," 402. Samuel Gompers believed the worker's living wage should "be sufficient to sustain himself and those dependent upon him in a manner to maintain his self-respect, to educate his children, supply his household with literature, with opportunities to spend a portion of his life with his family." In Samuel Gompers, "A Minimum Living Wage," *American Federationist,* 5 (April 1898), 26.

15. See, for example, the list compiled by F. Spencer Baldwin in Louise Bosworth, *The Living Wage of Women Workers* (New York: Longmans Green and Co., 1911), 7; see also Elizabeth Beardsley Butler, *Women and the Trades: Pittsburgh, 1907–1908* (Pittsburgh: University of Pittsburgh Press, 1984 [1909]), 346–47.

16. J. Laurence Laughlin, ed., *Principles of Political Economy by John Stuart Mill* (New York: D. Appleton and Company, 1885), 214.

17. Italics mine. Ryan, *Living Wage,* 107.

18. Lynn Y. Wiener, *From Working Girl to Working Mother: The Female Labor Force in the United States, 1820–1980* (Chapel Hill: University of North Carolina, 1985), 19, 26, 84.

19. Ryan, *Living Wage,* 107.

20. Ibid., 120.

21. Kellogg Durland, "Labor Day Symposium," *American Federationist* 12 (September 1905), 619.

22. Ryan, *Living Wage,* 107.

23. Ibid., 133.

24. Dorothy W. Douglas, *American Minimum Wage Laws at Work* (New York: National Consumers' League, 1920), 14.

25. Butler, *Women and the Trades,* 346; Bosworth, *Living Wage of Women Workers,* 9. The Women's Bureau estimated that the minimums in effect from 1913 to 1915 ranged from $8.50 to $10.74. See Bulletin no. 61, *The Development of Minimum Wage Laws in the United States: 1912–1927* (Washington, D.C.: Government Printing Office, 1928).

26. Thomas Herbert Russell, *The Girl's Fight for a Living: How to Protect Working Women from Dangers Due to Low Wages* (Chicago: M.A. Donahue, 1913), 108.

27. Elizabeth Brandeis, "Labor Legislation," vol. 3 of John Commons, *History of Labor in the United States* (New York: Macmillan, 1935), 524–25, makes the point that these budgets were calculated in one of two ways: on the basis of actual expenditures (a problem because women had to live on what they earned, however small) or on the basis of theoretical budgets (a problem because employer-members of boards resisted the inclusion of such items as recreation, "party dress," etc.). They were then "modified" by estimates of prevailing wages, consideration of the amounts of the proposed increases, and possible consequences for business conditions.

28. Sue Ainslee Clark and Edith Wyatt, "Working-Girls' Budgets: A Series of Articles Based upon Individual Stories of Self-Supporting Girls," *McClure's,* 35 (October 1910). Additional articles appeared in *McClure's* in vol. 36 in November and December 1910 and February 1911. They were published in book form under the title, *Making Both Ends Meet: The Income and Outlay of New York Working-Girls* (New York: Macmillan, 1911). The classic study is that of Louise Bosworth, cited above.

29. Clark and Wyatt, "Working-Girls' Budgets," *McClure's,* 35 (October 1910), 604. See the discussion of these budgets in Wiener, *From Working Girl to Working Mother,* 75–77; and Joanne Meyerowitz, *Women Adrift: Independent Wage Earners in Chicago, 1880–1930* (Chicago: University of Chicago Press, 1988), 33–35.

30. The magazine advertised for contributions in January 1908 and published from four to six contributions from February 1908 to January 1909. In September 1908 it announced that it was flooded with contributions and would no longer accept any more. There is no way of knowing how heavily these were edited, so they have been used here only to extract a broad gauge of opinion.

31. "The Girl Who Comes to the City," *Harper's Bazaar,* 42 (January 1908), 54.

32. "The Girl Who Comes to the City," 42 (October 1908), 1005; 42 (July 1908), 694.

33. "The Girl Who Comes to the City," 42 (August 1908),

776. The maximum achieved by any of these women was the $100 a month earned by a Washington D.C., civil servant (42[November 1908], 1141). That sum was sufficient for a single woman not only to live reasonably well but to save and invest some of her income. It was rarely achieved by women.

34. "The Girl Who Comes to the City," 42 (November 1908), 1141; see also October 1908, 1007.

35. See, for example, Alice Kessler-Harris, *Out to Work: A History of Wage Earning Women in the United States* (New York: Oxford, 1982), 99–101; Meyerowitz, *Women Adrift,* 34–36.

36. "The Girl Who Comes to the City," 42 (March 1908), 277; 42 (May 1908), 500. The widespread nature of this assumption is apparent in "Women's Wages," *Nation,* 108 (February 22, 1919), 270–71: "The employer of women today is in a large proportion of cases heavily subsidized; for there is a considerable gap between the $9 a week that is paid to a girl and her actual cost of maintenance. Who makes up the difference? In the employer's mind it is usually the girl's family—which is often mythical."

37. Smart, *Studies in Economics,* 115.

38. Butler, *Women and the Trades,* 346.

39. Meyerowitz, *Women Adrift,* 33.

40. Butler, *Women and the Trades,* 344.

41. FIC, Fourth Report, vol. 4, app. 3, 450.

42. Scott Nearing, "The Adequacy of American Wages," *Annals of the American Academy of Political and Social Sciences,* 59 (May 1915), 2.

43. "Women's Wages and Morality," *American Federationist,* 20 (June 1913), 467.

44. Smart, *Studies in Economics,* 125.

45. Russell, *Girl's Fight for a Living,* 21. On pay differences by race, see Meyerowitz, *Women Adrift,* 36; and Dolores Janiewski, *Sisterhood Denied: Race, Gender and Class in a New South Community* (Philadelphia: Temple University Press, 1985), 110–13.

46. FIC, Fourth Report, vol. 2, app. 3, 468; Don D. Lescohier, then a Minnesota statistician and later to become an eminent gatherer of labor statistics, commented at the same hearings that "custom . . . plays a far larger part in holding wages stationary than we have been accustomed to think" (ibid., 459).

47. Smart, *Studies in Economics,* 116. The radical Scott Nearing, in a minority opinion, held that the male wage was not determined by another principle at all. He protested industry's lack of attention to social relations: "The man with a family is brought into active competition with the man who has no family obligations. The native-born head of a household must accept labor terms which are satisfactory to the foreign-born single man. Industry does not inquire into a worker's social obligations" (Nearing, "Adequacy of American Wages," 123).

48. Which is not, of course, to imply that all males who earned wages were paid enough to support families. See

Janiewski, *Sisterhood Denied,* for illustrations of wages in the southern tobacco and textile industries that required the labor of three or more people to sustain a family.

49. Bosworth, *Living Wage,* 4.

50. Russell, *Girl's Fight for a Living,* 73.

51. Ibid., 108.

52. Ibid., 83.

53. Smart, *Studies in Economics,* 107.

54. Samuel Gompers, "Woman's Work, Rights and Progress," *American Federationist,* 20 (August 1913), 625.

55. Alfred Marshall, *Principles of Economics,* 8th ed. (New York: Macmillan, 1953), 685.

56. Quoted in Russell, *Girl's Fight for a Living,* 16; and see "Women's Wages and Morality," 465.

57. Russell, *Girl's Fight for a Living,* 38; cf. also the testimony of Ida Tarbell in ibid., 39.

58. Butler, *Women and the Trades,* 342–43.

59. Frances Amasa Walker, *The Wages Question: A Treatise on Wages and the Wages Class* (New York: Henry Holt and Company, 1876), 374.

60. Ibid., 378.

61. Quoted in Marjorie Shuler, "Industrial Women Confer," *Woman Citizen,* 8 (January 27, 1923), 25.

62. Such arguments were prefigured in the late nineteenth century by assertions that the greedy were taking jobs from the needy. See Kessler-Harris, *Out to Work,* 99ff.

63. "Women as Wage Earners," *New York Times,* January 28, 1923, 26.

64. Maurine Greenwald, *Women, War, and Work: The Impact of World War One on Women in the United States* (Westport, Conn.: Greenwood Press, 1980), 155. Greenwald notes that a female janitor who might have made $35 a month earned $75–80 a month as a conductor.

65. Daniel Nelson, *Managers and Workers: Origins of the New Factory System in the United States* (Madison: University of Wisconsin Press, 1975), 145.

66. Quoted in "Women and Wages," *The Woman Citizen,* 4 (June 7, 1919), 8. The article went on to report that one plant had "reckoned women's production as 20 per cent greater than that of the men preceding them. But this did not prevent the same plant from cutting down the women's pay one-third."

67. Typescript, "Memoranda Regarding Women's Bureau," in National Archives, Record Group 86, Box 4, File: WTUL Action on Policies. The bureau lost this battle. As a result, its professional staff tended to work more out of loyalty and commitment than for monetary gain. See Judith Sealander, *As Minority Becomes Majority: Federal Reaction to the Phenomenon of Women in the Work Force, 1920–1963* (Westport, Conn.: Greenwood Press, 1983), chap. 3, for the early days of the Women's Bureau.

68. Ronald W. Schatz, *The Electrical Workers: A History of Labor at General Electric and Westinghouse, 1923–60* (Urbana: University of Illinois Press, 1983), 32.

69. Quoted in Stephen Meyer III, *The Five Dollar Day: Labor Management and Social Control in the Ford Motor Company, 1908–1921* (Albany: State University of New York Press, 1981), 140.

70. Schatz, *Electrical Workers,* 20–21.

71. Quoted in Schatz, *Electrical Workers,* 21; Nelson, *Managers and Workers,* 118, confirms that the wage as welfare differed for men and women: "Manufacturers who employed large numbers of women usually emphasized measures to make the factory more habitable. Lunchrooms, restrooms, landscaping and other decorative features conveyed the idea of a home away from home. At the same time, the classes in domestic economy and child rearing, social clubs, outings and dances (women only) assured the worker that she need not sacrifice her femininity when she entered the male world of the factory. But, because the female operative was (or was thought to be) a secondary wage earner and probably a transient, she was not offered pensions, savings programs and insurance plans."

72. Meyer, *Five Dollar Day,* 140; implicit in the Ford policy was a quite conscious attempt to circumscribe the roles and self-perceptions of men as well as of women. Meyer quotes a Ford policy manual from the 1920s to the effect that "if a man wants to remain a profit sharer, his wife should stay at home and assume the obligations she undertook when married" (141). See the commentary on this issue in "Housework Wages," *The Woman Citizen,* 4 (October 4, 1919), 449.

73. Russell, *Girl's Fight for a Living,* 101; the same investigator asked an employer, "If you raised a little girl from $3 to $8 would a man getting $15 feel aggrieved?" (112)—a question that loads the dice by imagining women as no more than children.

74. Microfilm records, Western Electric Plant, Hawthorne Works, Operating Branch M., interviews, Reel 6, July 8, 1929. Records of individuals are not identified or tagged beyond the branch where the interviews were taken. The growing sense of entitlement to comparable wages was captured by an experienced female worker who declared herself satisfied with her work "because it was more interesting and I could make my rate" but nevertheless complained that "I don't see why they didn't raise me anyway like they did the other girls, every half year or every year." In ibid., July 9, 1929. This phenomenon was not specific to women alone. F. J. Roethlisberger and William Dickson, analyzing the Western Electric research, commented, "The results of the interviewing program show very clearly that the worker was quite as much concerned with these differentials, that is the relation of his wages to that of other workmen as with the absolute amount of his wages." See *Management and the Worker: An Account of a Research Program Conducted by the Western Electric Company, Hawthorne Works, Chicago* (Cambridge, Mass.: Harvard University Press, 1946), 543. But nothing in the interviews indicates that women compared their wages with those of men, nor did men with those of women.

75. Mary Schaill and Ethel Best to Mary Anderson, November 5, 1919, Virginia Survey, Bulletin no. 10, National Archives, Record Group 86: Records of the Women's Bureau, Box 2.

76. Pauline Newman, veteran trade unionist, challenged old notions of a living wage in "The 'Equal Rights' Amendment," *American Federationist,* 45 (August 1938), 815. She wrote, "It is not a wage which affords an opportunity for intellectual development; it is not a wage which allows for spiritual growth; it is not a wage on which wage-earning women can enjoy the finer things of life."

77. Ronald Edsforth, *Class Conflict and Cultural Consensus: The Making of a Mass Consumer Society in Flint, Michigan* (New Brunswick, N.J.: Rutgers University Press, 1987), 95.

78. Daniel T. Rodgers, *The Work Ethic in Industrial America: 1850–1920* (Chicago: University of Chicago Press, 1974), 196.

79. Theresa Wolfson, *The Woman Worker and the Trade Unions* (New York: International Publishers, 1926), 42.

80. Microfilm records, Western Electric Plant, Hawthorne Works, Operating Branch M., interviews, Reel 6, July 8, 1929.

81. Wolfson, *Woman Worker,* 42–43.

82. Microfilm records, Western Electric Plant, Hawthorne Works, Operating Branch M., interviews, Reel 6, Folder 1, Box 14, July 1, 1929.

83. Mary Anderson, "Industrial Standards for Women," *American Federationist,* 32 (July 1925), 565.

84. Jacquelyn Dowd Hall et al., *Like a Family: The Making of a Southern Cotton Mill World* (Chapel Hill: University of North Carolina Press, 1987), 255–56.

85. See interviews with Ada Mae Wilson, Mary Ethel Shockley, Ina Wrenn, and Gertrude Shuping in Southern Oral History Project Collection, Martin Wilson Library, University of North Carolina, Chapel Hill. Used with the kind help of Jacquelyn Dowd Hall.

86. The quotation is from FIC, Fourth Report, vol. 4, 440. The percentage of married black women working and supporting families was far higher than that for white women.

87. Shuler, "Industrial Women Confer," 12.

Bringing the Men Back In: Sex Differentiation and the Devaluation of Women's Work

BARBARA F. RESKIN

One of the most enduring manifestations of sex inequality in industrial and postindustrial societies is the wage gap.[1] In 1986, as in 1957, among full-time workers in the United States, men earned 50 percent more per hour than did women. This disparity translated to $8,000 a year in median earnings, an all-time high bonus for being male. Most sociologists agree that the major cause of the wage gap is the segregation of women and men into different kinds of work (Reskin and Hartmann 1986). Whether or not women freely choose the occupations in which they are concentrated, the outcome is the same: the more proportionately female an occupation, the lower its average wages (Treiman and Hartmann 1981). The high level of job segregation (Bielby and Baron 1984) means that the 1963 law stipulating equal pay for equal work did little to reduce the wage gap.[2]

This "causal model"—that the segregation of women and men into different occupations causes the wage gap—implies two possible remedies. One is to equalize men and women on the causal variable—occupation—by ensuring women's access to tradition-

From *Gender & Society,* vol. 2, no. 1, March 1988. Copyright © 1988 Sociologists for Women in Society. Reprinted by permission of Sage Publications, Inc.

Barbara F. Reskin is a Professor of Sociology at The Ohio State University. She has written extensively on sex inequality in science and sex segregation in the workplace, including *Women's Work, Men's Work: Sex Segregation on the Job* (with Heidi Hartmann, published by the National Academy Press, 1986). She is also studying men's responses to women's employment in typically male jobs with Irene Padavic and jurors' decisions in sexual-assault cases.

ally male occupations. The other is to replace occupation with a causal variable on which women and men differ less, by instituting comparable-worth pay policies that compensate workers for the "worth" of their job regardless of its sex composition.

I contend, however, that the preceding explanation of the wage gap is incorrect because it omits variables responsible for the difference between women and men in their distribution across occupations. If a causal model is incorrect, the remedies it implies may be ineffective. Lieberson's (1985, p. 185) critique of causal analysis as it is commonly practiced explicates the problem by distinguishing between *superficial* (or surface) causes that *appear to* give rise to a particular outcome and *basic* causes that *actually* produce the outcome. For example, he cites the belief that the black-white income gap is due to educational differences and thus can be reduced by reducing the educational disparity. As Lieberson pointed out, this analysis misses the fact that "the dominant group . . . uses its dominance to advance its own position" (p. 166), so that eliminating race differences in education is unlikely to reduce racial inequality in income because whites will find another way to maintain their income advantage. In other words, what appear in this example to be both the outcome variable (the black-white income gap) and the imputed causal variable (the black-white educational disparity) may stem from the same basic cause (whites' attempt to maintain their economic advantage). If so, then if the disparity in education were eliminated, some other factor would arise to produce the same economic consequence (Lieberson 1985, p. 164).

Dominant groups remain privileged because they write the rules, and the rules they write "enable them *to continue to write the rules*" (Lieberson 1985, p. 167; emphasis added). As a result, they can change the rules to thwart challenges to their position. Consider the following example. Because Asian American students tend to outscore occidentals on standard admissions tests, they are increasingly overrepresented in some university programs. Some universities have allegedly responded by imposing quotas for Asian students (Hechinger 1987, p. C1) or weighing more heavily admissions criteria on which they believe Asian Americans do less well.[3]

How can one tell whether a variable is a superficial or a basic cause of some outcome? Lieberson offered a straightforward test: Does a change in that variable lead to a change in the outcome? Applying this rule to the prevailing causal theory of the wage gap, we find that between 1970 and 1980 the index of occupational sex segregation declined by 10 percent (Beller 1984), but the wage gap for full-time workers declined by just under 2 percent (computed from data in Blau and Ferber 1986, p. 171). Although its meaning may be equivocal,[4] this finding is consistent with other evidence that attributing the wage gap to job segregation misses its basic cause: men's propensity to maintain their privileges. This claim is neither novel nor specific to men. Marxist and conflict theory have long recognized that dominant groups act to preserve their position (Collins 1975). Like other dominant groups, men are reluctant to give up their advantages (Goode 1982). To avoid having to do so, they construct "rules" for distributing rewards that guarantee them the lion's share (see also Epstein 1985, p. 30). In the past, men cited their need as household heads for a "family wage" (May 1982) and designated women as secondary earners. Today, when millions of women who head households would benefit from such a rule, occupation has supplanted it as the principle for assigning wages.

Neoclassical economic theory holds that the market is the mechanism through which wages are set, but markets are merely systems of rules (Marshall and Paulin n.d., p. 15) that dominant groups establish for their own purposes. When other groups, such as labor unions, amassed enough power, they modified the "market" principle.[5] Steinberg (1987) observed that when consulted in making comparable-worth adjust-

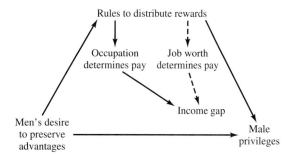

FIGURE 1   Heuristic model of the wage gap

ments, male-dominated unions tended to support management over changes that would raise women's salaries (see also Simmons, Freedman, Dunkle, and Blau 1975, pp. 115–36; Hartmann 1976).

In sum, the basic cause of the income gap is not sex segregation but men's desire to preserve their advantaged position and their ability to do so by establishing rules to distribute valued resources in their favor.[6] Figure 1 represents this more complete causal model. Note that currently segregation is a superficial cause of the income gap, in part through "crowding" (Bergmann 1974), but that some other distributional system such as comparable-worth pay could replace it with the same effect.

With respect to income, this model implies that men will resist efforts to close the wage gap. Resistance will include opposing equalizing women's access to jobs because integration would equalize women and men on the current superficial cause of the wage gap—occupation. Men may also try to preserve job segregation because it is a central mechanism through which they retain their dominance in other spheres, and because many people learn to prefer the company of others like them. My theory also implies that men will resist efforts to replace occupation with alternative principles for assigning pay that would mitigate segregation's effect on women's wages (as pay equity purports to do).

Before I offer evidence for these claims, let us examine how dominant groups in general and men in particular maintain their privileged position. I formulate my analysis with reference to dominant groups to emphasize that the processes I discuss are not specific to sex classes. It also follows that, were women the dominant sex, the claims I make about men's behavior should hold for women.

DIFFERENTIATION, DEVALUATION, AND HIERARCHY

Differentiation—the practice of distinguishing categories based on some attribute—is the fundamental process in hierarchical systems, a logical necessity for differential evaluation and differential rewards. But differentiation involves much more than merely acting on a preexisting difference. In a hierarchical context, differentiation assumes, amplifies, and even creates psychological and behavioral differences in order to ensure that the subordinate group differs from the dominant group (Epstein 1985, p. 36; Jagger 1983, pp. 109–10; MacKinnon 1987, p. 38; West and Zimmerman 1987, p. 137), "because the systematically differential delivery of benefits and deprivations require[s] making no mistake about who was who" (MacKinnon 1987, p. 40) and because "differences are inequality's post hoc excuse" (MacKinnon 1987, p. 8).

Differentiated status characteristics influence evaluations of people's behavior and their overall worth (Berger, Cohen, and Zelditch 1972; Pugh and Wahrman 1983). In hierarchical systems in which differentiation takes the form of an Aristotelian dichotomy, individuals are classified as either A ("the subject") or Not-A ("the other"). But these two classes are not construed as natural opposites that both have positive qualities; instead, A's characteristics are valued as normal or good and Not-A's as without value or negative (de Beauvoir 1953, p. xvi; Jay 1981).

The official response to the influx of south- and central-eastern European immigrants to the United States early in this century, when people assumed that each European country represented a distinct biological race (Lieberson 1980, p. 24), illustrates differentiation's central role in dominance systems. A congressionally mandated immigration commission concluded that "innate, ineradicable race distinctions separated groups of men from one another" and agreed on the

necessity of classifying these races to know which were most worthy of survival. The immediate problem was to ascertain "whether there may not be certain races that are inferior to other races . . . to discover some test to show whether some may be

better fitted for American citizenship than others." (Lieberson 1980, pp. 2–26)

Thus differentiation in all its forms supports dominance systems by demonstrating that superordinate and subordinate groups differ in essential ways and that such differences are natural and even desirable.

"Sex Differentiation" versus "Gender Differentiation": A Note on Terminology

Scholars speak of both "sex" and "gender" differentiation: the former when biological sex or the "sex category" into which people are placed at birth (West and Zimmerman 1987, p. 127) is the *basis for* classification and differential treatment; the latter to refer to the *result* of that differential treatment. In order to emphasize that the initial biological difference (mediated through sex category) is the basis for differential treatment, I use the terms *sex differentiation* and *sex segregation*. This usage should not obscure the fact that the process of converting sex category into gender is a social one or that most differences that are assumed to distinguish the sexes are socially created. I agree with Kessler and McKenna (1978) that the "gender attribution process" assumes dimorphism and seeks evidence of it to justify classifying people as male and female and treating them unequally. This article examines how and why those differences are produced.

Sex Differentiation and Devaluation

Probably no system of social differentiation is as extensive as that based on sex category. Its prevalence led anthropologist Gayle Rubin to claim that there is "a taboo against the sameness of men and women, a taboo dividing the sexes into two mutually exclusive categories, a taboo which exacerbates the biological differences between the sexes and thereby *creates* gender" (1975, p. 178). Moreover, although femaleness is not always devalued, its deviation from maleness in a culture that reserves virtues for men has meant the devaluation of women (Jay 1981). Bleier's research on biological scientists' study of sex differences illustrates this point: the "search for the truth about differences, [implies] that difference means *different from the white male norm and, therefore, inferior*" (1987, p. 2; emphasis added). In consequence, men's activities are typically valued above women's, regardless of their content or importance for group survival (Goode 1964; Mead 1949; Schur 1983, pp. 35–48), and both sexes come to devalue women's efforts (Major, McFarlin, and Gagnon 1984). Thus it should be no surprise that women's occupations pay less at least partly *because* women do them (Treiman and Hartmann 1981).

In short, differentiation is the sine qua non of dominance systems. Because of its importance, it is achieved through myriad ways:

> To go for a walk with one's eyes open is enough to demonstrate that humanity is divided into two classes of individuals whose clothes, faces, bodies, smiles, gaits, interests and occupations are manifestly different. (de Beauvoir 1953, p. xiv)

We differentiate groups in their location, appearance, and behavior, and in the tasks they do. Now let us turn to how these mechanisms operate to differentiate women and men.

PHYSICAL SEGREGATION

Dominant groups differentiate subordinate groups by physically isolating them—in ghettos, nurseries, segregated living quarters, and so on. Physical segregation fosters unequal treatment, because physically separate people can be treated differently and because it spares members of the dominant group the knowledge of the disparity and hides it from the subordinate group. Although women and men are integrated in some spheres, physical separation continues to differentiate them (e.g., see Goffman 1977, p. 316).

Cohn's (1985) vivid account of women's physical segregation in the British Foreign Office in the nineteenth century illustrates the extent to which organizations have gone to separate the sexes. The Foreign Office hid its first female typists in an attic, but it failed to rescind the requirement that workers collect their pay on the ground floor. When payday came, managers evacuated the corridors, shut all the doors, and then sent the women running down the attic stairs to get their checks and back up again. Only after they were out of sight were the corridors reopened to men.

This account raises the question of *why* managers segregate working men and women. What licentiousness did the Foreign Office fear would occur in integrated hallways? Contemporary answers are markedly similar to turn-of-the-century fears. Compare the scenario expressed in a 1923 editorial in the *Journal of Accountancy* ("any attempt at heterogeneous personnel [in after-hours auditing of banks] would hamper progress and lead to infinite embarrassment" [p. 151]) with recent reactions to the prospect of women integrating police patrol cars, coal mines, and merchant marine vessels (e.g., Martin 1980). At or just below the surface lies the specter of sexual liaisons. For years, McDonald's founder Ray Kroc forbade franchisees to hire women counter workers because they would attract "the wrong type" of customers (Luxenburg 1985). The U.S. Army ended sex-integrated basic training to "facilitate toughening goals" (National Organization for Women 1982), and the Air Force reevaluated whether women could serve on two-person Minuteman missile-silo teams because "it could lead to stress" (*New York Times* 1984).

My thesis offers a more parsimonious alternative to these ad hoc explanations—men resist allowing women and men to work together *as equals* because doing so undermines differentiation and hence male dominance.

BEHAVIORAL DIFFERENTIATION

People's behavior is differentiated on their status-group membership in far too many ways for me to review the differences adequately here. I concentrate in this section on differentiation of behaviors that occur in the workplace: task differentiation and social differentiation.

Task differentiation assigns work according to group membership. It was expressed in the extreme in traditional Hindu society in which caste virtually determined life work. Task assignment based on sex category—the sexual division of labor—both prescribes and proscribes assorted tasks to each sex, and modern societies still assign men and women different roles in domestic work (Pleck 1985), labor-market work (Reskin and Hartmann 1986), and emotional and interpersonal work (Fishman 1982; Hochschild 1983).[7] Task differentiation generally assigns to lower-status groups the least desirable, most poorly rewarded work: menial, tedious, and degraded tasks, such as cleaning, disposing of waste, and caring for the dying.[8] This practice symbolizes and legitimates the subordinate group's low status, while making it appear to have an affinity for these undesirable tasks. As an added benefit, members of the dominant group don't have to do them! Important to discussions of the wage gap, because modern law and custom permit unequal pay for different work, task differentiation justifies paying the subordinate group lower wages, thereby ensuring their economic inferiority. Women's assignment to child care, viewed as unskilled work in our society, illustrates these patterns. Women are said to have a "natural talent" for it and similar work; men are relieved from doing it; society obtains free or cheap child care; and women are handicapped in competing with men. As researchers have shown, sex-based task differentiation of both nonmarket and market work legitimates women's lower pay, hinders women's ability to succeed in traditionally male enterprises, and, in general, reinforces men's hegemony (Coverman 1983).

Social differentiation is achieved through norms that set dominant and subordinate groups apart in their appearance (sumptuary rules) or behavior (etiquette rules [van den Berghe 1960]). When applied to sex, Goffman's (1976) concept of "gender display" encompasses both. Sumptuary rules require certain modes of dress, diet, or life-style of members of subordinate groups as emblems of their inferior status, and reserve other modes to distinguish the dominant group. For example, Rollins (1985) discovered that white female employers preferred black domestic employees to dress shabbily to exaggerate their economic inferiority. Sex-specific sumptuary rules are epitomized in norms that dictate divergent dress styles that often exaggerate physical sex differences and sometimes even incapacitate women (Roberts 1977).[9] An extreme example is the *burqua* fundamentalist Muslim women wear as a symbol of their status and as a portable system of segregation (Papanek 1973).

Etiquette rules support differentiation by requiring subordinate group members to display ritualized deference toward dominants. Relations between enlistees and officers (van den Berghe 1960) or female domestic workers and their employers (Rollins 1985) illustrate their role. Although typically it is the subordinate group that must defer, gender etiquette that requires middle- and upper-class men to display deference to women of the same classes preserves differentiation by highlighting women's differentness. Women who do not express gratitude or who refuse to accept the deference are faced with hostility, shattering the fiction that women hold the preferred position.

Physical segregation, behavioral differentiation, social separation, and even hierarchy are functional alternatives for satisfying the need for differentiation in domination systems. For example, when their physical integration with the dominant group means that a subordinate group's status differences might otherwise be invisible, special dress is usually required of them, as servants are required to wear uniforms. Physical separation can even compensate for the absence of hierarchy, a point acknowledged in the black folk saying that southern whites don't care how close blacks get if they don't get too high, and northern whites don't care how high blacks get if they don't get too close (Lukas 1985).

This substitutability explains why men will tolerate women in predominantly male work settings if they work in "women's" jobs and accept women doing "men's" jobs in traditionally female settings, but resist women doing traditionally male jobs in male work settings (e.g., Schroedel 1985). Physical proximity per se is not threatening as long as another form of differentiation sets women apart. But the absence of *any* form of differentiation precludes devaluation and unequal rewards and hence threatens the sex-gender hierarchy. Because of the centrality of differentiation in domination systems, dominant groups have a considerable stake in maintaining it.

DOMINANTS' RESPONSE TO CHALLENGES

Dominants respond to subordinates' challenges by citing the group differences that supposedly warrant differential treatment (Jackman and Muha 1984). Serious challenges often give rise to attempts to demonstrate biological differences scientifically.

The nineteenth-century antislavery and women's rights movements led reputable scientists to try to prove that women's and blacks' brains were underdeveloped (Bleier 1987). The Great Migration to the United States in the first two decades of this century fueled a eugenics movement that purported to establish scientifically the inferiority of south- and central-eastern Europeans (Lieberson 1980, pp. 25–26). The civil rights movement of the 1960s stimulated renewed efforts to establish racial differences in intelligence. And we are once again witnessing a spate of allegedly scientific research seeking a biological basis for presumed sex differences in cognitive ability and, specifically, for boys' higher average scores on math questions in some standardized tests. As Bleier pointed out, "The implication if not purposes of [such] research is to demonstrate that the structure of society faithfully reflects the natural order of things" (1987, p. 11; see also Epstein 1985, pp. 32, 35, for a similar pattern in the social sciences). According to Bleier, reputable journals have published studies that violate accepted standards of proof, and the scientific press has given dubious findings considerable attention (as in the news story in *Science* that asked, "Is There a Male Math Gene?"). Although subsequently these studies have been discredited, the debate serves its purpose by focusing attention on how groups differ.[10]

MEN'S RESPONSE TO OCCUPATIONAL INTEGRATION

An influx of women into male spheres threatens the differentiation of men and women, and men resist (Goode 1982). One response is to bar women's entry. Women have had to turn to the courts to win entry into Little League sports, college dining clubs, private professional clubs, and the Rotary (Anderson 1987; Association of American Colleges 1985, p. 11; Schafran 1981). Recently, University of North Carolina trustees decried the fact that women are now a majority of UNC students, and some proposed changing the weights for certain admission criteria to restore the male majority (Greene 1987).[11] Twice since a shortage of male recruits forced the army to lift its quota on women, it has reduced the number of jobs open to women (Becraft 1987, p. 3).

Numerous studies have documented men's resistance to women entering "their" jobs (e.g., see Hartmann 1976 on cigar makers; Schroedel 1985 on a cross-section of trades). Sometimes the resistance is simply exclusion; at other times it is subtle barriers that block women's advancement or open harassment (Reskin 1978). Now that more women hold managerial jobs, one hears of "a glass ceiling" that bars middle-management women from top-level positions (e.g., Hymowitz and Schellhardt 1986), and Kanter (1987) claimed that organizations are changing the rules of what one must do to reach the top in order to make it more difficult for women to succeed.

My thesis implies that men will respond to women's challenge in the workplace by emphasizing how they differ from men. Especially common are reminders of

women's "natural" roles as wife, mother, or sexual partner. Witness the recent—and subsequently disputed-claims that women who postponed marriage and childbearing to establish their careers had a negligible chance of finding husbands and were running the risk that their "biological clocks" would prevent pregnancy, and accounts of women dropping out of middle management to spend more time with their children.[12]

Men who cannot bar women from "male" jobs can still preserve differentiation in other spheres. Their attempts to do so may explain why so few husbands of wage-working women share housework (Pleck 1985, p. 146), as well as elucidating Wharton and Baron's (1987) finding that among men working in sex-integrated jobs, those whose wives were employed were more dissatisfied than unmarried men or men married to homemakers.

Another response to women's challenge is to weaken the mechanisms that have helped women advance in the workplace. Since 1980, the Reagan administration has sought to undermine equal-opportunity programs and affirmative-action regulations, and the campaign has partly succeeded. Efforts to dilute or eliminate Equal Employment Opportunity (EEO) programs are advanced by claims that sex inequality has disappeared (or that men now experience "reverse discrimination"). For example, the *New York Times* (Greer 1987, pp. C1, 10) recently described the Department of Commerce announcement that women now compose the majority in professional occupations as a "historic milestone," adding that "the barriers have fallen."

THE ILLUSION OF OCCUPATIONAL INTEGRATION

If male resistance is so pervasive, how can we explain the drop in the index of occupational sex segregation in the 1970s and women's disproportionate gains in a modest number of male-dominated occupations (Rytina and Bianchi 1984)? In order to answer this question, Patricia Roos and I embarked on a study of the changing sex composition of occupations (Reskin and Roos forthcoming). The results of our case studies of a dozen traditionally male occupations in which women made disproportionate statistical gains during the 1970s cast doubt on whether many women can advance economically through job integration.

The case studies revealed two general patterns. First, within many occupations nominally being integrated, men and women remain highly segregated, with men concentrated in the highest-status and best-paying jobs. For example, although women's representation in baking grew from 25 percent in 1970 to 41 percent in 1980, men continue to dominate production baking. The increase in women bakers is due almost wholly to their concentration in proliferating "in-store" bakeries (Steiger 1987). Although women now make up the majority of residential real estate salespersons, men still monopolize commercial sales (Thomas and Reskin 1987).

The second pattern shows that women often gained access to these occupations after changes in work content and declines in autonomy or rewards made the work less attractive to men (Cockburn 1986, p. 76). In some occupations, the growth of functions already socially labeled as "women's work" (e.g., clerical, communications, or emotional work) spurred the change. For example, computerization and the ensuing clericalization prompted women's entry into typesetting and composing (Roos 1986) and insurance adjusting and examining (Phipps 1986). An increasing emphasis on communicating and interpersonal or emotional work contributed to women's gains in insurance sales (Thomas 1987), insurance adjusting and examining (Phipps 1987), systems analysis (Donato 1986), public relations (Donato 1987), and bank and financial management (Bird 1987).

Brief summaries of our findings for two occupations illustrate these processes.[13] First, women's disproportionate gains in pharmacy have been largely confined to the retail sector (male pharmacists work disproportionately in research and management) and occurred after retail pharmacists lost professional status and entrepreneurial opportunities. After drug manufacturers took over the compounding of drugs, pharmacists increasingly resembled retail sales clerks; their primary duties became dispensing and record keeping. As chain and discount-store pharmacies supplanted independently owned pharmacies, retail pharmacy no longer offered a chance to own one's own business, reducing another traditional attraction for men. The resulting shortages of male pharmacy graduates eased women's access to training programs and retail jobs (Phipps 1987).

Second, book editing illustrates how declining autonomy and occupational prestige contributed to feminization of an occupation. For most of this century, the cultural image of publishing attracted bright young men and women despite very low wages. But during the 1970s, multinational conglomerates entered book publishing, with profound results. Their emphasis on the bottom line robbed publishing of its cultural aura, and the search for blockbusters brought a greater role for marketing people in acquisition decisions, thereby eroding editorial autonomy. As a result, editing could no longer compete effectively for talented men who could choose from better opportunities. Because women's occupational choices are more limited than men's, editing still attracted them, and the occupation's sex composition shifted accordingly (Reskin 1987).

In sum, although sex integration appears to have occurred in the 1970s among census-designated detailed occupations (Beller 1984), our findings indicate that within these occupations, women are segregated into certain specialties or work settings and that they gained entry because various changes made the occupations less attractive to men. The nominal integration that occurred in the 1970s often masks within-occupation segregation or presages resegregation of traditionally male occupations as women's work. In short, the workplace is still overwhelmingly differentiated by sex. Moreover, our preliminary results suggest that real incomes in the occupations we are studying declined during the 1970s; so reducing segregation at the occupational level appears to have been relatively ineffective in reducing the wage gap—and certainly not the remedy many experts predicted. This brings us to the other possible remedy for the wage gap—comparable worth.

IMPLICATIONS FOR COMPARABLE WORTH

The comparable-worth movement calls for equal pay for work of equal worth. Worth is usually determined by job-evaluation studies that measure the skill, effort, and responsibility required, but in practice, assessing worth often turns on how to conceptualize and measure skill.

Although some objective criteria exist for assessing skill (e.g., how long it takes a worker to learn the job [see Spenner 1985, pp. 132–136]), typically the designation of work as skilled is socially negotiated. Workers are most likely to win it when they control social resources that permit them to press their claims, such as a monopoly over a labor supply or authority based on their personal characteristics such as education, training, or sex (Phillips and Taylor 1980). As a result, the evaluation of "skill" is shaped by and confounded with workers' sex (Dex 1985, p. 100).

Groups use the same power that enabled them to define their work as skilled to restrict competition by excluding women (among others) from training for and practicing their trade or profession (Dex 1985, p. 103; see also Hartmann 1976), as Millicent Fawcett recognized almost a hundred years ago when she declared, "Equal pay for equal work is a fraud for women." Because men use their power to keep women "from obtaining equal skills, their work [cannot be] equal" (Hartmann 1976, p. 157). Roos's (1986) case history of the effect of technological change on women's employment in typesetting illustrates these points. When a Linotype machine was developed that "female typists could operate," the International Typographical Union (ITU) used its labor monopoly to force employers to agree to hire as operators only skilled printers who knew *all* aspects of the trade. By denying women access to apprenticeships or other channels to become fully skilled and limiting the job of operating the Linotype to highly skilled printers, the ITU effectively barred women from the new Linotype jobs. In short, the ITU used its monopoly power both to restrict women's access to skills and credentials and to define its members as "uniquely skilled" to operate the Linotype.

Excluded from occupations male workers define as skilled, women are often unable, for several reasons, to press the claim that work in traditionally female occupations is skilled. First, as I have shown, the devaluation of women's work leads whatever work women do to be seen as unskilled. Second, women's powerlessness prevents their successfully defining their work—caring for children, entering data, assembling microelectronic circuits—as skilled. Third, because many female-dominated occupations require workers to acquire skills before employment, skill acquisition is less visible and hence unlikely to be socially credited. Fourth, the scarcity of apprenticeship programs for women's jobs and women's exclusion from other programs denies women a credential society recognizes as denoting skill (Reskin and Hartmann 1986). Finally, "much of women's work involves recognizing and responding to subtle cues" (Feldberg 1984, p. 321), but the notion of "women's intuition" permits men to define such skills as inborn and hence not meriting compensation. Thus women are both kept from acquir-

ing socially valued skills and not credited for those they do acquire (Steinberg 1984–85). As a result, the sex of the majority of workers in an occupation influences whether or not their work is classified as skilled (Feldberg 1984; Gregory 1987).

In view of these patterns, how effective can comparable worth be in reducing the wage gap? As with the Equal Pay Act, implementing it has symbolic value. Moreover, it would bar employers from underpaying women relative to their job-evaluation scores, the practice alleged in *AFSCME v. Washington State* (1985). But setting salaries according to an occupation's worth will reduce the wage gap only to the extent that (1) women have access to tasks that society values, (2) evaluators do not take workers' sex into account in determining a job's worth, and (3) implementers do not sacrifice equity to other political agendas.

Neither of the first two conditions holds. As I have shown, men already dominate jobs society deems skilled. Moreover, the tendency to devalue women's work is embedded in job-evaluation techniques that define job worth (Steinberg 1984–85); so such techniques may yield biased evaluations of traditionally female jobs and lower their job-evaluation scores (Treiman and Hartmann 1981; Marshall and Paulin n.d., p. 5). Beyond these difficulties is the problem of good-faith implementation. Acker (1987), Brenner (1987), and Steinberg (1987) have documented the problems in implementing comparable-worth pay adjustments. According to Steinberg (p. 8), New York State's proposed compensation model *negatively* values working with difficult clients, work performed in historically female and minority jobs (in other words, workers lose pay for doing it!), and Massachusetts plans to establish separate comparable-worth plans across sex-segregated bargaining units. For these reasons, the magnitude of comparable-worth adjustments have been about half of what experts expected—only 5 percent to 15 percent of salaries (Steinberg 1987).

Moreover, to the extent that equity adjustments significantly raise salaries in women's jobs, men can use their power to monopolize them. It is no accident that the men who integrated the female semiprofessions moved rapidly to the top (Grimm and Stern 1974). The recent experience of athletic directors provides an additional illustration. Title IX required college athletic programs to eliminate disparities in resources between women's and men's programs, including salaries. Within ten years the proportion of coaches for women's programs who were male grew from 10 percent to 50 percent (Alfano 1985). Finally, men as the primary implementers of job evaluation have a second line of defense—they can and do subvert the process of job evaluation.

CONCLUSION

Integrating men's jobs and implementing comparable-worth programs have helped some women economically and, more fully implemented, would help others. But neither strategy can be broadly effective because both are premised on a flawed causal model of the pay gap that assigns primary responsibility to job segregation. A theory that purports to explain unequal outcomes without examining the dominant group's stake in maintaining them is incomplete. Like other dominant groups, men make rules that preserve their privileges. With respect to earnings, the current rule—that one's job or occupation determines one's pay—has maintained white men's economic advantage because men and women and whites and nonwhites are differently distributed across jobs.[14]

Changing the allocation principle from occupation to job worth would help nonwhites and women if occupation were the pay gap's *basic* cause. But it is not. As long as a dominant group wants to subordinate others' interests to its own and is able to do so, the outcome—distributing more income to men than women—is, in a sense, its own cause, and tinkering with superficial causes will not substantially alter the outcome. Either the rule that one's occupation determines one's wages exists *because* men and women hold different occupations, or men and women hold different occupations because we allocate wages according to one's occupation. Obviously the dominant group will resist attempts to change the rules. In *Lemons v. City and County of Denver* (1980), the court called comparable worth "pregnant with the possibility of disrupting the entire economic system" (Steinberg 1987). "Disrupting the entire white-male dominance system" would have been closer to the mark.

If men's desire to preserve their privileges is the basic cause of the wage gap, then how can we bring about change? The beneficiaries of hierarchical reward systems yield their privileges only when failing to yield is more costly than yielding. Increasing the costs men pay to maintain the status quo or rewarding men for dividing resources more equitably may reduce their resistance.

As individuals, many men will gain economically if their partners earn higher wages. Of course, these men stand to lose whatever advantages come from outearning one's partner (Hartmann 1976; Kollock, Blumstein, and Schwartz 1985). But more important than individual adjustments are those achieved through organizations that have the power to impose rewards and penalties. Firms that recognize their economic stake in treating women equitably (or can be pressed by women employees or EEO agencies to act as if they do) can be an important source of pressure on male employees. Employers have effectively used various incentives to overcome resistance to affirmative action (e.g., rewarding supervisors for treating women fairly [Shaeffer and Lynton 1979; Walshok 1981]). Employers are most likely to use such mechanisms if they believe that regulatory agencies are enforcing equal-opportunity rules (Reskin and Hartmann 1986). We can attack men's resistance through political pressure on employers, the regulatory agencies that monitor them, and branches of government that establish and fund such agencies.

Analyses of sex inequality in the 1980s implicitly advance a no-fault concept of institutionalized discrimination rather than fixing any responsibility on men. But men *are* the dominant group, the makers and the beneficiaries of the rules. Of course, most men do not consciously oppose equality for women (Kluegel and Smith 1986) or try to thwart women's progress. When men and women work together, both can gain, as occurred when the largely male blue-collar union supported the striking Yale clerical and technical workers (Ladd-Taylor 1985; see also Glazer 1987). But as a rule, this silent majority avoids the fray, leaving the field to those who do resist to act on behalf of all men (Bergmann and Darity 1981). It is time to bring men back into our theories of economic inequality. To do so does not imply that women are passive agents. The gains we have made in the last two decades in the struggle for economic equality—redefining the kinds of work women can do, reshaping young people's aspirations, and amassing popular support for pay equity despite opponents' attempt to write it off as a "loony tune" idea—stand as testimony to the contrary. Just as the causal model I propose views the dominant group's self-interest as the source of unequal outcomes, so too does it see subordinate groups as the agents of change.

ACKNOWLEDGMENTS

Author's note: This article is a revised version of the Cheryl Allyn Miller Lecture on Women and Social Change, presented at Loyola University on May 1, 1987. I am grateful to Sociologists for Women in Society and the friends and family of Cheryl Allyn Miller who prompted me to develop these ideas. The present version owes a great deal to Judith Lorber and Ronnie Steinberg for their extensive comments. I also wish to thank James Baron, Cynthia Epstein, Lowell Hargens, Mary Jackman, Kathleen Much, Deborah Rhode, Patricia Roos, and an anonymous reviewer for their helpful suggestions, but I ask readers to remember that I did not always take their advice and that they will not necessarily agree with my final conclusions. This article was partly prepared while I was a Fellow at the Center for Advanced Study in the Behavioral Sciences, where I was supported in part by a grant from the John D. and Catherine T. MacArthur Foundation. Grants from the National Science Foundation (SES-85-12452) and the Rockefeller Foundation Program on the Long-Term Implications of Changing Gender Roles supported the larger study that contributed to my developing these ideas.

NOTES

1. Women's incomes are not depressed uniformly. Women of color continue to earn less than white women, particularly when their hours of work are controlled. As I indicate below, the same general social processes that subordinate women as a group—differentiation and devaluation—operate to preserve the advantages of white men *and women*.

2. Workplace segregation occurs across occupations and, within occupations, across jobs. For convenience, I speak primarily of occupational segregation because most segregation and income data are for occupations, but my remarks apply as well to jobs.

3. My informant said his campus now weighs the admissions essay more heavily for this reason.

4. For example, Smith and Ward (1984) attributed the wage gap's failure to narrow to the influx of less-experienced women into the labor force during the 1970s.

5. Some employers do reward productivity, as neoclassical economists predict, but for the most part, wages are attached to occupations—the proximate cause of workers' wages.

6. Of course, only a subset of men—predominantly upper-class whites—actually make rules, and the rules they make protect class- and race- as well as sex-based interests.

7. A full explanation of the specific forces that produce the sexual division of labor is beyond the scope of this article, but social-control systems, including gender ideology, "custom," socialization, and myriad institutionalized structures, shape the preferences of wives and husbands, workers and employers, women and men (Reskin and Hartmann 1986). These preferences in turn are played out in concert with institutional arrangements (training programs, personnel practices, child-care facilities, informal organization) to give rise to the task differentiation we observe in the home and workplace.

8. This is not to say that all tasks assigned to subordinate groups are unimportant or undesirable. Many, such as reproducing, socializing the young, and burying the dead, are essential. Others are more intrinsically pleasant (e.g., office work) than the work some dominant-group members do (which has led economists to argue that men's wages are higher than women's partly to compensate them for doing less desirable jobs [Filer 1985]).

9. This perspective elucidates the importance that the media attached to the wearing, spurning, and burning of bras in the early 1970s. Shedding or burning these symbols of women's sex (and hence their status) constituted insubordination.

10. For example, at the 1987 meetings of the American Educational Research Association, 25 sessions reported research on sex differences in interest or achievement in math and science (Holden 1987, p. 660).

11. Trustee John Pope remarked, "Any time you get over 50 percent, it's becoming more and more a girls' school . . . and I don't think favoritism should be given to the females" (Greene 1987). It apparently did not strike him as favoritism when the rules produced a male majority.

12. The return in the late 1970s of feminine dress styles following the entry of large numbers of women into professional and managerial jobs is probably not coincidental. Although caution is in order in drawing conclusions about changing dress styles, a quick trip through a department store should persuade readers that dresses and skirts have supplanted

pants for women (see Reskin and Roos 1987). Although fashion is ostensibly a woman's choice, most women are aware of the sanctions that await those who fail to dress appropriately.

13. Limited space forces me to condense sharply the causes of women's disproportional gains in these occupations. For a full account, see the complete studies.

14. It also serves the interest of the economically dominant classes by legitimating a wide disparity in income. Comparable-worth pay would largely preserve that disparity, in keeping with the class interests of its middle-class proponents and its implementers (Brenner 1987).

REFERENCES

Acker, Joan. 1987. "Sex Bias in Job Evaluation: A Comparable-Worth Issue." Pp. 183–96 in *Ingredients for Women's Employment Policy,* edited by Christine Bose and Glenna Spitze. Albany: SUNY University Press.

AFSCME v. State of Washington. 1985. 770 F.2d 1401. 9th Circuit.

Alfano, Peter. 1985. "Signs of Problems Amid the Progress." *New York Times* (December 14):25, 28.

Anderson, Susan Heller. 1987. "Men's Clubs Pressed to Open Doors for Women." *New York Times* (February 1).

Association of American Colleges. 1985. "Princeton's All-Male Eating Clubs Eat Crow." *Project on the Status and Education of Women* (Fall):11.

Becraft, Carolyn. 1987. "Women in the Military." Pp. 203–7 in *The American Woman: A Report in Depth,* edited by Sara Rix. New York: W. W. Norton.

Beller, Andrea. 1984. "Trends in Occupational Segregation by Sex and Race." Pp. 11–26 in *Sex Segregation in the Workplace: Trends, Explanations, Remedies,* edited by Barbara F. Reskin. Washington, DC: National Academy Press.

Berger, Joseph, Bernard P. Cohen, and Morris Zelditch. 1972. "Status Characteristics and Social Interaction." *American Sociological Review* 37:241–55.

Bergmann, Barbara R. 1974. "Occupational Segregation, Wages and Profits When Employers Discriminate by Race or Sex." *Eastern Economic Journal* 1:103–10.

Bergmann, Barbara R. and William Darity. 1981. "Social Relations, Productivity, and Employer Discrimination." *Monthly Labor Review* 104:47–9.

Bielby, William T. and James N. Baron. 1984. "A Woman's Place Is with Other Women." Pp. 27–55 in *Sex Segregation in the Workplace: Trends, Explanations, Remedies,* edited by Barbara F. Reskin. Washington, DC: National Academy Press.

Bird, Chloe. 1987. "Changing Sex Composition of Bank and Financial Managers." Unpublished manuscript. University of Illinois, Urbana.

Blau, Francine D. and Marianne A. Ferber. 1986. *The Economics of Women, Men and Work.* Englewood Cliffs, NJ: Prentice-Hall.

Bleier, Ruth. 1987. "Gender Ideology: The Medical and Scientific Construction of Women." Lecture presented at the University of Illinois, Urbana.

Brenner, Johanna. 1987. "Feminist Political Discourses: Radical vs. Liberal Approaches to the Feminization of Poverty and Comparable Worth." *Gender & Society* 1:447–65.

Cockburn, Cynthia. 1986. "The Relations of Technology: Implications for Theories of Sex and Class." Pp. 74–85 in *Gender and Stratification,* edited by Rosemary Crompton and Michael Mann. Cambridge, England: Polity Press.

Cohn, Samuel. 1985. *The Process of Occupational Sex Typing.* Philadelphia: Temple University Press.

Collins, Randall. 1975. *Conflict Sociology.* New York: Academic Press.

Coverman, Shelley. 1983. "Gender, Domestic Labor Time, and Wage Inequality." *American Sociological Review* 48:623–37.

de Beauvoir, Simone. 1953. *The Second Sex.* New York: Knopf.

Dex, Shirley. 1985. *The Sexual Division of Work.* New York: St. Martin's Press.

Donato, Katharine M. 1986. "Women in Systems Analysis." Paper presented at Annual Meetings, American Sociological Association, New York.

———. 1987. "Keepers of the Corporate Image: Women in Public Relations." Paper presented at Annual Meetings, American Sociological Association, Chicago.

Epstein, Cynthia F. 1985. "Ideal Roles and Real Roles or the Fallacy of the Misplaced Dichotomy." *Research in Social Stratification and Mobility* 4:29–51.

Feldberg, Roslyn L. 1984. "Comparable Worth: Toward Theory and Practice in the U.S." *Signs: Journal of Women in Culture and Society* 10:311–28.

Filer, Randall K. 1985. "Male-Female Wage Differences: The Importance of Compensating Differentials." *Industrial & Labor Relations Review* 38:426–37.

Fishman, Pamela. 1982. "Interaction: The Work Women Do." Pp. 170–80 in *Women and Work,* edited by Rachel Kahn-Hut and Arlene Kaplan Daniels. New York: Oxford University Press.

Glazer, Nona Y. 1987. "Where Are the Women? The Absence of Women as Social Agents in Theories of Occupational Sex Segregation." Paper presented at Annual Meetings, American Sociological Association, Chicago.

Goffman, Erving. 1976. "Gender Display." *Studies in the Anthropology of Visual Communication* 3:69–77.

———. 1977. "The Arrangement Between the Sexes." *Theory and Society* 4:301–31.

Goode, William C. 1964. *The Family.* Englewood Cliffs, NJ: Prentice-Hall.

———. 1982. "Why Men Resist." Pp. 121–50 in *Rethinking the Family,* edited by Barrie Thorne with Marilyn Yalom. New York: Longman.

Greene, Elizabeth. 1987. "Too Many Women? That's The Problem at Chapel Hill, Say Some Trustees." *Chronicle of Higher Education* (January 28):27–8.

Greer, William R. 1987. "In Professions, Women Now a Majority." *New York Times* (March 19):C1, 10.

Gregory, R. G. 1987. Lecture, Labor and Industrial Relations Institute, University of Illinois, Urbana.

Grimm, James W. and Robert N. Stern. 1974. "Sex Roles and Internal Labor Market Structures: The Female Semi-Professions." *Social Problems* 21:690–705.

Hartmann, Heidi. 1976. "Capitalism, Patriarchy, and Job Segregation by Sex." *Signs: Journal of Women in Culture and Society* 1, (Part 2):137–69.

Hechinger, Fred M. 1987. "The Trouble with Quotas." *New York Times* (February 10):C1.

Hochschild, Arlie. 1983. *The Managed Heart.* Berkeley, CA: University of California Press.

Holden, Constance. 1987. "Female Math Anxiety on the Wane." *Science* 236:660–61.

Hymowitz, Carol and Timothy D. Schellhardt. 1986. "The Glass Ceiling." *The Wall Street Journal* (March 24):Section 4, 1.

Jackman, Mary and Michael Muha. 1984. "Education and Intergroup Attitudes." *American Sociological Review* 49:751–69.

Jagger, Allison M. 1983. *Feminist Politics and Human Nature.* Totowa, NJ: Rowman & Allanheld.

Jay, Nancy. 1981. "Gender and Dichotomy." *Feminist Studies* 7:38–56.

Journal of Accountancy. 1984. "J of A Revisited: Women in Accountancy." 158:151–2.

Kanter, Rosabeth Moss. 1987. "Men and Women of the Change Master Corporation (1977–1987 and Beyond): Dilemmas and Consequences of Innovations of Organizational Structure." Paper presented at Annual Meetings, Academy of Management, New Orleans.

Kessler, Suzanne and Wendy McKenna. 1978. *Gender: An Ethnomethodological Approach.* New York: John Wiley.

Kluegel, James R. and Eliot R. Smith. 1986. *Beliefs about Inequality.* New York: Aldine de Gruyter.

Kollock, Peter, Philip Blumstein, and Pepper Schwartz. 1985. "Sex and Power in Interaction." *American Sociological Review* 50:34–46.

Ladd-Taylor, Molly. 1985. "Women Workers and the Yale Strike." *Feminist Studies* 11:464–89.

Lemon v. City and County of Denver. 1980. 620 F.2d 228. 10th Circuit.

Lieberson, Stanley. 1980. *A Piece of the Pie.* Berkeley: University of California Press.

———. 1985. *Making It Count.* Berkeley: University of California Press.

Lukas, J. Anthony. 1985. *Common Ground.* New York: Knopf.

Luxenberg, Stan. 1985. *Roadside Empires.* New York: Viking.

MacKinnon, Catharine. 1987. *Feminism Unmodified.* Cambridge, MA: Harvard University Press.

Major, Brenda, Dean B. McFarlin, and Diana Gagnon. 1984. "Overworked and Underpaid: On the Nature of Gender Differences in Personal Entitlement." *Journal of Personality and Social Psychology* 47:1399–1412.

Marshall, Ray and Beth Paulin. N.D. "Some Practical Aspects of Comparable Worth." Unpublished manuscript.

Martin, Susan E. 1980. *Breaking and Entering.* Berkeley: University of California Press.

May, Martha. 1982. "Historical Problems of the Family Wage: The Ford Motor Company and the Five Dollar Day." *Feminist Studies* 8:395–424.

Mead, Margaret. 1949. *Male and Female.* New York: Morrow.

National Organization for Women. 1982. *NOW Times,* July.

New York Times. 1984. "Air Force Studies Male-Female Missile Crews." December 12.

———. 1987. "Dispute on Sex Ratio Troubles Women at North Carolina University." March 22.

Papanek, Hanna. 1973. "Purdah: Separate Worlds and Symbolic Shelter." *Comparative Studies in Society and History* 15:289–325.

Phillips, Anne and Barbara Taylor. 1980. "Sex and Skill." *Feminist Review* 6:79–88.

Phipps, Polly. 1986. "Occupational Resegregation: A Case Study of Insurance Adjusters, Examiners and Investigators." Paper presented at Annual Meetings, American Sociological Association, New York.

———. 1987. "Women in Pharmacy: Industrial and Occupational Change." Paper presented at Annual Meetings, American Sociological Association, Chicago.

Pleck, Joseph H. 1985. *Working Wives, Working Husbands.* Beverly Hills, CA: Sage.

Pugh, M.D. and Ralph Wahrman. 1983. "Neutralizing Sexism in Mixed-Sex Groups: Do Women Have to Be Better than Men?" *American Journal of Sociology* 88:746–62.

Reskin, Barbara F. 1978. "Sex Differentiation and the Social Organization of Science." *Sociological Inquiry* 48:6–36.

———. 1987. "Culture, Commerce and Gender: The

Changing Sex Composition of Book Editors." Unpublished manuscript.

———. and Heidi I. Hartmann. 1986. *Women's Work, Men's Work, Sex Segregation on the Job.* Washington, DC: National Academy Press.

Reskin, Barbara F. and Patricia A. Roos. 1987. "Sex Segregation and Status Hierarchies." Pp. 1–21 in *Ingredients for Women's Employment Policy,* edited by Christine Bose and Glenna Spitze. Albany: SUNY University Press.

———. Forthcoming. *Gendered Work and Occupational Change.*

Roberts, Helene E. 1977. "The Exquisite Slave: The Role of Clothes in the Making of the Victorian Woman." *Signs: Journal of Women in Culture and Society* 2:554–69.

Rollins, Judith. 1985. *Between Women.* Philadelphia: Temple University Press.

Roos, Patricia A. 1986. "Women in the Composing Room: Technology and Organization as the Determinants of Social Change." Paper presented at Annual Meetings, American Sociological Association, New York.

Rubin, Gayle. 1975. "The Traffic in Women: Notes on the 'Political Economy' of Sex." Pp. 157–210 in *Toward an Anthropology of Women,* edited by Rayna R. Reiter. New York: Monthly Review Press.

Rytina, Nancy F. and Suzanne M. Bianchi. 1984. "Occupational Reclassification and Changes in Distribution by Gender." *Monthly Labor Review* 107:11–17.

Schafran, Lynn Hecht. 1981. *Removing Financial Support from Private Clubs that Discriminate Against Women.* New York: Women and Foundations Corporate Philanthropy.

Schroedel, Jean Reith. 1985. *Alone in a Crowd.* Philadelphia: Temple University Press.

Schur, Edwin M. 1983. *Labeling Women Deviant.* New York: Random House.

Shaeffer, Ruth Gilbert and Edith F. Lynton. 1975. *Corporate Experience in Improving Women's Job Opportunities.* Report no. 755. New York: The Conference Board.

Simmons, Adele, Ann Freedman, Margaret Dunkle, and Francine Blau. 1975. *Exploitation from 9 to 5.* Lexington, MA: Lexington.

Smith, James P. and Michael Ward. 1984. *Women's Wages and Work in the Twentieth Century.* R-3119 NICHD. Santa Monica, CA: Rand Corporation.

Spenner, Kenneth I. 1985. "The Upgrading and Downgrading of Occupations: Issues, Evidence, and Implications for Education." *Review of Educational Research* 55 (Summer):125–54.

Steiger, Thomas. 1987. "Female Employment Gains and Sex Segregation: The Case of Bakers." Paper presented at Annual Meetings, American Sociological Association, Chicago.

Steinberg, Ronnie J. 1984–85. "Identifying Wage Discrimination and Implementing Pay Equity Adjustments." In *Comparable Worth: Issues for the 80s.* Vol. 1. Washington, DC: U.S. Commission on Civil Rights.

———. 1987. "Radical Challenges in a Liberal World: The Mixed Successes of Comparable Worth." *Gender & Society* 1:466–75.

Thomas, Barbara J. 1987. "Changing Sex Composition of Insurance Agents." Unpublished manuscript.

———. and Barbara F. Reskin. 1987. "Occupational Change and Sex Integration in Real Estate Sales." Paper presented at the Annual Meetings, American Sociological Association, Chicago.

Treiman, Donald J. and Heidi Hartmann. 1981. *Women, Work and Wages.* Washington, DC: National Academy Press.

van den Berghe, Pierre. 1960. "Distance Mechanisms of Stratification." *Sociology and Social Research* 44:155–64.

Walshok, Mary Lindenstein. 1981. "Some Innovations in Industrial Apprenticeship at General Motors." Pp. 173–82 in *Apprenticeship Research: Emerging Findings and Future Trends* edited by Vernon M. Briggs, Jr., and Felician Foltman. Ithaca: New York State School of Industrial Relations.

West, Candace and Don H. Zimmerman. 1987. "Doing Gender." *Gender & Society* 1:125–51.

Wharton, Amy and James Baron. 1987. "The Impact of Gender Segregation on Men at Work." *American Sociological Review* 52:574–87.

Race, Sex, and Class: Black Female Tobacco Workers in Durham, North Carolina, 1920–1940, and the Development of Female Consciousness

BEVERLY W. JONES

This article examines how race, sex, and class affected the lives and consciousness of black female tobacco workers in Durham, North Carolina, and how they conceptualized work and its meaning in their lives. The research was based on 15 interviews. The interviewees fall into three broad age categories: five were born before 1908, seven between 1908 and 1916, and three between 1916 and 1930. All were born in the rural South. The majority migrated to Durham in the 1920s, subsequently entering the labor force.

Historically, black labor of both females and males has been critical to the tobacco manufacturing industry. As cigarette manufacture became mechanized, blacks were hired as stemmers, sorters, hangers, and pullers. These "dirty" jobs were seen as an extension of field labor and therefore as "Negro work" for which whites would not compete.[1] The rapidly expanding number of tobacco factories employed the thousands of black females and males migrating from the rural South. The pull of better paying jobs and the push of falling farm prices, perennial pests, and hazardous weather induced a substantial number of black sharecroppers, renters, and landowners to seek refuge in Durham.

Charlie Necoda Mack, the father of three future female tobacco workers, remembered the difficulties of making an adequate living out of farming in Manning,

Reprinted from *Feminist Studies,* vol. 10, no. 3 (Fall 1984): 441–51, by permission of the publisher, Feminist Studies, Inc., c/o Women's Studies Program, University of Maryland, College Park, MD 20742.

South Carolina. "I was a big cotton farmer; I made nine bales of cotton one year. Next year I made, I think, one or two, and the next year I didn't make none. I left in July, I had to leave. I borrowed money to get up here—Durham. I had six children and I know no jobs available. Well, then I came up here in July in 1922 and got a job at the factory. And by Christmas I had all my children with clothes and everything." Unlike the Mack family, who were pushed out of South Carolina, others were pulled into the city. Dora Miller, after marrying in 1925, left Apex, North Carolina, because she heard of the "better paying jobs in Durham." Mary Dove, at age 10 and accompanied by her family, left Roxboro, North Carolina, because a "Duke agent told us that a job in the factory at Liggett Myers was waiting for my daddy." Rosetta Branch, age eighteen and single, left Wilmington, North Carolina, because her mother had died, and "there were no other kinfolks."[2]

Thus, Durham's gainfully employed black population swelled from 6,869 in 1910 to 12,402 in 1930. (The city's total black population in 1930 was 23,481.) According to the census, the number of black female tobacco workers in 1930 was 1,979 out of a total black female population of 12,388. (See table 1.) Durham and Winston-Salem tobacco factories employed more black females than other cities: one-half of the number of women employed in tobacco factories in 1930 in these cities were black compared with the 19.7 in Petersburg and Richmond in Virginia.[3]

Upon disembarking at the central train station, the newly arrived southern migrants were immediately

TABLE I   TOBACCO INDUSTRY EMPLOYMENT BY RACE AND GENDER

DURHAM COUNTY: 1930			
White		Negro	
Male	Female	Male	Female
2,511	2,932	1,336	1,979

NORTH CAROLINA: 1940			
White		Negro	
Male	Female	Male	Female
6,517	3,175	5,899	5,898

SOURCE : U.S. Bureau of the Census, *Population: 1930* (Washington, D.C.: GPO, 1930), vol. 3, pt. 2, pp. 355, 378; *Labor Force: 1940* (Washington, D.C.: GPO, 1940), vol. 3, pt. 4, p. 566.

faced with race restrictions. Rigidly segregated communities were the dominant feature of Durham's black life. Many of the migrants settled in the dilapidated housing in the larger communities of East End and Hayti, a bustling commercial district of black businesses, and in the smaller areas of Buggy Bottom and Hickstown. Almost all black workers rented either from the company and white landlords or from black real estate agents. The comments of Annie Barbee, the daughter of Necoda Mack, reflect her first impressions of Durham.

We were renting in the southern part of Durham— the Negro section—on Popular Street, second house from the corner, across the railroad tracks. The house was small, two rooms, but somehow we managed. The street was not paved and when it rained it got muddy and in the fall, the wind blew all the dust into your eyes and face. There were no private family bathrooms. But it was an exciting life. See, in the country things were so dull—no movie houses. . . . Up here people were always fighting and going on all the time.[4]

Despite the exploitive living conditions described by Barbee, urban employment did have some liberating consequences for rural daughters.

Race restricted the black population to segregated neighborhoods and also determined the kinds of jobs

black females could get. Black female tobacco workers also faced discrimination as poor people and as females. Although class and sex restraints punctuated the lives of white female tobacco workers, their impact was reinforced by management policies. Although white females' wages were a fraction of white males' and inadequate to support a family, black females' wages were even lower. According to some black female tobacco workers, the wage inequity led many white women to consider black women inferior. This in turn led to an atmosphere of mistrust between black and white females. Management strengthened racial and class inequities in hiring practices, working conditions, and spatial organization of the factory, and therefore impeded the formation of gender bonds among working-class women.

Black females were usually hired as if they were on an auction block. "Foremen lined us up against the walls," one worker stated, "and chose the sturdy robust ones." Mary Dove recalled that she had "to hold up one leg at a time and then bend each backwards and forwards."[5] Once hired, black and white women were separated on different floors at the American Tobacco Company and in entirely different buildings at the Liggett & Myers Tobacco Company. In the 1920s and 1930s, according to a report by the Women's Bureau (the federal agency created in 1920), and confirmed by my interviews, 98 percent of these black females were confined to the prefabrication department, where they performed the "dirty" jobs—sorting, cleaning, and stemming tobacco.[6] White females had the "cleaner" jobs in the manufacturing and packing department as they caught, inspected, and packed the tobacco. However, both jobs were defined by the sex division of labor—jobs to be performed by women. Black men moved between the areas pushing 500-pound hogsheads of tobacco while white men worked as inspectors, safeguarding the sanctity of class and sex segregation.[7]

Reflecting on these blatant differences in working conditions, some 50 years later many black women expressed anger at the injustice. Annie Barbee recalled: "You're over here doing all the nasty dirty work. And over there on the cigarette side white women over there wore white uniforms. . . . You're over here handling all the old sweaty tobacco. There is a large difference. It ain't right!" Rosetta Branch spoke of her experience with anger. "They did not treat us Black folks right. They worked us like dogs. Put us in separate buildings . . . thinking maybe we were going to hurt those white women. Dirty work, dirty work we had to do. Them white women think they something working doing the lighter jobs."[8] These comments reflect both the effectiveness of management policies to aggravate racial and sexual differences in order to preclude any possible bonds of gender, but also illustrate the unhealthy working conditions to which black women were exposed.

In fact, the interviews indicate that the health of some black women suffered in the factories. Pansy Cheatham, another daughter of Necoda Mack, maintained that the Georgia leaf tobacco "was so dusty that I had to go to the tub every night after work. There was only one window and it got so hot that some women just fainted. The heat and smell was quite potent." Mary Dove recounted one of her fainting spells. "You know on the floor there was a salt dispenser, because it would get so hot. I did not feel so well when I came to work but I had to work. After about two hours standing on my feet, I got so dizzy—I fell out. My clothes was soaking wet from my head to my feet. When I woke up I was in the dispensary."[9]

Blanche Scott and another worker were forced to quit for health reasons. Scott, who began working for Liggett & Myers in 1919, quit four years later. "When I left the factory, it became difficult for me to breathe. The dust and fumes of the burly tobacco made me cough. The burly tobacco from Georgia had chicken feathers and even manure in it. Sometimes I would put an orange in my mouth to keep from throwing up. I knew some women who died of TB." The other worker had miscarried twice. Pregnant again, she decided not to return to the American Tobacco Company. "I felt that all that standing while I stemmed tobacco," she stated, "was the reason I lost my two children." Some women found momentary relief from the dust by retreating outside the confines of the factory complex to breathe the fresh air while sitting under trees or on the sidewalk during lunch.[10]

These comments on the poor, unhealthy working conditions were verified by research on Durham's death records between 1911 and 1930. In many instances, the records were imprecise and failed to provide information about race and occupation. Of the 105 certificates that identified black women as tobacco workers who died between 1911 and 1920, 48 (about 46 percent) died of tuberculosis, sometimes listed as phthisis and consumption. Of the 134 recorded deaths

of black female tobacco workers between 1920 and 1930, 86 (64.5 percent) died of tuberculosis. Because tuberculosis is caused by a bacillus that can be transmitted by a tubercular person through the cough, it is likely that poorly ventilated rooms and incessant coughing by workers, possibly by a carrier, made some workers susceptible to the disease, although deplorable living conditions for workers cannot be dismissed as a contributing factor.[11]

As studies have found in other cities, black females in Durham were more likely to work than white females.[12] Black females also earned lower wages than white females. In the early 1900s, wages for black tobacco workers, both female and male, ranked the lowest in the nation. In 1930, 45.5 percent of native-born white women in Durham were gainfully employed—27.7 percent in tobacco. While 44 percent of black women were working, 36.2 percent were employed in tobacco. From 1920 to 1930, Durham's white female tobacco workers averaged about 29 cents per hour, while black female hand stemmers earned about 11.9 cents an hour. However, black men, as well as black women who stemmed tobacco by machine, averaged about 27 cents an hour, still less than white women.[13]

Wage differentials continued and worsened throughout the 1930s. By the eve of the New Deal, a Women's Bureau survey reported figures for North Carolina which revealed an even higher wage discrepancy. White women working in the making and packing departments reported a median weekly wage of $15.35. Wages ranged from $14.10 earned as catchers to $20.50 on older packing machines. On the newest packing machines, the median wage was $18.15. Black women, working in the leaf department, reported a median weekly wage of $7.95. Hand stemmers earned a median wage of $6.50.[14]

The low wage was itself demeaning to black female workers. But the inadequate wages also forced many into the labor force at an early age. Black women thus worked for a longer part of their lives, and henceforth were more vulnerable to diseases and other health problems. Blanche Scott, for example, began working at the age of twelve. "Since my mother stayed so sick, I had to go to work. I worked at Liggett Myers after school got out. I attended West End School. I'd normally get out at 1:30 and worked from two o'clock to 6 P.M. I was just twelve years old. In the summer, they're let children come and work all day until four o'clock."

Pansy Cheatham began working at age thirteen. "My father talked to the foreman," she stated. "I worked because my sisters Mae and Annie worked; I stemmed tobacco by hand. But Papa did collect the money and use it for food and clothing." Cheatham's statement would indicate that at the top of the gender hierarchy of the black family was the father, who controlled the daughter's wages.[15]

Many women saw their employment as a means of "helping out the family." Better stated in the words of Margaret Turner, "that's what a family is all about, when we—the children—can help out our parents."[16] Out of the fifteen interviewees, the ten women who entered the work force at an early age all conceptualized the central meaning of their work in relation to their families.

By the late 1920s and early 1930s, the enforcement of the Child Labor Law of 1917 arrested the practice of employing children under the age of sixteen. "They began to ask for your birth certificate," one worker stated. A study done by Hugh Penn Brinton substantiated the decrease of child labor employment in Durham's factories. Brinton found that from 1919 to 1930 the percentage of black laboring-class households sending children into the labor force had decreased from 35 to 14 percent.[17]

However, the legislation against child labor did not force the wages up for black tobacco workers, and the constant low earning power of both female and male breadwinners continued to affect the lives of black female workers psychologically. Many women submitted to the demands of the foreman and other company officials. Viewed as short-term cheap labor, some females submitted to physical and verbal harassment, because in many instances defiance would have certainly resulted in the loss of jobs. Dora Miller asserted that "since the foreman knew you needed the job, you obeyed all of his demands without question. He called you dirty names and used foul language but you took it." Mary Dove recalled what it was like to work under one "of the toughest bosses." "Our foreman was a one-eyed fella named George Hill. He was tight! He was out of South Carolina, and he was tight! I mean tight! He'd get on top of them machines—they had a machine that altered the tobacco—he'd get on top of that machine and watch you, see if you was working all right and holler down and curse. Holler down and say, 'GD . . . get to work! GD . . . go to work there you

ain't doin' nothing.' Janie Mae Lyons remembered one who walked in on her while she "was in the sitting position on the stool" and told her "that if you ain't finished then you can pack up and leave. I was so embarrassed and that's what I did."[18]

Lyons's departure from the factory represented a form of militancy—a definitive stance against further harassment. Other women resisted verbally. Annie Barbee publicly castigated "women who allowed the foreman to fumble their behind" and further stated that if "one did that to me he would be six feet under." She indicated no one ever did. One worker resisted "by playing the fool." "The foreman thought I was crazy and left me alone."[19]

Constantly resisting physical and verbal abuse and trying to maintain their jobs, the workers were further threatened by increased mechanization. "I don't think it is right," one woman stated, "to put them machines to take away from us poor people." "Because of the strain we work under," another maintained, "they don't care nothing for us." One woman recalled crying at the machines because she could not quit in the face of high unemployment. "With them machines you have to thread the tobacco in. Them machines run so fast that after you put in one leaf you got to be ready to thread the other. If you can't keep pace the foreman will fire you right on the spot. Sometimes I get so nervous but I keep on going."[20]

The increased mechanization of the tobacco factories resulting in physical hardships of female workers can to some degree be attributed to Franklin D. Roosevelt's National Industrial Recovery Acts of 1933 and 1934. On the one hand, President Roosevelt's New Deal measures fostered economic stability for many black families by establishing standard minimum wages and maximum hours. On the other hand, this standardization exacerbated the job insecurity of black workers by indirectly catalyzing many companies to maximize profits by replacing hand labor with technology. During the latter part of the 1930s, Liggett & Myers closed its green leaf department, which had employed the majority of black women.[21]

The long-term insecurities of their jobs led black female stemmers to organize Local 194. The limited success of the union was reflected in the decline of its membership of two thousand in January 1935 to less than two hundred by May 1935. Black female union members found little support from either Local 208, black controlled, or Local 176, white controlled. In the eyes of the male unionists, the temporary nature of women's jobs excluded them from any serious consideration by the locals.[22] Conscious of their auxiliary position and the lack of support from male-led unions, black females chose not to support the April 16, 1939, strike at Liggett & Myers. Reporting for work on that day, they were turned away as management had no other recourse but to close the factory. Dora Miller recalled that the black stemmery workers "were never involved in the strike because demands for wage increases did not include us."[23] On April 26, 1939, the company capitulated. The contract indeed reaffirmed Miller's assessment because the stemmery workers were not mentioned.[24]

The factory policies of hiring, wages, working conditions, and spatial segregation, inherently reinforced by racism, the "cult of true white womanhood," and the inadvertent effect of New Deal governmental measures, all came together to touch the lives of black women tobacco workers with sex, race, and class exploitation. These practices further dissipated any possible gender bonds between black women and white women workers. As a race, black female tobacco workers were confined to unhealthy segregated areas either in separate buildings or on separate floors. As a working class, they were paid inadequate wages. As a sex, they were relegated to the worst, lowest paid, black women's jobs.

Black females conceptualized work as a means of "helping out the family." Denied self-respect and dignity in the factory, black female tobacco workers felt a need to validate themselves in other spheres. Victimized by their working conditions, female tobacco workers looked to the home as a preferred if not powerful arena. The home became the inner world that countered the factory control over their physical well-being. The duality of their lives—workers of production and nurturers of the family—could be assessed as a form of double jeopardy. But it was their role as nurturers, despite the hardship of work, that provided them with a sense of purpose and "joy." As Pansy Cheatham described her daily routine, "I get up at 5:30 A.M. I feed, clothe, and kiss my children. They stay with my sister while I work. At 7 A.M. I am on the job. A half-hour for lunch at about 12 noon. At 4 P.M. I quit work. At home about 4:30, then I cook, sometimes mend and wash clothes before I retire. About 11:30 I

go to bed with joy in my heart for my children are safe and I love them so."[25]

Black females who worked together in the tobacco factories also had the positive experience of creating networks of solidarity. Viewing their plight as one, black females referred to one another as "sisters." This sisterhood was displayed in the collection of money during sickness and death and celebration of birthdays. The networks established in the factory overlapped into the community and church. Many of these workers belonged to the same churches—Mount Vernon, Mount Gilead, and White Rock Baptist churches—and functioned as leaders of the usher boards, missionary circles, and Sunday School programs. These bonds were enhanced in the community by the development of clubs. These church groups and females' clubs overlapped the factory support networks and functioned in similar ways.

Finally, the resistance to the physical and verbal abuse that was a constant in the work lives of black women fostered among some a sense of autonomy, strength, and self-respect. Annie Barbee was one of those women. The assertiveness, dignity, and strength she developed through work became an intricate part of her private life. At age 40 and pregnant, she decided to obtain private medical assistance despite her husband's resistance. "When you know things ain't right God gave you a head and some sense. That's my body. I knew I wasn't going to Duke Clinic. And I was working and making my own money, I went where I wanted to go. You see, being married don't mean that your husband controls your life. That was my life and I was carrying his child, it's true, but I was going to look after myself."[26]

Although the work experience of black women tobacco workers was one of racial, sex, and class oppression, the early entrance into the labor force, the resistance to exploitation, and the longevity of work created a consciousness that fostered a sense of strength and dignity among some women in this working class. Management tactics of wage inequity, hiring practices, and racial-sexual division of labor pitted black women against white women economically as workers, and made the formation of gender bonds across race lines all but impossible. Yet among black women, the linkages of sisterhood engendered a consciousness of female strength, if not feminism.

ACKNOWLEDGMENTS

I am deeply grateful to North Carolina Central University for a Faculty Research Grant and for the excellent editorial comments of the *Feminist Studies* editors.

NOTES

1. For discussion of the historical involvement of black labor in tobacco manufacturing, see Joseph C. Robert, *The Tobacco Kingdom* (Durham, N.C.: Duke University Press, 1938).

2. Author's interviews with Charlie Necoda Mack, 22 May 1979; Dora Miller, 6 June 1979; Mary Dove, 7 July 1979; Rosetta Branch, 15 August 1981; all on file in the Southern Oral History Program, University of North Carolina, Chapel Hill, hereafter cited as SOHP/UNC.

3. The 1940 labor force figures do not include information for Durham County. U.S. Bureau of the Census, *Population: 1930* (Washington, D.C.: GPO, 1930), 3:341. In 1900, the major tobacco industries in the South were the American Tobacco Company and Liggett & Myers in Durham; R. J. Reynolds in Winston-Salem; and P. Lorillard in Richmond, Virginia.

4. Annie Barbee, interview, 28 May 1979, SOHP/UNC.

5. Mary Dove, interviews, 7 July 1971 and 30 May 1981.

6. Women's Bureau, *The Effects of Changing Conditions in the Cigar and Cigarette Industries,* Bulletin no. 110 (Washington, D.C.: GPO, 1932), 774–75. The Women's Bureau was established by Congress in 1920 under the aegis of the United States Department of Labor. Its purpose was to gather information and to provide advice to working women.

7. Mary Dove, interviews, 7 July 1971, 15 and 28 August 1981.

8. Annie Barbee and Rosetta Branch, interviews.

9. Pansy Cheatham, interview, 9 July 1979, SOHP/UNC; Mary Dove, interview, 7 July 1971.

10. Blanche Scott, interviews, 11 July 1979 (SOHP/UNC), 8 and 15 June, 1981; Mary Dove, Annie Barbee interviews.

11. Death certificates, 1911–1930, Durham County Health Department, Vital Records, Durham, North Carolina. I was also interested in the correlation of working conditions and female-related maladies such as stillbirths, miscarriages, and uterine disorders. Further perusal of death certificates of stillbirths was less valuable for there were no indications of mothers' occupations. Even hospital statistics lacked occupational data. This area of inquiry as it relates to the health of black female workers and working conditions needs further research. Further questions that will have to be explored include: Was there a higher percentage of female tobacco workers dying of tuberculosis than non-female tobacco workers? How long were stricken female workers employed in the factory? How much weight must be given to the working environment over that of home environs? Despite the lack of solid data on these questions, the interviews and death records clearly indicate that racial division of labor negatively impacted upon the health of many black female tobacco workers.

12. Elizabeth H. Pleck, "A Mother's Wage: Income Earning among Married Italian and Black Women, 1896–1911," in *The American Family in Social-Historical Perspective,* 2d ed, ed. Michael Gordon (New York: St. Martin's Press, 1978), 490–510; "Culture, Class, and Family Life among Low-Income Urban Negroes," in *Employment, Race, and Poverty,* ed. Arthur M. Ross and Herbert Hill (New York: Harcourt Brace & World, 1967), 149–72; "The Kindred of Veola Jackson: Residence and Family Organization of an Urban Black American Family," in *Afro-American Anthropology: Contemporary Perspectives,* ed. Norman E. Whitten, Jr., and John F. Szwed (New York: Free Press, 1970), chap. 16.

13. U.S. Bureau of the Census, *Population: 1930,* vols. 3 and 4; U.S. Department of Labor, Women's Bureau, *Hours and Earning in Tobacco Stemmeries,* Bulletin no. 127 (Washington, D.C.: GPO, 1934).

14. Women's Bureau, *Effects of Changing Conditions,* 172–75.

15. Blanche Scott and Pansy Cheatham, interviews.

16. Margaret Turner, interview with author, 25 September 1979, SOHP/UNC.

17. Interview, 8 June 1981; Hugh Penn Brinton, "The Negro in Durham: A Study in Adjustment to Town Life" (Ph.D. diss., University of North Carolina, Chapel Hill, 1930).

18. Dora Miller and Mary Dove, interviews; Janie Mae Lyons, interview with author, 4 August 1981.

19. Annie Barbee, interviews 28 May 1979, 10 July 1981.

20. Interviews, 4 and 15 June 1981.

21. For the best discussions of the National Industrial Recovery Act's impact on blacks, see Raymond Wolters, *Negroes and the Great Depression: The Problem of Economic Recovery,* ed. Stanley E. Kutler (Westport, Conn.: Greenwood, 1970); and Bernard Sternsher, ed., *The Negro in the Depression and War: Prelude to Revolution, 1930–45*

(Chicago: Quadrangle, 1969). Also see Dolores Janiewski, "From Field to Factory: Race, Class, and Sex and the Woman Worker in Durham, 1880–1940" (Ph.D. diss., Duke University, 1979).

22. *Durham* (N.C.) *Morning Herald,* 17, 18 April 1939, p. 1; Janiewski.

23. Dora Miller, interview.

24. For terms of contract, see *Durham Morning Herald* and *Durham Sun,* 27 April 1939, pp. 1, 2; Janiewski.

25. Pansy Cheatham, interview.

26. Annie Barbee, interview.

R E A D I N G   2 2

Occupation/Steelworker: Sex/Female

MARY MARGARET FONOW

Occupations in the United States fall into two categories: the *primary sector,* which is characterized by higher pay, union protection, fringe benefits, high rates of employment, high profits, and good chances for advancement, and the *secondary sector,* which is characterized by low pay, lack of union protection, few fringe benefits, higher rates of unemployment, few promotional opportunities, and lower profits. Women in the United States have been employed in the secondary sector, and consequently have received lower salaries and few benefits (Acker, 1980). Recent efforts to initiate affirmative action programs in the steel, communications, auto, mining, rubber, electrical, and other basic industries may represent an opportunity for women to break with the traditional pattern of female employment and substantially alter their socioeconomic status.

This article will examine the specific experiences of women steelworkers in their attempt to enter a male-dominated occupation. Although the primary method of data collection for this study was participant observation, a combination of methods was employed. First, I conducted an in-depth field study of one steel union local in a major steel-producing region of the Midwest. This local represented approximately 5,000 workers, 60 of whom were women. During the summer of 1977, I

Reprinted, with changes, from Mary Margaret Fonow, "Women in Steel: A Case Study of the Participation of Women in a Trade Union," Ohio State University, 1977 (Ph.D. diss.), by permission of the author.

was able to make observations of the routine day-to-day activities of the union local and interview union officials. Using the snowball sampling technique, I also conducted a total of 27 in-depth interviews with women steelworkers. Each interview lasted between one and one-half to two hours and all were tape-recorded. I did my own transcribing. In addition, I observed the 18th Constitutional Convention of the United Steelworkers of America, August 30–September 3, 1976, in Las Vegas, Nevada. At this event I conducted formal and informal interviews with 23 women participants (delegates, organizers, and observers). I also observed informal caucus meetings and strategy sessions on women's issues.

JOB ENTRY

On April 15, 1974, in the United States District Court in Birmingham, Alabama, an industry-wide consent decree was signed by nine of the "big ten" steel companies and the union, the United Steelworkers of America. The decree required an entire restructuring of the seniority system and an affirmative action plan for the hiring and promotion of women and minorities. Except for a brief period during World War II, women had been relegated to a sex-segregated unit in the plant, "tin inspection."

The flow of information about the new policy reflected the hierarchy of the work environment. News about the hiring of women in the mill traveled downward from management and its staff to union officials and finally to workers. Few women read about the openings in the newspaper; most relied on informal sources or "talk around town." Some of the women applied for jobs despite negative publicity about the new hiring policy. A waitress applied for a job after she overheard some of the supervisors from the mill discussing the new policy in her restaurant over breakfast. "I heard them talking about it. This one was saying, '. . . we are going to hire broads down there. The government is forcing us.'" Another woman, who had applied for a nontraditional job at the phone company, was told by the personnel director, "The steel mill is being forced to do this too." A third woman had heard about the new policy from a friend employed as a secretary by the mill. "When my friend told me about it, we all laughed. We thought it was ridiculous. Later, I had second thoughts and put my application on file." To apply for a job in a climate of negative or hostile public opinion indicates that these women were little influenced by the normative proscriptions concerning women's work roles.

Initially, management did not believe that women would be interested in jobs as steelworkers. One supervisor remarked, "We never expected them to even apply." Another said, "I was shocked that women would even want to work in the mill. I know this might sound like prejudice, but my idea of a woman is a step above a steelworker." Many of the women steelworkers believed that management deliberately tried to discourage their employment. During the intake interviews, personnel officials repeatedly emphasized the negative aspects of the job, particularly their perception of potential harassment from male co-workers. Typical were such remarks: "They kept stressing that men didn't want the women in there and they would be rough on me," "They kept emphasizing the harassment from men," "You are going to be working around some very vicious people." One woman reported that she was given her first assignment on a nonexistent work crew.

> I went in on a Sunday and was put on a labor gang. There is no labor gang on weekends. I didn't know what to do. It was very discouraging. At the interview I was told that I would be lifting 100-pound bags. He wanted you to say, I can't.

I asked union officials how the men in the mill first responded to the news that women were being hired. I received a variety of responses. One category of responses reflected the idea held by some, that women would expect special privileges because of their status as females. One official told me:

> You heard things like, we are getting those broads on the gang now; broads are coming to work in the mill and they are going to have preference over us; maybe I can get a good-looking helper.

According to union officials, there was widespread fear that women would not be able to do the job and that the men would have to work twice as hard. Some of the men resented a perceived threat to a territory they had exclusively staked out for themselves. One union official said, "Some of those who are hollering the most about women are the same ones who don't appreciate the blacks and other minorities achieving goals greater than theirs." Another male official said:

> Wow, at first there was a lot of resentment. Why don't they go home where they belong; they can't do a man's work; they are taking a man's job; they can't lift . . . a lot of them can't . . . A man is often threatened by a woman who holds her own as an individual.

Finally there was some concern that as good-paying jobs in the region were scarce, the men would no longer be able to secure jobs in the mills for their sons. It was not uncommon for two or even three generations of males from the same family to be employed in the mill. One official said the following about the hiring of women:

> I have mixed emotions about it. Given the employment picture in this country, I feel jobs should go first to heads of the family rather than to movements [women and blacks]. The society is based on the family.

THE JOB

The early years of employment in the mill are characterized by periodic cycles of unemployment and little choice in job assignments. Nearly all mill recruits are initially assigned to the "labor gang." These jobs involve general maintenance work, such as sweeping, shoveling, painting, washing walls, cleaning track, and some semiskilled work such as breaking up cement and laying concrete. Workers from the labor gang are also chosen on the basis of seniority, to fill in for vacationing or disabled workers in other departments. Most workers consider their stint on the labor gang as temporary, and once they have accumulated enough seniority, the workers may bid on more permanent positions. Women, particularly heads of households, are often limited in their choices of permanent jobs because child-care responsibilities may preclude changing shifts or working weekends. Many trade promotional opportunities for steady daylight work and weekends off. In addition, affirmative action requires that women be admitted to apprenticeship programs that lead to the skilled crafts within the industry. While some of the women qualify for training, very few skilled jobs have opened up in recent years.

Some women deliberately requested jobs that isolated them from other workers as a way to minimize hostile contacts with those male workers who do not approve of their presence. One woman reported, "I like it best when I work by myself or just one other person. It cuts down on all the hassles." Another woman preferred a particular department because it afforded her the opportunity to work alone and because the nature of the work minimized status distinctions.

You see, everybody over there is in the same class. Everybody is dirty and nobody is clean . . . so nobody really looks down on you. Everybody on the job over there mainly works by himself or else has one helper but you don't get a conglomeration of a lot of people in one department. In other departments there are people who never get dirty and they frown on people who do. You see those kind of people are in a different class from us.

Many women, in part because of low seniority, are assigned jobs in the coke plant or blast furnace. In general, these are the hardest, dirtiest, lowest-paying, and least safe jobs in the mill. However, some women cannot take advantage of transfers because of child-care responsibilities.

Work is also social and can be conceived as a network of interpersonal relationships (Richardson, 1981). How comfortable do the women feel about interaction with the other workers in such a male-dominated environment? Some felt it was difficult to communicate. Understanding the rules that govern conversation became problematic.

If the guys talk to me, I talk to them. But I never go out of my way to talk to the men. If you don't talk to the guys, they say you are stuck up, conceited, a bitch. If you do talk to them, they say you are a whore, so you can't win.

Others simply were not interested in the kinds of things men talk about at work: cars, sports, sex, etc. . . . However, another woman felt that sharing in the same work experience increased understanding between the sexes.

Everybody acts like men and women have never worked together until women came into the steel mills. All of a sudden it's a big deal . . . it's not new. The more we work together on this basic level, sweatin' and workin' the horrible shifts and going through all the suffering you go through, you really begin to understand each other.

Black workers do not always feel that they can be honest in their social relations with white workers in the mill. Attempting to converse across sex and race lines poses special problems for black women. One woman said:

I prefer to work with another black person 'cause it is hard to talk to a white person all day. You are afraid to say what you are doing . . . like fixing up your house or buying a new car. If it looks like you are getting on your feet, the white resents it. They think you are getting too far ahead of yourself. Black and white workers get along fine as long as the black person lets a white person feel as though they are still on top. There are times you would like to say something but you don't. The mill is not as bad as other places I've worked.

Although over time the relationship between men and women and black and white becomes easier to establish, for the most part getting along meant the absence of any overt hostility or conflict. Although they seldom had the opportunity, women preferred working with other women in the mill.

Sexism took a variety of forms within the plant. Job placement, job training, and promotional opportunities were cited as features of sex discrimination. One woman believed that the company deliberately tried to ensure the failure of women, by placing unqualified women in difficult positions.

They pick women for certain jobs that they know in advance will wash out. Placement is not done according to ability or aptitude. In order to fill the quotas, they pick women off the street rather than a woman already in the mill who has a little experience. They build in failure.

Another woman believed that the testing procedure for apprenticeships was biased and successfully argued the case with her employer.

I placed a bid for an apprenticeship program. I failed the mechanical aspect of the aptitude test that would qualify me for the job. I had to convince the company that failure on the aptitude test did not necessarily disqualify me for the apprenticeship. I explained that women are not given the opportunity to become familiar with mechanical principles. I threatened that I felt I was being discriminated against. They let me into the program. My work on the job was termed "above average" by my supervisors and my average in my school work is 89 [70 is passing].

Job evaluation also drew criticism from some of the women. Some believed that women were fired more quickly for mistakes or that the rules governing the performance of tasks were more strictly applied. When the rules were more narrowly interpreted, the men became more hostile and resentful of the presence of women. One woman related the following:

The rules were tightened specifically for women and the men lost some of the informal privileges won over the years. There was an informal agreement between the men working the blast furnace that they could exchange assignments if they didn't want to work a specific job that day. They traded jobs and took turns. In the rush to prove that women can't

do the job, the company came down hard and stopped allowing the workers to take turns. They showed us the rules from the book. This caused a lot of resentment toward the women. I think the company knew it would.

Some women even felt that they were assigned to departments where the men were particularly hostile and that men were assigned women helpers as punishment for work infractions.

In addition to the structural features of sexism, there is the tension and psychological strain associated with being the first women to cross occupational barriers. Because of their high visibility as "groundbreakers," the women faced incredible pressures to do an exemplary job. A sampling of comments: "I put in two parts to their one," "You have to prove yourself over and over," "You are constantly being watched." Sometimes they feel the pressure to be the standard bearer for the entire population of women. One woman explained:

While I was working on the lids [coke ovens] I was told to move these 100-pound lead boxes. I wanted to prove that I could do it. That all women could do it. After the third lift, I ripped open my intestines and had to be rushed to the hospital. It took surgery and a three-month recovery period. What I didn't know at the time was that no man would have lifted that much weight. They would have asked for a helper or simply refused.

There is also the constant pressure of interpreting male reaction to your presence. Women often hear the men say, "The mill is no place for a woman," "You are taking a job away from a man who needs the money to raise a family," "Women don't do their share," "Women get the easy jobs because they flirt with the foreman." Sometimes their sexuality is called into question. One woman remarked, "If you are too nice, you are a whore, if you aren't nice enough, you're a bitch." Even accepting help from male co-workers becomes problematic.

You are under so much pressure. If you walk out of the shanty and you are carrying this heavy bucket, the other workers come along and say, how come you let her carry all that? You should be carrying that for her. But if you let them help you, someone else says, see that, you're doing all her work.

One dimension of sexism in the mill is sexual harassment. According to Farley, sexual harassment is unsolicited nonreciprocal male behavior that values a woman's sex role over her function as worker and can include a wide range of behavior, from propositions for dates to touching to actual rape (1979: 33). The practice of sexual harassment is not limited to steel mills or to male-dominated occupations in general. Rather it occurs across the lines of age, marital status, physical appearance, race, class, occupation, pay range (MacKinnon, 1979: 28). Sexual harassment is rarely about sex. According to Farley (1978) the issue is power or dominance, and sexual harassment is one form of general dominance aimed at keeping women subordinate at work. Steel mill supervisors, who hold the power to reward or punish, are more likely to be perpetrators of sexual harassment. More often than not it is the implicit or explicit promise of a better job assignment or the threat of a worse one. One woman explained, "One foreman used to say, come work for my crew. You can sit in the office all day. Sure, I thought, but what would I have to give in return?" Another woman believed that she was given a particularly hard job because she refused to go out with her supervisor. In addition, the job was deliberately left for her to finish after her days off.

Last summer this foreman kept bugging me to go out with him. I refused. He stuck me in some of the dirtiest jobs. He put me in the oil pits. They had to lower me in this narrow hole. I was scared to death. I was new in the mill and I was petrified. I had to remove the oil with buckets. It must have been 110° down there. I came up crying; I was really scared. I was off the next two days but when I came back, he put me on the same job. Usually when you start a job the next crew on the next shift finishes it. You see, he saved it for me to finish after my days off.

Direct physical contact of a sexual nature was not prevalent but such incidents did happen.

Once a foreman grabbed my boob, under eight layers of thermal underwear. It scared the shit out of me 'cause the doors on the trailers aren't locked. What do you do? When it happens, it's a strange thing. At first you think, he doesn't know he is doing it or he didn't mean it . . . but he knew.

Sexual coercion or harassment was not limited solely to supervisory personnel. Some cases were reported

between women workers and their male co-workers. However, this type of harassment most often took the form of gossip, verbal remarks, graffiti, or persistent requests for dates.

Despite the hassles, women steelworkers were satisfied with their jobs because the alternatives were less desirable. During the interviews I asked women to compare their present job with previous jobs. Working in the mill is substantially more attractive than jobs that have been traditionally available to women, such as clerical, waitress, and sales jobs. Better pay, greater job security, health-care benefits, degree of supervision, union protection, pace of work were cited again and again as the difference between working in steel and previous jobs. Caught between strict supervision and customer demand, former sales clerks were the most dissatisfied with previous jobs.

It was tougher being a salesgirl. The stores have a strict dress code and for the money they pay, it's just not worth it. There is all this pressure to get a quota of sales. The customers don't understand this. Some would boss you around . . . "get me this, get me that." They feel as if you are their servant. I am the same as the person that comes in and I don't want to be treated like I am below them.

Another former sales clerk responded:

It sounds funny but sales was more difficult. I was hassled constantly, if not by my employer, then by the customers. We had to attack them when they come in and this makes some people belligerent. They treated you like you weren't there.

A factory worker from a nonunion shop compared her old work with her job in the mill.

On my old job, I had to stand on one foot all day. We worked a constant eight-hour day. It was like production but we got a straight hourly wage, no incentive rate. In the mill you can work at your own speed. At the factory they pushed you and pushed you. They didn't care if you lost your fingers in the press; they just wanted that production. I am now making double what I used to and the pressure is a lot less.

Overall the majority of women were much more satisfied with their jobs in the mill than with previous jobs. It seemed nobody wanted to return to the "pink-collar ghetto."

THE UNION

One way to cope with the problems associated with entering a traditional male occupation is union participation. The women in the mill, while often critical of union performance, were overwhelmingly in favor of unions. I asked one woman employed in the mill since 1934 to tell me what the mill was like before the union was established.

> Before the union came, they worked you harder and they treated you like you weren't human. They never called you by name, they just sissed at you like you were a cat.

She also reported that you never knew from one day to the next if you would even have a job. Workers were often forced to bribe mill supervisors in order to keep their jobs.

> At that time the ladies bought gifts so they could hold their jobs and the forelady treats them good. I did not go for that. At $2.44 a day I couldn't afford it.

Most of the women in the mill did not have to reach back in their memories to 1934 in order to recall what life was like without a union. Most had been employed in the nonunionized sector of the labor market prior to their employment in steel and most could make comparisons between the two. In fact, the number one response to the question "What surprised you the most about your new job?" was union protection and union benefits.

Although the number of women who are unionized and the percentage who participate in union affairs is small, their potential influence is far greater than their numbers suggest. In the case of women steelworkers, women are 8 percent of the union members covered by the basic steel agreement and 15 percent of the total membership, yet their impact can be felt on all levels. On the local level women are a source of new ideas and energy needed to revitalize the labor movement. In fact, their participation on the local level exceeds their proportion of the steel work force. At the district level women have formed networks, some publishing newsletters that lobby for the concerns of women steelworkers, the same concerns facing all working women. Their efforts to include child care, maternity leave, and other health and safety issues in the collective bargaining agreement can become a model for other unions. In fact, the steel contract in general is often the model for other industries. On the national level women in the United Steelworkers of America can place pressure on the AFL-CIO to organize the vast number of unorganized women workers. The potential to shape national policy on such work issues as flextime, job sharing, affirmative action, job training, CETA, insurance benefits, and retirement is unprecedented.

Another avenue for change is the Coalition of Labor Union Women (CLUW), a national organization of women trade unionists. Working women from a variety of industries have formed their own network to lobby the unions to promote the rights of women in the workplace and to help to organize the vast number of unorganized women workers in the United States. CLUW is also training women for leadership roles in the trade union movement. The efforts of women to make their unions more responsive to the concerns of working women are very likely to have an impact on the quality of work life for both men and women in the workplace.

REFERENCES

Acker, J. 1980. "Women and stratification: A review of recent literature." *Contemporary Sociology* 9:25–35.

Farley, L. 1979. *Sexual shakedown: The sexual harassment of women on the job*. New York: Warner.

MacKinnon, C. A. 1979. *Sexual harassment of working women*. New Haven: Yale University Press.

Richardson, L. W. 1981. *The dynamics of sex and gender: A sociological perspective*. Boston: Houghton Mifflin.

Peril and Promise: Lesbians' Workplace Participation

BETH SCHNEIDER

Lesbians must work. Put most simply, few lesbians will ever have, however briefly, the economic support of another person (man or woman); lesbians are dependent on themselves for subsistence. Thus, a significant portion of the time and energies of most lesbians is devoted to working. Working as a central feature of lesbian existence is, however, rarely acknowledged. As with any significant primary commitment by a woman to job or career, a lesbian's relationship to work is obscured, denied, or trivialized by cultural assumptions concerning heterosexuality.[1]

Moreover, the concept "lesbian" is so identified with sexual behavior and ideas of deviance, particularly in social science literature,[2] that it has been easy to ignore the fact that lesbians spend their time at other than sexual activities; for a lesbian, working is much more likely to be a preoccupation than her sexual or affectional relations. Given the limited research on the sexual behavior of lesbians over the course of their lives, it is no surprise that there is decidedly less known about the working lives and commitments of lesbians.

In asserting the centrality, if not the primacy, of a working life to lesbians, we assume that work provides both a means of economic survival and a source of personal integrity, identity, and strength. While lesbians are certainly not the only women whose identities are at least partially formed by their relationship to work, in a culture defined for women in terms of heterosexual relations and limited control over the conditions of motherhood, most lesbians are likely to have fewer of

the commitments and relations considered appropriate and necessary to the prevailing conceptions of women.

On the other hand, work and one's relationship to it is considered a major source of economic and social status, personal validation, and life purpose—certainly for men—in this society.[3] For lesbians then, whose lives will not necessarily provide or include the constraints or the comforts that other women receive ("heterosexual privileges"), working may well take on additional and special meaning. Thus, lesbians' workplace participation is shaped by the possibility of a unique commitment to working, an outsider status by dint of sexual identity, and the set of conditions common to all women workers. The conflicting aspects of these forces define the problematic and often paradoxical context within which lesbians work.

Being a woman worker has many implications for lesbians' material, social, and emotional well-being. Compared to their male counterparts, women employed full-time continue to receive significantly less pay.[4] Most do not have college degrees and enter occupations of traditional female employment where unionization is rare, benefits meager, and prestige lacking.[5] Continued employment in female-dominated occupations maintains women's disadvantage relative to men, since it is associated with lower wages; typically, lower wages keep women dependent on men—their husbands (when they have them) or their bosses.[6] In those situations in which women and men are peers at work, status distinctions remain, reflecting the realities of sexism in the workplace and the society.[7] In general, then, women are on the lower end of job and authority hierarchies. In addition, basic to the economic realities of all working women is the need to appear (through

Reprinted from *Women-Identified Women,* ed. Trudy Darty and Sandee Potter, published by Mayfield Publishing Company. Copyright © 1984 by Sandee Potter. Some notes have been renumbered.

dress and demeanor) sexually attractive to men, who tend to hold the economic position and power to enforce heterosexual standards and desires.[8]

Thus, as one portion of the female labor force, lesbians are in a relatively powerless and devalued position, located in workplaces occupied but not controlled by women. Herein lies one paradox of a great many lesbians' working lives. The world of women's labor—with its entrenched occupational and job segregation—creates a homosocial female environment, a milieu potentially quite comfortable for lesbians.

But lesbians must also manage their sexual identity difference at work.[9] As women whose sexual, political, and social activities are primarily with other women, lesbians are daily confronted with heterosexual assumptions at work. The nature and extent of heterosexual pressures (over and above those experienced by all women) condition the nature of their social relationships. Two markedly different dynamics simultaneously affect lesbians in their daily interactions at work.

Negative attitudes toward homosexuality are still widespread in the society. The statements and activities of New Right leaders and organizations and the research results of a number of studies on less politicized populations indicate that lesbians and male homosexuals must continue to be cautious in their dealings with the heterosexual world and to be wary of being open about their sexual identity in certain occupations—especially teaching.[10]

Directly related to these public attitudes, employment-related issues and articles tend to predominate in the lesbian and gay press. Either legislative and political efforts toward an end to discrimination are detailed and progress assessed, or some person or persons who have lost their jobs or personal credibility when their sexual identity has become known or suspected are written up. For example, recently readers of both the alternative press and mass media have seen accounts of the anticipated disastrous financial consequences of a publicly revealed lesbian relationship on the women's tennis tour, community censure of public officials who spoke in favor of antidiscrimination laws, lesbian feminists fired or not rehired at academic jobs, and a purge of suspected lesbians aboard a Navy missile ship, among others.[11]

Nevertheless, there is little systematic evidence that indicates how particular heterosexuals react to lesbians in concrete situations. It is these daily encounters and interactions with heterosexuals that are of crucial concern to lesbians; at work, the disclosure of one's sexual identity might have serious consequences. In a recent study of job discrimination against lesbians, fully 50 percent anticipated discrimination at work and 22 percent reported losing a job when their sexual identity became known.[12] But in addition, lesbians fear harassment and isolation from interpersonal networks; often they live under pressure or demands to prove they are as good or better workers than their coworkers.[13]

Whether anyone is fired or legislation is won or lost, the world of work is perceived and experienced by lesbians as troublesome, ambiguous, problematic. And while it is generally assumed that lesbians are more tolerated than gay men and therefore safer at work and elsewhere, a climate of ambivalence and disapproval pervades the world within which lesbians work; most are not likely to feel immediately comfortable about their relationships to coworkers.

Despite these significant disadvantages and potential troubles, a number of studies consistently show that lesbians have stable work histories, are higher achievers than comparable heterosexual women,[14] and have a serious commitment to work, giving it priority because they must support themselves.[15] These findings suggest, but do not describe or document, that lesbians' workplace survival results from a complicated calculation of the degree to which a particular work setting allows them freedom to be open and allows for the negotiation and development of a support network.

At work and elsewhere, lesbians want and have friendships and relationships with other women; while some research suggests that lesbians are no different than single heterosexuals in the extent of their friendship networks, others describe much greater social contacts for lesbians since they must negotiate two possibly overlapping worlds (work and social life) and most are free of familial constraints that pull other women away from work relationships.[16] Whatever the extent of their networks, it is these friendships and relationships that are a major source of workplace support—and complication—for lesbians, as well as an important facet of their emotional well-being and job satisfaction.

However, there is virtually no research that systematically explores lesbian work sociability, the creation of a support mechanism there, or the conditions under which lesbians are willing to make their sexual identity known. Most of what is known about these problems is based on findings from research on male homosexuals, and therefore does not take into account the greater

importance women as a group, and lesbians specifically, attach to emotional support and relationships.[17]
Nevertheless, this research indicates that the more a
male is known as a homosexual, the less stressful are
his relationships with heterosexuals because he does
not anticipate and defend against rejection.[18] But economic success frequently requires denying one's sexual
identity: research findings over the last decade are consistent in showing that high-status males are less open
than low-status males.[19] A combination of avoidance,
information control, and role distance are strategies
used by homosexuals to preserve secrecy; the result is
often the appearance of being boring, unfriendly, sexless, or heterosexual.[20]

In addition to focusing on men, many of these studies were completed prior to, or at the onset of, the gay
liberation movement, which has continued to encourage and emphasize "coming out" for reasons of either
political principle and obligation or personal health.[21]
Certainly, in the last decade many lesbians have taken
extraordinary risks in affirming their sexual identities
and defending their political and social communities.[22]

In sum, lesbians' relationship to the world of work
is both ordinary and unique. Based on findings from a
recent study of 228 lesbian workers, a number of previously unexamined aspects of the conditions of lesbian
participation at the workplace are explored here.
Following a brief description of the research project
from which these data are taken and a discussion of the
sample generation and characteristics, four aspects of
lesbian existence at work are discussed: (1) making
friends, (2) finding a partner, (3) coming out, and (4)
being harassed.

RESEARCH METHODS AND SAMPLE

The findings are part of a larger research project on
working women (both lesbian and heterosexual) and
their perspectives and experiences concerning sociability, sexual relationships, and sexual harassment at the
workplace.[23] The project was not explicitly designed to
directly examine instances of discrimination against
lesbians and cannot adequately address that problem.
It was designed to explore some of the more subtle
interpersonal terrain that all women are likely to
encounter at work, as well as those situations of particular concern to lesbians.

The lesbian sample was gathered with the assistance

of twenty-eight contacts who provided me with the
names, addresses, and approximate ages of women
who they thought were lesbians. The contacts provided
476 names. A self-administered questionnaire with 316
items was mailed to 307 of these contacts during the
period between January and March 1980. The letter
that accompanied the questionnaire did not assume
any knowledge of a particular woman's sexual identity.
Eighty-one percent of these women returned the questionnaire, a very high rate of return that seems to
reflect significant interest in all the topics covered.

There were 228 women who identified themselves
as either lesbian or homosexual or gay in the question
asking for current sexual identity. This sample of lesbians ranged in age from 21 to 58 (median = 29.4); 10
percent were women of color (most Afro-American).[24]
The sample was unique in that it was not a San
Francisco– or New York City–based population; 55
percent were from New England, 33 percent from
Middle Atlantic states, and the rest from other locations east of the Mississippi River.

The lesbians in this study were employed in all
kinds of workplaces.[25] More than half (57 percent)
were in professional or technical occupational categories (in such jobs as teaching and social work), with
the remaining distributed as follows: administrative
and managerial (10 percent), clerical (11 percent), craft
(7 percent), service (7 percent), operative (5 percent),
and sales (2 percent). Sixty-nine percent worked full-
time, 20 percent part-time, and the rest were unemployed at the time of the survey. Fifty-two percent
were employed in predominantly (55 to 100 percent)
female workplaces, 25 percent in workplaces with 80
percent or more females; 10 percent worked in units
with 80 percent or more males. While the educational
attainment of this group of lesbians was very high for a
population of adult women (82 percent were at least
college graduates), their median income was $8,800 (in
1979). The low income of the total group reflects a
combination of its relative youth and the proportion
with less than full-time or full-year employment.

Two questions were asked to determine lesbians'
openness about themselves at work, a matter of crucial
concern to any understanding of daily workplace experiences. The first asked: "How open would you say you
are about your lesbianism at your *present* job?" The
choices were: "Totally," "Mostly," "Somewhat," "Not
at all." The participants varied widely in the extent to
which they felt they were open at work: Only 16 per-

cent felt they were totally open, while 55 percent tended to be and 29 percent were closed about who they
were at work.

The second question asked the proportion of each
woman's coworkers who knew she was a lesbian.
Twenty-five percent estimated that *all* their coworkers
knew about their sexual identity,[26] half estimated that
at least one or "some" knew, and 14 percent stated that
"none knew." The remainder simply "didn't know" if
anyone knew they were lesbians, a difficult and often
anxiety-provoking situation.

MAKING FRIENDS

Most lesbians sampled believed it desirable to integrate their work and social lives in some ways.[27] Thus
the distinction between public and private life is not
terribly useful in describing their lives, despite its persistence as ideology throughout the culture.[28] For
example, only one-third maintained that they kept
their social life completely separate from their work
life, and 39 percent tried not to discuss personal matters with persons from work. Alternatively, 43 percent
believed that doing things socially with coworkers
makes relationships run more smoothly.

There obviously was variability in beliefs. Lesbians
who most consistently and strongly held the view that
work and social life should be integrated fell into two
categories: those who had to—that is, lesbians in professional employment whose jobs required a certain
level of sociability and collegiality; and those who had
nothing to lose—women in dead-end jobs with no
promise of advancement, those with few or no supervisory responsibilities, and those who were already open
with persons from work about their sexual identity.

On the other hand, women who could not or did not
believe these spheres could be easily or truly integrated were constrained by powerful forces that limited
and denied the possibility of such integration: lesbians
in male-dominated workplaces and those in worksites
with male supervisors and bosses, in which males bond
with each other, often to the exclusion and detriment
of the females.

The beliefs of the lesbians in the sample were quite
consistent with the actual extent of their social contacts
with persons from work. Most lesbians (in fact, most
women) maintained social ties with at least some per-

sons from work—at the job and outside it. Not surprisingly, 84 percent ate lunch with coworkers, but fewer
engaged in social activities outside the work setting.
For example, 9 percent visited frequently, 55 percent
visited occasionally at each other's homes, 8 percent
frequently and 47 percent occasionally went out socially with persons from work.

Two aspects of these findings merit further comment. First, the figures for the lesbians differ by less
than 1 percent from those of the heterosexual women
workers in the larger research project; if lesbians curtail contact or make certain judgments about coworkers as acquaintances or friends, they may do so for different reasons, but they do so to an extent similar to
heterosexual women.

Second, certain conditions determine both lesbians'
beliefs about and the extensiveness of their social contacts. Those in professional employment have more
social ties with persons from work than lesbians in
working-class jobs (which as a rule require less sociability); lesbians who are older, who have come to be
familiar with a particular job setting over a length of
time, and those who are open about their sexual identity are much more likely to maintain social contacts
with coworkers than their younger or more closeted
counterparts. In this particular study, there were no
differences of any significance between lesbians of
color and whites with regard to sociability; in fact, the
lesbians of color had, as a group, more contact with
coworkers. This is not surprising in that the networking
that produced the original sample reached only as far
as a particular group of lesbians of color, who were disproportionately employed in feminist workplaces such
as women's centers and women's studies programs,
locations that facilitate, however imperfectly, such
sociability. Those conditions in which a female culture
can develop (granted, often within the limits of a male
work world) allow lesbians greater possibilities for
being open about their sexual identity with at least
some coworkers. Familiar and supportive conditions
tend to foster friendships and, as will become clear in
the next section, provide the basis upon which more
intimate relationships may also develop.

When there is a need to be social, lesbians are; professional jobs require sociability, but very many also
require some degree of secrecy as well. This is particularly true for work in traditionally male occupations. In
addition, and more important given women's location

in the occupational structure, working with children (as teachers, nurses, social workers) can be cause for a relatively closeted existence. In this research, working with children did not seem to influence the extent of lesbian sociability, but it did affect how open they were about themselves at their workplaces. Here lies a classic instance of a highly contradictory situation, one common to many persons in human services and educational institutions. An ideology prevails that encourages (often demands) honesty, trust, and congenial nonalienating working relationships, but a lesbian's ability to actively involve herself in the prescribed ways is often limited or contorted. Frye's description of her experience in a women's studies program captures the essence of the difficulties:

> But in my dealings with my heterosexual women's studies colleagues, I do not take my own advice: I have routinely and habitually muffled or stifled myself on the subject of Lesbianism and heterosexualism . . . out of some sort of concern about alienating them. . . . Much more important to me is a smaller number who are my dependable political coworkers in the university, . . . the ones with some commitment to not being homophobic and to trying to be comprehending and supportive of Lesbians and Lesbianism. If I estrange these women, I will lose the only footing I have, politically and personally, in my long-term work-a-day survival in academia. They are important, valuable and respected allies. I am very careful, over-careful, when I talk about heterosexuality with them.[29]

More traditional workplaces provide even fewer possibilities for support than the one described above.

FINDING A PARTNER

In the last section, brief reference is made to lesbians' sexual relationships at work. The typical story of the office affair seems to have little to do with lesbians. It centers on a boss (the powerful person, the man) and his secretary (the powerless person, the woman); the consequences of this double-edged inequality of occupational status and gender are of prime concern. As the story would have it, the powerful one influences the other's (the woman's) career in such a way that she

is highly successful ("She slept her way to the top") or her work and career are permanently ruined. It is rarely acknowledged that relationships at work occur between coworkers or between persons of the same gender, or that the consequences may be close to irrelevant—at least with regard to the job. When acknowledged, it seems that heterosexual affairs are more tolerated than are lesbian or homosexual relations.[30]

But the facts tell another story.[31] Twenty-one percent of the lesbians in this study met their current partners at work; overall, 52 percent of the lesbians had had at least one sexual relationship with a person from work during their working lives. This amazingly high proportion makes sense when it is remembered that the vast majority of women (and lesbians) are employed in female-dominated workplaces. Such a work setting is a good location for a lesbian to find a potential lover. But in addition, there have traditionally been few places—other than bars—for lesbians to meet each other socially; most met, and still meet, through friendship networks (44 percent). While recently the women's and lesbians' communities have provided some alternatives—restaurants, clubs, political activities—employment plays such a significant part in lesbians' lives (and takes such a significant part of their time) that the workplace becomes an important, almost obvious, site for creating and having friendships and more intimate relationships.

Nineteen percent of the currently self-identified lesbians were heterosexual and 9 percent were married at the time of the sexual relationship they reported. This means that 81 percent were lesbians when they entered into at least a somewhat committed (and potentially risky) relationship with a person from work.

The chances that a lesbian will have a relationship with someone at work increase with age. To illustrate, while 79 percent of the sampled lesbians over forty had had a relationship with someone at work sometime in their lifetime, 59 percent in their thirties and 42 percent in their twenties had had such an involvement. In addition, the longer a woman has identified herself as a lesbian (whatever her age), the more likely she is to have an intimate relationship with a person at work. This certainly suggests that some part of the freedom to pursue an involvement in the work setting is an easiness with oneself as a lesbian and a flexibility and wisdom gained from years of managing the complexities of sexual identity difference at work.

Most of the relationships reported were not brief affairs; 60 percent of the lesbians had been or were currently in a relationship of a year or more duration. Having such a relationship can have many effects, many small and predictable, others large and less controllable. Perhaps most obviously, the longer a relationship lasts, the more likely are some people at work (in addition to friends outside work) to know of the involvement. (In contrast to the heterosexuals in the larger study, lesbians tended to be more secretive about the relationship with people from work.)

Since the "office affair" mythology assumes a heterosexual relationship and the dynamic of superior–subordinate, it is useful to examine who in fact the lesbian workers were involved with. Eighteen percent of the lesbians were involved with a man (most, but not all, were heterosexual at the time); the few self-identified lesbians who were nevertheless involved with a man were almost exclusively involved with their boss in relatively brief affairs. Overall, 75 percent were involved with coworkers, 14 percent with boss or supervisor, 6 percent with subordinates, and 5 percent with customers, clients, and the like. With the female boss still very much a rarity, lesbians are less likely to have the option of a relationship with a woman with institutionalized authority over their working lives. This is in contrast to heterosexual women, whose relationships at work tend to be unequal as a result of the mix of gender and status inequality.

There were only a few consistent and predictable patterns in the effects and consequences of these relationships for the lesbians as a group. Seventy-two percent enjoyed their work more than usual. Some involvements improved relationships with other coworkers (25 percent) while others caused problems with coworkers (35 percent) or trouble with a boss or supervisor (20 percent). Much of the difficulty during the course of the relationship seemed to stem from jealousies, irritation at undone work, or in attention on the part of one or both of the parties to others. Also, the involvements often highlighted the lesbians' sexual identity, forcing them to be less closeted. The data suggest that one of the conflicts a lesbian must face in having a relationship at work is a willingness to either engage in massive secrecy and denial of the situation or become more clear about who she is. Many lesbians (30 percent) reported relief at the end of their involvements in part because hostility or gossip was lessened,

in part because the pressures of enforced secrecy were removed.

The effects of being and becoming open about one's sexual identity as a consequence of the relationship are mixed and complicated, and often contradictory. For example, 62 percent of the more open lesbians compared to 19 percent of the more closed ones reported significantly greater friction with coworkers and some (22 percent) felt their chances for advancement were diminished. On the other hand, 31 percent of the more open lesbians reported improvement in workplace relations and improved advancement possibilities (10 percent); they enjoyed their work more than the closed lesbians. It is interesting to note that not one lesbian who was closed about her sexual identity at work believed that her chances for promotion were affected one way or the other by her involvement.

Almost everyone reported suffering the usual kinds of emotional problems at the termination of the relationship, obviously the longer the relationship the more so. The work-related consequences of lesbian involvements with women of similar job status are much simpler and less harmful than those with a superior. Thirteen percent of the lesbians resigned or quit because of the breakup; most of the lesbians who resigned were involved with a boss, rather than a coworker, some few of whom were women. A very few lesbians (4 percent) reported losing out on some career-related opportunity, such as a promotion or pay increase; none reported gaining any work benefit. In 15 percent of the instances, the other person left the job at the termination of the relationship; in all these cases, these were female coworkers.

In general, involvements at work are an integral part of a lesbian's emotional commitments to women. This extension of the prescribed limits of relationships beyond friendship is consistent with most other research on lesbians that similarly shows fluid boundaries between friends and lovers and friendship networks of former lovers.[32]

COMING OUT

Most lesbians are acutely aware that their openness about their lesbianism is not an all-or-nothing phenomenon at work or elsewhere but that it varies depending at the very least on the context and on the particular individuals involved. The lesbians in this study clearly varied in their own sense of how open they *felt* they were at work. As we already saw, being open allowed lesbians greater contact with coworkers, facilitating network-building and support as well as being a basis for (and a possible result of) having a sexual relationship with someone at work.

This study indicates that lesbians tend to be open about their sexual identity when their workplace has a predominance of women and most of their work friends are women, when they have a female boss or supervisor, when they are employed in small workplaces, when they have few supervisory responsibilities, when they have relatively low incomes, and when they are not dealing with children as either students, clients, or patients.

Two aspects of these findings require special comment. First, as noted earlier, the situation of professionally employed lesbians is terribly contradictory. Since the jobs require socializing and contacts with others either at work or in the business or professional communities, lesbians maintain those social contacts; on the other hand, high-income professional lesbians are likely to be closeted. The result of this predicament is a well-managed, manicured lie delivered to people with whom one is spending a great deal of time.

Second, the influence of gender proportions is crucial. For example, in workplaces that were heavily female-dominated (80 percent or more women as employees), 55 percent of the lesbians were totally or mostly open about their sexual identity. It is worth noting that this still means that 45 percent tended to be somewhat closeted even in these settings. In contrast, in heavily male-dominated workplaces (80 percent or more men as employees), only 10 percent of the lesbians were open.

A workplace with a predominance of women may include other lesbians to whom a lesbian can be open; they may also become friends or lovers. Of the lesbians who met another lesbian at work, almost all (94 percent) did in fact become friends. But even when there are not other lesbians at work, lesbians take certain risks, trusting at least one heterosexual woman not to react negatively to knowledge of her sexual identity. Moreover, most women are not in a structurally powerful position to affect the conditions under which lesbians work. When lesbians do have a female supervisor or boss, they are more often open about their sexual

identity than with a male boss. For example, only 21 percent of lesbians with a male boss were open, compared to 47 percent who were open with a female boss. When lesbians were themselves the boss or were self-employed, 88 percent were open about their sexual identity.

How open a lesbian is at her current job is not related to her age or race or the length of time she has been at that position. However, if she has lost a previous job because she is a lesbian, she is less sociable with people from work at her current job and tends to be more cautious about "coming out" at work. In this study 8 percent of the lesbians reported losing a job when their sexual identity became known and another 2 percent believed (but did not know for certain) they lost a job for this reason. The relatively young age of this sample may account for the lower proportion of job loss than in other studies. Whatever the extent of their openness, 75 percent of all lesbians were concerned that their lesbianism might cause damage to their job or career.

In summary, openness is most likely under conditions that are intimate and safe, free of potentially serious consequences for a lesbian's working life. That is, lesbians are most likely to be open in a small workplace, with a female boss, in a job with relatively little financial or social reward (and possibly few career risks).

The consequences of being open are substantial. Open lesbians have more friends and more social contact at work than closed lesbians; they are more willing to have, and do have, sexual relationships with women from their workplace. In contrast, and almost by definition, lesbians who are closed about their sexual identity at work are more likely to avoid certain situations with coworkers and feel reluctant to talk about their personal life.

While cause and effect is admittedly difficult to disentangle here, open and closed lesbians differ in the extent to which they feel that their sexual identity causes problems in many areas of their life. This research indicates that lesbians who remain closeted at work are obviously more concerned and afraid than open lesbians about losing their jobs. But in addition, closeted lesbians are much more concerned than open ones about losing their friends, harming their relationship with their parents, and where applicable, harming their lovers' careers or child custody situations. Consistent with this is the finding that openness at work is related to a general freedom to be open elsewhere as well: lesbians who are open at work are more likely to be open with parents and with both female and male heterosexual friends.

Not surprisingly, closed and open lesbians have uniquely different feelings about their positions at work. Closeted lesbians suffer from a sense of powerlessness and significant strain and anxiety at work, while open lesbians have greater emotional freedom. Eighty-four percent of the closed lesbians in the study felt they had no choice about being closeted; two-thirds felt uncomfortable about that decision, and 39 percent felt that the anxiety about being found out was "paralyzing." A significant 35 percent devoted time and emotion to maintaining a heterosexual front at work.

On the other hand, 94 percent of the open lesbians felt better since coming out, and while the strength of their feelings varied, most felt they were treated with respect because of their candor. Forty percent reported that their work relationships were a lot better than they were before coming out. Disclosure of one's sexual identity at work allows for the possibility of integrating into the workplace with less anxiety about who one is and how one is perceived. But there are some negative consequences to coming out. Twenty-nine percent of the open lesbians sensed that some coworkers avoided them and 25 percent admitted to working harder to keep the respect they had from their peers. While these consequences seem insignificant in contrast to the benefits of disclosure, it is good to remember that coming out often can be a quite limited communication to a quite limited number of persons; thus, protection is built into the very choice of context and relationship.

BEING HARASSED

Eighty-two percent of the lesbians studied experienced sexual approaches at work in the year of the study; that is, 33 percent were sexually propositioned, 34 percent were pinched or grabbed, 54 percent were asked for a date, and 67 percent were joked with about their body or appearance by someone at the workplace.[33] These figures are high for one year; they are, however, comparable to those for the heterosexual women in the larger research project who were of similar race and

age. Relatively young, unmarried women (this fits the description of most of the lesbians in the study) and those who worked in male-dominated work settings were most often the recipients of these sexual approaches. Ironically enough, the lesbians who tended to be secretive about their sexual identity (therefore presumed to be heterosexual) were more often sexually approached in these particular ways than the more open lesbians. For example, while 32 percent of the more closed lesbians were pinched or grabbed, only 12 percent of the more open were; likewise, 26 percent of the more closed in contrast to 13 percent of the more open were sexually propositioned.

In comments written to the researcher, it became evident that some lesbians were occasionally referring to both women and men in reporting on date requests and jokes, the more prevalent types of interactions. Unfortunately, the data for these experiences did not specify the gender of the initiator, thus making impossible a true profile of all interpersonal dynamics of this sort.

When asked their emotional response to these experiences ("like," "mixed," "dislike"), the great majority (more than 90 percent) reported disliking pinching or grabbing and sexual propositions—whoever initiated them; few lesbians in fact ever reported liking any such incident. The one exception was being asked for a date by a coworker, and even here only 9 percent said they liked this interaction, with 46 percent "mixed." Toleration (mixed feelings) was the main response to jokes and date requests. And in all cases, coworkers were the most tolerated group of initiators; some of these coworkers may well be women. Typically, coworkers do not have the institutionalized authority to affect each other's job or career standing though they may nevertheless make life more difficult in these kinds of ways.

We cannot directly infer from these data the meaning of these experiences to lesbian workers. Unwanted sexual approaches can be seen as harassment explicitly targeted at a lesbian because she is a lesbian or as harassment typically experienced by most working women. These sexual approaches highlight the disadvantages of lesbians in a working environment by emphasizing heterosexual norms of intimacy and behavior and accenting further the outsider position many lesbians feel at work. Research that compares lesbian workers with heterosexual women workers indicates that while lesbians and heterosexuals have a quite similar number of such approaches in their daily lives, these interactions are experienced quite differently. Lesbians are more sensitive to the problem of unwanted sexual approaches and are much more willing than heterosexuals to label behaviors of this type as sexual harassment.[34]

CONCLUSION

This research was an effort using quantitative data to describe the context of daily life at work for lesbians and to understand the sources of lesbian survival at work. It was not a definitive study of the prevalence of lesbian job loss or harassment.

The findings showed fewer difficulties at work than other studies seem to indicate, but like that research, it insufficiently explored the meanings lesbians attach to particular situations. One obvious question that remains is the extent to which a problem or harassment situation at work is attributed specifically to discrimination on the basis of sexual identity rather than understood as a reflection of the general condition of women. In this research (in which all but one of the lesbians indicated that she was a feminist), the interpretation of events is complicated and complex.

Applying a feminist interpretation to certain workplace situations could diminish or exaggerate the extent to which lesbians perceive those instances as resulting from, or in reaction to, their lesbianism. Sexual harassment is a particularly clear case. A lesbian may well wonder why she was hugged by a male coworker: was it a gesture of friendship, harassment specifically directed to her as a lesbian, or harassment similar to that most women encounter at work? If most lesbians considered the variety of harassing experiences at work discrimination against them as lesbians, the proportion reporting workplace problems would surely increase.

While a more complete picture of workplace problems awaits additional research, these findings underscore some important dimensions of lesbians' workplace participation. First, the experience of lesbians is both similar and different from that of heterosexual women workers. It is similar in (1) the creation of a supportive environment of work friends, (2) the experience of unwanted sexual approaches from various parties with whom they interact, and (3) the use of the workplace to meet sexual partners. It is different in (1) the necessity of strategizing in the face of fear of disclosure and possible job loss, and (2) the meanings attached to interactions and events in the workplace.

While the fear of job or career loss or damage is often uppermost in a recitation of workplace problems, most lesbians do not lose their jobs. Two mutually reinforcing aspects of a strategy seem to account for this general lack of this most serious and negative sanction. First, lesbians tend to remain closeted, keeping their sexual identity secret from most persons at work; at the same time, they create an environment that protects them, emotional ties with a few people who contribute to a sense of a less hostile and alienating work world.

Coming out is clearly a process; within any particular institutional context, such as work, an assessment is made as to the degree to which a lesbian can be open about who she is. The extent of disclosure varies, dependent on the particulars of personnel and place; it changes over time. Certainly few are the lesbians and fewer still the workplaces that can manage or tolerate complete disclosure. At the minimum, lesbians come out when they are ready and conditions are good, meaning in some workplaces and with some people. While the exact process is not detailed here, it is clear that coming out occurs when a woman believes that a person is trustworthy, sensitive, or politically aware. This is an assessment over which a lesbian has some control. When a lesbian is known as such at work, a congenial and supportive relationship has typically preceded disclosure.

The ease with which a lesbian is disclosing about her sexual identity reflects historically specific conditions as well. In this sample of highly politicized lesbian women workers in late 1979, 40 percent felt they were totally or most open about being lesbians; 75 percent were concerned that their lesbianism might affect their employment situation. In the current climate of conservatism reflected in recent efforts to defend and preserve the "sanctity of the family,"[35] lesbians are forced constantly to weigh the costs of disclosure. Thus, a combination of forces—personal choice, workplace characteristics, and political concerns—continues to define the options and limitations of the workplace environment.

Finally, female support systems at work—allies and

networks—can be seen as an integral part of lesbians' emotional commitments to women. While it is certainly ironic and contradictory to proclaim the virtues of "women's work," with its devalued economic and social worth, those workplaces do provide an easier, more congenial atmosphere than is immediately available in more highly paid, male-segregated locations. Many lesbians know these facts and in decisions regarding work may well take them into account.

While the fear and peril of lesbians' workplace situation cannot be denied or diminished, neither can the challenge. Lesbians' participation and relationship to work is similar to the kind of "double vision" shared by other groups who are outsiders:[36] an acute awareness of the strength and force of an oppressive ideology of heterosexuality and its structural manifestations, coupled with an active accommodation and creation of a livable working environment.

NOTES

1. The socioemotional climate of work is based on strong cultural assumptions of heterosexuality. An ideology of heterosexuality includes the following beliefs: (1) All persons are heterosexual. (2) All intimate relationships occur between persons of opposite gender. (3) Heterosexual relationships are better—healthier, more normal—than homosexual relations. With regard to employment, the ideology assumes that every woman is defined by, and in some way is the property of, a man (father, husband, boss); thus a woman's work is secondary, since she is, will be, or ought to be supported by a man. See the following for statements concerning the cultural and structural dimensions of heterosexuality: . . . Gayle Rubin, "The Traffic in Women: Notes on the 'Political Economy' of Sex," in Rayna Rapp, ed. Toward an Anthropology of Women (New York: Monthly Review Press, 1975), pp. 157–210; Catharine A. MacKinnon, *Sexual Harassment of Working Women: A Case of Sex Discrimination* (New Haven: Yale University Press, 1979); Adrienne Rich, "Compulsory Heterosexuality and Lesbian Existence," reading 18 in this volume; Lisa Leghorn and Katherine Parker, *Woman's Worth: Sexual Economics and the World of Women* (Boston: Routledge & Kegan Paul, 1981).

2. See Anabel Faraday, "Liberating Lesbian Research," and Kenneth Plummer, "Homosexual Categories: Some Research Problems in the Labelling Perspective of Homosexuality," in Kenneth Plummer, ed., *The Making of the Modern Homosexual* (Totowa, N.J.: Barnes & Noble, 1981).

3. For a review of the literature on the relationship of work to individual well-being, see Rosabeth Moss Kanter, *Work and Family in the United States: A Critical Review and Agenda for Research and Policy* (New York: Russell Sage, 1977).

4. U.S. Bureau of Labor Statistics, *Perspectives on Working Women: A Databook,* Bulletin 2080 (Washington, D.C.: U.S. Government Printing Office, 1980).

5. Louise Kapp Howe, *Pink-Collar Workers: Inside the World of Women's Work* (New York: G. P. Putnam, 1977).

6. Heidi Hartman, "Capitalism, Patriarchy, and Job Segregation by Sex," in Zillah Eisenstein, ed., *Capitalist Patriarchy and the Case for Socialist Feminism* (New York: Monthly Review Press, 1979), pp. 206–47.

7. Neal Gross and Anne Trask, *The Sex Factor and Management of Schools* (New York: Wiley, 1976); and Rosabeth Moss Kanter, *Men and Women of the Corporation* (New York: Basic Books, 1977).

8. MacKinnon (see n. 1 above).

9. Throughout this article, sexual identity, rather than sexual orientation or sexual preference, is the term used to describe and distinguish heterosexual and lesbian women. As a construct, sexual identity most adequately describes the process of creating and maintaining an identity as a sexual being. In contrast to sexual orientation, it does not assume an identity determined by the end of childhood; in contrast to sexual preference, it does not narrow the focus to the gender of one's partner or to particular sexual practices. See Plummer (n. 2 above) for a recent discussion of the issues and problems of homosexual categorization in the social sciences.

10. Amber Hollibaugh, "Sexuality and the State: The Defeat of the Briggs Initiative," *Socialist Review* 45 (May–June 1979): 55–72; Linda Gordon and Alan Hunter, "Sex, Family and the New Right," *Radical America* 11 November 1977–February 1978); George Gallup, "Report on the Summer 1977 Survey of Attitudes Toward Homosexuality," *Boston Globe,* September 10, 1977; Albert Klassen, Jr., and Eugene Levitt, "Public Attitudes Toward Homosexuality," *Journal of Homosexuality* 1 (1974): 29–43.

11. See any issue of *Gay Community News* and any newsletter of the National Gay Task Force for a more complete sampling of these types of stories; also see Judith McDaniel, "We Were Fired: Lesbian Experiences in Academe," *Sinister Wisdom* 20 (Spring 1982): 30–43; and J. R. Roberts, *Black Lesbians* (Tallahassee, Florida: Naiad Press, 1981), pp. 74–76.

12. Martin P. Levine and Robin Leonard, "Discrimination

Against Lesbians in the Workforce," paper presented at Annual Meetings of the American Sociological Association, September 1982.

13. Sasha Gregory Lewis, *Sunday's Women: A Report on Lesbian Life Today* (Boston: Beacon Press, 1979); Laud Humphreys, *Out of the Closets: The Sociology of Homosexual Liberation* (Englewood Cliffs, N.J.: Prentice-Hall, 1972).

14. Jack Hedblom, "The Female Homosexual: Social and Attitudinal Dimensions," in Joseph McCaffrey, ed., *The Homosexual Dialectic* (Englewood Cliffs, N.J.: Prentice-Hall, 1972); William Simon and John Gagnon, "The Lesbians: A Preliminary Overview," in W. Simon and J. Gagnon, eds., *Sexual Deviance* (New York: Harper & Row, 1967), pp. 247–82.

15. Fred A. Minnegerode and Marcy Adelman, "Adaptations of Aging Homosexual Men and Women," paper presented at Convention of the Gerontological Society, October 1976.

16. For an analysis that suggests a similarity of friendship networks between lesbians and single heterosexual women, see Andrea Oberstone and Harriet Sukoneck, "Psychological Adjustment and Lifestyles of Single Lesbians and Single Heterosexual Women," *Psychology of Women Quarterly* 1 (Winter 1976): 172–88; for one that suggests differences between these two groups, see Alan Bell and Martin Weinberg, *Homosexualities: A Study of Diversity Among Men and Women*.

17. E. M. Ettorre, *Lesbians, Women, and Society* (New York: Methuen, 1980).

18. Martin Weinberg and Colin Williams, *Male Homosexuals: Their Problems and Adaptations* (New York: Oxford University Press, 1975).

19. Joseph Harry, "Costs and Correlates of the Closet," paper presented at annual meeting of the American Sociological Association, September 1982; also, Humphreys (n. 13 above).

20. Kenneth Plummer, *Sexual Stigma: An Interactionist Account* (London: Routledge & Kegan Paul, 1977).

21. Karla Jay and Allen Young, eds., *Out of the Closets: Voices of Gay Liberation* (New York: Pyramid Books, 1972); Karla Jay and Allen Young, eds., *Lavender Culture* (New York: Jove, 1978). See particularly Barbara Grier, "Neither Profit Nor Salvation," in *Lavender Culture,* pp. 412–20.

22. William Paul et al., eds., *Homosexuality: Social, Psychological, and Biological Issues* (Beverly Hills, Calif.: Sage, 1972).

23. For those interested in more detailed statistical and analytical discussion of the findings of this research, see Beth E. Schneider, "Consciousness about Sexual Harassment Among Heterosexual and Lesbian Women Workers," *Journal of Social Issues* 38 (December 1982): 75–97; and Beth E. Schneider, "The Sexualization of the Workplace" (Ph.D. dissertation, University of Massachusetts, 1981).

24. It is difficult to assess the accuracy of the proportion of lesbians of color in this sample since the population is unknown. Moreover, because of racism in the feminist and lesbian communities as well as the varying extent to which sexual identity rather than race or class identity is most salient to lesbians of color, many may not be part of lesbian community networks. Thus, the sampling procedures used here—working through contacts (only two of whom were lesbians of color)—likely proved inadequate to reach them.

25. The only concern of this article is with lesbians in paid employment. Necessarily excluded are volunteer labor in political activities and unpaid labor of household maintenance and child care responsibilities. While there are 17 lesbians who are working for wages in consciously organized feminist workplaces, and they are included in the discussion, no effort is made to talk about the particular challenges of working in such locations.

26. Ninety-four percent of the lesbians who reported that *all* coworkers knew they were lesbians also reported being "totally" or "mostly open" about their sexual identity. They were employed in all occupations, but a disproportionate number were in human service jobs (40 percent), and 27 percent were in explicitly feminist work organizations. Thirty-one percent were self-employed, in a collective, or were the boss or owner of a workplace; of those who worked for someone else, almost all had a woman supervisor.

27. Women workers' beliefs about the integration of their public and private lives were measured using an index composed of four statements. These were: "The best policy to follow is to keep work separate from friendship," "You try to keep your social life completely separate from your work life," "Doing things socially with coworkers makes work relationships run more smoothly," and "You follow the general rule of not discussing personal matters with people from work." The sociability index combined four behaviors to measure the extent of social contact the women had with people at their current jobs. These four were eating lunch together, talking on the phone after work hours, visiting at each other's home, and going out socially.

28. For a discussion of these issues, see Kanter (n. 3 above) and Lydia Sargent, ed., *Women and Revolution: A Discussion of the Unhappy Marriage of Marxism and Feminism* (Boston: South End Press, 1981).

29. Marilyn Frye, "Assignment: NWSA-Bloomington-1980: Lesbian Perspectives on Women's Studies," *Sinister Wisdom* 14 (1980): 3–7, esp. 3.

30. For one effort to discuss this distinction, see Richard Zoglin, "The Homosexual Executive," in Martin P. Levine, ed., *Gay Men: The Sociology of Male Homosexuality* (New York: Harper & Row, 1979), pp. 68–77.

31. The results described here are in response to a series of questions about involvement in a sexual relationship at the workplace. The initial item—"Have you *ever* been involved in an intimate sexual relationship with someone from your

workplace?"—was followed by a series of descriptive questions about the relationship.

32. Ettorre (n. 17 above); Lewis (n. 13 above); Sidney Abbott and Barbara Love, *Sappho Was a Right-On Woman: A Liberated View of Lesbianism* (New York: Stein & Day, 1972); Del Martin and Phyllis Lyon, *Lesbian/Woman* (San Francisco: Glide, 1972).

33. Sixteen questions measured the frequency of experiences in the last year of requests for dates, jokes about body or appearance, pinches or grabs, and sexual propositions by four initiators (boss, coworker, subordinate, and recipient of service). Sixteen additional questions measured levels of dislike of these experiences. In the larger study, there were also questions concerning the general problem of unwanted sexual approaches at work and those behaviors that women most likely define as sexual harassment.

34. Schneider (n. 23 above).

35. Zillah Eisenstein, "Antifeminism in the Politics and Election of 1980," *Feminist Studies* 7 (Summer 1981): 187–205; Susan Harding, "Family Reform Movements," *Feminist Studies* 7 (Spring 1981): 57–75; Rosalind Pollack Petchesky, "Antiabortion, Antifeminism, and the Rise of the New Right," *Feminist Studies* 7 (Summer 1981): 206–246.

36. See Barry Adam, *The Survival of Domination: Inferiorization and Everyday Life* (New York: Elsevier, 1978); Dorothy E. Smith, "A Sociology for Women," in Julia A. Sherman and Evelyn Torton Beck, eds., *The Prism of Sex: Essays in the Sociology of Knowledge* (Madison: University of Wisconsin Press, 1977); Albert Memmi, *Dominated Man: Notes Toward a Portrait* (Boston: Beacon Press, 1968); Erving Goffman, *Stigma: Notes on the Management of Spoiled Identity* (Englewood Cliffs, N.J.: Prentice-Hall, 1963).

Families

The fundamental social unit is the family. In families we develop a sense of ourselves as individuals and as members of a primary group. We internalize messages about our position in our communities, nations, and the world. We are taught systems of belief, usually consistent with the society in which we live, about appropriate roles for particular kinds of people. For example, we learn to think differently about men and women, elders and children, and people of various races, classes, and social statuses. We also learn how we are expected to treat the people we encounter in the world around us.

Families come in many forms, even within one society. No matter the form a family assumes, it is within the family that members of a society first develop ideas and feelings about themselves as gendered individuals. The socialization we receive contains strong messages about the appropriate attitudes and behaviors for males and females. Families expect their members to assume interpersonal roles considered appropriate for people of one sex or the other.

Feminist scholars examine the family as a major source of the reproduction of sexism in society. Researchers ask questions about how the organization of family life supports women's oppression in society through its ideologies, economics, distribution of domestic tasks, and intimate relations. Reciprocally, researchers examine the impact of demographic, technological, economic, and political structures on women's power and positions in their families. Feminist family studies include considerations of the ways that race, ethnicity, sexuality, and class influence our family experiences. In contrast, earlier generalizations about "the family" glossed over important differences in the ways people organize their domestic and interpersonal lives and, in fact, tended to present one kind of familial organization pattern as "normal" and desirable while presenting others as "deviant" and dysfunctional.

In the first selection in Section Six, "Beyond Separate Spheres: Feminism and Family Research," Myra Marx Ferree analyzes the central issues of concern to a feminist analysis of family life. After discussing the limitation of the "sex roles" approach to understanding the family, Ferree describes a "gender theory" approach. Ferree discusses how families construct gender through symbolic and structural dimensions of paid labor, housework, and control over the family income. Her analysis breaks down the false dichotomies between public and private, home and work, love and money; it links the family, by class and race, to other institutions; and it theorizes the rewards and costs of family life to both women and men. She stresses that the family is inseparable from the larger system of male domination and is not automatically a site of solidarity or caring.

Arlie Hochschild observed and interviewed heterosexual couples in order to understand how women's increasing participation in the paid work force and changing gender ideologies have affected domestic life. According to this research, women's participation in the paid labor force does little to diminish families' perceptions of domestic responsibilities as "women's work." As a result, heterosexual couples adopt various strategies for mediating the tensions between rhetoric about "equal partnerships" and the reality of unequal burdens. In "The Second Shift: Working Parents and the Revolution at Home," Hochschild describes the social meanings assigned to household labor by different families, as well as what those meanings tell us about women's lives and social status.

The difficulties heterosexual couples experience because of men's reluctance to participate fully in the management of household labor and parenting tasks lead us to ask questions about the possible benefits for children and women of establishing families without adult male participation. Sandra Pollack discusses some parenting issues unique to lesbians in "Lesbian Parents: Claiming Our Visibility." Pollack argues that while focusing on the similarities between lesbian and heterosexual mothers may serve the purposes of lesbian mothers in custody cases, such comparisons generally promote lesbian invisibility and depoliticize lesbianism. She calls for feminist scholars to abandon research that focuses on how "typical" lesbian parents and their children are and instead to examine how children may benefit from having lesbian parents.

Women's power and positions in their families and communities change throughout the course of the life cycle, and those changes look different in the contexts of various regions and ethnicities. The interaction of age, ethnicity, and gender ideologies in family life is demonstrated in the final reading in this section. In "Puerto Rican Elderly Women: Shared Meanings and Informal Supportive Networks," Melba Sánchez-Ayéndez describes the interplay between behavior and values in family and community. She explores how the Puerto Rican values of family interdependence and sex-segregated roles have shaped elderly women's participation in family and community networks.

Beyond Separate Spheres: Feminism and Family Research

MYRA MARX FERREE

Over the past two decades, feminist scholarship has opened up many neglected topics to intensive scholarly exploration. As other essays in this issue demonstrate, feminist thinking now informs some of the best research on violence in the family, on single-parent families, on the relation between employment and family life, and on the impact of public policy on families. Because any comprehensive review of feminist influence in family studies would be too broad to be useful, this essay instead attempts to clarify recent developments in feminist theory and to use the emerging gender model to examine paid work, housework, and the control over household income in more detail.

FEMINIST THEORY

Feminist Premises

Although feminism offers an internally diverse and sometimes divisive set of theories, attention to the differences can obscure fundamental points of agreement (Jagger, 1983; Tong, 1989). Feminists agree that male dominance within families is part of a wider system of male power, is neither natural nor inevitable, and occurs at women's cost. In contrast, much conventional research on families treats them as more or less closed units that can be understood in isolation from other

"Beyond Separate Spheres: Feminism and Family Research" by Myra Marx Ferree, in *Journal of Marriage and the Family* 52 (November 1990). Copyright © 1990 by the National Council on Family Relations, 3989 Central Ave., N.E., Suite #440, Minneapolis, MN 55421. Reprinted by permission.

social institutions, such as politics or the economy. Feminism thus challenges family studies to rethink both the separateness and the solidarity of families.

By *separateness* I mean the conventional distinction between public and private, with family as the "haven in a heartless world" (Lasch, 1977), where fundamentally different social relations prevail than in the rest of society and where the "separation of spheres" allows women a distinct and complementary role. In this bifurcated view, politics and economics have only small and indirect influences on what happens within the borders of "the" family. Instrumental activity (work), being equated only with wage-earning and usually associated only with men, is rendered invisible. Within this supposedly private domain, women take center stage, appear to have unlimited power, and are held responsible for everything—the quality of the marital relationship, the mental health of children, even for preventing male violence (cf. Caplan and Hall-McCorquodale, 1985). Feminism questions every aspect of this privatized view.

By *solidarity* I mean the conventional conceptualization of "the family" as a unitary whole, a "glued-together family" (Sen, 1983), anthropomorphically treated as if it were a single actor with a single class position, standard of living, and set of interests. The myth of a unitary "family interest" permeates conventional models even in the matters of reproduction, where the differential costs to women and men should be apparent (Folbre, 1983), and of violence, where fundamental conflicts of interest by gender and generation are disregarded (cf. Breines and Gordon, 1983; Brush, 1990). Feminism also challenges this assumption of unity.

Although 1970s feminist research began to question these mainstream assumptions, new feminist scholarship in the 1980s has both sharpened its critique and developed a new approach that (*a*) defines families as fully integrated into wider systems of economic and political power and (*b*) recognizes the diverging and sometimes conflicting interests of each member (see reviews in Baca Zinn, 1990, Glenn, 1987, Osmond and Thorne, 1990, Smith, 1987b). To appreciate the significance of this new gender model requires understanding the limitations of the sex role approach that it is intended to replace.

Feminism and Sex Roles

Because sex role was a well-established concept in conventional family studies, feminist scholars in the 1960s and '70s at first adopted this term and only criticized the normative implications of its theoretical framework. By the late 1970s, however, a variety of theoretical and empirical problems became evident. In a trenchant critique, Lopata and Thorne (1978) noted that "sex role" was being used as a catchall term for everything from structural disadvantage to implied personality traits, even though a "role" should only imply specific behavioral prescriptions toward specified others. Supposedly dichotomous, internally consistent, and complementary, "sex roles" were presumed to be internalized early in life and expressed by individuals in a variety of social settings. The absurdity of a parallel concept, "race roles," they suggested, should alert us to the invisibility of social structure in this framework.

Connell (1985) emphasized role theory's static and ahistorical tendencies. Because role theory explains conformity as the result of sanctions applied by other individuals, its central focus is on individual socialization rather than social structures. This leads into an infinite regress: actors do unto others what was done to them, ad infinitum. Thus mothers socialize daughters to subordinate behaviors because they themselves have been socialized to them, not because they perceive the danger of insubordinate behavior in a male-dominated society. This logic replaces concrete, historically specific social structures with reified, impersonal norms, or "frozen descriptions" (Connell, 1985: 263). Even feminist descriptions of "sex roles" usually assumed that expected behavior was clear, consistent, and uniform, and they neglected evidence of contradiction and struggle (Stacey and Thorne, 1985).

Throughout the 1980s sex role theory came increasingly into question. First, the emergence of "sex role" as a unitary concept was recognized as a product of specific historical circumstances. Breines (1986) analyzed how Parsons, Riesman, and other sociologists of the 1950s reacted to actual changes in gender systems, such as the increasing education and employment of middle-class women and the loss of autonomy in middle-class men's jobs, by constructing ideal types of male and female behavior. The unity of personality traits, interpersonal behavior, and occupational choice that became crystallized in the concept "sex role" expressed this new idealization and wishfully asserted the existence of "traditional" arrangements as static and uniform, rather than as diverse and contested (cf. Pleck, 1987). Nonetheless, the ideological unity of the sex role label only temporarily disguised the weak or nonexistent empirical relationships between social statuses (i.e., nonemployed, housewife, mother), observable behaviors (i.e., expressing emotion, deferring to men), personality traits (i.e., passivity, conformity), and attitudes favoring the subordination of women (i.e., devaluation, fear of change). By the mid-1980s, the implicit unity in the concept of sex role began to dissolve (Vannoy-Hiller and Philliber, 1989).

Second, the concept of "sex role" placed within individuals what increasingly has come to be seen as an ongoing interaction between actors and structures. This critique takes seriously women's own reports of identity transformation in later life, claims such as "I am not the same person I was before I got married" (Acker, 1988). Gerson (1985) shows that many women see themselves as dramatically changing direction in adulthood, some in the direction of greater emphasis on paid work, some in turning unexpectedly toward motherhood. Structural opportunity is a better predictor than socialization for such later-life orientations. The instability of the traits and preferences that supposedly link playing with dolls and trucks with nurturing children and managing corporations increasingly led psychologists to more situational explanations of behavior (see review in Deaux and Kite, 1987).

Third, the association of socialization with early learning identified families as the primary focus of women's oppression, with sex roles acquired there thought to "spill over" into the labor market or educational system. Thus families often appear to be the one residue of tradition in a modernizing and increasingly egalitarian society, in which "traditional sex roles" could be defined as increasingly dysfunctional (e.g., Friedan, 1963). However, women in the working class and subordinated racial and ethnic groups argue that the emphasis on family as the central locus of oppression for women is misplaced (Jones, 1984; Rapp, 1982; Zavella, 1987). Families are also institutions of support and resistance for women as they confront other forms of social oppression, providing a cultural grounding for self-esteem as well as networks in which concrete resources can be traded (cf. reviews by Baca Zinn, 1990; Dill, 1988; Glenn, 1987). The sex role formulation fails to place family relationships in this wider structural context in which family ties support or undercut resistance to specific social arrangements.

In sum, the concept of "sex roles," rooted in socialization, internalized in individuals, and merely echoed in and exploited by other social institutions, cannot encompass the actual variation in men's and women's lives—individually over the life course and structurally in the historical context of race and class. The role approach also obscures the dimension of power and the ongoing processes of conflict associated with change. Feminist explorations of family relationships are therefore increasingly cast in a fundamentally different theoretical context, that of gender.

The Gender Perspective

The concept of gender emerged in the 1980s as the dominant feminist model. Joan Scott, a historian, defines gender as "a constitutive element of social relationships based on perceived differences between the sexes, and . . . a primary way of signifying relationships of power" (1986: 1067). Gender theory focuses upon how specific behaviors and roles are given gendered meanings, how labor is divided to express gender difference symbolically, and how diverse social structures—rather than just families—incorporate gender values and convey gender advantages (cf. Hess, 1989). While the sex role model *assumes* a certain packaging of structures, behaviors, and attitudes, the gender model analyzes the *construction* of such packages. Consequently, the gender perspective simultaneously emphasizes the symbolic and the structural, the ideological and the material, the interactional and the institutional levels of analysis (Smith, 1987a).

This conceptualization of gender highlights the process of the social construction of maleness and femaleness as oppositional categories with unequal social value. As Rubin (1975) argued, despite their differences, women and men are more like each other than like anything else in nature, so that the construction of gender as polarized dichotomies (reason and emotion, aggressive and nurturant, etc.) requires the suppression of natural similarities for social purposes by social means (p. 179). Because the active suppression of similarity and the construction of difference requires social power, the issue of domination is central to gender theory. While the basic dynamic of sex role theory is socialization, the central processes in the gender perspective are categorization and stratification (Reskin, 1988). The fundamental question is how the illusion of a gender dichotomy is constructed and maintained in the face of between-sex similarity and within-sex difference, and the answer is found in the constant and contentious process of en-gendering behavior as separate and unequal.

The proposition that gender is continuously being constructed and used to further a variety of individual and group goals is central to what West and Zimmerman (1987) call "doing gender," those interactional processes in which individuals claim a gender identity for themselves and convey it to others. Being a man or woman socially is not a natural or inevitable outgrowth of biological features but an achievement of situated conduct. Much of the work of doing gender is taken for granted and thus made invisible, but at boundaries and points of change these gender dynamics become open to explicit negotiation (Gerson and Peiss, 1985). Social structures provide the concrete resources and constraints that shape these ongoing interactions, and all sorts of objects and relationships, not only individual people, have gender meanings.

By separating the gender given to specific roles from the gender of the individuals who occupy them, the gender perspective provides a model for an authentically structural analysis of family relationships. Looking at parenthood, for example, Risman (1987) employs a "micro-structural" model to study men who "mother," that is, exercise primary parental responsibility on a day-to-day basis, and who come to think and behave in ways similar to women who mother. Barbara Katz Rothman (1989) discusses how new reproductive technologies allow women to be "fathers" more thoroughly than ever before; in addition to using (other) women to care for their children, (female) fathers can appropriate (other) women's labor to bear children from their "seed." She suggests that women, too, as "fathers" will devalue nurturing as unskilled contractual labor worth subminimum wages and define "mothers" as fungible service providers. Nelson (1989) finds evidence for this in the depersonalized view of child care providers expressed by their women employers but also points to the workers' view that they are more "feminine and motherly" than their employers as a sign of an active contest over the gender meaning and social value of their work.

From a gender perspective, the dynamics of categorization are closely associated with processes of stratification and social control (Reskin, 1988). The power to define is itself a means of social control, and this is evident even among children. Children—no less than adults—are actively engaged in working out the meaning of gender in response to the power relationships they perceive all around them. Joffe's (1973) study of an "alternative" preschool found that children who did not know the content of mainstream culture's stereotypes still used gender to manipulate other children's behavior (e.g., claiming that "girls can't play in sandboxes" to get other children to relinquish their place). Thorne (1986a) shows how children themselves actively structure gender into group games ("girls chase boys") and express their own group membership by adopting gender symbols (like Barbie dolls) and stigmatizing cross-gendered characteristics (like long eyelashes on boys).

Bem (1983) discusses the difficulty of raising children in what she calls a "gender-schematic" society, in which all sorts of objects and behaviors are imbued with gender meaning (cf. Paoletti, 1987, on the emergence of pink and blue as gender color codes in the 1920s). Bem illustrates her point about the "unnatural" nature of children's gender categorization in the story of her son wearing a barrette to nursery school, being confronted by a classmate who insisted he had to be a girl because "only girls wear barrettes." Her son's attempted demonstration that he was a boy "because he had a penis" was rejected by the other child: "anybody can have a penis, but only girls wear barrettes" (p. 612). Adult struggles over who or what is a "real" man or woman continue this dynamic.

Because "gender is relational and not essential, creating and recreating ourselves as gendered persons involves not a little struggle and ambivalence" (cf. Hess, 1989: 26; Connell, 1985). The internal conflict over what a "real" mother or father feels and does is one manifestation of this struggle. For example, studies of postpartum depression reveal the extensive "emotional work" that must be done by new mothers to produce socially appropriate feelings and repress inappropriate ones (Taylor and McCormick, 1989). External conflict over the meaning of motherhood can be seen in the varying evaluations of Mary Beth Whitehead, a so-called surrogate mother (Harrison, 1987), and in the controversy over a corporate "mommy track" (Schwartz, 1989); both issues highlight the importance of nonfamily power structures for family identities. Within a set of structural power relationships, the processes of categorization and resistance to categorization provide a lifelong dialectic of engendering identity.

In sum, the feminist critique of a unified and internalized "sex role" has matured into an alternative theoretical standpoint that defines gender as a lifelong process of situated behavior that both reflects and reproduces a structure of differentiation and control in which men have material and ideological advantages. The power that men (and adults, whites, employers, etc.) possess gives them certain advantages in using gender to advance and defend their interests, while gender itself associates maleness with power and authority, in and out of the family.

Gender and Family

Applying a gender perspective to families advances the feminist challenge to mainstream views of separateness and solidarity. First, because the gender system is theoretically distinguished from the particular family forms of a specific historical period, "family" is no longer seen as the primary focus of all women's oppression. The diversity of family forms by race and class, and what they offer to men and women in different economic circumstances, is explicitly recognized (Baca Zinn, 1990). Gender is, with race and class, a hierarchical structure of opportunity and oppression as well as an affective structure of identity and cohesion, and families are one of many institutional settings in which these structures become lived experience. To understand the diverse ways they structure the material conditions of people's lives, families need to be studied in relation to other political and economic institutions.

Second, attention to both the structural and ideological levels of analysis requires distinguishing between *households,* which are the coresidential units in which people empirically can be found, and *family,* the ideology of relatedness that explains who should live together, share income, and perform certain common tasks (Andersen, 1990; Rapp, 1982). An important contemporary example of the significance of distinguishing between family and household is the restructuring of family obligations and household composition after divorce. The extent to which fathers define their *family* obligation of support as ceasing when they are no longer in the same *household* as their children is a major public policy problem, as well as a source of economic crisis for women and children in mother-only households (Arendell, 1987).

Third, understanding family cohesion as a cultural prescription rather than as a natural fact helps to clarify its role in legitimating male dominance, while also recognizing that it can sometimes be invoked to mitigate or resist male power (Hartmann, 1981). The social construct "family," like gender, needs to be analyzed historically to identify whose claims it legitimates and how (Davidoff and Hall, 1987; Folbre, 1983). Families are not articulate actors and cannot make demands, but family members can and do make claims on each other, using the ideology of family to legitimate their appeals and justify self-sacrifice (Ferree, 1984; Stack, 1989). The notion of a unitary family interest represented by husbands and fathers (e.g., Geerken and Gove, 1983: 74) serves to conceal men's particular familial interests.

Fourth, this perspective assumes that gender relations are always contentious; change is actively sought and partially accomplished in all historical periods. The gender model thus acknowledges the diversity of conventional gender arrangements historically and today (Baca Zinn, 1990; Bose, 1987b; Kimmel, 1987). Unlike "traditional sex roles," gender *conventions* are not assumed to be melting away in the light of "modernity." In place of a linear, evolutionary view of "progress," the gender perspective focuses attention on the continual struggles to maintain and change gender relations (Scott, 1986). The term *convention* conceptually acknowledges more diversity than the word *tradition:* what is unconventional for working-class women (i.e., deferring childbearing) may be quite conventional in the middle class, while paid employment for mothers of preschool children may be less conventional for middle-class than for working-class mothers.

In sum, the development of a gender perspective reveals that the experience of gender in a family context cannot be limited to behavior within a household (DiLeonardo, 1987; but see Thompson and Walker, 1989, for an excellent review of marriage, work, and parenthood as gendered activities within households). As a system of obligation to specified others, family connects economic and kinship structures within and between households. Because these obligations and connections are deeply gendered, through processes that are historically developed in each particular culture, the interaction of gender with race and class is theoretically important (Baca Zinn, 1990). The gender perspective's attention to the boundary areas and points of conflict through time also makes greater methodological demands for historical specificity (Breines, 1986; Kimmel, 1987).

Because the gender perspective emphasizes the contingent historical construction of the link between households and the economy, much feminist research in the past decade has focused on families as the structural and symbolic place where this connection is forged, contested, and transformed in gender-specific ways (Hartmann, 1981). The issue of work, both paid and unpaid, is central to this model. As Hartmann puts it, "the creation of gender can be thought of as the creation of a division of labor between the sexes, the creation of two categories of workers who need each other" (1981: 393). Indeed, Berk (1985) considers the production of gender relations as such a major element of what families create in doing housework that she entitles her book on the division of household labor *The Gender Factory.* The relationship between labor and gender is a substantial portion of what family organizes, both in and out of the household.

The feminist attempt to analyze, rather than take for granted, the gendered nature of these work-family connections has created a new view of family, in which family-and-work is a single, historically variable, gendered system (e.g., collections by Benaria and Stimpson, 1987; Gerstel and Gross, 1987; Thorne with Yalom, 1982). Such volumes discuss how the ideology of "separate spheres" has obscured the links between work and family; these authors treat both men and women as family members and workers simultaneously, and recognize the gendered meaning and structural conditions of paid and unpaid work. Three issues that were marginal to mainstream views of families—waged work, housework, and the control over household

TEEN-AGE PREGNANCY

FAYE WATTLETON

In 1983 a 25-year-old woman with a 9-year-old daughter gave the following testimony before Congress:

In the tenth grade, my girlfriends and I were all sexually active, but none of us used birth control. I had hopes of a career and I wanted to go to college. One day my mother said, "Towanda, you're pregnant." I asked her how she knew. She said, "I can just tell."

My mother wouldn't even consider abortion. I had nothing to say about a decision that would alter my entire life. A few weeks after the baby was born, my mother said, "You'll have to get a job." The only job I could get was in a bar.

I spent two years dealing with the nightmare of welfare. Finally I went to the father of my child and asked him to take care of her while I went back to school. He agreed.

I am now making some progress. I went to business school and I now have a job working in an office in Washington. But my life has been very difficult . . . I had ambitions as a child, but my hopes and dreams were almost killed by the burden of trying to raise a child while I was still a child myself.

This young woman's story is relived around us every day. The United States has the dubious distinction of leading the industrialized world in its rates of teen-age pregnancy, teen-age childbirth and teen-age abortion. According to a study of thirty-seven developed nations published by the Alan Guttmacher Institute in 1985, the teen pregnancy rate in the United States is more than double the rate in England, nearly triple the rate in Sweden and

Faye Wattleton, "Teen-Age Pregnancy: The Case for National Action," *The Nation* magazine, The Nation Co., Inc., © 1989.

seven times the rate in the Netherlands. Throughout the 1970s, this rate rose in the United States, while it declined in such places as England, Wales and Sweden. Each year, more than 1 million American teen-agers become pregnant; about half of these young women give birth.

Teen pregnancy is both cause and consequence of a host of social ills. The teen-agers likeliest to become pregnant are those who can least afford an unwanted child: those who are poor, those who live with one parent, those who have poor grades in school and those whose parents did not finish high school. As the National Research Council points out, teen mothers face "reduced employment opportunities, unstable marriages (if they occur at all), low incomes, and heightened health and developmental risks to the children. . . . Sustained poverty, frustration, and hopelessness are all too often the long-term outcomes." Compounding the tragedy is the fact that children of teen-age mothers are more likely to become teen parents themselves. The burden is felt by the entire society: The national costs of health and social service programs for families started by teen-agers amount to more than $19 billion a year.

Media accounts have tended to represent teen-age pregnancy as primarily a problem of the black community, and implicitly—or explicitly, as in the case of the 1986 CBS Special Report on the "vanishing" black family by Bill Moyers—they have attempted to blame the problem on the so-called degeneracy of the black family. Such distortions of fact are particularly dangerous because they coincide all too neatly with the insensitivity to blacks and the blame-the-victim ideology that the Reagan Administration so disastrously fostered.

High rates of teen pregnancy actually are as all-American as apple pie. Even when the figures for "nonwhite" teens were subtracted from the calculations, the rate of teen pregnancy in the United States in 1981 (83 per 1,000) far exceeded the teen pregnancy rates in all other major industrialized nations. In England and Wales, our closest competitors, the rate for teens of all races was just 45 per 1,000.

The fact of the matter is that teen-age pregnancy rates in the United States have a great deal more to do with class than they do with race. The majority of poor people in this country are white, and so are the majority of pregnant teen-agers. In a report published in 1986, the Guttmacher Institute examined interstate differences in teen pregnancy rates. It found that the percentage of teens who are black is relatively unimportant as a determinant of overall state variations in teen-age reproduction. It is states with higher percentages of poor people and of people living in urban areas—whatever their race—that have significantly higher teen pregnancy and birth rates.

Teen pregnancy is as grave a problem within many black communities as are poverty and social alienation. One-third of all blacks, and one-half of all black children, live in poverty. And today the pregnancy rate among teens of color is double that of white teens. One of every four black children is born to a teen-age mother; 90 percent of these children are born to unwed mothers. Such patterns can only intensify the problems already facing the black community. Disproportionately poor, blacks are disproportionately affected by the social and economic consequences of teen-age pregnancy.

We need only look to other Western nations to recognize both the cause and the solutions to our teen pregnancy problem. American teens are no more sexually active than their counterparts in Europe; and teen-agers abroad resort to abortion far less often than do those in the United States. There is a major cause for our higher rates of teen pregnancy and childbirth: the fundamental discomfort of Americans with sexuality. Unlike other Western societies, we have not yet accepted human sexuality as a normal part of life. The result is that our children, and many adults as well, are confused, frightened and bombarded by conflicting sexual messages.

Most parents recognize their role as the first and most important sexuality educators their children will have, providing information and sharing family values from the time their children are born. Nevertheless, many parents are unable to talk with their children about such sensitive issues as sex and human relationships. Schools do not fill the gap. Only seventeen states and the District of Columbia mandate comprehensive sex education. As a result, many teen-agers are abysmally ignorant about their reproductive functions.

The mass media, particularly television, only exacerbate the problem. Many teen-agers spend more time in front of the television than they do in the classroom, and their sexual behavior in part reflects what they have learned from this thoroughly unreliable teacher. Nowhere is it more apparent than on television that America suffers from sexual schizophrenia: We exploit sex, and at the same time we try to repress it. Programs and advertisements bombard viewers with explicit sexual acts and innuendo. One study indicates that in a single year, television airs 20,000 sexual messages. Yet rarely is there any reference to contraception or to the consequences of sexual activity.

A substantial number of teens believe that what they see on television is a faithful representation of life. Many believe that television gives a realistic picture of pregnancy and the consequences of sex. And large numbers of teens say they do not use contraceptives because they are "swept away" by passion—surely a reflection of the romanticized view of sex that pervades the mass media.

Network executives, though they apparently have few qualms about exploiting the sexual sell twenty-four hours a day, have the hypocrisy to claim that good taste forbids them to carry ads for contraceptives. Some of the networks recently decided to accept condom ads, though not during prime time, and those ads promote condoms only as protection against AIDS, not against pregnancy. It should not surprise us, then, that America's youths are sexually illiterate, or that 67 percent of sexually active teens either never use contraceptives or use them only occasionally.

We have not failed to resolve this problem for lack of majority agreement on how to do it. A 1988 Harris public opinion survey done for Planned Parenthood found a strong consensus about both the severity of the teen pregnancy problem and about how to solve it:

- Ninety-five percent of Americans think that teen-age pregnancy is a serious problem in this country, up 11 percent from 1985.
- Seventy-eight percent of parents believe that relaxed discussions between parents and children about sex will reduce unintended teen-age pregnancy.
- Eighty-nine percent endorse school sex education.
- Eighty percent support school referrals of sexually active teens to outside family-planning clinics.
- Seventy-three percent favor making contraceptives available in school clinics.

School-linked clinics that offer birth control as part of general health care are growing in number in many areas of the country. Community support and involvement are crucial to their development, to insure that the programs are consistent with community values and needs.

Clearly the vast majority of Americans, regardless of racial, religious or political differences, strongly supports the very measures that have proven so effective in reducing teen pregnancy rates in other Western nations. Unfortunately, an extremist minority in this country has an entirely different outlook on sexuality—a minority that has a level of influence out of all proportion to its size. Eager to cultivate the anti-family planning, antiabortion fringe, the Reagan-Bush Administration and its cohorts in Congress sought to whittle down Federal funds for domestic and international family planning, limit sex education in the schools, eliminate confidentiality for birth control and abortion services and block the development of school-linked

clinics. These vocal opponents object to everything that has proven successful elsewhere in the industrialized world. Their one and only solution to the problem of teen-age pregnancy is, "Just say no!" But just saying no prevents teen-age pregnancy the way "Have a nice day" cures chronic depression.

There is nothing inherent in American life that condemns us permanently to having the highest teen pregnancy rate in the Western world—nothing that Sweden, England, France, the Netherlands and Canada have been able to do that we cannot.

Parents must talk with their children about all aspects of sexuality—openly, consistently and often—beginning in early childhood. Every school district in the country should provide comprehensive sex education, from kindergarten through twelfth grade. Community groups need to support the development of school-linked health clinics. The media must present realistic, balanced information about relationships and the consequences of sex. Television, in particular, must end the restrictions on contraceptives advertising. Government—at the local, state and Federal levels—must live up to its obligation to eliminate any financial barriers to family-planning education and services and to foster a community environment in which our children can flourish and aspire to a productive and fulfilling life.

But we must also recognize that the teen pregnancy problem cannot be solved through sexuality education and family-planning services alone. If our efforts are to succeed, society must provide all our young people with a decent general education, tangible job opportunities, successful role models and real hope for the future.

It is only by placing such a comprehensive national agenda at the top of the priority list that our society can protect the creative and productive potential of its youth.

income—emerge as central for understanding the historically specific structural context in which families construct gender in their daily operations. In the second half of this essay, these three issues are examined in greater detail for the light they can throw on the relation of gender to work-family systems as such.

WAGED WORK AND THE PROVIDER ROLE

The mainstream view of the family assumes that men have "traditionally" been the only paid workers and that they thus "provided" for their dependents. The feminist sex role model accepted the truth of this view but argued that it was unnecessary, unhealthy, and open to change. In contrast, the new gender perspective contests the reality of this version of the past and points to the damaging consequences for sociological research and for people's lives produced by this political myth.

Gendered Views of Employment

The sociological study of paid employment has tended to focus on (male) workers only in the context of the workplace and to place both women and families on the periphery (Acker, 1988; Delphy and Leonard, 1986). With regard to workplace behavior and job attitudes, the sociological models used have typically been gendered: men are explained in terms of their jobs, women in terms of their families and their "nature" (Feldberg and Glenn, 1979). Models of family functioning have also been gendered: women are assumed to be present and available to meet the needs of other family members, so that women's paid employment is considered a social problem or strain on the family and women's economic dependence unproblematic (Acker, 1988; DeVault, 1990). Men's paid employment has been taken for granted, the demands it may place on other family members normalized, and men excused from active participation when their jobs interfere (Pleck, 1977). Sociology's gendered view of families corresponds to the "domestic code" of 1950s popular culture (Breines, 1986; Moeller, 1989).

The gender perspective's demand for greater historical accuracy challenges two key elements of the male "provider" myth. First, it recognizes that women have always contributed significantly to the household economy, including through paid employment in and out of the home. Second, it brings men's work into view as part of a gendered structure of employment that has changed significantly over time.

Rethinking Women's Employment

Detailed historical studies show that economic structure and household composition interact in determining which household members go "out to work" and which contribute in other ways—by subsistence production, industrial outwork, home-based enterprises, or petty commodity trading (Bose, 1987b; Kessler-Harris, 1982; Tilly and Scott, 1978). Research on women in industrializing areas of the Third World

today shows broad similarities to patterns found a century or two before in Europe and America: daughters are an important part of the labor force, mothers tend to earn money in the shadow economy where work conditions and wages are worst, and few families are able to rely on a single "breadwinner," whether male or female, until industrialization is relatively advanced and unionization widespread (Boxer and Quataert, 1987; Matthaei, 1982; Tiano, 1987).

The gender model has been able to bring women's work out of the shadows by questioning the socially constructed definition of work itself. Even "objective" census statistics conceal assumptions about work and workers that tend to undercount women's paid employment, as Bose (1987a) shows in regard to the U.S. Census at the turn of the century and today. Deacon (1985) compares the British and Australian censuses in the political goals that made them more or less willing to count women among the employed and thus choose different ways of defining "employment." Because of the politics of counting, the extent to which recent rises in the labor force participation of married women overstate the degree of real change in women's work activities is unknown. Clearly, women's economic contributions have been substantial, despite the ideology that denies them; Rainwater (1979) estimated married women's cash contributions to the household economy as 25% at the turn of the century, which is not a great deal less than the 30% married women are estimated to earn today (Spitze, 1988).

Since women have always worked, the image of women's paid employment as a "nontraditional" activity "intruding" upon their "prior" responsibilities must be revised to reflect the fact that women's "traditional" responsibilities included providing income for the family when necessary (Beechey, 1988; Kessler-Harris, 1982). Black women and working-class immigrant women were especially likely to be economically active (Jones, 1984; Kessler-Harris, 1982). Despite Victorian fantasies about "man the hunter" and woman at the hearth, the historical reality was that households were productive units in which all members contributed, in gender- and generationally specific ways, and in which jointly produced resources were (unequally) controlled and redistributed (Boxer and Quataert, 1987; Dwyer and Bruce, 1988). A central element of the feminist research agenda is to recover a more accurate accounting of the variation in women's economic contributions across time, place, class, race, and culture.

Rethinking Men's Employment

The second challenge to the "provider" myth lies in the recognition that the social construction of men as employees, spending a significant portion of the day away from home and bringing back a wage that could support a nonemployed family, is only a phenomenon of the late industrial era. The social association of masculinity with the role of sole provider is new, not "traditional" (Bernard, 1981; Carrigan, Connell, and Lee, 1987; Pleck, 1987). For example, a single male provider role was actively constructed through Henry Ford's family wage plan (May, 1987). This benefited an elite of skilled male autoworkers only; Ford also intentionally used their families' economic dependence to make wives into his allies in imposing work discipline. In contrast, Turbin shows how the wage work of women in the collar industry and of men in the iron industry in Troy, New York, in the early 19th century allowed each to support the other's strikes and create family traditions of labor militance (1987). It was the social construction of a blue-collar "labor aristocracy" of white men with "skilled" and secure jobs that allowed the ideology of dual spheres—a male provider and a wife at home—to become a working-class ideal, even when the reality was quite different (Hareven, 1982; Parr, 1987).

At the end of the 18th century, domesticity, rather than occupational achievement, was the ideal for middle-class men. Davidoff and Hall (1987) examine English entrepreneurial families' emphasis on the home as the ideal for both sexes. Home was where male property owners could develop and exercise the new bourgeois values of citizenship, self-development, and moral responsibility. Women, men, and children of the working class were expected to labor to make such domesticity possible. However, the interaction of family and economy soon separated middle-class men from the home. Ryan (1981) describes the making of a managerial middle class in early 19th-century New York, and the ideals of motherhood and masculinity that were constructed along with it. Because education was the new means of passing on class position, mothers became charged with the responsibility for instilling certain educational values and work habits in their sons, especially competitiveness. In effect, mothers were now expected to create the "human capital" that potential employers valued. The "self-made man" thus

emerged as a new cultural ideal in the 19th century, but his making has been and remains a gendered process in which mothers and wives have clearly prescribed, supporting roles (Finch, 1983; Fowlkes, 1980; Ryan, 1981).

Consequences of the Gendered Provider Role

Recognition that the equation of masculinity with the provider role is a convention of modern industrial society throws new light on contemporary family dynamics. In the first place, it focuses attention on the nature and significance of women's paid and unpaid labor in making the "self-made man" and how this varies by class and ethnicity. Daniels (1989) and Ostrander (1984) examine the role of upper-class women as volunteers in the community, whose labor helps to legitimate the family's class position as "earned." At the other end of the economic spectrum, women's invisible and unremunerated work in "family-owned" but husband-controlled enterprises provides access to the middle class; Cuban, Korean, and Vietnamese family enterprises provide contemporary examples. In many disadvantaged groups, mothers labor in domestic service and sweatshops to keep their children in school and to make upward mobility possible (Dill, 1980; Glenn, 1985). Male professional success also depends on the status-production work of wives—what Papanek (1973) called the two-person career (cf. Finch, 1983; Fowlkes, 1980). Family structure, much invoked to explain poverty, should therefore also enter into sociological explanations of prosperity.

Second, understanding how paid employment has been constructed in industrial society as a gendered (male) form of work also helps explain why women's entry into the paid labor force could not be the panacea that feminist proponents of "role expansion" once expected (Crosby, 1987). Women who enter conventionally male-defined careers do "need a wife," as the complaint goes, because the expectations built into the structure of the job and the workplace take such a full-time support system for granted. Hunt and Hunt (1982) raise the possibility that the incorporation of women into "fast-track" professional and managerial careers can only succeed when both spouses are "husbands" who put minimal investment into family life. One way for "two-husband" families to manage is to hire a "wife," typically a woman of color and/or a new immigrant (Hertz, 1986; Hochschild, 1989). However, only a small proportion of employed married women have earnings high enough to make this feasible (Benenson, 1984).

Studies of two-income families support Hunt and Hunt's contention that sharing responsibility at home is facilitated if neither spouse places highest priority on their paid work, as may be more typical in working-class households (e.g., Hochschild, 1989; Hood, 1983). However, carrying responsibility for housework does have measurable occupational costs for men and women of all classes (Coverman, 1983; Shelton and Firestone, 1989). The kernel of truth, and hence popular appeal, in advocating a "mommy track" in the corporation (Schwartz, 1989) or rejecting feminist demands for equal opportunity in favor of special protection (Hewlett, 1986) lies in recognizing the gendered nature of the occupational system; these authors plead for accommodation to it, rather than transformation.

Finally, the development of gender theory helps to explain why the link between masculinity and the provider role is significant for two-income families today. In a majority of two-earner households, wives are supplemental earners rather than "co-providers" in their own and others' eyes (Ferree, 1988; Haas, 1986; Hood, 1986; Potuchek, 1989). Nearly half of all couples (43%) think income earning should be solely the husband's responsibility (Vannoy-Hiller and Philliber, 1989: 105). Because women's full-time year-round wages are still less than two-thirds of men's, the structural opportunity for married women to earn enough to share the provider role is limited. But when only husbands are seen as providers, only husbands are treated as entitled to the support that this role presumes (Ferree, 1984). Sharing the provider role can be threatening to men who have constructed their ideal of masculinity on this economic ground (Goode, 1982; Hunt and Hunt, 1987), so that even women who are providers lack the support systems at home for this role (Parr, 1987).

The provider role is not without its costs and conflicts. Working-class men have resisted and resented the pressure from their dependents that comes with the family wage. Luxton (1980: 67) notes how "some men see their wives as constantly nagging, forcing them to work when they hate it" and taking out their anger over their work on their wives. At the same time,

conventional gender ideology rationalizes the costs of exclusive devotion to paid employment as the price of achieving masculinity (Carrigan et al., 1987; Hunt and Hunt, 1987). For women, being a sole or co-provider is often experienced as a loss of "freedom of choice" and perceived as a failure of men to live up to their "proper" role. Black women lose no matter how they handle the provider role: blamed for not providing adequately for their families, and blamed for harming men by taking the best jobs they can get (Baca Zinn, 1989; Collins, 1989).

In sum, the gendering of waged work, as well as of the provider role within the household, creates obstacles to achieving equality in both domains, since both are part of a single, interlocking system. It is not confinement in the home so much as the historically constructed structural and ideological incompatibilities between home and workplace that limit women's efforts to gain equality. Rather than defining the agenda as giving women the opportunity to add more roles and enrich their lives (to the point of exhaustion), the gender perspective views both macro and micro structures of the work-family system as in need of reform (Gerstel and Gross, 1987; Moen, 1989). Thus changes in transportation systems, home design, normal work schedules, recruitment and promotion structures, and national job creation policies join traditional demands for affordable child care, more flexible work opportunities, and enforcement of equal opportunity policies for women. Because men's jobs and career paths are gendered and built upon a structure of family support that is also gendered, changes for women necessarily also imply changes for men, and men's reactions to change should be understood in these terms (Goode, 1982; Hunt and Hunt, 1987; Weiss, 1987).

HOUSEWORK

Housework is more than the invisible and unpaid labor that makes wage work possible (e.g., Brown, 1982). It is also gendered labor, that is, a set of culturally and historically specific tasks that convey social meanings about masculinity and femininity, and therefore about power (Berk, 1985). The gender perspective leads to an examination of both the material and the ideological dimensions of this work.

The Physical Labor of Housework

The label "housework" connects extremely diverse responsibilities. The nature of the work women do for their families in industrialized countries is quite unlike the work women do in many developing nations—hauling water, producing subsistence crops, processing raw materials—yet calling this labor "housework" has enabled development "experts" to ignore the needs of women workers and exclude their home production from calculations of GNP (Ciancanelli and Berch, 1987; Tiano, 1987). Even the history of housework in this country reveals important changes in the nature of the labor women provide (Cowan, 1983; Strasser, 1982). The physical labor of housework has been reduced by technology—more by such public conveniences as running water, sewer systems, and electricity than by purely domestic products (Strasser, 1982)—but it has also been increasingly concentrated in the person of an individual "housewife" (Cowan, 1983).

What is actually to be defined as housework is a methodological morass: tasks change in content and they move between paid and unpaid labor, in and out of the home, while still being seen as "housework." This confusion arises because the apparent unity in the conceptualization of housework comes from imposing culturally shared gender categories on a historically shifting domain. Among cultures and across time there is no one thing that can be consistently defined as housework. The idea of housework as a distinctive form of labor only emerges with industrialization; it is the cultural opposite of waged work, reflecting the much older idea of a gender division of labor (Deacon, 1985; Luxton, 1980). This distinction conveys value—as when the labor done by "the farmer's wife" is categorized as supposedly unproductive "housework," thus reducing her claim on family resources (Elbert, 1987; Kleinegger, 1987).

Some scholars (e.g., Glenn, 1985; Nelson, 1988; Saraceno, 1984) highlight the continuity between the work women did at home without pay and the jobs they hold in the paid labor force. Thus, nursing service was once part of housework, became a paid occupation, and is now being transferred back into the home as unpaid labor, as hospitals respond to cost-containment pressures by sending patients home "quicker and sicker" to be cared for by family members, primarily wives, daughters, and daughters-in-law (Abel, 1986; Glazer, 1988). Glenn (1985) points out how women of

color who did "housework" for pay as domestic servants are now channeled into similar cleaning and service jobs outside the private household. The definition of such jobs as dirty and demeaning, but "suited" for women of color, is significant (Rollins, 1985).

Looking at paid domestic labor from the vantage point of Asian, black, and Hispanic women illuminates the race and class dimensions of the division of household labor and the struggle over housework "between women" (Glenn, 1986; Kaplan, 1987; Rollins, 1985; Romero, 1988). The invisibility of the domestic worker's own family to the woman employer, the unbounded demands on time and energy created by the absence of any contract, the rituals of subordination demanded from domestic workers, and the absence of recognition of workers' skills are common themes in these studies. Rollins (1985) makes clear that wives who "hire help" are redistributing tasks for which their husbands continue to hold them personally accountable; this makes employers less rather than more sympathetic to their employees, since they get the credit for the quantity and quality of labor extracted from "their" domestic worker.

Along with recognizing the contributions of paid domestic workers, the gender perspective also directs attention to children as workers, whether paid or unpaid (Thorne, 1986b). Although the "role-sharing" focus of feminist sex role research formerly treated children as unimportant and invisible, the gender model recognizes that they may do significant quantities of unpaid labor (Goldscheider and Waite, 1989). Children contribute regularly to certain chores and may do more supplemental housework when their mothers are employed than their fathers do (Berk, 1985). Goldscheider and Waite (1989) argue for a reconceptualization of the division of labor as three-cornered, since the more children do, the less fathers contribute (and vice versa). Single mothers are especially likely to rely on children's housework (Michelson, 1985), and this may pose special problems for daughters, who are often expected to do the domestic work that their mothers cannot (Kaplan, 1987). Daughters are still more likely to be given housework than sons, and among sons and daughters who do housework, daughters do more hours of work (Berk, 1985). The nature of the tasks assigned to children still reflects cultural stereotypes of gender-appropriateness (White and Brinkerhoff, 1981).

Insofar as husbands and wives divide domestic

labor, the majority of the chores fall to the wives (see reviews in Berk, 1985; Spitze, 1988; and Thompson and Walker, 1989). Women do from 70% to 80% of the total housework hours and the majority of the most frequently repeated and time-consuming chores (Berk, 1985; Huber and Spitze, 1983). Single mothers suggest that losing a husband actually *decreases* time pressures in housework (Graham, 1987; Michelson, 1985: 97). Although global self-reports show some increases in men's housework in recent years (e.g., Ferree, 1990; Ross, Mirowsky, and Huber, 1983), all time-budget studies are now too dated to test this (Coleman, 1988). These clearly need replication in the next decade, both to check trends and to include new, detailed measures of children's domestic labor.

The Symbolic Meaning of Housework

The gender perspective attempts to explain why the rise in married women's paid employment has not led to large and dramatic changes in their husbands' domestic labor (Pleck, 1985). In contrast to the predictions of the resource model, "there is no simple trade-off of wage and family work hours between wives and husbands, nor do partners allocate family work based on time availability" (Thompson and Walker, 1989: 856). It is not an economic bargain, even when it is rationalized as such (Acker, 1988). At least for some households, it seems more acceptable to do without certain amounts or kinds of unpaid labor than to have it done by the person of the "wrong" gender.

Since the gender perspective highlights the significance of rigid categorization, it directs attention to variations among married couples in the extent to which men participate in housework and how tasks are divided (Ferree, 1988; Maret and Finlay, 1984). While time-budget and task-allocation measures have primarily been used to examine changes in the *mean* proportion of housework men do, little attention has been paid to changes in the *variability* in these measures. Studies of participation in gender-stereotypical household tasks tend not to report or compare the standard deviation among subgroups, although differences in the amount of variation would indicate change in the degree of gender categorization. If variation in men's participation in housework is greater when wives hold full-time jobs, this would suggest that housework is becoming a contentious, boundary-defining issue. Hood (1983) and Hochschild (1989) suggest that dif-

ferent meanings given to women's paid employment increase the variability among husbands in the amount of housework they do, with some reducing their "share" to sabotage their wives' attempt to gain independence, while others increase their housework to "help her out."

Although Hochschild (1989) finds considerable struggle between husbands and wives over the symbolic meaning of housework, especially when wives are employed, other studies find that both husbands and wives seem to collaborate in creating and sustaining economically irrational, gendered expectations for housework (Berk, 1985; Thompson and Walker, 1989). Housework remains a "natural" (culturally expected and legitimate) part of being a wife, part of the "project of constructing 'proper' families" (DeVault, 1990). Thus, the quality of housework can be a symbolic reaffirmation of women as "good" wives and mothers, as our culture defines these roles (Berk, 1985: 198–211). Whereas women define their responsibility as providing enough housework to satisfy their husbands, husbands are accorded the right to criticize what wives do (Berk, 1985: 206–207; DeVault, 1990).

While resource models tend to see housework as an unmitigated "bad" that anyone with power would avoid doing (Hood, 1983), from a gender perspective, doing housework is understood as an expression of love and care, but in unequal ways for men and women. Since housework supposedly flows out of her "natural" desire to care for her family, a woman may feel guilty about every unmet "need," while a man's contributions, however small, are a favor to her (DeVault, 1990; Luxton, 1980). In this gendered context, the reduction of time that women put into housework in the past two decades could be interpreted as a significant victory. However, it is important to study differences among women in their feelings about housework and perceptions of the division of labor as fair or not (Benin and Agostinelli, 1988; Ferree, 1987). When and how do women lower their standards for housework and challenge the equation between caring and cleaning?

The gendering of housework as female means the work also symbolizes subordination and can be either resisted or embraced for that reason (Hochschild, 1989). Housework-like chores are imposed in other institutions to instill discipline and deference (e.g., KP in the army: Wittner, 1980). The power symbolism in housework and class differences in the legitimacy of male authority in the family apparently lead working-class families to understate men's actual participation in chores, and middle-class couples to exaggerate it (Ferree, 1984; Hochschild, 1989). As Hochschild's case studies illustrate, when housework carries the meaning of subordination more than the meaning of caring, both partners in middle-class couples struggle to avoid it (cf. Hood, 1983; Goldscheider and Waite, 1989).

However, it is striking how little explicit conflict there is over housework in many families (Berk, 1985: 188). Despite the fact that wives clearly do most of the housework, even when employed full-time, only a minority (36%) express a desire to have their husbands do more (Pleck, 1985) or themselves do less (21%; Berk, 1985). Komter (1989) describes this as the result of the "hidden power" of gender ideology to suppress conflict by creating resignation, fear of disturbing the relationship, and denial of one's own feelings. In her study, legitimations of the status quo in the division of housework were made by invoking supposed differences in the characters of men and women ("he's not suited for it," "she enjoys it," etc.) as normal and right, and housework as something women just "have to get used to." Recognizing this suppression of conflict as an important power dynamic should lead scholars to look not only at "adjustment" and "satisfaction" but at their personal and emotional costs; for example, who is more likely to be depressed-employed women who are angry about how little housework their husbands do or those who are resigned to it?

In sum, the gender perspective on housework challenges three basic assumptions of resource models. First, housework is not allocated efficiently to the person with the most time to do it. Although the time demands of men's paid jobs explain some variation in the extent to which they participate in housework, even women's full-time employment does not reduce their domestic obligations equivalently. Second, housework is not necessarily something that either or both partners define as a "bad" to be avoided. Although women do not seem actually to like or enjoy housework more than men do, they often accept it as an expected element of being a wife, or the "price" of domestic harmony. Third, while differences in individual resources within the family influence the allocation of housework, gender influences it more: women from outside the household are hired, daughters are given more housework than sons, and employed women reduce their own housework more easily than they

seek or obtain increases in their husbands' contributions.

The gender perspective points to the symbolic construction of housework as "women's work" and as an expression of both love and subordination. This explains, as economic models fail to do, why women and men so often collaborate to maintain a system that objectively imposes unequal burdens on women. It could potentially begin to explain variation here as well, indicating ways in which the gender division of labor is *not* consistent and consensual. Conflict over housework might even be a good sign, indicating women's growing sense of entitlement to a more equal division of labor at home rather than a failure of "adjustment" to a power-imbalanced status quo.

INDIVIDUAL WAGES AND HOUSEHOLD INCOME

Since modern economic systems revolve around wages, control over a wage—in particular, the ability to command a wage adequate to meet household subsistence needs—is essential for family survival. Because wages are earned by individuals and redistributed to other family members, both within and across households (Rapp, 1982; Stack, 1974), money is a significant source of family power. However, both neoclassical and Marxist economic theorists lost interest in seeing what actually happened to money once it entered the supposedly private household (Folbre, 1988). Cracking the boundaries of the family "sphere" has meant an increased recognition of how money moves into and within households and the significance of which person(s) earns, controls, redistributes, and spends it (Bergmann, 1986). The gender perspective suggests that the actual control over money and how it is used are important dimensions of power inside the household, and that gendered family norms are essential to understanding these dynamics.

Controlling Money

Earning money is not the same thing as controlling income (Blumberg, 1988). The increase in women's earnings and the decline in married women's economic dependency over the past few decades have been impressive (Sorenson and McLanahan, 1987). But while this trend has certainly contributed to increasing women's family power (Bergmann, 1986), a woman's status in the rest of society remains crucial for her ability to control even her own income (Acker, 1988). Although it seems evident that gendered ideas about family obligation guide the sharing of individual income within and between households, surprisingly little attention has been paid to money transactions among family members. The discovery of just how much money matters is one of the most exiting frontiers in feminist family scholarship today.

In the first place, recognition of the existence of conflicts over allocation of goods within families makes the very concept of "family income" problematic. Even within the same household, family members do not necessarily share the same standard of living (Pahl, 1980). In developing nations, this can produce differential mortality and malnutrition for girls and women (Dwyer and Bruce, 1988); increasing household income exacerbates these differentials, since boys and men get more of the increase (Blumberg, 1988; Sen, 1983). Policies that raise women's income do more to improve the nutrition of children in their families than those that increase the income of male family members (Blumberg, 1988; Dwyer and Bruce, 1988).

Few studies have been done of the intrahousehold economy in highly industrialized, affluent nations, but the limited evidence indicates gender differences in allocational rules and outcomes for everything from meat at meals (Charles and Kerr, 1987) to pocket money for personal expenditure (Wilson, 1987). Jan Pahl (1980) led the way in exploring this issue when she found women whose "family incomes" dropped substantially after leaving a battering spouse were reporting that their income "really" rose. The premise that family income is shared equally among all members is clearly wrong in these families and doubtful in others; to some unknown extent, poverty among women and children is disguised by their residing in a household with a man whose "adequate" income is not being shared with them (Pahl, 1980; cf. Brannen and Wilson, 1987).

Second, household allocation systems are being studied for how they incorporate and express gender. Pahl (1983) finds that wives are most likely to have financial control at the lowest absolute income levels, where money management means "allocating shortages" and forestalling creditors; when income is high enough to allow a surplus, husbands typically control it (Brannen and Wilson, 1987; Zelizer, 1989). Not all of

men's earnings go into a common pot; gender norms still demand that men have "spending money," no matter how tight things are. In addition, raises and bonuses are often seen by men as "their" money that might or might not get put into the household budget (Zelizer, 1989). All monies that enter the household are not equal, but carry normative meanings that allow them to be earmarked; thus, "women's" money often goes for child care or is labeled "pin money" and kept out of the household budget (Zelizer, 1989).

Evidence from developing countries (Dwyer and Bruce, 1988) about men's propensity to spend money on themselves and women's tendency to use their "personal" money to buy things for their children (from shoes to college) has not yet been followed up by systematic empirical research in the United States (but see Gerson and Andrews, 1990, on gender and spending on food). Even though women do the work of consumption, they do not necessarily control the priorities that guide it (Blumberg, 1988; Weinbaum and Bridges, 1976). Nonetheless, large-scale economic surveys in the United States continue to treat households as economic black boxes, forcing investigators to make unrealistic assumptions about equal distribution.

Considerably more work on what happens to women's and men's money once it enters a household is desperately needed. Social policy continues to be driven by the implausible assumptions that all family members are equally well-off, that above-poverty-line household incomes imply no below-poverty-level individuals within them, and that increasing total family income has the same effect if it derives from a rise in male or female income (Acker, 1988; Blumberg, 1988). When individual income is redistributed to family members in two or more households, as in child support payments after divorce, gross inequities appear (Arendell, 1987; Weitzman, 1985). Gender and generational inequities within one household are probably less, but we have no reason to believe they are not real and consequential.

Family Bargaining

Wage-earning is an important source of family power for contemporary women, even though such power is undercut by legal structures and social norms that give women less claim on money they earn (Blumberg and Coleman, 1989; Folbre, 1988; Weitzman, 1990). Since gendered expectations about housework and childrearing mean that the cost of "replacement" domestic services and child care will be "deducted" from women's earnings rather than men's (Brannen and Moss, 1987; Parr, 1987; Zelizer, 1989), already unequal wages are more unequal in their impact on family entitlements. When and how women use their position as income-earners to improve their position within the family are questions that are only beginning to receive the empirical investigation they deserve (e.g., Hertz, 1990; Weitzman, 1990).

The theoretical model of "new home economics" suggests that such bargaining can be understood by treating the family as a two-person firm in which market transactions occur "in an imagined way at imagined prices and imagined wages" (Sen, 1983: 17). This produces an idealized account of the good of the whole emerging from self-interested calculations in which all current social constraints are taken as givens (Acker, 1988; England, 1989). Thus, when women get less, this can be (tautologically) explained by noting that they are "worth" less outside the household; this rationalizes inequality rather than acknowledging that family members also discriminate and act unjustly.

The gender perspective suggests an alternative approach in which bargaining is seen as a process that carries gender meanings. Curtis (1986) and England (1989) point out women's economic disadvantages if they follow social rules (and value connection) but trade with partners who follow market rules (and seek only personal advantage). Although marriage norms often define social rules as applying to both husbands and wives, by gender norms, women are defined as social-rule followers and men as market-rule driven. This may now be changing, as women recognize their disadvantage under the "double standard" of exchange (Curtis, 1986) and as market models become more generally legitimate in regulating personal relationships (DiLeonardo, 1987; Hunt and Hunt, 1982).

Sen (1983) suggests a model of "cooperative conflict" in which active bargaining over the choice among a set of equally efficient cooperative arrangements takes place within changing societal parameters. In each marriage, some set of (gendered) social and market rules are chosen for a reason other than efficiency. Thus, a cooperative conflict approach tries to define the conditions under which reciprocity and altruism emerge, rather than insisting that they are always or never characteristic of families (DiLeonardo, 1987;

Folbre, 1983), and suggests that conflict over the nature of the rules themselves, not merely their application, underlies marital bargaining processes. When and how spouses apply particular rules of evaluation, and what the women and men gain and lose thereby, deserves further investigation.

In sum, as Hartmann (1981) points out, the family is a locus of struggle, not of uncontested male power. The image of a unitary "family income" disguises the continued significance of money in this process. Differences in gender and generational interests within the household are important, and control over income after it enters a household still matters. The limited research to date suggests that there is an internal allocation process that produces unequal outcomes for individual family members, depending on generation and gender, and that it is conditioned by the societal allocation of power and value outside the household. Because of the gender meanings of income and bargaining, the extent to which women's income earning increases their power and decreases dependency is not directly proportional to their wage levels.

CONCLUSION

The new gender perspective has shifted emphasis away from socialization and toward processes of categorization and stratification. Gender models also explicitly theorize the connection between structural and ideological levels of analysis. The family, as a cultural system of obligation, a "tangle of love and domination," is distinguished from the household, a locus of labor and economic struggle. Neither families nor households can be conceptualized as separate or solidary "spheres" of distinctive relationships; both family and household are ever more firmly situated in their specific historical context, in which they take on diverse forms and significance. Race and class are understood as significant structural features underlying the diversity of family forms (Baca Zinn, 1990). Although specific family roles are gendered, the phrase "gender role" is a theoretical self-contradiction, for there is no distinct and dichotomous "role" that uniquely embodies the variety of gender norms and meanings.

Gendered kinship relationships are not just dependent variables, affected by economic structures, although they are that, too. Rather, gendered family ties exert an independent influence upon the structure of work opportunities, definitions of skill, and wages received for both women and men. Indeed, in this new view, men as family members become far more visible than ever before. Rather than insisting on a dichotomous view of families as either solidary or oppressive, the gender model suggests that family relationships may be altruistic, or self-seeking, or carry an inseparable mix of motivations; that they may be simultaneously supportive and oppressive for women in relation to diverse others; that there is not one dimension of family power, but many (Blumberg and Coleman, 1989).

Because gender theory highlights both categorization and stratification as important dynamics, analyzing struggle over gender within families requires a more political vocabulary. Creative borrowing of ideas from studies of the workplace (e.g., "contested terrain" in Elbert, 1987) and politics (e.g., the "third dimension of power" in Komter, 1989) can help to understand gender stratification processes within the family context. In a gender model, women as individual actors, agents with interests that are distinctive and meaningful, emerge out of history's shadows. Children as actors, negotiating identities, doing work (paid and unpaid), and contending for power, can be better conceptualized in this framework as well (Thorne, 1986b). The feminist perspective redefines families as arenas of gender and generational struggles, crucibles of caring and conflict, where claims for an identity are rooted, and separateness and solidarity are continually created and contested. Using a gender perspective to shatter such artificial dichotomies as work and home, money and love, self-interest and altruism, as well as their conventional associations with masculinity and femininity, may now begin to move family studies beyond separate spheres.

ACKNOWLEDGMENTS

Thanks are extended to Linda Haas, Beth Hess, Mary Alice Neubeck, Marie Withers Osmond, Jane Riblett Wilkie, Maxine Baca Zinn, all the members of the Women and Work Group, and two anonymous reviewers for their many helpful suggestions, and to the National Science Foundation, Grant No. SES 88-11944, which provided some support for the preparation of this article.

REFERENCES

Abel, Emily. 1986. "Adult daughters and care for the elderly." Feminist Studies 12:479–493.

Acker, Joan. 1988. "Class, gender, and the relations of distribution." Signs 13:473–497.

Andersen Margaret. 1990. "Feminism and the American family ideal." Journal of Comparative Family Studies. Forthcoming.

Arendell, Terry. 1987. "Women and the economics of divorce in the contemporary United States." Signs 13:121–135.

Baca Zinn, Maxine. 1989. "Family, race and poverty in the eighties." Signs 14:856–874.

Baca Zinn, Maxine. 1990. "Family, feminism and race in America." Gender and Society 4:68–82.

Beechey, Veronica. 1988. "Rethinking the definition of work: Gender and work." In J. Jenson, E. Hagen, and C. Reddy (eds.), Feminization of the Labor Force. New York: Oxford University Press.

Bem, Sandra. 1983. "Gender-schema theory and its implications for child development." Signs 8:598–616.

Benenson, Harold. 1984. "Women's occupational and family achievement in the U.S. class system." British Journal of Sociology 35:19–41.

Beneria, Lourdes, and Catherine Stimpson (eds.). 1987. Women, Households, and the Economy. New Brunswick, NJ: Rutgers University Press.

Benin, Mary, and Joan Agostinelli. 1988. "Husbands' and wives' satisfaction with the division of labor." Journal of Marriage and the Family 50:349–361.

Bergmann, Barbara. 1986. The Economic Emergence of Women. New York: Basic Books.

Berk, Sarah Fenstermaker. 1985. The Gender Factory: The

Apportionment of Work in American Households. New York: Plenum.

Bernard, Jessie. 1981. "The good provider role: Its rise and fall." American Psychologist 36:1–12.

Blumberg, Rae Lesser. 1988. "Income under female versus male control: Hypotheses from a theory of gender stratification and data from the Third World." Journal of Family Issues 9:51–84.

Blumberg, Rae Lesser, and Marion Coleman. 1989. "A theoretical look at the gender balance of power in American couples." Journal of Family Issues 10:225–250.

Bose, Christine. 1987a. "Devaluing women's work: The undercount of women's employment in 1900 and 1980." In C. Bose, R. Feldberg, and N. Sokoloff (eds.), Hidden Aspects of Women's Work. New York: Praeger.

Bose, Christine. 1987b. "Dual spheres." In Beth Hess and Myra Marx Ferree (eds.), Analyzing Gender. Beverly Hills, CA: Sage.

Boxer, Marilyn, and Jean Quataert. 1987. Connecting Spheres: Women in the Western World, 1500 to the Present. New York: Oxford University Press.

Brannen, Julia, and Peter Moss. 1987. "Dual earner households: Women's contributions after the birth of the first child." In Julia Brannen and Gail Wilson (eds.), Give and Take in Families: Studies in Resource Distribution. Boston: Allen and Unwin.

Brannen, Julia, and Gail Wilson (eds.). 1987. Give and Take in Families: Studies in Resource Distribution. Boston: Allen and Unwin.

Breines, Wini. 1986. "The 1950s: Gender and some social science." Sociological Inquiry 56:69–92.

Breines, Wini, and Linda Gordon. 1983. "The new scholarship on family violence." Signs 8:490–531.

Brown, Clair Vickery. 1982. "Home production for use in a market economy." In Barrie Thorne with Marilyn Yalom (eds.), Rethinking the Family: Some Feminist Questions. New York: Longman.

Brush, Lisa D. 1990. "Violent acts and injurious outcomes in married couples." Gender and Society 4:56–67.

Caplan, Paula, and Ian Hall-McCorquodale. 1985. "Mother-blaming in major clinical journals." American Journal of Orthopsychiatry 55:345–357.

Carrigan, Tim, Bob Connell, and John Lee. 1987. "Toward a new sociology of masculinity." In Harry Brod (ed.), The Making of Masculinities. Boston: Unwin Hyman.

Charles, Nicola, and Marion Kerr. 1987. "Just the way it is: Gender and age differences in food consumption." In Julia Brannen and Gail Wilson (eds.), Give and Take in Families: Studies in Resource Distribution. Boston: Allen and Unwin.

Ciancanelli, Penelope, and Bettina Berch. 1987. "Gender and the GNP." In Beth Hess and Myra Marx Ferree (eds.), Analyzing Gender. Beverly Hills, CA: Sage.

Coleman, Marion Tolbert. 1988. "The division of household labor: Suggestions for future empirical consideration and theoretical development." Journal of Family Issues 9:132–147.

Collins, Patricia Hill. 1989. "A comparison of two works on black family life." Signs 14:275–284.

Connell, Robert W. 1985. "Theorizing gender." Sociology 19:260–272.

Coverman, Shelley. 1983. "Gender, domestic labor time, and wage inequality." American Sociological Review 48:623–637.

Cowan, Ruth Schwartz. 1983. More Work for Mother. New York: Basic Books.

Crosby, Faye (ed.). 1987. Spouse, Parent, Worker. New Haven, CT: Yale University Press.

Curtis, Richard. 1986. "Household and family in theory on inequality." American Sociological Review 51:168–183.

Daniels, Arlene Kaplan. 1989. Invisible Careers: Women Civic Leaders. Chicago: University of Chicago Press.

Davidoff, Lenore, and Catherine Hall. 1987. Family Fortunes: Men and Women of the English Middle Class, 1780–1850. Chicago: University of Chicago Press.

Deacon, Desley. 1985. "Political arithmetic: The nineteenth century Australian census and the construction of the dependent woman." Signs 11:27–47.

Deaux, Kay, and Mary Kite. 1987. "Thinking about gender." In Beth Hess and Myra Marx Ferree (eds.), Analyzing Gender. Beverly Hills, CA: Sage.

Delphy, Christine, and Diane Leonard. 1986. "Class analysis, gender analysis and the family." In Rosemary Crompton and Michael Mann (eds.), Gender and Stratification. New York: Basil Blackwell.

DeVault, Marjorie. 1990. "Conflict over housework: A problem that (still) has no name." In L. Kriesberg (ed.), Research in Social Movements, Conflict, and Change. Greenwich, CT: JAI Press.

DiLeonardo, Micaela. 1987. "The female world of cards and holidays: Women, families, and the work of kinship." Signs 12:440–453.

Dill, Bonnie Thornton. 1988. "Our mothers' grief: Racial/ethnic women and the maintenance of families." Journal of Family History 13:415–431.

Dwyer, Judith, and Daisy Bruce (eds.). 1988. A Home Divided: Women and Income in the Third World. Stanford, CA: Stanford University Press.

Elbert, Sarah. 1987. "The farmer takes a wife: Women in America's farming families." In Lourdes Beneria and Catherine Stimpson (eds.), Women, Households, and the Economy. New Brunswick, NJ: Rutgers University Press.

England, Paula. 1989. "Rational choice models and feminist critiques: Implications for sociology." American Sociologist 20:14–28.

Feldberg, Roslyn, and Evelyn Nakano Glenn. 1979. "Male and female: Job versus gender models in the sociology of work." Social Problems 26:5524–5538.

Ferree, Myra Marx. 1984. "The view from below: Women's employment and gender equality in working class families." In Beth Hess and Marvin Sussman (eds.), Women and the Family: Two Decades of Change. New York: Haworth Press.

Ferree, Myra Marx. 1987. "The struggles of superwoman." In C. Bose, R. Feldberg, and N. Sokoloff (eds.), Hidden Aspects of Women's Work. New York: Praeger.

Ferree, Myra Marx. 1988. "Negotiating household roles and responsibilities: Resistance, conflict, and change." Paper presented at annual meeting of the National Council on Family Relations.

Ferree, Myra Marx. 1990. "The gender division of labor in two-earner marriages: Dimensions of variability and change." Paper presented at the annual meeting of the Eastern Sociological Society.

Finch, Janet. 1983. Married to the Job: Wives' Incorporation into Men's Work. London: Allen and Unwin.

Folbre, Nancy. 1983. "Of patriarchy born: The political economy of fertility decisions." Feminist Studies 9:261–284.

Folbre, Nancy. 1988. "The black four of hearts: Toward a new paradigm of household economics." In Judith Dwyer and Daisy Bruce, A Home Divided: Women and Income in the Third World. Stanford, CA: Stanford University Press.

Fowlkes, Martha. 1980. Behind Every Successful Man. New York: Columbia University Press.

Friedan, Betty. 1963. The Feminine Mystique. New York: Dell.

Geerken, Michael, and W. Gove. 1983. At Home and at Work. Beverly Hills, CA: Sage.

Gerson, Judith, and Margaret Andrews. 1990. "Household food budgets: Analyzing familial resources and power." Paper presented at the annual meeting of the Eastern Sociological Society.

Gerson, Judith, and Kathy Peiss. 1985. "Boundaries, negotiations, consciousness: Reconceptualizing gender relations." Social Problems 32:317–331.

Gerson, Kathleen. 1985. Hard Choices. Berkeley: University of California Press.

Gerstel, Naomi, and Harriet Engel Gross (eds.). 1987. Families and Work. Philadelphia: Temple University Press.

Glazer, Nona. 1988. "Overlooked, overworked: Women's unpaid and paid work in the health services' 'cost crisis'." International Journal of Health Services 18:119–137.

Glenn, Evelyn Nakano. 1985. "Racial ethnic women's labor: The intersection of race, gender, and class oppression." Review of Radical Political Economics 17:86–109.

Glenn, Evelyn Nakano. 1986. Issei, Nisei, Warbride. Philadelphia: Temple University Press.

Glenn, Evelyn Nakano. 1987. "Gender and the family." In Beth Hess and Myra Marx Ferree (eds.), Analyzing Gender. Beverly Hills, CA: Sage.

Goldscheider, Frances, and Linda Waite. 1989. "The domestic economy: Husbands, wives, children." Paper presented at annual meeting of the American Sociological Association.

Goode, William J. 1982. "Why men resist." In Barrie Thorne with Marilyn Yalom (eds.), Rethinking the Family: Some Feminist Questions. New York: Longman.

Graham, Hilary. 1987. "Being poor: Perceptions and strategies of lone mothers." In Julia Brannen and Gail Wilson (eds.), Give and Take in Families: Studies in Resource Distribution. Boston: Allen and Unwin.

Haas, Linda. 1986. "Wives' orientation to breadwinning." Journal of Family Issues 7:358–381.

Hareven, Tamara. 1982. Family Time and Industrial Time. Cambridge, MA: Harvard University Press.

Harrison, Michelle. 1987. "Social construction of Mary Beth Whitehead." Gender and Society 1:300–311.

Hartmann, Heidi. 1981. "The family as the locus of gender, class, and political struggle: The example of housework." Signs 6:366–394.

Hertz, Rosanna. 1986. More Equal than Others. Berkeley: University of California Press.

Hertz, Rosanna. 1990. "Financial arrangements among dual-earner couples." Paper presented at the annual meeting of the American Sociological Association.

Hess, Beth B. 1989. "Beyond dichotomy: Making distinctions and recognizing differences." Presidential address at the annual meeting of the Eastern Sociological Society.

Hewlett, Sylvia. 1986. A Lesser Life. New York: Morrow.

Hochschild, Arlie, with Anne Machung. 1989. The Second Shift. New York: Viking.

Hood, Jane. 1983. Becoming a Two-Job Family. New York: Praeger.

Hood, Jane. 1986. "The provider role: Its meaning and measurement." Journal of Marriage and the Family 48:349–359.

Huber, Joan, and Glenna Spitze. 1983. Sex Stratification: Children, Housework, Jobs. New York: Academic Press.

Hunt, Janet, and Larry Hunt. 1982. "Male resistance to role symmetry in dual-earner households." In Naomi Gerstel and Harriet Engel Gross (eds.), Families and Work. Philadelphia: Temple University Press.

Hunt, Janet, and Larry Hunt. 1982. "The dualities of careers and families: New integrations or new polarizations?" Social Problems 29:499–510.

Jagger, Alison. 1983. Feminist Politics and Human Nature. Totowa, NJ: Rowman and Allenheld.

Joffe, Carol. 1973. "Taking young children seriously." In Norman Denzin (ed.), Children and Their Caretakers. New Brunswick, NJ: Transaction Books.

Jones, Jacqueline. 1984. Labor of Love, Labor of Sorrow: Black Women, Work, and Family from Slavery to the Present. New York: Basic Books.

Kaplan, Elaine Bell. 1987. "'I don't do no windows': Competition between the domestic worker and the housewife." In Valerie Miner and Helen Longino (eds.), Competition: A Feminist Taboo? New York: Feminist Press.

Kessler-Harris, Alice. 1982. Out to Work: A History of Wage-Earning Women in the United States. New York: Oxford University Press.

Kimmel, Michael. 1987. "The contemporary crisis of 'masculinity' in historical perspective." In Harry Brod (ed.), The Making of Masculinities. Boston: Unwin Hyman.

Kleinegger, Christine. 1987. "Out of the barns and into the kitchens." In Barbara D. Wright et al. (eds.), Women, Work, and Technology. Ann Arbor: University of Michigan Press.

Komter, Aafke. 1989. "Hidden power in marriage." Gender and Society 3:187–216.

Lasch, Christopher. 1977. Haven in a Heartless World. New York: Basic Books.

Lopata, Helena, and Barrie Thorne. 1978. "On the term 'sex roles'." Signs 718–721.

Luxton, Meg. 1980. More than a Labour of Love: Three Generations of Women's Work in the Home. Toronto: Women's Press.

Maret, Elizabeth, and Barbara Finlay. 1984. "The distribution of household labor among women in dual earner families." Journal of Marriage and the Family 357–364.

Matthaei, Julie. 1982. An Economic History of Women in America. New York: Schocken Books.

May, Martha. 1987. "The historical problem of the family wage: The Ford Motor Company and the five-dollar day." In Naomi Gerstel and Harriet Engel Gross (eds.), Families and Work. Philadelphia: Temple University Press.

Michelson, William. 1985. From Sun to Sun. Totowa, NJ: Rowman and Allenheld.

Moeller, Robert. 1989. "Reconstructing the family in reconstruction Germany: Women and social policy, 1949–55." Feminist Studies 137–169.

Moen, Phyllis. 1989. Working Parents. Madison: University of Wisconsin Press.

Nelson, Margaret. 1988. "Providing family daycare: An analysis of home-based work." Social Problems 35:78–94.

Nelson, Margaret. 1989. "Negotiating care: Relationships between family daycare providers and mothers." Feminist Studies 15: 7–34.

Osmond, Marie Withers, and Barrie Thorne. 1990. "Feminist theories: The social construction of gender in families and society." In Pauline Boss et al. (eds.), Sourcebook of Family Theories and Methods. New York: Plenum.

Ostrander, Susan. 1984. Women of the Upper Class. Philadelphia: Temple University Press.

Pahl, Jan. 1980. "Patterns of money management within marriage." Journal of Social Policy 9:313–335.

Pahl, Jan. 1983. "The allocation of money and the structuring of inequality within marriage." Sociological Review 31:237–262.

Paoletti, Jo. 1987. "Clothing and gender in America, 1890–1920." Signs 13:136–143.

Papanek, Hanna. 1973. "Men, women, and work: Reflections on the two-person career." In Joan Huber (ed.), Changing Women in a Changing Society. Chicago: University of Chicago Press.

Parr, Joy. 1987. "Re-thinking work and kinship in a Canadian hosiery town, 1910–1950." Feminist Studies 13:137–162.

Pleck, Joseph. 1977. "The work-family role system." Social Problems 24:417–427.

Pleck, Joseph. 1985. Working Wives/Working Husbands. Beverly Hills, CA: Sage.

Pleck, Joseph. 1987. "The theory of male sex role identity: Its rise and fall, 1936 to the present." In Harry Brod (ed.), The Making of Masculinities. Boston: Allen and Unwin.

Potucheck, Jean. 1989. "Employed wives' orientation to the breadwinner role." Paper presented at the annual meeting of the American Sociological Association.

Rainwater, Lee. 1979. "Mothers' contribution to the family money economy in Europe and the United States." Journal of Family History 4:198–211.

Rapp, Rayna. 1982. "Family and class in contemporary America." In Barrie Thorne with Marilyn Yalom (eds.), Rethinking the Family: Some Feminist Questions. New York: Longman.

Reskin, Barbara. 1988. "Bringing the men back in: Sex differentiation and the devaluation of women's work." Gender and Society 2:58–81.

Risman, Barbara. 1987. "Intimate relationships from a microstructural perspective: Men who mother." Gender and Society 1:6–32.

Rollins, Judith. 1985. Between Women. Philadelphia: Temple University Press.

Romero, Mary. 1988. "Sisterhood and domestic service: Race, class, and gender in the mistress-maid relationship." Humanity and Society 12:318–346.

Ross, Catherine, John Mirowsky, and Joan Huber. 1983. "Dividing work, sharing work, and in-between." American Sociological Review 48:809–823.

Rothman, Barbara Katz. 1989. "Women as fathers: Motherhood and childcare under a modified patriarchy." Gender and Society 3:89–104.

Rubin, Gayle. 1975. "The traffic in women: Notes on the 'political economy' of sex." In R. Reiter (ed.), Toward an Anthropology of Women. New York: Monthly Review Press.

Ryan, Mary. 1981. Cradle of the Middle Class: Family in Oneida County, New York, 1790–1865. New York: Cambridge University Press.

Saraceno, Chiara. 1984. "Shifts in public and private boundaries: Women as mothers and service workers in Italian daycare." Feminist Studies 10: 7–30.

Schwartz, Felice. 1989. "Management women and the new facts of life." Harvard Business Review 67:65–76.

Scott, Joan. 1986. "Gender: A useful category of historical analysis." American Historical Review 91:1053–1075.

Sen, Amartya. 1983. "Economics and the family." Asian Development Review 1:14–26.

Shelton, Beth Anne, and Juanita Firestone. 1989. "Household labor time and the gender gap in earnings." Gender and Society 3:105–112.

Smith, Dorothy. 1987a. The Everyday World as Problematic. Boston: Northeastern University Press.

Smith, Dorothy. 1987b. "Women's inequality and the family." In Naomi Gerstel and Harriet Engel Gross (eds.), Families and Work. Philadelphia: Temple University Press.

Sorenson, Annemette, and Sarah McLanahan. 1987. "Married women's economic dependency, 1940–1980." American Journal of Sociology 93:659–687.

Spitze, Glenna. 1988. "Women's employment and family relations: A review." Journal of Marriage and the Family 50:595–618.

Stacey, Judith, and Barrie Thorne. 1985. "The missing feminist revolution in sociology." Social Problems 32:301–316.

Stack, Carol. 1974. All Our Kin. New York: Harper and Row.

Stack, Carol. 1989. "Kinscripts." Paper delivered at the conference, Status Passages and Risks in a Life Course Perspective, University of Bremen, West Germany.

Strasser, Susan. 1982. Never Done: A History of American Housework. New York: Pantheon.

Taylor, Verta, and Kelly McCormick. 1989. "Breaking the emotional rules of motherhood: The experience of postpartum depression." Paper presented at the annual meeting of the American Sociological Association.

Thompson, Linda, and Alexis Walker. 1989. "Gender in families: Women and men in marriage, work, and parenthood." Journal of Marriage and the Family 51:845–871.

Thorne, Barrie. 1986a. "Girls and boys together . . . but mostly apart: Gender arrangements in elementary schools." In W. Hartup and Z. Rubin (eds.), Relationships and Development. Hillsdale, NJ: Erlbaum.

Thorne, Barrie. 1986b. "Re-visioning women and social change: Where are the children?" Gender and Society 1:85–109.

Thorne, Barrie, with Marilyn Yalom (eds.). 1982. Rethinking the Family: Some Feminist Questions. New York: Longman.

Tiano, Susan. 1987. "Gender, work, and world capitalism: Third World women's role in development." In Beth Hess and Myra Marx Ferree (eds.), Analyzing Gender. Beverly Hills, CA: Sage.

Tilly, Louise, and Joan Scott. 1978. Women, Work, and Family. New York: Holt, Rinehart and Winston.

Tong, Rosemarie. 1989. Feminist Thought: A Comprehensive Introduction. San Francisco: Westview.

Turbin, Carole. 1987. "Reconceptualizing family, work, and labor organizing: Working Women in Troy, 1860–1890." In C. Bose, R. Feldberg, and N. Sokoloff (eds.), Hidden Aspects of Women's Work. New York: Praeger.

Vannoy-Hiller, Dana, and William Philliber. 1989. Equal Partners. Beverly Hills, CA: Sage.

Weinbaum, Batya, and Amy Bridges. 1976. "The other side of the paycheck: Monopoly capital and the structure of consumption." Monthly Review 28(3):88–103.

Weiss, Robert. 1987. "Men and their wives' work." In Faye Crosby (ed.), Spouse, Parent, Worker. New Haven, CT: Yale University Press.

Weitzman, Lenore. 1985. The Divorce Revolution. New York: Free Press.

Weitzman, Lenore. 1990. "Legal rules vs. norms of justice: The allocation of money and property in the family." Paper presented at the annual meeting of the American Sociological Association.

West, Candace, and Don Zimmerman. 1987. "Doing gender." Gender and Society 1:125–151.

White, Lynn, and David Brinkerhoff. 1981. "The sexual division of labor: Evidence from childhood." Social Forces 60:170–181.

Wilson, Gail. 1987. "Money: Patterns of responsibility and irresponsibility in marriage." In Julia Brannen and Gail Wilson (eds.), Give and Take in Families: Studies in Resource Distribution. Boston: Allen and Unwin.

Wittner, Judith. 1980. "Domestic labor as work discipline." In Sarah Fenstermaker Berk (ed), Women and Household Labor. Beverly Hills, CA: Sage.

Zavella, Patricia. 1987. Women's Work and Chicano Families. Ithaca, NY: Cornell University Press.

Zelizer, Viviana. 1989. "The social meaning of money: 'Special monies'." American Journal of Sociology 95:342–377.

READING 25

The Second Shift:
Working Parents and the Revolution at Home

ARLIE HOCHSCHILD

She is not the same woman in each magazine advertisement, but she is the same idea. She has that working-mother look as she strides forward, briefcase in one hand, smiling child in the other. Literally and figuratively, she is moving ahead. Her hair, if long, tosses behind her; if it is short, it sweeps back at the sides, suggesting mobility and progress. There is nothing shy or passive about her. She is confident, active, "liberated." She wears a dark tailored suit, but with a silk bow or colorful frill that says, "I'm really feminine underneath." She has made it in a man's world without sacrificing her femininity. And she has done this on her own. By some personal miracle, this image suggests, she has managed to combine what 150 years of industrialization have split wide apart—child and job, frill and suit, female culture and male.

When I showed a photograph of a supermom like this to the working mothers I talked to . . . many responded with an outright laugh. One daycare worker and mother of two, ages three and five, threw back her head: "Ha! They've got to be *kidding* about her. Look at me, hair a mess, nails jagged, twenty pounds overweight. Mornings, I'm getting my kids dressed, the dog fed, the lunches made, the shopping list done. That lady's got a maid." Even working mothers who did have maids couldn't imagine combining work and family in such a carefree way. "Do you know what a baby *does* to your life, the two o'clock feedings, the four o'clock feedings?" Another mother of two said: "They don't show it, but she's whistling"—she imitated a

whistling woman, eyes to the sky—"so she can't hear the din." They envied the apparent ease of the woman with the flying hair, but she didn't remind them of anyone they knew.

The women I interviewed—lawyers, corporate executives, word processors, garment pattern cutters, daycare workers—and most of their husbands, too—felt differently about some issues: how right it is for a mother of young children to work a full-time job, or how much a husband should be responsible for the home. But they all agreed that it was hard to work two full-time jobs and raise young children.

How well do couples do it? The more women work outside the home, the more central this question. The number of women in paid work has risen steadily since before the turn of the century, but since 1950 the rise has been staggering. In 1950, 30 percent of American women were in the labor force; in 1986, it was 55 percent. In 1950, 28 percent of married women with children between six and seventeen worked outside the home; in 1986, it had risen to 68 percent. In 1950, 23 percent of married women with children under six worked. By 1986, it had grown to 54 percent. We don't know how many women with children under the age of one worked outside the home in 1950; it was so rare that the Bureau of Labor kept no statistics on it. Today half of such women do. Two-thirds of all mothers are now in the labor force; in fact, more mothers have paid jobs (or are actively looking for one) than nonmothers. Because of this change in women, two-job families now make up 58 percent of all married couples with children.[1]

Since an increasing number of working women have small children, we might expect an increase in part-

From *The Second Shift* by Arlie Hochschild and Ann Machung. Copyright © 1989 by Arlie Hochschild. Used by permission of Viking Penguin, a division of Penguin Books USA Inc.

time work. But actually, 67 percent of the mothers who work have full-time jobs—that is, thirty-five hours or more weekly. That proportion is what it was in 1959.

If more mothers of young children are stepping into full-time jobs outside the home, and if most couples can't afford household help, how much more are fathers doing at home? As I began exploring this question I found many studies on the hours working men and women devote to housework and childcare. One national random sample of 1,243 working parents in forty-four American cities, conducted in 1965–66 by Alexander Szalai and his coworkers, for example, found that working women averaged three hours a day on housework while men averaged 17 minutes; women spent fifty minutes a day of time exclusively with their children; men spent twelve minutes. On the other side of the coin, working fathers watched television an hour longer than their working wives, and slept a half hour longer each night. A comparison of this American sample with eleven other industrial countries in Eastern and Western Europe revealed the same difference between working women and working men in those countries as well.[2] In a 1983 study of white middle-class families in greater Boston, Grace Baruch and R. C. Barnett found that working men married to working women spent only three-quarters of an hour longer each week with their kindergarten-aged children than did men married to housewives.[3]

Szalai's landmark study documented the now familiar but still alarming story of the working woman's "double day," but it left me wondering how men and women actually felt about all this. He and his coworkers studied how people used time, but not, say, how a father felt about his twelve minutes with his child, or how his wife felt about it. Szalai's study revealed the visible surface of what I discovered to be a set of deeply emotional issues: What should a man and woman contribute to the family? How appreciated does each feel? How does each respond to subtle changes in the balance of marital power? How does each develop an unconscious "gender strategy" for coping with the work at home, with marriage, and, indeed, with life itself? These were the underlying issues.

But I began with the measurable issue of time. Adding together the time it takes to do a paid job and to do housework and childcare, I averaged estimates from the major studies on time use done in the 1960s and 1970s, and discovered that women worked roughly fifteen hours longer each week than men. Over a year, they worked an *extra month of twenty-four-hour days a year*. Over a dozen years, it was an extra year of twenty-four-hour days. Most women without children spend much more time than men on housework; with children, they devote more time to both housework and childcare. Just as there is a wage gap between men and women in the workplace, there is a "leisure gap" between them at home. Most women work one shift at the office or factory and a "second shift" at home.

Studies show that working mothers have higher self-esteem and get less depressed than housewives, but compared to their husbands, they're more tired and get sick more often. In Peggy Thoits's 1985 analysis of two large-scale surveys, each of about a thousand men and women, people were asked how often in the preceding week they'd experienced each of twenty-three symptoms of anxiety (such as dizziness or hallucinations). According to the researchers' criteria, working mothers were more likely than any other group to be "anxious."

In light of these studies, the image of the woman with the flying hair seems like an upbeat "cover" for a grim reality, like those pictures of Soviet tractor drivers smiling radiantly into the distance as they think about the ten-year plan. The Szalai study was conducted in 1965–66. I wanted to know whether the leisure gap he found in 1965 persists, or whether it has disappeared. Since most married couples work two jobs, since more will in the future, since most wives in these couples work the extra month a year, I wanted to understand what the wife's extra month a year meant for each person, and what it does for love and marriage in an age of high divorce.

MY RESEARCH

With my research associates Anne Machung and Elaine Kaplan, I interviewed fifty couples very intensively, and I observed in a dozen homes. We first began interviewing artisans, students, and professionals in Berkeley, California, in the late 1970s. This was at the height of the women's movement, and many of these couples were earnestly and self-consciously struggling to modernize the ground rules of their marriages. Enjoying flexible job schedules and intense cultural support to do so, many succeeded. Since their circumstances were unusual they became our "comparison group" as we sought other couples more typical of mainstream America. In 1980 we located more typical couples by sending a questionnaire on work and family life to every thirteenth name—from top to bottom—of the personnel roster of a large, urban manufacturing company. At the end of the questionnaire, we asked members of working couples raising children under six and working full time jobs if they would be willing to talk to us in greater depth. Interviewed from 1980 through 1988, these couples, their neighbors and friends, their children's teachers, daycare workers and baby-sitters, form the heart of this [analysis].

When we called them, a number of baby-sitters replied as one woman did, "You're interviewing us? Good. We're human too." Or another, "I'm glad you consider what we do work. A lot of people don't." As it turned out, many daycare workers were themselves juggling two jobs and small children, and so we talked to them about that, too.

We also talked with other men and women who were not part of two-job couples; divorced parents who were war-weary veterans of two-job marriages, and traditional couples, to see how much of the strain we were seeing was unique to two-job couples.

I also watched daily life in a dozen homes during a weekday evening, during the week-end, and during the months that followed, when I was invited on outings, to dinner, or just to talk. I found myself waiting on the front doorstep as weary parents and hungry children tumbled out of the family car. I shopped with them, visited friends, watched television, ate with them, walked through parks, and came along when they dropped their children at daycare, often staying on at the baby-sitter's house after parents waved good-bye. In their homes, I sat on the living-room floor and drew pictures and played house with the children. I watched as parents gave them baths, read bedtime stories, and said good night. Most couples tried to bring me into the family scene, inviting me to eat with them and talk. I responded if they spoke to me, from time to time asked questions, but I rarely initiated conversations. I tried to become as unobtrusive as a family dog. Often I would base myself in the living room, quietly taking notes. Sometimes I would follow a wife upstairs or down, accompany a child on her way out to "help Dad" fix the car, or watch television with the other watchers. Sometimes I would break out of my peculiar role to join in the jokes they often made about acting like the "model" two-job couple. Or perhaps the joking was a subtle part of my role, to put them at ease so

they could act more naturally. For a period of two to five years, I phoned or visited these couples to keep in touch even as I moved on to study the daily lives of other working couples—black, Chicano, white, from every social class and walk of life.

I asked who did how much of a wide variety of household tasks. I asked who cooks? Vacuums? Makes the beds? Sews? Cares for plants? Sends Christmas or Hanukkah cards? I also asked: Who washes the car? Repairs household appliances? Does the taxes? Tends the yard? I asked who did most household planning, who noticed such things as when a child's fingernails need clipping, cared more how the house looked or about the change in a child's mood.

INSIDE THE EXTRA MONTH A YEAR

The women I interviewed seemed to be far more deeply torn between the demands of work and family than were their husbands. They talked with more animation and at greater length than their husbands about the abiding conflict between them. Busy as they were, women more often brightened at the idea of yet another interviewing session. They felt the second shift was *their* issue and most of their husbands agreed. When I telephoned one husband to arrange an interview with him, explaining that I wanted to ask him about how he managed work and family life, he replied genially, "Oh, this will *really* interest my *wife.*"

It was a woman who first proposed to me the metaphor, borrowed from industrial life, of the "second shift." She strongly resisted the *idea* that homemaking was a "shift." Her family was her life and she didn't want it reduced to a job. But as she put it, "You're on duty at work. You come home, and you're on duty. Then you go back to work and you're on duty." After eight hours of adjusting insurance claims, she came home to put on the rice for dinner, care for her children, and wash laundry. Despite herself her home life *felt* like a second shift. That was the real story and that was the real problem.

Men who shared the load at home seemed just as pressed for time as their wives, and as torn between the demands of career and small children. . . . But the majority of men did not share the load at home. Some refused outright. Others refused more passively, often offering a loving shoulder to lean on, an understanding ear as their working wife faced the conflict they both saw as hers. At first it seemed to me that the problem of the second shift was hers. But I came to realize that those husbands who helped very little at home were often indirectly just as deeply affected as their wives by the need to do that work, through the resentment their wives feel toward them, and through their need to steel themselves against that resentment. Evan Holt, a warehouse furniture salesman . . . did very little housework and played with his four-year-old son, Joey, at his convenience. Juggling the demands of work with family at first seemed a problem for his wife. But Evan himself suffered enormously from the side effects of "her" problem. His wife did the second shift, but she resented it keenly, and half-consciously expressed her frustration and rage by losing interest in sex and becoming overly absorbed with Joey. One way or another, most men I talked with do suffer the severe repercussions of what I think is a transitional phase in American family life.

One reason women take a deeper interest than men in the problems of juggling work with family life is that even when husbands happily shared the hours of work, their wives felt more *responsible* for home and children. More women kept track of doctors' appointments and arranged for playmates to come over. More mothers than fathers worried about the tail on a child's Halloween costume or a birthday present for a school friend. They were more likely to think about their children while at work and to check in by phone with the baby-sitter.

Partly because of this, more women felt torn between one sense of urgency and another, between the need to soothe a child's fear of being left at daycare, and the need to show the boss she's "serious" at work. More women than men questioned how good they were as parents, or if they did not, they questioned why they weren't questioning it. More often than men, women alternated between living in their ambition and standing apart from it.

As masses of women have moved into the economy, families have been hit by a "speed-up" in work and family life. There is no more time in the day than there was when wives stayed home, but there is twice as much to get done. It is mainly women who absorb this "speed-up." Twenty percent of the men in my study shared housework equally. Seventy percent of men did a substantial amount (less than half but more than a third), and 10 percent did less than a third. Even when couples share more equitably in the work at home,

women do two-thirds of the *daily* jobs at home, like cooking and cleaning up—jobs that fix them into a rigid routine. Most women cook dinner and most men change the oil in the family car. But, as one mother pointed out, dinner needs to be prepared every evening around six o'clock, whereas the car oil needs to be changed every six months, any day around that time, any time that day. Women do more childcare than men, and men repair more household appliances. A child needs to be tended daily while the repair of household appliances can often wait "until I have time." Men thus have more control over *when* they make their contributions than women do. They may be very busy with family chores but, like the executive who tells his secretary to "hold my calls," the man has more control over his time. The job of the working mother, like that of the secretary, is usually to "take the calls."

Another reason women may feel more strained than men is that women more often do two things at once—for example, write checks and return phone calls, vacuum and keep an eye on a three-year-old, fold laundry and think out the shopping list. Men more often cook dinner *or* take a child to the park. Indeed, women more often juggle three spheres—job, children, and housework—while most men juggle two—job and children. For women, two activities compete with their time with children, not just one.

Beyond doing more at home, women also devote *proportionately more* of their time at home to housework and proportionately less of it to childcare. Of all the time men spend working at home, more of it goes to childcare. That is, working wives spend relatively more time "mothering the house"; husbands spend more time "mothering" the children. Since most parents prefer to tend to their children than clean house, men do more of what they'd rather do. More men than women take their children on "fun" outings to the park, the zoo, the movies. Women spend more time on maintenance, feeding and bathing children, enjoyable activities to be sure, but often less leisurely or "special" than going to the zoo. Men also do fewer of the "undesirable" household chores: fewer men than women wash toilets and scrub the bathroom.

As a result, women tend to talk more intently about being overtired, sick, and "emotionally drained." Many women I could not tear away from the topic of sleep. They talked about how much they could "get by on" . . . six and a half, seven, seven and a half, less, more. They talked about who they knew who needed more or less. Some apologized for how much sleep they needed—"I'm afraid I need eight hours of sleep"—as if eight was "too much." They talked about the effect of a change in baby-sitter, the birth of a second child, or a business trip on their child's pattern of sleep. They talked about how to avoid fully waking up when a child called them at night, and how to get back to sleep. These women talked about sleep the way a hungry person talks about food.

All in all, if in this period of American history, the two-job family is suffering from a speed up of work and family life, working mothers are its primary victims. It is ironic, then, that often it falls to women to be the "time and motion expert" of family life. Watching inside homes, I noticed it was often the mother who rushed children, saying, "Hurry up! It's time to go," "Finish your cereal now," "You can do that later," "Let's go!" When a bath is crammed into a slot between 7:45 and 8:00 it was often the mother who called out, "Let's see who can take their bath the quickest!" Often a younger child will rush out, scurrying to be first in bed, while the older and wiser one stalls, resistant, sometimes resentful: "Mother is always rushing us." Sadly enough, women are more often the lightning rods for family aggressions aroused by the speed-up of work and family life. They are the "villains" in a process of which they are also the primary victims. More than the longer hours, the sleeplessness, and feeling torn, this is the saddest cost to women of the extra month a year. . . .

NOTES

1. U.S. Bureau of Labor Statistics, *Employment and Earnings, Characteristics of Families: First Quarter* (Washington, D.C.: U.S. Department of Labor, 1988).

2. Alexander Szalai, ed., *The Use of Time: Daily Activities of Urban and Suburban Populations in Twelve Countries* (The Hague: Mouton, 1972), p. 668, Table B. Another study found that men spent a longer time than women eating meals (Shelley Coverman, "Gender, Domestic Labor Time and Wage Inequality," *American Sociological Review* 48 [1983]:626). With regard to sleep, the pattern differs for men and women. The higher the social class of a man, the more sleep he's likely to get. The higher the class of a woman, the less sleep she's likely to get. (Upper-white-collar men average 7.6 hours sleep a night. Lower-white-collar, skilled and unskilled men all averaged 7.3 hours. Upper-white-collar women average 7.1 hours of sleep; lower-white-collar workers average 7.4; skilled workers 7.0 and unskilled workers 8.1.) Working wives seem to meet the demands of high-pressure careers by reducing sleep, whereas working husbands don't. . . .

3. Grace K. Baruch and Rosalind Barnett, "Correlates of Fathers' Participation in Family Work: A Technical Report," Working Paper no. 106 (Wellesley, Mass.: Wellesley College Center for Research on Women, 1983), pp. 80–81. Also see Kathryn E. Walker and Margaret E. Woods, *Time Use: A Measure of Household Production of Goods and Services* (Washington, D.C.: American Home Economics Association, 1976).

READING 26

Lesbian Parents: Claiming Our Visibility

SANDRA POLLACK

Very often in discussions and research on lesbian and straight parents, the focus is on the common factor of motherhood and on the ways lesbian parents and straight parents face some of the same difficulties. I would like us to think not so much about these similarities, but to redirect our thinking and focus more on the differences. I want to think with you about why a good deal of the initial research on lesbian mothers focused on the comparisons rather than the contrasts, why that research can have a negative impact on us as feminists, and why we need to encourage and support the research that is now beginning to be done on the differences. What I want to show is that the life situations/life experiences/realities for lesbian parents are not the same as those of heterosexuals and that it is not particularly advantageous to show that we are all the same.

You will notice that I often use the word "parent" rather than "mother." I do that because I believe that the terms parents and parenting are more inclusive and more easily incorporate the role of persons who are not the biological mothers, such as co-parents, step-parents, adoptive parents, and others who are bringing up children. The term mother too often tends to imply only the biological mother. Yet even as I explain this reasoning, I need to add that for lesbians, the whole question of naming and the terms we use to identify ourselves is more complex than it might be for straight women. For while I recognize the importance of using the term parent, I know that at times I intentionally use the term lesbian mother as a way of identifying

myself. On the one hand we want a term that reflects the fact that the care of the children is often done by other than the biological mother, and on the other hand, because, in the public mind, the term lesbian and mother are often seen as a contradiction, we intentionally, at times, want to put these two words together.

This perhaps is only one small example of what happens when we focus on the differences rather than the similarities. When we look specifically at a situation from the perspective of the lesbian, we see things that too easily get overlooked when we just look for the ways in which we are the same as straight women.

And yet, when we look at the literature, we see that many studies suggest that lesbian mothers are just like other mothers. While this might seem reassuring at first glance, such a conclusion is dangerous. It makes us once more invisible, and it obscures the radical alternative lesbian lives can model. Uncritical acceptance of such research may also lead us to the false conclusion that we will be accepted by the larger society because we have some of the same problems and concerns as other mothers. Research which focuses on the ways lesbians and their children resemble heterosexual mothers and their children may be important as part of custody courtroom strategy, but it negates the healthy and positive characteristics unique to lesbian parenting. In addition, most of the research on lesbian parents has focused on white lesbians. Yet it is not only the sexual or political, but also the racial differences that must be considered if we are to fully understand the realities of our lives.

Early research on sexual practices, etiology, and "cures," combined with a view of sexual preference as immutable, defined the lesbian mother out of existence. Before 1970, lesbian mothers were virtually

"Lesbian Parents: Claiming Our Visibility" by Sandra Pollack in *Woman-Defined Motherhood,* The Haworth Press, Inc., 10 Alice Street, Binghamton, NY 13904. Copyright © 1990.

invisible in the research on homosexuality, in the early research in women's studies, and in the literature on mothering.

In 1977 I was shocked into recognizing my own complicity in this process. A woman I worked with in organizing for the New York Women's Studies Association incredulously asked, "You are a mother?" While I had been open about being a lesbian during the two years of our work together, I had never mentioned my children. Suddenly I became conscious of being a "closet mother." I asked others in the room and discovered two other lesbian mothers. The time had come to acknowledge our full identities and to better understand the impact of raising children as lesbians in a patriarchal society.

The fact that we have been ignored in research, and that we, at times, have colluded in that invisibility, adds to the difficulty of knowing just how large a population we are talking about. In spite of this, estimates are that ten to twenty percent of adult women are lesbians, and that twenty to thirty percent of lesbians are mothers, a total of three to four million lesbian parents in the United States. Many might be more open if the legal system were not so weighted against them (Hunter & Polikoff, 1976; Martin & Lyon, 1972; Riley, 1975). As economic heads of households, lesbian parents often remain in the closet because they cannot afford to risk losing their jobs.

We begin to break that pattern of invisibility as we define ourselves. When we consciously claim the labels of lesbian and of parent, we assume the power to decide what we want them to mean in our lives. This self-definition and empowerment should anchor future research, legal defense strategies and work with clients in therapy.

The homophobia that pervades our society exhibits itself in a myriad of myths about lesbian parents—for example, lesbians will molest children, the children will grow up to be homosexuals, lesbians will engage in sexual activity in front of their children, the children will develop psychological problems and be stigmatized and ridiculed by society. Nowhere does this homophobia allow for the recognition that lesbian parenting can be a healthy, wholesome experience for adults and children.

An important link in my thinking about the need to claim our visibility as lesbian parents has been an understanding of lesbian mothers and the law. One of the most publicized lesbian mother custody battles was that of Mary Jo Risher. The 1975 case was covered by the mass media and turned into a prime-time television movie. In a comprehensive summary of this case, Lindsay Van Gelder (1976) showed that public sympathy was aroused (perhaps for the first time) when people saw how a thirty-nine-year-old white Texas mother lost custody of her nine-year-old son, despite the fact that she was a college graduate, nurse, a former Baptist Sunday school teacher, a P.T.A. President, and a Chaplain of the Order of the Eastern Star who had been living for the past three years in a stable committed relationship with her lover.

Both women had good jobs; they were solid members of their community. There was no question of alcoholism or drugs. They saw themselves as a family with two adults and three children (two boys from Mary Jo's previous marriage and one daughter from her lover Ann's previous marriage). They were each other's insurance beneficiaries, had joint checking accounts, co-owned property. The life Mary Jo and Ann lived was "straight" in most ways except that they were two women loving each other. According to several psychologists, Mary Jo's son had an "exceptionally loving stable family life." However, as one juror said, "We are taking him out of a good home to put him in a better one" (Van Gelder, 1976, p. 72).

Remarried Douglas Risher now had a new baby and a "full-time" wife to stay home with the children. One of Doug Risher's witnesses was a social worker who felt that nine-year-old Richard would be better off in a home "where the mother didn't work." Douglas and his wife could provide the proper father and mother image. This image was more important than the fact that Douglas Risher had a record of drunk driving, had broken Mary Jo's nose, had been accused of getting a nineteen-year-old woman pregnant, and had paid for her abortion.

The mass media coverage of this case may have caused some people to feel sorry for Mary Jo when she was ordered to give up her son on Christmas morning, but it barely began to challenge the assumption that the straight nuclear family is best. The question was never whether or not Mary Jo was a good mother; Mary Jo as a lesbian mother was on trial.

The Risher case is an important example of the futility of seeking safety in the argument that we are "all really the same"—that lesbian mothers and straight mothers are not so different after all.

Obviously I do not wish to imply that only lesbian

mothers lose custody of their children. Phyllis Chesler in *Mothers on Trial* (1987) certainly points out many examples of how heterosexual mothers face similar trauma in a male court system where too often the financial and material advantages of the father, or other males, are given precedent over a recognition of the parenting skills of women. The point I do wish to make, though, is that in spite of this shared anguish, there is a difference for lesbian mothers who not only may lose custody of their children in the courts, but who may also lose a sense of self-esteem and validation as they try to argue that their lives are really no different from those of heterosexual mothers.

Lesbians have always raised children in our society, but this fact has only recently come to the attention of the courts. With the consciousness stimulated by the women's liberation and gay liberation movements, more and more women are insisting on their right to be what they are: lesbians and mothers.

While there have been some lesbian mother court victories (Armanini v. Armanini, 1979; Medeiros v. Medeiros, 1982; Miller v. Miller, 1979; Schuster v. Schuster and Isaacson v. Isaacson, 1974), the overwhelming fear among lesbian mothers is that they will lose their children. That fear is based on reality. In a contested custody case, the courts will, in most instances, believe the mother is an unfit parent because she is a lesbian. Going to court is also an enormous psychological, emotional, and financial drain. And custody cases can always be reopened. The homophobic nature of the courts is shown in the child custody orders which grant the lesbian parent custody but include provisions that she is not permitted to live with a lover (Basile, 1974). One can never really feel safe as a lesbian mother.

Judges at times exhibit a voyeurism that belies their claim to objectivity. Such an attitude was evidenced in my own protracted custody case when my ex-husband's lawyer was describing a visit his client made to my house when my lover had been visiting me for the weekend. As the lawyer was reciting the events, the judge burst out with, "Where were they (the adult women) and what were they wearing?" What assumptions did this judge have about homosexuals? Was he assuming we were probably in bed or parading around naked? Would he ask those questions about a heterosexual man or woman? To have to explain that we were sitting in the living room wearing ordinary clothing, that my daughters and my lover's daughter were

watching TV, was an insult to our dignity. Yet lesbian mothers are frequently abused in this way. For too many people, the word lesbian or homosexual only conjures up images of sex.

In the words of another judge, "Ma'am, will you explain to the Court exactly what occurs—we talk here generally of a homosexual act. Just what does this entail? What do you do?" And again later, the same judge asked if there was "any potential that the lesbian mother might 'use' her child in sexual activity" (Hitchens & Price, 1978–9, p. 453).

Given the realities that many lesbian mother custody cases are lost, that the legal system is homophobic, and that court battles are long and expensive, the desire for research that would help the lesbian parent in court is understandable. This research though has largely been a reaction—an attempt to answer the fears and myths perpetuated by the very homophobic society we must now try to convince, and the form of that reaction has too often been to show that we are the same as straight mothers rather than dealing with the homophobic assumptions of the courts.

The fact that a mother is a lesbian is often so startling and offensive to a judge's value system that once this issue is brought into the case, it is omnipresent in the judge's mind. In a positive and important study, recognizing the particulars of lesbian custody cases, Donna Hitchens and Barbara Price (1978–79) argue that this problem should be dealt with directly by the mother's attorney, who should know the prejudices to be countered and the evidence to be used. The custody outcome, they state, depends more on the beliefs and attitudes of the judge about homosexuality than on the specific facts of the case.

Court transcripts studied by Hitchens and Price reveal three erroneous assumptions commonly held by judges and mental health professionals called in to testify. The first has to do with the sexual behavior of lesbians. Lesbians are assumed to be promiscuous, liable to sexually harm the children, and sexually maladjusted. The belief, then, is that allowing the mother to be both with her lover and her children would result in undesirable sexual behavior.

The second myth is that children of gay parents will grow up to be gay or will have confused sex-role identification. The third assumption is that the child could be socially stigmatized and therefore seriously harmed if the mother's lesbianism is widely known.

Expert testimony directed at countering these

myths rather than focusing only on the general stability of the mother and the mother's parenting ability appears to be essential.

Unlike the important Hitchens and Price research, most of the other early lesbian studies focused on showing how lesbian and straight families have few differences. This simply means that according to these researchers, neither lesbians nor their children have pathological problems that are very different from those of heterosexual single mothers (Golombok, Spencer, & Rutter, 1983; Kirkpatrick, Smith & Roy, 1981; Lewin & Lyons, 1982). It appears to me that an underlying assumption in these studies is that the lesbian mother will be judged on how well she compares to the heterosexual norm.

Demonstrating that we are the same may have seemed to be useful as a legal strategy, but these comparison studies often overlook serious questions and, therefore, present skewed results. For example, to study the ways lesbians and straight mothers rely on relationships with kin, particularly in child care and holiday celebrations, one must also ask questions related to the realities of lesbian life. Do lesbians go home for the holidays alone or with their lovers? Are children free to talk about the women in their mother's life when they are with relatives? What is the relationship between disclosure and employment for lesbian parents?

While the daily lives of both groups of mothers have many similarities, the specifics of the household must be examined to really find out about raising a child in this setting. Are lesbian posters, books, and records around as freely as heterosexual materials would be? Can lesbian conversations take place as freely as heterosexual conversations? Probing these areas will uncover differences that mark lesbian lives more deeply than questions about whom they can turn to for child care, or how to cope with the low salaries all women receive, or the fact that few women get adequate financial support from ex-husbands.

There are differences in the way lesbian and heterosexual women take charge of and plan for their futures—be it in home ownership, self-employment, or life-long planning (Pagelow, 1980). So, too, when we show lesbian and straight mothers functioning as caregivers, the myth that heterosexual mothers are more child-oriented than lesbian mothers comes under serious challenge (Miller, Jacobson, & Bigner, 1981). These differences, rather than the similarities, must be emphasized both in court and in the larger world to show the benefits of lesbian parenting and to reinforce a positive self-image among lesbians.

Some comparison studies focus on the sex roles of children and conclude that the two groups have similar sex-role behavior and attitudes toward ideal child behavior (Kweskin & Cook, 1982). Again, my reservation is the underlying assumption that there are appropriate sex roles for boys and girls. What these studies really examine is whether the children conform to acceptable societal norms. Yet this very assumption of appropriate roles is what feminists are committed to eliminating. The consequences of not conforming weigh heavily, however.

In the Mary Jo Risher case, much was made of the apparent heterosexual orientation of the children. Ann's daughter, Judie Ann, was described as an "especially pretty child, very charming who espoused a traditional feminine role." Mary Jo's son, Richard, said he wanted to be a policeman. Despite all this backward bending, even the slightest deviations were seized upon. Apparently, Mary Jo allowed Richard to appear at the psychologist's office "wearing unsuitable clothing"—a YWCA T-shirt and a jacket that belonged to Judie Ann. Upon cross-examination, the psychologist acknowledged that since Richard was taking a gym course at the Y, the shirt was hardly high drag (Van Gelder, 1976, p. 73). No matter, Mary Jo was a lesbian and therefore should be more sensitive to Richard's appearance.

Researchers often feel it necessary to show that the children are "all right," that they are not contaminated by lesbianism, and that they will grow up to be "proper boys and girls." Kirkpatrick et al. (1981) tested children ages five to twelve and concluded that the gender development of the children of heterosexual and homosexual mothers was not identifiably different. While we might use these studies as a courtroom tactic because the children "do just fine," we must remain aware of the acceptance of sex-role stereotyping on which such an argument is based.

Our strategies would be very different if we chose to emphasize the value of the independent model provided by lesbians (Berzins, Willing, & Wetter, 1978 in Riddle, 1978). Dorothy Riddle says it strongly: "Rather than posing a menace to children, gays may actually facilitate important developmental learning . . . children have the possibility of learning that it is possible to resist traditional sex-role socialization. . . .

Children become exposed to the concept of cultural and individual diversity as positive rather than threatening" (pp. 39–50).

Studies that look at the actual lives of the children of lesbians may be more useful than those focusing on sex-role identities. Karen Gail Lewis (1980) encouraged children of lesbians to talk about how their mother's lifestyles have influenced their lives. Lewis concludes that "the children do want to be accepting of their mother's lifestyles, and . . . the gay community and the therapeutic community owe it to the children to provide the opportunity for them to work towards a realistic assessment and acceptance of their feelings" (pp. 198–203).

Lewis raises an important point rarely addressed by the research: the possible benefits of being a child of a lesbian mother. The children of lesbians may become aware (perhaps more so than other children) of their responsibility for themselves and their own choices. So too Marjorie Hill in "Child-Rearing Attitudes of Black Lesbian Mothers" (1987), focuses on the positive aspects of difference. Poet Audre Lorde says it clearly, "There are certain basic requirements of any child— food, clothing, shelter, love. So what makes our children different? We do. Gays and Lesbians of Color are different because we are embattled by reason of our sexuality and our Color, and if there is any lesson we must teach our children, it is that difference is a creative force for change, that survival and struggle for the future is not a theoretical issue. It is the very texture of our lives . . ." (1986, p. 313). This message should be repeated frequently.

We need to convince the courts that the child's interests are often best served by living with a lesbian parent who can be open rather than leading a double and secret life. We need to recognize that concern over the absence of a male model is a bogus issue, that the problem often is not the lack of a male presence, but the lack of a male income. A lesbian parent who can live openly, and who can share income and household expenses with other women, has a better chance of maintaining a standard of living that is beneficial for the child.

While this issue, like the decision of whether we use the term parent or mother to identify ourselves, is more complex than it might be for straight women, I also do not want to imply that if we simply stood up in court and shouted the benefits of lesbian parenting, we would fare much better in the courts. I would like to

hope that such may be the direction for the future, and there may be some indications of that in the successful lesbian mother decisions, but it is premature to make too much of these victories. We can though, at this point, at least identify it as an area that needs more research.

When we begin to listen to the voices of lesbians, what kind of call for new research do we hear?

At lesbian parent workshops women say they want a stop to the neutralizing of their lives. They want to portray the positive aspects and specialness of their lives. They want research on the relationship of adolescents to lesbian mothers, as there is little in the adolescent literature that pertains to them. They are concerned with the role of co-parents and with ways to provide their children with skills to counter homophobia. They want help in developing support groups for children. They want to know how to get support for lesbians choosing to have children via alternative fertilization and how to better validate lesbians who do not live with their children. They want to find ways to recognize second-generation lesbians and gay men, individuals whose lives are often kept invisible because their existence feeds into the homophobic fear that children will turn out gay.

When we listen, we hear of the ways in which lesbian parents have issues to deal with that are not generally found in the straight community. Marilyn Murphy shares her pain as she reaches the decision not to attend her son's wedding because she feels the unfairness of an institution that recognizes the love a man and a women share, but not the love two women share. "After all," she says, "what kind of a mother has to stop and think about whether or not to attend her child's wedding? A lesbian mother does" (1987, p. 198).

Our relationships are not recognized in a myriad of ways.

- In many states our relationships are illegal, and it is not against the law to discriminate against us. We have no formal recognition of our unions, our separations, our births, our deaths. This reality has an impact on our families. Our situation is not the same as it is for straight women.
- Our children have been taken from us—by religious doctrine, by the courts, by the pressures imposed upon us to make us choose between our children and our lovers.

GAY COUPLES MAKE IT LEGAL AS DOMESTIC PARTNERS UNDER SAN FRANCISCO LAW

San Francisco (AP)—Chris Minor and Richard Mulholland, sporting matching leather jackets and boots, beat the Valentine's Day rush and became the city's first domestic partners.

"It's a real milestone, not only in our relationship, but for the gay community," said Minor, who had waited since 5:30 a.m. on the steps of City Hall.

His chilly vigil paid off when the couple became the city's first legal domestic partners shortly after 8 a.m. on the first day that unwed couples could officially register their romances with the city.

About a dozen couples were waiting when City Hall opened for an expected Valentine's Day deluge of gays, lesbians and unwed heterosexuals taking advantage of the first opportunity to sign up.

Among the first wave were Christmas Leubrie, a 41-year-old nurse, and her lover of six years, Alice Heimsoth, 39, a city health worker. They wore pastel silk outfits and flowers in their hair.

"We worked hard on this," said Leubrie, who was active in the campaign to get the law approved by voters in November. "It's about love and recognition of relationships."

City Hall already had 100 weddings scheduled for Valentine's Day, and no one was sure how many

domestic partners would show up. Estimates ranged from 50 to 5,000.

By 11 a.m. about 70 couples had paid the $35 fee to file their declaration with the county clerk.

A multidenominational ceremony was planned to recognize each registered couple, with their names announced as they strolled down City Hall's stairway.

The San Francisco law potentially affects more people. While homosexuals in the national population are estimated at one in 10, they are estimated at 15 to 20 percent of San Francisco's population.

The new law in San Francisco is narrower in scope than the earlier proposals. It does not provide any benefits for domestic partners, only letting them declare that they have an intimate relationship, that they have lived together at least six months and that they will be jointly responsible for living expenses.

San Francisco Supervisor Harry Britt's staff handed out thousands of fliers about the law in the city's predominantly gay Castro district.

Voters passed the law in November after narrowly rejecting a similar initiative in 1989.

The city's Board of Supervisors had adopted a domestic partners ordinance in 1982, but former Mayor Dianne Feinstein vetoed it as too costly.

Other cities, including Seattle, West Hollywood and Santa Cruz, Calif., and Madison, Wis., have similar laws.

From *The Columbus Dispatch,* February 1991. Reprinted by permission of Associated Press.

- As co-parents we have no assurance that we will be allowed to continue to raise our children at the death of the birth mother.
- Lesbian parents agonize with the internalized oppression that often makes it impossible for them to tell their child that their mother is a lesbian.

While many of the day to day tasks of raising a child may be the same for straight and lesbian women, the reality of prejudice against the family for the parents' sexual orientation is a major difference—lesbians must

deal with this with day care workers, teachers, and relatives.

What might this mean to therapists and researchers? Recognizing the differences and the particular stresses they entail may be more helpful to the client than dealing with her as if she were like any other "single mother." Sally Crawford in her essay in *Lesbian Psychologies* (1987) does an important job of identifying some of the particular stresses for lesbians in the family-building process. And as Nancy Polikoff says (1987), "In the courts too often, a lesbian mother must portray herself as being as close to the All-American norm as possible—the spitting image of her ideal heterosexual counterpart—and preferably asexual . . . the necessity of assuming a role that contradicts her identity has important consequences . . . the toll on the client is obviously enormous. She is forced to deny any pride in her lesbianism, any solidarity with other lesbians; she may even be compelled to deny or alter her sexual relationships. There is no guarantee that, at the end of this ordeal, she will be allowed to keep her children."

As a lawyer, Polikoff tells how she has encouraged lesbian mothers not to see themselves as having more in common with heterosexual mothers than with other lesbians. She urges them to resist, in every conceivable forum, the presumption of heterosexuality that attaches to motherhood. "When we constantly assert in the public arena that we will raise our children to be heterosexual, and that we will protect them from the manifestations of our sexuality and from the larger lesbian and gay community . . . we essentially concede it is preferable to be heterosexual, thereby foreclosing an assertion of pride and of the positive value in homosexuality" (p. 326). This sense of pride and positive self-identity may often need to be reinforced in the client's therapy.

The biological mother and the co-parents may need help to stay focused on positive aspects and the specialness of their situation. The co-parent, regardless of her role within the family, can be easily disenfranchised. As therapists, you may be called to testify in custody disputes. We will need help to support our families in an alien legal framework. For example, today, a known sperm donor, who originally intended to remain uninvolved but who later changes his mind can gain full parental rights. A minimally involved father of a child raised by a lesbian couple will almost certainly obtain custody if the legal mother dies. Under the law, after all, he is the sole surviving parent. At present we do not have legal recognition of parenthood for both mothers. But in some states, before sympathetic judges, there may be room to take the offensive and gain this recognition by presenting a positive picture of the role played by the co-parent.

As lesbian parents we are a diverse group. I would hope that you will hear our varied voices. It is our strength to be able to share our differences. Research and therapy that recognizes these differences will be more empowering to lesbian parents than showing that we are the same as, or that it is desirable when we or our children are the same as, heterosexual families.

REFERENCES

Armanini v. Armanini (1979). *5 family law reporter,* 2501 (N.Y. Sup.Ct.)

Basile, R. (1974). Lesbian mothers. *Women's Rights Law Reporter, 2,* 3–5.

Chesler, P. (1987). *Mothers on trial: The battle for children and custody.* Seattle, WA: Seal Press.

Crawford, S. (1987). Lesbian families: Psychosocial stress and the family-building process. In Boston Lesbian Psychologies Collective, (Eds.), *Lesbian psychologies: Explorations and challenges* (pp. 195–214). Urbana: University of Illinois Press.

Golombok, S., Spencer, A., & Rutter, M. (Oct. 1983). Children in lesbian and single parent households: Psychosexual and psychiatric appraisal. *Journal of Child Psychology and Allied Disciplines, 24,* 551–572.

Hill, M. (1987). Child-rearing attitudes of black lesbian mothers. In Boston Lesbian Psychologies Collective, (Eds.), *Lesbian Psychologies: Explorations and challenges* (pp. 215–226). Urbana: University of Illinois Press.

Hitchens, D. J., & Price, B. (1978–9). Trial strategy in lesbian mother custody cases: The use of expert testimony, *Golden Gate University Law Review, 9,* 451–453.

Hunter, N. D., & Polikoff, N. D. (1976). Custody rights of lesbian mothers: Legal theory and litigation strategy. *Buffalo Law Review, 25,* 691–733.

Kirkpatrick, M., Smith, C., & Roy, R. (1981). Lesbian mothers and their children: A comparative study. *American Journal of Orthopsychiatry, 51,* 545–551.

Kweskin, S., & Cook, A. (1982). Heterosexual and homosexual mothers: Self-described sex-role behavior and ideal and sex-role behavior in children. *Sex Roles, 8,* 967.

Lewin, E., & Lyons, T. A. (1982). Everything in its place: The co-existence of lesbianism and motherhood. In W. Paul, J. D. Weinrich & M. Hotvedt (Eds.), *Homosexuality: Social, psychological and biological issues.* Beverly Hills: Sage Publications.

Lewis, K. G. (May, 1980). Children of lesbians: Their point of view. *Social Work, 25,* 198–203.

Lorde, A. (1986). Turning the beat around: Lesbian parenting 1986. In S. Pollack, & J. Vaughn (Eds.), *Politics of the heart: A lesbian parenting anthology* (pp. 310–315). Ithaca, NY: Firebrand Books.

Martin, D., & Lyon, P. (1972). *Lesbian/Women.* San Francisco: Glide Publications.

Medeiros v. Medeiros (1982). *8 family law reporter,* 2372 (Vt. Sup.Ct.)

Miller, J. A., Jacobson, R. B., & Bigner, H. J. (1981). The child's home environment for lesbian vs. heterosexual mothers: A neglected area of research. *Journal of Homosexuality, 7,* 49–56.

Miller v. Miller (1979). *405 Michigan reporter,* 809.

Murphy, M. (1987). Mother of the groom. In S. Pollack & J. Vaughn (Eds.), *Politics of the heart: A lesbian parenting anthology* (pp. 198–211). Ithaca, NY: Firebrand Books.

Pagelow, M., (1980). Heterosexual and lesbian single mothers: A comparison of problems, coping, and solutions. *Journal of Homosexuality, 5,* 189–203.

Polikoff, N. D. (1987). Lesbian mothers, lesbian families: Legal obstacles, legal challenges. In S. Pollack & J. Vaughn (Eds.), *Politics of the heart: A lesbian parenting anthology* (pp. 325–332). Ithaca, NY: Firebrand Books.

Riddle, D. (1978). Relating to children: Gays as role models. *Journal of Social Issues, 34,* 39–50.

Riley, M. (1975). The avowed lesbian mother and her right to child custody. *San Diego Law Review, 12,* 799–864.

Schuster v. Schuster & Isaacson v. Isaacson (1974) 585 P. 2d 130 (Wash. Sup. Ct.) in R. A. Basile. *Women's rights law reporter, 2,* 3–5.

Van Gelder, L. (Sept. 1976). Lesbian custody: A tragic day in court. *MS., 72*–73.

R E A D I N G   2 7

Puerto Rican Elderly Women: Shared Meanings and Informal Supportive Networks

MELBA SÁNCHEZ-AYÉNDEZ

INTRODUCTION

Studies of older adults' support systems have seldom taken into account how values within a specific cultural context affect expectations of support and patterns of assistance in social networks. Such networks and supportive relations have a cultural dimension reflecting a system of shared meanings. These meanings affect social interaction and the expectations people have of their relationships with others.

Ethnicity and gender affect a person's adjustment to

Reprinted with the permission of The Free Press, a Division of Macmillan, Inc., from *All American Women: Lines that Divide, Ties that Bind* by Johnnetta B. Cole. Copyright © 1986 by The Free Press.

old age. Although sharing a "minority" position produces similar consequences among members of different ethnic minority groups, the groups' diversity lies in their distinctive systems of shared meanings. Studies of older adults in ethnic minority groups have rarely focused on the cultural contents of ethnicity affecting the aging process, particularly of women (Barth, 1969). Cultural value orientations are central to understanding how minority elders approach growing old and how they meet the physical and emotional changes associated with aging.

This article describes the interplay between values and behavior in family and community of a group of older Puerto Rican women living on low incomes in Boston.[1] It explores how values emphasizing family interdependence and different roles of women and men shape the women's expectations, behavior, and supportive familial and community networks.

BEING A WOMAN IS DIFFERENT FROM BEING A MAN

The women interviewed believe in a dual standard of conduct for men and women. This dual standard is apparent in different attributes assigned to women and men, roles expected of them, and authority exercised by them.

The principal role of men in the family is viewed as that of provider; their main responsibility is economic in nature. Although fathers are expected to be affectionate with their children, child care is not seen to be a man's responsibility. Men are not envisioned within the domestic sphere.

The "ideal" man must be the protector of the family, able to control his emotions and be self-sufficient. Men enjoy more freedom in the public world than do women. From the women's perspective, the ideal of maleness is linked to the concept of *machismo*. This concept assumes men have a stronger sexual drive than women, a need to prove virility by the conquest of women, a dominant position in relation to females, and a belligerent attitude when confronted by male peers.

The women see themselves as subordinate to men and recognize the preeminence of male authority. They believe women ought to be patient and largely forbearing in their relations with men, particularly male family members. Patience and forbearance, however, are not confused with passivity or total submissiveness. The elderly Puerto Rican women do not conceive of themselves or other women as "resigned females" but as dynamic beings, continually devising strategies to improve everyday situations within and outside the household.

Rosa Mendoza,[2] now sixty-five, feels no regrets for having decided at thirty years of age and after nine years of marriage not to put up with her husband's heavy drinking any longer. She moved out of her house and went to live with her mother.

I was patient for many years. I put up with his drunkenness and worked hard to earn money. One day I decided I'd be better off without him. One thing is to be patient, and another to be a complete fool. So I moved out.

Although conscious of their subordinate status to their husbands, wives are also aware of their power and the demands they can make. Ana Fuentes recalls when her husband had a mistress. Ana was thirty-eight.

I knew he had a mistress in a nearby town. I was patient for a long time, hoping it would end. Most men, sooner or later, have a mistress somewhere. But when it didn't end after quite a time and everyone in the neighborhood knew about it, I said "I am fed up!" He came home one evening and the things I told him! I even said I'd go to that woman's house and beat her if I had to. . . . He knew I was not bluffing; that this was not just another argument. He tried to answer back and I didn't let him. He remained silent. . . . And you know what? He stopped seeing her! A woman can endure many things for a long time, but the time comes when she has to defend her rights.

These older Puerto Rican women perceive the home as the center around which the female world revolves. Home is the woman's domain; women generally make decisions about household maintenance and men seldom intervene.

Family relations are considered part of the domestic sphere and therefore a female responsibility. The women believe that success in marriage depends on the woman's ability to "make the marriage work."

A marriage lasts as long as the woman decides it will last. It is us who make a marriage work, who put up with things, who try to make ends meet, who yield.

The norm of female subordination is evident in the view that marriage will last as long as the woman "puts up with things" and deals with marriage from her subordinate status. Good relations with affinal kin are also a woman's responsibility. They are perceived as relations between the wife's domestic unit and other women's domestic units.

Motherhood

Motherhood is seen by these older Puerto Rican women as the central role of women. Their concept of motherhood is based on the female capacity to bear children and on the notion of *marianismo,* which presents the Virgin Mary as a role model (Stevens, 1973). *Marianismo* presupposes that it is through motherhood that a woman realizes herself and derives her life's greatest satisfactions.

A woman's reproductive role is viewed as leading her toward more commitment to and a better understanding of her children than is shown by the father. One of the women emphasized this view:

> It is easier for a man to leave his children and form a new home with another woman, or not to be as forgiving of children as a mother is. They will never know what it is like to carry a child inside, feel it growing, and then bring that child into the world. This is why a mother is always willing to forgive and make sacrifices. That creature is a part of you; it nourished from you and came from within you. But it is not so for men. To them, a child is a being they receive once it is born. The attachment can never be the same.

The view that childrearing is their main responsibility in life comes from this conceptualization of the mother–child bond. For the older women, raising children means more than looking after the needs of offspring. It involves being able to offer them every possible opportunity for a better life, during childhood or adulthood, even if this requires personal sacrifices.

As mother and head of the domestic domain, a woman is also responsible for establishing the bases for close and good relations among her children. From childhood through adulthood, the creation and maintenance of family unity among offspring is considered another female responsibility.

FAMILY UNITY AND INTERDEPENDENCE

Family Unity

Ideal family relations are seen as based on two interrelated themes, family unity and family interdependence. Family unity refers to the desirability of close and intimate kin ties, with members getting along well and keeping in frequent contact despite dispersal.

Celebration of holidays and special occasions are seen as opportunities for kin to be together and strengthen family ties. Family members, particularly grandparents, adult children, and grandchildren, are often reunited at Christmas, New Year's, Mother's and Father's days, Easter, and Thanksgiving. Special celebrations like weddings, baptisms, first communions, birthdays, graduations, and funerals occasion reunions with other family members. Whether to celebrate happy or sad events, the older women encourage family gatherings as a way of strengthening kinship ties and fostering family continuity.

The value the women place on family unity is also evident in their desire for frequent interaction with kin members. Visits and telephone calls demonstrate a caring attitude by family members which cements family unity.

Family unity is viewed as contributing to the strengthening of family interdependence. Many of the older women repeat a proverb when referring to family unity: *En la unión está la fuerza.* ("In union there is strength.") They believe that the greater the degree of unity in the family, the greater the emphasis family members will place on interdependence and familial obligation.

Family Interdependence

Despite adaptation to life in a culturally different society, Puerto Rican families in the United States are still defined by strong norms of reciprocity among family members, especially those in the immediate kinship group (Cantor, 1979; Carrasquillo, 1982; Delgado, 1981; Donaldson & Martínez, 1980; Sánchez-Ayéndez, 1984). Interdependence within the Puerto Rican symbolic framework "fits an orientation to life that stresses that the individual is not capable of doing everything and doing it well. Therefore, he should rely on others for assistance" (Bastida, 1979:70). Individualism and self-reliance assume a different meaning from the one prevailing in the dominant U.S. cultural tradition. Individuals in Puerto Rican families will expect and ask for assistance from certain people in their social networks without any derogatory implications for self-esteem.

Family interdependence is a value to which these older Puerto Rican women strongly adhere. It influences patterns of mutual assistance with their children as well as expectations of support. The older women expect to be taken care of during old age by their adult children. The notion of filial duty ensues from the value orientation of interdependence. Adult children are understood to have a responsibility toward their aged parents in exchange for the functions that parents performed for them throughout their upbringing. Expected reciprocity from offspring is intertwined with the concept of filial love and the nature of the parent–child relationship.

Parental duties of childrearing are perceived as inherent in the "parent" role and also lay the basis for long-term reciprocity with children, particularly during old age. The centrality that motherhood has in the lives of the older women contributes to creating great expectations among them of reciprocity from children. More elderly women than men verbalize disappointment when one of their children does not participate in the expected interdependence ties. Disappointment is unlikely to arise when an adult child cannot help due to financial or personal reasons. However, it is bound to arise when a child chooses not to assist the older parent for other reasons.

These older Puerto Rican women stress that good offspring ought to help their parents, contingent upon available resources. Statements such as the following are common:

Of course I go to my children when I have a problem! To whom would I turn? I raised them and worked very hard to give them the little I could. Now that I am old, they try to help me in whatever they can. . . . Good offspring should help their aged parents as much as they are able to.

Interdependence for Puerto Rican older parents also means helping their children and grandchildren. Many times they provide help when it is not explicitly requested. They are happy when they can perform supportive tasks for their children's families. The child who needs help, no matter how old, is not judged as dependent or a failure.

Reciprocity is not based on strictly equal exchanges. Due to the rapid pace of life, lack of financial resources, or personal problems, adult children are not always able to provide the care the elder parent needs. Many times, the older adults provide their families with more financial and instrumental assistance than their children are able to provide them. Of utmost importance to the older women is not that their children be able to help all the time, but that they visit or call frequently. They place more emphasis on emotional support from their offspring than on any other form of support.

Gloria Santos, for example, has a son and a daughter. While they do not live in the same state as their mother, they each send her fifty to seventy dollars every month. Yet she is disappointed with her children and explains why:

They both have good salaries but call me only once or twice a month. I hardly know my grandchildren. All I ask from them is that they be closer to me, that they visit and call me more often. They only visit me once a year and only for one or two days. I've told my daughter that instead of sending me money she could call me more often. I was a good mother and worked hard in order for them to get a good education and have everything. All I expected from them was to show me they care, that they love me.

The importance that the older women attach to family interdependence does not imply that they constantly require assistance from children or that they do not value their independence. They prefer to live in their own households rather than with their adult children. They also try to solve as many problems as possible by themselves. But when support is needed, the adult children are expected to assist the aged parent to the degree they are able. This does not engender conflict or lowered self-esteem for the aged adult. Conflict and dissatisfaction are caused when adult children do not offer any support at all.

SEX ROLES AND FAMILIAL SUPPORTIVE NETWORKS

The family is the predominant source of support for most of these older women, providing instrumental and emotional support in daily life as well as assistance during health crises or times of need. Adult children play a central role in providing familial support to old parents. For married women, husbands are also an important component of their support system. At the same time, most of the older women still perform functional roles for their families.

Support from Adult Children

The support and helpfulness expected from offspring is related to perceptions of the difference between men and women. Older women seek different types of assistance from daughters than from sons. Daughters are perceived as being inherently better able to understand their mothers due to their shared status and qualities as women; they are also considered more reliable. Sons are not expected to help as much as daughters or in the same way. When a daughter does not fulfill the obligations expected of her, complaints are more bitter than if the same were true of a son: "Men are different; they do not feel as we feel. But she is a woman; she should know better." Daughters are also expected to visit and/or call more frequently than are sons. As women are linked closely to the domestic domain, they are held responsible for the care of family relations.

Motherhood is perceived as creating an emotional bond among women. When daughters become mothers, the older women anticipate stronger ties and more support from them.

Once a daughter experiences motherhood, she understands the suffering and hardships you underwent for her. Sons will never be able to understand this.

My daughter always helped me. But when she became a mother for the first time, she grew much closer to me. It was then she was able to understand how much a mother can love.

Most of the older women go to a daughter first when confronted by an emotional problem. Daughters are felt to be more patient and better able to understand them as women. It is not that older women never discuss their emotional problems with their sons, but they prefer to discuss them with their daughters. For example, Juana Rivera has two sons who live in the same city as she and a daughter who resides in Puerto Rico. She and her sons get along well and see each other often. The sons stop by their mother's house every day after work, talk about daily happenings, and assist her with some tasks. However, when a physical exam revealed a breast tumor thought to be malignant, it was to her daughter in Puerto Rico that the old woman expressed her worries. She recalls that time of crisis:

Eddie was with me when the doctor told me of the possibility of a tumor. I was brave. I didn't want him to see me upset. They [sons] get nervous when I get upset or cry. . . . That evening I called my daugh-

ter and talked to her. . . . She was very understanding and comforted me. I can always depend on her to understand me. She is the person who better understands me. My sons are also understanding, but she is a woman and understands more.

Although adult children are sources of assistance during the illnesses of their mothers, it is generally daughters from whom more is expected. Quite often daughters take their sick parents into their homes or stay overnight in the parental household in order to provide better care. Sons, as well as daughters, take the aged parent to the hospital or doctors' offices and buy medicines if necessary. However, it is more often daughters who check on their parents, provide care, and perform household chores when the parent is sick.

When the old women have been hospitalized, adult children living nearby tend to visit the hospital daily. Daughters and daughters-in-law sometimes cook special meals for the sick parent and bring the meals to the hospital. Quite often, adult children living in other states or in Puerto Rico come to help care for the aged parent or be present at the time of an operation. When Juana Rivera had exploratory surgery on her breast, her daughter came from Puerto Rico and stayed with her mother throughout the convalescence. Similarly, when Ana Toledo suffered a stroke and remained unconscious for four days, three of her six children residing in other states came to be with her and their siblings. After her release from the hospital, a daughter from New Jersey stayed at her mother's house for a week. When she left, the children who live near the old woman took turns looking after her.

Most adult children are also helpful in assisting with chores of daily living. At times, offspring take their widowed mothers grocery shopping. Other times, the older women give their children money to do the shopping for them. Daughters are more often asked to do these favors and to also buy personal care items and clothes for their mothers. Some adult offspring also assist by depositing Social Security checks, checking post office boxes, and buying money orders.

Support from Elderly Mothers

The Puerto Rican older women play an active role in providing assistance to their adult children. Gender affects the frequency of emotional support offered as well as the dynamics of the support. The older women offer advice more often to daughters than to sons on matters related to childrearing. And the approach used differs according to the children's gender. For example, one older woman stated,

> I never ask my son openly what is wrong with him. I do not want him to think that I believe he needs help to solve his problems; he is a man. . . . Yet, as a mother I worry. It is my duty to listen and offer him advice. With my daughter it is different; I can be more direct. She doesn't have to prove to me that she is self-sufficient.

Another woman expressed similar views:

> Of course I give advice to my sons! When they have had problems with their wives, their children, even among themselves, I listen to them, and tell them what I think. But with my daughters I am more open. You see, if I ask one of my sons what is wrong and he doesn't want to tell me, I don't insist too much; I'll ask later, maybe in a different way; and they will tell me sooner or later. With my daughters, if they don't want to tell me, I insist. They know I am a mother and a woman like them and that I can understand.

Older mothers perceive sons and daughters as in equal need of support. Daughters, however, are understood to face additional problems in areas such as conjugal relations, childrearing, and sexual harassment, due to their status as women.

Emotional support to daughters-in-law is also offered, particularly when they are encountering marriage or childrearing problems. Josefina Montes explains the active role she played in comforting her daughter-in-law, whose husband was having an extramarital affair.

> I told her not to give up, that she had to defend what was hers. I always listened to her and tried to offer some comfort. . . . When my son would come to my home to visit I would ask him "What is wrong with you? Don't you realize what a good mother and wife that woman is?" . . . I made it my business that he did not forget the exceptional woman she is. . . . I told him I didn't want to ever see him with the other one and not to mention her name in front of me. . . . I was on his case for almost two years.

> . . . All the time I told her to be patient. . . . It took time but he finally broke up with the other one.

When relations between mother and daughters-in-law are not friendly, support is not usually present. Eulalia Valle says that when her son left his wife and children to move in with another woman, there was not much she could do for her daughter-in-law.

> There was not much I could do. What could I tell him? I couldn't say she was nice to me. . . . Once I tried to make him see how much she was hurting and he replied: "Don't defend her. She has never been fond of you and you know it." What could I reply to that? All I said was, "That's true but, still, she must be very hurt." But there was nothing positive to say about her!

Monetary assistance generally flows from the older parent to the adult children, although few old people are able to offer substantial financial help. Direct monetary assistance, rarely exceeding fifty dollars, is less frequent than gift-giving. Gift-giving usually takes the form of monetary contributions for specific articles needed by their children or children's families. In this way the older people contribute indirectly to the maintenance of their children's families.

The older women also play an active role in the observance of special family occasions and holidays. On the days preceding the celebration, they are busy cooking traditional Puerto Rican foods. It is expected that those in good health will participate in the preparation of foods. This is especially true on Christmas and Easter, when traditional foods are an essential component of the celebrations.

Cooking for offspring is also a part of everyday life. In many of the households, meals prepared in the Puerto Rican tradition are cooked daily "in case children or grandchildren come by." Josefina Montes, for example, cooks a large quantity of food every day for herself, her husband, and their adult children and grandchildren. Her daughters come by after work to visit and pick up their youngest children, who stay with grandparents after school. The youngest daughter eats dinner at her parents' home. The oldest takes enough food home to serve her family. Doña[3] Josefina's sons frequently drop by after work or during lunch and she always insists that they eat something.

The older women also provide assistance to their

children during health crises. When Juana Rivera's son was hospitalized for a hernia operation, she visited the hospital every day, occasionally bringing food she had prepared for him. When her son was released, Doña Juana stayed in his household throughout his convalescence, caring for him while her daughter-in-law went off to work.

The aged women also assist their children by taking care of grandchildren. Grandchildren go to their grandmother's house after school and stay until their parents stop by after work. If the children are not old enough to walk home by themselves, the grandparent waits for them at school and brings them home. The women also take care of their grandchildren when they are not old enough to attend school or are sick. They see their role as grandmothers as a continuation or reenactment of their role as mothers and childrearers.

The women, despite old age, have a place in the functional structure of their families. The older women's assistance is an important contribution to their children's households and also helps validate the women's sense of their importance and helpfulness.

Mutual Assistance in Elderly Couples

Different conceptions of women and men influence interdependence between husband and wife as well as their daily tasks. Older married women are responsible for domestic tasks and perform household chores. They also take care of grandchildren, grocery shopping, and maintaining family relations. Older married men have among their chores depositing Social Security checks, going to the post office, and buying money orders. Although they stay in the house for long periods, the men go out into the community more often than do their wives. They usually stop at the *bodegas*,[4] which serve as a place for socializing and exchange of information, to buy items needed at home and newspapers from Puerto Rico.

Most married couples have a distinctive newspaper reading pattern. The husband comments on the news to his wife as he reads or after he has finished. Sometimes, after her husband finishes reading and commenting on the news, the older woman reads about it herself. Husbands also inform their wives of ongoing neighborhood events learned on their daily stops at the *bodegas*. Wives, on the other hand, inform husbands of familial events learned through their daily telephone conversations and visits from children and other kin members.

The older couple escort each other to service-pro-

viding agencies, even though they are usually accompanied by an adult child, adolescent grandchild, or social worker serving as translator. An older man still perceives himself in the role of "family protector" by escorting the women in his family, particularly his wife.

Older husbands and wives provide each other with emotional assistance. They are daily companions and serve as primary sources of confidence for each other, most often sharing children's and grandchildren's problems, health concerns, or financial worries. The couple do not always agree on solutions or approaches for assisting children when sharing their worries about offspring. Many times the woman serves as a mediator in communicating her husband's problems to adult children. The men tend to keep their problems, particularly financial and emotional ones, to themselves or tell their wives but not their children. This behavior rests upon the notion of men as financially responsible for the family, more self-sufficient, and less emotional than women.

Among the older couples, the husband or wife is generally the principal caregiver during the health crises of their spouse. Carmen Ruiz, for example, suffers from chronic anemia and tires easily. Her husband used to be a cook and has taken responsibility for cooking meals and looking after the household. When Providencia Cruz's husband was hospitalized she spent many hours each day at the hospital, wanting to be certain he was comfortable. She brought meals she had cooked for him, arranged his pillows, rubbed him with bay leaf rubbing alcohol, or watched him as he slept. When he was convalescing at home, she was his principal caregiver. Doña Providencia suffers from osteoarthritis and gastric acidity. When she is in pain and spends the day in bed, her husband provides most of the assistance she needs. He goes to the drugstore to buy medicine or ingredients used in folk remedies. He knows how to prepare the mint and chamomile teas she drinks when not feeling well. He also rubs her legs and hands with ointments when the arthritic pain is more intense than usual. Furthermore, during the days that Doña Providencia's ailments last, he performs most of the household chores.

While both spouses live, the couple manages many of their problems on their own. Assistance from other family members with daily chores or help during an illness is less frequent when the woman still lives with her husband than when she lives alone. However, if one or both spouses is ill, help from adult children is more common.

FRIENDS AND NEIGHBORS AS COMMUNITY SOURCES OF SUPPORT

Friends and neighbors form part of the older women's support network. However, the women differentiate between "neighbors" and "friends." Neighbors, unlike kin and friends, are not an essential component of the network which provides emotional support. They may or may not become friends. Supportive relations with friends involve being instrumental helpers, companions, and confidants. Neighbors are involved only in instrumental help.

Neighbors as Sources of Support

Contact with neighbors takes the form of greetings, occasional visits, and exchanges of food, all of which help to build the basis for reciprocity when and if the need arises. The establishment and maintenance of good relations with neighbors is considered to be important since neighbors are potentially helpful during emergencies or unexpected events. Views such as the following are common: "It is good to get acquainted with your neighbors; you never know when you might need them."

Josefina Rosario, a widow, has lived next door to an older Puerto Rican couple for three years. Exchange of food and occasional visits are part of her interaction with them. Her neighbor's husband, in his mid-sixties, occasionally runs errands for Doña Josefina, who suffers from rheumatoid arthritis and needs a walker to move around. If she runs out of a specific food item, he goes to the grocery store for her. Other times, he buys stamps, mails letters, or goes to the drugstore to pick up some medicines for her. Although Doña Josefina cannot reciprocate in the same way, she repays her neighbors by visiting every other week and exchanging food. Her neighbors tell her she is to call them day or night if she ever feels sick. Although glad to have such "good neighbors," as she calls them, she stresses she does not consider them friends and therefore does not confide her personal problems to them.

Supportive Relationships among Friends

Although friends perform instrumental tasks, the older women believe that a good friend's most important quality is being able to provide emotional support. A friend is someone willing to help during the "good" and "bad" times, and is trustworthy and reserved.

Problems may be shared with a friend with the certainty that confidences will not be betrayed. A friend provides emotional support not only during a crisis or problem, but in everyday life. Friends are companions, visiting and/or calling on a regular basis.

Friendship for this group of women is determined along gender lines. They tend to be careful about men. Relationships with males outside the immediate familial group are usually kept at a formal level. Mistrust of men is based upon the women's notion of *machismo*. Since men are conceived of as having a stronger sexual drive, the women are wary of the possibility of sexual advances, either physical or verbal. None of the women regards a male as a confidant friend. Many even emphasize the word *amiga* ("female friend") instead of *amigo* ("male friend"). Remarks such as the following are common:

> I've never had an *amigo*. Men cannot be trusted too much. They might misunderstand your motives and some even try to make a pass at you.

The few times the women refer to a male as a friend they use the term *amigo de la familia* ("friend of the family"). This expression conveys that the friendly relations are not solely between the woman and the man. The expression is generally used to refer to a close friend of the husband. *Amigos de la familia* may perform instrumental tasks, be present at family gatherings and unhappy events, or drop by to chat with the respondent's husband during the day. However, relations are not based on male–female relationships.

Age similarity is another factor that seems to affect selection of friends. The friendship networks of the older women are mainly composed of people sixty years of age and older. Friends who fill the role of confidant are generally women of a similar age. The women believe that younger generations, generally, have little interest in the elders. They also state that people their own age are better able to understand their problems because they share many of the same difficulties and worries.

Friends often serve as escorts, particularly in the case of women who live alone. Those who know some English serve as translators on some occasions. Close friends also help illiterate friends by reading and writing letters.

Most of the support friends provide one another is of an emotional nature, which involves sharing personal problems. Close friends entrust one another with family and health problems. This exchange occurs when friends either visit or call each other on the telephone. A pattern commonly observed between dyads of friends is daily calls. Many women who live alone usually call the friend during the morning hours, to make sure she is all right and to find out how she is feeling.

Another aspect of the emotional support the older women provide one another is daily companionship, occurring more often among those who live alone. For example, Hilda Montes and Rosa Mendoza sit together from 1:00 to 3:00 in the afternoon to watch soap operas and talk about family events, neighborhood happenings, and household management. At 3:00 P.M., whoever is at the other's apartment leaves because their grandchildren usually arrive from school around 4:00 P.M.

Friends are also supportive during health crises. If they cannot come to visit, they inquire daily about their friend's health by telephone. When their health permits, some friends perform menial household chores and always bring food for the sick person. If the occa-

sion requires it, they prepare and/or administer home remedies. Friends, in this sense, alleviate the stress adult children often feel in assisting their aged mothers, particularly those who live by themselves. Friends take turns among themselves or with kin in taking care of the ill during the daytime. Children generally stay throughout the night.

Exchange ties with female friends include instrumental support, companionship, and problem sharing. Friends, particularly age cohorts, play an important role in the emotional well-being of the elders.

The relevance of culture to the experience of old age is seen in the influence of value orientations on the expectations these Puerto Rican women have of themselves and those in their informal support networks. The way a group's cultural tradition defines and interprets relationships influences how elders use their networks to secure the support needed in old age. At the same time, the extent to which reality fits culturally based expectations will contribute, to a large extent, to elders' sense of well-being.

NOTES

1. The article is based on a nineteen-month ethnographic study. The research was supported by the Danforth Foundation; Sigma Xi; the Scientific Research Society; and the Delta Kappa Gamma Society International.

2. All names are fictitious.

3. The deference term *Doña* followed by the woman's first name is a common way by which to address elderly Puerto Rican women and the one preferred by those who participated in the study.

4. Neighborhood grocery stores, generally owned by Puerto Ricans or other Hispanics, where ethnic foods can be purchased.

REFERENCES

Barth, F. 1969. Introduction to F. Barth, ed., *Ethnic groups and boundaries*. Boston: Little, Brown.

Bastida, E. 1979. "Family integration and adjustment to aging among Hispanic American elderly." Ph.D. dissertation, University of Kansas.

Cantor, M. H. 1979. "The informal support system of New York's inner city elderly: Is ethnicity a factor?" In D. L. Gelfand & A. J. Kutzik, eds., *Ethnicity and aging*. New York: Springer.

Carrasquillo, H. 1982. "Perceived social reciprocity and self-esteem among elderly barrio Antillean Hispanics and their familial informal networks." Ph.D. dissertation, Syracuse University.

Delgado, M. 1981. "Hispanic elderly and natural support systems: A special focus on Puerto Ricans." Paper presented at the Scientific Meeting of the Boston Society for Gerontological Psychiatry, November, Boston.

Donaldson, E., & Martínez, E. 1980. "The Hispanic elderly of East Harlem." *Aging* 305–306:6–11.

Sánchez-Ayéndez, M. 1984. "Puerto Rican elderly women: Aging in an ethnic minority group in the United States." Ph.D. dissertation, University of Massachusetts at Amherst.

Stevens, E. P. 1973. "Marianismo: The other face of machismo in Latin America." In A. Pescatello, ed., *Female and male in Latin America*. Pittsburgh: University of Pittsburgh Press.

Intimacy and Sexuality

The processes of socialization encourage women to develop strong interpersonal skills in preparation for roles as wives, mothers, and keepers of the hearth, and for employment in professions associated with nurturance, like teaching and nursing. As a consequence, many women assign great importance and devote much energy to creating satisfying interpersonal relationships in the context of partnerships, families, and communities. Despite women's common interests in interpersonal relationships, the forms those relationships take vary widely. Situated in particular historical, social, and economic contexts, women's beliefs and practices concerning love, intimacy, and sexuality reflect broader social trends. In this section, articles offer glimpses of women's experiences with intimacy and sexuality in particular settings, pointing out that even ideas and feelings about sex are *socially constructed*.

In "'Charity Girls' and City Pleasures: Historical Notes on Working-Class Sexuality, 1880–1920," Kathy Peiss examines the work and social lives of white heterosexual single women in New York City at the turn of the century. In her analysis, Peiss reveals how economics and gender ideologies affect sexuality, including dating patterns.

The association of women with domesticity and emotion may also result in a particular definition of what counts as affection. Francesca M. Cancian considers gender-limited approaches to heterosexual affection in "The Feminization of Love." She argues that the relegation of men and women to separate spheres has produced a widespread and lopsided vision of love which overemphasizes the expressive elements and undervalues instrumental aspects of caring. Cancian calls us to remedy the imbalance by integrating both expressive and material support into our definitions of heterosexual love.

Women's relegation to "private spheres," combined with changing expectations for how women conduct themselves in relationships, makes historical revelations and interpretations of women's lives difficult for feminist scholars. Leila J. Rupp's article, "Imagine My Surprise: Women's Relationships in Mid-Twentieth Century America," explores the difficulty of identifying women's relationships as lesbian or heterosexual, given changing definitions of lesbianism, as well as the social creation of a distinctive lesbian identity. By allowing the letters and other documents of mid-twentieth-century women to speak for themselves, Rupp offers us insight on our foremothers' lives and provides an example of a woman-centered historical analysis.

In addition to partnerships and dyadic friendships, many scholars study communities as sites of emotional attachments. In the twentieth century in the United States a visible lesbian community emerged. In this section's concluding article, "Oral History and the Study of Sexuality in the Lesbian Community: Buffalo, New York, 1940–1960," Madeline Davis and Elizabeth Lapovsky Kennedy document the sexual, social, and political evolution of a lesbian community. In the construction of that community, lesbians created sexual roles that validated women's sexuality and served as precursors of the feminist and gay liberation movements.

279

"Charity Girls" and City Pleasures: Historical Notes on Working-Class Sexuality, 1880–1920

KATHY PEISS

Uncovering the history of working-class sexuality has been a particularly intractable task for recent scholars. Diaries, letters, and memoirs, while a rich source for studies of bourgeois sexuality, offer few glimpses into working-class intimate life. We have had to turn to middle-class commentary and observations of working people, but these accounts often seem hopelessly moralistic and biased. The difficulty with such sources is not simply a question of tone or selectivity, but involves the very categories of analysis they employ. Reformers, social workers, and journalists viewed working-class women's sexuality through middle-class lenses, invoking sexual standards that set "respectability" against "promiscuity." When applied to unmarried women, these categories were constructed foremost around the biological fact of premarital virginity, and secondarily by such cultural indicators as manners, language, dress, and public interaction. Chastity was the measure of young women's respectability, and those who engaged in premarital intercourse, or, more importantly, dressed and acted as though they had, were classed as promiscuous women or prostitutes. Thus labor investigations of the late nineteenth century not only surveyed women's wages and working conditions, but delved into the issue of their sexual virtue, hoping to resolve scientifically the question of working women's respectability.[1]

Nevertheless, some middle-class observers in city missions and settlements recognized that their standards did not always reflect those of working-class

youth. As one University Settlement worker argued, "Many of the liberties which are taken by tenement boys and girls with one another, and which seem quite improper to the 'up-towner,' are, in fact, practically harmless."[2] Working women's public behavior often seemed to fall between the traditional middle-class poles: they were not truly promiscuous in their actions, but neither were they models of decorum. A boarding-house matron, for example, puzzled over the behavior of Mary, a "good girl": "The other night she flirted with a man across the street," she explained. "It is true she dropped him when he offered to take her into a saloon. But she does go to picture shows and dance halls with 'pick up' men and boys."[3] Similarly, a city missionary noted that tenement dwellers followed different rules of etiquette, with the observation: "Young women sometimes allow young men to address them and caress them in a manner which would offend well-bred people, and yet those girls would indignantly resent any liberties which they consider dishonoring."[4] These examples suggest that we must reach beyond the dichotomized analysis of many middle-class observers and draw out the cultural categories created and acted on by working women themselves. How was sexuality "handled" culturally? What manners, etiquette, and sexual style met with general approval? What constituted sexual respectability? Does the polarized framework of the middle class reflect the realities of working-class culture?

Embedded within the reports and surveys lie small pieces of information that illuminate the social and cultural construction of sexuality among a number of working-class women. My discussion focuses on one set of young, white working women in New York City

From *Passion and Power: Sexuality in History* by Kathy Peiss and Christina Simons, eds. Reprinted by permission of Temple University Press.

in the years 1880 to 1920. Most of these women were single wage earners who toiled in the city's factories, shops, and department stores, while devoting their evenings to the lively entertainment of the streets, public dance halls, and other popular amusements. Born or educated in the United States, many adopted a cultural style meant to distance themselves from their immigrant roots and familial traditions. Such women dressed in the latest finery, negotiated city life with ease, and sought intrigue and adventure with male companions. For this group of working women, sexuality became a central dimension of their emergent culture, a dimension that is revealed in their daily life of work and leisure.[5]

These New York working women frequented amusements in which familiarity and intermingling among strangers, not decorum, defined normal public behavior between the sexes. At movies and cheap theaters, crowds mingled during intermission, shared picnic lunches, and commented volubly on performances. Strangers at Coney Island's amusement parks often involved each other in practical jokes and humorous escapades, while dance halls permitted close interaction between unfamiliar men and women. At one respectable Turnverein ball, for example, a vice investigator described closely the chaotic activity in the barroom between dances:

> Most of the younger couples were hugging and kissing, there was a general mingling of men and women at the different tables, almost everyone seemed to know one another and spoke to each other across the tables and joined couples at different tables, they were all singing and carrying on, they kept running around the room and acted like a mob of lunatics let lo[o]se.[6]

As this observer suggests, an important aspect of social familiarity was the ease of sexual expression in language and behavior. Dances were advertised, for example, through the distribution of "pluggers," small printed cards announcing the particulars of the ball, along with snatches of popular songs or verse; the lyrics and pictures, noted one offended reformer, were often "so suggestive that they are absolutely indecent."[7]

The heightened sexual awareness permeating many popular amusements may also be seen in working-class dancing styles. While waltzes and two-steps were common, working women's repertoire included "pivoting" and "tough dances." While pivoting was a wild, spinning dance that promoted a charged atmosphere of physical excitement, tough dances ranged from a slow shimmy, or shaking of the hips and shoulders, to boisterous animal imitations. Such tough dances as the grizzly bear, Charlie Chaplin wiggle, and the dip emphasized bodily contact and the suggestion of sexual intercourse. As one dance investigator commented, "What particularly distinguishes this dance is the motion of the pelvic portions of the body."[8] In contrast, middle-class pleasure-goers accepted the animal dances only after the blatant sexuality had been tamed into refined movement. While cabaret owners enforced strict rules to discourage contact between strangers, managers of working-class dance halls usually winked at spieling, tough dancing, and unrestrained behavior.[9]

Other forms of recreation frequented by working-class youth incorporated a free and easy sexuality into their attractions. Many social clubs and amusement societies permitted flirting, touching, and kissing games at their meetings. One East Side youth reported that "they have kissing all through pleasure time, and use slang language, while in some they don't behave nice between [sic] young ladies."[10] Music halls and cheap vaudeville regularly worked sexual themes and suggestive humor into comedy routines and songs. At a Yiddish music hall popular with both men and women, one reformer found that "the songs are suggestive of everything but what is proper, the choruses are full of double meanings, and the jokes have broad and unmistakable hints of things indecent."[11] Similarly, Coney Island's Steeplechase amusement park, favored by working-class excursionists, carefully marketed sexual titillation and romance in attractions that threw patrons into each other, sent skirts flying, and evoked instant intimacy among strangers.[12]

In attending dance halls, social club entertainments, and amusement resorts, young women took part in a cultural milieu that expressed and affirmed heterosocial interactions. As reformer Belle Israels observed, "No amusement is complete in which 'he' is not a factor."[13] A common custom involved "picking up" unknown men or women in amusement resorts or on the streets, an accepted means of gaining companionship for an evening's entertainment. Indeed, some amusement societies existed for this very purpose. One vice investigator, in his search for "loose" women, was advised by a waiter to "go first on a Sunday night to 'Hans'l & Gret'l Amusement Society' at the Lyceum 86th Str & III Ave, there the girls come and men pick them up."[14] The waiter carefully stressed that these were respectable working women, not prostitutes. Nor was the pickup purely a male prerogative. "With the men they 'pick up,'" writer Hutchins Hapgood observed of East Side shop girls, "they will go to the theater, to late suppers, will be as jolly as they like."[15]

The heterosocial orientation of these amusements made popularity a goal to be pursued through dancing ability, willingness to drink, and eye-catching finery. Women who would not drink at balls and social entertainments were often ostracized by men, while cocktails and ingenious mixtures replaced the five-cent beer and helped to make drinking an acceptable female activity. Many women used clothing as a means of drawing attention to themselves, wearing high-heeled shoes, fancy dresses, costume jewelry, elaborate pompadours, and cosmetics. As one working woman sharply explained, "If you want to get any notion took of you, you gotta have some style about you."[16] The clothing that such women wore no longer served as an emblem of respectability. "The way women dress today they all look like prostitutes," reported one rueful waiter to a dance hall investigator, "and the waiter can some times get in bad by going over and trying to put some one next to them, they may be respectable women and would jump on the waiter."[17]

Underlying the relaxed sexual style and heterosocial interaction was the custom of "treating." Men often treated their female companions to drinks and refreshments, theater tickets, and other incidentals. Women might pay a dance hall's entrance fee or carfare out to an amusement park, but they relied on men's treats to see them through the evening's entertainment. Such treats were highly prized by young working women; as Belle Israels remarked, the announcement that "he treated" was "the acme of achievement in retailing experiences with the other sex."[18]

Treating was not a one-way proposition, however, but entailed an exchange relationship. Financially unable to reciprocate in kind, women offered sexual favors of varying degrees, ranging from flirtatious companionship to sexual intercourse, in exchange for men's treats. "Pleasures don't cost girls so much as they do young men," asserted one saleswoman. "If they are agreeable they are invited out a good deal, and they are not allowed to pay anything." Reformer

Lillian Betts concurred, observing that the working woman held herself responsible for failing to wangle men's invitations and believed that "it is not only her misfortune, but her fault; she should be more attractive."[19] Gaining men's treats placed a high premium on allure and personality, and sometimes involved aggressive and frank "overtures to men whom they desire to attract," often with implicit sexual proposals. One investigator, commenting on women's dependency on men in their leisure time, aptly observed that "those who are unattractive, and those who have puritanic notions, fare but ill in the matter of enjoyments. On the other hand those who do become popular have to compromise with the best conventional usage."[20]

Many of the sexual patterns acceptable in the world of leisure activity were mirrored in the workplace. Sexual harassment by employers, foremen, and fellow workers was a widespread practice in this period, and its form often paralleled the relationship of treating, particularly in service and sales jobs. Department store managers, for example, advised employees to round out their meager salaries by finding a "gentleman friend" to purchase clothing and pleasures. An angry saleswoman testified, for example, that "one of the employers has told me, on a $6.50 wage, he don't care where I get my clothes from as long as I have them, to be dressed to suit him."[21] Waitresses knew that accepting the advances of male customers often brought good tips, and some used their opportunities to enter an active social life with men. "Most of the girls quite frankly admit making 'dates' with strange men," one investigator found. "These 'dates' are made with no thought on the part of the girl beyond getting the good time which she cannot afford herself."[22]

In factories where men and women worked together, the sexual style that we have seen on the dance floor was often reproduced on the shop floor. Many factories lacked privacy in dressing facilities, and workers tolerated a degree of familiarity and roughhousing between men and women. One cigar maker observed that his workplace socialized the young into sexual behavior unrestrained by parental and community control. Another decried the tendency of young boys "of thirteen or fourteen casting an eye upon a 'mash.'" Even worse, he testified, were the

many men who are respected—when I say respected and respectable, I mean who walk the streets and are respected as working men, and who would not under any circumstances offer the slightest insult or disrespectful remark or glance to a female in the streets, but who, in the shops, will whoop and give expressions to "cat calls" and a peculiar noise made with their lips, which is supposed to be an endearing salutation.[23]

In sexually segregated workplaces, sexual knowledge was probably transmitted among working women. A YWCA report in 1913 luridly asserted that "no girl is more 'knowing' than the wage-earner, for the 'older hands' initiate her early through the unwholesome story or innuendo."[24] Evidence from factories, department stores, laundries, and restaurants substantiates the sexual consciousness of female workers. Women brought to the workplace tales of their evening adventures and gossip about dates and eligible men, recounting to their co-workers the triumphs of the latest ball or outing. Women's socialization into a new shop might involve a ritualistic exchange about "gentlemen friends." In one laundry, for example, an investigator repeatedly heard this conversation:

"Say, you got a feller?"
"Sure. Ain't you got one?"
"Sure."[25]

Through the use of slang and "vulgar" language, heterosexual romance was expressed in a sexually explicit context. Among waitresses, for example, frank discussion of lovers and husbands during breaks was an integral part of the work day. One investigator found that "there was never any open violation of the proprieties but always the suggestive talk and behavior." Laundries, too, witnessed "a great deal of swearing among the women." A 1914 study of department store clerks found a similar style and content in everyday conversation:

While it is true that the general attitude toward men and sex relations was normal, all the investigators admitted a freedom of speech frequently verging upon the vulgar, but since there was very little evidence of any actual immorality, this can probably be likened to the same spirit which prompts the telling of risqué stories in other circles.[26]

In their workplaces and leisure activities, many working women discovered a milieu that tolerated, and

at times encouraged, physical and verbal familiarity between men and women, and stressed the exchange of sexual favors for social and economic advantages. Such women probably received conflicting messages about the virtues of virginity, and necessarily mediated the parental, religious, and educational injunctions concerning chastity, and the "lessons" of urban life and labor. The choice made by some women to engage in a relaxed sexual style needs to be understood in terms of the larger relations of class and gender that structured their sexual culture.

Most single working-class women were wage earners for a few years before marriage, contributing to the household income or supporting themselves. Sexual segmentation of the labor market placed women in semi-skilled, seasonal employment with high rates of turnover. Few women earned a "living wage," estimated to be $9.00 or $10.00 a week in 1910, and the wage differential between men and women was vast. Those who lived alone in furnished rooms or boarding houses consumed their earnings in rent, meals, and clothing. Many self-supporting women were forced to sacrifice an essential item in their weekly budgets, particularly food, in order to pay for amusements. Under such circumstances, treating became a viable option. "If my boy friend didn't take me out," asked one working woman, "how could I ever go out?"[27] While many women accepted treats from "steadies," others had no qualms about receiving them from acquaintances or men they picked up at amusement places. As one investigator concluded, "The acceptance on the part of the girl of almost any invitation needs little explanation when one realizes that she often goes pleasureless unless she does accept 'free treats.'"[28] Financial resources were little better for the vast majority of women living with families and relatives. Most of them contributed all of their earnings to the family, receiving only small amounts of spending money, usually 25¢ to 50¢ a week, in return. This sum covered the costs of simple entertainments, but could not purchase higher priced amusements.[29]

Moreover, the social and physical space of the tenement home and boarding house contributed to freer social and sexual practices. Working women living alone ran the gauntlet between landladies' suspicious stares and the knowing glances of male boarders. One furnished-room dweller attested to the pressure placed on young, single women: "Time and again when a male lodger meets a girl on the landing, his salutation usually ends with something like this: 'Won't you step into my place and have a glass of beer with me?'"[30]

The tenement home, too, presented a problem to parents who wished to maintain control over their daughters' sexuality. Typical tenement apartments offered limited opportunities for family activities or chaperoned socializing. Courtship proved difficult in homes where families and boarders crowded into a few small rooms, and the "parlor" served as kitchen, dining room, and bedroom. Instead, many working-class daughters socialized on street corners, rendezvoused in cafes, and courted on trolley cars. As one settlement worker observed, "Boys and girls and young men and women of respectable families are almost obliged to carry on many of their friendships, and perhaps their love-making, on tenement stoops or on street corners."[31] Another reformer found that girls whose parents forebade men's visits to the home managed to escape into the streets and dance halls to meet them. Such young women demanded greater independence in the realm of "personal life" in exchange for their financial contribution to the family. For some, this new freedom spilled over into their sexual practices.[32]

The extent of the sexual culture described here is particularly difficult to establish, since the evidence is too meager to permit conclusions about specific groups of working women, their beliefs about sexuality, and their behavior. Scattered evidence does suggest a range of possible responses, the parameters within which most women would choose to act and define their behavior as socially acceptable. Within this range, there existed a subculture of working women who fully bought into the system of treating and sexual exchange, by trading sexual favors of varying degrees for gifts, treats, and a good time. These women were known in underworld slang as "charity girls," a term that differentiated them from prostitutes because they did not accept money in their sexual encounters with men. As vice reformer George Kneeland found, they "offer themselves to strangers, not for money, but for presents, attention, and pleasure, and most important, a yielding to sex desire."[33] Only a thin line divided these women and "occasional prostitutes," women who slipped in and out of prostitution when unemployed or in need of extra income. Such behavior did not result in the stigma of the "fallen woman." Many working women apparently acted like Dottie: "When she needed a pair of shoes she had found it easy to 'earn' them

in the way that other girls did." Dottie, the investigator reported, was now known as a respectable married woman.[34]

Such women were frequent patrons of the city's dance halls. Vice investigators note a preponderant number of women at dances who clearly were not prostitutes, but were "game" and "lively"; these charity girls often comprised half or more of the dancers in a hall. One dance hall investigator distinguished them with the observation, "Some of the women . . . are out for the coin, but there is a lot that come in here that are charity."[35] One waiter at La Kuenstler Klause, a restaurant with music and dancing, noted that "girls could be gotten here, but they don't go with men for money, only for good time." The investigator continued in his report, "Most of the girls are working girls, not prostitutes, they smoke cigarettes, drink liquers and dance dis[orderly] dances, stay out late and stay with any man, that pick them up first."[36] Meeting two women at a bar, another investigator remarked, "They are both supposed to be working girls but go out for a good time and go the limit."[37]

Some women obviously relished the game of extracting treats from men. One vice investigator offered to take a Kitty Graham, who apparently worked both as a department store clerk and occasional prostitute, to the Central Opera House at 3 A.M.; he noted that "she was willing to go if I'd take a taxi; I finally coaxed her to come with me in a street car."[38] Similarly, Frances Donovan observed waitresses "talking about their engagements which they had for the evening or for the night and quite frankly saying what they expected to get from this or that fellow in the line of money, amusement, or clothes."[39] Working women's manipulation of treating is also suggested by this unguarded conversation overheard by a journalist at Coney Island:

> "What sort of a time did you have?"
> "Great. He blew in $5 on the blow-out."
> "You beat me again. My chump only spent $2.50."[40]

These women had clearly accepted the full implications of the system of treating and the sexual culture surrounding it.

While this evidence points to the existence of charity girls—working women defined as respectable, but who engaged in sexual activity—it tells us little about their numbers, social background, working lives, or relationships to family and community. The vice reports indicate that they were generally young women, many of whom lived at home with their families. One man in a dance hall remarked, for example, that "he sometimes takes them to the hotels, but sometimes the girls won't go to [a] hotel to stay for the night, they are afraid of their mothers, so he gets away with it in the hallway."[41] While community sanctions may have prevented such activity within the neighborhood, the growth of large public dance halls, cabarets, and metropolitan amusement resorts provided an anonymous space in which the subculture of treating could flourish.

The charity girl's activities form only one response in a wide spectrum of social and sexual behavior. Many young women defined themselves sharply against the freer sexuality of their pleasure-seeking sisters, associating "respectability" firmly with premarital chastity and circumspect behavior. One working woman carefully explained her adherence to propriety: "I never go out in the evenings except to my relatives because if I did, I should lose my reputation and that is all I have left." Similarly, shop girls guarded against sexual advances from co-workers and male customers by spurning the temptations of popular amusements. "I keep myself to myself," said one saleswoman. "I don't make friends in the stores very easily because you can't be sure what anyone is like."[42] Settlement workers also noted that women who freely attended "dubious resorts" or bore illegitimate children were often stigmatized by neighbors and workmates. Lillian Betts, for example, cites the case of working women who refused to labor until their employer dismissed a co-worker who had borne a baby out of wedlock. To Betts, however, their adherence to the standard of virginity seemed instrumental, and not a reflection of moral absolutism: "The hardness with which even the suggestion of looseness is treated in any group of working girls is simply an expression of self-preservation."[43]

Other observers noted an ambivalence in the attitudes of young working women toward sexual relations. Social workers reported that the critical stance toward premarital pregnancy was "not always unmixed with a certain degree of admiration for the success with the other sex which the difficulty implies." According to this study, many women increasingly found premarital intercourse acceptable in particular situations: "'A girl can have many friends,' explained one of them,

'but when she gets a "steady," there's only one way to have him and to keep him; I mean to keep him long.'"[44] Such women shared with charity girls the assumption that respectability was not predicated solely on chastity.

Perhaps few women were charity girls or occasional prostitutes, but many more must have been conscious of the need to negotiate sexual encounters in the workplace or in their leisure time. Women would have had to weigh their desire for social participation against traditional sanctions regarding sexual behavior, and charity girls offered to some a model for resolving this conflict. This process is exemplified in Clara Laughlin's report of an attractive but "proper" working woman who could not understand why men friends dropped her after a few dates. Finally she receives the worldly advice of a co-worker that social participation involves an exchange relationship: "Don't yeh know there ain't no feller goin' t'spend coin on yeh fer nothin'? Yeh gotta be a good Indian, Kid—we all gotta!"[45]

For others, charity girls represented a yardstick against which they might measure their own ideas of respectability. The nuances of that measurement were expressed, for example, in a dialogue between a vice investigator and the hat girl at Semprini's dance hall. Answering his proposal for a date, the investigator noted, she "said she'd be glad to go out with me but told me there was nothing doing (i.e., sexually). Said she didn't like to see a man spend money on her and then get disappointed." Commenting on the charity girls that frequented the dance hall, she remarked that "these women get her sick, she can't see why a woman should lay down for a man the first time they take her out. She said it wouldn't be so bad if they went out with the men 3 or 4 times and then went to bed with them but not the first time."[46]

For this hat girl and other young working women, respectability was not defined by the strict measurement of chastity employed by many middle-class observers and reformers. Instead, they adopted a more instrumental and flexible approach to sexual behavior. Premarital sex *could* be labeled respectable in particular social contexts. Thus charity girls distinguished their sexual activity from prostitution, a less acceptable practice, because they did not receive money from men. Other women, who might view charity girls as promiscuous, were untroubled by premarital intimacy with a steady boyfriend.

This fluid definition of sexual respectability was

embedded within the social relations of class and gender, as experienced by women in their daily round of work, leisure, and family life. Women's wage labor and the demands of the working-class household offered daughters few resources for entertainment. At the same time, new commercial amusements offered a tempting world of pleasure and companionship beyond parental control. Within this context, some young women sought to exchange sexual goods for access to that world and its seeming independence, choosing not to defer sexual relations until marriage. Their notions of legitimate premarital behavior contrast markedly with the dominant middle-class view, which placed female sexuality within a dichotomous and rigid framework. Whether a hazard at work, fun and adventure at night, or an opportunity to be exploited, sexual expression and intimacy comprised an integral part of these working women's lives.

NOTES

1. See, for example, Carroll D. Wright, *The Working Girls of Boston* (1889; rpt. New York: 1969).

2. "Influences in Street Life," University Settlement Society *Report* (1900), 30.

3. Marie S. Orenstein, "How the Working Girl of New York Lives," New York State, Factory Investigating Commission, *Fourth Report Transmitted to Legislature,* 15 February 1915, Senate Doc. 43, vol. 4, app. 2 (Albany: 1915), 1697.

4. William T. Elsing, "Life in New York Tenement-Houses as Seen by a City Missionary," *Scribner's* 11 (June 1892): 716.

5. For a more detailed discussion of these women, and further documentation of their social relations and leisure activities, see my Ph.D. dissertation, "Cheap Amusements: Gender Relations and the Use of Leisure Time in New York City, 1880 to 1920," (Brown University, 1982). [See also my book *Cheap Amusements: Working Women and Leisure in Turn-of-the-Century New York* (Philadelphia: 1986).]

6. Investigator's Report, Remey's, 917 Eighth Ave., 11 February 1917, Committee of Fourteen Papers, New York Public Library Manuscript Division, New York.

7. George Kneeland, *Commercialized Prostitution in New York City* (New York: 1913), 68; Louise de Koven Bowen, "Dance Halls," *Survey* 26 (3 July 1911): 384.

8. Committee on Amusements and Vacation Resources of Working Girls, two-page circular, in Box 28, "Parks and Playgrounds Correspondence," Lillian Wald Collection, Rare Book and Manuscripts Library, Columbia University, New York.

9. See, for example, Investigator's Report, Princess Cafe, 1206 Broadway, 1 January 1917; and Excelsior Cafe, 306 Eighth Ave., 21 December 1916, Committee of Fourteen Papers. For an excellent discussion of middle- and upper-class leisure activities, see Lewis A. Erenberg, *Steppin' Out: New York Nightlife and the Transformation of American Culture, 1890–1930* (Westport, Conn.: 1981).

10. "Social Life in the Streets," University Settlement Society *Report* (1899), 32.

11. Paul Klapper, "The Yiddish Music Hall," *University Settlement Studies* 2, no. 4 (1905): 22.

12. For a description of Coney Island amusements, see Edo McCullough, *Good Old Coney Island: A Sentimental Journey into the Past* (New York: 1957), 309–13; and Oliver Pilot and Jo Ransom, *Sodom by the Sea: An Affectionate History of Coney Island* (Garden City, N.J.: 1941).

13. Belle Lindner Israels, "The Way of the Girl," *Survey* 22 (3 July 1909): 486.

14. Investigator's Report, La Kuenstler Klause, 1490 Third Ave., 19 January 1917, Committee of Fourteen Papers.

15. Hutchins Hapgood, *Types from City Streets* (New York: 1910), 131.

16. Clara Laughlin, *The Work-A-Day Girl: A Study of Some Present Conditions* (1913; rpt. New York: 1974), 47, 145. On working women's clothing, see Helen Campbell, *Prisoners of Poverty: Women Wage-Earners, Their Trades and Their Lives* (1887; rpt. Westport, Conn.: 1970), 175; "What It Means to Be a Department Store Girl as Told by the Girl Herself," *Ladies Home Journal* 30 (June 1913): 8; "A Salesgirl's Story," *Independent* 54 (July 1902): 1821. Drinking is discussed in Kneeland, *Commercialized Prostitution,* 70; and Belle Israels, "Diverting a Pastime," *Leslie's Weekly* 113 (27 July 1911): 100.

17. Investigator's Report, Weimann's, 1422 St. Nicholas Ave., 11 February 1917, Committee of Fourteen Papers.

18. Israels, "Way of the Girl," 489; Ruth True, *The Neglected Girl* (New York: 1914), 59.

19. "A Salesgirl's Story," 1821; Lillian Betts, *Leaven in a Great City* (New York: 1902), 251–52.

20. New York State, Factory Investigating Commission, *Fourth Report,* vol. 4, 1585–86; Robert Woods and Albert Kennedy, *Young Working-Girls: A Summary of Evidence from Two Thousand Social Workers* (Boston: 1913), 105.

21. New York State, Factory Investigating Commission,

Fourth Report, vol. 5, 2809; see also Sue Ainslie Clark and Edith Wyatt, *Making Both Ends Meet: The Income and Outlay of New York Working Girls* (New York: 1911), 28. For an excellent analysis of sexual harassment, see Mary Bularzik, *Sexual Harassment at the Workplace: Historical Notes* (Somerville, Mass.: 1978).

22. Consumers' League of New York, *Behind the Scenes in a Restaurant: A Study of 1017 Women Restaurant Employees* (1916), 24; Frances Donovan, *The Woman Who Waits* (1920; rpt. New York: 1974), 42.

23. New York Bureau of Labor Statistics, *Second Annual Report* (1884), 153, 158; *Third Annual Report* (1885), 150–51.

24. Report of Commission on Social Morality from the Christian Standpoint, Made to the Fourth Biennial Convention of the Young Women's Christian Associations of the U.S.A., 1913, Records File Collection, Archives of the National Board of the YWCA of the United States of America, New York, N.Y.

25. Clark and Wyatt, *Making Both Ends Meet,* 187–88; see also Dorothy Richardson, *The Long Day, in Women at Work,* ed. William L. O'Neill (New York: 1972); Amy E. Tanner, "Glimpses at the Mind of a Waitress," *American Journal of Sociology* 13 (July 1907): 52.

26. Committee of Fourteen in New York City, *Annual Report for 1914,* 40; Clark and Wyatt, *Making Both Ends Meet,* 188; Donovan, *The Woman Who Waits,* 26, 80–81.

27. Esther Packard, "Living on Six Dollars a Week," New York State, Factory Investigating Commission, *Fourth Report,* vol. 4, 1677–78. For a discussion of women's wages in New York, see *ibid.,* vol. 1, 35; and vol. 4, 1081, 1509. For an overview of working conditions, see Barbara Wertheimer, *We Were There: The Story of Working Women in America* (New York: 1977), 209–48.

28. Packard, "Living on Six Dollars a Week," 1685.

29. New York State, Factory Investigating Commission, *Fourth Report,* vol. 4, 1512–13, 1581–83; True, *Neglected Girl,* 59.

30. Marie Orenstein, "How the Working Girl of New York Lives," 1702. See also Esther Packard, *A Study of Living Conditions of Self-Supporting Women in New York City* (New York: 1915).

31. "Influences in Street Life," 30; see also Samuel Chotzinoff, *A Lost Paradise* (New York: 1955), 81.

32. On the rejection of parental controls by young women, see Leslie Woodcock Tentler, *Wage-Earning Women: Industrial Work and Family Life in the United States, 1900–1930* (New York: 1979), 110–13. For contemporary accounts, see True, *Neglected Girl,* 54–55, 62–63, 162–63; Lillian Betts, "Tenement House Life and Recreation," *Outlook* (11 February 1899): 365.

33. "Memoranda on Vice Problem: IV. Statement of George J. Kneeland," New York State, Factory Investigating Commission, *Fourth Report,* vol. 1, 403. See also Committee of Fourteen, *Annual Report* (1917), 15, and *Annual Report* (1918), 32; Woods and Kennedy, *Young Working-Girls,* 85.

34. Donovan, *The Woman Who Waits,* 71; on occasional prostitution, see U.S. Senate, *Report on the Condition of Women and Child Wage-Earners in the United States,* U.S. Sen. Doc. 645, 61st Cong., 2nd Sess. (Washington, D.C.: 1911), vol. 15, 83; Laughlin, *The Work-A-Day Girl,* 51–52.

35. Investigator's Report, 2150 Eighth Ave., 12 January 1917, Committee of Fourteen Papers.

36. Investigator's Report, La Kuenstler Klause, 1490 Third Ave., 19 January 1917, Committee of Fourteen Papers.

37. Investigator's Report, Bobby More's, 252 W. 31st Street, 3 February 1917, Committee of Fourteen Papers.

38. Investigator's Report, Remey's, 917 Eighth Ave., 23 December 1916, Committee of Fourteen Papers.

39. Donovan, *The Woman Who Waits,* 55.

40. Edwin Slosson, "The Amusement Business," *Independent* 57 (21 July 1904): 139.

41. Investigator's Report, Clare Hotel and Palm Gardens/ McNamara's, 2150 Eighth Ave., 12 January 1917, Committee of Fourteen Papers.

42. Marie Orenstein, "How the Working Girl of New York Lives," 1703; Clark and Wyatt, *Making Both Ends Meet,* 28–29.

43. Betts, *Leaven in a Great City,* 81, 219.

44. Woods and Kennedy, *Young Working-Girls,* 87, 85.

45. Laughlin, *The Work-A-Day Girl,* 50.

46. Investigator's Report, Semprini's, 145 W. 50th Street, 5 October 1918, Committee of Fourteen Papers.

The Feminization of Love

FRANCESCA M. CANCIAN

A feminized and incomplete perspective on love predominates in the United States. We identify love with emotional expression and talking about feelings, aspects of love that women prefer and in which women tend to be more skilled than men. At the same time we often ignore the instrumental and physical aspects of love that men prefer, such as providing help, sharing activities, and sex. This feminized perspective leads us to believe that women are much more capable of love than men and that the way to make relationships more loving is for men to become more like women.[1] This paper proposes an alternative, androgynous perspective on love, one based on the premise that love is both instrumental and expressive.[2] From this perspective, the way to make relationships more loving is for women and men to reject polarized gender roles and integrate "masculine" and "feminine" styles of love.

THE TWO PERSPECTIVES

"Love is active, doing something for your good even if it bothers me" says a fundamentalist Christian. "Love is sharing, the real sharing of feelings" says a divorced secretary who is in love again. In ancient Greece, the ideal love was the adoration of a man for a beautiful young boy who was his lover. In the thirteenth century, the exemplar of love was the chaste devotion of a knight for another man's wife. In Puritan New England, love between husband and wife was the ideal, and in Victorian times, the asexual devotion of a mother for her child seemed the essence of love.[3] My purpose is to focus on one kind of love: long-term heterosexual love in the contemporary United States.

What is a useful definition of enduring love between a woman and a man? One guideline for a definition comes from the prototypes of enduring love—the relations between committed lovers, husband and wife, parent and child. These relationships combine care and assistance with physical and emotional closeness. Studies of attachment between infants and their mothers emphasize the importance of being protected and fed as well as touched and held. In marriage, according to most family sociologists, both practical help and affection are part of enduring love, or "the affection we feel for those with whom our lives are deeply intertwined."[4] Our own informal observations often point in the same direction: if we consider the relationships that are the prototypes of enduring love, it seems that what we really mean by love is some combination of instrumental and expressive qualities.

Historical studies provide a second guideline for defining enduring love, specifically between a woman and a man.[5] In precapitalist America, such love was a complex whole that included work and feelings. Then it was split into feminine and masculine fragments by the separation of home and workplace. This historical analysis implies that affection, material help, and routine cooperation all are parts of enduring love.

Consistent with these guidelines, my working definition of enduring love between adults is a relationship wherein a small number of people are affectionate and emotionally committed to each other, define their collective well-being as a major goal, and feel obliged to provide care and practical assistance for each other. People who love each other also usually share physical contact; they communicate with each other frequently and cooperate in some routine tasks of daily life. My discussion is of enduring heterosexual love only; I will for the sake of simplicity refer to it as "love."

From *Signs: Journal of Women in Culture and Society*, 1986, vol. 11, no. 4. Copyright © 1986 by The University of Chicago Press. All rights reserved.

In contrast to this broad definition of love, the narrower, feminized definition dominates both contemporary scholarship and public opinion. Most scholars who study love, intimacy, or close friendship focus on qualities that are stereotypically feminine, such as talking about feelings.[6] For example, Abraham Maslow defines love as "a feeling of tenderness and affection with great enjoyment, happiness, satisfaction, elation and even ecstasy." Among healthy individuals, he says, "there is a growing intimacy and honesty and self-expression."[7] Zick Rubin's "Love Scale," designed to measure the degree of passionate love as opposed to liking, includes questions about confiding in each other, longing to be together, and sexual attraction as well as caring for each other. Studies of friendship usually distinguish close friends from acquaintances on the basis of how much personal information is disclosed, and many recent studies of married couples and lovers emphasize communication and self-disclosure. A recent book on marital love by Lillian Rubin focuses on intimacy, which she defines as "reciprocal expression of feeling and thought, not out of fear or dependent need, but out of a wish to know another's inner life and to be able to share one's own."[8] She argues that intimacy is distinct from nurturance or caretaking and that men are usually unable to be intimate.

Among the general public, love is also defined primarily as expressing feelings and verbal disclosure, not as instrumental help. This is especially true among the more affluent; poorer people are more likely than they to see practical help and financial assistance as a sign of love.[9] In a study conducted in 1980, 130 adults from a wide range of social classes and ethnic backgrounds were interviewed about the qualities that make a good love relationship. The most frequent response referred to honest and open communication. Being caring and supportive and being tolerant and understanding were the other qualities most often mentioned.[10] Similar results were reported from Ann Swidler's study of an affluent suburb: the dominant conception of love stressed communicating feelings, working on the relationship, and self-development.[11] Finally, a contemporary dictionary defines love as "strong affection for another arising out of kinship or personal ties" and as attraction based on sexual desire, affection, and tenderness.[12]

These contemporary definitions of love clearly focus on qualities that are seen as feminine in our culture. A study of gender roles in 1968 found that warmth, expressiveness, and talkativeness were seen as appropriate for women and not for men. In 1978 the core features of gender stereotypes were unchanged although fewer qualities were seen as appropriate for only one sex. Expressing tender feelings, being gentle, and being aware of the feelings of others were still ideal qualities for women and not for men. The desirable qualities for men and not for women included being independent, unemotional, and interested in sex.[13] The only component perceived as masculine in popular definitions of love is interest in sex.

The two approaches to defining love—one broad, encompassing instrumental and affective qualities, one narrow, including only the affective qualities—inform the two different perspectives on love. According to the androgynous perspective, both gender roles contain elements of love. The feminine role does not include all of the major ways of loving; some aspects of love come from the masculine role, such as sex and providing material help, and some, such as cooperating in daily tasks, are associated with neither gender role. In contrast, the feminized perspective on love implies that all of the elements of love are included in the feminine role. The capacity to love is divided by gender. Women can love and men cannot.

SOME FEMINIST INTERPRETATIONS

Feminist scholars are divided on the question of love and gender. Supporters of the feminized perspective seem most influential at present. Nancy Chodorow's psychoanalytic theory has been especially influential in promoting a feminized perspective on love among social scientists studying close relationships. Chodorow's argument—in greatly simplified form—is that as infants, both boys and girls have strong identification and intimate attachments with their mothers. Since boys grow up to be men, they must repress this early identification, and in the process they repress their capacity for intimacy. Girls retain their early identification since they will grow up to be women, and throughout their lives females see themselves as connected to others. As a result of this process, Chodorow argues, "girls come to define and experience themselves as continuous with others; . . . boys come to define themselves as more separate and distinct."[14] This theory implies that love is feminine—women are more open to love than men—and that this gender difference will remain as long as women are the primary caretakers of infants.

Scholars have used Chodorow's theory to develop the idea that love and attachment are fundamental parts of women's personalities but not of men's. Carol Gilligan's influential book on female personality development asserts that women define their identity "by a standard of responsibility and care." The predominant female image is "a network of connection, a web of relationships that is sustained by a process of communication." In contrast, males favor a "hierarchical ordering, with its imagery of winning and losing and the potential for violence which it contains." "Although the world of the self that men describe at times includes 'people' and 'deep attachments,' no particular person or relationship is mentioned. . . . Thus the male 'I' is defined in separation."[15]

A feminized conception of love can be supported by other theories as well. In past decades, for example, such a conception developed from Talcott Parsons's theory of the benefits to the nuclear family of women's specializing in expressive action and men's specializing in instrumental action. Among contemporary social scientists, the strongest support for the feminized perspective comes from such psychological theories as Chodorow's.[16]

On the other hand, feminist historians have developed an incisive critique of the feminized perspective on love. Mary Ryan and other social historians have analyzed how the separation of home and workplace in the nineteenth century polarized gender roles and feminized love.[17] Their argument, in simplified form, begins with the observation that in the colonial era the family household was the arena for economic production, affection, and social welfare. The integration of activities in the family produced a certain integration of expressive and instrumental traits in the personalities of men and women. Both women and men were expected to be hard working, modest, and loving toward their spouses and children, and the concept of love included instrumental cooperation as well as expression of feelings. In Ryan's words, "When early Americans spoke of love they were not withdrawing into a female byway of human experience. Domestic affection, like sex and economics, was not segregated into male and female spheres." There was a "reciprocal ideal of conjugal love" that "grew out of the day-to-day cooperation, sharing, and closeness of the diversified home economy."[18]

Economic production gradually moved out of the home and became separated from personal relation-

ships as capitalism expanded. Husbands increasingly worked for wages in factories and shops while wives stayed at home to care for the family. This division of labor gave women more experience with close relationships and intensified women's economic dependence on men. As the daily activities of men and women grew further apart, a new worldview emerged that exaggerated the differences between the personal, loving feminine sphere of the home and the impersonal, powerful, masculine sphere of the workplace. Work became identified with what men do for money while love became identified with women's activities at home. As a result, the conception of love shifted toward emphasizing tenderness, powerlessness, and the expression of emotion.[19]

This partial and feminized conception of love persisted into the twentieth century as the division of labor remained stable: the workplace remained impersonal and separated from the home, and married women continued to be excluded from paid employment. According to this historical explanation, one might expect a change in the conception of love since the 1940s, as growing numbers of wives took jobs. However, women's persistent responsibility for child care and housework, and their lower wages, might explain a continued feminized conception of love.[20]

Like the historical critiques, some psychological studies of gender also imply that our current conception of love is distorted and needs to be integrated with qualities associated with the masculine role. For example, Jean Baker Miller argues that women's ways of loving—their need to be attached to a man and to serve others—result from women's powerlessness, and that a better way of loving would integrate power with women's style of love.[21] The importance of combining activities and personality traits that have been split apart by gender is also a frequent theme in the human potential movement.[22] These historical and psychological works emphasize the flexibility of gender roles and the inadequacy of a concept of love that includes only the feminine half of human qualities. In contrast, theories like Chodorow's emphasize the rigidity of gender differences after childhood and define love in terms of feminine qualities. The two theoretical approaches are not as inconsistent as my simplified sketches may suggest, and many scholars combine them;[23] however, the two approaches have different implications for empirical research.

EVIDENCE ON WOMEN'S "SUPERIORITY" IN LOVE

A large number of studies show that women are more interested and more skilled in love than men. However, most of these studies use biased measures based on feminine styles of loving, such as verbal self-disclosure, emotional expression, and willingness to report that one has close relationships. When less biased measures are used, the differences between women and men are often small.

Women have a greater number of close relationships than men. At all stages of the life cycle, women see their relatives more often. Men and women report closer relations with their mothers than with their fathers and are generally closer to female kin. Thus an average Yale man in the 1970s talked about himself more with his mother than with his father and was more satisfied with his relationship with his mother. His most frequent grievance against his father was that his father gave too little of himself and was cold and uninvolved; his grievance against his mother was that she gave too much of herself and was alternately over-protective and punitive.[24]

Throughout their lives, women are more likely to have a confidant—a person to whom one discloses personal experiences and feelings. Girls prefer to be with one friend or a small group, while boys usually play competitive games in large groups. Men usually get together with friends to play sports or do some other activity, while women get together explicitly to talk and to be together.[25]

Men seem isolated given their weak ties with their families and friends. Among blue-collar couples interviewed in 1950, 64 percent of the husbands had no confidants other than their spouses, compared to 24 percent of the wives.[26] The predominantly upper-middle-class men interviewed by Daniel Levinson in the 1970s were no less isolated. Levinson concludes that "close friendship with a man or a woman is rarely experienced by American men."[27] Apparently, most men have no loving relationships besides those with wife or lover; and given the estrangement that often occurs in marriages, many men may have no loving relationships at all.

Several psychologists have suggested that there is a natural reversal of these roles in middle age, as men become more concerned with relationships and women turn toward independence and achievement; but there seems to be no evidence showing that men's relationships become more numerous or more intimate after middle age, and some evidence to the contrary.[28]

Women are also more skilled than men in talking about relationships. Whether working class or middle class, women value talking about feelings and relationships and disclose more than men about personal experiences. Men who deviate and talk a lot about their personal experiences are commonly defined as feminine and maladjusted.[29] Working-class wives prefer to talk about themselves, their close relationships with family and friends, and their homes, while their husbands prefer to talk about cars, sports, work, and politics. The same gender-specific preferences are expressed by college students.[30]

Men do talk more about one area of personal experience: their victories and achievements; but talking about success is associated with power, not intimacy. Women say more about their fears and disappointments, and it is disclosure of such weaknesses that usually is interpreted as a sign of intimacy.[31] Women are also more accepting of the expression of intense feelings, including love, sadness, and fear, and they are more skilled in interpreting other people's emotions.[32]

Finally, in their leisure time women are drawn to topics of love and human entanglements while men are drawn to competition among men. Women's preferences in television viewing run to daytime soap operas, or if they are more educated, the high-brow soap operas on educational channels, while most men like to watch competitive and often aggressive sports. Reading tastes show the same pattern. Women read novels and magazine articles about love, while men's magazines feature stories about men's adventures and encounters with death.[33]

However, this evidence on women's greater involvement and skill in love is not as strong as it appears. Part of the reason that men seem so much less loving than women is that their behavior is measured with a feminine ruler. Much of this research considers only the kinds of loving behavior that are associated with the feminine role and rarely compares women and men in terms of qualities associated with the masculine role. When less biased measures are used, the behavior of men and women is often quite similar. For example, in a careful study of kinship relations among young adults in a southern city, Bert Adams found that women were much more likely than men to say that their parents and relatives were very important to their

THE MYTH OF THE PERFECT BODY

ROBERTA GALLER

A woman was experiencing severe abdominal pain. She was rushed to the emergency room and examined, then taken to the operating room, where an appendectomy was performed. After surgery, doctors concluded that her appendix was fine but that she had VD. It never occurred to them that this woman had a sexual life at all, because she was in a wheelchair.

I saw a woman who had cerebral palsy at a neuromuscular clinic. She was covered with bruises. After talking with her, it became clear that she was a battered wife. I brought her case to the attention of the medical director and social worker, both progressive practitioners who are knowledgeable about resources for battered women. They said, "But he supports her. Who else will take care of her? And besides, if she complains, the court might take custody of her children."

As a feminist and psychotherapist I am politically and professionally interested in the impact of body image on a woman's self-esteem and sense of sexuality. However, it is as a woman with a disability that I am personally involved with these issues. I had polio when I was 10 years old, and now with arthritis and some new aches and pains I feel in a rather exaggerated fashion other effects of aging, a progressive disability we all share to some degree.

Although I've been disabled since childhood, until the past few years I didn't know anyone else with a disability and in fact *avoided* knowing anyone with a disability. I had many of the same fears and anxieties which many of you who are currently able-bodied might feel about close association with anyone with a disability. I had not opted for, but in fact rebelled against the prescribed role of dependence expected of women growing up when I did

Excerpts from "The Myth of the Perfect Body" by Roberta Galler, in *Pleasure and Danger* edited by Carole S. Vance. Copyright © 1984 by Roberta Galler. Reprinted by permission of HarperCollins Ltd.

and which is still expected of disabled women. I became the "exceptional" woman, the "super-crip," noted for her independence. I refused to let my identity be shaped by my disability. I wanted to be known for *who* I am and not just by what I physically cannot do.

Although I was not particularly conscious of it at the time, I was additionally burdened with extensive conflicts about dependency and feelings of shame over my own imperfections and realistic limitations. So much of my image and definition of myself had been rooted in a denial of the impact of my disability. Unfortunately, my values and emphasis on independence involved an assumption that any form of help implied dependence and was therefore humiliating.

As the aging process accelerated the impact of my disability, it became more difficult to be stoic or heroic or ignore my increased need for help at times. This personal crisis coincided in time with the growing national political organization of disabled persons who were asserting their rights, demanding changes in public consciousness and social policy, and working to remove environmental and attitudinal barriers to the potential viability of their lives.

Disabled women also began a dialogue within the feminist community. On a personal level it has been through a slow process of disability consciousness-raising aided by newly-found "sisters in disability," as well as through profoundly moving discussions with close, non-disabled friends that we, through mutual support and self-disclosure, began to explore our feelings and to shed the shame and humiliation associated with needing help. We began to understand that to need help did not imply helplessness nor was it the opposite of independence. This increased appreciation of mutual interdependence as part of the human condition caused us to reexamine the feminist idea of autonomy versus dependence.

Feminists have long attacked the media image of "the Body Beautiful" as oppressive, exploitative, and objectifying. Even in our attempts to create alternatives, however, we develop standards which oppress some of us. The feminist ideal of autonomy does not take into account the realistic needs for help that disabled, aging—and, in fact, most—women have. The image of the physically strong "superwoman" is also out of reach for most of us.

As we began to develop disability consciousness, we recognized significant parallels to feminist consciousness. For example, it is clear that just as society creates an ideal of beauty which is oppressive for us all, it creates an ideal model of the physically perfect person who is not beset with weakness, loss, or pain. It is toward these distorted ideals of perfection in form and function that we all strive and with which we identify.

The disabled (and aging) woman poses a symbolic threat by reminding us how tenuous that model, "the myth of the perfect body," really is, and we might want to run from this thought. The disabled woman's body may not meet the standard of "perfection" in either image, form, or function. On the one hand, disabled women share the social stereotype of women in general as being weak and passive, and in fact are depicted as the epitome of the incompetent female. On the other hand, disabled women are not viewed as women at all, but portrayed as helpless, dependent children in need of protection. She is not seen as the sexy, but the sexless object, asexual, neutered, unbeautiful and unable to find a lover. This stigmatized view of the disabled woman reflects a perception of assumed inadequacy on the part of the non-disabled.

For instance, disabled women are often advised by professionals not to bear children, and are (within race and class groupings) more likely to be threatened by or be victims of involuntary sterilization. Concerns for reproductive freedom and child custody, as well as rape and domestic violence often exclude the disabled woman by assuming her to be an asexual creature. The perception that a disabled woman couldn't possibly get a man to care for or take care of her underlies the instances where professionals have urged disabled women who have been victims of brutal battery to stay with abusive males. Members of the helping professions often assume that no other men would want them.

Disability is often associated with sin, stigma and a kind of "untouchability." Anxiety, as well as a sense of vulnerability and dread, may cause others to respond to the "imperfections" of a disabled woman's body with terror, avoidance, pity and/or guilt. In a special *Off Our Backs* issue on disabled women, Jill Lessing postulated that it is "through fear and denial that attitudes of repulsion and oppression are acted out on disabled people in ways ranging from our solicitous good intentions to total invisibility and isolation."*

Even when the disabled woman is idealized for surmounting all obstacles, she is the recipient of a distancing admiration, which assumes her achievement to be necessary compensation for a lack of sexuality, intimacy, and love. The stereotype of the independent "super-crip," although embodying images of strength and courage, involves avoidance and denial of the realities of disability for both the observer and the disabled woman herself.

These discomforts may evoke a wish that disabled women remain invisible and that their sexuality be a hidden secret. However, disabled (and aging) women are coming out; we are beginning to examine our issues publicly, forcing other women to address not only the issues of disability but to reexamine their attitudes toward their own limitations and lack of perfection, toward oppressive myths, standards, and social conditions which affect us all. . . .

*Jill Lessing, "Denial and Disability," *Off Our Backs,* vol. xi, no. 5, May 1981, p. 21.

lives (58 percent of women and 37 percent of men). In measures of actual contact with relatives, though, there were much smaller differences: 88 percent of women and 81 percent of men whose parents lived in the same city saw their parents weekly. Adams concluded that "differences between males and females in relations with parents are discernible primarily in the subjective sphere; contact frequencies are quite similar."[34]

The differences between the sexes can be small even when biased measures are used. For example, Marjorie Lowenthal and Clayton Haven reported the finding, later widely quoted, that elderly women were more likely than elderly men to have a friend with whom they could talk about their personal troubles—clearly a measure of a traditionally feminine behavior. The figures revealed that 81 percent of the married women and 74 percent of the married men had confidants—not a sizable difference.[35] On the other hand, whatever the measure, virtually all such studies find that women are more involved in close relationships than men, even if the difference is small.

In sum, women are only moderately superior to men in love: they have more close relationships and care more about them, and they seem to be more skilled at love, especially those aspects of love that involve expressing feelings and being vulnerable. This does not mean that men are separate and unconcerned with close relationships, however. When national surveys ask people what is most important in their lives, women tend to put family bonds first while men put family bonds first or second, along with work.[36] For both sexes, love is clearly very important.

EVIDENCE ON
THE MASCULINE STYLE OF LOVE

Men tend to have a distinctive style of love that focuses on practical help, shared physical activities, spending time together, and sex.[37] The major elements of the masculine style of love emerged in Margaret Reedy's study of 102 married couples in the late 1970s. She showed individuals statements describing aspects of love and asked them to rate how well the statements described their marriages. On the whole, husband and wife had similar views of their marriage, but several sex differences emerged. Practical help and spending time together were more important to men. The men were more likely to give high ratings to such statements as: "When she needs help I help her," and "She would rather spend her time with me than with anyone else." Men also described themselves more often as sexually attracted and endorsed such statements as: "I get physically excited and aroused just thinking about her." In addition, emotional security was less important to men than to women, and men were less likely to describe the relationship as secure, safe, and comforting.[38] Another study in the late 1970s showed a similar pattern among young, highly educated couples. The husbands gave greater emphasis to feeling responsible for

the partner's well-being and putting the spouse's needs first, as well as to spending time together. The wives gave greater importance to emotional involvement and verbal self-disclosure but also were more concerned than the men about maintaining their separate activities and their independence.[39]

The difference between men and women in their views of the significance of practical help was demonstrated in a study in which seven couples recorded their interactions for several days. They noted how pleasant their relations were and counted how often the spouse did a helpful chore, such as cooking a good meal or repairing a faucet, and how often the spouse expressed acceptance or affection. The social scientists doing the study used a feminized definition of love. They labeled practical help as "instrumental behavior" and expressions of acceptance or affection as "affectionate behavior," thereby denying the affectionate aspect of practical help. The wives seemed to be using the same scheme; they thought their marital relations were pleasant that day if their husbands had directed a lot of affectionate behavior to them, regardless of their husbands' positive instrumental behavior. The husbands' enjoyment of their marital relations, on the other hand, depended on their wives' instrumental actions, not on their expressions of affection. The men actually saw instrumental actions as affection.[40] One husband who was told by the researchers to increase his affectionate behavior toward his wife decided to wash her car and was surprised when neither his wife nor the researchers accepted that as an "affectionate" act.

The masculine view of instrumental help as loving behavior is clearly expressed by a husband discussing his wife's complaints about his lack of communication: "What does she want? Proof? She's got it, hasn't she? Would I be knocking myself out to get things for her—like to keep up this house—if I didn't love her? Why does a man do things like that if not because he loves his wife and kids? I swear, I can't figure what she wants." His wife, who has a feminine orientation to love, says something very different: "It is not enough that he supports us and takes care of us. I appreciate that, but I want him to share things with me. I need for him to tell me his feelings."[41] Many working-class women agree with men that a man's job is something he does out of love for his family,[42] but middle-class women and social scientists rarely recognize men's practical help as a form of love. (Indeed, among upper-middle-class men whose jobs offer a great deal of intrinsic gratification, their belief that they are "doing it for the family" may seem somewhat self-serving.)

Other differences between men's and women's styles of love involve sex. Men seem to separate sex and love while women connect them,[43] but, paradoxically, sexual intercourse seems to be the most meaningful way of giving and receiving love for many men. A twenty-nine-year-old carpenter who had been married for three years said that, after sex, "I feel so close to her and the kids. We feel like a real family then. I don't talk to her very often, I guess, but somehow I feel we have really communicated after we have made love."[44]

Because sexual intimacy is the only recognized "masculine" way of expressing love, the recent trend toward viewing sex as a way for men and women to express mutual intimacy is an important challenge to the feminization of love. However, the connection between sexuality and love is undermined both by the "sexual revolution" definition of sex as a form of casual recreation and by the view of male sexuality as a weapon—as in rape—with which men dominate and punish women.[45]

Another paradoxical feature of men's style of love is that men have a more romantic attitude toward their partners than do women. In Reedy's study, men were more likely to select statements like "we are perfect for each other."[46] In a survey of college students, 65 percent of the men but only 24 percent of the women said that, even if a relationship had all of the other qualities they desired, they would not marry unless they were in love.[47] The common view of this phenomenon focuses on women. The view is that women marry for money and status and so see marriage as instrumentally, rather than emotionally, desirable. This of course is at odds with women's greater concern with self-disclosure and emotional intimacy and lesser concern with instrumental help. A better way to explain men's greater romanticism might be to focus on men. One such possible explanation is that men do not feel responsible for "working on" the emotional aspects of a relationship, and therefore see love as magically and perfectly present or absent. This is consistent with men's relative lack of concern with affective interaction and greater concern with instrumental help.

In sum, there is a masculine style of love. Except for romanticism, men's style fits the popularly conceived masculine role of being the powerful provider.[48] From the androgynous perspective, the practical help and physical activities included in this role are as much a part of love as the expression of feelings. The feminized perspective cannot account for this masculine style of love; nor can it explain why women and men are so close in the degrees to which they are loving.

NEGATIVE CONSEQUENCES OF THE FEMINIZATION OF LOVE

The division of gender roles in our society that contributes to the two separate styles of love is reinforced by the feminized perspective and leads to political and moral problems that would be mitigated with a more androgynous approach to love. The feminized perspective works against some of the key values and goals of feminists and humanists by contributing to the devaluation and exploitation of women.

It is especially striking how the differences between men's and women's styles of love reinforce men's power over women. Men's style involves giving women important resources, such as money and protection that men control and women believe they need, and ignoring the resources that women control and men need. Thus men's dependency on women remains covert and repressed, while women's dependency on men is overt and exaggerated; and it is overt dependency that creates power, according to social exchange theory.[49] The feminized perspective on love reinforces this power differential by leading to the belief that women need love more than do men, which is implied in the association of love with the feminine role. The effect of this belief is to intensify the asymmetrical dependency of women on men.[50] In fact, however, evidence on the high death rates of unmarried men suggests that men need love at least as much as do women.[51]

Sexual relations also can reinforce male dominance insofar as the man takes the initiative and intercourse is defined either as his "taking" pleasure or as his being skilled at "giving" pleasure, either way giving him control. The man's power advantage is further strengthened if the couple assumes that the man's sexual needs can be filled only by any attractive woman while the woman's sexual needs can be filled only by the man she loves.[52]

On the other hand, women's preferred ways of loving seem incompatible with control. They involve admitting dependency and sharing or losing control, and being emotionally intense. Further, the intimate talk about personal troubles that appeals to women requires of a couple a mutual vulnerability, a willingness to see oneself as weak and in need of support. It is true that a woman, like a man, can gain some power by providing her partner with services, such as understanding, sex, or cooking; but this power is largely unrecognized because the man's dependency on such services is not overt. The couple may even see these services as her duty or as her response to his requests (or demands).

The identification of love with expressing feelings also contributes to the lack of recognition of women's power by obscuring the instrumental, active component of women's love just as it obscures the loving aspect of men's work. In a culture that glorifies instrumental achievement, this identification devalues both women and love.[53] In reality, a major way by which women are loving is in the clearly instrumental activities associated with caring for others, such as preparing meals, washing clothes, and providing care during illness; but because of our focus on the expressive side of love, this caring work of women is either ignored or redefined as expressing feelings. Thus, from the feminized perspective on love, child care is a subtle communication of attitudes, not work. A wife washing her husband's shirt is seen as expressing love, even though a husband washing his wife's car is seen as doing a job.

Gilligan, in her critique of theories of human development, shows the way in which devaluing love is linked to devaluing women. Basic to most psychological theories of development is the idea that a healthy person develops from a dependent child to an autonomous, independent adult. As Gilligan comments, "Development itself comes to be identified with separation, and attachments appear to be developmental impediments."[54] Thus women, who emphasize attachment, are judged to be developmentally retarded or insufficiently individuated.

The pervasiveness of this image was documented in a well-known study of mental health professionals who were asked to describe mental health, femininity, and masculinity. They associated both mental health and masculinity with independence, rationality, and dominance. Qualities concerning attachment, such as being tactful, gentle, or aware of the feelings of others, they associated with femininity but not with mental health.[55]

Another negative consequence of a feminized per-spective on love is that it legitimates impersonal, exploitive relations in the workplace and the community. The ideology of separate spheres that developed in the nineteenth century contrasted the harsh, immoral marketplace with the warm and loving home and implied that this contrast is acceptable.[56] Defining love as expressive, feminine, and divorced from productive activity maintains this ideology. If personal relationships and love are reserved for women and the home, then it is acceptable for a manager to underpay workers or for a community to ignore a needy family. Such behavior is not unloving; it is businesslike or shows a respect for privacy. The ideology of separate spheres also implies that men are properly judged by their instrumental and economic achievements and that poor or unsuccessful men are failures who may deserve a hard life. Levinson presents a conception of masculine development itself as centering on achieving an occupational dream.[57]

Finally, the feminization of love intensifies the conflicts over intimacy between women and men in close relationships. One of the most common conflicts is that the woman wants more closeness and verbal contact while the man withdraws and wants less pressure.[58] Her need for more closeness is partly the result of the feminization of love, which encourages her to be more emotionally dependent on him. Because love is feminine, he in turn may feel controlled during intimate contact. Intimacy is her "turf," an area where she sets the rules and expectations. Talking about the relationship, as she wants, may well feel to him like taking a test that she made up and that he will fail. He is likely to react by withdrawing, causing her to intensify her efforts to get closer. The feminization of love thus can lead to a vicious cycle of conflict where neither partner feels in control or gets what she or he wants.

CONCLUSION

The values of improving the status of women and humanizing the public sphere are shared by many of the scholars who support a feminized conception of love; and they, too, explain the conflicts in close relationships in terms of polarized gender roles. Nancy Chodorow, Lillian Rubin, and Carol Gilligan have addressed these issues in detail and with great insight. However, by arguing that women's identity is based on attachment while men's identity is based on separation, they reinforce the distinction between feminine expressiveness and masculine instrumentality, revive the ideology of separate spheres, and legitimate the popular idea that only women know the right way to love. They also suggest that there is no way to overcome the rigidity of gender roles other than by pursuing the goal of men and women becoming equally involved in infant care. In contrast, an androgynous perspective on love challenges the identification of women and love with being expressive, powerless, and nonproductive and the identification of men with being instrumental, powerful, and productive. It rejects the ideology of separate spheres and validates masculine as well as feminine styles of love. This viewpoint suggests that progress could be made by means of a variety of social changes, including men doing child care, relations at work becoming more androgynous. Changes that equalize power within close relationships by equalizing the economic and emotional dependency between men

and women may be especially important in moving toward androgynous love.

The validity of an androgynous definition of love cannot be "proven": the view that informs the androgynous perspective is that both the feminine style of love (characterized by emotional closeness and verbal self-disclosure) and the masculine style of love (characterized by instrumental help and sex) represent necessary parts of a good love relationship. Who is more loving: a couple who confide most of their experiences to each other but rarely cooperate or give each other practical help, or a couple who help each other through many crises and cooperate in running a household but rarely discuss their personal experiences? Both relationships are limited. Most people would probably choose a combination: a relationship that integrates feminine and masculine styles of loving, an androgynous love.

ACKNOWLEDGMENTS

I am indebted to Frank Cancian, Steven Gordon, Lillian Rubin, and Scott Swain for helpful comments and discussions.

NOTES

1. The term "feminization" of love is derived from Ann Douglas. *The Feminization of Culture* (New York: Alfred A. Knopf, 1977).

2. The term "androgyny" is problematic. It assumes rather than questions sex-role stereotypes (aggression is masculine, e.g.,); it can lead to a utopian view that underestimates the social causes of sexism; and it suggests the complete absence of differences between men and women, which is biologically impossible. Nonetheless, I use the term because it best conveys my meaning: a combination of masculine and feminine styles of love. The negative and positive aspects of the concept "androgyny" are analyzed in a special issue of *Women's Studies* (vol. 2, no. 2 [1974]), edited by Cynthia Secor. Also see Sandra Bem, "Gender Schema Theory and Its Implications for Child Development: Raising Gender-aschematic Children in a Gender-schematic Society," *Signs: Journal of Women in Culture and Society* 8, no. 4 (1983): 598–616.

3. The quotations are from a study by Ann Swidler, "Ideologies of Love in Middle Class America" (paper presented at the annual meeting of the Pacific Sociological

Association, San Diego, 1982). For useful reviews of the history of love, see Morton Hunt, *The Natural History of Love* (New York: Alfred A. Knopf, 1959): and Bernard Murstein, *Love, Sex and Marriage through the Ages* (New York: Springer, 1974).

4. See John Bowlby, *Attachment and Loss* (New York: Basic Books, 1969), on mother-infant attachment. The quotation is from Elaine Walster and G. William Walster, *A New Look at Love* (Reading, Mass.: Addison-Wesley Publishing Co., 1978), 9. Conceptions of love and adjustment used by family sociologists are reviewed in Robert Lewis and Graham Spanier, "Theorizing about the Quality and Stability of Marriage," in *Contemporary Theories about the Family,* ed. W. Burr, R. Hill, F. Nye, and I. Reiss (New York: Free Press, 1979), 268–94.

5. Mary Ryan, *Womanhood in America,* 2d ed. (New York: New Viewpoints, 1979), and *The Cradle of the Middle Class: The Family in Oneida County, N.Y., 1970–1865* (New York: Cambridge University Press, 1981); Barbara Ehrenreich and Deirdre English, *For Her Own Good: 150 Years of Experts' Advice to Women* (New York: Anchor Books,

1978); Barbara Welter, "The Cult of True Womanhood: 1820–1860," *American Quarterly* 18, no. 2 (1966): 151–74; Carl N. Degler, *At Odds* (New York: Oxford University Press, 1980).

6. Alternative definitions of love are reviewed in Walster and Walster; Clyde Hendrick and Susan Hendrick, *Liking, Loving and Relating* (Belmont, Calif.: Wadsworth Publishing Co., 1983); Ira Reiss, *Family Systems in America,* 3d ed. (New York: Holt, Rinehart & Winston, 1980), 113–41; Margaret Reedy, "Age and Sex Differences in Personal Needs and the Nature of Love" (Ph.D. diss., University of Southern California, 1977).

7. Abraham Maslow, *Motivation and Personality,* 2d ed. (New York: Harper & Row, 1970). 182–83.

8. Zick Rubin's scale is described in his article "Measurement of Romantic Love," *Journal of Personality and Social Psychology* 16, no. 2 (1970): 265–73; Lillian Rubin's book on marriage is *Intimate Strangers* (New York: Harper & Row, 1983), quote on 90.

9. The emphasis on mutual aid and instrumental love among poor people is described in Lillian Rubin, *Worlds of Pain* (New York: Basic Books, 1976); Rayna Rapp, "Family and Class in Contemporary America," in *Rethinking the Family,* ed. Barrie Thorne (New York: Longman, Inc., 1982), 168–87; S. M. Miller and F. Riessman, "The Working-Class Subculture," in *Blue-Collar World,* ed. A. Shostak and W. Greenberg (Englewood Cliffs, N.J.: Prentice-Hall, Inc., 1964), 24–36.

10. Francesca Cancian, Clynta Jackson, and Ann Wysocki, "A Survey of Close Relationships" (University of California, Irvine, School of Social Sciences, 1982, typescript).

11. Swidler.

12. *Webster's New Collegiate Dictionary* (Springfield, Mass.: G. C. Merriam Co., 1977).

13. Paul Rosencrantz, Helen Bee, Susan Vogel, Inge Broverman, and Donald Broverman, "Sex Role Stereotypes and Self-Concepts in College Students," *Journal of Consulting and Clinical Psychology* 32, no. 3 (1968): 287–95; Paul Rosencrantz, "Rosencrantz Discusses Changes in Stereotypes about Men and Women," *Second Century Radcliffe News* (Cambridge, Mass., June 1982), 5–6.

14. Nancy Chodorow, *The Reproduction of Mothering* (Berkeley: University of California Press, 1978), 169. Dorothy Dinnerstein presents a similar theory in *The Mermaid and the Minotaur: Sexual Arrangements and Human Malaise* (New York: Harper & Row, 1976; Freudian and biological dispositional theories about women's nurturance are surveyed in Jean Stockard and Miriam Johnson, *Sex Roles* (Englewood Cliffs, N.J.: Prentice-Hall, Inc., 1980.

15. Carol Gilligan, *In a Different Voice* (Cambridge, Mass.: Harvard University Press, 1982). 32, 159–61; see also L. Rubin, *Intimate Strangers.*

16. Talcott Parsons and Robert F. Bales, *Family, Socialization and Interaction* (Glencoe, Ill.: Free Press, 1955).

For a critical review of family sociology from a feminist perspective, see Arlene Skolnick, *The Intimate Environment* (Boston: Little, Brown & Co., 1978). Radical feminist theories also support the feminized conception of love, but they have been less influential in social science; see, e.g., Mary Daly, *Gyn/Ecology: The Metaethics of Radical Feminism* (Boston: Beacon Press, 1979).

17. I have drawn most heavily on Ryan, *Womanhood* (n. 5 above); Ryan, *Cradle* (n. 5 above); Ehrenreich and English (n. 5 above); Welter (n. 5 above).

18. Ryan, *Womanhood,* 24–25.

19. Similar changes occurred when culture and religion were feminized, according to Douglas (n. 1 above). Conceptions of God's love shifted toward an image of a sweet and tender parent, a "submissive, meek and forgiving" Christ (149).

20. On the persistence of women's wage inequality and responsibility for housework, see Stockard and Johnson (n. 14 above).

21. Jean Baker Miller, *Toward a New Psychology of Women* (Boston: Beacon Press, 1976). There are, of course, many exceptions to Miller's generalization, e.g., women who need to be independent or who need an attachment with a woman.

22. In psychology, the work of Carl Jung, David Bakan, and Bem are especially relevant. See Carl Jung, "Anima and Animus," in *Two Essays on Analytical Psychology. Collected Works of C.G. Jung* (New York: Bollinger Foundation, 1953), 7:187–209; David Bakan, *The Duality of Human Existence* (Chicago: Rand McNally & Co., 1966). They are discussed in Bem's paper, "Beyond Androgyny," in *Family in Transition,* 2d ed., ed. A. Skolnick and J. Skolnick (Boston: Little, Brown & Co., 1977), 204–21. Carl Rogers exemplifies the human potential theme of self-development through the search for wholeness. See Carl Rogers, *On Becoming a Person* (Boston: Houghton Mifflin Co., 1961).

23. Chodorow (n. 14 above) refers to the effects of the division of labor and to power differences between men and women, and the special effects of women's being the primary parents are widely acknowledged among historians.

24. The data on Yale men are from Mirra Komarovsky, *Dilemma of Masculinity* (New York: W. W. Norton & Co., 1976). Angus Campbell reports that children are closer to their mothers than to their fathers, and daughters feel closer to their parents than do sons, on the basis of large national surveys, in *The Sense of Well-Being in America* (New York: McGraw-Hill Book Co., 1981), 96. However, the tendency of people to criticize their mothers more than their fathers seems to contradict these findings; e.g., see Donald Payne and Paul Mussen, "Parent-Child Relations and Father Identification among Adolescent Boys," *Journal of Abnormal and Social Psychology* 52 (1956); 358–62. Being "closer" to one's mother may refer mostly to spending more time together and knowing more about each other rather than to feeling more comfortable together.

25. Studies of differences in friendship by gender are reviewed in Wenda Dickens and Daniel Perlman. "Friendship over the Life Cycle," in *Personal Relationships,* vol. 2, ed. Steve Duck and Robin Gilmour (London: Academic Press, 1981), 91–122; and Beth Hess, "Friendship and Gender Roles over the Life Course," in *Single Life,* ed. Peter Stein (New York: St. Martin's Press, 1981), 104–15. While almost all studies show that women have more close friends, Lionel Tiger argues that there is a unique bond between male friends in *Men in Groups* (London: Thomas Nelson, 1969).

26. Komarovsky, *Blue-Collar Marriage* (New York: Random House, 1962), 13.

27. Daniel Levinson, *The Seasons of a Man's Life* (New York: Alfred A. Knopf, 1978). 335.

28. The argument about the middle-age switch was presented in the popular book *Passages.* by Gail Sheehy (New York: E. P. Dutton, 1976), and in more scholarly works, such as Levinson's. These studies are reviewed in Alice Rossi, "Life-Span Theories and Women's Lives," *Signs* 6, no. 1 (1980): 4–32. However, a survey by Claude Fischer and S. Oliker reports an increasing tendency for women to have more close friends than men beginning in middle age, in "Friendship, Gender and the Life Cycle," Working Paper no. 318 (Berkeley: University of California, Berkeley, Institute of Urban and Regional Development, 1980).

29. Studies on gender differences in self-disclosure are reviewed in Letitia Peplau and Steven Gordon, "Women and Men in Love: Sex Differences in Close Relationships," in *Women, Gender and Social Psychology,* ed. V. O'Leary, R. Unger, and B. Wallston (Hillsdale, N.J.: Lawrence Erlbaum Associates, 1985). 257–91. Also see Zick Rubin, Charles Hill, Letitia Peplau, and Christine Dunkel-Schetter, "Self-Disclosure in Dating Couples," *Journal of Marriage and the Family* 42, no. 2 (1980): 305–18.

30. Working-class patterns are described in Komarovsky, *Blue Collar Marriage.* Middle-class patterns are reported by Lynne Davidson and Lucille Duberman. "Friendship: Communication and and Interactional Patterns in Same-Sex Dyads," *Sex Roles* 8. no. 8(1982):809–22 Similar findings are reported in Robert Lewis, "Emotional Intimacy among Men." *Journal of Social Issues* 34, no. 1(1978): 108–21.

31. Rubin et al., "Self-Disclosure."

32. These studies, cited below, are based on the self-reports of men and women college students and may reflect norms more than behavior. The findings are that women feel and express affective and bodily emotional reactions more often than do men, except for hostile feelings. See also Jon Allen and Dorothy Haccoun, "Sex Differences in Emotionality," *Human Relations* 29, no. 8 (1976): 711–22; and Jack Balswick and Christine Avertt, "Gender, Interpersonal Orientation and Perceived Parental Expressiveness," *Journal of Marriage and the Family* 39, no. 1(1977):121–28. Gender differences in interaction styles are analyzed in Nancy Henley, *Body Politics: Power, Sex and Non-verbal Communication*

(Englewood Cliffs, N.J.: Prentice-Hall, Inc., 1977). Also see Paula Fishman, "Interaction: The Work Women Do," *Social Problems* 25. no. 4 (1978): 397–406.

33. Gender differences in leisure are described in L. Rubin, *Worlds of Pain* (n. 9 above), 10. Also see Margaret Davis, "Sex Role Ideology as Portrayed in Men's and Women's Magazines" (Stanford University, typescript).

34. Bert Adams, *Kinship in an Urban Setting* (Chicago: Markham Publishing Co., 1968), 169.

35. Marjorie Lowenthal and Clayton Haven, "Interaction and Adaptation: Intimacy as a Critical Variable," *American Sociological Review* 33, no. 4 (1968): 20–30.

36. Joseph Pleck argues that family ties are the primary concern for many men, in *The Myth of Masculinity* (Cambridge, Mass.: MIT Press, 1981).

37. Gender-specific characteristics also are seen in same-sex relationships. See M. Caldwell and Letitia Peplau, "Sex Differences in Same Sex Friendship," *Sex Roles* 8, no. 7 (1982): 721–32; see also Davidson and Duberman (n. 30 above), 809–22. Part of the reason for the differences in friendship may be men's fear of homosexuality and of losing status with other men. An exploratory study found that men were most likely to express feelings of closeness if they were engaged in some activity such as sports that validated their masculinity (Scott Swain, "Male Intimacy in Same-Sex Friendships: The Impact of Gender-validating Activities" [paper presented at annual meeting of the American Sociological Association, August 1984]). For discussions of men's homophobia and fear of losing power, see Robert Brannon, "The Male Sex Role," in *The Forty-nine Percent Majority,* ed. Deborah David and Robert Brannon (Reading, Mass.: Addison-Wesley Publishing Co., 1976), 1–48. I am focusing on heterosexual relations, but similar gender-specific differences may characterize homosexual relations. Some studies find that, compared with homosexual men, lesbians place a higher value on tenderness and verbal self-disclosure and engage in sex less frequently. See, e.g., Alan Bell and Martin Weinberg, *Homosexualities* (New York: Simon & Schuster, 1978).

38. Unlike most studies, Reedy (n. 6 above) did not find that women emphasized communication more than men. Her subjects were upper-middle-class couples who seemed to be very much in love.

39. Sara Allison Parelman, "Dimensions of Emotional Intimacy in Marriage" (Ph.D. diss., University of California, Los Angeles, 1980).

40. Both spouses thought their interaction was unpleasant if the other engaged in negative or displeasurable instrumental or affectional actions. Thomas Wills, Robert Weiss, and Gerald Patterson, "A Behavioral Analysis of the Determinants of Marital Satisfaction," *Journal of Consulting and Clinical Psychology* 42, no. 6 (1974): 802–11.

41. L. Rubin, *Worlds of Pain* (n. 9 above), 147.

42. See L. Rubin, *Worlds of Pain;* also see Richard Sennett

and Jonathan Cobb, *Hidden Injuries of Class* (New York: Vintage, 1973).

43. For evidence on this point, see Morton Hunt, *Sexual Behavior in the 1970s* (Chicago: Playboy Press, 1974), 231; and Alexander Clark and Paul Wallin, "Women's Sexual Responsiveness and the Duration and Quality of Their Marriage," *American Journal of Sociology* 21, no. 2 (1965): 187–96.

44. Interview by Cynthia Garlich, "Interviews of Married Couples" (University of California, Irvine, School of Social Sciences, 1982).

45. For example, see Catharine MacKinnon, "Feminism, Marxism, Method, and the State: An Agenda for Theory," *Signs* 7, no. 3 (1982): 515–44. For a thoughtful discussion of this issue from a historical perspective, see Linda Gordon and Ellen Dubois, "Seeking Ecstacy on the Battlefield: Danger and Pleasure in Nineteenth Century Feminist Thought," *Feminist Review* 13, no. 1 (1983): 42–54.

46. Reedy (n. 6 above).

47. William Kephart, "Some Correlates of Romantic Love," *Journal of Marriage and the Family* 29, no. 3 (1967): 470–74. See Peplau and Gordon (n. 29 above) for an analysis of research on gender and romanticism.

48. Daniel Yankelovich, *The New Morality* (New York: McGraw-Hill Book Co., 1974), 98.

49. The link between love and power is explored in Francesca Cancian, "Gender Politics: Love and Power in the Private and Public Spheres," in *Gender and the Life Course,* ed. Alice S. Rossi (New York: Aldine Publishing Co., 1984), 253–64.

50. See Jane Flax, "The Family in Contemporary Feminist Thought," in *The Family in Political Thought,* ed. Jean B. Elshtain (Princeton, N.J.: Princeton University Press, 1981), 223–53.

51. Walter Gove, "Sex, Marital Status and Mortality," *American Journal of Sociology* 79, no. 1 (1973): 45–67.

52. This follows from the social exchange theory of power, which argues that person A will have a power advantage over B if A has more alternative sources for the gratifications she or he gets from B than B has for those from A. See Peter Blau, *Exchange and Power in Social Life* (New York: John Wiley & Sons, 1964), 117–18.

53. For a discussion of the devaluation of women's activities, see Michelle Rosaldo, "Woman, Culture and Society: A Theoretical Overview," in *Woman, Culture and Society,* ed. Michelle Rosaldo and Louise Lamphere (Stanford, Calif.: Stanford University Press, 1973), 17–42.

54. Gilligan (n. 15 above), 12–13.

55. Inge Broverman, Frank Clarkson, Paul Rosenkrantz, and Susan Vogel, "Sex-Role Stereotypes and Clinical Judgments of Mental Health," *Journal of Consulting Psychology* 34, no. 1 (1970): 1–7.

56. Welter (n. 5 above).

57. Levinson (n. 27 above).

58. L. Rubin, *Intimate Strangers* (n. 8 above); Harold Rausch, William Barry, Richard Hertel, and Mary Ann Swain, *Communication, Conflict and Marriage* (San Francisco: Jossey-Bass, Inc., 1974). This conflict is analyzed in Francesca Cancian, "Marital Conflict over Intimacy," in *The Psychosocial Interior of the Family,* 3d ed., ed. Gerald Handel (New York: Aldine Publishing Co., 1985), 277–92.

"Imagine My Surprise": Women's Relationships in Mid-Twentieth Century America*

LEILA J. RUPP

When Carroll Smith-Rosenberg's article, "The Female World of Love and Ritual," appeared in the pages of *Signs* in 1975, it revolutionized the way in which women's historians look at nineteenth-century American society and even served notice on the historical profession at large that women's relationships would have to be taken into account in any consideration of Victorian society.[1] Since then we have learned more about relationships between women in the past, but we have not reached consensus on the issue of characterizing these relationships.

Debate within the women's movement has centered around the work of two writers. In 1980, Adrienne Rich published "Compulsory Heterosexuality and Lesbian Existence," in which she argued for the concept of a lesbian continuum based on solidarity among women and resistance to patriarchy rather than on identity or sexual behavior.[2] The next year, Lillian

From *Frontiers: A Journal of Women Studies,* vol. 5, no. 3, Fall 1980. Reprinted by permission of Frontiers Editorial Collective.

*Holly Near's song, "Imagine My Surprise," celebrates the discovery of women's relationships in the past. The song is recorded on the album, *Imagine My Surprise,* Redwood Records. I am grateful to Holly Near and Redwood Records for their permission to use the title here.

This is a revised version of an article originally published in *Frontiers: A Journal of Women Studies 5* (Fall 1980). The original research was made possible by a fellowship from the Radcliffe Research Scholars Program. Additional research, funded by the National Endowment for the Humanities, was undertaken jointly with Verta Taylor for our book, *Survival in the Doldrums: The American Women's Rights Movement* (1987).

Faderman's *Surpassing the Love of Men,* which traced the history of women's relationships, suggested that the nineteenth-century phenomenon of romantic friendship involved a deep commitment and sensuality but not, ordinarily, genital sexuality.[3] As a result of the controversy that has swirled around these works, we have no simple answer to the question, asked of a variety of historical figures: Was she a lesbian?

Meanwhile, outside the feminist world, Smith-Rosenberg's work has increasingly been misused to deny the sexual aspect of relationships between prominent women in the past. In response, feminist scholars have reacted to such distortions by bestowing the label "lesbian" on women who would themselves not have used the term. The issue goes beyond labels, however, because the very nature of women's relationships is so complex. The problem of classification becomes particularly thorny in twentieth-century history with the establishment of a lesbian identity. I would like to consider here the issue of women's relationships in the twentieth century by reviewing the conflicting approaches to lesbian labeling, by tracing the continuity of romantic friendship into the mid-century, and, finally, by suggesting a conceptual approach that recognizes the complexity of women's relationships without denying the common bond shared by all women who have committed their lives to other women in the past.

Looking first at what Blanche Cook proclaimed "the historical denial of lesbianism," we find the most publicized and most egregious example in Doris Faber's *The Life of Lorena Hickok: E. R.'s Friend,* the story of the relationship of Eleanor Roosevelt and reporter Lorena Hickok.[4] Author Doris Faber presented page after page of evidence that delineated the growth and development of a love affair between the two women, yet she steadfastly maintained that a woman of Eleanor Roosevelt's "stature" could not have *acted* on the love that she expressed for Hickok. This attitude forced Faber to go to great lengths with the evidence before her. For example, she quoted a letter Roosevelt wrote to Hickok and asserted that it is "particularly susceptible to misinterpretation." Roosevelt's wish to "lie down beside you tonight and take you in my arms," Faber claimed, represented maternal—"albeit rather extravagantly" maternal— solicitude. For Faber, "there can be little doubt that the final sentence of the above letter does not mean what it appears to mean" (p. 176).

Faber's book received far more public attention than serious works of lesbian history because the idea of a famous and well-respected—even revered—woman engaging in lesbian acts was titillating. An article about the Hickok book was even carried in the *National Enquirer* which, for a change, probably presented the material more accurately, if more leeringly, than the respectable press.[5]

Faber's interpretation, unfortunately, is not an isolated one. She acknowledged an earlier book, *Miss Marks and Miss Woolley,* for reinforcing her own views "regarding the unfairness of using contemporary standards to characterize the behavior of women brought up under almost inconceivably different standards."[6] Anna Mary Wells, the author of the Marks and Woolley book, set out originally to write a biography of Mary Woolley, a president of Mount Holyoke, but almost abandoned the plan when she discovered the love letters of the two women. Ultimately Wells went ahead with a book about the relationship, but only after she decided, as she explained in the preface, that there was no physical relationship between them.

Another famous women's college president, M. Carey Thomas of Bryn Mawr, received the same sort of treatment in a book that appeared at the same time as the Hickok book, but to less fanfare.[7] The discovery of the Woolley-Marks letters sparked a mild panic among Mount Holyoke alumnae and no doubt created apprehension about what might lurk in Thomas's papers, which were about to be microfilmed and opened to the public.[8] But Marjorie Dobkin, editor of *The Making of a Feminist: Early Journals and Letters of M. Carey Thomas,* insisted that there was nothing to worry about. Thomas admittedly fell for women throughout her life. At fifteen, she wrote: "I think I

must feel towards Anna for instance like a boy would, for I admire her so . . . and then I like to touch her and the other morning I woke up and she was asleep and I admired her hair so much that I kissed it. I never felt so much with anybody else." And at twenty: "One night we had stopped reading later than usual and obeying a sudden impulse I turned to her and asked, 'Do you love me?' She threw her arms around me and whispered, 'I love you passionately.' She did not go home that night and we talked and talked." At twenty-three, Thomas wrote to her mother: "If it were only possible for women to elect women as well as men for a 'life's love!' . . . It is possible but if families would only regard it in that light!" (pp. 72, 118, 229).

Thomas did in fact choose women for her "life's loves," but Dobkin, who found it "hard to understand why anyone should very much care" about personal and private behavior and considered the question of lesbianism "a relatively inconsequential matter," assured us that "physical contact" unquestionably played a part in Thomas's relationships with women, but, making a labored distinction, insisted that "sexuality" just as unquestionably did not (pp. 79, 86).

The authors of these three books were determined to give us an "acceptable" version of these prominent women's relationships in the past, and they seized gratefully on Smith-Rosenberg's work to do it. Likewise, Arthur Schlesinger, Jr., in *The New York Times Book Review,* found the question of whether Hickok and Roosevelt were "lovers in the physical sense" an "issue of stunning inconsequence," but cited Smith-Rosenberg's work to conclude that the two women were "children of the Victorian age" which accepted celibate love between women.[9]

As Blanche Cook pointed out in her review of Faber's book, however, it is absurd to pretend that the years 1932 to 1962 now belong to the nineteenth century.[10] Although it is vitally important not to impose modern concepts and standards on the past, we have gone entirely too far with the notion of an idyllic Victorian age in which chaste love between people of the same sex was possible and acceptable.

It is not surprising, in light of such denials of sexuality, that many feminist scholars have chosen to claim as lesbians all women who have loved women in the past. Blanche Cook has concluded firmly that "women who love women, who choose women to nurture and support and to create a living environment in which to work creatively and independently, are lesbians."[11]

Cook named as lesbians Jane Addams, the founder of Hull House who lived for forty years with Mary Rozet Smith; Lillian Wald, also a settlement house pioneer, who left evidence of a series of intense relationships with women; and Jeannette Marks and Mary Woolley. All, Cook insisted, in the homophobic society in which we live, must be claimed as lesbians.

In the simplest terms, we are faced with a choice between labelling women lesbians who might have violently rejected the notion or glossing over the significance of women's relationships by considering them asexual and Victorian.[12] But what is problematic enough when we are dealing with a period in which the concept of lesbianism did not exist becomes even more troubling when we turn to the twentieth century.

What the research increasingly suggests is that two separate largely class-bound forms of relationships between women existed. We seem to have little trouble identifying the working-class phenomena—"crossing" women who dressed and worked as men and who married women, and lesbian communities that grew up around the bars and, eventually, in the military—as sexual and, therefore, lesbian. But what about the middle- and upper-class romantic friends? It is not a question of nineteenth-century romantic friends becoming lesbians in the twentieth century. Despite the sexualization of American society at the turn of the century and the concomitant "discovery of lesbianism," romantic friendship and "Boston marriage" continued to exist.[13] I would like to illustrate this continuity, and therefore the complexity of women's relationships in historical perspective, with examples from the American women's rights movement in the late 1940s and 1950s.

I have found evidence of a variety of relationships in collections of women's papers and in the records of women's organizations from this period. I do not have enough information about many of these relationships to characterize them in any definitive way, nor can I even offer much information about some of the women. But we cannot afford to overlook whatever evidence women have left us, however fragmentary. Since my research focuses on feminist activities, the women I discuss here are by no means a representative group of women. The women's rights movement in the period after the Second World War was composed primarily of white, privileged women who maintained a preexisting commitment to feminism by creating an isolated and homogeneous feminist community.[14]

Within the women's rights movement were two distinct phenomena—couple relationships and intense devotion to a charismatic leader—that help clarify the problems that face us if we attempt to define these relationships in any cut-and-dried fashion. None of the women who lived in couple relationships and belonged to the women's rights movement in the post-1945 period would, as far as can be determined, have identified themselves as lesbians. They did, however, often live together in long-term committed relationships, which were accepted in the movement, and they did sometimes build a community with other women like themselves. Descriptions of a few relationships that come down to us in the sources provide some insight into their nature.

Jeannette Marks and Mary Woolley, subjects of the biography mentioned earlier, met at Wellesley College in 1895 when Marks began her college education and Woolley arrived at the college as a history instructor. Less than five years later they made "a mutual declaration of ardent and exclusive love" and "exchanged tokens, a ring and a jeweled pin, with pledges of lifelong fidelity."[15] They spent the rest of their lives together, including the many years at Mount Holyoke where Woolley served as president and Marks taught English. Mary Woolley worked in the American Association of University Women and the Women's International League for Peace and Freedom. Jeannette Marks committed herself to suffrage and, later, through the National Woman's Party, to the Equal Rights Amendment. It is clear from Mark's correspondence with women in the movement that their relationship was accepted as a primary commitment. Few letters to Marks in the 1940s fail to inquire about Woolley, whose serious illness clouded Mark's life and work. One married woman, who found herself forced to withdraw from Woman's Party work because of her husband's health, acknowledged in a letter to Marks the centrality of Marks's and Woolley's commitment when she compared her own reason for "pulling out" to "those that have bound you to Westport," the town in which the two women lived.[16] Mary Woolley died in 1947, and Jeannette Marks lived on until 1964, devoting herself to a biography of Woolley.

Lena Madesin Phillips, the founder of the International Federation of Business and Professional Women's Clubs, lived for some thirty years with Marjory Lacey-Baker, an actress whom she first met in 1919. In an unpublished autobiography included in Phillips's

IN PRAISE OF "BEST FRIENDS": THE REVIVAL OF A FINE OLD INSTITUTION

BARBARA EHRENREICH

All the politicians, these days, are "profamily," but I've never heard of one who was "profriendship." This is too bad and possibly shortsighted. After all, most of us would never survive our families if we didn't have our friends.

I'm especially concerned about the fine old institution of "best friends." I realized that it was on shaky ground a few months ago, when the occasion arose to introduce my own best friend (we'll call her Joan) at a somewhat intimidating gathering. I got as far as saying, "I am very proud to introduce my best friend, Joan . . . " when suddenly I wasn't proud at all: I was blushing. "Best friend," I realized as soon as I heard the words out loud, sounds like something left over from sixth-grade cliques: the kind of thing where if Sandy saw you talking to Stephanie at recess, she might tell you after school that she wasn't going to be your best friend anymore, and so forth. Why couldn't I have just said "my good friend Joan" or something *grown-up* like that?

But Joan is not just any friend, or even a "good friend"; she is my best friend. We have celebrated each other's triumphs together, nursed each other through savage breakups with the various men in our lives, discussed the Great Issues of Our Time, and cackled insanely over things that were, objectively speaking, not even funny. We have quarreled and made up; we've lived in the same house and we've lived thousands of miles apart. We've learned to say hard things, like "You really upset me when . . . " and even "I love you." Yet, for all this, our relationship has no earthly weight or status. I can't even say the name for it without sounding profoundly silly.

Why is best friendship, particularly between women, so undervalued and unrecognized? Partly, no doubt, because women themselves have always been so undervalued and unrecognized. In the

Western tradition, male best friendships are the stuff of history and high drama. Reread Homer, for example, and you'll realize that Troy did not fall because Paris, that spoiled Trojan prince, loved Helen, but because Achilles so loved Patroclus. It was Patroclus' death, at the hands of the Trojans, that made Achilles snap out of his sulk long enough to slay the Trojans' greatest warrior and guarantee victory to the Greeks. Did Helen have a best friend, or any friend at all? We'll never know, because the only best friendships that have survived in history and legend are man-on-man: Alexander and Hephaestion, Orestes and Pylades, Heracles and Iolas.

Christianity did not improve the status of female friendship. "Every woman ought to be filled with shame at the thought that she is a woman," declaimed one of the early church fathers, Clement of Alexandria, and when two women got together, the shame presumably doubled. Male friendship was still supposed to be a breeding ground for all kinds of upstanding traits—honor, altruism, courage, faith, loyalty. Consider Arthur's friendship with Lancelot, which easily survived the latter's dalliance with Queen Guinevere. But when two women got together, the best you could hope for, apparently, was bitchiness, and the worst was witchcraft.

Yet, without the slightest encouragement from history, women have persisted in finding best friends. According to recent feminist scholarship, the 19th century seems to have been a heyday of female best friendship. In fact, feminism might never have gotten off the ground at all if it hadn't been for the enduring bond between Elizabeth Cady Stanton, the theoretician of the movement, and Susan B. Anthony, the movement's first great pragmatist.

And they are only the most famous best friends. According to Lillian Faderman's book *Surpassing the Love of Men*, there were thousands of anonymous female couples who wrote passionate letters

Reprinted from *Ms.* magazine (January 1987) by permission of the author.

to each other, exchanged promises and tokens of love, and suffered through the separations occasioned by marriage and migration. Feminist scholars have debated whether these great best friendships were actually lesbian, sexual relationships—a question that I find both deeply fascinating (if these were lesbian relationships, were the women involved conscious of what a bold and subversive step they had taken?) and somewhat beside the point. What matters is that these women honored their friendships, and sought ways to give them the kind of coherence and meaning that the larger society reserved only for marriage.

In the 20th century, female best friendship was largely eclipsed by the new ideal of the "companionate marriage." At least in the middle-class culture that celebrated "togetherness," your *husband* was now supposed to be your best friend, as well, of course, as being your lover, provider, coparent, housemate, and principal heir. My own theory (pro-family politicians please take note) is that these expectations have done more damage to the institution of marriage than no-fault divorce and the sexual revolution combined. No man can be all things to even one woman. And the foolish idea that one could has left untold thousands of women not only divorced, but what is in the long run far worse—friendless.

Yet even feminism, when it came back to life in the early seventies, did not rehabilitate the institution of female best friendship. Lesbian relationships took priority, for the good and obvious reason that they had been not only neglected, but driven underground. But in our zeal to bring lesbian relationships safely out of the closet, we sometimes ended up shoving best friendships further out of sight. "Best friends?" a politically ever-so-correct friend once snapped at me, in reference to Joan, "why aren't you lovers?" In the same vein, the radical feminist theoretician Shulamith Firestone wrote that after the gender revolution, there would be no asexual friendships. The coming feminist Utopia, I realized sadly, was going to be a pretty lonely place for some of us.

Then, almost before we could get out of our jeans and into our corporate clone clothes, female friendship came back into fashion—but in the vastly attenuated form of "networking." Suddenly we are supposed to have dozens of women friends, hundreds if time and the phone bill allow, but each with a defined function: mentors, contacts, connections, allies, even pretty ones who might be able to introduce us, now and then, to their leftover boyfriends. The voluminous literature on corporate success for women is full of advice on friends: whom to avoid ("turkeys" and whiners), whom to cultivate (winners and potential clients), and how to tell when a friend is moving from the latter category into the former. This is an advance, because it means we are finally realizing that women are important enough to be valued friends and that friendship among women is valuable enough to write and talk about. But in the pushy new dress-for-success world, there's less room than ever for best friendships that last through thick and thin, through skidding as well as climbing.

Hence my campaign to save the institution of female best friendship. I am not asking you to vote for anyone, to pray to anyone, or even to send me money. I'm just suggesting that we all begin to give a little more space, and a little more respect, to the best friendships in our lives. To this end, I propose three rules:

1. Best friendships should be given social visibility. If you are inviting Pat over for dinner, you would naturally think of inviting her husband, Ed. Why not Pat's best friend, Jill? Well, you may be thinking, how childish! They don't have to go everywhere together. Of course they don't, but neither do Pat and Ed. In many settings, including your next dinner party or potluck, Pat and Jill may be the combination that makes the most sense and has the most fun.

2. Best friendships take time and nurturance, even when that means taking time and nurturance away from other major relationships. Everyone knows that marriages require "work." (A ghastly concept, that. "Working on a marriage" has always sounded to me like something on the order of lawn maintenance.) Friendships require effort, too, and best friendships require our very best efforts. It should be possible to say to husband Ed or whomever, "I'm sorry I can't spend the evening with you because I need to put in some quality time with Jill." He will be offended only if he is a slave to heterosexual couple-ism—in which case you shouldn't have married him in the first place.

3. Best friendship is more important than any work-related benefit that may accrue from it, and should be treated accordingly. Maybe your best friend will help you get that promotion, transfer, or new contract. That's all well and good, but the real question is: Will that promotion, transfer, or whatever help your best friendship? If it's a transfer to San Diego and your best friend's in Cincinnati, it may not be worth it. For example, as a writer who has collaborated with many friends, including "Joan," I am often accosted by strangers exclaiming, "It's just amazing that you got through that book [article, or other project] together and you're still friends!" The truth is, in nine cases out of ten, that the friendship was always far more important than the book. If a project isn't going to strengthen my friendship—and might even threaten it—I'd rather not start.

When I was thinking through this column—out loud of course, with a very good friend on the phone—she sniffed, "So what exactly do you want—formal legalized friendships, with best-friend licenses and showers and property settlements in case you get in a fight over the sweaters you've been borrowing from each other for the past ten years?" No, of course not, because the beauty of best friendship, as opposed to, say, marriage, is that it's a totally grass-roots creative effort that requires no help at all from the powers-that-be. Besides, it would be too complicated. In contrast to marriage—and even to sixth-grade cliques—there's no rule that says you can have only one "best" friend.

---

papers, she straightforwardly wrote about her lack of interest in men and marriage. As a young girl, she wrote that she "cared little for boys," and at the age of seven she wrote a composition for school that explained: "There are so many little girls in the school and the thing i [sic] like about it there are no boys in school. i [sic] like that about it."[17] She noted that she had never taken seriously the idea of getting married. "Only the first of the half dozen proposals of marriage which came my way had any sense of reality to me. They made no impression because I was wholly without desire or even interest in the matter." Phillips seemed unperturbed by possible Freudian and/or homophobic explanations of her attitudes and behavior. She explained unabashedly that she wanted to be a boy and suffered severe disappointment when she learned that, contrary to her father's stories, there was no factory in Indiana that made girls into boys. She mentioned in her autobiography the "crushes" she had on girls at the Jessamine Female Institute—nothing out of the ordinary for a young woman of her generation, but perhaps a surprising piece of information chosen for inclusion in the autobiography of a woman who continued to devote her emotional energies to women.

In 1919, Phillips attended a pageant in which Lacey-Baker performed and she inquired about the identity of the woman who had "[t]he most beautiful voice I ever heard."[18] Phillips "lost her heart to the sound of that voice," and the two women moved in together in the 1920s. In 1924, according to Lacey-Baker's notes for a biography of Phillips, the two women went different places for Easter; recording this caused Lacey-Baker to quote from *The Prophet:* "Love knows not its own depth until the hour of separation."[19] Phillips described Lacey-Baker in her voluminous correspondence as "my best friend," or noted that she "shares a home with me."[20] Phillips's friends and acquaintances regularly mentioned Lacey-Baker. One male correspondent, for example, commented that Phillips's "lady-friend" was "so lovely, and so devoted to you and cares for you."[21] Phillips happily described the tranquillity of their life together to her many friends: "Marjory and I have had a lovely time, enjoying once more our home in summertime. . . . Marjory would join in the invitation of this letter and this loving greeting if she were around. Today she is busy with the cleaning woman, while I sit with the door closed working in my study."[22] "We have had a happy winter, with good health for both of us. We have a variety of interests and small obligations, but really enjoy most the quiet and comfort of Apple Acres."[23] "We read and talk and work."[24]

Madesin Phillips's papers suggest that she and Marjory Lacey-Baker lived in a world of politically active women friends. Phillips had devoted much of her energy to international work with women, and she kept in touch with European friends through her correspondence and through her regular trips to Europe accompanied by Lacey-Baker. Gordon Holmes, of the British Federation of Business and Professional Women, wrote regularly to "Madesin and Maggie." In a 1948 letter she teased Phillips by reporting that "two other of our oldest & closest Fed officers whom you know could get married but are refusing—as they are both more than middle-aged (never mind their looks) it suggests 50–60 is about the new dangerous age for women (look out for Maggie!)."[25] Phillips reported to Holmes on their social life: "With a new circle of friends around us here and a good many of our overseas members coming here for luncheon or tea with us the weeks slip by."[26] The integral relationship between Phillips's social life and her work in the movement is suggested by Lacey-Baker's analysis of Phillips's personal papers from the year 1924: "There is the usual crop of letters to LMP following the Convention [of the BPW] from newly-met members in hero-worshipping mood—most of whom went on to be her good friends over the years."[27] Lacey-Baker was a part of Phillips's movement world, and their relationship received acceptance and validation throughout the movement, both national and international.

The lifelong relationship between feminist biographer Alma Lutz and Marguerite Smith began when they roomed together at Vassar in the early years of the twentieth century. From 1918 until Smith's death in 1959, they shared a Boston apartment and a summer home, Highmeadow, in the Berkshires. Lutz and Smith, a librarian at the Protestant Zion Research Library in Brookline, Massachusetts, worked together in the National Woman's Party. Like Madesin Phillips, Lutz wrote to friends in the movement of their lives together: "We are very happy here in the country— each busy with her work and digging in the garden."[28] They traveled together, visiting Europe several times in the 1950s. Letters to one of them about feminist work invariably sent greetings or love to the other. When Smith died in 1959, Lutz struggled with her grief. She wrote to her acquaintance Florence Kitchelt, in response to condolences: "I am at Highmeadow trying to get my bearings. . . . You will understand how hard it is. . . . It has been a very difficult anxious time for me."[29] She thanked another friend for her note and added, "It's a hard adjustment to make, but one we all have to face in one way or another and I am remembering that I have much to be grateful for."[30] In December she wrote to one of her regular correspondents that she was carrying on but it was very lonely for her.[31]

The fact that Lutz and Smith seemed to have many friends who lived in couple relationships with other women suggests that they had built a community of women within the women's rights movement. Every year Mabel Vernon, a suffragist and worker for peace, and her friend and companion Consuelo Reyes, whom Vernon had met through her work with the Inter-American Commission of Women, spent the summer at Highmeadow. Vernon, one of Alice Paul's closest associates during the suffrage struggle, had met Reyes two weeks after her arrival in the United States from Costa Rica in 1942. They began to work together in Vernon's organization, People's Mandate, in 1943, and they shared a Washington apartment from 1951 until Vernon's death in 1975.[32] Reyes received recognition in Vernon's obituaries as her "devoted companion" or "nurse-companion."[33] Two other women who also maintained a life-long relationship, Alice Morgan Wright and Edith Goode, also kept in contact with Lutz, Smith, Vernon, and Reyes. Sometimes they visited Highmeadow in the summer.[34] Wright and Goode had met at Smith and were described as "always together" although they did not live together.[35] Like Lutz and Smith, they worked together in the National Woman's Party, where they had also presumably met Vernon. Both Wright and Goode devoted themselves to two causes, women's rights and humane treatment for animals. Wright described herself as having "fallen between two stools—animals and wimmin."[36] The two women traveled together and looked after each other as age began to take its toll.

These examples illustrate what the sources provide: the bare outlines of friendship networks made up of woman-committed women. Much of the evidence must be pieced together, and it is even scantier when the women did not live together. Alma Lutz's papers, for example, do not include any personal correspondence from the post-1945 period, so what we know about her relationship with Marguerite Smith comes from the papers of her correspondents. Sometimes a relationship surfaces only upon the death of one of the women. For example, Agnes Wells, chairman of the National Woman's Party in the late 1940s, explained to an acquaintance in the Party that her "friend of forty-one years and house-companion for twenty-eight years" had just died.[37] When Mabel Griswold, executive secretary of the Woman's Party, died in 1955, a family member suggested that the Party send the telegram of sympathy to Elsie Wood, the woman with whom

Griswold had lived.[38] This kind of reference tells us little about the nature of the relationship involved, but we do get a sense of acceptance of couple relationships within the women's rights movement.

A second important phenomenon found in the women's rights movement—the charismatic leader who attracted intense devotion—also adds to our understanding of the complexity of women's relationships. Alice Paul, the founder and leading light of the National Woman's Party, inspired devotion that bordered on worship. One woman even addressed her as "My Beloved Deity."[39] But, contrary to both the ideal type of the charismatic leader and the portrait of Paul as it exists now in historical scholarship, Paul maintained close relationships with a number of women she had first met in the suffrage struggle.[40] Paul's correspondence in the National Woman's Party papers does not reveal much about the nature of her relationships, but it does make it clear that her friendships provided love and support for her work.

It is true that many of the expressions of love, admiration, and devotion addressed to Paul seem to have been one-sided, from awe-struck followers, but this is not the only side of the story. Paul maintained close friendships with a number of women discussed earlier who lived in couple relationships with other women. She had met Mabel Vernon when they attended Swarthmore College together, and they maintained contact throughout the years, despite Vernon's departure from the Woman's Party in the 1930s.[41] Of Alice Morgan Wright, she said that, when they first met, they ". . . just became sisters right away."[42] Jeannette Marks regularly sent her love to "dear Alice" until a conflict in the Woman's Party ruptured their relationship.[43] Other women, too, enjoyed a closer relationship than the formal work-related one for which Paul is so well known.

Paul obviously cared deeply, for example, for her old friend Nina Allender, the cartoonist of the suffrage movement. Allender, who lived alone in Chicago, wrote to Paul in 1947 of her memories of their long association: "No words can tell you what that [first] visit grew to mean to me & to my life. . . . I feel now as I did then—only more intensely—I have never changed or doubted—but have grown more inspired as the years have gone by. . . . There is no use going into words. I believe them to be unnecessary between us."[44] Paul wrote that she thought of Allender often and sent her "devoted love."[45] She worried about Allender's

loneliness and gently encouraged her to come to Washington to live at Belmont House, the Woman's Party headquarters, where she would be surrounded by loving friends who appreciated the work she had done for the women's movement.[46] Paul failed to persuade her to move, however. Two years later Paul responded to a request from Allender's niece for help with the cost of a nursing home with a hundred-dollar check and a promise to contact others who might be able to help.[47] But Allender died within a month at the age of eighty-five.

Paul does not seem to have formed an intimate relationship with any one woman, but she did live and work within a close-knit female world. When in Washington, she lived, at least some of the time, at Belmont House; when away she lived either alone or with her sister, Helen Paul, and later with her lifelong friend Elsie Hill. It is clear that Alice Paul's ties—whether to her sister or to close friends or to admirers—served as a bond that knit the Woman's Party together. That Paul and her network could also tear the movement asunder is obvious from the stormy history of the Woman's Party.[48]

Alice Paul is not the only example of a leader who inspired love and devotion among women in the movement. One senses from Marjory Lacey-Baker's comment, quoted above—that "newly met members in hero-worshipping mood" wrote to Lena Madesin Phillips after every BPW convention—that Phillips too had a charismatic aura. But the best and most thoroughly documented example of a charismatic leader is Anna Lord Strauss of the League of Women Voters, an organization that in the post-1945 years distanced itself from women's rights.

Strauss, the great-granddaughter of Lucretia Mott, came from an old and wealthy family; she was prominent and respected, a staunch liberal who rejected the label of "feminist." She never married and her papers leave no evidence of intimate relationships outside her family. Yet Strauss was the object of some very strong feelings on the part of the women with whom she worked. She, like Alice Paul and Madesin Phillips, received numerous hero-worshipping letters from awe-struck followers. But in her case we also have evidence that some of her coworkers fell deeply in love with her. It is hard to know how the women discussed here would have interpreted their relationship with Strauss. The two women who expressed their feelings explicitly were both married women, and in one case

Strauss obviously had a cordial relationship with the woman's husband and children. Yet there can be no question that this League officer fell in love with Strauss. She found Strauss "the finest human being I had ever known" and knowing her "the most beautiful and profound experience I have ever had."[49] Loving Strauss—she asked permission to say it—made the earth move and "the whole landscape of human affairs and nature" take on a new appearance.[50] Being with Strauss made "the tone and fiber" of her day different; although she could live without her, she could see no reason for having to prove it all the time.[51] She tried to "ration and control" her thoughts of Strauss, but it was small satisfaction.[52] When Strauss was recovering from an operation, this woman wrote: "I love you! I can't imagine the world without you. . . . I love you. I need you."[53]

Although our picture of this relationship is completely one-sided—for Strauss did not keep copies of most of her letters—it is clear that Strauss did not respond to such declarations of love. This woman urged Strauss to accept her and what she had to say without "the slightest sense of needing to be considerate of me because I feel as I do." She understood the "unilateral character" of her feelings, and insisted that she had more than she deserved by simply knowing Strauss at all.[54] But her hurt, and her growing suspicion that Strauss shunned intimacy, escaped on occasion. She asked: "And how would it hurt you to let someone tell you sometime how beautiful—how wonderful you are? Did you ever let anyone have a decent chance to try?"[55] She realized that loving someone did not always make things easier—that sometimes, in fact, it made life more of a struggle—but she believed that to withdraw from love was to withdraw from life. In what appears to have been a hastily written note, she expressed her understanding—an understanding that obviously gave her both pain and comfort— that Strauss was not perfect after all: "Way back there in the crow's nest (or at some such time) you decided not to become embroiled in any intimate human relationship, except those you were, by birth, committed to. I wonder. . . . There is something you haven't mastered. Something you've been afraid of after all."[56]

This woman's perception that Strauss avoided intimacy is confirmed elsewhere in Strauss's papers. One old friend was struck, in 1968, by Strauss's ability to "get your feelings out and down on paper!" She contin-

ued: "I know you so well that I consider this great progress in your own inner state of mental health. It is far from easy for you to express your feelings. . . ."[57] This aspect of Strauss's personality fits with the ideal type of the charismatic leader. The other case of a woman falling in love with Strauss that emerges clearly from her papers reinforces this picture. This woman, also a League officer, wrote in circuitous fashion of her intense pleasure at receiving Strauss's picture. In what was certainly a reference to lesbianism, she wrote that she hoped Strauss would not think that she was "one of those who had never outgrown the emotional extravaganzas of the adolescent." Before she got down to League business, she added:

> But, Darling, as I softly close the door on all this— as I should and as I want to—and as I must since all our meetings are likely to be formal ones in a group—as I go back in the office correspondence to "Dear Miss Strauss" and "Sincerely Yours," . . . as I put myself as much as possible in the background at our March meeting in order to share you with the others who have not been with you as I have—as all these things happen, I want you to be very certain that what is merely under cover is still there—as it most surely will be—and that if all the hearts in the room could be exposed there'd be few, I'm certain, that would love you more than . . . [I].[58]

Apparently Strauss never responded to this letter, for a month later, this woman apologized for writing it: "I have had qualms, dear Anna, about that letter I wrote you. (You knew I would eventually of course!)." Continuing in a vein that reinforces the previously quoted perception of Strauss's inability to be intimate, she wrote of imagining the "recoil . . . embarrassment, self-consciousness and general discomfort" her letter must have provoked in such a "reserved person." She admitted that the kind of admiration she had expressed, "at least in certain classes of relationships (of which mine to you is one)—becomes a bit of moral wrong-doing."[59] She felt ashamed and asked forgiveness.

What is clear is that this was a momentous and significant relationship to at least one of the parties. Almost twenty years later, this woman wrote of her deep disappointment in missing Strauss's visit to her city. She had allowed herself to dream that she could persuade Strauss to stay with her awhile, even though she knew that others would have prior claims on Strauss's time. She wrote:

> I have not seen you since that day in Atlantic City when you laid the gavel of the League of Women Voters down. . . . I do not look back on that moment of ending with any satisfaction for my own behavior, for I passed right by the platform on which you were still standing talking with one of the last persons left in the room and shyness at the thought of expressing my deep feeling about your going—and the fact that you were talking with someone else led me to pass on without even a glance in your direction as I remember though you made some move to speak to me! . . . But if I gave you a hurt it is now a very old one and forgotten, I'm sure—as well as understood.[60]

Whatever the interpretation these two women would have devised to explain their feelings for Strauss, it is clear that the widely shared devotion to this woman leader could sometimes grow into something more intense. Strauss's reserve and her inability to express her feelings may or may not have had anything to do with her own attitude toward intimate relationships between women. One tantalizing letter from a friend about to be married suggests that Strauss's decision not to marry had been made early: "I remember so well your answer when I pressed you, once, on why you had never married. . . . Well, it is very true, one does not marry unless one can see no other life."[61] A further fragment, consisting of entries in the diary of Doris Stevens—a leading suffragist who took a sharp swing to the right in the interwar period—suggests that at least some individuals suspected Strauss of lesbianism. Stevens, by this time a serious redbaiter and, from the evidence quoted here, a "queerbaiter" as well, apparently called a government official in 1953 to report that Strauss was "not a bit interested in men."[62] She seemed to be trying to discredit Strauss, far too liberal for her tastes, with a charge of "unorthodox morals."[63]

Stevens had her suspicions about other women as well. She recorded in her diary a conversation with a National Woman's Party member about Jeannette Marks and Mary Woolley, noting that the member, who had attended Wellesley with Marks, "Discreetly indicated there was 'talk.'"[64] At another point she reported a conversation with a different Woman's

Party member who had grown disillusioned about Alice Paul. Stevens noted that her informant related "weird goings on at Wash. hedquts wherein it was clear she thought Paul a devotee of Lesbos & afflicted with Jeanne d'Arc identification."[65] Along the same lines, the daughter of a woman who had left the National Woman's Party complained that Alice Paul and another leader had sent her mother a telegram that "anybody with sense" would think "was from two people who were adolescent [sic] or from two who had imbied [sic] too much or else Lesbians to a Lesbian."[66]

Such comments suggest that the intensity of women's relationships and the existence and acceptance of couple relationships in women's organizations had the potential, particularly during the McCarthy years, to attract denunciation. Doris Stevens herself wrote to the viciously right-wing and anti-Semitic columnist Westbrook Pegler to "thank you for knowing I'm not a queerie" despite the fact that she considered herself a feminist.[67] Although the association between feminism and lesbianism was not new in the 1950s, the McCarthyite connection between political deviance and homosexuality seemed to fuel suspicion.[68] How real the threat was for women is suggested by two further incidents involving opposition to the appointment of women, both described in the memoirs of India Edwards, a top woman in the Truman administration.[69]

In 1948, opposition to tax court judge Marion Harron's reappointment to the bench arose from Harron's fellow judges, who cited her lack of judicial temperament and "unprovable charges of an ethical nature." Although Edwards did not specify the nature of the charges, we know from *The Life of Lorena Hickok* that Harron had written letters to "E. R.'s friend" that even Doris Faber had to admit were love letters. The other case that Edwards described left no doubt about what ethical and moral charges were involved. When Truman appointed Kathryn McHale, long-time executive director of the American Association of University Women, to the Subversive Activities Control Board, Senator Pat McCarran advised Truman to withdraw her name and threatened to hold public hearings during which "information would be brought out that she was a lesbian."

On the whole, though, the feminists who lived in couple relationships managed to do so respectably, despite the emergence of a lesbian culture and the occasional charges of lesbianism. This was because they worked independently or in professional jobs, had the money to buy homes together, and enjoyed enough status to be beyond reproach in the world in which they moved. Women who later identified as lesbians but did not attach an identity to their emotions and behaviors in the 1950s describe that period as one in which women might live together without raising any eyebrows, but it is important to remember that even the class privilege that protected couple relationships would not necessarily suffice if women sought to enter powerful male-dominated institutions.[70]

What exactly should we make of all this? In one way it is terribly frustrating to have such tantalizingly ambiguous glimpses into women's lives. In another way, it is exciting to find out so much about women's lives in the past. I think it is enormously important not to read into these relationships what we want to find, or what we think we should find. At the same time, we cannot dismiss what little evidence we have as insufficient when it is all we have; nor can we continue to contribute to the conspiracy of silence that urges us to ignore what is not perfectly straightforward. Thus, although it is tempting to try to speculate about the relationships I have described here in order to impose some analysis on them, I would rather simply lay them out, fragmentary as they are, in order to suggest a conceptual approach that recognizes the complexities of the issue.

It is clear, I think, that none of these relationships can be easily categorized. There were women who lived their entire adult lives in couple relationships with other women, and married women who fell in love with other women. Were they lesbians? Probably they would be shocked to be identified in that way. Alice Paul, for example, spoke scornfully of *Ms.* magazine as "all about homosexuality and so on."[71] Another woman who lived in a couple relationship distinguished between the (respectable) women involved in the ERA struggle in the old days and the "lesbians and bra-burners" of the contemporary movement.[72] Sasha Lewis, in *Sunday's Women,* reported an incident we would do well to remember here. One of her informants, a lesbian, went to Florida to work against Anita Bryant and stayed with an older cousin who had lived for years in a marriagelike relationship with another woman. When Lewis's informant saw the way the two women lived—sharing everything, including a bedroom—she remarked about the danger of Bryant's campaign for their lives. They were aghast that she

would think them lesbians, since, they said, they did not do anything sexual together.[73] If even women who chose to share beds with other women would reject the label "lesbian," what about the married women, or the women who avoided intimate relationships?

What is critical here, I would argue, is that these women lived at a time during which some women *did* identify as lesbians. The formation of a lesbian identity, from both an individual and historical perspective, is enormously significant. So far, most of the historical debate over the use of the term "lesbian" has focused on earlier periods.[74] Passionate love between women has existed, but it has not always been named. Since it *has* been named in the twentieth century, and since there *was* such a thing as a lesbian culture, we need to distinguish between women who identify as lesbians and/or who are part of a lesbian culture, where one exists, and a broader category of women-committed women who would not identify as lesbians but whose primary commitment, in emotional and practical terms, was to other women. There is an important difference between, on the one hand, butch-fem couples in the 1950s who committed what Joan Nestle has aptly called an act of "sexual courage" by openly proclaiming the erotic aspect of their relationships, and, on the other, couples like Eleanor Roosevelt and Lorena Hickok or Alma Lutz and Marguerite Smith.[75]

We know that identity and sexual behavior are not the same thing.[76] There are lesbians who have never had a sexual relationship with another woman and there are women who have had sexual experiences with women but do not identify as lesbians. This is not to suggest that there is no difference between women who loved each other and lived together but did not make love (although even that can be difficult to define, since sensuality and sexuality, "physical contact" and "sexual contact" have no distinct boundaries) and those who did. But sexual behavior—something about which we rarely have historical evidence anyway—is only one of a number of relevant factors in a relationship. Blanche Cook has said everything that needs to be said about the inevitable question of evidence: "Genital 'proofs' to confirm lesbianism are never required to confirm the heterosexuality of men and women who live together for twenty, or fifty, years." Cook reminds us of the publicized relationship of General Eisenhower and Kay Summersby during the Second World War: They "were passionately involved with each other. . . . They were inseparable.

But they never 'consummated' their love in the acceptable, traditional, sexual manner. Now does that fact render Kay Summersby and Dwight David Eisenhower somehow less in love? Were they not heterosexual?"[77]

At this point, I think, the best we can do as historians is to describe carefully and sensitively what we do know about a woman's relationships, keeping in mind both the historical development of a lesbian identity (Did such a thing as a lesbian identity exist? Was there a lesbian culture?) and the individual process that we now identify as "coming out" (Did a woman feel attachment to another woman or women? Did she act on this feeling in some positive way? Did she recognize the existence of other women with the same commitment? Did she express solidarity with those women?). Using this approach allows us to make distinctions among women's relationships in the past—intimate friendships, supportive relationships growing out of common political work, couple relationships—without denying their significance or drawing fixed boundaries. We can recognize the importance of friendships among a group of women who, like Alma Lutz, Marguerite Smith, Mabel Vernon, Consuelo Reyes, Alice Morgan Wright, and Edith Goode built a community of women but did not identify it as a lesbian community. We can do justice to both the woman-committed woman who would angrily reject any suggestion of lesbianism and the self-identified lesbian without distorting their common experiences.

This approach does not solve all the problems of dealing with women's relationships in the past, but it is a beginning. The greatest problem remains the weakness of sources. Not only have women who loved women in the past been wisely reluctant to leave evidence of their relationships for the prying eyes of a homophobic society, but what evidence they did leave was often suppressed or destroyed.[78] Furthermore, as the three books discussed at the beginning show, even the evidence saved and brought to light can be savagely misinterpreted.

How do we know if a woman felt attachment, acted on it, recognized the existence of other women like her, or expressed solidarity? There is no easy answer to this, but it is revealing, I think, that both Doris Faber and Anna Mary Wells are fairly certain that Lorena Hickok and Jeannette Marks, respectively, did have "homosexual tendencies" (although Faber insists that even Hickok cannot fairly be placed in the "contemporary gay category"), even if the admirable figures in each book, Eleanor Roosevelt and Mary Woolley, certainly did not. That is, both of these authors, as hard as they try to deny lesbianism, find evidence that forces them to discuss it, and both cope by pinning the "blame" on the women they paint as unpleasant—fat, ugly, pathetic Lorena Hickok and nasty, tortured, arrogant Jeannette Marks.

So we present what evidence we have, being careful to follow Linda Gordon's advice and "listen quietly and intently" to the women who speak to us from the sources.[79] In the case of twentieth-century history, we may also have the opportunity to listen to women speak in the flesh. We may privately believe that all the evidence suggests that a woman was a lesbian, but what do we do if she insisted, either explicitly or implicitly, that she was not? That is why the process of coming out is so important to us as historians. In a world in which some women claimed a lesbian identity and built lesbian communities, the choice to reject that identification has a meaning of its own. It is imperative that we not deny the reality of any woman's historical experience by blurring the distinctions among different kinds of choices. At the same time, recognition of the common bond of commitment to women shared by diverse women throughout history strengthens our struggle against those who attempt to divide and defeat us.

NOTES

1. Carroll Smith-Rosenberg, "The Female World of Love and Ritual: Relations between Women in Nineteenth Century America," *Signs* 1 (1975): 1–29.

2. Adrienne Rich, "Compulsory Heterosexuality and Lesbian Existence," *Signs* 5 (1980): 631–60. See also Ann Ferguson, Jacquelyn N. Zita, and Kathryn Pyne Addelson,

"On Compulsory Heterosexuality and Lesbian Existence: Defining the Issues," *Signs* 7 (1981): 158–99.

3. Lillian Faderman, *Surpassing the Love of Men: Romantic Friendship and Love between Women from the Renaissance to the Present* (New York: William Morrow, 1981). See also Faderman's *Scotch Verdict* (New York: Quill,

1983), a compelling re-creation of the trial of two Edinburgh school-teachers accused of having sex together (the model for Lillian Hellman's *The Children's Hour*). Faderman argues against a sexual component in the two women's relationship, suggesting that "for many women, what *ought* to be, in fact *was*" (p. 126).

For examples, of reviews that discussed the controversial nature of Faderman's argument, see the Muriel Haynes's review of *Surpassing the Love of Men* in *Ms.* 9 (June 1981): 36; and reviews of *Scotch Verdict* by Karla Jay in *Women's Review of Books* 1 (December 1983):9–10 and by Terry Castle in *Signs* 9 (1984): 717–20.

4. Blanche Wiesen Cook, "The Historical Denial of Lesbianism," *Radical History Review* 20 (1979): 60–65; Doris Faber, *The Life of Lorena Hickok: E.R.'s Friend* (New York: William Morrow, 1980).

5. Edward Sigall, "Eleanor Roosevelt's Secret Romance—the Untold Story," *National Enquirer,* November 13, 1979, pp. 20–21.

6. Anna Mary Wells, *Miss Marks and Miss Woolley* (Boston: Houghton Mifflin, 1978); Faber, *Lorena Hickok,* p. 354. Cook, "Historical Denial," is a review of the Wells book.

7. Marjorie Housepian Dobkin, *The Making of a Feminist: Early Journals and Letters of M. Carey Thomas* (Kent, Ohio: Kent State University Press, 1980).

8. *The New York Times,* August 21, 1976, p. 22.

9. Arthur Schlesinger, Jr., "Interesting Women," *The New York Times Book Review,* February 17, 1980, p. 31.

10. Cook, review of *The Life of Lorena Hickok, Feminist Studies* 6 (1980): 511–16.

11. Cook, "Female Support Networks and Political Activism: Lillian Wald, Crystal Eastman and Emma Goldman," *Chrysalis* 3 (1977): 48.

12. In a review of books on Frances Willard, Alice Paul, and Carrie Chapman Catt, Gerda Lerner criticized the denial of sexuality in relationships in which women shared their lives "in the manner of married couples." In an attempt to bridge the two approaches, Lerner suggested that perhaps Paul, Willard, Catt, along with Susan B. Anthony, Anna Dickinson, and Jane Addams, were "simply what Victorian 'lesbians' looked like." Gerda Lerner, "Where Biographers Fear to Tread," *Women's Review of Books* 11 (September 1987): 11–12.

13. On the significance of class, see Myriam Everard, "Lesbian History: A History of Change and Disparity," *Journal of Homosexuality* 12 (1986): 123–37 and "Lesbianism and Medical Practice in the Netherlands, 1897–1930," paper presented at the Berkshire Conference of Women Historians, Wellesley, Massachusetts, 1987. Not all the lesbian communities we know of prior to the 1950s were working class, however. There were middle- and upper-class communities in Europe and, to a lesser extent, among American bohemians at the turn of the century. On "crossing" women, see Jonathan Katz, *Gay American History* (New York: Thomas

Y. Crowell, 1976), and *Gay/Lesbian Almanac* (New York: Harper and Row, 1983). On the emergence of a lesbian community, see Madeline Davis and Elizabeth Lapovsky Kennedy, "Oral History and the Study of Sexuality in the Lesbian Community: Buffalo, New York, 1940–1960," in this volume; Joan Nestle, "Butch-Fem Relationships: Sexual Courage in the 1950's," *Heresies: The Sex Issue* 12 (1981): 21–24; Allan Bérubé, "Coming Out Under Fire," *Mother Jones* (February/March 1983): 23–45; and John D'Emilio, *Sexual Politics, Sexual Communities: The Making of a Homosexual Minority in the U.S. 1940–1970* (Chicago: University of Chicago Press, 1983).

On the "discovery of lesbianism," see Nancy Sahli, "Smashing: Women's Relationships Before the Fall," *Chrysalis* 8 (1979): 17–27; George Chauncey, Jr., "From Sexual Inversion to Homosexuality: Medicine and the Changing Conceptualization of Female Deviance," *Salmagundi* 58/59 (Fall 1982/Winter 1983): 114–46; Christina Simmons, "Women's Sexual Consciousness and Lesbian Identity, 1900–1940" (paper presented at the Berkshire Conference of Women Historians, Northhampton, Massachusetts, 1984); Esther Newton, "The Mythic Mannish Lesbian: Radclyffe Hall and the New Woman," in this volume.

14. See Leila J. Rupp and Verta Taylor, *Survival in the Doldrums: The American Women's Rights Movement, 1945 to the 1960s* (New York: Oxford University Press, 1987).

15. Wells, *Miss Marks and Miss Woolley,* p. 56.

16. Caroline Babcock to Jeannette Marks, February 12, 1947, Babcock papers, box 8 (105), Schlesinger Library, Radcliffe College, Cambridge, Massachusetts. I am grateful to the Schlesinger Library for permission to use the material quoted here.

17. "The Unfinished Autobiography of Lena Madesin Phillips," Phillips papers, Schlesinger Library.

18. "Chronological Records of Events and Activities for the Biography of Lena Madesin Phillips, 1881–1955," Phillips papers, Schlesinger Library.

19. "Chronological Records of Events and Activities for the Biography of Lena Madesin Phillips, 1881–1955," Phillips papers, Schlesinger Library.

20. Lena Madesin Phillips to Audrey Turner, January 21, 1948, Phillips papers, Schlesinger Library; Phillips to Olivia Rossetti Agresti, April 26, 1948, Phillips papers, Schlesinger Library.

21. Robert Heller to Phillips, September 26, 1948, Phillips papers, Schlesinger Library.

22. Phillips to Mary C. Kennedy, August 20, 1948, Phillips papers, Schlesinger Library.

23. Phillips to Gordon Holmes, March 28, 1949, Phillips papers, Schlesinger Library.

24. Phillips to [Ida Spitz], November 13, 1950, Phillips papers, Schlesinger Library.

25. Holmes to Madesin & Maggie, December 15, 1948, Phillips papers, Schlesinger Library.

26. Phillips to Holmes, March 28, 1949, Phillips papers, Schlesinger Library.

27. "Chronological Record of Events and Activities for the Biography of Lena Madesin Phillips, 1881–1955," Phillips papers, Schlesinger Library.

28. Alma Lutz to Florence Kitchelt, July 1, 1948, Kitchelt papers, box 6 (177), Schlesinger Library.

29. Lutz to Kitchelt, July 29, 1959, Kitchelt papers, box 7 (178), Schlesinger Library.

30. Lutz to Florence Armstrong, August 26, 1959, Armstrong papers, box 1 (17), Schlesinger Library.

31. Lutz to Rose Arnold Powell, December 14, 1959, Powell papers, box 3 (43), Schlesinger Library.

32. Mabel Vernon, "Speaker for Suffrage and Petitioner for Peace," an oral history conducted in 1972 and 1973 by Amelia R. Fry, Regional Oral History Office, University of California, 1976. Courtesy, the Bancroft Library.

33. Press release from Mabel Vernon Memorial Committee, Vernon, "Speaker for Suffrage"; obituary in the *Wilmington Morning News,* September 3, 1975, Vernon, "Speaker for Suffrage."

34. Alice Morgan Wright to Anita Pollitzer, July 9, 1946, National Woman's Party papers, reel 89. The National Woman's Party papers have been microfilmed and are distributed by the Microfilming Corporation of America. I am grateful to the National Woman's Party for permission to quote the material used here.

35. Alice Paul, "Conversations with Alice Paul: Woman Suffrage and the Equal Rights Amendment," an oral history conducted in 1972 and 1973 by Amelia R. Fry, Regional Oral History Office, University of California, 1976, p. 614. Courtesy, the Bancroft Library. Nora Stanton Barney to Alice Paul, n.d. [received May 10, 1945], National Woman's Party papers, reel 86.

36. Wright to Pollitzer, n.d. [July 1946], National Woman's Party papers, reel 89.

37. Agnes Wells to Pollitzer, August 24, 1946, National Woman's Party papers, reel 89.

38. Paul to Dorothy Griswold, February 2, 1955, National Woman's Party papers, reel 101.

39. Lavinia Dock to Paul, May 9, 1945, National Woman's Party papers, reel 86.

40. See, for example, Susan D. Becker, *The Origins of the Equal Rights Amendment: American Feminism Between the Wars* (Westport, Conn.: Greenwood Press, 1981), and Christine A. Lunardini, *From Equal Suffrage to Equal Rights: Alice Paul and the National Woman's Party, 1910–1928* (New York: New York University Press, 1986).

41. Vernon, "Speaker for Suffrage."

42. Paul, "Conversations," p. 197.

43. Jeannette Marks to Paul, March 25, 1945, National Woman's Party papers, reel 85; Marks to Paul, March 30, 1945, National Woman's Party papers, reel 85; Marks to Paul, April 27, 1945, National Woman's Party papers, reel 85.

44. Nina Allender to Paul, January 5, 1947, National Woman's Party papers, reel 90.

45. Paul to Allender, March 9, 1950, National Woman's Party papers, reel 96.

46. Paul to Allender, November 20, 1954, National Woman's Party papers, reel 100; Kay Boyle to Paul, December 5, 1954, National Woman's Party papers, reel 100; Paul to Nina, December 6, 1954, National Woman's Party papers, reel 100.

47. Boyle to Paul, February 13, 1957, National Woman's Party papers, reel 103; Paul to Boyle, March 5, 1957, National Woman's Party papers, reel 103.

48. See Leila J. Rupp, "The Women's Community in the National Woman's Party, 1945 to the 1960s," *Signs* 10 (1985): 715–40.

49. Letter to Anna Lord Strauss, December 22, 1945, Strauss papers, box 6 (118), Schlesinger Library. Because of the possibly sensitive nature of the material reported here, I am not using the names of the women involved.

50. Letter to Strauss, September 19, 1946, Strauss papers, box 6 (119), Schlesinger Library.

51. Letter to Strauss, May 9, 1947, Strauss papers, box 6 (121), Schlesinger Library.

52. Letter to Strauss, June 28, 1948, Strauss papers, box 6 (124), Schlesinger Library.

53. Letter to Strauss, February 26, 1951, Strauss papers, box 1 (15), Schlesinger Library.

54. Letter to Strauss, December 22, 1945, Strauss papers, box 6 (118), Schlesinger Library.

55. Letter to Strauss, May 9, 1947, Strauss papers, box 6 (121), Schlesinger Library.

56. "Stream of consciousness," March 10, 1948, Strauss papers, box 6 (124), Schlesinger Library.

57. Augusta Street to Strauss, n.d. [1968], Strauss papers, box 7 (135), Schlesinger Library.

58. Letter to Strauss, February 11, 1949, Strauss papers, box 6 (125), Schlesinger Library.

59. Letter to Strauss, March 3, 1949, Strauss papers, box 6 (125), Schlesinger Library.

60. Letter to Strauss, March 8, 1968, Strauss papers, box 7 (135), Schlesinger Library.

61. Lilian Lyndon to Strauss, April 23, 1950, Strauss papers, box 1 (14), Schlesinger Library.

62. Diary entries, August 30, 1953 and September 1, 1953, Doris Stevens papers, Schlesinger Library.

63. Diary entry, August 24, 1953, Doris Stevens papers, Schlesinger Library.

64. Diary entry, February 4, 1946, Doris Stevens papers, Schlesinger Library.

65. Diary entry, December 1, 1945, Doris Stevens papers, Schlesinger Library.

66. Katharine Callery to Stevens, Aug. 17, 1944, Stevens papers, Schlesinger Library.

67. Stevens to Westbrook Pegler, May 3, 1946, Stevens papers, Schlesinger Library.

68. See Margaret Jackson, "Sexual Liberation or Social Control? Some Aspects of the Relationship between Feminism and the Social Construction of Sexual Knowledge in the Early Twentieth Century," *Women's Studies International Forum* 6 (1983): 1–17; Carroll Smith-Rosenberg, "Discourses of Sexuality and Subjectivity: The New Woman, 1870–1936," in this volume; and John D'Emilio, "The Homosexual Menace: The Politics of Sexuality in Cold War America," unpublished paper presented at the Organization of American Historians Conference, Philadelphia, 1982.

69. India Edwards, *Pulling No Punches* (New York: Putnam's 1977), pp. 189–90.

70. Interviews by Leila J. Rupp and Verta Taylor; see Rupp and Taylor, *Survival in the Doldrums*.

71. Paul, "Conversations," pp. 195–96.

72. Interview conducted by Taylor and Rupp, December 10, 1979.

73. Sasha Gregory Lewis, *Sunday's Women: A Report on Lesbian Life Today* (Boston: Beacon Press, 1979), p. 94.

74. See, for an example, the discussion in Judith C. Brown, *Immodest Acts: The Life of a Lesbian Nun in Renaissance Italy* (New York: Oxford University Press, 1986), pp. 171–73.

75. Nestle, "Butch-Fem Relationships."

76. Much of the literature on lesbianism emphasizes this crucial distinction between identity and experience. See, for example, Barbara Ponse, *Identities in the Lesbian World: The Social Construction of Self* (Westport, Conn.: Greenwood Press, 1978); and E.M. Ettore, *Lesbians, Women and Society* (London: Routledge & Kegan Paul, 1980).

77. Cook, "Historical Denial," p. 64.

78. The Mount Holyoke administration closed the Marks-Woolley papers when Wells discovered the love letters, and the papers are only open to researchers now because an American Historical Association committee, which included Blanche Cook as one of its members, applied pressure to keep the papers open after Wells, to her credit, contacted them. Faber describes her unsuccessful attempts to persuade the archivists at the FDR Library to close the Lorena Hickok papers.

79. Linda Gordon, "What Should Women's Historians Do: Politics, Social Theory, and Women's History," *Marxist Perspectives* 3 (1978), 128–36.

R E A D I N G   3 1

Oral History and the Study of Sexuality in the Lesbian Community: Buffalo, New York, 1940–1960

MADELINE DAVIS and ELIZABETH LAPOVSKY KENNEDY

We began a study of the history of the Buffalo lesbian community, 1940–1960, to determine that community's contribution to the emergence of the gay liberation movement of the 1960s.[1] Because this community centered around bars and was highly role defined, its members often have been stereotyped as low-life societal discards and pathetic imitators of heterosexuality. We suspected instead that these women were heroines

Reprinted from *Feminist Studies*, vol. 12, no. 1 (Spring 1986): 7–26, by permission of the publisher, Feminist Studies, Inc., c/o Women's Studies Program, University of Maryland, College Park, MD 20742.

who had shaped the development of gay pride in the twentieth century by forging a culture for survival and resistance under prejudicial conditions and by passing this sense of community on to newcomers; in our minds, these are indications of a movement in its prepolitical stages.[2] Our original research plan assumed the conceptual division between the public (social life and politics) and the private (intimate life and sex), which is deeply rooted in modern consciousness and which feminism has only begun to question. Thus we began our study by looking at gay and lesbian bars—the public manifestations of gay life at the time—and relegated sex to a position of less importance, viewing it as only incidentally relevant. As our research progressed we came to question the accuracy of this division. This article records the transformation in our thinking and explores the role of sexuality in the cultural and political development of the Buffalo lesbian community.

At first, our use of the traditional framework that separates the public and private spheres was fruitful.[3] Because the women who patronized the lesbian and gay bars of the past were predominantly working class and left no written records, we chose oral history as our method of study. Through the life stories of over forty narrators, we found that there were more bars in Buffalo during the forties and fifties than there are in that city today. Lesbians living all over the city came to socialize in these bars, which were located primarily in the downtown area. Some of these women were born and raised in Buffalo; others had migrated there in search of their kind. In addition, women from nearby cities, Rochester and Toronto, came to Buffalo bars on weekends. Most of the women who frequented these bars had full-time jobs. Many were factory workers, taxi drivers, bartenders, clerical workers, hospital technicians; a few were teachers or women who owned their own businesses.[4]

Our narrators documented, beyond our greatest expectations, the truth of our original hypothesis that this public bar community was a formative predecessor to the modern gay liberation movement. These bars not only were essential meeting places with distinctive cultures and mores, but they were also the central arena for the lesbian confrontation with a hostile world. Participants in bar life were engaged in constant, often violent, struggle for public space. Their dress code announced them as lesbians to their neighbors, to strangers on the streets, and of course to all who entered the bars. Although confrontation with the straight world was a constant during this period, its nature changed over time. In the forties, women braved ridicule and verbal abuse, but rarely physical conflict. One narrator of the forties conveys the tone: "There was a great difference in looks between a lesbian and her girl. You had to take a streetcar—very few people had cars. And people would stare and such."[5] In the fifties, with the increased visibility of the established gay community, the concomitant postwar rigidification of sex roles, and the political repression of the McCarthy era, the street dyke emerged. She was

a full-time "queer," who frequented the bars even on week nights and was ready at any time to fight for her space and dignity. Many of our fifties' narrators were both aware and proud that their fighting contributed to a safer, more comfortable environment for lesbians today.

> Things back then were horrible, and I think that because I fought like a man to survive I made it somehow easier for the kids coming out today. I did all their fighting for them. I'm not a rich person; I don't even have a lot of money; I don't even have a little money. I would have nothing to leave anybody in this world, but I have that that I can leave to the kids who are coming out now, who will come out into the future, that I left them a better place to come out into. And that's all I have to offer, to leave them. But I wouldn't deny it; even though I was getting my brains beaten up I would never stand up and say, "No, don't hit me, I'm not gay, I'm not gay." I wouldn't do that.

When we initially gathered this material on the growth and development of community life, we placed little emphasis on sexuality. In part we were swept away by the excitement of the material on bars, dress, and the creation of public space for lesbians. In addition, we were part of a lesbian feminist movement that opposed a definition of lesbianism based primarily on sex. Moreover, we were influenced by the popular assumption that sexuality is natural and unchanging and the related sexist assumption of women's sexual passivity—both of which imply that sexuality is not a valid subject for historical study. Only recently have historians turned their attention to sexuality, a topic that used to be of interest mainly to psychologists and the medical profession. Feminists have added impetus to this study by suggesting that women can desire and shape sexual experience. Finally, we were inhibited by the widespread social reluctance to converse frankly about sexual matters. Thus for various reasons, all stemming, at least indirectly, from modern society's powerful ideological division between the public and the private, we were indisposed to consider how important sexuality might have been to the women we were studying.

The strength of the oral history method is that it enables narrators to shape their history, even when their views contradict the assumptions of historians. As our work progressed, narrators volunteered information about their sexual and emotional lives, and often a shyly asked question would inspire lengthy, absorbing discourse. By proceeding in the direction in which these women steered us, we came to realize that sexuality and sexual identity were not incidental but were central to their lives and their community. Our narrators taught us that although securing public space was indeed important, it was strongly motivated by the need to provide a setting for the formation of intimate relationships. It is the nature of this community that it created public space for lesbians and gay men, while at the same time it organized sexuality and emotional relationships. Appreciation of this dynamic interconnection requires new ways of thinking about lesbian history.

What is an appropriate framework for studying the sexual component of a lesbian community's history and for revealing the role of sexuality in the evolution of twentieth-century lesbian and gay politics? So little research has been done in this area that our work is still exploratory and tentative. At present, we seek primarily to understand forms of lesbian sexual expression and to identify changes in sexual norms, experiences, and ideas during the 1940s and 1950s. We also look for the forces behind these changes in the evolving culture and politics of the lesbian community. Our goal has been to ascertain what part, if any, sexuality played in the developing politics of gay liberation. As an introduction to this discussion, we shall present our method of research because it has been crucial in our move to study sexuality, and so little has been written on the use of oral history for research on this topic.

USING ORAL HISTORY TO CONSTRUCT THE HISTORY OF THE BUFFALO LESBIAN COMMUNITY

The memories of our narrators are colorful, illuminating, and very moving. Our purpose, however, was not only to collect individual life stories, but also to use these as a basis for constructing the history of the community. To create from individual memories a historically valid analysis of this community presented a difficult challenge. The method we developed was slow and painstaking.[6] We treated each oral history as a historical document, taking into account the particular social position of each narrator and how that might affect her

memories. We also considered how our own point of view influenced the kind of information we received and the way in which we interpreted a narrator's story. We juxtaposed all interviews with one another to identify patterns and contradictions and checked our developing understanding with other sources, such as newspaper accounts, legal cases, and labor statistics.

As mentioned earlier, we first focused on understanding and documenting lesbian bar life. From the many vibrant and humorous stories about adventures in bars and from the mountains of seemingly unrelated detail about how people spent their time, we began to identify a chronology of bars and to recognize distinctive social mores and forms of lesbian consciousness that were associated with different time periods and even with different bars. We checked and supplemented our analysis by research into newspaper accounts of bar raids and closings and actions of the State Liquor Authority. Contradictions frequently emerged in our material on bars, but, as we pursued them, we found they were rarely due to idiosyncratic or faulty memory on the part of our narrators but to the complexity of bar life. Often the differences could be resolved by taking into account the different social positions of our narrators or the kinds of questions we had asked to elicit the information we received. If conflicting views persisted, we tried to return to our narrators for clarification. Usually we found that we had misunderstood our narrators or that contradictions indeed existed in the community at the time. For instance, narrators consistently told us about the wonderful times in bars as well as how terrible they were. We came to understand that both of these conditions were part of the real experience of bar life.

When we turned our attention to sexuality and romance in this community, we were at first concerned that our method would not be adequate. Using memories to trace the evolution of sexual norms and expression is, at least superficially, more problematic than using them to document social life in bars. There are no concrete public events or institutions to which the memories can be linked. Thus, when a narrator talks about butch–fem sexuality in the forties, we must bear in mind the likelihood that she has modified her view and her practice of butch–fem sexuality in the fifties, sixties, seventies, and eighties. In contrast, when a narrator tells about bars in the forties, even though social life in bars might have changed over the last forty years, she can tie her memories to a concrete place like

Ralph Martin's bar, which existed during a specific time period. Although not enough is known about historical memory to fully evaluate data derived from either type of narrative, our guess is that, at least for lesbian communities, they are equally valid.[7] The vividness of our narrators' stories suggests that the potential of oral history to generate full and rich documents about women's sexuality might be especially rich in the lesbian community. Perhaps lesbian memories about sexual ideals and experiences are not separated from the rest of life because the building of public communities is closely connected with the pursuit of intimate relationships. In addition, during this period, when gay oppression marked most lesbians' lives with fear of punishment and lack of acceptance, sexuality was one of the few areas in which many lesbians found satisfaction and pleasure. This was reinforced by the fact that, for lesbians, sexuality was not directly linked with the pain and/or danger of women's responsibility for child-bearing and women's economic dependence on men. Therefore, memories of sexual experience might be more positive and more easily shared. But these ideas are tentative. An understanding of the nature of memory about sexuality must await further research.

The difficulty of tying memories about sexual or emotional life to public events does present special problems. We cannot identify specific dates for changes in sexual and emotional life, such as when sex became a public topic of conversation or when role-appropriate sex became a community concern. We can talk only of trends within the framework of decades. In addition, we are unable to find supplementary material to verify and spark our narrators' memories. There are no government documents or newspaper reports on lesbian sexuality. The best one can find are memoirs or fiction written about or by residents in other cities, and even these don't exist for participants in working-class communities of the forties.[8] In general, we have not found these problems to require significant revision of our method.

Our experience indicates that the number of people interviewed is critical to the success of our method, whether we are concerned with analyzing the history of bar life or of emotional and sexual life. We feel that between five and ten narrators' stories need to be juxtaposed in order to develop an analysis that is not changed dramatically by each new story. At the present time, our analysis of the white lesbian community of the fifties is based on oral histories from over fifteen narrators. In contrast, we have only five narrators who participated in the white community of the forties, four for the black community of the fifties, and one from the black community of the forties. Therefore, we emphasize the fifties in this article and have the greatest confidence in our analysis of that decade. Our discussion of the forties must be viewed as only tentative. Our material on the black community is not yet sufficient for separate treatment; so black and white narrators' memories are interspersed throughout the article. Ultimately, we hope to be able to write a history of each community.

SEXUALITY AS PART OF THE CULTURAL POLITICAL DEVELOPMENT OF THE BUFFALO LESBIAN COMMUNITY

Three features of lesbian sexuality during the forties and fifties suggest its integral connection with the lesbian community's cultural-political development. First, butch–fem roles created an authentic lesbian sexuality appropriate to the flourishing of an independent lesbian culture. Second, lesbians actively pursued rich and fulfilling sexual lives at a time when sexual subjectivity was not the norm for women. This behavior was not only consistent with the creation of a separate lesbian culture, but it also represented the roots of a personal and political feminism that characterized the gay liberation movement of the sixties. Third, although butch–fem roles and the pursuit of sexual autonomy remained constant throughout this period, sexual mores changed in relation to the evolving forms of resistance to oppression.

Most commentators on lesbian bar life in the forties and fifties have noted the prominence of butch–fem roles.[9] Our research corroborates this; we found that roles constituted a powerful code of behavior that shaped the way individuals handled themselves in daily life, including sexual expression. In addition, roles were the primary organizer for the lesbian stance toward the straight world as well as for building love relationships and for making friends.[10] To understand butch–fem roles in their full complexity is a fundamental issue for students of lesbian history; the particular concern of this article is the intricate connection between roles and sexuality. Members of the community, when explaining how one recognized a person's role, regularly referred to two underlying determinants: image, including dress and mannerism, and sexuality.[11] Some people went so far as to say that one never really knew a woman's role identity until one went to bed with her. "You can't tell butch–fem by people's dress. You couldn't even really tell in the fifties. I knew women with long hair, fem clothes, and found out they were butches. Actually I even knew one who wore men's clothes, haircuts and ties, who was a fem."

Today, butch–fem roles elicit deep emotional reactions from many heterosexuals and lesbians. The former are affronted by women assuming male prerogatives; the latter by lesbians adopting male-defined role models. The hostility is exemplified by the prevalent ugly stereotype of the butch–fem sexual dyad: the butch with her dildo or penis substitute, trying to imitate a man, and the simpering passive fem who is kept in her place by ignorance. This representation evokes pity for lesbians because women who so interact must certainly be sexually unfulfilled; one partner cannot achieve satisfaction because she lacks the "true" organ of pleasure, and the other is cheated because she is denied the complete experience of the "real thing." Our research counters the view that butch–fem roles are solely an imitation of sexist heterosexual society.

Inherent in butch–fem relationships was the presumption that the butch is the physically active partner and the leader in lovemaking. As one butch narrator explains, "I treat a woman as a woman, down to the basic fact it'd have to be my side doin' most of the doin'." Insofar as the butch was the doer and the fem was the desired one, butch–fem roles did indeed parallel the male/female roles in heterosexuality. Yet unlike the dynamics of many heterosexual relationships, the butch's foremost objective was to give sexual pleasure to a fem; it was in satisfying her fem that the butch received fulfillment. "If I could give her satisfaction to the highest, that's what gave me satisfaction." As for the fem, she not only knew what would give her physical pleasure, but she also knew that she was neither object or nor receptacle for someone else's gratification. The essence of this emotional/sexual dynamic is captured by the ideal of the "stone butch," or untouchable butch, that prevailed during this period. A "stone butch" does all the "doin'" and does not ever allow her lover to reciprocate in kind. To be untouchable meant to gain pleasure from giving pleasure. Thus, although these women did draw on models in heterosexual society, they transformed those models into an authentically lesbian interaction. Through role-playing they developed distinctive and fulfilling expressions of women's sexual love for women.

The archetypal lesbian couple of the 1940s and 1950s, the "stone butch" and the fem, poses one of the most tantalizing puzzles of lesbian history and possibly of the history of sexuality in general.[12] In a culture that viewed women as sexually passive, butches developed a position as sexual aggressor, a major component of which was untouchability. However, the active or "masculine" partner was associated with the giving of sexual pleasure, a service usually assumed to be "feminine." Conversely, the fem, although the more passive partner, demanded and received sexual pleasure and in this sense might be considered the more self-concerned or even more "selfish" partner. These attributes of butch–fem sexual identity remove sexuality from the realm of the "natural," challenging the notion that sexual performance is a function of biology and affirming the view that sexual gratification is socially constructed.

Within this framework of butch–fem roles, individual lesbians actively pursued sexual pleasure. On the one hand, butch–fem roles limited sexual expression by imposing a definite structure. On the other hand, this structure ordered and gave a determinant shape to lesbian desire, which allowed individuals to know and find what they wanted. The restrictions of butch–fem sexuality, as well as the pathways it provided for satisfaction, are best captured and explored by examining what it meant for both butch and fem that the butch was the doer; how much leeway was there before the butch became fem, or the fem became butch?

Although there was complete agreement in the community that the butch was the leader in lovemaking, there was a great deal of controversy over the feasibility or necessity of being a "stone butch." In the forties, most butches lived up to the *ideal* of "the untouchable." One fem, who was in a relationship with an untouchable butch at that time, had tried to challenge her partner's behavior but met only with resistance. Her butch's whole group—those who hung out at Ralph Martin's—were the same. "Because I asked her one time, I said, 'Do you think that you might be just the only one?' 'Oh no,' she said. 'I know I'm not, you know, that I've discussed with . . . different people.' [There were] no exceptions, which I thought was ODD, but, I thought, well, you know. This is how it is."

In the fifties, the "stone butch" became a publicly discussed model for appropriate sexual behavior, and it was a standard that young butches felt they had to achieve to be a "real" or "true" butch. In contrast to the forties, a fifties' fem, who was out in the community, would not have had to ask her butch friend why she was untouchable, and if there were others like her. She would have known it was the expected behavior for butches. Today our narrators disagree over whether it was, in fact, possible to maintain the ideal and they are unclear about the degree of latitude allowed in the forties or fifties before a butch harmed her reputation. Some butches claim that they were absolutely untouchable; that was how they were, and that's how they enjoyed sex. When we confronted one of our narrators, who referred to herself as an "untouchable," with the opinion of another narrator, who maintained that "stone butches" had never really existed, she replied, "No, that's not true. I'm an 'untouchable.' I've tried to have my lover make love to me, but I just couldn't stand it. . . . I really think there's something physical about that." Like many of our butch narrators, this woman has always been spontaneously orgasmic; that is, her excitement level peaks to orgasm while making love to another woman. Another "stone butch" explains: "I wanted to satisfy them [women], and I wanted to make love—I love to make love. I still think that's the greatest thing in life. But I don't want them to touch me. I feel like that spoils the whole thing—I am the way I am. And I figure if a girl is attracted to me, she's attracted to me because of what I am."

Other butches who consider themselves, and have the reputation of being, untouchable claim that it is, as a general matter, impossible to be completely untouchable. One, when asked if she were really untouchable, replied, "Of course not. How would any woman stay with me if I was? It doesn't make any sense. . . . I don't believe there was ever such a class—other than what they told each other." This woman preferred not to be touched, but she did allow mutual lovemaking from time to time during her long-term relationships. A first time in bed, however:

> There's no way in hell that you would touch me . . if you mean untouchable like that. But if I'm living with a woman, I'd have to be a liar if I said that she hadn't touched me. But I can say that I don't care for it to happen. And the only reason it does happen is because she wants it. It's not like something I desire or want. But there's no such thing as an untouchable butch—and I'm the finest in Buffalo and I'm telling you straight—and don't let them jive you around it—no way.

This narrator's distinction between her behavior on a first night and her behavior in long-term relationships appeared to be accepted practice. The fact that some—albeit little—mutuality was allowed over the period of a long relationship did not affect one's reputation as an untouchable butch, nor did it counter the presumption of the butch as the doer.

This standard of untouchability was so powerful in shaping the behavior of fifties' butches that many never experienced their fems making love to them. By the seventies, however, when we began our interviewing, norms had changed enough so that our butch narrators had had opportunities to experience various forms of sexual expression. Still, many of them—in fact all of those quoted above on "stone butches"—remained untouchable. It was their personal style long after community standards changed. Today these women offer explanations for their preference that provide valuable clues about both the personal importance and the social "rightness" of untouchability as a community norm in the forties and fifties. Some women, as indicated in one of the above quotes, continue to view their discomfort with being touched as physical or biological. Others feel that if a fem were allowed the physical liberties usually associated with the butch role, distinctions would blur and the relationship would become confusing. "I feel that if we're in bed and she does the same thing to me that I do her, we're the same thing." Another narrator, reflecting on the fact that she always went to bed with her clothes on, suggests that "what it came to was being uncomfortable with the female body. You didn't want people you were with to realize the likeness between the two." Still other butches are hesitant about the vulnerability implicit in mutual lovemaking. "When the first girl wanted to make a mutual exchange sexually, . . . I didn't want to be in the position of being at somebody's disposal, or at their command that much—maybe that's still inside me. Maybe I never let loose enough."

But many untouchables of the fifties did try mutual lovemaking later on, and it came as a pleasant surprise when they found they enjoyed being touched. "For some reason . . . I used to get enough mental satisfaction by satisfying a woman . . . then it got to the point where this one woman said, 'Well, I'm just not gonna accept that,' and she started venturing, and at first I said, 'No, no,' and then I said, 'Well, why not?' and I got to enjoy it." This change was not easy for a woman who had spent many years as an "untouchable." At first she was very nervous and uncomfortable about mutual sex, but "after I started reaching physical climaxes instead of just mental, it went, that little restlessness about it. It just mellowed me right out, y'know." The social pressure of the times prevented some women from experiencing expanded forms of sexual expression they might have enjoyed, and it also put constraints upon some women who had learned mutual sex outside of a structured community. One of our narrators had begun her sex life with mutual relations and enjoyed it immensely, but in order to conform to the community standard for butches, adopted untouchability as her sexual posture. She accepted to this behavioral change willingly and saw it as a logical component of her role during this period.

How was a community able to monitor the sexual activities of its members, and how might people come to know if a butch "rolled over"—the community lingo for a butch who allowed fems to make love to her? The answer was simple: fems talked! A butch's reputation was based on her performance with fems.

Despite the fact that sexual performance could build or destroy a butch's reputation, some butches of the fifties completely ignored the standard of untouchability. Our narrators give two reasons for this. One reason is the opinion that a long-term relationship requires some degree of mutuality to survive. One butch, a respected leader of the community because of her principles, her affability, and her organizational skills, was not only "touchable" but also suspects that most of the butches she knew in the fifties were not "stone butches." "Once you get in bed or in your bedroom and the lights go out, when you get in between those sheets, I don't think there's any male or there's any female or butch or fem, and it's a fifty–fifty thing. And I think that any relationship . . . any true relationship that's gonna survive has got to be that way. You can't be a giver and can't be a taker. You've gotta both be givers and both gotta be takers." The second reason is the pleasure of being touched. Some women experienced this in the fifties and continued to follow the practice.

When it came to sex [in the fifties] butches were untouchable, so to speak. They did all the lovemaking, but love was not made back to them. And after I found out how different it was, and how great it was, I said, "What was I missing?" I remember a friend of mine, that I had, who dressed like a man all her life . . . and I remember talking to [her] and

saying to her, you know you've got to stop being an untouchable butch, and she just couldn't agree. And I remember one time reaching over and pinching her and I said, "Did you feel that?" and she said, "Yes," and I said, "It hurt, didn't it? Well, why aren't you willing to feel something that's good?"

We do not know if in the forties, as in the fifties, butches who preferred a degree of mutuality in lovemaking existed side by side with the ideal of untouchability because we have considerably less information on that decade. Therefore, we cannot judge whether there was in fact a development toward mutual sexuality, the dominant form of lesbian lovemaking of the sixties and seventies, or whether the "stone butch" prescribed ideal and mutual lovemaking couples existed side by side consistently throughout the forties and fifties.

Our information on fem sexuality is not as extensive as that on butch sexuality because we have been able to contact fewer fem narrators. Nevertheless, from the fems we have interviewed and from comments by butches who sought them out and loved them, we do have an indication that fems were not passive receivers of pleasure, but for the most part knew what they wanted and pursued it.[13] Many butches attributed their knowledge of sex to fems, who educated them by their sexual responsiveness as well as by their explicit directions in lovemaking.

As implied by our discussion of butch sexuality, many fems had difficulty accepting "untouchability." One fem narrator of the forties had a ten-year relationship with an untouchable butch, and the sexual restrictions were a source of discomfort for her. "It was very one-sided, you know, and . . . you never really got a chance to express your love. And I think this kind of suppressed . . . your feelings, your emotions. And I don't know whether that's healthy. I don't think so." But at the same time the majority of these fems appreciated being the center of attention; they derived a strong sense of self-fulfillment from seeking their own satisfaction and giving pleasure—by responding to their butches. "I've had some that I couldn't touch no parts of their bodies. It was all about me. Course I didn't mind! But every once in a while I felt like, well, hey, let me do something to you. I could NEVER understand that. 'Cause I lived with a girl. I couldn't touch any part of her, no part. But boy, did she make me feel good, so I said . . . All right with me . . . I don't mind laying down."

What emerges from our narrators' words is in fact a

range of sexual desires that were built into the framework of role-defined sexuality. For butches of the period, we found those who preferred untouchability; those who learned it and liked it; those who learned it and adjusted to it for a time; those who preferred it, but sensed the need for some mutuality; and those who practiced mutuality regularly. For fems, we found those who accepted pleasure, thereby giving pleasure to their lovers; usually such women would aggressively seek what they wanted and instruct their lovers with both verbal and nonverbal cues. Some fems actively sought to make love to their butches and were successful. And finally, we found some women who were not consistent in their roles, changing according to their partners. In the varied sex lives of these role-identified women of the past, we can find the roots of "personal-political" feminism. Women's concern with the ultimate satisfaction of other women is part of a strong sense of female and potentially feminist agency and may be the wellspring for the confidence, the goals, and the needs that shaped the later gay and lesbian feminist movement. Thus, when we develop our understanding of this community as a predecessor to the gay liberation movement, our analysis must include sexuality. For these lesbians actively sought, expanded, and shaped their sexual experience, a radical undertaking for women in the 1940s and 1950s.

Although butch–fem roles were the consistent framework for sexual expression, sexual mores changed and developed throughout this period; two contradictory trends emerged. First, the community became more open to the acceptance of new sexual practices, the discussion of sexual matters, and the learning about sex from friends as well as lovers. Second, the rules of butch–fem sexuality became more rigid, in that community concern for the role-appropriate behavior increased.

In the forties there were at least two social groups, focused in two prominent bars, Ralph Martin's and Winters. According to our narrators, the sexual mores of these two groups differed: the former group was somewhat conservative; the latter group was more experimental, presaging what were to become the accepted norms of the fifties. The lesbian patrons of Ralph Martin's did not discuss sex openly, and oral sex was disdained. "People didn't talk about sex. There was no intimate conversation. It was kind of hush, hush . . . I didn't know there were different ways." By way of contrast, this narrator recalls a visit to Winters,

where other women were laughing about "sixty-nine." "I didn't get it. I went to [my partner] and said, 'Somebody says "sixty-nine" and everybody gets hysterical.'" Finally her partner learned what the laughter was all about. At that time our narrator would have mentioned such intimacies only with a lover. It wasn't until later that she got into bull sessions about such topics. Not surprisingly, this narrator does not recall having been taught about sex. She remembers being scared during her first lesbian experience, then found that she knew what to do "naturally." She had no early affairs with partners older than herself.

The Winters' patrons had a more open, experimental attitude toward sex; they discussed it unreservedly and accepted the practice of oral sex. These women threw parties in which women tried threesomes and daisy chains. "People would try it and see how it worked out. But nothing really happened. One person would always get angry and leave, and they would end up with two." Even if their sexual adventures did not always turn out as planned, these women were unquestionably innovative for their time. Our narrator from the Winters' crowd reminisced that it was always a contrast to go home to the serene life of her religious family. She also raved about two fems who were her instructors in sexual matters, adding, "I was an apt pupil."

During the fifties the picture changed, and the mores of the Ralph Martin's group virtually disappeared. Sex came to be a conversation topic among all social groups. Oral sex became an accepted form of lovemaking, so that an individual who did not practice it was acting on personal preference rather than on ignorance or social proscription. In addition, most of our fifties' butch narrators recall having been teachers or students of sex. As in the Winters' group in the forties, an important teacher for the butch was the fem. "I had one girl who had been around who told me. I guess I really frustrated the hell out of her. And she took a piece of paper and drew me a picture and she said, 'Now you get this spot right here.' I felt like a jerk. I was embarrassed that she had to tell me this." According to our narrator, the lesson helped, and she explains that "I went on to greater and better things."

The fifties also saw the advent of a completely new practice—experienced butches teaching novice butches about sex. One narrator remembers that younger women frequently approached her with questions about sex: "There must be an X on my back. They just pick me out. . . ." She recalls one young butch who "had to know every single detail. She drove me crazy. Jesus Christ, y'know, just get down there and do it—y'get so aggravated." The woman who aggravated her gives the following account of learning about sex:

And I finally talked to a butch buddy of mine. . . . She was a real tough one. I asked her "What do you do when you make love to a woman?" And we sat up for hours and hours at a time. . . . "I feel sexually aroused by this woman, but if I take her to bed, what am I gonna do?" And she says, "Well, what do you feel like doing?" and I says "Well, the only thing I can think of doing is . . . all I want to do is touch her, but what is the full thing of it . . . you know." So when [she] told me I says, "Really," well there was this one thing in there, uh . . . I don't know if you want me to state it. Maybe I can . . . well, I won't . . . I'll put in terms that you can understand. Amongst other things, the oral gratification. Well, that kind of floored me because I never expected something like that and I thought, well, who knows, I might like it.

She later describes her first sexual experience in which she was so scared that her friend had to shove her into the bedroom where the girl was waiting.

At the same time that attitudes toward discussions of and teachings about sexuality relaxed, the fifties' lesbian community became stricter in enforcing role-appropriate sexuality. Those who deviated from the pattern in the forties might have identified themselves as "lavender butch" and might have been labeled by others as "comme ci, comme ca." Although their divergence from the social norm would have been noticed and discussed, such women were not stigmatized. But the community of the fifties left little room to deviate. Those who did not consistently follow one role in bed were considered "ki-ki" (neither–nor), or more infrequently, "AC/DC," both pejorative terms imposed by the community. Such women were viewed as disruptive of the social order and not to be trusted. They not only elicited negative comments, but they also were often ostracized from social groups. From the perspective of the 1980s, in which mutuality in lovemaking is emphasized as a positive quality, it is important to clarify that "ki-ki" did not refer to an abandonment of role-defined sex but rather to a shifting of sexual posture depending upon one's bed partner. Therefore, it was

grounded absolutely in role playing. One of our narrators in fact defined "ki-ki" as "double role playing."[14]

These contradictory trends in attitudes and norms of lesbian sexuality parallel changes in the heterosexual world. Movement toward open discussion of sex, the acceptance of oral sex, and the teaching about sex took place in the society at large, as exemplified by the publication of and the material contained in the Kinsey reports.[15] Similarly, the lesbian community's stringent enforcement of role-defined behavior in the fifties occurred in the context of straight society's postwar move toward a stricter sexual division of labor and the ideology that accompanied it.[16] These parallels indicate a close connection between the evolution of heterosexual and homosexual cultures, a topic that requires further research.[17] At this point, we wish to stress that drawing parallels with heterosexuality can only partially illuminate changes in lesbian sexual mores. As an integral part of lesbian life, lesbian sexuality undergoes transformations that correspond with changing forms of the community's resistance to oppression.

Two developments occurred in this prepolitical period that are fundamental for the later emergence of the lesbian and gay liberation movement of the sixties. The first development was the flourishing of a lesbian culture; the second was the evolving stance of public defiance. The community of the forties was just beginning to support places for public gatherings and socializing, and during this period lesbians were to be found in bars only on weekends. Narrators of the forties do not remember having role models or anyone willing to instruct them in the ways of gay life. The prevalent feeling was that gay life was hard, and if people wanted it, they had to find it for themselves. In the fifties, the number of lesbian bars increased, and lesbians could be found socializing there every night of the week. As bar culture became more elaborate and open, lesbians more freely exchanged information about all aspects of their social lives, including sexuality. Discussion of sex was one of the many dimensions of an increasingly complex culture. The strengthening of lesbian culture and the concomitant repression of gays in the fifties led the community to take a more public stance. This shift toward public confrontation subsequently generated enough sense of pride to counter the acknowledged detriments of gay life so that members of the community were willing to instruct newcomers both socially and sexually. Almost all our narrators who came out in the fifties remember a butch who served as a role model or remember acting as a role model themselves. Instruction about sexuality was part of a general education to community life that developed in the context of expanding community pride.

However, the community's growing public defiance was also related to its increased concern for enforcing role-appropriate behavior in the fifties. Butches were key in this process of fighting back. The butches alone, or the butch–fem couple, were always publicly visible as they walked down the street, announcing themselves to the world. To deal effectively with the hostility of the straight world, and to support one another in physical confrontations, the community developed, for butches in particular, rules of appropriate behavior and forms of organization and exerted pressure on butches to live up to these standards. Because roles organized intimate life, as well as the community's resistance to oppression, sexual performance was a vital part of these fifties' standards.

From the vantage point of the 1980s and twenty more years of lesbian and gay history, we know that just as evolving community politics created this tension between open discussion and teaching about sex and strict enforcement of role-appropriate sexual behavior, it also effected the resolution. Our research suggests that in the late sixties in Buffalo, with the development of the political activities of gay liberation, explicitly political organizations and tactics replaced butch–fem roles in leading the resistance to gay oppression. Because butch–fem roles were no longer the primary means for organizing the community's stance toward the straight world, the community no longer needed to enforce role-appropriate behavior.[18] This did not mean that butch–fem roles disappeared. As part of a long tradition of creating an authentic lesbian culture in an oppressive society, butch–fem roles remain, for many lesbians, an important code of personal behavior in matters of either appearance, sexuality, or both.

ACKNOWLEDGMENTS

This article is a revision of a paper originally presented at the "International Conference on Women's History and Oral History," Columbia University, New York, 18 November 1983. We want to thank Michael Frisch, Ellen DuBois, and Bobbi Prebis for reading the original version and offering us helpful comments. We also want to thank Rayna Rapp and Ronald Grele for their patience throughout the revision process.

NOTES

1. This research is part of the work of the Buffalo Women's Oral History Project, which was founded in 1978 with three goals: (1) to produce a comprehensive, written history of the lesbian community in Buffalo, New York, using as the major source oral histories of lesbians who came out prior to 1970; (2) to create and index an archive of oral history tapes, written interviews, and relevant supplementary materials; and (3) to give this history back to the community from which it derives. Madeline Davis and Elizabeth (Liz) Kennedy are the directors of the project. Avra Michelson was an active member from 1978 to 1981 and had a very important influence on the development of the project. Wanda Edwards

has been an active member of the project since 1981, particularly in regard to research on the black lesbian community and on racism in the white lesbian community.

2. This hypothesis was shaped by our personal contact with Buffalo lesbians who came out in the 1940s and 1950s, and by discussion with grass roots gay and lesbian history projects around the country, in particular, the San Francisco Lesbian and Gay History Project, the Boston Area Gay and Lesbian History Project, and the Lesbian Herstory Archives. Our approach is close to and has been influenced by the social constructionist tendency of lesbian and gay history. See in particular, Jonathan Katz, *Gay American History: Lesbians*

and *Gay Men in the U.S.A.* (New York: Crowell, 1976); Gayle Rubin, Introduction to *A Woman Appeared to Me,* by Renée Vivien (Nevada: Naiad Press, 1976), iii–xxxvii; Jeffrey Weeks, *Coming Out: Homosexual Politics in Britain from the Nineteenth Century to the Present* (London: Quartet Books, 1977). We want to thank all these sources which have been inspirational to our work.

3. The Buffalo Women's Oral History Project has written two papers on bar life, both by Madeline Davis, Elizabeth (Liz) Kennedy, and Avra Michelson: "Buffalo Lesbian Bars in the Fifties," presented at the National Women's Studies Association, Bloomington, Indiana, May 1980, and "Buffalo Lesbian Bars: 1930–1960," presented at the Fifth Berkshire Conference on the History of Women, Vassar College, Poughkeepsie, N.Y., June 1981. Both papers are on file at the Lesbian Herstory Archives, P.O. Box 1258, New York, New York 10116.

4. We think that this community could accurately be designated as a working-class lesbian community, but this is not a concept many members of this community would use; therefore, we have decided to call it a public bar community.

5. All quotes are taken from the interviews conducted for this project between 1978 and 1984. The use of the phrase "lesbian and her girl" in this quote reflects some of our butch narrators' belief that the butch member of a couple was the lesbian and the fem member's identity was less clear.

6. A variety of sources were helpful for learning about issues and problems of oral history research. They include the Special Issue on Women's Oral History, *Frontiers* 2 (Summer 1977); Willa K. Baum, *Oral History for the Local Historical Society* (Nashville, Tenn.: American Association for State and Local History, 1975); Michael Frisch, "Oral History and *Hard Times:* A Review Essay," *Oral History Review* (1979): 70–80; Ronald Grele, ed., *Envelopes of Sound: Six Practitioners Discuss the Method, Theory, and Practice of Oral History and Oral Tradition* (Chicago: Precedent Publishing, 1975); Ronald Grele, "Can Anyone over Thirty Be Trusted: A Friendly Critique of Oral History," *Oral History Review* (1978): 36–44; "Generations: Women in the South," *Southern Exposure* 4 (Winter 1977); "No More Moanin'," *Southern Exposure* 1 (Winter 1974); Peter Friedlander, *The Emergence of a UAW Local, 1936–1939* (Pittsburgh: University of Pittsburgh Press, 1975); William Lynwood Montell, *The Saga of Coe Ridge: A Study in Oral History* (Knoxville: University of Tennessee Press, 1970); Studs Terkel, *Hard Times: An Oral History of the Great Depression* (New York: Pantheon Books, 1970); Martin B. Duberman, *Black Mountain: An Exploration in Community* (Garden City, N.Y.: Doubleday, 1972); Sherna Gluck, ed., *From Parlor to Prison: Five American Suffragists Talk about Their Lives* (New York: Vintage, 1976); and Kathy Kahn, *Hillbilly Women* (New York: Doubleday, 1972).

7. For a helpful discussion of memory, see John A. Neuenschwander, "Remembrance of Things Past: Oral His-

torians and Long-Term Memory," *Oral History Review* (1978): 46–53; Many sources cited in the previous note also have relevant discussions of memory; in particular, see Frisch; Grele, *Envelopes of Sound;* Friedlander; and Montell.

8. See for instance, Joan Nestle, "Esther's Story: 1960," *Common Lives/Lesbian Lives* 1 (Fall 1981):5–9; Joan Nestle, "Butch–Fem Relationships: Sexual Courage in the 1950s," *Heresies* 12 (1981): 21–24; Audre Lorde, "Tar Beach," *Conditions,* no. 5 (1979): 34–47 and Audre Lorde, "The Beginning," in *Lesbian Fiction,* ed. Elly Bulkin (Watertown, Mass.: Persephone Press, 1981), 225–74. Lesbian pulp fiction can also provide insight into the emotional and sexual life of this period; see, for instance, Ann Bannon's *I Am a Woman* (Greenwich, Conn.: Fawcett, 1959) and *Beebo Brinker* (Greenwich, Conn.: Fawcett, 1962).

9. See, for instance, Nestle, "Butch–Fem Relationships"; Lorde, "Tar Beach"; Del Martin and Phyllis Lyon, *Lesbian/Woman* (New York: Bantam, 1972); John D'Emilio, *Sexual Politics, Sexual Communities: The Making of a Homosexual Minority in the United States 1940–1970* (Chicago: University of Chicago Press, 1983).

10. For a full discussion of our research on butch–fem roles, see Madeline Davis and Elizabeth (Liz) Kennedy, "Butch–Fem Roles in the Buffalo Lesbian Community, 1940–1960" (paper presented at the Gay Academic Union Conference, Chicago, October 1982). This paper is on file at the Lesbian Herstory Archives.

11. These two main determinants of roles are quite different from what would usually be considered as indicators of sex roles in straight society; they do not include the sexual division of labor.

12. The origins of the "stone butch" and fem couple are beyond the scope of this paper. For an article that begins to approach these issues, see Esther Newton, "The Mythic Mannish Lesbian: Radclyffe Hall and the New Woman," *Signs* 9 (Summer 1984): 557–75.

13. Our understanding of the fem role has been enhanced by the following: Nestle's "Butch–Fem Relationships" and "Esther's Story"; Amber Hollibaugh and Cherrie Moraga, "What We're Rolling Around in Bed With: Sexual Silences in Feminism: A Conversation toward Ending Them," *Heresies* 12 (1981):58–62.

14. For indications that "ki-ki" was used nationally in the lesbian subculture, see Jonathan Katz, *Gay/Lesbian Almanac: A New Documentary* (New York: Harper & Row, 1983), 15, 626.

15. Alfred C. Kinsey, Wardell B. Pomeroy, and Clyde E. Martin, *Sexual Behavior in the Human Male* (Philadelphia: W. B. Saunders, 1948); and Alfred Kinsey et al., *Sexual Behavior in the Human Female* (Philadelphia: W. B. Saunders, 1953). Numerous sources document this trend; see, for instance, Ann Snitow, Christine Stansell, and Sharon Thompson, eds., *Powers of Desire: The Politics of Sexuality* (New York:

Monthly Review Press, 1983), in particular, Introduction, sec. 2, "Sexual Revolutions," and sec. 3, "The Institution of Heterosexuality," 9–47, 115–71, 173–275; and Katz, *Gay/Lesbian Almanac.*

16. See Mary P. Ryan, *Womanhood in America: From Colonial Times to the Present* (New York: Franklin Watts, 1975).

17. A logical result of the social constructionist school of gay history is to consider that heterosexuality is also a social construction. Katz, in *Gay/Lesbian Almanac,* begins to explore this idea.

18. Although national homophile organizations began in the fifties, no such organizations developed in Buffalo until the formation of the Mattachine Society of the Niagara Frontier in 1969. But we do not think that the lack of early homophile organizations in this city made the bar community's use of roles as an organizer of its stance toward the straight world different from that of cities where homophile organizations existed. In general, these organizations, whether mixed or all women, did not draw from or affect bar communities. Martin and Lyon in chap. 8, "Lesbians United," *Lesbian/Woman* (238–79), present Daughters of Bilitis (DOB) as an alternative for those dissatisfied with bar life, not as an organization to coalesce the forces and strengths of the bar community. Gay liberation combined the political organization of DOB and the defiance and pride of bar life and therefore affected and involved both communities.

Health and Medicine

Much feminist scholarship and activism focuses on women's health issues. Women's rights to control their reproductive lives, to live and work in conditions not injurious to their health, and to receive safe, effective, and affordable medical care are central to women's welfare. Feminists have devoted considerable energy to changing public policy on women's behalf during the last two decades.

In the 1970s a women's health movement developed in the United States as an outgrowth of the feminist and consumer health movements. Women's health advocates criticized and challenged the tendency of the existing medical establishment to view women as abnormal and inherently diseased simply because the female reproductive cycle deviates from the male's. Women today across the world are asserting the right to control their own bodies by exposing and resisting the medical abuse of women in forms ranging from forced sterilization and sex selection against females to pharmaceutical experimentation. Women are also increasing their control over their own health care by enhancing women's access to information and specialized training that allow them to more accurately assess their health care needs and make informed decisions about medical treatment.

This section explores the role of medicine in the maintenance of gender inequality, as well as issues related to women's health, including what illness tells us about women's position in society.

In "Hormonal Hurricanes: Menstruation, Meno-

pause, and Female Behavior," Anne Fausto-Sterling examines traditional research on menstruation and menopause and finds that it reflects a deep bias against women by advancing the view that women are "slaves of their reproductive physiologies." Reviewing recent feminist studies on premenstrual syndrome and menopause, Fausto-Sterling suggests other approaches to women's health issues. Her work forces us to realize that social contexts deeply affect medical interpretations of the female reproductive cycle.

Women's right to control sexual reproduction, to practice safe contraception and abortion, and to make informed decisions on general health care matters have been central concerns of the women's movement and of the feminist health movement that emerged in the United States. The articles in this section focus on abortion, reproductive technologies, and the differences in meaning these issues have for women, depending upon their economic situations and ethnic identities.

In "Racism, Birth Control, and Reproductive Rights," Angela Y. Davis discusses the history of the birth control movement and the contemporary abortion rights movement, pointing out that white women in these movements have failed to understand the experiences and interests of women of color and have frequently used blatantly racist premises to advance their cause. While white women have struggled for individual rights to birth control, women of color have faced forced sterilization as the dominant white culture's primary means of reducing population growth among "less desirable" groups. Davis's analysis explicates why women have failed to unite around the issue of birth control, despite its importance to women's struggle for equality.

New reproductive technologies allowing women to become pregnant with children conceived by other women raise complex and compelling questions for feminist thinkers. In "Women as Fathers: Motherhood and Child Care under a Modified Patriarchy," Barbara Katz Rothman notes the importance of analyzing the new reproductive technologies from feminist perspectives informed by understandings of race, class, and economic issues. Do new technologies serve women by addressing problems of infertility and impaired health, or do they perpetuate women's oppression and increase wealthy and white women's exploitation of poor women and women of color? Are we as a society willing to accept the latter for the sake of the former? Such reproductive issues will surely come to occupy an important place on the feminist agenda in coming decades.

Hormonal Hurricanes:
Menstruation, Menopause, and Female Behavior

ANNE FAUSTO-STERLING

Woman is a pair of ovaries with a human being attached, whereas man is a human being furnished with a pair of testes.

—*Rudolf Virchow, M.D. (1821–1902)*

Estrogen is responsible for that strange mystical phenomenon, the feminine state of mind.

—*David Reuben, M.D., 1969*

In 1900, the president of the American Gynecological Association eloquently accounted for the female life cycle:

> Many a young life is battered and forever crippled in the breakers of puberty; if it crosses these unharmed and is not dashed to pieces on the rock of childbirth, it may still ground on the ever-recurring shadows of menstruation and lastly upon the final bar of the menopause ere protection is found in the unruffled waters of the harbor beyond the reach of the sexual storms.[1]

Since then we have amassed an encyclopedia's worth of information about the existence of hormones, the function of menstruation, the regulation of ovulation,

Adapted from "Hormonal Hurricanes: Menstruation, Menopause, and Female Behavior" in *Myths of Gender* by Anne Fausto-Sterling. Copyright © 1986 by Basic Books, Inc. Reprinted by permission of BasicBooks, a division of HarperCollins Publishers Inc.

and the physiology of menopause. Yet many people, scientists and nonscientists alike, still believe that women function at the beck and call of their hormonal physiology. In 1970, for example, Dr. Edgar Berman, the personal physician of former Vice President Hubert Humphrey, responded to a female member of Congress:

> Even a Congresswoman must defer to scientific truths . . . there just are physical and psychological inhibitants that limit a female's potential. . . . I would still rather have a male John F. Kennedy make the Cuban missile crisis decisions than a female of the same age who could possibly be subject to the curious mental aberrations of that age group.[2]

In a more grandiose mode, Professor Steven Goldberg, a university sociologist, writes that "men and women differ in their hormonal systems . . . every society demonstrates patriarchy, male dominance and male attainment. The thesis put forth here is that the hormonal renders the social inevitable."[3]

At the broadest political level, writers such as Berman and Goldberg raise questions about the competency of *any and all* females to work successfully in positions of leadership, while for women working in other types of jobs, the question is, Should they receive less pay or more restricted job opportunities simply because they menstruate or experience menopause? And further, do women in the throes of premenstrual frenzy frequently try to commit suicide? Do they really suffer from a "diminished responsibility" that should exempt them from legal sanctions when they beat their children or murder their boyfriends?[4] Is the health of large numbers of women threatened by inappropriate and even ignorant medical attention—medical diagnoses that miss real health problems, while resulting instead in the prescription of dangerous medication destined to create future disease?

The idea that women's reproductive systems direct their lives is ancient. But whether it was Plato, writing about the disruption caused by barren uteri wandering about the body,[5] Pliny, writing that a look from a menstruating woman will "dim the brightness of mirrors, blunt the edge of steel and take away the polish from ivory,"[6] or modern scientists writing about the changing levels of estrogen and progesterone, certain messages emerge quite clearly. Women, by nature emotionally erratic, cannot be trusted in positions of responsibility. Their dangerous, unpredictable furies warrant control by the medical profession,* while ironically, the same "dangerous" females also need protection because their reproductive systems, so necessary for the procreation of the race, are vulnerable to stress and hard work.

"The breakers of puberty," in fact, played a key role in a debate about higher education for women, a controversy that began in the last quarter of the nineteenth century and still echoes today in the halls of academe. Scientists of the late 1800s argued on physiological grounds that women and men should receive different types of education. Women, they believed, could not survive intact the rigors of higher education. Their reasons were threefold: first, the education of young women might cause serious damage to their reproductive systems. Energy devoted to scholastic work would deprive the reproductive organs of the necessary "flow of power," presenting particular problems for pubescent women, for whom the establishment of regular menstruation was of paramount importance. Physicians cited cases of women unable to bear children because they pursued a course of education

designed for the more resilient young man.[7] In an interesting parallel to modern nature-nurture debates, proponents of higher education for women countered biological arguments with environmental ones. One anonymous author argued that, denied the privilege afforded their brothers of romping actively through the woods, women became fragile and nervous.[8]

Opponents of higher education for women also claimed that females were less intelligent than males, an assertion based partly on brain size itself but also on the overall size differences between men and women. They held that women cannot "consume so much food as men . . . [because] their average size remains so much smaller; so that the sum total of food converted into thought by women can never equal the sum total of food converted to thought by men. It follows, therefore, that *men will always think more than women.*"[9] One respondent to this bit of scientific reasoning asked the thinking reader to examine the data: Aristotle and Napoleon were short, Newton, Spinoza, Shakespeare, and Comte delicate and of medium height, Descartes and Bacon sickly, "while unfortunately for a theory based upon superior digestion, Goethe and Carlyle were confirmed dyspeptics."[10] Finally, as if pubertal vulnerability and lower intelligence were not enough, it seemed to nineteenth-century scientists that menstruation rendered women "more or less sick and unfit for hard work" "for one quarter of each month during the best years of life."[11]

Although dated in some of the particulars, the turn-of-the-century scientific belief that women's reproductive functions make them unsuitable for higher education remains with us today. Some industries bar fertile women from certain positions because of workplace hazards that might cause birth defects, while simultaneously deeming equally vulnerable men fit for the job.* Some modern psychologists and biologists suggest that women perform more poorly than do men on mathematics tests because hormonal sex differences alter male and female brain structures; and many people believe women to be unfit for certain professions because they menstruate. Others argue that premenstrual changes cause schoolgirls to do poorly in their studies, to become slovenly and disobedient, and even to develop a "nymphomaniac urge [that] may be responsible for young girls running away from home . . . only to be found wandering in the park or following boys."[12]

---

*In the nineteenth century, control took the form of sexual surgery such as ovariectomies and hysterectomies, while twentieth-century medicine prefers the use of hormone pills. The science of the 1980s has a more sophisticated approach to human physiology, but its political motives of control and management have changed little. For an account of medicine's attitudes toward women, see Barbara Ehrenreich and Deidre English, *For Her Own Good: 150 Years of Experts' Advice to Women* (New York: Doubleday, 1979); and G. J. Barker-Benfield, *The Horrors of the Half-Known Life* (New York: Harper & Row, 1977).

*The prohibited work usually carries a higher wage.

If menstruation really casts such a dark shadow on women's lives, we ought certainly to know more about it—how it works, whether it can be controlled, and whether it indeed warrants the high level of concern expressed by some. Do women undergo emotional changes as they progress through the monthly ovulatory cycle? And if so do hormonal fluctuations bring on these ups and downs? If not—if a model of biological causation is appropriate—how else might we conceptualize what happens?

THE SHADOWS OF MENSTRUATION: A READER'S LITERATURE GUIDE

The Premenstrual Syndrome

SCIENCE UPDATE: PREMENSTRUAL STRAIN LINKED TO CRIME

—Providence Journal

ERRATIC FEMALE BEHAVIOR TIED TO PREMENSTRUAL SYNDROME

—Providence Journal

VIOLENCE BY WOMEN IS LINKED TO MENSTRUATION

—National Enquirer

Menstruation makes news, and the headlines summarize the message. According to Dr. Katharina Dalton, Premenstrual Syndrome (PMS) is a medical problem of enormous dimensions. Under the influence of the tidal hormonal flow, women batter their children and husbands, miss work, commit crimes, attempt suicide, and suffer from up to 150 different symptoms, including headaches, epilepsy, dizziness, asthma, hoarseness, nausea, constipation, bloating, increased appetite, low blood sugar, joint and muscle pains, heart palpitations, skin disorders, breast tenderness, glaucoma, and conjunctivitis.[13] Although the great concern expressed in the newspaper headlines just quoted may come from a single public relations source,[14] members of the medical profession seem eager to accept at face value the idea that "70 to 90% of the female population will admit to recurrent premenstrual symptoms and that 20 to 40% report some degree of mental or physical incapacitation."[15]

If all this is true, then we have on our hands nothing less than an overwhelming public health problem, one that deserves a considerable investment of national resources in order to develop understanding and treatment. If, on the other hand, the claims about premenstrual tension are cut from whole cloth, then the consequences are equally serious. Are there women in need of proper medical treatment who do not receive it? Do some receive dangerous medication to treat nonexistent physiological problems? How often are women refused work, given lower salaries, taken less seriously because of beliefs about hormonally induced erratic behavior? In the game of PMS the stakes are high.

The key issues surrounding PMS are so complex and interrelated that it is hard to know where to begin. There is, as always, the question of evidence. To begin with we can look, in vain, for credible research that defines and analyzes PMS. Despite the publication of thousands of pages of allegedly scientific analyses, the most recent literature reviews simultaneously lament the lack of properly done studies and call for a consistent and acceptable research definition and methodology.[16] Intimately related to the question of evidence is that of conceptualization. Currently held theoretical views about the reproductive cycle are inadequate to the task of understanding the emotional ups and downs of people functioning in a complex world. Finally, lurking beneath all of the difficulties of research design, poor methods, and muddy thinking is the medical world's view of the naturally abnormal woman. Let's look at this last point first.

If you're a woman you can't win. Historically, females who complained to physicians about menstrual difficulties, pain during the menstrual flow, or physical or emotional changes associated with the premenstruum heard that they were neurotic. They imagined the pain and made up the tension because they recognized menstruation as a failure to become pregnant, to fulfill their true role as a woman.[17] With the advent of the women's health movement, however, women began to speak for themselves.[18] The pain is real, they said; our bodies change each month. The medical profession responded by finding biological/hormonal causes, proposing the need for doctor-supervised cures. A third voice, however, entered in: that of feminists worried about repercussions from the idea that women's natural functions represent a medical problem capable of preventing women from competing in the world outside the home. Although this multisided discussion continues, I currently operate on the premise that some women probably do require medical attention

IF MEN COULD MENSTRUATE—

GLORIA STEINEM

A white minority of the world has spent centuries conning us into thinking that a white skin makes people superior—even though the only thing it really does is make them more subject to ultraviolet rays and to wrinkles. Male human beings have built whole cultures around the idea that penis-envy is "natural" to women—though having such an unprotected organ might be said to make men vulnerable, and the power to give birth makes womb-envy at least as logical.

In short, the characteristics of the powerful, whatever they may be, are thought to be better than the characteristics of the powerless—and logic has nothing to do with it.

What would happen, for instance, if suddenly, magically, men could menstruate and women could not?

The answer is clear—menstruation would become an enviable, boast-worthy, masculine event:

Men would brag about how long and how much.

Boys would mark the onset of menses, that longed-for proof of manhood, with religious ritual and stag parties.

Congress would fund a National Institute of

Copyright © Gloria Steinem, *MS*. Magazine, October 1978. Used with permission

Dysmenorrhea to help stamp out monthly discomforts.

Sanitary supplies would be federally funded and free. (Of course, some men would still pay for the prestige of commercial brands such as John Wayne Tampons, Muhammad Ali's Rope-a-dope Pads, Joe Namath Jock Shields—"For Those Light Bachelor Days," and Robert "Barretta" Blake Maxi-Pads.)

Military men, right-wing politicians, and religious fundamentalists would cite menstruation ("*men*-struation") as proof that only men could serve in the Army ("you have to give blood to take blood"), occupy political office ("can women be aggressive without that steadfast cycle governed by the planet Mars?"), be priests and ministers ("how could a woman give her blood for our sins?"), or rabbis ("without the monthly loss of impurities, women remain unclean").

Male radicals, left-wing politicians, and mystics, however, would insist that women are equal, just different; and that any woman could enter their ranks if only she were willing to self-inflict a major wound every month ("you *must* give blood for the revolution"), recognize the preeminence of menstrual issues, or subordinate her selfness to all men in their Cycle of Enlightenment.

Street guys would brag ("I'm a three-pad man")

---

for incapacitating physical changes that occur in synchrony with their menstrual cycle. Yet in the absence of any reliable medical research into the problem it is impossible to diagnose true disease or to develop rational treatment. To start with, we must decide what is normal.

The tip-off to the medical viewpoint lies in its choice of language. What does it mean to say "70 to 90% of the female population will admit to recurrent premenstrual symptoms"?[19] The word *symptom* carries two rather different meanings. The first suggests a disease or an abnormality, a condition to be cured or rendered normal. Applying this connotation to a statistic suggest-

ing 70 to 90 percent symptom formation leads one to conclude that the large majority of women are by their very nature diseased. The second meaning of *symptom* is that of a sign or signal. If the figure of 70 to 90 percent means nothing more than that most women recognize signs in their own bodies of an oncoming menstrual flow, the statistics are unremarkable. Consider then the following, written in 1974 by three scientists:

> It is estimated that from 25% to 100% of women experience some form of premenstrual or menstrual emotional disturbance. Eichner makes the discerning point that the few women who do not admit to

or answer praise from a buddy ("Man, you lookin' *good!* ") by giving fives and saying, "Yeah, man, I'm on the rag!"

TV shows would treat the subject at length. ("Happy Days": Richie and Potsie try to convince Fonzie that he is still "The Fonz," though he has missed two periods in a row.) So would newspapers. (SHARK SCARE THREATENS MENSTRUAT- ING MEN. JUDGE CITES MONTHLY STRESS IN PARDONING RAPIST.) And movies. (New- man and Redford in "Blood Brothers"!)

Men would convince women that intercourse was *more* pleasurable at "that time of the month." Lesbians would be said to fear blood and therefore life itself—though probably only because they need- ed a good menstruating man.

Of course, male intellectuals would offer the most moral and logical arguments. How could a woman master any discipline that demanded a sense of time, space, mathematics, or measurement, for instance, without that in-built gift for measuring the cycles of the moon and planets—and thus for measuring anything at all? In the rarefied fields of philosophy and religion, could women compen- sate for missing the rhythm of the universe? Or for their lack of symbolic death-and-resurrection every month?

Liberal males in every field would try to be kind: the fact that "these people" have no gift for measur- ing life or connecting to the universe, the liberals would explain, should be punishment enough.

And how would women be trained to react? One can imagine traditional women agreeing to all these arguments with a staunch and smiling masochism. ("The ERA would force housewives to wound themselves every month": Phyllis Schlafly. "Your husband's blood is as sacred as that of Jesus—and so sexy, too!": Marabel Morgan.) Reformers and Queen Bees would try to imitate men, and *pretend* to have a monthly cycle. All feminists would explain endlessly that men, too, needed to be liberated from the false idea of Martian aggressiveness, just as women needed to escape the bonds of menses-envy. Radical feminists would add that the oppression of the nonmenstrual was the pattern for all other oppressions. ("Vampires were our first freedom fighters!") Cultural feminists would develop a bloodless imagery in art and literature. Socialist feminists would insist that only under capitalism would men be able to monopolize menstrual blood. . . . In fact, if men could menstruate, the power jus- tifications could probably go on forever.

If we let them.

premenstrual tension are basically unaware of it but one only has to talk to their husbands or co-workers to confirm its existence.[20]

Is it possible that up to 100 percent of all menstruating women regularly experience emotional disturbance? Compared to whom? Are males the unstated standard of emotional stability? If there is but a single definition of what is normal and men fit that definition, then women with "female complaints" must by definition be either crazy or in need of medical attention. A double bind indeed.

Some scientists explicitly articulate the idea of the naturally abnormal female. Professor Frank Beach, a pioneer in the field of animal psychology and its rela- tionship to sexuality, suggests the following evolution-

ary account of menstruation. In primitive hunter-gath- erer societies adult women were either pregnant or lac- tating, and since life spans were so short they died well before menopause; low-fat diets made it likely that they did not ovulate every month; they thus experi- enced no more than ten menstrual cycles. Given cur- rent life expectancies as well as the widespread use of birth control, modern women may experience a total of four hundred menstrual cycles. He concludes from this reasoning that "civilization has given women *a physio- logically abnormal status* which may have important implications for the interpretation of psychological responses to periodic fluctuations in the secretion of ovarian hormones"—that is, to menstruation (empha- sis added).[21] Thus the first problem we face in evaluat- ing the literature on the premenstrual syndrome is figuring out how to deal with the underlying assumption that women have "a physiologically abnormal status."

Researchers who believe in PMS hold a wide variety of viewpoints (none of them supported by scientific data) about the basis of the problem. For example, Dr. Katharina Dalton, the most militant promoter of PMS, says that it results from a relative end-of-the-cycle deficiency in the hormone progesterone. Others cite deficiencies in vitamin B-6, fluid retention, and low blood sugar as possible causes. Suggested treatments range from hormone injection to the use of lithium, diuretics, megadoses of vitamins, and control of sugar in the diet[22] (see Table 1 for a complete list). Although some of these treatments are harmless, others are not. Progesterone injection causes cancer in animals. What will it do to humans? And a recent issue of *The New England Journal of Medicine* contains a report that large doses of vitamin B-6 damage the nerves, causing a loss of feeling in one's fingers and toes.[23] The wide variety of PMS "causes" and "cures" offered by the experts is confusing, to put it mildly. Just what *is* this syndrome that causes such controversy? How can a woman know if she has it?

TABLE I ALLEGED CAUSES AND PROPOSED TREATMENTS OF PMS

Hypothesized Causes of Premenstrual Syndrome	Various PMS Treatments (used but not validated)
Estrogen excess	Oral contraceptives
Progesterone deficiency	(combination estrogen
Vitamin B deficiency	and progesterone pills)
Vitamin A deficiency	Estrogen alone
Hypoglycemia	Natural progesterone
Endogenous hormone	Synthetic progestins
allergy	Valium or other
Psychosomatic	tranquilizers
Fluid retention	Nutritional supplements
Dysfunction of the	Minerals
neurointermediate lobe	Lithium
of the pituitary	Diuretics
Prolactin metabolism	A prolactin inhibitor/
	dopamine agonist
	Exercise
	Psychotherapy, relaxation,
	education, reassurance

SOURCES: Robert L. Reid and S. S. Yen, "Premenstrual Syndrome," *American Journal of Obstetrics and Gynecology* 139 (1981): 85–104; and Judith Abplanalp, "Premenstrual Syndrome: A Selective Review," *Women and Health* 8 (1983): 107–24.

With a case of the measles it's really quite simple. A fever and then spots serve as diagnostic signs. A woman said to have PMS, however, may or may not have any of a very large number of symptoms. Furthermore, PMS indicators such as headaches, depression, dizziness, loss or gain of appetite show up in everyone from time to time. Their mere presence cannot (as would measle spots) help one to diagnose the syndrome. In addition, whether any of these signals connote disease depends upon their severity. A slight headache may reflect nothing more than a lack of sleep, but repeated, severe headaches could indicate high blood pressure. As one researcher, Dr. Judith Abplanalp, succinctly put it: "There is no one set of symptoms which is considered to be the hallmark of or standard criterion for defining the premenstrual syndrome."[24] Dr. Katharina Dalton agrees but feels one can diagnose PMS quite simply by applying the term to "any symptoms or complaints which regularly come just before or during early menstruation but are absent at other times of the cycle."[25] Dalton contrasts this with men suffering from potential PMS "symptoms," because, she says, they experience them randomly during the month while women with the same physical indications acknowledge them only during the premenstruum.

PMS research usually bases itself on an ideal, regular, twenty-eight-day menstrual cycle. Researchers eliminate as subjects for study women with infrequent, shorter, or longer cycles. As a result, published investigations look at a skewed segment of the overall population. Even for those women with a regular cycle, however, a methodological problem remains because few researchers define the premenstrual period in the same way. Some studies look only at the day or two preceding the menstrual flow, others look at the week preceding, while workers such as Dalton cite cases that begin two weeks before menstruation and continue for one week after. Since so few investigations use exactly the same definition, research publications on PMS are difficult to compare with one another.[26] On this score if no other, the literature offers little useful insight, extensive as it is.

Although rarely stated, the assumption is that there is but *one* PMS. Dalton defines the problem so broadly that she and others may well lump together several phenomena of very different origins, a possibility heightened by the fact that investigators rarely assess the severity of the symptoms. Two women, one suffer-

TABLE 2   TOWARD A DEFINITION OF PREMENSTRUAL SYNDROME

Experimental criteria (rarely met in PMS studies):
 Premenstrual symptoms for at least six preceding cycles
 Moderate to severe physical and psychological symptoms
 Symptoms *only* during the premenstrual period with
   marked relief at onset of menses
 Age between 18 and 45 years
 Not pregnant
 Regular menses for six previous cycles
 No psychiatric disorder; normal physical examination
   and laboratory test profile
 No drugs for preceding four weeks
 Will not receive anxiolytics, diuretics, hormones,
   or neuroleptic drugs during the study

*Minimal descriptive information to be offered
in published studies of PMS (rarely offered in
the current literature):*
 Specification of the ways in which subjects
   were recruited
 Age limitations
 Contraception and medication information
 Marital status
 Parity
 Race
 Menstrual history data
 Assessment instruments
 Operational definition of PMS
 Psychiatric history data
 Assessment of current psychological state
 Criteria for assessment of severity of symptoms
 Criteria for defining ovulatory status of cycle
 Cut-off criteria for "unacceptable" subjects

SOURCE: Judith Abplanalp, "Premenstrual Syndrome: A Selective Review," *Women and Health* 8 (1983): 107–24.

ing from a few low days and the other from suicidal depression, may both be diagnosed as having PMS. Yet their difficulties could easily have different origins and ought certainly to receive different treatments. When investigators try carefully to define PMS, the number of people qualifying for study decreases dramatically. In one case a group used ten criteria (listed in Table 2) to define PMS only to find that no more than 20 percent of those who had volunteered for their research project met them.[27] In the absence of any clearly agreed-upon definition(s) of PMS, examinations of the topic should at least state clearly the methodology used; this would enable comparison between publications, and allow us to begin to accumulate some knowl-

edge about the issues at hand (Table 2 lists suggested baseline information). At the moment the literature is filled with individual studies that permit neither replication nor comparison with one another—an appropriate state, perhaps, for an art gallery but not for a field with pretensions to the scientific.

Despite the problems of method and definition, the conviction remains that PMS constitutes a widespread disorder, a conviction that fortifies and is fortified by the idea that women's reproductive function, so different from that of "normal" men, places them in a naturally diseased state. For those who believe that 90 percent of all women suffer from a disease called PMS, it becomes a reasonable research strategy to look at the normally functioning menstrual cycle for clues about the cause and possible treatment. There are, in fact, many theories but no credible evidence about the origins of PMS. In Table 1 I've listed the most frequently cited hypotheses, most of which involve in some manner the hormonal system that regulates menstruation. Some of the theories are ingenious and require a sophisticated knowledge of human physiology to comprehend. Nevertheless, the authors of one recent review quietly offer the following summary: "To date no one hypothesis has adequately explained the constellation of symptoms composing PMS."[28] In short, PMS is a disease in search of a definition and cause.

PMS also remains on the lookout for a treatment. That many have been tried is attested to in Table 1. The problem is that only rarely has the efficacy of these treatments been tested with the commonly accepted standard of a large-scale, double-blind study that includes placebos. In the few properly done studies "there is usually (1) a high placebo response and (2) the active agent is usually no better than a placebo."[29] In other words, women under treatment for PMS respond just as well to sugar pills as to medication containing hormones or other drugs. Since it is probable that some women experience severe distress caused by malfunctions of their menstrual system, the genuinely concerned physician faces a dilemma. Should he or she offer treatment until the patient says she feels better even though the drug used may have dangerous side effects; or should a doctor refuse help for as long as we know of no scientifically validated treatment for the patient's symptoms? I have no satisfactory answer. But the crying need for some scientifically acceptable research on the subject stands out above all. If we continue to assume that menstruation is itself pathological, we cannot establish a baseline of health against which to define disease. If, instead, we accept in theory that a range of menstrual normality exists, we can then set about designing studies that define the healthy female reproductive cycle. Only when we have some feeling for *that* can we begin to help women who suffer from diseases of menstruation.

Many of those who reject the alarmist nature of the publicity surrounding PMS believe nevertheless that women undergo mood changes during their menstrual cycle. Indeed, most Western women would agree. But do studies of large segments of our population support this generality? And if so, what causes these ups and downs? In trying to answer these questions we confront another piece of the medical model of human behavior, the belief that biology is primary, that hormonal changes cause behavioral ones, but not vice versa. Most researchers use such a linear, unicausal model without thinking about it. Their framework is so much a part of their belief system that they forget to question it. Nevertheless it is the model from which they work, and failure to recognize and work skeptically with it often results in poorly conceived research combined with implausible interpretations of data. Although the paradigm of biological causation has until very recently dominated menstrual cycle research, it now faces serious and intellectually stimulating challenge from feminist experts in the field. . . .

MENOPAUSE: THE STORM BEFORE THE CALM

An unlikely specter haunts the world. It is the ghost of former womanhood . . . "unfortunate women abounding in the streets walking stiffly in twos and threes, seeing little and observing less. . . . The world appears [to them] as through a grey veil, and they live as docile, harmless creatures missing most of life's values." According to Dr. Robert Wilson and Thelma Wilson, though, one should not be fooled by their "vapid cowlike negative state" because "there is ample evidence that the course of history has been changed not only by the presence of estrogen, but by its absence. The untold misery of alcoholism, drug addiction, divorce and broken homes caused by these unstable estrogen-starved women cannot be presented in statistical form."[30]

Rather than releasing women from their monthly

emotional slavery to the sex hormones, menopause involves them in new horrors. At the individual level one encounters the specter of sexual degeneration, described so vividly by Dr. David Reuben: "The vagina begins to shrivel, the breasts atrophy, sexual desire disappears. . . . Increased facial hair, deepening voice, obesity . . . coarsened features, enlargement of the clitoris, and gradual baldness complete the tragic picture. Not really a man but no longer a functional woman, these individuals live in the world of intersex."[31] At the demographic level writers express foreboding about women of the baby-boom generation, whose life span has increased from an average forty-eight years at the turn of the century to a projected eighty years in the year 2000.[32] Modern medicine, it seems, has played a cruel trick on women. One hundred years ago they didn't live long enough to face the hardships of menopause but today their increased longevity means they will live for twenty-five to thirty years beyond the time when they lose all possibility of reproducing. To quote Dr. Wilson again: "The unpalatable truth must be faced that all postmenopausal women are castrates."[33]

But what medicine has wrought, it can also rend asunder. Few publications have had so great an effect on the lives of so many women as have those of Dr. Robert A. Wilson, who pronounced menopause to be a disease of estrogen deficiency. At the same time in an influential popular form, in his book *Feminine Forever,* he offered a treatment: estrogen replacement therapy (ERT).[34] During the first seven months following publication in 1966, Wilson's book sold one hundred thousand copies and was excerpted in *Vogue* and *Look* magazines. It influenced thousands of physicians to prescribe estrogen to millions of women, many of whom had no clinical "symptoms" other than cessation of the menses. As one of his credentials Wilson lists himself as head of the Wilson Research Foundation, an outfit funded by Ayerst Labs, Searle, and Upjohn, all pharmaceutical giants interested in the large potential market for estrogen. (After all, no woman who lives long enough can avoid menopause.) As late as 1976 Ayerst also supported the Information Center on the Mature Woman, a public relations firm that promoted estrogen replacement therapy. By 1975 some six million women had started long-term treatment with Premarin (Ayerst Labs' brand name for estrogen), making it the fourth or fifth most popular drug in the United States. Even today, two million of the forty million postmenopausal women in the United States contribute to the $70 million grossed each year from the sale of Premarin-brand estrogen.[35] The "disease of menopause" is not only a social problem: it's big business.[36]

The high sales of Premarin continue despite the publication in 1975 of an article linking estrogen treatment to uterine cancer.[37] Although in the wake of that publication many women stopped taking estrogen and many physicians became more cautious about prescribing it, the idea of hormone replacement therapy remains with us. At least three recent publications in medical journals seriously consider whether the benefits of estrogen might not outweigh the dangers.[38] The continuing flap over treatment for this so-called deficiency disease of the aging female forces one to ask just what *is* this terrible state called menopause? Are its effects so unbearable that one might prefer to increase, even ever so slightly, the risk of cancer rather than suffer the daily discomforts encountered during "the change of life"?

Ours is a culture that fears the elderly. Rather than venerate their years and listen to their wisdom, we segregate them in housing built for "their special needs," separated from the younger generations from which we draw hope for the future. At the same time we allow millions of old people to live on inadequate incomes, in fear that serious illness will leave them destitute. The happy, productive elderly remain invisible in our midst. (One must look to feminist publications such as *Our Bodies, Ourselves* to find women who express pleasure in their postmenopausal state.) Television ads portray only the arthritic, the toothless, the wrinkled, and the constipated. If estrogen really is the hormone of youth and its decline suggests the coming of old age, then its loss is a part of biology that our culture ill equips us to handle.

There is, of course, a history to our cultural attitudes toward the elderly woman and our views about menopause. In the nineteenth century physicians believed that at menopause a woman entered a period of depression and increased susceptibility to disease. The postmenopausal body might be racked with "dyspepsia, diarrhea . . . rheumatic pains, paralysis, apoplexy . . . hemorrhaging . . . tuberculosis . . . and diabetes," while emotionally the aging female risked becoming irritable, depressed, hysterical, melancholic, or even insane. The more a woman violated social laws (such as using birth control or promoting female suf-

frage), the more likely she would be to suffer a disease-ridden menopause.[39] In the twentieth century, psychologist Helene Deutsch wrote that at menopause "woman has ended her existence as a bearer of future life and has reached her natural end—her partial death—as a servant of the species."[40] Deutsch believed that during the postmenopausal years a woman's main psychological task was to accept the progressive biological withering she experienced. Other well-known psychologists have also accepted the idea that a woman's life purpose is mainly reproductive and that her postreproductive years are ones of inevitable decline. Even in recent times postmenopausal women have been "treated" with tranquilizers, hormones, electroshock, and lithium.[41]

But should women accept what many see as an inevitable emotional and biological decline? Should they believe, as Wilson does, that "from a practical point of view a man remains a man until the end," but that after menopause "we no longer have the 'whole woman'—only the 'part woman'"?[42] What is the real story of menopause?

The Change: Its Definition and Physiology

In 1976 under the auspices of the American Geriatric Society and the medical faculty of the University of Montpellier, the First International Congress on the Menopause convened in the south of France. In the volume that emerged from that conference, scientists and clinicians from around the world agreed on a standard definition of the words *menopause* and *climacteric*. "Menopause," they wrote, "indicates the final menstrual period and occurs during the climacteric. The climacteric is that phase in the aging process of women marking the transition from the reproductive stage of life to the non-reproductive stage."[43] By consensus, then, the word *menopause* has come to mean a specific event, the last menstruation, while *climacteric* implies a process occurring over a period of years.*

During the menstrual cycle the blood levels of a number of hormones rise and fall on a regular basis.

---

*There is also a male climacteric, which entails a gradual reduction in production of the hormone testosterone over the years as part of the male aging process. What part it plays in that process is poorly understood and seems frequently to be ignored by researchers, who prefer to contrast continuing male reproductive potency with the loss of childbearing ability in women.[44]

At the end of one monthly cycle, the low levels of estrogen and progesterone trigger the pituitary gland to make follicle stimulating hormone (FSH) and luteinizing hormone (LH). The FSH influences the cells of the ovary to make large amounts of estrogen, and induces the growth and maturation of an oocyte. The LH, at just the right moment, induces ovulation and stimulates certain ovarian cells to form a progesterone-secreting structure called a corpus luteum. When no pregnancy occurs the life of the corpus luteum is limited and, as it degenerates, the lowered level of steroid hormones calls forth a new round of follicle stimulating and luteinizing hormone synthesis, beginning the cycle once again. Although the ovary produces the lion's share of these steroid hormones, the cells of the adrenal gland also contribute and this contribution increases in significance after menopause.

What happens to the intricately balanced hormone cycle during the several years preceding menopause is little understood, although it seems likely that gradual changes occur in the balance between pituitary activity (FSH and LH production) and estrogen synthesis.[45] One thing, however, is clear: menopause does not mean the *absence* of estrogen, but rather a gradual lowering in the availability of *ovarian* estrogen. Table 3 summarizes some salient information about changes in steroid hormone levels during the menstrual cycle and after menopause. In looking at the high point of cycle synthesis and then comparing it to women who no longer menstruate, the most dramatic change is seen in the estrogenic hormone estradiol.* The other estrogenic hormones, as well as progesterone and testosterone, drop off to some extent but continue to be synthesized at a level comparable to that observed during the early phases of the menstrual cycle. Instead of concentrating on the notion of estrogen deficiency, however, it is more important to point out that (1) postmenopausally the body makes different kinds of estrogen; (2) the ovaries synthesize less and the adrenals more of these hormones; and (3) the monthly ups and downs of these hormones even out following menopause.

While estrogen levels begin to decline, the levels of FSH and LH start to increase. Changes in these

hormones appear as early as eight years before menopause.[46] At the time of menopause and for several years afterward, these two hormones are found in very high concentrations compared to menstrual levels (FSH as many as fourteen times more concentrated than premenopausally, and LH more than three times more). Over a period of years such high levels are reduced to about half their peak value, leaving the postmenopausal woman with one-and-one-half times more LH and seven times more FSH circulating in her blood than when she menstruated regularly.

It is to all of these changes in hormone levels that the words *climacteric* and *menopause* refer. From these alterations Wilson and others have chosen to blame estrogen for the emotional deterioration they believe appears in postmenopausal women. Why they have focused on only one hormone from a complex system of hormonal changes is anybody's guess. I suspect, however, that the reasons are (at least) twofold. First, the normative biomedical disease model of female physiology looks for simple cause and effect. Most researchers, then, have simply assumed estrogen to be a "cause" and set out to measure its "effect." The model or framework out of which such investigators work precludes an interrelated analysis of all the different (and closely connected) hormonal changes going on during the climacteric. But why single out estrogen? Possibly because this hormone plays an important role in the menstrual cycle as well as in the development of "feminine" characteristics such as breasts and overall body contours. It is seen as the quintessential female hormone. So where could one better direct one's attention if, to begin with, one views menopause as the loss of true womanhood?

Physical changes do occur following menopause. Which, if any, of these are caused by changing hormone levels is another question. Menopause research comes equipped with its own unique experimental traps.[47] The most obvious is that a postmenopausal population is also an aging population. Do physical and emotional differences found in groups of postmenopausal women have to do with hormonal changes or with other aspects of aging? It is a difficult matter to sort out. Furthermore, many of the studies on menopause have been done on preselected populations, using women who volunteer because they experience classic menopausal "symptoms" such as the hot flash. Such investigations tell us nothing about average

---

*Estrogens are really a family of structurally similar molecules. Their possibly different biological roles are not clearly delineated.

TABLE 3   HORMONE LEVELS AS A PERCENTAGE OF MID-MENSTRUAL-CYCLE HIGH POINT

Stage of Menstrual Cycle	TYPE OF ESTROGEN			Progesterone	Testosterone	Androstenedione
	Estrone	Estradiol	Estriol			
Premenopausal stage						
Early (menses)	20%	13%	67%	100%	55%	87%
Mid (ovulation)	100	100	—	—	100	100
Late (premenstrual)	49	50	100	—	82	—
Postmenopausal stage	17	3	50	50	23	39

SOURCE: Wulf H. Utian, *Menopause in Modern Perspectives* (New York: Appleton-Century-Crofts, 1980), 32.

changes within the population as a whole. In the language of the social scientist, we have no baseline data, nothing to which we can compare menopausal women, no way to tell whether the complaint of a particular woman is typical, a cause for medical concern, or simply idiosyncratic.

Since the late 1970s feminist researchers have begun to provide us with much-needed information. Although their results confirm some beliefs long held by physicians, these newer investigators present them in a more sophisticated context. Dr. Madeleine Goodman and her colleagues designed a study in which they drew information from a large population of women ranging in age from thirty-five to sixty. All had undergone routine multiphasic screening at a health maintenance clinic, but none had come for problems concerning menopause. From the complete clinic records they selected a population of women who had not menstruated for at least one year and compared their health records with those who still menstruated, looking at thirty-five different variables, such as cramps, blood glucose levels, blood calcium, and hot flashes, to see if any of these symptoms correlated with those seen in postmenopausal women. The results are startling. They found that only 28 percent of Caucasian women and 24 percent of Japanese women identified as postmenopausal "reported traditional menopausal symptoms such as hot flashes, sweats, etc., while in nonmenopausal controls, 16% in Caucasians and 10% in Japanese also reported these same symptoms."[48] In other words, 75 percent of menopausal women in their sample reported no remarkable menopausal symptoms, a result in sharp contrast to earlier studies using women who identified themselves as menopausal.

In a similar exploration, researcher Karen Frey found evidence to support Goodman's results. She wrote that menopausal women "did not report significantly greater frequency of physical symptoms or concern about these symptoms than did pre- or postmenopausal women."[49] The studies of Goodman, Frey, and others[50] draw into serious question the notion that menopause is generally or necessarily associated with a set of disease symptoms. Yet at least three physical changes—hot flashes, vaginal dryness and irritation, and osteoporosis—and one emotional one—depression—remain associated in the minds of many with the decreased estrogen levels of the climacteric. Goodman's work indicates that such changes may be far less widespread than previously believed, but if they are troublesome to 26 percent of all menopausal women they remain an appropriate subject for analysis.

We know only the immediate cause of hot flashes: a sudden expansion of the blood flow to the skin. The technical term to describe them, *vasomotor instability,* means only that nerve cells signal the widening of blood vessels allowing more blood into the body's periphery. A consensus has emerged on two things: (1) the high concentration of FSH and LH in blood probably causes hot flashes, although exactly how this happens remains unknown; and (2) estrogen treatment is the only currently available way to suppress the hot flashes. One hypothesis is that by means of a feedback mechanism, artificially raised blood levels of estrogen signal the brain to tell the pituitary to call off the FSH and LH. Although estrogen does stop the hot flashes, its effects are only temporary; remove the estrogen and the flashes return. Left alone, the body eventually adjusts to the changing levels of FSH and LH. Thus a premenopausal woman has two choices in dealing with hot flashes: she can either take estrogen as a permanent medication, a course Wilson refers to as embarking "on the great adventure of preserving or regaining your full femininity,"[51] or suffer some discomfort while nature takes its course. Since the longer one takes estrogen, the greater the danger of estrogen-linked cancer, many health-care workers recommend the latter.[52]

Some women experience postmenopausal vaginal dryness and irritation that can make sexual intercourse painful. Since the cells of the vaginal wall contain estrogen receptors, it is not surprising that estrogen applied locally or taken in pill form helps with this difficulty. Even locally applied, however, the estrogen enters into the bloodstream, presenting the same dangers as when taken in pill form. There are alternative treatments, though, for vaginal dryness. The Boston Women's Health Collective, for example, recommends the use of nonestrogen vaginal creams or jellies, which seem to be effective and are certainly safer. Continued sexual activity also helps—yet another example of the interaction between behavior and physiology.

Hot flashes and vaginal dryness are the *only* climacteric-associated changes for which estrogen unambiguously offers relief. Since significant numbers of women do not experience these changes and since for many of those that do the effects are relatively mild, the wisdom of ERT must be examined carefully and on an individual basis. Both men and women undergo certain changes as they age, but Wilson's catastrophic vision of postmenopausal women—those ghosts gliding by "unnoticed and, in turn, notic[ing] little"[53]—is such a far cry from reality that it is a source of amazement that serious medical writers continue to quote his work.

In contrast to hot flashes and vaginal dryness, osteoporosis, a brittleness of the bone which can in severe cases cripple, has a complex origin. Since this potentially life-threatening condition appears more frequently in older women than in older men, the hypothesis of a relationship with estrogen levels seemed plausible to many. But as one medical worker has said, a unified theory of the disease "is still non-existent, although sedentary life styles, genetic predisposition, hormonal imbalance, vitamin deficiencies, high-protein diets, and cigarette smoking all have been implicated."[54] Estrogen treatment seems to arrest the disease for a while, but may lose effectiveness after a few years.[55]

Even more than in connection with any physical changes, women have hit up against a medical double bind whenever they have complained of emotional problems during the years of climacteric. On the one

hand physicians dismissed these complaints as the imagined ills of a hormone-deficient brain, while on the other they generalized the problem, arguing that middle-aged women are emotionally unreliable, unfit for positions of leadership and responsibility. Women had two choices: to complain and experience ridicule and/or improper medical treatment, or to suffer in silence. Hormonal changes during menopause were presumed to be the cause of psychiatric symptoms ranging from fatigue, dizziness, irritability, apprehension, and insomnia to severe headaches and psychotic depression. In recent years, however, these earlier accounts have been supplanted by a rather different consensus now emerging among responsible medical researchers.

To begin with, there are no data to support the idea that menopause has any relationship to serious depression in women. Postmenopausal women who experience psychosis have almost always had similar episodes premenopausally.[56] The notion of the hormonally depressed woman is a shibboleth that must be laid permanently to rest. Some studies have related irritability and insomnia to loss of sleep from nighttime hot flashes. Thus, for women who experience hot flashes, these emotional difficulties might, indirectly, relate to menopause. But the social, life history, and family contexts in which middle-aged women find themselves are more important links to emotional changes occurring during the years of the climacteric. And these, of course, have nothing whatsoever to do with hormones. Quite a number of studies suggest that the majority of women do not consider menopause a time of crisis. Nor do most women suffer from the so-called "empty nest syndrome" supposedly experienced when children leave home. On the contrary, investigation suggests that women without small children are less depressed and have higher incomes and an increased sense of well-being.[57] Such positive reactions depend upon work histories, individual upbringing, cultural background, and general state of health, among other things.

In a survey conducted for *Our Bodies, Ourselves,* one which in no sense represents a balanced cross section of U.S. women, the Boston Women's Health Collective recorded the reactions of more than two hundred menopausal or postmenopausal women, most of whom were suburban, married, and employed, to a series of questions about menopause. About two-thirds of them felt either positively or neutrally about a variety of changes they had undergone, while a whopping 90 percent felt okay or happy about the loss of childbearing ability![58] This result probably comes as no surprise to most women, but it flies in the face of the long-standing belief that women's lives and emotions are driven in greater part by their reproductive systems.

No good account of adult female development in the middle years exists. Levinson,[59] who studied adult men, presents a linear model of male development designed primarily around work experiences. In his analysis, the male climacteric plays only a secondary role. Feminist scholars Rosalind Barnett and Grace Baruch have described the difficulty of fitting women into Levinson's scheme: "It is hard to know how to think of women within this theory—a woman may not enter the world of work until her late thirties, she seldom has a mentor, and even women with life-long career commitments rarely are in a position to reassess their commitment pattern by age 40," as do the men in Levinson's study.[60]

Baruch and Barnett call for the development of a theory of women in their middle years, pointing out that an adequate one can emerge only when researchers set aside preconceived ideas about the central role of biology in adult female development and listen to what women themselves say. Paradoxically, in some sense we will remain unable to understand more about the role of biology in women's middle years until we have a more realistic *social* analysis of women's postadolescent psychological development. Such an analysis must, of course, take into account ethnic, racial, regional, and class differences among women, since once biology is jettisoned as a universal cause of female behavior, it no longer makes sense to lump all women into a single category.

Much remains to be understood about menopause. Which biological changes, for instance, result from ovarian degeneration and which from other aspects of aging? How does the aging process compare in men and women? What causes hot flashes and can we find safe ways to alleviate the discomfort they cause? Do other aspects of a woman's life affect the number and severity of menopausally related physical symptoms? What can we learn from studying the experience of menopause in other, especially non-Western cultures? A number of researchers have proposed effective ways of finding answers to these questions.[61] We need only time, research dollars, and an open mind to move forward.

CONCLUSION

The premise that women are by nature abnormal and inherently diseased dominates past research on menstruation and menopause. While appointing the male reproductive system as normal, this viewpoint calls abnormal any aspect of the female reproductive life cycle that deviates from the male's. At the same time such an analytical framework places the essence of a woman's existence in her reproductive system. Caught in her hormonal windstorm, she strives to attain normality but can do so only by rejecting her biological uniqueness, for that too is essentially deformed: a double bind indeed. Within such an intellectual structure no medical research of any worth to women's health can be done, for it is the blueprint itself that leads investigators to ask the wrong questions, look in the wrong places for answers, and then distort the interpretation of their results.

Reading through the morass of poorly done studies on menstruation and menopause, many of which express deep hatred and fear of women, can be a discouraging experience. One begins to wonder how it can be that within so vast a quantity of material so little quality exists. But at this very moment the field of menstrual-cycle research (including menopause) offers a powerful antidote to that disheartenment in the form of feminist researchers (both male and female) with excellent training and skills, working within a new analytical framework. Rejecting a strict medical model of female development, they understand that men and women have different reproductive cycles, *both* of which are normal. Not binary opposites, male and female physiologies have differences *and* similarities. These research pioneers know too that the human body functions in a social milieu and that it changes in response to that context. Biology is not a one-way determinant but a dynamic component of our existence. And, equally important, these new investigators have learned not only to *listen* to what women say about themselves but to *hear* as well. By and large, these researchers are not in the mainstream of medical and psychological research, but we can look forward to a time when the impact of their work will affect the field of menstrual-cycle research for the better and for many years to come.

NOTES

1. Carroll Smith-Rosenberg and Charles Rosenberg, "The Female Animal: Medical and Biological Views of Woman and Her Role in 19th Century America," *Journal of American History* 60(1973):336.

2. Edgar Berman, Letter to the Editor, *New York Times,* 26 July 1970.

3. Steven Goldberg, *The Inevitability of Patriarchy* (New York: William Morrow, 1973), 93.

4. Herbert Wray, "Premenstrual Changes," *Science News* 122(1982):380–81.

5. Ilza Veith, *Hysteria: The History of a Disease* (Chicago: University of Chicago Press, 1965).

6. Pliny the Elder, quoted in M. E. Ashley-and Montagu, "Physiology and Origins of the Menstrual Prohibitions," *Quarterly Review of Biology* 15(1940):211.

7. Smith-Rosenberg and Rosenberg, "The Female Animal"; Henry Maudsley, "Sex in Mind and in Education," *Popular Science Monthly* 5(1874):200; and Joan Burstyn, "Education and Sex: The Medical Case Against Higher Education for Women in England 1870–1900," *Proceeds of the American Philosophical Society* 177(1973):7989.

8. Carroll Smith-Rosenberg, "The Hysterical Woman: Sex Roles and Role Conflict in 19th Century America," *Social Research* 39(1972):652–78.

9. M. A. Hardaker, "Science and the Woman Question," *Popular Science Monthly* 20(1881):583.

10. Nina Morais, "A Reply to Ms. Hardaker on: The Woman Question," *Popular Science Monthly* 21(1882):74–75.

11. Maudsley, "Sex in Mind and in Education," 211.

12. Katharina Dalton, *Once a Month* (Claremont, Calif.: Hunter House, 1983), 78.

13. Ibid.; Katharina Dalton, *The Premenstrual Syndrome* (London: William Heinemann Medical Books, 1972).

14. Andrea Eagan, "The Selling of Premenstrual Syndrome," *Ms.* Oct. 1983, 26–31.

15. Robert L. Reid and S. S. Yen, "Premenstrual Syndrome," *American Journal of Obstetrics and Gynecology* 139(1981):86.

16. J. Abplanalp, R. F. Haskett, and R. M. Rose, "The Premenstrual Syndrome," *Advances in Psychoneuroendocrinology* 3(1980):327–47.

17. Dalton, *Once a Month.*

18. Boston Women's Health Collective, *Our Bodies, Ourselves* (New York: Simon and Schuster, 1979).

19. Reid and Yen, "Premenstrual Syndrome," 86.

20. John O'Connor, M. Shelley Edward, and Lenore O. Stern, "Behavioral Rhythms Related to the Menstrual Cycle," in *Biorhythms and Human Reproduction,* ed. M. Fern et al. (New York: Wiley, 1974), 312.

21. Frank A. Beach, Preface to chapter 10, in *Human Sexuality in Four Perspectives* (Baltimore: Johns Hopkins University Press, 1977), 271.

22. M. B. Rosenthal, "Insights into the Premenstrual Syndrome," *Physician and Patient* (April 1983):46–53

23. Herbert Schaumberg et al., "Sensory Neuropathy from Pyridoxine Abuse," *New England Journal of Medicine* 309(1983):446–48.

24. Judith Abplanalp, "Premenstrual Syndrome: A Selective Review," *Women and Health* 8(1983):110.

25. Dalton, *Once a Month,* 12.

26. Abplanalp, Haskett, and Rose, "The Premenstrual Syndrome"; and Abplanalp, "Premenstrual Syndrome: A Selective Review."

27. Abplanalp, "Premenstrual Syndrome: A Selective Review."

28. Reid and Yen, "Premenstrual Syndrome," 97.

29. G. A. Sampson, "An Appraisal of the Role of Progesterone in the Therapy of Premenstrual Syndrome," in *The Premenstrual Syndrome,* ed. P. A. vanKeep and W. H. Utian (Lancaster, England: MTP Press Ltd. International Medical Publishers, 1981), 51–69; and Sampson, "Premenstrual Syndrome: A Double-Bind Controlled Trial of Progesterone and Placebo," *British Journal of Psychiatry* 135 (1979):209–15.

30. Robert A. Wilson and Thelma A. Wilson, "The Fate of the Nontreated Postmenopausal Woman: A Plea for the Maintenance of Adequate Estrogen from Puberty to the Grave," *Journal of the American Geriatric Society* 11(1963):352–56.

31. David Reuben, *Everything You Always Wanted to Know about Sex but Were Afraid to Ask* (New York: McKay, 1969), 292.

32. Wulf H. Utian, *Menopause in Modern Perspectives* (New York: Appleton-Century-Crofts, 1980).

33. Wilson and Wilson, "The Fate of the Nontreated Postmenopausal Woman," 347.

34. Robert A. Wilson, *Feminine Forever* (New York: M. Evans, 1966).

35. Marilyn Grossman and Pauline Bart, "The Politics of Menopause," in *The Menstrual Cycle,* vol. 1, ed. Dan, Graham, and Beecher.

36. Kathleen MacPherson, "Menopause as Disease: The Social Construction of a Metaphor," *Advances in Nursing Science* 3(1981):95–113; A. Johnson, "The Risks of Sex Hormones as Drugs," *Women and Health* 2(1977):8–11.

37. D. Smith et al., "Association of Exogenous Estrogen Endometrial Cancer," *New England Journal of Medicine* 293(1975):1164–67.

38. H. Judd et al., "Estrogen Replacement Therapy," *Obstetrics and Gynecology* 58(1981):267–75; M. Quigley, "Postmenopausal Hormone Replacement Therapy: Back to Estrogen Forever?" *Geriatric Medicine Today* 1(1982):78–85; and Thomas Skillman, "Estrogen Replacement: Its Risks and Benefits," *Consultant* (1982):115–27.

39. C. Smith-Rosenberg, "Puberty to Menopause: The Cycle of Femininity in 19th Century America," *Feminist Studies* 1(1973):65.

40. Helene Deutsch, *The Psychology of Women* (New York: Grune and Stratton, 1945), 458.

41. J. H. Osofsky and R. Seidenberg, "Is Female Menopausal Depression Inevitable," *Obstetrics and Gynecology* 36(1970):611.

42. Wilson and Wilson, "The Fate of the Nontreated Postmenopausal Woman," 348.

43. P. A. vanKeep, R. B. Greenblatt, and M. Albeaux-Fernet, eds., *Consensus on Menopause Research* (Baltimore: University Park Press, 1976), 134.

44. Marcha Flint, "Male and Female Menopause: A Cultural Put-on," in *Changing Perspectives on Menopause,* ed. A. M. Voda, M. Dinnerstein, and S. O'Donnell (Austin: University of Texas Press, 1982).

45. Utian, *Menopause in Modern Perspectives.*

46. Ibid.

47. Madeleine Goodman, "Toward a Biology of Menopause," *Signs* 5(1980):739–53.

48. Madeleine Goodman, C. J. Stewart, and F. Gilbert, "Patterns of Menopause: A Study of Certain Medical and Physiological Variables among Caucasian and Japanese Women Living in Hawaii," *Journal of Gerontology* 32(1977):297.

49. Karen Frey, "Middle-Aged Women's Experience and Perceptions of Menopause," *Women and Health* 6(1981):31.

50. Eve Kahana, A. Kiyak, and J. Liang, "Menopause in the Context of Other Life Events," in *The Menstrual Cycle,* vol. 1, ed. Dan, Graham, and Beecher, 167–78.

51. Wilson, *Feminine Forever,* 134.

52. A. Voda and M. Eliasson, "Menopause: The Closure of Menstrual Life," *Women and Health* 8(1983):137–56.

53. Wilson and Wilson, "The Fate of the Nontreated Postmenopausal Woman," 356.

54. Louis Avioli, "Postmenopausal Osteoporosis: Prevention vs. Cure," *Federation Proceedings* 40(1981):2418.

55. Voda and Eliasson, "Menopause: The Closure of Menstrual Life."

56. G. Winokur and R. Cadoret, "The Irrelevance of the Menopause to Depressive Disease," in *Topics in Psychoendocrinology,* ed. E. J. Sachar (New York: Grune and Stratton, 1975).

57. Rosalind Barnett and Grace Baruch, "Women in the Middle Years: A Critique of Research and Theory," *Psychology of Women Quarterly* 3(1978):187–97.

58. Boston Women's Health Collective, *Our Bodies, Ourselves.*

59. D. Levinson et al., "Periods in the Adult Development of Men: Ages 18–45," *The Counseling Psychologist* 6(1976):21–25.

60. Barnett and Baruch, "Women in the Middle Years," 189.

61. Ibid.; Goodman, "Toward a Biology of Menopause"; and Voda, Dinnerstein, and O'Donnell, eds., *Changing Perspectives on Menopause.*

R E A D I N G   3 3

*A Call for Our Language: Anorexia from Within**†

TAKAYO MUKAI

PREFACE

I am a recovered anorectic. And I am a feminist. As a feminist, I view my anorexia and my recovery in ways I explore in this thesis.

Excerpt from "A Call for Our Language: Anorexia from Within," by Takayo Mukai, in *Women's Studies International Forum,* vol. 12, no. 6, 1989. Reprinted by permission of the author.

I became anorexic eleven years ago. I lost 10 kg within six months and stayed at that lowest weight for one and half years, after which I started eating. During that process, I had never heard of the term "anorexia,"

*Thesis submitted to the Graduate School of West Virginia University, in partial fulfillment of the requirements for The Degree of Master of Arts.
†*Dedication:* To my mother, Katsuko Mukai, and her mother, Sakae Hyodo.

nor did I ever think of myself as being *ill*. About three years after I started to eat, I began to associate the term with my past experience of a thin body. However, a sense of "disorderedness" was still detached from the sound and the spelling of the word "anorexia." The eight-letter-word was just an empty envelope, unstamped and unaddressed.

Meanwhile, I had become involved in the feminist movement, first in Japan, and then in the U.S. This social, intellectual, and spiritual experience changed my viewpoint of the world drastically. Everything that I had taken for granted before was now re-visioned, re-examined. I was beginning to un-learn who I had been and then to re-learn new ways to relate to everything and everybody with care and honesty.

At the intellectual level, feminism is a challenge to the traditional disciplines including their assumptions, methods, and findings. At the spiritual level, it connects my life to that of all women both past and present, by reclaiming women's experiences which have previously been shared only in masculine versions or that have not been shared at all.

It was from the feminist standpoint and especially with the impact of French feminism that I realized that while anorexia has been experienced by many women, it has not been truly *shared* by these women or with anyone else through these women's perspective. I'm afraid it will never be, as long as we keep authorities over us and listen to how they (authority) translate *our* experiences. As some of the French feminists—Helene Cixous, Luce Irigaray, and Monique Wittig, for example—state, in order to *share* our bodies' experiences, we need to share the language. The language which is not entrapped by the net of the patriarchy. The language in which a word means what we co-experience instead of what we are supposed to experience. The language which shall never restrict our experiences into its own structures/rules but instead, the language which lets the experiences be re-vived in its dynamics and delivers them in its flow. The flow that contains the velosity, the viscosity, and the warmth of our experiences, of our bodies experiences.

This is what I call "our language.". . .

Noises are becoming bigger in my ears.

The mother? The mother's body? The "bad-me"? The taboos in contemporary society?

My whole body, from the core, startled, turning into a stone. I cover my ears with my hands. I try to keep the voices from getting tangled up again. I must keep the flow from clotting. No. Never again!

I need to go back to the inside of me, into my flesh, into my fat, my muscle, my bones, my veins. I need to listen to my body. Let my body talk of itself. Let my body tell me its story, about its pain, its rage, its tears, and about its love.

What have I just said?
Was it my word?   Were they my words?
The story of my body?   The body would tell a story?
Its story?
What, then, bridges the gap between me and my body?
What is the 'gap'?
What, please, am I trying to say? Or, is it my body that is trying to say something?

I look at my hand. I look at a tiny mark on my right palm. I remember exactly how I got it. It's been here for fifteen years. I touch the mark with my finger. I feel it. It's hollow. It is there. It's been with me all the time. It's been everywhere with me. . . .

In spring, it played with falling cherry
  blossoms.
In summer, it startled at the burned sand
  on beach.
In fall, it helped me to make clumsy rice
  balls for a picnic.
In winter, it always wanted to curl up in a
  mitten.

Yes, it has its story.
The mark does.   The hand does.
  The veins the muscles the bones. . . .
Oh, my body wants to speak!
Please, let it speak.   Let them speak.

My body needs a language.
And I need to share it in order to listen to
  my body, to listen to what it needs to
  say, what it means to say, without
  translating, without being translated.
  We need languages in order to hear "I
  love you," when our bodies say, "I love
  you."

in order to feel "I love you."
in order to resonate with "I love you."
in order to return "I love you, too."

Tears run down my cheeks. And yet, I am smiling. I am
at peace now. There is a dynamic flow in me now.

Once we listen to our bodies
without translating, without being translated,
would it also be possible to share it with
   each other?
without editing, without being edited,
without summarizing, without being summarized.

Once we acquire "our language(s),"
our way(s) of connecting sensations to
   ourselves,
our way(s) of articulating feelings and
   thoughts,
would it also be possible to be tied with
   each other? between us?
even with doubts? with conflicts? or with
   hesitations?
across the boundaries, across the vacuum,
and across the "gap" both within and out
   of ourselves.

Where there are thousands of anorectics
   and recovered anorectics, there are
   thousands of different stories, thousands
   of stories of pleasure, of rejection,
   and of acceptance.

It does not really matter whether the
   source of the voice is objective, or
   subjective.
What is more important is how much,
   with what intensity the voice is echoed,
   by trembling lips, by tightened fists,
   and by tearful eyes.

We have to begin
to listen,
to talk,
and to write.
But, how?

The story is not completed. There is no conclusion,
nor ending remarks. There will be no main story, nor
side story. There will be no footnotes, nor format, no
rules. There will be no distinction between the subject
and the object, nor between the teller and the listener,
nor between the written and the read. Boundaries will
have been dissolved. The speaker and the listener will
work together to generate a story. The writer and the
reader will invite each other to re-live the story, together. It will be a story in the style without a style.
Rather, it is passionate encounters and dynamic rapport between people—between the writer and the
character—that we would like to hear about. We
would like to resonate together.

Racism, Birth Control, and Reproductive Rights

ANGELA Y. DAVIS

When nineteenth-century feminists raised the demand for "voluntary motherhood," the campaign for birth control was born. Its proponents were called radicals and they were subjected to the same mockery as had befallen the initial advocates of woman suffrage. "Voluntary motherhood" was considered audacious, outrageous and outlandish by those who insisted that wives had no right to refuse to satisfy their husbands' sexual urges. Eventually, of course, the right to birth control, like women's rights to vote, would be more or less taken for granted by U.S. public opinion. Yet in 1970, a full century later, the call for legal and easily accessible abortions was no less controversial than the issue of "voluntary motherhood" which had originally launched the birth control movement in the United States.

Birth control—individual choice, safe contraceptive methods, as well as abortions when necessary—is a fundamental prerequisite for the emancipation of women. Since the right of birth control is obviously advantageous to women of all classes and races, it would appear that even vastly dissimilar women's groups would have attempted to unite around this issue. In reality, however, the birth control movement has seldom succeeded in uniting women of different social backgrounds, and rarely have the movement's leaders popularized the genuine concerns of working-class women. Moreover, arguments advanced by birth control advocates have sometimes been based on blatantly racist premises. The progressive potential of birth control remains indisputable. But in actuality, the historical record of this movement leaves much to be desired in the realm of challenges to racism and class exploitation.

From *Women, Race and Class* by Angela Davis. Copyright © 1981 by Angela Davis. Reprinted by permission of Random House, Inc.

The most important victory of the contemporary birth control movement was won during the early 1970s when abortions were at last declared legal. Having emerged during the infancy of the new Women's Liberation movement, the struggle to legalize abortions incorporated all the enthusiasm and the militancy of the young movement. By January, 1973, the abortion rights campaign had reached a triumphant culmination. In *Roe* v. *Wade* (410 U.S.) and *Doe* v. *Bolton* (410 U.S.), the U.S. Supreme Court ruled that a woman's right to personal privacy implied her right to decide whether or not to have an abortion.

The ranks of the abortion rights campaign did not include substantial numbers of women of color. Given the racial composition of the larger Women's Liberation movement, this was not at all surprising. When questions were raised about the absence of racially oppressed women in both the larger movement and the abortion rights campaign, two explanations were commonly proposed in the discussions and literature of the period: women of color were overburdened by their people's fight against racism; and/or they had not yet become conscious of the centrality of sexism. But the real meaning of the almost lily-white complexion of the abortion rights campaign was not to be found in an ostensibly myopic or underdeveloped consciousness among women of color. The truth lay buried in the ideological underpinnings of the birth control movement itself.

The failure of the abortion rights campaign to conduct a historical self-evaluation led to a dangerously superficial appraisal of Black people's suspicious attitudes toward birth control in general. Granted, when some Black people unhesitatingly equated birth control with genocide, it did appear to be an exaggerated—even paranoiac—reaction. Yet white abortion rights activists missed a profound message, for underlying these cries of genocide were important clues about the history of the birth control movement. This movement, for example, had been known to advocate involuntary sterilization—a racist form of mass "birth control." If ever women would enjoy the right to plan their pregnancies, legal and easily accessible birth control measures and abortions would have to be complemented by an end to sterilization abuse.

As for the abortion rights campaign itself, how could women of color fail to grasp its urgency? They were far more familiar than their white sisters with the murderously clumsy scalpels of inept abortionists seeking profit in illegality. In New York, for instance, during the several years preceding the decriminalization of abortions in that state, some 80 percent of the deaths caused by illegal abortions involved Black and Puerto Rican women.[1] Immediately afterward, women of color received close to half of all the legal abortions. If the abortion rights campaign of the early 1970s needed to be reminded that women of color wanted desperately to escape the back-room quack abortionists, they should have also realized that these same women were not about to express pro-abortion sentiments. They were in favor of *abortion rights,* which did not mean that they were proponents of abortion. When Black and Latina women resort to abortions in such large numbers, the stories they tell are not so much about their desire to be free of their pregnancy, but rather about the miserable social conditions which dissuade them from bringing new lives into the world.

Black women have been aborting themselves since the earliest days of slavery. Many slave women refused to bring children into a world of interminable forced labor, where chains and floggings and sexual abuse for women were the everyday conditions of life. A doctor practicing in Georgia around the middle of the last century noticed that abortions and miscarriages were far more common among his slave patients than among the white women he treated. According to the physician, either Black women worked too hard or

as the planters believe, the blacks are possessed of a secret by which they destroy the fetus at an early stage of gestation. . . . All country practitioners are aware of the frequent complaints of planters [about the] . . . unnatural tendency in the African female to destroy her offspring.[2]

Expressing shock that "whole families of women fail to have any children,"[3] this doctor never considered how

"unnatural" it was to raise children under the slave system. The episode of Margaret Garner, a fugitive slave who killed her own daughter and attempted suicide herself when she was captured by slavecatchers, is a case in point.

She rejoiced that the girl was dead—"now she would never know what a woman suffers as a slave"—and pleaded to be tried for murder. "I will go singing to the gallows rather than be returned to slavery!"[4]

Why were self-imposed abortions and reluctant acts of infanticide such common occurrences during slavery? Not because Black women had discovered solutions to their predicament, but rather because they were desperate. Abortions and infanticides were acts of desperation, motivated not by the biological birth process but by the oppressive conditions of slavery. Most of these women, no doubt, would have expressed their deepest resentment had someone hailed their abortions as a stepping-stone toward freedom.

During the early abortion rights campaign it was too frequently assumed that legal abortions provided a viable alternative to the myriad problems posed by poverty. As if having fewer children could create more jobs, higher wages, better schools, etc., etc. This assumption reflected the tendency to blur the distinction between *abortion rights* and the general advocacy of *abortions.* The campaign often failed to provide a voice for women who wanted the *right* to legal abortions while deploring the social conditions that prohibited them from bearing more children.

The renewed offensive against abortion rights that erupted during the latter half of the 1970s has made it absolutely necessary to focus more sharply on the needs of poor and racially oppressed women. By 1977 the passage of the Hyde Amendment in Congress had mandated the withdrawal of federal funding for abortions, causing many state legislatures to follow suit. Black, Puerto Rican, Chicana and Native American Indian women, together with their impoverished white sisters, were thus effectively divested of the right to legal abortions. Since surgical sterilizations, funded by the Department of Health, Education and Welfare, remained free on demand, more and more poor women have been forced to opt for permanent infertility. What is urgently required is a broad campaign to defend the reproductive rights of all women—and especially those women whose economic circumstances

WHEN THE POLITICAL BECOMES THE PERSONAL OR AN ABORTION THAT WASN'T AN ABORTION; A RIGHT THAT HARDLY SEEMS SUCH

ELEANOR MILLER

I never thought I'd need an abortion. In 1980 we were referred to New York Hospital's Infertility Clinic. I remember Dale and I sitting in the waiting room; each man held a small container through which one could see the semen he had just collected in the bathroom. The next year we moved to Milwaukee. A lay midwife referred us to *the* infertility expert in town, one of the few physicians who would provide backup for the lay midwives who practice illegally here. Sounded like someone I would like, and I did.

He immediately noticed my congenital heart defect. No reason not to try to have a baby; we just needed to be careful. This next part of the story is a well-known one: invasive tests, temperature charts, dashes home followed by post-coital exams, clomid. Finally, in August of 1983, Samantha was born (with the crash cart outside my door in case of heart failure and intravenous antibiotics to reduce the risk of endocarditis). I was 36.

When Sam was eight months old we discovered that Dale had thyroid cancer. Given my age and history of infertility and the fact that Dale's prognosis was good, we decided that it was now or never if we wanted a second child. Radiation has a distinctive impact on male fertility, however. I remember staring at bent and pinheaded sperm through our ob/gyn's microscope. We had the same experiences we had the first time—miscarriage in my office, followed within the hour by a D&C without anesthesia in my ob/gyn's office. In 1987 Jill was born. I was very tired, but very happy.

Given my age and health and Dale's, we were sure we didn't want any more children. Then in

Copyright © 1991, Midwest Sociologists for Women in Sociology. Reprinted by permission from *Midwest Feminist Papers,* New Series, Vol. I, edited by Michael R. Hill and Mary Jo Deegan.

September of 1989, noticing that I was feeling exhausted and nauseous, I realized I was pregnant. I called Dale. He said he would be right home. After I hung up, I called my ob/gyn's office. A nurse who knew me answered. "I'm pregnant," I said. "I need. . . ." "Congratulations," says she. "No," I reply. "I want to arrange to have an abortion." She says she will have the doctor call me, nothing more.

He tells me that I am not too old to have another child. He volunteers that he could do a tubal ligation at the same time. But I'm too exhausted, I argue, and I still have a baby in diapers (not to mention that I have a good chance of soon being elected President of SWS and chair of my Department). He jokes that his wife and he will raise the child until it's three and then, becoming more serious, asks me whether I've really thought long and hard about this decision and whether I've discussed it with Dale. I can't believe this conversation. He says finally, "You know, I don't do abortions; but I will refer you to a friend I trust who does." He gives me the person's name; he's on the staff of an abortion clinic. We hang up. I feel betrayed, angry, silly. Why did I think it would be easy? Why did I trust this man?

I call the abortion clinic to set up an appointment. I notice that it is in the heart of Milwaukee's poorest, most segregated area; in fact it is the area in which I do my research. When I arrive there three days later, I'm grateful that there aren't any protesters. We park in the unpaved, litter-strewn lot beside the two-story cinder-block building that houses the abortion clinic. The first story has large aqua and orange plastic squares decorating it. There is no sign. When we enter, we approach a glass-enclosed office and I fill out a sheet that asks for basic demographic information as well as insurance information. I am then asked for $200. I begin to write a check. The receptionist looks askance. Don't I know they only accept cash? I tell her that I wasn't told. "Oh, you're Dr. So-and-so's patient; I guess it's alright." I write my check and am asked to wait in the basement of the building. I descend the stairs, holding Dale's hand.

There are four or five couples seated in orange plastic chairs, all silently staring into space or looking at a TV chained to the wall. An African-American woman is standing. She and a very young looking African-American couple are the only non-whites in the room. With one exception, the white couples are older and appear to be married. Dale and I wait there a long time, two hours to be exact. During that time I am called to have a brief medical history taken and to have some bloodwork done. The nurse who pricks my finger to take the blood says: "I see you're a doctor; well, let's make this clear. I'll be your nurse today; you do what I say; you're my patient." I am puzzled by this obvious exercise of social control and status jockeying. I had given no indication that I thought any other situation existed. The interesting thing is that I never see her again.

I am later called into a tiny office off the small main waiting room. Here a rosy-cheeked social worker inquires as to whether I really know what I am doing and asks me whether or not my decision has been coerced. She asks me what form of birth control I had been using and looks critical when I say that I had been using none. I don't try to explain. She also asks me what sort I intend to use when I leave that day. I tell her that my husband will probably have a vasectomy, but I feel intruded upon by her questions. In fact, I hadn't thought about birth control at all, either in the past or for the future.

At about 11:00, I am ushered upstairs into a small, green room where I am asked to undress. I put on a hospital gown and a nurse helps me onto the table and into the stirrups. She turns on the vacuum aspirator; she says it would be good for me to hear what it sounds like, so as not to be alarmed later. She records my blood pressure in my chart and notes that I have been referred by Dr. So-and-so. She ventures that she is in the market for a fertility expert since she is having difficulty conceiving. I describe my ob/gyn in vaguely positive terms and then I pour out my story to her. I tell her what a

cruel trick I think it is that someone with my history should find herself pregnant. I feel human for a moment.

The doctor, pale, bespectacled, enters the room. He seems embarrassed. He says his name. He looks at my chart, puts it down and inserts the speculum. He says, "You're starting to have a spontaneous abortion; it often happens in women your age." "Look," he says to the nurse, stepping back, "see the tissue." "I am going to give you an injection of lidocaine; it will make your mouth [sic] numb." At this point the nurse took my right arm. I thought she was trying to hold my hand, but, as I groped for hers, it became clear that she was actually pinning my right arm to the table. I hear the vacuum switch on and the procedure is over in about two or three minutes. The nurse rolls me over to my left side, away from the vacuum aspirator, and tells me to bring my knees up. A brief time later, I feel something moving swiftly up my legs as she puts on my underpants to which she has attached a sanitary napkin. She tells me to dress and then leads me to the recovery room.

Three or four women are on the other cots, but most of the women who had been in the basement are in an adjoining room having soda and cookies. The nurse takes my blood pressure and massages my uterus several times. After a while she says she needs to see how much I am bleeding. I tell her I didn't think much, but she hauls me to my feet and asks me to take down my pants so she can see. While I am doing this, she holds a blanket between me and the other women. I am shocked as she goes from cot to cot doing this. She gives us instructions on aftercare and announces to the group that we should not call unless we are passing big clots or are filling, she emphasizes filling, four pads an hour. She says that we will have to listen to a talk about how to take birth control pills and participate in a question and answer period before we can be discharged. She walks us into the room where the first women to have had abortions that morning are talking, eating and reading magazines. They have apparently been detained there until all the abortions are completed. I listen to the lecture. Afterwards, there is only one question. A woman asks: "When will it be safe to lift a baby." Dale is waiting for me. He has witnessed two C-sections, but has not been allowed into the room where I have just had my D&C. Yes, somehow my abortion had been magically transformed into a D&C, at least that's how my ob/gyn subsequently refers to what happened that morning when I next meet him.

As we ride home, I feel sad and angry. The whole process has been such a degradation ceremony. I chide myself for having panicked, for trusting my infertility specialist, for not having the presence of mind to think that I would have been better off at "Bread and Roses," a feminist clinic. I am angry about the stereotypes of the abortion seeker, particularly the one of the professional woman who is too self-absorbed to want to be bothered with children.

The next time I visit my internist, I ask him if he can recommend a gynecologist, someone who does abortions. He looks rather puzzled. I describe my experience. I make it clear that my request is a matter of politics, not immediate medical need. He replies, "Most gynecologists here don't do abortions; you know, they picket your house and things." I thought, "'They' aren't the only ones who can picket."

---

often compel them to relinquish the right to reproduction itself.

Women's desire to control their reproductive system is probably as old as human history itself. As early as 1844 the *United States Practical Receipt Book* contained, among its many recipes for food, household chemicals and medicines, "receipts" for "birth preventive lotions." To make "Hannay's Preventive Lotion," for example,

> take pearlash, 1 part; water, 6 parts. Mix and filter. Keep it in closed bottles, and use it, with or without soap, immediately after connexion.[5]

For "Abernethy's Preventive Lotion,"

> take bichloride of mercury, 25 parts; milk of almonds, 400 parts; alcohol, 100 parts; rosewater, 1000 parts. Immerse the glands in a little of the mixture. . . . Infallible, if used in proper time.[6]

While women have probably always dreamed of infallible methods of birth control, it was not until the issue of women's rights in general became the focus of an organized movement that reproductive rights could emerge as a legitimate demand. In an essay entitled "Marriage," written during the 1850s, Sarah Grimke argued for a "right on the part of women to decide *when* she shall become a mother, how often and under what circumstances."[7] Alluding to one physician's humorous observation, Grimke agreed that if wives and husbands alternatively gave birth to their children,

"no family would ever have more than three, the husband bearing one and the wife two."[8] But, as she insists, "the *right* to decide this matter has been almost wholly denied to woman."[9]

Sarah Grimke advocated women's right to sexual abstinence. Around the same time the well-known "emancipated marriage" of Lucy Stone and Henry Blackwell took place. These abolitionists and women's rights activists were married in a ceremony that protested women's traditional relinquishment of their rights to their persons, names and property. In agreeing that as husband, he had no right to the "custody of the wife's person,"[10] Henry Blackwell promised that he would not attempt to impose the dictates of his sexual desires upon his wife.

The notion that women could refuse to submit to their husband's sexual demands eventually became the central idea of the call for "voluntary motherhood." By the 1870s, when the woman suffrage movement had reached its peak, feminists were publicly advocating voluntary motherhood. In a speech delivered in 1873, Virginia Woodhull claimed that

> the wife who submits to sexual intercourse against her wishes or desires, virtually commits suicide; while the husband who compels it, commits murder, and ought just as much to be punished for it, as though he strangled her to death for refusing him.[11]

Woodhull, of course, was quite notorious as a proponent of "free love." Her defense of a woman's right to abstain from sexual intercourse within marriage as a means of controlling her pregnancies was associated with Woodhull's overall attack on the institution of marriage.

It was not a coincidence that women's consciousness of their reproductive rights was born within the organized movement for women's political equality. Indeed, if women remained forever burdened by incessant childbirths and frequent miscarriages, they would hardly be able to exercise the political rights they might win. Moreover, women's new dreams of pursuing careers and other paths of self-development outside marriage and motherhood could be realized only if they could limit and plan their pregnancies. In this sense, the slogan "voluntary motherhood" contained a new and genuinely progressive vision of womanhood. At the same time, however, this vision was rigidly bound to the lifestyle enjoyed by the middle classes and the bourgeoisie. The aspirations underlying the demand for "voluntary motherhood" did not reflect the conditions of working-class women, engaged as they were in a far more fundamental fight for economic survival. Since this first call for birth control was associated with goals which could be achieved only by women possessing material wealth, vast numbers of poor and working-class women would find it rather difficult to identify with the embryonic birth control movement.

Toward the end of the nineteenth century the white birth rate in the United States suffered a significant decline. Since no contraceptive innovations had been publicly introduced, the drop in the birth rate implied that women were substantially curtailing their sexual activity. By 1890 the typical native-born white woman was bearing no more than four children.[12] Since U.S. society was becoming increasingly urban, this new birth pattern should not have been a surprise. While farm life demanded large families, they became dysfunctional within the context of city life. Yet this phenomenon was publicly interpreted in a racist and anti-working-class fashion by the ideologues of rising monopoly capitalism. Since native-born white women were bearing fewer children, the specter of "race suicide" was raised in official circles.

In 1905 President Theodore Roosevelt concluded his Lincoln Day Dinner speech with the proclamation that "race purity must be maintained."[13] By 1906 he blatantly equated the falling birth rate among native-born whites with the impending threat of "race suicide." In his State of the Union message that year Roosevelt admonished the well-born white women

who engaged in "willful sterility—the one sin for which the penalty is national death, race suicide."[14] These comments were made during a period of accelerating racist ideology and of great waves of race riots and lynchings on the domestic scene. Moreover, President Roosevelt himself was attempting to muster support for the U.S. seizure of the Philippines, the country's most recent imperialist venture.

How did the birth control movement respond to Roosevelt's accusation that their cause was promoting race suicide? The President's propagandistic ploy was a failure, according to a leading historian of the birth control movement, for, ironically, it led to greater support for its advocates. Yet, as Linda Gordon maintains, this controversy "also brought to the forefront those issues that most separated feminists from the working class and the poor."[15]

This happened in two ways. First, the feminists were increasingly emphasizing birth control as a route to careers and higher education—goals out of reach of the poor with or without birth control. In the context of the whole feminist movement, the race-suicide episode was an additional factor identifying feminism almost exclusively with the aspirations of the more privileged women of the society. Second, the pro-birth control feminists began to popularize the idea that poor people had a moral obligation to restrict the size of their families, because large families create a drain on the taxes and charity expenditures of the wealthy and because poor children were less likely to be "superior."[16]

The acceptance of the race-suicide thesis, to a greater or lesser extent, by women such as Julia Ward Howe and Ida Husted Harper reflected the suffrage movement's capitulation to the racist posture of Southern women. If the suffragists acquiesced to arguments invoking the extension of the ballot to women as the saving grace of white supremacy, then birth control advocates either acquiesced to or supported the new arguments invoking birth control as a means of preventing the proliferation of the "lower classes" and as an antidote to race suicide. Race suicide could be prevented by the introduction of birth control among Black people, immigrants and the poor in general. In this way, the prosperous whites of solid Yankee stock could maintain their superior numbers within the population. Thus class bias and racism crept into the birth control movement when it was still in its infancy. More and more, it was assumed within birth control circles that poor women, Black and immigrant alike, had a "moral obligation to restrict the size of their families."[17] What was demanded as a "right" for the privileged came to be interpreted as a "duty" for the poor.

When Margaret Sanger embarked upon her lifelong crusade for birth control—a term she coined and popularized—it appeared as though the racist and anti-working-class overtones of the previous period might possibly be overcome. For Margaret Higgens Sanger came from a working-class background herself and was well acquainted with the devastating pressures of poverty. When her mother died, at the age of forty-eight, she had borne no less than eleven children. Sanger's later memories of her own family's troubles would confirm her belief that working-class women had a special need for the right to plan and space their pregnancies autonomously. Her affiliation, as an adult, with the Socialist movement was a further cause for hope that the birth control campaign would move in a more progressive direction.

When Margaret Sanger joined the Socialist party in 1912, she assumed the responsibility of recruiting women from New York's working women's clubs into the party.[18] *The Call*—the party's paper—carried her articles on the women's page. She wrote a series entitled "What Every Mother Should Know," another called "What Every Girl Should Know," and she did on-the-spot coverage of strikes involving women. Sanger's familiarity with New York's working-class districts was a result of her numerous visits as a trained nurse to the poor sections of the city. During these visits, she points out in her autobiography, she met countless numbers of women who desperately desired knowledge about birth control.

According to Sanger's autobiographical reflections, one of the many visits she made as a nurse to New York's Lower East Side convinced her to undertake a personal crusade for birth control. Answering one of her routine calls, she discovered that twenty-eight-year-old Sadie Sachs had attempted to abort herself. Once the crisis had passed, the young woman asked the attending physician to give her advice on birth prevention. As Sanger relates the story, the doctor recommended that she "tell [her husband] Jake to sleep on the roof."[19]

I glanced quickly to Mrs. Sachs. Even through my sudden tears I could see stamped on her face an expression of absolute despair. We simply looked at each other, saying no word until the door had closed behind the doctor. Then she lifted her thin, blue-veined hands and clasped them beseechingly. "He can't understand. He's only a man. But you do, don't you? Please tell me the secret, and I'll never breathe it to a soul. Please!"[20]

Three months later Sadie Sachs died from another self-induced abortion. That night, Margaret Sanger says, she vowed to devote all her energy toward the acquisition and dissemination of contraceptive measures.

I went to bed knowing that no matter what it might cost, I was finished with palliatives and superficial cures; I resolved to seek out the root of evil, to do something to change the destiny of mothers whose miseries were as vast as the sky.[21]

During the first phase of Sanger's birth control crusade, she maintained her affiliation with the Socialist party—and the campaign itself was closely associated with the rising militancy of the working class. Her staunch supporters included Eugene Debs, Elizabeth Gurley Flynn and Emma Goldman, who respectively represented the Socialist party, the International Workers of the World and the anarchist movement. Margaret Sanger, in turn, expressed the anti-capitalist commitment of her own movement within the pages of its journal, *Woman Rebel,* which was "dedicated to the interests of working women."[22] Personally, she continued to march on picket lines with striking workers and publicly condemned the outrageous assaults on striking workers. In 1914, for example, when the National Guard massacred scores of Chicano miners in Ludlow, Colorado, Sanger joined the labor movement in exposing John D. Rockefeller's role in this attack.[23]

Unfortunately, the alliance between the birth control campaign and the radical labor movement did not enjoy a long life. While Socialists and other working-class activists continued to support the demand for birth control, it did not occupy a central place in their overall strategy. And Sanger herself began to underestimate the centrality of capitalist exploitation in her analysis of poverty, arguing that too many children caused workers to fall into their miserable predicament. Moreover, "women were inadvertently perpetu-ating the exploitation of the working class," she believed, "by continually flooding the labor market with new workers."[24] Ironically, Sanger may have been encouraged to adopt this position by the neo-Malthusian ideas embraced in some socialist circles. Such outstanding figures of the European socialist movement as Anatole France and Rosa Luxemburg had proposed a "birth strike" to prevent the continued flow of labor into the capitalist market.[25]

When Margaret Sanger severed her ties with the Socialist party for the purpose of building an inde-pendent birth control campaign, she and her followers became more susceptible than ever before to the anti-Black and anti-immigrant propaganda of the times. Like their predecessors, who had been deceived by the "race suicide" propaganda, the advocates of birth control began to embrace the prevailing racist ideolo-gy. The fatal influence of the eugenics movement would soon destroy the progressive potential of the birth control campaign.

During the first decades of the twentieth century the rising popularity of the eugenics movement was hardly a fortuitous development. Eugenic ideas were perfectly suited to the ideological needs of the young monopoly capitalists. Imperialist incursions in Latin America and in the Pacific needed to be justified, as did the intensi-fied exploitation of Black workers in the South and immigrant workers in the North and West. The pseu-doscientific racial theories associated with the eugenics campaign furnished dramatic apologies for the conduct of the young monopolies. As a result, this movement won the unhesitating support of such leading capitalists as the Carnegies, the Harrimans and the Kelloggs.[26]

By 1919 the eugenic influence on the birth control movement was unmistakably clear. In an article pub-lished by Margaret Sanger in the American Birth Control League's journal, she defined "the chief issue of birth control" as "more children from the fit, less from the unfit."[27] Around this time the ABCL heartily welcomed the author of *The Rising Tide of Color Against White World Supremacy* into its inner sanctum.[28] Lothrop Stoddard, Harvard professor and theoretician of the eugenics movement, was offered a seat on the board of directors. In the pages of the ABCL's journal, articles by Guy Irving Birch, director of the American Eugenics Society, began to appear. Birch advocated birth control as a weapon to

prevent the American people from being replaced by alien or Negro stock, whether it be by immigra-tion or by overly high birth rates among others in this country.[29]

By 1932 the Eugenics Society could boast that at least twenty-six states had passed compulsory sterilization laws and that thousands of "unfit" persons had already been surgically prevented from reproducing.[30] Margaret Sanger offered her public approval of this development. "Morons, mental defectives, epileptics, illiterates, paupers, unemployables, criminals, prosti-tutes and dope fiends" ought to be surgically sterilized, she argued in a radio talk.[31] She did not wish to be so intransigent as to leave them with no choice in the mat-ter; if they wished, she said, they should be able to choose a lifelong segregated existence in labor camps.

Within the American Birth Control League, the call for birth control among Black people acquired the same racist edge as the call for compulsory ster-ilization. In 1939 its successor, the Birth Control Federation of America, planned a "Negro Project." In the Federation's words,

the mass of Negroes, particularly in the South, still breed carelessly and disastrously, with the result that the increase among Negroes, even more than among whites, is from that portion of the popu-lation least fit, and least able to rear children properly.[32]

Calling for the recruitment of Black ministers to lead local birth control committees, the Federation's pro-posal suggested that Black people should be rendered as vulnerable as possible to their birth control propa-ganda. "We do not want word to get out," wrote Margaret Sanger in a letter to a colleague,

that we want to exterminate the Negro population and the minister is the man who can straighten out that idea if it ever occurs to any of their more rebel-lious members.[33]

This episode in the birth control movement confirmed the ideological victory of the racism associated with eugenic ideas. It had been robbed of its progressive potential, advocating for people of color not the indi-vidual right to *birth control,* but rather the racist strate-

RIGHT TO LIFE

MARGE PIERCY

Saille

A woman is not a pear tree
thrusting her fruit in mindless fecundity
into the world. Even pear trees bear
heavily one year and rest and grow the next.
An orchard gone wild drops few warm rotting
fruit in the grass but the trees stretch
high and wiry gifting the birds forty
feet up among inch long thorns
broken atavistically from the smooth wood.

A woman is not a basket you place
your buns in to keep them warm. Not a brood
hen you can slip duck eggs under.
Not the purse holding the coins of your
descendants till you spend them in wars.
Not a bank where your genes gather interest
and interesting mutations in the tainted
rain, any more than you are.

You plant corn and you harvest
it to eat or sell. You put the lamb
in the pasture to fatten and haul it in
to butcher for chops. You slice
the mountain in two for a road and gouge
the high plains for coal and the waters
run muddy for miles and years.
Fish die but you do not call them yours
unless you wished to eat them.

Now you legislate mineral rights in a woman.
You lay claim to her pastures for grazing,
fields for growing babies like iceberg
lettuce. You value children so dearly
that none ever go hungry, none weep
with no one to tend them when mothers
work, none lack fresh fruit,
none chew lead or cough to death and your
orphanages are empty. Every noon the best
restaurants serve poor children steaks.

At this moment at nine o'clock a partera
is performing a table top abortion on an
unwed mother in Texas who can't get Medicaid
any longer. In five days she will die
of tetanus and her little daughter will cry
and be taken away. Next door a husband
and wife are sticking pins in the son
they did not want. They will explain
for hours how wicked he is,
how he wants discipline.

We are all born of woman, in the rose
of the womb we suckled our mother's blood
and every baby born has a right to love
like a seedling to sun. Every baby born
unloved, unwanted is a bill that will come
due in twenty years with interest, an anger
that must find a target, a pain that will
beget pain. A decade downstream a child
screams, a woman falls, a synagogue is torched,
a firing squad is summoned, a button
is pushed and the world burns.

I will choose what enters me, what becomes
flesh of my flesh. Without choice, no politics,
no ethics lives. I am not your cornfield,
not your uranium mine, not your calf
for fattening, not your cow for milking.
You may not use me as your factory.
Priests and legislators do not hold
shares in my womb or my mind.
This is my body. If I give it to you
I want it back. My life
is a non-negotiable demand.

From *The Moon Is Always Female* by Marge Piercy.
Copyright © 1979 by Marge Piercy. Reprinted by permission of Alfred A. Knopf, Inc.

gy of *population control.* The birth control campaign would be called upon to serve in an essential capacity in the execution of the U.S. government's imperialist and racist population policy.

The abortion rights activists of the early 1970s should have examined the history of their movement. Had they done so, they might have understood why so many of their Black sisters adopted a posture of suspicion toward their cause. They might have understood how important it was to undo the racist deeds of their predecessors, who had advocated birth control as well as compulsory sterilization as a means of eliminating the "unfit" sectors of the population. Consequently, the young white feminists might have been more receptive to the suggestion that their campaign for abortion rights include a vigorous condemnation of sterilization abuse, which had become more widespread than ever.

It was not until the media decided that the casual sterilization of two Black girls in Montgomery, Alabama, was a scandal worth reporting that the Pandora's box of sterilization abuse was finally flung open. But by the time the case of the Relf sisters broke, it was practically too late to influence the politics of the abortion rights movement. It was the summer of 1973 and the Supreme Court decision legalizing abortions had already been announced in January. Nevertheless, the urgent need for mass opposition to sterilization abuse became tragically clear. The facts surrounding the Relf sisters' story were horrifyingly simple. Minnie Lee, who was twelve years old, and Mary Alice, who was fourteen, had been unsuspectingly carted into an operating room, where surgeons irrevocably robbed them of their capacity to bear children.[34] The surgery had been ordered by the HEW-funded Montgomery Community Action Committee after it was discovered that Depo-Provera, a drug previously administered to the girls as a birth prevention measure, caused cancer in test animals.[35]

After the Southern Poverty Law Center filed suit on behalf of the Relf sisters, the girls' mother revealed that she had unknowingly "consented" to the operation, having been deceived by the social workers who handled her daughters' case. They had asked Mrs. Relf, who was unable to read, to put her "X" on a document, the contents of which were not described to her. She assumed, she said, that it authorized the continued Depo-Provera

injections. As she subsequently learned, she had authorized the surgical sterilization of her daughters.[36]

In the aftermath of the publicity exposing the Relf sisters' case, similar episodes were brought to light. In Montgomery alone, eleven girls, also in their teens, had been similarly sterilized. HEW-funded birth control clinics in other states, as it turned out, had also subjected young girls to sterilization abuse. Moreover, individual women came forth with equally outrageous stories. Nial Ruth Cox, for example, filed suit against the state of North Carolina. At the age of eighteen—eight years before the suit—officials had threatened to discontinue her family's welfare payments if she refused to submit to surgical sterilization.[37] Before she assented to the operation, she was assured that her infertility would be temporary.[38]

Nial Ruth Cox's lawsuit was aimed at a state which had diligently practiced the theory of eugenics. Under the auspices of the Eugenics Commission of North Carolina, so it was learned, 7,686 sterilizations had been carried out since 1933. Although the operations were justified as measures to prevent the reproduction of "mentally deficient persons," about 5,000 of the sterilized persons had been Black.[39] According to Brenda Feigen Fasteau, the ACLU attorney representing Nial Ruth Cox, North Carolina's recent record was not much better.

> As far as I can determine, the statistics reveal that since 1964, approximately 65% of the women sterilized in North Carolina were Black and approximately 35% were white.[40]

As the flurry of publicity exposing sterilization abuse revealed, the neighboring state of South Carolina had been the site of further atrocities. Eighteen women from Aiken, South Carolina, charged that they had been sterilized by a Dr. Clovis Pierce during the early 1970s. The sole obstetrician in that small town, Pierce had consistently sterilized Medicaid recipients with two or more children. According to a nurse in his office, Dr. Pierce insisted that pregnant welfare women "will have to submit [sic!] to voluntary sterilization" if they wanted him to deliver their babies.[41] While he was "tired of people running around and having babies and paying for them with my taxes,"[42] Dr. Pierce received some $60,000 in taxpayers' money for the sterilizations he performed. During his trial he was supported by the

South Carolina Medical Association, whose members declared that doctors "have a moral and legal right to insist on sterilization permission before accepting a patient, if it is done on the initial visit."[43]

Revelations of sterilization abuse during that time exposed the complicity of the federal government. At first the Department of Health, Education and Welfare claimed that approximately 16,000 women and 8,000 men had been sterilized in 1972 under the auspices of federal programs.[44] Later, however, these figures underwent a drastic revision. Carl Schultz, director of HEW's Population Affairs Office, estimated that between 100,000 and 200,000 sterilizations had actually been funded that year by the federal government.[45] During Hitler's Germany, incidentally, 250,000 sterilizations were carried out under the Nazis' Hereditary Health Law.[46] Is it possible that the record of the Nazis, throughout the years of their reign, may have been almost equaled by U.S. government-funded sterilization in the space of a single year?

Given the historical genocide inflicted on the native population of the United States, one would assume that Native American Indians would be exempted from the government's sterilization campaign. But according to Dr. Connie Uri's testimony in a Senate committee hearing, by 1976 some 24 percent of all Indian women of childbearing age had been sterilized.[47] "Our blood lines are being stopped," the Choctaw physician told the Senate committee. "Our unborn will not be born. . . . This is genocidal to our people."[48] According to Dr. Uri, the Indian Health Services Hospital in Claremore, Oklahoma, had been sterilizing one out of every four women giving birth in that federal facility.[49]

Native American Indians are special targets of government propaganda on sterilization. In one of the HEW pamphlets aimed at Indian people, there is a sketch of a family with *ten children* and *one horse* and another sketch of a family with *one child* and *ten horses*. The drawings are supposed to imply that more children mean more poverty and fewer children mean wealth. As if the ten horses owned by the one-child family had been magically conjured up by birth control and sterilization surgery.

The domestic population policy of the U.S. government has an undeniably racist edge. Native American, Chicana, Puerto Rican and Black women continue to be sterilized in disproportionate numbers. According to a National Fertility Study conducted in 1970 by Princeton University's Office of Population Control, 20 percent of all married Black women have been permanently sterilized.[50] Approximately the same percentage of Chicana women had been rendered surgically infertile.[51] Moreover, 43 percent of the women sterilized through federally subsidized programs were Black.[52]

The astonishing number of Puerto Rican women who have been sterilized reflects a special government policy that can be traced back to 1939. In that year President Roosevelt's Interdepartmental Committee on Puerto Rico issued a statement attributing the island's economic problems to the phenomenon of overpopulation.[53] This committee proposed that efforts be undertaken to reduce the birth rate to no more than the level of the death rate.[54] Soon afterward an experimental sterilization campaign was undertaken in Puerto Rico. Although the Catholic Church initially opposed this experiment and forced the cessation of the program in 1946, it was converted during the early 1950s to the teachings and practice of population control.[55] In this period over 150 birth control clinics were opened, resulting in a 20 percent decline in population growth by the mid-1960s.[56] By the 1970s over 35 percent of all Puerto Rican women of childbearing age had been surgically sterilized.[57] According to Bonnie Mass, a serious critic of the U.S. government's population policy,

> if purely mathematical projections are to be taken seriously, if the present rate of sterilization of 19,000 monthly were to continue, then the island's population of workers and peasants could be extinguished within the next 10 or 20 years . . . [establishing] for the first time in world history a systematic use of population control capable of eliminating an entire generation of people.[58]

During the 1970s the devastating implications of the Puerto Rican experiment began to emerge with unmistakable clarity. In Puerto Rico the presence of corporations in the highly automated metallurgical and pharmaceutical industries had exacerbated the problem of unemployment. The prospect of an ever-larger army of unemployed workers was one of the main incentives for the mass sterilization program. Inside the United States today, enormous numbers of people of color—and especially racially oppressed youth—have become part of a pool of permanently unemployed workers. It is hardly coincidental, considering the Puerto Rican example, that the increasing incidence of sterilization has kept pace with the high rates of unemployment. As growing numbers of white people suffer the brutal consequences of unemployment, they can also expect to become targets of the official sterilization propaganda.

The prevalence of sterilization abuse during the latter 1970s may have been greater than ever before. Although the Department of Health, Education and Welfare issued guidelines in 1974, which were ostensibly designed to prevent involuntary sterilizations, the situation nonetheless deteriorated. When the American Civil Liberties Union's Reproductive Freedom Project conducted a survey of teaching hospitals in 1975, they discovered that 40 percent of those institutions were not even aware of the regulations issued by HEW.[59] Only 30 percent of the hospitals examined by the ACLU were even attempting to comply with the guidelines.[60]

The 1977 Hyde Amendment has added yet another dimension to coercive sterilization practices. As a result of this law passed by Congress, federal funds for abortions were eliminated in all cases but those involving rape and the risk of death or severe illness. According to Sandra Salazar of the California Department of Public Health, the first victim of the Hyde Amendment was a twenty-seven-year-old Chicana woman from Texas. She died as a result of an illegal abortion in Mexico shortly after Texas discontinued government-funded abortions. There have been many more victims—women for whom sterilization has become the only alternative to the abortions which are currently beyond their reach. Sterilizations continue to be federally funded and free, to poor women, on demand.

The struggle against sterilization abuse has continued to be waged primarily by Puerto Rican, Black, Chicana and Native American women. Their cause has not yet been embraced by the women's movement as a whole. Within organizations representing the interests of middle-class white women, there has been a certain reluctance to support the demands of the campaign against sterilization abuse, for these women are often denied their individual rights to be sterilized when they desire to take this step. While women of color are urged, at every turn, to become permanently infertile, white women enjoying prosperous economic conditions are urged, by the same forces, to reproduce themselves. They therefore sometimes consider the "waiting period" and other details of the demand for "informed consent" to sterilization as further inconveniences for women like themselves. Yet whatever the inconveniences for white middle-class women, a fundamental reproductive right of racially oppressed and poor women is at stake. Sterilization abuse must be ended.

NOTES

1. Edwin M. Gold et al., "Therapeutic Abortions in New York City: A Twenty-Year Review," in *American Journal of Public Health* 55 (July 1965):964–72, quoted in Lucinda Cisla, "Unfinished Business: Birth Control and Women's Liberation," in Robin Morgan, ed., *Sisterhood Is Powerful: An Anthology of Writings from the Women's Liberation Movement* (New York: Vintage Books, 1970), p. 261. Also quoted in Robert Staples, *The Black Woman in America* (Chicago: Nelson Hall, 1974), p. 146.

2. Herbert Gutman, *The Black Family in Slavery and Freedom, 1750–1925* (New York: Pantheon 1976), pp. 80–81 (note).

3. Ibid.

4. Herbert Aptheker, "The Negro Woman," *Masses and Mainstream* 11 (no. 2) (February 1948):12.

5. Quoted in Rosalyn Baxandall, Linda Gordon, & Susan Reverby, eds., *America's Working Women: A Documentary History—1600 to the Present* (New York: Random House, 1976), p. 17.

6. Ibid.

7. Gerda Lerner, *The Female Experience: An American Documentary* (Indianapolis: Bobbs-Merrill, 1977), p. 91.

8. Ibid.

9. Ibid.

10. "Marriage of Lucy Stone under Protest" appeared in *History of Woman Suffrage*, vol. 1, quoted in Miriam Schneir, ed., *Feminism: The Essential Historical Writings* (New York: Vintage, 1972), p. 104.

11. Speech by Virginia Woodhull, "The Elixir of Life," quoted in Schneir, p. 153.

12. Mary P. Ryan, *Womanhood in America from Colonial Times to the Present* (New York: Franklin Watts, 1975), p. 162.

13. Melvin Steinfeld, *Our Racist Presidents* (San Ramon, Calif.: Consensus Publishers, 1972), p. 212.

14. Bonnie Mass, *Population Target: The Political Economy of Population Control in Latin America* (Toronto: Women's Educational Press, 1977), p. 20.

15. Linda Gordon, *Woman's Body, Woman's Right: Birth Control in America* (New York: Penguin, 1976), p. 157.

16. Ibid., p. 158.

17. Ibid.

18. Margaret Sanger, *An Autobiography* (New York: Dover Press, 1971), p. 75.

19. Ibid., p. 90.

20. Ibid., p. 91.

21. Ibid., p. 92.

22. Ibid., p. 106.

23. Mass, *Population Target,* p. 27.

24. Bruce Dancis, "Socialism and Women in the United States, 1900–1912," *Socialist Revolution,* No. 27, vol. vi, No. 1 (January–March, 1976), p. 96.

25. David M. Kennedy, *Birth Control in America: The Career of Margaret Sanger* (New Haven and London: Yale University Press, 1976), pp. 21–22.

26. Mass, *Population Target,* p. 20.

27. Gordon, *Woman's Body,* p. 281.

28. Mass, *Population Target,* p. 20.

29. Gordon, *Woman's Body,* p. 283.

30. Herbert Aptheker, "Sterilization, Experimentation and Imperialism," *Political Affairs* 53 (no. 1) (January 1974): 44.

31. Gena Corea, *The Hidden Malpractice* (New York: Jove, 1977), p. 149.

32. Gordon, *Woman's Body,* p. 332.

33. Ibid, pp. 332–333.

34. Aptheker, "Sterilization," p. 38. See also Anne Braden, "Forced Sterilization: Now Women Can Fight Back," *Southern Patriot,* September 1973.

35. Ibid.

36. Jack Slater, "Sterilization, Newest Threat to the Poor," *Ebony* 28 (no. 12) (October 1973):150.

37. Braden, "Forced Sterilization."

38. Les Payne, "Forced Sterilization for the Poor?" *San Francisco Chronicle,* February 26, 1974.

39. Harold X., "Forced Sterilization Pervades South," *Muhammed Speaks,* October 10, 1975.

40. Slater, "Sterilization."

41. Payne, "Forced Sterilization."

42. Ibid.

43. Ibid.

44. Aptheker, "Sterilization," p. 40.

45. Payne, "Forced Sterilization."

46. Aptheker, "Sterilization," p. 48.

47. Arlene Eisen, "They're Trying to Take Our Future—Native American Women and Sterilization," *The Guardian,* March 23, 1972.

48. Ibid.

49. Ibid.

50. Quoted in a pamphlet issued by the Committee to End Sterilization Abuse, Box A244, Cooper Station, New York 10003.

51. Ibid.

52. Ibid.

53. Gordon, *Woman's Body,* p. 338.

54. Ibid.

55. Mass, *Population Target,* p. 92.

56. Ibid., p. 91.

57. Gordon, *Woman's Body,* p. 401.

58. Mass, *Population Target,* p. 108.

59. Rahemah Aman, "Forced Sterilization," *Union Wage,* March 4, 1978.

60. Ibid.

READING 35

Women as Fathers: Motherhood and Child Care under a Modified Patriarchy

BARBARA KATZ ROTHMAN

Patriarchal kinship is the core of patriarchy: Paternity is the central social relationship. A very clear statement of patriarchal kinship is found in the book of Genesis, in the "begats." Each man, from Adam onward, is described as having "begot a son in his likeness, after his image." After the birth of this first-born son, the men are described as having lived so many years and begot sons and daughters. The text then turns to that first-born son and, in turn, his first-born son. Women appear as the "daughters of men who bore them offspring." In a patriarchal kinship system, children are reckoned as being born to men, out of women. Women, in this system, bear the children of men.

The essential concept here is the *seed,* the part of men that grows into the children of their likeness within the bodies of women. Such a system is inevitably male dominated, but it is a particular kind of male domination. Men control women as daughters, much as they control their sons, but they also control women as the mothers of men's children. It is women's motherhood in particular that men have to control to maintain patriarchy. In a patriarchy, because what is valued is the relationship of a man to his sons, women are a vulnerability that men have: To beget these sons, men must pass their seed through the body of a woman.

In matrilineal societies, where a shared mother produces the lineage or family group, men may still rule the women and children who are related to them through their mother's line, but they do not rule as

From *Gender & Society,* vol. 3, no. 1, March 1989. Copyright © 1989 Sociologists for Women in Society. Reprinted by permission of Sage Publications, Inc.

fathers. Women in such a system are not a vulnerability, but a source of connection. As anthropologist Glenn Petersen says, in a matrilineal system "women, rather than infiltrating and subverting patrilines, are acknowledged to produce and reproduce the body of society itself" (1982, p. 141).

The modern American kinship system is not classically patriarchal, though remnants of patriarchy can be seen in such things as the strong pressure to give children their father's surname. Modern American kinship is a bilateral system, in that individuals are considered to be equally related to their mother's and their father's kin. Yet the very definition of kin is based on the principles of patriarchy. A patriarchal kinship tie is, by definition, a connection by seed. Kinship through fathers is based on the act of impregnating and therefore glorifies genetic connections. In a mother-based system, a "blood" relative does not mean simply a genetic relative; the blood tie is the mingled blood of mothers and their children; children grow out of the blood of their mothers, of their bodies and being. When the shared bond of kinship comes through mothers, the tie is based on *the growing of children,* a social connection.

Each type of kinship system leads to different ideas about kin identity and what a person is. In a mother-based system, a person is what mothers grow—people are made of the care and nurturance that brings a baby forth into the world and turns the baby into a member of the society, intimately related to those who had the same care and nurturance. In a patriarchal system, a person is what grows out of men's seed. The belief that the essence of the person is there in the seed when it is planted in the mother still persists as the various forms of genetic determinism. And of course remnants of the classical patriarchal valuing of men's seed also persist. In 1987, the director of a California sperm bank distributed T-shirts with a drawing of sperm swimming on a blue background and the words "Future People." Using the principles of a patriarchal system, shared identity—or kinship—comes from shared genes.

THE SEEDS OF WOMEN

Modern procreative technology has been forced to go beyond the sperm as seed. Modern science has had to confront the *egg* as seed also. Modern scientific thinking cannot possibly hold onto old notions of women as nurturers of men's seeds. The doctor who has spent time "harvesting" eggs from women's bodies for *in vitro* fertilization fully understands the significance of women's seed.

The old patriarchal kinship system had a clear place for women: the nurturers of men's seeds, the soil in which seeds grow, the daughters of men who bear them offspring. When forced to acknowledge that women's genetic contribution is equal to men's genetic contribution, Western patriarchy could have foundered. *But the central concept of patriarchy, the importance of the seed, was kept by extending it to women.* Valuing the seed of women, the genetic material women also have, extends to women some of the privileges of patriarchy. That is, when the significance of woman's seed is acknowledged in her relationship with her children, women too have paternity rights in their children.

In this modified system based on the older ideology of patriarchy, women can be seen to own their children, just as men do. Unlike what happens in a mother-based system, this relationship between a woman and her children is not based on motherhood *per se,* not on the unique nurturance, the long months of pregnancy, the intimate connections with the baby as it grows and moves inside her body, passes through her genitals, and sucks at her breasts. Instead, women are said to own their babies, have "rights" to them, just as men do: based on their seed.

This modification does not end patriarchy, and it does not end the domination of the children of women by men. Instead, by maintaining the centrality of the seed, the ideology maintains the rights of men in their children, even as it recognizes something approaching equal rights of women in their children. Since men's control over women and the children of women is no longer based simply on their (no longer) unique seed, their economic superiority and the other privileges of a male-dominated social system become increasingly important. Children are, based on the seed, presumptively "half his, half hers"—and might as well have grown in the backyard. Women do not gain their rights to their children in this society as *mothers,* but as *father-equivalents,* sources of seed.

And if the nurturance of mothers is discounted, so too is the nurturance of fathers. There are men who mother, who intensively, actively, intimately nurture children, as prime parents in families in which the mother's role is reduced (Pruett 1987), or as single fathers (Risman 1987), or in families in which parenting is shared equally (Ehrensaft 1987). In our society their fatherhood has no more legal weight than that of men whose paternity is based entirely on a single sexual encounter. The principles of a patriarchal kinship system denigrate all nurturance, that of women and that of men, in favor of genetic ties.

THE GENETIC TIE

What precisely is the physical nature of this highly valued genetic connection between parent and child? The closest genetic connection a human being can have is an identical twin. Identical twins have the same chromosomes, the same genes. The next closest relations are those between parent and child and between full siblings. If an individual carries a certain gene, the chances that a sibling will carry the same gene are fifty-fifty, the same as the parent-child relationship. Genetically, "there is nothing special about the parent-offspring relationship except its close degree and a certain fundamental asymmetry. The full-sib relationship is just as close" (Hamilton 1978 p. 191).

Genetic connections exist as percentages: the 100 percent connection of identical twins, the 50 percent connection of siblings and of parents to children, the 25 percent connection of grandparents to grandchildren and of half-siblings to each other, and the 12.5 percent connection of cousins, and so on. In strictly genetic terms, your sister might as well be your mother. The genetic connection is the same.

But parenthood is not just a genetic connection, a

genetic relationship. And it is more than the age difference that distinguishes the parent-child relationship: The social relationship of a 17-year-old sibling to a newborn baby is quite different from the relationship of a 17-year-old parent to a newborn baby. It may be six-of-one and a half-dozen of the other genetically, but socially these are not interchangeable relationships.

The parent-child relationship is invested with social and legal rights and claims that are not recognized, in patriarchal societies, in any other genetic relationship, because that genetic connection was the basis for men's control over the children of women. The contemporary modification of traditional patriarchy has been to recognize the genetic parenthood of women as the equivalent of the genetic parenthood of men. Genetic parenthood replaces paternity in determining who a child is, who it belongs to. I believe it is time to move beyond the patriarchal concern with genetic relationships.

We can recognize and appreciate the genetic tie without its being a determinative connection. We do so in most of our genetic relations. American society recognizes no special claims of a sibling on a sibling, or of aunts and uncles on nieces and nephews. We recognize the relationship, we allow people to make what they will of it, but it carries no legal weight. If my brother does not like the way I am raising his niece, so it goes. Even though he is closely related to her genetically, even if she were to look more like him than like me, it gives him no legal claim to her. He has no basis to challenge my claim as parent, short of showing me to be unfit—and even then, no assurance that the child would be turned over to him. And if my son doesn't like the way I am raising my daughter, even though he is just as closely related to her genetically as I am, there is no way he can challenge my custody, and that will still be true when he is over 21. But my husband, as her father, can challenge my custody, without showing me to be unfit, as I can challenge his custody. We are parents, and that gives us special legal rights over the child.

While not denying the reality of genetic relationships, the question I am asking is: Just how much weight do we need to give this one genetic tie? How much can it hold? Stripped of all the social supports, is that genetic tie sufficient to define a person, to establish a kinship? Am I my mother's daughter because of our chromosomes? If a woman donates an egg, or a man turns over to a lab technician a vial of semen, does

that make the person a *parent* to the child created with those chromosomes?

PATRIARCHAL IDEOLOGY AND NEW PROCREATIVE TECHNOLOGY

The new procreative technology being developed is based on the patriarchal focus on the seed. The seed, the genetic material, is the one absolutely irreplaceable part of procreation, as science now approaches it. The procreative technology continues to substitute for one after another of the nurturing tasks, but makes no substitute for the seed. Breasts became unnecessary quite some time ago, as artificial formula substituted for human milk. The act of giving birth becomes increasingly unnecessary, as doctors work on surgical removal of babies to the point that now one of five American babies is born by cesarean section. The nurturance of late pregnancy becomes increasingly unnecessary as neonatal intensive care units develop the skill to maintain younger and younger, smaller and smaller premature babies or "extrauterine fetuses" in incubation. And the nurturing environment of the Fallopian tube becomes replaceable by the nurturance of the glass dish, the *in vitro* environment. None of these techniques of artificial nurturance works as well as the natural mothering experience, though as one or another becomes "faddish" there is a tendency for doctors to proclaim its superiority over the natural mother.

But once a substitute for a thing is possible, the thing itself loses its mystique. By their very existence, substitutes denigrate the original. What is the value of penmanship in a world with typewriters? Who needs to do long division in a world with calculators? What happened to oral history in a world that learned to write? Once a substitute, or just a "man-made" alternative is available, what's so "special" about the original? Think about how the mystical meaning of flight changed once airplanes streaked over eagles.

That is what is happening to mothering—as a physical and as a psychological experience—as we offer substitute after substitute, surrogate after surrogate. What's so *special* about motherhood?

I recently listened to a group of lawyers trying to figure out if there was anything special or unique about a mother's relationship to her fetus, compared with anyone else's relationship to that fetus. The context was the issue of prenatal torts—the ever-present legal question of who can sue whom for what. The question was: If a child can sue someone—for example, a manufacturer of a chemical—for harm that was done to that child when it was a fetus, then is there any reason that the child cannot sue the mother for harm she did to the child when it was a fetus? Is there anything that makes a mother's relationship to her fetus unique? They had a hard time thinking of anything.

We have focused on the seed, on the embryo, and then on the fetus, and reduced all of the nurturance, all of the intimacy, all of the *mothering,* to background, environmental factors. And so as we substitute for this and for that environmental factor, substitute for this or for that mothering experience, we wonder what is so special about the original, what is so unique about the mother's relationship.

The problem has been brought to a head with the new procreative technology, which forces us to confront questions about mothering and the mother-child relationship. But these are not new problems or new questions. People in our society have been substituting for aspects of mothering for a long time, always along the same patterns. Upper-class women have bought the services of lower-class women to provide one or another mothering service for their children. Or, it might more accurately be said in some circumstances, upper-class men have bought the services of lower-class women to supplement the services of their wives. Some societies have let men have mistresses while their wives mothered; some have let men hire servants to do the mothering so that their wives could be reserved for their sexual and social uses.

Wet nurses are the earliest example of such a biological substitution of one woman for another in mothering. Sometimes wet-nursing has been done in an exchange among women—two or more women occasionally nursing each other's babies, substituting for one another. "Commercializing" wet-nursing meant putting a price tag on that service. When the wet nurses were slave mammies, the price was factored into the cost of the slave. In the case of a hired wet nurse, the cost was per feeding, per hour, or per week. In these cash exchanges, the "breast-feeding relationship" was considered unimportant. Milk became a product to be bought and sold, not the basis of an intimate relationship. Once one buys the milk, the producer of the milk is reduced in status—her relationship is not a mothering relationship, not a relationship to the child, but a relationship to her product, her milk. Her value lies in the quality of her milk, not the quality of her relationship with the child. And so wet nurses were inspected, like animals, for the quality of their product.

In a patriarchal society, men use women to have their children. A man can use this woman or that woman to have *his* children. He can hire this woman or that woman to substitute for one or another aspect—biological, social, or psychological—of the mothering his child needs. From the view of the man, his seed is irreplaceable; the mothering, the nurturance, is substitutable.

And from the woman's point of view? We can use this man's sperm or that man's to have our children. With this or that man as father, our bellies will swell, life will stir, milk will flow. We may prefer one man's seed to another, just as a man may prefer one woman's nurturance to another for his child. For men, the nurturers are substitutable, interchangeable. For men, what makes the child *his* is his seed. For women, what makes the child ours is the nurturance, the work of our bodies. Wherever the sperm came from, it is in our bodies that our babies grow, and our physical presence and nurturance that makes our babies ours.

But is that inevitable? Did not some women substitute other women's bodies when they hired wet nurses? Don't some women substitute other women's arms, other women's touch, when they hire housekeepers and baby-sitters and day-care workers? And now the new procreative technology lets us cut our seeds loose from our bodies and plant them in other women's bodies. Now the seed, the egg, of one woman can be brought to term in the body of another.

Then who is the mother? The person who supplied the egg or the person in whose body the fetus grows and is nurtured? Our answer depends on where we stand when we ask the question.

When we accept the patriarchal valuing of the seed, there is no doubt—the real mother, like the real father, is the genetic parent. When we can contract for pregnancy at the now-going rate of $10,000, we can choose which women to substitute for us in the pregnancy.

For which women are these substitutes available? Who can afford to hire substitutes for the various parts of mothering? The situation today is exactly what it has been historically: women of privilege, wealthy or fairly wealthy women, hiring the services of poor, or fairly poor women. Upper-class women can have some of the privileges of patriarchy. Upper-class women can have, can buy, some of the privileges of their paternity, using the bodies of poorer women to "bear them offspring." And upper-class women can, as they so often have, be bought off with these privileges, and accept men's worldview as their own. And so we have women, right along with men, saying that what makes a child one's own is the seed, the genetic tie, the "blood." And the blood they mean is not the real blood of pregnancy and birth, not the blood of the pulsing cord, the bloody show, the blood of birth, but the metaphorical blood of the genetic tie.

This is the ultimate meaning of patriarchy for mothers: Seeds are precious. Mothers are fungible.

Today we are more familiar with the nonbiological services that we hire from mother-substitutes. We hire baby-sitters, day-care workers, nannies, housekeepers, to "watch" our children. The tasks are the traditional tasks of mothering—feeding, tending, caring, the whole bundle of social and psychological and physical tasks involved in the care of young children. When performed by mothers, we call this mothering. When performed by fathers, we have sometimes called it fathering, sometimes parenting, sometimes helping the mother. When performed by hired hands, we called it unskilled.

We devalue these nurturing tasks when we contract for them. When we do them ourselves because we want to do them, we see them as precious, as special, as treasured moments in life. That is the contradiction that allows us to value the children so highly, to value our special time with them, to speak lovingly of the child's trust, the joys of that small hand placed in ours—and hire someone to take that hand, at minimum wage.

In sum, the ideology of a patriarchal society goes much deeper than male dominance. It means far more than just having men in charge, or men making more decisions than women do. The ideology of patriarchy is a basic worldview, and in a patriarchal system that view permeates all of our thinking. In our society, even as a modified patriarchy, the ideology of patriarchy provides us with an understanding not only of the relations between men and women but also of the relations between mothers and their children.

MOTHERWORKS AND THE NEW OEDIPUS COMPLEX

There's a new kind of mother-manual out these days. The old ones told us how to mix formula, or how many minutes on a breast, how to be firm, be gentle, protect the baby, toughen the baby, let it cry, never let it cry—how to mother by the current rules of the game. The new how-to tells us all that, and also how to find, use, train, supervise, relate to, (not) compete with, our children's caregivers.

I find reading through such books, listening to such conversations, deeply troubling. It's not just the "good-help-is-so-hard-to-find" elitism of it all. What troubles me is listening to women talking about the mothering work of other women in a way that sounds to me like Victorian fathers must have talked about their wives. Maybe this is indeed the way rich people have always talked, and I am just new to the world of servants. But whether historically rooted or a new variant, this is not what I thought the women's movement was about.

First of all, as in every other discussion of child care, it is focused entirely on the mother. The slipping in and out of nonsexist language and assumptions is extraordinary. The *Big Apple Parent's Paper* ran a multi-part series, "In Search of Mary Poppins." It was Part III that happened to come my way, "Training and Supervising Your Caregiver" (Morin and Davis 1987). The article began, "The time has come for you to go back to work—and to turn your baby over to someone else to be the mother all day." So much for nonsexist assumptions. The "parent" reading is a woman, and the caregiver is also a woman. The reader is quite specifically told, "First get your husband's agreement that only one person—namely you—will be supervising the caregiver. Any suggestions or complaints on his part about her performance should go through you." It is not just being patronizing, saying that caregivers "perform" and employers' suggestions or complaints need to come from one person only. It is specifically saying that one person, "namely you," is the mother. Parents genuinely sharing child care, as they are apparently sharing responsibility for earning money, are not addressed.

And how are we to treat Mary Poppins? "The general principle here is to relate to your caregiver in the way you want her to relate to your baby." That sentence is in italics. We are to relate to her as we do to the baby, but fortunately, it is a good era for babies: "Give her the feeling that you respect her and have confidence in her. Praise her for the things she does well. Don't attack or criticize her for mishaps or mistakes." Just what is meant by doing well, what are the standards for performance? Apparently, making sure that she is doing things "your way." The reader, presumably not an old hand at raising babies or she would not be looking for direction, will begin the relationship with the caregiver by taking three days off and "training her to take care of your baby by letting her see how YOU do it." The caregiver, never quite described here, is actually not Mary Poppins, or even a trained nanny, who would have flown off the job, but more likely a mother, maybe a grandmother, a woman who has herself raised children, her "own" or others on her previous jobs. But we will not learn from her, not even work with her, not even teach her. We will train her.

As I read this—and similar articles are appearing monthly in women's magazines and books for new parents—I am reminded of the centuries of child-rearing advice from male experts to mothers (Ehrenreich and English 1979). I think specifically of the control exercised by fathers, who without actually taking care of children, set the boundaries, the moral tone, the values, under which mothers could rear the children of men.

But unlike the Victorian father who was assured of his control, and did not want or expect intimacy or expressions of love from the child, women today want good child care, want deeply to have someone the child can feel secure with, feel love for—and yet feel threatened by that love. The mother needs to be reassured of her control, her very motherhood. Barbara Berg, for example, in *Crisis of the Working Mother,* tells the reader, "Knowing that you are in control—that your values and standards are being transmitted to the child even in your absence—will reinforce the feeling that YOU are the mother even if you are away at work" (1986, p. 74).

But something more disturbing than the "transmission of values and standards" is happening. The pull and tug for the child's affection, as it is described today, reads like the Oedipal drama, stripped bare of sex, and left with the naked power issue. The mother wants the child to identify with her, not with the caregiver. The child expresses its attachment to the caregiver. Berg describes her own feelings of distress when her child spoke of the babysitter as his other mother. She describes other women firing a caregiver precisely because the child grew to love her "too much." But as Freud showed us, if the child has access to power, it will turn to power, just as sons turned to fathers.

In the Oedipal situation as described by Freud, sons begin by loving their mothers, their caregivers, more than their fathers—the attachment, the identification, is with the nurturant, caring mother. The father, unlike the mother, is a distant and frightening figure who has power over the child and over the mother. Once the boy-child learns of the physical difference between the sexes, Freud hypothesized, he fears the powerful father will mutilate the son just as the boy believes the mother has been mutilated, by the loss of the treasured penis. Eventually the boy resolves his dilemma and fear by changing his identification to his father. The boy comes to want to grow up to be a man like his father, possessing for himself a woman like his mother.

In the modern American family drama I am describing, both mother and father are sources of power—but it may be that neither is the daily care giver. The child is asked to switch identification from the nurturant care giver to the powerful parent, mother or father. And so, in this situation, the source of power is not sex, but class.

Berg says she was comforted by someone assuring her that "just as you can't feel the same way about another person's child as you do about your own, your child can't feel the same way about a caretaker as he or she feels toward you." But what does "own" mean here? Berg is no biological determinist. Her child was adopted (Berg 1986). What makes this mother-child bond so sure, so irreplaceable? It is not biology. It is not sex. It is power. We won't be "vulnerable to our children's declarations that they love their baby-sitters more than they love us" (1986, p. 73), because we will remember who is in control: "Remember that they are really our assistants rather than our substitutes" (1986, p. 73). And so might Freud have reassured the Victorian father who left his son in the care of the mother all day: The young child may profess his love of his mother, but he will grow up to walk in his father's footsteps.

If we are the fathers here, setting the tone, controlling the mothers, what are we looking for in these mothers? Compliance, certainly, is always important if we are going to remain in control. But there are other qualities, too, that vary with the age of the child. Berg describes Sara's search for a suitable replacement caregiver for 3-year-old Gary. It is a discussion I've heard in playgrounds, school lobbies, kitchens, and offices for years. Lucy, the first caregiver, "had been wonderful with Gary when he was a baby. She was warm, nurturing, honest, neat and willing to follow directions. But she was not really interested in engaging Gary in intellectual or creative activities, and Sara felt these to be increasingly important as Gary grew older" (1986, p. 75).

These qualities of Lucy are distinctively, stereotypically feminine qualities. Sara, and the dozens of women like her I know, are doing what men have long done. Men left the babies and little children to the warm, neat, nurturant, compliant care of women. Men took their sons, as they outgrew the world of women, the private world, and sent them off to schools, apprenticeships, the world of men, the public world. The new mother, the managerial mother, is doing the same thing, only she wants her daughters too to leave the world of nurturant women and enter into the world of intellect and creativity.

Racism and classism enter into this equation, too. Poor women, women of color, are often valued for their nurturant qualities. I've been told it is "Island women," or "old Southern Black women," or "Mexican women" who are especially motherly. But by the age of 3 or 4—just the age the "Oedipal" drama begins—these aren't the qualities being sought, just as these feminine qualities were inappropriate for the Victorian boy. At this point, European, American, middle-class caregivers are wanted, class and ethnicity replacing sex in this revised Oedipal drama. Given the expense of a trained English-type nanny, or even a graduate student live-in, preschool and "enriched" day-care programs become the choice for entry into the world of intellect, what used to be the world of men, the public world.

What happens to the discarded outgrown caregiver? Some move from job to job, home to home, child to child. One friend told me about firing the baby-sitter her child had outgrown. A responsible employer, she found another job for the woman, in a household with a baby, and for more money. The child took it well, the mother told me—didn't seem more than passingly sad to hear the baby-sitter was leaving. But the baby-sitter—she cried. She said she'd miss the child. She'd cared for her for four years. She'd grown to love her.

In *The Managed Heart: Commercialization of Human Feeling*, Hochschild describes the work of flight attendants. In the work that they do, "processing people, the product is a state of mind" (1983, p. 6). They are paid for what she calls emotional labor:

This labor requires one to induce or suppress feeling in order to sustain the outward countenance that produces the proper state of mind in others—in this case, the sense of being cared for in a convivial and safe place. This kind of labor calls for a coordination of mind and feeling, and it sometimes draws on a source of self that we honor as deep and integral to our individuality. (1983, p. 7)

The emotional work of mothers done without pay, or the emotional work of hired caregivers done for a salary, is a more intense version of the flight attendant's work, with the similar goal of creating a state of mind in others—just that sense of being safe and cared for. To do such work, Hochschild shows, calls for "deep acting," as Stanislavski described it: We must call forth the emotion from our very selves. To soothe a child, we must make it feel cared for, nurtured, loved. To make the child feel that way, the caregiver must act as if she indeed loves the child. To act so convincingly—and children are a tough audience—requires calling forth her own feelings of love, of tenderness.

What do caregivers *feel* when they rock an infant to sleep, kiss a boo-boo to make it better, play peek-a-boo, settle a playground spat? What did slave mammies feel as they nursed these white babies, lullabied them with songs of their own children's suffering, sale, even death? Perhaps it is not so surprising that child caregivers, from Roman slave nurses (Joshel 1986) to the American black slave and on to today's minimum wage caregivers are so often remembered with affection by their grown charges. At unknown costs to themselves, they were mothers.

CHILD CARE AND MIDREVOLUTIONARY MORES

Is the moral of the story that no one should ever hire anyone to do child care? Maybe, in a better world, it would be. Maybe, in a better world, communities of people, not just mothers, would be responsible for children. I haven't the imagination to envision how such a world would work. The highly imaginative author, Ursula LeGuin, says that she could only make that work in a novel by having the people live in small communities (1988). Small communities of like-minded people have no great appeal for me personally, a resident by choice in one of the largest and probably the most diverse city on the planet. So maybe, in a better world, there would be no need of paid child care—but

I don't even know what such a world would, could, or even should look like.

In this world, something has to be done about child care, and paying for it is an inevitable part of what needs to be done. Some would like to see all child care institutionalized, with marvelous, state-subsidized or state-run day-care centers for children from birth on up. I'm not so sure. I worry about what values state-run, or worse yet, corporate-run day care, might teach children. I wonder about maintaining intimacy, warmth, individuality, nurturance in an institutional setting. I know it has been done in some fine centers, with a committed, excited staff developing wonderful programs. But on a large scale? For all children?

For now, we need to keep our options open. We need a variety of child-care arrangements: cooperatives or communes of mothers and fathers sharing child care, small in-home child-care centers; housekeepers; baby-sitters, parental leave time, day-care centers—all of that, and whatever else our imaginations can conjure up. And it all takes money.

Child care is either going to have to be provided in a fundamental rearrangement of the way we live—for starters, flexible time and households and shared responsibility for children beyond just one or even two harried parents—or with a rearrangement of our money. We cannot go on calling for "affordable child care" if what is meant is that one person's salary must be big enough to cover another's. That inevitably sets the salary to be made in child care as too low for that person in turn to be able to afford good child care. If children are to be something other than a burden, the costs must be a societally shared responsibility. Monetary subsidies for child care would help us break out of the class- and race-based pattern, in which the children of the rich are cared for by the poor, and the children of the poor too often go untended.

But it's not just money. *Someone* has to watch the children. *Someone* has to actually, truly, literally be there with them. Whoever that person is—mother, father, adoptive parent, sibling, housekeeper, teacher, baby-sitter, day-care worker, grandparent—*whoever* is with that child, that person must never be thought of as being there in place of someone else. The person who is there, is there. The person is not a substitute-some-one-else. The person caring for a child is in a first-person, one-on-one, direct relationship to that child.

That relationship deserves respect, just as that work deserves to be valued. And respect, as we know from what has happened to mothers historically, is not adequately taken care of with politeness and a Mother's Day card. It must come with legally recognized rights. Someone who has been raising a child has moral rights invested in that child. At a minimum, we have to protect child-care workers from arbitrary firing, from loss of visitation rights to the children they raise, from having the relationship with the child used as a source of exploitation.

We must move beyond patriarchal definitions of the relations between parents and children, and beyond modifications that simply extend to some women, most often at cost to other women, some of the privileges of patriarchy. Otherwise we seem to be caught in a trap of endlessly remaking the world in the same image: some people in the public sphere, the world of power, of importance, and some people in the private sphere, rocking the cradle but never really ruling the world.

ACKNOWLEDGMENTS

Author's note: *Portions of this article appear in* Recreating Motherhood: Ideology and Technology in a Patriarchal Society *(W. W. Norton, 1989). I want to thank Maren Lockwood Carden, Betty Leyerle, Eileen Moran, Wendy Simonds, and Mary White, for their helpful discussions of these issues, and Mary Cunnane and Judith Lorber, for both substantive and editorial assistance.*

REFERENCES

Berg, Barbara. 1983. *Nothing to Cry About.* New York: Bantam.

———1986. *Crisis of the Working Mother: Resolving the Conflicts Between Family and Work.* New York: Summit Books.

Ehrenreich, Barbara and Deirdre English. 1979. *For Her Own Good: 150 Years of the Experts' Advice to Women.* Garden City, NY: Doubleday Anchor.

Ehrensaft, Diane. 1987. *Parenting Together: Men and Women Sharing the Care of Their Children.* New York: Free Press.

Hamilton, W. D. 1978. "The Genetic Evolution of Social Behavior." In *The Sociobiology Debate: Readings on Ethical and Scientific Issues,* edited by Arthur L. Caplan. New York: Harper & Row.

Hochschild, Arlie Russell. 1983. *The Managed Heart: Commercialization of Human Feeling.* Berkeley: University of California Press.

Joshel, Sandra. 1986. "Nurturing the Master's Child: Slavery and the Roman Child-Nurse." *Signs: Journal of Women in Culture and Society* 12:3–22.

LeGuin, Ursula K. 1988. Anthropology Department Colloquium, University of Rochester, January 12.

Morin, Eleanor and Harold Davis. 1987. "In Search of Mary Poppins: Part III. Training and Supervising Your Caregiver." *Big Apple Parent's Paper* 2(4):10–11.

Petersen, Glenn. 1982. "Ponepean Matriliny: Production, Exchange and the Ties That Bind." *American Ethnologist* 9:140–50.

Pruett, Kyle D. 1987. *The Nurturing Father: Journey Toward the Complete Man.* New York: Warner Books.

Risman, Barbara. 1987. "Intimate Relationships from a Microstructural Perspective: Men Who Mother." *Gender & Society* 1:6–32.

Violence against Women

Violence against women manifests itself in many forms. Verbal harassment, sexual imposition, sexual assault, rape, domestic battering, and lesbian bashing all contribute to a social climate that encourages women to comply with men's desires or to restrict their activities in order to avoid assault. The threat of violence against women is pervasive across cultures. Feminist analyses of violence against women focus on the extent to which violence serves as a means for the institutionalized social control of women by men. The articles in this section analyze various forms of violence against women and contrast beliefs and actualities about various kinds of male violence. Often, male-controlled ideologies encourage us to accept violence against women as either harmless or deserved. Feminist analyses take the position that this violence constitutes a system through which men frighten and therefore control and dominate women.

Sexual harassment is a form of sexual coercion that affects women's ability to function appropriately in work and academic settings. In "The Lecherous Professor: A Portrait of the Artist," Billie Wright Dziech and Linda Weiner describe the process of sexual harassment on college campuses. This article does more than simply provide an analysis of the problem; it offers practical information, such as how to recognize early warning signs of harassment and how to differentiate harassers from their nonharassing colleagues.

The second article in this section, "'The Man in the Street': Why He Harasses," by Cheryl Benard and Edit Schlaffer, points out just how common harassing assaults on women are; they occur not only at work but in many public places—in coffee shops, in self-service laundries, and on the street. Benard and Schlaffer interviewed men on the streets who harassed them and found that what feminists have suggested is indeed accurate. Street harassment is not a way to flatter women but a form of male bonding through which men aggrandize their egos. Although some may consider the street harasser a minor offender, this article suggests his role as "an accomplice in the more massive forms of violence against women."

Patricia Yancey Martin and Robert A. Hummer also explore the implications of heterosexual male bonding in "Fraternities and Rape on Campus." Fraternity members' negative attitudes toward women, rigid ideas about masculinity, and pressures to demonstrate simultaneously their heterosexuality and their utter loyalty to the "brotherhood" create fraternity cultures in which men use women to demonstrate their masculinity and worth.

Popular ideologies about rape include the belief that women enjoy rape or at least deserve it when they violate male-prescribed values and standards. This attitude is apparent among the men Diana Scully and Joseph Marolla interviewed for their article "'Riding the Bull at Gilley's': Convicted Rapists Describe the Rewards of Rape." The men who

369

talked to Scully and Marolla reported the use of rape as retaliation against the perceived transgressions of particular women in their lives as well as against womankind in general. Such admissions support the feminist analysis of rape as a means of social control.

Pauline B. Bart and Patricia H. O'Brien make an empirical examination of women's likelihood of escaping attackers by fighting back. In "Stopping Rape: Effective Avoidance Strategies," we discover that women who resist assault escape more often than women who follow popular advice to submit to an assailant. Bart and O'Brien's research also offers an analysis of the particular strategies that women have used effectively against male assailants.

Hate crimes are crimes motivated by prejudice against particular groups. Because violence against women is so widespread, we sometimes fail to recognize it as a crime of hate. By situating the murders of women in a sexist control context in "'Femicide': Speaking the Unspeakable," Jane Caputi and Diana E. H. Russell demonstrate that we can usefully regard such murders as crimes

against women as a group, not just individual and apolitical assaults by deranged men.

In some of the preceding articles we have encountered ideas about strategies women can use to resist men's violent efforts to control them: Bart and O'Brien name specific self-defense approaches women use successfully; Caputi and Russell encourage us to withdraw support from the oppressors and their patriarchal social structures. In "Female Slave Resistance: The Economics of Sex," Darlene Hine and Kate Wittenstein present particular historical examples of African-American women's strategies for resisting racist, sexist domination. Their account suggests that even in the face of incredible oppression, women find ways to resist for the sake of their freedom and personal dignity. Equally as striking is the authors' insight on women's use of violence as resistance, particularly in cases of slave mothers killing their children to spare their offspring the tortures of slavery and to deprive white slave holders of the opportunity to exploit them.

The Lecherous Professor: A Portrait of the Artist

BILLIE WRIGHT DZIECH and LINDA WEINER

"When I use a word," Humpty Dumpty said, in a rather scornful tone, "it means just what I choose it to mean—neither more nor less." "The question is," said Alice, "whether you can make words mean so many different things." "The question is," said Humpty Dumpty, "which is to be the master—that's all."

Lewis Carroll, *Alice in Wonderland*

In a recent *Cosmopolitan* article on sexual harassment, Adrian L., a student at a large Midwestern state university, described Tom, one of her professors:

[He's] like a rabid wolf hovering at the edge of a sheep pack—the incoming class of freshmen.

When he's selected a girl who's unusually attractive, intelligent, and naive, he moves right in. Believe me, he's *predatory*—I've seen him in action. First, he'll "rap and relate" with the freshman over drinks at the college bar. In a couple of weeks, he has her dizzy with the "existential nihilism of Sartre" or "archetypal patterns of Jung." All this may sound exciting, but the results are tragicomic. Two years ago, he "shared" a girl with a friend of his, another faculty member. The three of them made it while watching a particularly beautiful sunrise—very aesthetic, you know. His current ploy is backgammon. You see him shaking those dice at a table in the rathskeller with this hazy-eyed kid. Several dormitory assistants have seen him leaving

From *The Lecherous Professor* by Billie Wright Dziech and Linda Weiner. Copyright © 1984 by Billie Wright Dziech and Linda Weiner. Beacon Press, Boston.

her room at six in the morning, and the campus security guard once caught him with a student in the stacks of the library. You can guess what he found.

Is Tom exploiting his pupils? You bet he is. Does he know what he's doing? Of course. Is the administration aware of what he's up to? Sure they are, but these days, to get fired for what they used to call "moral turpitude," you'd have to rape an entire cheerleading squad at half time. Tom's like a pot-head turned loose in a Twinkies factory.[1]

Although there is limited evidence of the number of harassers who may be "loose" on the nation's campuses, one point is clear. They are tolerated because society doubts that men are capable of sexual restraint. Sexual harassers are often defended with the shrugged observation, "After all, they're only human." A middle-aged professor, notorious for pursuing sexual relations with female students, offered a variation on this view. "If you put me at a table with food (with coeds), I eat."

The appeal to "human nature" is a reminder that even in an era of ostensible sexual liberalism and freedom, both men and women suffer and stereotypes die hard. Even in the 1980s, society has not freed itself of the Victorian notion that men are creatures barely capable of controlling their bestial appetites and aggressions. All the contemporary rhetoric about liberating the sexes from stereotypes has done little to change the popular view of the male as a kind of eternal tumescence, forever searching and forever unsatisfied.

Such an attitude demeans the notion of "human." To be human does not mean that a man is at the mercy of his genitalia. Whatever it is that constitutes "human-

371

ness" is located in the mind and heart, not the libido. "Human" implies reason, compassion, control—all the qualities that distinguish college professors from their cats and dogs. Without these, they are "only animal," a defense few find appealing. Sexual harassment unquestionably harms females, but men are equally debased when it is allowed to flourish. On the college campus, a very small number of men damage the reputations of colleagues who perform difficult tasks for relatively low wages without "succumbing" to the "irresistible" temptations of women students.

The professor-as-lecher is so much a part of the folklore of higher education that it appears consistently in popular writing. One of the most telling examples is Anna Sequoia's *The Official J.A.P. Handbook.* The work is intended as a parody of the Jewish American Princess stereotype, but in order to accomplish the parody, the author relies on the universally familiar stereotype of the lecherous professor. According to Sequoia, Marsha Lynn, the typical J.A.P., "looks for love in all the wrong places." One of the most predictable is college:

Marsha Lynn and the Professor. Marsha Lynn often meets her professor during the first term of her freshman year. Usually, Professor Maisel is teaching an art-survey course or a freshman English course. He may be a painter or a poet: probably the first real painter or poet Marsha Lynn's met. Professor Maisel, of course, won't put the touch on Marsha Lynn that term: he'll wait until she has her (well-deserved) A, but they'll become friends. Perhaps they'll have long, passionate conversations about Faulkner. Perhaps Professor Maisel will introduce Marsha Lynn to *Roethke: Collected Poems,* or *The Selected Poems of Margaret Atwood.* Maybe when Adrienne Rich or David Ignatow come to read on campus, Professor Maisel will invite Marsha Lynn to the party afterward and get her as drunk on the proximity to Real Poets as on the cheap white wine. Little by little, Marsha Lynn will become incorporated into Professor Maisel's world, visiting him in the afternoons in his office, perhaps stopping by on occasion—usually with two or three other bright students—for a dinner of homemade pasta and intelligent conversation.

And coming from what Marsha Lynn will perceive as her intellectually limited suburb, in (temporary) rebellion against her parents' milieu of con-

spicuous (even if tasteful) consumption, hungry for the stimulation and surface glamour of the Literary Life, Marsha Lynn will fall into Professor Maisel's carefully laid trap. Poor Marsha Lynn really has no adequate defense. Professor Maisel is an old hand at seducing students and makes a regular, if moderately discreet, practice of it.

JAP parents have few resources against the Predatory Professor. If they withdraw Marsha Lynn from that college, she may refuse to leave and move in with her Older Man. If Daddy goes to talk to the professor, he'll embarrass himself and have no effect. Usually, the dean or chairman of the department or even the president of the college will do nothing: they know that every campus has its share of Professor Maisels, and they choose to do nothing about it. Usually, the only resource is to have a powerful friend on the college's board of trustees: sometimes that works.

But generally it's just a question of time. Sooner or later, Marsha Lynn will realize that Professor Maisel drinks too much, or sleeps with other students, or is just too old for her (even though he may be in his late thirties or early to middle forties), or too condescending.[2]

Popular fiction also perpetuates the lecherous stereotypes. Jacob Horner, John Barth's protagonist in *The End of the Road,* described his opening day of classes:

Indeed! One hundred spelling words dictated rapidly enough to keep their heads down, and I, perched high on my desk, could diagnose to my heart's content every bump of femininity in the room (praised be American grade schools, where little girls learn to sit up front!). Then, perhaps, having ogled my fill, I could get on with the business of the course. For as a man must grow used to the furniture before he can settle down to read in his room, this plentitude of girlish appurtenances had first to be assimilated before anyone could concentrate attention on the sober prescriptions of English grammar.

Four times I repeated the ritual pronouncements—at eight and nine in the morning and at two and three in the afternoon. Between the two sessions I lounged in my office with a magnificent erection, wallowing in my position, and watched with proprietary eye the parade of young things passing my door. I had nothing at all to do but spin indolent daydreams of absolute authority—neurotic, Caligular authority of the sort that summons up officefuls of undergraduate girls, hot and submissive—leering professorial dreams![3]

Horner's adventures may sell books, but they miss the point about everyday life in higher education. The truth is that most faculty probably lack the time and energy required for "leering professorial dreams." Literary characters can afford the luxury of "magnificent erection[s]," whereas real-life college professors spend their working hours juggling time between classes, meetings, research, writing, and professional conferences. Those who fit the Jacob Horner stereotype are the exception, not the rule, but lecherous professors repeat their offenses on multiple victims and do so much damage that they claim more attention than professors who simply do their jobs.

A crucial concern for both students and academicians is learning to recognize the characteristics that differentiate the lecherous professor from his colleagues. There are no infallible predictors for recognizing sexual harassment. The most pernicious behavior can occur exclusive of "giveaways," or isolated actions can be misinterpreted as sinister when they are simply examples of clumsy professional or social style. However, a tentative list of warning signs might include the following:

- *Staring, leering, ogling.* These behaviors may be surreptitious or very obvious. In any case, college faculty should possess knowledge of social decorum, and must avoid such activities.
- *Frequently commenting on personal appearance of the student.* In the academic setting, most professors refrain from discussing the apparel and physical traits of their students.
- *Touching out of context.* Every physical gesture should be appropriate to the occasion, setting, and need and character of the individual student. Professional educators may legitimately be expected to possess the ability to make such determinations.
- *Excessive flattery and praise of the student.* This behavior, exhibited with others present, is especially seductive to students with low self-esteem *or* high aspirations. By convincing a student that she is intellectually and/or physically exceptional, the lecherous professor gains psychological access to her.

- *Deliberately avoiding or seeking encounters with the student in front of colleagues.* Depending on the type of harasser, he may either attempt to hide from or to perform for colleagues in interactions with the student. The key is that in either case his behavior with the student changes when he is being observed.
- *Injecting a "male versus female" tone into discussions with the students or colleagues.* A frequent behavior of verbal harassers, this conduct signals a generally disparaging attitude toward women. Its initial effect is to make them feel outsiders in the academic environment, but it may also be an indicator of other potential forms of abuse.
- *Persistently emphasizing sexuality in all contexts.* Pervasive, inordinate emphasis on sex can occur in class or outside. For the lecherous professor, sexuality becomes, in effect, the prism through which all topics are focused. Students, male and female, can usually detect this behavior readily, and such professors often acquire a reputation for "being fixated on sex" in papers, tests, and discussions.

Such behaviors can serve as signals to the student. Another key to understanding the lecherous professor is assessing the setting or context in which he works. There are both public and private harassers, and they act in very different fashions. The public harasser engages in observable, flagrant posturing toward women. He is the most likely to intimidate or seek control through sexist remarks and advances that may be offensive but are essentially free from sanctions. Students sometimes refer to him as "hands," "touchy-feely," or "mouth." Colleagues describe him as "patronizing," "always performing," "convinced of his own cuteness." He frequently costumes himself by extreme dressing up or down and seldom employs standard academic vocabulary—except to punctuate a witticism. He is articulate, glib, sarcastic and/or funny. His general image is that of a casual "good guy" or an imposing man of the world.

The public harasser appears always available, always approachable. He spends enormous amounts of time with students—in his office, in the halls during breaks, in the student union or at a nearby bar when the day or week ends. His informality is a welcome contrast to the authoritarian style of most of his colleagues. The more perceptive of them detect but hesitate to question his intentions. This was the position of a male philosophy professor:

I'm really not particularly comfortable with ———'s style. Perhaps because it's so different from mine and so unlike what we were taught to emulate in graduate school. I do feel a sense of unease when I see him several times a week huddled with a group of young women over coffee in the Union. I have other colleagues who are just as concerned about students and spend equal amounts of time with them, but they don't seem to need to flaunt those relationships before others.

The high profile of the public harasser is his defense. It deters observers or victims from protesting when he touches too often or cracks one joke too many. Even male students hesitate to criticize public harassers. A sophomore at a college in Michigan explained:

Sure, I was afraid to say anything to anyone about Mr. ———. They all laughed every time he made some stupid remark. You would have thought he was a burlesque comedian or something. What I really couldn't get, what really floored me was why the girls laughed at him too. He was supposed to be teaching psychology, and there he was making these gross remarks that should have embarrassed them half to death (they sure as hell embarrassed me) and they just kept on laughing all year.

When an individual's remarks to and about women or his physical contact with them appears open, he can easily contend, "I have nothing to hide. There's nothing malevolent in my intentions. Everything I say or do is right out there for everyone to see." The difficulty is that an institution's ability to restrain a public harasser depends upon the level of awareness of those within the environment. Some "see" malevolent intentions and others do not, but the harasser's reputation as communicative, friendly, and open provides a sure defense. Thus he is free to perform and be observed but not challenged or chastized for his behavior.

The style and intent of the private harasser are directly opposite. He may be the more genuinely "lecherous" of the two, for he uses his authority to gain private access to the student. Unlike his counterpart, he deliberately avoids notoriety. He not only seeks but depends upon privacy because he requires a domain in which there are no witnesses to his behavior. He is the harasser of greatest interest to the public and the media, the one who demands sexual favors of students,

the one most readily cast in the image of despoiler of innocence and molester of youth.

His personal and professional styles lend credence to the epithets. The private harasser often adheres to academic stereotypes. He usually dresses conservatively. His language and demeanor are generally formal, perhaps even intimidating, to the student. Because he appears so circumspect, he is the last to be suspected by colleagues. The Levi-clad professor who sits casually before the class seems more culpable than the imposing man with the resonant voice who stands behind the lectern.

The lectern symbolizes the private harasser's teaching style. Characteristically removed and aloof, he lectures while the class listens. Just as the public harasser uses his openness to move the student to compliance, the private offender employs authority to lure her into acquiescence. The ability to control the setting gives him special access to the women under his power. He can seduce them into his private domain with a simple oral or written directive. "Please see me" or "I would like a conference with you" are familiar demands.

But, few are prepared for the deception that occurs when the professor closes the office door and sheds the professorial for the male role. Whether he begins with overt sexual advances or the more subtle verbal approach ("My wife doesn't love me anymore," "Young women like you are so lovely"), his sudden role change causes the student surprise and confusion. Her role submissiveness, female self-doubt, and shock combine with the privacy of the interaction to provide a cover for the harasser. When there are no witnesses and the student experiences extreme disorientation, there are seldom sexual harassment grievances.

Another way of understanding sexual harassers is to describe the roles they most commonly assume:

- *The counselor-helper.* This type of professor uses the guise of nurturer and caretaker to gain access to the student. If she feels lonely and anonymous on campus, she may be flattered or consoled by his interest. He invites her confidence and uses information about her private life to discover her vulnerabilities, commitments, and attitudes about men and sex. Then he can tailor his "line" to her specific need. One professor, after encouraging a student's anguished account of rejection by a boyfriend, replied earnestly, "I'd never treat you like that." To her, it was a terribly moving assertion. To the witness to the incident, it was far less compelling because she had observed the professor making the statement to at least three other female students from whom he later sought sexual favors.

The counselor-helper may act as a go-between in male–female relationships of students. This behavior, described by one ombudsman as "pimping," encourages the student to see the professor as a broker or gatekeeper in her relationship with a significant male. The professor's intent can be to derive vicarious sexual pleasure from thus involving himself or to use the male as a foil to increase his own stature in the eyes of the female. One administrator describes this as "seduction with an agent." An accomplished harasser in one university was fond of acting as go-between and then reporting to the female that he had advised her boyfriend, "She's a real woman. Are you prepared to satisfy her?" The motive was to win the seduction when the student became attracted to the professor's image of her as experienced and voluptuous.

- *The confidant.* This individual approaches the student not as a superior who can help her but as an equal and friend. Sharing is an essential element in their interaction. He may invite her confidences, but he also offers his own. In an attempt to impress or win sympathy from the student, he may relate or invent stories about his private and professional life. Placed in this role, the student often feels that he values and trusts her, so she becomes an involuntary confidante. Without genuine mutual agreement, the relationship is moved to an intimate domain from which she may find it difficult to extricate herself.

Another method a harasser may employ is creating indebtedness through gestures of friendship. Offers from a professor to lend the student books, money, notes, a place to study or providing her with free tickets or rides may signal an attempt to make her feel obligated.

- *The intellectual seducer.* Called "mind fucking" or "intellectual intercourse" by some, this kind of seduction results from the professor's ability to impress students with his skill and knowledge. He may use class content to gain access to personal information about the student. Self-disclosure on the part of the student is often invited in disciplines like psychology, sociology, philosophy, and literature where personal values, beliefs, and experiences are easily related to course content. At one college, stu-

dents told of being required to write about their sex fantasies. Such information may be used to identify areas of vulnerability and/or accessibility in the student. A psychology professor bragged to a colleague about requiring students to take personality inventories. He told them the demonstrated uses of the test, but his real motivation was to gain personal information about respondents in whom he was interested.

A professor's avocations may also be engaging or dangerous. A common example is the faculty member who uses his knowledge of books or movies to move the student into discussions of erotic topics. Another is that of the professor who hypnotizes students outside the classroom. While some use hypnosis appropriately, it can be dangerous when done by a sexual harasser. Finally, there is the case of the art professor who employs female students as nude models for private studio work.

- *The opportunist.* This person takes advantage of the physical setting and unusual or occasional circumstances to obscure his inappropriate behavior and to gain intimacy with students. He may rely on equipment or subject matter to gain physical access to the student. A serious problem in clinical, laboratory, counseling, performance, and vocational-technical settings, this behavior is often described by students as stealing "cheap feels." The lecherous professor discovers ways to touch the student by using proximity to equipment as an excuse or by employing parts of her body in class demonstrations. One student complained that her woodwind professor persisted in touching her breasts while telling her he was illustrating the movements of her diaphragm; another that her nursing instructor "felt [her] up" while using her body to demonstrate physical disabilities in patients.

The opportunist may also use field trips, meetings, and conventions as occasions to escape institutional restraints. The problem for the student is that these are often described as scholastic or professional honors and/or necessities, and she feels compelled to attend.

- *The power broker.* The most familiar type of harasser, the power broker, trades on his ability to control grades, credentials, recommendations, or jobs. The assumption that he works only through crude and raw assertions of power is inaccurate. Direct promises of rewards or threats of punishment can exert enormous influence on students, but they feel equally victimized by promises and threats that are implied rather than stated openly. Because so much may be at stake, the student is unlikely to risk a complaint unless the harasser has been very overt about his intentions.

Regardless of the role he assumes or the type of harassment in which he engages, the lecherous professor always controls the circumstances surrounding the student victim. Sexual harassment is a power issue, and the power of the professoriate is enormous. It is easy for some college professors to deceive themselves about the relationship between their power and students' responses to them. Reviewing a number of studies on sexual harassment, Marilyn B. Brewer commented in "Further Beyond Nine to Five: An Integration and Future Directions":

> In general, the participant in a high power position is likely to perceive an interaction—especially one involving positive expressions—as motivated by interpersonal attraction, and to assume that flattering remarks, compliance, and agreement are sincere and attributable to internal causes. The lower-power participant, on the other hand, is more likely to be aware of the external constraints imposed by the threat of abuse of power and consciously to use flattery and compliance as strategies to win approval and/or to avoid the displeasures of persons in high power positions. The low-power participant is also likely to *assume* that the high-power individual is aware of these external causes to a greater extent than is actually the case.[4]

In *Power and Innocence,* Rollo May commented on the environment of higher education:

> If we take the university as the setting, we need only ask any graduate student whether his professors have power over him, and he will laugh at our naiveté. Of course professors have power; the perpetual anxiety of some graduate students as to whether they will be passed or not is proof enough. The professor's power is even more effective because it is clothed in scholarly garb. It is the power of prestige, status, and the subtle coercion of others that follow from these. This is not due to the professor's conscious aims; it has more to do with the organization of the university and the teacher's unconscious motivations for being part of it.[5]

Sexual harassers are people who misuse the power of their positions to abuse members of the opposite sex. Higher education tends to discuss their behavior in the abstract—as if it were unrelated to real-life human beings. But sexual harassment cannot be understood or curtailed until professors are subjected to the same scrutiny as students. What motivates a man with so much education and power over others to act abusively toward women?

Obviously, there are no simple cause–effect relationships to explain so complex a behavior. There is an infinite number of variables that may intervene in the experiences of individuals to influence their actions, and there is little reliable, verifiable information on the psychology of sexual harassers or college professors in general. There is also no means to gather from individual faculty the enormous retrospective data necessary to establish an image of a prototypic sexual harasser.

What *can* be examined are some relevant questions about contemporary male professors: What traits are generally associated with male academics? Are there knowable similarities in the developmental cycles of a significant number of men who choose the academic profession? How might one or a combination of these contribute to the aberrant professor's decision to harass women students? Although there is currently little information to aid in analyzing the sexual harasser's motivations, this speculation may be valuable in raising the consciousness of the academic community and encouraging new perspectives on the issue. To anyone attempting to understand the problem of professors who harass women, analyses of the developmental cycles of human beings are particularly interesting. Perhaps most worth consideration at this point are unresolved adolescent crisis, professional crisis, and midlife crisis.

ADOLESCENT CRISIS

The socialization that underlies sexual harassment by men is easy to recognize and understand. It would be heartening and convenient to find that the harassers of academe are freaks and outcasts, true outlaws in society where men value equality, compassion, intimacy, and authenticity in relation to women. But the reality, however painful, is that the code of sexual ethics that harassers follow is simply a crude extension of the norms some consider acceptable for males.

By the time the average male reaches school age, he already believes that "real boys" must be assertive, aggressive, competitive, and physically strong. Peers, parents, and society in general influence boys to behave in traditionally masculine ways. The elementary school setting presents them with a serious dilemma, which Herb Goldberg described in *The Hazards of Being Male:*

> While there is great peer pressure to act like a boy, the teacher's coveted classroom values are traditionally "feminine" ones. The emphasis is on politeness, neatness, docility, and cleanliness, with not much approved room being given for the boy to flex his muscles. Teacher's greatest efforts often go into keeping the boys quiet and in their seats.

> A recent study of 12,000 students produced some interesting findings along this line. The researcher correlated masculinity scores of boys on the California Psychological Inventory with their school grades. She found that the higher the boy scored on the masculine scale, the lower his report card average tended to be.

> Of the 277 students with a D or F average, 60 percent were boys. Of the two boys with the most distinguished scholastic records, one was noted to be markedly effeminate in speech and gesture while the other "gave the strong impression of being more feminine than effeminate." Both boys had very low scores in physical fitness.[6]

The male experience may become especially traumatic during adolescence, which is the period when the masculine stereotype exerts its greatest influence. Adolescence is the bridge between childhood and adulthood, the period during which biological, sociological, and psychological forces converge to produce self-concept and identity. Psychologists like Robert Havighurst and Erik Erikson used various terms to describe the tasks essential to healthy transition into adulthood. Whatever the language, almost all developmental theories stress the importance of adolescence as the time during which one crystallizes a sex role, develops satisfying relationships with peers of the same sex, forms adequate heterosexual relationships, and lays the foundation for a career choice. Asserting that an identity crisis occurs in its purest form in adolescence, Erikson maintained that if the crisis was not resolved during this period, the conflicts of adulthood would be greater and more difficult.[7]

Although many have studied adolescence in the abstract, few have examined the real-life arena in which it takes place. The American high school is the most significant setting in which the developmental tasks of adolescence are carried out or left uncompleted. Whether it works through formal or informal mechanisms, the high school experience influences adults. Oddly, or perhaps predictably, college professors who study adolescence often limit their observations to issues such as "socioeconomic influences on achievement" and "intellectual-cognitive development." But high school graduates usually recall that the primary effect of the high school is not educational but social. Long after the last geometry theorem has been forgotten, graduates remember the captain of the football team, the prom queen, and their own positions in the status quo of adolescence.

In *Is There Life after High School?* Ralph Keyes stated colloquially a concept similar to more erudite theories about ego-identity formation during adolescence. Arguing that adult values grow directly out of high school, Keyes contended that the imprinting of adolescent peer acceptance remains with Americans throughout life. In other words, people go through life seeing themselves socially as they did in high school—as "innies" or "outies." High school "innies" and "outies" differ from one another solely on the basis of status or power. Keyes reported surprise at discovering, "Power is central to innie status. . . . I always thought status in high school had to do with being well-liked, and liking yourself. . . . That isn't what status is all about. What it's about is power."[8] And lack of power can leave indelible marks on the self-images of those unfortunate enough to be among the outies.

What constitutes the power and status for which adolescent American males strive? *The Adolescent Society,* James Coleman's classic 1957–1958 study of this subject, provided impressive empirical data to prove what most Americans already knew. Coleman contended that desire for status was the controlling force in the adolescent society and that for males athletic stardom was the highest symbol of success, the surest guarantee of entry into the leading crowd, and the most reliable means of gaining popularity with females.[9]

The masculine myth rests in large part upon equating athletic achievement and physical prowess with masculinity and success. Early in American history frontiersmen and farm and factory workers defined manliness as having the strength and stamina to endure the rigors of physical labor. As conditions changed during the twentieth century and intellectual achievement became more important, the value system incorporated the new without discarding the old. The playing field became the testing ground for masculinity, and American faith in the importance of physical superiority remained so unwavering that no one raised an eyebrow when Robert F. Kennedy, Attorney General of the United States, declared in the early 1960s, "Except for war, there is nothing in American life—nothing—which trains a boy better for life than football."[10]

Males learn very early what Marc Feigen Fasteau in *The Male Machine* described as

a skewing of values which tends to make sports a compulsion for many boys, the mandated center of their lives. Some boys can live with this. . . . Boys who can't conform easily to the athletic ideal are made to feel inadequate. They either quit completely, developing a compensatory disdain for sports as a result, or they keep trying, setting standards for themselves that have nothing to do with their own talents or desires.[11]

Burt Avedon in *Ah, Men* expressed a similar point:

The pressure on boys is most intense during their teens. . . . The demands of rapidly budding masculinity reach their heights for the boy in high school (perhaps earlier now), where the laurels of success adorn the competitive athlete, the masculine ideal. (Schools often seem geared toward elevation of athletic endeavor over all activities, including academic achievement.)[12]

James Coleman's findings corroborated this. In his studies, scholastic achievement was ambiguously regarded by adolescents. In some institutions it was respected; in others, it was a source of embarrassment. However, it was never in any of his research settings ranked above athletic ability, the primary determinant of recognition and respect.

The recognition awarded athletes over scholars comes not only from other males. Coleman and his colleagues found that adolescent girls overwhelmingly preferred athletes. Avedon supported this view: "In high school, boys find that only those who fit the ideal male image, principally through sports, are able to achieve another conquest of growing importance for adolescents reaching adulthood: the attraction of beautiful, desirable females."[13]

To the adolescent, physical attractiveness in males means looking "athletic," and Coleman found "good looks" to be another key to status and power within the adolescent society. Very early, but reaching a culmination in adolescence, the body becomes a primary symbol of self. A recent poll of sixty thousand *Psychology Today* readers found that "adults who thought they were unattractive teenagers currently have lower self-esteem than those who felt beautiful, even adults who blossomed in maturity."[14] The relationship between physical appearance and self-image is clear. The male who sees himself as unattractive in adolescence does not often acquire physical self-confidence as an adult and may never forget his failure to achieve the masculine ideal in the difficult world of high school and youth. It is, after all, as Keyes quoted one female, a time when "nothing didn't matter."[15]

Keyes, a self-acknowledged "outie," is firm in his view of the placement of college professors in the adolescent status system:

Here is how the sides break down: we give the innies all of pro sports and its cheerleaders; we concede them the military, insurance agencies, PE departments, and heavy equipment. Politics and show business are divided zones, but we write everybody's lines because outies control America's means of communication. We write the speeches, publish the books, produce the movies, make the music, do the research, report for the paper and comment on reports. . . .

Teaching is a field shared by innies, but we tell them how to do it. Our strategy here is to take over the colleges of education [i.e., higher education], control research, and write all the books about how to teach high school. In these books we never take seriously any of the values innies used to keep us down. "Popularity" is a topic we're very condescending about and brush under the heading of "Peer Relations." Sports generally get ridiculed, and activities such as cheerleading and homecoming are reduced to "Student Culture: Ceremony and Ritual."[16]

The future professor might easily be recognized in *Fear of Flying,* when Erica Jong described the "brainy boys" at Columbia:

> [They wore] flannel shirts with twenty-five leaky ballpoint pens in their breast pockets, [and had] flesh-colored frames on their thick glasses, blackheads in their ears, pustules on their necks, pleated trousers, greasy hair. . . . They commuted by subway from their mothers' [kitchens] in the Bronx to the classrooms of Moses Hadas and Gilbert Highet on Morningside Heights, where they learned enough literature and philosophy to get straight A's, but never seemed to lose their gawkiness, their schoolboy defensiveness, their total lack of appeal.[17]

Jong is not the only one to notice the phenomenon. Students, alumni, staff, and women faculty often recognize it too. They hesitate to say that they, like men, observe and evaluate the appearance of the opposite sex; they are also uncomfortable because the idea of characterizing an entire profession as "plain" seems so outlandish. Yet two women professors and a university secretary were among a number of women who admitted to finding male professors physically unappealing:

> I'm embarrassed to say this but I really do find most of my colleagues unattractive physically. When I began teaching eight years ago, I thought my standards were probably adolescent or too demanding; but after all this time, I'm still not impressed. If I had to depend on the university for attractive male companionship, I might never have married.

> The assumptions that college professors who are women are sexless is absurd. Of course, I look at men; and what I see here is not what you'd call encouraging. There are more short men, more men with glasses, more men with bad skin, more unkempt men here than in any single place I've ever been. Don't ask me to explain. I just know it's true.

> When I first became a secretary at the college, my husband was upset because he knew I would be around men so much of the time. If I ever thought it would cause a strain, I know now how silly I was. There isn't a man here anyone would want to look at once—let alone twice. There are days when I honestly wonder where these people come from. I probably sound like a sex fiend, but you can't help noticing things like that. I've had three secretarial jobs, and I've never worked anywhere else where there were so many sexless men.

A woman dean explained the situation more graphically:

> You're asking me what I think of the way these guys look? I *don't.* You work with the same types. You must understand why.

It is difficult to determine how the media developed the image of the sexy college professor with the corduroy jacket and the ever-present pipe. He may be alive and well on the silver screen and in the pages of best sellers, but he is not in abundance at the Faculty Club or meetings of the American Association of University Professors. The typical professor does not resemble Fred MacMurray, Elliott Gould, Donald Sutherland, or any other of the Hollywood types who have portrayed him over the years. If there is a star who most resembles the typical accounting, art history, or seventeenth-century literature professor, it would have to be Woody Allen.

Some college professors have been critical of organized team sports on the campus. This faculty hostility probably results from a conviction that sports receive excessive emphasis and financial support from institutions and seem at odds with academic priorities. But sometimes the fervor appears personal as well as political. Is it possible that student athletes can become surrogates for former classmates who captured attention denied the future college professor? One college coach, countering criticism of the athletic program, inadvertently touched on this possibility. While hardly unbiased, his point of view is a reminder that faculty criticism of athletic programs may be motivated by many factors.

> You want to know the truth? I don't think these guys [faculty] are upset about these boys' grades at all. I don't think they know or care what happens to them. I think what bothers them, what really makes them come down on these kids is they're jealous. You take a look at them—most of them almost pass out once a week on the racquetball court. You think

they like seeing these younger men in top physical condition when they probably couldn't even make manager for the high school team? I don't think they ever forgot that or forgive it, and all the rest of the talk about standards is just that—talk.

A woman professor also noticed how male members of her department raised dubious objections to the football program:

I have to admit when I sit in faculty meetings and listen to the assault on the football program, I detect a certain adolescent hysteria. It's as if the skeletons have come out of the closet, and some of these men are foolish enough to believe they can clothe them with flesh and make them pay for the defeats of the past. If you listen carefully, the debate hinges as much on the perceived ills of athletic types as it does on the economics of football. If I could be certain their opposition to the football program was really based on academic and economic concerns rather than on some perverse need to resurrect and redo the past, my own position would be easier to decide.

There are women professors who are quick to maintain that adolescent attitudes and behaviors color their colleagues' interactions with them. Sometimes they are frustrated and angry for themselves as well as for their students. Jackie T., an instructor in a community college, exclaimed:

There are days when I just want to scream! If I'm late to a faculty meeting, it's like running the goddamned gauntlet or something. There are maybe a hundred people in the room, but all the men in business and math sit together, and having to squeeze past them is a nightmare. These are forty- and fifty-year-old men and they're saying things like, "Hey, you can sit on my lap" or "We've got room for you here, if you don't mind a tight fit." I feel like I'm a sophomore in high school having to pass the greased-up motorcycle gang that used to stand outside until the last bell rang. I really dislike the way they all chuckle and guffaw after one of these remarks—as if to imply that they have some secret bond. They're no different with the students. They make the same kind of disgusting remarks to them in front of other people; and when they talk about

some of the attractive ones, it's even worse. Back to sophomorics. I've seen them stand in a group and do everything but whistle when an attractive student walks by. Two weeks ago I walked into a conversation three of my educated colleagues were having, and it turned out to be a discussion about "what a piece of ass" a student in the economics class of one of them was. The thing that makes me most angry is that I was embarrassed, and they couldn't have cared less.

These are subjective impressions, and there should be caution about opinions unsubstantiated by statistics. In this case, however, there are previously unpublished data to support the thesis that, as adolescents, a majority of male academicians did not fit the masculine stereotype. Coleman's 1957–1958 study, which was replicated several times, included approximately 9,000 male and female students. In 1975, Lloyd Temme, who was then with the Bureau of Social Science Research, composed *The History and Methodology of "The Adolescent Society" Follow-up Study.* Temme was able to locate a remarkably high number of the original participants in the Coleman survey—approximately 85 percent. In his own exhaustive study of these adults, Temme gathered considerable data on their vocational experiences. These records enabled him and his associate Jere Cohen to isolate from the original Coleman sample those individuals who became college professors. They found 120 males who were actively working in the profession.

The results of their findings are significant. One of the questions asked of Coleman's male adolescents was "What do you and the fellows you go around with here at school have most in common? What are the things you do together?" Out of several choices, the most relevant here was "Organized outdoor sports—including football, basketball, tennis, etc." Of those who became college professors, 94.2 percent replied they did not share with friends participation in organized athletics.[18]

Coleman provided five responses to the query "Suppose you had an extra hour in school and could either take some course of your own choosing, or use it for athletics or some other activity, or use it for study hall. How would you use it?" The choices were (1) course, (2) athletics, (3) club or activity, (4) study hall, to study, (5) study hall, to do something else. Future college professors differed most significantly from their peers on the first two items. Most, 41 percent, preferred to use the extra time for a course; only 17.2 percent of the general population selected this item. While 42.6 percent of the total group indicated they would spend the time in athletic activity, 31.6 percent of the subgroup chose this option.

Another item in the Coleman survey read, "Suppose the circle below represented the activities that go on here at school. How far out from the center of things are you?" The number 1 was the center, and 6 the periphery. As adolescents, most academicians viewed themselves at the fringes of the "innie" group: 9.4 percent saw themselves at the center (1), 31.6 percent at point 2, 41.0 percent at point 3, and the remainder in the outer three categories. Keyes and Temme had interesting observations on adolescents who were just beyond the center of status in high school. Keyes reported:

Temme says it's important to distinguish between those who were at the bottom of the social ladder and those who stood on the "second tier," one rung below the top. Those lower in the pecking order get used to being dumped on over time, he speculates, and are less resentful of it. But those on the second tier aren't accustomed to being excluded and resent it bitterly. Adults from the second rung don't lose this resentment after graduation.[19]

Another set of statistics from the sample was college professors' responses to the question "If you could be remembered here at school for one of three things below, which one would you want it to be? Brilliant student, athletic star, most popular." Their responses were the following: brilliant student, 51.0 percent; athletic star, 22.3 percent; most popular, 25.0 percent. These are considerably different from the aggregate responses of 3,696 adolescent boys of whom they are a part: brilliant student, 31.3 percent; athletic star, 43.6 percent; and most popular, 25.0 percent.

Although the future college professors very early defined themselves as different from their male peers, their attitudes toward females were quite typical. Asked whether they would prefer dating a cheerleader, the best-looking girl in class, or the best student in class, their interest in intellectual pursuits lessened considerably. By a majority of 54.5 percent, they preferred the best-looking girl; the cheerleader received the next highest vote, 32.7 percent; and only 12.7 percent were enthusiastic about dating the best female student. The aggregate responses were very similar: best-looking girl, 63.1 percent; cheerleader, 26.1 percent; best female student, 10.8 percent.

When they have been fully analyzed, the Coleman-Temme materials provide fascinating insights into the relationships between adolescence and adult choices, behaviors, and opinions. They serve as a reminder that adults—even the aberrant ones—may not be as mysterious as most choose to believe. Some sexually harassing behavior may logically have roots in adolescence if Temme's assertion is valid: "I think the rest of our lives are spent making up for what we did or didn't do in high school."[20]

This is not to suggest that all college professors were adolescent failures or that high school stereotypes are necessarily desirable. On the contrary, achievement of status in the adolescent society can be seriously detrimental to those who cannot adjust to the demands of the adult world. Emotionally healthy adults translate the superficial standards of adolescence into mature values. But there are some people who never recover from its trauma, and some sexual harassers may be among them.

If physical attractiveness and athletic achievement are the access to status with adolescent females, what is the long-term effect upon the individual outside the high school mainstream? Education is one of the few vocations in which adult males are exposed for extended periods to large groups of very young women at the height of physical desirability. For the few who have never resolved the ego problems developed in adolescent society, this may become a serious difficulty. How do a professor's recollections of adolescence influence his behaviors and attitudes toward the women over whom he exercises power? If he has painful memories of adolescent females, what are his behaviors when the tables are turned and scholarship is finally a symbol of prestige and authority? Is it likely that the past will trigger misuse of power in the present?

Unresolved adolescent conflict may contribute to the motivation of the harasser seeking sex from students. For him, as for other promiscuous men, young women can represent a means of remaking the past. To the professor denied status in high school, the prospect of a relationship with an attractive, desirable student may be especially enticing. It offers not only sexual gratification but also an opportunity to prove, if only to himself, that he can "score" as successfully as any musclebound jock.

A 1980 *Glamour* article paraphrased the statement of a psychiatrist who refused to use her name because "so many of [her] patients [were] involved in [student–professor] relationship[s], and not happily."[21] She believed that such relationships "arise because of the professor's need to take advantage of a younger person who looks for his approval and is probably quite vulnerable. Consciously or not, he is bolstering his ego by choosing from a crop of 'subjects' who are readily attracted to him—thanks to the showmanship of teaching—and readily available to him." In the same article, Dr. Maj-Britt Rosenbaum, associate clinical professor of psychiatry at Albert Einstein College of Medicine, stated, "The male-teacher is the dominant man on campus and . . . has the chance to preen and show off because of the nature of his position."[22]

Arrested adolescent development may also influence the verbal or gender harasser. In high school, football heroes dominate the spotlight and the fantasies of females, but the academic harasser learns that when the setting changes his image can be altered. In *Ah, Men* Burt Avedon emphasized the male's concern about image:

The desire for an image of sexual prowess inheres in almost all males no matter what their income or social position. . . . Sexual conquest is an essential part of the masculine persona. Sexual prowess, or at least the image of sexual prowess, is the goal. Sex is part of a game men play, much like the games they played as boys. The aim is to score. Once they won on the field of play; now they score and win in the great pastures of prurience.[23]

Those denied the recognition that comes from victory "on the field of play" may discover later in life that power is an aphrodisiac and that words aimed at the right audience can be as much of an ego trip as scoring a touchdown. Some professors use sarcasm and repartee about gender and sex to demonstrate that despite their bookishness, they are nevertheless virile and exciting. Others employ words as a way of asserting control and putting women in their place.

Sue W., a senior at a college in Texas, saw both motivations in the verbal harassment of a psychology professor who was "fixated on the parts of girls' bodies":

He was always saying these dumb, off-color things

he thought were real cute. I don't know if he thought they were going to make us like him or if he just wanted to watch us squirm. I *do* know I've heard funnier remarks and seen more grown-up behavior from my fourteen-year-old brother.

A botany major at a large university described the behavior of a verbal harasser even more explicitly:

I was standing in the hall just outside of the student lounge carrying on a discussion with a senior botany major when Dr.——— walked past, stood by the window and called out my name. He motioned for me to come over and I did. He had a roll of lifesavers. He took a green lifesaver from the pack, placed it in the palm of my hand and said, "The green ones make you want to screw." He then gave me a red lifesaver and said, "The red ones make you want to fuck." I tried to put both lifesavers back into his hand; however, he was laughing and refused them, so I put them on his briefcase and said, "That's okay, you can have your lifesavers." He acted surprised and somewhat taken aback, but I walked away and continued to talk with my friend.

Verbal harassment can also be related to insecurities about male bonding. The adolescent boy whose interests are intellectual rather than athletic has a more difficult time feeling a part of the peer group. In adulthood, he may assume that the way to gain peer acceptance is to "be cool" with the women. Whistles, insistence on eye contact, nonreciprocal touching, jokes, and off-color remarks are standard tactics that unsophisticated men suppose to be masculine behaviors. A well-known professor at a large Midwestern university was fond of beginning his first class with a sweeping glance at the women and an injunction to them to "cross your legs and close the gates to hell." It was his way of declaring to the male community his place in the order of things, and he was said to take pride in his reputation. A similar motivation inspired the language of a business instructor whose department head described him as having "locker-room humor." The department head claimed that the professor needed to "feel himself one of the boys" and mistakenly assumed that salacious remarks to and about women were a way of "making the grade with the group."

Bonding can assume more ominous tones, however.

Sometimes protection of turf and preservation of conventions and the status quo are the primary forces underlying harassment. This is the reason that women who enter nontraditional fields suffer so much verbal abuse. Consciously or subconsciously, instructors may try to punish females for invading their ranks, for entering the locker room uninvited. The perpetrators of such offenses claim a standard defense. A law professor stated matter-of-factly:

> Lawyers must learn the element of give and take. Women are no exception to the rule. If they're not prepared to withstand classroom pressure, they don't belong in the courtroom.

A similar view was expressed by an engineering professor:

> If you're going to enter a man's profession, you had better be prepared to take harassment and learn to defend yourself. Engineering has been male territory for years, and our job is to teach these young ladies how to live in it with dignity and calm.

PROFESSIONAL CRISIS

Arrested adolescent development is only one concept that can help explain the behaviors of men who harass. Another is the professional crisis contemporary college professors face. The financial crises facing most campuses in the 1980s mean that college professors, especially those who are younger, confront harsh realities over which they have no control. In the foreseeable future, mobility in most disciplines will be limited, promotion and tenure will be harder to achieve, and salaries will not improve significantly. Since the financial rewards of higher education have never been good, such bleak forecasts only add to the professor's dilemma. Because society sees the academic profession as prestigious, rewarding, and influential, there is widespread confusion about the realities of the profession.

College professors pay thousands of dollars for educations that, at best, qualify them economically for inclusion in the middle class. *The Chronicle of Higher Education* reported that in 1982–1983, the average salary for faculty in all types of higher education institutions was $26,063. The survey did not include instructors, who receive the lowest pay. Its breakdown of average pay for the other three ranks demonstrated

the limited financial mobility of academics: assistant professors, $20,636; associate professors, $24,876; professors, $32,258.[24]

In a 1980 article in *Academe,* Walter F. Abbot, Associate Professor of Sociology at the University of Kentucky, presented a painstaking analysis of recent trends in academic salaries. His thesis confirmed the gravity of the college professor's professional crisis:

> The working poor comprise those who are employed but receive incomes that provide a marginal level of existence. An academic career has traditionally been considered a middle-class occupation that will provide neither an upper-level nor a poverty-level income. . . . [H]owever, if 1970–1977 trends in academic salaries and the poverty-level threshold persist, lower-ranking American academicians may expect to enter the ranks of the working poor in the eighties and faculty in the professor rank will receive an income in 2000 that compares about as well with the poverty threshold as assistant professors at the present time.[25]

In popular myth and movies, college professors live in Victorian houses with wood-burning fireplaces, oak staircases, and paneled, book-lined studies. In reality, many drive secondhand cars, consider themselves fortunate to afford tract housing, and wonder how they will accumulate enough money to send their own children to college. A party of professors often means moving the department or college meeting to someone's basement family room to nibble cheddar cheese and drink wine from Styrofoam cups. This scenario is not all that bleak unless one considers the discrepancy between the ideal and actual worlds of academics. College professors are the people who teach others to appreciate expensive and sophisticated equipment, books, art, theater, and music—all that society recognizes as manifestations of "the good life"—and who cannot readily afford them for themselves or their families.

In *The Male Mid-Life Crisis,* Nancy Mayer pointed out that "in America success has always meant making money and translating it into status or fame,"[26] and the relationship between financial success, power, and sexuality is a frequent topic of psychologists and organization specialists. In their article "The Executive Man and Woman: The Issue of Sexuality," Bradford, Sargent, and Sprague observed:

An important aspect of the sense of self-identity for both males and females is their masculinity and femininity. . . . How do males assert their sexuality? Teenagers resort to fistfighting . . . playing football, and competing against one another to see who can consume more beer or have more dates. While this may do for youth, an educated adult must find more discreet and indirect proofs. . . . For many men, work serves as the major vehicle defining their identity, including sexual identity. . . . Status and pay of the job also bear an element of sexuality. . . . [Men] strive to advance, build up their programs, and compete in meetings partially to obtain status and financial records that connote masculine success, but also to affirm their masculinity more directly.[27]

A professor who sees himself in a static or unsuccessful professional and financial position may choose to exert his masculinity in negative ways. Feelings of frustration and defeat can be displaced onto the women students under his control. He can affirm his authority by being openly abusive to them, or he can turn to them for solace and ego-gratification. The dean of students at a very selective liberal arts college considered such displacement significant in some sexual harassment:

I guess you might say that many men consider access to females one of the perks of the profession. If you don't make a lot of money, if you can't go to Europe without scrimping and sacrificing, if publication of your dream book seems less and less a reality and even promotion becomes a vain hope, life looks fairly dim. It's also not hard to see why some of these men turn to students for comfort or excitement or whatever it is their egos need. Sometimes they're abusive to students because that's a way to deal with their own anger and despair. It's not right, but it's one of the realities we have to live with.

MIDLIFE CRISIS

The frustration and confusion inherent in professional crisis are similar to and sometimes synonymous with those of midlife crisis. Not surprisingly, midlife crisis is the most frequently—if not the only—explanation offered for sexually harassing behavior. Peter A., professor at a large Massachusetts university, voiced this common defense:

Another problem, and one not easily dismissed, is the fact that many of us are in our thirties and forties and are watching our youth slip away at the very time we're in extremely close contact with women who are just coming into bloom. Let me tell you, it's not easy to hit the beginning of a midlife crisis when you're surrounded by nubile twenty-year-olds.[28]

If a man is going to follow the traditional pattern for male midlife crisis, academe is the best of all possible worlds in which to be. Mayer described this period in the male's life:

In response to wrenching change, a man at this stage of life is struggling to revise his own self-image and find dignity in the face of undeniable limitations. More than ever, he needs the confirmation of being seen as a powerful and desirable man—a need that the nubile girl is uniquely suited to satisfy. Our culture's most obvious symbol of hot-blooded sexuality, she can meet the aging male's intensified need for reassurance both in public and in private. . . .

Seeking refuge from the harsh assaults of this midlife period and release from heightened anxieties that haunt and perplex them, [some men in middle age] confirm their manhood through the worshipful gaze of a nubile girl—who mirrors back an image of their most potent self. Contrary to popular wisdom, men in their middle years are generally drawn to younger women not because they want to recapture their youth, but because they need to reconfirm their maturity. . . .

This, then, is the single most seductive reason for the appeal of the nubile girl: A yielding innocent on whom a man can project whatever fantasy he craves, she makes him feel not merely potent, but also omnipotent. A soothing balm indeed. Where else, after all, can the aging male find a sexual partner who will offer applause and adulation without demanding reciprocal attentions? Who will satisfy his emotional needs without requiring him to cater to hers? Only the young can afford to be so selfless.[29]

The enormous advantage that college professors have over men in similar situations is that for them, the stage is already set. Not only are there more than enough "nubile girls" from whom to choose, but they are women who have already been conditioned to regard the teacher as intellectually omnipotent. As individual desires and needs change over time, a wife who is a peer may become intellectually, professionally, or emotionally menacing; the attraction to a younger woman may lie in her lack of competition or threat. A person with whom the professor has no shared history is cleaner, less complicated. If she is also a student, she exhibits all of the deference that comes with discrepancies in roles, experience, and sophistication. A male confused about responding to an older woman's demands may find those of female students more manageable and less intense.

The middle-aged professor suffering from sexual insecurity may find college women especially appealing sexually. Older women may pose not only intellectual and professional threats but also—and perhaps more important—very real sexual pressure. Their sexual demands are greater, and they increase the anxiety of the male in crisis. One man explained to Mayer:

> One thing that's true, though, I think you can get a younger woman to respond to you very strongly. She's going to be less appraising than an older woman. She's had less experience. There are fewer men in her life to which she can compare you. You can dominate her more, sort of impose your myth on her. And you can feel you're initiating her into all sorts of things and blowing her mind and enslaving her—or whatever the hell it is that you want to do with a woman.[30]

The professor whose sexual insecurity contributes to his harassment of students can easily delude himself. He has heard that women students today are freer and engage in intercourse earlier, so taboos about despoiling or deflowering the innocent can be rationalized. At the same time, women students are, by and large, young and lacking the sexual experience of older, more demanding women. Thus the student seems "safe," a novice flattered by the attentions of the professor who can introduce her to the mysterious pleasures of adult sexuality. And the harasser can delude himself into believing that he has done no harm and that the student is responding to his sexuality rather than his position.

Even when sexual activity with the student is the end of harassment, it is not the only motivation. Mayer

noted that contemporary social scientists, "in contrast to Freud, who said all human actions were shaped by sexual needs . . . now suggest the opposite: that sexual activity is often motivated by other needs. Non sexual needs."[31] At any point in a man's life cycle, but especially during midlife, one such need may be competition with other males. The college professor at forty is in an unusual position: he is surrounded by physically desirable young women, as well as by young men in their physical prime. If he has been reared in traditional fashion, he knows that beyond all the myths about male friendships, the truth is that males are taught to relate to one another in one way—competition. Fasteau was clear on this point:

> Competition is the principal mode by which men relate to each other—at one level because they don't know how else to make contact, but more basically because it is the way to demonstrate, to themselves, and others, the key masculine qualities of unwavering toughness and the ability to dominate and control. The result is that they inject competition into situations which don't call for it.[32]

The classroom may be one such situation. Male students represent youth, virility, vigor, uncircumscribed futures—everything the man in midlife crisis may feel himself lacking. Added to this may be the professor's doubts about the masculinity of his profession. The males he teaches in the 1980s are interested in careers in high technology, business, engineering, law, and medicine. His own profession is not especially popular—not only because it does not pay well but also because many men do not view it as particularly masculine. A study by David F. Aberle and Kaspar Naegele found, for instance, that middle-class fathers rejected academic careers for their sons because they did "not consider the academic role to exemplify appropriate masculine behavior."[33] The exception was a father who replied that such a role would be appropriate for his son, who was shy, bookish, and needed women to care for him.

One way a professor can assert his masculinity in such a situation is to prove himself and other males that he is attractive to and can control women. Dean Z., a basketball player at a small college in the Midwest, seemed aware of this possibility:

> Sometimes I think my English prof is trying to tell us something when he tries to make it with the girls.

I could care less if they like him. He's so over the hill he's not really any competition, but he makes a big deal out of trying to show us that he can get our girls.

The harasser in midlife crisis may also be influenced by curiosity about contemporary youth and their lifestyles. The young women who populate the nation's campuses in the 1980s may appear terribly exotic to men who began dating in the 1950s. Alison Lurie's *The War Between the Tates* depicted this condition. Brian Tate, the middle-aged political science professor in the novel, temporarily abandoned his family for Wendy, a seductive student who not only bolstered his ego but also introduced him to a new way of life. Wendy's attraction for Brian resulted in part from her membership in a culture that appeared alien to him:

Brian had known for some time that he and his colleagues were not living in the America they had grown up in; it was only recently though that he had realized they were also not living in present-day America, but in another country or city state with somewhat different characteristics. The important fact about this state, which can for convenience sake be called "University," is that the great majority of its population is aged eighteen to twenty-two. Naturally the physical appearance, interests, activities, preferences and prejudices of this majority are the norm in University. Cultural and political life is geared to their standards, and any deviation from them is a social handicap.

Brian had started life as a member of the dominant class in America, and for years had taken this position for granted. Now, in University, he finally has the experience of being among a depressed minority.[34]

If some sexual harassment is influenced by adolescent, professional, and/or midlife crises, others spring from more disturbing roots that only in-depth analyses of individuals could explain. An undergraduate art student felt that one of her professors was "deeply troubled":

At first I wasn't so scared of him because I figured his line was just like that of all the other guys I knew, even if he was older. I started to get upset when he started saying crazy things to me—like he would like to smear me with grape jelly and paint

me naked. One day he told me that if I was his girlfriend he would tie me up to the bed, and I don't know why but all I could think of was getting the hell out of there. I never went back to his class. And I'm not sorry.

A respondent to the National Advisory Council reported an experience that indicated that harassment is seldom a simple case of "boys will be boys":

All the incidents with this professor share a pattern: indecent exposure. Although the precise circumstances vary, this faculty member (young, supposedly socially conscious) would initiate the incidents by tucking his shirt in, "fixing his belt," or otherwise rearranging his clothing. He is also known to verbally sexually abuse students by initiating discussion on penis size, how he has overcome his inferiority complex about his small penis size and following this with a verbal offer to expose his penis to view. This faculty member has also exposed himself in his home to at least one other graduate student in another department.[35]

Obviously, in such cases only individuals skilled in the study of psychology and familiar with the histories of individual subjects should analyze such behaviors. But most sexual harassment follows a more familiar pattern and is easier to understand. Higher education needs to use its resources to learn more about common causes for the behavior and the motivations of those who engage in it. When that happens, people will recognize that sexual harassment is more controllable than most realize.

If the problem is to be understood, there are a number of issues that researchers need to consider. If, for example, the physical appearance of a woman student is relevant in a discussion of sexual harassment, that of her professor is no less important. If the culture and socialization of contemporary women students is worthy of discussion, that of their instructors must also be taken into account. If students' motivations and self-concepts warrant consideration, those of their teachers are equally relevant. If sex stereotyping influences women's behavior, it must also affect men and must be considered in attempts to analyze the behaviors of harassers. There also needs to be more research on the relationships between sexual attitudes and vocational choice and experiences. Are there preestablished sexual attitudes, behaviors, and opportunities within specific occupational groups that attract certain types of men? How do work experiences and relationships affect men's perceptions of the opposite sex?

To an extent, of course, the motivations of professors who harass will always be enigmatic. Like their colleagues, most are products of traditional sex stereotyping; they are schooled in similar attitudes toward women and sexual codes of ethics. Yet harassers act on their impulses and assumptions when others do not. Harassers either cannot or will not subordinate personal drives and desires to professional ethics. Nonharassers can and do.

If responsible college professors have anything to fear as a result of students' and the public's learning about sexual harassment, it is not that women will make unjust or capricious accusations. The real fear should be that students will hold the institution and the faculty accountable for transgressions of which they *are* guilty. Sexual harassment is deviant behavior, and while those within the institution probably cannot alter the personal psychologies of individual academicians, they *can* influence the campus environment. Aberrant organizational activity may be impossible to eliminate, but it can be curtailed if colleagues refuse to tolerate improprieties.

The behaviors of harassers and nonharassers have become much easier to differentiate as awareness has grown. Many professors, often grudgingly, now monitor their behaviors and avoid questionable interactions with students. They hesitate before making certain kinds of statements or engaging in physical gestures; they pause before placing themselves in questionable situations. And none of that really is so bad. It may be annoying, but it is not wrong or oppressive. If men and women had treated one another with greater sensitivity in the first place, sexual harassment would not be such a problem today. If teachers had approached students with greater sensitivity in the past, students would not seem such enigmas.

The harasser lives by an outlaw code. Relying upon colleagues' reluctance to intervene in student–faculty relationships and the romantic notion that eccentricity is tolerable in academe, he has failed to read the signs of change. Higher education may accept idiosyncratic dress, manners, speech, and interests, but sexual harassment is different from these—less superficial and more threatening to the profession. Once professors realize that their own reputations suffer with that of the harasser, male college professors are likely to find the "eccentricity" of the lecherous professor less tolerable and less deserving of defense.

NOTES

1. Harry Zehner, "Love and Lust on Faculty Row," *Cosmopolitan,* April 1982, pp. 271–72.

2. Anna Sequoia, *The Official J.A.P. Handbook* (New York: New American Library, 1982), pp. 114–15.

3. John Barth, *The End of the Road* (New York: Doubleday, 1958), p. 98.

4. Marilyn B. Brewer, "Further Beyond Nine to Five: An Integration and Future Directions," *Journal of Social Issues* 38 (1982): 155.

5. Rollo May, *Power and Innocence* (New York: Dell, 1972), p. 102.

6. Herb Goldberg, *The Hazards of Being Male* (New York: New American Library, 1976), p. 175.

7. Erik Erikson, *Identity, Youth and Crisis* (New York: Norton, 1968).

8. Ralph Keyes, *Is There Life After High School?* (Boston: Little, Brown, 1976), pp. 94–95.

9. James S. Coleman, *The Adolescent Society* (New York: The Free Press, 1961).

10. Quoted in Nancy G. Clinch, *The Kennedy Neurosis* (New York: Grosset & Dunlap, 1973), p. 266.

11. Marc Feigen Fasteau, *The Male Machine* (New York: McGraw-Hill, 1974), p. 105.

12. Burt Avedon, *Ah, Men* (New York: A & W Publishers, 1980), p. 72.

13. Avedon, p. 45.

14. Ellen Berscheid, Elaine Walster, and George Behrnstedt, "Body Image," *Psychology Today,* November 1973, p. 250.

15. Keyes, p. 10.

16. Keyes, pp. 97, 98.

17. Erica Jong, *Fear of Flying* (New York: Holt, Rinehart and Winston, 1974), p. 188.

18. The data on college professors are derived from James Coleman's *The Adolescent Society* and Lloyd Temme's *"Adolescent Society" Follow-up Study* (Washington, D.C.: Bureau of Social Science, 1976). Temme and his associate Jere Cohen made this previously unreported information available for use in *The Lecherous Professor.* This particular question was selected for analysis to demonstrate that college professors were not among Coleman's athletic "elite." It should be noted that the responses of the total sample were

similar to those of men who became professors; 92 percent of the total gave negative responses to this query.

19. Keyes, p. 56.

20. Keyes, p. 57.

21. Mopsy Strange Kennedy, "'A' for Affairs with the Professor: What Happens When a Student Falls in Love with Her Teacher?" *Glamour,* August, 1980, p. 237.

22. Kennedy, p. 241.

23. Avedon, p. 72.

24. American Association of University Professors, "9-Month Salaries for 1982–83," Fact File, *The Chronicle of Higher Education,* June 22, 1983, p. 20.

25. Walter F. Abbot, "Commentary: When Will Academicians Enter the Ranks of the Working Poor?" *Academe* 66 (October 1980): 349.

26. Nancy Mayer, *The Male Mid-Life Crisis* (New York: New American Library, 1978), p. 164.

27. David Bradford, Alice Sargent, and Melinda Sprague, "The Executive Man and Woman: The Issue of Sexuality," *Bringing Women Into Management,* eds. Francine Gordon and Myra Strober (New York: McGraw-Hill, 1975), pp. 18–19.

28. Zehner, p. 273.

29. Mayer, pp. 107, 111–13.

30. Mayer, p. 108.

31. Mayer, p. 107.

32. Fasteau, p. 11.

33. David F. Aberle and Kaspar Naegele, "Middle-Class Fathers' Occupational Role and Attitudes Toward Children," *American Journal of Orthopsychiatry* 22 (1952): 366.

34. Alison Lurie, *The War Between the Tates* (New York: Warner Books, 1975), p. 40.

35. Frank J. Till, *Sexual Harassment: A Report on the Sexual Harassment of Students,* Report of the National Advisory Council on Women's Education Programs (Washington, D.C.: 1980), p. 23.

R E A D I N G   3 7

"The Man in the Street": Why He Harasses

CHERYL BENARD and EDIT SCHLAFFER

It is a violation of my natural external freedom not to be able to go where I please, and to experience other restrictions of this kind. . . . Even though the body and life are something external, just like property, nevertheless my personality is wounded by such experiences, because my most immediate identity rests in my body.

Hegel, *Texte zur philosophischen Propaedeutik*

I am standing at Wittenbergplatz waiting for the light to turn green, in my left hand I am

carrying a bag filled with groceries . . . behind me I sense the approach of two men and turn my head, at that moment the man on my left reaches for my hair which falls to my shoulders colored with henna, he runs his fingers through my hair experimentally and says to his friend: great hair. . . . An ordinary everyday experience for the colonized in a city of the First World.

Verena Stefan, *Haeutungen*

By the time we are in our twenties we have become accustomed to the laws of the street. The abrupt but regular interruptions of our daily movements have become familiar, we have acquired the habit of overhearing comments, we are graceful at dodging straying

Reprinted from Cheryl Benard and Edit Schlaffer, "'The Man in the Street': Why He Harasses," by permission of the authors.

hands, we have the skill of a general in making rapid strategic evaluations, we can usually tell at a glance whether that group of young men leaning against a car door might use physical intimidation or just jokes, whispered comments, laughter, whether it's worth crossing over to the other side of the street or enough to act nonchalant and cultivate deafness. It's no longer frightening, just annoying, sometimes jolting when one is called abruptly out of a train of thought or a moment of absentmindedness. One gets used to it.

Is all of this normal, inevitable? It was a question I had stopped asking myself by the time I spent a year abroad at the university in Beirut. In the dorm I shared a room with Widad from Bahrein, an 18-year-old who wanted to be a teacher. At home, Widad always wrapped an abaya around her jeans and T-shirt when she went out of the house, and to Widad, the behavior of men on the street was news. Not yet hardened by long experience, Widad spent her first week in Beirut in tears. Sobbing with anger and confusion, she would report on the insulting and unbelievable things that had been said to her, the grabbing, the pushing, the comments, the aggressive looks, the smacking lips, the hissing in her ear. The abaya, she would conclude, has nothing to do with women. In Bahrein we wear it because of the men, someday maybe we won't have to but right now, this is how they are, and who can stand it? The final outcome, I am sorry to report, was not that Widad became hardened and militant, schooled in the martial arts and an example to us all, but that she was instrumental in organizing a group of Bahreini men, so that for the rest of the academic year the women from Bahrein moved through the city like a convoy flanked by a string of guards ready to fight at the sign of a covetous glance.

For the American women, this was an occasion to think again about the kind of world we have learned to accept as normal. On public streets, we plan our routes and our timing as if we were passing through a mine field. We are touched, harassed, commented upon in a stream of constant small-scale assaults, and in a culture which values privacy and anonymity in crowds these intimacies are considered inevitable. Secretly, women like it, popular opinion believes, and posters of men whistling after a woman are thought by advertising agencies to sell their product. Besides, popular opinion goes on to explain, women provoke it, with their fashions, their manner of walking, their behavior. These are familiar arguments; we hear them whenever the

subject of violence against women comes up. There are few facts to hold up against them. Stamped as trivial, the harassment of women has received no attention from sociology, and cities that regulate almost everything from bicycles and dogs to the use of roller skates in order to keep the traffic moving have no ordinances or rules to guarantee women the right to free passage.

What kinds of men harass women, what do they think they are doing, how do women feel about it? Diaries and essays by women, and reports from other times and cultures, give some very sketchy information. For a more systematic picture, we observed the behavior of men in four cities (Berlin, Los Angeles, Rome, and Vienna) over the period of a year, allowing for differences in season, time of day, and part of town. Interviews with women provided information on how the victims feel. Some of the results were surprising and some were depressingly predictable.

That the behavior of the "man on the street" has received so little attention is odd, because it captures in quintessential, almost primordial form the combination of the ordinary and the bizarre which we have learned to regard as normal. The "man on the street" is a synonym for everyone, which in our society means every man. The behavior he casually accords to randomly passing women he has never seen before serves to identify him as a member of the ruling group, to whom the streets and the society belong. And at the same time this behavior, looked at with an analytic eye, is very peculiar. The anthropologist from outer space, that popular device for viewing the world with a bit more perspective, would be very astonished to find adult males moaning, jumping, whistling, singing, honking, winking, contorting face and body, hissing obscenities, laughing hysterically, and mumbling hoarse endearments to perfect strangers without apparent provocation. However odd, though, these single and seemingly irrational instances add up to a pattern, and the pattern spells intimidation.

Women are assigned, in this interaction, an inevitably passive part. They have a number of available responses, but their response makes little difference. A woman can ignore what she sees or hears, she can reply, she can curse, keep walking, stop, try for a disarming smile, get angry, start a discussion. What she does has little influence. A friendly answer may stop the man, or it may encourage him to further intimacies; threats and curses may silence him, or they may prompt genuine aggression. The language itself puts us at a permanent disadvantage; it is hard to exchange serious insults without using sexual putdowns that invariably go against women. And passers-by, far from supporting a woman who defends herself, will shed their former indifference to disapprove of feminine vulgarity.

It is commonly supposed that certain countries and cultures display this behavior more than others; the Mediterranean cultures, particularly, are assumed to be swarming with papagallos dedicated to the female foreign tourist. In fact, this form of male behavior is distributed quite evenly across the continents, races, and generations. The nationalist author Qasim Amin deplored the harassment of the heavily veiled Egyptian women at the turn of the century and in fact attributed masculine aggression to the veil. As a sign of women's inferior status, he argued, it encouraged men to treat them with disrespect and take liberties. This interpretation comes very close to the truth. Like other forms of sexual violence, harassment has little to do with the individual woman and nothing to do with sex; the issue is power.

Whether you wear a slit skirt or are covered from head to foot in a black chador, the message is not that you are attractive enough to make a man lose his self-control but that the public realm belongs to him and you are there by his permission as long as you follow his rules and as long as you remember your place. Badr-al-Moluk Bamdad recalls in her book on growing up in Iran that there was no way for a woman to win this game; if, in the opinion of any passing male, one's veil was not wrapped with sufficient modesty, one could be insulted, reprimanded, and threatened, while if obediently covered one would be followed and taunted by boys and young men shouting that one looked like a "black crow or an inkwell."*

Harassment of women is timeless, but the notion that women really like it and feel flattered is a refinement that has been added more recently. Women's own accounts have always shown a clear awareness of the essential hostility implied by these male attentions, even when they didn't put that awareness into the context of any more general picture of sexist structures. Descriptions have been handed down to us from many different sources. Evelyn Scott, an American woman who later was to become a successful author, spent the

year of 1916 in Brazil with her lover. They were poor, she was pregnant. In her diary, she wrote that, in Rio, "something objectionable always occurred" when she went outdoors unaccompanied. "Perhaps it is because I am only 20 years old," she wrote. "Perhaps it is because I am shabbily dressed. I know perfectly well that I am not particularly pretty. Inwardly shrinking and cold with an obscure fear, I make it a point to look very directly at all the men who speak to me. I want to shame them by the straightforwardness of my gaze. Perhaps I am ridiculous. If I could consider sex more factually and with less mystical solemnity I might find amusement in the stupidity of these individuals who can't be so sinister after all."*

Anger and an "obscure fear" are the most common responses of women, and those feelings are all the greater when the situation seems too intimidating to allow a reply. Pretending to have heard nothing, looking away, hoping the men will get bored and stop or will be too busy with the woman walking in front of you to attend to you are calculations that increase the impact of the experience. A 22-year-old law student remembered one pivotal incident in her life: "I was 17, and just walking around downtown with my friend Marie. Two men started talking to us, making jokes and telling us to come with them. They grabbed our arms and tried to pull us along. Marie got angry and told them to let us go. The men pushed her against a building and started shaking her and saying she was unfriendly and stuck up and should watch out. Finally they left. It was afternoon and there were a lot of people around, but nobody said anything. At the time I learned from that that it was better to ignore men who talked to you like that. If you act like you don't care, they usually let you go without any trouble. I don't think that's a very good conclusion to draw, but I still don't know how to act in situations like that without getting into trouble."

What is going on in the minds of the men who do this? Not much, judging from their difficulties in articulating their intentions. We interviewed 60 men, choosing a range of age groups out of those who addressed us on the street. (Incidentally, this was the only female response we found that genuinely and predictably disarms the harassing male, so if you want to transform a lewdly smirking man into a politely confused one

---

*Badr-al-Moluk Bamdad, *Women's Emancipation in Iran* (New York, 1977).

*Mary Jane Moffat and Charlotte Painter, eds., *Revelations: Diaries of Women* (New York: Vintage, 1974), p. 100.

within a matter of seconds you need only pull a mimeographed questionnaire out of your bag and inform him that he is part of a research project. This method, however, is rather time-consuming.) Pressed for an explanation of their behavior, most of the men initially played it down. Boredom and a feeling of youthful camaraderie that came over them when discussing women with other men emerged as the most frequent feelings prompting harassment. The notion that women disliked this and felt infringed upon in their freedom of movement was a novel one for most men, not because they had another image of the woman's response but because they had never given it any thought at all. Only a minority, around 15%, explicitly set out to anger or humiliate their victims. This is the same group that employs graphic sexual commentary and threats. Other forms of antagonism often become mixed up with the sexual. Some migrant laborers or construction workers insult not so much the woman as the snobbish privileged class she symbolizes to them. Another minority of men believes with firm conviction that women enjoy receiving their attention. One 45-year-old construction worker portrayed himself as a kind of benefactor to womanhood and claimed to specialize in older and less attractive women to whom, he was sure, his display of sexual interest was certain to be the highlight in an otherwise drab and joyless existence. A significant group of men, around 20%, said that they would not engage in this behavior when alone, but only in the company of male friends. This supports the explanation that the harassment of women is a form of male bonding, of demonstrating solidarity and joint power.

The symbolic nature of the behavior is its most important attribute. A surprising finding was that harassment declines in the late evening and during the night, and that men are then more likely to display the kind of behavior typical of the avoidance usually shown to strangers in public or crowded situations: averting one's eyes, accelerating the pace of walking to keep a distance, etc. At first glance, this finding is sur-

prising. It would seem that harassment would be even more effective at night, even more intimidating to the woman. Probably, this is precisely the reason it declines during the night; on a deserted street, it would be *too* effective. The woman, not merely annoyed or unnerved but genuinely alarmed, might well be driven to an "extreme" response (such as calling for help) that the good citizen would not like to have to explain. In the daytime, he takes no such risk. The age, education, and income of the man make little difference; in their street behavior, they revert to a primordially uniform condition across the lines of class and generation. Younger men tend to be more aggressive, and older men to lower their voices and whisper hastily as they pass you. Some areas are exempt altogether: small villages, where all the inhabitants know each other, and residential suburban areas.

The genuinely *public* world is the main arena for harassment. The street, as a place where strangers encounter each other, is also the place where societies have always taken care to clearly mark the lines of order and status. It is on the streets that members of subordinate groups have to wear special clothing or identifying marks, that they must salute, take off their hat, or jump down from the sidewalk to make way for the members of the superior group. Harassment is a way of ensuring that women will not feel at ease, that they will remember their role as sexual beings available to men and not consider themselves equal citizens participating in public life. But the ritual of harassment does more than that. By its seeming harmlessness and triviality, it blurs the borders of women's right to personal integrity, and encourages men who would never commit a violent crime against a strange woman to participate in minor transgressions against her right to move freely, to choose which interactions to participate in and which people to communicate with. By making of the "man on the street," the average man, a minor sex offender, it also makes him an accomplice in the more massive forms of violence against women.

Fraternities and Rape on Campus

PATRICIA YANCEY MARTIN and ROBERT A. HUMMER

Rapes are perpetrated on dates, at parties, in chance encounters, and in specially planned circumstances. That group structure and processes, rather than individual values or characteristics, are the impetus for many rape episodes was documented by Blanchard (1959) 30 years ago (also see Geis 1971), yet sociologists have failed to pursue this theme (for an exception, see Chancer 1987). A recent review of research (Muehlenhard and Linton 1987) on sexual violence, or rape, devotes only a few pages to the situational contexts of rape events, and these are conceptualized as potential risk factors for individuals rather than qualities of rape-prone social contexts.

Many rapes, far more than come to the public's attention, occur in fraternity houses on college and university campuses, yet little research has analyzed fraternities at American colleges and universities as rape-prone contexts (cf. Ehrhart and Sandler 1985). Most of the research on fraternities reports on samples of individual fraternity men. One group of studies compares the values, attitudes, perceptions, family socioeconomic status, psychological traits (aggressiveness, dependence), and so on, of fraternity and nonfraternity men (Bohrnstedt 1969; Fox, Hodge, and Ward 1987; Kanin 1967; Lemire 1979; Miller 1973). A second group attempts to identify the effects of fraternity membership over time on the values, attitudes, beliefs, or moral precepts of members (Hughes and Winston 1987; Marlowe and Auvenshine 1982; Miller 1973; Wilder, Hoyt, Doren, Hauck, and Zettle 1978; Wilder, Hoyt, Surbeck, Wilder, and Carney 1986). With minor exceptions, little research addresses the group and organizational context of fraternities or the social

From *Gender & Society*, vol. 3, no. 4, December 1989. Copyright © 1989 Sociologists for Women in Society. Reprinted by permission of Sage Publications, Inc.

construction of fraternity life (for exceptions, see Letchworth 1969; Longino and Kart 1973; Smith 1964).

Gary Tash, writing as an alumnus and trial attorney in his fraternity's magazine, claims that over 90 percent of all gang rapes on college campuses involve fraternity men (1988, p. 2). Tash provides no evidence to substantiate this claim, but students of violence against women have been concerned with fraternity men's frequently reported involvement in rape episodes (Adams and Abarbanel 1988). Ehrhart and Sandler (1985) identify over 50 cases of gang rapes on campus perpetrated by fraternity men, and their analysis points to many of the conditions that we discuss here. Their analysis is unique in focusing on conditions in fraternities that make gang rapes of women by fraternity men both feasible and probable. They identify excessive alcohol use, isolation from external monitoring, treatment of women as prey, use of pornography, approval of violence, and excessive concern with competition as precipitating conditions to gang rape (also see Merton 1985; Roark 1987).

The study reported here confirmed and complemented these findings by focusing on both conditions and processes. We examined dynamics associated with the social construction of fraternity life, with a focus on processes that foster the use of coercion, including rape, in fraternity men's relations with women. Our examination of men's social fraternities on college and university campuses as groups and organizations led us to conclude that fraternities are a physical and sociocultural context that encourages the sexual coercion of women. We make no claims that all fraternities are "bad" or that all fraternity men are rapists. Our observations indicated, however, that rape is especially probable in fraternities because of the kinds of organizations they are, the kinds of members they have, the practices their members engage in, and a virtual absence of university or community oversight. Analyses that lay blame for rapes by fraternity men on "peer pressure" are, we feel, overly simplistic (cf. Burkhart 1989; Walsh 1989). We suggest, rather, that fraternities create a sociocultural context in which the use of coercion in sexual relations with women is normative and in which the mechanisms to keep this pattern of behavior in check are minimal at best and absent at worst. We conclude that unless fraternities change in fundamental ways, little improvement can be expected.

METHODOLOGY

Our goal was to analyze the group and organizational practices and conditions that create in fraternities an abusive social context for women. We developed a conceptual framework from an initial case study of an alleged gang rape at Florida State University that involved four fraternity men and an 18-year-old coed. The group rape took place on the third floor of a fraternity house and ended with the "dumping" of the woman in the hallway of a neighboring fraternity house. According to newspaper accounts, the victim's blood-alcohol concentration, when she was discovered, was .349 percent, more than three times the legal limit for automobile driving and an almost lethal amount. One law enforcement officer reported that sexual intercourse occurred during the time the victim was unconscious: "She was in a life-threatening situation" (*Tallahassee Democrat,* 1988b). When the victim was found, she was comatose and had suffered multiple scratches and abrasions. Crude words and a fraternity symbol had been written on her thighs (*Tampa Tribune,* 1988). When law enforcement officials tried to investigate the case, fraternity members refused to cooperate. This led, eventually, to a five-year ban of the fraternity from campus by the university and by the fraternity's national organization.

In trying to understand how such an event could have occurred, and how a group of over 150 members (exact figures are unknown because the fraternity refused to provide a membership roster) could hold rank, deny knowledge of the event, and allegedly lie to a grand jury, we analyzed newspaper articles about the case and conducted open-ended interviews with a variety of respondents about the case and about fraternities, rapes, alcohol use, gender relations, and sexual activities on campus. Our data included over 100 newspaper articles on the initial gang rape case; open-ended

interviews with Greek (social fraternity and sorority) and non-Greek (independent) students (N = 20); university administrators (N = 8, five men, three women); and alumni advisers to Greek organizations (N = 6). Open-ended interviews were held also with judges, public and private defense attorneys, victim advocates, and state prosecutors regarding the processing of sexual assault cases. Data were analyzed using the grounded theory method (Glaser 1978; Martin and Turner 1986). In the following analysis, concepts generated from the data analysis are integrated with the literature on men's social fraternities, sexual coercion, and related issues.

FRATERNITIES AND THE SOCIAL CONSTRUCTION OF MEN AND MASCULINITY

Our research indicated that fraternities are vitally concerned—more than with anything else—with masculinity (cf. Kanin 1967). They work hard to create a macho image and context and try to avoid any suggestion of "wimpishness," effeminacy, and homosexuality. Valued members display, or are willing to go along with, a narrow conception of masculinity that stresses competition, athleticism, dominance, winning, conflict, wealth, material possessions, willingness to drink alcohol, and sexual prowess vis-à-vis women.

Valued Qualities of Members

When fraternity members talked about the kind of pledges they prefer, a litany of stereotypical and narrowly masculine attributes and behaviors was recited and feminine or woman-associated qualities and behaviors were expressly denounced (cf. Merton 1985). Fraternities seek men who are "athletic," "big guys," good in intramural competition, "who can talk college sports." Males, "who are willing to drink alcohol," "who drink socially," or "who can hold their liquor" are sought. Alcohol and activities associated with the recreational use of alcohol are cornerstones of fraternity social life. Nondrinkers are viewed with skepticism and rarely selected for membership.[*]

[*]Recent bans by some universities on open-keg parties at fraternity houses have resulted in heavy drinking before coming to a party and an increase in drunkenness among those who attend. This may aggravate, rather than improve, the treatment of women by fraternity men at parties.

Fraternities try to avoid "geeks," nerds, and men said to give the fraternity a "wimpy" or "gay" reputation. Art, music, and humanities majors, majors in traditional women's fields (nursing, home economics, social work, education), men with long hair, and those whose appearance or dress violate current norms are rejected. Clean-cut, handsome men who dress well (are clean, neat, conforming, fashionable) are preferred. One sorority woman commented that "the top ranking fraternities have the best looking guys."

One fraternity man, a senior, said his fraternity recruited "some big guys, very athletic" over a two-year period to help overcome its image of wimpiness. His fraternity had won the interfraternity competition for highest grade-point average several years running but was looked down on as "wimpy, dancy, even gay." With their bigger, more athletic recruits, "our reputation improved; we're a much more recognized fraternity now." Thus a fraternity's reputation and status depends on members' possession of stereotypically masculine qualities. Good grades, campus leadership, and community service are "nice" but masculinity dominance—for example, in athletic events, physical size of members, athleticism of members—counts most.

Certain social skills are valued. Men are sought who "have good personalities," are friendly, and "have the ability to relate to girls" (cf. Longino and Kart 1973). One fraternity man, a junior, said: "We watch a guy [a potential pledge] talk to women . . . we want guys who can relate to girls." Assessing a pledge's ability to talk to women is, in part, a preoccupation with homosexuality and a conscious avoidance of men who seem to have effeminate manners or qualities. If a member is suspected of being gay, he is ostracized and informally drummed out of the fraternity. A fraternity with a reputation as wimpy or tolerant of gays is ridiculed and shunned by other fraternities. Militant heterosexuality is frequently used by men as a strategy to keep each other in line (Kimmel 1987).

Financial affluence or wealth, a male-associated value in American culture, is highly valued by fraternities. In accounting for why the fraternity involved in the gang rape that precipitated our research project had been recognized recently as "the best fraternity chapter in the United States," a university official said: "They were good-looking, a big fraternity, had lots of BMWs [expensive, German-made automobiles]." After the rape, newspaper stories described the fraternity members' affluence, noting the high number of members who owned expensive cars (*St. Petersburg Times,* 1988).

The Status and Norms of Pledgeship

A pledge (sometimes called an associate member) is a new recruit who occupies a trial membership status for a specific period of time. The pledge period (typically ranging from 10 to 15 weeks) gives fraternity brothers an opportunity to assess and socialize new recruits. Pledges evaluate the fraternity also and decide if they want to become brothers. The socialization experience is structured partly through assignment of a Big Brother to each pledge. Big Brothers are expected to teach pledges how to become a brother and to support them as they progress through the trial membership period. Some pledges are repelled by the pledging experience, which can entail physical abuse; harsh discipline; and demands to be subordinate, follow orders, and engage in demeaning routines and activities, similar to those used by the military to "make men out of boys" during boot camp.

Characteristics of the pledge experience are rationalized by fraternity members as necessary to help pledges unite into a group, rely on each other, and join together against outsiders. The process is highly masculinist in execution as well as conception. A willingness to submit to authority, follow orders, and do as one is told is viewed as a sign of loyalty, togetherness, and unity. Fraternity pledges who find the pledge process offensive often drop out. Some do this by openly quitting, which can subject them to ridicule by brothers and other pledges, or they may deliberately fail to make the grades necessary for initiation or transfer schools and decline to reaffiliate with the fraternity on the new campus. One fraternity pledge who quit the fraternity he had pledged described an experience during pledgeship as follows:

This one guy was always picking on me. No matter what I did, I was wrong. One night after dinner, he and two other guys called me and two other pledges into the chapter room. He said, "Here, X, hold this 25 pound bag of ice at arms' length 'til I tell you to stop." I did it even though my arms and hands were killing me. When I asked if I could stop, he grabbed me around the throat and lifted me off the floor. I thought he would choke me to death. He cussed me and called me all kinds of names. He took one of my fingers and twisted it until it nearly broke. . . . I stayed in the fraternity for a few more days, but then I decided to quit. I hated it. Those guys are sick. They like seeing you suffer.

Fraternities' emphasis on toughness, withstanding pain and humiliation, obedience to superiors, and using physical force to obtain compliance contributes to an interpersonal style that de-emphasizes caring and sensitivity but fosters intragroup trust and loyalty. If the least macho or most critical pledges drop out, those who remain may be more receptive to, and influenced by, masculinist values and practices that encourage the use of force in sexual relations with women and the covering up of such behavior (cf. Kanin 1967).

Norms and Dynamics of Brotherhood

Brother is the status occupied by fraternity men to indicate their relations to each other and their membership in a particular fraternity organization or group. Brother is a male-specific status; only males can become brothers, although women can become "Little Sisters," a form of pseudomembership. "Becoming a brother" is a rite of passage that follows the consistent and often lengthy display by pledges of appropriately masculine qualities and behaviors. Brothers have a quasi-familial relationship with each other, are normatively said to share bonds of closeness and support, and are sharply set off from nonmembers. Brotherhood is a loosely defined term used to represent the bonds that develop among fraternity members and the obligations and expectations incumbent upon them (cf. Marlowe and Auvenshine [1982] on fraternities' failure to encourage "moral development" in freshman pledges).

Some of our respondents talked about brotherhood in almost reverential terms, viewing it as the most valuable benefit of fraternity membership. One senior, a business-school major who had been affiliated with a fairly high-status fraternity throughout four years on campus, said:

Brotherhood spurs friendship for life, which I consider its best aspect, although I didn't see it that way when I joined. Brotherhood bonds and unites. It instills values of caring about one another, caring about community, caring about ourselves. The values and bonds [of brotherhood] continually develop over the four years [in college] while normal friendships come and go.

Despite this idealization, most aspects of fraternity practice and conception are more mundane. Brotherhood often plays itself out as an overriding concern with masculinity and, by extension, femininity. As a consequence, fraternities comprise collectivities of highly masculinized men with attitudinal qualities and behavioral norms that predispose them to sexual coercion of women (cf. Kanin 1967; Merton 1985; Rapaport and Burkhart 1984). The norms of masculinity are complemented by conceptions of women and femininity that are equally distorted and stereotyped and that may enhance the probability of women's exploitation (cf. Ehrhart and Sandler 1985; Sanday 1981, 1986).

Practices of Brotherhood

Practices associated with fraternity brotherhood that contribute to the sexual coercion of women include a preoccupation with loyalty, group protection and secrecy, use of alcohol as a weapon, involvement in violence and physical force, and an emphasis on competition and superiority.

Loyalty, Group Protection, and Secrecy Loyalty is a fraternity preoccupation. Members are reminded constantly to be loyal to the fraternity and to their brothers. Among other ways, loyalty is played out in the practices of group protection and secrecy. The fraternity must be shielded from criticism. Members are admonished to avoid getting the fraternity in trouble and to bring all problems "to the chapter" (local branch of a national social fraternity) rather than to outsiders. Fraternities try to protect themselves from close scrutiny and criticism by the Interfraternity Council (a quasi-governing body composed of representatives from all social fraternities on campus), their fraternity's national office, university officials, law enforcement, the media, and the public. Protection of the fraternity often takes precedence over what is procedurally, ethically, or legally correct. Numerous examples were related to us of fraternity brothers' lying to outsiders to "protect the fraternity."

Group protection was observed in the alleged gang rape case with which we began our study. Except for one brother, a rapist who turned state's evidence, the entire remaining fraternity membership was accused by university and criminal justice officials of lying to protect the fraternity. Members consistently failed to cooperate even though the alleged crimes were felonies, involved only four men (two of whom were not even members of the local chapter), and the victim of the crime nearly died. According to a grand jury's findings, fraternity officers repeatedly broke appointments with law enforcement officials, refused to provide police with a list of members, and refused to cooperate with police and prosecutors investigating the case (*Florida Flambeau*, 1988).

Secrecy is a priority value and practice in fraternities, partly because full-fledged membership is premised on it (for confirmation, see Ehrhart and Sandler 1985; Longino and Kart 1973; Roark 1987). Secrecy is also a boundary-maintaining mechanism, demarcating in-group from out-group, us from them. Secret rituals, handshakes, and mottoes are revealed to pledge brothers as they are initiated into full brotherhood. Since only brothers are supposed to know a fraternity's secrets, such knowledge affirms membership in the fraternity and separates a brother from others. Extending secrecy tactics from protection of private knowledge to protection of the fraternity from criticism is a predictable development. Our interviews indicated that individual members knew the difference between right and wrong, but fraternity norms that emphasize loyalty, group protection, and secrecy often overrode standards of ethical correctness.

Alcohol as Weapon   Alcohol use by fraternity men is normative. They use it on weekdays to relax after class and on weekends to "get drunk," "get crazy," and "get laid." The use of alcohol to obtain sex from women is pervasive—in other words, it is used as a weapon against sexual reluctance. According to several fraternity men whom we interviewed, alcohol is the major tool used to gain sexual mastery over women (cf. Adams and Abarbanel 1988; Ehrhart and Sandler 1985). One fraternity man, a 21-year-old senior, described alcohol use to gain sex as follows: "There are girls that you know will fuck, then some you have to put some effort into it. . . . You have to buy them drinks or find out if she's drunk enough. . . ."

A similar strategy is used collectively. A fraternity man said that at parties with Little Sisters: "We provide them with 'hunch punch' and things get wild. We get them drunk and most of the guys end up with one." "'Hunch punch,'" he said, "is a girls' drink made up of

overproof alcohol and powdered Kool-Aid, no water or anything, just ice. It's very strong. Two cups will do a number on a female." He had plans in the next academic term to surreptitiously give hunch punch to women in a "prim and proper" sorority because "having sex with prim and proper sorority girls is definitely a goal." These women are a challenge because they "won't openly consume alcohol and won't get openly drunk as hell." Their sororities have "standards committees" that forbid heavy drinking and easy sex.

In the gang rape case, our sources said that many fraternity men on campus believed the victim had a drinking problem and was thus an "easy make." According to newspaper accounts, she had been drinking alcohol on the evening she was raped; the lead assailant is alleged to have given her a bottle of wine after she arrived at his fraternity house. Portions of the rape occurred in a shower, and the victim was reportedly so drunk that her assailants had difficulty holding her in a standing position (*Tallahassee Democrat,* 1988a). While raping her, her assailants repeatedly told her they were members of another fraternity under the apparent belief that she was too drunk to know the difference. Of course, if she was too drunk to know who they were, she was too drunk to consent to sex (cf. Allgeier 1986; Tash 1988).

One respondent told us that gang rapes are wrong and can get one expelled, but he seemed to see nothing wrong in sexual coercion one-on-one. He seemed unaware that the use of alcohol to obtain sex from a woman is grounds for a claim that a rape occurred (cf. Tash 1988). Few women on campus (who also may not know these grounds) report date rapes, however; so the odds of detection and punishment are slim for fraternity men who use alcohol for "seduction" purposes (cf. Byington and Keeter 1988; Merton 1985).

Violence and Physical Force   Fraternity men have a history of violence (Ehrhart and Sandler 1985; Roark 1987). Their record of hazing, fighting, property destruction, and rape has caused them problems with insurance companies (Bradford 1986; Pressley 1987). Two university officials told us that fraternities "are the third riskiest property to insure behind toxic waste dumps and amusement parks." Fraternities are increasingly defendants in legal actions brought by pledges subjected to hazing (Meyer 1986; Pressley 1987) and by women who were raped by one or more members. In a recent alleged gang rape incident at another Florida university, prosecutors failed to file charges but the victim filed a civil suit against the fraternity nevertheless (*Tallahassee Democrat,* 1989).

Competition and Superiority   Interfraternity rivalry fosters in-group identification and out-group hostility. Fraternities stress pride of membership and superiority over other fraternities as major goals. Interfraternity rivalries take many forms, including competition for desirable pledges, size of pledge class, size of membership, size and appearance of fraternity house, superiority in intramural sports, highest grade-point averages, giving the best parties, gaining the best or most campus leadership roles, and, of great importance, attracting and displaying "good looking women." Rivalry is particularly intense over members, intramural sports, and women (cf. Messner 1989).

FRATERNITIES' COMMODIFICATION OF WOMEN

In claiming that women are treated by fraternities as commodities, we mean that fraternities knowingly, and intentionally, *use* women for their benefit. Fraternities use women as bait for new members, as servers of brothers' needs, and as sexual prey.

Women as Bait

Fashionably attractive women help a fraternity attract new members. As one fraternity man, a junior, said, "They are good bait." Beautiful, sociable women are believed to impress the right kind of pledges and give the impression that the fraternity can deliver this type of woman to its members. Photographs of shapely, attractive coeds are printed in fraternity brochures and videotapes that are distributed and shown to potential pledges. The women pictured are often dressed in bikinis, at the beach, and are pictured hugging the brothers of the fraternity. One university official says such recruitment materials give the message: "Hey, they're here for you, you can have whatever you want," and, "we have the best looking women. Join us and you can have them too." Another commented: "Something's wrong when males join an all-male organization as the best place to meet women. It's so illogical."

Fraternities compete in promising access to beautiful women. One fraternity man, a senior, commented

that "the attraction of girls [i.e., a fraternity's success in attracting women] is a big status symbol for fraternities." One university official commented that the use of women as a recruiting tool is so well entrenched that fraternities that might be willing to forgo it say they cannot afford to unless other fraternities do so as well. One fraternity man said, "Look, if we don't have Little Sisters, the fraternities that do will get all the good pledges." Another said, "We won't have as good a rush [the period during which new members are assessed and selected] if we don't have these women around."

In displaying good-looking, attractive, skimpily dressed, nubile women to potential members, fraternities implicitly, and sometimes explicitly, promise sexual access to women. One fraternity man commented that "part of what being in a fraternity is all about is the sex" and explained how his fraternity uses Little Sisters to recruit new members:

> We'll tell the sweetheart [the fraternity's term for Little Sister], "You're gorgeous; you can get him." We'll tell her to fake a scam and she'll go hang all over him during a rush party, kiss him, and he thinks he's done wonderful and wants to join. The girls think it's great too. It's flattering for them.

Women as Servers

The use of women as servers is exemplified in the Little Sister program. Little Sisters are undergraduate women who are rushed and selected in a manner parallel to the recruitment of fraternity men. They are affiliated with the fraternity in a formal but unofficial way and are able, indeed required, to wear the fraternity's Greek letters. Little Sisters are not full-fledged fraternity members, however; and fraternity national offices and most universities do not register or regulate them. Each fraternity has an officer called Little Sister Chairman who oversees their organization and activities. The Little Sisters elect officers among themselves, pay monthly dues to the fraternity, and have well-defined roles. Their dues are used to pay for the fraternity's social events, and Little Sisters are expected to attend and hostess fraternity parties and hang around the house to make it a "nice place to be." One fraternity man, a senior, described Little Sisters this way: "They are very social girls, willing to join in, be affiliated with the group, devoted to the fraternity." Another member, a sophomore, said: "Their sole purpose is social—attend parties, attract new members, and 'take care' of the guys."

Our observations and interviews suggested that women selected by fraternities as Little Sisters are physically attractive, possess good social skills, and are willing to devote time and energy to the fraternity and its members. One undergraduate woman gave the following job description for Little Sisters to a campus newspaper:

> It's not just making appearances at all the parties but entails many more responsibilities. You're going to be expected to go to all the intramural games to cheer the brothers on, support and encourage the pledges, and just be around to bring some extra life to the house. [As a Little Sister] you have to agree to take on a new responsibility other than studying to maintain your grades and managing to keep your checkbook from bouncing. You have to make time to be a part of the fraternity and support the brothers in all they do. (*The Tomahawk*, 1988)

The title of Little Sister reflects women's subordinate status; fraternity men in a parallel role are called Big Brothers. Big Brothers assist a sorority primarily with the physical work of sorority rushes, which, compared to fraternity rushes, are more formal, structured, and intensive. Sorority rushes take place in the daytime and fraternity rushes at night so fraternity men are free to help. According to one fraternity member, Little Sister status is a benefit to women because it gives them a social outlet and "the protection of the brothers." The gender-stereotypic conceptions and obligations of these Little Sister and Big Brother statuses indicate that fraternities and sororities promote a gender hierarchy on campus that fosters subordination and dependence in women, thus encouraging sexual exploitation and the belief that it is acceptable.

Women as Sexual Prey

Little Sisters are a sexual utility. Many Little Sisters do not belong to sororities and lack peer support for refraining from unwanted sexual relations. One fraternity man (whose fraternity has 65 members and 85 Little Sisters) told us they had recruited "wholesale" in the prior year to "get lots of new women." The structural access to women that the Little Sister program

provides and the absence of normative supports for refusing fraternity members' sexual advances may make women in this program particularly susceptible to coerced sexual encounters with fraternity men.

Access to women for sexual gratification is a presumed benefit of fraternity membership, promised in recruitment materials and strategies and through brothers' conversations with new recruits. One fraternity man said: "We always tell the guys that you get sex all the time, there's always new girls. . . . After I became a Greek, I found out I could be with females at will." A university official told us that, based on his observations, "no one [i.e., fraternity men] on this campus wants to have 'relationships.' They just want to have fun [i.e., sex]." Fraternity men plan and execute strategies aimed at obtaining sexual gratification, and this occurs at both individual and collective levels.

Individual strategies include getting a woman drunk and spending a great deal of money on her. As for collective strategies, most of our undergraduate interviewees agreed that fraternity parties often culminate in sex and that this outcome is planned. One fraternity man said fraternity parties often involve sex and nudity and can "turn into orgies." Orgies may be planned in advance, such as the Bowery Ball party held by one fraternity. A former fraternity member said of this party:

> The entire idea behind this is sex. Both men and women come to the party wearing little or nothing. There are pornographic pinups on the walls and usually porno movies playing on the TV. The music carries sexual overtones. . . . They just get schnockered [drunk] and, in most cases, they also get laid.

When asked about the women who come to such a party, he said: "Some Little Sisters just won't go. . . . The girls who do are looking for a good time, girls who don't know what it is, things like that."

Other respondents denied that fraternity parties are orgies but said that sex is always talked about among the brothers and they all know "who each other is doing it with." One member said that most of the time, guys have sex with their girlfriends "but with socials, girlfriends aren't allowed to come and it's their [members'] big chance [to have sex with other women]." The use of alcohol to help them get women into bed is a routine strategy at fraternity parties.

CONCLUSIONS

In general, our research indicated that the organization and membership of fraternities contribute heavily to coercive and often violent sex. Fraternity houses are occupied by same-sex (all men) and same-age (late teens, early twenties) peers whose maturity and judgment is often less than ideal. Yet fraternity houses are private dwellings that are mostly off-limits to, and away from scrutiny of, university and community representatives, with the result that fraternity house events seldom come to the attention of outsiders. Practices associated with the social construction of fraternity brotherhood emphasize a macho conception of men and masculinity, a narrow, stereotyped conception of women and femininity, and the treatment of women as commodities. Other practices contributing to coercive sexual relations and the cover-up of rapes include excessive alcohol use, competitiveness, and normative support for deviance and secrecy (cf. Bogal-Allbritten and Allbritten 1985; Kanin 1967).

Some fraternity practices exacerbate others. Brotherhood norms require "sticking together" regardless of right or wrong; thus rape episodes are unlikely to be stopped or reported to outsiders, even when witnesses disapprove. The ability to use alcohol without scrutiny by authorities and alcohol's frequent association with violence, including sexual coercion, facilitates rape in fraternity houses. Fraternity norms that emphasize the value of maleness and masculinity over femaleness and femininity and that elevate the status of men and lower the status of women in members' eyes undermine perceptions and treatment of women as persons who deserve consideration and care (cf. Ehrhart and Sandler 1985; Merton 1985).

Androgynous men and men with a broad range of interests and attributes are lost to fraternities through their recruitment practices. Masculinity of a narrow and stereotypical type helps create attitudes, norms, and practices that predispose fraternity men to coerce women sexually, both individually and collectively (Allgeier 1986; Hood 1989; Sanday 1981, 1986). Male athletes on campus may be similarly disposed for the same reasons (Kirshenbaum 1989; Telander and Sullivan 1989).

Research into the social contexts in which rape crimes occur and the social constructions associated with these contexts illumine rape dynamics on campus. Blanchard (1959) found that group rapes almost always have a leader who pushes others into the crime. He also found that the leader's latent homosexuality, desire to show off to his peers, or fear of failing to prove himself a man are frequently an impetus. Fraternity norms and practices contribute to the approval and use of sexual coercion as an accepted tactic in relations with women. Alcohol-induced compliance is normative, whereas, presumably, use of a knife, gun, or threat of bodily harm would not be because the woman who "drinks too much" is viewed as "causing her own rape" (cf. Ehrhart and Sandler 1985).

Our research led us to conclude that fraternity norms and practices influence members to view the sexual coercion of women, which is a felony crime, as sport, a contest, or a game (cf. Sato 1988). This sport is played not between men and women but between men and men. Women are the pawns or prey in the interfraternity rivalry game; they prove that a fraternity is successful or prestigious. The use of women in this way encourages fraternity men to see women as objects and sexual coercion as sport. Today's societal norms support young women's right to engage in sex at their discretion, and coercion is unnecessary in a mutually desired encounter. However, nubile young women say they prefer to be "in a relationship" to have sex while young men say they prefer to "get laid" without a commitment (Muehlenhard and Linton 1987). These differences may reflect, in part, American puritanism and men's fears of sexual intimacy or perhaps intimacy of any kind. In a fraternity context, getting sex without giving emotionally demonstrates "cool" masculinity. More important, it poses no threat to the bonding and loyalty of the fraternity brotherhood (cf. Farr 1988). Drinking large quantities of alcohol before having sex suggests that "scoring" rather than intrinsic sexual pleasure is a primary concern of fraternity men.

Unless fraternities' composition, goals, structures, and practices change in fundamental ways, women on campus will continue to be sexual prey for fraternity men. As all-male enclaves dedicated to opposing faculty and administration and to cementing in-group ties, fraternity members eschew any hint of homosexuality. Their version of masculinity transforms women, and men with womanly characteristics, into the out-group. "Womanly men" are ostracized; feminine women are used to demonstrate members' masculinity. Encouraging renewed emphasis on their founding values (Longino and Kart 1973), service orientation and activities (Lemire 1979), or members' moral development

(Marlowe and Auvenshine 1982) will have little effect on fraternities' treatment of women. A case for or against fraternities cannot be made by studying individual members. The fraternity qua group and organization is at issue. Located on campus along with many vulnerable women, embedded in a sexist society, and caught up in masculinist goals, practices, and values, fraternities' violation of women—including forcible rape—should come as no surprise.

ACKNOWLEDGMENTS

Author's note: We gratefully thank Meena Harris and Diane Mennella for assisting with data collection. The senior author thanks the graduate students in her fall 1988 graduate research methods seminar for help with developing the initial conceptual framework. Judith Lorber and two anonymous *Gender & Society* referees made numerous suggestions for improving our article and we thank them also.

REFERENCES

Allgeier, Elizabeth. 1986. "Coercive Versus Consensual Sexual Interactions." G. Stanley Hall Lecture to American Psychological Association Annual Meeting, Washington, DC, August.

Adams, Aileen and Gail Abarbanel. 1988. *Sexual Assault on Campus: What Colleges Can Do.* Santa Monica, CA: Rape Treatment Center.

Blanchard, W. H. 1959. "The Group Process in Gang Rape." *Journal of Social Psychology* 49:259–66.

Bogal-Allbritten, Rosemarie B. and William L. Allbritten. 1985. "The Hidden Victims: Courtship Violence Among College Students." *Journal of College Student Personnel* 43:201–4.

Bohrnstedt, George W. 1969. "Conservatism, Authoritarianism and Religiosity of Fraternity Pledges." *Journal of College Student Personnel* 27:36–43.

Bradford, Michael. 1986. "Tight Market Dries Up Nightlife at University." *Business Insurance* (March 2):2, 6.

Burkhart, Barry. 1989. Comments in Seminar on Acquaintance/Date Rape Prevention: A National Video Teleconference, February 2.

Burkhart, Barry R. and Annette L. Stanton. 1985. "Sexual Aggression in Acquaintance Relationships." Pp. 43–65 in *Violence in Intimate Relationships,* edited by G. Russell. Englewood Cliffs, NJ: Spectrum.

Byington, Diane B. and Karen W. Keeter. 1988. "Assessing Needs of Sexual Assault Victims on a University Campus." Pp. 23–31 in *Student Services: Responding to Issues and Challenges.* Chapel Hill: University of North Carolina Press.

Chancer, Lynn S. 1987. "New Bedford, Massachusetts, March 6, 1983–March 22, 1984: The 'Before and After' of a Group Rape." *Gender & Society* 1:239–60.

Ehrhart, Julie K. and Bernice R. Sandler. 1985. *Campus Gang Rape: Party Games?* Washington, DC: Association of American Colleges.

Farr, K. A. 1988. "Dominance Bonding Through the Good Old Boys Sociability Network." *Sex Roles* 18:259–77.

Florida Flambeau. 1988. "Pike Members Indicted in Rape." (May 19):1, 5.

Fox, Elaine, Charles Hodge, and Walter Ward. 1987. "A Comparison of Attitudes Held by Black and White Fraternity Members." *Journal of Negro Education* 56:521–34.

Geis, Gilbert. 1971. "Group Sexual Assaults." *Medical Aspects of Human Sexuality* 5:101–13.

Glaser, Barney G. 1978. *Theoretical Sensitivity: Advances in the Methodology of Grounded Theory.* Mill Valley, CA: Sociology Press.

Hood, Jane. 1989. "Why Our Society Is Rape-Prone." *New York Times,* May 16.

Hughes, Michael J. and Roger B. Winston, Jr. 1987. "Effects of Fraternity Membership on Interpersonal Values." *Journal of College Student Personnel* 45:405–11.

Kanin, Eugene J. 1967. "Reference Groups and Sex Conduct Norm Violations." *The Sociological Quarterly* 8:495–504.

Kimmel, Michael, ed. 1987. *Changing Men: New Directions in Research on Men and Masculinity.* Newbury Park, CA: Sage.

Kirshenbaum, Jerry. 1989. "Special Report, An American Disgrace: A Violent and Unprecedented Lawlessness Has

Arisen Among College Athletes in all Parts of the Country." *Sports Illustrated* (February 27):16–19.

Lemire, David. 1979. "One Investigation of the Stereotypes Associated with Fraternities and Sororities." *Journal of College Student Personnel* 37:54–57.

Letchworth, G. E. 1969. "Fraternities Now and in the Future." *Journal of College Student Personnel* 10:118–22.

Longino, Charles F., Jr., and Cary S. Kart. 1973. "The College Fraternity: An Assessment of Theory and Research." *Journal of College Student Personnel* 31:118–25.

Marlowe, Anne F. and Dwight C. Auvenshine. 1982. "Greek Membership: Its Impact on the Moral Development of College Freshmen." *Journal of College Student Personnel* 40:53–57.

Martin, Patricia Yancey and Barry A. Turner. 1986. "Grounded Theory and Organizational Research." *Journal of Applied Behavioral Science* 22:141–57.

Merton, Andrew. 1985. "On Competition and Class: Return to Brotherhood." *Ms.* (September):60–65, 121–22.

Messner, Michael. 1989. "Masculinities and Athletic Careers." *Gender & Society* 3:71–88.

Meyer, T. J. 1986. "Fight Against Hazing Rituals Rages on Campuses." *Chronicle of Higher Education* (March 12):34–36.

Miller, Leonard D. 1973. "Distinctive Characteristics of Fraternity Members." *Journal of College Student Personnel* 31:126–28.

Muehlenhard, Charlene L. and Melaney A. Linton. 1987. "Date Rape and Sexual Aggression in Dating Situations: Incidence and Risk Factors." *Journal of Counseling Psychology* 34:186–96.

Pressley, Sue Anne. 1987. "Fraternity Hell Night Still Endures." *Washington Post* (August 11):B1.

Rapaport, Karen and Barry R. Burkhart. 1984. "Personality and Attitudinal Characteristics of Sexually Coercive College Males." *Journal of Abnormal Psychology* 93:216–21.

Roark, Mary L. 1987. "Preventing Violence on College Campuses." *Journal of Counseling and Development* 65:367–70.

Sanday, Peggy Reeves. 1981. "The Socio-Cultural Context of

Rape: A Cross-Cultural Study." *Journal of Social Issues* 37:5–27.

———. 1986. "Rape and the Silencing of the Feminine." Pp. 84–101 in *Rape,* edited by S. Tomaselli and R. Porter. Oxford: Basil Blackwell.

St. Petersburg Times. 1988. "A Greek Tragedy." (May 29):1F, 6F.

Sato, Ikuya. 1988. "Play Theory of Delinquency: Toward a General Theory of 'Action.'" *Symbolic Interaction* 11:191–212.

Smith, T. 1964. "Emergence and Maintenance of Fraternal Solidarity." *Pacific Sociological Review* 7:29–37.

Tallahassee Democrat. 1988a. "FSU Fraternity Brothers Charged" (April 27):1A, 12A.

———. 1988b. "FSU Interviewing Students About Alleged Rape" (April 24):1D.

———. 1989. "Woman Sues Stetson in Alleged Rape" (March 19):3B.

Tampa Tribune. 1988. "Fraternity Brothers Charged in Sexual Assault of FSU Coed." (April 27):6B.

Tash, Gary B. 1988. "Date Rape." *The Emerald of Sigma Pi Fraternity* 75(4):1–2.

Telander, Rick and Robert Sullivan. 1989. "Special Report, You Reap What You Sow." *Sports Illustrated* (February 27):20–34.

The Tomahawk. 1988. "A Look Back at Rush, A Mixture of Hard Work and Fun" (April/May):3D.

Walsh, Claire. 1989. Comments in Seminar on Acquaintance/Date Rape Prevention: A National Video Teleconference, February 2.

Wilder, David H., Arlyne E. Hoyt, Dennis M. Doren, William E. Hauck, and Robert D. Zettle. 1978. "The Impact of Fraternity and Sorority Membership on Values and Attitudes." *Journal of College Student Personnel* 36:445–49.

Wilder, David H., Arlyne E. Hoyt, Beth Shuster Surbeck, Janet C. Wilder, and Patricia Imperatrice Carney. 1986. "Greek Affiliation and Attitude Change in College Students." *Journal of College Student Personnel* 44:510–19.

"Riding the Bull at Gilley's": Convicted Rapists Describe the Rewards of Rape*

DIANA SCULLY and JOSEPH MAROLLA

Over the past several decades, rape has become a "medicalized" social problem. That is to say, the theories used to explain rape are predicated on psychopathological models. They have been generated from clinical experiences with small samples of rapists, often the therapists' own clients. Although these psychiatric explanations are most appropriately applied to the atypical rapist, they have been generalized to all men who rape and have come to inform the public's view on the topic.

Two assumptions are at the core of the psychopathological model; that rape is the result of idiosyncratic mental disease and that it often includes an uncontrollable sexual impulse (Scully and Marolla, 1985). For example, the presumption of psychopathology is evident in the often cited work of Nicholas Groth (1979). While Groth emphasizes the nonsexual nature of rape (power, anger, sadism), he also concludes, "Rape is always a symptom of some psychological dysfunction, either temporary and transient or chronic and repetitive" (Groth, 1979:5). Thus, in the psychopathological view, rapists lack the ability to

*This research was supported by a grant (R01 MH33013) from the National Center for the Prevention and Control of Rape, National Institute of Mental Health. We are indebted to the Virginia Department of Corrections for their cooperation and assistance in this research. Correspondence to: Scully, Department of Sociology/Anthropology, Virginia Commonwealth University, 312 Shafer Street, Richmond, Virginia 23284.

Copyright © 1985 by the Society for the Study of Social Problems. Reprinted from *Social Problems*, vol. 32, no. 3, February 1985, pp. 251–263, by permission.

control their behavior; they are "sick" individuals from the "lunatic fringe" of society.

In contradiction to this model, empirical research has repeatedly failed to find a consistent pattern of personality type or character disorder that reliably discriminates rapists from other groups of men (Fisher and Rivlin, 1971; Hammer and Jacks, 1955; Rada, 1978). Indeed, other research has found that fewer than 5 percent of men were psychotic when they raped (Abel et al., 1980).

Evidence indicates that rape is not a behavior confined to a few "sick" men but many men have the attitudes and beliefs necessary to commit a sexually aggressive act. In research conducted at a midwestern university, Koss and her coworkers reported that 85 percent of men defined as highly sexually aggressive had victimized women with whom they were romantically involved (Koss and Leonard, 1984). A recent survey quoted in *The Chronicle of Higher Education* estimates that more than 20 percent of college women are the victims of rape and attempted rape (Meyer, 1984). These findings mirror research published several decades earlier which also concluded that sexual aggression was commonplace in dating relationships (Kanin, 1957, 1965, 1967, 1969; Kirkpatrick and Kanin, 1957).[1] In their study of 53 college males, Malamuth, Haber and Feshback (1980) found that 51 percent indicated a likelihood that they, themselves, would rape if assured of not being punished.

In addition, the frequency of rape in the United States makes it unlikely that responsibility rests solely with a small lunatic fringe of psychopathic men. Johnson (1980), calculating the lifetime risk of rape to girls and women aged twelve and over, makes a similar observation. Using Law Enforcement Assistance Association and Bureau of Census Crime Victimization Studies, he calculated that, excluding sexual abuse in marriage and assuming equal risk to all women, 20 to 30 percent of girls now 12 years old will suffer a violent sexual attack during the remainder of their lives. Interestingly, the lack of empirical support for the psychopathological model has not resulted in the de-medicalization of rape, nor does it appear to have diminished the belief that rapists are "sick" aberrations in their own culture. This is significant because of the implications and consequences of the model.

A central assumption in the psychopathological model is that male sexual aggression is unusual or strange. This assumption removes rape from the realm of the everyday or "normal" world and places it in the category of "special" or "sick" behavior. As a consequence, men who rape are cast in the role of outsider and a connection with normative male behavior is avoided. Since, in this view, the source of the behavior is thought to be within the psychology of the individual, attention is diverted away from culture or social structure as contributing factors. Thus, the psychopathological model ignores evidence which links sexual aggression to environmental variables and which suggests that rape, like all behavior, is learned.

CULTURAL FACTORS IN RAPE

Culture is a factor in rape, but the precise nature of the relationship between culture and sexual violence remains a topic of discussion. Ethnographic data from pre-industrial societies show the existence of rape-free cultures (Broude and Green, 1976; Sanday, 1979), though explanations for the phenomena differ.[2] Sanday (1979) relates sexual violence to contempt for female qualities and suggests that rape is part of a culture of violence and an expression of male dominance. In contrast, Blumberg (1979) argues that in pre-industrial societies women are more likely to lack important life options and to be physically and politically oppressed where they lack economic power relative to men. That is, in pre-industrial societies relative economic power enables women to win some immunity from men's use of force against them.

Among modern societies, the frequency of rape varies dramatically, and the United States is among the most rape-prone of all. In 1980, for example, the rate of reported rape and attempted rape for the United States was eighteen times higher than the corresponding rate for England and Wales (West, 1983). Spurred by the Women's Movement, feminists have generated an impressive body of theory regarding the cultural etiology of rape in the United States. Representative of the feminist view, Griffin (1971) called rape "The All American Crime."

The feminist perspective views rape as an act of violence and social control which functions to "keep women in their place" (Brownmiller, 1975; Kasinsky, 1975; Russell, 1975). Feminists see rape as an extension of normative male behavior, the result of conformity or overconformity to the values and prerogatives which define the traditional male sex role. That is, traditional socialization encourages males to associate power, dominance, strength, virility and superiority with masculinity, and submissiveness, passivity, weakness, and inferiority with femininity. Furthermore, males are taught to have expectations about their level of sexual needs and expectations for corresponding female accessibility which function to justify forcing sexual access. The justification for forced sexual access is buttressed by legal, social, and religious definitions of women as male property and sex as an exchange of goods (Bart, 1979). Socialization prepares women to be "legitimate" victims and men to be potential offenders (Weis and Borges, 1973). Herman (1984) concludes that the United States is a rape culture because both genders are socialized to regard male aggression as a natural and normal part of sexual intercourse.

Feminists view pornography as an important element in a larger system of sexual violence; they see pornography as an expression of a rape-prone culture where women are seen as objects available for use by men (Morgan, 1980; Wheeler, 1985). Based on his content analysis of 428 "adults only" books, Smith (1976) makes a similar observation. He notes that, not only is rape presented as part of normal male/female sexual relations, but the woman, despite her terror, is always depicted as sexually aroused to the point of cooperation. In the end, she is ashamed but physically gratified. The message—women desire and enjoy rape—has more potential for damage than the image of the violence *per se*.[3]

The fusion of these themes—sex as an impersonal act, the victim's uncontrollable orgasm, and the violent infliction of pain—is commonplace in the actual accounts of rapists. Scully and Marolla (1984) demonstrated that many convicted rapists denied their crime and attempted to justify their rapes by arguing that their victim had enjoyed herself despite the use of a weapon and the infliction of serious injuries, or even death. In fact, many argued, they had been instrumental in making *her* fantasy come true.

The images projected in pornography contribute to a vocabulary of motive which trivializes and neutralizes rape and which might lessen the internal controls that otherwise would prevent sexually aggressive behavior. Men who rape use this culturally acquired vocabulary to justify their sexual violence.

Another consequence of the application of psychopathology to rape is it leads one to view sexual violence as a special type of crime in which the motivations are subconscious and uncontrollable rather than overt and deliberate as with other criminal behavior. Black (1983) offers an approach to the analysis of criminal and/or violent behavior which, when applied to rape, avoids this bias.

Black (1983) suggests that it is theoretically useful to ignore that crime is criminal in order to discover what such behavior has in common with other kinds of conduct. From his perspective, much of the crime in modern societies, as in pre-industrial societies, can be interpreted as a form of "self help" in which the actor is expressing a grievance through aggression and violence. From the actor's perspective, the victim is deviant and his own behavior is a form of social control in which the objective may be conflict management, punishment, or revenge. For example, in societies where women are considered the property of men, rape is sometimes used as a means of avenging the victim's husband or father (Black, 1983). In some cultures rape is used as a form of punishment. Such was the tradition among the puritanical, patriarchal Cheyenne where men were valued for their ability as warriors. It was Cheyenne custom that a wife suspected of being unfaithful could be "put on the prairie" by her husband. Military confreres then were invited to "feast" on the prairie (Hoebel, 1954; Llewellyn and Hoebel, 1941). The ensuing mass rape was a husband's method of punishing his wife.

Black's (1983) approach is helpful in understanding rape because it forces one to examine the goals that some men have learned to achieve through sexually violent means. Thus, one approach to understanding why some men rape is to shift attention from individual psychopathology to the important question of what rapists gain from sexual aggression and violence in a culture seemingly prone to rape.

In this paper, we address this question using data from interviews conducted with 114 convicted, incarcerated rapists. Elsewhere, we discussed the vocabulary of motive, consisting of excuses and justifications, that these convicted rapists used to explain themselves and their crime (Scully and Marolla, 1984).[4] The use of these culturally derived excuses and justifications allowed them to view their behavior as either idiosyncratic or situationally appropriate and thus it reduced their sense of moral responsibility for their actions. Having disavowed deviance, these men revealed how they had used rape to achieve a number of objectives. We find that some men used rape for revenge or punishment while, for others, it was an "added bonus"—a last minute decision made while committing another crime. In still other cases, rape was used to gain sexual access to women who were unwilling or unavailable, and for some it was a source of power and sex without any personal feelings. Rape was also a form of recreation, a diversion or an adventure and, finally, it was something that made these men "feel good."

METHODS[5]

Sample

During 1980 and 1981 we interviewed 114 convicted rapists. All of the men had been convicted of the rape or attempted rape (n = 8) of an adult woman and subsequently incarcerated in a Virginia prison. Men convicted of other types of sexual offense were omitted from the sample.

In addition to their convictions for rape, 39 percent of the men also had convictions for burglary or robbery, 29 percent for abduction, 25 percent for sodomy, 11 percent for first or second degree murder and 12 percent had been convicted of more than one rape. The majority of the men had previous criminal histories but only 23 percent had a record of past sex offenses and only 26 percent had a history of emotional problems. Their sentences for rape and accompanying crimes ranged from ten years to seven life sentences plus 380 years for one man. Twenty-two percent of the rapists were serving at least one life sentence. Forty-six percent of the rapists were white, 54 percent black. In age, they ranged from 18 to 60 years but the majority were between 18 and 35 years. Based on a statistical profile of felons in all Virginia prisons prepared by the Virginia Department of Corrections, it appears that this sample of rapists was disproportionately white and, at the time of the research, somewhat better educated and younger than the average inmate.

All participants in this research were volunteers. In constructing the sample, age, education, race, severity of current offense and past criminal record were balanced within the limitations imposed by the characteristics of the volunteer pool. Obviously the sample was not random and thus may not be typical of all rapists, imprisoned or otherwise.

All interviews were hand recorded using an 89-page instrument which included a general background, psychological, criminal, and sexual history, attitude scales and 30 pages of open-ended questions intended to explore rapists' own perceptions of their crime and themselves. Each author interviewed half of the sample in sessions that ranged from three to seven hours depending on the desire or willingness of the participant to talk.

Validity

In all prison research, validity is a special methodological concern because of the reputation inmates have for "conning." Although one goal of this research was to understand rape from the perspective of men who have raped, it was also necessary to establish the extent to which rapists' perceptions deviated from other descriptions of their crime. The technique we used was the same others have used in prison research; comparing factual information obtained in the interviews, including details of the crime, with reports on file at the prison (Athens, 1977; Luckenbill, 1977; Queen's Bench Foundation, 1976). In general, we found that rapists' accounts of their crime had changed very little since their trials. However, there was a tendency to understate the amount of violence they had used and, especially among certain rapists, to place blame on their victims.

HOW OFFENDERS VIEW THE REWARDS OF RAPE

Revenge and Punishment

As noted earlier, Black's (1983) perspective suggests that a rapist might see his act as a legitimized form of

revenge or punishment. Additionally, he asserts that the idea of "collective liability" accounts for much seemingly random violence. "Collective liability" suggests that all people in a particular category are held accountable for the conduct of each of their counterparts. Thus, the victim of a violent act may merely represent the category of individual being punished.

These factors—revenge, punishment, and the collective liability of women—can be used to explain a number of rapes in our research. Several cases will illustrate the ways in which these factors combined in various types of rape. Revenge-rapes were among the most brutal and often included beatings, serious injuries and, even murder.

Typically, revenge-rapes included the element of collective liability. That is, from the rapist's perspective, the victim was a substitute for the woman they wanted to avenge. As explained elsewhere, (Scully and Marolla, 1984), an upsetting event, involving a woman, preceded a significant number of rapes. When they raped, these men were angry because of a perceived indiscretion, typically related to a rigid, moralistic standard of sexual conduct, which they required from "their woman" but, in most cases, did not abide by themselves. Over and over these rapists talked about using rape "to get even" with their wives or other significant woman.[6] Typical is a young man who, prior to the rape, had a violent argument with his wife over what eventually proved to be her misdiagnosed case of venereal disease. She assumed the disease had been contracted through him, an accusation that infuriated him. After fighting with his wife, he explained that he drove around "thinking about hurting someone." He encountered his victim, a stranger, on the road where her car had broken down. It appears she accepted his offered ride because her car was out of commission. When she realized that rape was pending, she called him "a son of a bitch," and attempted to resist. He reported flying into a rage and beating her, and he confided,

> I have never felt that much anger before. If she had resisted, I would have killed her. . . . The rape was for revenge. I didn't have an orgasm. She was there to get my hostile feelings off on.

Although not the most common form of revenge rape, sexual assault continues to be used in retaliation against the victim's male partner. In one such case, the offender, angry because the victim's husband owed him money, went to the victim's home to collect. He confided, "I was going to get it one way or another." Finding the victim alone, he explained, they started to argue about the money and,

> I grabbed her and started beating the hell out of her. Then I committed the act,[7] I knew what I was doing. I was mad. I could have stopped but I didn't. I did it to get even with her and her husband.

Griffin (1971:33) points out that when women are viewed as commodities, "In raping another man's woman, a man may aggrandize his own manhood and concurrently reduce that of another man."

Revenge-rapes often contained an element of punishment. In some cases, while the victim was not the initial object of the revenge, the intent was to punish her because of something that transpired after the decision to rape had been made or during the course of the rape itself. This was the case with a young man whose wife had recently left him. Although they were in the process of reconciliation, he remained angry and upset over the separation. The night of the rape, he met the victim and her friend in a bar where he had gone to watch a fight on TV. The two women apparently accepted a ride from him but, after taking her friend home, he drove the victim to his apartment. At his apartment, he found a note from his wife indicating she had stopped by to watch the fight with him. This increased his anger because he preferred his wife's company. Inside his apartment, the victim allegedly remarked that she was sexually interested in his dog, which he reported, put him in a rage. In the ensuing attack, he raped and pistol-whipped the victim. Then he forced a vacuum cleaner hose, switched on suction, into her vagina and bit her breast, severing the nipple. He stated:

> I hated at the time, but I don't know if it was her (the victim). (Who could it have been?) My wife? Even though we were getting back together, I still didn't trust her.

During his interview, it became clear that this offender, like many of the men, believed men have the right to discipline and punish women. In fact, he argued that most of the men he knew would also have beaten the victim because "that kind of thing (referring to the dog) is not acceptable among my friends."

Finally, in some rapes, both revenge and punishment were directed at victims because they represented women whom these offenders perceived as collectively responsible and liable for their problems. Rape was used "to put women in their place" and as a method of proving their "manhood" by displaying dominance over a female. For example, one multiple rapist believed his actions were related to the feeling that women thought they were better than he was.

> Rape was a feeling of total dominance. Before the rapes, I would always get a feeling of power and anger. I would degrade women so I could feel there was a person of less worth than me.

Another, especially brutal, case involved a young man from an upper middle class background, who spilled out his story in a seven-hour interview conducted in his solitary confinement cell. He described himself as tremendously angry, at the time, with his girl friend whom he believed was involved with him in a "storybook romance," and from whom he expected complete fidelity. When she went away to college and became involved with another man, his revenge lasted eighteen months and involved the rape and murder of five women, all strangers who lived in his community. Explaining his rape-murders, he stated:

> I wanted to take my anger and frustration out on a stranger, to be in control, to do what I wanted to do. I wanted to use and abuse someone as I felt used and abused. I was killing my girl friend. During the rapes and murders, I would think about my girl friend. I hated the victims because they probably messed men over. I hated women because they were deceitful and I was getting revenge for what happened to me.

An Added Bonus

Burglary and robbery commonly accompany rape. Among our sample, 39 percent of rapists had also been convicted of one or the other of these crimes commited in connection with rape. In some cases, the original intent was rape and robbery was an after-thought. However, a number of the men indicated that the reverse was true in their situation. That is, the decision to rape was made subsequent to their original intent which was burglary or robbery.

This was the case with a young offender who stated

that he originally intended only to rob the store in which the victim happened to be working. He explained that when he found the victim alone,

> I decided to rape her to prove I had guts. She was just there. It could have been anybody.

Similarly, another offender indicated that he initially broke into his victim's home to burglarize it. When he discovered the victim asleep, he decided to seize the opportunity "to satisfy an urge to go to bed with a white woman, to see if it was different." Indeed, a number of men indicated that the decision to rape had been made after they realized they were in control of the situation. This was also true of an unemployed offender who confided that his practice was to steal whenever he needed money. On the day of the rape, he drove to a local supermarket and paced the parking lot, "staking out the situation." His pregnant victim was the first person to come along alone and "she was an easy target." Threatening her with a knife, he reported the victim as saying she would do anything if he didn't harm her. At that point, he decided to force her to drive to a deserted area where he raped her. He explained:

> I wasn't thinking about sex. But when she said she would do anything not to get hurt, probably because she was pregnant, I thought, 'why not.'

The attitude of these men toward rape was similar to their attitude toward burglary and robbery. Quite simply, if the situation is right, "why not." From the perspective of these rapists, rape was just another part of the crime—an added bonus.

Sexual Access

In an effort to change public attitudes that are damaging to the victims of rape and to reform laws seemingly premised on the assumption that women both ask for and enjoy rape, many writers emphasize the violent and aggressive character of rape. Often such arguments appear to discount the part that sex plays in the crime. The data clearly indicate that from the rapists' point of view rape is in part sexually motivated. Indeed, it is the sexual aspect of rape that distinguishes it from other forms of assault.

Groth (1979) emphasizes the psychodynamic function of sex in rape arguing that rapists' aggressive

needs are expressed through sexuality. In other words, rape is a means to an end. We argue, however, that rapists view the act as an end in itself and that sexual access most obviously demonstrates the link between sex and rape. Rape as a means of sexual access also shows the deliberate nature of this crime. When a woman is unwilling or seems unavailable for sex, the rapist can seize what isn't volunteered. In discussing his decision to rape, one man made this clear.

> All the guys wanted to fuck her . . . a real fox, beautiful shape. She was a beautiful woman and I wanted to see what she had.

The attitude that sex is a male entitlement suggests that when a woman says "no," rape is a suitable method of conquering the "offending" object. If, for example, a woman is picked up at a party or in a bar or while hitchhiking (behavior which a number of the rapists saw as a signal of sexual availability), and the woman later resists sexual advances, rape is presumed to be justified. The same justification operates in what is popularly called "date rape." The belief that sex was their just compensation compelled a number of rapists to insist they had not raped. Such was the case of an offender who raped and seriously beat his victim when, on their second date, she refused his sexual advances.

> I think I was really pissed off at her because it didn't go as planned. I could have been with someone else. She led me on but wouldn't deliver. . . . I have a male ego that must be fed.

The purpose of such rapes was conquest, to seize what was not offered.

Despite the cultural belief that young women are the most sexually desirable, several rapes involved the deliberate choice of a victim relatively older than the assailant.[8] Since the rapists were themselves rather young (26 to 30 years of age on the average), they were expressing a preference for sexually experienced, rather than elderly, women. Men who chose victims older than themselves often said they did so because they believed that sexually experienced women were more desirable partners. They raped because they also believed that these women would not be sexually attracted to them.

Finally, sexual access emerged as a factor in the accounts of black men who consciously chose to rape white women.[9] The majority of rapes in the United

States today are intraracial. However, for the past 20 years, according to national data based on reported rapes as well as victimization studies, which include unreported rapes, the rate of black on white (B/W) rape has significantly exceeded the rate of white on black (W/B) rape (La Free, 1982).[10] Indeed, we may be experiencing a historical anomaly, since, as Brownmiller (1975) has documented, white men have freely raped women of color in the past. The current structure of interracial rape, however, reflects contemporary racism and race relations in several ways.

First, the status of black women in the United States today is relatively lower than the status of white women. Further, prejudice, segregation and other factors continue to militate against interracial coupling. Thus, the desire for sexual access to higher status, unavailable women, an important function in B/W rape, does not motivate white men to rape black women. Equally important, demographic and geographic barriers interact to lower the incidence of W/B rape. Segregation as well as the poverty expected in black neighborhoods undoubtedly discourages many whites from choosing such areas as a target for housebreaking or robbery. Thus, the number of rapes that would occur in conjunction with these crimes is reduced.

Reflecting in part the standards of sexual desirability set by the dominant white society, a number of black rapists indicated they had been curious about white women. Blocked by racial barriers from legitimate sexual relations with white women, they raped to gain access to them. They described raping white women as "the ultimate experience" and "high status among my friends. It gave me a feeling of status, power, macho." For another man, raping a white woman had a special appeal because it violated a "known taboo," making it more dangerous, and thus more exciting, to him than raping a black woman.

Impersonal Sex and Power

The idea that rape is an impersonal rather than an intimate or mutual experience appealed to a number of rapists, some of whom suggested it was their preferred form of sex. The fact that rape allowed them to control rather than care encouraged some to act on this preference. For example, one man explained,

Rape gave me the power to do what I wanted to do without feeling I had to please a partner or respond to a partner. I felt in control, dominant. Rape was the ability to have sex without caring about the woman's response. I was totally dominant.

Another rapist commented:

Seeing them laying there helpless gave me the confidence that I could do it. . . . With rape, I felt totally in charge. I'm bashful, timid. When a woman wanted to give in normal sex, I was intimidated. In the rapes, I was totally in command, she totally submissive.

During his interview, another rapist confided that he had been fantasizing about rape for several weeks before committing his offense. His belief was that it would be "an exciting experience—a new high." Most appealing to him was the idea that he could make his victim "do it all for him" and that he would be in control. He fantasized that she "would submit totally and that I could have anything I wanted." Eventually, he decided to act because his older brother told him, "forced sex is great, I wouldn't get caught and, besides, women love it." Though now he admits to his crime, he continues to believe his victim "enjoyed it." Perhaps we should note here that the appeal of impersonal sex is not limited to convicted rapists. The amount of male sexual activity that occurs in homosexual meeting places as well as the widespread use of prostitutes suggests that avoidance of intimacy appeals to a large segment of the male population. Through rape men can experience power and avoid the emotions related to intimacy and tenderness. Further, the popularity of violent pornography suggests that a wide variety of men in this culture have learned to be aroused by sex fused with violence (Smith, 1976). Consistent with this observation, recent experimental research conducted by Malamuth et al. (1980) demonstrates that men are aroused by images that depict women as orgasmic under conditions of violence and pain. They found that for female students, arousal was high when the victim experienced an orgasm and *no* pain, whereas male students were highly aroused when the victim experienced an orgasm and pain. On the basis of their results, Malamuth et al. (1980) suggest that forcing a woman to climax despite her pain and abhorrence of the assailant makes the rapist feel powerful, he has gained control over the only source of power historically associated with women, their bodies. In the final analysis, dominance was the objective of most rapists.

Recreation and Adventure

Among gang rapists, most of whom were in their late teens or early twenties when convicted, rape represented recreation and adventure, another form of delinquent activity. Part of rape's appeal was the sense of male camaraderie engendered by participating collectively in a dangerous activity. To prove one's self capable of "performing" under these circumstances was a substantial challenge and also a source of reward. One gang rapist articulated this feeling very clearly,

> We felt powerful, we were in control. I wanted sex and there was peer pressure. She wasn't like a person, no personality, just domination on my part. Just to show I could do it—you know, macho.

Our research revealed several forms of gang rape. A common pattern was hitchhike-abduction rape. In these cases, the gang, cruising an area, "looking for girls," picked up a female hitchhiker for the purpose of having sex. Though the intent was rape, a number of men did not view it as such because they were convinced that women hitchhiked primarily to signal sexual availability and only secondarily as a form of transportation. In these cases, the unsuspecting victim was driven to a deserted area, raped, and in the majority of cases physically injured. Sometimes, the victim was not hitchhiking; she was abducted at knife or gun point from the street usually at night. Some of these men did not view this type of attack as rape either because they believed a woman walking alone at night to be a prostitute. In addition, they were often convinced "she enjoyed it."

"Gang date" rape was another popular variation. In this pattern, one member of the gang would make a date with the victim. Then, without her knowledge or consent, she would be driven to a predetermined location and forcibly raped by each member of the group. One young man revealed this practice was so much a part of his group's recreational routine, they had rented a house for the purpose. From his perspective, the rape was justified because "usually the girl had a bad reputation, or we knew it was what she liked."

During his interview, another offender confessed to participating in twenty or thirty such "gang date" rapes because his driver's license had been revoked making it difficult for him to "get girls." Sixty percent of the time, he claimed, "they were girls known to do this kind of thing," but "frequently, the girls didn't want to

have sex with all of us." In such cases, he said, "It might start out as rape but, then, they (the women) would quiet down and none ever reported it to the police." He was convicted for a gang rape, which he described as "the ultimate thing I ever did," because unlike his other rapes, the victim, in this case, was a stranger whom the group abducted as she walked home from the library. He felt the group's past experience with "gang date" rape had prepared them for this crime in which the victim was blindfolded and driven to the mountains where, though it was winter, she was forced to remove her clothing. Lying on the snow, she was raped by each of the four men several times before being abandoned near a farm house. This young man continued to believe that if he had spent the night with her, rather than abandoning her, she would not have reported to the police.[11]

Solitary rapists also used terms like "exciting," "a challenge," "an adventure," to describe their feelings about rape. Like the gang rapists, these men found the element of danger made rape all the more exciting. Typifying this attitude was one man who described his rape as intentional. He reported:

> It was exciting to get away with it (rape), just being able to beat the system, not women. It was like doing something illegal and getting away with it.

Another rapist confided that for him "rape was just more exciting and compelling" than a normal sexual encounter because it involved forcing a stranger. A multiple rapist asserted, "it was the excitement and fear and the drama that made rape a big kick."

Feeling Good

At the time of their interviews, many of the rapists expressed regret for their crime and had empirically low self-esteem ratings. The experience of being convicted, sentenced, and incarcerated for rape undoubtedly produced many, if not most, of these feelings. What is clear is that, in contrast to the well-documented severity of the immediate impact, and in some cases, the long-term trauma experienced by the victims of sexual violence, the immediate emotional impact on the rapists is slight.

When the men were asked to recall their feelings immediately following the rape, only eight percent indicated that guilt or feeling bad was part of their emotional response. The majority said they felt good, relieved or simply nothing at all. Some indicated they had been afraid of being caught or felt sorry for themselves. Only two men out of 114 expressed any concern or feeling for the victim. Feeling good or nothing at all about raping women is not an aberration limited to men in prison. Smithyman (1978), in his study of "undetected rapists"—rapists outside of prison—found that raping women had no impact on their lives nor did it have a negative effect on their self-image.

Significantly a number of men volunteered the information that raping had a positive impact on their feelings. For some the satisfaction was in revenge. For example, the man who had raped and murdered five women:

It seems like so much bitterness and tension had built up and this released it. I felt like I had just climbed a mountain and now I could look back.

Another offender characterized rape as habit forming: "Rape is like smoking. You can't stop once you start." Finally one man expressed the sentiments of many rapists when he stated,

After rape, I always felt like I had just conquered something, like I had just ridden the bull at Gilley's.

CONCLUSIONS

This paper has explored rape from the perspective of a group of convicted, incarcerated rapists. The purpose was to discover how these men viewed sexual violence and what they gained from their behavior.

We found that rape was frequently a means of revenge and punishment. Implicit in revenge-rapes was the notion that women were collectively liable for the rapists' problems. In some cases, victims were substitutes for significant women on whom the men desired to take revenge. In other cases, victims were thought to represent all women, and rape was used to punish, humiliate, and "put them in their place." In both cases women were seen as a class, a category, not as individuals. For some men, rape was almost an after-thought, a bonus added to burglary or robbery. Other men gained access to sexually unavailable or unwilling women through rape. For this group of men, rape was a fantasy come true, a particularly exciting form of impersonal sex which enabled them to dominate and

control women, by exercising a singularly male form of power. These rapists talked of the pleasures of raping—how for them it was a challenge, an adventure, a dangerous and "ultimate" experience. Rape made them feel good and, in some cases, even elevated their self image.

The pleasure these men derived from raping reveals the extreme to which they objectified women. Women were seen as sexual commodities to be used or conquered rather than as human beings with rights and feelings. One young man expressed the extreme of the contemptful view of women when he confided to the female researcher.

Rape is a man's right. If a woman doesn't want to give it, the man should take it. Women have no right to say no. Women are made to have sex. It's all they are good for. Some women would rather take a beating, but they always give in; it's what they are for.

This man murdered his victim because she wouldn't "give in."

Undoubtedly, some rapes, like some of all crimes, are idiopathic. However, it is not necessary to resort to pathological motives to account for all rape or other acts of sexual violence. Indeed, we find that men who rape have something to teach us about the cultural roots of sexual aggression. They force us to acknowledge that rape is more than an idiosyncratic act committed by a few "sick" men. Rather, rape can be viewed as the end point in a continuum of sexually aggressive behaviors that reward men and victimize women.[12] In the way that the motives for committing any criminal act can be rationally determined, reasons for rape can also be determined. Our data demonstrate that some men rape because they have learned that in this culture sexual violence is rewarding. Significantly, the overwhelming majority of these rapists indicated they never thought they would go to prison for what they did. Some did not fear imprisonment because they did not define their behavior as rape. Others knew that women frequently do not report rape and of those cases that are reported, conviction rates are low, and therefore they felt secure. These men perceived rape as a rewarding, low risk act. Understanding that otherwise normal men can and do rape is critical to the development of strategies for prevention.

We are left with the fact that all men do not rape. In

view of the apparent rewards and cultural supports for rape, it is important to ask why some men do not rape. Hirschi (1969) makes a similar observation about delinquency. He argues that the key question is not "Why do they do it?" but rather "Why don't we do it?" (Hirschi, 1969:34). Likewise, we may be seeking an answer to the wrong question about sexual assault of women. Instead of asking men who rape "Why?" perhaps we should be asking men who don't "Why not?"

NOTES

1. Despite the fact that these data have been in circulation for some time, prevention strategies continue to reflect the "lunatic fringe" image of rape. For example, security on college campuses, such as bright lighting and escort service, is designed to protect women against stranger rape while little or no attention is paid to the more frequent crime—acquaintance or date rape.

2. Broude and Green (1976) list a number of factors which limit the quantity and quality of cross-cultural data on rape. They point out that it was not customary in traditional ethnography to collect data on sexual attitudes and behavior. Further, where data do exist, they are often sketchy and vague. Despite this, the existence of rape-free societies has been established.

3. This factor distinguishes rape from other fictional depictions of violence. That is, in fictional murder, bombings, robberys, etc., victims are never portrayed as enjoying themselves. Such exhibits are reserved for pornographic displays of rape.

4. We also introduced a typology consisting of "admitters" (men who defined their behavior as rape) and "deniers" (men who admitted to sexual contact with the victim but did not define it as rape). In this paper we drop the distinction between admitters and deniers because it is not relevant to most of the discussion.

5. For a full discussion of the research methodology, sample, and validity, see Scully and Marolla (1984).

6. It should be noted that significant women, like rape victims, were also sometimes the targets of abuse and violence and possibly rape as well, although spousal rape is not recognized in Virginia law. In fact, these men were abusers. Fifty-five percent of rapists acknowledged that they hit their significant woman "at least once," and 20 percent admitted to inflicting physical injury. Given the tendency of these men to under-report the amount of violence in their crime, it is probably accurate to say, they under-reported their abuse of their significant women as well.

7. This man, as well as a number of others, either would not or could not, bring himself to say the word "rape." Similarly, we also attempted to avoid using the word, a technique which seemed to facilitate communication.

8. When asked towards whom their sexual interests were primarily directed, 43 percent of rapists indicated a preference for women "significantly older than themselves." When those who responded, "women of any age" are added, 65 percent of rapists expressed sexual interest in women older than themselves.

9. Feminists as well as sociologists have tended to avoid the topic of interracial rape. Contributing to the avoidance is an awareness of historical and contemporary social injustice. For example, Davis (1981) points out that fictional rape of white women was used in the South as a post-slavery justification to lynch black men. And LaFree (1980) has demonstrated that black men who assault white women continue to receive more serious sanctions within the criminal justice system when compared to other racial combinations of victim and assailant. While the silence has been defensible in light of historical racism, continued avoidance of the topic discriminates against victims by eliminating the opportunity to investigate the impact of social factors on rape.

10. In our sample, 66 percent of black rapists reported their victim(s) were white, compared to two white rapists who reported raping black women. It is important to emphasize that because of the biases inherent in rape reporting and processing, and because of the limitations of our sample, these figures do not accurately reflect the actual racial composition of rapes committed in Virginia or elsewhere. Furthermore, since black men who assault white women receive more serious sanctions within the criminal justice system when compared to other racial combinations of victim and assailant (LaFree, 1980), B/W rapists will be overrepresented within prison populations as well as over-represented in any sample drawn from the population.

11. It is important to note that the gang rapes in this study were especially violent, resulting in physical injury, even death. One can only guess at the amount of hitchhike-abduction and "gang-date" rapes that are never reported or, if reported, are not processed because of the tendency to disbelieve the victims of such rapes unless extensive physical injury accompanies the crime.

12. It is interesting that men who verbally harass women on the street say they do so to alleviate boredom, to gain a sense of youthful camaraderie, and because it's fun (Benard and Schlaffer, 1984)—the same reason men who rape give for their behavior.

REFERENCES

Abel, Gene, Judith Becker, and Linda Skinner 1980 "Aggressive behavior and sex." Psychiatric Clinics of North America 3:133–51.

Athens, Lonnie 1977 "Violent crime: a symbolic interactionist study." Symbolic Interaction 1:56–71.

Bart, Pauline 1979 "Rape as a paradigm of sexism in society—victimization and its discontents." Women's Studies International Quarterly 2:347–57.

Benard, Cheryl and Edit Schlaffer 1984 "The man in the street: why he harasses." Pp. 70–73 in Alson M. Jaggar and Paula S. Rothenberg (eds.), Feminist Frameworks. New York: McGraw-Hill.

Black, Donald 1983 "Crime as social control." American Sociological Review 48:34–45.

Blumberg, Rae Lesser 1979 "A paradigm for predicting the position of women: policy implications and problems." Pp. 113–42 in Jean Lipman-Blumen and Jessie Bernard (eds.), Sex Roles and Social Policy. London: Sage Studies in International Sociology.

Broude, Gwen and Sarah Greene 1976 "Cross-cultural codes on twenty sexual attitudes and practices." Ethnology 15:409–28.

Brownmiller, Susan 1975 Against Our Will. New York: Simon and Schuster.

Davis, Angela 1981 Women, Race and Class. New York: Random House.

Fisher, Gary and E. Rivlin 1971 "Psychological needs of rapists." British Journal of Criminology 11:182–85.

Griffin, Susan 1971 "Rape: the all American crime." Ramparts, September 10:26–35.

Groth, Nicholas 1971 Men Who Rape. New York: Plenum Press.

Hammer, Emanuel and Irving Jacks 1955 "A study of Rorschack flexnor and extensor human movements." Journal of Clinical Psychology 11:63–67.

Herman, Dianne 1984 "The rape culture." Pp. 20–39 in Jo Freeman (ed.), Women: A Feminist Perspective. Palo Alto: Mayfield.

Hirschi, Travis 1969 Causes of Delinquency. Berkeley: University of California Press.

Hoebel, E. Adamson 1954 The Law of Primitive Man. Boston: Harvard University Press.

Johnson, Allan Griswold 1980 "On the prevalence of rape in the United States." Signs 6:136–46.

Kanin, Eugene 1957 "Male aggression in dating-courtship relations." American Journal of Sociology 63:197–204. 1965 "Male sex aggression and three psychiatric hypotheses." Journal of Sex Research 1:227–29. 1967 "Reference groups and sex conduct norm violation." Sociological Quarterly 8:495–504. 1969 "Selected dyadic aspects of male sex aggression." Journal of Sex Research 5:12–28.

Kasinsky, Renee 1975 "Rape: a normal act?" Canadian Forum, September:18–22.

Kirkpatrick, Clifford and Eugene Kanin 1957 "Male sex aggression on a university campus." American Sociological Review 22:52–58.

Koss, Mary P. and Kenneth E. Leonard 1984 "Sexually aggressive men: empirical findings and theoretical implications." Pp. 213–32 in Neil M. Malamuth and Edward Donnerstein (eds.), Pornography and Sexual Aggression. New York: Academic Press.

LaFree, Gary 1980 "The effect of sexual stratification by race on official reactions to rape." American Sociological Review 45:824–54. 1982 "Male power and female victimization: towards a theory of interracial rape." American Journal of Sociology 88:311–28.

Llewellyn, Karl N., and E. Adamson Hoebel 1941 The Cheyenne Way: Conflict and Case Law in Primitive Jurisprudence. Norman: University of Oklahoma Press.

Luckenbill, David 1977 "Criminal homicide as a situated transaction." Social Problems 25:176–87.

Malamuth, Neil, Scott Haber and Seymour Feshback 1980 "Testing hypotheses regarding rape: exposure to sexual violence, sex difference, and the 'normality' of rapists." Journal of Research in Personality 14:121–37.

Malamuth, Neil, Maggie Heim, and Seymour Feshback 1980 "Sexual responsiveness of college students to rape depictions: inhibitory and disinhibitory effects." Social Psychology 38:399–408.

Meyer, Thomas J. 1984 "'Date rape': a serious problem that few talk about." Chronicle of Higher Education, December 5.

Morgan, Robin 1980 "Theory and practice: pornography and rape." Pp. 134–40 in Laura Lederer (ed.), Take Back the Night: Women on Pornography. New York: William Morrow.

Queen's Bench Foundation 1976 Rape: Prevention and Resistence. San Francisco: Queen's Bench Foundation.

Rada, Richard 1978 Clinical Aspects of Rape. New York: Grune and Stratton.

Russell, Diana 1975 The Politics of Rape. New York: Stein and Day.

Sanday, Peggy Reeves 1979 The Socio-Cultural Context of Rape. Washington, DC: United States Department of Commerce, National Technical Information Service.

Scully, Diana and Joseph Marolla 1984 "Convicted rapists' vocabulary of motive: excuses and justifications." Social Problems 31:530–44. 1985 "Rape and psychiatric vocabulary of motive: alternative perspectives." Pp. 294–312 in Ann Wolbert Burgess (ed.), Rape and Sexual Assault: A Research Handbook. New York: Garland Publishing.

Smith, Don 1976 "The social context of pornography." Journal of Communications 26:16–24.

Smithyman, Samuel 1978 The Undetected Rapist. Unpublished Dissertation: Claremont Graduate School.

West, Donald J. 1983 "Sex offenses and offending." Pp. 1–30

in Michael Tonry and Norval Morris (eds.), Crime and Justice: An Annual Review of Research. Chicago: University of Chicago Press.

Weis, Kurt and Sandra Borges 1973 "Victimology and rape: the case of the legitimate victim." Issues in Criminology 8:71–115.

Wheeler, Hollis 1985 "Pornography and rape: a feminist perspective." Pp. 374–91 in Ann Wolbert Burgess (ed.), Rape and Sexual Assault: A Research Handbook. New York: Garland Publishing.

R E A D I N G   4 0

Stopping Rape: Effective Avoidance Strategies

PAULINE B. BART and PATRICIA H. O'BRIEN

Try and fight him . . . it's more natural to be angry, if you let yourself feel the anger, maybe that'll give you strength . . . I used to think you could give him some kind of Jesus rap . . . I used to think you could reason 'em out of it, and talk to them like a human being, say "OK you don't want to do this, what are you doing?" . . . He seemed to listen to anger, yelling.

INTERVIEWER: What methods do you think would be ineffective, once a man tries to accost a woman?
INTERVIEWEE: Crying and pleading and begging. [Interview with a raped woman]

Women threatened with rape are in a double bind. On the one hand we are told, "Fighting back will only excite him. Fighting back will only get him angry," advice which assumes that the assailant is not already angry and that immediate retaliation is the most dangerous strategy. We are warned as well that resistance will result in serious injury, if not mutilation and death; our mangled bodies will turn up in garbage cans and under park benches.

On the other hand, rape has traditionally and legally been defined as an adult man's carnal knowledge of

a woman *by force and against her will* (the man must be over fourteen and the woman must not be his wife).[1] According to this definition, it is not enough that a man used or threatened to use force for the act to be considered rape; a man can compel a woman to have sex and still not legally be acting against her will. Therefore, in order to prove legally that what happened was rape, the woman has to prove that it was indeed against her will. The best way to prove that she is not willing to be forced to have sex is *not* by saying "Please don't," or "I have my period." The best way to prove that the act is not mutually consensual is by physically resisting.[2] In this article we describe the strategies that have prevented rape and the conditions under which they were effective. The 1976 Queen's Bench study was the first to show that "acting like a lady" was more likely to result in rape than in rape avoidance.[3] More recently, William Sanders, Jennie McIntyre, and Richard Block and Wesley Skogan—the latter using national victimization data—have come to similar conclusions.[4] All the studies based on interviews with raped women and women who prevented their rapes, as well as Block and Skogan's work, find that active strategies, notably fighting back, are effective in rape avoidance.

Our study also addresses important theoretical issues. For many years the question whether situational or personality factors have most influence in determining behavior has been central in social psychology, with sociologists leaning toward the former and psycholo-

Adapted from *Signs: Journal of Women in Culture and Society* 10, no. 1 (1984). Copyright © 1984 by The University of Chicago Press. All rights reserved.

gists and psychiatrists toward the latter. In this study, we do not deal with personality per se, partly because we do not think there are valid and reliable ways of measuring personality in interviews. More important, we do not use personality variables because research looking at the association of personality and victimization neglects variables such as autonomy training, independence, and competence.[5]

METHODOLOGY

This report is based on an analysis of 94 interviews with women eighteen or older who had been attacked and who had either avoided being raped ($N = 51$) or been raped ($N = 43$) in the two years prior to the interview. We limited the sample to women who experienced either force or the threat of force. The interview consisted of a self-report dealing with demographic variables, and answers to unstructured and semistructured questions about situational and background factors. Because of the exploratory nature of the research, we added questions when unanticipated patterns emerged—for instance, on incest, sexual assault in childhood, or other violence in the woman's life, or on whether the woman was primarily concerned with being killed or mutilated or primarily concerned with not being raped. The first part of the interview addressed such situational variables as the presence of a weapon, the number of assailants, the response of the woman, the acts that occurred during the assault, the degree of acquaintance with the assailant. The second part dealt with background variables, with questions about a woman's sense of competence and autonomy and about her socialization as a child and an adult into a traditional female role. We asked the raped woman about how her significant others responded to the assault and about interaction with institutions such as the police, hospitals, and therapists. We also examined the negotiation process between the woman and her assailant(s) if such negotiation took place.

Eighty percent of the interviews were conducted by the principal investigator (Pauline Bart) and 20 percent by a female clinical psychologist (Marlyn Grossman). The interviews lasted from one-and-a-half to six hours, depending on the subject's desire to talk and on the history of violence in her individual life. These interviews were transcribed.

Because of the nature of our major research ques-

tion, we could not obtain a random sample. Therefore, following a pretest, we launched a campaign to find respondents and recruited 94 women through newspaper ads (including major Black and Hispanic papers), press releases, public service announcements (the radio announcements were in both English and Spanish), appearances on radio and television, flyers, and contacts initiated through friendship networks of the project staff.

The resulting purposive, that is, nonrandom sample, when compared to the female population of the Chicago standard metropolitan statistical area (SMSA), which includes Cook and the surrounding counties, was disproportionately white, young, and unmarried

TABLE 1 DEMOGRAPHIC CHARACTERISTICS

	%	N
Race:		
White	81	76
Black	15	14
Hispanic	4	4
Religion:		
Protestant	38	35
Catholic	35	33
Jewish	19	18
No religion	6	. . .
Other	2	. . .
Marital status:		
Never married	58	54
Married, living with husband	15	14
Married, not living with husband	6	6
Divorced	19	18
Married, divorcing	1	. . .
Missing information	1	. . .
Education:		
High school or less	12	11
Some college	44	41
Four-year degree	19	18
Some graduate work	26	24
Occupation:		
Dependent	2	2
Homemaker	2	2
Blue-collar worker	10	9
Clerical worker	33	32
Professional	31	29
Student	9	8
Interim employment (usually student)	12	11
Missing information	1	. . .

NOTE: Interviewees ranged in age from 18 to 72. The mean age was 28.14 years.

TABLE 2   COMPARISON OF DATA ON SEXUALLY ASSAULTED WOMEN

	Bart and O'Brien (N = 94) (%)	McIntyre (N = 32) (%)	Queen's Bench (N = 108) (%)	National Victimization Surveys[a] (N = approx. 22,000) (%)
Age:				
Under 25	36	66[b]	71	59
Over 35	10	. . .	7	15
Race:				
White	81	75	79	69
Nonwhite	19	. . .	21	31
Marital status:				
Single	57	68	80	58
Married	16	. . .	10	22
Separated or divorced	27	. . .	11	17
Widowed	. . .	. . .	. . .	3
Work status:				
Employed full-time	62	46	39	46
Employed part-time	13	. . .	. . .	. . .
Student	12	35	37	15
Unemployed	8	. . .	13	6
Homemaker	4	. . .	1	33
Missing information	1	. . .	. . .	. . .
Attacked by stranger	78[c]	77	81	82
Rape completed	46	60	63	33
Weapon present	46	. . .	33	40
Attacked by multiple assailants	13	14	15	16
Reported attack to police	66	. . .	. . .	56

SOURCES: Jennie J. McIntyre, "Victim Response to Rape: Alternative Outcomes" (final report to National Institute of Mental Health, grant R01MH29045); Queen's Bench Foundation, "Rape: Prevention and Resistance" (Queen's Bench Organization, 1255 Post St., San Francisco, California, 1976); Joan McDermott, "Rape Victimization in 26 American Cities" (Washington, D.C.: Department of Justice, Law Enforcement Assistance Administration, Government Printing Office, 1979).
[a]All percentages (except for the percent attacked by strangers) are calculated for attacks by strangers only.
[b]Percentage calculated for women under 26, not 25.
[c]Includes 71 percent raped by total strangers and 7 percent raped by men known by sight or met on a casual first encounter.

(either single or divorced). Also none of the women who responded was engaged only in domestic labor at the time of the interview; all were either working outside the home or attending school. However, while the sample is not representative of women in the Chicago SMSA, it is not very different from the population of raped women and rape avoiders in national victimization data, except for an overrepresentation of white women (tables 1 and 2).[6] In addition to the demographic bias, the sample is shaped by the fact that the participants were volunteers.[7] A final source of possible bias in our sample was the very high proportion of women who had been raped by strangers or near strangers (approximately 80 percent).[8] An additional

10 percent were attacked by men they had met for the first time just prior to the assault.

Actually, we currently have no way of knowing what the "real" population of women who have been sexually assaulted looks like. On the one hand, rapes reported to the police are known to be gross undercounts of total rapes and to involve a disproportionate number of rapes by strangers.[9] On the other hand, victimization researchers have found that some respondents fail to tell interviewers about rapes actually reported to the police.[10] The problem of defining rape adds further complications; many women who agree that they have been forced to have sex do not label the act as rape.[11]

We paid the women $25.00 for their time; moreover, all their expenses—including babysitting and travel for those who were from outside Chicago—were reimbursed. When the women telephoned us initially, we told them of the remuneration, and we asked for their own definition of the situation. Specifically, we asked them to tell us whether they had been raped or had been attacked but had avoided being raped. In this way, the women defined themselves into the two parts of the sample: rape avoiders and raped women.

A serendipitous finding was that while there was no problem in differentiating rape from seduction, there was no hard and fast line differentiating rape from rape avoidance.[12] Since we can conceptualize rape as a continuum starting with the first approach, verbal or physical, and ending with the rapist's penetration and intercourse to orgasm, any interruption in the continuum before the rapist's orgasm could theoretically be considered an avoidance.

In order to address this issue, we examined the data in three ways: the woman's perception of herself as either a raped woman or one who had avoided rape, the nature of the acts that occurred, and the legal definition of them.[13] The acts consisted of genital intercourse, sodomy, fellatio, interfemoral penetration (the assailant masturbating himself between the woman's thighs), cunnilingus, digital penetration, fondling and touching, and kissing. The possible legal definitions coded (using Illinois statutes at that time) were rape, attempted rape, and deviant sexual assault. When we examined the relationship between self-perception and the acts that had occurred, we learned that, for the most part, the women define rape by what is done with a man's penis (genital intercourse, sodomy, fellatio), not by what is done to a woman's genitals (digital penetration, fondling and touching, cunnilingus) (see table 3).[14]

FINDINGS

Defense Strategies

When the women described their assaults, distinct types of defense techniques emerged that were classified in the following way. A woman could

1. flee or try to flee.
2. scream, yell, or talk loudly—usually in an effort to attract attention.

TABLE 3   SELF-PERCEPTION AS RAPED WOMAN OR RAPE AVOIDER, BY OCCURRENCE OF PHALLIC SEX (%)

	SELF-PERCEPTION	
	Raped Woman	Rape Avoider
Phallic sex occurred[a] (N = 45)	93	7
Phallic sex did not occur[b] (N = 49)	2	98

NOTE:—This table was constructed by Kim Scheppele.
[a]Phallic sex includes any one or any combination of the following: penile-vaginal penetration, sodomy, fellatio, interfemoral penetration, or female masturbation of assailant.
[b]Phallic sex is considered not to have occurred if only the following took place: digital penetration, cunnilingus, fondling, touching and kissing. It is considered not to have occurred as well in situations where the attack was thwarted before any overt sexual acts took place.

3. use "affective verbal" techniques such as begging and pleading with the assailant in order to gain his sympathy.
4. use "cognitive verbal" techniques, which included attempting to reason with the assailant, "conning" him, trying to make him "see her as a person," and stalling.
5. take advantage of environmental intervention—someone or something in the surroundings that intruded on the scene and either caused the assailant to stop the assault or gave her an opportunity to escape.
6. respond with physical force, the possibilities ranging from a simple push to self-defense techniques to use of a weapon.

Avoiders used a substantially greater number of strategies than raped women. All of the five respondents who employed *no* strategies were raped; these made up 11.6 percent of the raped women in the sample. Of the respondents who used only one strategy, 30 percent (13) were raped women and 18 percent (9) were avoiders. Of the respondents who used two kinds of strategies, 28 percent (12) were raped women and 29 percent (15) were avoiders. The difference between raped women and avoiders sharply increases after this. Twenty-one percent (9) of the raped women and 35 percent (18) of the avoiders used three types of strategies; 9 percent (4) of the raped women and 18 percent

TABLE 4   STRATEGIES OF RAPE AVOIDANCE, BY OUTCOME OF ATTACK (%)

	Raped Women (N = 43)	Rape Avoiders (N = 51)
Fled or tried to flee	9	33
Screamed	35	49
Used physical force	33	59
Used cognitive verbal strategies	72	67
Used affective verbal strategies	33	22
Benefited from environmental intervention	5	20
Used no strategy	12	. . .

(9) of the avoiders used four types of strategies. The modal number of strategies for raped women was one, while for avoiders it was three. The mean number of types of strategies for raped women was 1.86 and for avoiders was 2.53, consistent with the results reported in the Queen's Bench study.[15]

Not only did avoiders use more types of strategies, the strategies they used differed from the strategies of the raped women. Avoiders were more likely to flee or try to flee, to talk loudly or scream, to use physical force, and to be aided by environmental intervention. Raped women were more likely to plead. Both were about equally likely to use cognitive verbal techniques, the strategy most frequently used (see table 4).

Because we have qualitative data, we can also study the sequence of strategies. Our analysis took particular note of women who used physical strategies since most debates revolve around this response. Six women who stopped their rapes first used physical strategies and then yelled or screamed. Another effective sequence of strategies for women who stopped their rapes involved using cognitive verbal strategies, and when those proved ineffective, changing to physical strategies. Such strategies, then, can convince the assailant that the woman is serious, not just feigning resistance.[16] The modal strategy for women who stopped their rapes was a combination of screaming/yelling and physical resistance. The correlation between the two strategies was +0.42 for avoiders.

Avoiding Death or Avoiding Rape

A woman's primary focus emerged during the interviews as a factor sharply differentiating raped women from rape avoiders: the women whose primary concern lay in avoiding death or mutilation have been less likely to avoid rape than those who had a gut reaction of rage and were primarily determined not to be raped. Because of the exploratory nature of this study, we were able to add a question to the interview schedule addressing this point after the pattern emerged. Twenty-eight women who were raped and 19 women who avoided rape expressed fear of death or mutilation as their foremost concern, while 3 women who were raped and 26 women who avoided rape were primarily determined not to be raped.

For example, the first woman we interviewed, a college student, was able to stop her rape even though her assailant was armed. She said, "We circled for a while; he had a knife. I was wearing some loose clothing . . . he knocked me to the ground, so he managed to get the top half of all of my clothes off and there's sort of a blank. I remember clearly wanting to fight this, not want this . . . not wanting to allow this to happen and I just thought, 'Well, I'm not going to stand for this, you know.' And I didn't. . . . He did have a knife and he did slash my coat. I didn't have any clothes on. I had an acute sense of being vigorous, stronger, and more overpowering in myself and then there was sort of a brief flurry or something . . . or sliding away." (She had, in fact, slid away from her attacker.)

This response was surprising since we had originally thought that if there were a weapon no resistance would be possible. At the same time, the women who feared death should in no way be blamed, since descriptions of rape in the media emphasize the more lurid rape/murders and give scant attention to the women who stopped their rapes.

Psychological and Bodily Consequences of Physical Resistance

The effectiveness of using physical force to resist rape proved to be our most controversial finding, albeit one that is replicated in other studies.[17] We have suggested above that its effectiveness may lie in its communicating a clear message to the assailant, in addition to any physical injury he might receive or be in danger of receiving. Some assailants were not convinced by other strategies, presumably because they subscribed to the ideology prevalent in pornography and other media that women, whatever they might say, really want to be sexually assaulted. But what of the effect of this strategy on the women? We found that raped women who used physical strategies were less likely to be depressed than raped women who did not. The largest number of women who said they were depressed or who had symptoms of depression such as insomnia and weight loss were among those who were raped but did not use physical strategies. There was no difference in frequency of depression among women who avoided rape by fighting back and those who avoided rape without using physical strategies. Thus we can say that one of the most important functions of physical resistance is to keep women from feeling depressed even if they have been raped.[18]

If what we are tapping were merely personality differences between those who physically resisted and those who did not, then we would not find differences in depression only for those women who were raped. We think the results stem from the traditional vocabulary of motives used in our society to account for rape, a vocabulary many women have internalized.[19] In this vocabulary, rape is provoked by women through their dress, their carelessness, their foolhardiness in going to a "forbidden" place, such as a bar. Women are told, moreover, that they cannot be raped against their will—that, indeed, women really want to be raped and enjoy it. By resisting rape, however, women demonstrate to themselves and to others that this vocabulary does not apply to them. They are less likely to attribute their rape to their "personality defects"—weakness, cowardice, ineffectiveness—and thus less likely to say, "If only I had fought back it wouldn't have happened."[20] They are less likely to blame themselves and to feel depressed, more likely to gain strength from the belief that they did everything they could in that situation.

We are told that if we fight back, if we physically resist, we will pay the price through severe injury or death. This admonition is not supported by our findings or in the studies reported above. Furthermore, advising women to comply or risk injury assumes that rape in itself does not result in injury, physical as well as mental. Several women who talked to us reported serious injury from rape. One woman had a psychotic breakdown which resulted in her hospitalization. Her rapist also tore the area between her vagina and her anus so badly that it required surgical repair. In addition she became pregnant and had an abortion. Since she was not conscious during the attack, the injury did not stem from her resistance. Another contracted venereal disease, which led to pelvic inflammatory disease; she is now permanently sterile. She screamed

and tried to reason with her assailant but did not resist physically.

We know that women who resist physically are more likely to avoid rape. We also know that there is little relationship between women's use of physical resistance and rapists' use of additional physical force over and above the attempted rape. True, sexual assault does not usually produce serious physical harm, while physical resistance often results in minor injuries such as bruises and scratches. Some women who used physical force were moderately or seriously injured. One such woman while arguing with her assailant, who was trying to enter her apartment, was punched in the eye and pushed into her apartment where she continued to struggle. Her screams alerted the neighbors who called the police. They arrived in time to stop the rape. A second woman screamed while being attacked in a cornfield and tried to strike her assailant. He pulled a knife, hit her twice with his fist, knocked her unconscious, and raped her. A woman who had decided to submit to rape, rather than be choked to death with a telephone cord, couldn't yield "because he was so dirty." The would-be rapist beat her, but when she yanked at his penis he hurriedly left.

Women who fought back sustained the following kinds of injuries: bruises and bite marks on the neck, soreness for a few days, strained muscles, bruises and minor cuts, more serious cuts, back injury, and aching the next morning. While we asked the women about the assailant's tactics including physical abuse, we did not systematically ask about their own injuries and so there may have been minor injuries not reported. It is likely, however, that all the women who had serious injuries told us of them.

To judge the correlation between injury and physical resistance we must consider the interviews of the 5 women who were brutally beaten or suffered serious injury. Three were raped and 2 avoided being raped. Both avoiders' injuries resulted from their having fought back. However, for one of them, the resistance delayed the rape long enough for a train to pull into the platform where the assault was taking place, and the assailants fled. A third woman who was raped fought back even though her assailant had an ice pick as a weapon. It is unclear whether her beating was in response to her fighting back or to her screams. A raped virgin, attacked by two armed assailants, fought back and was seriously injured. But the injury was a result not of her struggle but of her seven rapes and her escape method. The last woman became sterile, as we described above.

These experiences suggest that by fighting back a woman significantly increases her chances of rape avoidance and somewhat increases her chance of rough treatment. However, not resisting is no guarantee of humane treatment.

Degree of Acquaintance with Assailant

Do women respond differently when attacked by men they know than when attacked by strangers? If so, is such difference in response associated with whether the outcome of the attack is rape or rape avoidance? Being assaulted by a stranger results in different patterns of response than does being assaulted by an acquaintance (see table 5). Both groups of women were more likely to yell or scream as well as to use both cognitive and affective verbal strategies when the assailant was a stranger than when he was someone they knew. In addition, there was environmental intervention more often among women who were not raped.

Environmental intervention, in general, occurred more frequently for women who avoided rape. In only two instances did raped women experience environmental intervention, and in both of these the assailant was a stranger. It should be noted that the mere occurrence of environmental intervention was not always sufficient to thwart attack. Sometimes the assailant(s)

fled. But sometimes the woman had to be able to utilize such an opportunity in order to escape. One woman, for instance, who had been pinned against an alley wall, was able to flee when the sudden noise of a fire engine's siren caused her assailant to loosen his grip. On another occasion a woman had negotiated with her assailant to rape her in his van rather than in the alley where he first attacked her. While walking with him to the van, she saw a strange man approach and asked him to help her. Although he never actually intervened, she used this opportunity to break away and run to a nearby tavern.

Presence of a Weapon

Conventional wisdom would suggest that the most important variable in a woman's response to attack is the assailant's possession of a weapon. And indeed, presence of a weapon does influence the outcome.[21] Of the group of women who were attacked by an unarmed assailant, 37 percent (19) were raped and 63 percent (32) avoided rape. Of the group of women who were attacked when an assailant had a weapon, when a weapon was presumed to be present, or when the assailant used a weapon to threaten or wound the woman, 56 percent (24) were raped and 44 percent (19) stopped the rape. The last point needs emphasis, however; even where there was some indication of a weapon, 44 percent of the women avoided being raped.

When the assailant had a weapon, 2 raped women

TABLE 5   STRATEGIES OF RAPE AVOIDANCE, BY OUTCOME OF ATTACK AND DEGREE OF ACQUAINTANCE*

	RAPED WOMEN (N = 43)		RAPE AVOIDERS (N = 51)	
	Known Assailant (N = 13) (%)	Stranger (N = 30) (%)	Known Assailant (N = 14) (%)	Stranger (N = 37) (%)
Fled or tried to flee	—	13.3	14.3	40.5
Screamed	23.1	40.0	42.8	51.3
Used physical force	38.5	30.0	57.1	59.5
Used cognitive verbal strategies	46.2	83.3	57.1	75.7
Used affective verbal strategies	30.7	33.3	21.4	21.6
Benefited from environmental intervention	—	6.7	21.4	18.9

*Percentages are based on the number of women in a given category who knew/did not know their assailant(s) and employed a particular strategy.

fled, and 16 did not; 8 rape avoiders fled, and 6 did not. When the assailant had a weapon, 6 raped women screamed, and 12 did not; 4 avoiders screamed and 10 did not. When a weapon was present, 4 raped women used physical force, and 14 did not; 5 avoiders used that strategy, and 9 did not. When the assailant was armed, 13 raped women and 11 avoiders used cognitive verbal strategies. Five raped women and 3 avoiders did not use such strategies. Four raped women faced with weapons used affective verbal strategies and 12 did not, while 4 avoiders used this strategy and 10 did not. Of the 5 victims who used no strategies, 3 were faced with armed assailants, and in 2 cases the assailant was not armed.

Since much of the debate about rape avoidance focuses on whether women should use physical force, it is important that one of the most striking differences between raped women and rape avoiders occurred in the case where the assailant did not have a weapon. In such situations, three-quarters (24) of the avoiders used physical strategies while one-quarter (8) did not; about half (9) of the raped women used such strategies, and about half (10) did not.

Being Attacked While Asleep

We have already seen that the most obvious situational variable, presence of a weapon, is associated with victimization rather than with avoidance. But we have also seen that even under such circumstances some women avoid rape. We will now turn to another variable that makes appropriate defense difficult and, in fact, according to Ann Burgess and Lynda Holmstrum, has particularly long-lasting effects: being attacked while asleep.[22] Two of the 5 women who were asleep used no strategies. How did the women who were not raped manage to avoid the assault? None pleaded, although all used cognitive verbal strategies. One, whom we call the "Super Negotiator," screamed, talked, and fought. Another talked, used physical force, and took advantage of environmental intervention. Their assailants were armed in both cases, and yet both women physically resisted. A third screamed and used cognitive verbal strategies, while a fourth was one of the few women who was able to avoid rape simply by persuading the man that she was not interested. The latter case is particularly striking because the assailant was later apprehended on numerous rape charges. While in prison, he wrote a letter to one of the women he raped in which he mentioned that, while he really

liked her, he did not like another woman he tried to assault. We interviewed this second woman for our study. But he asked the woman to whom he wrote the letter why he was being charged with assault when he actually was raping.[23]

Two case histories give a sense of the kinds of strategies that can be employed in difficult situations. One of them involves the five-foot eight-inch tall Super Negotiator. She awoke to find herself pinned beneath the covers of her bed by a naked, armed man who was straddling her. She made an attempt to reach the phone but agreed to give up this bid for assistance in return for his removing a knife from her throat. She told the assailant she was menstruating and feigned embarrassment at the thought of removing her tampon in his presence. He agreed to allow her to go to the bathroom. However, once there, he would not allow her to close the door and scream for help. After removing her tampon, she refused to return to the bedroom, claiming that the knife, which was still in the room, frightened her. At this point, the assailant removed the knife from the nightstand and threw it down the hallway. She had attempted unsuccessfully to convince him to throw it outdoors, but he claimed that walking through the living room might cause him to be seen. Returning to the bedroom, he began to fondle her breasts and digitally penetrate her vagina. In response she feigned hysteria, in an effort to make him think that she was "going crazy." Finding this strategy unsuccessful, she asked if she could smoke some hash in order to relax. The hash pipe was big and heavy, and initially she planned on using it as a weapon; however, she was unable to work up enough nerve. After pretending to smoke for awhile, she asked if it would be all right if she went to the kitchen for a beer, as the hash had not had the desired effect. He refused and shoved her on her back on the bed. She responded by jumping and throwing him on his back, grabbing his hair and yanking his head as hard as she could over the footboard of the bed. The assailant began to whimper. She reprimanded him for being "pushy" and for hurting her, and once again made her request for a beer and cigarette. The assailant complied, but retrieved his knife and followed her to the kitchen, pressing the knife to her back.

Once in the kitchen, she had hoped to make her escape, but she found that this was not possible. Not having any beer in the refrigerator, she successfully passed off a can of soda as a beer. As they were walking back to the bedroom she feigned anger at their return to the initial scenario—being in the bedroom with an armed man. In order to appease her, he placed the knife on the bookcase in the living room. For the first time since the start of the incident, she knew exactly where the knife was; thus, it would be accessible if she could somehow maneuver away from him. After smoking her cigarette and drinking the "beer," she clutched her stomach, pretending nausea, and ran out of the room. When he realized that she wasn't heading for the bathroom, he began to pursue her, but by this time she had reached the knife. He reached for a nearby lamp, which he intended to use as a weapon, but discovered that it was far too light to be useful. At this point she was moving toward the door and he said, "All right, that's it, I'm leaving. I was gonna try to be nice, but I'm leaving. Forget it." She ran out the back door and screamed for help. He made a couple of attempts to run out after her, but every time he did, she'd raise the knife to threaten him. Finally, he made a dash out the door, still naked from the waist down, carrying his pants. Less than a week after the attack, he parked his car behind her building after following her home from work. She flagged down a police car and he was apprehended.

Another case in which a woman was faced with seemingly impossible odds against avoiding assault involved a five-foot-ten-inch worker in a drug rehabilitation center. After completing her duties one evening, she crawled into her sleeping bag and fell asleep. Not long afterward, one of the residents came in asking for the time. In her stupor, she yelled at him and he appeared to leave. The next thing she knew "he was on top of" her with a knife pressed to her neck. Initially she froze, but then she fought him. Somehow she managed to get him off and get to the door, all the while screaming at the top of her lungs. After escaping from the room, she ran into a very large fellow female worker. Two women were too much for this assailant and he took off. Returning from the hospital, the avoider and a female companion spotted the assailant on the highway and reported his presence to the police. He was apprehended.

While both of these women were comparatively tall, we do not think it was simply their size that made the difference, although women five feet seven inches and over proved more likely to avoid rape. Rather, we suggest that short and tall women are treated differently in this society. Tall women do not have the option of being "cute" or acting helpless. They are less likely than short women to have a trained incapacity to be

competent and assertive. Therefore, they are less likely to have the option of assuming the traditional "feminine" role, which rape analysts such as Susan Brownmiller and Susan Griffin suggest is conducive to being a rape victim.[24]

Much of what occurs in any assault depends on the woman's interaction with her assailant. In our interviews we discovered that women were able to negotiate parts of the scenario. Although it was difficult to avoid genital intercourse itself through negotiation, some of the women whom we interviewed were able to negotiate their way out of other sex acts after intercourse was completed; several through argument avoided sodomy, fellatio, and multiple acts of intercourse. Women also made bargains involving money or credit cards, negotiated regarding the place of assault, and modified some of the conditions of their assaults—arranged to be tied up in a more comfortable position, got assistance in walking from one place to another. The Super Negotiator superbly illustrates the range of individual negotiations.[25]

CONCLUSIONS AND POLICY IMPLICATIONS

Women who avoided rape used more kinds of strategies in response to the assault than women who were raped. They also used different strategies. Strategies associated with avoidance were fleeing or trying to flee, yelling, and using physical force. In cases where rape was avoided, there was also more likely to be environmental intervention. Women who were raped were more likely to use no strategies (no woman who avoided rape fell into this category) or to rely on affective verbal strategies. The most common strategies used were cognitive verbal—reasoning, verbally refusing, threatening, and conning. Use of such tactics, though they are frequently advised, did not differentiate raped women from those who avoided rape, and those strategies alone were rarely effective. The modal response which resulted in avoidance was a combination of yelling and using physical force. While the assailant's having a weapon made rape the more probable outcome, 37 percent of the women who avoided rape did so when the assailant was armed or claimed to be armed.

Because of the exploratory nature of the study and because ours was not a random sample, caution should be used in interpreting these results. Nonetheless, four empirical studies comparing the strategies of raped women and rape avoiders came up with similar findings. It is no accident that these findings, which suggest that women should physically resist their assailants, run counter to official ideology that women can avoid rape by behaving in ways more consonant with traditional socialization. Since rape is, after all, a paradigm of sexism in society,[26] it is not surprising that male advice to women on how to avoid rape also reflects that paradigm.

The tactics that women are usually advised to employ—verbal strategies, feigning insanity, or appealing to the assailant's humanity—are relatively ineffective. One might well conclude not only that the traditional ideology regarding rape is a form of social control over women,[27] but that traditional advice on rape avoidance also functions in this manner. This advice, when not such simple caveats about restricting one's behavior as "don't go out at night," suggests coping strategies consistent with the conventional female role, particularly use of verbal skills to manipulate the situation rather than confrontational behavior and fighting back. One police official is quoted as saying, "We recommend passive resistance, like getting a person's confidence by talking and doing what you were taught to do as girls growing up, to help resist attack."[28]

The importance of the policy implications of our study is augmented by Diana Russell and Nancy Howell's report of an intensive interview survey in San Francisco. They demonstrated the pervasiveness of the problem of sexual assault, contending "that there is at least a 26 percent probability that a woman in that city will become the victim of completed rape at some time in her life, and a 46 percent probability that she will become a victim of rape *or* attempted rape."[29] They conclude that the feminist analysis of rape, which states that sexual violence against women is endemic, is supported by research.

Feminist analysis has succeeded in making the point that rape is not a joke, that it has detrimental effects not only on the particular woman who is assaulted but on all women. For even though not all women are raped, fear of rape causes women generally to constrict their behavior.[30] Thus, it is clearly important to have data-based advice on which strategies are most effective in stopping a sexual assault. Indeed, since the National Institute of Mental Health released our findings, not only have the media been interested in disseminating our results—albeit in simplified form—but rape crisis centers and police departments have asked for our reports and papers so that they could be incorporated into their programs. We thus have the privilege of knowing that the pain our respondents endured not only during their assaults but in anticipation of their interviews, and the stress we experienced while listening to them and while analyzing the data, have not been in vain.

ACKNOWLEDGMENTS

This paper is based on research funded by the Center for the Prevention and Control of Rape of the National Institute of Mental Health, grant MH 29311-0. An earlier version was presented at the annual meetings of the American Sociological Association, New York, 1980, entitled "How to Say No to Storaska and Survive: Rape Avoidance Strategies." Frederick Storaska is the author of a book that is demeaning to women and is full of misinformation (*How to Say No to a Rapist and Survive* [New York: Random House, 1975]).

NOTES

1. Wallace D. Lok, "What Has Reform of Rape Legislation Wrought?" *Journal of Social Issues* 37, no. 4 (1981): 28–52. The Illinois sexual assault statute that went into effect in July 1984 omits the phrase "against her will." Catharine MacKinnon suggests that consent should be proven by the defense rather than disproven by the prosecution, making consent an "affirmative defense." See "Feminism, Marxism, Method, and the State: Toward Feminist Jurisprudence," *Signs: Journal of Women in Culture and Society* 8, no. 4 (1983):635–58, esp. 648, n. 29.

2. In fact, the People v. Joel Warren, 446 N.W. 2d 591, 1983, Illinois Appellate Court Fifth District (no. 82–180), reversed an original decision that found an assailant guilty of two counts of deviate sexual assault. The court reasoned that the complainant's "failure to resist when it was within her power to do so conveys the impression of consent regardless of her mental state, amounts to consent and removes from the act performed an essential element of the crime." The defendant maintained "that once complainant became aware that defendant intended to engage in sexual relations, it was incumbent upon her to resist." This decision was rendered even though the woman was five feet two inches and weighed one hundred pounds and the assailant was over six feet and weighed 185 pounds, the attack took place in an isolated area, and the woman was afraid that physically assaulting the man would anger him.

3. Queen's Bench Foundation, "Rape: Prevention and Resistance" (Queen's Bench Organization, 1255 Post St., San Francisco, 1976). See also Greer Litton Fox, "'Nice Girl': Social Control of Women through a Value Construct," *Signs* 2, no. 4(1977):805–17.

4. William B. Sanders, *Rape and Woman's Identity* (Beverly Hills, Calif.: Sage, 1980); Jennie J. McIntyre, "Victim Response to Rape: Alternative Outcomes" (final report to National Institute of Mental Health, grant R01MH29045); Richard Block and Wesley G. Skogan, "Resistance and Outcome in Robbery and Rape: Non-fatal, Stranger to Stranger Violence" (Center for Urban Affairs and Policy Research, Northwestern University, 1982).

5. Elsewhere we have addressed childhood and adult socialization as well as background and situational variables: Pauline B. Bart and Ellen Perlmutter, "Socialization and Rape Avoidance" (paper presented at the Association for Women in Psychology, Santa Monica, Calif., 1980); Bart, "A Study of Women Who Both Were Raped and Avoided Rape," *Journal of Social Issues* 37, no. 4(1981):123–37; Bart and Patricia H. O'Brien, "Stopping Rape: Strategies for Success" (Department of Psychiatry, University of Illinois at Chicago Health Sciences Center, 1983).

6. Joan McDermott, "Rape Victimization in 26 American Cities" (Washington, D.C.: Government Printing Office, 1979).

7. We attempted to allow for bias through the use of vol-

unteers in two ways: we first asked women why they volunteered (the two primary motives proved to be altruism and catharsis, often in combination); and we then asked them where they had learned about the study. Our inquiries revealed no substantial bias from a single source.

8. While rapes reported to the police and McDermott's secondary analysis of a "representative sample of 10,000 households" also show similarly high rates of rape by strangers, other studies have found that as many as half the rapes involved assailants known to the woman: Pauline B. Bart, "Rape Doesn't End with a Kiss," *Viva*, June 1975, pp. 39–41, 100–101; Joseph J. Peters, *The Philadelphia Rape Victim Project in Forcible Rape: The Crime, the Victim, and the Offender* (New York: Columbia University Press, 1977); Menachem Amir, *Patterns of Forcible Rape* (Chicago: University of Chicago Press, 1971).

9. Bart, "Rape Doesn't End."

10. McDermott (n. 6 above).

11. Irene Hanson Frieze et al., "Psychological Factors in Violent Marriages" (Department of Psychology, University of Pittsburgh, 1979); Frieze, "Investigating the Causes and Consequences of Marital Rape," *Signs* 8, no. 3(1983):532–53.

12. It has become increasingly apparent that the concept of seduction is itself a male ideology. We have found that much, if not all, of what men perceive as seduction is in fact the result of women's having decided "to put up with it" or having planned in advance to "allow" themselves to be seduced. Bart has further refined the continuum as follows: consensual sex/altruistic sex/compliant sex/rape. In consensual sex both partners are sexually aroused. In altruistic sex the man wants sex and the woman goes along with it. When men engage in altruistic sex they use the pejorative term "mercy fucking." In complaint sex one person, usually the female, engages in the act because of the adverse consequences that follow if she doesn't, although there is no threat of force. We define rape as sexual behavior the woman engages in because of force or threat of force.

13. Pauline B. Bart and Kim Scheppele, "There Ought to Be a Law: Self-Definition and Legal Definitions of Sexual Assault" (paper presented at the meetings of the American Sociological Association, New York, 1980).

14. Kim Lane Scheppele and Pauline B. Bart, "Through Women's Eyes: Defining Danger in the Wake of Sexual Assault," *Journal of Social Issues* 39, no. 2(1983):63–80.

15. Queen's Bench Foundation (n. 3 above).

16. See Roseann Giarusso et al., "Adolescents' Cues and Signals: Sex and Assault" (paper presented at the annual meeting of the Western Psychological Association, San Diego, California, April 1979) for an analysis of the differences in the way in which males and females perceive the world.

17. Queen's Bench Foundation (n. 3 above); Sanders, McIntyre, and Block and Skogan (all n. 4 above).

18. Pauline B. Bart and Patricia H. O'Brien, "The After-

math of Rape and Rape Avoidance: Behaviors, Attitudes, Ideologies and Response of Significant Others" (paper presented at the International Sociological Association meeting, Mexico City, August 1982).

19. Pauline B. Bart, "Social Structures and Vocabularies of Discomfort: What Happened to Female Hysteria?" *Journal of Health and Social Behavior* 9 (September 1968):188–93, esp. 189.

20. Ronnie Janoff-Bulman, "Characterological versus Behavioral Self-Blame: Inquiries into Depression and Rape," *Journal of Personality and Social Psychology* 37(1979): 1798–1809.

21. This finding is also reported in McDermott (n. 6 above). According to our study, this relationship does not hold for Black women.

22. Ann Wolbert Burgess and Lynda L. Holmstrum, *Rape: Crisis and Recovery* (Bowie, Md.: Robert J. Brady, 1979).

23. Personal communication with Mary Pennington Anderson, attorney in the case.

24. Susan Brownmiller, *Against Our Will: Men, Women and Rape* (New York: Simon & Schuster, 1975); Susan Griffin, "Rape: The All-American Crime."

25. While we have been focusing on rape avoidance strategies as a way of coping with assault, there were additional ways in which women coped. Depersonalization—feeling as if it were happening to someone else, as if it were not really happening, as if one were dreaming—was a relatively common response, although, as one might expect, it was more common among raped women. Thus, 44 percent (19) of the raped women mentioned they experienced depersonalization, while 22 percent (11) of the avoiders had this response.

26. Pauline B. Bart, "Rape as a Paradigm of Sexism in Society," *Women's Studies International Quarterly* 2, no. 3(1979):347–57.

27. Stephanie Riger and Margaret T. Gordon, "The Fear of Rape: A Study in Social Control," *Journal of Social Issues* 37, no. no.4(1981):71–92.

28. Quoted in Tacie Dejanikus, "New Studies Support Active Resistance to Rape," *Off Our Backs,* February 1981, pp. 9, 23.

29. Diana E. H. Russell and Nancy Howell, "The Prevalence of Rape in the United States Revisited," *Signs* 8, no. 4(1983):688–95, esp. 695.

30. Riger and Gordon (n. 27 above).

R E A D I N G   4 1

"Femicide": Speaking the Unspeakable

JANE CAPUTI and DIANA E. H. RUSSELL

Canadian novelist Margaret Atwood once asked a male friend why men feel threatened by women. He replied: "They are afraid women will laugh at them." She then asked a group of women why they feel threatened by men. They answered: "We're afraid of being killed."

However disproportionate, these fears are profoundly linked, as was demonstrated on December 6,

From "'Femicide': Speaking the Unspeakable", *Ms.* Magazine 1, no. 2 (September–October 1990):34–37.

The authors would like to thank Joan Balter, Sandy Butler, Candida Ellis, Marny Hall, and Helene Vann for their invaluable comments on this article.

1989, at the University of Montreal. That day, 25-year-old combat-video aficionado Marc Lépine suited up for war and rushed the school of engineering. In one classroom, he separated the women from the men, ordered the men out, and, shouting "You're all fucking feminists," opened fire on the women. During a half-hour rampage, he killed 14 young women, wounded nine other women and four men, then turned his gun on himself. A three-page suicide note blamed all of his failures on women, whom he felt had scorned him. Also found was a hit list of 15 prominent Canadian women.

Unable to complete an application to the school of engineering, Lépine felt humiliated by women he defined as "feminists" because they had entered traditional male territory. His response to the erosion of white male exclusivity was a lethal one. It was also an eminently political one.

In the massacre's aftermath, media reports regularly denied the political nature of the crimes, citing such comments as Canadian novelist Mordecai Richler's: "It was the act of an absolutely demented man [which does not] lend itself to any explanation." This despite Lépine's clear explanation of his actions. *Whether individual hate killers are demented is beside the point.* In a racist and sexist society, psychotics as well as so-called normals frequently act out the ubiquitous racist and misogynist attitudes they repeatedly see legitimized.

Lépine's murders were hate crimes targeting victims by gender, not race, religion, ethnicity, or sexual orientation. When racist murders—lynchings and pogroms—occur, no one wonders whether individual perpetrators are crazy or have had bad personal experiences with African Americans and Jews. Most people understand that lynchings and pogroms are motivated by political objectives: preserving white and gentile supremacy. Similarly, the aim of violence against women—conscious or not—is to preserve male supremacy.

Early feminist analysts of rape exposed the myths that it is a crime of frustrated attraction, victim provocation, or uncontrollable biological urges, perpetrated only by an aberrant fringe. Rather, rape is a direct expression of sexual politics, an assertion of masculinist norms, and a form of terrorism that preserves the gender status quo.

Like rape, the murders of women by husbands, lovers, fathers, acquaintances, and strangers are not the products of some inexplicable deviance. Murder is simply the most extreme form of sexist terrorism. A new word is needed to reflect this political understanding. We think *femicide* best describes the murders of women by men motivated by hatred, contempt, pleasure, or a sense of ownership of women. Femicide includes mutilation murder, rape murder, battery that escalates into murder; historical immolation of witches in Europe; historical and contemporary immolation of brides and widows in India; and "honor crimes" in some Latin and Middle Eastern countries, where women believed to have lost their virginity sometimes are killed by male relatives.

General male identification with killers demonstrates how rooted femicide is in sexist culture. For example, engineering student Celeste Brosseau, who

had complained about the sexism of the engineering faculty at the University of Alberta, was subjected to hundreds of her "fellow" students chanting "Shoot the bitch!" when she participated in an engineering society skit-night shortly after Lépine's assassinations.

The misogyny motivating violence against women also distorts press coverage of such crimes. Rape, femicide, and battery are variously ignored or sensationalized in the media, depending on the victim's race, class, and "attractiveness." Police, media, and public response to crimes against women of color, poor women, lesbian women, women working as prostitutes, and drug users, is particularly abysmal—usually apathy laced with pejorative stereotyping and victim-blaming. Moreover, public interest is disproportionately focused on cases involving nonwhite assailants and white middle-class victims, such as the uproar over the 1989 Boston murder of Carol Stuart, a pregnant white woman who, her husband falsely claimed, was shot by a black robber. (She had been murdered by her affluent, white husband.)

Femicide is the ultimate end of a continuum of terror that includes rape, torture, mutilation, sexual slavery (particularly in prostitution), incestuous and extrafamilial child sexual abuse, physical and emotional battery; sexual harassment; genital mutilations (clitoridectomies, infibulations); unnecessary gyneco-

FEMICIDE: RELATED CIRCUMSTANCES
California, 1988
(Out of 689 willful femicides where related circumstances are known)

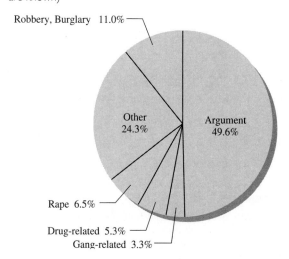

A LETTER FROM CLAUDIA BRENNER

January 1991

Dear Friend,

On May 13, 1988, my lover, Rebecca, was murdered. I survived, with five bullet wounds.

At the trial of the attacker, it was proven that we were attacked because of who we were—two lesbians, two women living our lives and our love for each other.

There is no way to lessen the horror of that moment. . . .

On May 13, Rebecca and I were hiking on the Appalachian trail in Adams County, Pennsylvania. At our campsite that morning, Rebecca was stopped by a man who asked her for a cigarette. He hadn't been there when we arrived at the site the previous evening, and must have arrived very late at night.

Later that day, we broke camp and continued our hike. As we checked a map at a fork in the trail, we were surprised to see the same man walking behind us. He had a rifle.

He asked us if we were lost. We said no, and turned left, onto a side trail. He continued along the main trail. The encounter made both Rebecca and

Reprinted by permission of Claudia Brenner

me uneasy. We kept looking behind to see if the man was following us, but we never saw him again.

Late that afternoon, Rebecca and I stopped and made camp near a stream. It was a secluded spot, some distance from the trail. We ate, made love and rested.

Suddenly, there were gunshots. The shots were *so* sudden, *so* loud, *so* violent, *so* world-changing that at first I didn't even realize that they were gunshots and that we were the targets—except there was so much blood.

Because I was between the attacker and Rebecca, I was hit first. I was shot in the upper arm, twice in the neck, in the head and face. Rebecca told me to run behind a nearby tree. As she followed me, Rebecca was shot in the head and back.

The shooting finally stopped. We were both behind a large tree. In my frantic shock and fear, I didn't understand how badly hurt we were. But Rebecca had the presence of mind to tell me what to do. She told me to stop the bleeding. I believe she saved my life.

My only thought was to get us out of there and get help. I brought Rebecca her sneakers, but she couldn't see them. She was losing her vision. I tried to lift her, but she kept slumping to the ground.

Someplace deep within me, I began to understand how badly hurt Rebecca was. If the situation could get worse, it came with the realization that I

---

logical operations (gratuitous hysterectomies), forced heterosexuality, forced sterilization, forced motherhood (criminalizing contraception and abortion), psychosurgery, abusive medical experimentation (e.g., some efforts to create new reproductive technologies), denial of protein to women in some cultures, cosmetic surgery and other mutilations in the name of beautification. Whenever these forms of terrorism result in death, they become femicides.

Federal statistics do not reveal the scope of violence against women. Surveys by independent researchers show rates of female victimization that should shatter

us all. For example, in Diana Russell's random sample survey of 930 San Francisco women: 44 percent reported being victimized by rape or attempted rape, 38 percent by child sexual abuse, 16 percent by incestuous abuse, 14 percent by wife rape, and 21 percent by marital violence.

As with rape and child sexual abuse, femicide is most likely to be perpetrated by a male family member, friend, or acquaintance. Ironically, the patriarchy's ideal domestic arrangement (heterosexual coupling) is the most potentially femicidal situation. Husbands (including common-law) account for 33 percent of had to go for help alone. I covered Rebecca, gave her all the first aid I could think of, and started out for help.

Before I left, Rebecca was unconscious. We never had a chance to say goodbye.

Soaked in blood, I walked on the rugged trail about two miles to a forest road. I was completely terrified that whoever had attacked us might be following and attack again. I walked on the road another two miles before I finally saw a car. I stopped the car, and the driver rushed me to the police in nearby Shippensburg.

All I could think about was Rebecca. The State Police immediately began a search for her.

That evening, I was airlifted to the Hershey Medical Center trauma unit. I had emergency surgery that night. The next day I learned that the police had found Rebecca's body. She died from the bullet wound that hit her back and exploded in her liver.

But my ordeal did not end with the horror of Rebecca's death.

The State Police caught the man who murdered Rebecca—the same man who had followed us on the trail—Stephen Roy Carr. We now know that Stephen Roy Carr stalked us, hid eighty-five feet away in the woods while we made camp, shot to kill and left us for dead.

During the legal proceedings that followed, it became clear that Carr had attacked us because we were lesbians. Carr's lawyer even implied—during the trial and the appeal—that Rebecca and I had provoked the attack.

The implication that Rebecca and I had "teased" Carr with our sexuality, and that we were responsible for this man stalking us, spying on us, and shooting to kill us was not only outrageous, it was disgusting.

Fortunately, the trial judge refused to allow this line of argument. On October 27, 1988, Stephen Roy Carr was convicted of first degree murder and later sentenced to life in prison without parole.

I survived the attack, but in the months that followed I was consumed with grief and fear. My world centered on the knowledge that Rebecca was dead and that somehow I was alive.

I had always known that the world was not a safe place for lesbians. But somehow, I believed that nothing this terrible would ever happen to me.

I believed that all I needed to do was not to look like a stereotypical lesbian and be discreet about my expressions of affection to other women. That security was shattered by the bullets. . . .

Sincerely,

Claudia Brenner

all women murdered between 1976 and 1987 in the United States.

Violent crimes against women have escalated in recent decades. Some believe this increase is due to women reporting them more. But Russell's research on (largely unreported) rape, for example, establishes a dramatic escalation during the last 50 years. Although it is not yet possible to assess the number of sex murders in any given year, virtually all experts agree there has been a substantial rise since the early 1960s. A surge in serial murder is recognized by criminologists to have begun in the 1950s, and has become a characteristic phenomenon of the late 20th century in the U.S. The vast majority of serial killers are white men and most of their victims are women.

We see this escalation of violence against females as part of a male backlash against feminism. This doesn't mean it's the *fault* of feminism: patriarchal culture terrorizes women whether we fight back or not. Still, when male supremacy is challenged, that terror is intensified. While women who stepped out of line in early modern Europe were tortured and killed as witches (estimates range from 200,000 to 9 million killed), today such women are regarded as cunts or bitches, deserving whatever happens to them. "Why is it wrong to get rid of some fuckin' cunts?" Kenneth Bianchi, convicted "Hillside Strangler," demanded to know. "Kill Feminist Bitches!" is a revealing graffito found on the Western Ontario campus after the Montreal massacre.

Law enforcement officials have noted the growing viciousness in slayings. Justice Department official Robert Heck said: "We've got people [sic] now killing 20 and 30 people [sic] and more, and some of them just don't kill. They torture their victims in terrible ways and mutilate them before they kill them." For example:

Teenager Shirley Ledford screamed for mercy while Roy Norris and Lawrence Bittaker of Los Angeles raped and mutilated her with a pair of locking pliers, hit her with a sledgehammer, and jabbed her in her ear with an ice pick. The men audiotaped the torture femicide from beginning to end.

In 1987, police found three half-naked, malnourished African American women "shackled to a sewer pipe in a basement that doubled as a secret torture chamber" in the home of Gary Heidnik, a white Philadelphian; 24 pounds of human limbs were stockpiled in a freezer and other body parts were found in an oven and a stew pot.

Such atrocities also are enacted upon women by their male intimates. The case of Joel Steinberg, who murdered his adopted daughter, Lisa, and tortured his companion, Hedda Nussbaum, for years, is extreme but not unique. In 1989, a California man was sentenced to 32 years in prison for torturing his wife in a 10-hour attack. After she refused anal sex, Curtis Adams handcuffed his wife, repeatedly forced a bottle and then a broomstick into her anus, and hung her naked out the window—taking breaks to make her read Bible passages adjuring women to obey their husbands.

A sense of entitlement is a major cause of sexist terrorism. Many males believe they have a right to get what they want from females. Consider the hatred exhibited in response to a trivial challenge to male dominance: female students at the University of Iowa complained about the loud stereos of male students on the floor above. A response in graffiti titled "The Top 10 Things To Do To The Bitches Below" was found in the men's bathroom and then published in the university newspaper, including exhortations to beat the women "into a bloody pulp with a sledgehammer and laugh" and instructions on "how to mutilate female genitalia with an electric trimmer, pliers, and a 'red-hot soldering iron.'" Similarly, a suggestion was made in the University of Toronto engineering students' newspaper that women "cut off their breasts if they were sick of sexual harassment."

To see where these students get such gruesome ideas, we only need look to pornography and mass media "gorenography." An FBI study of 36 sex serial killers found that pornography was ranked highest of many sexual interests by an astonishing 81 percent.

MURDER: RELATIONSHIP OF VICTIM TO OFFENDER (TEXAS, 1988)

Relationship	Number	% of Total
Acquaintance	572	42.2
Stranger	250	18.5
Wife/common-law wife	89	7.3
Friend	88	5.8
Other—known to victim	68	5.8
Husband/common-law husband	55	4.1
Other family	51	3.8
Son/stepson	34	2.5
Girlfriend	33	2.4
Neighbor	28	2.1
Brother	20	1.5
Father/stepfather	18	1.3
Boyfriend	15	1.1
Ex-wife	15	1.1
Daughter/stepdaughter	11	0.8
Mother/stepmother	8	0.4
Homosexual relationship	5	0.4
Sister	5	0.4
Ex-husband	2	0.1
TOTAL	1,355	100.0

*Relationship was known in 1,355 of 2,053 murder cases.

Such notorious killers as Edmund Kemper (the "Coed Killer"), Ted Bundy, David Berkowitz (the "Son of Sam"), and Kenneth Bianchi and Angelo Buono (the "Hillside Stranglers") were all heavy pornography consumers. Bundy maintained that pornography "had an impact on me that was just so central to the development of the violent behavior that I engaged in." His assessment is consistent with testimony from many other sex offenders, as well as research on the effects of pornography.

Femicidal atrocity is everywhere normalized, explained as "joking," and rendered into standard fantasy fare, from comic books through Nobel prizewinning literature, box-office smashes through snuff films. Meanwhile, the FBI terms sex killings "recreational murder."

Just as many people denied the reality of the Nazi Holocaust, most people refuse to recognize the gynocidal period in which women are living—and dying—today. Some husbands and fathers act as full-time guards who threaten to kill if defied. "Dedicated Bible reader" John List was convicted this year in New Jersey for mass murder, after escaping detection for 18 years. List complained that his wife refused to attend church, an action he "knew would harm the children." His daughter wanted to pursue an acting career, making him "fearful as to what that might do to her continuing to be a Christian." In a rage over his loss of control, this godly man slaughtered his wife, daughter, mother, and two sons.

If all femicides were recognized as such and accurately counted, if the massive incidence of nonlethal sexual assaults against women and girls were taken into account, if incest and battery were recognized as torture (frequently prolonged over years), if the patriarchal home were seen as the inescapable prison it so frequently becomes, if pornography and gorenography were recognized as hate literature, then this culture might have to acknowledge that we live in the midst of a reign of sexist terror comparable in magnitude, intensity, and intent to the persecution, torture, and annihilation of women as witches from the 14th to the 17th centuries in Europe.

It is unspeakably painful for most women to think about men's violence against us, as individuals and collectively, because the violence we encounter, and the

RAPE: RELATIONSHIP OF VICTIM TO OFFENDER (KANSAS, 1988)

Relationship	Number	% of Total
Acquaintance	217	28.5
Stranger	213	28.0
Friend	47	8.2
Wife/common-law wife	32	4.2
Ex-girlfriend	31	4.1
Girlfriend	19	2.5
Ex-wife	15	2.0
Daughter/stepdaughter	20	2.8
Other family/in-law	14	1.8
Sister	8	1.0
Granddaughter	2	0.3
Niece	1	0.1
Baby-sitter	1	0.1
Neighbor	1	0.1
Unknown	141	18.5
TOTAL	782	100.0

DOMESTIC VIOLENCE: REASONS FOR ASSAULT
Maryland, 1988

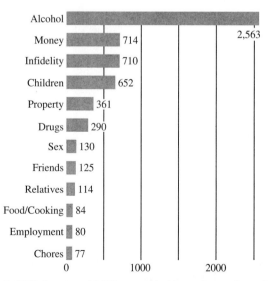

In 1988, there were 14,521 reported incidents of spousal assault in Maryland. In 5,988 cases, reasons for the assaults were given. These are the 12 most commonly cited.

disbelief and contempt with which we are met when we do speak out, is often so traumatic and life-threatening that many of us engage in denial or repression of our experiences.

In November 1989, 28-year-old Eileen Franklin-Lipsker of Foster City, California, suddenly remembered having witnessed her father sexually abuse her eight-year-old school friend, Susan Nason, then bludgeon her to death. Twenty years later, she turned her father in to the police. Such remembrance and denunciation is the work of the entire feminist movement against violence against women: to disobey the fathers' commandments to forget, deny, maintain silence, and, instead, to turn in our abusive fathers, husbands, brothers, lovers, sons, friends.

The recollection and acknowledgement of history/ experience that has been so profoundly repressed is what Toni Morrison in her masterpiece *Beloved* calls *rememory*. In an interview, Morrison noted that there is virtually no remembrance—no lore, songs, or dances—of the African people who died during the Middle Passage: "I suspect . . . it was not possible to survive on certain levels and dwell on it. . . . There is a necessity for remembering the horror, but . . . in a manner in which the memory is not destructive." Morrison's concept of rememory is crucial as well for all women grappling with the torment of living in a femicidal world. We too must be able to face horror in ways that do not destroy, but save us.

THE CYCLE OF DOMESTIC VIOLENCE

DAGMAR CELESTE

During her tenure as the first lady of Ohio, Dagmar Celeste championed many civil rights causes, and they included the concerns of women. Celeste was instrumental in Ohio's move to accept Battered Women's Syndrome as an admissible legal defense in cases involving a woman's fighting back against an abusive domestic partner, and in the award of clemency to women incarcerated for such actions. The following is the text of a speech Celeste delivered on this issue.

Experts call woman battering the most underreported crime in the nation. It is ironic that the same house a man calls his castle may be for his wife or lover a virtual prison. Women's experience of domestic violence remains shrouded in shame and secrecy. . . . What we call "the battered woman syndrome" is in fact a cycle of male violence against women. Men batter women. And as we focus on women's experience of that abuse, we must remember that women are not responsible for their victimization; women do not ask to be beaten or abused or tortured. . . .

. . . Researchers and clinicians, as well as survivors of battering, have codified its processes into a pattern called the cycle of violence [that occurs in three stages].

1. *The tension-building phase.* In this phase the man engages in emotional abuse and harassment, as well as less severe physical assaults like kicks and blows, pinching, spitting, and other behavior designed to degrade and humiliate the woman.

2. *The acute battering incident.* In this phase, the tension which began to build in the previous stage peaks. The batterer loses restraint and inhibition. His assault becomes more physical. He chokes her. He punches her. He kicks her. He beats her. He may crush her jaw and break her bones with his bare hands. Or he may be careful, abusing her so that the wounds don't show, though the beating is severe.

3. *The contrition phase.* After the acute battering incident, the man becomes repentant. He swears he will not "lose control" again. He becomes the romantic courtier. He brings flowers and candy and promises. She has been socialized to stand by her man. She does. She stays or goes back to the home she left after the acute battering incident.

Build up. Beat up. Make up. Time and time again, until he kills her or she kills him or someone dies or someone leaves. Men rarely voluntarily stop battering. Women rarely successfully extricate themselves from battering situations. The battering cycle encourages the woman's dependence upon her batterer; frequently battered women are not "allowed" to work outside the home, to have friends or contact with family, or to manage their own finances. Certainly, batterers pressure their victims to remain silent about the violence. Without strong support systems, and reluctant to fight back, women in battering situations commonly regard suicide as their best possible means of escape. . . .

. . . When incidents of domestic violence come to the attention of the judicial system, these same forces, which are not woman-centered, collide again to work against the interests, support, and protection of battered women. Laws, made largely by men to deal with typically male situations, often do not address the needs of women, let alone in cases where the killing or attacking of an abuser by his victim is justified by a history of abuse and a current threat of harm or death. We need to not only make sure that laws, such as those dealing with self-defense, address the specific situation of women who kill or attack their abusers, but we need to ensure that women who enter the legal system under such circumstances are able to present their experiences and to make full use of laws allowing battered woman syndrome as a defense. . . .

Woman battering is an endemic phenomenon in Western culture [that has its origins] in institutionalized patriarchy. In essence, socialization which trains men to control others through any means necessary, socialization which encourages women to allow others to define their realities, socialization which dictates that a woman must attach herself to a man at any cost in order to enjoy the full benefits of society, these processes set the context which fosters domestic violence. . . .

From text of a speech presented by Dagmar Celeste to Action Ohio Battered Women's Coalition, Spring 1990.

Canadian feminists are working to have December 6 declared a national day of remembrance for the slaughtered women. We encourage women worldwide to claim December 6 as an international day of mourning and rage, a "Rememory Day" for all women everywhere who have been victims of sexual violence.

Such rituals are modes of healing, but not cures. Feminists, collectively and internationally, must take on the task of formulating strategies of resistance as massive and formidable as the horrors that confront us.

Progressive people rightly favor an international boycott of South Africa so long as apartheid reigns; why do they/we so rarely consider the potential efficacy of boycotting violent and abusive men and *their* cul-

ture? In 1590, Iroquois women gathered in Seneca to demand the cessation of war among the nations. We must now demand an end to the global patriarchal war on women. The femicidal culture is one in which the male is worshiped. This worship is obtained through tyranny, subtle and overt, over our bruised minds, our battered and dead bodies, our co-optation into supporting even batterers, rapists, and killers. "Basically, I worshiped him," said Hedda Nussbaum. "We do not worship them . . . we do not trust them," wrote Alice Walker. In a myriad of ways, let us refuse nurture, solace, support, and approval. Let us withdraw our worship.

R E A D I N G   4 2

Female Slave Resistance: The Economics of Sex

DARLENE HINE and KATE WITTENSTEIN

The question of the extent and nature of black resistance to slavery has been the subject of a number of recent historical studies.[1] These works, concentrating as they do on the examination of black male resistance to the slave system, have demonstrated that such resistance was carried on both overtly in the form of slave rebellions and covertly in indirect attacks on the system through resistance to the whip, feigning of illness, conscious laziness, and other means of avoiding work and impeding production. None of these studies, however, has considered in depth the forms of black female resistance to slavery, although they have suggested a methodology for attempting such an investigation. This paper is concerned with uncovering the means through which female slaves expressed their political and economic opposition to the slave system. What behavior patterns did enslaved black women adopt to protect

"Female Slave Resistance: The Economics of Sex," by Darlene Hine and Kate Wittenstein in *The Black Women Cross-Culturally,* edited by Filomina Chioma Steady. Copyright © 1981 by Schenkman Books, Inc.

themselves and their children and to undermine the system which oppressed and exploited them?

Unlike male slaves, female slaves suffered a dual form of oppression. In addition, to the economic exploitation which they experienced along with black males, females under slavery were oppressed sexually as well. Sexual oppression and exploitation refer not only to the obvious and well-documented fact of forced sexual intercourse with white masters, but also to those forms of exploitation resulting from the very existence of their female biological systems. For example, the female slave in the role of the mammy was regularly required to nurse white babies in addition to, and often instead of, her own children. In his *Roll, Jordan, Roll: The World the Slaves Made,* Eugene Genovese acknowledges the uniquely difficult position in which this practice placed the mammy:

More than any other slave, she had absorbed the paternalist ethos and accepted her place in a system of reciprocal obligations defined from above. In so doing, she developed pride, resourcefulness, and a high sense of responsibility to white and black people alike. . . . She did not reject her people in order to identify with stronger whites, but she did place herself in a relationship to her own people that reinforced the paternalist social order.[2]

While Genovese gives evidence of the mammy's manipulation of her favored position, the pivotal question of how it must have felt to be forced to nurse and raise her future oppressors remains unexamined.

Another major aspect of the sexual oppression of black women under slavery took the form of the white master's consciously constructed view of black female sexuality. This construct, which was designed by the white master to justify his own sexual passion toward her, also blamed the female slave for the sexual exploitation which she experienced. Winthrop Jordan comments in his *White Over Black: American Attitudes Toward the Negro 1550–1812* that white men

> . . . by calling the Negro woman passionate . . . were offering the best possible justifications for their own passions. Not only did the Negro woman's warmth constitute a logical explanation for the white man's infidelity, but, much more important, it helped shift responsibility from himself to her. If she was *that* lascivious—well, a man could scarcely be blamed for succumbing against overwhelming odds.[3]

It is clear from several slave narratives that the female slave was well aware of the image of her sexuality which was fostered among the white male population. In her narrative *Incidents in the Life of a Slave Girl,* Linda Brent offers a revealing observation on the effect of this image on the female slave: "If God has bestowed beauty upon her, it will prove her greatest curse. That which commands admiration in the white woman only hastens the degradation of the female slave."[4] In his article "New Orleans: The Mistress of the Slave Trade," Frederic Bancroft documents Brent's observation and shows how this image of black female sexuality gave rise to a section of the slave trade specifically designed to profit from the sale of attractive black women, or as they were known at the time, "fancy girls."[5] Bancroft points out that slave traders frequently took pride in the numbers of such women they had for sale, and on the high prices commanded by their physical appearance. Often, these women sold

for prices which far exceeded that which planters were willing to pay for a field laborer. In 1857, for example, the *Memphis Eagle and Enquirer* ran an editorial in which it was observed that "a slave woman is advertized to be sold in St. Louis who is so surpassingly beautiful that $5000 has already been offered for her, at private sale, and refused."[6]

How, then, did the female slave resist both the economic and sexual oppressions which were a part of her daily life? Three intimately related forms of resistance peculiar to the female slave emerge from the narratives. The first method can be called sexual abstinence. This ranged from refusing or attempting to avoid sexual intercourse with the white master to a strong wish to delay marriage to a male slave while hope remained that marriage and childbirth could occur in a free state. Elizabeth Keckley who, toward the end of her life became a seamstress for Mrs. Abraham Lincoln, discusses this form of resistance in her narrative *Behind the Scenes: Thirty Years a Slave and Four Years in the White House.* Her story is typical in outlining the extent and duration of her attempt to avoid the designs of her licentious master. She recalls that she was "regarded as fair-looking for one of my race,"[7] and that as a result of her appearance her master pursued her for four years:

> I do not care to dwell upon this subject, for it is fraught with pain. Suffice it to say, that he persecuted me for four years, and I—I—became a mother. The child of which he was the father was the only child I ever brought into the world. If my poor boy ever suffered any humiliating pangs on account of birth, he could not blame his mother, for God knows that she did not wish to give him life; he must blame the edicts of that society which deemed it no crime to undermine the virtue of girls in my then position.[8]

Presumably, Mrs. Keckley found this experience so upsetting that she could not bring herself to have another child, not even after she had gained her freedom.

Similarly, Linda Brent described her prolonged attempts to avoid sexual relations with her master, Dr. Flint. She recalls that she was able to use the presence of her grandmother on the plantation to avoid her master's advances because "though she had been a slave, Dr. Flint was afraid of her. He dreaded her scorching rebukes. Moreover, she was known and patronized by many people; and he did not wish to have his villainy made public."[9]

Ellen Craft along with her future husband, William, escaped slavery in a most ingenious fashion. Mrs. Craft was so reluctant to have children while she remained in slavery that she and William agreed to delay their marriage until they reached the North. In their narrative *Running a Thousand Miles for Freedom,* William Craft perceptively explains his wife's motivations:

My wife was torn from her mother's embrace in childhood, and taken to a distant part of the country. She had seen so many other children separated from their parents in this cruel manner, that the mere thought of her ever becoming a mother of a child, to linger out a miserable existence under the wretched system of American slavery, appeared to fill her very soul with horror; and as she had taken what I felt to be an important view of her condition, I did not, at first, press the marriage, but agreed to assist her in trying to devise some plan by which we might escape from our unhappy condition, and then be married.[10]

A second method of female resistance to slavery, in general, and to sexual exploitation, in particular, took the form of abortion. Because abortion appears to have been less common than sexual abstinence, it seems fair to assume that destruction of the fetus exacted a higher psychological toll than did abstinence. In his recent study of the black family, Herbert Gutman observes that the conscious decision on the part of the slave woman to terminate her pregnancy was one act that was totally beyond the control of the master of the plantation. Gutman offers evidence of several southern physicians who commented upon abortion and the use of contraceptive methods among the slave population:

The Hancock County, Georgia, physician E. M. Pendleton reported in 1849 that among his patients 'abortion and miscarriage' occurred more frequently among slave than white free women. The cause was either 'slave labor (exposure, violent exercise, & c.')' or 'as the planters believe, that the blacks are possessed of a secret by which they destroy the fetus at an early stage of gestation. All county practitioners', he added, 'are aware of the frequent complaints of planters' about the 'unnatural tendency in the African female population to destroy her off-

spring. Whole families of women . . . fail to have any children.'[11]

Gutman also recounts a situation in which a planter had kept between four and six slave women "of the proper age to breed" for twenty-five years and that "only two children had been born on the place at full term." It was later discovered that the slaves had concocted a medicine with which they were able to terminate their unwanted pregnancies.[12] Gutman found evidence as well of a master who claimed that an older female slave had discovered a remedy for pregnancies and had been "instrumental in all . . . abortions on his place."[13]

This last instance suggests that even those women who did not resist slavery through actually having an abortion themselves, resisted even more covertly by aiding those who desired them. It is therefore possible that a sort of female conspiracy existed on the southern plantation which requires further study. In an interesting twist to the apparently chronic problem of unwanted and forced pregnancies, there is evidence that female slaves recognizing the importance of their role of procreation to the maintenance of the slave system, often feigned pregnancy as a method of receiving lighter work loads. The limited success of this kind of ploy would also require the aid of other female slaves on the plantation—a midwife, for example, who might testify to the master that one of his female slaves was indeed pregnant.

In their illuminating article "Day to Day Resistance to Slavery," Raymond and Alice Bauer note that "pretending to be pregnant was a type of escape in a class by itself, since the fraud must inevitably have been discovered."[14] The following contemporary report is contained in their article:

I will tell you of a most comical account Mr._____ has given of the prolonged and still protracted pseudo-pregnancy of a woman called Markie, who for many more months than are generally required for the process of continuing the human species, pretended to be what the Germans pathetically and poetically call 'in good hope' and continued to reap increased rations as the reward of her expectation, till she finally had to disappoint the estate and receive a flogging.[15]

Apparently, the increased allotment of food and the possibility of lighter work was enough inducement for this woman to risk the punishment which she must have known would follow. In this case, the slave woman was perceptive enough of the importance of her procreative function for the maintenance of the slave system to manipulate to her own advantage the precise function for which she was most valued by the master.

Possibly the most psychologically devastating means for undermining the slave system which the slave parent had at his or her disposal was infanticide. The frequency with which this occurred is by no means clear. Several historians have contended that infanticide was quite rare and Genovese writes that "slave abortions, much less infanticide, did not become a major problem for the slave holders or an ordinary form of 'resistance' for the slaves. Infanticide occurred, but so far as the detected cases reveal anything, only in some special circumstances."[16] The subject of infanticide under slavery is clearly in need of further study, but for our purposes it is important to note that the relatively small number of documented cases of infanticide is not as significant as the fact that it occurred at all as possibly the ultimate statement, with the exception of suicide, of opposition to both sexual and economic exploitation which was available to the slave. Raymond and Alice Bauer reveal how both infanticide and suicide were combined in the following account:

> Not only were slaves known to take the lives of their masters or overseers, but they were now and then charged with the murder of their own children, sometimes to prevent them growing up in bondage. In Covington, a father and mother, shut up in a slave baracoon and doomed to the southern market, 'when there was no eye to pity them and no arm to save,' did by mutual agreement 'send the souls of their children to heaven rather than have them descend to the hell of slavery,' then both parents committed suicide.[17]

Genovese notes one instance in which "the white citizens of Virginia petitioned in 1882 to spare a slave condemned to death for killing her infant. The child's father was a respectable white man, and the woman insisted that she would not have killed a child of her own color."[18] There are numerous instances in which slave women simply preferred to end their children's lives rather than allow the children to grow up enslaved. When Genovese writes that "for the most part,

however, the slaves recognized infanticide as murder. They loved their children too much to do away with them; courageously, they resolved to raise them as best they could, and entrusted their fate to God,"[19] he does not appear to be acknowledging the motivations for infanticide offered repeatedly by the slave parents themselves. Far from viewing such actions as murder, and therefore indicative of a lack of love, slave parents who took their children's lives may have done so out of a higher form of love and a clear understanding of the living death that awaited their children under slavery. Since this is the explanation that is offered most frequently in the narratives, there does not seem to be any evidence, at this time, not to accept the slaves' statements as reflective of their true motivations.

It is also possible that there were other motivations behind infanticide. It may have occurred as a response to rape or forced pregnancy and it was an act which, along with sexual abstinence and abortion, had economic implications as well. The narratives reveal that slave children were sometimes used as pawns in a power struggle between plantation owners and their slaves. Owners used the sale or the threat of sale of slave children as a means for manipulating their recalcitrant or troublesome slaves, and the slaves in turn used their children to manipulate the behavior of their masters. There is one documented instance, for example, in which a particularly rebellious female slave, Fannie, was told that she would have to be sold following an incident in which she physically attacked her mistress. To increase the harshness of the punishment, she was informed by her master that her infant would remain on the plantation: One of her older daughters recalls her mother's response:

> At this, Ma took the baby by its feet, a foot in each hand, and with the Baby's head swinging downward, she vowed to smash its brains out before she'd leave it. Tears were streaming down her face. It was seldom that Ma cried and everyone knew that she meant every word. Ma took her baby with her. . . .[20]

In this instance the threat of infanticide on the part of the slave mother was transformed into an effective means for gaining power over the planter and control over at least a part of her life. Thus, it seems that there were complex motivations involved in both infanticide and the threat of infanticide.

In attempting to evaluate the consequences for the slave system of these acts of resistance, Genovese's definition of paternalism is most helpful. He writes that "Paternalism in any historical setting defines relations of superordination and subordination. Its strength as a prevailing ethos increases as the members of the community accept—or feel compelled to accept—these relations as legitimate."[21] As was pointed out above, slave women were expected to serve a dual function in this system and therefore suffered a dual oppression. They constituted an important and necessary part of the work force and they were, through their childbearing function, the one group most responsible for the size and indeed the maintenance of the slave labor pool. Therefore, when they resisted sexual exploitation through such means as sexual abstention, abortion and infanticide, they were, at the same time, rejecting their vital economic function as breeders. This, of course, became especially important after 1808 when it was no longer legal to import slaves into the United States from Africa.

The slave woman's resistance to sexual, and therefore to economic exploitation, posed a potentially severe threat to paternalism itself, for implicit in such action was the slave woman's refusal to accept her designated responsibilities within the slave system as legitimate. This acceptance of mutual responsibility on the part of both the slaves and the masters was, as Genovese points out, at the heart of the maintenance of the paternalistic world view. The female slave, through her sexual resistance, attacked the very assumptions upon which the slave order was constructed and maintained.

Resistance to sexual exploitation, therefore, had major political and economic implications. A woman who elected not to have children or, to put it another way, to engage in sexual abstinence, abortion, or infanticide, negated through individual or group action her role in the maintenance of the slave pool. To the extent that in so doing she redefined her role in the system, she introduced a unit of psychological heterogeneity into a world view which depended, for its survival, on homogeneity at least with respect to the assumptions of its ideology.

The examples quoted above strongly indicate that the slave woman's decision to participate in these particular forms of resistance was made consciously and with full awareness of the potential political and economic ramifications involved. In rejecting her role in

the economic advancement of the slave system, she could reduce the numbers of slaves available for the slave trade and undermine her master's effort to profit from exploiting her sexually. Since the master had a dual stake in the female slave as worker and as breeder, the woman who engaged in these activities impeded the economic advantage of the sale and transfer of her child accruing to the master through the slave traders. The planters were the only beneficiaries of the increase in the numbers of slaves: $1,500 for a good, strong buck; $1,200 for a hardworking, childbearing wench, with no large-scale investment necessary to insure future profit. The master could, presumably, simply sit back and wait for the children to be born. If there was no black male available, he could engage in the procreative process himself. The result was the same, made conveniently so, by laws which stipulated that the child inherited the condition of the mother.

In his *Once a Slave: The Slaves' View of Slavery* Stanley Feldstein notes that, in his narrative, Frederick Douglass makes explicit the importance of breeding slaves even for the less wealthy planters:

> . . . Frederick Douglass told of the case of a master who was financially able to purchase only one slave. Therefore, he bought her as a 'breeder,' and then hired a married man to live with her for one year. Every night he would place the man and woman together in a room, at the end of the year, the woman gave birth to twins. The children were regarded by the master as an important addition to his wealth, and his joy was such that the breeder was kept in the finest of material comfort in the hope that she would continue providing good fortune to the master and his family.[22]

Perhaps the most revealing example of the female slaves' awareness of the sexual and economic nexus inherent in her dual role in the slave system is offered by Jane Black in her narrative *Memoirs of Margaret Jane Blake.* She comments that many slave women resisted pregnancy because they did not want their children to grow up in a state of bondage and that if "all the bond women had been of the same mind, how soon the institution could have vanished from the face of the earth, and all the misery belonging to it, been lifted from the hearts of the holders of slaves."[23]

One of the more striking aspects of the subject of female slave resistance is its complex nature. The decision to resist in the three ways which have been out-lined involved sexual, emotional, economic, and politi-cal concerns. The examination of the strategies which were developed by the female slave to resist sexual and economic exploitation represents a legitimate and nec-essary field of inquiry if we are to understand slave resistance in general. In connection with this, it is important to note that we need to know much more about the role which the male slave played in helping the slave woman to resist both sexual and economic exploitation. The dynamics of female slave behavior cannot be fully understood if examined in a vacuum.

Instances of sexual abstinence, abortion, and infan-ticide are important for the same reasons that we study the three major slave rebellions of the nineteenth cen-tury. Like the rebellions, the important point with respect to these modes of female resistance is not the infrequency with which they occurred, if indeed they were infrequent, but the fact that these methods were used at all. Through a closer examination of the responses of black women to slavery, we can gain fur-ther insight into the interaction of males and females of both races on the southern plantation.

NOTES

1. See, for example, Herbert Aptheker, *American Negro Slave Revolts* (New York: International Publishers, 1963); Eugene Genovese, *Roll, Jordan, Roll: The World The Slaves Made* (New York: Random House, 1972); Herbert Gutman, *The Black Family in Slavery and Freedom, 1750–1925;* Gerald Mullin, *Flight and Rebellion* (New York: Oxford University Press, 1972); and Peter Wood. *Black Majority* (New York: W. W. Norton and Co. Inc., 1974).

2. Genovese, pp. 360–361.

3. Winthrop Jordan, *White Over Black: American Atti-tudes Toward the Negro, 1550–1812* (Baltimore: Penguin Books Inc., 1969), pp. 151.

4. Linda Brent. *Incidents in the Life of a Slave Girl* (New York: Harcourt Brace Jovanovich, Inc., 1973), p. 27.

5. Frederic Bancroft, "New Orleans: The Mistress of the Slave Trade," in Irwin Unger and David Reimers (eds.), *The Slavery Experience in the United States* (New York: Holt, Rinehart and Winston, Inc., 1970), pp. 77.

6. Quoted in Bancroft, p. 77.

7. Elizabeth Keckley, *Behind the Scenes: Thirty Years a Slave and Four Years in the White House* (New York: Arno Press and the New York Times, 1968), pp. 38–39.

8. Keckley, p. 39.

9. Brent, p. 28.

10. William and Ellen Craft, "Running a Thousand Miles for Freedom," in Arna Bontemps ed., *Great Slave Narratives* (Boston: Beacon Press, 1969), pp. 285.

11. Gutman, pp. 80–81.

12. Gutman, p. 81.

13. Gutman, pp. 81–82.

14. Raymond and Alice Bauer, "Day to Day Resistance to Slavery," in Unger and Reimers. p. 186.

15. Bauer, p. 186.

16. Genovese, p. 497.

17. Bauer, p. 190.

18. Genovese, p. 497.

19. Genovese, p. 497.

20. Quoted in Gerda Lerner ed., *Black Women in White America* (New York: Vintage Books, 1973), p. 38.

21. Genovese, p. 6.

22. Stanley Feldstein, *Once a Slave: The Slaves' View of Slavery* (New York: William Morrow and Co., Inc., 1970), p. 90.

23. Quoted in Feldstein, p. 90.

P A R T   F O U R

Social Change

Thus far we have emphasized the *stability* of gender inequality. We have examined how socialization, social definitions of gender, and the structure and content of all the major institutional arenas of social life converge to produce a world in which males and females are differentially valued and differentially rewarded. The forces that perpetuate gender inequality are so intricately interwoven into the social fabric and so deeply embedded in the self-concepts and personalities of individuals that to effect change is beyond the power of the individual, no matter how well-intentioned that individual may be.

Yet societies can and do *change*. Anyone who has lived through the past three decades in the United States cannot help but notice that there has been substantial change in the roles, behaviors, and consciousness of women and men. In earlier readings, we discussed some of the dynamic forces that have *unintentionally* recast gender consciousness and behavior, including technological innovations, demographic processes, and economic factors. In order to understand fully how systems of gender inequality change, it is also necessary to examine the ways that women have sought collectively and *intentionally* to reduce their disadvantage. Certainly every society or group contains individuals who are nonconformists, but significant and lasting social change is ultimately the result of collective action rather than individual action.

In Part Four, we turn our attention to women's struggle for equality in two arenas linked to the transformation of culture and social institutions in modern industrialized societies. Section Ten focuses on the politicization of gender in state and international politics. The readings in Section Eleven document the rich history and diversity of the women's movement and demonstrate continuity and change in the history of American feminism. Understanding the part that women themselves have played in improving their status requires that we focus, on the one hand, on women's actions "within the system" through the use of conventional and orderly means and, on the other, on women's collective actions "outside the system" through the use of unconventional and disorderly means.

Politics is generally thought to refer to the institutionalized or authoritative system by which a society makes decisions, allocates power, and distributes resources. According to the traditional view, voting, campaigning, lobbying, organizational activities, office holding, and involvement in political parties are classified as politics because they take place in the context of the formal governmental structure. Feminist scholars have pointed out that the standard definition of politics is too narrow, however, for understanding women's political participation. It not only assumes a particular type of state and political system but ignores the fact that in most industrialized societies women have been denied access to the formal political process until fairly recently.

In the United States, women were not allowed to vote, hold office, or sit on juries until the first decades of the twentieth century. Even after women were enfranchised with the passage of the Nineteenth Amendment to the U.S. Constitution in 1920, their participation in electoral politics, involvement in the major political parties, and election to public offices lagged significantly behind men's. It was not until a half century later in the 1970s that the gap between men's and women's party involvement and office holding began to shrink, and even today women fare better in local and state politics than in the national arena. Voting turnout differences between women and men finally disappeared in 1976. But it took until 1980 for women to use the electoral process to express their collective dissatisfaction by voting in line with their interests in women's equality, creating for the first time what has come to be known as the "gender gap."

Elections, participation in party politics, running for office, and lobbying are not, however, the only means of expressing grievances, influencing public policy, and using politics to achieve social change. Scholars have recently defined politics more broadly to include social movements, protests, and other group actions intended to influence the distribution of power and other resources in a state or community. This definition is broad enough to encompass women's long history of participation in collective action on their own behalf through the feminist movement, as well as in pursuit of other human rights causes through female reform societies, women's church groups, alternative religious societies, women's clubs, and other social movements.

Social movements can be thought of as collective attempts to bring about change. They originate outside of the established political system, are based on collective discontent, forge linkages between individuals and groups who share common concerns, and mobilize the people and resources necessary to pursue collective goals. In democratic societies, social movements and the tactics they employ—marches, boycotts, strikes, demonstrations, and protests—are a regular part of the democratic process and have proved to be an effective avenue to social change. Movements act as pressure groups on behalf of people excluded from routine decision-making processes and the dominant power structure and are a major source of new social patterns and cultural understandings.

Because participants in social movements typically challenge conventional ideas and behaviors, they are often stereotyped by the larger society as deviant and irrational and are accused of exaggerating their claims. If we take a historical perspective on social movements, we will often find, however, that today's social institution is likely to have been yesterday's social movement. Thus, scholars generally agree that social movement participants are not qualitatively different from other kinds of social actors and that their actions are governed by the same norms of rationality that underlie other groups.

Although popular opinion often presents the women's movement as a relatively recent phenomenon, its roots are well-grounded historically. Indeed, the similarities between the views of contemporary feminists and earlier feminists are remarkable. More than 200 years ago, for example, Abigail Adams gave this warning to her husband, John, when he was fashioning the Constitution of the United States:

In the new code of laws which I suppose will be necessary for you to make, I desire you would remember the ladies and be more generous and favorable to them than your ancestors. Do not put such unlimited power in the hands of husbands. Remember, all men would be tyrants if they could. If particular care and attention is not paid to the ladies, we are determined to foment a rebellion, and will not hold ourselves bound by any laws in which we have no voice or representation.

John Adams, nonetheless, failed to take his wife's warning seriously. He urged her to be patient, noting that there were more important issues than "ladies" rights.

As this example illustrates, in the United States, as in much of the industrialized world, the history of feminist activism is long and rich. Until the past two decades, however, knowledge of the women's movement remained mostly buried. Initially most scholars studying the women's movement held that there have been two waves of feminism in the United States. The first began in the nineteenth century as a broad attack on male domination, continued for almost a century, and then died precipitously in 1920 with the passage of the suffrage amendment granting women the right to vote, which by then had become the movement's major goal. Supposedly, a forty-year lull followed before the second wave, or new feminist movement, erupted in the mid-1960s.

Recently, as a result of new research, a different interpretation of the history of the American women's movement has emerged that emphasizes the continuity and universality of women's resistance to oppression. The newer work recognizes two great waves of mass feminist activism, but also points to the survival of feminism in less highly mobilized periods. It focuses not only on the continuity of the movement but on changes in the movement's ideology, goals, constituency, tactics, and organizational style. We have, then, a long history in this society of feminist activism. Any analysis of contemporary feminism and the backlash against it must consider recent events in the larger context of an enduring and progressive struggle to redress gender inequality by dismantling the complex structures that are the foundation of male dominance.

During the 1960s, when the new feminist movement emerged, the country was witnessing a spate of social movement activities focused on a variety of issues: civil rights, the Vietnam war, and student rights in higher education. The women's movement of this period grew from the discontent of two distinct groups of women: older college-educated professional women who experienced intense discrimination in employment and dissatisfaction with traditional family roles; and younger women enrolled in college or immersed in the university community who found themselves cast into the traditional roles of "chicks," secretaries, dishwashers, and cooks by the male leadership of the antiwar, civil rights, and student movements of the day. Not surprisingly, these two social bases created different forms of movement organizations and developed different goals and strategies. The older professional women moved toward a moderate ideology and more bureaucratic organizational form, establishing such groups as the National Organization for Women (NOW), the Women's Equity Action League (WEAL), and the National Women's Political Caucus. The younger women claimed a more radical vision and organized smaller collectivities based on consciousness-raising and geared toward political activism around a variety of issues: women's health and reproductive rights; the media portrayal of women; marriage and sexuality; violence against women, including rape, sexual harassment, incest, pornography, and battering; and lesbian rights. To accomplish their goals, the younger branch established alternative structures within which a distinctively feminist women's culture flourished, such as women's recording companies, bookstores, theater groups, restaurants, poetry groups, spirituality groups, self-help groups, and publishing companies.

Although the media have recently proclaimed the present period the "postfeminist generation" and many young women disavow the feminist label, as we shall see, the women's movement is very much alive today. The contemporary movement continues to comprise many separate and diverse organizations, each with its own strategies, style, membership base, leadership, and specific goals. Supporting ideologies that may be moderate or radical, these smaller movement organizations are held together by overlapping membership, occasional participation in common political activities (such as the struggle for reproductive rights), and a shared feminist culture that justifies resisting the dominant society. Disputes over ideology and strategy are sometimes bitter among the various branches, but such conflicts are in no way unique to the women's movement. To some extent, all social movements thrive when they are heterogeneous and diverse in their goals and ideologies. Scholars have shown that broad-based social movements, whatever their focus, need radicals to define the group's ultimate political utopia and to sustain commitment against the odds. Ironically, a movement benefits from extremists because they serve to demonstrate to the larger society the reasonableness of the reforms sought by moderates.

The readings thus far suggest the depth, pervasiveness, and persistence of gender inequality. It is not surprising, then, that the ultimate vision of contemporary feminism is so broad as to include a fundamental restructuring of all institutions that perpetuate and sustain male dominance. Feminist groups can be found within every major institution: in the professions, in academia, in labor, in religion, in politics, in the arts, in music, and in literature. Furthermore, separate feminist groups have mobilized around practically every issue imaginable, including employment and equal pay issues, pornography, prostitution, abortion rights, health, depression, substance abuse, spirituality, disability rights, child care, nuclear power, lesbianism, incest, battering, racism, and older women's rights. Feminist groups have splintered on the basis of sexual, racial and ethnic, and class identities so that black women, Native-American women, Jewish women, Cuban-American, Mexican-American, Japanese-American, Chinese-American, and lesbian women often form their own separate groups. Nevertheless, we do not believe that diversification indicates that the movement is about to crumble for lack of unity. Rather, because feminism permeates every facet of social life, it is having a major and hopefully a lasting impact not only on economic, political, and cultural institutions but on the consciousness and lives of individual women and men as well.

In Part Four, we examine the diversity of the contemporary feminist movement, emphasizing the continuity and global nature of the feminist challenge as well as changes and differences in feminist goals, constituencies, and tactics. The readings document the multiple forms that feminist resistance can take, recognizing that protest can be directed at the structural, cultural, or individual levels. We conclude with an overview of the American women's movement and a look to the future.

SECTION TEN

The State and International Politics

National governments exert wide-ranging influence on the lives of women. Government-controlled economies dictate women's wages, the prices of woman-produced goods, and women's cost-of-living expenses. In market economies, federal policies on education, welfare, health, and various forms of violence against women affect women's daily lives in profound ways. Because governmental policies frequently reflect dominant sexist ideologies, they often serve to reinforce the disadvantaged position assigned to women in most countries.

The increasing interdependence of the world's countries means that the governmental policies restricting women's lives may reflect not only individual national cultures and economics but international politics and global economics as well. As a result, a complex web of interrelationships between states, groups within states, gender, class, racial, ethnic, and religious ideologies, geography, and technology shapes relations between women, states, and global politics. In this section, contributors provide examples of relationships between women and the governments of particular countries, as well as demonstrations of the relationships between international politics and women's lives.

The AIDS crisis provides a troubling example of state neglect of women. Marcia Ann Gillespie's "HIV: The Global Crisis" explicates the processes through which cultural beliefs about sex and gender, coupled with international economics and the racism of wealthy nations, contribute to the spread of AIDS among women in poor nations.

The issue of women's treatment by state welfare systems receives thorough examination in Nancy Fraser's article, "Women, Welfare, and the Politics of Need Interpretation." Fraser argues that U.S. welfare policy, like the welfare policies of other states, reflects cultural gender ideologies, perpetuates women's poverty, and inhibits women's abilities to challenge the systems oppressing them. In effect, we have two systems designed to assist people outside the labor market: "welfare" for women and "unemployment benefits" for men.

Some early suffragists speculated that women's oppression by the state would end with women's access to the vote, a symbol of political participation. Only in the 1980s in the United States, however, has there emerged a "gender gap" between male and female voting patterns. In that decade, women came to vote more often than men, and their votes differed from men's in ways consistent with their interests in women's equality. Carol Mueller analyzes the implications of this phenomenon in "The Gender Gap and Women's Political Influence."

Sometimes women use votes to challenge the state; other times women use guns. In "Women

441

in Revolution: The Mobilization of Latin American Women in Revolutionary Guerrilla Movements," Linda Lobao discusses major factors that affect women's mobilization in guerrilla struggles and applies them to case studies of movements that have occurred over the last three decades in five Latin American nations: Cuba, Colombia, Uruguay, Nicaragua, and El Salvador.

The processes by which revolutionary movements take advantage of the structure and solidarity of women's support networks are examined in Emily Honig's "Burning Incense, Pledging Sisterhood: Communities of Women Workers in the Shanghai Cotton Mills, 1919–1949." Honig's analysis demonstrates again the differences which divide women within national boundaries, and the difficulties of bridging such differences in efforts to create gender-based challenges to state or capitalist oppression.

The readings in this section emphasize that, despite national, ethnic, racial, and cultural differences, gender inequality subjects women around the world to many of the same concerns. The oppression of women in Third World countries is compounded, however, by the fact that wealthy countries and poor countries occupy very different positions in the global economic system. In "When the Oppressors Are Us," Amber Ault and Eve Sandberg present a case study to illustrate that the oppression of women in Third World countries is connected to the self-interested practices of wealthier countries, like the United States.

READING 43

HIV: The Global Crisis

MARCIA ANN GILLESPIE*

It's been little more than a decade since we first began to hear disquieting rumors of a new, deadly communicable disease in our midst. At first erroneously and homophobicly labeled the "gay men's disease," or dismissed out of ignorance and bias as an African or Haitian scourge, it would eventually be recognized for what it always was: a deadly viral disease, primarily sexually transmitted, that could place all sexually active people at risk. Sadly, the racism, sexism, classism, and homophobia that so distort our society—overlaid with fear, mass hysteria, and denial—continue to slow our response to and understanding of this disease.

Today, with 157 countries reporting AIDS cases, the world has come to accept the terrible fact that the human immunodeficiency virus (HIV) along with the acquired immune deficiency syndrome (AIDS) that it creates is of pandemic proportions. The World Health Organization (WHO) estimated that at the end of the last decade 8 to 10 million people were HIV-infected, and most of those infections occurred in the early to mid-1980s.

Still, what far too many people fail to understand is that HIV/AIDS has become a family disease, affecting both genders, all ages, the sick and the well.

First, the numbers—as best we know them. During the first decade of the HIV-AIDS pandemic there were about 500,000 cases of AIDS in women and children, most of which went unrecognized. By early 1990, the WHO conservatively estimates that more than 3 million females, most of them women of childbearing age, were infected with HIV. Approximately 80 per-

From Ms. Magazine (January–February 1991):17–22

*Marcia Ann Gillespie, a "*Ms.*" contributing editor, is editing a book on the future global impact of the HIV epidemic for the United Nations Development Programme.

cent of them are in sub-Saharan Africa, where there are cities in central Africa with up to 40 percent of the 30- to 34-year-olds infected and countries with a higher incidence of infection among women ages 15 to 24 than among their male counter-parts. While many in the United States may view HIV and AIDS as something that only happens to other people, no such illusion of safety exists for millions of the world's women and children, the WHO cautions that its projections may fall far short of the actual scope of infection.

Even so, numbers don't begin to address the epidemic's potential impact if it goes unchecked. At best, they only begin to tell the story of the many ways women's lives will be forfeited, put at risk, and dramatically changed. Here we have a disease that is not curable and only marginally treatable, with treatments often unavailable to most of those in need. All that we do know is that by drastically reducing high-risk behaviors, its spread can be contained.

In the best of circumstances, discussion of sexual behavior can open a Pandora's box. How we perceive ourselves as sexual beings and how we act upon the impulse—with whom, the endless variety of positions and erotic locations—has as much to do with social conditioning, mores, economics and power, belief systems, and habit as it does with biological urge. It also varies from situation to situation within a culture. Today, because of HIV, our need to understand sexual practices has never been more acute, but the very labels used in the Western world—hetero-, homo-, and bisexual—often obscure rather than illuminate. Human sexuality is far more complex and fluid than such labels would allow. But in any culture where the concept of manhood has been tied to heterosexuality, men find it difficult if not often impossible to admit to any "deviation." Therefore it should come as no surprise that current AIDS research indicates that bisexuality is far more widespread than had been previously thought. Unfortunately, those men who refuse to acknowledge their homosexual encounters, particularly those in Western countries where the incidence of infection among homosexual men is high, may place women at risk.

So much of the male behavior that puts women at risk—multiple partners, bisexuality, reluctance or refusal to wear condoms—cannot be changed by women alone. And so many of the attitudes that pervade societies about women's worth and place and men's rights make effective prevention campaigns extremely difficult to achieve. That women are often denied equal access to education, training, health care, property and legal rights, and independent incomes increases our vulnerability. Even when informed of the risk, women too rarely have the power to protect themselves. In every society, women are subservient to men. Depending on the degree of pressure on her to be submissive in sexual and social matters, a woman who tries to use information to prevent infection may become the target of mockery, rejection, stigmatization, economic reprisal, violence, and death.

In a country like Brazil, a husband can cite an offense to his honor as justification for the murder of his wife. A woman may know that her husband's behavior puts her at risk, but she also knows that her attempts to intervene could be met with charges of unfaithfulness, physical violence, and death. A recent story in the New York Times detailing the travails of one Ugandan woman gave poignant proof of the possible economic and social repercussions. Because she refused to have sex with her HIV-positive husband, she was treated as a pariah by his family. After his death, they stripped her of all her possessions and evicted her and her children from their home.

A layer of risk to women comes from the need to blame someone or some group that continues to haunt those caught in this epidemic. Sexually transmitted diseases (STDs) are almost universally thought of as women's diseases, a fact that increases the potential for scapegoating and violence as does the generally misplaced focus of so much attention on "prostitutes." The term carries negative, antifemale bias and fails to recognize economic and power realities of women's lives; it is sometimes used inappropriately to describe female sexual behavior in societies where there is a very real distinction between "free" women and women working in prostitution. For example, it is not uncommon to find women living independent of men in many of the

urban African settings where HIV is prevalent. These women, who are often denied job opportunities or consigned to low-paying jobs, may at times seek payment for sexual favors from their lovers to keep themselves and their children afloat. And it is customary in parts of Africa for a man to give a woman he's sexually involved with gifts of goods or money; this is not more or less a sign of prostitution than what happens when voluntary sex follows a dinner date in the U.S.A.

Almost invariably women described as prostitutes are targeted as disease carriers and blamed for the spread of HIV. Already there have been reports of groups of such women being forced out of several African cities, while in India, women working in prostitution who tested HIV positive have been thrown in jail. Although one can find prevention campaigns targeting these women in almost all countries reporting cases of AIDS, the fact remains that rarely do they have the power to insist on condom usage. The more fragile their economic situation, the less likely they are to refuse to have sex with clients who won't wear condoms. Meanwhile, only a few programs even try to provide economically viable alternatives.

Given the feminization of poverty and the limited economic options available to nations already overburdened with debt, prostitution increasingly becomes the sole means of survival for many of the world's poorest women. As a recent United Nations report concluded, "Even when prostitution seemed to have been freely chosen, it was actually the result of [economic] coercion." Such women, and the growing legions of street children who are also ensnared in the sex industry, easily fall prey to this epidemic. But it is these women and children, the weakest among us, who become targets for condemnation, not their male clients who may be the source of infection and who may spread the virus to their families and other sex partners. In addition, as one report stated: "The comparatively new phenomenon of international sex tourism, associated as it is not only with the power of men over vulnerable women, but also with the power of men from rich countries to purchase sexual activities from poor women in developing countries, adds an international dimension to the spread of HIV infection." One should not assume that the women in the developing world targeted for sex tours are the source of the infection. For example, HIV infection among women and children in prostitution in the Philippines has been traced to the U.S. military and other foreign clients.

In Bangkok, it is unofficially estimated that there

are one million prostitutes, of whom some five to eight hundred thousand are women. And studies indicate that in some Thai cities, the increase in HIV among females in prostitution has been as much as 50 percent. Chantawipa Apisuk, the head of EMPOWER (Education Means Protection of Women in Recreation), is all too aware of the realities that these women face. "Of course it is better for women to become prostitutes than to live in poverty, suffer from hunger in the villages, or be raped by relatives. AIDS or no AIDS, these women have to earn a living; you cannot eat a plate of morals." She has concluded, with a certain fatalism, that "prostitution is here to stay. What we want to do is minimize the suffering."

The precarious state of women's reproductive health in so many of the world's poorer countries also increases their chance of infection. The lifetime risk of dying of causes related to pregnancy in the developing world is 200 times that for women in the industrialized nations. And in the developing world, most of the blood transfusions go to women, usually in connection with obstetric complications, and to children. But the resources and equipment needed for routine screening of blood supplies are not readily available, especially in rural areas. As a result, women can be caught in a deadly cycle. Not only is there the risk of HIV infection due to contaminated blood, but because pregnancy, studies have indicated, may act to accelerate the disease, the combination of pregnancy and HIV leads to ever higher mortality rates.

There is also strong evidence to suggest that the presence of other STDs—such as syphilis, herpes, and cancroid that often cause genital ulcers and sores—leaves one more susceptible to HIV. Not only are we seeing dramatic increases in such diseases among teenagers and young adults in the U.S., but they are widespread throughout Africa in countries with insufficient resources to treat infection. Vaginal tears, abrasions, and lesions may also increase risk; these are common among women where the lack of female lubrication during sex, or an extremely tight vaginal passage, is thought to heighten male pleasure, as well as where female circumcision is practiced.

Terrible as rape is under any circumstance, the threat of HIV makes it even more ominous. The more violent the attack, the more likely it is that a woman will suffer internal bruising, lacerations, and bleeding. Just how many women become infected this way is not known, but given how frequently rape occurs and how widespread this particular form of violence is, the risk

is clear. Adolescent girls may become particular targets for rape. The low incidence of HIV among girls may encourage some men to seek them out, and it is not unheard of for young girls to be seduced or raped by men who believe that sex with a virgin cures sexually transmitted diseases.

Too often rape and war go hand in hand, and in many countries, HIV infection rates within the military are alarmingly high. According to a recent report in AIDS and Society, "military units in some central African states are reported to be over 50 percent seropositive." As a result, the recent invasion of the central African nation of Rwanda by a rebel force of exiled Rwandans out of Uganda carried the very real threat of HIV transmission to women, both through consensual sex and rape. Similarly, the presence of large standing armies in so much of the world where the incidence of HIV is high poses an ongoing threat. Africa Analysis reported last year that throughout sub-Saharan Africa, "armies are regarded as being the main disseminators of the AIDS virus"; and that up to half of Zimbabwe's 46,000-strong army is HIV positive.

Although pregnancy may hasten the progression of illness caused by HIV infection, abortion is often neither available to or chosen by women. In much of the world, a woman's identity and status are tied to her ability to bear healthy children, and, to many African and Asian people, children are considered necessary to maintain ancestral ties. A woman may well risk HIV infection by having unprotected sex in order to become pregnant. She may not learn that she is infected with the virus until pregnancy or until her child falls ill. Even if she knows she is infected, she may still attempt pregnancy in the hopes of having an uninfected baby. And wherever the Catholic church holds sway—in the Philippines, for example, or countries in the Caribbean and Central and South America—abortion is even less of an option and deep resistance to the use of contraception is prevalent.

As of the end of the last decade it's estimated that 2.5 million African women were HIV-infected. These women gave birth to 2 million infants, of whom about 500,000 are thought to be infected. The WHO estimates that worldwide, by the end of 1992, about 4 million babies will have been born to HIV-infected women; one million of these babies are expected to be infected, and in some areas of the continent, there will be more children than women with AIDS. The majority of children born infected are not expected to survive beyond their fifth birthdays. But the early deaths of

HIV-infected mothers place their children both the well and the sick, in terribly precarious situations. In Africa, the numbers of orphans may overwhelm the extended family that traditionally provided for them. In one section of Uganda, there are reports of some 40,000 children orphaned, many as a result of this epidemic. And throughout the developing world, nations will be hard pressed to provide facilities and care. Given that the world already allows some 100 million children and adolescents to live most of the time in its streets, it seems almost inevitable that many AIDS orphans will end up joining their ranks.

This epidemic also increases the burden on women who are the primary caretakers of children, the sick, and the dying. Although older women are less likely to become infected, it is they who often must shoulder the responsibilities of caregiving. They nurse and bury their children and kin: they take in their orphaned grandchildren. In those parts of Africa where the epidemic has made its most serious inroads, roles have been reversed. Older women who once relied on their children now provide the support; invariably increased poverty results.

The situation for adolescent girls may become increasingly difficult. Because the incidence levels among children five to 15 are still low, older men may begin to seek ever younger wives, thus increasing the risk of infection among the young. The epidemic may also decrease a girl's chances for education due to early marriage, or, as families become increasingly impoverished by AIDS, the tendency to spend whatever school fees are available for the education of her brothers.

Increased poverty is the one inevitable outcome of this epidemic. AIDS has taken its greatest toll among people in the prime of their lives, the sole or major providers of family income. The very people forced by poverty to make extreme choices—the Caribbean farm workers who toil in the U.S., the men who migrate from all over southern Africa to work in South Africa's mines, the women in prostitution—become the first casualties. The absence of their incomes, no matter how meager, endangers whole families. The disease also takes its toll among the developing world's educated and skilled urban populations, depriving nations of valued workers and leaving large networks of families destitute. Its spread into rural areas in nations already struggling and failing to feed themselves raises the specter of increased starvation.

The levels of risk for women are clear to anyone who cares to look at these worldwide patterns. In a speech delivered in Paris in 1989, Dr. Jonathan Mann, the former director of the WHO Global Programme on AIDS, spoke pointedly: "For women, AIDS is just the tip of the iceberg—of poverty, lack of access to adequate health care, disenfranchisement, and discrimination." And yet, as a recent article in Lancet noted: "The social, economic, and demographic impacts on women and children have until now been largely neglected. Only recently has the growing magnitude of HIV infection in women and children been recognized outside a few geographic areas. Economic studies of the HIV infection/AIDS pandemic have paid little or no attention to the special problems of women, especially mothers and children." The rationale often given for this neglect is that during the early states of the epidemic the majority of the cases were among men. But such neglect comes as no surprise, given that the plight of the world's women and children, the issues as they affect our lives, are too often given low priority, misaddressed, or ignored. Yet any success in arresting the spread of HIV can only come as a result of profound change in the condition of women's lives.

At some point in time, historians may look back and see this epidemic as a turning point in human history. Perhaps they will speculate about what might have happened if the numbers had been reversed, with heterosexuals in North America and Europe the ones most at risk. Despite the work of dedicated people in this and other industrialized nations, a cynicism taints public discussion and policy. From time to time the suffering of African, Asian, Caribbean, Central and South American people moves us—"We Are the World"—but too many of us have come to see death and poverty in the developing world as fated, an ugly but acceptable reality. It's a notion fueled by the unspoken assumptions of racial and cultural superiority.

While we seek vaccines—"magic bullets"—that no doubt will be tested on the very people we so distance ourselves from, we expend no concurrent effort to make today's treatments accessible to them. No public cry is raised to fund and field a massive drive to eliminate all the other curable sexually transmitted diseases that facilitate HIV infection. And even if by some stroke of luck or genius, a shot guaranteeing immunity is perfected, a cure found and made readily available to the world's people, all the underlying conditions will still remain.

HIV/AIDS has been described as a disease of development, its spread in so much of the developing world spawned by rapid urbanization and the attendant deterioration of living conditions and changes in behavior. It is in these cities that the epidemic has made its most dramatic impact. Some think that this is but the first of many such developmentally linked infectious diseases. If that's true, then unless there is a concerted effort to redress the economic imbalance between rich and poor nations, we may see untold millions of people die. And if all the factors that impoverish women, that silence and render them invisible, are not seriously addressed, the overwhelming majority of those who suffer will be brown, beige, and yellow women and children.

HOW HIV SPREADS

As part of its global watch, the World Health Organization describes three rather broad patterns of HIV infection as they pertain to particular regions:

- Western Europe, North America, Australia, New Zealand, and Oceania are classified as "Pattern I." In these areas gay men and IV drug users are the most affected. Although heterosexual spread of HIV is increasing, so far it accounts for relatively few new infections.

As a result, the number of pediatric AIDS cases remains comparatively low. It is believed that extensive HIV spread began in the late 1970s and early 1980s.

- Parts of sub-Saharan Africa and the Caribbean are described as "Pattern II" areas. Here HIV infection and AIDS predominate among sexually active heterosexuals and perinatal transmission is a major and growing problem. Extensive spread is thought to have begun in the mid-to-late 1970s.

- Although Latin America was originally classified as "Pattern I," sexual transmission among heterosexuals has increased to such an extent that the region is now classified "Pattern I/II."

- Asia, most Pacific countries, Eastern Europe, North Africa, and the Middle East are currently classified as "Pattern III." Here HIV was introduced in the early-to-mid 1980s, but the prevalence of AIDS cases and HIV infection was still low by the end of the decade. The situation is changing rapidly in a few countries. HIV infection has greatly increased among IV drug users in southeast Asia, most notably Thailand, where it is now 50 percent, and increases have also been reported among women in prostitution in several Indian and Thai cities.

—M.A.G.

R E A D I N G   4 4

Women, Welfare, and the Politics of Need Interpretation

NANCY FRASER

What some writers are calling "the coming welfare wars" will be largely wars about, even against, women. Because women constitute the overwhelming majority

From *Unruly Practices: Power, Discourse, and Gender in Contemporary Social Theory.* Copyright © 1989. Reprinted by permission of the University of Minnesota Press.

of social-welfare program recipients and employees, women and women's needs will be the principal stakes in the battles over social spending likely to dominate national politics in the coming period. Moreover, the welfare wars will not be limited to the tenure of Reagan or even of Reaganism. On the contrary, they will be protracted, both in time and in space. What

James O'Connor theorized over fifteen years ago as "the fiscal crisis of the state" is a long-term, structural phenomenon of international proportions.[1] Not just the United States but every late capitalist welfare state in Western Europe and North America is facing some version of it. And the fiscal crisis of the welfare state coincides everywhere with a second long-term, structural tendency: the feminization of poverty. This is Diana Pearce's term for the rapidly increasing proportion of women in the adult poverty population, an increase tied to, among other things, the rise in "female-headed households."[2] In the U.S. this increase is so pronounced and so steep that analysts project that should it continue, the poverty population will consist entirely of women and their children before the year 2000.[3]

This conjunction of the fiscal crisis of the state and the feminization of poverty suggests that struggles around social welfare will and should become increasingly focal for feminists. But such struggles raise a great many problems, some of which can be thought of as structural. To take one example, increasing numbers of women depend directly for their livelihoods on social-welfare programs; and many other women benefit indirectly, since the existence of even a minimal and inadequate "safety net" increases the leverage of women who are economically dependent on individual men. Thus, feminists have no choice but to oppose social-welfare cuts. However, economists like Pearce, Nancy Barrett, and Steven Erie, Martin Rein, and Barbara Wiget have shown that programs like Aid to Families with Dependent Children actually institutionalize the feminization of poverty.[4] The benefits they provide are system-conforming ones that reinforce rather than challenge basic structural inequalities. Thus, feminists cannot simply support existing social-welfare programs. To use the suggestive but ultimately too simple terms popularized by Carol Brown: If to eliminate or to reduce welfare is to bolster "private patriarchy," then simply to defend it is to consolidate "public patriarchy."[5]

Feminists also face a second set of problems in the coming welfare wars. These problems, seemingly more ideological and less structural than the first set, arise from the typical way in which issues get framed, given the institutional dynamics of the political system.[6] Typically, social-welfare issues are posed like this: Shall the state undertake to satisfy the social needs of a given constituency, and if so, to what degree? Now, this

way of framing issues permits only a relatively small number of answers, and it tends to cast debates in quantitative terms. More importantly, it takes for granted the definition of the needs in question, as if that were self-evident and beyond dispute. It therefore occludes the fact that the interpretation of people's needs is itself a political stake, indeed sometimes *the* political stake. Clearly, this way of framing issues poses obstacles for feminist politics, since at the heart of such politics lie questions about what various groups of women really need and whose interpretations of women's needs should be authoritative. Only in terms of a discourse oriented to the *politics of need interpretation*[7] can feminists meaningfully intervene in the coming welfare wars. But this requires a challenge to the dominant policy framework.

Both sets of problems, the structural and the ideological, are extremely important and difficult. In what follows, I shall not offer solutions to either of them. Rather, I want to attempt the much more modest and preliminary task of exploring how they might be thought about in relation to one another. Specifically, I want to propose a framework for inquiry that can shed light on both of them simultaneously.

Consider that in order to address the structural problem it will be necessary to clarify the phenomenon of "public patriarchy." One type of inquiry that is useful here is the familiar sort of economic analysis alluded to earlier, analysis that shows, for example, that "workfare" programs function to subsidize employers of low-wage "women's work" in the service sector and thus to reproduce the sex-segmented, dual labor market. Now, important as such inquiry is, it does not tell the whole story, since it leaves out of focus the discursive or ideological dimension of social-welfare programs. By the discursive or ideological dimension, I do not mean anything distinct from, or epiphenomenal to, welfare practices; I mean, rather, the tacit norms and implicit assumptions that are constitutive of those practices. To get at this dimension requires a meaning-oriented sort of inquiry, one that considers welfare programs as, among other things, institutionalized patterns of interpretation.[8] Such inquiry would make explicit the social meanings embedded within welfare programs, meanings that tend otherwise simply to go without saying.

In spelling out such meanings, the inquiry I am proposing could do two things simultaneously. First, it could tell us something important about the structure of the U.S. welfare system, since it might identify some underlying norms and assumptions that lend a measure of coherence to diverse programs and practices. Second, it could illuminate what I called "the politics of need interpretation," since it could expose the processes by which welfare practices construct women and women's needs according to certain specific—and, in principle, contestable—interpretations, even as they lend those interpretations an aura of facticity that discourages contestation. Thus, this inquiry could shed light on both the structural and ideological problems identified earlier.

The principal aim of this paper is to provide an account of this sort for the present U.S. social-welfare system. The account is intended to help clarify some key structural aspects of male dominance in late capitalist welfare state societies. At the same time, it is meant to point the way to a broader, discourse-oriented focus that can address political conflicts over the interpretation of women's needs.

The paper proceeds from some relatively "hard," uncontroversial facts about the U.S. social-welfare system (section 1) through a series of increasingly interpreted accounts of that system (sections 2 and 3). These culminate (in section 4) in a highly theorized characterization of the welfare system as a "juridical-administrative-therapeutic state apparatus." Finally, (in section 5) the paper situates that apparatus as one force among others in a larger and highly contested political field of discourse about needs that also includes the feminist movement.

I

Long before the emergence of welfare states, governments have defined legally secured arenas of societal action. In so doing, they have at the same time codified corresponding patterns of agency or social roles. Thus, early modern states defined an economic arena and the corresponding role of an economic person capable of entering into contracts. More or less at the same time, they codified the "private sphere" of the household and the role of head of the household. Somewhat later, governments were led to secure a sphere of political participation and the corresponding role of citizen with (limited) political rights. In each of these cases, the original and paradigmatic subject of the newly codified social role was male. Only secondarily, and much later, was it conceded that women, too, could occupy these

subject-positions, without, however, entirely dispelling the association with masculinity.

Matters are different, however, with the contemporary welfare state. When this type of government defined a new arena of activity—call it "the social"—and a new societal role—the welfare client—it included women among its original and paradigmatic subjects. Today, in fact, women have become the principal subjects of the welfare state. On the one hand, they make up the overwhelming majority both of program recipients and of paid social-service workers. On the other hand, they are the wives, mothers, and daughters whose unpaid activities and obligations are redefined as the welfare state increasingly oversees forms of caregiving. Since this beneficiary/social worker/caregiver nexus of roles is constitutive of the social-welfare arena, one might even call this arena a feminized terrain.

A brief statistical overview confirms women's greater involvement with and dependence on the U.S. social-welfare system. Consider, first, women's greater dependence as program clients and beneficiaries. In each of the major "means-tested" programs in the U.S., women and the children for whom they are responsible now comprise the overwhelming majority of clients. For example, more than 81 percent of households receiving Aid to Families with Dependent Children (AFDC) are headed by women, more than 60 percent of families receiving food stamps or Medicaid are headed by women, and 70 percent of all households in publicly owned or subsidized housing are headed by women.[9] High as they are, these figures actually underestimate the representation of women. As Barbara Nelson notes, in the androcentric reporting system, households counted as female-headed contain by definition no healthy adult men.[10] But healthy adult women live in most households counted as male-headed. Such women may directly or indirectly receive benefits going to "male-headed" households, but they are invisible in the statistics, even though they usually do the work of securing and maintaining program eligibility.

Women also predominate in the major U.S. "age-tested" programs. For example, 61.6 percent of all adult beneficiaries of Social Security are women, and 64 percent of those covered by Medicare are women.[11] In sum, because women as a group are significantly poorer than men—indeed, women now compose nearly two-thirds of all U.S. adults below the official poverty line—and because women tend to live longer than men, women depend more on the social-welfare system as clients and beneficiaries.

But this is not the whole story. Women also depend more on the social-welfare system as paid human-service workers—a category of employment that includes education and health as well as social work and services administration. In 1980, 70 percent of the 17.3 million paid jobs in this sector in the U.S. were held by women. This accounts for one-third of U.S. women's total paid employment and a full 80 percent of all professional jobs held by women. The figures for women of color are even higher than this average, since 37 percent of their total paid employment and 82.4 percent of their professional employment is in this sector.[12] It is a distinctive feature of the U.S. social-welfare system—as opposed to, say, the British and Scandinavian systems—that only 3 percent of these jobs are in the form of direct federal government employment. The rest are in state and local government, in the "private non-profit" sector, and in the "private" sector. However, the more decentralized and privatized character of the U.S. system does not make paid welfare workers any less vulnerable in the face of federal program cuts. On the contrary, the level of federal social-welfare spending affects the level of human-service employment in *all* sectors. State and local government jobs depend on federal and federally financed state and local government contracts, and private profit and nonprofit jobs depend on federally financed transfer payments to individuals and households for the purchase in the market of services like health care.[13] Thus, reductions in social spending mean the loss of jobs for women. Moreover, as Barbara Ehrenreich and Frances Fox Piven note, this loss is not compensated when spending is shifted to the military, since only one-half of 1 percent of the entire female paid workforce is employed in work on military contracts. In fact, one study they cite estimates that with each one-billion-dollar increase in military spending, ninety-five hundred jobs are lost to women.[14]

Finally, women are subjects of and subject to the social-welfare system in their traditional capacity as unpaid caregivers. It is well known that the sexual division of labor assigns women primary responsibility for the care of those who cannot care for themselves. (I leave aside women's traditional obligations to provide personal services to adult males—husbands, fathers, grown sons, lovers—who can very well care for themselves.) Such responsibility includes child care, of course, but also care for sick and/or elderly relatives, often parents. For example, a British study conducted in 1975 and cited by Hilary Land found that three times as many elderly people live with married daughters as with married sons and that those without a close female relative were more likely to be institutionalized, irrespective of degree of infirmity.[15] Thus, as unpaid caregivers, women are more directly affected than men by the level and character of government social services for children, the sick, and the elderly.

As clients, paid human-service workers and unpaid caregivers, then, women are the principal subjects of the social-welfare system. It is as if this branch of the state were in effect a Bureau of Women's Affairs.

II

Of course, the welfare system does not deal with women on women's terms. On the contrary, it has its own characteristic ways of interpreting women's needs and positioning women as subjects. In order to understand these, we need to examine how gender norms and meanings are encoded in the structure of the U.S. social-welfare system.

This issue is quite complicated. On the one hand, nearly all U.S. social-welfare programs are officially gender-neutral. Nevertheless, the system as a whole is a dual or two-tiered one, and it has an unmistakable gender subtext.[16] One set of programs is oriented to *individuals* and tied to participation in the paid work force—for example, unemployment insurance and Social Security. This set of programs is designed to supplement and compensate for the primary market in paid labor power. A second set of programs is oriented to *households* and tied to combined household income—for example, AFDC, food stamps, and Medicaid. This set of programs is designed to compensate for what are considered to be family failures, in particular the absence of a male breadwinner.

What integrates the two sets of programs is a common core of assumptions concerning the sexual division of labor, domestic and nondomestic. It is assumed that families do or should contain one primary breadwinner who is male and one unpaid domestic worker (homemaker and mother) who is female. It is further assumed that when a woman undertakes paid work outside the home, this is or should be in order to supplement the male breadwinner's wage and neither does nor should override her primary housewifely and maternal responsibilities. It is assumed, in other words, that society is divided into two separate spheres of home and outside work and that these are women's and men's spheres, respectively.[17]

These assumptions are increasingly counterfactual. At present, fewer than 15 percent of U.S. families conform to the normative ideal of a domicile shared by a husband who is the sole breadwinner, a wife who is a full-time homemaker, and their offspring. Nonetheless, the "separate spheres" norms determine the structure of the social-welfare system. They determine that it contains one subsystem related to the primary labor market and another subsystem related to the family or household. Moreover, they determine that these subsystems be gender-linked, that the primary-labor-market-related system be implicitly "masculine" and the family-related system be implicitly "feminine." Consequently, the normative, ideal-typical recipient of primary-labor-market-oriented programs is a (white) male, whereas the normative, ideal-typical adult client of household-based programs is a female.

This gender subtext of the U.S. welfare system is confirmed when we take a second look at participation figures. Consider again the figures just cited for the "feminine" or family-based programs, which I referred to earlier as "means-tested" programs: more than 81 percent of households receiving AFDC are female-headed, as are more than 70 percent of those receiving housing assistance and more than 60 percent of those receiving Medicaid and food stamps. Now recall that these figures do not compare female *individuals* with male *individuals* but, rather, female-headed *households* with male-headed *households.* They therefore confirm four things: (1) these programs have a distinctive administrative identity in that their recipients are not individualized but *familialized;* (2) they serve what are considered to be defective families, overwhelmingly families without a male breadwinner; (3) the ideal-typical (adult) client is female; and (4) she makes her claim for benefits on the basis of her status as an unpaid domestic worker, a homemaker, and mother, not as a paid worker based in the labor market.

Now, contrast this with the case of a typical labor-market-based and thus "masculine" program, namely, unemployment insurance. Here the percentage of female claimants drops to 38 percent, a figure that contrasts female and male *individuals,* as opposed to female-headed and male-headed households. As Diana Pearce notes, this drop reflects at least two different circumstances.[18] First, and most straightforwardly, it reflects women's lower rate of participation in the paid work force. Second, it reflects the fact that many women wageworkers are not eligible to participate in this program, for example, paid household service workers, part-time workers, pregnant workers, and workers in the "irregular economy" such as prostitutes, baby-sitters, and home typists. The exclusion of these female wageworkers testifies to the existence of a gender-segmented labor market, divided into "primary" and "secondary" employment. It reflects the more general assumption that women's earnings are "merely supplementary," not on a par with those of the primary (male) breadwinner. Altogether, then, the figures tell us four things about programs like unemployment insurance: (1) they are administered in a way that *individualizes* rather than familializes recipients; (2) they are designed to compensate primary-labor-market effects, such as the temporary displacement of a primary breadwinner; (3) the ideal-typical recipient is male, and (4) he makes his claim on the basis of his identity as a paid worker, not as an unpaid domestic worker or parent.

One final example will round out the picture. The Social Security system of retirement insurance presents the interesting case of a hermaphrodite or androgyne. I shall soon show that this system has a number of characteristics of "masculine" programs in virtue of its link to participation in the paid work force. However, it is also internally dualized and gendered, and thus stands as a microcosm of the entire dual benefit welfare system. Consider that whereas a majority—61.6 percent—of adult beneficiaries are female, only somewhat more than half of these—or 33.3 percent of all recipients—claim benefits on the basis of their own paid work records.[19] The remaining female recipients claim benefits on the basis of their husbands' records, that is, as wives or unpaid domestic workers. By contrast, virtually no male recipients claim benefits as husbands. On the contrary, they claim benefits as paid workers, a labor-market-located as opposed to family-located identity. So the Social Security system is hermaphroditic or androgynous; it is internally divided between family-based, "feminine" benefits, on the one hand, and labor-market-based, "masculine" benefits, on the other hand. Thus, it too gets its structure from gender norms and assumptions.

III

So far, I have established the dualistic structure of the U.S. social-welfare system and the gender subtext of that dualism. Now I can better tease out the system's implicit norms and tacit assumptions by examining its mode of operation. To see how welfare programs interpret women's needs, we must consider what benefits consist in. To see how programs position women as subjects, we need to examine administrative practices. In general, we shall see that the "masculine" and "feminine" subsystems are not only separate but also unequal.

Consider that the "masculine" social-welfare programs are social insurance schemes. They include unemployment insurance, Social Security (retirement insurance), Medicare (age-tested health insurance), and Supplemental Social Security Insurance (disability insurance for those with paid work records). These programs are contributory (wageworkers and their employers pay into trust funds), they are administered on a national basis, and benefit levels are uniform across the country. Though bureaucratically organized and administered, they require less, and less demeaning, effort on the part of beneficiaries in qualifying and maintaining eligibility than do "feminine" programs. They are far less subject to intrusive controls and in most cases lack the dimension of surveillance. They also tend to require less of beneficiaries in the way of actual efforts to collect their benefits, with the notable exception of unemployment insurance.

In sum, "masculine" social insurance schemes position recipients primarily as *rights-bearers*. The beneficiaries of these programs are in the main not stigmatized. Neither administrative practice nor popular discourse constitutes them as "on the dole." They are constituted rather as receiving what they deserve; what they, in "partnership" with their employers, have already "paid in" for, what they, therefore, have a *right* to. Moreover, these beneficiaries are also positioned as *purchasing consumers*. They often receive cash as opposed to "in kind" benefits and so are positioned as having "the liberty to strike the best bargain they can in purchasing services of their choice on the open market." In sum, these beneficiaries are what C. B.

MacPherson calls "possessive individuals."[20] Proprietors of their own persons who have freely contracted to sell their labor power, they become participants in social insurance schemes and, thence, paying consumers of human services. They therefore qualify as *social citizens* in virtually the fullest sense that term can acquire within the framework of a male-dominated, capitalist society.

All this stands in stark contrast to the "feminine" sector of the U.S. social-welfare system. This sector consists in relief programs, such as AFDC, food stamps, Medicaid, and public-housing assistance. These programs are not contributory but are financed out of general tax revenues (usually with one-third of the funds coming from the federal government and two-thirds coming from the states); and they are not administered federally but rather by the states. As a result, benefit levels vary dramatically, though they are everywhere inadequate, deliberately pegged below the official poverty line. The relief programs are notorious for the varieties of administrative humiliation they inflict upon clients. They require considerable work in qualifying and maintaining eligibility, and they have a heavy component of surveillance.

These programs do not in any meaningful sense position their subjects as rights-bearers. Far from being considered as having a right to what they receive, recipients are defined as "beneficiaries of governmental largess" or "clients of public charity."[21] Moreover, their actual treatment fails to live up to even that definition, since they are treated as "chiselers," "deviants," and "human failures." In the androcentric administrative framework, "welfare mothers" are considered not to work and so are sometimes required—that is to say, coerced—to "work off" their benefits via "workfare." They thus become inmates of what Diana Pearce calls a "workhouse without walls."[22] Indeed, the only sense in which the category of rights is relevant to these clients' situation is the somewhat dubious one according to which they are entitled to treatment governed by the standards of formal bureaucratic procedural rationality. But if that right is construed as protection from administrative caprice, then even it is widely and routinely disregarded.

Moreover, recipients of public relief are generally not positioned as purchasing consumers. A significant portion of their benefits is "in kind," and what cash they receive comes already carved up and earmarked for specific, administratively designated purposes.

These recipients are therefore essentially *clients,* a subject-position that carries far less power and dignity in capitalist societies than does the alternative position of purchaser. In these societies, to be a client (in the sense relevant to relief recipients) is to be an abject dependent. Indeed, this sense of the term carries connotations of a fall from autonomy, as when we speak, for example, of "the client states of empires or superpowers." As clients, then, recipients of relief are *the negatives of possessive individuals.* Largely excluded from the market both as workers and as consumers, claiming benefits not as individuals but as members of "failed" families, these recipients are effectively denied the trappings of social citizenship as it is defined within male-dominated, capitalist societies.[23]

Clearly, this system creates a double bind for women raising children without a male breadwinner. By failing to offer these women day care for their children, job training, a job that pays a "family wage," or some combination of these, it constructs them exclusively as mothers. As a consequence, it interprets their needs as maternal needs and their sphere of activity as that of "the family." Now, according to the ideology of separate spheres, this should be an honored social identity. Yet the system does not honor these women. On the contrary, instead of providing them a guaranteed income equivalent to a family wage as a matter of right, it stigmatizes, humiliates, and harasses them. In effect, it decrees simultaneously that these women must be and yet cannot be normative mothers.

Moreover, the way in which the U.S. social-welfare system interprets "maternity" and "the family" is both race-specific and culture-specific. The bias is made plain in Carol Stack's study, *All Our Kin.*[24] Stack analyzes domestic arrangements of very poor black welfare recipients in a midwestern city. Where conservative ideologues see the "disorganization of *the* black family," she finds complex, highly organized kinship structures. These include kin-based networks of resource pooling and exchange, which enable those in direct poverty to survive economically and communally. The networks organize delayed exchanges or "gifts," in Mauss's sense,[25] of prepared meals, food stamps, cooking, shopping, groceries, furniture, sleeping space, cash (including wages and AFDC allowances), transportation, clothing, child care, even children. They span several physically distinct households and so transcend the principal administrative category that organizes relief programs. It is significant

that Stack took great pains to conceal the identities of her subjects, even going so far as to disguise the identity of their city. The reason, though unstated, is obvious: these people would lose their benefits if program administrators learned that they did not utilize them within the confines and boundaries of a "household."

We can summarize the separate and unequal character of the two-tiered, gender-linked, race- and culture-biased U.S. social-welfare system in the following formulas: Participants in the "masculine" subsystem are positioned as *rights-bearing beneficiaries* and *purchasing consumers of services,* thus as *possessive individuals.* Participants in the "feminine" subsystem, on the other hand, are positioned as *dependent clients,* or *the negatives of possessive individuals.*

IV

Clearly, the identities and needs that the social-welfare system fashions for its recipients are interpreted identities and needs. Moreover, they are highly political interpretations and, as such, are in principle subject to dispute. Yet these needs and identities are not always recognized as interpretations. Too often, they simply go without saying and are rendered immune from analysis and critique. Doubtless one reason for this "reification effect" is the depth at which gender meanings and norms are embedded in our general culture. But there may also be another reason more specific to the welfare system.

Let me suggest yet another way of analyzing the U.S. social-welfare system, this time as a "juridical-administrative-therapeutic state apparatus" (JAT).[26] The point is to emphasize a distinctive style of operation. Qua JAT, the welfare system works by linking together a series of juridical, administrative, and therapeutic procedures. As a consequence, it tends to translate political issues concerning the interpretation of people's needs into legal, administrative, and/or therapeutic matters. Thus, the system executes political policy in a way that appears nonpolitical and tends to be depoliticizing.

Considered abstractly, the subject-positions constructed for beneficiaries of *both* the "masculine" and the "feminine" components of the system can be analyzed as combinations of three distinct elements. The first element is a *juridical* one, which positions recipients vis-à-vis the legal system by according or denying them various *rights.* Thus, the subject of the "masculine" subsystem has a right to benefits and is protected from some legally sanctioned forms of administrative caprice, whereas the subject of the "feminine" subsystem largely lacks rights.

This juridical element is then linked with a second one, an *administrative* element. In order to qualify to receive benefits, subjects must assume the stance of petitioners with respect to an administrative body; they must petition a bureaucratic institution empowered to decide their claims on the basis of administratively defined criteria. In the "masculine" subsystem, for example, claimants must prove their "cases" meet administratively defined criteria of entitlement; in the "feminine" subsystem, on the other hand, claimants must prove conformity to administratively defined criteria of need. The enormous qualitative differences between the two sets of procedures notwithstanding, both are variations on the same administrative moment. Both require claimants to translate their experienced situations and life problems into administrable needs, to present their predicaments as bona fide instances of specified generalized states of affairs that could in principle befall anyone.[27]

If and when they qualify, social-welfare claimants get positioned either as purchasing consumers or dependent clients. In either case, their needs are redefined as correlates of bureaucratically administered satisfactions. This means they are quantified, rendered as equivalents of a sum of money.[28] Thus, in the "feminine" subsystem, clients are positioned passively to receive monetarily measured, predefined, and prepackaged services; in the "masculine" subsystem, on the other hand, beneficiaries receive a specified, predetermined amount of cash.

In both subsystems, then, people's needs are subject to a sort of rewriting operation. Experienced situations and life problems are translated into administrable needs; and since the latter are not necessarily isomorphic to the former, the possibility of a gap between them arises. This possibility is especially likely in the "feminine" subsystem, for there, as we saw, clients are constructed as deviant, and service provision has the character of normalization—albeit normalization designed more to stigmatize than to "reform."

Here, then, is the opening for the third, *therapeutic,* moment of the JAT's modus operandi. Especially in the "feminine" subsystem, service provision often includes an implicit or explicit therapeutic or quasi-therapeutic dimension. In AFDC, for example, social

workers concern themselves with the "mental health" aspects of their clients' lives, often construing these in terms of "character problems." More explicitly and less moralistically, municipal programs for poor unmarried pregnant teenage women include not only prenatal care, mothering instruction, and tutoring or schooling but also counseling sessions with psychiatric social workers. As observed by Prudence Rains, such sessions are intended to bring girls to acknowledge what are considered to be their true, deep, latent, emotional problems, on the assumption that this will enable them to avoid future pregnancies.[29] Ludicrous as this sounds, it is only an extreme example of a more pervasive phenomenon, namely, the tendency of especially "feminine" social-welfare programs to construct gender-political and political-economic problems as individual, psychological problems. In fact, some therapeutic or quasi-therapeutic welfare services can be regarded as second-order services to compensate for the debilitating effects of first-order services. In any case, the therapeutic dimension of the U.S. social-welfare system encourages clients to close gaps between their culturally shaped lived experience and their administratively defined situation by bringing the former into line with the latter.

Clearly, this analysis of the U.S. welfare system as a "juridical-administrative-therapeutic state apparatus" lets us see both "feminine" and "masculine" subsystems more critically. It suggests that the problem is not only that women are disempowered by the *denial* of social citizenship in the "feminine" subsystem— although they are—but also that women and men are disempowered by the *realization* of an androcentric, possessive individualist form of social citizenship in the "masculine" subsystem. In both subsystems, even the "masculine" one, the JAT positions its subjects in ways that do not empower them. It personalizes them as "cases" and so militates against their collective identification. It imposes monological, administrative definitions of situation and need and so preempts dialogically achieved self-definition and self-determination. It positions its subjects as passive client or consumer recipients and not as active co-participants involved in shaping their life conditions. Lastly, it construes experienced discontent with these arrangements as material for adjustment-oriented, usually sexist therapy and not as material for empowering processes of consciousness-raising.

All told, then, the form of social citizenship constructed even in the *best* part of the U.S. social-welfare system is a degraded and depoliticized one. It is a form of passive citizenship in which the state preempts the power to define and satisfy people's needs. This form of passive citizenship arises in part as a result of the JAT's distinctive style of operation. The JAT treats the interpretation of people's needs as pregiven and unproblematic, while itself redefining them as amenable to system-conforming satisfactions. Thus, the JAT shifts attention away from the question, Who interprets social needs and how? It tends to substitute the *juridical, administrative, and therapeutic management of need satisfaction* for the *politics of need interpretation.* That is, it tends to substitute *monological, administrative processes of need definition* for *dialogical, participatory processes of need interpretation.*[30]

V

Usually, analyses of social complexes as "institutionalized patterns of interpretation" are implicitly or explicitly functionalist. They purport to show how culturally hegemonic systems of meaning are stabilized and reproduced over time. As a result, such analyses often screen out "dysfunctional" events like micro- and macro-political resistances and conflicts. More generally, they tend to obscure the active side of social processes, the ways in which even the most routinized practice of social agents involves the active construction, deconstruction, and reconstruction of social meanings. It is no wonder, then, that many feminist scholars have become suspicious of functionalist methodologies, for when applied to gender issues, these methods occult female agency and construe women as mere passive victims of male dominance.

In order to avoid any such suggestion here, I want to conclude by situating the foregoing analysis in a broader, nonfunctionalist perspective. I want to sketch a picture according to which the social-welfare apparatus is one force among others in a larger and highly contested political arena.

Consider that the ideological (as opposed to economic) effects of the JAT's mode of need interpretation operate within a specific and relatively new societal arena. I call this arena "the social" in order to mark its noncoincidence with the familiar institutionalized spaces of family and official economy. As I conceive it, the social is not exactly equivalent to the traditional public sphere of political discourse defined by

Jürgen Habermas,[31] nor is it coextensive with the state. Rather, the social is a site of discourse about people's needs, specifically about those needs that have broken out of the domestic and/or official economic spheres that earlier contained them as "private matters." Thus, the social is a site of discourse about problematic needs, needs that have come to exceed the apparently (but not really) self-regulating domestic and official economic institutions of male-dominated, capitalist societies.[32]

As the site of this excess, the social is by definition a terrain of contestation. It is a space in which conflicts among rival interpretations of people's needs are played out. "In" the social, then, one would expect to find a plurality of competing ways of talking about needs. And, in fact, what we do find here are at least three major kinds: (1) "expert" needs discourses of, for example, social workers and therapists, on the one hand, and welfare administrators, planners, and policy makers, on the other, (2) oppositional movement needs discourses of, for example, feminists, lesbians and gays, people of color, workers, and welfare clients, and (3) "reprivatization" discourses of constituencies seeking to repatriate newly problematized needs to their former domestic or official economic enclaves. Such discourses, and others, compete with one another in addressing the fractured social identities of potential adherents.[33]

Seen from this vantage point, the social has a twofold character. It is simultaneously a new arena of state activity and, equally important, a new terrain of wider political contestation. It is both the home turf of the JAT and a field of struggle on which the JAT acts as simply one contestant among others. It would be a mistake, then, to treat the JAT as the undisputed master of the terrain of the social. In fact, much of the growth and activity of the social branch of the state has come in response to the activities of social movements, especially the labor, black, feminist, and Progressive movements. Moreover, as Theda Skocpol has shown, the social state is not simply a unified, self-possessed political agent.[34] It is, rather, in significant respects a resultant, a complex and polyvalent nexus of compromise formations in which are sedimented the outcomes of past struggles as well as the conditions for present and future ones. In fact, even when the JAT does act as an agent, the results are often unintended. When it takes responsibility for matters previously left to the family and/or the official economy, it tends to denaturalize those matters and thus risks fostering their further politicization.

In any case, social movements, too, act on the terrain of the social (as do, on a smaller scale, clients who engage the JAT in micropolitical resistances and negotiations). In fact, the JAT's monological, administrative approach to need definition can also be seen as a strategy to contain social movements. Such movements tend by their very nature to be dialogic and participatory. They represent the emergent capacities of newly politicized groups to cast off the apparently natural and prepolitical interpretations that enveloped their needs in the official economy and/or family. In social movements, people come to articulate alternative, politicized interpretations of their needs as they engage in processes of dialogue and collective struggle. Thus, the confrontation of such movements with the JAT on the terrain of the social is a confrontation between conflicting logics of need definition.

Feminists too, then, are actors on the terrain of the social. Indeed, from this perspective, we can distinguish several analytically distinct but practically intermingled kinds of feminist struggles worth engaging in the coming welfare wars. First, there are struggles to secure the political status of women's needs, that is, to legitimate women's needs as genuine political issues as opposed to "private" domestic or market matters. Here, feminists would engage especially antiwelfarist defenders of privatization. Second, there are struggles over the interpreted content of women's needs, struggles to challenge the apparently natural, traditional interpretations still enveloping needs only recently sprung from domestic and official economic enclaves of privacy. Here, feminists would engage all those forces in the culture that perpetuate androcentric and sexist interpretations of women's needs, including, but not only, the social state. Third, there are struggles over the who and how of need interpretation, struggles to empower women to interpret their own needs and to challenge the antiparticipatory, monological practices of the welfare system qua JAT. Fourth, there are struggles to elaborate and win support for policies based on feminist interpretations of women's needs, policies that avoid both the Scylla of private patriarchy and the Charybdis of public patriarchy.

In all these cases, the focus would be as much on need interpretation as on need satisfaction. This is as it should be, since any satisfactions we are able to win will be problematic to the degree we fail to fight and win the battle of interpretation.

ACKNOWLEDGMENTS

I am grateful for the helpful comments, suggestions, and criticisms of Sandra Bartky, John Brenkman, Jane Collier, Ann Garry, Virginia Held, Thomas McCarthy, Carole Pateman, Birte Siim, Howard Winant, Terry Winant, Iris Young, and the members of the Midwest Society for Women in Philosophy. I also thank Drucilla Cornell and Betty Safford for the invitations that provided occasions for developing the essay, The Stanford Humanities Center for a congenial working environment and financial support, and Dee Marquez and Marina Rosiene for crackerjack word processing.

NOTES

1. James O'Connor, *The Fiscal Crisis of the State* (New York, 1973).

2. Diana Pearce, "Women, Work, and Welfare: The Feminization of Poverty," in *Working Women and Families,* ed. Karen Wolk Feinstein (Beverly Hills, Calif., 1979).

3. Barbara Ehrenreich and Frances Fox Piven, "The Feminization of Poverty," *Dissent* 31, no. 2 (Spring 1984): 162–70.

4. Pearce, "Women, Work, and Welfare"; Nancy S. Barrett, "The Welfare Trap" (American Economic Association, Dallas, Texas, 1984); and Steven P. Erie, Martin Rein, and Barbara Wiget, "Women and the Reagan Revolution: Thermidor for the Social Welfare Economy," in *Families, Politics, and Public Policies: A Feminist Dialogue on Women and the State,* ed. Irene Diamond (New York, 1983).

5. Carol Brown, "Mothers, Fathers, and Children: From

Private to Public Patriarchy," in *Women and Revolution: A Discussion of the Unhappy Marriage of Marxism and Feminism,* ed. Lydia Sargent (Boston, 1981). I believe that Brown's terms are too simple on two counts. First, for reasons elaborated by Gayle Rubin ("The Traffic in Women: Notes on the 'Political Economy' of Sex," in *Towards an Anthropology of Women,* ed. Rayna R. Reiter [New York, 1975]), I prefer not to use 'patriarchy' as a generic term for male dominance but rather as the designation of a specific historical social formation. Second, Brown's public/private contrast oversimplifies the structure of both laissez-faire and welfare state capitalism, since it posits two major societal zones where there are actually four (family, official economy, state, and sphere of public political discourse) and conflates two distinct public/private divisions. (For a discussion of this second problem, see "What's Critical about Critical Theory? The Case of Habermas and Gender," Chapter 6 of this volume.) These problems notwithstanding, it remains the case that Brown's terms are immensely suggestive and that we currently have no better terminology. Thus, in what follows I occasionally use 'public patriarchy' for want of an alternative.

6. For an analysis of the dynamics whereby late capitalist political systems tend to select certain types of interests while excluding others, see Claus Offe, "Political Authority and Class Structure: An Analysis of Late Capitalist Societies," *International Journal of Sociology* 2, no. 1 (Spring 1982: 73–108; "Structural Problems of the Capitalist State: Class Rule and the Political System—On the Selectiveness of Political Institutions," in *German Political Studies,* ed. Klaus von Beyme (London, 1974); and "The Separation of Form and Content in Liberal Democratic Politics," *Studies in Political Economy* 3 (Spring 1980): 5–16. For a feminist application of Offe's approach, see Drude Dahlerup, "Overcoming the Barriers: An Approach to the Study of How Women's Issues are kept from the Political Agenda," in *Women's Views of the Political World of Men,* ed. Judith H. Stiehm (Dobbs Ferry, N.Y., 1984).

7. This phrase owes its inspiration to Jürgen Habermas, *Legitimation Crisis,* trans. Thomas McCarthy (Boston, 1975).

8. I owe this phrase to Thomas McCarthy (personal communication).

9. Erie, Rein, and Wiget, "Women and the Reagan Revolution"; and Barbara J. Nelson, "Women's Poverty and Women's Citizenship: Some Political Consequences of Economic Marginality." *Signs: Journal of Women in Culture and Society* 10, no. 2 (Winter 1984):209–31.

10. Nelson, "Women's Poverty and Women's Citizenship."

11. Erie, Rein, and Wiget, "Women and the Reagan Revolution"; and Nelson, "Women's Poverty and Women's Citizenship."

12. Erie, Rein, and Wiget, "Women and the Reagan Revolution."

13. Ibid.

14. Ehrenreich and Piven, "The Feminization of Poverty."

15. Hilary Land, "Who Cares for the Family?" *Journal of Social Policy* 7, no. 3 (July 1978):257–84.

16. I owe the phrase "gender subtext" to Dorothy Smith "The Gender Subtext of Power" (Ontario Institute for Studies in Education, Toronto, 1984). A number of writers have noticed the two-tiered character of the U.S. social-welfare system. Andrew Hacker ("'Welfare': The Future of an Illusion," *New York Review of Books,* 28 February 1985, 37–43) correlates the dualism with class but not with gender. Diana Pearce ("Women, Work, and Welfare") and Erie, Rein, and Wiget ("Women and the Reagan Revolution") correlate the dualism with gender and with the dual labor market, itself gender-correlated. Barbara Nelson ("Women's Poverty and Women's Citizenship") correlates the dualism with gender, the dual labor market, and the sexual division of paid *and unpaid* labor. My account owes a great deal to all of these writers, especially to Barbara Nelson.

17. Hilary Land ("Who Cares for the Family?") identifies similar assumptions at work in the British social-welfare system. My formulation of them is much indebted to her.

18. Pearce, "Women, Work, and Welfare."

19. Nelson, "Women's Poverty and Women's Citizenship"; and Erie, Rein, and Wiget, "Women and the Reagan Revolution."

20. C. B. MacPherson, *The Political Theory of Possessive Individualism: Hobbes to Locke* (New York, 1964).

21. I owe these formulations to Virginia Held (personal communication).

22. Pearce, "Women, Work, and Welfare."

23. It should be noted that I am here taking issue with the view of some left theorists that "decommodification" in the form of in kind social-welfare benefits represents an emancipatory or progressive development. In the context of a two-tiered welfare system like the one described here, this assumption is clearly false, since in kind benefits are qualitatively and quantitatively inferior to the corresponding commodities and since they function to stigmatize those who receive them.

24. Carol B. Stack, *All Our Kin: Strategies for Survival in a Black Community* (New York, 1974).

25. Marcel Mauss, *The Gift: Forms and Functions of Exchange in Archaic Societies,* trans. Ian Cunnison (New York, 1967).

26. This term echoes Louis Althusser's term, "ideological state apparatus" ("Ideology and Ideological State Apparatuses: Notes towards an Investigation," in *Essays on Ideology,* trans. Ben Brewster [London, 1984]). Certainly, the U.S. social-welfare system as described in the present section of this paper counts as an "ISA" in Althusser's sense. However, I prefer the term 'juridical-administrative-therapeutic state apparatus' as more concrete and descriptive of the specific ways in which welfare programs produce and reproduce ideology. In general, then, a JAT can be understood as a subclass of an ISA. On the other hand, Althusserian-like ter-

minology aside, readers will find that the account in this section owes more to Michel Foucault *(Discipline and Punish: The Birth of the Prison,* trans. Alan Sheridan [New York, 1979]) and Jürgen Habermas *(Theorie des kommunikativen Handelns,* vol. 2, *Zur Kritik der funktionalistischen Vernunft* [Frankfurt on Main, 1981]) than to Althusser. Of course, neither Habermas nor Foucault is sensitive to the gendered character of social-welfare programs. For a critique of Habermas in this respect, see Chapter 6 of this volume. For my views about Foucault, see Chapters 1, 2, and 3.

27. Habermas, *Theorie des kommunikativen Handelns,* vol. 2.

28. Ibid.

29. Prudence Mors Rains, *Becoming an Unwed Mother: A Sociological Account* (Chicago, 1971).

30. These formulations owe much to Jürgen Habermas, *Legitimation Crisis,* and *Theorie des Kommunikativen Handelns,* vol. 2.

31. Habermas, *Legitimation Crisis,* and *Theorie des Kommunikativen Handelns,* vol. 2.

32. I borrow the term 'social' from Hannah Arendt (*The Human Condition* [Chicago, 1958]). However, my use of it differs from hers in several important ways. First, Arendt and I both understand the social as a historically emergent societal space specific to modernity. And we both understand the emergence of the social as tending to undercut or blur an earlier, more distinct separation of public and private spheres. But she treats the emergence of the social as a fall or lapse, and she valorizes the earlier separation of public and private as a preferred state of affairs appropriate to "the human condition." I, on the other hand, make no assumptions about the human condition; nor do I regret the passing of the private/public separation; nor do I consider the emergence of the social a fall or lapse. Second, Arendt and I agree that one salient, defining feature of the social is the emergence of heretofore "private" needs into public view. Arendt, however, treats this as a violation of the proper order of things: she assumes that needs are wholly natural and are forever doomed to be things of brute compulsion. Thus, she supposes that needs can have no genuinely political dimension and that their emergence from the private sphere into the social spells the death of authentic politics. I, on the other hand, assume that needs are irreducibly interpretive and that need interpretations are in principle contestable. It follows from my view that the emergence of needs from the "private" into the social is a generally positive development, since such needs thereby lose their illusory aura of naturalness as their interpretations become subject to critique and contestation. I, therefore, suppose that this represents the (possible) flourishing of politics, rather than the (necessary) death of politics. Finally, Arendt assumes that the emergence of the social and of public concern with needs necessarily means the triumph of administration and instrumental reason. I, on the other hand, assume that instrumental reason represents only one possible way of defining and addressing social needs and that administration represents only one possible way of institutionalizing the social. Thus, I would argue for the existence of another possibility: an alternative socialist-feminist, dialogical mode of need interpretation and a participatory-democratic institutionalization of the social.

33. See Chapter 8 of this volume for a fuller development of these ideas.

34. Theda Skocpol, "Political Response to Capitalist Crisis: Neo-Marxist Theories of the State and the Case of the New Deal," *Politics and Society* 10 (1980):155–201.

The Gender Gap and Women's Political Influence

CAROL MUELLER

The 1980 presidential campaign between Jimmy Carter and Ronald Reagan marked a turning point in women's political influence. For the first time since women won the suffrage, a significant proportion of women voted differently from the way men did. Eight percent fewer women than men voted for the Republican candidate, a difference that was to be sustained with only slight variation through the 1984 and 1988 presidential elections. This voting difference, later labeled the "gender gap" by the National Organization for Women (NOW), coincided with another breakthrough in women's political participation. A higher proportion of women voted than did men, another gap that grew throughout the 1980s. The two changes, a pattern of voting that differs significantly from that of men and a higher turnout rate, together have provided the potential for a new level of political influence for women.[1]

GROUP VOTING AND WOMEN'S POLITICAL INFLUENCE

Group voting has historically been a major component of American interest group politics. Thus it was taken for granted by public officials, candidates for office, and party bosses that the extension of suffrage to women in 1920 would lead to the creation of a women's voting bloc. It was widely assumed, for instance, that the National League of Women Voters, created in 1919 to replace the National American Women's Suffrage Association, represented a thinly disguised women's party. Women's influence peaked in the years

From *The Annals of the American Academy of Political and Social Sciences,* May 1991. Copyright © 1991. Reprinted by permission of Sage Publications, Inc.

immediately before and after 1920 in anticipation of an organized bloc of women voters that would pursue the suffrage campaign's Progressive agenda.[2]

This early influence garnered national committee and delegate positions for women from the two major parties. Parties and candidates endorsed much of the National League of Women Voters' platform in 1920. Wilson and Harding appointed women to state and federal regulatory boards, the foreign service, and judgeships. Congress passed an unprecedented amount of legislation proposed by the women's lobbying organization, the Women's Joint Congressional Committee, representing organizations with a combined membership of over 10 million.[3]

This influence had eroded by the mid-1920s, when the women's voting bloc failed to emerge. Because the passage of the Nineteenth Amendment paralleled an overall downturn in voting, the women's vote after 1920 was the lowest recorded in the Western democracies. While women may have voted differently from men—and there is some evidence to suggest this may have happened—it was not reported in surveys and polls and, thus, went unrecorded. Whether women voted differently or not, if men voted at a rate estimated at 30 to 45 percent higher, only very close elections could have been influenced by a women's vote.[4]

During the period from 1920 to 1960, as women's voting turnout was gradually increasing, women's political influence was primarily exerted through insider lobbying. From Molly Dewson and the social feminists of the New Deal to Alice Paul and the Women's Party's advocacy of the Equal Rights Amendment (ERA), the political goals of women were voiced in the administrative offices of the White House and the hearing rooms of Congress. The formation of NOW in 1966, however, and the proliferation of local women's liberation groups led to a massive wave of women's rights legislation and the creation of an expanded lobbying presence for women in Washington.[5]

Yet, both waves of legislative success were achieved without a women's voting bloc. The first wave of political influence was associated with the mass mobilization of the suffrage campaign, intensive lobbying by women's organizations, and the threat of a women's voting bloc. The second wave was similarly based on mass mobilization and lobbying but had the added impact of women in Congress such as Martha Griffiths (Democrat from Michigan), Margaret Heckler (Republican from Massachusetts), and Patricia Schroeder (Democrat from Colorado) who could personally guide legislative passage of the feminist agenda. Although the presence of women in Congress and in the party hierarchies reflected the growing women's vote, their vote was not acknowledged as a significant component of political calculation until 1980.

In the elections immediately following 1980, feminist organizations, particularly NOW, attempted to use the gender gap to win political support for key feminist issues such as the ERA in 1982 and the nomination of a woman for vice president in 1984. While the 1984 Democratic nomination did go to Geraldine Ferraro, NOW strategists in the ERA campaign had difficulty targeting the women's vote in specific states where ratification campaigns had a chance of success. Moreover, even though the Ferraro nomination was an important symbolic victory for feminists, it made little contribution to the unsuccessful Democratic ticket headed by Walter Mondale. These results contributed to a post-election atmosphere in which the Democratic Party sought to distance itself from special interests such as feminists. Many feminists also were disillusioned about the value of electoral strategies.[6]

Although the gender gap was brought to public attention by feminists, it has become a generalized political resource that is accessible to any candidate with the polling data to pinpoint media and campaign appeals to specific groups of women. The discovery of the gender gap and the media campaign orchestrated by NOW to make it public were paralleled by a less visible analysis by successive Republican polling consultants of gender differences in candidate, party, and issue preferences. Richard Wirthlin, polling consultant for Ronald Reagan, discovered these differences late in the 1980 campaign but became more concerned as the gap increased with the 1982 downturn in the economy and the greater decline in women's presidential

approval ratings. By the 1984 campaign, the Republicans had responded with the nomination of Sandra Day O'Connor to the Supreme Court, the appointment of Jeane Kirkpatrick as ambassador to the United Nations and of Margaret Heckler and Elizabeth Dole to cabinet positions. With large numbers of women also placed prominently in the presidential campaign, polling consultants devised a strategy to reach out to potential subgroups of women voters with special media appeals emphasizing the economic advantage of the Republican administration.[7]

Although analyses of the 1984 election have not sought to evaluate the campaign directed at women, the campaign seems to have made little difference in the final outcome. Thus there was little reason to credit the gender gap with playing a major role in either Reagan's victory or Mondale's defeat.[8] This is not the case with the 1988 election. A 20 percent gender gap favored the Democrats at the end of the primaries in May, with the likely Republican nominee, George Bush, seriously falling behind his Democratic opponent, Michael Dukakis, in the overall ratings. These polling results led to a Republican campaign that witnessed a new and qualitatively different kind of presidential campaign for a "kinder, gentler nation." As organized feminists played a secondary role to older women's organizations like the Federation of Business and Professional Women's Clubs—now BPW/USA—the focus also shifted from status issues like the ERA and a vice presidential candidate to the hopes and fears of the average woman voter.

THE GENDER GAP IN THE 1988 CAMPAIGN

In mid-October 1988, the *Washington Post* carried a story headlined, "Dukakis' Gender Gap Advantage, Once Formidable, Has Vanished." A week later *Newsweek* carried a similar story entitled, "Closing the Gender Gap: How Dukakis Squandered His Lead Among Women." The 5 percent difference between women and men in their anticipated voting choices in early October was a far cry from the twenty-point difference of late spring.[9]

The unprecedented gender gap had led many political columnists to speculate on the hidden meaning of the often told joke that "George Bush reminds every woman of her first husband." By fall, no one was telling jokes about George Bush, particularly jokes about his problems with women. At that stage of the campaign, *Newsweek* writers reported a reversal in campaign humor. The October version of the story ran that "Bush may remind some women of a bad first marriage, but for others, Dukakis seems to rekindle memories of a disastrous first date."[10]

The change in the object of women's chagrin from May to October reflected not only the precipitous decline in the gender gap but also the campaign issues that brought about the decline. Dukakis, the blind date, unknown in the spring, had been revealed by the fall as weak on crime, patriotism, and national security. Dukakis's image as a political leader had been so badly shaken that even those who were most concerned about the economy, his strongest issue, gave him only lukewarm support on election day.[11]

In the actual vote, the gender gap was still visible, with 7 percent more men than women supporting Bush and 8 percent more women than men backing Dukakis.[12] Yet, the gender gap had been diffused as a threat to the Republican candidate. Unlike the election of 1984, the campaign leading to the 1988 election had not been irrelevant; images and symbols such as the blind date had been central to the Republican victory.[13]

The Campaign and Political Influence

Surprisingly, perhaps, many feminist leaders did not show the keen disappointment in the outcome of the 1988 election that had accompanied the defeat of Mondale and Ferraro in 1984. In the fall of 1988, the women's candidate, Dukakis, was clearly losing, but women leaders already seemed to sense a different kind of victory. For the first time, women's issues were playing a significant role in a presidential campaign.

As early as October, Irene Natividad, president of the bipartisan National Women's Political Caucus, had noted approvingly the effect of the women's vote on the tenor of the campaign. Whether it was political expediency or genuine commitment hardly mattered. What was important was placing issues of child care alongside foreign policy as a campaign issue.[14]

In January 1989, during the week of George Bush's inauguration as the nation's forty-first president, one thousand women leaders gathered in Kansas City to evaluate the campaign and plan for the future. Political consultants and political scientists were called together by BPW/USA to address the Women's Agenda Conference II, representing a coalition of fifty national

women's organizations with a combined bipartisan membership of 10 million. The counsel of these illustrious consultants and women's leaders was simple: both the campaign and the election were proof of the growing influence of women voters. Vince Breglio, polling consultant for the Bush-Quayle campaign, offered perhaps the most compelling evidence for the influence of women voters when he told the conference that the major accomplishment of Bush-Quayle had been that of closing the gender gap. Although it had been as high as 15 to 20 percent in the late spring, by the end of the campaign it was down to a more reasonable level of 6 to 8. Closing the gap had been critical to winning the campaign.[15]

The campaign indeed was important. As the primaries came to a close in late spring, Dukakis led Bush in the CBS News/*New York Times* polls by 10 percent, his lead swelling to 17 points—50 to 33 percent—in the interlude following the Democratic Convention (see Table 1). Bush so dramatically altered the tone of the campaign at the Republican Convention in early August, however, that Dukakis never again held the

TABLE 1   EXPECTED VOTES FOR GEORGE BUSH (R) AND MICHAEL DUKAKIS (D), CBS NEWS/*NEW YORK TIMES* POLLS

Date of Poll	N	PERCENTAGE VOTING FOR		Percentage Difference
		Dukakis	Bush	
May 9–12	1056	49	39	10
July 5–8	947	47	39	8
July 31–August 3	941	50	33	17
August 19–21	N.A.	40	46	−6
September 8–11	1159	39	47	−8
September 21–23	1020	41	46	−5
October 1–3	744	43	45	−2
October 8–10	N.A.	42	47	−5
October 21–24	1827	38	51	−13
November 2–4	N.A.	40	48	−8
November 4–5	1585	42	51	−9

SOURCES: Data are from the *New York Times* issues of 18 May 1988, 12 July 1988, 7 Aug. 1988, 14 Sept. 1988, 30 Sept. 1988, 7 Oct. 1988, 18 Oct. 1988, 26 Oct. 1988, and 7 Nov. 1988. The sources for the data concerning the poll of 19–21 Aug., however, are the CBS News polls cited in these issues of the *New York Times*.

lead. Dukakis was only twice within striking distance: in early October, when the difference between the candidates was 2 percent, after Dukakis's strong showing in the first debate; and in the last two weeks before the election, when the Dukakis campaign took a populist turn based on economic issues and Bush's lead was narrowed from 13 to 8 points.[16]

The decline of the gender gap was a major factor in the dramatic transformation that saw an overall 10-point Dukakis lead become an 8-point advantage for Bush. CBS News/*New York Times* polls showed an 18-point difference favoring Dukakis among women in May (53 to 35 percent) and virtually no difference among men between Bush and Dukakis (43 to 44 percent). In late September, however, Bush held a slight advantage among women (43 to 41 percent) and a 16-point lead among men (53 to 37 percent). Although Bush's campaign made gains with both men and women, the greater gain was with women.[17]

The Republican Campaign

The successful Republican campaign that deflated the gender gap was a carefully researched combination of policy proposals on substantive issues of interest to women, such as child care and equal opportunity, with more symbolic issues touching women's fears and insecurities about crime and violence, patriotism and subversion. One of the major sources of the campaign's success was this careful blending of substantive policies directed to the practical realities of women's lives and symbols that touched deep emotional responses.

The story of William Horton, Jr., a black man who had raped a white Maryland woman and stabbed her boyfriend while participating in a Massachusetts prison furlough program, linked Dukakis with fear of crime, racism, and threats to personal safety.[18] Dukakis's veto, on constitutional grounds, of a Massachusetts bill that would have required public school teachers to lead students in reciting the Pledge of Allegiance merged with images of flag burning, liberalism—the *L* word—and Dukakis's membership in the American Civil Liberties Union. Together, the images provided a linked set of negative symbols threatening patriotism and fueling fears of internal subversion and threats to national security.[19]

The symbolic campaign was dramatically effective. Before the nominating convention, women were more likely than men either to view Dukakis as tougher than

Bush on crime (27 to 18 percent) or, if they thought the candidates were equally tough, to favor Dukakis. By October, a plurality of both men and women had been convinced that Dukakis would not be tough enough in dealing with criminals, and this group supported Bush overwhelmingly: 86 to 6 percent for men; 79 to 10 percent for women.[20]

The patriotism issue also served the Republican cause well, particularly with women. By mid-October, an ABC/*Washington Post* poll found that the Pledge of Allegiance figured into the voting calculations of 46 percent of women compared to only 31 percent of men. The CBS News/*New York Times* poll found in the fall that women who felt the pledge was an important issue favored Bush—52 to 31 percent; women who felt it was not important favored Dukakis—49 to 37 percent.

While Willie Horton and the Pledge of Allegiance represented appeals to women's anxieties and fears, the Republican campaign also suggested policy initiatives to address women's concerns about economic insecurity and stresses on the modern family. Proposals on child care, parental leave, and education followed rapidly after Bush received the Republican nomination. His acceptance speech invoked the vision of a "kinder, gentler America" and told women that two of every three jobs created during the current expansion had been filled by "the women of America." He reassured these women, "You know better than anyone that equality begins with economic empowerment. You're gaining economic power, and I'm not going to let them take it away from you." It was now the Republican candidate who seemed more concerned about the social agenda.[21]

After the nomination, Bush's appearances at the ubiquitous factory gates gave way to carefully selected visits at day-care centers and at the hospitals and offices where women work. Bush, the military man and leader of the Central Intelligence Agency, emerged after the convention as a warm and loving husband, father, and grandfather.

His acceptance speech reached out to place women's concerns at the center of national political discourse. Rather than rattling sabers as his predecessor had done, he voiced national dreams in a domestic vocabulary:

It seems to me the presidency provides an incomparable opportunity for gentle persuasion. . . . Prosperity with a purpose means taking your idealism and making it concrete by certain acts of goodness. . . . It means teaching troubled children through your presence that there is such a thing as reliable love. Some would say it's soft and insufficiently tough to care about these things. But where is it written that we must act as if we do not care, as if we are not moved? Well, I am moved. I want a kinder and gentler nation.

Throughout the Republican Convention, Bush showed that he understood and would place a high priority on family issues.

Bush also developed a new interest in women's groups and their programs. Although five Democratic candidates had accepted the invitation of the BPW to attend its first National Women's Agenda Conference in January 1988, it was not until six months later that George Bush, the Republican Party candidate, appeared at the annual convention of the BPW with a program for women on pay equity, child care, and equal opportunity.[22] In early October, Bush put more substance into his campaign slogan, "Invest in our children," by unveiling proposals to encourage adoption, improve child support collection, and use Medicaid to help high-risk poor children.[23]

The Democratic Campaign

Dukakis also had a program for women and families, but it was poorly dramatized and often upstaged by his opponent during the campaign. The low-key unveiling of his prenatal care program in a local Boston hospital, for instance, compared poorly with the high-profile image of Bush arriving in Boston the same day to receive the endorsement of the Boston Police Patrolman's Association and to emphasize his anticrime position. On his visit to Boston's Brigham and Women's Hospital, Dukakis called for a national version of the Massachusetts program known as Healthy Start. He also called for a national prenatal-care program for pregnant women based on a health insurance program in Massachusetts. Despite the success of the Massachusetts program in reducing the state's infant-mortality rate, despite the cost effectiveness of the program in paying for itself in savings from reduced costs for intensive care of premature and low-birthweight babies, it was Bush's police association endorsement that stole the headlines.[24]

The differences in the two candidates' programs for

women and children represented the differences typical of the Democratic and Republican parties. For family and medical leave, for health benefits, and for child care, Bush supported tax incentives and voluntary private sector involvement, while Dukakis supported mandatory requirements on the private sector for benefits coupled with federal enforcement and financial support. To deal with domestic violence and child abuse, the Republican candidate promised to appoint judges committed to stronger sentencing; the Democratic candidate supported awareness and training programs for families, judges, and police. Bush opposed and Dukakis supported the feminist positions on the ERA and abortion issues.[25] There are few surprises in these partisan approaches to the issues of interest to women. What was surprising, however, was the greater success of the Republican candidate in making women's issues his issues, in becoming personally associated with women's concerns about education, child care, and child health.

As consultants pointed out before and after the campaign, the key issue that might have made the difference for Dukakis was women's economic vulnerability. Women are disproportionately more likely than men to be single parents, marginally employed, unmarried, and elderly. A bipartisan group of 150 women leaders, calling themselves the "Super Saturday Group," had gathered in Atlanta in December 1987 to plan for the Super Tuesday primaries in the South by encouraging politicians to learn how to address issues of women's economic vulnerability. Jeanne Howes, executive director of the Women's Vote Project in Washington, D.C., advised politicians to take a more personal approach in talking to women by addressing issues such as paying the bills or finding health care for children.[26]

As the campaign began, women were considerably less confident than men about the country's economic future and more likely to favor a candidate who would bring about change. In late spring, women thought that that candidate was Dukakis. At the end of the campaign, women were evenly split on which candidate would bring about the change they wanted. The proportion of men who feared that the economy would get worse decreased from 29 percent in May to 18 percent in October. Over the same period, the proportion of women with such fears dropped only slightly, from 37 percent to 33 percent, indicating that these fears represented a source of political support among women for the candidate who could address them.

LESBIANS CLEAR HURDLES
TO GAIN LEADERSHIP POSTS

KATHERINE BISHOP

SAN FRANCISCO, Dec. 29—After two decades of perfecting their political skills in the feminist movement and in the mainstream parties, after years of fighting for better health care programs amid the AIDS crisis, lesbians are increasingly being elected to office. And they are becoming leaders of gay organizations that have historically been run by men.

From Los Angeles to Maine, voters in the November elections showed more willingness to elect lesbians to city and state offices, often for the first time. And in large gay organizations lesbians, who were once eclipsed by gay men, are emerging in highly-visible jobs, positioning themselves as possible candidates of the future.

While it is difficult to determine numbers of lesbians in elective office around the country, five of the six acknowledged lesbians running for public office were elected in November. Their successes followed years of toiling as volunteers before conquering attitudes that have slowed the political advancement of all women.

"In part, it's a matter of the traditional issue of women thinking they have to do a lot more work before they can ask to be elected, while every man comes out of law school thinking he can be a senator," said Deborah Glick, 39 years old, who in November became the first openly gay person to be elected to the New York Assembly. Her district is in lower Manhattan.

Fading as an Issue?

Other lesbian candidates, especially those who had previously made unsuccessful attempts at elective office, say the question of sexual orientation is fading as an issue to voters.

From *The New York Times,* December 30, 1990. Copyright © 1990 by The New York Times Company. Reprinted by permission.

"Most people said, 'Thank goodness, you're not a lawyer or an incumbent,'" said Carole Migden, who with another gay woman, Roberta Achtenberg, was elected in November to the San Francisco Board of Supervisors. "Roberta and I were seen first of all as smart, capable, affirmative and new."

Dale McCormick, who became the first acknowledged lesbian to be elected to the State Senate of Maine, said she thinks lesbians have made progress in politics. Ms. McCormick, 43, the former president of the Maine Lesbian-Gay Political Alliance, said she rode her bicycle on country roads to visit 6,000 homes in her district.

"People said, 'You'll never win, you have all this political baggage, you're too outspoken,'" Ms. McCormick said, "But the voters were willing." She won in 10 of 12 towns in Southern Maine.

Agendas Were Different

The women also cite the recent support by homosexual men of lesbians in leadership roles in gay organizations as an important ingredient in their current success.

Until recently, personal and political conflicts between homosexual men and women was serious enough to drive them into separate communities. While gay men were delighting in their sexual liberation and creating their own power bases, lesbians promoted a broader feminist agenda of child custody, child care and women's health issues, often in a context of long-term partnerships.

The AIDS crisis prompted a healing of long-standing rifts that had prevented men from supporting leadership by women, they say.

"AIDS meant that suddenly there were bigger fights to fight than protecting the old boys' club and preserving the newfound network of power brokers who ran gay rights organizations," said Torie Osborn, 40. She is the first woman to serve as executive director of the Gay and Lesbian Community

Services Center in Los Angeles since its founding 20 years ago. In 1985, all the women in the organization walked out for two years because the board refused to consider a woman for the position.

Many women cite Urvashi Vaid, the executive director of the 17,000-member National Gay and Lesbian Task Force in Washington, who was named "Woman of the Year" this month by The Advocate, the national news magazine for gay people. The Advocate said that for Ms. Vaid, a 32-year-old lawyer of Indian descent, to be selected to head a major lesbian and gay lobbying group "is a stunning coup for lesbians, who have been made as invisible in the gay rights movement as in mainstream society."

Homosexual men and women acknowledge that some people may believe that the current success of lesbians in leadership positions in public life is a result of the death of homosexual men from AIDS. But they reject that conclusion.

"AIDS has killed many gay men who were leaders, but it's also the case that the women have been extraordinary in the crisis," said David Scondras, a homosexual who is a member of the Boston City Council.

"Women's sense of community was touched by the horror, and it led them to fight a crusade for funding for health care and to find a cure," said Mr. Scondras, who organized the sixth annual Conference of Lesbian and Gay Elected Officials in November in Boston.

Ms. Glick agrees: "It's not simply that men are dying and now there are openings for women. It's that men are now more open to power sharing."

In November, Ms. Migden and Ms. Achtenberg were two of the first three openly gay candidates to be elected in a citywide race in San Francisco without having first been appointed to their respective offices. The third was Tom Ammiano, a teacher who was elected to the Board of Education.

Ms. Migden, 42, who serves on the State Health Commission and has headed two community mental health organizations, enters office with a strong background in Democratic Party politics. The party's San Francisco chairwoman since 1986, she was elected to the Democratic National Committee in 1988.

"There is no question the Democratic Party was a strong component of my campaign," Ms. Migden said. "I had a host of contacts and constituents that one builds up over the years."

AIDS Changes Thinking

Ms. Migden also served two terms as president of the Harvey Milk Lesbian/Gay Democratic Club here. She said her candidacy for the Board of Supervisors was backed by homosexual men as well as lesbians, in part because of her emphasis on health care issues.

"The divisions in our community began to evaporate with the AIDS emergency," she said. "There is a positive outcome of any catastrophe, and this one made gay men aware of a whole range of health care issues from medical insurance to access to specialized care that we as a society are justifiably already nervous about."

Ms. Achtenberg, a 40-year-old civil rights lawyer who headed the National Center for Lesbian Rights here, recalled that times were not always so harmonious. "The gay community has been dominated by white men, like the community at large," she said.

Health care issues are only part of the broader family agenda for lesbians. Because many are mothers, issues like affordable child care have been among their political goals, something they said also appealed to voters. Ms. Achtenberg said voters here found no dissonance in her being both a lesbian and a parent. She and her partner, Judge Mary C. Morgan of San Francisco Municipal Court, are raising a child borne by Judge Morgan. The judge, the nation's first acknowledged lesbian jurist, was appointed to the bench in 1981 by Gov. Edmund G. Brown Jr.

Ms. Vaid said openly lesbian elected officials remain a small fraction of the gay women in public service. But, she said, "voters are showing they are not going to reject you for sexual orientation if you have the background. That is huge progress for a community that has just begun to come out of hiding."

When Dukakis made a last-minute appeal on economic issues during the final weeks of the campaign, both men and women concerned about the economy responded favorably. On election day, men were more likely than women to say they were better off than in 1980 (55 to 42 percent). These men were more likely to vote for Bush. Women were somewhat more likely than men to say they were worse off than in 1980 (33 to 35 percent) and were more likely to vote for Dukakis. These women were an important component of Dukakis's remaining advantage among women on election day.[27]

The gender gap on election day reflected the extreme differences in the economic circumstances of some categories of men and women who are otherwise very similar. As shown in the CBS News/*New York Times* exit polls measuring the Democratic vote for Dukakis (see Table 2), the gap was greatest among men and women with less than a high school education (12 percent), unmarried men and women (10 percent), adults in middle age (12 percent), and Easterners (11 percent). The difference between men and women with the highest level of education produced a gender gap of 15 percent. Unmarried working women remained economically marginal, desirous of change, and favorable to the Democratic candidate. Their voting difference from married men was an impressive 18 percent. Significant gaps that had not existed before were also visible between black women and men (9 percent) and between married women and men (7 percent). Married women were significantly more likely than married men to have long-term economic anxieties. These differences presumably reflected the nature of the Democratic constituency among men and women, but the campaign did little to address the hopes and fears of women inclined toward the Democratic Party.

The Undecided Woman Voter

Although a gender gap of 7 to 8 percent remained in November and a majority of women—52 percent—voted for Dukakis, the gender gap declined by at least 10 points between the end of the primaries and the election, and the women's candidate of late spring did not win. An important factor in the election outcome was the women who changed their support from Dukakis to Bush over the course of the campaign. In the absence of panel data tracking the decision-making process for individuals during the campaign, it is not

TABLE 2   GENDER GAP, BY SUBGROUP: PERCENTAGE VOTING FOR DUKAKIS, BASED ON EXIT POLL DATA, 8 NOVEMBER 1988

	Women	Men	Gender Gap
Democrat	84	80	4
Independent	46	40	6
Republican	9	8	1
White	43	36	7
Black	90	81	9
Unmarried	57	47	10
Married	46	39	7
Less than high school	62	50	12
High school	50	49	1
Some college	45	38	7
College	51	36	15
18–29 years	50	43	7
30–44 years	49	40	9
45–59 years	48	36	12
60+ years	52	46	6
East	54	43	11
Midwest	49	43	6
South	44	38	6
West	56	48	8

SOURCE: Data from CBS News/*New York Times* exit polls and made available by Celinda Lake, Vice President, The Analysis Group, Inc., Washington, D.C.

possible to provide more than suggestive hypotheses about who these women were and how they made their voting decisions. Given the importance of understanding women's increasingly important role in electoral politics, however, even circumstantial evidence on who they were and what their concerns were may be useful.

In looking for women who shifted from Dukakis to Bush, it is not the Democratic loyalists who are of interest but rather those women who were willing to consider the alternative. In January 1988, the CBS News/*New York Times* poll showed that 30 percent of males with Democratic leanings were not certain that they would vote for their party's choice, compared with 40 percent of women. A much smaller proportion of Republicans were undecided in January, including only 17 percent of men and 25 percent of women.

Five months later, as the primary campaign came

to a close, the undecideds assumed an increasingly important role in the planning for the Republican Convention and the campaign against Dukakis. It was not only the large size of the gender gap that shaped the campaign but also the large proportion of undecided women voters who could potentially be shifted into the Republican column with the proper appeals. These undecided women voters were characterized by *MS* magazine in April as "women who have an open mind." As market researchers went to work, however, they viewed the undecideds more in terms of "the occasional woman voter"—women who vote only in presidential elections who are less involved and who are less likely to follow politics regularly.[28]

Barbara Kaplan, vice president of the Gene Reilly Groups, a marketing research firm in Darien, Connecticut, described the occasional women voters to the readers of the *Wall Street Journal* as distinctive from other women voters in terms of the remoteness of politics from their lives and their particular perspective on public policy. In words very much like those of the Super Saturday Group that had gathered in Atlanta during December, Kaplan cautioned that the occasional woman voter talks about politics in a highly personal language that does not include terms such as "the economy," "competitiveness," and the "budget" that characterize much of the usual campaign rhetoric.[29]

Occasional women voters are preoccupied with their kids and making ends meet, according to Kaplan. They do not belong to unions, church groups, or political parties. Yet, despite their lack of integration into the public sphere, they are concerned about public policy. Kaplan argued that their link to public policy is through their children. The drug issue is important because it is critical to the family's survival; child care is important because it enables women to help provide an income for their family. Occasional women voters can be drawn into politics if issues are framed in terms of their effect on children. Kaplan felt that either candidate who talked about his personal concerns for family and kids would have a greater chance of winning more of the occasional women voters.[30] Her advice for reaching the occasional woman voter read like a blueprint for Bush's acceptance speech and for the Republican campaign.

Information on the large proportion of women voters who are undecided and the characteristics of women who are occasional voters should be joined with recent research about persisting gender differences in attentiveness to politics. Despite the fact that women now vote at a rate exceeding that of men, women continue to be less interested and less informed about politics.[31] Since it has previously been assumed that voting is based on political interest, it has seemed paradoxical to some observers that women's voting turnout has increased more rapidly than their interest and information have. For men, political attentiveness is by far the best predictor of turnout. For women, however, turnout is tied to a sense of citizen duty and partisanship as well as to income and education.[32]

This finding is interesting in light of the uncertainty many women felt regarding their voting decision in 1988 and in earlier elections as well. If women's increased voting turnout stems from civic duty and party membership rather than from attentiveness to politics and a sense of comprehending world affairs, it is not surprising that women may take longer to make decisions. It also seems quite likely that they are more susceptible to campaigns waged through highly charged emotional symbols that appeal both to deeply felt fears and to hopes than they are to position papers and technical explanations of the cost-effectiveness of policy alternatives. The Republican candidate also took to heart the counsel that many women want to hear policy and national goals framed in terms of their concerns about caring for children and providing for a family's basic needs. It was not only the issues of the 1988 campaign that addressed women's concerns but also the language in which these issues were addressed.

CONCLUSION

The gender gap of 6–8 percent between men's and women's votes in the three presidential elections of the 1980s does not constitute the long-awaited women's voting bloc according to most standards of group politics. Sears and Huddy note that group mobilization of women based on a model derived from the group politics of ethnic groups would include "bloc voting, preferential voting for female candidates, unified support for government policies benefiting women, and support for political candidates based on the degree of their support for women's issues."[33]

Numerous scholars have argued, however, that most of these conditions do not exist for women in the United States. They emphasize that there are more differences between women than between women and men on a variety of values, attitudes, and policy positions such as support for women in public office or support for the key feminist issues of the ERA and abortion. Women also do not differ significantly from men on basic underlying political values such as egalitarianism, individualism, symbolic racism, position on the liberal-conservative spectrum, moral traditionalism, or sex-role orientations. Others have argued that even the partisan differences that have emerged in the elections of the 1980s reflect not an increasing support for the Democratic Party among women but a decline in Democratic support and greater increases in Republican preferences among men.[34]

Yet, persisting value, attitude, and policy differences between women and men continue to be found and may account for the longevity of the partisan differences in electoral outcomes. The most long-standing are women's greater opposition to the use of force and their greater support for public policies of a compassionate nature. Also, among some subgroups of women at opposite ends of the economic ladder, self-interest seems to differentiate their policy and party preferences from similarly situated men. Finally, it is increasingly argued that the gender gap should be attributed to the 25–30 percent of women who are strong feminists, the reason being that nonfeminist women do not differ significantly from men on domestic or foreign policy.[35]

These findings are not necessarily inconsistent, although the political implications inferred appear to differ considerably from one scholar to another. Two findings drawn from this research seem key to understanding the future of the gender gap and its implications for women's influence in electoral politics. The first involves the greater decline among men in voting turnout and in support for the Democratic Party and its candidates. Second is the association of a distinctive set of values and policy preferences with those women who have a feminist identity. Together, these factors suggest that women's current influence on electoral politics is based on the disaffection of men from voting as well as from the Democratic Party. They also suggest that feminists, like African Americans, probably provide the solid core of support for the Democratic Party, unlike the swing voters, who are wooed with media campaigns and policy proposals during election campaigns.

Because of the firmness of their commitment to the Democratic Party candidates, feminists may well be taken for granted by both parties or receive symbolic rewards like the nomination of Geraldine Ferraro in an election where neither the vice presidential candidate nor the campaign mattered. Thus it is perhaps not surprising that NOW, the major feminist organization at the national level, played a more minor role in the 1988 election than in the campaign of 1984 and that it was BPW/USA that called the two National Women's Agenda Conferences to first review candidates and then evaluate the 1988 campaign.

The gender gap and the increasing preponderance of women voters have made a difference in presidential campaigns and, perhaps, even in who holds the presidency. Women's concerns and women's language for talking about their concerns are now closer to the mainstream of electoral politics than ever before. Yet, these concerns are not articulated exclusively by either party or by any specific organization. If this is group politics, it is a species that is new and still little understood.

NOTES

1. The CBS News/*New York Times* poll's gender gap of 8 percent in 1980 was most widely quoted, although the National Election Study (NES) showed 10 percent. In 1984, CBS News and the *New York Times* initially reported only 4 percent, which was later upgraded to 6 percent. The NES reported 9 percent. For details of the gender gap reporting controversy, see Harold Brackman and Steven P. Erie, "The Future of the Gender Gap," *Social Policy,* 16:5–11 (Winter 1986). For NES voting results, see Ethel Klein, *Gender Politics* (Cambridge, MA: Harvard University Press, 1984); Arthur Miller, "Gender and the Vote: 1984," in *The Politics of the Gender Gap,* ed. Carol Mueller (Newbury Park, CA: Sage, 1988), pp. 258–82. See also Kathy Bonk, "The Selling of the 'Gender Gap,'" in ibid., pp. 82–101.

2. On group voting, see Angus Campbell et al., *The American Voter* (New York: John Wiley, 1960), pp. 295–332. The rise and fall of women's political influence around 1920 is described in William H. Chafe, *The American Woman* (New

York: Oxford University Press, 1972); J. Stanley Lemons, *The Woman Citizen* (Urbana: University of Illinois Press, 1973).

3. Lemons, *Woman Citizen*, pp. 73–95; Chafe, *American Woman*, pp. 22–30.

4. On the overall decline, see Frances Fox Piven and Richard Cloward, *Why Americans Don't Vote* (New York: Pantheon, 1988). The inflation of the estimates on women's failure to vote is accounted for in Paul Kleppner, "Were Women to Blame? Female Suffrage and Voter Turnout," *Journal of Interdisciplinary History,* 12:621–43 (Spring 1982).

5. Insider lobbying is described for the New Deal in Susan Ware, *Beyond Suffrage* (Cambridge, MA: Harvard University Press, 1981). For the Women's Party, see Leila Rupp and Verta Taylor, *Survival in the Doldrums* (New York: Oxford University Press, 1988). On feminist mobilization and legislation, see Jo Freeman, *The Politics of Women's Liberation* (New York: McKay, 1975); Klein, *Gender Politics;* Anne N. Costain, "Women's Claims as a Special Interest," in *Politics,* ed. Mueller, pp. 150–72. On interest group politics, see Joyce Gelb and Marian Lief Palley, *Women and Public Policies,* rev. ed. (Princeton, NJ: Princeton University Press, 1987). Costain, in particular, notes that women lobbyists in the early 1970s had no conception of a women's vote.

6. See Bonk, "Selling of the 'Gender Gap'"; Kathleen Frankovic, "The Election of 1984: The Irrelevance of the Campaign," *PS,* 18:39–47 (Winter 1985). Miller, "Gender and the Vote: 1984," discusses the impact of the Ferraro candidacy on the vote.

7. Bonk, "Selling of the 'Gender Gap'"; Brackman and Erie, "Future of the Gender Gap"; Bill Peterson, "Reagan Did Understand Women," *Washington Post,* 3 Mar. 1985.

8. Frankovic, "Election of 1984"; Miller, "Gender and the Vote: 1984."

9. Gwen Ifill, "Dukakis' Gender Gap," *Washington Post,* 17 Oct. 1988; James Baker, Howard Fineman, and Timothy Noah, "Closing the Gender Gap," *Newsweek,* 24 Oct. 1988, p. 22. Voting differences between men and women are taken from Celinda C. Lake and Nikki Heidepriem, "The Gender Gap and the 1988 Elections," *The Polling Report,* 21 Nov. 1988, pp. 2–3. An earlier headline was "The Coming Showdown at Gender Gulch: Why Women Voters Don't Like George Bush or His Party," the title of Gloria Berger's article in *U.S. News and World Report,* 4 July 1988, p. 25; the Harris poll of late July still showed that 15 percent more women than men supported Dukakis, leading to media coverage with headlines like "Shoot-Out at Gender Gap: Why Don't Women Take a Liking to Bush," the title of Margaret Carlson's article in *Time,* 8 Aug. 1988, p. 132–33.

10. In June, *Newsweek* carried the story, "Bush Reminds Every Woman of Her First Husband," 13 June 1988, p. 30. Fred Barnes, "A Fine Romance," *The New Republic,* 13 July 1988, attributed the joke to Bruce Babbitt, Ellen Goodman, and Art Buchwald. *The New Republic* offered a free year's gift subscription or extension for the best explanation of "what this remark means and why it's funny." By September, writer Jane O'Reilly confessed in an article for the *New York Times Magazine* that the widely attributed remark was, in fact, her own. When writing it in 1984, she had not really meant it to be funny. O'Reilly, "Talking about Women, Not to Them," *New York Times Magazine,* 11 Sept. 1988, pp. 32–33.

11. Election-voting analysis comes from Barbara G. Farah and Ethel Klein, "Public Opinion Trends," in *The Election of 1988: Reports and Interpretation,* ed. Gerald M. Pomper (Chatham, NJ: Chatham House, 1989), pp. 103–26.

12. Lake and Heidepriem, "Gender Gap."

13. On the 1984 campaign, see Frankovic, "1984 Election."

14. Ifill, "Dukakis' Gender Gap."

15. Maralee Schwartz, "Bush's Narrowing of the Gender Gap Was 'Critical,' Conference Told," *Washington Post,* 8 Jan. 1988.

16. Farah and Klein, "Public Opinion Trends." ABC/*Washington Post* polls taken every week after the conventions showed actual cross-over points on 31 Aug. and 14 Sept. when Dukakis's support exceeded Bush's. "Washington Post-ABC News Weekly Poll," *Washington Post,* 16 Oct. 1988.

17. Farah and Klein, "Public Opinion Trends"; Lake and Heidepriem, "Gender Gap."

18. Anthony Lewis, "Who Is George Bush?" *New York Times,* 6 Nov. 1988.

19. Lake and Heidepriem, "Gender Gap"; Farah and Klein, "Public Opinion Trends."

20. Farah and Klein, "Public Opinion Trends."

21. "Elusive Gender Gap," *Christian Science Monitor,* 7 Nov. 1988, p. 15.

22. Ann Lewis, "Would You Buy a Presidency from This Man?" *MS,* 17:81 (Oct. 1988).

23. David Hoffman, "Bush Details Child-Aid Plan," *Washington Post,* 6 Oct. 1988.

24. David Hoffman and Edward Walsh, "Bush Bound for Boston to Accept Police Support," *Washington Post,* 22 Sept. 1988.

25. Erika Reider Mark, "Good Housekeeping Preelection Poll," *Good Housekeeping* (Oct. 1988).

26. Marilyn Gardner, "Women Seek to Win More Attention in 1988," *Christian Science Monitor,* 7 Dec. 1987; "Elusive Gender Gap."

27. Celinda Lake, "The Gender Gap in the 1988 Election" (Paper from the Analysis Group, Washington, DC, n.d.); Farah and Klein, "Public Opinion Trends"; Kathleen Hendrix, "What Gender Gap?" *Los Angeles Times,* 16 Jan. 1989.

28. "Agenda '88: Women and the Presidency," *MS,* 16:78 (Apr. 1988).

29. Barbara Kaplan, "Target the Occasional Voter," *Wall Street Journal,* 22 June 1988, p. 24.

30. Ibid.

31. Stephen E. Bennett, *Apathy in America, 1960–1984* (Ardsley-on-Hudson, NY: Transnational, 1986).

32. Linda L. M. Bennett and Stephen E. Bennett, "Enduring Gender Differences in Political Interest," *American Politics Quarterly,* 17:105–22 (Jan. 1989).

33. David O. Sears and Leonie Huddy, "On the Origins of Political Disunity among Women," in *Women, Politics, and Change,* ed. Louise A. Tilly and Patricia Gurin (New York: Russell Sage Foundation, 1990), p. 249.

34. Sears and Huddy, "On the Origins"; Keith T. Poole and L. Harmon Zeigler, *Women, Public Opinion, and Politics* (New York: Longman, 1985); Pamela Johnston Conover, "Feminists and the Gender Gap," *Journal of Politics,* 50: 985–1010 (Nov. 1988); Daniel Wirls, "Reinterpreting the Gender Gap," *Public Opinion Quarterly,* 50:316–30 (Fall 1986). Wirls is quite correct to note that the long-term trend is for women to leave the Democratic Party less quickly than men or, in different language, to remain loyal longer. Although Wirl's data cover only the three elections of 1976, 1980, and 1984, Kenski's longer time series based on NES and census data shows that Democratic Party preference declined from 56 to 46 percent among men and 56 to 53 percent among women from 1952 to 1984. Over the same time period, men's preference for the Republican Party increased from 33 to 46 percent and women's from 36 to 41 percent. Henry C. Kenski, "The Gender Factor in a Changing Electorate," in *Politics,* ed. Mueller, p. 43.

35. Tom W. Smith, "The Polls: Gender and Attitudes toward Violence," *Public Opinion Quarterly,* 48:384–96 (Spring 1984); Robert Y. Shapiro and Harpreet Mahajan, "Gender Differences in Policy Preferences: A Summary of Trends from the 1960's to the 1980's," *Public Opinion Quarterly,* 50:42–61 (Spring 1986); Cynthia Deitz, "Sex Differences in Support for Government Spending," in *Politics,* ed. Mueller, pp. 192–216; Sears and Huddy, "On the Origins"; Miller, "Gender and the Vote: 1984"; Conover, "Feminists and the Gender Gap."

R E A D I N G   4 6

Women in Revolution: The Mobilization of Latin American Women in Revolutionary Guerrilla Movements

LINDA LOBAO

Guerrilla movements have long been considered a male domain of political contest. Latin American women have historically participated in guerrilla movements, but not in extensive numbers until recently (Chinchilla, 1982; Vitale, 1981; Jaquette, 1973; Rowbotham, 1972). The influx of women into modern revolutionary movements in Nicaragua, El Salvador, and Guatemala has forced analysts to acknowledge and reconsider women's contributions to armed struggle.

Guerrillas are members of political organizations

This paper is drawn from Linda Lobao Reif, "Women in Latin America Guerrilla Movements: A Comparative Perspective," *Comparative Politics* 18 (January 1986). Reprinted by permission of the author.

operating in both rural and urban areas which use armed warfare for the purpose of changing societal structure (Kohl & Litt, 1974; Jaquette, 1973; Gilio, 1970; Guevara, 1969). In contrast to the regular warfare employed by large armies, guerrillas possess "a much smaller number of arms for use in defense against oppression" (Guevara, 1969:4). Rather than try to outfight government forces, guerrillas concentrate on breaking down the legitimacy of the regime by morally isolating it from popular support (Chailand, 1982:240). Past revolutionary struggles in Latin America have been directed at colonial regimes as well as at internal political elites. These struggles have arisen from each nation's pattern of "dependent" development—development shaped by the domination of the United States, Britain, France, and earlier colonial powers (Cardoso & Faletto, 1979).

BARRIERS TO POLITICAL PARTICIPATION

Latin American women are limited in their involvement in nondomestic spheres of national life (Vitale, 1981; Chaney, 1979; Schmidt, 1976). The subordinate position of women in Latin American society is a major barrier to women's participation in nondomestic activities, including revolutionary struggle. Recent Marxian and feminist theory argue that the sphere of reproduction must be taken into account in order to explain women's roles, relegation to domestic activities, and historical subordination (Brenner & Ramas, 1984; Chodorow, 1979). Women are the primary directors of the household reproductive activities that are necessary for the reproduction of labor power. Such activities include childbearing, socialization of children, and the care of family members. Women are thus first located in the private sphere of the home by the sexual division of labor, while men are first located in the public sphere outside the home (Chodorow, 1979; López de Piza, 1977).

The sexual division of labor in production builds upon women's subordination in the sphere of reproduction (Deere & León de Leal, 1982). Women are socialized not to perform or to become expert at tasks that are incompatible with their reproductive roles. Further, in the occupational sphere, as well as in all areas of social organization, the energy, time, and freedom of movement available to most women is greatly limited by their role in reproductive activities (Chaney, 1979; Schlegel, 1977). Most men do not face the double burden of participating in nondomestic areas while taking primary responsibility for the domestic area.

In Latin America, patriarchal attitudes reflect and reinforce the subordination of women. These attitudes, which represent "ideal" configurations held by both sexes, include beliefs that women are "childlike" and "apolitical," and achieve "their highest fulfillment as wives and mothers" (Schmidt, 1976:244). While traditional patriarchal ideals are undermined by women who head households or who are professionals in charge of men, at the national level the formal pattern of male dominance still prevails. The legal status of women in most Latin American civil codes is based on

patria potestas, the patriarchal right of the father to control his family. Women are legally "equated with idiots and children" (Kinzer, 1973:304).

In addition to the subordinate roles that limit women's political involvement, class differences affect women's ability to participate. The classes that support revolutionary movements depend on the specific historical conditions experienced by each nation. Urban and rural workers, potentially the most radical classes, face the greatest barriers toward political involvement. Historically they have been marginalized from formal political participation. They are vulnerable to employer threats, and political participation can take away from paid work time (Nash, 1977). Working-class women in the labor force face even greater obstacles as a result of their role in the reproductive activities of the household. Their work is exhausting and pays little, and is likely to restrict them to domestic areas (two out of five Latin American women in the labor force are domestic servants) where class and gender consciousness are not likely to arise (Safa, 1977). Working-class women who do not work outside the home still share the disadvantages of their class and gender—low education, low income, few marketable skills, and major domestic responsibilities.

Should the middle classes (or, in some cases, segments of the elite) also support a revolutionary movement, such women would have greater ability to participate than working-class women. Although patriarchal ideology pervades the middle class (Chaney, 1979), these women have been less marginalized from formal political processes, education, and other important areas of national life. Political involvement is more feasible for middle-class women, as they are not burdened by the basic problems of family survival faced by working-class women. While middle-class women still face major domestic responsibility, they are able to escape much of the drudgery of housework and child care through their exploitation of lower-class women as domestic servants (Chaney, 1973). Thus, although middle-class women face gender barriers to participation, working-class women are doubly burdened by class and gender.

MOBILIZING WOMEN: REVOLUTIONARY STRATEGY AND IDEOLOGY

While women confront greater barriers than men and lower-class women face particular difficulties, certain factors can mitigate them and facilitate women's participation. Since the early 1970s, revolutionary strategy and ideology have undergone changes that have particularly encouraged women's involvement (Chinchilla, 1982). Before this period, a small group of revolutionaries relying on military action, in contrast to mass-based political organization, formed the center of struggle (Chinchilla, 1982). By the early 1970s, the failure of this strategy became apparent and pointed to the increased necessity for popular support in the face of greater repression from the right. According to Chinchilla (1982:20), women's mobilization is an important component of the "prolonged people's war" (gradual organization of all mass sectors) which has been adopted as current revolutionary strategy in Central America.

Increasing awareness of feminist issues and their incorporation into movement ideology have also encouraged participation (Chinchilla, 1982). The women's liberation movement that began in the late 1960s, primarily in developed nations, sensitized activists to feminist issues (Chinchilla, 1982; Flynn, 1980). From the 1970s onward, the "problems of gender oppression" were integrated with those of class oppression in leftist ideology (Flora, 1984:71). Women's liberation issues diffused not only to the socialist left but also to emergent feminist movements (Flora, 1984; Molyneux, 1985) and to the mass media (Chinchilla, 1982). Thus changes in guerrilla strategy and the diffusion of feminist thought have encouraged recent efforts to recruit women at a time when Latin American women have become receptive to the idea of their own liberation.

Socioeconomic and political conditions related to family survival can also mobilize women (Molyneux, 1985; Flora, 1984; Chinchilla, 1982). Because large numbers of men are unemployed or work only sporadically as agricultural migrants, large numbers of Central American households are dependent on female breadwinners (Chinchilla, 1982:9–11). Such women may join guerrilla movements when they perceive government as threatening and guerrilla movements as bolstering their joint roles of mother and wage earner.

Internal organizational characteristics, such as the way revolutionary goals are formulated, and male–female relationships within guerrilla groups, can foster women's participation (Chinchilla, 1982). Maxine Molyneux (1985) defines two major ways—strategic and practical—in which women's interests may be ar-

ticulated by movements seeking their support. Strategic gender interests involve long-term, essentially feminist objectives toward ending women's subordination, such as abolishing the sexual division of labor and institutionalized forms of gender discrimination. Practical gender interests arise in response to an immediate need, such as domestic provision and public welfare, and "do not generally entail a strategic goal such as women's emancipation or gender equality" (Molyneux, 1985:233). Practical gender interests are closely intertwined with class and family interests, as economic necessity most directly motivates poorer women. According to Molyneux (1985), movements must be perceived as supporting women's short-term practical interests first, before they will gain the mass support of women for longer-term strategic objectives.

Male–female relations within the guerrilla movements can also encourage women's participation, when egalitarian relationships in the division of labor and in the opportunity for leadership are promoted. An indication that earlier guerrillas held patriarchal attitudes, despite their otherwise radical orientations, is found in Che Guevara's handbook on guerrilla warfare (1969:87):

> But also in this stage [of the guerrilla struggle] a woman can perform her habitual tasks of peacetime; it is very pleasing to a soldier subjected to the extremely hard conditions of life to be able to look forward to a seasoned meal which tastes like something. . . . The woman as cook can greatly improve the diet and, furthermore, it is easier to keep her in these domestic tasks; . . . [such duties] are scorned by those [males] who perform them; they are constantly trying to get out of those tasks in order to enter into forces that are actively in combat.

WOMEN IN GUERRILLA MOVEMENTS: CASE STUDIES

Data about women in guerrilla movements are inherently limited by the nature of the subject. This is an area outside conventional politics where censorship and political reprisals may silence reports. Latin America is such a highly gender-stratified society that literature on women is sparse. Information about earlier guerrilla movements is impressionistic and fragmentary. Only one study presents a systematic comparative investigation of women's participation in the movements of several Latin American nations (see Jaquette, 1973).

Cuba

Armed struggle in Cuba was first aimed at overthrowing the regime of Fulgencio Batista, who had seized power in 1952 (Blasier, 1967). Cubans' outrage over the corruption and repressiveness of the regime, inequalities of wealth and living conditions, high unemployment, and Batista's policies toward U.S. investment in Cuba contributed to the dictator's downfall (Laquer, 1977; Blasier, 1967). The Cuban Revolution succeeded through the efforts of a core group of revolutionaries rather than through mass-based struggle.

The Cuban government under Fidel Castro has been lauded for the mobilization it achieved among women (Jaquette, 1973:347). They were mobilized generally after the insurgent period, however, and do not appear to have been extensively involved in the armed struggle itself. Jane S. Jaquette (1973:346–47) mentions only three women, all linked to male leaders, who participated in the guerrilla struggle in the Sierra Maestra: Celia Sánchez (Fidel's secretary), Vilma Espín (wife of Rául Castro), and Haydee Santamaría (wife of a party leader). Sheila Rowbotham (1972:223) notes that although a women's Red Army battalion was formed, "the conditions of guerrilla fighting did not encourage the emergence of women." Men took control of the revolution. They "were not accustomed to taking orders from a woman," according to Che Guevara (quoted in Rowbotham, 1972:224). Dickey Chapelle (1962:327) estimates that by December 1958, one in twenty revolutionary troops was a woman.

While there is disagreement over the social origins of those who participated in the insurgency, analysts acknowledge the important contributions made by the middle class and the peasantry (Blasier, 1967:45–46). Evidence that middle-class women participated is suggested by the backgrounds of the women who have been named and the existence of student guerrilla organizations, which sometimes included women (Franqui, 1980:186, 526–27, 532; López, 1976:111). Peasant women were generally not organizationally active until they were mobilized after the insurgency period (Purcell, 1973:263).

Through letters and interviews with Cuban revolutionaries, Carlos Franqui (1980:215, 219, 229) indicates

that women performed mainly support rather than combat duties. Women were "mobilized" to obtain a guerrilla's corpse from the police, delivered secret correspondence, and were active in street demonstrations. According to Olga López (1976:112), women were combatants, nurses, messengers, scouts, and teachers, and withstood battle conditions "to perform domestic tasks on guerrilla fronts." Che Guevara (1969) noted, however, that women were not routinely combatants, but sometimes substituted for relief purposes in these positions. Chapelle (1962:327) observed that with the exception of one sniper platoon, women in the guerrilla army did housekeeping and supply assignments. Celia, Haydee, and Vilma are exceptional in that they held actual combat positions. Fidel Castro "commended" Celia's work in a letter: "Even when a woman goes around the mountains with a rifle in hand, she always makes our men tidier, more decent, more gentlemanly" (Franqui, 1980:192).

While the Castro government early recognized the incompatibility between gender inequality and commitment to a classless, egalitarian society, women do not appear to have been actively recruited during the insurgency itself. Widespread mobilization of women came after revolutionary victory, with the establishment of the Federation of Cuban Women in 1960. Vilma Espín's comments reveal the initial lack of awareness of women's issues. When asked by Fidel Castro to organize the Federation, she responded: "Precisely why do we have to have a women's organization? I had never been discriminated against. I had my career as a chemical engineer. I never suffered, I never had any difficulty" (quoted in Azicri, 1979:29).

Columbia

Revolutionary struggle in Columbia during the mid-1960s was directed against an oligarchic regime that allowed political competition only between two indistinguishable parties serving elite interests (Gott, 1971). Few women appear to have participated in two important guerrilla organizations of the mid-1960s: the Army of National Liberation (ELN) of Camilo Torres and the People's Liberation Army (EPL) (Jaquette, 1973; Gott, 1971; Gómez, 1967). The goals of both groups included an end to oligarchic rule and imperialism and institution of agrarian reform (Gott, 1971:525–34). Jaquette (1973:348) notes that "progressively educated" women in Torres' movement researched condi-

REINVENTING THE WHEEL

MS. MAGAZINE, GULF DISPATCH

One fateful day last November, 47 Saudi women decided to drive a few yards in their own country (see Ms., January/February 1991). Now we have an eye-witness/participatory report on what actually took place in Riyadh, and on the aftermath. The author, a Saudi herself, must remain anonymous for her own safety.

3:00 P.M. Cars arrive in parking lot at Safeway supermarket on King Abdulaziz Road. Women sit beside male relatives or in the back of chauffeur-driven cars.

3:15 Fourteen women slide behind the wheels of as many cars. The men step away. Thirty-two other women join the 14, as passengers. None speak; they all move swiftly, as one black mass—wearing the traditional *gitwa* (head covering) and *abaya* (robe); all but five have their faces covered as well, with only their eyes showing.

3:22 The excitement in the air is overpowering. It is the first time the women have driven on their native soil. Furthermore, this is a country that does not favor public demonstrations of any kind, so this is a precedent. The convoy begins to move. Steady hands, heads held high.

3:25 Convoy moves out of the parking lot, turning north on King Abdulaziz Road. Some male relatives drive discreetly behind and alongside in support.

3:31 Turn west at the corner onto Mursalat Road. Two of the cars pull over by the Sheraton Hotel. People on the roads: a variety of expressions. Shock, horror, admiration. Some thumbs-up signals in encouragement, some smiles and fists held up in the air in solidarity, a few horns beeping in support.

3:35 Turn left, south on Olaya Road. Cars with curious (male) drivers begin to follow the convoy.

3:45 Another left. Four cars stopped at the traffic light are caught and pulled over by the police. The rest of the cars continue.

From *Ms.* Magazine (March–April 1991): 13–16.

3:48 Back onto King Abdulaziz Road. En masse they decide to make the round one more time.

3:53 Stopped by police at the traffic light in front of the mosque. Afternoon prayers have just ended. The police don't know what to do. One officer leaves to call his superiors for instruction. They in turn call City Hall.

3:55 The imam of the mosque comes out to ask the police about the situation, then goes back in. Within minutes, about 30 *mutawa* (fundamentalists) emerge, screaming epithets: "Whores! Prostitutes! Sinners!" They surround the cars and pound on the windows and doors. The women sit silently inside.

4:00 The police move in. They ask the women what they think they are doing. "Driving," is the simple reply. "Why?" "In time of war mobilization and national emergency we need to, for the safety of our families." The police seem strangely awed, filled with respect. More *mutawa* appear, screaming and cursing, demanding that the women be taken to their own (religious) prisons. The police refuse, saying this is a secular matter.

4:30 The eight cars and the other two cars are allowed to drive to where the other four cars are parked. Now numbering well over 50, the *mutawa* follow, becoming more abusive. The women no longer answer questions; they sit with the car windows rolled up while the fundamentalists surround and batter the cars.

5:15 Finally, a policeman takes the wheel of each car, with a *mutawa* sitting alongside him, haranguing the women. Only one carful of women refuses to permit the *mutawa* inside. The cars are driven to the Olaya police station, and the women are told to enter. They refuse to do so until a government representative is present.

5:50 The women are finally escorted into the police station. Seven *mutawa* insist on entering, and only after repeated requests by the police that they leave do they comply. The questioning begins.

Q: "Did your husbands or fathers or brothers know you were planning to do this?" A: "Does it matter?" Q: "Is this demonstration politically motivated?" A: "Why, no, it is a matter of safety during a time of national crisis." The women are polite and peaceable, courteous in giving the necessary information. One woman, assumed to be the ringleader, is taken to another room and questioned intensely. The other women chant, "We want her back with us. She is not our leader. This is a collective act." She is brought back, but later again sequestered for more interrogation. This continues for at least three hours.

9:30 Some of the husbands of the women appear. They are told to wait in an adjoining room.

12 MIDNIGHT Interrogation of the men begins— about a half hour each.

1:00 A.M. A government representative appears. The male relatives are urged to sign a document declaring that the women will never again participate in such an action, will never again drive or even speak of this matter, under threat of punishment or imprisonment. Only then will the women be released.

2:30 All the male relatives comply except one, who refuses as a matter of principle. Finally, so much pressure is put on him that he signs. Another male relative is so angered at his wife that he refuses to come to the police station at all; at last he too appears and complies. One of the women is single; her father is dead, and her brothers are in another city. Since she is not permitted to sign for herself, she names a male friend who appears to sign for her, so that she can be released. (Later, this man is harassed and called a criminal for having helped.)

3:30 The entire group is finally permitted to leave the police station and go to their homes.

The Next Day

Handwritten copies of "police reports" (bearing no official stamps) appear as leaflets; these are distributed in government offices, pasted or nailed to the walls of public buildings, left on the front windows of cars, passed out in the streets. These so-called reports claim that the women in the driving demonstration were wearing shorts; that they hurled insults at religious men and condemned the government. Included in the allegations: the women were sluts; their husbands were secularist, Westernized, communist pimps. . . .

Aftermath

The women and their families have been ceaselessly harassed, threatened, cursed—by telephone, mail, and in person. Some of the women are educators; their university offices were broken into and ransacked by fundamentalist students who believed the allegations. . . . The women have been fired from or suspended from their jobs, and they (and their husbands) are banned from traveling abroad. . . .

Postscript

January 15: Today I rang up my neighborhood civil defense office. I said that my brother is in the army, my father is dead, and my driver is too scared to drive me anywhere—he wants to stay in his room or go back to the Philippines right away. I told the civil defense office that I need tape and plastic to seal the windows against possible chemical warfare. I need bread and bottled water and basic supplies. May I have special dispensation to drive in this emergency?

"No," was the reply, "Call 999 emergency and they will bring you what you need." I called. They gave me another number. I have been trying to get through to this other number now for days. The line is continually busy.

Late January

We are at war.

In the midst of all this horror and uncertainty, last night a group of *mutawa* climbed over a fence to throw stones through the windows of the home of one of the women. They shouted threats for an hour before departing.

In a time of national crisis, they have nothing better to do than terrorize women?

tions of women in various areas of Colombia so that policies could be developed toward these groups. When Torres was killed by the army in 1966, a female comrade was presumed to be firing at the troops (Jaquette, 1973:348). The EPL, which was formed after Torres' death, encouraged women to join an auxiliary, but there is no evidence of women's involvement in this unit.

The women who participated in Torres' group were most likely middle-class, if we may judge by the support Torres received from students in general and the reference to "progressively educated" women (Broderick, 1975). Peasants also comprised part of Torres' organization, but in somewhat lesser numbers than students (Gott, 1971:227). The EPL purportedly had "real peasant support," though its organizers seem to have been educated and middle-class (Gott, 1971:303–4). The role women may have performed in the two movements is unclear. Participation in combat activities is alluded to only in the "presumed" account of an armed *guerrillera* at Torres' death.

Both Torres and the EPL seem to have made no real attempt to mobilize women (Broderick, 1975; Jaquette, 1973; Gott, 1971). Torres' platform (Gott, 1971:528) stated that "protection for women and children [would] be provided by the law by means of effective sanction," and that both men and women would be drafted into civic rather than military service. The EPL offered women branches to join but presented little rationale as to why they should join them (Gott, 1971:533). Platforms and policies thus addressed few of women's concerns and, correspondingly, women were not highly involved in the movements.

Uruguay

The Tupamaros arose as a response to a national economic crisis that resulted in stagnating production and rising unemployment and inflation. Uruguayans protested with strikes and riots in full stride during the late 1960s. The government responded by declaring states of seize and engaging in repression (Kohl & Litt, 1974; Porzencanski, 1973). The Tupamaros, founded in 1962, advocated an end to foreign hegemony, oligarchic rule, and government repression, and called for the establishment of socialism (Movimiento de Liberación Nacional, 1974:293–96).

A higher proportion of women were members of the Tupamaros than of the Cuban and Colombian guerrilla movements. A study of Tupamaro arrest records indicates that at the onset of the movement, in 1966, women composed approximately 10 percent of the group (Porzencanski, 1973:31). By 1972 they were over one-quarter of all Tupamaro members. A variety of other sources have also noted the importance of women to the movement (Wilson, 1974; Madruga, 1974; Jaquette, 1973).

The Tupamaros recruited members from all classes of society, but primarily from the middle class. Arrest records reveal that middle-class professionals and students outnumbered working-class members by about 2 to 1 (Porzencanski, 1973:28–31). Uruguay is a middle-class and highly urbanized nation, and the movement reflected this fact (Kohl & Litt, 1974:191).

Women seem to have filled both support and combat roles. All active Tupamaro squads had one or two female members, but emphasis was placed on such support activities as liaison, logistics, and operation of safe houses (Halperin, 1976:45). Women guarded prisoners and passed out leaflets (Gilio, 1970). Tupamaro reports indicated large numbers of women involved in robberies and kidnappings, often as decoys (Jaquette, 1973; Gilio, 1970). To distract government troops, women would strike a provocative pose and feign accidents and helplessness. The Tupamaros thus used women in important tactical roles that often capitalized on the patriarchal attitudes of government troops.

According to Jane Jaquette (1973:351), the Tupamaros were the only group (as of 1973) to have developed a detailed position on "revolutionary women." This position stressed an end to cultural and educational discrimination against women and advocated complementary rather than differential performance of guerrilla tasks. The Tupamaros also developed a program for revolutionary government which would seem to appeal to women. They called for, among other things, free education, equitable distribution of income, and state control of the health industry and wholesale food enterprises (Movimiento de Liberación Nacional, 1974). As the proportion of women in the Tupamaro movement was substantial and continually increasing, Tupamaro strategies appear to have been effective in recruiting women. Though this movement never achieved a mass base of support, it arose at a period when educated, middle-class Uruguayans had increased exposure to gender issues. Tupamaro women soon filled both combat and support positions, in contrast with women in Cuba and Colombia, where their low rates of participation were associated with basically noncombatant performance.

Nicaragua

Revolution in Nicaragua followed the pattern of a protracted people's war, with mass-based mobilization (Chinchilla, 1982). The immediate aim of the revolution was to overthrow Anastasio Somoza and his National Guard, who brutally repressed the population in an attempt to maintain the privileges of a small elite (FSLN, 1983:139). The process of dependent "development" in Nicaragua meant the dispossession of small farmers, the creation of a landless proletariat, high unemployment, a low standard of living, and a short life expectancy (Ramirez-Horton, 1982). It also meant the destabilization of family life, as men abandoned families and migrated in search of seasonal or other employment (Ramirez-Horton, 1982; Chinchilla, 1982). The number of female-headed households has thus been high, an estimated one-third of all families in 1978 (Chinchilla, 1982:11). Women have also participated in large numbers in the labor force (in comparison with women in other Latin American nations), as so many of them have had to work to support their families (AMNLAE, 1982:24). Thus, according to Norma Stoltz Chinchilla, "capitalist development in Nicaragua made impossible the realization of bourgeois ideals of the nuclear family and economically dependent women" (1982:14).

Female membership in the Sandinista movement during the final offensive in mid-1979 has been estimated at 30 percent (Flynn, 1980:29). A central factor in the large proportion of women in the Sandinista movement was active recruitment by AMPRONAC, the Association of Women Confronting the National Problem, founded in 1977 by FSLN cadres (Chinchilla, 1982:24). The earliest organizers of AMPRONAC had been mainly middle- and upper-class women, such as lawyers, journalists, and bureaucrats (Ramirez-Horton, 1982:151; Flynn, 1980:29). Susan E. Ramirez-Horton (1982:147) interviewed one woman, for example, who "decided to use her university education and leave her daughter with the maid, over the strong protests of her husband, to begin organizing women in the urban areas in defense of human rights." By 1978 the organization had achieved mass support, incorporating women of all social classes opposed to the dictatorship: peasants, workers, students, as well as the middle class and seg-

ments of the upper class (AMPRONAC, 1982; Booth, 1982; Randall, 1978).

Women initially participated in the Sandinista struggle in support operations, but later took combat roles. They secured positions of leadership in combat operations, commanding "everything from small units to full battalions" (Flynn, 1980:29). At the major battle at León, four of the seven Sandinista commanders were women (Schultz, 1980:38).

The organizational conditions created by the Sandinistas are an important reason that so many women participated in the movement. As Chinchilla (1982:14) notes, women's commitment to their families, which had been a traditional barrier to their participation in revolutionary movements, actually facilitated participation under the Sandinistas. The FSLN responded to the immediate problems faced by women under Somoza. First, it attempted to counter the repression felt sharply and uniquely by women: women were expected to protect their children, but their children had increasingly become targets of repression; and many women needed to work outside the home, but they, too, were subjected to harassment from Somoza's troops (Chinchilla, 1982:11). Second, the FSLN incorporated in its formal platform longer-term objectives important to women. It called for a "struggle to end discrimination against women," particularly in the forms of prostitution and domestic servitude, and encouraged women to organize "in defense of their rights" under the dictatorship (FSLN, 1979:112). AMPRONAC's (1982:4–5) 1978 platform included among its major demands: "Better living conditions, improved housing, education. Equal salary for equal work. . . . An end to prostitution and the usage of women as economic commodities. . . . Abolishment of all laws that discriminate against women." FSLN goals were thus oriented toward more immediate, social-welfare issues as well as the long-term end to discrimination. Such goals bolstered rather than undercut the familial roles of many women and tended to promote family survival, especially for lower-class and female-headed households.

The FSLN also created internal organizational conditions conducive to female participation. According to Chinchilla (1982:17), it stressed "correct relationships" among members, based advancement on merit and skill, and cultivated respect and support for women—all of which sharply contrasted with the sexism outside the movement. This organizational climate was not easily achieved. The first women recruited into the FSLN during the 1960s encountered isolation and an undervaluing of their achievements. As more women entered the movement, however, sexism began to break down. The opportunity for respect based on merit provided important motivation for women to join the movement (Chinchilla, 1982).

Nicaragua clearly demonstrates the possibility of women's mass mobilization despite class and gender barriers. The FSLN gained extensive support and ultimate victory by focusing on issues relevant throughout the society, on the overthrow of a repressive regime, and on gender issues that specifically addressed the role of working-class women. It created an organization, AMPRONAC, to mobilize women and the internal organizational conditions conducive to their participation.

El Salvador

El Salvador has had a history of military rule and corrupt and repressive regimes supported by the oligarchy, big business, and right-wing military officials. Recent government by the moderate Christian Democrats has not succeeded in curbing the power of the oligarchy and its allies, and repression by the right continues (NACLA, 1984). The major opposition to right-wing forces now consists of the joint opposition fronts of the FMLN/FDR (Martí Front for National Liberation/Democratic Revolutionary Front). Their present platform includes demands for direct power sharing, extensive agrarian reform, reform of the financial system and foreign trade, a mixed economy, and a pluralistic polity (NACLA, 1984:16). At this time, the position of women is not specifically mentioned among the principal objectives of the struggle (NACLA, 1984:16; Balyora, 1982:165).

Women make up a great part of the popular organizations that comprise the FMLN/FDR (Thomson, 1986: Herrera, 1983: Montgomery, 1982). The FMLN is a coalition of four political-military organizations and the Communist Party of El Salvador. Two of the organizations within the FMLN have high-ranking female *commandantes* (Armstrong, 1982:28) and female participation has been estimated to be as high as 40 percent (Armstrong & Shenk, 1980:20). The FDR is an umbrella organization for socialist, social democratic, student, and worker parties. Women are prominent

among its leadership, with 40 percent of the Revolutionary Council composed of women (Central American Information Office, 1982:57).

The FMLN/FDR has a broad base of support and includes individuals from the middle and working classes: students, union members, and professionals (WIRE, 1982a; Armstrong & Shenk, 1980). In rural areas, local peasants play a key part in guerrilla operations (NACLA, 1981). Middle-class women, particularly teachers and students, were the first to be drawn into political/military organizations in the late 1960s. Rural and then urban working-class women followed (Castillo, 1982:8).

Women are involved in both support and combat operations (AMES, 1982; Castillo, 1982; WIRE, 1982b, 1982c). Interviews with guerrilla troops suggest a strong attempt to promote egalitarian relations between men and women. One guerrilla notes that women are encouraged to assume nontraditional roles: "We have some peasant women who join us as cooks but they soon realize that they have opportunities to do other things. They become combatants, medics, or leaders" (NACLA, 1981:13). Another (Montgomery, 1982:151) states that fighting beside women, he and his fellow guerrillas learned "to see women as *compañeras* and not as sex objects." Two-thirds of the combatants in his unit were women, and there was great concern "to destroy *machismo.*" A female guerrilla, however, states that despite the great organizational commitment to equality, "even now, a woman has to be triply brave, triply astute on missions to win the recognition a man would receive" (Thomson, 1986:127).

The FMLN/FDR has no unified mass organization for women on the scale of the Sandinista AMPRONAC. Rather various smaller organizations affiliated with the FMLN/FDR deal with gender-related issues, such as AMES (Association of Salvadoran Women), which incorporates housewives, professionals, teachers, students, and previously unorganized groups; organizations of peasant women in the zones of FMLN Control; the Committee of Mothers and Relatives of the Disappeared, Assassinated, and Political Prisoners; and women's trade and professional associations (Latin American Working Group, 1983; WIRE, 1982a; Castillo, 1982).

The FMLN/FDR tacitly supports women's issues and encourages women to share tasks and leadership with men. While it has no formal platform on women's issues comparable to that of Nicaragua's FSLN, it does advocate goals important to women, such as the development of social services, literacy programs, and low-cost housing programs (Armstrong & Shenk, 1980:31–33). The Association of Salvadoran Women (AMES, 1982:19) has noted that the movements of the left have "not dealt with the problems of women with the same consistency with which they confront other social problems. Their pronouncements in this regard are limited to the realm of class struggle . . . they do not make reference to the specific condition of women." The various women's organizations affiliated with the FMLN/FDR therefore have the major task of organizing women around gender- as well as class-based issues. The AMES platform, for example, includes an end to forced sterilization; safe family planning; free child care; and the right to education and training (WIRE, 1982c:3). As in Nicaragua, the number of female-headed households is high (because of employment patterns), so that issues of family support are critical.

In sum, the FMLN/FDR has formally tended to focus on class-based issues, which appeal to women as well as men, and has created internal organizational conditions conducive to women's participation on an egalitarian basis. Women's organizations in the FMLN/FDR have the major task of addressing gender-based issues.

DISCUSSION AND CONCLUSIONS

The conclusions drawn from these case studies must be regarded as tentative because of the paucity of information about the *guerrillera*. The structural constraints of women's roles in reproductive activities and the patriarchal nature of Latin American society are barriers against women's participation in political movements. While it is impossible to ascertain directly to what extent these factors constrained women's participation, a statement by the Association of Salvadoran Women (AMES, 1982:18–19) acknowledges women's structural role in reproductive activities and the attitudes associated with this role as major limiting factors:

If men have, for centuries, devoted themselves to political work . . . it is because they have always had the support of one or several women who have provided them with children, with affection, with domestic services; to these women are diverted all psychological tensions, thereby freeing men from the small and large problems of domestic life.

We women, on the other hand, do not have such support systems available to us, and in order to utilize our intellectual potential we must organize ourselves in such a way that the private sphere does not interfere with our specific political work. It is indeed dramatic to organize ourselves physically and psychologically to exercise this role without experiencing guilt vis-à-vis the "neglected" roles of mother and wife which relegate us to the domestic sphere. . . . This situation is aggravated by the fact that until now it has not appeared that men have the intention of truly assuming some of the responsibility which for centuries has been delegated to women. It is not easy for men, even with good intentions, to raise their consciousness concerning the privileges conveyed by masculinity and to relinquish their role as the star members of the cast, becoming instead comrades who share daily life and struggle.

The analysis of the five movements indicates that middle-class women probably face fewer barriers to participation than working-class women do. Middle-class women are more likely to have been earlier participants in political struggles. Such activities may be linked to their higher education and perhaps greater awareness of political issues. Even *campesino* and working-class women who recognized the benefits of involvement, however, still faced the burdens of class as well as gender. As these women pay the highest costs for political participation, it is not surprising that they would enter movements later, when they have become conscious of fundamental interests, such as those related to household survival, and when revolutionary groups have provided the means to address these interests. The Nicaraguan and Salvadoran movements, for example, mobilized working-class and *campesino* women through attention to their specific class and gender interests. Practical gender interests, such as social welfare and child care, are critical because of the many female-headed households in both nations.

The historical location of a movement, social-structural impacts on women's roles, and the movement's internal organizational characteristics to a great extent determine the extent of women's participation. The Colombian and Cuban struggles, occurring before the 1970s, did not follow the mass-based mobilization strategy or prolonged "people's war" of Nicaragua and El Salvador. These movements also occurred before feminist thought had begun to diffuse throughout Latin America. The two earlier groups thus did not develop special platforms for women, nor did they direct efforts to their recruitment. They likewise overlooked gender egalitarianism as an essential component of internal organizational relations. There was, correspondingly, only a small degree of female involvement in the Cuban and Colombian movements.

In contrast, the three later movements with high female participation occurred during a period of increasing awareness of feminist issues and of women's contributions to other national struggles, which encouraged women's recruitment. The Sandinista and Salvadoran movements were also based on the current revolutionary strategy of protracted, mass-based struggle, which increases the possibility that women (as well as men) from all segments of society will participate.

Social-structural characteristics related to women's roles in Uruguay, Nicaragua, and El Salvador seem to have fostered women's participation. All three nations have high rates of female labor force participation (Wilkie & Haber, 1982:174), and Nicaragua and El Salvador also had many female-headed households. In the latter two nations, issues of family sustenance and government repression seemed particularly threatening to women's roles as family nurturers and protectors.

The Tupamaros, Sandinistas, and Salvadorans promoted routine policies of egalitarian relations between men and women. They also employed platforms attractive to women which seemed to be of two types. First, in opposition to patriarchalism, women were offered some feminist objectives, in line with long-term, strategic gender interests—an end to discrimination in such areas as the work force, the polity, and education. Second, they advocated programs stressing shorter-

term, practical gender interests, such as child care, health care, and literacy, which maximized social welfare and facilitated women's roles in the workplace and household. The Tupamaros and Sandinistas formally offered women both types of platforms. In the Salvadoran case, the FMLN/FDR offers social welfare policies in conjunction with the feminist planks offered by its affiliated women's organization. According to Molyneux (1985), the latitude that revolutionary movements possess in addressing gender issues depends in part on the severity of the struggle and the need for popular support. Advocacy of feminist or strategic gender interests in patriarchal societies becomes more problematic when the need for mass support is great. This may explain why the Salvadorans have formally made little reference to women, except through their affiliated women's organizations.

As women's revolutionary participation increased, the division of labor by gender became less rigid and women began to occupy combat as well as support positions. The diffusion of feminist thought and examples of women's previous successes in combat undoubtedly contributed to the broadening of women's roles. The sheer numbers of women in the three later movements also made them a visible force that served to break down patriarchal attitudes and the division of labor by gender.

While women have historically faced enormous obstacles to participation in revolutionary activity, the Tupamaro, Sandinista, and Salvadoran movements reveal how a number of interrelated factors fostered women's involvement. The mass-based mobilization of women and their greater role in combat indicate new patterns of Latin American revolutionary struggle. Women will continue to play important roles in future struggles, particularly since the Sandinista victory and other guerrilla successes can be attributed directly to their involvement. The critical task facing Sandinista and future revolutionary women is to expand and institutionalize the gender egalitarianism created in the context of struggle to the new revolutionary society.

ACKNOWLEDGMENTS

The author gratefully acknowledges the helpful comments made on a previous draft of this paper by Maxine Atkinson, Norma Chinchilla, Barbara Risman, Michael Schulman, and Richard Slatta.

REFERENCES

AMES (Association of Salvadoran Women). 1982. "Participation of Latin American women in social and political organizations: Reflections of Salvadoran women." *Monthly Review* 34 (June):11–23.

AMNLAE (Luisa Amanda Espinoza Association of Nicaraguan Women). 1982. "Our participation in the economy." In Women's International Resource Exchange, ed., *Nicaraguan woman and the revolution,* pp. 23–25. New York.

AMPRONAC (Association of Women Confronting the National Problem). 1982. "Nicaraguan women: Struggle for a free homeland." In Women's International Resource Exchange, ed., *Nicaraguan women and the revolution,* pp. 3–4. New York.

Armstrong, R. 1982. "The revolution stumbles." *NACLA Report on the Americas* 16 (March–April):23–30.

Armstrong, R., & Shenk, J. 1980. "There's a war going on." *NACLA Report on the Americas* 14 (July–August):20–30.

Azicri, M. 1979. "Women's development through revolutionary mobilization: A study of the Federation of Cuban Women." *International Journal of Women's Studies* 2 (January–February):27–30.

Balyora, E. 1982. *El Salvador in transition.* Chapel Hill: University of North Carolina Press.

Blasier, C. 1967. "Studies of social revolution: Origins in Mexico, Bolivia, and Cuba." *Latin American Research Review* 2 (3):28–62.

Booth, J. A. 1982. *The end and the beginning: The Nicaraguan revolution.* Boulder: Westview.

Brenner, J., & Ramas, M. 1984. "Rethinking women's oppression." *New Left Review* 144 (March–April):33–71.

Broderick, W. J. 1975. *Camilo Torres: A biography of the priest-guerrillero.* New York: Doubleday.

Cardoso, F. H., & Faletto, E. 1979. *Dependency and development in Latin America.* Berkeley: University of California Press.

Castillo, C. 1982. "The situation of women in El Salvador." In Women's International Resource Exchange, ed., *Women and war: El Salvador,* pp. 5–9. New York.

Central American Information Office. 1982. *El Salvador: Background to the crisis.* Cambridge, Mass.: Central America Information Office.

Chailand, G. 1982. *Guerrilla strategies.* Berkeley: University of California Press.

Chaney, E. M. 1973. "Old and new feminists in Latin America." *Journal of Marriage and the Family* 35 (May):331–43.

Chaney, E. M. 1979. *Supermadre: Women in politics in Latin America.* Austin: University of Texas Press.

Chapelle, D. 1962. "How Castro won." In F. M. Osand, ed., *Modern guerrilla warfare,* pp. 325–35. New York: Free Press.

Chinchilla, N. S. 1982. "Women in revolutionary movements: The case of Nicaragua." Paper presented at the annual meetings of the American Sociological Society, San Francisco.

Chodorow, N. 1979. "Mothering, male dominance, and capitalism." In Z. R. Eisenstein, ed., *Capitalist patriarchy and the case for socialist feminism,* pp. 83–106. New York: Monthly Review Press.

Deere, C. D., & León de Leal, M. 1982. "Peasant production, proletarianization, and the sexual division of labor in the Andes." In L. Beneria, ed., *Woman and development,* pp. 65–93. New York: Praeger.

Flora, C. B. 1984. "Socialist feminism in Latin America." *Women and Politics* 4 (Spring):69–93.

Flynn, P. 1980. "Women challenge the myth." *NACLA Report on the Americas* 14 (September–October):20–32.

Franqui, C. 1980. *Diary of the Cuban revolution.* New York: Viking.

FSLN (Frente Sandinista de Liberación Nacional). 1979. "Why the FSLN struggles in unity with the people." *Latin American Perspectives* 6 (Winter):108–13.

FSLN. 1983. "The historic program of the FSLN." In P. Rosset & J. Vandermeer, eds., *The Nicaragua reader,* pp. 139–47. New York: Grove Press.

Gilio, M. E. 1970. *La guerrilla tupamara.* Havana: Casas de las Américas.

Gómez, A. 1967. "The revolutionary forces of Colombia and their perspectives." *World Marxist Review* 10 (April):59–67.

Gott, R. 1971. *Guerrilla movements in Latin America.* Garden City, N.Y.: Doubleday.

Guevara, Che. 1969. *Guerrilla warfare.* New York: Vintage.

Halperin, E. 1976. *Terrorism in Latin America.* Beverly Hills, Calif.: Sage.

Herrera, N. 1983. *La mujer en la revolución salvadoreña.* Morelos, Mexico: CCOPEC/CECOPE.

Jaquette, J. S. 1973. "Women in revolutionary movements in Latin America." *Journal of Marriage and the Family* 35(May):344–54.

Jaquette, J. S. 1976. "Female political participation in Latin America." In J. Nash & H. Safa, eds., *Sex and class in Latin America,* pp. 221–44. New York: Praeger.

Kinzer, N. S. 1973. "Priests, machos, and babies." *Journal of Marriage and the Family* 35 (May):300–311.

Kohl, J., & Litt, J. 1974. "Urban guerrilla warfare: Uruguay." In J. Kohn & J. Litt, eds., *Urban guerrilla warfare in Latin America,* pp. 173–95. Cambridge: MIT Press.

Laquer, W. 1977. *Guerrilla: A historical and critical study.* London: Weidenfeld & Nicolson.

Latin American Working Group. 1983. "El Salvador." In *Central American women speak for themselves,* pp. 35–55. Toronto.

López, O. 1976. "Las guerrilleras cubanas." In M. Flouret, ed., *La guerrilla en Hispano America.* Paris: Masson.

López de Piza, E. 1977. "La labor doméstica como fuente importante de valor de plusvalía en los paises dependientes." *Revista de Ciencias Sociales* 14 (October):19–29.

Madruga, L. 1974. "Interview with Urbano." In J. Kohl & J. Litt, eds., *Urban guerrilla warfare in Latin America,* pp. 266–92. Cambridge: MIT Press.

Molyneux, M. 1985. "Mobilization without emancipation? Women's interests, the state, and revolution in Nicaragua." *Feminist Studies* 11 (Summer):227–54.

Montgomery, T. S. 1982. *Revolution in El Salvador.* Boulder: Westview.

Movimiento de Liberación Nacional. 1974. "The Tupamaros' program for revolutionary government." In J. Kohl & J. Litt, eds., *Urban guerrilla warfare in Latin America,* pp. 293–96. Cambridge: MIT Press.

NACLA (North American Congress on Latin America). 1981. "No easy victory." *NACLA Report on the Americas* 15 (May–June):8–17.

NACLA. 1984. "El Salvador 1984: Locked in battle." *NACLA Report on the Americas* 18 (March–April):14–17.

Nash, J. 1977. "Women in development: Dependency and exploitation." *Development and Change* 8 (2):161–82.

Porzencanski, A. C. 1973. *Uruguay's Tupamaros: The urban guerrilla.* New York: Praeger.

Purcell, S. K. 1973. "Modernizing women for a modern society: The Cuban case." In Ann Pescatello, ed., *Female and male in Latin America,* pp. 257–71. Pittsburgh: University of Pittsburgh Press.

Ramirez-Horton, S. E. 1982. "The role of women in the Nicaraguan revolution." In T. W. Walker, ed., *Nicaragua in revolution,* pp. 147–59. New York: Praeger.

Randall, M. 1978. *Doris Tijerino: Inside the Nicaraguan revolution.* Vancouver: New Star.

Rowbotham, S. 1972. *Women, resistance, and revolution.* New York: Random House.

Safa, H. I. 1977. "The changing class composition of the female labor force in Latin America." *Latin American Perspectives* 4 (Fall):126–36.

Schlegel, A. 1977. "Toward a theory of sexual stratification." In A. Schlegel, ed., *Sexual stratification,* pp. 1–40. New York: Columbia University Press.

Schmidt, S. W. 1976. "Political participation and development: The role of women in Latin America." *Journal of International Affairs* 30 (Fall–Winter):243–60.

Schultz, V. 1980. "Organizer! Women in Nicaragua." *NACLA Report on the Americas* 14 (March–April):36–39.

Thomson, M. 1986. *Women of El Salvador: The price of freedom.* Philadelphia: Institute for the Study of Human Issues.

Vitale, L. 1981. *Historia y sociología de la mujer latinoamericana.* Barcelona: Fontamara.

Wilkie, J. W., & Haber, S., eds. 1982. *Statistical abstract of Latin America,* vol. 22. Los Angeles: UCLA Latin American Center for Publications.

Wilson, C. 1974. *The Tupamaros.* Boston: Branden Press.

WIRE (Women's International Resource Exchange). 1982a. "An interview with Sister Margarita Navarro, member of Human Rights Commission for El Salvador." In Women's International Resource Exchange, ed., *Women and war: El Salvador,* pp. 34–35. New York.

WIRE. 1982b. "Reconciliation is no longer possible: An interview with Ana Guadalupe Martínez, member of FMLN and FDR." In Women's International Resource Exchange, ed., *Women and war: El Salvador,* pp. 23–24. New York.

WIRE. 1982c. "Women's lives in El Salvador: An interview with Miriam Galdeméz, an El Salvadoran refugee." In Women's International Resource Exchange, ed., *Women and war: El Salvador,* pp. 1–3. New York.

R E A D I N G   4 7

Burning Incense, Pledging Sisterhood: Communities of Women Workers in the Shanghai Cotton Mills, 1919–1949

EMILY HONIG

When we swore sisterhood we would go to a temple and burn incense. Everyone would have to make a pledge. We pledged to be loyal through life and death. And if someone was halfhearted in their loyalty, then we prayed that when they got on a boat, that boat would turn over.

A woman who worked in the Shanghai cotton mills in the 1920s

During the thirty years between the end of World War I and Liberation in 1949, it was common for women who worked in the cotton mills of Shanghai to form sisterhood societies *(jiemei hui)*. After working together for several years, six to ten women would formalize their relationship with one another by pledging sisterhood. Sometimes this simply involved going to a restaurant, eating a meal together, drinking a cup of "one-heart wine," and toasting their loyalty to one another. Because large numbers of women workers were Buddhists, it was more common for those forming sisterhoods to go to a Buddhist temple, burn incense before the statue of a deity, and pledge to be loyal to one another "through life and death."

I would like to thank Margery Wolf, Lisa Rofel, and Marilyn Young for discussions of the ideas developed in this article as well as for comments on earlier drafts.

From *Signs: Journal of Women in Culture and Society*, vol. 10, no. 4, 1985. Copyright © 1985 by The University of Chicago Press. All rights reserved.

Once they had formed a sisterhood, the members would call each other by kinship terms based on their age: the oldest was "Big Sister," the next oldest "Second Sister," and so forth. Often members of the sisterhoods contributed money to buy a cloth in order to make each member an identical Chinese-style, long blue cotton gown. They wore the gowns when they went out together to express their unity.[1]

Women displayed their loyalty to one another both inside and outside the mills. Members of sisterhoods walked together to work in order to protect each other from hoodlums on the street. During the twelve-hour shifts they worked in the factory, one woman would do the work of two while the other ate lunch, went to the bathroom, or hid in a yard bin to take a nap. They defended each other if a male worker or overseer threatened one of them. Often the sisterhoods functioned as an economic mutual aid society: in order to avoid borrowing from "stamp-money lenders" who charged over 100 percent in interest, women paid a monthly "sisterhood fee." Then if one of the members faced an extraordinary expense such as a wedding, a funeral, or an illness, she could draw on this fund.[2] Members of sisterhoods socialized together: they would get together at one member's house to chat on Sundays, to go window-shopping, or to hear performances of local opera, a favorite form of entertainment among women workers in Shanghai.

These sisterhoods are scarcely mentioned in contemporary surveys of working-class life in Shanghai. This is not because those conducting the surveys failed to observe and record the conditions of women cotton-mill workers, whose number represented over one-third of the ranks of the famed Shanghai proletariat.[3] Historians have used these contemporary records to describe the transformation of women workers from passive, ever-suffering victims of industrial poverty to heroines of the organized labor movement and, in some cases, to class-conscious revolutionaries.

The interviews I conducted with women who had worked in Shanghai cotton mills during the three decades before 1949 suggest that the majority of women working in Shanghai were not lonely, isolated individuals; but neither were they members of trade unions, political organizations, or the Chinese Communist Party (CCP).[4] They survived by forming ties with other women workers who helped and protected them. These informal groups in time formalized as sisterhoods.

Although all women can recall in great detail the ways in which they depended on each other, questions about the sisterhoods provoked a number of seemingly contradictory answers. Some said that only women who had worked for many years pledged sisterhood, while others disdainfully described the sisterhoods as a phenomenon most prevalent among young women workers who liked to go out shopping, dress up, and hear local opera. Some said they were hoodlum organizations, while others insisted they were formed by women who wanted to protect themselves against hoodlums. Some remembered that only the most ideologically "backward" women pledged sisterhood, while others said the sisterhoods had been organized by the CCP. And finally, there were women who, when asked about the sisterhoods, exclaimed, "We women mill workers—we *all* used to pledge sisterhood!"

This variety of explanations suggests that there was no single type of sisterhood, that sisterhoods were formed for a host of reasons, and that they engaged in many different kinds of activities. There were some sisterhoods, however, that encompassed all these contradictory aspects, and one purpose of this article is to explain this phenomenon.

The major focus of this article, though, is to evaluate the significance of the sisterhoods. It would be tempting when studying these organizations formed by women workers, largely to serve the needs of women workers, to assume that they represent members' development of a consciousness as women and as workers. By looking more closely at these sisterhoods—at the women who formed them and at their activities—this article will suggest that associations constituted solely of workers are not necessarily an expression of working-class consciousness and that neither are autonomous women's groups inherently an expression of female consciousness. When examined in their cultural and historical context, working women's organizations, such as the Chinese sisterhoods, may as easily confirm and perpetuate traditional social relationships as challenge them.

WHO ARE OUR SISTERS?

In order to understand the development of sisterhoods, we must first look at the conditions inside the cotton mills and working-class districts that made it necessary for women workers to depend on one another. It was this need for mutual aid that led to the development of a sense of community among women workers and, ultimately, to the sisterhoods.

The daily work routine in the mills—if women had adhered to the rules—would have been grueling. They were required to work twelve-hour shifts with only a ten-minute break for lunch. Even while they ate, the machines continued to run. But women did not passively accept these rules. They often made work-sharing arrangements with those who labored beside them. "Those who got along well," a worker named Gu Lianying recalled, "one would help the other work, so that the other could eat." If a woman was exhausted and wanted to sleep for a few hours, another worker watched her machine and woke her up when the overseer made his rounds through the workshop. Sometimes women had to leave the mill for several hours to take care of a child. Since requesting formal permission would have jeopardized their jobs, they instead asked a friend to guard their machine while they were gone.

The world outside the mills was equally threatening, and women were compelled to help each other if they were to survive. Local toughs—many of whom belonged to Shanghai's powerful gang organizations—gathered at the mill gates, then flirted with and even pursued women walking home from work. On payday they seized women's wages, and on ordinary days they collected some cash by engaging in an activity called "stripping a sheep"—robbing a woman of her clothes, which they then sold.[5] While sexual abuse by male hoodlums was the most common problem, women mill workers had reason to be equally fearful of female gangsters, who specialized in the lucrative business of kidnapping young girls for sale to brothels or as future daughters-in-law.[6] All women workers had family members or friends who had been raped, beaten, or kidnapped by neighborhood hoodlums. For protection they almost always walked to and from the mills in groups—accompanied by parents when they were young and by siblings and neighbors as they grew older.

Part of the experience of growing up in the mills, for girls who had begun working when they were ten or eleven, was developing a network of "sisters" on whom they could depend for both help and protection. "We younger workers would not help each other in the workshop," one woman recalled, "but when I was older, I also had 'little sisters.' Then when I would eat, one of them would tend my machine. It was the girls in the lane next to me—we would help each other. This started when I was about fifteen." As women developed such relationships in the mills, they began to socialize with these other women workers as well. "After working a long time, then you'd start to have friends," the same woman continued. "And on Sundays, if you had time, you could go visit their house. Maybe that started when I was seventeen or eighteen. All of my friends then were cotton-mill workers." These relationships often continued after women were married. "We used to love to go see Subei operas," Chen Zhaodi recalled. "We would go in the evening, from seven to eleven. We almost never went with our husbands or children. It was usually some of us women who worked together who would go. But I would not tell my family where I was going. My mother-in-law would never have let me go. I just went secretly, with my 'sisters.'"

These relationships often remained casual, but frequently they were formalized as sisterhoods. One woman described this process: "Originally we would go to work together, and leave work together, because then it was not good to walk alone. After a while we would get to know each other. Then, if I thought that person was very decent, I would say to her, 'Why don't we pledge loyalty? Then if you have some problems I'll help you, and if I have some problems you can help me.'" It was at this point that they would go to a Buddhist temple and burn incense to establish their sisterhood. Women who pledged sisterhood were thus formalizing relationships with people outside their families as they began to perceive the women with whom they worked in the factory as their sisters.

This does not mean, however, that individual women perceived *all* other women mill workers, or even all other women who worked in the same mill, as potential sisters. In fact, most of the relationships of work sharing and mutual assistance that I have described were based on traditional connections between those from the same native place. In order to understand the nature of communities formed by women workers—and ultimately the nature of the sisterhoods—we must look briefly at the workers' origins and the extent to which their native place determined their experience in Shanghai, both inside and outside the mills.

Although some women who worked in the cotton mills were natives of Shanghai, throughout this thirty-year period the overwhelming majority of women came from rural villages in the provinces of Jiangsu and Zhejiang. (Shanghai is located at the southeastern corner of Jiangsu, on the border of Zhejiang.) They came from villages with almost every kind of economy imaginable—from places that relied on salt production to ones that depended on rice cultivation to ones where cotton was the major crop, from areas where handicraft industries such as silk or cotton spinning and weaving were a vital part of the peasant household economy to ones where handicrafts were almost nonexistent. They came from locales where foot-binding was still common in the 1930s as well as from places where the practice had long since ceased.

The villages from which women came can be roughly divided into two groups: those located in Subei, the part of Jiangsu Province north of the Yangzi River, and those located in the Jiangnan, the area south of the river. (The Yangzi River flows just north of Shanghai.) The Jiangnan has historically been one of the richest agricultural areas in China. Although no systematic research has considered the role of women in the rural economy, it appears that most peasant women in this area engaged in handicraft work. The places in the Jiangnan from which the mill workers came, such as Wuxi and Changzhou, had also exported many mill owners and technicians to Shanghai.

Subei was a much poorer area. Handicraft industries were less developed than in the south, and most peasant women played an active role in agricultural work. Throughout the early twentieth century vast numbers of families fled villages in the north that had been devastated by floods. Ever since that time, refugees from northern Jiangsu had performed the coolie jobs—such as collecting night soil and pulling rickshaws—that locals considered too demeaning to do themselves.[7]

These basic differences in the rural economies north and south of the river were replicated and perpetuated in the mills of Shanghai. In general, women from Subei, considered strong, robust, and accustomed to dirt, were channeled into the mill workshops, where the labor was most arduous and dirty. Often they did the jobs that in earlier stages of industrialization had been performed by male workers and that women from Shanghai proper or from villages of Jiangnan were not willing to do. Women from Jiangnan concentrated in the workshops where the labor was lighter and better paying. They also had the possibility of being promoted to supervisory positions.

Individual departments in the cotton mills were usually staffed by workers from a particular village.[8] This does not appear to have been the result of a management strategy to create divisions in the labor force, even though it had that effect. Hiring in the Shanghai mills was not controlled by a central personnel office but rather was the prerogative of the "Number Ones" (forewomen) in the workshops, and women secured jobs by dint of their "connections" with a Number One. When women who had migrated from the countryside arrived in Shanghai in search of work, they sought out people from their hometown who could introduce them to a Number One, usually someone from the same town. People from the same native place considered it their duty to help others from their district.[9]

The cotton mills were the only enterprise in Shanghai that brought several thousand women of disparate origins together under one roof. But they did not necessarily provide a setting where traditional patterns of localism were dissolved. Women from the same village were likely to be employed in the same workshop, surrounded by relatives and neighbors who came from their town, shared their customs, and spoke their particular dialect of Chinese. Furthermore, in the course of a working day, women had little reason to leave their workshop and have contact with women from others.

This localism pervaded the lives of women outside the mills as well. They usually lived in neighborhoods where people from their hometown had gathered.[10] Their hairstyles and eating habits often reflected the traditions of their native villages, and, as Chen Zhaodi observed:

> People from each place had different styles of dress. People from Subei liked to wear red, brightly colored clothes. People from Wuxi, Changzhou, and Tongzhou had their own looms, so they wore clothing they had woven themselves. They had little square scarves they would wrap on their heads. They also had long aprons. People from Nantong liked to wear long aprons. People from Yangzhou liked to dress up their hair. They would wear a bun. People from Changzhou and Wuxi liked to wear hairpins.

When they socialized on Sundays or holidays, they almost always did so with friends from their native place. Women from Zhejiang socialized with relatives and other people from Zhejiang and "did not bother too much with other people." When attending performances of local opera, Subei women went to theaters where they could hear Yangzhou opera, women from Wuxi went to hear Wuxi opera, and those from Zhejiang attended performances of Shaoxing (a city in Zhejiang) opera. When they married, their spouses were inevitably from the same district.

Place of origin was the major way in which women perceived themselves as similar to or different from others. Their attitude toward women from other villages was indifferent, at best, and sometimes overtly hostile. Women from Shanghai and from villages in the Jiangnan were contemptuous of women from Subei and often swore at them, "You Jiangbei swine!" It was not unheard of for a Subei woman to dump a bucket of night soil on the head of a fellow worker from Jiangnan or to shove a woman from Jiangnan into one of the rivers or canals that crisscrossed Shanghai.[11] Regional animosity—often the cause of bloody battles between male laborers—was also expressed by women who worked in the mills.[12]

When women pledged sisterhood, they were perpetuating both intraregional bonds and interregional divisions. No systematic information about the membership of sisterhoods is available. Yet based on what we know about patterns of migration to and settlement in Shanghai and about hiring practices, which usually resulted in concentrations of people from the same village in particular workshops, it seems safe to assume that, when women pledged sisterhood, it was with women from the same village. This is confirmed by the comment of a woman from Wuxi who, when asked whether she had ever joined a sisterhood, replied, "There was no one else in my workshop from Wuxi, so with whom could I pledge sisterhood?"

Thus the sisterhoods were not organizations that drew and bonded all women workers together. The women who joined them by no means perceived themselves as sisters to all women who shared their predicament. The important commonality was a shared native place. Yet the sisterhoods involved something more than traditional relationships. It is important to remember that new workers did not have a group of sisters on whom they could depend. To some degree the relationships embodied in the sisterhoods were ones that developed during the time women worked in the mills, and in that sense they were indeed a product of factory life.

SISTERS, NOT BROTHERS

Even if women in the Shanghai cotton mills did not perceive themselves as sisters to all women workers, they did indeed enter into formal organizations with some of their fellow laborers. They could have simply continued to help each other at work, walk with one another to and from the mill, and socialize together without bothering to go to Buddhist temples, burn incense, and pledge sisterhood. Thus we must return to the question, What does it mean that women mill workers formed autonomous female organizations?

Before confronting this question, I must point out that there is some evidence that the sisterhoods were not exclusively female. In describing the sisterhoods, one woman explained, "When ten of us women workers pledged sisterhood, we usually included one male worker and two or three tough women workers. Otherwise our group would not have power for defense." That this was not an atypical situation is suggested by a similar phenomenon among prostitutes in Shanghai. "Wild chickens," the lowest class of prostitutes in Shanghai, and the only ones who went out onto the streets to attract customers, also formed sisterhood societies. Their sisterhoods are described as consisting of nine prostitutes plus one male, usually a petty gang-ster who had connections with the local police, who was supposed to help protect the women if anyone tried to abuse them while they were out at night.[13]

Unfortunately, we do not know if the practice of including men in the sisterhoods of women mill workers was widespread. Nor do we know what role the men played. It is possible, for example, that they were part of the sisterhood simply to give physical protection when necessary but did not participate in the other functions of the sisterhood such as work sharing, providing economic mutual aid, and socializing.

While the evidence of men's inclusion in the sisterhoods is perplexing, what we know about male membership at this point is not enough to negate our consideration of the sisterhoods as organizations formed primarily for and by women. This is confirmed by the simultaneous existence of "brotherhoods" among male workers in the mills. Groups of eight to ten male workers pledged loyalty to each other by burning incense, and members of brotherhoods referred to each other as "Oldest Brother," "Second Brother," and so forth. If women did not intend to form separate, autonomous organizations, then why did they not form "brother-sister societies" or simply "workerhoods"? The answer to this question, I would argue, is found in the historical and cultural context in which sisterhoods developed.

During the three decades before Liberation, it was socially acceptable for women to participate in activities or associations with other women but not with men. This was a reality that even radical organizers in the CCP—who would have preferred to develop organizations that included both men and women—had to accept in order to mobilize women. "Although I am an extreme supporter of the belief that men and women should study together," Xiang Jingyu, head of the Women's Bureau of the CCP, wrote in 1924, "when it comes to establishing workers' schools, I am an absolute advocate of male and female separatism. . . . It is only by setting up schools especially for women that women will be willing to come, and that their fathers and husbands will be willing to let them come and study."[14] That year, the first Party-sponsored workers' schools were established in one of Shanghai's cotton-mill districts: one for men and one for women.[15] A year later Xiang Jingyu extended this principle to unions, suggesting that, in order to attract female members, there would have to be separate unions for women.[16] As late as 1941, when the Party was trying to organize underground during the Japanese occupation, the person responsible for organizing in the cotton mills lamented that it was still necessary to establish separate Party branches for women workers.[17]

In this context, forming a mixed-gender group may have presented a more profound challenge to traditional social relationships than forming a women's organization. Or, more modestly put, establishing a women's association and calling it a sisterhood did not necessarily indicate that women desired autonomy from men. In Shanghai (and in most of China) separate female organizations were traditional, not radical.

This does not mean, however, that the formation of autonomous women's groups was inherently conservative. It would have been equally possible for women to have established organizations that expressed their determination to challenge the existing social order. This is in fact what happened in the Canton delta during the late nineteenth and early twentieth centuries, according to Marjorie Topley. Many peasant women in this area, who played a critical role in sericulture, formed sisterhoods to resist marriage. Groups of women pledged loyalty to one another before a deity in a Buddhist temple and made vows never to marry. This was possible because they could support themselves through the wages they earned as silk workers.[18]

Although women in the Shanghai mills, like peasant women in Canton, enjoyed independent incomes, there is little similarity between the two types of sisterhoods besides the name and ceremony of pledging loyalty. The women in Shanghai were not coming together to demand change in their status either as women or as workers. The majority of women who joined sisterhoods in Shanghai accepted what they probably considered to be their fate: they would work twelve hours a day in a mill only to return home to face the task of maintaining a household; they were vulnerable to sexual abuse by overseers inside the mills and thugs on the streets; they would marry the person who had been chosen for them by their parents, often when they were only children. The purpose of the sisterhoods was not to advocate change or express resistance but simply to help each other survive within the context of traditional social relationships.

Sisterhoods were not the only associations women workers formed to ensure their survival in Shanghai. To protect themselves from the wrath of the Number Ones in the mills and from attacks by hoodlums outside, many women workers also "pledged godmothers" *(bai ganniang)*. "For protection from the gangs, you could make arrangements with one gang member,"

Zhu Fanu recalled. "Male workers would find a male gang leader, and women workers would find a woman. This was called pledging a godmother. When you found the person who would protect you, you would send her presents. Then if another gangster ever bothered you, you could go tell your godmother, and she would take care of you, because she had power." Often women mill workers pledged loyalty to the Number One in their workshop as their godmother. Most of the Number Ones not only had the power commensurate with their position in the mills but also were members of the gangs (or were married to gang members) and therefore were influential in the neighborhood as well. With such godmothers, women workers had protection both on and off the job.

Like pledging sisterhood, pledging loyalty to a godmother also involved a ceremony: burning incense, kneeling, and reciting a vow in front of an altar. Once a woman had a godmother, she was expected to demonstrate her appreciation by periodically sending gifts, preferably cash. Whenever the godmother had a pretext—such as a birthday or holiday—she would send invitations to all her "godchildren" to partake in a celebration *(chi jiu)*. "You had to go, and when you went, you had to send them money. That was the main purpose," one worker commented.

Sometimes the distinction between pledging sisterhoods and pledging a godmother blurred. While individual women may have chosen either to pledge sisterhood or to pledge a godmother, some may have pledged both. More important, there is some evidence that the two practices sometimes merged—that some sisterhoods included a godmother. One woman, for example, described the sisterhoods as including "one male and two or three tough women." More compelling evidence comes from a description of organizing strategies developed by the CCP during the Anti-Japanese War (1937–45). According to this account, the Party, in an attempt to adapt organizational forms familiar to women workers, established sisterhoods that included several ordinary mill workers, a woman who was a Number One, and an older woman who was married to a gang leader.[19] In these cases women of different ages and of different status in the mill were bonded together in the sisterhoods.

This information affects how we ultimately assess the relationships among the members of sisterhoods. The term "sisterhood" usually evokes the notion of equality, and it is appealing to think of the associations as ones composed of women who saw themselves as sisters, hence equals. Even if these "hybrid" sister-hoods were the exception, not the rule, they caution us not to assume uncritically that sisterhoods are egalitarian organizations.

SISTERS IN REVOLUTION

Although the sisterhoods were not self-consciously political, they often took actions that had political implications. This was particularly evident when groups of sisters, banding together to protect one member, opposed—or even physically attacked—their employers. "One time a girl worker was being harassed by an overseer," one woman remembered. "She told us sisters, and we all attacked that overseer and beat him up." Sometimes their commitment to mutual protection put them in strikelike situations. If a Number One threatened to fire a woman who belonged to a sisterhood, her sisters would refuse to work until the Number One revoked her threat. These were common, spontaneous incidents, but it does not require much stretch of the imagination to recognize how these loyalties might be appropriated in an organized labor movement. If one member of a sisterhood shut off the motor of her spinning frame or loom as part of a strike, her sisters could be expected to shut off their machines too, even if for no reason other than personal loyalty.

The most vivid example of how the sisterhoods were used to advocate principles very different from those that characterized their original purpose comes from CCP actions during the Anti-Japanese War and during the Civil War from 1946 to 1949. The political situation during both conflicts made only the most covert means of organizing possible, and Party members began to pay closer attention to preexisting social networks among workers, such as sisterhoods, viewing them as potentially revolutionary organizations. In one of the only available reports on this phenomenon, the Party in 1941 instructed local organizers:

> Because of the subjective and objective circumstances of women's lives, they must often help each other. In order to prevent strangers from flirting with them, or thieves from trying to take away their wages, they often walk together. On their time off, when they go buy things, they also usually go in groups of seven or eight. In all of these groups there is always one or two people who are at the center. If we can attract them, then it is easy to attract the

others in their group. More and more of these groups are developing in the areas occupied by the Japanese, where women want to protect themselves. So, it is not just important to unite with these elements in struggle, but also important to do this in their everyday organizations.[20]

Thus, instead of encouraging the members of sisterhoods to read progressive literature, to participate in discussions of the workers' movement, or to go to secret screenings of Russian movies, organizers initially went shopping with their "sisters" or played in parks with them. "First we just tried to develop friendships," a woman who was active in the Party underground in the late 1930s and 1940s recalled, "and then later we could talk about the conditions of women workers."

In some cases Party activists did not simply join sisterhoods that already existed but actually began forming sisterhoods themselves. In order to do so, however, they had to adhere to the practices that made pledging sisterhood meaningful to ordinary women workers, no matter how far they may have diverged from the principles upheld by the Party. Thus, when the CCP formed sisterhoods, the Party activists had to go along with the other members to a Buddhist temple, where they all burned incense, knelt in front of a statue of a deity, and took oaths to "be loyal to each other through life and death."[21]

If these new sisterhoods differed from the traditional ones, the differences were small, almost imperceptible. At the Da Kang mill, for instance, after a group of women pledged such a Party-supported sisterhood, they each contributed a small sum of money to buy a piece of white cloth. They cut the cloth into squares, sewed handkerchiefs, and on each one embroidered the words "working together with one heart." Each member of the sisterhood kept a handkerchief as a souvenir.[22] While members of traditional sisterhoods occasionally made identical gowns—or may even have made identical handkerchiefs—to symbolize their relationship, they were not likely to have expressed their common interests as workers as did the new sisters with their embroidered emblem.

Similarly, it had always been common for members of sisterhoods to get together on Sundays, to go out window-shopping, or to go to a park. Party members encouraged and participated in these activities and gradually introduced new dimensions. When they went to parks, for example, Party members spent part of the time telling their sisters about the progress women had made through the Russian Revolution and about the work of the CCP in Yanan.[23] Women who were sympathetic to these ideas were enlisted by the Party organizers to attend schools for women workers run by the YWCA.[24] Some eventually joined the CCP themselves.[25]

This strategy was apparently successful, for during the Civil War, unprecedented numbers of women workers continuously participated in strikes, for the first time demanding and winning benefits specifically for women, such as maternity leave and nurseries. For some women, the potential for the development of worker and female solidarity that had been inherent in the sisterhoods was finally realized.

CONCLUSION

The significance of the sisterhoods, then, is that they indicate the ways in which women were not passive vic-

tims of industrial poverty. They demonstrate women's resistance to unbearably long work hours, beatings by overseers, and physical abuse by neighborhood gangsters. They also characterize the communities formed by women workers in Shanghai—communities in which women drew on traditional social relationships to survive in a new, unfamiliar, and threatening environment. The Shanghai sisterhoods suggest that organizations formed by women workers are not necessarily expressions of working-class or feminist consciousness. And once formed, the sisterhoods did not inevitably lead their members to see that by acting collectively they could change their circumstances. Nevertheless, the sisterhoods do provide a critical link in the story of how some women became revolutionaries. It was only when Communist Party organizers burned incense and pledged sisterhood that women workers, as sisters, became active participants in the Chinese revolution.

NOTES

1. Materials provided by the Institute for Historical Research, Shanghai Academy of Social Sciences. These materials include unpublished factory histories, transcripts of interviews, and accounts of strikes collected as part of an effort undertaken in the 1950s to chronicle the history of the pre-Liberation labor movement in Shanghai. The documents are not labeled or cataloged. Further information about these materials can be obtained by contacting me [at Yale University].

2. Cora Deng, "The Economic Status of Women in Industry in China, with Special Reference to a Group in Shanghai" (M.A. thesis, New York University, 1941), p. 73.

3. In 1929, when the industry was close to its peak of development, there were sixty-one cotton mills in Shanghai, employing 110,882 workers. Of these, 84,270 (76 percent) were women (Shanghai Bureau of Social Affairs, *Wages and Hours of Labor, Greater Shanghai, 1929* [Shanghai, 1929]). Throughout the period from World War I through Liberation in 1949, Shanghai was the largest industrial center in China, and the cotton industry was Shanghai's major industry.

4. I conducted these interviews during two research trips to Shanghai. Under the auspices of the Committee on Scholarly Communication with the People's Republic of China and the Social Science Research Council, I was an exchange scholar at Fudan University in Shanghai from 1979 to 1981. I returned to conduct follow-up research in September and October of 1982. The interviews with women workers were

almost all arranged by Fudan University and usually took place at the cotton mills. I interviewed approximately fifty women. Often these interviews were set up as "round-table discussions," in which I questioned four or five women during a single three-hour session. There was almost no opportunity to conduct follow-up interviews with individual women. Unless otherwise cited, all quotations in the text are from these interviews.

5. For a discussion of these problems, see Liu Ta-chun, *The Growth and Industrialization of Shanghai* (Shanghai: China Institute of Pacific Relations, 1936), p. 169; and Shanghai shehui kexueyuan, jingji yanjiusuo (Institute for Economic Research, Shanghai Academy of Social Sciences), ed., *Shanghai penghuqude bianyi* (Changes in the squatter settlements of Shanghai) (Shanghai: Shanghai renmin chubanshe, 1965), p. 24.

6. Mary Ninde Gamewell, *Gateway to China: Pictures of Shanghai* (New York: Fleming H. Revell Co., 1916), p. 210. See also *Shanghai heimo yiqian zhong* (A thousand kinds of shady plots in Shanghai) (Shanghai: Shanghai chunming shudian yinxing, 1939), pp. 1–31

7. For a more detailed discussion of the workers' origins, see Emily Honig, "Women Cotton Mill Workers in Shanghai, 1919–1949" (Ph.D. diss., Stanford University, 1982).

8. See, e.g., Zhongguo fangzhi jianshe gongsi (China Textile Reconstruction Corp.), *Shanghai dishisi fangzhichang*

sanshiwuniande gongzuo nianbao (Yearly report on the work at the Shanghai Number Fourteen Textile Mill, 1946) (Shanghai, 1946), pp. 63–65. See also *Xin qingnian* (New youth) (Beijing), vol. 7, no. 6 (May 1920). This segregation of workers by place of origin is also documented by the retirement cards from one of the largest cotton mills in Shanghai. These cards—filled out when a worker retires—are part of the personnel records at each mill. They indicate the worker's name, place and date of birth, and work history.

9. For a more extensive discussion of hiring practices in the cotton mills, see Honig, pp. 95–104. See also Jean Chesneaux, *The Chinese Labor Movement, 1919–1927* (Stanford, Calif.: Stanford University Press, 1968). These patterns of people from the same hometown helping each other are not unique to workers. See, e.g., Susan Mann Jones, "The Ningpo Pang and Financial Power at Shanghai," in *The Chinese City between Two Worlds,* ed. Mark Elvin and G. W. Skinner (Stanford, Calif.: Stanford University Press, 1974), pp. 73–96.

10. This observation is based on interviews as well as on Herbert Lamson, "The Problem of Housing for Workers in China," *Chinese Economic Journal* 11, no. 2 (August 1932): 139–62.

11. *Shen Bao* (The Huangpu Daily) (Shanghai) (May 6, 1924).

12. For a discussion of regional rivalries in Shanghai, see Chesneaux, p. 123; and Leung Yuen Sang, "Regional Rivalry in Mid-Nineteenth Century Shanghai: Cantonese vs Ningpo Men." *Ch'ing shih wen-t'i* 4, no. 8 (December 1982):29–50.

13. Materials provided by the Institute for Historical Research, Shanghai Academy of Social Sciences. The source does not explain the relationship of the men to the sisterhoods of prostitutes. Since the men who acted as pimps are discussed in a separate section of the article, it seems safe to assume that these men were not pimps.

14. *Xiang Jingyu wenji* (The collected works of Xiang Jingyu) (Changsha: Hunan renmin chubanshe, 1980), pp. 146–47.

15. Shanghai shehui kexueyuan lishi yanjiusuo (Institute for Historical Research, Shanghai Academy of Social Sciences), ed., *Wusa yundong shiliao* (Historical materials on the May Thirtieth Movement) (Shanghai: Shanghai renmin chubanshe, 1981), 1:270.

16. *Xiang Jingyu wenji,* p. 216.

17. Materials provided by the Institute for Historical Research, Shanghai Academy of Social Sciences.

18. Marjorie Topley, "Marriage Resistance in Rural Kwangtung," in *Women in Chinese Society,* ed. Margery Wolf and Roxane Witke (Stanford, Calif.: Stanford University Press, 1975), pp. 67–68.

19. Materials provided by the Institute for Historical Research, Shanghai Academy of Social Sciences.

20. Ma Chunji, "Shanghai nugong gongzuo baogao" (Report on work among women workers in Shanghai) (Yanan, 1941), reprinted by Zhonghua quanguo zonggonghui ziliaoshi (Materials Department of the All-China Federation of Labor) (1954).

21. Materials provided by the Institute for Historical Research, Shanghai Academy of Social Sciences.

22. Ibid.

23. Ibid.

24. Tang Guifen, "Huxi shachang gongren douzhengde gaikuang" (General conditions of the cotton workers' struggle in western Shanghai), in *Shanghai gongren yundong lishi ziliao* (Materials on the history of the Shanghai workers' movement) (Shanghai, 1956, mimeographed). Starting in the 1920s, the YWCA operated a number of night schools for women industrial workers. Ostensibly the schools taught literacy, but they were known for teaching women workers to understand their position in the social and economic system. They also taught women skills, such as public speaking, that were useful in labor organizing. By the 1940s, the CCP began using the schools to organize women workers, and many teachers in them were Party members (interview with Cora Deng, Shanghai, 1980; Robin Porter, "The Christian Conscience and Industrial Welfare in China, 1919–1941" [Ph.D. diss., University of Montreal, 1977]; Wang Zhijin et al., "Huiyi Shanghai nuqingnianhuide nugong yexiao" [Recalling the YWCA night schools for women workers in Shanghai], *Shanghai wenshi ziliao xuanji* [Selected materials on Shanghai culture and history], no. 5 [Shanghai, 1979], pp. 83–93).

25. Shanghai gongren yundong shiliao weiyuanhui (Shanghai Labor History Committee), ed., *Shanghai guomian shichang gongren douzheng lishi ziliao* (Materials on the history of the workers' struggles at the Number Ten Textile Mill in Shanghai) (Shanghai, 1954, mimeographed).

READING 48

When the Oppressors Are Us

AMBER AULT and EVE SANDBERG

Women around the globe share many concerns, including meeting basic subsistence needs, improving the prevention and treatment of diseases like AIDS, providing for reproductive health and freedom, reducing infant mortality and childhood illness, preventing violence against women, ensuring gender equity in labor, law, and education, and increasing women's ability to exercise sexual self-determination. Because wealthy countries and poor countries occupy very different positions in the global economic system, however, the social, economic, and political oppression experienced by women of poor countries differs in form from that experienced by women in wealthy countries. Furthermore, the oppression of women in Third World countries does not exist in a vacuum that begins and ends at national borders. Indeed, much of the poverty, discrimination, disease, and violence experienced by Third World women results from the exploitation of their countries by wealthier countries and the international organizations that they control. As feminist scholars and activists in wealthy Western countries, we must educate ourselves about our roles in supporting the systems of domination which perpetuate the exploitation of women elsewhere.

We do not argue that all women in industrialized nations enjoy vast, substantial advantages over all women in Third World countries. Indeed, many women in the United States live in extreme poverty, without decent housing, steady health care, stable employment, or any assurance of personal safety, while some women in poor nations enjoy relatively high standards of living. Nonetheless, because wealthy Western countries benefit from the labor of exploited Third World workers, Western feminists need to understand the roles their governments play in women's oppression in other countries.

In this brief report, we use a case study to demonstrate how the self-interested practices of wealthier countries in one international organization exacerbate and sometimes create the oppression of Third World women as women, citizens, and workers. To explicate the connections between the United States government, one powerful international organization, and the lives of women in Third World countries, we recount the impact of an International Monetary Fund (IMF) Structural Adjustment Program in the African country of Zambia.

The International Monetary Fund constitutes an international agency designed to promote a stable world economy. As part of its mission, it provides loans to countries with failing economies. Capital for such loans comes from deposits made by the countries participating in the International Monetary Fund. The conditions each borrowing country must meet to secure a loan are contingent on the ultimate approval by the Board of Directors of the Fund, which includes representatives of the member states, whose votes are weighted relative to their countries' financial contributions; wealthy nations like the United States make large contributions and therefore enjoy great influence over the contingencies attached to loans the agency makes, as well as its policies and actions. Not surprisingly, the terms of loans to Third World countries reflect the economic and political interests and values of the world's wealthiest nations.

The "Structural Adjustment Program" constitutes one kind of loan package managed by this organization. The International Monetary Fund makes financial assistance to Third World countries contingent upon

Reprinted by permission of the authors, Amber Ault and Eve Sandberg.

borrower countries' willingness to make significant adjustments in their economic systems. The adjustments required by the International Monetary Fund reflect Western capitalist economic ideologies. In addition, they often reflect a disregard for the structural, cultural, social, and technological features of the borrowing country. As a result, Structural Adjustment Programs administered by the International Monetary Fund frequently result in dramatic and devastating changes in the countries that adopt them. Nonetheless, because the International Monetary Fund constitutes one of the few sources of loan capital to which an indebted country can turn, countries suffering severe economic difficulty often accept the terms of Structural Adjustment Programs.

Such was the case of Zambia, a Black-governed country in South-Central Africa that implemented an IMF Structural Adjustment Program in October, 1985 and wrestled with it in various forms until its termination in May, 1987. Before we describe the policies and outcomes of the Structural Adjustment Program in Zambia, we offer a brief description of some features of the country, so that readers may more fully grasp the ramifications of the program on the lives of citizens in general and women in particular.

At the time it instituted its IMF Structural Adjustment Program, Zambia reported that its population numbered about 6.7 million citizens. About 3.81 million Zambians over the age of 11 were working or actively seeking work, but only about 71% of these people could find jobs. While some urban Zambian women worked as teachers, nurses, secretaries, and waitresses, many more were self-employed as food sellers, street vendors, and charcoal producers, or in other jobs in the "informal sector"; in rural areas, women usually worked as farmers.

Then, as now, Zambia imported many goods. Government controls on foreign exchange rates held in check the cost to consumers of food and other goods imported by retailers before the implementation of the Structural Adjustment Program. Such controls helped to allow families in both urban and rural areas to meet their basic subsistence needs, and were especially beneficial for women upon whom rests most of the responsibility of supporting the family.

Other government policies and programs helped to make life in Zambia manageable for its citizens before the Structural Adjustment Program. For example, the Zambian government made heavily subsidized health care available to all citizens, and ensured access to basic education. Zambian governmental policies also kept domestic tensions in check by equitably distributing government-subsidized resources to the four separate geographic areas occupied by the country's four major ethnic groups.

Before it would disburse a loan to Zambia, the IMF required the Zambian government to promise to make major changes in the structure of its economy. According to the IMF, the required changes would allow the country to participate more successfully in the world market and, as a result, would allow it to repay its loan. Although many of the wealthy countries with controlling interests in the IMF do not have balanced national budgets, the IMF's Structural Adjustment Program packages are designed around the idea that Third World countries should achieve balanced budgets, and that they should do this in part by suspending support to domestic programs.

The International Monetary Fund required Zambia to devalue its currency, discontinue its subsidization of food, health, and education, suspend social welfare programs, lay-off federal employees, and turn its attention to both diversifying and increasing its exports for international markets. The result: a socio-economic nightmare for the country's people. The changes required by the IMF produced widespread unemployment; inflation of astronomical proportions; the suspension of the education of many people, especially girls; a dramatic decrease in access to health care; an increase in violence; conflict between the country's ethnic groups; and increased class stratification. While these problems affected most citizens, they made life especially arduous for women.

Over night, the devaluation of Zambian currency and the suspension of government subsidies on imported goods produced massive inflation. The consumer prices of domestically produced products and services, including health care, school fees, and transportation, rose by 50%; the prices of many imported goods doubled. Women and girls were especially hard-hit by inflation. For example, because women are primarily responsible for feeding and clothing their children, the dramatic increases in the cost of food and household goods took a great toll on their limited incomes; with the increase in household expenses, and the end of nationally subsidized health care and education, medicine and schooling became increasingly beyond the means of most families. As a result, families made difficult decisions about who would receive the benefit of increasingly limited resources, and those decisions reflected entrenched patriarchal values. In the case of education, for example, families often reverted to traditions that promoted the education of male children over that of girls.

Sudden, massive unemployment exacerbated the problems resulting from inflation. The IMF required the Zambian government to lay-off scores of government workers as a means of reducing expenditures. As a result of reduced consumer spending, private businesses and industry also let large numbers of workers go. In both spheres, women suffered great losses because their positions were frequently regarded as the most expendable. Joblessness, coupled with inflation, left Zambians destitute; sexist social structures disadvantaged women, even relative to men who were suffering greatly.

For example, while the inflated price of gasoline made the cost of public transportation beyond most citizens' means and forced those who retained jobs to walk long distances to and from work, after-work hours were very different for men and women. Because they are responsible for feeding their families, many women had to extend their days with either extra income-producing activities or by obtaining land on which to create family gardens. Women's "double burden" of work and child-care became even greater under the hardships of the Structural Adjustment Program.

Women also suffered directly at the hands of men as a result of the social stress the country experienced during the Structural Adjustment Program. Men, pressed to their limits, took advantage of women's resources and patriarchal social structures which allowed them to succeed in such efforts. For example, one woman farmer interviewed recounted how her brother had stolen from her: their father had willed them an ox to share, and every year she and her brother took turns using the animal to plough their fields; in the first year of the Structural Adjustment Program, the brother took the ox, refused to return it, and rented it to others for extra income, saying that his family could not survive if he did otherwise; the woman, in turn, could not plant enough to feed her family that year, and since customary law in the area did not recognize women's right to property, had no recourse. Such situations were not uncommon.

Nor was physical violence. In the years of the Structural Adjustment Program, the rate of violent crime in Zambia rose sharply. Women's increased activity away from home, as a result of their need to have extra income-generating activities, made them increasingly vulnerable to attack; women walking to and from work or their gardens, often distant from their homes, were fearful of being assaulted. At home, too, people were wary. One interviewee described how she and her husband took turns staying awake at night to protect themselves from prospective robbers.

These problems were further exacerbated by increasing conflict between groups in Zambia. As a result of IMF conditions, the government suspended its policy of distributing agricultural resources equitably throughout the country. Some areas of the country began to receive more and better supplies, setting the stage for conflicts between the ethnic groups living in different geographic regions. The Structural Adjustment Program also indirectly produced increased stratification among the country's women: those women farmers who happened to live along the country's supply roads received many more resources than those who lived in remote territories. While such women were among the few to benefit financially from the Structural Adjustment Program in Zambia, their prosperity rested on the deprivation of others.

Clearly, the imposition of the conditions of the IMF Structural Adjustment Program in Zambia wreaked havoc on the lives of the country's people. Similar IMF Structural Adjustment Programs throughout the Third World have produced equally devastating effects. We note that some IMF Structural Adjustment Programs in other impoverished countries have included a feature missing from the Zambian program: special encouragement for multinational corporations to promote exports. The mistreatment of women workers by such corporations has been well documented by other feminist scholars. (Nash and Fernandez-Kelly, 1983; Fuentes and Ehrenreich, 1983; Ward, 1990)

A small number of women entrepreneurs benefit from the free-market conditions created by IMF adjustment programs, and some women find empowerment and forge coalitions with other women in their efforts to resist the hardships the programs impose. Generally, however, throughout the Third World, people suffer greatly as a result of the conditions their governments must accept in order to procure loans designed to relieve the economic instability of their countries.

As voting members in the IMF, western governments, including that of the United States, condone and encourage the policies that so disrupt the lives of so many millions in Third World states. The United Nations Economic Social and Cultural Organization (UNESCO) and the United Nations Africa Economic Committee (UNAEC) have criticized the extraordinary toll that citizens in Third World states, especially women, are paying for their governments' Structural Adjustment Programs. In the 1990s, other organizations and individual citizens in Western countries are also attempting to alter IMF policies. Friends of the Earth, for example, a Washington, D.C. based nongovernmental organization concerned primarily with the environment, began a campaign in 1991 to urge the U.S. Congress to use the U.S. voting position in the International Monetary Fund to alter IMF Structural Adjustment Programs.

Western feminists can join or initiate efforts to alter the IMF's programs. Women from wealthy countries must recognize our collaboration in the global system that oppresses women. As citizens of the countries intimately involved with the implementation of international policies which foster the exploitation of women in the Third World, we can seek to change the system. Indeed, we must: to fail to act on behalf of the women suffering as a result of our government's involvement in the IMF is to perpetuate the oppression of others, even as we seek to relieve our own.

REFERENCES

Fuentes, Annette and Ehrenreich, Barbara, eds.: *Women in the Global Factory.* Boston: South End Press, 1983.

Nash, June and Fernandez-Kelly, Patricia, eds.: *Women, Men, and the International Division of Labor.* Albany: State University of New York Press, 1983.

Ward, Kathryn, ed.: *Women Workers and Global Restructuring.* Ithaca: Cornell University Press, 1990.

Social Protest and the Feminist Movement

Patriarchal culture asserts itself against women in many ways. Throughout *Feminist Frontiers III* we have begun to understand the breadth and magnitude of the social forces working to disadvantage women. Socialization, the organization of social institutions, and social and economic policies all come together to prevent women from achieving full political participation and from leading lives of self-determination, let alone lives in which health and safety can be taken for granted.

Despite the ubiquitous nature of sexism, racism, classism, nationalism, homophobia, and the other forms of prejudice embedded in our social institutions, women resist. As we have seen, women often fight to undermine forces of oppression in individual ways. Women also come together to take collective action to effect social change. This section explores contemporary feminist movements, noting that feminist issues look different in particular cultural and historical contexts.

Bell Hooks's "Black Women and Feminism" examines some major conflicts facing the women's movement. Hooks analyzes tensions between black women and men in the 1950s and 1960s, as well as the racist neglect of concerns of women of color by the women's movement. Her analysis opens the way for meaningful dialogue between women of different races, ethnicities, and classes.

Gloria Anzaldúa's article, "En rapport, In Opposition: Cobrando cuentas a las nuestras," analyzes

the danger of infighting among women of color in the name of ethnic correctness. Examining the divisiveness of this conflict and its roots in the ideological systems of white dominance, Anzaldúa calls for a rejection of white values and the development of visions of change not based in opposition to male whiteness but centered instead in the women's self-defined ethnic realities.

The "triple burden" of being black, female, and lesbian becomes clear in an interview between Jewelle L. Gomez and Barbara Smith, both black lesbian feminists. "Taking the *Home* out of *Homophobia*" points out the connection between sexism and homophobia, and explores the politics of invisibility and coming out in communities antagonistic toward lesbians.

Judith Stacey examines the relationship between the feminist movement, the transition to a service-oriented economy, and women's strategies for managing their daily lives in "Postindustrial Conditions and Postfeminist Consciousness in the Silicon Valley." Stacey asserts that the feminist movement may have served as unwitting midwife to the birth of new family and work situations that, ironically, perpetuate gender stratification and limit possibilities for feminist consciousness and practice.

In the anthology's final article, Verta Taylor and Nancy Whittier present an overview of the new feminist movement from its emergence in the 1960s to the present. Their article, "The New Feminist

Movement," traces three stages in the contemporary women's movement: the period of resurgence, 1966–1971; the feminist heyday, 1972–1982; and the period of abeyance, 1983 through the present. Taylor and Whittier discuss the transformations and ideologies driving each stage and, in contrast to other descriptions of the 1980s and 1990s as a "postfeminist era," suggest that the women's movement in the 1990s is continuous, and exists with a new focus and new strategies for change. Feminism, they argue, has a long and continuous past and strong prospects for the future.

Black Women and Feminism

BELL HOOKS

A large number of black women, many who were young, college-educated, and middle class, were seduced in the 60s and 70s by the romanticized concept of idealized womanhood first popularized during the Victorian age. They stressed that woman's role was that of a helpmate to her man. And for the first time in the history of black civil rights movements, black women did not struggle equally with black men. Writing of the 60s black movement in *Black Macho and the Myth of the Superwoman,* Michelle Wallace comments:

> Misogyny was an integral part of Black Macho. Its philosophy, which maintained that black men had been more oppressed than black women, that black women had, in fact, contributed to that oppression, that black men were sexually and morally superior and also exempt from most of the responsibilities human beings had to other human beings, could only be detrimental to black women. But black women were determined to believe—even as their own guts were telling them it was not so—that they were finally on the verge of liberation from the spectre of the omnipotent blonde with the rosebud lips and the cheesecake legs. They would no longer have to admire another woman on the pedestal. The pedestal would be theirs. They would no longer have to do their own fighting. They would be fought for. The knight in white armor would ride for them. The beautiful fairy princess would be black.

The women of the Black Movement had little sense of the contradictions in their desire to be models of fragile Victorian womanhood in the midst of revolution. They wanted a house, a picket fence around it, a chicken in the pot, and a man. As they saw it, their only officially designated revolutionary responsibility was to have babies.

Not all black women succumbed to the sexist brainwashing that was so much a part of black liberation rhetoric, but those who did not received no attention. People in the U.S. were fascinated with the image of the black female—strong, fierce, and independent—meekly succumbing to a passive role, in fact longing to be in a passive role.

Although Angela Davis became a female heroine of the 60s movement, she was admired not for her political commitment to the Communist party, not for any of her brilliant analyses of capitalism and racial imperialism, but for her beauty, for her devotion to black men. The American public was not willing to see the "political" Angela Davis; instead they made of her a poster pinup. In general, black people did not approve of her communism and refused to take it seriously. Wallace writes of Angela Davis:

> For all her achievements, she was seen as the epitome of the selfless, sacrificing "good woman"—the only kind of black woman the Movement would accept. She did it for her man, they said. A woman in a woman's place. The so-called political issues were irrelevant.

Contemporary black women who supported patriarchal dominance placed their submission to the status quo in the context of racial politics and argued that they were willing to accept a subordinate role in relationship to black men for the good of the race. They

Reprinted from *Ain't I a Woman: Black Women and Feminism* by Bell Hooks with permission from the publisher, South End Press, 116 St. Botolph Street, Boston, Massachusetts 02115.

were indeed a new generation of black females—a generation that had been brainwashed not by black revolutionaries but by white society, by the media, to believe that woman's place was in the home. They were the first generation of black women to face competition with white women for the attention of black men. Many of them accepted black male sexism solely because they were afraid of being alone, of not having male companions. The fear of being alone, or of being unloved, had caused women of all races to passively accept sexism and sexist oppression. There was nothing unique or new about the black woman's willingness to accept the sexist-defined female role. The 60s black movement simply became a background in which their acceptance of sexism, or patriarchy, could be announced to the white public that was so convinced that black women were more likely to be assertive and domineering than white women.

Contrary to popular opinion, the sexual politics of the 50s socialized black women to conform to sexist-defined role patterns—not the black macho of the 70s. Black mothers of the 50s had taught their daughters that they should not be proud to work, that they should educate themselves in case they did not find that man who would be the most important force in their lives, who would provide for and protect them. With such a legacy it was not surprising that college-educated black women were embracing patriarchy. The 60s black movement simply exposed a support of sexism and patriarchy that already existed in the black community—it did not create it. Writing of the black woman's response to the 60s civil rights struggle, Michelle Wallace comments:

> The black woman never really dealt with the primary issues of the Black movement. She stopped straightening her hair. She stopped using lighteners and brighteners. She forced herself to be submissive and passive. She preached to her children about the glories of the black man. But then, suddenly, the Black movement was over. Now she has begun to straighten her hair again, to follow the latest fashions in *Vogue* and *Mademoiselle,* to rouge her cheeks furiously, and to speak, not infrequently, of what a disappointment the black man has been. She has little contact with other black women, and if she does, it is not of a deep sort. The discussion is generally of clothes, makeup, furniture, and men. Privately she does whatever she can to stay out of that surplus of black women (one million) who will never find mates. And if she doesn't find a man, she might just decide to have a baby anyway.

Now that an organized black civil rights movement no longer exists, black women do not find it necessary to place their willingness to assume a sexist-defined role in the context of black liberation; so it is much more obvious that their support of patriarchy was not engendered solely by their concern for the black race but by the fact that they live in a culture in which the majority of women support and accept patriarchy.

When the movement toward feminism began in the late 60s, black women rarely participated as a group. Since the dominant white patriarchy and black male patriarchy conveyed to black women the message that to cast a vote in favor of social equality of the sexes, i.e. women's liberation, was to cast a vote against black liberation, they were initially suspicious of the white woman's call for a feminist movement. Many black women refused to participate in the movement because they had no desire to fight against sexism. Theirs was not an unusual stance. The great majority of women in the U.S. did not participate in the women's movement for the same reason. White men were among the first observers of the women's movement to call attention to the absence of black women participants, but they did so solely to mock and ridicule the efforts of white feminists. They smugly questioned the credibility of a women's liberation movement that could not attract women from the most oppressed female groups in American society. They were among the first critics of feminism to raise the question of white female racism. In response, white women liberationists urged black and other non-white women to join their ranks. Those black women who were most vehemently anti-feminist were the most eager to respond. Their stance came to be depicted as *the* black female position on women's liberation. They expressed their views in essays like Ida Lewis' "Women's Rights, Why the Struggle Still Goes On," Linda LaRue's "Black Liberation and Women's Lib," "Women's Liberation Has No Soul," first published in *Encore* magazine, and Renee Fergueson's "Women's Liberation Has a Different Meaning for Blacks." Linda LaRue's comments on women's liberation were often quoted as if they were the definitive black female response to women's liberation:

> Let it be stated unequivocally that the American white women has had a better opportunity to live a free and fulfilling life, both mentally and physically,

than any other group in the United States, excluding her white husband. Thus any attempt to analogize black oppression with the plight of American white women has all the validity of comparing the neck of a hanging man with the rope-burned hands of an amateur mountain climber.

In their essays, black female anti-feminists revealed hatred and envy of white women. They expended their energy attacking white women liberationists, not by offering any convincing evidence that would support their claim that black women had no need of women's liberation. Black sociologist Joyce Ladner expressed her views on women's liberation in her study of black women, *Tomorrow's Tomorrow:*

> Many black women who have traditionally accepted the white models of femininity are now rejecting them for the same general reasons that we should reject the white middle-class lifestyle. Black women in this society are the only ethnic or radical group which has had the opportunity to be women. By this I simply mean that much of the current focus on being liberated from the constraints and protectiveness of the society which is proposed by women's liberation groups has never applied to Black women, and in that sense, we have always been "free," and able to develop as individuals even under the most harsh circumstances. This freedom, as well as the tremendous hardships from which black women suffered, allowed for the development of a personality that is rarely described in the scholarly journals for its obstinate strength and ability to survive. Neither is its peculiar humanistic character and quiet courage viewed as the epitome of what the American model of femininity should be.

Ladner's assertion that black women were "free" became one of the accepted explanations for black female refusal to participate in a women's liberation movement. But such an assertion merely reveals that black women who were most quick to dismiss women's liberation had not thought seriously about feminist struggle. For while white women may have seen feminism as a way to free themselves from the constraints imposed upon them by idealized concepts of femininity, black women could have seen feminism as a way to free themselves from constraints that sexism clearly imposed on their behavior. Only a very naive unenlightened person could confidently state that black

women in the U.S. are a liberated female group. The black women who patted themselves on the back for being "already liberated" were really acknowledging their acceptance of sexism and their contentment with patriarchy.

The concentrated focus on black anti-feminist thought was so pervasive that black women who supported feminism and participated in the effort to establish a feminist movement received little attention, if any. For every black anti-feminist article written and published, there existed a pro-feminist black female position. Essays like Cellestine Ware's "Black Feminism," Shirley Chisholm's "Women Must Rebel," Mary Ann Weather's "An Argument for Black Women's Liberation as a Revolutionary Force," and Pauli Murray's "The Liberation of Black Women" all expressed black female support of feminism.

As a group, black women were not opposed to social equality between the sexes but they were not eager to join with white women to organize a feminist movement. The 1972 Virginia Slims American Women's Opinion Poll showed that more black women supported changes in the status of women in society than white women. Yet their support of feminist issues did not lead them as a collective group to actively participate in the women's liberation movement. Two explanations are usually given for their lack of participation. The first is that the 60s black movement encouraged black women to assume a subservient role and caused them to reject feminism. The second is that black women were, as one white women liberationist put it, "repelled by the racial and class composition of the women's movement." Taken at face value, these reasons seem adequate. Examined in a historical context in which black women have rallied in support of women's rights despite pressure from black men to assume a subordinate position, and despite the fact that white middle and upper class women have dominated every women's movement in the U.S., they seem inadequate. While they do provide justification for the anti-feminist black female position, they do not explain why black women who support feminist ideology refuse to participate fully in the contemporary women's movement.

Initially, black feminists approached the women's movement white women had organized eager to join the struggle to end sexist oppression. We were disappointed and disillusioned when we discovered that white women in the movement had little knowledge of or concern for the problems of lower class and poor women or the particular problems of non-white women from all classes. Those of us who were active in women's groups found that white feminists lamented the absence of large numbers of non-white participants but were unwilling to change the movement's focus so that it would better address the needs of women from all classes and races. Some white women even argued that groups not represented by a numerical majority could not expect their concerns to be given attention. Such a position reinforced the black female participants' suspicion that white participants wanted the movement to concentrate not on the concerns of women as a collective group, but on the individual concerns of the small minority who had organized the movement.

Black feminists found that sisterhood for most white women did not mean surrendering allegiance to race, class, and sexual preference, to bond on the basis of the shared political belief that a feminist revolution was necessary so that all people, especially women, could reclaim their rightful citizenship in the world. From our peripheral position in the movement we saw that the potential radicalism of feminist ideology was being undermined by women who, while paying lip service to revolutionary goals, were primarily concerned with gaining entrance into the capitalist patriarchal power structure. Although white feminists denounced the white male, calling him an imperialist, capitalist, sexist, racist pig, they made women's liberation synonymous with women obtaining the right to fully participate in the very system they identified as oppressive. Their anger was not merely a response to sexist oppression. It was an expression of their jealousy and envy of white men who held positions of power in the system while they were denied access to those positions.

Individual black feminists despaired as we witnessed the appropriation of feminist ideology by elitist, racist white women. We were unable to usurp leadership positions within the movement so that we could spread an authentic message of feminist revolution. We could not even get a hearing at women's groups because they were organized and controlled by white women. Along with politically aware white women, we, black feminists, began to feel that no organized feminist struggle really existed. We dropped out of groups, weary of hearing talk about women as a force that could change the world when we had not changed ourselves. Some black women formed "black feminist"

groups which resembled in almost every way the groups they had left. Others struggled alone. Some of us continued to go to organizations, women's studies classes, or conferences, but were not fully participating.

For ten years now I have been an active feminist. I have been working to destroy the psychology of dominance that permeates Western culture and shapes female/male sex roles and I have advocated reconstruction of U.S. society based on human rather than material values. I have been a student in women's studies classes, a participant in feminist seminars, organizations, and various women's groups. Initially I believed that the women who were active in feminist activities were concerned about sexist oppression and its impact on women as a collective group. But I became disillusioned as I saw various groups of women appropriating feminism to serve their own opportunistic ends. Whether it was women university professors crying sexist oppression (rather than sexist discrimination) to attract attention to their efforts to gain promotion; or women using feminism to mask their sexist attitudes; or women writers superficially exploring feminist themes to advance their own careers, it was evident that eliminating sexist oppression was not the primary concern. While their rallying cry was sexist oppression, they showed little concern about the status of women as a collective group in our society. They were primarily interested in making feminism a forum for the expression of their own self-centered needs and desires. Not once did they entertain the possibility that their concerns might not represent the concerns of oppressed women.

Even as I witnessed the hypocrisy of feminists, I clung to the hope that increased participation of women from different races and classes in feminist activities would lead to a reevaluation of feminism, radical reconstruction of feminist ideology, and the launching of a new movement that would more adequately address the concerns of both women and men. I was not willing to see white women feminists as "enemies." Yet as I moved from one women's group to another trying to offer a different perspective, I met with hostility and resentment. White women liberationists saw feminism as "their" movement and resisted any efforts by non-white women to critique, challenge, or change its direction.

During this time, I was struck by the fact that the ideology of feminism, with its emphasis on transforming and changing the social structure of the U.S., in no way resembled the actual reality of American feminism. Largely because feminists themselves, as they attempted to take feminism beyond the realm of radical rhetoric into the sphere of American life, revealed that they remained imprisoned in the very structures they hoped to change. Consequently, the sisterhood we talked about has not become a reality. And the women's movement we envisioned would have a transformative effect on U.S. culture has not emerged. Instead, the hierarchical pattern of sex-race relationships already established by white capitalist patriarchy merely assumed a different form under feminism. Women liberationists did not invite a wholistic analysis of woman's status in society that would take into consideration the varied aspects of our experience. In their eagerness to promote the idea of sisterhood, they ignored the complexity of woman's experience. While claiming to liberate women from biological determinism, they denied women an existence outside that determined by our sexuality. It did not serve the interest of upper and middle class white feminists to discuss race and class. Consequently, much feminist literature, while providing meaningful information concerning women's experiences, is both racist and sexist in its content. I say this not to condemn or dismiss. Each time I read a feminist book that is racist and sexist, I feel a sadness and an anguish of spirit. For to know that there thrives in the very movement that has claimed to liberate women endless snares that bind us tighter and tighter to old oppressive ways is to witness the failure of yet another potentially radical, transformative movement in our society.

Although the contemporary feminist movement was initially motivated by the sincere desire of women to eliminate sexist oppression, it takes place within the framework of a larger, more powerful cultural system that encourages women and men to place the fulfillment of individual aspirations above their desire for collective change. Given this framework, it is not surprising that feminism has been undermined by the narcissism, greed, and individual opportunism of its leading exponents. A feminist ideology that mouths radical rhetoric about resistance and revolution while actively seeking to establish itself within the capitalist patriarchal system is essentially corrupt. While the contemporary feminist movement has successfully stimulated an awareness of the impact of sexist discrimination on the social status of women in the U.S., it has done little to eliminate sexist oppression. Teaching women how to

defend themselves against male rapists is not the same as working to change society so that men will not rape. Establishing houses for battered women does not change the psyches of the men who batter them, nor does it change the culture that promotes and condones their brutality. Attacking heterosexuality does little to strengthen the self-concept of the masses of women who desire to be with men. Denouncing housework as menial labor does not restore to the woman houseworker the pride and dignity in her labor she is stripped of by patriarchal devaluation. Demanding an end to institutionalized sexism does not ensure an end to sexist oppression.

The rhetoric of feminism with its emphasis on resistance, rebellion, and revolution created an illusion of militancy and radicalism that masked the fact that feminism was in no way a challenge or a threat to capitalist patriarchy. To perpetuate the notion that all men are creatures of privilege with access to a personal fulfillment and a personal liberation denied women, as feminists do, is to lend further credibility to the sexist mystique of male power that proclaims all that is male is inherently superior to that which is female. A feminism so rooted in envy, fear, and idealization of male power cannot expose the de-humanizing effect of sexism on men and women in American society. Today, feminism offers women not liberation but the right to act as surrogate men. It has not provided a blueprint for change that would lead to the elimination of sexist oppression or a transformation of our society. The women's movement has become a kind of ghetto or concentration camp for women who are seeking to attain the kind of power they feel men have. It provides a forum for the expression of their feelings of anger, jealousy, rage, and disappointment with men. It provides an atmosphere where women who have little in common, who may resent or even feel indifferent to one another, can bond on the basis of shared negative feelings toward men. Finally, it gives women of all races who desire to assume the imperialist, sexist, racist positions of destruction men hold with a platform that allows them to act as if the attainment of their personal aspirations and their lust for power is for the common good of all women.

Right now, women in the U.S. are witnessing the demise of yet another women's rights movement. The future of collective feminist struggle is bleak. The women who appropriated feminism to advance their own opportunistic causes have achieved their desired

BLACK WOMEN AS DO-ERS: THE SOCIAL RESPONSIBILITY OF BLACK WOMEN

JOYCE A. LADNER

When I think of social responsibility, I think of Bill and Camille Cosby, whose gift of $20 million to Spelman College is one of the most extraordinary examples of duty and commitment and faith and hope for Black women. When I think of the social responsibility of Black women, I think of the generations of our foremothers and forefathers who instilled within us the idea and value that it is our duty to help those in need. I think about the women who have gone before us who although poor, understood that the only way they could assure progress for the race would be through the dint of their own efforts. I think of Harriet Tubman who risked her life while helping other Blacks escape to freedom, because she understood the importance of duty. I think of Sojourner Truth who understood that it was she who had to take responsibility for interpreting the plaintive cries for freedom of enslaved Blacks. I think of Ida B. Wells Barnett, who took the responsibility to advocate against lynching. I think of Anna Julia Cooper who knew she had to take responsibility to educate Black youths. I think of Mary Church Terrell who understood the relationship between advocacy and race. I think of Mary McLeod Bethune who took up the mantle of responsibility to educate, to advocate, to lobby, to pester—because she knew that if she didn't, there would be few others who could.

When I think of social responsibility, I think of Zola Jackson, my first teacher in Hattiesburg, Mississippi, who believed every child has something to give, and that it is up to us to help them to develop. I think of Ruby Doris Robinson, a Spelman student who was one of the founders of the Student Nonviolent Coordinating Committee—who spent weeks in jail, who was a tireless organizer, strategist and leader within the civil rights movement. Ruby D., who walked this campus, sat in these classrooms, and left her indomitable courage and relentless efforts to bring equality to Blacks—here on this campus to be passed on to another generation. And

From *Sage*, vol. 6, Summer 1989. Copyright © 1989. Reprinted by permission of Sage Publications, Inc.

yes, I think of Fannie Lou Hamer, the short, stout woman from the Delta of Mississippi, who stands alone as the voice and spirit of grassroots social change in America. I think of Ella Jo Baker, the spirited civil rights activist who had the moral courage to try to change America. I think of Mother Hale, the Harlem woman who soothes the cries of babies born addicted to drugs; I think of the Black woman who operates "Grandma's House" in Washington, D.C., where Black babies born with AIDS are given a chance to grow and develop, to play and to be normal, for whatever period they live. Ruby Doris Robinson once sat here in Sisters Chapel, pondering the relationship between education and social responsibility. In a real sense, it was her model that women of my generation, women of Johnnetta Cole's generation, followed in defining ourselves, defining our sense of duty and obligation.

The women I have talked about inherited a noble tradition for being "do-ers"; that is, they were brought up to believe they could do anything. They were taught that they had to learn to be flexible, they had to learn to wash, cook, sew, get an education, raise children, work in their churches and clubs, establish orphanages, relief societies, become presidents of colleges, start colleges, and everything else that needed to be done.

Being a "do-er" was normal and expected. Being a "do-er" meant that you saw what had to be done, and you simply went out and tried to do it. No task was too small, no reward too minimal to do what had to be done. All around us the idea was hammered into our heads that social responsibility was a normal part of life—it was not something that was tucked off to the side as a special volunteer activity. It was part of the way you defined your identity, your sense of purpose, your values, your reason for being. Our religious upbringing reinforced this concept of obligation, this sense of helping the needy, giving something back to the community, or in the words of my mother, "earning your space in the world."

What does all of this mean today? How do we, how should we, define social responsibility? How do we get more women involved? How do we pass these values and this sense of duty on to the next generation, especially at a time when the tasks before us seem impossible?

Our communities are so fragmented, our families are under such stress and many poor families are suffering the effects of such acute crisis and devastation that it is easy to become discouraged—it is easy to think that there is nothing we can do to help people who have such tremendous need. Over the past twenty years Black families have experienced a record number of problems. Since 1960 we have seen the number of Black families become so fractured that today, 52 percent are headed by women. The majority of children in such families are living in poverty. Black infant mortality rates continue to increase, as the gap between Blacks and whites widens.

The school drop-out rate continues to increase. The numbers of homeless individuals and families (600,000 to 3 million) escalate by the day. Blacks now have a disproportionate number of the AIDS cases. Teenage pregnancy continues to be a huge problem with Black women becoming grandmothers as young as 24 years old. The rates of child abuse and neglect escalate, especially among drug addicted mothers and teenage mothers. Crime and violence have torn many communities apart, undermining stable neighborhoods where people are now afraid for their safety. And drugs have come to symbolize a modern day plague—a plague in its seriousness and its proportions. In Washington, D.C., drug-related violence has caused almost three-hundred deaths this year. Most of them involve young Black men in their late teens and early twenties—young Black men who are cut down in the prime of their lives—long before they have had the opportunity to become husbands, fathers, workers in productive jobs, and socially responsible citizens. More enter prison than enter college each year. A similar pattern has developed among young Black women, whose futures are just as dim, who see their prospects for a bright future with a college degree, a good career, a good marriage with children—as something that is absolutely impossible. They don't value life very much because they don't feel they will live very long.

What do we do? How do we intervene? How do we help these young people to get off their destructive courses? How do we help to restore a sense of normalcy to our communities so that elderly men and women can walk the streets safely? How do we keep children in school long enough to graduate? How do we stop children from having children? How do we inspire hope and trust, and a desire to achieve? Whose responsibility is it to do these things?

I do not pretend to have the answers to all these questions. I do know that if we fail to act, if we fail to try to find solutions to these problems, we will have failed the sense of mission and the sense of history that our foremothers charted for us. We will have failed to be this generation of "do-ers," a generation that is blessed with more wealth, more education, more skills than any before us. It is our obligation to become involved. It is our obligation to teach this sense of responsibility to solve problems to the young women who are now entering adulthood. It is our responsibility to use our social and civic clubs, our professional organizations, our churches, our workplaces—and everywhere else—to organize for change. Black women need to establish a National Corps of 'Do-ers', an army of concerned citizens who can reclaim our legacy and chart new courses in these seemingly impossible muddy waters.

There are no easy answers; there are no magical and quick-fix solutions to these extraordinary problems. One might ask, why do WE have to assume the responsibility to fix the problems of others? Why shouldn't the Federal government, or the people themselves, fix their own problems. *We* have to fix them because no one else is trying to do it. *We* have to fix them because we care. *We* have to help to fix them because they are also our problems. *We* have to be concerned about drugs and child care because these are problems that also affect middle class kids. *We* have to fix them because we have to insure that there will be a wholesome and healthy generation of young Black people to take over the reins after we have stepped aside. *We* have to fix them because, in my mother's words, *we* have to earn our space in this world.

Whether we are aerospace engineers, social workers, professors, day care providers, or homemakers, we have to take up the do-er mantle of our heritage of social responsibility, for there is no contradiction between being a good and competent professional and a "do-er."

The voice of Ruby Doris Robinson, my friend Ruby D., speaks softly, gently but firmly as she, like Meridian, the heroine of the Alice Walker novel, by the same name, guides us toward regeneration and renewal as we go forth in our challenging tasks—as we become the do-ers in the spirit of our foremothers.

ends and are no longer interested in feminism as a political ideology. Many women who remain active in women's rights groups and organizations stubbornly refuse to critique the distorted analysis of woman's lot in society popularized by women's liberation. Since these women are not oppressed they can support a feminist movement that is reformist, racist, and classist because they see no urgent need for radical change. Although women in the U.S. have come closer to obtaining social equality with men, the capitalist-patriarchal system is unchanged. It is still imperialist, racist, sexist, and oppressive.

The recent women's movement failed to adequately address the issue of sexist oppression, but that failure does not change the fact that it exists, that we are victimized by it to varying degrees, nor does it free any of us from assuming responsibility for change. Many black women are daily victimized by sexist oppression. More often than not we bear our pain in silence, patiently waiting for a change to come. But neither passive acceptance nor stoic endurance lead to change. Change occurs only when there is action, movement, revolution. The 19th century black female was a woman of action. Her suffering, the harshness of her lot in a racist, sexist world, and her concern for the plight of others motivated her to join feminist struggle. She did not allow the racism of white women's rights advocates or the sexism of black men to deter her from political involvement. She did not rely on any group to provide her with a blueprint for change. She was a maker of blueprints. In an address given before an audience of women in 1892 Anna Cooper proudly voiced the black woman's perspective on feminism:

Let woman's claim be as broad in the concrete as in the abstract. We take our stand on the solidarity of humanity, the oneness of life, and the unnaturalness and injustice of all special favoritism, whether of sex, race, country, or condition. If one link of the chain is broken, the chain is broken. A bridge is no stronger than its weakest part, and a cause is not worthier than its weakest element. Least of all can woman's cause afford to decry the weak. We want, then, as toilers for the universal triumph of justice and human rights, to go to our homes from this Congress demanding an entrance not through a gateway for ourselves, our race, our sex, or our sect, but a grand highway for humanity. The colored

woman feels that woman's cause is one and universal; and that not till the image of God whether in parian or ebony, is sacred and inviolable; not till race, color, sex, and condition are seen as accidents, and not the substance of life; not till the universal title of humanity to life, liberty, and the pursuit of happiness is conceded to be inalienable to all; not till then is woman's cause won—not the white woman's, nor the black woman's, nor the red woman's, but the cause of every man and of every woman who has writhed silently under a mighty wrong. Woman's wrongs are thus indissolubly linked with all undefended woe, and the acquirement of her "rights" will mean the final triumph of all right over might, the supremacy of the moral forces of reason, and justice, and love in the government of the nations of earth.

Cooper spoke for herself and thousands of other black women who had been born into slavery, who because they had been severely victimized, felt a compassion and a concern for the plight of all oppressed peoples. Had all women's rights advocates shared their sentiments, the feminist movement in the U.S. would be truly radical and transformative.

Feminism is an ideology in the making. According to the Oxford English Dictionary, the term "feminism" was first used in the latter part of the 19th century and it was defined as having the "qualities of females." The meaning of the term has been gradually transformed and the 20th century dictionary definition of feminism is a "theory of the political, economic, and social equality of the sexes." To many women this definition is inadequate. In the introduction to *The Remembered Gate: Origins of American Feminism* Barbara Berg defines feminism as a "broad movement embracing numerous phases of woman's emancipation." She further states:

It is the freedom to decide her own destiny; freedom from sex-determined role; freedom from society's oppressive restrictions; freedom to express her thoughts fully and to convert them freely to actions. Feminism demands the acceptance of woman's right to individual conscience and judgment. It postulates that woman's essential worth stems from her common humanity and does not depend on the other relationships of her life.

Her expanded definition of feminism is useful but limited. Many women have found that neither the struggle for "social equality" nor the focus on an "ideology of woman as an autonomous being" are enough to rid society of sexism and male domination. To me feminism is not simply a struggle to end male chauvinism or a movement to ensure that women will have equal rights with men; it is a commitment to eradicating the ideology of domination that permeates Western culture on various levels—sex, race, and class, to name a few—and a commitment to reorganizing U.S. society so that the self-development of people can take precedence over imperialism, economic expansion, and material desires. Writers of a feminist pamphlet published anonymously in 1976 urged women to develop political consciousness:

In all these struggles we must be assertive and challenging, combating the deep-seated tendency in Americans to be liberal, that is, to evade struggling over questions of principle for fear of creating tensions or becoming unpopular. Instead we must live by the fundamental dialectical principle: that progress comes only from struggling to resolve contradictions.

It is a contradiction that white females have structured a women's liberation movement that is racist and excludes many non-white women. However, the existence of that contradiction should not lead any woman to ignore feminist issues. Oftentimes I am asked by black women to explain why I would call myself a feminist and by using that term ally myself with a movement that is racist. I say, "The question we must ask again and again is how can racist women call themselves feminists." It is obvious that many women have appropriated feminism to serve their own ends, especially those white women who have been at the forefront of the movement; but rather than resigning myself to this appropriation I choose to re-appropriate the term "feminism," to focus on the fact that to be "feminist" in any authentic sense of the term is to want for all people, female and male, liberation from sexist role patterns, domination, and oppression.

Today masses of black women in the U.S. refuse to acknowledge that they have much to gain by feminist struggle. They fear feminism. They have stood in place so long that they are afraid to move. They fear change. They fear losing what little they have. They are afraid to openly confront white feminists with their racism or black males with their sexism, not to mention confronting white men with their racism and sexism. I have sat in many a kitchen and heard black women express a belief in feminism and eloquently critique the women's movement, explaining their refusal to participate. I have witnessed their refusal to express these same views in a public setting. I know their fear exists because they have seen us trampled upon, raped, abused, slaughtered, ridiculed and mocked. Only a few black women have rekindled the spirit of feminist struggle that stirred the hearts and minds of our 19th century sisters. We, black women who advocate feminist ideology, are pioneers. We are clearing a path for ourselves and our sisters. We hope that as they see us reach our goal—no longer victimized, no longer unrecognized, no longer afraid—they will take courage and follow.

REFERENCES

Berg, B. 1979. *The remembered gate: Origins of American feminism.* New York: Oxford University Press.

Chisholm, S. 1970. "Racism and anti-feminism." *The Black Scholar,* pp. 40–45.

Cooper, J. 1892. *A voice from the South.* Xenia, Ohio.

Ladner, J. 1972. *Tomorrow's tomorrow.* New York: Anchor Books.

Wallace, M. 1978. *Black macho and the myth of the super woman.* New York: Dial Press.

Ware, C. 1970. *Woman power.* New York: Tower.

En rapport, In Opposition:
Cobrando cuentas a las nuestras

GLORIA ANZALDÚA

WATCH FOR FALLING ROCKS

The first time I drove from El Paso to San Diego, I saw a sign that read *Watch for Falling Rocks*. And though I watched and waited for rocks to roll down the steep cliff walls and attack my car and me, I never saw any falling rocks. Today, one of the things I'm most afraid of are the rocks we throw at each other. And the resultant guilt we carry like a corpse strapped to our backs for having thrown rocks. We colored women have memories like elephants. The slightest hurt is recorded deep within. We do not forget the injury done to us and we do not forget the injury we have done another. For unfortunately we do not have hides like elephants. Our vulnerability is measured by our capacity for openness, intimacy. And we all know that our own kind is driven through shame or self-hatred to poke at all our open wounds. And we know they know exactly where the hidden wounds are.

> *I keep track of all distinctions. Between past and present. Pain and pleasure. Living and surviving. Resistance and capitulation. Will and circumstances. Between life and death. Yes. I am scrupulously accurate. I have become a keeper of accounts.*
>
> *Irena Klepfisz[1]*

From "En Rapport, In Opposition: Cobrando Cuentas a las Nuestras" by Gloria Anzaldúa, in *Making Face, Making Soul: Haciendo Caras* edited by Gloria Anzaldúa. Copyright © 1990. Reprinted by permission of aunt lute books.

One of the changes that I've seen since *This Bridge Called My Back* was published[2] is that we no longer allow white women to efface us or suppress us. Now we do it to each other. We have taken over the missionary's "let's civilize the savage role," fixating on the "wrongness" and moral or political inferiority of some of our sisters, insisting on a profound difference between oneself and the *Other*. We have been indoctrinated into adopting the old imperialist ways of conquering and dominating, adopting a way of confrontation based on differences while standing on the ground of ethnic superiority.

In the "dominant" phase of colonialism, European colonizers exercise direct control of the colonized, destroy the native legal and cultural systems, and negate non-European civilizations in order to ruthlessly exploit the resources of the subjugated with the excuse of attempting to "civilize" them. Before the end of this phase, the natives internalize Western culture. By the time we reach the "neocolonialist" phase, we've accepted the white colonizers' system of values, attitudes, morality, and modes of production.[3] It is not by chance that in the more rural towns of Texas Chicano neighborhoods are called *colonias* rather than *barrios*.

There have always been those of us who have "cooperated" with the colonizers. It's not that we have been "won" over by the dominant culture, but that it has exploited pre-existing power relations of subordination and subjugation within our native societies.[4] The great White ripoff and they are still cashing in. Like our exploiters who fixate on the inferiority of the natives, we fixate on the fucked-upness of our sisters. Like them we try to impose our version of "the ways things should be"; we try to impose one's self on the *Other* by making her the recipient of one's negative elements, usually the same elements that the Anglo projected on us. Like them, we project our self-hatred on her; we stereotype her; we make her generic.

JUST HOW ETHNIC ARE YOU?

One of the reasons for this hostility among us is the forced cultural penetration, the rape of the colored by the white, with the colonizers depositing their perspective, their language, their values in our bodies. External oppression is paralleled with our internalization of that oppression. And our acting out from that oppression. They have us doing to those within our own ranks what they have done and continue to do to us—*Othering* people. That is, isolating them, pushing them out of the herd, ostracizing them. The internalization of negative images of ourselves, our self-hatred, poor self-esteem, makes our own people the *Other*. We shun the white-looking Indian, the "high yellow" Black woman, the Asian with the white lover, the Native woman who brings her white girl friend to the Pow Wow, the Chicana who doesn't speak Spanish, the academic, the uneducated. Her difference makes her a person we can't trust. *Para que sea "legal,"* she must pass the ethnic legitimacy test we have devised. And it is exactly our internalized whiteness that desperately wants boundary lines (this part of me is Mexican, this Indian)

marked out and woe to any sister or any part of us that steps out of our assigned places, woe to anyone who doesn't measure up to our standards of ethnicity. *Si no cualifica,* if she fails to pass the test, *le aventamos mierda en la cara, le aventamos piedras, la aventamos.* We throw shit in her face, we throw rocks, we kick her out. *Como gallos de pelea nos atacamos unas a las otras— mexicanas de nacimiento contra* the born-again *mexicanas.* Like fighting cocks, razor blades strapped to our fingers, we slash out at each other. We have turned our anger against ourselves. And our anger is immense. *Es un acido que corroe.*

INTERNAL AFFAIRS
o las que niegan a su gente

> *Tu traición yo la llevo aquá muy dentro,*
> *la llevo dentro de mi alma*
> *dentro de mi corazón.*
> *Tu traicón.*
>
> Cornelio Reyna[5]

I get so tired of constantly struggling with my sisters. The more we have in common, including love, the greater the heartache between us, the more we hurt each other. It's excruciatingly painful, this constant snarling at our own shadows. Anything can set the conflict in motion: the lover getting more recognition by the community, the friend getting a job with higher sta-

---

SISTERSONG

GAY HADLEY

If we should turn against each other now
If we should turn
   to little wars of envy
   seizing castoffs
   cutting patterns from old cloths
   satisfied with remnants from the sun

If we should turn against each other now
If we should turn
   from our own stars
   our primal energy
   pale moonbeams vying
   for a sunken light
What will there be left for us if we should
   turn
Save one more endless, separated night?

Reprinted from Gay Hadley, "Sistersong," by permission of the author. Copyright © 1978 by Gay Hadley.

tus, a break-up. As one of my friends said, "We can't fucking get along."

So we find ourselves *entreguerras*,[6] a kind of civil war among intimates, an in-class, in-race, in-house fighting, a war with strategies, tactics that are our coping mechanisms, that once were our survival skills and which we now use upon one another,[7] producing intimate terrorism—a modern form of *las guerras floridas,* the war of flowers that the Aztecs practiced in order to gain captives for the sacrifices. Only now we are each other's victims, we offer the *Other* to our politically correct altar.

El deniego. The hate we once cast at our oppressors we now fling at women of our own race. Reactionary—we have gone to the other extreme—denial of our own. We struggle for power, compete, vie for control. Like kin, we are there for each other, but like kin we come to blows. And the differences between us and this new *Other* are not racial but ideological, not metaphysical but psychological. *Nos negamos a si mismas y el deniego nos causa daño.*

BREAKING OUT OF THE FRAME

> *I'm standing at the sea end of the truncated Berkeley pier. A boat had plowed into the black posts gouging out a few hundred feet of structure, cutting the pier in two. I stare at the sea, surging silver-plated, between me and the lopped-off corrugated arm, the wind whipping my hair. I look down, my head and shoulders, a shadow on the sea. Yemaya pours strings of light over my dull jade, flickering body, bubbles pop out of my ears. I feel the tension easing and, for the first time in months, the litany of work yet to do, of deadlines, that sings incessantly in my head, blows away with the wind.*
>
> > *Oh, Yemaya, I shall speak the words*
> > *you lap against the pier.*
>
> *But as I turn away I see in the distance a ship's fin fast approaching. I see fish heads lying listless in the sun, smell the stench of pollution in the waters.*

From where I stand, *queridas carnalas*—in a feminist position—I see, through a critical lens with variable focus, that we must not drain our energy breaking down the male/white frame (the whole of Western culture) but turn to our own kind and change our terms of reference. As long as we see the world and our experiences through white eyes—in a dominant/subordinate way—we're trapped in the tar and pitch of the old manipulative and strive-for-power ways.

Even those of us who don't want to buy in get sucked into the vortex of the dominant culture's fixed oppositions, the duality of superiority and inferiority, of subject and object. Some of us, to get out of the internalized neocolonial phase, make for the fringes, the Borderlands. And though we have not broken out of the white frame, we at least see it for what it is. Questioning the values of the dominant culture which imposes fundamental difference on those of the "wrong" side of the good/bad dichotomy is the first step. Responding to the *Other* not as irrevocably different is the second step. By highlighting similarities, downplaying divergences, that is, by *rapprochement* between self and *Other* it is possible to build a syncretic relationship. At the basis of such a relationship lies an understanding of the effects of colonization and its resultant pathologies.

We have our work cut out for us. Nothing is more difficult than identifying emotionally with a cultural alterity, with the *Other. Alter:* to make different; to castrate. *Altercate:* to dispute angrily. *Alter ego:* another self or another aspect of oneself. *Alter idem:* another of the same kind. Nothing is harder than identifying with an interracial identity, with a mestizo identity. One has to leave the permanent boundaries of a fixed self, literally "leave" oneself and see oneself through the eyes of the *Other.* Cultural identity is "nothing more nor less than the mean between selfhood and otherness. . . ."[8] Nothing scares the Chicana more than a quasi Chicana; nothing disturbs a Mexican more than an acculturated Chicana; nothing agitates a Chicana more than a Latina who lumps her with the *norteamericanas.* It is easier to retreat to the safety of difference behind racial, cultural and class borders. Because our awareness of the *Other* as object often swamps our awareness of ourselves as subject, it is hard to maintain a fine balance between cultural ethnicity and the continuing survival of that culture, between traditional culture and an evolving hybrid culture. How much must remain the same, how much must change.

For most of us our ethnicity is still the issue. Ours continues to be a struggle of identity—not against a white background so much as against a colored background. *Ya no estamos afuera o atras del marco de la pintura*—we no longer stand outside nor behind the frame of the painting. We are both the foreground, the background and the figures predominating. Whites are not the central figure, they are not even in the frame, though the frame of reference is still white, male and heterosexual. But the white is still there, invisible, under our skin—we have subsumed the white.

El desengaño / DISILLUSIONMENT

And yes I have some criticism, some self-criticism. And no I will not make everything nice. There is shit among us we need to sift through. Who knows, there may be some fertilizer in it. I've seen collaborative efforts between us end in verbal abuse, cruelty and trauma. I've seen collectives fall apart, dumping their ideals by the wayside and treating each other worse than they'd treat a rabid dog. My momma said, "Never tell other people our business, never divulge family secrets." Chicano dirt you do not air out in front of white folks, nor lesbian dirty laundry in front of heterosexuals. The cultural things stay with la Raza. Colored feminists must present a united front in front of white and other groups. But the fact is we are not united. (I've come to suspect that unity is another Anglo invention like their one sole god and the myth of the monopole.[9]) We are not going to cut through *la mierda* by sweeping the dirt under the rug.

We have a responsibility to each other, certain commitments. The leap into self-affirmation goes hand in hand with being critical of self. Many of us walk around with reactionary, self-righteous attitudes. We preach certain political behaviors and theories and we do fine with writing about them. Though we want others to live their lives by them, we do not live them. When we are called on it, we go into a self-defensive mode and denial just like whites did when we started asking them to be accountable for their race and class biases.

Las opuestas / THOSE IN OPPOSITION

In us, intra- and cross-cultural hostilities surface in not so subtle put-downs. *Las no comprometidas, las que negan a sus gente. Fruncemos las caras y negamos toda responsabilidad.* Where some of us racially mixed peo-

ple are stuck in now is denial and its damaging effects. Denial of the white aspects that we've been forced to acquire, denial of our sisters who for one reason or another cannot "pass" as 100% ethnic—as if such a thing exists. Racial purity, like language purity, is a fallacy. Denying the reality of who we are destroys the basis needed from which to talk honestly and deeply about the issues between us. We cannot make any real connections because we are not touching each other. So we sit facing each other and before the words escape our mouths the real issues are blanked in our consciousness, erased before they register because it hurts too much to talk about them, because it makes us vulnerable to the hurt the *carnala* may dish out, because we've been wounded too deeply and too often in the past. So we sit, a paper face before another paper face—two people who suddenly cease to be real. *La no compasiva con la complaciente, lo incomunicado atorado en sus gargantas.*

We, the new Inquisitors, swept along with the "swing to the right" of the growing religious and political intolerance, crusade against racial heretics, mow down with the sickle of righteous anger our dissenting sisters. The issue (in all aspects of life) has always been when to resist changes and when to be open to them. Right now, this rigidity will break us.

Recobrando / RECOVERING

Una luz fria y cenicienta bañada en la plata palida del amanecer entra a mi escritorio y I think about the critical stages we feminists of color are going through, chiefly that of learning to live with each other as carnalas, parientes, amantes, as kin, as friends, as lovers. Looking back on the road that we've walked on during the last decade, I see many emotional, psychological, spiritual, political gains—primarily developing an understanding and acceptance of the spirituality of our root ethnic cultures. This has given us the ground from which to see that our spiritual lives are not split from our daily acts. En recobrando our affinity with nature and her forces (deities), we have "recovered" our ancient identity, digging it out like dark clay, pressing it to our current identity, molding past and present, inner and outer. Our clay-streaked faces acquiring again images of our ethnic self and self-respect taken from us by the colonizadores. And if we've suffered losses, if often in the process we have momentarily "misplaced" our *car-*

*nala*hood, our sisterhood, there beside us always are the women, las mujeres. And that is enough to keep us going.

By grounding in the earth of our native spiritual identity, we can build up our personal and tribal identity. We can reach out for the clarity we need. Burning sage and sweetgrass by itself won't cut it, but it can be a basis from which we act.

And yes, we are elephants with long memories, but scrutinizing the past with binocular vision and training it on the juncture of past with present, and identifying the options on hand and mapping out future roads will ensure us survival.

So if we won't forget past grievances, let us forgive. Carrying the ghosts of past grievances *no vale la pena.* It is not worth the grief. It keeps us from ourselves and each other; it keeps us from new relationships. We need to cultivate other ways of coping. I'd like to think that the in-fighting that we presently find ourselves doing is only a stage in the continuum of our growth, an offshoot of the conflict that the process of biculturation spawns, a phase of the internal colonization process, one that will soon cease to hold sway over our lives. I'd like to see it as a skin we will shed as we are born into the 21st century.

And now in these times of the turning of the century, of harmonic conversion, of the end of *El Quinto Sol* (as the ancient Aztecs named our present age), it is time we began to get out of the state of opposition and into *rapprochment,* time to get our heads, words, ways out of white territory. It is time that we broke out of the invisible white frame and stood on the ground of our own ethnic being.

NOTES

1. Irena Klepfisz, *Keeper of Accounts* (Montpelier, VT: Sinister Wisdom, 1982), 85.

2. According to Chela Sandoval, the publication of *Bridge* marked the end of the second wave of the women's movement in its previous form. *U.S. Third World Feminist Criticism: The Theory and Method of Oppositional Consciousness,* a dissertation in process.

3. Abdul R. JanMohamed, "The Economy of Manichean Allegory: The Function of Racial Difference in Colonialist Literature," *"Race," Writing, and Difference,* ed. Henry Louis Gates, Jr. (Chicago: University of Chicago Press, 1985), 80–81.

4. JanMohamed, 81.

5. A Chicano from Texas who sings and plays *bajo-sexto* in his *música norteña/conjunto. "Tu Traición"* is from the album *15 Exitasos,* Reyna Records, 1981.

6. *Entreguerras, entremundos/Inner Wars Among the Worlds* is the title of a forthcoming book of narratives/novel.

7. Sarah Hoagland, "Lesbian Ethics: Intimacy & Self-Understanding," *Bay Area Women's News,* May/June 1987, vol. 1, no. 2, 7.

8. Nadine Gordimer is quoted in JanMohamed's essay, 88.

9. Physicists are searching for a single law of physics under which all other laws will fall.

Taking the Home *Out of* Homophobia

A dialogue between JEWELLE L. GOMEZ and BARBARA SMITH

Barbara: One of the challenges we face in trying to raise the issue of lesbian and gay identity within the Black community is to try to get our people to understand that they can indeed oppress someone after having spent a life of being oppressed. That's a very hard transition to make.

Jewelle: At this point, it seems almost impossible because the issue of sexism has become such a major stumbling block for the Black community. I think we saw the beginning of it in the 1970s with Ntozake Shange's play *For Colored Girls Who Have Considered Suicide When the Rainbow Is Enuf.* The play really prompted Black women to embrace the idea of independent thinking; to begin looking to each other for sustenance and to start appreciating and celebrating each other in ways that we've always done naturally. I think that the Black male community was so horrified to discover that they were not at the center of Black women's thoughts, that they could only perceive the play as a negative attack upon them. I think that, for the first time, that play made the Black community look at its sexism. And many people rejected Ntozake Shange and things having to do with feminism, in a very cruel way. So years later, when we got the Central Park incident with the white woman being beaten and raped by a group of young Black males, all people could talk about was the role racism played in the attack.

Barbara: There was an article in *The Village Voice* in which some Black women were asked what they thought about the Central Park rape, and most of them

"Taking the *Home* Out of *Homophobia*," by Jewelle L. Gomez and Barbara Smith, in *Out/Look,* Spring 1990. Reprinted by permission of the authors

came down very hard on sexual violence and sexism in the Black community. They indeed cited sexism as a cause of the rape. This incident is not a mysterious fluke. It is part and parcel of what African-American women face on the streets and in their homes every day. There was a Black woman standing in a supermarket line right here in New York City and they were talking about the rape. There was a Black man behind her and he was apparently wondering why they had to beat the white woman, why they had to do her like that. And then he said, "Why didn't they just rape her?" As if that would have been okay. So you see, we have a lot to contend with.

Jewelle: I think that the sexism continues to go unacknowledged and even praised as part of the Black community's survival technique. The subsequent acceptance of homophobia that falls naturally with that kind of thinking will be the thing that cripples the Black community. So I don't think we should be surprised about homophobia. It sneaks in, in a very subtle and destructive way, even though homosexuality has always been an intrinsic part of the Black community.

Barbara: Absolutely.

Jewelle: When I was growing up, everyone always knew who was gay. When the guys came to my father's bar, I knew which ones were gay, it was clear as day. For instance, there was Miss Kay, who was a big queen, and Maurice. These were people that everybody knew. They came and went in my father's bar just like everybody else. This was a so-called lower-class community—the working poor in Boston. It was a community in which people did not talk about who was gay, but I knew who the lesbians were. It was always unspoken and I think that there's something about leaving it unspoken that leaves us unprepared.

Barbara: That's the break point for this part of the 20th century as far as I'm concerned. There've been lesbian and gay men, Black ones, as long as there've been African people. So that's not even a question. You know how they say that the human race was supposed to have been started by a Black woman. Well, since she had so many children, some of them were undoubtedly queer. *(Laughter)* Writer Ann Allen Shockley has a wonderful line that I use often: "Play it, but don't say it." That's the sentiment that capsulizes the general stance of the Black community on sexual identity and orientation. If you're a lesbian, you can have as many women as you want. If you're a gay man, you can have all the men you want. But just don't say anything about it or make it political. The difference today is that the lesbian and gay movement prides itself on being out, verbalizing one's identity and organizing around our oppression. With the advent of this movement, the African-American community has really been confronted with some stuff that they've never had to deal with before.

Jewelle: I was thinking as you were saying that, that if one embraces the principles of liberation—gay liberation and feminism—then you have to assault the sexual stereotype that young Black girls have been forced to live out in the African-American community. The stereotype that mandates that you develop into the well-groomed girl who pursues a profession and a husband.

Barbara: High achiever.

Jewelle: Or the snappy baby machine. You tend to go one way or the other. You're either fast or you're well-groomed. I think that for so many young Black women, the idea of finding their place in society has been defined by having a man or a baby. So if you begin to espouse a proud lesbian growth, you find yourself going against the grain. That makes embracing your lesbianism doubly frightening, because you then have to discard the mythology that's been developed around what it means to be a young Black woman.

Barbara: And that you gotta have a man. The urgency of which probably can't even be conveyed on the printed page. *(Laughter)* I was just going to talk about when I was younger, people would want to know about me. Not so much about my sexual orientation, because they weren't even dealing with the fact that somebody could be a lesbian. But I always noticed they were more surprised to find out I didn't have children than that I wasn't married.

Jewelle: Right. They had no understanding at all that you could reach a certain age and not have any children.

Barbara: And not having children doesn't mean we're selfish. It means we're self-referenced. Many Black lesbians and gay men have children. Those of us who don't may not have had the opportunity. Or we may have made the conscious choice not to have children. One of the things about being a Black lesbian is that we're very conscious. At least those of us who are politicized about what we will and will not have in our lives. Coming out is such a conscious choice that the process manifests itself in other areas of our lives.

Jewelle: Yes, it's healthy. Having grown up with a lot of Black women who had children at an early age, I've noticed a contradictory element in that that's the way many of them come into their own. I have younger cousins who have two, three, four children and are not married and will probably never be married. It seems that the moment they have the baby is when they come into their own and their identity after that becomes the "long-suffering Black mother." I think it re-creates a cycle of victimization because a lot of these young women carry the burden of being on a road that wasn't really a conscious choice. On the other hand, when I look at Black lesbian mothers, I see that yes, many of them are struggling with their children. But there is also a sense of real choice because they've made a conscious decision to be out and have children. They are not long-suffering victims. They are not women who have been abandoned by their men. They are lesbian mothers who have made a place in the world that is not a victim's place. Now that doesn't necessarily mean that things are any easier or simpler for them. But there is a psychological difference because most Black lesbian mothers have made a choice and have a community they can look to for support.

Barbara: I think that conscious lesbianism lived in the context of community is a positive thing. It can be a really affirming choice for women. The connection to sexism is deep, though. Homophobia is a logical extension of sexual oppression because sexual oppression is about roles—one gender does this, the other does that. One's on top, the other is on the bottom.

Jewelle: I didn't really come out through the women's movement. For me, my sexuality didn't have a political context until later. I always had a sexual identity that I tried to sift out, but I was most concerned about how I was going to fit it in with being a Black Catholic, which was very difficult. Once I realized that one of them had to go—sexuality or Catholicism—it took me about five or ten minutes to drop Catholicism. *(Laughter)* Then I focused on racism, to the exclusion of homophobia and everything else. That left me unprepared. I had a woman lover very early. Then I slept with men until my mid-20s. They were kind of like the entertainment until I found another girlfriend and got my bearings. I didn't have the political context to deal with what it meant to want to sleep with both men and women. I skipped past the feminism until much later. So homophobia came as a total shock to me because I had never experienced it. Nobody seemed to be homophobic in my community, because no one ever talked about it. I hadn't experienced it because I wasn't out. I didn't know that I wasn't out. But I wasn't.

Barbara: Because you weren't out, you weren't really experiencing homophobia consciously.

Jewelle: Right. I thought it was an aberration. I didn't quite understand what it meant. But looking for an apartment in Jersey City with my then lover, who was Black, we'd be dealing with people who had two-family homes and were looking to rent one of the units. I remember we called this one place, and I was in stark terror. In my mind, I was thinking about a white couple looking at us and seeing two Black people that they were going to potentially bring into their home. It terrified me because I could see them insulting us or even possibly slamming the door in our face. And then just as we were about to get out of the car, it occurred to me that this white couple would also look at us and see two lesbians. *(Laughter)* I was literally shaking. I had been so focused on them seeing two Black women, that it hadn't occurred to me that they would also see two lesbians. They'd see the quintessential butch-femme couple, both of us going into our 40s.

Barbara: Yes. Well beyond the college roommate stage.

Jewelle: It terrified me. But as it turns out, they would have rented to us if we had decided to take the place, which we didn't. But the anxiety I suffered during those minutes before we rang the doorbell was devastating and definitely scarred me internally.

Barbara: Of course. It's deep. This is one of the permutations of how homophobia and heterosexism overshadow our lives. One of the things that I'm very happy about now is that I live in Albany, New York. And they did allow me to buy a house there. I don't know how many Chase Manhattans I would have had to rob down here in New York City in order to get enough money to buy a house. *(Laughter)* My house is in the heart of Albany's Black community. And one of the really nice things about it is that I know that nobody can put me out of my house because of what I have on my walls, who I bring in there, or whatever. That's very refreshing. Of course, it's the first time I've ever felt that way. What I'd always done before, because of homophobia and racism, was to be pretty low-key wherever I lived. I just felt that around my house, I had to try to be very cautious, even though I'm known to be a very out lesbian, both politically and in print. I didn't want anybody following me into my house who thought that bulldaggers shouldn't be allowed to live. Because I own my house in Albany, I feel less threatened. I feel like I have more safety and control over my life.

This is very important for all people, especially Black people in this country, to understand: We pay a heavy toll for being who we are and living with integrity. Being out means you are doing what your grandmother told you to do, which is not to lie. Black lesbians and gays who are out are not lying. But we pay high prices for our integrity. People really need to understand that there is entrenched violence against lesbians and gay men that is much like and parallel to the racial violence that has characterized Black people's lives since we've been in this country. When we then say that we are concerned about fighting homophobia and heterosexism, and changing attitudes, we're not talking about people being pleasant to us.

Jewelle: Right. My lover and I went camping in New Mexico recently. One day we camped on the Rio Grande in a fairly isolated area. We put up our tent and went away for a while. When we returned, there were these guys fishing nearby and it made us really nervous. In fact, we had a long, serious discussion about our mutual terror of being a lesbian couple in an isolated area with these men nearby. I was especially conscious of us being an interracial couple and how much that might enrage some people.

Barbara: Oh yes, absolutely. Speaking from experi-

THE BRIDGE POEM

KATE RUSHIN

I've had enough
I'm sick of seeing and touching
Both sides of things
Sick of being the damn bridge for everybody

Nobody
Can talk to anybody
Without me
Right?

I explain my mother to my father my father to my
    little sister
My little sister to my brother my brother to the white
    feminists
The white feminists to the Black church folks the
    Black church folks
To the ex-hippies the ex-hippies to the Black
    separatists the
Black separatists to the artists the artists to my
    friends' parents . . .

Then
I've got to explain myself
To everybody

I do more translating
Than the Gawdamn U.N.

Forget it
I'm sick of it

I'm sick of filling in your gaps

Sick of being your insurance against
The isolation of your self-imposed limitations

"The Bridge Poem" by Kate Rushin, in *This Bridge Called
My Back: Writings by Radical Women of Color* edited by
Cherríe Moraga and Gloria Anzaldúa. Copyright © 1983
by Kate Rushin. Reprinted by permission of the author
and Kitchen Table: Women of Color Press, P. O. Box 908,
Latham, N.Y. 12110.

Sick of being the crazy at your holiday dinners
Sick of being the odd one at your Sunday Brunches
Sick of being the sole Black friend to 34 individual
    white people

Find another connection to the rest of the world
Find something else to make you legitimate
Find some other way to be political and hip

I will not be the bridge to your womanhood
Your manhood
Your human-ness

I'm sick of reminding you not to
Close off too tight for too long

I'm sick of mediating with your worst self
On behalf of your better selves

I am sick
Of having to remind you
To breathe
Before you suffocate
Your own fool self

Forget it
Stretch or drown
Evolve or die

The bridge I must be
Is the bridge to my own power
I must translate

My own fears
Mediate
My own weaknesses

I must be the bridge to nowhere
But my true self
And then
I will be useful

ence, I think it's easier for two Black women who are lovers to be together publicly than it is for a mixed couple. To me, that's a dead giveaway because this is such a completely segregated society. Whenever I had a lover of a different race, I felt that it was like having a sign or a billboard over my head that said—"These are dykes. Right here." Because you don't usually see people of different races together in this country, it was almost by definition telling the world that we were lesbians. I think the same is true for interracial gay male couples. So, you see, the terror you were feeling was based on fact. Just recently a lesbian was murdered while she and her lover were on the Appalachian Trail in Pennsylvania [see the boxed insert, "Letter from Claudia Brenner," on page 426]. This is what colors and affects our lives in addition to Howard Beach and Bernhard Goetz.

Jewelle: The guy who murdered the lesbian on the Appalachian Trail claimed his defense was that he had been enraged by seeing their blatant lesbianism. He believed he had a right to shoot them because he had been disturbed by their behavior.

Barbara: What is that defense called? The homophobic panic?

Jewelle: To me, it's equivalent to [Dan White's use of] the Twinkie defense [to rationalize his murder of Harvey Milk and George Moscone].

Barbara: Yes. There's a term of defense they try to trot out that suggests that the mere existence of gay people is so enraging to some that they are then justified in committing homicide.

Jewelle: It's sort of like saying that because you are scared of the color black you are justified in running over Black people in Howard Beach.

Barbara: Right. We as a race of people would generally find that kind of thinking ludicrous. Yet there are Black people who would say that those murdered lesbians got what they deserved. I think that some Black men abhor Black lesbians because we are, by definition, women they are never going to control. I think something snaps in their psyche when they realize that Black lesbians are saying, "No way. I'm with women and that's that." But the real question is: Why should they be bothered? There are plenty of heterosexual Black women.

Jewelle: I think it's a psychological thing. Black women are perceived as property and they are the means by which Black men define themselves. It's another way they are like white men. They use female flesh to define themselves. They try to consume us to prove themselves as men because they're afraid to look inside of themselves. The final note about our terror in New Mexico was that it was both a positive and negative thing. It was positive because we refused to give up ground. We decided to stay where we were because we liked the spot. Of course, it meant that I slept with a large rock in my hands and she with her knife open. But I'll tell you, I slept very well and she did too.

Barbara: I'm glad you said that about not giving up ground because as out Black lesbians we have to live and do live with an incredible amount of courage. I attended a conference several years ago for women organizing around poverty and economic issues in the deep South. The Black women who came to the conference were wonderful and they treated me gloriously. As usual, I was out as a lesbian at this conference. Homophobia was the one issue they had not considered as a barrier to women's leadership. Funny thing, they skipped that. *(Laughter)* But there was a little quorum of white and Black lesbians and we raised the issue. We got up on the stage and read a statement about homophobia. Then we invited other lesbians and people in solidarity with us, to stand up. Almost everybody in the room stood up. Later we were talking about the incident in our small groups and a woman said something I'll never forget. She said that what we'd done had taken a lot of courage. And I have never forgotten those words because they came from a woman who was in a position to know the meaning of courage. She knew what it meant because she had been hounded by crazy white people all her life. For her to recognize our being out as courage meant a lot to me.

Jewelle: That's a very important point. I think that for those of us in Manhattan, Brooklyn, Albany, we have a certain leeway in being out. We have a diverse women's community that supports us in our efforts to be honest about being lesbians. I find it sad that there is a larger proportion of Black lesbians in small rural communities who won't and can't come out because they don't have this support. I think they suffer an isolation and even a kind of perversion of their own desires. That's one of the things that Ann Allen Shockley writes about so well—the Black lesbian who is isolated and psychically destroyed because she doesn't have a positive reflection of herself. These are the stories that aren't often told. Such Black lesbians don't get many opportunities to share what is going on for them.

Barbara: Yes. Class is a factor, too.

Jewelle: Certainly. Your whole view about what it means to be lesbian is colored by whether you were able to get an education—to read different things about the experience.

Barbara: Another point I want to make is that the people who are not out and have the privilege of good education and jobs need to be more accountable. It really bothers me that there are closeted people who are perceived as leaders within the Black community. This is something I find very annoying, because I think they are skating. We also need to discuss some of the young Black men who are so prominent today in the Hollywood movie and television industry. People like Arsenio Hall, Eddie Murphy, etc. I think they are homophobic to their hearts.

Jewelle: And sexist. I think it's telling that Spike Lee, the most popular Black filmmaker in the country today, includes the rape of a Black woman in his films. Sexism is so pervasive in our community that we don't even think of this as awful. Imagine what it feels like to sit in a movie theater watching his film *School Daze,* in which a Black woman is raped. The so-called Black brothers in the movie are saying, "Yeah, bone her. Bone her." And the Black women in the audience are giggling.

Barbara: They were probably giggling because they knew they had to go back home with those kinds of guys. This gets back to the Central Park rape that obsessed and terrorized me so much. The question I was raising at that time is: Do men understand that they can kill a woman by raping her? Do they understand that rape is torture and terror for us?

Jewelle: I think that as Black lesbians, in some ways, we are very fortunate. This is because we are in a community that supports us in growing past racism, sexism, and homophobia. But as you've said, our heterosexual sisters have to go home with these guys.

Barbara: We have to acknowledge that there are heterosexual Black females who are not putting up with

that stuff. There are definitely Black heterosexual feminists who are saying—"No way. I'm not taking that kind of abuse, negation, or suppression." But that means that most of those women are without mates. From what I can see, many Black heterosexual women who stand up for their rights go without long-term partners. And my impression is that there used to be more cooperation between Black men and Black women. Back when lynching was a daily American pastime and the crazed white man was our common enemy, we were not as inclined to lash out against each other as we are today. For instance, there was an article recently in *Publishers Weekly* about Black writers. The thrust of the piece was that Black male writers are suffering because Black women writers are getting lots of attention. This kind of thinking is based on the scarcity model that says there is only so much approval for Black writers within the mainstream white publishing industry. And that may be true. But there should be infinite approval within a Black context. Everybody who wants to write should write so we can all keep moving up a little higher.

Jewelle: I'd like to close by saying that homophobia is particularly dangerous for Black lesbians because it is so insidious. There have always been acceptable places for gay Black men to retreat and escape from danger—look at the choir queen or those who embrace the white gay male community. But as Black gay women, we haven't been interested in removing ourselves from our families or communities because we understand the importance of that connection. The insidiousness of the homophobia lies in the fact that we've been forced to find ways to balance our contact with the community with our need to continue to grow as Black lesbians. We straddle the fence that says we cannot be the uplifters of the race and lesbians at the same time—that's what makes it so dangerous for our emotional health as Black lesbians. But you know, I think that our ability to see the need to keep the family intact is what is going to be our savior and help preserve the Black community. As lesbians, we have so much to teach the Black community about survival.

Barbara: I'm very glad that you said that about family. One of the myths that's put out about Black lesbians and gay men is that we go into the white gay community and forsake our racial roots. People say that to be lesbian or gay is to be somehow racially denatured. I have real problems with that because that's never been where I was coming from. And that's not the place that the Black lesbians and gays I love, respect, and work with are coming from either. We are as Black as anybody ever thought about being. Just because we are committed to passionate and ongoing relationships with members of our own gender does not mean that we are not Black. In fact, the cultural and political leadership of the Black community has always had a very high percentage of lesbian and gay men. Although

closeted in many cases, Black lesbians and gays have been central in building our freedom.

Jewelle: Yes. It's very important that all our voices be heard. Everyone asks: Why do we have to talk about homophobia? Why can't we be quiet about it? The fact that we have to talk about it means that a lot of people don't want to hear it. And as soon as there's something they don't want to hear, it's very important that we say it. I learned that as a Black person.

R E A D I N G 5 2

Postindustrial Conditions and Postfeminist Consciousness in the Silicon Valley

JUDITH STACEY

When I moved here, there were orchards all around, and now there are integrated-circuit manufacturing plants all around. . . . That's been the thrill, because I've been part of it, and it's the most exciting time in the history of the world, I think. And the center of it is here in Silicon Valley.

> *Female engineer at Hewlett-Packard, quoted in* San Jose Mercury News, *February 19, 1985*

During the past three decades profound changes in the organization of family, work, and gender have occurred in the United States, coincident with the rise of second wave feminism.* Feminist scholars have

*By "second wave" feminism I refer to the resurgence of feminist politics and ideology that began in the mid-1960s, peaked in the early 1970s, and has been a major focus of social and political backlash since the late 1970s.

demonstrated that an important relationship exists between the development of the earlier feminist movement and that of capitalist industrialization in the West. In the United States, for example, the disintegration of the agrarian family economy and the reorganization of family, work, and gender relationships that took place during the nineteenth century provided the major impetus for the birth of American feminism.[1] Although the more recent history of feminism and social change is equally intimate, it has received far less attention.

This essay explores a number of connections between the recent transition to an emergent "postindustrial" stage of capitalist development and the simultaneous rise and decline of a militant and radical phase of feminism in the US.[2] First I reflect on an ironic role second-wave feminism has played as an unwitting midwife to the massive social transformations of work and family life that have occurred in the post-World War II

Reprinted from *Socialist Review,* vol. 17 (Nov./Dec. 1987).

era. Secondly I draw from my field research on family life in California's "Silicon Valley"—a veritable postindustrial hothouse—to illustrate some of the effects of this ironic collaboration in fostering emergent forms of "postfeminist" consciousness.

Let me begin, however, by explaining my use of the troubling term "postfeminist," a concept offensive to many feminists who believe that the media coined it simply "to give sexism a subtler name."[3] Whatever the media's motives, I find the concept useful in describing the gender consciousness and the family and work strategies of many contemporary women. I view the term postfeminist as analogous to "postrevolutionary" and use it not to indicate the death of the women's movement, but to describe the simultaneous incorporation, revision, and depoliticization of many of the central goals of second wave feminism.[4] I believe postfeminism is distinct from antifeminism and sexism, for it aptly describes the consciousness and strategies increasing numbers of women have developed in response to the new difficulties and opportunities of postindustrial society. In this sense the diffusion of postfeminist consciousness signifies both the achievements of, and challenges for, modern feminist politics.

FEMINISM AS MIDWIFE TO POSTINDUSTRIAL SOCIETY

Hindsight allows us to see how feminist ideology helped legitimate the massive structural changes in American work and family that invisibly accompanied the transition to postindustrial society in the 1960s and early 1970s.[5] I believe this period of postindustrialization should be read as the unmaking of a gender order rooted in the modern nuclear family system, the family of male breadwinner, female homemaker and dependent children that was grounded in the male family wage and stable marriage, at least for the majority of white working class and middle class families. Family and work relations in the emergent postindustrial order, by contrast, have been transformed by the staggering escalation of divorce rates and women's participation in paid work. As the US changed from having an industrial to a "service" dominated occupational structure,[6] unprecedented percentages of women entered the labor force and the halls of academe, while unprecedented percentages of marriages entered the divorce courts.[7] Unstable, and often incompatible, work

and family conditions have become the postindustrial norm as working class occupations become increasingly "feminized."

This process generated an extreme disjuncture between the dominant cultural ideology of domesticity, an ideology that became particularly strident in the 1950s, and the simultaneous decline in the significance placed on marriage and motherhood and the rise of women's employment.

The gap between the ideology of domesticity and the increasingly nondomestic character of women's lives helped generate feminist consciousness in the 1960s. As that consciousness developed, women launched an assault on traditional domesticity, an assault, that is, on a declining institution and culture.[*] Therefore this feminist movement was backward looking in its critique, and unwittingly forward looking (but not to the future of our fantasies) in its effects.

Feminism developed a devastating critique of the stultifying, infantilizing, and exploitative effects of female domesticity on women, especially of the sort available to classes that could afford an economically dependent housewife. Although the institutions of domesticity and its male beneficiaries were the intended targets of our critique, most housewives felt themselves on the defensive. Feminist criticism helped undermine and delegitimize the flagging but still celebrated nuclear family and helped promote the newly normative double-income (with shifting personnel) middle- and working-class families. We also provided ideological support for the sharp rise of single mother families generated by the soaring divorce rates.[8] Today fewer than 10 percent of families in the US consist of a male breadwinner, a female housewife, and their dependent children.[9]

Millions of women have derived enormous, tangible benefits from these changes in occupational patterns and family life and from the ways in which feminist ideology encouraged women to initiate and cope with these changes. Yet it is also true that since the mid-1970s, when the contours of the new postindustrial society began to be clear, economic and personal life has worsened for many groups of women, perhaps for the majority. The emerging shape of postindustrial society seems to have the following, rather disturbing

---

[*] Betty Friedan's *The Feminine Mystique* was one of the earliest, most successful polemical examples of this assault.

characteristics: As unionized occupations and real wages decline throughout the economy, women are becoming the postindustrial "proletariat," performing the majority of "working-class," low-skilled, low-paying jobs.[10] Because the overall percentage of jobs that are secure and well-paying has declined rapidly, increasing numbers of men are unemployed or under-employed. Yet the majority of white, male workers still labors at jobs that are highly skilled and comparatively well-paid.[11] Family instability is endemic with devastating economic effects on many women, as the "feminization of poverty" literature has made clear.[12] Increasing percentages of women are rearing children by themselves, generally with minimal economic contributions from former husbands and fathers.[13] Yet rising numbers of those single mothers who work full time, year-round do not earn wages sufficient to lift their families above the official poverty line.[14]

In the emerging class structure, marriage is becoming a major axis of stratification because it structures access to a second income. The married female as "secondary" wage-earner lifts a former working-class or middle-class family into comparative affluence, while the loss or lack of access to a male income can force women and their children into poverty.[15] In short, the drastic increase in female employment during the past several decades has meant lots more work for mother, but with very unevenly distributed economic benefits and only a slight improvement in relative income differentials between women and men.[16]

This massive rise in female employment also produces a scarcely visible, but portentous social effect through the drastic decline in the potential pool of female volunteers, typically from the middle class, who have sustained much of family and community life in the United States since the nineteenth century. The result of this decline may be a general deterioration of domesticity and social housekeeping that, in turn, is fueling reactionary nostalgia for traditional family life among leftists and feminists as well as among right wing forces.[17]

In light of these developments, many women (and men) have been susceptible to the appeals of the antifeminist backlash, and especially to profamily ideologies. Because of its powerful and highly visible critique of traditional domesticity, and because of the sensationalized way the media disseminated this critique, feminism has taken most of the heat for family

and social crises that have attended the transition from an industrial to a postindustrial order in the US. Despite efforts by feminists like Barbara Ehrenreich to portray men as the real family deserters, many continue to blame feminism for general decline of domesticity and nurturance within families and communities.[18] Feminism serves as a symbolic lightning rod for the widespread nostalgia and longing for "lost" intimacy and security that presently pervades social and political culture in the United States.[19] Not by accident do 1950s fashions and symbols dominate popular culture in the 1980s.

It is in this context, I believe, that we can best understand why during the late 1970s and the 1980s, even many feminists began to retreat from the radical critique of conventional family life of the early second wave.[20] The past decade, during which postindustrial social patterns became firmly established, has been marked instead by the emergence of various forms of postfeminist consciousness and family strategies.

FAMILY AND WORK IN THE SILICON VALLEY

Material from my current study of family and work experience in California's "Silicon Valley" highlights a number of features of postindustrial society and several of the diverse postfeminist strategies that contemporary women have devised to cope with them. After briefly describing the major postindustrial contours of the region, I will draw from my fieldwork to illustrate some of these strategies.

As the birthplace and international headquarters of the electronics industry, the "Silicon Valley"—Santa Clara County, California—is popularly perceived as representing the vanguard of postindustrialism. Until the early 1950s the region was a sparsely populated agricultural area, one of the major fruit baskets in the United States. But in the three decades since the electronics industry developed there, its population has grown by 350 percent and its economy, ecology, and social structure have been dramatically transformed.[21]

During this period, electronics, the vanguard postindustrial industry, feminized (and "minoritized") its production work force. In the 1950s and 1960s, when the industry was young, most of its production workers were men, for whom there were significant opportunities for advancement into technical and, at times, engi-

ECOFEMINISM: ANIMA, ANIMUS, ANIMAL

CAROL J. ADAMS

Feminists, building on women's experiences, have emphasized such values as connectedness, responsibility, attentive love, an embodied ethic incorporating body-mediated knowledge. If we were to touch, hear, and see animals whom we eat, wear, or otherwise use, we might replace current exploitation with a respectful relationship.

Notions of human nature exaggerate differences and minimize similarities between the other animals and ourselves. We talk about animals as if we were not animals ourselves. This permits humans in the United States alone to imprison almost six billion animals in intensive farming systems that violate the animals' basic physical and behavioral needs; to tolerate the killing of as many as three animals a second in laboratories; to purchase fur garments that require the suffering and death of at least 70 million animals each year; to hunt and kill 200 million animals annually for "sport"; and to exhibit millions of animals in circuses, rodeos, and zoos, where they endure boredom, mistreatment, lack of privacy, and deprivation of their natural environment.

Parallels between women's experiences and those of other animals have been made repeatedly in feminist literature and theory. Animals are meat, experimental guinea pigs, and objectified bodies; women are treated like meat, guinea pigs, and objectified bodies. We see pornographic pictures of "beaver hunters" who "bag" a woman, or of women put through meat grinders. Batterers have forced their victims to watch the killing of a favorite animal. Sexually abused children are sometimes threatened with a pet's death to ensure their compliance. "Why Can't This Veal Calf Walk?" by performance artist Karen Finley is a poem about rape and incest. (Well, why can't she or he walk? Kept in small crates, "veal" calves are unable to turn around, since exercise would increase muscle development, toughen the flesh, and slow weight gain. Standing on slatted floors causes a constant strain. Diarrhea, resulting from an improper diet that fosters anemia to produce pale flesh, causes the slats to become slippery; the calves often fall, getting leg injuries. When taken to be slaughtered, many can hardly walk.)

Raised in enclosed, darkened, or dimly lit buildings, other intensively farmed animals fare as poorly, their lives characterized by little extraneous stimuli, restricted movement, no freedom to choose social interactions, intense and unpleasant fumes, and ingestion of subtherapeutic doses of antibiotics (50 percent of the antibiotics in the U.S. go to livestock). Hens are kept as many as five to a cage with dimensions only slightly larger than this magazine. When being cooked in an oven, the chicken has four times more space than when she was alive.

Many feminists have noted that women's oppression and animal exploitation are interrelated. Rosemary Ruether has established a connection between the domestication of animals, the development of urban centers, the creation of slavery, and the inequality of the sexes. Some anthropologists correlate male domination with hunting economies. One ecofeminist, Sally Abbott, speculates that patriarchal religion resulted from the guilt of consuming animals. Another, Elizabeth Fisher, proposes that the breeding of animals suggested ways to control women's reproductivity. Gena Corea shows how embryo transfer was applied to women after being developed in the cattle industry. Andrée Collard and others argue that the beast slain in hero mythologies represents the once powerful goddess.

Feminist philosophers have exposed the methodology of science as arising from and valorizing human male (usually white, heterosexual, and upperclass) experience. They say that how science defines or selects research problems, how it defines *why* these are problems, how it designs experiments, constructs and confers meaning—all aspects of science also used to defend animal experimentation—are sexist, racist, homophobic, and classist. Animal rights adds speciesism to this analysis.

From *Ms.* Magazine 1, no. 6 (May–June 1991):62–63.

Yet for many, feminism and animal rights are antithetical, partly because of approaches adopted by the animal rights movement. Who isn't offended by a poster of a woman that declares, "It takes up to 40 dumb animals to make a fur coat. But only one to wear it"? Why have farm animals—who represent at least 90 percent of the exploited animals—not been the focus of animal activism, rather than such women-identified consumer objects as cosmetics and furs? No law requires the testing of cosmetics on animals, and so, like fur, cosmetics are equated with vanity, and are seen as more expendable than animal foods. Furthermore, women are seen as more caring about animals. The animal rights movement seems to sense that women will identify with the exploited animal because of our own exploitation.

Some feminists fear that animal rights would set a precedent for the rights of fetuses. Ironically, antiabortionists agree, assailing activists for caring about animals but not fetuses. But it is disingenuous to compare a fetus with a living, breathing animal. A fetus has potential interests; an animal has actual interests. Speciesism is perhaps nowhere more pronounced than in the protestation about the fate of the human conceptus, while the sentience of other animals is declared morally irrelevant because they are not human. Some antiabortionists define meaningful life so broadly as to encompass a newly fertilized egg, yet so narrowly that fully grown animals with well-developed nervous systems and social sensibilities are excluded. Extending the feminist understanding of reproductive freedom, we see that both women and other female animals experience enforced pregnancies.

Animal rights is charged with being antihuman. (This is reminiscent of "antimen" charges against feminists.) It is convenient to divide the issue of animal rights from human rights issues, to complain that we are concerned about animals when humans are starving. But this division is perpetuated out of ignorance; animal agriculture greatly *contributes* to the devastation of the environment and to inequity in food distribution. Frances Moore Lappé describes how half of all water consumed in the United States, much of it from unrenewable resources, is used for crops fed to livestock. More than 50 percent of water pollution is due to wastes from the livestock industry (including manure, eroded soil, and synthetic pesticides and fertilizers). "Meat" production also places demands on energy sources: the 500 calories of food energy from one pound of cooked "steak" requires 20,000 calories of fossil fuel. Some environmentalists argue that 40 percent of our imported oil requirements would be cut if we switched to a vegetarian diet (because of the energy used in growing food for animals, keeping them alive, killing them, and processing their bodies). Livestock are responsible for 85 percent of topsoil erosion, and methane gas, much of it being emitted by cows being raised to be our food, accounts for at least 20 percent of the human contribution to the greenhouse effect.

Actually, animal *exploitation* is antihuman. In positing animal suffering as essential to human progress and conceptualizing morality so that this suffering is deemed irrelevant, a deformed definition of humanity prevails. Besides environmental degradation, many human illnesses are linked to eating animals (on a pure vegetarian diet the risk of death by heart attack is reduced from 50 percent to 4 percent, and the risk of breast and ovarian cancer is three times lower). Animal research now wastes billions of tax dollars yielding misleading results because it fails to use models that could produce information more quickly, more reliably, and for less cost than animal "models."

Charges that animal rights is antihuman really mean: "The animal rights movement is against what I am doing and so is against me." If animal rights arguments are persuasive, personal change becomes necessary. As with feminism, if you accept the arguments, the consequences are immediate. You can't go on living the way you have, for suddenly you understand your complicity with an immense amount of exploitation. This can be very discomforting if you enjoy eating or wearing dead animals, or accept the premises of animal experimentation.

I know: that described me. For the first half of my life I ate animals and benefited in other ways from their exploitation. But feminism predisposed me to wonder if this was right or necessary. It equipped me to challenge language that removes agency and cloaks violence: "Someone kills animals so I can eat their corpses as meat" becomes "animals are killed to be eaten as meat," then "animals are meat," and finally "meat animals," thus "meat." Something *we do to animals* has become instead something that is a part of animals' nature, and we lose consideration of our role entirely. Alice Walker regained understanding of this role through a horse, recalling that "human animals and nonhuman animals can communicate quite well," and perceiving in eating "steak," "I am eating misery."

If the model for humanity was, say, a vegetarian feminist, rather than a male meat eater, our idea of human nature would be fundamentally challenged—animals would be seen as kin, not as prey, "models," or "animal machines"; *we* would be seen as radically in relationship with these kin, not as predators, experimenters, or owners. Reconstructing human nature as feminists includes examining how we as humans interact with the nonhuman world. Animal rights is not antihuman; it is antipatriarchal.

neering ranks even for those with very limited schooling. But as the industry matured, it turned increasingly to female, ethnic minority, and recent migrant workers to fill production positions that offered fewer and fewer advancement opportunities.[22] By the late 1970s, the industry's occupational structure was crudely stratified by gender, as well as by race and ethnicity. At the top was an unusually high proportion (25 percent) of the most highly educated and highly paid salaried employees in any industry—the engineers and professionals employed in research and design. As in traditional industries, the vast majority were white males (89 percent males, 89 percent non-Hispanic whites). At the bottom, however, were the women, three-fourths of the very poorly paid assembly workers and operatives who performed the tedious, often health-threatening work assigned to 45 percent of the employees. In between were the moderately well-paid technicians and craft workers, also primarily Anglo males, but into whose ranks women and Asians were making gradual inroads.[23]

In the heady days of technological triumph and economic expansion, when the Silicon Valley was widely portrayed as the mecca of the new intellectual entrepreneurs and as a land where factories resembled college campuses, its public officials also liked to describe it as a feminist capital. Indeed San Jose, the county seat, had a feminist mayor in the late 1970s and was one of the first public employers in the nation to implement a comparable worth standard of pay for city employees.

What is less widely known is that the area is also the site of a significant degree of family turbulence. Much of the data on local family change represent an exaggeration of national and even California trends, which tend to be more extreme than the national averages. For example, whereas the national divorce rate has doubled since 1960, in Santa Clara County it nearly tripled so that by 1977, divorces exceeded marriages. Likewise the percentage of "non-family households" grew faster than in the nation, and abortion rates were one and one-half times the national figures. And although the percent of single-parent households was not quite as high as in the US as a whole, the rate of increase has been far more rapid.[24] Thus the coincidence of path-breaking changes in both economic and family patterns makes the Silicon Valley an ideal site for examining women's responses to these transformations.

During the past three years I have conducted intermittent fieldwork in the Valley concentrating on an in-depth study of two kinship networks of people, which mainly consist of non-ethnic caucasians who have lived in the region during the period of postindustrialization. My key informant in each network is a white woman now in her late forties who married in the 1950s and became a homemaker for a white man who was to benefit from the unusual electronics industry opportunities of the 1960s. Both of these marriages and careers proved to be highly turbulent, however, and in response both women and several of their daughters have devised a variety of postfeminist survival strategies. At first glance their strategies appear to represent a simple retreat from feminism, but closer study has convinced me that these women are selectively blending and adapting certain feminist ideas to traditional and modern family and work strategies. Vignettes from their

their family histories suggest the texture and purpose of such strategies as well as important generational variations.

PATHS TO POSTFEMINISM

Let me first introduce Pam, currently a staff analyst in a municipal agency.* We became friendly in 1984 when I was interviewing clients at a feminist-inspired social service program where Pam was then an administrator. From various informal conversations, lunches, and observations of her work goals and relations, I had pegged Pam as a slightly cynical divorcee who came to feminist consciousness through divorce and a women's reentry program at a local community college. I had learned that Pam's first husband Don, to whom she was married for twelve years and with whom she had three children, was one of those white male electronics industry success stories. A telephone repair worker with an interest in drafting when they married, Don entered the electronics industry in the early 1960s and proceeded to work and job-hop his way up to a career as a packaging engineer, a position which currently earns him $50,000 annually.

I had heard too that Don's route to success had been arduous and stormy, entailing numerous setbacks, failures, and lay-offs, and requiring such extraordinary work hours that Don totally neglected Pam and their children. This and other problems led to Pam's divorce fifteen years ago, resulting in the normative female impoverishment. Pam became a single mother on welfare, continued her schooling (eventually through the master's level), developed feminist consciousness, experimented with sexual freedom, cohabited with a couple of lovers, and began to develop an administrative career in social services. Before the 1984 election Pam made many scornful remarks about Reagan, Reaganomics, and the military build-up. Therefore, I was quite surprised when, four months after meeting Pam, I learned that she was now married to Al, a construction worker with whom she earlier had cohabited. I also learned that they both were recent converts to charismatic, evangelical Christianity, and that they were participating in Christian marriage counseling to improve their relationship. Pam had

been separated from, but was on a friendly basis with her second husband, Al, when he had an automobile accident followed by a dramatic conversion experience. Al "accepted Jesus into his life," and Pam suddenly accepted Al and Jesus back into hers.

Pam acknowledges the paradoxes and contradictions of her participation in "Christian marriage"* and Christian marriage counseling, based, as they are, on patriarchal doctrines. Pam, however, credits the conversion experience and the counseling with helping her achieve a more intimate, positive marital relationship than she had experienced before. The conversion, she claims, changed Al from a defensive, uncommunicative, withholding male into a less guarded, more trusting, loving, and committed mate.[†] Although Pam and Al's marriage is not as communicative, nurturant, and intimate as Pam would like, she believes their shared faith is leading them in this direction. And she believes that "if you can work out that kind of relationship, then who would care who's in charge, because it's such a total wonderful relationship?" Moreover, Pam cedes Al dominance only in the "spiritual realm"; financially, occupationally, interpersonally, and politically, she retains strong independence, or even control.

Pam's selective adaptation and blending of feminist and fundamentalist ideologies first struck me as rather unique as well as extremely contradictory. I have gradually learned, however, that a significant tendency in contemporary fundamentalist thought incorporates some feminist criticisms of patriarchal men and marriage into its activism in support of patriarchal profamilialism. Quite a few evangelical ministers urge Christian wives to make strong emotional demands on their husbands for communication, commitment, and nurturance within the framework of patriarchal marriage, and they actively counsel Christian husbands to meet these demands.[25]

Feminism served Pam well as an aid for leaving her unsatisfactory first marriage and for building a career and sense of individual identity. But Pam failed to form successful, satisfying, intimate relationships to replace her marriage. Struggling alone with the emotional and social crises to which two of her three children were

---

* I have given pseudonyms to all the individuals described in this essay.

* Pam, like many evangelical and fundamentalist Christians, uses the term "Christian" to designate only born-again Christians.
[†] Al, as well as Pam's children, agree with this description.

prone, Pam describes herself as desperately unhappy much of the time. Although Pam received support from several intense friendships with women, neither this nor feminism seemed to offer her sufficient solace or direction. Her retreat from feminism and her construction of an extreme form of postfeminist consciousness took place in this context.

Dotty Lewison, one of the key informants in the other kinship network I studied, has a more complex story. I first sought out Dotty because of her early experience in electronics assembly work and because of her intact thirty-year marriage to Lou Lewison, another white male electronics industry success story. Dotty had been a teenager in 1954 when she met and married Lou, a sailor who had dropped out of school in the ninth grade. Although Dotty primarily had been a homemaker for Lou and the five children she bore at two-year intervals during her first decade of marriage, she also had made occasional forays into the world of paid work, including one two-year stint in the late 1950s assembling semiconductors. But Dotty neither perceived nor desired significant opportunities for personal advancement in electronics or any occupation at that time. Instead several years later she pushed Lou to enter the industry. This proved to be a successful strategy for *family* economic mobility, although one which was to have contradictory effects on their marital and family relationships as well as on Dotty's personal achievement goals. With his mechanical aptitude and naval background, Lou was able to receive on-the-job training and advance to the position of line maintenance engineer. Then, as Lou told me, "the companies didn't have many choices. No one even knew what a circuit looked like. . . . [But] you can't find many engineers starting out now who don't enter with degrees . . . because the companies have a lot more choices now."

When I first arrived at the Lewison's modest, cluttered, tract home, Dotty was opening a delivery from a local gadgets sale. A "knick-knack junkie" by her own description, Dot unpacked various porcelain figures and a new, gilded Bible. My social prejudices cued me to expect Dot to hold somewhat conservative and antifeminist views, but I was wrong again. She reported a long history of community and feminist activism, including work in the anti-battering movement. And she still expressed some support for feminism, "depending," she said, "on what you mean by feminism."

Later I learned that Dotty's intact marriage had

been broken by numerous short-term separations, and one of two year's duration that almost became permanent. During that separation Dot too was a welfare mother, who hated being on welfare, and who had a serious live-in love affair. Dot does not repudiate very many of her former feminist ideas, but she has not been active since the late 1970s. She specifically distances herself from the "militant man-hating types."

Dotty is a feisty, assertive woman who had protofeminist views long before she (or most of us) had heard of the women's liberation movement. Yet for twenty years, Dotty tolerated a marriage in which she and her husband fought violently. Her children were battered, sometimes seriously, most often by Lou, but occasionally by Dotty as well. Before I learned about the violence, Dotty and Lou both led me to believe that their near-divorce in the mid-1970s was caused by Lou's workaholicism as an upwardly mobile employee in the electronics industry. They spoke of the twelve- to fourteen-hour days and the frequent three-day shifts that led Lou to neglect his family completely. Later I came to understand the dynamic relationships between that workaholicism and their marital hostilities. Dotty had become a feminist and community activist by then, involved in antibattering work and many other community issues. Partly due to her involvement with feminism (again, some of it encountered in a college women's reentry program), Dotty was beginning to shift the balance of power in her marriage. In this situation, I suspect Lou's escape into work was experienced more as relief than neglect on all sides. Although now Dotty blames the work demands of the electronics industry for Lou's heart disease and his early death last year at the age of 52, at the time Lou's absence from the family gave Dotty the "space" to develop her strength and the willingness to assume the serious economic and emotional risks of divorce and an impoverished life as a single-parent.

Dotty kicked Lou out, although she did not file for divorce. Two years later she took him back, but only after his nearly fatal, and permanently disabling, heart attack, and after her live-in lover left her. Even then she took him back on her own rather harsh terms. She was to have total independence with her time and relationships. Despite the economic inequality between them, Dotty now held the undeniable emotional balance of power in the relationship, but only because she had proven she could survive impoverishment and live without Lou. And, of course, Lou's disability contributed to the restructuring of the division of labor and power in their household. Lou did most of the housework and gardening, while Dotty participated in the paid labor force. Nonetheless, Dotty remained economically dependent on Lou, and she regrets her limited career options. Indeed this was one crucial factor in her decision to resume her marriage with Lou.

By the late 1970s Dotty was no longer active in feminist or community causes. She says she "got burned out" and "turned off by the 'all men are evil' kind of thinking." More importantly, I believe, Dotty's life stage and circumstances had changed so that she did not feel she needed or benefited from feminism any more. In the mid-1970s, she "needed to have my stamp validated," to be reassured that her rebellious and assertive feelings and her struggles to reform her marriage were legitimate. But, partly due to the feminist-assisted success of those struggles, Dotty came to feel less need for reassurance from feminists. Dotty also finds she has no room for feminism today. She is "too tired, there's too much other shit to deal with." These days she has been trying to maintain her precarious hold on her underpaid job at a cable television service, while heroically struggling to cope with the truly staggering series of family tragedies that befell the Lewisons this year. Lou and two of the adult Lewison children died and one son spent four months in prison. Under these circumstances Dotty too has found more comfort from organized religion than from feminism. After the death of their first son, Dotty and Lou left a spiritualist church they had been attending and returned to the neighborhood Methodist church in which Dotty once had been active. Since Lou's death last fall, Dotty's oldest daughter Lyn and Dotty's mother have joined her in attending this church regularly.

Parallels and idiosyncracies in the life histories just described illustrate some of the complex, reciprocal effects of the family and work dynamics and gender consciousness that I have been observing in the Silicon Valley. Pam and Dotty both were young when they married. They both entered their marriages with conventional "Parsonsian" gender expectations about family and work responsibilities and "roles." For a significant period of time, they and their husbands conformed to the then culturally prescribed pattern of "instrumental" male breadwinner and "expressive" female housewife/mother. Assuming primary responsibility for rearing the children they began to bear imme-

diately after marriage, Pam and Dotty supported their husbands' successful efforts to develop middle to upper-middle class careers as electronics engineers. In the process, both men became workaholics, increasingly uninvolved with their families.

As their marriages deteriorated, both Pam and Dotty enrolled in a women's reentry program where they were affected profoundly by feminist courses. Eventually both women left their husbands and became welfare mothers, an experience each of them found to be both liberating and debilitating. Each experienced an initial "feminist high," a sense of enormous exhilaration and strength in her new independent circumstances. One divorced her husband, developed a viable career, experimented with the single life, and gradually became desperately unhappy. The other did not develop a career, lost her lover, and only then decided to take back her newly disabled husband (with his pension). Their rather different experiences with failed intimacy and their different occupational resources, I believe, help explain their diverse postfeminist strategies.

POSTFEMINIST DAUGHTERS

Between them Pam and Dotty had five daughters who, reckoning by the calendar, were members of the quintessential postfeminist generation.[26] (One died recently at the age of twenty-six; the surviving four range in age from twenty-three to thirty-one.) To varying degrees, all of the daughters have distanced themselves from feminist identity and ideology, in some cases in conscious reaction against what they regard as the excesses of their mothers' earlier feminist views. At the same time, however, most of the daughters have semiconsciously incorporated feminist principles into their expectations and strategies for family and work. A brief description of the family and work histories and gender consciousness of Dotty's and Pam's oldest, and most professionally succesful daughters illustrates this depoliticized incorporation of feminist thought.

Pam's oldest daughter Lanny is twenty-three. Like Dotty's oldest daughter Lyn, she is a designer-drafter who received her initial training in a feminist-inspired skills program. She is now in her second marriage, with one child from each marriage. Lanny dropped out of high school and at seventeen married a truck driver who moves electronics equipment, and who she describes as addicted to drugs and totally uncommunicative. Staying home with their baby, she found herself isolated and unbearably lonely. Pam encouraged Lanny's entry into a drafting course sponsored by a county agency, and Lanny soon found ready employment in electronics via various temporary agencies.[27] After she discovered her husband's narcotics addiction and convinced him to enter a residential detox program, Lanny spent a brief period as a welfare mother. Although she hated drafting, she job-shopped frequently to raise her income sufficiently to support herself and her daughter. She was earning 14 dollars an hour, without benefits, in 1985 when she met her present husband, Ken, at one of these jobs where he worked as an expediter in the purchasing department for eight dollars an hour until a recent lay-off.

Lanny does not consider herself a feminist and has never been active or interested in politics. She also hates her work, but has no desire to be a homemaker and is perfectly willing to support her husband if he wants to stay home and take care of the children, or if, as they hope, she can afford to send him back to engineering school. She would like to become an interior designer.

Although Lanny started out in a rather traditional working-class marriage, she is an authentic postfeminist. She was not able to tolerate the isolation, boredom and emotional deprivation of that traditional marriage. Lanny's goals are to combine marriage to a nurturant, communicative, coparenting man (the way she perceives Ken) with full-time work at a job she truly enjoys. There is an ease to Lanny's attitudes about the gender division of labor at home and at work, and about gender norms more generally that is decidedly postfeminist. These are not political issues to Lanny, nor even conscious points of personal struggle. She did actively reject her traditionally gendered first marriage, but without conceptualizing it that way. Lanny takes for granted the right to be flexible about family and work priorities. Remarkably, Ken appears to be equally flexible and equally oblivious to feminist influences on his notably enlightened attitudes.

The postfeminism of Dotty's oldest daughter Lyn, however, represents a somewhat more conscious and ambivalent response to feminism. Like Lanny, Lyn was a high school drop-out who took a variety of low-wage service sector jobs. But, unlike Lanny, the father of her child with whom she cohabited left during her pregnancy, making Lyn an unwed welfare mother. Lyn got

off welfare by moonlighting at an electronics security job while developing her successful career in drafting. She is now a hybrid designer at one of the world's major semiconductor companies. Unlike Lanny, Lyn loves her work in drafting, although she is constantly anxious, exhausted, and deeply frustrated by the extreme demands, stress, and unpredictability of her working conditions, and by their incompatibility with her needs as a single mother. There have been long periods when Lyn hardly saw her son and depended upon her parents and friends to fill in as babysitters.

Lyn's desire for a father for her son was a major motive for her brief marriage to a man who quickly abused her. She has lived alone with her son since she divorced her husband five years ago. Although Lyn is proud and fiercely independent, during the past two years she has somewhat ambivalently pursued a marital commitment from her somewhat resistant boyfriend, Tom. Tom, like Lanny's husband Ken, appears both unthreatened by Lyn's greater career drive and income and quite flexible about gender norms generally. He, however, seems much less willing or able than Ken to commit himself to the long-term responsibilities of marriage and parenthood.

Lyn is aware of sex discrimination at work and of issues of gender injustice generally and will occasionally challenge these by herself. Yet more explicitly than Lanny, Lyn distances herself from a feminist identity which she regards as an unnecessarily hostile and occasionally petty one: "I do not feel like a feminist, because to me my mother is a perfect feminist. . . . If someone asks her to make coffee, she first has to determine if it is because she is a woman." Upon reflection Lyn acknowledges that it is the word "feminist" that she does not like, "because of the way I was brought up with it. It meant slapping people in the face with it. . . . I do what I think is right, and if I am asked, I tell them why. . . . Honestly I guess I am a very strong feminist, but I don't have to beat people with it."

I consider Lyn a stronger postfeminist than feminist because of her thoroughly individual and depoliticized relationship to feminist issues. She cannot imagine being active politically on any issue, not even one like battering which she experienced: "I leave them for people like my mother who can make issues out of that, because I don't see it that way. I'll help the neighbor next door whose husband is beating her to death . . . but I do it my way. My way is not in a public form. I am very different from my mother." Equally postfeminist are the ways Lyn fails both to credit feminist struggles for the career opportunities for women she has grown up taking for granted, or to blame sexism or corporation for the male-oriented work schedules and demands that jeopardize her family needs. For example, she would like to have a second child, but accepts the "fact" that a second child does not fit with a successful career. Lyn shares Lanny's postfeminist expectations for family and work, that is, the desire to combine marriage to a communicative, egalitarian man with motherhood and a successful, engaging career. While Lanny has achieved more of the former, Lyn has more of the latter.

The emergent relationships between postindustrialism, family turbulence and postfeminism are nuanced and dynamic. Crisis in the family, as manifested in escalating rates of divorce and single-mother households, contributes both to the peculiar gender stratification of this postindustrial workforce, and to a limited potential for feminist consciousness. Marital instability continually refuels a large, cheap female labor pool which underwrites the feminization of both the postindustrial proletariat and of poverty.[28] But this crudely gender-stratified and male-oriented occupational structure helps to further destabilize gender relationships and family life. Moreover, the skewed wages and salaries available to white men help to inflate housing costs for everyone, thereby contributing to the rapid erosion of the working class breadwinner and the family wage.[29]

One consequence of family instability in such an environment seems to have been an initial openness on the part of many women, like Dotty and Pam, to feminist ideas. Feminism served many mothers of the postfeminist generation well as an ideology for easing the transition from an unhappy, 1950s-style marriage and for providing support for efforts to develop independent career goals. Neither feminism nor other progressive movements have been as successful, however, in addressing either the structural inequalities of postindustrial occupational structure, or the individualist, fast-track culture that makes all too difficult the formation of stable intimate relations on an egalitarian, or, for that matter, any other basis. Organized religion, and particularly evangelical groups, may offer more effective support to troubled family relationships in these circumstances.

I believe this explains the attractiveness of various kinds of postfeminist ideologies and strategies for achieving intimacy, or for just surviving in a profoundly insecure milieu. Postfeminist strategies correspond to different generational and individual experiences of feminism as well as postindustrial family and work conditions. For many women of the "mother" generation, feminism has become as much a burden as a means of support. Where once it helped them to reform or leave unsatisfactory relationships, now it can intensify the pain and difficulty of the compromises most women must make in order to mediate the destructive effects of postindustrial society on family and personal relationships. Too seldom today can women find committed mates, let alone those who also would pass feminist muster.

Perhaps this helps to account for Pam's simultaneous turn to religion and her subtle adaptation of patriarchal, evangelical Christian forms to feminist ends and for Dotty's return to, but also reform of, a previously unsatisfactory marriage coupled with her shift from political engagement to paid work and organized religion. In a general climate and stage of their lives characterized by diminished expectations, both seek support for the compromises with and commitments to family and work they have chosen to make, rather than for greater achievement or independence. Without repudiating feminism, both Dotty and Pam have distanced themselves from feminist identity or activism. On the other hand, their postfeminist, oldest daughters take for granted the gains in female career opportunities and male participation in child rearing and domestic work for which feminists of their mothers' generation struggled. Lanny and Lyn do not conceptualize their troubling postindustrial work and family problems in political terms. To them feminism and politics appear irrelevant or threatening.

These diverse forms of postfeminism, I believe, are semiconscious responses to feminism's unwitting role as midwife to the new family and work conditions in postindustrial America. Some versions are more reactionary, some more progressive, but all, I believe, differ from *anti*feminism. They represent women's attempts to both retain and depoliticize the egalitarian family and work ideals of the second wave. This is an inherently contradictory project, and one that presents feminists with an enigmatic dilemma. Is it possible to devise a personal politics that respects the political and personal anxieties and the exhaustion of women contending with the destabilized family and work conditions of the postindustrial era? To do so without succumbing to conservative nostalgia for patriarchal familial and religious forms is a central challenge for contemporary feminism.

ACKNOWLEDGMENTS

I wish to thank Linda Gordon, Carole Joffe, David Plotke, Rayna Rapp, and Barrie Thorne for their challenging and supportive responses to earlier drafts of this article.

NOTES

1. Historians have argued that the establishment of separate spheres for the sexes had as one of its paradoxical consequences the development of feminist consciousness and activity. See, for example, Nancy Cott, *The Bonds of Womanhood: "Woman's Sphere" in New England, 1750–1835,* (New Haven: Yale University Press, 1976); Mary Ryan, *Womanhood in America* (New York: Franklin Watts, 1983). There were similar developments in Europe. By contrast, feminism has been weak in most preindustrial and "underdeveloped" societies, including even revolutionary societies with explicit commitments to gender equality.

2. As with the term "postfeminist," which I discuss below, I use the term "postindustrial" with trepidation as it carries a great deal of ideological charge. I use it here exclusively in a descriptive sense to designate a form and period of capitalist social organization in which traditional industrial occupations supply a small minority of jobs to the labor force, and the vast majority of workers labor in varieties of clerical, sales, and service positions. Daniel Bell claims to have formulated the theme of postindustrial society in 1962 in an essay, "The Post-Industrial Society." See his *The Coming of Post-Industrial Society. A Venture in Social Forecasting* (New York: Basic Books, 1973), p. 145.

3. Thus Geneva Overholser concludes a *New York Times* editorial opinion titled "What 'Post-Feminism' Really Means," 19 September 1986, p. 30.

4. My appreciation to Steven Buechler for first suggesting this analogy to me.

5. For an analogous argument about the relationship between feminism and deindustrialization in modern England, see Juliet Mitchell, "Reflections on Twenty Years of Feminism," in *What is Feminism?,* Juliet Mitchell and Ann Oakley, eds. (Oxford: Basil Blackwell, 1986), pp. 34–48.

6. There is considerable debate among economists concerning the accuracy of labeling the US as a service economy. For example, see Richard Walker's challenge to this characterization, "Is There a Service Economy? The Changing Capitalist Division of Labor," *Science & Society* 49, no. 1 (Spring 1985):42–83. The debate involves the politics of semantics. Few disagree, however, that significant occupational changes have occurred in the past few decades, or that these involve the decline of unions and real wages and the rise of female employment. For a synthetic analysis of occupational trends, see Bennett Harrison and Barry Bluestone, "The

Dark Side of Labor Market 'Flexibility': Falling Wages and Growing Income Inequality in America," International Labor Office, File IL02 (June 1987).

7. Labor force participation rates for women increased steadily but slowly between 1900 and 1940, climbing from 20.5 percent to 25.4 percent. However, this pattern accelerated rapidly in the post-1940 period. In 1950 29 percent of women 14 years and older were in the labor force; in 1960 this percentage grew to 34.5 percent; in 1984 63 percent of all women ages 18–64 were in the labor force. See, Valerie Kincade Oppenheimer, *The Female Labor Force in the United States,* Population Monograph Series, No. 5, Institute of International Studies, University of California, Berkeley, 1970; and Barbara F. Reskin and Heidi I. Hartmann, eds., *Women's Work, Men's Work* (Washington, D.C.: National Academy Press, 1986). The dramatic rise in female enrollment in colleges occurred in the 1960s and 70s, rising from 38 to 48 percent of enrollees between 1960 and 1979. Rosalind Petchesky, *Abortion and Woman's Choice* (Boston: Northeastern University Press, 1984), US marriage rates peaked at 16.4 per 1,000 people in 1946, declined sharply to 9.9 in 1952, and have fluctuated around 10 ever since, while divorce rates have increased steadily to 5.0 in 1985. National Center for Health Statistics, Annual Summary of Births, Marriages, Divorces and Deaths, *Monthly Vital Statistics Reports.* More significantly, the age of women at their first marriage has risen and their rate of marriage has declined steadily since 1960. Fertility rates peaked at 3.6 per 1000 women during the famous mid-1950s baby boom and declined steadily thereafter to 1.8 in 1976. See Petchesky, *Abortion and Women's Choice,* pp. 103–107. Even more striking are the rising proportions of women who never marry or bear children. The cohort of women born between 1935–39 had the lowest rate of childlessness in the twentieth century—10 percent. The Census Bureau projects a childless rate of 20–25 percent, however, for women born in the 1960s, and it estimates that 40 percent of college-educated women born in this decade never will bear children. "The Birth Question," *USA Today,* 28 February 1986, p. 1.

8. In 1960 one out of every eleven children lived with only one parent, but by 1986 one out of four children lived in a single-parent household, and 90 percent of these lived with their mothers. Tim Schreiner, "US Family Eroding, Says Census Bureau," *San Francisco Chronicle,* 10 December 1986.

9. "A Mother's Choice," *Newsweek,* 31 March 1986, p. 47.

10. See Harrison and Bluestone, "Dark Side of Labor Market 'Flexibility'."

11. These are among the findings of a study that attempted to operationalize Marxist criteria for assigning class categories to workers in the US. Even though the study excluded housewives from its sample, it found "that the majority of the working class in the United States consists of women (53.6 percent)." See, Erik Olin Wright, et al, "The American Class Structure," *American Sociological Review* 47 (December 1982), p. 22. For additional data on female occupational patterns and earnings and an astute analysis of the paradoxical relationship between female employment and poverty, see Joan Smith, "The Paradox of Women's Poverty: Wage-Earning Women and Economic Transformation," *Signs* 10, no. 2 (Winter 1984).

12. The concept "feminization of poverty" also misrepresents significant features of contemporary poverty, particularly the worsening conditions for minority men. See Pamela Sparr, "Reevaluating Feminist Economics: 'Feminization of Poverty' Ignores Key Issues," and Linda Burnham, "Has Poverty Been Feminized in Black America?" in Rochelle Lefkowitz and Ann Withorn, eds., *For Crying Out Loud: Women and Poverty in the United States* (New York: The Pilgrim Press, 1986).

13. As the much publicized findings from Lenore Weitzman's study of no-fault divorce in California underscore. In the first year after divorce women and minor children in their care suffer a 73 percent decline in their standard of living while husbands enjoy a 42 percent gain. *The Divorce Revolution: The Unexpected Social and Economic Consequences for Women and Children in America,* Lenore J. Weitzman (New York: Free Press, 1985). For a qualitative study which focuses on the plight of divorced, single mothers, see Terry Arendell, *Mothers and Divorce: Legal, Economic, and Social Dilemmas* (Berkeley: University of California Press, 1986).

14. In 1980, households headed by fully employed women had a poverty rate almost three times greater than husband-wife households and twice that of households headed by unmarried men. The number of female-headed families doubled between 1970 and 1980. By 1981, women headed almost one fifth of all families with minor children. Smith, "Paradox of Women's Poverty," p. 291.

15. Households with working wives accounted for 60 percent of all family income in 1985, which made it possible for 65 percent of all families to earn more than $25,000 per year, compared with only 28 percent of families who achieved comparable incomes 20 years ago. In 1981 the median earnings of full-time year-round women workers was $12,001, 59 percent of the $20,260 that men earned. That year married women contributed a median of 26.7 percent of family income. The lower the family's annual income, however, the higher the proportion contributed by women. Paradoxically, however, there is an inverse relationship between family income and the percentage of wives working. See *The Working Woman: A Progress Report* (Washington D.C.: The Conference Board, 1985), and Reskin and Hartmann, *Women's Work, Men's Work,* p. 4. The combined effects of these trends are acute for black women, for whom astronomical divorce rates have overwhelmed the effects of their relative gains in earnings, forcing them increasingly into poverty. For data see US Department of Labor, *Time of Change: 1983 Handbook on Women Workers* (Washington D.C.: Dept. of Labor, Women's Bureau Bulletin 298, 1983), p. 29; Paula Giddings, *When and Where I Enter: The Impact of Black Women on Race and Sex in America* (Toronto: Bantam Books, 1985), p. 353.

16. For a more optimistic evaluation of the economic and social effects of these changes on women, see Heidi I. Hartmann, "Changes in Women's Economic and Family Roles in Post World War II United States," in Lourdes Beneria and Catherine Stimpson, eds., *Women, Households, and Structural Transformation* (New Brunswick: Rutgers University Press, 1987).

17. It seems plausible that there has been a concomitant decline in political activism as well. Note, for example, the stark contrast in the amount of time available for politics for women active on opposing sides of the abortion controversy. In a recent study of this conflict, most of the antiabortion activists were housewives who spent at least thirty hours per week on antichoice politics, whereas most of the prochoice activists were career women, few of whom spent more than five hours per week on this issue. See Kristin Luker, *Abortion & the Politics of Motherhood* (Berkeley and Los Angeles: University of California Press, 1984). Although there are problems with Luker's prochoice sample that may exaggerate its career and income levels, it seems unlikely that the contrast is spurious.

18. Barbara Ehrenreich, *The Hearts of Men: American Dreams and the Flight from Commitment* (Garden City: Anchor Press/Doubleday, 1983).

19. Christopher Lasch has made a sideline industry out of this sort of attack on feminists. For some of his most recent polemics on this subject, see "What's Wrong with the Right?" *Tikkun* 1, no. 1 (1986); and "Why the Left Has No Future," *Tikkun* 1, no. 2 (1986). The latter was his response to critics of the former, including Lillian Rubin's "A Feminist Response to Lasch." The most comprehensive and popular recent book to scapegoat feminism in this way is probably Sylvia Ann Hewlett's, *A Lesser Life: The Myth of Women's Liberation in America* (New York: William Morrow, 1986). For a critical discussion of this book that does not deny the power of its approach, see Deborah Rosenfelt and Judith Stacey, "Second Thoughts on the Second Wave," *Feminist Studies* 13, no. 2 (Summer 1987).

20. The most conspicuous representatives of this backlash within feminist thought are Betty Friedan, Jean Bethke Elshtain, and Germaine Greer. For critical discussions of their writings see my "Are Feminists Afraid to Leave Home? The

Challenge of Conservative Pro-family Feminism," in Juliet Mitchell & Ann Oakley, eds., *What is Feminism?* (London: Basil Blackwell 1986), and Zillah Eisenstein, *Feminism and Sexual Equality: Crisis in Liberal America* (New York: Monthly Review Press, 1984).

21. The county population grew from 290,547 in 1950 to 1,295,071 in 1980. US Bureau of the Census. *Census of Population: 1950,* Vol. 2, *Characteristics of the Population* pt. 5, California, 1952; and *Census of Population: 1980* Vol. I. *Characteristics of the Population, General Population Characteristics,* pt. 6, California, 1982.

22. For data and a superb ethnographic and analytical account of this transition, see John Frederick Keller, "The Production Worker in Electronics: Industrialization and Labor Development in California's Santa Clara Valley," (Ph.D. dissertation, University of Michigan, 1981).

23. For data on the occupational structure of the electronics industry, see Keller, "Production Worker in Electronics;" Marcie Axelrad, *Profile of the Electronics Workforce in the Santa Clara Valley* (San Jose: Project on Health and Safety in Electronics, 1979); Lennie Siegel and Herb Borock, "Background Report on Silicon Valley," prepared for the US Commission on Civil Rights (Mountain View, CA: Pacific Studies Center, 1982).

24. For the data on divorce rates and household composition for Santa Clara County in comparison with California and the US as a whole, see Bureau of the Census, *Census of Population,* 1960, 1970, and 1980. During the 1970s Santa Clara County recorded 660 abortions for every 1000 births, compared with a statewide average of 489.5 and a ratio of less than 400 for the nation. See Bureau of the Census, *Statistical Abstract of the United States,* 1981.

25. The most influential representative of this tendency may be James Dobson, founder and president of Focus on the Family, "a nonprofit corporation dedicated to the preservation of the home." Focus produces a radio talk show on family issues aired as much as three times daily on hundreds of Christian stations throughout the US and abroad. The organization also produces and distributes Christian films, tapes, and audio-cassettes on family topics. Dobson, who served on the recent Meese Commission on Pornography, has also authored scores of advice books and pamphlets on family and personal relationships, most of which advocate the doctrine of "tough love." The uneasy fusion of patriarchal and feminist thought is marked in his advice book on marital crisis, *Love Must Be Tough* (Waco, Texas: Word Books, 1983). For a discussion of the infusion of the female sexual revolution into fundamentalist culture, see Barbara Ehrenreich, Elizabeth Hess, and Gloria Jacobs, *Re-Making Love: The Feminization of Sex* (New York: Anchor Press, 1986), chapter 5.

26. Indeed the first media use of the term "postfeminist" to catch my attention was in the title of an essay about women in their late twenties. Susan Bolotin, "Voices From the Post-Feminist Generation," *New York Times Magazine,* 17 October 1982.

27. The very concept of "temporary" employment is being reshaped by postindustrial labor practices. High tech industries in the Silicon Valley make increasing use of temporary agencies to provide "flexible staffing" and to cut employee benefits. In 1985 one of every 200 workers in the US was a "temp," but one of 60 workers in the Silicon Valley held a "temporary" job. See David Beers, "'Temps': A High-Tech's Ace in The Hole," *San Bernadino Sun,* 28 May 1985.

28. Nor are the effects of the relationship between marital instability, female production work, and poverty confined to the US. As many have noted, in the postindustrial economy, women work on a "global assembly line." Maria Patricia Fernandez-Kelly discusses the effects of these international processes on Mexican women who work in electronics and garment factories on the Mexican-US border in "Mexican Border Industrialization, Female Labor Force Participation, and Migration," in June Nash and Maria Patricia Fernandez-Kelly, eds., *Women, Men, and the International Division of Labor,* (Albany: SUNY Press, 1983), pp. 205–223.

29. More work needs to be done on ways in which the practice of one pattern of family life by some constrains options for others. The most obvious of the asymmetrical relationships among family patterns available to different social classes today is that between affluent dual-career couples and the poorly-paid women who provide the child care and domestic services upon which their egalitarian marriages depend. For a valuable study of the former, see Rosanna Hertz, *More Equal Than Others: Women and Men in Dual-Career Marriages* (Berkeley: University of California Press, 1986). For a sensitive analysis of other kinds of unanticipated feedback effects of the electronics industry on the social ecology of the Silicon Valley, see AnnaLee Saxenian, "Silicon Chips and Spacial Structure: the Industrial Basis of Urbanization in Santa Clara County, California," (Masters thesis, University of California Berkeley, 1980).

The New Feminist Movement

VERTA TAYLOR and NANCY WHITTIER

Popular authors and scholars alike have described the 1980s and 90s as a "post-feminist" era of political apathy during which former feminists traded their political ideals for career mobility and Cuisinarts, and younger women single-mindedly pursued career goals and viewed feminism as an anachronism. While there is a kernel of truth to these stereotypes, by and large they fail to recognize the continuity of the women's movement. Although feminism has changed form in the late 1980s and 90s, neither the movement nor the injustices that produced it have vanished. Of all the manifestations of social activism in the 1960s, feminism is one of the few that continued to flourish in the 1970s and 80s and remains active in the 1990s. Yet few authors have studied the women's movement of the late 1980s and 90s, and the transformations that the movement has undergone in recent years have not been documented. We attempt here to trace the ideology and structure of the most recent wave of the American women's movement into the 1990s, using existing studies and our own research to outline the movement's primary characteristics and changes from the 1960s to the present.

From a social movement perspective, women in the United States have always had sufficient grievances to create the context for feminist activity. Indeed, instances of collective action on the part of women abound in history, especially if one includes female reform societies, women's church groups, alternative religious societies, and women's clubs. However, collective activity on the part of women directed specifically toward improving their own status has flourished primarily in periods of generalized social upheaval, when sensitivity to moral injustice, discrimination, and

social inequality has been widespread in the society as a whole (Chafe 1977). The first wave of feminism in this country grew out of the abolitionist struggle of the 1830s and peaked during an era of social reform in the 1890s, and the contemporary movement emerged out of the general social discontent of the 1960s. Although the women's movement did not die between these periods of heightened activism, it varied greatly in form and intensity.

Structural conditions underlie the emergence of protest (Oppenheimer 1973; Huber and Spitze 1983; Chafetz and Dworkin 1986). Chafetz and Dworkin (1986), for example, propose that as industrialization and urbanization bring greater education for women, expanding public roles create role and status conflicts for middle class women, who then develop the discontent and gender consciousness necessary for a women's movement. The changing shape and size of women's movements depend on the opportunities for women to organize on their own behalf, the resources available to them, and their collective identity and interpretation of their grievances. All of these vary for different groups of women and at different times and places (West and Blumberg 1990). Thus, it is to be expected that the ideology, structure, and strategies adopted by the women's movement are quite different depending on when, where, and by what groups of women it is organized.

Most scholarly analyses of the women's movement of the late 1960s—the "new feminist movement"— divide it into two wings, with origins in the grievances and pre-existing organizations of two groups of women: older professional women who formed bureaucratic organizations with a liberal ideology, and younger women from the civil rights and New Left movements

Written expressly for this edition.

who formed small collective organizations with radical ideology (Freeman 1975; Cassell 1977; Ferree and Hess 1985; Buechler 1990).

The organizations and ideologies developed by these two factions have not, however, remained separate and distinct since the 1970s. Our analysis divides the contemporary wave of feminist activism into three stages: resurgence (1966–1971), the feminist heyday (1972–1982), and abeyance (1983–1991).

Scholars generally mark the feminist resurgence with the founding of the National Organization for Women (NOW) in 1966 (Buechler 1990; Ryan forthcoming). During the resurgence period, the movement established itself, forming organizations and ideologies and moving into the public eye. We place the end of this stage in 1971. By this time, major segments of feminism had crystallized: liberal feminism with the formation of groups such as NOW, the Women's Equity Action League (WEAL) in 1967, and the National Women's Political Caucus (NWPC) in 1971; radical feminism and socialist feminism with the development of consciousness raising groups, theory groups, and small action groups such as Redstockings and the Feminists in 1969; and lesbian feminism with the establishment of groups such as Radicalesbians in 1970 and the Furies (initially called "Those Women") in 1971 (Echols 1989).

The year 1972 was pivotal both for the movement's success and for its opposition. The Equal Rights Amendment (ERA) passed the Congress and Phyllis Schafly launched her first attacks, signifying the transition to a second phase of feminist activism that lasted until the defeat of the ERA in 1982 (Mansbridge 1986). While some authors argue that this period saw a decline in the women's movement and a retreat from radicalism (Echols 1989), we think it should be considered the movement's heyday because the feminist revolution seemed to be on the move. The campaign to ratify the ERA in the states brought mass mobilization, fostering female solidarity and enlisting women into feminism, women's studies programs were introduced on college campuses, the number and variety of feminist organizations proliferated, and the movement entered the political arena and encountered active opposition (Matthews and DeHart 1990; Ryan forthcoming). Not only did feminism flourish in the ratification campaign but it spread into the political mainstream while radical and lesbian feminist organizing heightened outside it.

Following the ERA's defeat in 1982, we argue that the women's movement has entered a period of abeyance, in which it has developed new structural forms in order to survive a shrinking membership and an increasingly nonreceptive environment. The 1980s saw a turning away from the values of equality, human rights, and social justice and even a deliberate backlash against the feminist momentum of the 1970s (O'Reilly, 1980; Yankelovich 1981). Rights won by feminists in the 1960s and 70s—from affirmative action to legal abortion—have been under siege throughout the 1980s and 90s.

Yet in the United States, the feminist challenge lives on. The 1980s and 90s are not the first hostile period in which feminism has endured. In the period following World War II, when strict gender roles and social and political conservatism flourished, the women's movement adopted a tight-knit abeyance structure that enabled it to survive (Rupp and Taylor 1987; Taylor 1989). The so-called "postfeminist" era of the 1980s and 90s no more marks the death of the women's movement than did the 1950s. In fact, although the women's movement of the 1990s takes a different form than it did twenty years earlier, it remains vital and influential.

IDEOLOGY

While ideas do not necessarily cause social movements, ideology is a central component in the life of any social movement. The new feminist movement, like most social movements, is not ideologically monolithic. In the 1970s, it was commonplace to characterize the women's movement as consisting of three ideological strands: liberal feminism, socialist feminism, and radical feminism (Ryan 1989; Buechler 1990). Feminist ideology today continues to be a mix of several orientations that differ in the scope of change sought, the extent to which gender inequality is linked to other systems of domination, especially class, race/ethnicity, and sexuality, and the significance attributed to gender differences. Our analysis here explores the diversity of feminism by focusing on the evolution of the dominant ideologies that have motivated participants in the two major branches of the new feminist movement from its inception, liberal feminism and radical feminism.

The first wave of the women's movement was by and large a liberal feminist reform movement. It asked for equality within the existing social structure and, indeed, in many ways functioned like other reform movements to reaffirm existing values within the society (Ferree and Hess 1985). Nineteenth-century feminists believed that if they obtained the right to an education, the right to own property, the right to vote, employment rights—in other words, equal civil rights under the law—they would attain equality with men.

The basic ideas identified with contemporary liberal or "mainstream" feminism have changed little since their formulation in the nineteenth century when they seemed progressive, even radical (Eisenstein 1981). Contemporary liberal feminist ideology holds that women lack power simply because we are not, as women, allowed equal opportunity to compete and succeed in the male-dominated economic and political arenas but, instead, are relegated to the subordinate world of home, domestic labor, motherhood, and family. Its major strategy for change is to gain legal and economic equalities and to obtain access to elite positions in the workplace and in politics while, at the same time, making up for the fact that women's starting place in the "race of life" is unequal to men's (Eisenstein 1981). Thus, liberal feminists tend to place as much emphasis on changing individual women as they do on changing society. For instance, teaching women managerial skills or instructing rape victims in "survival" strategies strikes a blow at gender social definitions that channel women into traditionally feminine occupations or passive behaviors that make them easy targets of male aggression. Liberal feminists likewise tend to define patriarchy in individualistic rather than structural terms—as a problem of certain men oppressing certain women, for example (Friedan 1963).

In sum, the liberal concept of equality involves equality under the law, in the workplace, and in the public arena, and fails to recognize how deeply women's inequality is rooted in their responsibility for the care of children and the home (Hartmann 1981; Huber and Spitze 1983), their dependence on men in the context of traditional heterosexual marriage (Rich 1980), and in men's use of their dominant status to preserve male advantage by establishing the rules that distribute rewards (Reskin 1988). As several scholars have recently noted, liberal feminism ironically provided ideological support through the 1970s and 80s for the massive transformation in work and family life that was occurring as the United States underwent the transition to a postindustrial order (Mitchell 1986;

Stacey 1987). By urging women to enter the workplace and adopt a male orientation, the equal opportunity approach to feminism unwittingly contributed to a host of problems that further disadvantaged women, especially working-class women and women of color, including the rise in divorce rates, the "feminization" of working-class occupations, and the devaluation of motherhood and traditionally-female characteristics (Gordon 1991).

Radical feminist ideology dates to Simone de Beauvior's early 1950s theory of "sex class," which was developed further in the late 1960s among small groups of radical women who fought the subordination of women's liberation within the New Left, and which flourished in the feminist movement in the 1970s (Beauvior 1952; Firestone 1970; Millett 1971; Atkinson 1974; Rubin 1975; Rich 1976, 1980; Griffin 1978; Daly 1978; Eisenstein 1978; Hartmann 1981; Frye 1983; Hartsock 1983; MacKinnon 1983). The radical approach recognizes women's identity and subordination as a "sex class," views gender as the primary contradiction and foundation for the unequal distribution of a society's rewards and privileges, and recasts relations between women and men in political terms (Echols 1989). Defining women as a "sex class" means no longer treating patriarchy in individual terms but acknowledging the social and structural nature of women's subordination. Radical feminists hold that in all societies, institutions and social patterns are structured to maintain and perpetuate gender inequality and that female disadvantage permeates virtually all aspects of sociocultural and personal life. Further, through the gender division of labor, social institutions are linked so that male superiority depends upon female subordination (Acker 1980; Hartmann 1981; Chafetz 1990). In the United States, as in most industrialized societies, power, prestige, and wealth accrue to those who control the distribution of resources outside the home in the economic and political spheres. The sexual division of labor that assigns childcare and domestic responsibilities to women not only ensures gender inequality in the family system but perpetuates male advantage in political and economic institutions as well.

In contrast to the liberal position, radical feminists do not deny that men are privileged as men and that they benefit as a group from their privilege—not just in the public arena but also in relation to housework, reproduction, sexuality, and marriage. Rather, they

THE ROCK WILL WEAR AWAY

MEG CHRISTIAN and HOLLY NEAR

For someone who usually composes in total isolation, never uttering a public peep until every note, every word is perfectly polished and practiced, the experience of co-writing a song was fairly traumatic. But it was real wonderful to learn to share creative processes, and then to even like the result!

The theme of the chorus is a common one: many small, weak entities joining together to defeat a larger, stronger one. Holly heard the rock-water imagery in a Vietnamese poem, while I fondly recall the flies in the elephant's nose in Judy Grahn's poem. You haven't really heard this song until you've sung it yourself with a whole roomful of women. For me, that experience is one of those moments when I feel our growing collective strength and purpose, and I know we can win.

Sixteen-year-old virgin
Springtime takes her to the park
Where the moon shines down like the future
calling her out of the dark
But her nightmare finds her freedom

"The Rock Will Wear Away," lyrics by Holly Near and music by Meg Christian. Reprinted by permission of Holly Near. Music of Holly Near available at 1-800-888-SONG.

And leaves her lying wounded, worn from
invasion
Light as a feather floating by
Landing, then covered with soot
Waiting now, watching now for rain
To wash clean her pain

CHORUS:
Can we be like drops of water falling on the
stone
Splashing, breaking, dispersing in air
Weaker than the stone by far
But be aware that as time goes by
The rock will wear away
And the water comes again

Thirty-year-old mother
Autumn finds her pregnant once more
And the leaves like gold and copper reminding
her that she is poor
And her children often are hungry
And she hungers too, for knowledge, time and
choices

CHORUS:
Eighty-year-old poet
Winter keeps her home and alone
Where she freezes and darkness keeps her from
writing her final wisdom
But she lights her last red candle
And as it is melting, tilting it, writing now

view patriarchy as a system of power that structures and sustains male advantage in every sphere of life, in economic, political, and family institutions, in the realms of religion, law, science and medicine, and in the interactions of everyday life. To unravel the complex structure on which gender inequality rests requires, from a radical feminist perspective, a fundamental transformation of all institutions in society and the existing relations among them. To meet this challenge, radical feminists have formulated influential cri-

tiques of the family, marriage, love, motherhood, heterosexuality, rape, battering, and other forms of sexual violence, capitalism, the medicalization of childbirth, reproductive policies, the media, science, language and culture, the beauty industry, politics and the law, and technology and its impact on the environment. Thus, radical feminism is a transformational politics engaged in a fight against female disadvantage and the masculinization of culture. Its ultimate vision is revolutionary in scope: a fundamentally new social order that eliminates the sex-class system and replaces it with new ways of defining and structuring experience.

Central to the development of radical feminist ideology was the strategy of forming small groups for the purpose of "consciousness-raising." Pioneered initially among New Left women, consciousness raising can be understood as a kind of conversion in which women come to view experiences previously thought of as personal and individual, such as sexual exploitation or employment discrimination, as social problems that are the result of gender inequality and sexism. Because it enables women to view the "personal as political," for most women, consciousness-raising is an identity-altering experience. Becoming a feminist can transform a woman's entire self-concept and way of life: her biography, appearance, beliefs, behavior, and relationships (Cassell 1977).

A major consequence of the strategy of seeing the personal as political is that, ideologically, the new feminist movement has become increasingly more radical in the decades since its inception. By the mid-1970s, the distinction between liberal and radical feminism was becoming less clear (Carden 1978). Ideological shift took place at both the individual and organizational levels. Participation in liberal feminist reform and service organizations working on such "women's issues" as rape, battering, abortion, legal and employment discrimination, and women's health problems raised women's consciousness, increased their feminist activism, and contributed to their radicalization as they came to see connections between these issues and the larger system of gender inequality (Schlesinger and Bart 1983; Sparks 1979). Women were also radicalized by working through their own personal experiences. Whether through sexual harassment, divorce, rape, abortion, incest, alcoholism, drug addiction, depression, or discrimination in the workplace, women have become aware of the political rather than the personal nature of their problems (Huber 1973; Keuck 1980; Klein 1984).

Radicalization has also occurred at the group level. By the end of the 1970s, liberal feminist organizations, such as the National Organization for Women (NOW), the Women's Equity Action League, the Women's Legal Defense Fund, and the National Abortion Rights Action League, which had been pursuing equality within the law, began to adopt strategies and goals consistent with a more radical stance. NOW included in its 1979 objectives not only such legal strategies as the Equal Rights Amendment (ERA) and reproductive choice, but broader issues such as the threat of nuclear energy to the survival of the species, lesbian and gay rights, homemakers' rights, the exploitation of women in the home, sex-segregation in the workplace, and the influence of corporate, patriarchal, and hierarchical models of organization on the activities and strategies of NOW (Eisenstein 1981). If there is a single objective that reflected the extent to which the dichotomy between liberal and radical feminism had blurred by the 1980s, it was the Equal Rights Amendment. Although the ERA asked for equality for women within the existing legal and economic structure, it was based on the fact that women are discriminated against as a "sex class" (Mansbridge 1986). Recognizing the radical potential of feminism, sociologist Jessie Bernard in 1975 described the "restructuring of sex roles as no less epochal than the restructuring of the class system which was one of the first consequences of the industrial revolution."

By the 1980s, feminism had become, as activist and writer Charlotte Bunch (1987) put it, more than just a "laundry list of women's issues" or areas for social reform. Neither was feminism merely a constituency of women. There were and always will be women organized against feminism (Marshall 1984). Rather, feminism was becoming a transformational politics, a comprehensive ideology that addressed nearly every social issue, from international peace and the economic policy of the United States to animal rights. It is precisely because feminist ideology has become a tool for linking such a wide range of social issues and multiple forms of domination that it poses such a fundamental challenge to the established order. The belief in woman's right to control her body that underlies the campaign for reproductive rights, for example, raises the questions not only of rape, incest, battering, and sexual harassment, but also of job safety, environmental illness, chemical dumping, nuclear proliferation, the exporting of unsafe drugs and food additives banned in the U.S. to the Third World, and world hunger.

Radical feminism is premised on the belief that there are underlying or "essential" differences between women and men. Early radical feminists sought equality by striving to eradicate gender differentiation (Echols 1989). More recently, lesbian feminists have pursued an end to gender inequality by celebrating or affirming femaleness and glorifying that which is different or "special" about women. Even though most radical feminists believe that women's differences are socially constructed as a result of gender stratification and socialization, the notion of "woman" as a social category mobilized women to organize on behalf of common issues during the height of the new feminist movement. Beginning in the mid-1980s, with the defeat of the unifying issue of the ERA and the growing diversification of the movement, radical feminism entered a new stage of "deconstructing" the term "woman." Shifting the emphasis away from gender oppression, women of color, Jewish women, lesbians, and working class women challenged radical feminists' idea of a "sex class" that implied a distinctive and essential female condition. In reality, women are distributed throughout all social classes, racial and ethnic groupings, sexual communities, subcultures, and religions. Thus, disadvantage for women varies and is multidimensional. The recognition that the circumstances of women's oppression differ has given way to a new feminist paradigm that views race, class, gender, ethnicity, and sexuality as interlocking systems of oppression, forming what Patricia Hill-Collins (1990) refers to as a "matrix of domination." Pointing out that the unity on which feminism has been based is largely a white middle-class heterosexual unity, much of contemporary feminist ideology focuses on women's differences from one another as a way of seeing the connections among as well as the additive effects of multiple systems of domination (Hill-Collins 1990).

Some scholars have charged that focusing on women's differences has resulted in the demise of radical feminism and a retreat into "identity politics" (Echols 1989) and that ideological debates among feminists have undermined the unity of the movement (Ryan 1989). To the contrary, we think that by linking the oppression of women to other systems of human domination, such as race and ethnicity, class, sexuality, religion, and subcultural differences, contemporary radical feminism poses a fundamentally more radical critique of society predicated on resisting all forms of human domination at every level of exchange, whether individual, cultural, or structural. In some ways, as an ideology feminism has come full circle; by focusing on women's differences based on race, class, and sexuality, it is renewing its alliance with other movements for human rights from which it has emerged in this country and around the world. While the feminists of the late 1960s and the 1970s viewed the "woman problem" primarily from the perspective of the wrongs that have

been done to women and the discrimination we have borne, feminists now are asking a much larger question: How can United States society be changed according to feminist principles so that it is just and fair for all people regardless of sex, race, class, sexual orientation, or any other social characteristic?

Although the new feminist movement appears to be moving toward an increasingly radical position ideologically, ideas alone are an incomplete explanation of either the direction or the consequences of a social movement (Marx and Wood, 1975; McCarthy and Zald 1977). Much depends on a movement's structure, as well as on the larger political context.

STRUCTURE

Social movements do not generally have a single, central organization or unified direction. Rather, the structure of any general and broad-based social movement is more diffuse—composed of a number of relatively independent organizations that differ in ideology, structure, goals, and tactics—is characterized by decentralized leadership, and is loosely connected by multiple and overlapping memberships, friendship networks, and cooperation in working toward common goals (Gerlach and Hine 1970). The organizational structure of the new feminist movement has conformed to this model from its beginnings (Freeman 1975; Cassell 1977). While the movement as a whole is characterized by a decentralized structure, the various organizations that comprise it vary widely in structure. The diversity of feminist organizational forms reflects both ideological differences and, as Freeman (1979) points out, the movement's diverse membership base (for example, differences in members' prior organizational expertise, experience in other movements, expectations, social status, age or generation, and relations with different target groups).

There have been two main types of organizational structure in the new feminist movement since its resurgence, reflecting the two main sources of feminist organizing in the late 1960s: bureaucratically structured movement organizations with hierarchical leadership and democratic decision-making procedures, such as the National Organization for Women (NOW); and smaller collectively structured groups that formed a more diffuse social movement community held together by a feminist political culture. It is important to recognize, however, that while these two strands emerged separately, they have not remained distinct and opposed to each other. On the contrary, the two structures have converged as bureaucratic organizations adopted some of the innovations of collectivism, and feminist collectives became more formally structured (Staggenborg 1988, 1989; Martin 1990; Ryan forthcoming). In addition, many individual activists are involved in a variety of organizations with differing structures.

The bureaucratically structured and professionalized movement organizations initially adopted by liberal groups such as NOW were well suited to work within the similarly-structured political arena and to members' previous experience in professional organizations. The structures that radical feminist groups initially adopted, on the other hand, built on their prior involvement experiences in the New Left (Evans 1979). Collectivist organizations grew from radical feminists' attempt to structure relations among members, processes of decision making, and group leadership in a way that reflected or prefigured the values and goals of the movement (Rothschild-Whitt 1979; Breines 1982). Put differently, the belief that "the personal is political" dictated collective structure. Feminist collectivist organizations made decisions by consensus, rotated leadership and other tasks among members, and shared skills to avoid hierarchy and specialization. As Jo Freeman (1972/3) and others have noted, such groups often failed to meet their ideals and did, in fact, spawn unacknowledged hierarchies. Nevertheless, the conscious effort to build a feminist collective structure has had a lasting impact on the women's movement and has led to the growth of what Steven Buechler (1990), in a study of women's movements in the United States, calls a social movement community.

Buechler proposes that movements consist not only of formal organizations, but that they also include more informally organized communities, made up of networks of people who share the movement's political goals and outlook and work toward common aims. The collectivist branch of the women's movement initially sparked the growth of a feminist social movement community in which alternative structures guided by a distinctively feminist women's culture flourished—including bookstores, theater groups, music collectives, poetry groups, art collectives, publishing and recording companies, spirituality groups, vacation resorts, self-help groups, and a variety of feminist-run businesses. This "women's culture," though it includes feminists of diverse political persuasions, has been largely maintained by lesbian feminists in the 1980s and 90s. It nurtures a feminist collective identity that is important to the survival of the women's movement as a whole (Taylor and Whittier forthcoming).

Both bureaucratic organizations working within mainstream politics and the alternative feminist culture have expanded since the movement's emergence in the 1960s. Following 1972, the scope of feminist goals broadened as the ideology of the movement as a whole grew more radical, and the decentralized structure of the movement made it possible for feminist groups to proliferate. Feminism flourished throughout the 1970s, and the issue of gender took center stage in American politics and in other arenas. Membership in NOW reached 250,000 in 1982, an increase from 35,000 in the mid-70s (Ryan forthcoming), and uncounted numbers of small independent feminist groups formed in cities and towns across the country. Structural distinctions between the bureaucratic and collectivist branches of the movement diminished along with ideological distinctions, as small and large groups alike became institutionalized, and the thriving women's movement community drew participants from both traditions of feminist activism. As a result of feminist values of egalitarianism and avoidance of hierarchy, organizations such as NOW and the National Abortion Rights Action League (NARAL) incorporated some of the innovations of collectivism, including CR groups, modified consensus decision-making, and the use of direct action tactics and civil disobedience. A host of structural variations emerged, including formally-structured groups that use consensus decision-making, organizations with deliberately democratic structures, and groups that officially operate by majority-rule democracy but in practice make most decisions by consensus (Tierney 1982; Staggenborg 1988, 1989; Martin 1990; Ryan forthcoming; Taylor forthcoming). At the same time, feminist collectives shifted their focus from consciousness-raising and radical feminist critique to the development of feminist self-help and service organizations, such as rape crisis centers, shelters for battered women (Tierney 1982), job training programs for displaced homemakers, lesbian peer counseling groups, support for single mothers, and the presentation of women's theatrical and musical productions. At the same time, many feminist collectives revised their structure to depend less on consensus decision making, and permit specialization of skills. In short, some groups that identified themselves as part of the radical branch of the movement assumed a more reform-oriented stance and adopted relatively institutionalized structures and strategies for change.

During the period from 1972 to 1982, the campaign for ratification of the ERA, the struggle to win and maintain abortion rights, and the candidacies of women for political office galvanized feminists of diverse persuasions into cooperation with one another. Coalition efforts brought notable successes in the early 1970s. The ERA passed through Congress in 1972 and was ratified by 22 states within the first year, and the Supreme Court handed down the Roe v. Wade decision in 1973 legalizing abortion. In the late 1970s, more bureaucratically structured organizations such as NOW, the National Women's Political Caucus (NWPC), and NARAL came to function as interest groups aligned with the Democratic party. The culmination of this trend was the nomination of a woman, Geraldine Ferraro, for Vice President, on the Democratic ticket in 1984, as the Democratic party sought the endorsement of feminist groups (Klein 1984; Mueller 1987; Frankovic 1988). The necessity of working as an interest group on Capitol Hill brought further structural developments to this wing of the movement, with the creation of Political Action Committees, the adoption of mass mailing techniques to gain supporters and contributors, and the further professionalization of movement organizations (Boles 1991; Staggenborg forthcoming; Ryan forthcoming).

Institutionalization and professionalization were not limited to liberal feminist groups. Even groups that developed out of the radical branch have gained access to the established political structure and won support for their goals. Feminist anti-rape groups, for example, have received financial support from government agencies and private foundations to provide rape-prevention and treatment services in public schools and universities. The widespread acceptance of the feminist analysis of rape as an act of violence and power rather than a strictly sexual act further attests to the impact of the feminist anti-rape movement. Likewise, the movement to provide shelters for battered women has grown from a small group of radical feminists to a project supported by such agencies as the United Way and, in some states, by a tax on marriage licenses (Tierney 1982). In addition, the movement to integrate feminist research and study into the academy has led to the establishment of women's studies programs at most colleges and universities and the proliferation of jour-

nals dealing with women and feminism. The distinction between "working outside the system" and "working within the system," so important in the late 1960s, no longer has the same significance.

The women's movement community also became institutionalized and flourished in the late 1970s and 1980s. National cultural events such as the Michigan Womyn's Music Festival, which draws from between 5,000 and 10,000 women annually, and a multitude of local events such as "Take Back the Night" marches against rape, feminist concerts, lesbian writers' workshops, and conferences on topics ranging from feminist spirituality to substance abuse, proliferated. As the liberal branch of the women's movement retreated from protest and disruptive tactics and focused instead on actions within the political arena, the network of feminist counter-institutions grew more elaborate. It is within the structure of the women's movement community that the ideologies and goals of radical feminism and lesbian feminism have continued to flourish (Taylor and Whittier forthcoming).

The women's movement remained relatively homogenous in terms of race, class, and ethnicity throughout the 1970s and 1980s. Although individual women of color and working-class women had participated in the founding of NOW and in the early protests against sexism in the civil rights movement, the women's movement attracted primarily white middle-class women. Buechler (1990) proposes that because white middle-class women are oppressed on the basis of gender and not on the basis of class or race, they are the most likely to be drawn to a movement that focuses on eliminating sexism. Certainly, it is not that women of color and working class or poor women experience no oppression as women or oppose feminist goals. A 1989 *New York Times*/CBS News poll, for example, showed that, while only 64% of white women saw a need for a women's movement, 85% of African American women and 76% of Hispanic women thought the women's movement was needed (Sapiro 1991). Yet the feminist movement has remained predominantly white both because of the continuation of its tradition of defining its goals with an eye to the concerns of white middle-class women and because black women and other women of color place a priority on working with men of their own communities to advance their collective interests. Independent organizing by women of color did occur during the 1970s, and when African American activists in the women's movement formed the National Black Feminist Organization in 1973 it grew to a membership of 1,000 within its first year (Deckard 1983). Several anthologies of feminist writings by women of color in the early 1980s called attention to the ways in which white-dominated feminist organizations continued to marginalize and overlook women of color, despite increased rhetorical commitment to anti-racism (Moraga and Anzaldúa 1981; Hull, Scott, and Smith 1982; Smith 1983). In response, women of color have persistently formed active caucuses within pre-dominantly white feminist organizations, such as the National Women's Studies Association, to work against racism within the women's movement. Likewise, Jewish women, who had historically played important roles within the women's movement, began to organize their own groups and speak out against anti-Semitism within the movement (Beck 1980; Bulkin, Pratt, and Smith 1984).

Although the class bias of the women's movement has made working-class and poor women unlikely to participate in sizable numbers, class boundaries have been more permeable than race boundaries (Buechler 1990). Union women played a significant role in the formation of NOW in 1966; they supported the fledgling organization by providing office space and clerical services until the group's endorsement of the ERA in 1967 forced the women of the United Auto Workers, an organization that at the time opposed the ERA, to withdraw such support. Women committed to both feminism and the union movement eventually formed their own organization, the Coalition of Labor Union Women (CLUW) in 1974 (Balser 1987). CLUW claimed 16,000 members by 1982 and had made progress in its fight to win AFL-CIO support for feminist issues. While the women's movement had been criticized in the early 1980s for neglecting issues relevant to working women (Hewlett 1986), working-class and middle-class feminists cooperated throughout the 80s on issues of economics and childcare such as comparable worth, daycare tax credits, and parental leave (Gelb and Paley 1982). The basic class and race composition of the movement may have changed little throughout the 70s and 80s, but feminists began to recognize the need to expand the definition of "women's issues" to include problems of central concern to women of color, working-class and poor women, and lesbian women. In sum, as Buechler (1990:158) puts it, the new feminist awareness of race and class means that "a movement that began as unconsciously class-bound and race-bound has now become consciously class-bound and race-bound."

The fact that collective action by the women's movement has both created new institutions and moved into almost every major institution of our society suggests that the feminist challenge has had a significant impact on every facet of social life and on the lives of many individuals as well. However, in direct proportion to the successes of the women's movement, a countermovement has developed that has successfully reversed some feminist gains, stalled progress on others, and has changed the face of the women's movement.

FROM HEYDAY TO ABEYANCE

The early 1980s saw a rapid decrease in the number of feminist organizations and a transformation in the form and activities of the women's movement. In part, this was a response to the successes of the New Right: so powerful were antifeminist sentiments and forces that members of a major political party, the Republican party, were elected in 1980 on a platform developed explicitly to "put women back in their place." After forty years of faithful support of the ERA, the Republican party dropped it from its platform, called for a constitutional amendment to ban abortion, and aligned itself with the economic and social policies of the New Right. After the election of the conservative Reagan administration in 1980, federal funds and grants were rarely available to feminist service organizations, and because other social service organizations were also hard hit by budget cuts, competition increased for relatively scarce money from private foundations. As a result, many feminist programs such as rape crisis centers, shelters for battered women, and job training programs were forced to close or limit their services.

The failure of the ERA in 1982 seemed to reflect the changed political climate, setting the stage for other setbacks throughout the 1980s. Abortion rights, won in 1973 with the Supreme Court's decision in Roe v. Wade, were reduced in 1989 by the Supreme Court's decision in Webster v. Reproductive Services permitting states to enact restrictions on abortion (Staggenborg forthcoming:137–8). Following the Webster decision, state governments enacted increasingly tight restrictions on abortion, ranging from "informed consent" laws that required a waiting period before women could have abortions, to parental consent laws for underage women, to outright bans on abortion unless the mother's life was in danger. In 1991, the Supreme Court further limited abortion rights by ruling that federally-funded family planning clinics could be barred from providing information on abortion. The anti-abortion movement also escalated and hardened its tactics in the late 80s: it bombed abortion clinics, picketed doctors who performed abortions, and attempted to dissuade women entering clinics from having abortions (Staggenborg forthcoming).

Further, Women's Studies programs in colleges and universities, which had been established in the 1970s in response to feminist agitation, have come under attack by conservatives in the late 1980s and early 90s. A backlash against "multiculturalism" and "political correctness" in academia seeks to restore the traditional academic focus on the "great thinkers" of Western European thought, and thus to maintain the primacy of white, male perspectives and experiences. Women's Studies, Black Studies, Latin American Studies, Lesbian and Gay Studies, and other curricula that focus on minority perspectives, diversity, or oppression are ridiculed for, as a critical article in *New York* magazine put it, "their conviction that Western culture and American society are thoroughly and hopelessly racist, sexist, oppressive" (Taylor 1991:34) and for their preoccupation with such "insignificant" questions as the terminology used to refer to ethnic groups, or the relationship between subtle coercion in heterosexual relations and date rape (Will 1991).

The women's movement has suffered not only from opposition, but also from its apparent success. Overt opposition to the feminist movement had been muted in the mid- to late 1970s. Elites in politics, education, and industry gave the appearance of supporting feminist aims through largely ineffectual affirmative action programs and the appointment of a few token women to high positions in their respective areas. Meanwhile, the popular image of feminism advanced by the mass media suggested that the women's movement had won its goals, making feminism an anachronism. Despite the real-life difficulties women encountered trying to balance paid employment and a "second shift" of housework and childcare (Hochschild 1989), the image of the working woman became the feminine ideal. The public discourse implied that since women had already achieved equality with men, they no longer needed a protest movement, unless they happened to be lesbians and man haters. Both popular and scholarly writers, in short, declared the 1980s and 90s a "post-feminist" era.

In addition to external obstacles, the movement's shift from heyday to abeyance has been marked by internal divisions and conflict. Some scholars have argued that these internal factors are largely responsible for the decline of mass feminist activism. Alice Echols (1989), tracing the demise of radical feminism, contends that when feminist ideology began to emphasize the essentialist nature of sex differences in the early 1970s, idealizing the feminine and denigrating the masculine, the women's movement lost its radical potential and impetus. In her view, the move toward building an alternative feminist culture represented a feminist retreat from confronting and changing social institutions. In a similar vein, Barbara Ryan (1989) argues that internal debates over the correctness of competing feminist theories and the political implications of personal choices—which she terms "ideological purity"—along with the rise of lesbian feminism and its emphasis on separatism and criticism of men and heterosexual relationships, tore the women's movement apart. It cannot be disputed that the task of building a movement of such a diverse group of women has proven difficult and has, at times, distracted activists from the important work of confronting social institutions.

As feminists increasingly question the notion of women as a unified sex class, the emphasis on women's differences from each other has sometimes fragmented the movement. Identity politics, then, has been both a strength of the women's movement and an obstacle, as women with different allegiances struggle to find common ground. Battles over heterosexism, homophobia, and lesbianism strained the women's movement in the 1970s and early 80s, but during the late 1980s and 90s, it was the issues of race and racism that most divided the movement. Major organizations such as the National Women's Studies Association (NWSA) were split by accusations of racism leveled by women of color caucuses and the defensive reactions of white women (Ruby, et al. 1990). Participants at the first national lesbian conference held in Atlanta in 1991 decided that they were unable to found a national lesbian organization because lesbians' differences from each other made it difficult to find common ground (Sharon, et al. 1991). Other differences among women have also become points of contention: fat women, disabled women, women with environmental illnesses, old women, young women, women with seizure disorders, women confronting substance abuse, and numerous other groups have met at conferences, proposed their own agendas, and demanded changes in policies and culture at feminist events in order to accommodate their needs and prevent their oppression (see Sharon, et al. 1991 for a sample account of such proceedings). While some scholars argue that such debates are counterproductive and divisive (Ryan 1989, forthcoming), others point out that the problem that divides the movement is racism itself, not the criticism of it (Smith 1983; Hill-Collins 1990). Because the women's movement has been based on the common identity of "woman," it faces difficult and far-reaching challenges as it attempts to recognize differences and divisions among women.

We are suggesting here that the women's movement of the late 1980s and 90s is in abeyance. Verta Taylor (1989), building on research on the women's movement of the 1950s (Rupp and Taylor 1987), suggests that movements adopt abeyance structures in order to survive in hostile political climates. Movements in abeyance are in a "holding pattern," during which activists from an earlier period maintain the ideology and structural base of the movement, but few new recruits join. A movement in abeyance is primarily oriented toward maintaining itself rather than confronting the established order directly. Focusing on building an alternative culture, for example, is a means of surviving when external resources are not available and the political structure is not amenable to challenge. The structure of the women's movement has changed as mass mobilization and confrontation of the social system have declined. Nevertheless, feminist resistance continues in different forms. Patricia Hill-Collins suggests that resistance can occur at three levels: the individual level of consciousness, the cultural level, and the social structural level (1990:227). This conceptualization allows us to recognize that protest takes many forms and to acknowledge the role of social movements in changing consciousness and culture.

The women's movement has sought to make profound changes in the lives of women. At the level of consciousness and individual actions, women who were active in the women's movement of the 1960s and 70s have continued to shape their lives around their feminist beliefs in the 1980s and 90s, even when they are not involved in organized feminist activity. For example, many feminists hold jobs in government, social service organizations, or Women's Studies and other academic programs that allow them to incorporate their political goals into their work, and continue to choose leisure activities, significant relationships, and dress and presentation of self that are consistent with feminist ideology (Whittier unpublished). The consciousness and lives of women who do not identify as feminist have also been altered by the women's movement. In a study of gender and family life in the Silicon Valley of California [see Reading 52, pages 519 to 532], Judith Stacey (1987) argues that in the 1980s some women have incorporated portions of feminism into family and work structures that are otherwise traditional, combining a feminist emphasis on developing satisfying careers, sharing household work with hus-

DREAMWEAVERS—FINDING OUR TREASURE

MOUNTAINGROVE

We wanted to have a dream circle around what was the future of the women's movement, so we gathered on this land and we kept close to the middle of the circle. We were all going to sleep in the dream circle. And from the coast we brought rope to make weavings, and everyone wove a weaving that she was going to sleep under, in her sleeping bag. Some women wove very beautiful weavings. Now mine was a symbolic weaving. It lasted through the night. Some women wove beautiful weavings with shells and feathers.

One of the dreams I remember was dreaming of a woman who was going down a spiral, down, down, down, into a forgotten city where there was treasure. She was going down to find her treasure, which I think is what we have been doing in this second wave of feminism, finding our treasure.

From *Center for the Study of Women in Society Review,* copyright © 1988. Eugene, Oregon: University of Oregon, Center for the Study of Women in Society.

bands, and increasing men's emotional expressiveness, with fundamentalist Christianity and its focus on the importance of the family. In short, even some segments of fundamentalist Christianity have adopted elements of the feminist critique of men's absence from families and lack of emotional expression, and are encouraging men to broaden their gender roles. In an example of these changes, President George Bush received applause when he broke masculine conventions and wept as he spoke to a Southern Baptist conference about his emotional decision to send troops to the Persian Gulf war (*Columbus Dispatch*, 6/7/91:2A). While many feminists may not rejoice at such changes in traditional religion, it is nevertheless apparent that the effects of the women's movement stretch far beyond policies and practices that are explicitly labelled feminist.

At the cultural level, the feminist social movement community has continued to thrive into the 1990s, with such events as, for example, an "annual multicultural multiracial conference on aging" for lesbians (*Off Our Backs* 1991:12), feminist cruises, several annual women's music festivals and a women's comedy festival in different parts of the country. Gatherings and conferences in 1990 included groups such as Jewish lesbian daughters of holocaust survivors, women motorcyclists, fat dykes, practitioners of Diannic Wicca, Asian lesbians, practitioners of herbal medicine, and survivors of incest. Newsletters and publications exist for groups including women recovering from addictions, women's music professionals and fans, lesbian separatists, disabled lesbians, lesbian couples, feminists interested in sadomasochism, feminists opposed to pornography, and a multitude of others. The growth of the feminist community underscores the flowering of lesbian feminism in the late 1980s and 90s. A wide variety of lesbian and lesbian feminist books and anthologies have been published on topics ranging from lesbian feminist ethics, to separatism, to sexuality, to commitment ceremonies for lesbian couples (see, for example, Hoagland 1988, Hoagland and Penelope 1988, Loulan 1990, Butler 1990), reflecting diverse perspectives that have been hotly debated in the pages of lesbian publications and at conferences and festivals. For example, a series of letters to the editor in a national lesbian newsletter argued over the correct lesbian feminist response to lesbians serving in the armed forces in the Persian Gulf War: some readers held that the war was a manifestation of patriarchy and that lesbians in the military should not be celebrated; others argued that lesbian soldiers should be supported be-

cause they are lesbians in a homophobic institution, regardless of support or opposition to the war; still others argued that the Gulf War was justified and that lesbian servicewomen should be celebrated for their patriotic service (*Lesbian Connection* 1991). Clearly, the task of building a community based on the identity "lesbian" has proven complex, if not impossible. Nevertheless, the institutional structure of the social movement community has continued to expand, and within the community feminists construct and reinforce a collective identity based on opposition to dominant conceptions of women and lesbians (Taylor and Whittier forthcoming).

At the social structural level, the feminist movement has not been unresponsive to the conservative backlash. In fact, the gains of the New Right in the late 1980s sparked some of the largest feminist demonstrations and actions in years. In April, 1989, NOW and abortion rights groups organized a national demonstration in Washington, DC, that drew between 300,000 and 600,000 women and men to protest restrictions on abortion. Additional national and local demonstrations followed, and pro-choice activists organized electoral lobbying, defense of abortion clinics, and conferences, and attempted to form coalitions across racial and ethnic lines and among women of different ages (Staggenborg forthcoming; Ryan forthcoming). The National Abortion Rights Action League (NARAL) experienced a growth in membership from 200,000 in 1989 to 400,000 in 1990 (Staggenborg forthcoming: 138), and membership in NOW also continued to grow in the late 1980s and 90s after a decline in the early 1980s, with a membership of 250,000 in 1989.

The women's movement has also had a substantial impact on other social movements of the 1980s and 90s. Movements such as the gay and lesbian movement, AIDS movement, recovery from addictions, New Age spirituality, and the animal rights movement have been profoundly influenced by feminist values and ideology, including the emphasis on collective structure and consensus, the notion of the personal as political, goddess-worship, and the critique of patriarchal mistreatment of animals and ecological resources. The women's movement also trained a large number of feminist activists in the 1970s, particularly lesbians, who have participated in new social movements and integrated feminism into them (Cavin 1990; Whittier unpublished). For example, the gay and lesbian movement has begun expanding its health concerns to include breast cancer as well as AIDS and has adopted strategies of the feminist anti-rape movement to confront violence against gays and lesbians. The recovery movement discusses the ways that gender socialization makes women co-dependent. Many women's self-help groups, such as the postpartum depression movement, sprung directly out of the early women's health movement and continue to model support groups on feminist consciousness-raising groups. In addition, feminists have renewed coalitions with the peace, environmental, socialist, anti-U.S. intervention in Latin America and anti-apartheid movements, transforming these movements both by forming separate feminist organizations that address these issues and by moving into mixed-sex organizations (Whittier unpublished). In a sense the women's movement has come full circle, rejoining the 1990s versions of the movements that composed the New Left in the 1960s when feminists split off to form a separate women's movement.

Given the scope and size of women's movement activity in the late 1980s and 90s, why do we argue that the movement is in abeyance? We think that, although the movement may resurge in the mid 1990s, the level of mass mobilization and confrontation of the social structural system clearly declined following 1982. Because feminism in the late 80s and 90s is focused more on consciousness and culture and has established roots in other social movements of the period, feminist protest is less visible than it was during the heyday of the women's movement. Notably, in keeping with the patterns that characterize movements in abeyance (Taylor 1989), the most active feminists in the late 1980s and 90s have been women who became involved with the movement during the late 1960s and 1970s, were transformed by their involvement, and formed a lasting commitment to feminist goals. Despite support for feminist goals, many young women do not identify themselves as feminists, apparently because the identity of feminist is stigmatized. A feminist is seen as someone who deviates from gender norms by being unattractive, aggressive, hostile to men, opposed to marriage and motherhood, lesbian, and seeking to imitate men (Schneider 1988, Dill unpublished). Despite the

gains made by women in some areas, gender norms are still so rigid and deeply internalized that they successfully deter many women who otherwise support the feminist agenda from participating in the movement.

Yet, some younger women have joined the women's movement in the late 1980s and 90s despite the risks entailed in identifying with a stigmatized and unpopular cause. In a study of young feminist activists in the 1990s, Kim Dill has found that a new generation of women has been recruited to feminism primarily through Women's Studies courses and through the transmission of feminism from mothers to daughters (unpublished). In short, the institutionalized gains of the heyday of feminist activism in the 1970s are enabling the women's movement to survive and to spread its ideology to new recruits.

The history of the women's movement, and its present survival despite the challenges it has confronted from within its own ranks and from a conservative political climate, suggest that because feminism is a response to the fundamental social cleavage of gender it will continue to exist (Rupp and Taylor unpublished). As one generation of feminists fades from the scene with its ultimate goals unrealized, another takes up the challenge (Rossi 1982). But each new generation of feminists does not simply carry on where the previous generation left off. Rather, it speaks for itself and defines its own objectives and strategies, often to the dismay and disapproval of feminists from earlier generations. The activism of a new generation of feminists may take the form of distributing condoms and dental dams to women for AIDS prevention, or organizing "Kiss-Ins" with Queer Nation, or organizing a "warm line" for women suffering postpartum depression (Taylor forthcoming), or sponsoring recycling drives. While earlier generations of activists may not view such endeavors as feminist, as Myra Ferree and Beth Hess (1985:182) point out, "feminism is not simply a form of received wisdom" but something that evolves with each new cycle of feminist activism. Both continuity and change, then, will characterize the feminism of the twenty-first century.

ACKNOWLEDGMENTS

We would like to thank Leila Rupp and Kate Weigand for their insightful contributions, careful readings of earlier drafts of this paper, and steadfast support.

REFERENCES

Acker, J. 1980. "Women and stratification: A review of recent literature." *Contemporary Sociology* 9:25–35.

Atkinson, T. G. 1974. *Amazon odyssey.* New York: Links.

Balser, Diane. 1987. *Sisterhood and solidarity: Feminism and labor in modern times.* Boston: South End Press.

Beauvoir, S. de. 1952. *The second sex.* New York: Bantam.

Beck, E. T. 1980. *Nice Jewish girls: A lesbian anthology.* Watertown, MA: Persephone.

Boles, Janet. 1979. *The politics of the equal rights amendment.* New York: Longman.

Breines, 1982. *Community and organization in the New Left, 1962–68.* New York: Praeger.

Buechler, Steven M. 1990. *Women's movements in the United States.* New Brunswick, NJ: Rutgers.

Bulkin, Elly, Minnie Bruce Pratt, and Barbara Smith. 1984. *Yours in struggle: Three feminist perspectives on anti-Semitism and racism.* New York: Long Haul Press.

Bunch, C. 1987. *Passionate politics.* New York: St. Martin's.

Butler, Becky. 1991. *Ceremonies of the heart: Celebrating lesbian unions.* Seattle, WA: The Seal Press.

Carden, Maren. 1978. "The proliferation of a social movement." Pp. 179–196 in *Research in social movements, conflict, and change,* vol. 1, edited by Louis Kriesberg. Greenwich, CT: JAI Press.

Cassell, J. 1977. *A group called women: Sisterhood and symbolism in the feminist movement.* New York: David McKay.

Cavin, Susan. 1990. "The invisible army of women: Lesbian social protests, 1969–88." Pp. 321–332 in *Women and social protest,* edited by Guida West and Rhoda Blumberg. New York: Oxford University Press.

Chafe, W. H. 1977. *Women and equality: Changing patterns in American culture.* New York: Oxford University Press.

Chafetz, Janet and Gary Dworkin. 1986. *Female revolt.* Totowa, NJ: Rowman and Allenheld.

Chafetz, Janet. 1990. *Gender equity: An integrated theory of stability and change.* Newbury Park, CA: Sage.

Columbus Dispatch. 1991. "Bush cries as he tells Baptists of his prayers, tears before war." Friday, June 7: 2A.

Daly, Mary. 1978. *Gyn/ecology.* Boston: Beacon.

Deckard, Barbara Sinclair. 1983. *The women's movement.* New York: Harper and Row.

Dill, Kim. Unpublished. "Feminism in the nineties: The influence of collective identity and community on young feminist activists." Master's thesis, The Ohio State University, 1991.

Echols, Alice. 1989. *Daring to be bad: Radical feminism in America 1967–1975.* Minneapolis: University of Minnesota Press.

Eisenstein, Z. 1981. *The radical future of liberal feminism.* New York: Longman.

Evans, Sarah. 1979. *Personal politics.* New York: Knopf.

Ferree, Myra Marx, and Beth B. Hess. 1985. *Controversy and coalition: The new feminist movement.* Boston: Twayne.

Firestone, S. 1970. *The dialectic of sex.* New York: William Morrow.

Frankovic, Kathleen A. "The Ferraro factor: The women's movement, the polls, and the press." Pp. 102–123 in *The politics of the gender gap: The social construction of political influence,* edited by Carol M. Mueller. Newbury Park, CA: Sage.

Freeman, Jo. 1972/3. "The tyranny of structurelessness." *Berkeley Journal of Sociology* 17:151–164.

———— . 1975. *The politics of women's liberation.* New York: David McKay.

———— . 1979. "Resource mobilization and strategy: A model for analyzing social movement organization actions." Pp. 167–89 in *The dynamics of social movements,* edited by M. N. Zald and J. D. McCarthy. Cambridge, MA: Winthrop.

Friedan, B. 1963. *The feminine mystique.* New York: Norton.

Frye, Marilyn. 1983. *The politics of reality: Essays in feminist theory.* Trumansburg, NY: Crossing Press.

Gelb, Joyce and Marian Lief Paley. 1982. *Women and public policy.* Princeton: Princeton University Press.

Gerlach, L. P., and V. H. Hine. 1970. *People, power, change: Movements of social transformation.* Indianapolis: Bobbs-Merrill.

Gordon, Suzanne. *Prisoners of men's dreams.* New York: Little, Brown.

Griffin, S. 1978. *Women and nature.* New York: Harper & Row.

Hartmann, H. 1981. "The family as the locus of gender, class, and political struggle: The example of housework." *Signs* 6 (Spring):366–94.

Hartsock, N.C.M. 1983. *Money, sex, and power: Toward a feminist historical materialism.* New York: Longman.

Hewlett, Sylvia. 1987. *A lesser life.* New York: Morrow.

Hill-Collins, Patricia. 1990. *Black feminist thought.* Boston: Unwin Hyman.

Hoagland, Sarah Lucia. 1988. *Lesbian ethics: Toward new value.* Palo Alto, CA: Institute of Lesbian Studies.

———— and Julia Penelope, eds. 1988. *For lesbians only.* London: Onlywomen Press.

Hochschild, Arlie. 1989. *The second shift.* New York: Avon.

Huber, J. 1973. "From sugar and spice to professor." In *Academic women on the move,* edited by A. S. Rossi and A. Calderwood. New York: Russell Sage Foundation.

Hull, Gloria T., Patricia Bell Scott, and Barbara Smith. 1982. *But some of us are brave: Black women's studies.* New York: The Feminist Press.

Keuck, D. 1980. "Community action to prevent rape." A class presentation in Sociology of Women course, Ohio State University, Columbus.

Klein, Ethel. 1984. *Gender politics.* Cambridge, MA: Harvard University Press.

Lesbian connection 1991. Vols. 13 and 14. Lansing, MI: Ambitious Amazons.

Loulan, JoAnn. 1990. *The lesbian erotic dance.* San Francisco: Spinsters Book Company.

McCarthy, J. D., and M. N. Zald. 1977. "Resource mobilization and social movements: A partial theory." *American Journal of Sociology* 82 (May):1212–1239.

MacKinnon, C. A. 1983. "Feminism, Marxism, method, and the state: Toward feminist jurisprudence." *Signs* 8(4):635–58.

Mansbridge, Jane. 1986. *Why we lost the ERA.* Chicago: University of Chicago Press.

Marshall, S. 1984. "Keep us on the pedestal: Women against feminism in twentieth-century America." Pp. 568–81 in *Women: A feminist perspective,* edited by Jo Freeman. Palo Alto: Mayfield.

Martin, Patricia Yancey. 1990. "Rethinking feminist organizations." *Gender and Society* 4(2):182–206.

Marx, G. T., and J. L. Wood. 1975. "Strands of theory and research in collective behavior." Pp. 363–428 in *Annual review of sociology,* vol. 1, edited by A. Inkeles, J. Coleman, and N. Smelser.

Mathews, Donald G. and Jane Sherron DeHart. 1990. *Sex, gender, and the politics of ERA: A state and the nation.* New York: Oxford.

Millett, K. 1971. *Sexual politics.* New York: Avon.

Mitchell, Juliet. 1986. "Reflections on twenty years of feminism." Pp. 34–48 in *What is feminism?* edited by Juliet Mitchell and Ann Oakley. Oxford: Basil Blackwell.

Moraga, Cherrie, and Gloria Anzaldúa. 1981. *This bridge called my back: Writings by radical women of color.* Watertown, MA: Persephone.

Mueller, Carol McClurg. 1987. "Collective consciousness, identity transformation, and the rise of women in public office in the United States." Pp. 89–108 in *The women's movement of the United States and Western Europe,* edited by M. F. Katzenstein and C. M. Mueller. Philadelphia: Temple University Press.

O'Reilly, J. 1980. "To fight them, we've got to understand what they're saying." *Savvy,* October.

Off Our Backs 1991. "Passages 7—Beyond the barriers." Vol. 21(6):12.

Oppenheimer, Valerie Kincade. 1973. "Demographic influence on female employment and the status of women." Pp. 184–199 in *Changing women in a changing society,* edited by Joan Huber. Chicago: University of Chicago Press.

Reskin, Barbara. 1988. "Bringing the men back in: Sex differentiation and the devaluation of women's work." *Gender and Society* 2:58–81.

Rich, Adrienne. 1976. *Of woman born.* New York: Norton.

———. 1980. "Compulsory heterosexuality and lesbian existence." *Signs* 5:631–60.

Rothschild-Whitt, Joyce. 1979. "The collectivist organization: An alternative to rational-bureaucratic models." *American Sociological Review* 44:509–527.

Rossi, A. S. 1982. *Feminists in politics.* New York: Academic Press.

Rubin, G. 1975. "The traffic in women: Notes on the 'political economy' of sex." In *Toward an anthropology of women,* edited by Rayne Reiter. New York: Monthly Review Press.

Ruby, Jennie, Farar Elliott, and Carol Anne Douglas. 1990. "The National Women's Studies Association conference." *Off Our Backs* 20(8).

Rupp, Leila J. and Verta Taylor. 1987. *Survival in the doldrums: The American women's rights movement, 1945 to 1960s.* New York: Oxford University Press.

———. Unpublished. "Women's culture and the persisting women's movement." Paper presented at the Annual Meeting of the American Sociological Association, Washington, DC, August, 12, 1990.

Ryan, Barbara. 1989. "Ideological purity and feminism: The U.S. women's movement from 1966 to 1975." *Gender and Society* 3:239–257.

———. Forthcoming. *Feminism and the women's movement.* London: Harper Collins Academic.

Sapiro, V. 1991. In *The annals of the American Academy of Political and Social Science* 515 (May), edited by Janet Boles.

Sharon, Tanya, Farar Elliott, and Cecile Latham. 1991. "The National Lesbian Conference: For, by and about lesbians." *Off Our Backs* 21(6):1–4, 18–23.

Schlesinger, M. B., and P. Bart. "Collective work and self-identity: The effect of working in a feminist illegal abortion collective." In *Feminist frontiers,* edited by L. Richardson and V. Taylor. Reading, MA: Addison-Wesley.

Schneider, Beth. 1988. "Political generations in the contemporary women's movement." *Sociological Inquiry* 58:4–21.

Smith, Barbara. 1983. *Home girls: A black feminist anthology.* New York: Kitchen Table Women of Color Press.

Sparks, C. H. 1979. "Program evaluation of a community rape prevention program." Ph.D. diss., Ohio State University, Columbus.

Stacey, Judith. 1987. "Sexism by a subtler name? Post-industrial conditions and postfeminist consciousness." *Socialist Review* 17(6).

Staggenborg, Suzanne. 1988. "The consequences of professionalization and formalization in the pro-choice movement." *American Sociological Review* 53:585–606.

———. 1989. "Stability and innovation in the women's movement: A comparison of two movement organizations." *Social Problems* 36:75–92.

———. Forthcoming, 1991. *The pro-choice movement.* New York: Oxford University Press.

Taylor, John, 1991. "Are you politically correct?" *New York Magazine.* January 21:33–40.

Taylor, Verta. 1989. "Social movement continuity: The women's movement in abeyance." *American Sociological Review* 54:761–775.

———. Forthcoming. "The movement to combat postpartum depression: Self help and feminist consciousness."

——— and Nancy Whittier. Forthcoming. "Collective identity in social movement communities: Lesbian feminist mobilization." In *Frontiers of social movement theory,* edited by Aldon Morris and Carol Mueller. New Haven, CT: Yale University Press.

Tierney, K. J. 1982. "The battered women movement and the creation of the wife beating problem." *Social Problems* 29:207–20.

West, Guida and Rhoda Lois Blumberg. 1990. *Women and social protest.* New York: Oxford University Press.

Whittier, Nancy E. Unpublished. "Collective identity and social movement continuity: The impact of the women's movement on social movements of the 1990s." Ph.D. diss., The Ohio State University, 1991.

Will, George F. 1991. "Yes, teach complete history, but curriculums of group grievances are divisive." *Philadelphia Inquirer,* Monday, July 15.

Yankelovich, D. 1981. *New rules.* New York: Random House.